THE OXFORD HANDBOOK OF

GREEK AND ROMAN COMEDY

THE OXFORD HANDBOOK OF

GREEK AND

ROMAN

COMEDY

Edited by

MICHAEL FONTAINE

and

ADELE C. SCAFURO

OXFORD

UNIVERSITY PRESS

OXFORD
UNIVERSITY PRESS

Oxford University Press is a department of the University of Oxford.
It furthers the University's objective of excellence in research, scholarship,
and education by publishing worldwide.

Oxford   New York
Auckland   Cape Town   Dar es Salaam   Hong Kong   Karachi
Kuala Lumpur   Madrid   Melbourne   Mexico City   Nairobi
New Delhi   Shanghai   Taipei   Toronto

With offices in
Argentina   Austria   Brazil   Chile   Czech Republic   France   Greece
Guatemala   Hungary   Italy   Japan   Poland   Portugal   Singapore
South Korea   Switzerland   Thailand   Turkey   Ukraine   Vietnam

Oxford is a registered trademark of Oxford University Press
in the UK and certain other countries.

Published in the United States of America by
Oxford University Press
198 Madison Avenue, New York, NY 10016

Library of Congress Cataloging-in-Publication Data
The Oxford handbook of Greek and Roman comedy / edited by Michael Fontaine and Adele C. Scafuro.
pages. cm
Includes index.
ISBN 978-0-19-974354-4
1. Greek drama (Comedy)—History and criticism.   2. Latin drama (Comedy)—History and criticism.
I. Fontaine, Michael.   II. Scafuro, Adele C.
PA3028.O87 2013
882'.0109—dc23
2013004230

1 3 5 7 9 8 6 4 2
Printed in the United States of America
on acid-free paper

Contents

List of Contributors   xi
List of Abbreviations   xiii

Introduction. Ancient Comedy: The *longue durée*   1
ADELE C. SCAFURO

PART ONE: GREEK COMEDY

I. BEGINNINGS

1. In Search of the Essence of Old Comedy: From Aristotle's *Poetics* to Zieliński, Cornford, and Beyond   33
   JEFFREY RUSTEN

2. Performing Comedy in the Fifth through Early Third Centuries   50
   ERIC CSAPO

3. Dionysiac Festivals in Athens and the Financing of Comic Performances   70
   ANDRONIKE MAKRES

II. THE GREEK COMEDIANS AND THEIR PLAYS

4. The First Poets of Old Comedy   95
   IAN STOREY

5. The Last Laugh: Eupolis, Strattis, and Plato against Aristophanes   113
   MARIO TELÒ

6. Aristophanes   132
   BERNHARD ZIMMERMANN

7. Comedy in the Fourth Century I: Mythological Burlesques   160
   IOANNIS M. KONSTANTAKOS

8. Comedy in the Fourth Century II: Politics and Domesticity   181
   JEFFREY HENDERSON

9. Comedy in the Late Fourth and Early Third Centuries BCE   199
   ADELE C. SCAFURO

10. Menander   218
    ADELE C. SCAFURO

11. Reconstructing Menander   239
    ALAIN BLANCHARD

12. Crossing Genres: Comedy, Tragedy, and Satyr Play   258
    JOHANNA HANINK

13. Crossing Conceptual Worlds: Greek Comedy and Philosophy   278
    DAVID KONSTAN

III. ATTIC COMEDY AND SOCIETY

14. The Politics of Comic Athens   297
    DAVID ROSENBLOOM

15. Law and Greek Comedy   321
    EMILIANO J. BUIS

16. Religion and the Gods in Greek Comedy   340
    SCOTT SCULLION

IV. THE DIFFUSION OF COMEDY IN THE
HELLENISTIC WORLD

17. The Diffusion of Comedy from the Age of Alexander to the
    Beginning of the Roman Empire   359
    BRIGITTE LE GUEN

18. Hellenistic Mime and Its Reception in Rome   378
    COSTAS PANAYOTAKIS

PART TWO: ROMAN COMEDY

I. BEGINNINGS

19. The Beginnings of Roman Comedy   401
    PETER G. McC. BROWN

20. Festivals, Producers, Theatrical Spaces, and Records   409
    GEORGE FREDRIC FRANKO

21. Plautus between Greek Comedy and Atellan Farce: Assessments and
    Reassessments   424
    ANTONIS K. PETRIDES

II. THE ROMAN COMEDIANS AND THEIR PLAYS

22. Plautus's Dramatic Predecessors and Contemporaries in Rome   447
    WOLFGANG DAVID CIRILO DE MELO

23. Plautus and Terence in Performance   462
    ERICA M. BEXLEY

24. Metrics and Music   477
    MARCUS DEUFERT

25. Prologue(s) and *Prologi*   498
    BORIS DUNSCH

26. Between Two Paradigms: Plautus   516
    MICHAEL FONTAINE

27. The Terentian Reformation: From Menander to Alexandria   538
    MICHAEL FONTAINE

28. The Language of the *Palliata*   555
    EVANGELOS KARAKASIS

29. Tragedy, Paratragedy, and Roman Comedy   580
    GESINE MANUWALD

III. ROMAN COMEDY AND SOCIETY

30. Roman Comedy and the Social Scene   601
    ERICH GRUEN

31. Law and Roman Comedy   615
    JAN FELIX GAERTNER

32. Religion in Roman Comedy   634
    BORIS DUNSCH

PART THREE: TRANSMISSION AND ANCIENT RECEPTION

33. The Transmission of Aristophanes   655
    NIGEL WILSON

34. Later Greek Comedy in Later Antiquity   667
    HEINZ-GÜNTHER NESSELRATH

35. The Rebirth of a Codex: Virtual Work on the Ambrosian Palimpsest
    of Plautus   680
    WALTER STOCKERT

36. The Transmission of Terence   699
    BENJAMIN VICTOR

37. Graphic Comedy: Menandrian Mosaics and Terentian Miniatures   717
    SEBASTIANA NERVEGNA

38. Greek Comedy, the Novel, and Epistolography   735
    REGINA HÖSCHELE

39. Roman Comedy in the Second Sophistic   753
    REGINE MAY

40. The Reception of Plautus in Antiquity   767
    ROLANDO FERRI

41. Aelius Donatus and His Commentary on Terence's Comedies   782
    CHRYSANTHI DEMETRIOU

Appendices
1. *New Texts: Greek Comic Papyri 1973–2010*   803
    EFTYCHIA BATHRELLOU
2. *Post-Menandrian Comic Poets: An Overview of the Evidence
    and a Checklist*   871
    BENJAMIN MILLIS

Index   885

LIST OF CONTRIBUTORS

Eftychia Bathrellou is Teaching Fellow in Classics at the University of Edinburgh.

Erica M. Bexley is Visiting Research Fellow at the Australian National University.

Alain Blanchard is Professor at Université Paul Sabatier.

Peter G. McC. Brown is Emeritus Fellow of Trinity College, University of Oxford.

Emiliano J. Buis is Professor in International Law at the University of Buenos Aires Law School.

Wolfgang David Cirilo de Melo is University Lecturer in Classical Philology at Wolfson College, University of Oxford.

Eric Csapo is Professor of Classics and Ancient History at the University of Sydney.

Marcus Deufert is Professor of Classics at the University of Leipzig.

Chrysanthi Demetriou is Adjunct Tutor of Hellenic Culture at the Open University of Cyprus.

Boris Dunsch is Associate Professor of Classical Studies at the University of Marburg.

Rolando Ferri is Professor of Classical Philology at the University of Pisa.

Michael Fontaine is Associate Professor of Classics at Cornell University.

George Fredric Franko is Professor of Classics at Hollins University.

Jan Felix Gaertner is Lecturer on the Classics at Harvard University.

Erich Gruen is Wood Professor Emeritus at the University of California, Berkeley.

Johanna Hanink is Assistant Professor of Classics at Brown University.

Jeffrey Henderson is William Goodwin Aurelio Professor of Greek Language and Literature at Boston University.

Regina Höschele is Associate Professor of Classics at the University of Toronto.

Evangelos Karakasis is Lecturer of Latin Language and Literature at the University of Ioannina.

David Konstan is Professor of Classics at New York University.

Ioannis M. Konstantakos is Assistant Professor, Faculty of Philology, University of Athens.

Brigitte Le Guen is Professor of Greek History at Université Paris 8.

Andronike Makres is Academic Director of the Hellenic Education & Research Center (HERC).

Gesine Manuwald is Professor of Latin at University College London.

Regine May is Lecturer in Classics at the University of Leeds.

Benjamin Millis is Research Associate at the University of Oxford.

Sebastiana Nervegna is ARC Postdoctoral Research Fellow at the University of Sydney.

Heinz-Günther Nesselrath is Professor of Classics at the University of Göttingen.

Costas Panayotakis is Reader in Classics at the University of Glasgow.

Antonis K. Petrides is Lecturer at the Open University of Cyprus.

David Rosenbloom is Associate Professor of Ancient Studies at the University of Maryland, Baltimore County.

Jeffrey Rusten is Professor of Classics at Cornell University.

Adele C. Scafuro is Professor of Classics at Brown University.

Scott Scullion is Tutor in Classics at Worcester College, University of Oxford.

Ian Storey is Professor Emeritus of Classics at Trent University.

Walter Stockert is Lecturer in Classical Philology at the University of Vienna.

Mario Telò is Assistant Professor of Classics at the University of California, Los Angeles.

Benjamin Victor is Associate Professor of Classical Studies at the Université de Montréal.

Nigel Wilson is Emeritus Fellow at Lincoln College, University of Oxford.

Bernhard Zimmermann is Dean of Studies at University College Freiburg.

LIST OF ABBREVIATIONS

APF Davies, J. K. 1971. *Athenian Propertied Families*. Oxford: Clarendon Press.

BOC Rusten, J. 2011. *The Birth of Comedy. Texts, Documents, and Art from Athenian Comic Competitions, 486–280*. Translations by J. Henderson, D. Konstan, R. Rosen, J. Rusten, and N. W. Slater. Baltimore: Johns Hopkins University Press.

CAD Csapo, E. and W. J. Slater. 1995. *The Context of Ancient Drama*. Ann Arbor: University of Michigan Press.

CGFP Austin, C. 1973. *Comicorum Graecorum Fragmenta in Papyris Reperta*. Berlin: de Gruyter.

*DFA*² Pickard-Cambridge, A. 1968. *The Dramatic Festivals of Athens*. 2nd ed., rev. by J. Gould and D. M. Lewis. Reissued with supplement, 1988. Oxford: Clarendon Press. [First edition 1953.]

FGrHist F. Jacoby. 1923–. *Die Fragmente der griechischen Historiker*. Berlin and Leiden: Weidmann, Brill.

IG Deutsche Akademie der Wissenschaften zu Berlin. 1913–. *Inscriptiones Graecae*. Berlin: Reimer, de Gruyter.

K-A Kassel, R. and C. Austin. 1983–. *Poetae Comici Graeci*. 8 vols. Berlin: de Gruyter.

Koster Koster, W. J. W. 1975. *Scholia in Aristophanem*. Fascicule 1A: *Prolegomena de Comoedia*. Groningen: Bouma.

*MNC*³ T. B. L. Webster. 1995. *Monuments Illustrating New Comedy*, Vol. 1, 3rd ed., rev. and enlarged by J. R. Green and A. Seeberg. *BICS* Suppl. 50. London: Institute of Classical Studies.

PA Kirchner, J. 1901–1903. *Prosopographia Attica*. 2 vols. Berlin: Reimer.

PCG See K-A, above.

PhV² Trendall, A. D. 1967. *Phlyax Vases*. 2nd ed. *BICS* Supplement 19. London: Institute of Classical Studies.

Stephanis Stephanis, I. E. 1988. *Dionysiakoi Technitai*. Heraklion: Panepistemiakes Ekdoseis Kretes.

TrGF Snell, B., S. L. Radt, and R. Kannicht. 1971–2004. *Tragicorum Graecorum Fragmenta*. 5 vols. Göttingen: Vandenhoeck & Ruprecht.

INTRODUCTION

Ancient Comedy: The longue durée

ADELE C. SCAFURO

NOT quite arbitrarily, a glance at the 1960s and '70s is the starting point for reflection. Baby boomers might recall, firsthand and vividly, the escalation of the Vietnam War with the Tet Offensive in January 1968 and the ensuing spring as the season of student revolt, when members of SDS and SAS took over buildings at Columbia University, when students rioted angrily in Paris streets, and Malraux suggested, by way of explanation, God was dead. The Beatles produced *Sgt. Pepper's Lonely Hearts Club Band* in 1968, *Abbey Road* in 1969, and broke up in 1970. Martin Luther King Jr. promoted black workers, equality, civil disobedience and, not yet forty, was assassinated on April 4, 1968, in Memphis, Tennessee. The Black Panther Party, endorsing a socialist agenda, engaged in confrontational activities; in Oakland, California, its seventeen-year-old treasurer Bobby Hutton was killed by police on April 6, 1968. In Los Angeles, Robert F. Kennedy, Attorney General of the United States, was assassinated on June 5, 1968. Responding to student demands, universities in the United States expanded curricula to include Departments of Black Studies and African-American Studies.

At the same time, the "sexual revolution" was in full swing in the United States; sexual mores were rapidly changing and sexual experimentation on the rise, well beyond the gates of college campuses. In 1962, Helen Gurley Brown published *Sex and the Single Girl*; Masters and Johnson's scientific study *Human Sexual Response* appeared in 1966; both were blockbuster sellers. "Pornography" proliferated, was prosecuted in the courts, and defied definition. In 1957, the Supreme Court had issued a groundbreaking ruling about a bookseller who sent erotic literature through the mail: obscenity was not protected by the First Amendment; Congress could ban material that was "utterly without redeeming social importance," meaning "whether to the average person, applying contemporary community standards, the dominant theme of the material, taken as a whole, appeals to prurient interest" (Roth v. United States 354 U.S. 476 [1957]). In 1959, Grove Press sued Robert K. Christenberry, the postmaster of New York City, for restricting its use of the postal service to send unexpurgated versions of D.H. Lawrence's 1928 novel *Lady Chatterley's Lover*;[1] the press won the case in the U.S. District Court for the Southern District of New York and the ruling was affirmed on appeal by the Second Circuit Court of Appeals.[2] The court found that the book was not obscene, since the sexual content was not its central purpose: "In short, all these passages to which the Postmaster General takes exception—in bulk only a portion of the book—are subordinate, but highly useful, elements to the development of the author's central purpose. And that is not prurient" (excerpt from the Court of Appeals decision). In 1964, Grove Press appealed to the U.S. Supreme Court a Florida decision banning the sale of Henry Miller's 1934 novel *Tropic of Cancer* and won the case.[3] And in 1965, G. P. Putnam's Sons appealed to the Supreme Court a Massachusetts decision banning John Cleland's *Memoirs of a Woman of Pleasure* (*Fanny Hill*) and won.[4] In all three cases, the judges who reversed lower-court decisions provided different definitions or tests for obscenity. In the Grove Press case for *Tropic of Cancer*, the judges had cited the opinions they gave on the same day in *Jacobellis v. Ohio*. In that case, the majority held that the First Amendment, as applied through the Fourteenth, protected a movie theater manager from being prosecuted for showing a film that was not obscene;[5] insofar as the film *Les Amants* was not obscene, it was constitutionally protected. The most famous opinion in that case was Justice Potter Stewart's, that the Constitution protected all obscenity except "hard core pornography"; he continued:

> I shall not today attempt further to define the kinds of material I understand to be embraced within that shorthand description; and perhaps I could never succeed in intelligibly doing so. But I know it when I see it, and the motion picture involved in this case is not that.[6]

Obviously, debate on the definition of obscenity continued. In *Miller v. California*, 413 U.S. 15 (1973), the Supreme Court took up the case of Marvin Miller, convicted for mailing illustrated brochures advertising "adult" books. The Justices now imposed a more clearly defined test for obscenity that is not offered protection by the First Amendment. The decision was neither unanimous nor greeted with universal acclaim; it has been modified and expanded; nevertheless, it has not been overturned.

---

[1] The press had published Lawrence's third manuscript version of the novel, which had been privately distributed in Florence; it was "a sumptuous edition selling for $6.00, with a prefatory letter of commendation by Archibald MacLeish, poet, playwright, and Boylston Professor of Rhetoric and Oratory at Harvard University, and with an extensive Introduction and a concluding Bibliographical Note by Mark Schorer, Professor of English Literature at the University of California and a Lawrence scholar," Grove Press, Inc. v. Robert K. Christenberry 276 F.2d 433, (1960), para. 1.

[2] Grove Press, Inc. v. Christenberry, 175 F.Supp. 488 (decided July 21, 1959) and 276 F.2d 433 (decided March 25, 1960).

[3] Grove Press v. Gerstein, 378 U.S. 577 (1964).

[4] Memoirs v. Massachusetts, 383 U.S. 413 (1966).

[5] Jacobellis v. Ohio, 378 U.S. 184 (1964).

[6] *Jacobellis*, v. Ohio, 378 U.S. 184, 197 (1964).

While the sexual revolution flourished, while "make love not war" became a younger generation's slogan for the policy of now, and while the Supreme Court adjusted its rulings, concurrences, and dissents on obscenity to changing community values, feminists in the women's liberation movement campaigned for equal pay and equal opportunity; universities responded by expanding curricula to include Departments of Women's Studies. The Women's Classical Caucus, an affiliate of the American Philological Association founded in 1972, promoted feminist studies of the ancient world and diversity in the profession. The "Other" was being talked about—and institutionalized.

In 1973, Steve Jobs dropped out of Reed College; in spring 1976, he began assembling Apple computers with Steve Wozniak in the family garage.

FROM POLITICS TO LITERARY INTERPRETATION

Elsewhere in the academic universe, in the pre-Twitter, pre-Facebook, pre-Google, pre-blog, pre–word search, pre-laptop period, some areas of published literary scholarship, traditionally a few years behind the present, were now running with the pack. New waves of criticism followed quickly one upon another: New Criticism, reacting against the "Old Criticism" of the nineteenth century that had looked to the biography of the author and the circumstances of his times to explain a text, now studied the "autonomous text," examining its intrinsic units apart from the world that once had been thought to produce it; by the early sixties, New Criticism was itself being washed away by a structuralism that imported much from linguistics and social anthropology; that, in turn was washed away by deconstructionism, and that by poststructuralism. Other critical waves, not successor but simultaneous ones, showed durable resistance—Marxist, psychoanalytic, feminist, and reader-response theories. Speech act theory, having roots (misplaced or not) in J. L. Austin's *How to Do Things with Words* (1962) in combination with works by John Searle, inspired new linguistic approaches to literary and dramatic texts. These and other linguistic and anthropological theories (whether recently untied from the fundamentals of structuralism or never tied there at all) spawned new, or remanipulated older, theories of language and sociolinguistics, revising approaches to literary evolution and ritual and welcoming visual semiotics and proxemics. New critical approaches would come later—e.g., the New Historicism in the eighties, returning, to some degree, to the pre–New Criticism stage. But that is later, and we are looking at the sixties and seventies.

Many literary critics among classicists (some of whom would, decades later, designate themselves "cultural historians") kept pace. In the field of Roman comedy, however, traditional studies of analytic critics maintained healthy production levels during the '60s and '70s. Often, the titles of their works were dead giveaways: e.g., *Das Original des plautinischen Persa* (Mueller 1957); "The *Curculio* of Plautus: An Illustration of

Plautine Methods in Adaptation" (Fantham 1965); "The *Poenulus* of Plautus and Its Attic Original" (Gratwick 1969); "Die plautinische *Cistellaria* und das Verhältnis von Gott und Handlung bei Menander" (Ludwig 1970); *Der Miles gloriosus des Plautus und sein griechisches Original: Ein Beitrag zur Kontaminationsfrage* (Schaaf 1977).[7] Change did come. Toward the end of this period ('60s and '70s), in the realm of comedy and drama criticism, Elaine Fantham published a pioneering essay, "Sex, Status, and Survival in Hellenistic Athens. A Study of Women in New Comedy" (1975), and E. Schuhmann at the same time published *Die soziale Stellung der Frau in den Komödien des Plautus* (1975). A few years later, Helene P. Foley edited a landmark anthology called *Reflections of Women in Antiquity* (1981), including her own essay, "The Concept of Women in Athenian Drama" and one by Froma Zeitlin titled "Travesties of Gender and Genre in Aristophanes' *Thesmophoriazousae*." The first edition of Eva Keuls's *The Reign of the Phallus: Sexual Politics in Ancient Athens* appeared in 1985, adding visual testimony to the classicist/feminist's arsenal. Alan Sommerstein published "The Naming of Women in Greek and Roman Comedy" in 1980 and David Bain "Female Speech in Menander" in 1984. Jeffrey Henderson's *Maculate Muse* with its examination of obscenity in Aristophanes had appeared almost a decade earlier (1975), bringing the language of sodomy and coitus interruptus out of the Latin tongue and into the joyful translating classroom.[8] His doctoral thesis (Harvard 1972, directed by Zeph Stewart) on the topic had been hard enough to pull off; while he could write in the preface to the second edition of the 1975 study (1991) that "scorn of the old taboos about human sexuality and its social expressions had become socially fashionable among members of my generation" (vii), few in the older generation of the professoriate had been fired with similar enthusiasm. Nonetheless, the U.S. Supreme Court had cleared the way with the decisions mentioned earlier, in 1957 (*Roth v. United States*), 1959 (*Grove Press, Inc. v. Christenberry*), 1964 (*Grove Press v. Gerstein* and *Jacobellis v. Ohio*, with Potter Stewart's defining moment: "I know it when I see it"), 1966 (*Memoirs v. Massachusetts*), and 1973 (*Miller v. California*).

On the Latin side, gender issues often transmogrified into studies of linguistic characterization. W. G. Arnott in the early '70s illustrated such characterization specifically in Roman comedy (1970 and 1972); so did J. N. Adams in 1972 with "Latin Words for Woman and Wife" and in 1984 with "Female Speech in Latin Comedy"; R. Maltby followed suit in 1979 with "Linguistic Characterization of Old Men in Terence." M. Gilleland provided a statistical method for such studies in a 1979 dissertation and

---

[7] Sometimes such works appear with less obvious titles but nevertheless are easily identifiable to the knowing reader, e.g., "Micio und Demea in den terenzischen *Adelphen*" (Tränkle 1972) and "Plautus-Studien: I: Der doppelte Geldkreislauf im *Pseudolus*" (Lefèvre 1977). The titles here and in the text above are a mere sampling. Lefèvre and his Freiburg colleagues in the last two decades have become energetic advocates for the influence of the improvisatory techniques of Atellan farce on Plautus (see Fontaine and Petrides, this volume).

[8] Comparable work in Latin studies appeared in the eighties: J. N. Adams, *The Latin Sexual Vocabulary* (1982), and Amy Richlin, *The Garden of Priapus: Sexuality and Aggression in Roman Humor* (1983).

followed this in 1980 with "Female Speech in Greek and Latin." On a broader playing field, Niall Slater introduced an expansive notion of metatheatrics into modern discussions of ancient drama with *Plautus in Performance* (1985; PhD thesis 1981), distinguishing his view from Lionel Abel's restrictive one as formulated in his 1963 study *Metatheatre: A New View of Dramatic Form*. The latter had argued that metatheater had come to replace tragedy as a genre in the Renaissance; for Slater, metatheater "is theatrically self-conscious theatre, i.e., theatre that demonstrates an awareness of its own theatricality" (1985:10). Moreover, Plautus had incorporated the improvisatory traditions of native Italian theater by characters who *simulate* improvisation in scripted plays. Plautine studies were especially receptive; Plautus's originality, brilliantly articulated in 1922 in Eduard Fraenkel's *Plautinisches im Plautus* (Berlin: Weidmann), reproduced and revised in the Italian edition of 1960, *Elementi plautini in Plauto* (Florence: La Nuova Italia Editrice), had now been reinvigorated. Arnott (*Gnomon* 59 [1987]:18) shot back, reminding readers that carefully scripted pieces simulating improvisational spontaneity (as in the pirate tale at *Bacch.* 251–347) were likely to be Menandrian in origin. The Greek vs. Roman originality contest continued.

Beyond the Literary Critique

The sixties and seventies were a period of tremendous scholarly activity in the broad field of classical antiquity, some of it taking place in libraries, some in archaeological excavations and museums, and some onstage, where it often served as a frame for theater experiments and political agendas, whether one thinks of Burt Shevelove's "splashy" production of *Frogs* by the Yale Repertory Theater in the swimming pool of Payne Whitney Gymnasium on May 21, 1974 (with the not-so-famous-at-the-time Meryl Streep, Sigourney Weaver, and Christopher Durang in the chorus) or the *first* public performance of *Lysistrata* in Britain in 1957[9] and the spate of performances of that same comedy in the late '60s and '70s on college campuses in the United States in protest of the Vietnam War,[10] or Richard Schechner's production *Dionysus in 69* which premiered on June 6, 1968 (a day after the assassination of Robert F. Kennedy). Indeed, Edith Hall, in her introduction to a volume on the reception of Greek tragedy (Edith Hall, Fiona MacIntosh, and Amanda Wrigley, eds., *Dionysus since 69: Greek Tragedy at the Dawn of the Third Millenium*, Oxford University Press, 2004) argues that the end of the '60s with

---

[9] The British theatre was under the control of the Lord Chamberlain, who served as censor until 1968 (Walton 2010, 15–16). The production of *Lysistrata* by the English Stage Company in 1957, under the direction of Minos Volonakis and using Dudley Fitts's translation, was the first allowed. Walton (ibid.) reports that it "was condemned as 'savagely pornographic' by the monthly periodical *Theatre World*."

[10] See Hardwick 2010 for an account of the "Lysistrata Project of 2003," involving over a thousand "coordinated readings" all over the globe on March 3, 2003, as a protest against the imminent attack on Iraq by the US-led coalition.

"its seismic and cultural shifts" (p. 1) produced, inter alia, a revival of interest in Greek tragedy heralded by Schechner's production; 1968–1969 was a "watershed" after which new performances of Greek tragedies increased by quantum leaps (cf. Revermann 2008, 177 col. 1). Here, a bit differently, the '60s and '70s are envisioned as a Janus-like gateway to past and future scholarship on ancient comedy.[11] During those decades, many significant scholarly books were produced and significant scholarly projects (or simply trends) initiated, with long tentacles reaching to the present and some notable ones straddling both sides of the date-gate, instantiated by the appearances of "second editions" in the '60s and "third editions" decades later. Many of the initiators of important projects are dead, in retirement, or nearing that moment.[12] This introduction is, in some ways, a salute to their work, but it also presents the case, in brief, not only for their collective achievement in amalgamating the interdisciplinary studies of comedy in classics but also for the vision of comedy produced by that amalgamation, namely its own *longue durée*. The 2010s are a watershed moment in the history of comedy scholarship.

Contributions to comedy scholarship in the '60s and '70s ranged over numerous subfields and topics, and many are treated in this volume. Performance studies (of Greek and Roman plays, tragedies and comedies, even satyr plays and mimes), for example, have blossomed, some looking to the ancient text to provide directions for the ways it was performed onstage, others incorporating knowledge of material finds in their envisioning of performance, still others looking to the experience of performing, and some combining two or three of these approaches at once. These, along with reception studies of performance, are possibly the biggest growth industries in the field of Classics.[13] Let me focus here for a moment on performance studies that are "text-derived." From earliest times (i.e., from early scholia and early modern commentators), learned readers and scholars have used texts to envisage performance (see, e.g. Demetriou, this volume, on Donatus). In the modern era, it would be a rare commentator, indeed, who showed no curiosity to find links between text and stage.[14] To take a well-known example from

---

[11] As the author was writing this introduction, the announcement arrived of a work by James T. Patterson (Emeritus Professor of History at Brown University), *The Eve of Destruction: How 1965 Transformed America* (2012). The title alludes to the plaintive song of protest written by P. F. Sloan and sung by Barry McGuire in 1965.

[12] Eric Handley died soon after this Introduction was written, on January 17, 2013; Colin Austin died on August 13, 2010 (see n. 34 below); Geoffrey Arnott on December 1, 2010.

[13] In this volume, one may consult especially chapters 2, 3, 7, 9, 17, 18, 20, 21, 23, 24, 41 and appendices 1 and 2 in which, while not always a main topic, performance is certainly touched upon in meaningful ways; ancient reception is discussed in chapters 5, 18, 22, 27 and more particularly in chapters 34 and 37–41.

[14] A beautiful early modern example of a "text-derived" study emerged from the debate over the stage in the the the theatre of Dionysus: J. W. White's (1891) "The 'Stage' in Aristophanes," *HSCPh* 2: 159–205, masterfully composed with the knowledge of Dörpfeld's then provocative theory that there was no stage (actors and chorus performed on the same level in the orchestra) but before it was fully published. White criss-crossed the fields of archaeology (the first chairman of the Managing Committee of the American School of Classical Studies at Athens) and philology with ease, publishing works of lasting value, e.g., *The Verse of Greek Comedy* (1912) and *The Scholia on the Aves of Aristophanes* (1914) and essays in *HSCPh* 29 (1918) and 30 (1919) coauthored with E. Cary.

tragedy, all one need do is to read carefully the pages of Fraenkel's grand commentary on *Agamemnon* (1950) to realize how often he ponders stage action, as when, for example, the question of the timing of Clytemnestra's first entrance arises: is she onstage when the Elders pose questions of her at *Agamemnon* 83–87 and does she then remain silent for some 165 verses, or does she only enter at the end of the long *parodos*, immediately before she speaks (255–258)? For anyone reading the play and imagining it played (as we must), the question begs for an answer and has exercised dozens of scholars (for references, see Fraenkel 1950, Vol. 2, 83–84; Taplin 1972: 89–94 and 1977: 280–285). Such text-derived considerations of performance have produced numerous studies that focus on exits and entrances, on "asides" and "eavesdropping scenes," the "three-actor rule," scene structure, and act division. Oliver Taplin's *Stagecraft of Aeschylus* published in 1977 and *Greek Tragedy in Action* in the following year, as well as David Bain's *Actors and Audience* in 1977, seemed almost to herald a new age: e.g., D. J. Mastronarde's *Contact and Discontinuity: Some Conventions of Speech and Action on the Greek Stage* appeared in 1979; Bain's *Masters, Servants and Orders in Greek Tragedy: A Study of some Aspects of Dramatic Technique and Convention* in 1982; David Seale's *Vision and Stagecraft in Sophocles* in the same year; and K. B. Frost's *Exits and Entrances in Menander* in 1988. Taplin's later work would incorporate more of the material world as he sought to show the spread of Greek drama, first in South Italy in *Comic Angels: And Other Approaches to Greek Drama through Vase Painting* (1993), more broadly in *Pots and Plays: Interactions between Tragedy and Greek Vase-Painting of the Fourth Century B.C.* (2007), and more recently in a multiauthored volume of essays edited with Rosie Wyles, *The Pronomos Vase and its Content* (2010).

This last little sketch, beginning with text-derived performance studies, has brought us well beyond the '60s and '70s, to a time when the study of material artifacts had already twined with numerous text-driven studies of drama, when performance studies seemed less and less the fringe of classics (compare, e.g., responses to Rush Rehm's *Greek Tragic Theatre* in 1992 and *The Play of Space, Spatial Transformation in Greek Tragedy* in 2001), and when a reviewer of Martin Revermann's *Comic Business* (2006), speaking of the author's perspective on performance and stagecraft, could say that it "could only have been written in a post-Taplin era" (Rosen, *BMCR* 2007.04.69)—which is not exactly right but not absolutely wrong, either: it simply elides the generation that was Taplin's rocket ship.

PERFORMANCE AND THEATER ARTIFACTS

The contribution of T. B. L. Webster (1905–1974) to the study of ancient theater texts and practice is monumental. Though our formal starting point is the '60s, some dots in the trajectory of his early years call for connection to his later career, especially as his active engagement with art and drama spanned more than half a century—if we start with his student days at Oxford in the early twenties when he studied, inter alia, Greek vases with John Beazley and later, in 1928 in Leipzig, when he studied Menander *and* theater artifacts with Alfred Körte.[15] Thereafter, in the thirties and forties, Webster made numerous contributions to *The Classical Review*, often reviews of Ciceronian texts or works on Greek tragedy or vases and sculpture, but also original contributions on different aspects of Greek drama (such as plot structure and "preparation and motivation"); he also began publishing books on other dramatists (thus, a Clarendon *Introduction to Sophocles* in 1936) and works linking art and literature (see n. 18 below). Webster reports in the preface to his 1950 *Studies in Menander* that its form owes something to its period of gestation: "When I went on military service in 1940, texts of Menander, Plautus, and Terence were compact enough to take with me. The stimulus to publish the results of my reading was given by Dr. H. Guppy when he invited me to lecture in the Rylands Library in December 1944." One of the immediate publications in the *Bulletin of the John Rylands Library* was a short pamphlet titled *Restorations in Menander* (Vol. 30, Manchester, 1946), elegantly rebuffed by Gomme the following year (*CR* 61 [1947]: 94–95) on grounds that would become a familiar refrain among his literary critics over the years: his reconstructions of scenes were too mechanical, relying on parallels in other comedies, Greek or Roman, and without internal support. Undeterred, Webster would continue to write about fragmentary Greek drama; after the first monograph on Menander, he published *Studies in Later Greek Comedy* in 1953 (treating comedy from 400–370 and from 370–321, followed by New Comedy). His *Tragedies of Euripides* appeared in 1967; here he lavished attention on the fragmentary plays, reconstructing plots and scenes and hypothesizing not only plot structures but rules of dramatic competition to explain changes in those structures. His *Introduction to Menander* appeared posthumously in 1974. Of this work, one laudatory reviewer exuberantly remarked: "Webster has written a book which, almost as far as is possible, will transform a modern reader into an Athenian citizen sitting in the theater of Lykourgos, complete with the knowledge and expectation of the kind of play he will see in the newest Menandrean work" (J. N. Grant, *CW* 71 [1977]: 199).

Those words have an eerie ring, resonating as they do with contemporary emphasis in performance studies of Greek and Roman drama, where it has become almost formulaic to set the scene, to recreate the moment of original performance, no matter how impossible everyone knows that is, but nevertheless, to use every legitimate means possible to understand the size and shape of the acting space, a matter of great controversy in the nineteenth (see n. 14 above) and twentieth centuries (even as late as the 1970s: Gebhard 1974), to envision how it was used, and to locate it in a city or countryside; to envision costumes and masks and of course the actors who wore them and how they may have used them, and to conjecture their number in any given production (or scene), their rehearsals, scripts (and actors' interpolations), voicings, gestures,

[15] E.W. Handley (2003: 450–451) points out in his short and informative biography of Webster that "[t]his was then a twofold meeting of minds. It is still the case, as it was throughout the Webster years, that the publication and study of new papyri and new archaeological material have gone on in parallel, with gains to knowledge that neither master nor pupil in Leipzig would have dared to dream of while some of the foundations of future work were being laid."

onstage arrivals and departures (or "exits and entrances"), fees, and fame.[16] The audience is also envisioned: its size, its composition, and the gradient of its intelligence and expertise.[17] And now it is not only the Athenian citizen who is imagined as spectator, but the Corinthian in Corinth or Alexander's mercenaries in Susa and elsewhere (references in *DFA*²: 280). The economics of performance are set out, too—not only the cost of attendance but of performance itself, and where all that funding came from. And beyond these topics, the meaning of theater to the lives of polis inhabitants all around the Mediterranean is reflected upon through different media (Green 1994, Green 2000). Among epigraphic texts, we can look, for example, at the honorary decrees for actors, playwrights, and *choregoi* (the funding sponsors of choruses: Makres 1994 and this volume, chapter 3; Wilson 2000) that are inscribed on statue bases or stone pillars, and at leases for theaters or contracts for their repair, and we can ask: what social values do such documents unveil? We can examine literary texts, treatises like Plato's *Symposium* in which both Agathon and Aristophanes appear, orations like Antiphon 6 *On the Chorus Boy* and Demosthenes 21 *Against Meidias* in which *choregoi* appear, and works such as Athenaeus's *Dinner of the Sophists* with long discussions of and quotations from comedy; and again, we can ask: what social values do these texts unveil? We can study archaeological finds; in addition to considering the theaters themselves and their spread throughout the Greco-Roman world, we can examine theater tickets and consider the proliferation of vase paintings of actors and choruses, actor figurines, terracotta masks, and glorious mosaics of once famous theater scenes, and we can ask: what does all this theater paraphernalia and decorative art suggest about the societies that produced it (see, e.g. Nervegna, this volume, chapter 37)? And we can study papyrus texts over time and consider what they have to tell us not only about the tastes of the reading public or of school studies and the evolution of a canon, but also what they might tell us about contemporary readings and possibly performance (consider no. 76 in Bathrellou's discussion of a third-century CE papyrus, in Appendix 1 in this volume).

Much of this (by no means all, but especially the evaluation of archaeological finds) owes something to Webster, who early on saw the importance of vases and other material artifacts for reconstructing the theater scene. As alluded to earlier, Webster had begun to publish more directly about connections between literature and objects in the

---

[16] See, e.g., on the Greek side: E. Csapo and W. J. Slater, *The Context of Ancient Drama* (1995), and bibliographies by J. R. Green, "Theatre Production," *Lustrum* 31 (1989): 7–95, 273–278; *Lustrum* 37 (1995, for 1987–1995): 7–202, 309–318; *Lustrum* 50 (2008, for 1996–2006): 7–302 and 367–391; among recent works highlighting theatre performance, M. Revermann, *Comic Business: Theatricality, Dramatic Technique, and Performance Contexts of Aristophanic Comedy* (2006); D. Stuttard (ed.), *Looking at Lysistrata* (2010); R. K. Roselli, *Theater of the People: Spectators and Society in Ancient Athens*. On the Roman side: W. Beare, *The Roman Stage* (1950, 2d ed. 1955, 3d ed. 1965 [completed by N. G. L. Hammond]); R. C. Beacham, *The Roman Theatre and Its Audience* (1991, 2d ed. 1995); T. Moore, *The Theater of Plautus: Playing to the Audience* (1998); C. W. Marshall, *The Stagecraft and Performance of Roman Comedy* (2006).

[17] See, e.g., on the Greek side, Revermann 2006, and on the Roman side, Goldberg 1998 and Fontaine 2010.

late thirties, especially on vases that illustrated drama, theater masks, and comic costume.[18] In 1956, the first edition of *Greek Theatre Production* was published, a precursor of his later volumes that would catalogue the material artifacts of Greek theater, with some 1,500 monuments used as its foundation for research and with a select list of some 270 items for discussion.[19] The triadic first edition of *Monuments* arrived in 1960, 1961, and 1962: *Monuments Illustrating Old and Middle Comedy* (*MMC*[1]); *Monuments Illustrating New Comedy* (*MNC*[1]); *Monuments Illustrating Tragedy and Satyr-Play* (*MTS*[1]). A second edition of the triad appeared at the end of the decade (1967 *MTS*[2], 1969 *MMC*[2] and *MNC*[2]). A more general reference work, in collaboration with A. D. Trendall, appeared in 1971, *Illustrations of Greek Drama*. The third edition of *Monuments* came later, posthumously, in 1978 (*MMC*[3], revised by J. R. Green) and in 1995 (*MNC*[3], two vols. including material published up to late 1986, revised by J. R. Green once again, and now with A. Seeberg).[20] The catalogues that formed the basis of *Monuments* grew steadily through the editions; approximately 600 items had been catalogued in *MMC*[1], about 150 new pieces were added to *MMC*[2], and another 250 to *MMC*[3]. The greatest number of finds belonged to New Comedy, with over 1,400 items catalogued in *MNC*[1] and some 375 items added to *MNC*[2], and, remarkably, over 3,500 items catalogued in the third edition. New finds (terracotta actor figurines and masks) from the Lipari Islands increased the totals in the later editions of both *MMC* and *MNC*, and in the latter, mosaics also added significantly. L. Bernabó-Brea and M. Cavalier in 1965 had published the first theatrical terracotta masks and actor figurines from the Contrada Diana necropolis with its (then excavated) 565 tombs dating from the sixth century BCE to the second century CE; Trendall had contributed a chapter on the Lipari vases to that volume, and Webster a commentary on the theatrical items. It was the 1981 Lipari materials, however, that especially contributed to the greater nuancing of interpretation, taxonomy, and chronology, especially of masks, in the latest edition of *MNC* in 1995 (see the Museum Index in 1.172–174). A like interval between excavation and dissemination in *MNC* transpired in the case of the now well-known third-century CE mosaics from "the house of Menander" in Mytilene. These had been excavated in the early sixties by S. Charitonides, announced by

[18] See, e.g., essays by Webster in 1948, 1949, 1951, 1952, 1954, 1955. A series of books began in 1939, connecting Greek art and literature: *Greek Art and Literature 530–400 BC*; *Art and Literature in Fourth Century Athens* (1956); *From Mycenae to Homer* (1958, repr. 1960); *Greek Art and Literature 700–530 BC* (1959); *Hellenistic Poetry and Art* (1964).

[19] The large catalogue was based on M. Bieber's *Denkmäler zum Theaterwesen* (1920) and *The History of the Greek and Roman Theater* (1939, 2d ed. 1961) and A. Simon's *Comicae Tabellae* (1938), but with a great many additions.

[20] The practice of passing on editions to "surviving" scholars is not so unusual, but is nevertheless prominent for, in some cases, large-scale revision among works on ancient theatre. Webster, at the end of 1951, on Pickard-Cambridge's request, took over the manuscript of the first edition of *The Dramatic Festivals of Athens* (1953) and "saw it through the press." Webster made only minor alterations here. Pickard-Cambridge for his part had revised the third edition of A. E. Haigh's *The Attic Theatre* ("revised and in part re-written") in 1907, where, aside from much else, he vastly expanded the second appendix on dramatic inscriptions and added the third on the original place of the Lenaea. Other examples are mentioned in the text above and in n. 31.

Webster in the preface to the second edition of *MNC* in 1969, published posthumously in 1970 after the Greek excavator's death in a motor accident (S. Charitonides, L. Kahil, and R. Ginouvès, *Les mosaïques de la maison du Ménandre à Mytilène*, Bern: Francke), reviewed that same year by Webster (*JHS* 91: 210–211), but only integrated into discussion in the third edition of *MNC* by Green and Seeberg (1995, Vol. 2, 469–471), though widely discussed before then as testimony to Menander's plays and aids to reconstructing the fragmentary remains.

What is immediately evident in *MNC*³ is the broader geographical distribution of material all over the Greek and Roman world, as well as the diachronic span of that material, beginning ca. 250 BCE and extending (through *six* periods) to ca. CE 180 and later. While items in the last period are exceedingly difficult to date, two ivory consular diptychs may be among the latest: one shows an "actor as youth" (6DI 1) and the other an "actor disrobing" and receiving applause from those watching the games (6DI 2); both date to the early sixth century CE. Green and Seeberg have suggested, regarding the latter diptych (St. Petersburg ω 263 [Byz 925/16]), that if the youth's Phrygian cap indicates Act IV of the Menandrian *Eunuchus*, then the applause occurs before the end of the play; and if so, the dramatic implication is quite important: "the ivory could be taken to mean that what the consul put on at the games was not the staging of a complete Menander play, but a speech or speeches from Menander rendered in stage dress by a *cantor*. This at least agrees with the fact that Menander was handed down in the main Byzantine tradition not as a playwright, but as an author of set speeches and quotations" (*MNC*³1.76; cf. Nervegna 2007: 23–41, esp. 38). The transitions and alterations of theater stagings over the centuries are a mirror of cultural preoccupations.

The twin phenomena of ancient theater's long diachronic span and broad geographical spread were already becoming evident in the '60s but were given ever more material proof in publications as the end of the century approached. As was said earlier, the '60s and '70s were a gateway to the past and future. One reviewer of Webster's second edition of *MMC* pointed to the '60s as a decade when "an astonishing number of books on theatre have gone into a second edition" (B. A. Sparkes, *JHS* 91 [1971]: 210): indeed, the '60s saw not only the first and second editions of Webster's *Monuments*, but additionally, in the same year as *MMC*¹ (1960) appeared, Webster published a second edition of *Studies in Menander*, and in the same year as *MTS*¹ (1962), he produced a much revised second edition of Pickard-Cambridge's (1927) *Dithyramb, Tragedy, and Comedy*. J. Gould and D. M. Lewis extensively revised Pickard-Cambridge's *Festivals* in 1968 (with "generous assistance in the choice and collection of illustrations" from Beazley and Webster: p. x). The second edition of M. Bieber's *The History of the Greek and Roman Theater* (1939) appeared in 1961, the second edition of A. D. Trendall's *Phlyax Vases* (*BICS* Suppl. 19) in 1969, and in that same year the second edition, with additional material, of Webster's *Sophocles* (Methuen). In 1963, Webster published *Griechische Bühnenaltertümer*, a short history of Greek theater production from its beginnings to late imperial times, updating earlier work and summarizing more recent; and in 1970, he published a second edition of *Greek Theatre Production*—as well as a revised edition of *Studies in Later Greek*

Comedy.[21] Second editions look not only backwards to the now meager appearance of predecessor editions, but also robustly forward into the promising future.

All the while, the study of ancient Greek drama was becoming a much broader and more interdisciplinary study, exemplified, e.g., by the work of E. W. Handley and J. R. Green. Over the last three decades of the twentieth century and into the current one, the latter has brought expert knowledge of vases into the theater realm in grand ways, insisting on a broader understanding of the meaning of theater in the lives of the Greeks not only by carrying on and vastly expanding Webster's *Monuments,* but additionally with a protreptic agenda evident in collaborative works such as *Images of the Greek Theatre* (with Handley in 1995), in bibliographies on theater production (n. 16 above), and in various articles on vases, mosaics, and the theater world (e.g. 1985, 1991, 2001). Handley himself, for a longer period (beginning in the fifties), has so frequently crossed between art, archaeology, stage history, papyrology, and philology that it hardly makes sense to speak of boundaries at all. This is evident in numerous works, among them other collaborations with Green (2000, 2001), as well as in edited volumes (e.g. 1990, 1993) and essays (e.g., 2000, 2001, 2002). No finer heir could have written the brief and eloquent biography of Webster that appeared in the *Proceedings of the British Academy* in 2003.

TEXTS AND SCHOLIA

Elsewhere in the '60s and '70s, our starting point, classical scholarship stepped cautiously forward. In the world of Aristophanic studies, new critical texts of the scholia, later known as the "Groningen edition,"[22] began to appear in 1960. Paleographer and metrician W. J. K. Koster served as its first general editor; D. Holwerda succeeded him in 1975 and brought the enterprise, divided into four parts and composed of eighteen fascicles produced by eight contributors, to its conclusion in 2007. This was the first complete edition since Dindorf's three volumes (1838) and Dübner's singleton in 1842. Some of the scholia had never been edited before (e.g., the greater part of the commentaries of Tzetzes and many scholia belonging to the *vetera*). The quality of material varies; the *Prolegomena de Comoedia* (ed. Koster), for example, are mostly useless, though anecdotal material such as the story of Eupolis's drowning by Alcibiades after the production of *Baptai* is not without interest, and, on the more serious side, there is good reason to think that parts

---

[21] Webster's Cambridge edition, *Sophocles Philoctete*s, and also *The Greek Chorus* were published the same year (1970).

[22] The project was sponsored by what was subsequently called NWO, *Nederlandse Organisatie voor Wetenschappelijk Onderzoek* (Netherlands Organization for Scientific Research). Part IV was published first, but its four fascicles appeared over a number of years. Similarly the other volumes, so that, for example, Part I appeared as follows: (1A) *Prolegomena* on Comedy, ed. W. J. W. Koster (1975); (1B) Scholia to *Acharnians,* ed. N. G. Wilson (1975); (2) Scholia to *Knights,* ed. D. Mervyn Jones, N. G. Wilson (1969); (3.1) Ancient Scholia to *Clouds,* ed. D. Holwerda (1977); (3.2) Recent Scholia to *Clouds,* ed. W. J. W. Koster

of *Prolegomenon* III go back to Aristophanes of Byzantium, with useful information on numbers of plays assigned to poets and duration of poetic careers (Nesselrath 1990: 43–51; 172–187). Not surprisingly, some manuscripts of the scholia yield alternative readings or emendations for Aristophanes's plays (and also for other authors) that are helpful for editors of texts, as well as miscellaneous interpretive information such as explanations of jokes and topical allusions.[23]

Nearly coinciding with the initial publications of the new volumes of scholia, the Oxford Clarendon series of commentaries on Aristophanes got underway. This was envisioned to be, eventually, a complete series of critical editions with commentary, and as such, would be the first since Van Leeuwen's twelve volumes (including prolegomena, Leiden 1893–1906) and Rogers's volumes with less commentary and less reliable texts (London 1902–1916) nearly fifty years earlier. M. Platnauer's edition of *Peace* appeared in 1963, followed by K. J. Dover's *Clouds* in 1968, D. MacDowell's *Wasps* in 1971, and R. G. Ussher's *Ecclesiazusae* in 1973; since then, six more have been published, including a new edition of *Peace* to replace Platnauer's inaugural one, J. Henderson's *Lysistrata* (1987, 1989), K. J. Dover's *Frogs* (1993), N. Dunbar's *Birds* (1995), S. D. Olson's *Peace* (1999) and *Acharnians* (2002), and C. Austin and Olson's *Thesmophoriazusae* (2004).[24] Most of these texts were major advances on predecessors' editions; thus, e.g., Henderson, before producing his text of *Lysistrata*, collated its eight pre-sixteenth-century MSS in situ. During this same "Clarendon period," A. Sommerstein began producing his critical editions of the comedies of Aristophanes for Aris and Phillips commencing with *Acharnians* (Vol. 1) in 1980 and ending in 2002 (Indexes, Vol. 12). Henderson published the first volume of the (long-awaited) second Loeb edition of Aristophanes in 1998 and finished with *The Fragments* (Vol. V) in 2007.[25] Both Sommerstein and Henderson continue a tradition of endorsing translations that are readable *and* actable; stage versions and versions for the study are a false opposition. Thus Sommerstein: "Although Aristophanes, like his tragic contemporaries, wrote primarily for the stage, neither he nor they can have been unaware that their works would be read as well, and there is no evidence that the reading texts differed in any way from the acting texts" (1973: 142–143, with n. 1). Henderson, pointing to an archival custom of preserving scripts, likewise sees Aristophanes as writing "with both performers and readers in mind" (1992, 81–82). The sentiment is articulated by earlier translators as well, e.g. by P. Dickinson in the Introduction to his 1957 translation of three Aristophanic comedies: "Aristophanes

---

(1974). A full listing of the contents of the four parts appears in *CR*, n.s., 51, 2001: 18–19 (C. Austin) and *BMCR* 2008.09.24 (R. Tordoff).

[23] For a quick survey of the contents of these and other publications of Aristophanic scholia, see Dickey (2007: 28–31). Special mention should be made of Ada Adler's magnificent critical edition of the Suda (*Suidae Lexicon I–V* (1928–1938 Leipzig) with an apparatus that, inter alia, gives references to direct sources that in certain cases are Aristophanic scholia.

[24] A new edition of *Wasps* is now underway by Olson and Z. Biles to replace MacDowell's 1971 edition.

[25] The first editors of the series (E. Capps, T. E. Page, and W. H. D. Rouse) had wanted to appoint the great Aristophanic scholar J. W. White (see n. 14 above) to the task in the 1910s, but he died in 1917 before composing the critical edition of the eleven plays that he had planned. The editors subsequently decided to use B. B. Rogers's texts and translations, filling in the parts that Rogers had omitted as being

wrote for the theatre, words for actors to speak, just as Shakespeare did. It is therefore no use translating him into language that cannot be spoken on a stage." No doubt debate will continue over the best way to translate comedy for contemporary audiences (e.g., whether to compose in prose or verse, whether to use anachronisms, stage directions, and explanations as notes or somehow tucked into the translation) and that debate will include assessments of particular audiences for particular translations; in this respect, it is apt to point out that both Sommerstein and Henderson wrote about the "actable/readable script" before publishing translations with Greek on one side of the page and English on the other (or rather, British-English in the one case and American-English in the other). On both sides of the pond, obscenity is in, euphemism and Latin obfuscation out.

In most instances, the Greek texts (in the Oxford Clarendon series as well as Sommerstein's editions for Aris and Phillips and Henderson's editions in the Loeb series), replaced both Hall and Geldart's long obsolete Oxford texts (1900, 1906) and also the more reliable Budé of V. Coulon (1923–1930).[26] A new collective edition, however, was in the making. N. G. Wilson, who had edited two fascicles in the Groningen series of scholia in 1969 and 1975,[27] produced a new Aristophanes (2 vols., OCT) in 2007 (see chapter 33), but one with neither *stemmata codicum* for the plays nor a fresh collation of MSS (which to some extent had been carried out by the individual editors in the Clarendon series). Naturally, this is not the end of the story of today's text of Aristophanes (as if the telos of the Groningen edition were to be the near-simultaneous publication of Wilson's Aristophanes and the completion of Sommerstein's and Henderson's separate editions with translations—spectacular as that quadruple near-simultaneity is); but as this is not a story about the text of Aristophanes but an essay that reflects both on the massive scholarly work undertaken in the last fifty or sixty years and on its substantive consequences, a rerouting must be made.

obscene (often with Latin) and abridging introductions and notes; this was published in 1924, five years after Rogers's death. Sommerstein successfully approached the later series editor (E. H. Warmington) in 1972 with a notion for a new edition, but in 1978 the series, on financial grounds, had to postpone his publication for a five-year period. Handley and G. Goold (both at UCL, and the latter now Loeb series editor) brought the situation to the attention of Aris and Phillips—and so Sommerstein's editions found a home there (see Sommerstein 2006: 130–134). Henderson, who would become general editor of the Loeb series in 1999, had undertaken the second edition of Aristophanes in the early 1990s under Goold's headship. The series itself had now been reinvigorated after the financial woes of the '70s, and a new policy prevailed: "the seemingly harmless edict included in the early contracts to alter or omit licentious and obscene passages—anything that 'might give offense'—is now considered to be shabby scholarship" (from the *History of the Loeb Classical Library*, www.hup.harvard.edu/features/loeb/history. html, accessed Dec. 27, 2012). It should be noted that the "new policy" regarding "licentious and obscene passages" could hardly have been inaugurated legally in the US or UK before the late '60s or early '70s.

[26]   Two other omnibus editions (including text, commentary, and Italian translation) since the 1960s are: (1) G. Mastromarco's and P. Totaro's: Mastromarco, *Commedie di Aristofane, I* (Turin 1983), including *Acharnians –Peace*; Mastromarco and Totaro, *Commedie di Aristofane, II* (Turin 2006), including *Birds–Frogs*. The texts are based on existing editions but with departures. (2) B. Marzullo, *Aristofane: Le commedie* (Rome 1968, 1982², 1989³, 2003⁴).

[27]   In 1969, with D. M. Jones, the scholia to *Knights* (Part I.2); in 1975, the scholia to *Acharnians* (Part I B).

A papyrus codex of Menander "discovered" in Egypt and acquired by Martin Bodmer after World War II originally contained three plays. *Dyskolos,* almost in its entirety (thus a first for Menander), was published in 1958 by the Swiss papyrologist Victor Martin as *Papyrus Bodmer IV*; Handley's important edition was published in 1965. *Samia* and *Aspis,* with mutilated text at the beginning of the former and at the end of the latter, were published by Kasser and Austin in 1969 as *Papyrus Bodmer XXV* and *XXVI*; Austin published a critical edition of the two plays in the Kleine Texte series that same year. Discoveries made in Paris from a different papyrus led to an editio princeps of *Sikyonios* in 1964 by A. Blanchard and A. Bataille. These, of course, were the "second wave" of grand Menandrian discoveries in the twentieth century—the earlier one arrived with Lefebvre's publication of the Cairo codex in 1907 (see Blanchard, chapter 11, and Bathrellou, appendix 1, this volume). First appraisals of *Dyskolos* that stepped beyond the important critique of text are especially good reminders of the sometimes long digestive period required for the absorption of a new work (e.g., how it fits into the corpus, or how it illumines New Comedy dramaturgy generally) and a learning tool for reimagining a territory once unmarked and whose early routes and trailblazers have sometimes been forgotten. P. W. Harsh, writing a review of Victor Martin's editio princeps in 1959, found the play vastly inferior to *Epitrepontes,* dramaturgically flawed, and, on the basis of comparison with Terence's *Adelphoe* (modeled on a "developed" Menandrian original), argued that *Dyskolos's* inferiority was due to the playwright's inexperience (*Gnomon* 31: 577–86). L. A. Post, writing a review of the same edition in the same year, was more enthralled; far from seeing dramaturgic flaws, he could exclaim, "Each episode is not only a surprise itself but leads to future surprises and delights" (*AJPh* 80: 402–15 at 405). *Dyskolos* is a brilliant, fast-moving play, calling for agile acting, something that contemporary audiences (of the mid-twentieth century), accustomed, as Post put it, to such slow-paced reflective plays as Beckett's *Waiting for Godot,* might incorrectly associate with farce (ibid. 404–405). Still, Post seemed to think the play would not have been to everyone's taste in the late fourth century, and so he pondered, "Was Menander's victory, his first, due to the plaudits of the multitude, or had Demetrius introduced a reform urged by Plato (*Laws,* II, 659 A–C) and emboldened the judges to disregard applause and decide the merits of the play by philosophic standards?"(ibid. 402).[28] Post opted for Demetrius's legislative intervention; the audience may not have enjoyed the play, but the judges knew better. Political interpretation, via an extraneous door (a soaring inference based on Plato's *Laws* to explain an imagined negative audience response to a play that only the morally attuned minds of imaginary finer men might appreciate!), stood at the head of the hermeneutic enterprise. More sophisticated interpretations would arrive by the end of the next decade.[29] Nonetheless, here at the outset, we see an interest in the original

---

[28] Similarly, Barigazzi 1959 had seen the influence of Demetrius of Phalerum.

[29] E.g., Keuls's "Mystery Elements in Menander's *Dyscolus*" (1969), with its focus on the δίκελλα (double-pronged hoe) as symbol of rustic hard labor with "overtones of penance or moral improvement" (213); the double-pronged hoe is found on Hellenistic gems and is often combined with shackles, an aspect of the Eros and Psyche myth that, in Menander's play, establishes a tie with the dream vision of Sostratus's mother as well as with mystery and cultic symbolism (214).

spectators, even if without any attempt to sort out methodically who those spectators might have been.

F. H. Sandbach would publish in 1972 a new critical edition (Oxford Classical Text) of the longer extant plays and fragments found in the direct (papyri) and indirect (book quotations) traditions.[30] His commentary followed in the next year; in it, he used but heavily revised Gomme's notes and typescript of a commentary on *Heros, Epitrepontes, Perikeiromene*, and *Samia* (Gomme died in 1959—he had seen the text of *Dyskolos* but not written on it: Sandbach 1973, p. v),[31] and he extended its reach to include new finds not only from the Bodmer Papyri (*Dyskolos, Samia, Aspis*) but also from new papyri sources (e.g., *Sikyonioi, Dis Exapaton*). In 1990, Sandbach published a revised edition with an Appendix comprised of recently discovered and important fragments (esp. of *Epitrepontes* and *Misoumenos*). Arnott in his three-volume critical edition with verse translation for the Loeb series (1979, 1996, 2000) added *Leukadia*, scraps of *Synaristosai* (from recent papyrus finds), and *Encheiridion* (from earlier papyrus finds, but with argument for ascription in 1979: 358–64); he also added nine *Fabulae Incertae* (Sandbach had included but one), newly ascribed to Menander though with varying degrees of likelihood. This major accrual to Menander's oeuvre that had begun in the late fifties (and that has now been published together with new finds in Arnott's Loeb volumes) is not the end of the story—and not least because new finds (e.g., additions to *Epitrepontes*) have been discovered since then (see Bathrellou's Appendix to this volume), but also because, once again, this is not a story (only) about the text of Menander; another rerouting is warranted.

For this, we turn to interesting developments that were taking place in Plautine studies in Italy. After writing a number of essays in the late 1950s and early '60s on textual and metrical matters in Menander, Plautus, and Terence, C. Questa published in 1967 what soon became a standard reference work on Plautine meters, *Introduzione alla metrica di Plauto* (Bologna); forty years later (a span that has become familiar in the course of this essay!), he produced an amplified work, *La metrica di Plauto e di Terenzio* (Urbino 2007), and this, too, has quickly become a standard work of reference. In the interval between the two (in fact, a bit before the publication of the first), Questa and colleagues undertook detailed studies of the text of Plautus. Questa supervised editions with Italian

---

[30] Other important editions of Menandrian plays appeared after the editio princeps of *Dyskolos*; thus, e.g.: D. del Corno, vol. I (Milan 1967), without *Samia* and *Aspis*, with Italian prose translation; J. M. Jacques (Budé) I.1 *Samia*, 1971; I. 2 *Dyskolos*, 2nd ed. 1976.

[31] See also M. F. McGregor's review of Gomme's commentary on Thucydides, vols. I–III, "completed the day before the news came of A. W. Gomme's death, after a long illness, on January 18 [1959]": *Phoenix* 13 [1959]: 58–68.); A. Andrewes and K. J. Dover completed the commentary (vols. IV and V, 1970, 1981). This is an apt point to observe the profound hybrid proficiency of these and other scholars (historians/philologists) and the length of their careers: Gomme (publications begin in 1925); Dover (in 1950); MacDowell (in 1959). D. M. Lewis, primarily an epigraphist and historian (1952 dissertation, "Towards an Historian's Text of Thucydides"), revised *DFA* with J. Gould and wrote occasional reviews and learned notes on "literary" texts (1983, 1984, 1987).

translations of *Pseudolus* (1983), *Casina* (1988), *Trinummus* (1993), *Asinaria* (1994), *Amphitryo* (2002), *Persa* (2003), *Mercator* (2004), and *Stichus* (2008), all published by the Biblioteca Universale Rizzoli; he also inaugurated the important and critical Sarsina series in 2001 with an edition of *Casina* that has now been followed by six Plautine texts, including his own text of *Bacchides* in 2008. This was the third edition that Questa had produced of the play; the first appeared in 1965 (Florence: Sansoni)—interestingly, the very same year as Handley had published his edition of *Dyskolos*. As every classical scholar knows, a remarkable—nay, an absolutely sensational—event had taken place a few years after the appearance of Questa's 1965 edition of *Bacchides*, namely, Handley's first but partial publication of *Dis Exapaton* ("Twice a Swindler") in *Menander and Plautus: A Study in Comparison* (Inaugural Lecture, University College, London, 1968); surely here is an "aha!" moment in the history of Menandrian/Plautine scholarship. The recovered verses (lines 11–30 and 91–112) provided the most extended piece of extant Greek text for which a Roman adaptation is available (it is the model for *Bacchides* 494–562: see Fontaine, chapter 26, this volume for discussion and references).[32] Questa published a review of Handley's text that same year (*RFIC* 96: 502) and followed with a second edition of *Bacchides* in 1975 (Florence: Sansoni), reprinting Sandbach's (i.e., Handley's) text in an appendix with minor changes and a much expanded introduction to Plautus's play. A quarter of a century later, R. Raffaelli and A. Tontini edited a volume of essays on *Bacchides* in the Sarsina series (*Bacchides: Sarsina, 9 settembre 2000*, Lecturae Plautinae Sarsinates 4, Urbino: QuattroVenti, 2001). It is not surprising to find the names of two Englishmen among the contributors, E. W. Handley and J. A. Barsby—the latter, inter alia, had published an Aris and Phillips edition of *Bacchides* in 1986 with the new text of *Dis Exapaton* tucked into an appendix at the end. Given Questa's publication of the third edition of *Bacchides* (in the Sarsina series) and its dedication to Handley in 2008, one can't help but wonder: what went on behind the scenes before, during, and after the colloquium that spawned the volume that appeared in 2001? Whatever it may have been, the exchange of scholarship has been a boon to classical studies.

FRAGMENTS

Another "monumental project" commenced in 1974 with the publication of C. Austin's *Comicorum graecorum fragmenta in papyris reperta* (*CGFP*, Berlin: de Gruyter). This was a collection of papyri fragments of Greek comedy, serving as a prelude to a

---

[32] Handley provided Sandbach with a lengthier provisional text for the 1972 OCT, adding lines 47–63 and 89–90; Handley published the "definitive" text in 1997 (P.Oxy. 4407, with altered readings of already published verses and additions to fragmentary lines 1–10, 31–46, 64–88, and 113). Before the first publication of *Dis Exapaton* in 1968, the previous "record holder" (lengthiest extant Greek text with Roman adaptation) was Menander *Plokion* K-A fr. 296, with sixteen verses of Caecilius's fragmentary play (both preserved by Aulus Gellius 2.23.8).

completely modernized corpus that would replace the earlier collections: A. Meineke's *Fragmenta Comicorum Graecorum* (*FCG*, Berlin 1839–1857), T. Kock's *Comicorum Atticorum Fragmenta* (*CAF*, Leipzig 1880–1888), and J. Edmonds's *The Fragments of Attic Comedy* (*FAC*, Leiden 1957–1961). The first of these early editions was outstanding for its day; the second was much beholden to Meineke but had the independent virtue, at least, of supplying the fragments with continuous numbers; Edmonds's text, alleged apparatus criticus, and notes were appalling—nonetheless, its English verse translation drew followers, especially among those unacquainted with the Greek language.[33] The first volume of the new collective edition *Poetae Comici Graeci* (*PCG*, but abbreviated in this volume as K-A when associated with a particular ancient author or text), was edited by C. Austin and R. Kassel and appeared in 1983 (Vol. IV). There were to be eleven fascicles in all; so far, eight have appeared, all edited by the same twosome: *PCG* IV Aristophon–Crobylus (1983); III.2 fragments of Aristophanes (1984); V Damoxenous–Magnes (1986); VII Menecrates–Xenophon (1989); II Agathenor–Aristonymus (1991); VIII *Adespota* (1995); VI.2 fragments of Menander (1998); I *Comoedia dorica, mimi, phlyaces* (2001). In most volumes, the comic authors appear in alphabetic rather than in a (largely unattested and unverifiable) chronological order; Epicharmus and Sicilian poets comprise the first volume. Each has its standouts, by quantity and quality of material: thus Alexis, Antiphanes, and Archedicus in Vol. II; Cratinus and Crates in Vol. IV; Diphilus, Eubulus, and Eupolis in Vol. V; Pherecrates, Platon, Philemon, and that dynamic political duo Philippides and Timocles in Vol. VII. The *Adespota* in Vol. VIII beckon for identification, not only of author, but even as comedy: twenty texts in the volume stand with an asterisk before their number, indicating the editors' doubts. By the original plan, the volume of fragments of Aristophanes in III.2 was to be complemented, eventually, by III.1, the extant plays of Aristophanes; and VI.2, the fragments of Menander, by VI.1, an edition of the more fully preserved plays.[34] A volume of Indices was planned to conclude

[33] See Kassel's review, *Gnomon* 34 [1962]: 554–556, and the general overview of the three editions in Hunter, *JHS* 104 [1984]: 224–225. Another projected "collective" edition had a premature finish: Georg Kaibel only completed the first fascicle of his *Comicorum Graecorum Fragmenta* I.1 (1899) before his death in 1901; this provided exemplary treatment of Doric comedy and especially Epicharmus. His unpublished notes on the fragments of Old Comedy were made available to Kassel and Austin (Wilson *CR*, n.s., 26 [1976]: 15) and served well in *PCG* III.2 Aristophanes. J. Demiańczuk's *Supplementum Comicorum* (Krakow: Nakładem Akademii Umiejętności, 1912) provided additions to Kock and Kaibel. Earlier publications of *single* fragmentary authors or fragmentary plays (e.g., Pieters 1946 and Luppe 1963 on Cratinus; Plepelits 1970 on the *Demoi* of Eupolis; Hunter 1983 on Eubulus) were available before *PCG* but do not appear to have been numerous; see the useful bibliography (supervised by Prof. Lucía Rodríguez-Noriega Guillén from the University of Oviedo in Spain) at www.lnoriega.es/comedy.html ("Bibliography on the Greek fragmentary fifth-century comedy"), beginning with a list of editions and translations, followed by works on individual fragmentary authors (accessed Dec. 18, 2012).
[34] *PCG* VI.2 replaces Koerte-Thierfelder, that is, vol. II of A. Koerte's Teubner edition of Menander, revised after his death by A. Thiefelder in 1953, with a second edition in 1959. At the time of Colin Austin's death in 2010, he was working on a new edition of Menander that would include all the plays not included in *PCG* VI 2. He was able to complete his version of eleven shorter pieces and that edition appeared in 2013 (see bibliography); it includes an autobiographical preface recounting the renowned scholar's first acquaintance with Menander. An editorial group plans to complete his work (Austin

the project. The publication of *PCG* has quickly and effectively become both goad and anchor for subsequent studies such as Arnott's commentary on Alexis, published in 1996 (which, not surprisingly, as reported in the preface, he began researching in 1953), and more recent studies, including Aristophanes's rivals (Harvey and Wilkins 2000, Storey 2003, Telò 2007, Napolitano 2012), later comic authors (Papachrysostomou 2008, Orth 2009, Pirrotta 2009, Bruzzese 2011), and both earlier and later poets combined (Belardinelli 1998, Olson 2007).[35]

The quality and exemplary presentation of the fragments in *PCG* has moreover encouraged new translations. Henderson's volume of Aristophanes's fragments in the Loeb series has already been mentioned (2007). I. C. Storey's three-volume edition of the fragments of Old Comedy (excepting Aristophanes) in the same series (2011) is another offshoot. Both editors retain *PCG*'s numbering of the fragments, so that the projects are interconnected. Another new translation source (without Greek text) is the monumental singleton *The Birth of Comedy: Texts, Documents, and Art from Athenian Comic Competitions, 486–20*, edited by J. Rusten with translations of his own and also many contributed by J. Henderson, D. Konstan, R. Rosen, and N. Slater. This is a remarkable florilegium of fragmentary and tantalizing tidbits small and large from scores of comic poets, with plenty of commentary (ancient and modern) and illustrations to envision performance; it is a book of the times, capturing the trends and industry of the scholarship of this and the last century.[36]

An edition of the fragments of tragedy, *Tragicorum Graecorum Fragmenta (TrGF)*, must also be mentioned: its publication parallels that of the fragments of comedy over the last three decades of the twentieth century (*CGFP* in 1974 and the volumes of *PCG* spanning 1983–2001). It began with B. Snell's volume of (inter alia) didascalic notices for tragedy and fragments of "minor tragic poets" in 1971 and concluded with Kannicht's two fascicles of Euripides in 2004. A revised edition of Snell's first volume appeared in 1986,[37] and second editions of other volumes appeared later (Sophocles in 1999, *Adespota* in 2007, Aeschylus in 2008). Translations of tragic fragments in the Loeb series were not long to follow: Sophocles in 1996 (Lloyd-Jones), Euripides in two volumes in 2008 and 2009 (Collard and Cropp); Aeschylus in 2009 (Sommerstein). The number of attested

---

2013, "Editorial note," iii). Austin's final publication appeared after the essays in this volume had been submitted to the press.

[35] A new "monumental project" called Kommentierung der Fragmente der griechischen Komödie is another offshoot of *PCG* and is now underway in Freiburg under the direction of Bernhard Zimmermann under the auspices of the Heidelberger Akademie der Wissenschaften; it aims to produce a series (named *Studia Comica*) of commentaries on the fragments of Greek comedies. Thus far, four volumes have been published: those by Pirotta, Orth, and Napolitano mentioned in the text above, as well as one by S. Schirru (2009).

[36] Plautus's fragments have now appeared in vol. 5 (2012) of the Loeb edition translated by W. de Melo. The same press is spearheading a "new Warmington," to be called *Fragmentary Republican Latin*, planned for nine volumes, with Gesine Manuwald as editor of the new series.

[37] A new edition of the *Didascaliae*, the Fasti, and the Victors Lists was published by B. Millis and S. D. Olson in 2012: *Inscriptional Records for the Dramatic Festivals in Athens: IG II2 2318–2325 and Related Texts* (Brill).

"minor tragic poets" is comparable to the number of comic poets, though the fragments themselves are lesser in extent. The near parity of projects in tragedy and comedy could be extended beyond the collections of fragmentary texts and translations: there have been new editions of Aeschylus, Sophocles, and Euripides throughout these decades, as well as a vigorous interest in performance (including theater paraphernalia) and reception. When we think of future grand projects, we should be thinking of comedy and tragedy together.[38] And we should also be considering the implications of the vast fragmentary terrain and ways to incorporate it into our map of ancient drama.

THE *LONGUE DURÉE*

The absence of a definitive chronology for texts in *PCG* is both provocative and cautious: it beckons future users to discover ways to date its unanchored poets and plays and to heed new finds that may provide assistance, and it cautions against arbitrary and precipitate assignments. B. Millis (Appendix 2, this volume), working with the epigraphic tradition and literary dates provided in *PCG,* points out that whereas "almost exactly half of the ca. 250 poets in *PCG* postdate Menander," yet our modern "understanding of the genre's trends and development is focused on barely a quarter of a tradition that lasted nearly a millennium" (similarly Henderson 1995, 175). Of those many post-Menandrian comic poets, Millis can signal a handful of names of comic writers who composed in the first two centuries CE (Amphichares, Antiochus, Antiphon, Anubion, Onesicles).[39] This provides important emphasis: that comedies were being newly composed and performed so long after the deaths of Menander and Philemon and Philippides in the third century BCE, and that comedy remained a thriving genre for centuries (and tragedy as well: Jones 1993)—even if not in Athens, where attestation of dramatic competitions at the Dionysia are secure for 155/4 but almost certainly lasted until the mid-140s or 130s.[40] Important, too, is Millis's observation that our critical

---

[38] Two projects have been funded by the Australian Research Council at the University of Sydney: "Accounting for the Ancient Theatre: A New Social and Economic History of Classical Greek Drama" (2005–5009) and "The Theatrical Revolution: The Expansion of Theatre outside Athens" (2010–2014). The principal researchers, Eric Csapo and Peter Wilson, plan eventually to publish a two- or three-volume collection of documents (edited, translated, and with full commentary) called *Historical Documents for the Greek Theatre Down to 300 BC.*

[39] The ballpark dates are based on epigraphic attestations in *PCG* for Amphichares, Antiphon, Anubion, and Onesicles (all four for performances); additionally, there is literary attestation for the posthumous production of a play composed by Germanicus (Suet. *Cal.* 3.2; *Claud.* 11.2). Another poet, Apollonaris, is given literary attestation (Sozem. *Hist. eccl.* 5.18.2 [p. 222.5 Bidez]) for the fourth century CE, but no attestation for the staging of his work. See Millis Appendix 2, below.

[40] The calculation is based on the number of entries missing in the text of IG II² 2323.524–582 compared with IG II² 2325C (comic poets victorious at the Dionysia), Millis and Olson 2012: 76, 84,144). A similar dating for the Lenaea is suggested by IG II² 2325E (comic poets victorious at the Lenaea) and,

view of comedy has been distorted by focusing on a mere quarter of its production. Such observations on the long tradition of drama from epigraphic and literary evidence are consonant, of course, with the picture of the tradition that has emerged from archaeological finds, including the study of vases, figurines, and other objects where the material survives into the sixth century.[41] It is, indeed, a *longue durée*.

The establishment of this period with all its rich furniture of texts and artifacts is the legacy of the projects that commenced in the fiercely kinetic decades of the '60s and '70s or of important published volumes that got a second hurrah (e.g., the triadic edition of Webster's *Monuments* in 1960–1962 and Pickard-Cambridge 1968, to name just two) during those decades. The grand vista, temporal and geographical, has been observed by specialists now and again for decades (Webster 1948, Csapo 1986, Taplin 1987a and 1987b, Henderson 1995, Green 2000, Csapo 2000, Le Guen 2001, Aneziri 2003). From these perspectives, does periodization still make sense? We can put a magnifying glass on fragmentary comic texts of the fourth century BCE, we can point to a heyday for the predominance of mythological themes and for extension of the role of cooks, we can chart the rise and fall and once again the rise and fall of political invective, and we can make observations here and there about the use of meter and less certain ones on the disappearance (and late [re]appearance) of the chorus and willy-nilly make a case for an evolution from Old to Middle to New Comedy. Now this might suffice, as apparently it did for Aristophanes of Byzantium, for comedy as it was composed from ca. the 480s until ca. 210 (when the Byzantine scholar may have been ca. fifty years old); it might suffice, if one stopped looking at comedy then and there. We might then recognize these designations as some kind of "Old Speak." But from a tradition of drama that extends for another 500 years, what are we to make of it?

Many of the authors in this volume address this and like questions. Some do so when they query canon formation or when they notice continuities and predominant styles in different periods rather than abrupt changes, or when they see Roman comedy in much greater proximity to Greek. Surely one feature to think more about in the future is the significance of revival productions. Should we consider Roman comedy a particular type of "revival comedy" of enormous creativity? And what do revival performances

---

to a lesser extent, IG II² 2325F (comic actors victorious at the Lenaea). Le Guen (chapter 17) cites a new composition performed at the Rhomaia festival at Magnesia-on-Maeander in the first half of the first century BCE (p. 562), as well as later Greek performances well into the second century CE in the West (pp. 569–570).

[41] These late materials probably do not correspond to productions of plays—theater performances are not attested this late—but rather other forms of entertainment (e.g., recitations, solo singers). I. E. Stefanis, Διονυσιακοὶ Τεχνῖται. Συμβολὲς στὴν προσωπογραφία τοῦ θεάτρου καὶ τῆς μουσικῆς τῶν ἀρχαίων Ἑλλήνων (Heraklion, 1988) is an annotated catalogue in alphabetical order of 3,023 persons (nos. 2994–3023 are anonymous) who performed in Greek theatrical *and* musical contests and as ἀκροάματα ("entre-act" performers) in the period 500 BCE–500 CE in the Greek and Roman world; see SEG 38 1934. For detailed study of the Dionysiac *technitai* in the Hellenistic era, see Aneziri 2003 and Le Guen 2001; Le Guen in this volume considers evidence for an agonistic circuit in the time of Hadrian.

mean for contemporary artistic enterprises? How do they fit with the production of "theater art"—the commercialization or memorialization of drama on vases and mosaics and terracotta figurines? Do their meanings shift in time?

The 2010s are a watershed moment in the history of comedy scholarship. Comedy's 2,500th birthday is at hand. Celebrate!

* * *

This volume of essays is the first comprehensive introduction and reference work that presents the *longue dureé* of comedy, from its beginnings in Greece to its end in Rome, as well as its Hellenistic and Imperial receptions. Roman comedy is vitally connected to Greek comedy, by temporal and geographical proximities that permitted cultural and commercial exchanges that surely extended in both directions. Transmission and reception are an important part of this story, and not only in later ages but from its beginnings. Evidence for reception is discussed from a variety of perspectives, e.g., Eric Csapo, Andronike Makres, Brigitte Le Guen, and Benjamin Millis discuss different theatrical venues in Attica and elsewhere (and thus the early "reception" of Greek comedy outside Athens). Both Le Guen and Millis offer detailed studies of the evidence for the continuous existence and "travel" of comedy in the Mediterranean. Other authors examine Greek comedy's own reception of other genres: Johanna Hanink considers its absorption of tragedy and satyr play, David Konstan its absorption of contemporary philosophy, and Costas Panayotakis the reception of Hellenistic mime in Rome.

Indeed, the reception of Greek comedy in Rome has been a controversial question forever, or so it seems. Antonis Petrides offers a fresh analysis of previous scholarship on the question of Plautus's relationship both to Greek comedy and Atellan farce and uses Plautus's deployment of masks to suggest a corrective to current views on the "triadic" model (Plautus's originality, and his use of Greek and Italian models). Michael Fontaine takes up these issues in his chapters on Plautus and Terence and offers a new way of seeing Terence, that is, through a Hellenistic and neoteric lens. Gesine Manuwald examines Roman comedy's reception of tragedy and paratragedy.

Emphasis on reception is of a piece with the times, and so it is that the final segment of the volume puts together essays both on the transmission of comedy texts from their first appearance as scripts and also on their reception in later eras. Nigel Wilson's "Introduction" to his *Aristophanea* appears here (exceptionally, as the other pieces in this volume are here published for the first time) and provides a short history of the text of Aristophanes. Heinze-Günther Nesselrath discusses the reception of both Attic Middle and New Comedy in Hellenistic and Imperial times, with special attention to Athenaeus as a principal conduit. Walter Stockert literally examines the Ambrosian Palimpsest of Plautus, and Benjamin Victor presents the textual history of Terence. Two authors present the reception of comedy during the Second Sophistic: Regina Höschele discusses the reception of Greek comedy in the novel and epistolography and Regine May the reception of Roman comedy in both grammarians and literary authors, above all Apuleius. Sebastiana Nervegna presents a lively discussion of New Comedy's "graphic reception" in Menandrian mosaics and Terentian miniatures. The segment ends with two complementary essays, one on Plautus's reception in antiquity by Rolando Ferri and the other on Donatus's commentary on Terence's comedies by Chrysanthi Demetriou—a fit finale, as Demetriou puts at the forefront of her essay the controversial question of Donatus's familiarity with contemporary theater, and thus shows the vibrancy of reception studies.

Also consonant with contemporary trends is the number of authors who pursue studies of performance and the economics of performance in this volume. Eric Csapo, Andronike Makres, George Frederick Franko, and Erica Bexley all make important contributions to these subjects for both Greek and Roman comedy.

It would be a mistake to think that all is reception and performance, pervasive as those strands of comedy scholarship are today. As noted earlier, some authors examine canon formation (Mario Telò), others notice continuities and predominant styles in different periods rather than abrupt changes (Ian Storey, Ioannis Konstantakos, Jeffrey Henderson, Adele Scafuro, Wolfgang de Melo). The origins of Greek and Roman comedy are examined by Jeffrey Rusten and Peter Brown, respectively. Major and not-so-major playwrights are discussed (Storey, Telò, Zimmermann, Konstantakos, Henderson, Scafuro, de Melo, Fontaine). Metrics, music, and language are given significant hearings not only in separate chapters devoted to those topics by Marcus Deufert and Evangelos Karakasis but also in the chapters devoted to major playwrights (Zimmermann, Scafuro, Fontaine). Alain Blanchard's chapter discusses the difficulties of the varied evidence for reconstructing Menander's plays and the perilous foundations for determining the playwright's theatrical practices.

Social, political, and religious spheres are not neglected: David Rosenbloom discusses the politicians who figure in Greek comedy, while Erich Gruen presents the "social scene" of Roman comedy; Emiliano Buis discusses law and Greek comedy, while Jan Felix Gaertner discusses law and Roman comedy; Scott Scullion discusses religion in Greek comedy, and Boris Dunsch discusses it in Roman comedy.

Eftychia bathrellou provides an informative appendix, noting comic papyri texts found between 1973 and 2010 and annotating some of the most interesting finds. Benjamin Millis' appendix provides a checklist of Greek comic poets who postdate Menander; the significance of this list and of Millis's observations about it has been mentioned earlier in this introduction.

Adele C. Scafuro
January 1, 2013
Spring Lake Heights, NJ

BIBLIOGRAPHY

Bibliographic note: Books that have been cited by title, author, and year of publication in the course of this essay are not repeated here; likewise articles that are fully cited (esp. reviews). J. T. Hooker has provided a list of 341 items written by Webster in Studies in Honour of T. B. L. Webster, Vol. I (eds. J. H. Betts, J. T. Hooker, and J. R. Green), 1986: xiii– xxiii (Bristol).

Adams, J. N. 1972. "Latin Words for Woman and Wife." *Glotta* 50: 234–255.

——. 1984. "Female Speech in Latin Comedy." *Antichthon* 18: 43–77.

Aneziri, S. 2003. *Die Vereine der dionysischen Techniten im Kontext der hellenistischen Gesellschaft: Untersuchungen zur Geschichte, Organisation und Wirkung der hellenistischen Technitenvereine.* Historia Einzelschriften 163. Stuttgart: F. Steiner.

Arnott, W. G. 1970. "'*Phormio Parasitus*': A Study in Dramatic Methods of Characterization." *G&R*, 2nd ser., 17: 32–57.

——.1972. "Targets, Techniques and Traditions in Plautus' *Stichus.*" *BICS* 19: 54–79.

——.1996a. *Alexis: The Fragments: A Commentary.* Cambridge, UK: Cambridge University Press.

Austin, C. 2013. *Menander: Eleven Plays.* Cambridge: Proceedings of the Cambridge Philological Society, Suppl. volume 37.

Bain, D. 1984. "Female Speech in Menander." *Antichthon* 18: 24–42.

Barigazzi, A. 1959. "Il *Dyscolos* di Menandro o la commedia della solidarietà umana." *Athenaeum* 37: 184–195.

Barsby, J. A. "Improvvisazione, metateatro, decostruzione." In *Bacchides (Sarsina, 9 settembre 2000),* edited by R. Raffaelli and A. Tontini, 51–70. Lecturae Plautinae Sarsinates 4. Urbino: QuattroVenti.

Belardinelli, A. M., O. Imperio, G. Mastromarco, M. Pellegrino, and P. Totaro. 1998. *Tessere: Frammenti della commedia greca: Studi e commenti.* Bari: Adriatica.

Tessere: Frammenti della commedia greca: Studi e commenti. Bari: Adriatica.

Bruzzese, L. 2011. *Studi su Filemone comico.* Lecce: Pensa Multimedia.

Csapo, E. 1986. "A Note on the Würzburg Bell-Crater H5697 ('Telephus Travestitus')." *Phoenix* 40: 379–392.

——. 2000. "From Aristophanes to Menander? Genre Transformation in Greek Comedy." In *Matrices of Genre: Authors, Canons, and Society,* edited by M. Depew and D. Obbink, 115–133 and 271–276. Cambridge, MA: Harvard University Press.

Dickey, E. 2007. *Ancient Greek Scholarship: A Guide to Finding, Reading, and Understanding Scholia, Commentaries, Lexica and Grammatical Treatises, from their Beginnings to the Byzantine Period.* New York and Oxford: Oxford University Press.

Dickinson, P. 1957. *Aristophanes against War: The Acharnians, The Peace, Lysistrata.* Oxford: Oxford University Press.

Fantham, E. 1965. "The *Curculio* of Plautus: An Illustration of Plautine Methods in Adaptation." *CQ* 15: 84–100.

——. 1975. "Sex, Status, and Survival in Hellenistic Athens: A Study of Women in New Comedy." *Phoenix* 29: 44–74.

Foley, H. P. 1981. "The Concept of Women in Athenian Drama." In *Reflections of Women in Antiquity,* edited by H. P. Foley, 117–168. New York: Gordon and Breach Science Publishers.

Fontaine, M. 2010. *Funny Words in Plautine Comedy.* Oxford: Oxford University Press.

Fraenkel, E. 1950. *Agamemnon, I, II, III,* Oxford: Clarendon Press.

Gebhard, E. 1974. "The Form of the Orchestra in the Early Greek Theater." *Hesperia* 4: 428–440.

Gilleland, M. 1979. "The Linguistic Differentiation of Character Type and Sex in the Comedies of Plautus and Terence." PhD diss., University of Virginia. (*Non vidi.*)

——. 1980. "Female Speech in Greek and Latin." *AJPh* 101: 180–183.

Goldberg, S. M. 1998. "Plautus on the Palatine." *JRS* 88: 1–20.

Gratwick, A. S. 1969. "The *Poenulus* of Plautus and Its Attic Original." PhD diss., University of Oxford.

Green, J. R. 1985. "Drunk Again: A Study in the Iconography of the Comic Theater." *AJA* 89: 465–473.

——1991. "On Seeing and Depicting the Theatre in Classical Athens." *GRBS* 32: 15–50.

——1994. *Theatre in Ancient Greek Society*. London: Routledge.

——. 2000. "Forty Years of Theatre Research and Its Future Directions." In *Theatre: Ancient and Modern: Selected Proceedings of a Two-Day International Research Conference Hosted by the Department of Classical Studies, Faculty of Arts, the Open University, Milton Keynes, 5th and 6th January 1999*, edited by L. Hardwick, P. Easterling, S. Ireland, N. Lowe, and F. MacIntosh, 1–20. Milton Keynes, UK: The Open University. Available online at www2.open.ac.uk/ClassicalStudies/GreekPlays/Conf99/index.htm (accessed Dec. 12, 2012).

——. 2001. "Comic Cuts: Snippets of Action on the Greek Comic Stage." *BICS* 45: 37–64.

Green, J. R., and E. W. Handley. 1995. *Images of the Greek Theatre*. London: British Museum Publications.

——. 2000. "Gnomic Gnathia." In *Skenika: Beiträge zum antiken Theater und seiner Rezeption: Festschrift zum 65. Geburtstag von Horst-Dieter Blume*, edited by S. Gödde and Th. Heinze, 247–252. Darmstadt: Wissenschaftliche Buchgesellschaft.

——. 2001. "The Rover's Return: A Literary Quotation on a Pot in Corinth." *Hesperia* 70: 367–371.

Handley, E. W. 1990. "The Bodmer Menander and the Comic Fragments." In *Relire Ménandre*, edited by E. W. Handley and A. Hurst, 123–148. Geneva: Droz.

——. 1993. "Aristophanes and his Theatre." In *Aristophane: Sept exposés suivis de discussions*, by Enzo Degani, et al., 97–123. Entretiens sur l'antiquité classique 38. Geneva: Fondation Hardt.

——. 2000. "The Ancient Greek Theatre: Tradition, Image and Reality." *BAB*, 6th ser., 11: 269–301.

——. 2001. "*Actoris opera*: Words, Action and Acting in *Dis Exapaton* and *Bacchides*." In *Bacchides (Sarsina, 9 settembre 2000)*, edited by R. Raffaelli and A. Tontini, 13–36. Lecturae Plautinae Sarsinates 4. Urbino: QuattroVenti.

——. 2002. "Acting, Action and Words in New Comedy." In *Greek and Roman Actors: Aspects of an Ancient Profession*, edited by P. Easterling and E. Hall, 165–188. Cambridge, UK: Cambridge University Press.

——.2003. "Thomas Bertram Lonsdale Webster 1905–1974." *Proceedings of the British Academy* 120: 445–67.

Hardwick, L. 2010. "*Lysistratas* on the Modern Stage." In *Looking at Lysistrata: Eight Essays and a New Version of Aristophanes' Provocative Comedy*, edited by D. Studdard, 80–89. London: Bristol Classical Press.

Harvey, D., and J. Wilkins, eds. 2000. *The Rivals of Aristophanes: Studies in Athenian Old Comedy*. London: Duckworth and the Classical Press of Wales.

Henderson, Jeffrey. 1993. "Translating Aristophanes for Performance." In *Intertextualität in der griechisch-römischen Komödie*, edited by N. W. Slater and B. Zimmermann, 81–92. Stuttgart: M & P.

——_. 1995. Beyond Aristophanes." In *Beyond Aristophanes: Tradition and Diversity in Greek Comedy*, ed. G.W. Dobrov, 175–83. Atlanta: Scholars Press.

Hunter, R. L. 1983. *Eubulus: The Fragments*. Cambridge, UK: Cambridge University Press.

Jones, C. P. 1993. "Greek Drama in the Roman Empire." In *Theater and Society in the Classical World*, edited by R. Scodel, 39–52. Ann Arbor: University of Michigan Press.

Keuls, E. 1969. "Mystery Elements in Menander's *Dyscolus*." *TAPhA* 100: 209–220.

Lefèvre, E. 1977. "Plautus-Studien: I: Der doppelte Geldkreislauf im Pseudolus." *Hermes* 105: 441–454.

Lewis, D. M. 1983. Review of *The Comedies of Aristophanes*, Vol. 2: *Knights*, by A. Sommerstein. *CR*, n.s., 33: 175–177.

——. 1984. "Further Notes on Page, *Further Greek Epigrams.*" *JHS* 104: 179–180.

——. 1987. "Bowie on Elegy: A Footnote." *JHS* 107: 188.

Ludwig, W. 1970. "Die plautinische *Cistellaria* und das Verhältnis von Gott und Handlung bei Menander." In *Ménandre: Sept exposés suivis de discussions,* edited by E. G. Turner, 43–110. Geneva: Fondation Hardt.

Le Guen, B. 2001. *Les associations de technites dionysiaques à l'époque hellénistique.* 2 vols. Nancy: Association pour la diffusion de la recherche sur l'antiquité.

Luppe, W. 1963. *Fragmente des Kratinos: Texte und Kommentar.* Halle: Martin-Luther-Universität.

Makres, A. 1994. "The Institution of *Choregia* in Classical Athens." PhD diss., University of Oxford.

Maltby, R. 1979. "Linguistic Characterization of Old Men in Terence." *CPh* 74: 136–147.

Millis, B. W., and S. D. Olson. 2012. *Inscriptional Records for the Dramatic Festivals in Athens:* IG II² 2318–2325 and Related Texts. Leiden and Boston: Brill.

Mueller, G. L. 1957. "Das Original des plautinischen Persa." PhD diss., Johann-Wolfgang-Goethe-Universität zu Frankfurt am Main.

Napolitano, M. 2012. *I Kolakes di Eupoli: Introduzione, traduzione, commento.* Studia Comici 4. Berlin: Verlag Antike.

Nervegna, S. 2007. "Staging Scenes or Plays? Theatrical Revivals of 'Old' Greek Drama in Antiquity." *ZPE* 162: 14–42.

Olson, S. D. 2007. *Broken Laughter: Select Fragments of Greek Comedy.* Oxford: Oxford University Press.

Orth, C. 2009. *Strattis: Die Fragmente: Ein Kommentar.* Studia Comica 2. Berlin: Verlag Antike.

Papachrysostomou, A. 2008. *Six Comic Poets: A Commentary on Selected Fragments of Middle Comedy.* Tübingen: Narr.

Pieters J. Th. M. F. 1946. *Cratinus. Bijdrage tot de geschiedenis der vroeg-attische comedie.* Leiden: Brill.

Pirrotta, S. 2009. *Plato Comicus: Die fragmentarischen Komödien: Ein Kommentar.* Studia Comica 1. Berlin: Verlag Antike.

Plepelits, K. 1970. *Die Fragmente der Demen des Eupolis.* Vienna: Verlag Notring.

Revermann, M. 2006. "The Competence of Theatre Audiences in Fifth- and Fourth-Century Athens." *JHS* 126: 99–124.

——. 2008. "Review Article: Reception Studies of Greek Drama." *JHS* 128: 175–178.

Schaaf, L. 1977. *Der Miles gloriosus des Plautus und sein griechisches Original: Ein Beitrag zur Kontaminationsfrage.* Munich: W. Fink.

Schirru, S. 2009. *La favola in Aristofane.* Studia Comica 3. Berlin: Verlag Antike.

Sommerstein, A. H. 1973. "On Translating Aristophanes: Ends and Means." *G&R* 20: 140–154.

——. 2006. "How Aristophanes Got His A&P." In *Playing around Aristophanes: Essays in Celebration of the Completion of the Edition of the Comedies of Aristophanes by Alan Sommerstein,* edited by L. Kozak and J. Rich, 126–139. Oxford: Aris & Phillips.

——. 2009. "The Language of Athenian Women." In *Talking about Laughter: And Other Studies in Greek Comedy,* by A. H. Sommerstein, 15–42 (with Addenda). Oxford. First published in 1995.

Storey, I. C. 2003. *Eupolis: Poet of Old Comedy.* Oxford: Oxford University Press.

Studdard, D. 2010. (ed.) *Looking at Lysistrata:Eight Essays and a New Version of Aristophanes' Provocative Comedy*. London: Bristol Classical Press.

Taplin, O. 1972. "Aeschylean Silences and Silences in Aeschylus." *HSCP* 76: 57–97.

——. 1987a. "*Phallology*, Phlyakes, Iconography and Aristophanes." *PCPhS* 33: 92–104.

——. 1987b. "Classical Phallology, Iconographic Parody, and Potted Aristophanes." *Dioniso* 57: 95–109.

Telò, M. 2007. *Eupolidis Demi*. Florence: F. Le Monnier.

Tränkle, H. 1972. "Micio und Demea in den terenzischen *Adelphen*." *MH* 29: 241–255.

Walton, J. M. 2010. "Where is the Spine?" In *Looking at Lysistrata Eight Essays and a New Version of Aristophanes' Provocative Comedy*, edited by D. Studdard, 11–19. London: Bristol Classical Press.

Webster, T. B. L. 1948. "South Italian Vases and Attic Drama." *CQ* 42: 15–27.

——. 1949. "The Masks of Greek Comedy." *Bulletin of the John Rylands Library* 32: 97–133.

——. 1951. "Masks on Gnathia Vases." JHS 7: 222–232.

——. 1952. "Notes on Pollux' List of Tragic Masks." In *Festschrift Andreas Rumpf, zum 60. Geburtstag dargebracht von Freunden und Schülern*, edited by T. Dohrn, 141–150. Krefeld: Scherpe.

——. 1954. "Greek Comic Costume." Bulletin of the John Rylands Library 36: 563–588.

——. 1955. "The Costume of the Actors in Aristophanic Comedy." *CQ*, n.s., 5: 94–95.

White, J. W. 1918. "Collations of the Manuscripts of Aristophanes' *Aves*." *HSCPh* 29: 77–131.

——. 1919. "Collations of the Manuscripts of Aristophanes' *Aves*, Part II." *HSCPh* 30: 1–35.

Wilson, P. 2000. *The Athenian Institution of the Khoregia: The Chorus, the City and the Stage*. Cambridge, UK: Cambridge University Press.

Zeitlin, F. 1981. "Travesties of Gender and Genre in Aristophanes' *Thesmophoriazousae*." In *Reflections of Women in Antiquity*, edited by H. P. Foley, 169– 217. New York: Gordon and Breach Science Publishers.

PART ONE

....

GREEK COMEDY

....

I

....

Beginnings

....

IN SEARCH OF THE ESSENCE OF OLD COMEDY: FROM ARISTOTLE'S *POETICS* TO ZIELIŃSKI, CORNFORD, AND BEYOND

JEFFREY RUSTEN

INTRODUCTION

THOUGH the history of tragedy as a genre is usually considered without reference to other genres, when it comes to comedy, whose very name is a derivative of tragedy's, scholars ancient and modern often seem unable to examine it as a genre except in tragedy's shadow. But right from its origins, the evidence for Athenian comedy shows some important differences from that for tragedy:

Its starting date, at the Dionysia in March 486 BCE, is precisely known (Rusten 2006: 37n3);

Old Comedy is far more commonly depicted in art, including its early stages;

Its extant plays are all those of a single author, at a much later period than for the first preserved tragedy;

Old Comedy was not in itself stable—its form changed even within the lifetime of Aristophanes, and did not become fixed until the age of Menander (first production 321, died 290/1 BCE).

The *historical* basis of the precursors of Greek comedy is in fact better documented today than for tragedy, and its history in outline of this period through three stages—"Old," "Middle," and "New" Comedy—is the basis of near-universal agreement. Furthermore, the last of these stages is well recognized as forming the basis, through its adaptations by Plautus and Terence, of a fairly homogeneous western tradition of dramatic comedy. But in contrast to what comes before and after, capturing the essence of "Old Comedy," a mixture of narrative chaos and formal complexity, grotesque obscenity and naive innocence, savage satire and high-minded optimism, is a greater challenge and has been undertaken in vastly different ways.

What are the assumptions that underlie both the Aristotelian and modern attempts to explain the appeal of Old Comedy? While certainly worth pursuing, universalizing theories of "comedy" or "the comic" in general are not at issue here. Rather, I will describe how various critics have tried to isolate the animating principle of Old Comedy and the extent to which their hypotheses account for—or fail to account for—the genre as we know it today.

1. ARISTOTLE'S APPROACH TO OLD COMEDY

The comic authors mentioned in the *Poetics* (apart from Epicharmus, Chionides, and Magnes as the earliest) are Aristophanes and Crates, and they are what we would call Old Comedy; but the tripartite division of authors into Old, New, and "Middle" Comedy would not at all suit Aristotle's methods, and he does not use the terms *archaios* or *neos* even for their relative dating.[1] This partition seems not to predate Hellenistic scholarship, perhaps having been framed by Aristophanes of Byzantium (Nesselrath 1990, Rusten 1991, and in this volume).[2]

In the *Poetics*, no literary genre remains completely independent (see especially Heath 1989b); each is connected by succession or opposition to every other. Old Comedy, despite seeming to us the most eccentric of genres, is nonetheless frequently subordinated to others in Aristotle's analysis. Here are the ways in which the *Poetics* considers comedy primarily as parallel or in opposition to tragedy:

1. Tragedy's *difference* from comedy can be seen in the sort of characters it depicts: better than real versus worse than real.
   (1448a16–19: ἐν αὐτῇ δὲ τῇ διαφορᾷ καὶ ἡ τραγῳδία πρὸς τὴν κωμῳδίαν διέστηκεν· ἡ μὲν γὰρ χείρους ἡ δὲ βελτίους μιμεῖσθαι βούλεται τῶν νῦν. "This very distinction separates tragedy from comedy: the latter tends to represent people inferior, the former superior, to existing humans.")[3]
2. Homer hinted at the form of comedy in dramatizing the ridiculous; *Margites* is to comedy as the *Iliad* and *Odyssey* are to tragedy.

---

[1] See *BOC* 579 Nr. 1. Aristotle does however use ἀρχαῖος/νέος of tragedy, *Poetics* 1450a25, 1450b7.

[2] For Old Comedy's authors and characteristics see *BOC* 81–92.

[3] This and all other translations from the *Poetics* are from Halliwell (1995).

(1448b35–a6: ὥσπερ δὲ καὶ τὰ σπουδαῖα μάλιστα ποιητὴς Ὅμηρος ἦν…οὕτως καὶ τὸ τῆς κωμῳδίας σχῆμα πρῶτος ὑπέδειξεν, οὐ ψόγον ἀλλὰ τὸ γελοῖον δραματοποιήσας· ὁ γὰρ Μαργίτης ἀνάλογον ἔχει, ὥσπερ Ἰλιὰς καὶ ἡ Ὀδύσσεια πρὸς τὰς τραγῳδίας, οὕτω καὶ οὗτος πρὸς τὰς κωμῳδίας. "Just as Homer was the supreme poet of elevated subjects…so too he was the first to delineate the forms of comedy, by dramatizing not invective but the laughable; thus *Margites* stands in the same relation to comedies as do the *Iliad* and *Odyssey* to tragedies.")

3. Iambic poets took up comedy, whereas epic poets took up tragedy.

(1449a2–6: παραφανείσης δὲ τῆς τραγῳδίας καὶ κωμῳδίας οἱ ἐφ' ἑκατέραν τὴν ποίησιν ὁρμῶντες κατὰ τὴν οἰκείαν φύσιν οἱ μὲν ἀντὶ τῶν ἰάμβων κωμῳδοποιοὶ ἐγένοντο, οἱ δὲ ἀντὶ τῶν ἐπῶν τραγῳδοδιδάσκαλοι, διὰ τὸ μείζω καὶ ἐντιμότερα τὰ σχήματα εἶναι ταῦτα ἐκείνων. "And when tragedy and comedy had been glimpsed, those whose own natures gave them an impetus towards either type of poetry abandoned iambic lampoons to become comic poets, or epic to become tragedians, because these newer forms were grander and more esteemed than the earlier.")

4. Just as tragedy was improvised by dithyramb singers in the cult of Dionysus, so comedy was improvised by performers of the phallic songs there.[4]

(1449a9–14: γενομένη δ' οὖν ἀπ' ἀρχῆς αὐτοσχεδιαστικῆς—καὶ αὐτὴ καὶ ἡ κωμῳδία, καὶ ἡ μὲν ἀπὸ τῶν ἐξαρχόντων τὸν διθύραμβον, ἡ δὲ ἀπὸ τῶν τὰ φαλλικὰ ἃ ἔτι καὶ νῦν ἐν πολλαῖς τῶν πόλεων διαμένει νομιζόμενα—κατὰ μικρὸν ηὐξήθη προαγόντων ὅσον ἐγίγνετο φανερὸν αὐτῆς. "Anyhow, when it came into being from an improvisatory origin (that is, both tragedy and comedy, the former from the leaders of dithyrambs, the other from the leaders of the phallic songs which remain even now a custom in many cities), it was gradually enhanced as poets developed the potential they saw in it."

5. Plots that end happily for the good and unhappily for the bad are more characteristic of comedy than tragedy.

(1453a35–39: ἔστιν δὲ οὐχ αὕτη ἀπὸ τραγῳδίας ἡδονὴ ἀλλὰ μᾶλλον τῆς κωμῳδίας οἰκεία· ἐκεῖ γὰρ οἳ ἂν ἔχθιστοι ὦσιν ἐν τῷ μύθῳ, οἷον Ὀρέστης καὶ Αἴγισθος, φίλοι γενόμενοι ἐπὶ τελευτῆς ἐξέρχονται, καὶ ἀποθνῄσκει οὐδεὶς ὑπ' οὐδενός. "Yet this is not the pleasure to expect from tragedy, but is more appropriate to comedy, where those who are deadliest enemies in the plot, such as Orestes and Aegisthus, exit at the end as new friends, and no one dies at anyone's hands.")

Thus for Aristotle in *Poetics*, which is overwhelmingly concerned with tragedy, comedy is frequently just a convenient foil for illustrating his contentions.

---

[4] See Csapo forthcoming on the history of *phallica*. As he points out, I should not have implied in Rusten (2006) that phallic processions stopped after 486; not only the evidence he cites, but also Aristotle himself (*Poetics* 1449 a12) specifically attests that they continued.

Furthermore, there are three features in the *Poetics* that the discussion of comedy, in contrast to tragedy, completely lacks:

1. The discussion of its parts, techniques, and ultimate function: this is promised also for hexameter poetry, but not preserved in the extant *Poetics*.[5]
(1449b21–22: περὶ μὲν οὖν τῆς ἐν ἑξαμέτροις μιμητικῆς καὶ περὶ κωμῳδίας ὕστερον ἐροῦμεν· "We shall later discuss the art of mimesis in hexameters, as well as comedy.")

2. An account of its early development.
(1449a37–b6: αἱ μὲν οὖν τῆς τραγῳδίας μεταβάσεις καὶ δι' ὧν ἐγένοντο οὐ λελήθασιν, ἡ δὲ κωμῳδία διὰ τὸ μὴ σπουδάζεσθαι ἐξ ἀρχῆς ἔλαθεν· καὶ γὰρ χορὸν κωμῳδῶν ὀψέ ποτε ὁ ἄρχων ἔδωκεν, ἀλλ' ἐθελονταὶ ἦσαν. ἤδη δὲ σχήματά τινα αὐτῆς ἐχούσης οἱ λεγόμενοι αὐτῆς ποιηταὶ μνημονεύονται. τίς δὲ πρόσωπα ἀπέδωκεν ἢ προλόγους ἢ πλήθη ὑποκριτῶν καὶ ὅσα τοιαῦτα, ἠγνόηται. "Now, tragedy's stages of development, and those responsible for them, have been remembered, but comedy's early history was forgotten because no serious interest was taken in it: only at a rather late date did the archon grant a comic chorus; previously performers were volunteers. It is from a time when the genre already had some formal features that the first named poets of comedy are remembered. Who introduced masks, prologues, various numbers of actors, and everything of that kind, has been lost.")

3. A description of comedy as reaching its own proper "nature" (*physis*, cf. 1449a15 for tragedy): perhaps this was supplied in a lost later discussion, but it cannot have consisted in New Comedy (*pace* Segal [1973], who however at least sees the problem), since Aristotle died in 322, before Menander's first production in 321.

Finally, there are three occasions in *Poetics* where Aristotle seems to find comedy distinctive, and more interesting than other genres:

1. *There are forms of comedy that predate the Athenian one and have influenced it* (1448a31–8): The invention of comedy is claimed by Dorian Megarians from the Peloponnese under a democracy, and by Sicilian Megarians because the oldest comic writer, Epicharmus, was from Sicily. They reject the genre's obvious derivation from *komos*, the group of revelers depicted on numerous vases in sixth-century Attica and Corinth (see note 12 below).
(1448a29–b3 διὸ καὶ ἀντιποιοῦνται τῆς τε τραγῳδίας καὶ τῆς κωμῳδίας οἱ Δωριεῖς (τῆς μὲν γὰρ κωμῳδίας οἱ Μεγαρεῖς οἵ τε ἐνταῦθα ὡς ἐπὶ τῆς παρ'

---

[5] This does not necessarily imply a lost section; it might be an "unfulfilled promise," on which see Vander Waerdt (1991). On the claim of Richard Janko to have found this lost discussion in an anonymous treatise called the *Tractatus Coislinianus* see the convincing objections of Nesselrath (1990) (not even mentioned by Janko in his 2002 update) and the review of Nesselrath by Rusten (1991).

αὐτοῖς δημοκρατίας γενομένης καὶ οἱ ἐκ Σικελίας, ἐκεῖθεν γὰρ ἦν Ἐπίχαρμος ὁ ποιητὴς πολλῷ πρότερος ὢν Χιωνίδου καὶ Μάγνητος· καὶ τῆς τραγῳδίας ἔνιοι τῶν ἐν Πελοποννήσῳ) ποιούμενοι τὰ ὀνόματα σημεῖον· αὐτοὶ μὲν γὰρ κώμας τὰς περιοικίδας καλεῖν φασιν, Ἀθηναίους δὲ δήμους, ὡς κωμῳδοὺς οὐκ ἀπὸ τοῦ κωμάζειν λεχθέντας ἀλλὰ τῇ κατὰ κώμας πλάνῃ ἀτιμαζομένους ἐκ τοῦ ἄστεως· καὶ τὸ ποιεῖν αὐτοὶ μὲν δρᾶν, Ἀθηναίους δὲ πράττειν προσαγορεύειν. περὶ μὲν οὖν τῶν διαφορῶν καὶ πόσαι καὶ τίνες τῆς μιμήσεως εἰρήσθω ταῦτα. "Hence the assertion some people make, that dramas are so called because they represent people in action. Thus, the Dorians actually lay claim to tragedy and comedy (comedy being claimed by the Megarians both here on the mainland, contending it arose during their democracy, and in Sicily, the homeland of the poet Epicharmus, a much earlier figure than Chionides and Magnes; and tragedy being claimed by some of those in the Peloponnese); and they cite the names as evidence. They say that they call villages *komoi*, while the Athenians call them *demoi*; their contention is that comic performers [*komoidoi*] got their name not from reveling [*komazein*] but from wandering through villages when banned from the city. And they say their own word for acting is *dran*, while the Athenians' is *prattein*. So much, then, by way of discussion of the number and nature of the distinctions within mimesis.")

2. The quality that makes comedy laughable is the *aischron* (1449a32–b27): Comedy imitates people who are worse (*phauloteroi, cheirones*), not by every standard of evil (*kata pasan kakian*) but by only one, the *aischron*, which is aesthetically "ugly" and morally "disgraceful," and it is of this that the laughable (*to geloion*) is a component. The laughable is any fault or instance of the *aischron* which is not pain-inducing or destructive; for example, a mask represents the laughable when it is *aischron* and distorted without pain.

   (1449a32–b27: ἡ δὲ κωμῳδία ἐστὶν ὥσπερ εἴπομεν μίμησις φαυλοτέρων μέν, οὐ μέντοι κατὰ πᾶσαν κακίαν, ἀλλὰ τοῦ αἰσχροῦ ἐστι τὸ γελοῖον μόριον. τὸ γὰρ γελοῖόν ἐστιν ἁμάρτημά τι καὶ αἶσχος ἀνώδυνον καὶ οὐ φθαρτικόν, οἷον εὐθὺς τὸ γελοῖον πρόσωπον αἰσχρόν τι καὶ διεστραμμένον ἄνευ ὀδύνης. "Comedy, as we said, is mimesis of baser but not wholly vicious characters: rather, the laughable is one category of the shameful. For the laughable comprises any fault or mark of shame which involves no pain or destruction: most obviously, the laughable mask is something ugly and twisted, but not painfully.")

3. Comedy's independence from previous stories (1449b2–8, 1451b12). Since tragedians begin from the preexisting names of myth and iambic poets write about an individual (*ton kath' ekaston*), comedy, which makes up its plots and uses any names it wishes (*katholou*),[6] is the least "fact-dependent" of all poetic

---

[6] See especially Lowe (2000). Heath (1989a, 350) ingeniously argues that *katholou* refers to the plausibility of comic plots, which, however, forces him into the conclusion that "Aristotle's requirement of causal connection in comic plots should not be taken so rigidly as to exclude designed inconsequentiality" (352).

genres (see the often-cited fragment of Antiphanes K-A fr. 189, which says that comic writers have to be much more inventive than tragedians), and it is in this respect that Crates is mentioned as a pioneer (over Epicharmus, at least some of whose plots we know to have been mythological).[7]

(1449b5–9: τὸ δὲ μύθους ποιεῖν [Ἐπίχαρμος καὶ Φόρμις] τὸ μὲν ἐξ ἀρχῆς ἐκ Σικελίας ἦλθε, τῶν δὲ Ἀθήνησιν Κράτης πρῶτος ἦρξεν ἀφέμενος τῆς ἰαμβικῆς ἰδέας καθόλου ποιεῖν λόγους καὶ μύθους. "The composition of plots originally came from Sicily; of Athenian poets Crates was the first to relinquish the iambic manner and to create stories and plots with an overall structure." And 1451b11–15: ἐπὶ μὲν οὖν τῆς κωμῳδίας ἤδη τοῦτο δῆλον γέγονεν· συστήσαντες γὰρ τὸν μῦθον διὰ τῶν εἰκότων οὕτω τὰ τυχόντα ὀνόματα ὑποτιθέασιν, καὶ οὐχ ὥσπερ οἱ ἰαμβοποιοὶ περὶ τὸν καθ’ ἕκαστον ποιοῦσιν. "In comedy, this point has by now become obvious: the poets construct the plot on the basis of probability, and only then supply arbitrary names, they do not, like iambic poets, write about a particular person.")

From all the observations noted above, but especially from this last triad, we may speculatively deduce some elements of an Aristotelian theory of comedy.

1. The goal of comedy for Aristotle seems to be laughter, an emotional response that Plato's *Philebus* 48a–50b criticizes, just as he does the emotional response to tragedy in *Republic* 2–3.

2. Political satire, since it deals in specific targets (even when allegorical) and intends to cause pain to them,[8] probably does not have a place in his theory; neither Epicharmus nor Crates (both mentioned as "firsts") seem to have engaged in it.

3. Since what comedy imitates is *aischron*, obscenity and scatology probably *do* have an essential place in it, and this seems to be clinched by Aristotle's derivation of the genre from the phallic processions, as well as the fact that his strictures on avoiding obscenity in civic education (*Politics* 7 1336b4–23) include a ban on watching *iamboi* or comedies (well discussed by Heath [1989a: 344–345]). This suggests he might even find the comedies of his own day a falloff, since they have abandoned *aischrologia* (*EN* 1128a22), which produced the desired result, analogous to his complaints about tragedies that have happy endings.[9]

4. For Aristotle, the chorus may not have been an essential part of comedy. The Dorian derivation from *kome* that he cites would eliminate the *komos* from its name and evidently substitute (individual?) exiles (*atimazomenous*);

---

[7] Aristotle's contrast is between *ta genomena* "actual" (including transmitted mythical names) and *tuchonta* "coincidental, random" names and actions.

[8] I cannot agree with Heath (1989a, 353) that *anôdunon* in 1449a35 is "not meant to be prescriptive."

[9] Halliwell (2008, 326–327, 394) puts these three Aristotelian texts on *aischra* together in a very different way.

furthermore, the extensive fragments of Epicharmus, whom Aristotle accepts as the inventor of comic plots, show no evidence of a chorus or any lyric meters (see *BOC* 59). Is it possible that Aristotle thought that, whereas tragedy was originally a chorus out of which dramatic space was created for actors (citing dithyramb as its precursor, Aeschylus's invention of more actors), pre-comedy had individual performers (his "volunteers" and "singers of the phallic songs"), into which a chorus was integrated when it was accepted into the dramatic festival? Such a scheme would fly in the face of the numerous archaic artistic depictions of *komoi*,[10] but it might explain why, as we shall see in 2.A below, the participation of the chorus in comedy is so different from that in tragedy.

4. From this list of possible attributes of Aristotle's ideal comedy, one item, the absence of political satire of specific individuals, is certainly not true of the most famous comedies of Aristophanes, and yet this author himself seems to have represented for Aristotle the classic comic writer (1448a25–27, on the categories of imitation: ὥστε τῇ μὲν ὁ αὐτὸς ἂν εἴη μιμητὴς Ὁμήρῳ Σοφοκλῆς, μιμοῦνται γὰρ ἄμφω σπουδαίους, τῇ δὲ Ἀριστοφάνει, πράττοντας γὰρ μιμοῦνται καὶ δρῶντας ἄμφω, "in one respect Sophocles is the same class of imitator as Homer, because they both imitate serious people, in another as Aristophanes, because it is men in action and performance that they both imitate").

Without some retrospective Procrustean refitting of them ("Aristotle could not possibly have meant…he *must* rather have meant…"), it looks as if the attempt to unify Aristotle's various comments on the essence of comedy cannot succeed. That is true of most modern attempts as well.

2. Formalism, Folklore, Religion, Generic Parasitism: Modern Ideas about the Essence of Old Comedy

Most modern scholars bypass Aristotle's *Poetics* to seek the essence of Old Comedy largely from the eleven preserved plays of Aristophanes—this despite the fact that these plays postdate by more than half a century the first comic performances at the Dionysia, and, though by a single author in a single lifetime, display much greater diversity (some would say "development") than do the extant tragedies of three different authors over nearly three-quarters of a century.

Such theories differ widely according to how critics frame their inquiries, the scholarly tendencies they presuppose, and the aspects of comedy they emphasize.

---

[10] Rusten (2006); important studies since then include Rothwell (2007), Smith (2010), Csapo (2013).

Furthermore, in their attempts to account for evidence at odds with their hypotheses, they often become extremely complex, so that most of the books described below are quite lengthy. What follows is not a full description but more of an aerial view of the warring camps pitched on the field of comic origins, chiefly as orientation for those who might want to descend for a closer look. None of these theories is a direct descendent or adaptation of any other, but they might be classified broadly, omitting much detail, into four approaches (the order is roughly chronological).

A. Metrical Form as Essence

Aristotle says (1449b2–4), "It was only when comedy already has some of its features (*schemata*) that its recorded poets are mentioned." He notes characters, prologues, number of actors, and "things like that" as already established when poets were first recorded in 486, and since Aristotle himself compiled *didascaliai*, "Victories at the Dionysia in the City and the Lenaea" (see *BOC* 739), we can assume that he is speaking of records of the festivals. "Things like that" could also have included structural forms that predate 486 and might be thought to give clues to its core. And in fact Old Comedy has a very complex metrical and dramatic structure, perhaps the one "thing" about it that is absolutely unique and sui generis, owing nothing to any previous known genre. Any reader of Aristophanic comedy, even in translation, will immediately notice some features that are surprising in a drama:

> The prologue often breaks the dramatic illusion by addressing the audience, with the characters of the scene sometimes even acknowledging that they are actors in a play.
> The chorus is not a bystander to the action, but enters with its own distinct agenda (the *parodos*).
> The greatest conflict in the play is in the middle (the agon).
> After this conflict, the stage is cleared for the chorus, which addresses the audience directly on behalf of the playwright, sometimes evidently "stripping" (*apoduntes*), which may even mean that it removes its costume (the *parabasis*).
> The rest of the comedy is usually a series of episodes separated by choral strophes, as in tragedy.

Those reading closely in the original will further observe that the metrical structure is different from tragedy, and more complex: tetrameters are as frequent as trimeters; lyric meters are mixed with stichic ones; more precisely, response (metrical symmetry between groups of verses) is not "strophic" (AB AB AB), but "epirrhematic" (ABC ABC D), and its components include stichic (trimeter, tetrameter, other units) as well as lyric verses.

The ancient metrical writer Hephaestion and the scholia note some of these features, and in the late nineteenth century they began to be studied intensively. The most widely accepted treatment was that of Tadeusz Zieliński in 1885 (at the age of twenty-six), who argued comprehensively that Old Comedy was a unique form of composition, and assumed that its structure (prologue, *parodos*, agon, and *parabasis*) was the key to its origins as an "Ionic" choral form as opposed to the traditional "Doric" one (a hypothesis he based on the "Doric" comedy of the *Poetics*). Unfortunately, he went still further: since the agon as he defined it (either metrically or dramatically or both) comes after the *parabasis* in *Knights* and *Frogs*, and is absent entirely not only from the late plays (*Ecclesiazusae* and *Plutus*) but also from *Clouds*, *Acharnians*, *Peace*, and *Women at the Thesmophoria*, he found it necessary to argue that all these comedies had been revised (as we know was the case for *Clouds*) or distorted in the process of displacing or omitting an original agon. He also argued that the *parabasis*, when the chorus takes off its costume, must originally have been the conclusion of the comedy, implying that Aristophanes's post-*parabasis* episodes were his own experiments in the genre. Much of this was encapsulated in a colorful chart created by Zieliński and reproduced here in monochrome as Figure 1.1.

Zieliński (1885: 215–216) explained the chart in this way (slightly modified to reflect the monochrome chart reproduced here):

> The uniqueness of comic composition will become even more striking if the reader consults the attached lithographic chart. I hope little effort will be required to become familiar with the graphic symbols applied there. The three shades of black signify the three different types of composition of ancient poetry, that is stichic composition (black), strophic (light grey), and συστήματα ἐξ ὁμοίων ["systems of similar lines"[11]] (dark grey). Within the stichic composition, trimeters are differentiated from longer verse forms (anapaests, tetrameters, Eupolideans, and other long stichic forms) by the lower height of their lines. (This meant the lyric parts as well as the hypermetric ones had to be adjusted to the height of the στίχοι of the section to which they belong.) The horizontal length of each section corresponds exactly to its number of verses (which can be checked by the general guidelines placed at 200-verse intervals). Vertical strokes indicate that the corresponding parts occur outside of symmetries, whereas an antistrophic relationship is represented by the slanting of the strokes against each other; this enables a syzygy to be instantly recognizable.
>
> Seven of the Aristophanic comedies have been illustrated in this way. For *Assemblywomen* and *Wealth*, the artlessness of the composition scarcely needs visual representation; for *Clouds* and *Women at the Thesmophoria* on the other hand, whose composition has been obscured by διασκευή ["reworking"], a color diagram would be of no value. Instead, three tragedies have been brought in for comparison, which represent three chronologically different periods of the development of the art of tragedy: *Persians*, *Antigone*, and *Bacchae*.
>
> Merely a quick glance at the chart allows us to discern the following fundamental principle for the composition of dialogue: *episodes occur only in the second half of the*

---

[11] The Greek term is from Hephaestion *On Poems*, ch. 3, but Zieliński uses it differently, to indicate shorter anapaestic, iambic, or trochaic stichic blocks.

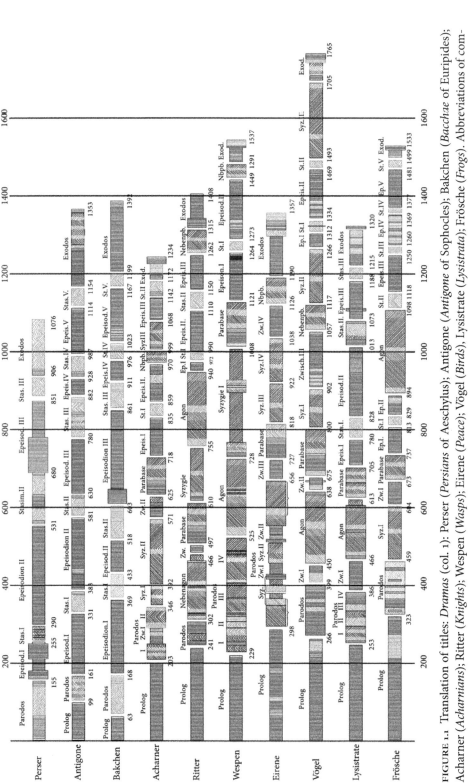

FIGURE 1.1 Translation of titles: *Dramas* (col. 1): Perser (*Persians* of Aeschylus); Antigone (*Antigone* of Sophocles); Bakchen (*Bacchae* of Euripides); Acharner (*Acharnians*); Ritter (*Knights*); Wespen (*Wasps*); Eirene (*Peace*); Vögel (*Birds*); Lysistrate (*Lysistrata*); Frösche (*Frogs*). Abbreviations of comedy components not readily recognizable: Epeis. or Epeisod. = Epeisodion; Nebenagon = "secondary agon"; Nbpb. or Nebenpb. = Nebenparabase ("secondary *parabasis*"); Stas. = Stasimon; Zw. or Zwisch. = Zwischenszenen ("in-between scenes"); Syz. = Syzygie.

drama, which follows the parabasis. Therefore, the Doric forms do not penetrate the original form of Ionic comedy; to this extent, Aristophanic comedy is conscious of its origins.

Zwischenszenen ("in-between scenes") do of course occur, but their occurrence has a good technical reason. Think of a comedy of the old style, where the *parodos* is followed by the agon, and the agon by the *parabasis*. No matter which form the *parodos* might be composed in, its last part was left for the chorus (either as *antode* or *antepirrhema*). The agon began with an ode, thus once again with a choral contribution. At the time of purely choral comedy, of course, such an unending claim on the chorus was unavoidable, but on the one hand, the comedies at that time were not as long; on the other, one can probably assume that a rest period was allowed to the speakers. Once actors were being used, it made sense to fill this rest period with dialogue. Thus was born the *proagon*, perhaps the earliest of the dialogue sections. It too immediately took in the content which would become a canonical position in comic composition; we have already said about its place what was necessary. For this application of *Zwischenszenen*, the *Lysistrata* offers a good example…

Zieliński's general description of comedy's structure is standard today,[12] though his detailed attempts to explain away any deviation are not. They were critiqued as overly rigid in the 1904 dissertation of Paul Mazon, who analyzed each preserved play to argue that Aristophanes felt free to adapt comedy's preexisting structures to suit his dramatic purposes (though Mazon's own account of what these purposes were is sometimes less than convincing), but that certain principles were more or less followed in all but the final two plays (as well as *Clouds*, which he regards as a daring experiment):

> The prologue consists of three parts, the "parade," the "patter," and the start of the action (sometimes explained by the characters themselves).
> The agon is expanded from a physical combat into a verbal debate.
> The part of the comedy after the *parabasis* is much more conventional and adopts the form of tragedy, being a series of repetitive episodes separated by choral lyrics that stop the action (which, in the first part, had been continuous); in the second half of the play, the chorus loses its identity.

Metrically speaking, Mazon notes that 1) the action never stops for a choral ode in the first half of the play; 2) tetrameters are never found outside of the *parodos*, agon, and *parabasis*; and 3) scenes that are not one of these three types are written in iambic trimeters. He concludes that this unique form was derived from the archaic *komos*, in which a group of revelers attacked an individual who then defended himself vigorously, leading to a celebratory conclusion. Aristophanes's main innovation is to insert, between the *parabasis* and the komastic conclusion, the working-out in detail of his comic plot.

---

[12] Subsequent outlines for all eleven comedies are in an appendix to Pickard-Cambridge and Webster (1962), and in greatest detail in Zimmermann (1984–1987). Zieliński (1931) provides a retrospective on the book's impact and some corrections of detail.

Zieliński's and Mazon's formalist approach to comic origins is open to the objection that its structures are constantly being reconfigured, but opponents must admit that its traditional structures remained largely unchanged, and lasted until their complete disappearance marked the end of Old Comedy itself. Analysts of Aristophanic structure and metrics today are no longer troubled by the variety of their appearance, perhaps because they do not see them as evidence for comic essence or origins (these include Sifakis 1971, Zimmermann 1984–1987, Gelzer 1993, Parker 1997).

B. Folklore

A natural conception of comedy is to view it as an opposition to high, urban, literary culture: low, popular, rural, subliterary, authentic. Here too Zieliński was a pioneer. In the same year as his book cited above, he also produced an emotional description of a subgenre of Old Comedy—the *Märchen-* or folktale comedy. In contrast to the purely mythological comedy that he calls (appropriating for his own purposes Aristotle's variant) "Doric," he derives the folktale comedy from an Ionic tradition of popular stories that the audience would know well, and he offers examples from modern Greek and other European folktale collections. His paradigmatic case is the tale of the Eagle brother-in-law (Thompson 1946 type 552, p. 55) who alone can tell a young prince the location of the distant city where he can find his runaway bride, which he argues is reproduced (with much adaptation) in Aristophanes's *Birds*. His other examples come from fragmentary plays, especially those whose titles indicate animals or alien beings, like the very early comic poet Magnes as recalled in the *parabasis* of *Knights* (*BOC* 133 7A), or the *Beasts* of Crates, the *Fish* of Archippus, or numerous candidates by Pherecrates (*Ant-men, Savages, Persians, Mine-workers*). Zieliński's reconstructions are especially bold: in most cases, neither the Greek comedy nor the ancient folktale behind it is extant—both have to be reconstructed. His stated aim is, however, to rescue from oblivion the stories that relieved the otherwise joyless existence of the ancient lower classes (his conclusion seems to be evoking the end of Russian serfdom).

Süss (1905 and 1908) changed the focus from animals to humans, arguing that the prototypic figures of all comic plots are, first, the *alazon*, an intellectual or military imposter, and in opposition to him the *bomolochos*, the mocking respecter of no one; these popular types did not remain static, as in the masks of the commedia dell'arte, but were developed into lampoons of actual figures such as Euripides in *Acharnians, Women at the Thesmophoria* and *Frogs* and Socrates in *Clouds*, or else fulfilled their familiar functions under new identities. Sifakis (1992) made these functions central to his own comic folktale model, which, however, follows neither Zieliński nor Süss but applies the analytical categories of Vladimir Propp to reduce each comic plot to a limited number of folktale functions, which each character is charged to fulfill.

A more targeted and less ideological comparison of folktale motifs is Davies (2004), noting classic folktale patterns (especially of an initial "lack" and a quest for it, ending in marriage and feast), especially in *Peace*, but also in *Birds, Acharnians, Frogs* and even to some extent in *Clouds*; but also that, whereas the questing heroes in folktale are always young, those in Aristophanes are elderly.

C. Religion

Although it is increasingly seen as misguided, ritual is still a widely accepted model for all dramatic origins (see Rozik [2002], Scullion [2002], and Nesselrath, chapter 34 in this volume). That comedies were performed in the context of the festival of Dionysus is a fact, as it is that the plays of Aristophanes are pervaded with undisguised religious expression in the form of rituals, prayers, hymns, and festival-settings. But proponents of religious origins do not stop there: they seek comic origins and audience appeal in rituals that lie submerged underneath the apparent plot and exist only in the subconscious of the spectators.

The most-cited such theory is that of F. M. Cornford's *Origin of Attic Comedy* (1914, often reprinted).[13] Rather than critiquing any previous work, he makes room for all of it—Zieliński on comic structure and Süss on characters are both incorporated into the mix, as well as Aristotle on phallic processions and Dorian comedy; but he moves the discussion decisively away from metrical forms to an impassioned argument ("es liest sich teilweise selbst wie ein Drama" [Zieliński 1935: 7]), under the influence of a collaboration with colleagues Jane Harrison and Gilbert Murray in *Themis: A Study in the Social Origins of Greek Religion* (see Beard 2000: 129–160 and Versnel 1990), that all Greek drama is inspired by rituals of the calendar, borrowing from the "year king" model of Frazer's *Golden Bough*. He takes the structures defined by Zieliński as stages in a ritual drama, and adapts Süss's three archetypal characters into aspects of the "sacred hero," who concludes the play in triumph with a sacred marriage, as in *Peace* and *Birds*. The presentation is bracing, with much comparative material (fertility rituals, feasts, and sacred marriage), and ahead of its time in positing Near Eastern influence on Greek culture; but as Henderson points out in his Introduction (xxiv–xxvi, see also Webster in *DTC²* 193–194), it is precisely his central concept of the year king that cannot be traced in Dionysiac or even Greek myth or cult.

Bowie 1993 (cf. 2010) also sees Greek myths and rituals underlying comic plots, but not in an overt way—mythological comedy about the gods and heroes themselves is largely lost, or from a later period—but rather through patterns or archetypes for the apparently nonmythical plots. Furthermore, many comedies evoke festivals that would stir in the audience a number of emotions not explicitly articulated: *Knights* hints at a divine succession myth known from Hesiod's *Theogony*; *Clouds* suggests the punishment of Ixion, who attempted to rape Hera but assaulted only a cloud-figment; *Women at the Thesmophoria* recalls the punishment of Miltiades (a historical figure) for invading a shrine of Demeter. Aspects of *Knights, Wasps*, and *Clouds* can be compared to rites of

---

[13] Its publication on the eve of the First World War meant that the most interesting review, that of Zieliński himself, did not appear until many years later (Zieliński 1935).

passage; *Peace* and *Wealth* figure rituals of divine return. *Lysistrata* can suggest the myth of the Lemnian women who murdered their husbands (one of several backgrounds which can problematize an apparently happy ending). The fact that these patterns are by their very nature nearly invisible to the modern reader makes them impossible to verify, and puts them in tension with the definition of comedy, ever since Aristotle, as the least mythical and least factual form of composition. But searching for deep religious patterns in comic plots is certainly a healthy corrective to the search for a comic author's underlying political point of view, against which Bowie (1992, Introduction) offers cogent arguments.

Bierl (2009) makes comedy essentially religious through a new conception of the comic chorus: if every choral performance is (as he argues) a ritual celebration for a god, then comedy's chorus, too, is engaged in creating a ritual environment for performance. This is argued initially on a theoretical level (with the support of modern anthropological and performance criticism and recent studies of the tragic chorus), then with a detailed commentary on a single chorus which is actually composed of ritual celebrants, that of *Women at the Thesmophoria* (*Frogs* also has such a chorus, briefly). Such an argument involves, as he recognizes (49), rejecting the trends traced above that differentiate the comic chorus's involvement in the action from that of tragedy; he goes on to assert (54) that the structure of the comedy mimics that of the Dionysia: the *parodos* of the chorus is like the initial *pompe* (procession), the agon is like the central choral competitions, and then comes the concluding celebration. As ingenious and energetic as is the argument, one cannot overlook some similarities of methodology with Cornford: starting with deductions from contemporary theory (rather than inductively from the comedies themselves); the imposition of an abstract, external, theoretical model; and the minimization of the difference between comedy and tragedy.

Halliwell (2008: 207) disclaims any interest in comic origins, but does remind us (chapters 4–5) of the ritual basis of what we have seen was probably for Aristotle a central feature of Old Comedy, viz., its frequent obscenity. He surveys thoroughly the numerous Greek instances of "aischrology" (mandated obscenity in certain religious cults) and argues that it is a uniquely Greek phenomenon, one which Aristophanes in the *parodos* of *Frogs* makes a chorus of Eleusinian initiates reenact and assimilate to his own style of obscene mockery.

D. Generic Inheritance, Parody, and Appropriation

Comedy is the last of the classical genres to be created, and, as we have noticed, Aristotle largely views its origins in relation to its predecessor genres. It also often snatches its own contents from these generic rivals, in particular tragedy (see Hanink, chapter 12), which is extensively parodied for different purposes in *Acharnians*, *Women at the Thesmophoria*, and *Frogs*; Aristophanes's intimate relationship with tragedy is specially studied by Silk (2000, among his other publications). Cratinus (K-A fr. 342, *BOC* 216) documents the connection in his coinage of the verb "Euripidaristophanize," but he himself is even more obsessed with other genres, employing characters, meters, and stories from epic, iambic, and satyr play, as documented by Rosen (2013) and Bakola (2010). But the most recent approaches to the essence of Old Comedy adopt what Bakhtin (1981) said about the novel—that it alone could appropriate other genres while remaining itself—and apply it to Old Comedy (Platter 2007).

Until now, all the seekers of Old Comedy's essence have had to admit that their candidates do not fit all the plays alike; there are major discrepancies that have to be explained away. But in today's theories of generic imitation and rivalry, the animating spirit of Old Comedy is to elude any permanent identity and refashion itself, which ensures its continuing diversity and lack of homogeneity. The newest book on the subject (Bakola, Prauscello, and Telò 2013) finds its generic interaction not only "essential" (ix), but also the means of rescuing Old Comedy from essentialism (x). After so many attempts to pin down Old Comedy to a single model that fall short, then, an approach that embraces its contradictions, and views Old Comedy's permanent carnival as an endless masquerade, is perhaps the best way to come to confront a genre that seems never to have progressed to its Aristotelian literary adulthood.

BIBLIOGRAPHY

Bakhtin, M. 1981. "Epic and Novel: Towards a Methodology for the Study of the Novel." In *The Dialogic Imagination: Four Essays*, translated by C. Emerson and M. Holquist (Russian original 1941), 3–40. Austin: University of Texas Press.

Bakola, E. 2010. *Cratinus and the Art of Comedy*. Oxford: Oxford University Press.

Bakola, E., L. Prauscello and M. Telò. 2013. *Greek Comedy and the Discourse of Genres*. Oxford: Oxford University Press.

Beard, M. 2000. *The Invention of Jane Harrison*. Cambridge, MA: Harvard University Press.

Bierl, A. 2009. *Ritual and Performativity: The Chorus in Old Comedy*. Translated by Alexander Hollmann. Washington, DC: Center for Hellenic Studies.

Bowie, A. M. 1993. *Aristophanes: Myth, Ritual, and Comedy*. Cambridge, UK, and New York: Cambridge University Press.

———. 2010. "Myth and Ritual in Comedy." In *Brill's Companion to the Study of Greek Comedy*, edited by G. W. Dobrov, 143–176. Leiden and Boston: Brill.

Cornford, F. M. 1993. *The Origin of Attic Comedy*, edited by Theodor H. Gaster. Ann Arbor: University of Michigan Press. Originally published Cambridge, UK: Cambridge University Press, 1914.

Csapo, E. 2013. "Comedy and the *pompê*: Dionysian Genre-Crossing." In *Greek Comedy and the Discourse of Genres*, edited by E. Bakola, L. Prauscello and M. Telò, 40–80. Oxford: Oxford University Press.

Davies, M. 2004. "Aristophanes and the folk-tale." *Studi italiani di filologia classica* 4: 28-41.

Dobrov, G. W. 2010. *Brill's Companion to the Study of Greek Comedy*. Leiden and Boston: Brill.

Pickard-Cambridge, A. W., and T. B. L. Webster. 1962. 2d rev. ed. *Dithyramb, Tragedy and Comedy*. Oxford: Clarendon Press (referred to as *DTC²*).

Edwards, A. T. 2002. "Historicizing the Popular Grotesque: Bakhtin's *Rabelais and his World* and Attic Old Comedy." In *Bakhtin and the Classics*, edited by R. Bracht Branham, 27–55. Evanston, IL: Northwestern University Press.

Gelzer, T. 1993. "Feste Strukturen in der Komödie des Aristophanes." In *Aristophane: Sept exposés suivis de discussions*, edited by J. M. Bremer and E. W. Handley, 51–96. Entretiens sur l'Antiquité classique 38. Geneva: Fondation Hardt.

Halliwell, S. 2008. *Greek Laughter: A Study of Cultural Psychology from Homer to Early Christianity*. Cambridge, UK, and New York: Cambridge University Press.

Halliwell, S., W. H. Fyfe, D. A. Russell, and D. C. Innes, tr. 1995. *Aristotle, Poetics; Longinus, On the Sublime; Demetrius, On Style*. Cambridge, MA: Harvard University Press.

Heath, Ma. 1989a. "Aristotelian Comedy." *CQ* 39: 344–54.

——. 1989b. *Unity in Greek Poetics*. Oxford: Clarendon Press.

Herter, H. 1947. *Vom dionysischen Tanz zum komischen Spiel*. Iserlohn, Germany: Silva-Verlag.

Janko, R. 2002. *Aristotle on Comedy: Towards a Reconstruction of Poetics II*. London: Duckworth. First published 1984.

Lowe, N. J. 2000. "Comic Plots and the Invention of Fiction." In *The Rivals of Aristophanes: Studies in Athenian Old Comedy*, edited by D. Harvey and J. Wilkins, 259–272. London: Duckworth.

Mazon, P. 1904. *Essai sur la composition des comédies d'Aristophane*. Paris: Hachette.

Moellendorff, P. von. 1995. *Grundlagen einer Ästhetik der alten Komödie: Untersuchungen zu Aristophanes und Michail Bachtin*. Tübingen, Germany: Narr.

Nesselrath, H.-G. 1990. *Die attische Mittlere Komödie: Ihre Stellung in der antiken Literaturkritik und Literaturgeschichte*. Untersuchungen zur antiken Literatur und Geschichte 36. Berlin and New York: W. de Gruyter.

Parker, L. P. E. 1997. *The Songs of Aristophanes*. Oxford: Clarendon Press.

Pickard-Cambridge, Arthur Wallace and T. B. L Webster. 1962. *Dithyramb, tragedy and comedy*. Oxford: Clarendon Press. 2d ed. rev.

Platter, C. 2007. *Aristophanes and the Carnival of Genres*. Baltimore: Johns Hopkins University Press.

Rosen, R. 2013. "Iambos, comedy and the question of generic affiliation." In *Greek Comedy and the Discourse of Genres*, edited by E. Bakola, L. Prauscello and M. Telò, 81–100. Oxford: Oxford University Press.

Rothwell, K. S. 2006. *Nature, Culture, and the Origins of Greek Comedy: A Study of Animal Choruses*. Cambridge, UK: Cambridge University Press.

Rotstein, A. 2010. *The Idea of Iambos*. Oxford and New York: Oxford University Press.

Rozik, E. 2002. *The Roots of Theatre: Rethinking Ritual and Other Theories of Origin*. Iowa City: University of Iowa Press.

Rusten, J. 1991. Review of *Die attische mittlere Komödie: Ihre Stellung in der antiken Literaturkritik und Literaturgeschichte*, by H.-G. Nesselrath, *BMCR* 12 (2): 2.

——. 2006. "Who 'Invented' Comedy? The Ancient Candidates for the Origins of Comedy and the Visual Evidence." *AJP* 127: 37–66.

Rusten, J. 2011. *The Birth of Comedy: Texts, Documents, and Art from Athenian Comic Competitions*, 486–280. Baltimore: Johns Hopkins University Press (referred to as *BOC*).

Scullion, S. 2002. "'Nothing to Do With Dionysus': Tragedy Misconceived as Ritual." *CQ* 52: 102–137.

Segal, E. 1973. "The Physis of Comedy." *HSCP* 77: 129–136.

Sifakis, G. M. 1971. *Parabasis and Animal Choruses: A Contribution to the History of Attic Comedy*. London: Athlone Press.

——. 1988. "Towards a Modern Poetics of Old Comedy." *Métis* 3: 53–67.

——. 1992. "The Structure of Aristophanic Comedy." *JHS* 112: 123–142.

——. 2006. "From Mythological Parody to Political Satire: Some Stages in the Evolution of Old Comedy." *C&M* 57: 19–48.

Silk, M. J. 2000. *Aristophanes and the Definition of Comedy*. Oxford: Oxford University Press.

Smith, T. J. 2010. *Komast Dancers in Archaic Greek Art*. Oxford: Oxford University Press.

Süss, W. 1905. "De personarum antiquae comoediae Atticae usu atque origine." PhD diss., University of Bonn.

——. 1908. "Zur Komposition der altattischen Komoedie." *RhMus*, n.s., 63: 12–38.

——. 1911. *Aristophanes und die Nachwelt*. Leipzig: Dieterich.

Thompson, S. 1946. *The Folktale*. New York: Dryden Press.

Vander Waerdt, P. A. 1991. "The Plan and Intention of Aristotle's Ethical and Political Writings." *Illinois Classical Studies* 16: 231–253.

Versnel, H. S. 1990. "What Is Sauce for the Goose Is Sauce for the Gander: Myth and Ritual, Old and New." In *Inconsistencies in Greek & Roman Religion*. Vol. 2: *Transition and Reversal in Myth& Ritual*, by H. S. Versnel, 15–88. Leiden and New York: E. J. Brill. First published in different form in *Approaches to Greek Myth*, edited by L. Edmunds, 23–92 (Baltimore: Johns Hopkins Press, 1990).

Zieliński, T. 1885. *Die Gliederung der altattischen Komödie*. Leipzig: Teubner.

——. 1885. *Die Märchenkomödie in Athen*. St. Petersburg: Buchdruckerei der Kaiserlichen Akademie der Wissenschaften. Reprinted with introductory note in *Iresione: Dissertationes ad comoediam et tragoediam spectantes continens*, by T. Zieliński, 8–75 (Lvov: Societas philologa Polonorum).

——. 1931. "Zur 'Gliederung der altattischen Komödie' (1885): Retraktationen." In *Iresione: Dissertationes ad comoediam et tragoediam spectantes continens*, by T. Zieliński, 456–468. Lvov: Societas philologa Polonorum.

——.1935. Review of Cornford, *Origin of Attic Comedy* (1934). *Gnomon* 11: 6–9.

Zimmermann, B. 1984–1987. *Untersuchungen zur Form and dramatischen Technik der aristophanischen Komödien*. Königstein im Taunus, Germany: A. Hain.

——. 2010. "Structure and Meter." In *Brill's Companion to the Study of Greek Comedy*, edited by G. W. Dobrov, 455–469. Leiden; Boston: Brill.

CHAPTER 2

PERFORMING COMEDY IN THE FIFTH THROUGH EARLY THIRD CENTURIES

ERIC CSAPO

I. CHORUS AND ACTOR

IN Athens, performance in a dramatic chorus was regarded as a civic duty. Participation was (at least in theory) unpaid, but not altogether voluntary. Athens had elaborate legal mechanisms to force ordinary people to serve their term in performing choreutic service (MacDowell 1989). Dramatic choruses therefore embodied the broad public and frequently spoke with the voice of the common Athenian. Choral duty was restricted to (male) citizens for the Dionysia and to citizens or metics for the Lenaea. This helps explain both the initial importance and the eventual decline of the chorus. Comedy, as we know it, was probably never a ritual form, but it was in part modeled after the various "funny" choruses that participated in the Parade (*Pompe*), a carnival-type sacrificial procession that opened the Dionysia. It was the professionalization of the other performers, the actors and the musicians, that left the chorus behind, precipitating its decline over the course of the fifth and fourth centuries and its eventual segregation from the dramatic narrative; there is no evidence to suggest that the chorus ever disappeared from the performance of Greek comedy (as it did in Roman).

Athenian official discourse continued to regard the chorus as the core of comedy long after it had ceased to be so. When a poet, called the "teacher" (*didaskalos*) of a chorus, wished to perform a comedy, he went to the archon and "asked for a chorus" (Cratinus K-A fr. 17). The archon "granted a chorus" (Pl. *Rep.* 383c, *Laws* 817d7; Arist. *Poet.* 1449b1–2). At the competition, the herald invited the poet to "bring on your chorus" (Aristophanes *Acharnians* 11). The oath of the festival judges enjoined them to award the prize "to the chorus that sang well" (Wilson 2000: 99). The success of the chorus determined the success of the poet. The dramatic genres are regularly referred to as "the tragedians," "the satyrs," and "the comedians," meaning precisely "the chorus" (Pickard-Cambridge 1968: 127).

The comic chorus, with twenty-four choreuts, was bigger than the tragic (twelve or fifteen) and initially more important to its drama (Pickard-Cambridge 1968: 234–236). Aristophanes structures his plays around the chorus and designs his plots to motivate its set pieces. Typically, a hero with a big idea overcomes obstruction by the chorus (*parodos*); persuades the chorus to support him (*agon*); departs as the chorus comments on his plan (*parabasis*); and then, after various episodes in which characters react to the implementation of his plan, each separated by short choral odes, is escorted out of the theater in a triumphant procession (*komos*). No other Old Comic playwright survives well enough to permit certainty, but the fragments suggest that Aristophanes's rivals sometimes used these choral movements differently, often placing them closer to the margins of the performance in order to develop more intricate plots. Aristophanes's political comedy may have been uniquely chorocentric.

As music grew more complex and actors more accomplished in the late fifth century, the musical burden gradually shifted from chorus to actor. The shift is large and swift in tragedy, but comedy was more conservative. It is only in Aristophanes's fourth-century plays that we can measure diminution in the importance of choral music. Perhaps a more decisive factor was the growth in market demand for drama (see below), as well as a recognition that contacts between actors, who traveled, and choruses, which were locally recruited, might be minimal, so that efficiency was best served by a compartmentalization of their parts.

By the time of Menander, the comic chorus is completely marginalized. It only ever appears in our manuscripts in the form of a one-word note meaning "choral song" where a choral performance occurred. Otherwise, the texts acknowledge its existence at most with a line announcing its approach. Menander probably did not write the choral lyrics that were performed in his plays (cf. Revermann 2006: 274–281).

Vase paintings show lively and obscene choruses from the late seventh century but it does not help to call these "comedy." Certainly Sicily and probably Megara had comedy from the beginning of the fifth century. At Athens, we have no good evidence for a chorus and at least one actor performing together until the introduction of tragedy in the last decade of the sixth century (and probably right after the building of the theater). The introduction of a comic competition to the Athenian Dionysia is attested for about 486 (see Rusten chapter 1, p. 40 and Makres chapter 3, p. 72). It had sophisticated models in tragedy and Sicilian comedy, and Aristotle does claim to know that "writing [comic] plots first came from Sicily" (*Poetics* 1449b5–9). Aristotle inferred evolutionary stages, such as a gradual increase in the number of actors, as happened in tragedy, but he admits that he could discover nothing about the early period. Despite Aristotle, comedy may have developed rapidly. The comedies of the 430s, the earliest for which we have adequate remains, reveal none of the awkwardness in the use of actors that we can detect in early tragedy. Unlike tragedy, however, comedy had no fixed number of actors until the time of New Comedy. Extant Menander can be performed with only three actors.

Aristophanes, by contrast, frequently requires four actors and can require as many as six (we cannot be sure of other Old Comedy). This may be another industry norm that was imposed to facilitate reperformance.

The early years were run by theatrical families (Csapo 2010: 88–89). Different families may have dominated production, providing the Athenian theater with both playwrights and actors for either tragedy or comedy (but never both). Ancient tradition maintains that many fifth-century poets also acted in their plays. We hear of comic poet-actors much longer than their tragic equivalents. One might wonder if Dicaeopolis in *Acharnians* slipped so easily into the persona of Aristophanes (501–518) because the actor was the poet himself, or if Cratinus played the main role in his autobiographical fantasy, the *Wineflask (Pytine)*. Talented outsiders are not clearly visible in comedy's professional ranks until the early forth century. In professional development, comedy lagged behind tragedy. The Athenian Dionysia instituted a prize for tragic acting in about 449, but no prize for comic acting until sometime between 329 and 312. It is also true that while some tragic actors attained international celebrity as early as 420, comic actors do not achieve stardom (Satyrus, Lycus, Philemon, Parmenon) until the mid-fourth century. On the other hand, the Lenaean contests seem to have had prizes for comic as well as tragic actors from their inception, about 432, and artifacts reveal that the comic actors captured the popular imagination from the 420s onwards (see section III).

II. Audience and Theater

Even in his lifetime, the plays of Aristophanes might have been performed at any one of thirty-two known theaters throughout the Greek world. By Menander's day, we know over one hundred. Our evidence is serendipitous; doubtless many more existed. Despite this, our texts only ever mention the Athenian theater; e.g., *Acharnians* 504 tells us the play was performed at the Lenaea, and the *parabasis* of *Clouds* tells us that "because I judged you [Athenians] a clever audience, I deemed you worthy of first sampling this cleverest of all my comedies" (21–23). But this last example should put us on our guard: it implies that as early as 423 there were other audiences that Aristophanes might have preferred. The production records that survive only record first performances at the Athenian festivals, not necessarily premieres. The often-repeated creed that Old Comedy, or at least Aristophanes, was too Athenocentric to be produced anywhere but Athens is challenged by West Greek vases (Figures 2.3, 2.4, 7.1, 7.2), all produced for local markets, that show scenes of Old Comedy in performance, among them plays of Aristophanes. They date to the first half of the fourth century. It is even less likely that all the plays of Menander were performed first in Athens, yet even they are set, by preference, in Athens. Greeks evidently liked their comedy to be "Athenian" in much the same way that Romans liked it to be "Greek," and indeed by preference "Athenian" (Pl. *Men.* 7–9).

Even in Athens, the audience for the Dionysia (though not the Lenaea) had a large international component. The Dionysia, held at the beginning of the sailing season, attracted not only tourists but merchants eager to exploit the large markets attracted by the event. Hermippus (K-A fr. 63) lists goods that Dionysus, figured as the captain of a merchant ship, brought from all corners of the Mediterranean ("from Cyrene silphium and cowhides, from the Hellespont mackerel and salt fish, from Thessaly barley flakes and sides of beef… from Sicily pork and cheese," etc., etc.). Aristophanes did the same in *Merchant Ships* (K-A fr. 425–431). Official delegates from the cities of the empire must have numbered well over a thousand. Allies and colonies (roughly 200 at the peak of the empire) were required to bring to the Dionysia, along with their tribute, choruses (probably twelve to fifteen men) to process a phallus pole in the Parade. The tribute, about 500 talents of silver, was displayed in the theater to a populace feasting on bread and beef (also in large part contributed by the allies). Wealthy citizens might add free distributions of wine. The theme of the Dionysia was inclusivity, plenitude, and a "Golden Age" abundance, a Dionysian theme we find frequently echoed in the comedies.

Plenitude and inclusivity applied to people as well as goods. In addition to the Athenian population of some 30,000 adult citizen males, boys and slaves attended the festival. Some scholars deny the presence of women, though the ambiguities they claim for the evidence point more to ideological than physical exclusion. Even poorer citizens were provided with distributions of money (*theorika*) to help pay for seating in the theater and extras for the feast. Pericles seems to have initiated one-off distributions during the fifth century, but they became regular for much of the fourth.

The number of people who could attend the theater was always therefore much greater than the theater could accommodate. The fifth-century Theater of Dionysus probably seated about 6,000 people. The population of residents and visitors might have numbered forty times that figure. Until the early fourth century the city appears to have leased the construction of the *theatron* (i.e., seating area of the theater) to entrepreneurs who built wooden benches and charged 2 obols a sitting (Dem. 18.28.6–7). If we can draw a crude equation, watching all the plays might cost an individual the equivalent of one and a third times the daily wage of a skilled workman in Athens in the late fifth century, not an altogether inconsiderable sum.[1] Above the *theatron* on the south slope of the acropolis there was space for perhaps another 2,000 to stand. Seating was therefore always sociologically layered: the first row of seats (*prohedria*) consisted of chairs with backs (Figure 2.1) for elite officials and recipients of special honors (Dionysus's icon and priest sat front center); there followed some twenty rows of wooden benches for those who could afford it; above that, standing room.

Because the benchwork was simple and temporary, it formed three straight sides around a dancing ground (*orchestra*) of about 28 × 30 m. All early *orchestrai*—we know twelve—have a rectilinear (or more properly "trapezoidal") shape, with at best slight

---

[1] 2 obols × 4 days = 1.33 drachmas. One drachma per day is a typical daily wage of a skilled workman in Athens in the late fifth century

curvature as in the case of the theater at Thoricus, which uniquely had a stone *theatron*. The far end of the *orchestra* was bordered by the stage-building, the *skene,* erected by 458 (we know this from Aeschylus's *Oresteia*, where the building is not only necessary but virtually a main character). The *skene* was probably not permanent. We may suppose that it could be fitted with as many operational doors as required by any festival. From the 420s we have iconographic evidence (Figures 2.1, 2.3, 7.1) for a low stage (ca. 1 m. high) that stood in front of the *skene*. In the extant plays (with few exceptions), the chorus never departs the *orchestra* until the very end of the play; actors, on the other hand, used all available spaces (which is why Figure 2.1 shows a ladder descending into the orchestra), even the *skene* roof.

Because the Greek theater was open to the air, the vertical realm is often incorporated into the production, most particularly in the appearance of gods or airborne heroes on the *skene* roof or hanging from the crane *(mekhane).* Comedy used the crane for paratragic effect, e.g. in *Peace* (110–176) in a parody of Euripides's *Bellerophon,* or in Cratinus's *Seriphioi* in a generic parody of Perseus tragedy (Bakola 2010, 164–168, contemporary with our Figure 2.1, which shows a comic Perseus), or in a "tragic mode" to add pomp and grace to the grand entrances of gods and supermen (*Clouds* 218; *Birds* 1196–1261; Strattis *Phoenissai* K-A fr. 46). Even the subterranean realm cannot be excluded: tunnels leading from inside the *skene* to the center of the *orchestra,* called "Charon's stairs," are reported in fourteen ancient theaters, though none of them date from earlier than the third century.

FIGURE 2.1 Audience, abbreviated orchestra, stage and actor. Attic red-figured chous, Painter of the Perseus Dance, ca. 420 BCE, Athens BΣ 518. Drawing by E. Malyon. © E. Csapo.

Comedy is still freer in the use of the horizontal space from the *skene* interior out into the *theatron*. Tragedy used the *ekkyklema* or "out-roller," probably a shallow platform on wheels, to bring out interior tableaux, usually corpses, through the central doors of the *skene*. The tragic audience was to think of this device as revealing an interior scene, as if viewed through the open doors. In *Clouds* 183–201, however, the effect is more like walking into Socrates's Thinkery along with Strepsiades and glimpsing in succession the varied activities of its occupants. Sometimes the *ekkyklema* adds tragic grandeur to an entrance, e.g., Euripides's entrance in *Acharnians* or Agathon's in *Women at the Thesmophoria* or the tragically injured Cnemon's in *Dyskolos* 758. Comedy also engages the interior of the *skene* in ways unknown to tragedy; think of the various apertures from which Philocleon attempts to escape from the house in *Wasps* or the duets with the young woman at the window in *Assemblywomen*! Unlike tragedy, comedy can also breach the boundaries of its playing space and enter into the world of its audience. At the beginning of *Wasps*, for example, the two prologue slaves banter with the audience. In *Peace* 960–965, they throw them nuts and sweetmeats. Dionysus at *Frogs* 297 enters the front row of seats to seek protection from his priest. *Peace* 871–908 most expansively sends the actors into the section of the *theatron* reserved for the Council, where they deposit the gynecomorphic "Festival" on the lap of a red-faced city official. Old Comedy is particularly famous for addressing the audience, singling out individual audience members for mockery, or even briefly assigning the audience a role in the drama (e.g., *Frogs* 275–276).

The "fourth wall" did not exist for Old Comedy, and remained permeable for New. The audience is so regularly drawn into Old Comedy that it could never generate enough dramatic illusion to allow us to speak meaningfully of its rupture. For its part, the Athenian audience was far from passive. It clapped and shouted approval. If it was not satisfied it whistled, clucked, and banged its heels against the wooden seats. Sometimes it forced a drama to withdraw from the competition. It did not help that much of the audience was intoxicated: the Early Hellenistic historian of Athens, Philochorus (*FGrH* 328 F 171), informs us that stewards regularly poured wine for the audience (probably at the *choregos*'s expense) at the beginning and end of each drama. Old Comic performers hoped to elicit not just laughter but a show of partisan support. Attacking politicians or espousing popular causes was evidently not enough. The chorus made direct appeals for audience support (e.g., *Peace* 765–773). Some ancient sources suggest that the contest judges were swayed by the will of the crowd and others that the judges were obliged to be swayed by the will of the crowd. Plato tells us that in South Italy and Sicily the prize was determined by a direct show of hands by the audience (*Laws* 695a–c). Philemon is said to have engaged claques (Aul. Gel. 17.4, probably a malicious report, but doubtless a Hellenistic practice; cf. Plaut. *Amph.* 65–85). In general, it would appear that Old Comedy learned to manage those unruly energies of the festival crowd that other genres endured as random and dangerous disruptions.

Recent discoveries show that Athens began to build its earliest round theater (known to modern scholarship as "Lycurgan") in the early fourth century. Athens clearly felt the need for a more capacious theater. But while the theater became more inclusive by midcentury (the date of the completion of the *theatron*, now holding about 16,000), it became less inclusive in the late fourth century. The disenfranchisement and expulsion of a significant sector of the poorest Athenians after 322, as well as the probable abolition of the distribution of festival money sometime afterwards, are likely to have changed the demographics of the audience, pushing it somewhat higher on the socioeconomic scale.

A new *skene* was built for the Lycurgan theater, but it remained a single story. By the middle of Menander's career, however, there were many theaters in Greece with a *proskenion*. This was a single-story building placed directly in front of a two-story *skene* so that the roof (*episkenion*) of the one-story building (*proskenion*) might then be used as a very high stage against the backdrop of the *skene*'s second story. At Athens, however, the earliest *proskenion* appears to have been built only in the second century. Here actors must have continued to perform at *orchestra* level. From the 320s, we have evidence of Athens' concern to maintain the priority of its dramatic festival by trading on its cultural heritage as the home of the classics. The spatial configuration of the Athenian theater probably remained conservative to permit "authentic" reperformances of Aeschylus, Sophocles, and Euripides in which actors and chorus met at *orchestra* level. Nevertheless, scholars are frequently tempted to link the separation of chorus and actor in New Comedy with the gulf separating *orchestra* and *episkenion* in the Hellenistic theater. If this is correct, it shows the degree to which the topography of the Athenian theater had become irrelevant to dramatic performance. Poets like Menander must have had an eye to performance conditions elsewhere when they took the final step in severing the chorus from the dramatic narrative.

III. Costume and Mask

We know quite a lot about comic costume, thanks to a rich tradition of producing characters and whole scenes from comedy in art. A few highly realistic representations of tragic and satyric choruses (performing, dressing for performance, or undressing after performance) appear in vase painting as early as about 490. There survive only two (Attic) vase paintings that imitate or take inspiration from the paintings or reliefs dedicated by successful comic *choregoi* (some of which also survive). One of these is reconstructed in Figure 2.2.

By contrast, depictions of comic actors become very popular. In Attica, only a few small wine pots (such as that in Figure 2.1), produced 430–400, show comic actors. But from about 410, Athenian coroplasts begin to produce comic figurines and clay masks, probably for sale as souvenirs to visitors attending the Athenian Dionysia. These figurines are found throughout the Greek world, and were soon imitated by coroplasts from Spain to Egypt. The figurines are particularly important for describing the evolution of comic costume because they form a continuous series through to late antiquity. In addition, from 400–320 West Greek vase painters working in Southern Italy and Sicily take a major interest in Old Comedy, apparently inspired by local performances

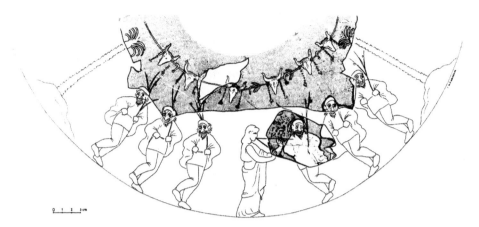

FIGURE 2.2 Abbreviated comic chorus in performance. Fragmentary Attic red-figured chous, 380–360 BCE, Benaki Museum 30895. Reconstruction by S. Pingiatoglou. Drawing by M. Miltsakakis. Reproduced courtesy of S. Pingiatoglou.

(Figures 2.3–4, 7.1–2). After 300, comic artifacts are produced in all media through-out the Mediterranean and they continue to be copied until the sixth century AD. New Comedy is therefore better attested iconographically than any dramatic or literary genre, with more than 3,500 surviving artifacts (Figures 2.5–9).

The artifacts show that the most basic costume of the Old Comic performer consisted of tights and a comic body that, unless covered by other costume, represented naked flesh. These appear most clearly on the central actor of Figure 2.3, which carefully ren-ders the wrinkles of the loose tights on upper and lower body, leaving only the head, hands, and feet uncovered. On top of these is an apparently one-piece padded leather torso (*somation*). This *somation* included full breasts, protruding buttocks, a large beer belly, and, hanging below the belly, a large phallus. Sometimes the whole *somation* is painted red (Figure 2.4), though frequently only the phallus is singled out in this way. The *somation* was apparently put on over the head and then fastened tight to the actor's body (note the buckle, visible on the actor's right side). None of the four surviving depic-tions of comic choruses allow us to decide if choreuts wore a phallus, but it is clear that they shared the rest of the comic body with the actors (Figure 2.2).

Old Comedy's hermaphrodite body may have its roots in Dionysian ritual, but the combination of feminine breasts and buttocks with masculine belly and phallus had the added benefit of permitting actors to switch from male to female characters without changing bodies. The contours of the old woman on stage in Figure 2.3 reveal the same body shape as the "naked" men. Female clothing always covered the entire body down to the ankles, so that the uncompromisingly gender-diagnostic phallus never confused the audience about the character's intended gender. Nude females, who do sometimes appear in comedy (e.g. Festival in *Peace*), were never played by actors but by mute extras. The term "actor" was reserved in antiquity for performers who spoke—there was never any limit to the number of nonspeaking parts in either tragedy or comedy.

FIGURE 2.3 Scene from Old Comedy with actors in orchestra and on stage. Apulian red-figured calyx krater, Tarporley Painter, ca. 400. The Metropolitan Museum of Art, Fletcher Fund, 1924 (24.97.104). Image © The Metropolitan Museum of Art.

The other essential component of comic costume was a full three-quarter mask (such as is seen floating near the top center of Figure 2.3). It left nothing of the actor's head exposed beyond teeth, lips (when closed), and the pupils of his eyes (the masks even included irises). The typology of Old Comic masks is known only from artifacts. There are some thirty recurrent types, and they are remarkably consistent between Attic and West Greek artifacts. One mask is used only for the character of Heracles. A mask consistently used for Zeus also seems to serve for other self-important men. Old Comedy seems to have used "portrait masks" to represent real individuals, though the crucial testimony, *Knights* 230–233, is just ambiguous enough to allow for dispute. In general, the repertoire of Old Comic masks revealed by the artifacts is strongly biased in favor of age and ugliness (in the Webster-Green typology, for example, apart from gods, heroes, and portrait masks of famous individuals like Socrates, we have among male masks only two young men, seven middle-aged men, and seven old men). It is also usually difficult to tell free men from slaves, unless the latter are carrying baggage or being beaten. Male characters regularly wore unconventionally short chitons in order to expose the phallus.

The art and literature of the fourth century are marked by an increased interest in human character. The development of the "science" of physiognomy had a particularly profound impact on rhetoric, drama, and the plastic arts. Physiognomics, a realm of philosophical speculation in which Aristotle's school took a particular interest, was premised upon a belief in the formal interdependence of mind and body, with the corollary that moral character and physical appearance are so closely correlated that one could learn to "read" character from examining a person's physical appearance. While advances in ethical philosophy encouraged growth and variation in comedy's range of characters, advances in physiognomics encouraged differentiation in the comic body and mask. Forms of comic ugliness that in Old Comedy had been evenly shared by all characters were in the later fourth century very unevenly redistributed across an ethical (and ultimately social) grid.

Variations in body shape emerge by the second half of the fourth century. The (for male characters) improbably prominent breasts and buttocks gradually disappear. Big bellies increasingly distinguish slaves from free men. The phallus, or rather its visibility, begins to mark social and characterological distinctions; the garments of free men grow decently longer (Figure 2.4). By the time of New Comedy, only slaves (and occasionally pimps) still have large bellies. Citizen "gentlemen" (i.e., the independently wealthy) wear shin-length garments, distinguishing them from the dependent or laboring classes, whose chitons descend to just below the knee, and from slaves, whose garments rise well above the knee, making the phallus comically visible when the actor sits down facing the audience. If Roman comedy can be used as evidence for its Greek prototypes, New Comic slaves still withdraw the phallus for an occasional joke (Marshall 2006: 62–64).

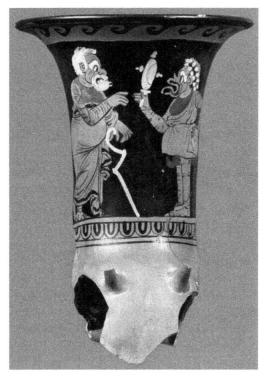

FIGURE 2.4 Master (left) and slave (right). Paestan red-figured rhyton, Asteas, 340–330 BCE, Museo Archeologico Regionale "Paolo Orsi," Syracuse 29966. By permission of the Assessorato Beni Culturali e dell'Identità Siciliana della Regione Sicilia.

But it is perhaps significant that the plays in question (*Rudens* 428–429, *Mostellaria* 324–331) are based on originals by Diphilus and Philemon, not Menander. Differentiation of body shape made quick changes more difficult for actors, and one might speculate that this encouraged one of the actors (probably the protagonist) to specialize in the depiction of characters who still shared comedy's traditional body fat: slaves, old women, and the nastier varieties of working men and urban poor—these tended also to be the more colorful and challenging roles.

The typology of New Comic masks is well known because of both the abundance of New Comic artifacts and the preservation of a list by the second-century AD rhetorician Julius Pollux (the list is copied from a much older source). The striking difference between the masks of New and Old Comedy, as between the comic bodies, is the uneven distribution of comic ugliness. Most of the young men and young women of New Comedy (now the majority) have naturalistic and often even attractive bodies and faces. Old men, old women, and particularly slaves retain something of the traditionally distorted facial features, but they do so differentially. Pollux lists forty-four mask types, with a short physical description; most of them can easily be matched with recurrent types found in the art.

A few examples will show how the New Comic mask, under the influence of physiognomic theory, fused physical with moral qualities. It is important to New Comedy that a given mask create expectations of certain forms of behavior, both in the mind of the audience and in the minds of the other characters in the drama. These expectations are, moreover, sometimes unfair or misleading—if we can judge from Menander's comedy, New Comic physiognomics was never strictly deterministic. False inferences about behavior or morality on the basis of appearance or social standing, when made by other characters in the drama, contribute to the misunderstandings around which so many New Comic plots revolve. False inferences by the audience permit the plot to generate surprising turns. We will restrict ourselves to a few examples taken from New Comedy's "heroes," the class of free young men.

Mask 10, the Excellent Youth (*Panchrestos*), comes close to the elite ideal (Figure 2.5). Pollux (4.146) says the mask "has a ruddy complexion, is athletic, and has a few wrinkles on his forehead, a wreath of hair, and raised eyebrows." The physiognomic literature indicates that a ruddy complexion shows a man to be good-natured, intelligent, quick, and athletic. The wrinkles show seriousness. The raised brows show agitation. He is the sort of comic youth who gets more sympathy than laughs as he actively seeks to rectify the misdeeds of others. He is, for example, very likely to be the main character of the play by Diphilus that served as model for Plautus's *Rudens* (where he is described, 314, as "strong, ruddy-complexioned, and intense"). Several Excellent Youth masks retain their reddish-brown paint.

Also of good family, but of much weaker moral fiber, is mask 13, the Delicate Youth (Figure 2.6). Pollux says the Delicate Youth, "with hair like the Excellent Youth, is the youngest of all the young men and white-skinned, brought up in the shade, intimating delicacy." His face appears pudgy with residual baby fat. The Aristotelian *Physiognomica* (812a 13–14) makes white skin a sign of timidity and effeminacy. The Delicate Youth

FIGURE 2.5 Terracotta Mask of Excellent Youth, Würzburg H 4613. Courtesy Martin von Wagner Museum der Universität Würzburg. Photo: Peter Neckermann.

FIGURE 2.6 Terracotta Mask of Delicate Youth, 2nd c. BCE, Munich 5401. Courtesy Staatliche Antikensammlungen und Glyptothek, Munich.

has had a protected upbringing, with always a slave or pedagogue to look after him. Sostratus in the *Dyskolos* probably wears this mask. Sostratus is white-skinned, and gives the immediate impression of being soft, lazy, and dependent on others. He initially relies on others to win his girl for him (though her father, unknown to him, prizes rugged self-reliance). He gains some self-reliance in the course of the play, even does hard work and acquires a bit of tan. This proves instrumental in gaining Cnemon's approval.

The Delicate Youth usually wears a festive wreath; he likes parties. He is also musical, and plays cymbals in *Theophoroumene*. He easily loses control. Frequently he is a rapist. The character behind Diniarchus in the original of Plautus's *Truculentus* was probably a Delicate Youth. He is described as "a soft adulterer, a curly-haired shadeling, a tambourine banger" (609–610). Against this background we are to understand Gorgias's alarm at the attention Sostratus pays his sister in *Dyskolos*. Because of his youth and uncontrolled friskiness, the wearer of mask 13 is frequently called "Moschion" ("Little calf"; e.g., *Sikyonios*, esp. 200 and 258; *Perikeiromene*).

Lower down the social scale is the poor but respectable Rustic Youth. Pollux's description of mask 14 lists the attributes "dark-skinned, thick lips, a snub nose, and a wreath of hair" (Figure 2.7). These features draw upon satyr and faun iconography. The physiognomic literature associates the snub nose with lasciviousness. Thick lips and a broad forehead are signs of stupidity. The rustic is dark from working the fields. He knows little leisure and consequently shows no grace or cultivation. To Theophrastus, rusticity is "a disfiguring sort of ignorance." Because he appears coarse, dirty, and poor, he is often treated with contempt by urban upper-class characters. As a result, he is suspicious, quick to take offence, and fierce in the assertion of his rights. The physiognomists make flaring nostrils a sign of a quick temper. One anticipates an explosion of wrath and resentment when Gorgias first confronts Sostratus in *Dyskolos*, especially after he accuses Sostratus of perpetrating a crime "deserving many deaths" (292). Pollux says the rustic wears a goatskin and carries a leather bag and a crook (4.119–120). He is likely to have a speaking name like Gorgias (*georgos* means "farmer").

New Comic masks were not invariable; it appears to have been up to the poet or mask-maker to emphasize different features. The Toady (mask 17) and Parasite (mask

FIGURE 2.7 Terracotta Mask of Rustic Youth, Late 4th—Early 3rd c., Louvre MNB 506. © RMN / Hervé Lewandowski.

FIGURE 2.8 Terracotta Figurine of Toady, 2nd c., National Archeological Museum, Athens 5027. © Hellenic Ministry of Culture and Tourism/Archaeological Receipts Fund.

18) both belong to young men pursuing the same "profession" (flattering and sponging off rich patrons), and both have the same basic features. Many masks, while easily identifiable as either a Parasite or Toady, allow no clearer determination and would best be mapped at various locations along a continuum stretching from one mask to the other, depending on the impression of harmlessness or malevolence that each particular example evokes. According to Pollux: "The Toady and the Parasite are dark-skinned—but not more so than befits the wrestling-ground—and hook-nosed; they aspire to live the good life. The Parasite has more broken ears and is more cheerful, whereas the Toady raises his eyebrows more maliciously" (4.149). Figure 2.8 is only a six or seven on the scale of malevolence: his right eyebrow is raised, but not his left (clearer "Toadies" raise both). Contrast the more relaxed and good-natured appearance of Figure 2.9. The physiognomy of the raised brows shows mischievousness and vehemence; the hook nose indicates shamelessness; the short neck shows a treacherous nature; the hunched shoulders indicate an unfree disposition. This last points to the Parasite/Toady's ambiguous social status: he spends his time in the gymnasium and in the company of gentlemen, dining with the wealthy, but is entirely dependent upon their good will and usually performs servile duties. He carries an oil bottle and a strigil (the former still visible in the left hand, the latter lost from the right hand of Figure 2.8) in order to rub down his patron after a day at the gymnasium. His ears are broken because frequently boxed by

FIGURE 2.9 Terracotta Mask of Parasite, Early 3rd c., Lipari 11188. By permission of the Archaeological Museum "Luigi Bernabò Brea"—Lipari (Eolian Island—Italy).

his patron. He flatters his patron and endures mockery and insults but secretly despises him. The more toadyish of his tribe will betray their patrons the moment they have anything to gain by it. The best Parasites/Toadies are preserved in Roman comedy, where they are given names like Jawbone (Gnatho), Breadgnawer (Artotrogus), and Little Sponge (Peniculus), often explaining how they acquired the nickname in an entrance monologue.

IV. ACTING

Old Comic acting was not illusionistic. Everything tended towards artifice: the padding, the oversized phallus, the grotesquely distorted mask, the absurd presuppositions and movements of the plot, even the manner of delivery. Old Comedies are half musical. The chorus's lines, normally a quarter of the play, were always delivered to the music of a piper who remained conspicuously visible in the *orchestra* or on stage from the time the chorus entered until the end of the drama. Actors too spoke barely half their lines: iambic trimeter, the meter of dialogue, was in comedy especially loose and close to natural speech, but the rest was sung to pipes (lyric meters), or chanted (regular meters other than iambic trimeter). Movement was also often unnatural. The chorus danced as it sang, or it performed a stylized march as it chanted (Figure 2.2). This was probably also often true of the actors. Finally, the texts show little concern to make the action believable or the characters consistent. Plutarch justly complained that Aristophanes did nothing to distinguish the language of one character from another. Although Plutarch should have made some allowance for Aristophanes's imitation of the inherently and immediately ridiculous speech of foreigners, or of tragic and dithyrambic poets, this had more to do with mimicry than character acting. Parmenon, the most famous comic actor of the mid-fourth century, was best remembered for his imitation of a squealing pig (Plut. *Mor.* 18c, 674b–c).

Old Comic acting tends to staginess and virtuoso display, not the illusionism and naturalism that became increasingly popular in tragedy. Just as the plot could be loosely strung between set choral pieces, the acting was sometimes loosely strung between set routines, calculated crowd-pleasers. These are often prepared, carefully "framed" moments that mark off the discrete segments in the action that invite the audience to admire the actor's virtuosity and to give applause. For this reason Old Comedy is particularly fond of narrative modes that frame the artifice (metatheater, self-reference, paratragedy) and the related plot devices that "stage" it (disguise scenes, rehearsals, impersonations). There is indeed room for illusionistic acting in this kind of regime, but only when it is bracketed off as artifice, because illusionistic acting was hostile to Old Comedy's purpose, which was not to create a "suspension of disbelief" but to draw attention to the skill with which it aped other activities, genres, and cultural practices. Figure 2.3 nicely exemplifies how the action is arranged to showcase the actor's mimic talents.

Figure 2.3 shows an abbreviated and foreshortened theater filled by four characters. On the far left and on a higher plane, occupying the space of the audience and simply watching, we see a young man without mask or costume; he is mysteriously labeled *tragoidos* (tragedic poet, actor, or choreut). The other three characters represent actors: they wear masks and comic costume. Letters issue from their mouths, representing lines from the comedy. The old woman on the stage to the right says "I hand him over," the man in the *orchestra* on his tiptoes with raised arms says "he has tied up my hands," and the thuggish-looking character on the left says "Noraretteblo," which is not Greek, and which may indicate that he is a policeman, since in Athens the police function was performed by Scythians. The old woman's phrase is perfectly intelligible and is a formula by which she releases her slave for interrogation or punishment (which in Athenian law were the same thing, since the evidence of slaves was only admissible when extracted under torture). The old man is about to get a beating from the thug with the stick: it was also customary to suspend slaves before whipping them, in order to inflict maximum damage.

For a long time, however, it bothered iconographers that no ropes were visible upon or above the old man's wrists. They suggested that the phrase he speaks meant "he has bound up my hands [with a magical curse]." This presupposes the standard of illusionistic performance that I have just denied for the Old Comic theater; indeed, such a scene could never have been performed in the middle of the *orchestra*, where there is nothing to hang a man from. And yet there is a high degree of (pointedly non-naturalistic) illusionism. The old man is creating the illusion of being suspended (this is why the painter shows him on tiptoes and not actually hanging in the air). The line of his words also suggests, like a wake, the sudden movement as he rises up as if being hoisted by invisible men pulling invisible ropes. But it is what must follow that is of particular interest. He will be beaten, and he must sway his back violently to and fro while continuing to dance *en pointe* in order to create the illusion of one suspended while beaten. The scene was evidently a favorite precisely because of the bravura performance involved (we have the same kind of beating scene at *Frogs* 632–671). But the important point is that these scenes are not illusionism for its own sake: if believability were important, the scene would either have been omitted or the old man would have been suspended from the *skene*. Attention is deliberately drawn to the absence of ropes, not away from the "unreal." He is beaten in order to show off the extraordinary body control that creates the illusion of a tortured man dangling in the air.

Old Comic actors needed an enormous range of talents. In addition to the gymnastic and balletic skills noted above, they needed an operatic singing voice; actor's monody became increasingly popular in the last two decades of the fifth century, largely because it became increasingly popular in tragedy. Many comic songs are paratragic, but even the parodic songs could be highly original compositions, like the song of the Hoopoe in *Birds,* requiring an extraordinary vocal range and expertise. Breath control was not the least of the necessary vocal and musical talents. The "choker" (*pnigos*) or "long song" (*makron*), a type of patter-song in anapaestic dimeters, usually containing lists, was meant to be delivered without pausing for breath (cf. Pollux 4.112, Σ Ar. *Ach.* 659; Σ Ar. *Eq.* 507, etc.). It is invariably quite short when delivered by the chorus, and one wonders how it acquired its name, but the same form of song when delivered by actors can stretch to extraordinary lengths precisely to create an opportunity for a bravura performance: twenty-eight lines in *Peace* 987–1015, forty-one lines in Mnesimachus's *Hippotrophos,* and an amazing menu of sixty-six lines recited by a cook in Anaxandrides's *Protesilaus* in just one (or two?) breath(s).

New Comedy, by contrast, did pursue illusionism and naturalism for their own sake. All aspects of production point this way. New Comedy dispensed with most of the "unreal" aspects of Old Comedy: *phalloi* and body fat, grotesque masks, highly poetic language, the *mekhane*. It severed the connection with the chorus and virtually got rid of all but the spoken forms of delivery. Its vocabulary was drawn from common speech, a choice praised by Aristotle as most illusionistic ("it deceives well")—Aristotle most admired it in his contemporary, the tragedian Theodorus (*Rhetoric* 1404b: "his seems the voice of natural speech, others' artificial"). The function of drama was, like that of rhetoric, to persuade (or, as Aristotle put it, to "deceive"), and this, Aristotle says, can only be done when words, voice, and character match one another (*Rhetoric* 1408b). Many studies have in fact shown the care with which Menander tailored the vocabulary, expressions, syntax, and contents of speech, not just to specific types but to individual characters, even endowing them with recurrent tics of speech, and sometimes allowing them to be flustered and, as in transcripts of real unrehearsed speech, ungrammatical.

It is surprising, given this context, that controversy could exist over whether (in accordance with Aristotle's prescription) voices were modulated to suit different characters. The surest proof is the frequent direct quotation of other characters in narrative monologues. Quintilian complains that "even if [comic actors] play the part of a youth they nonetheless speak with a quavering or effeminate voice when reporting the speech of an old man, as for example in the prologue of [Menander's] *Hydria,* or of a woman, as in [Menander's] *Georgos*" (*Inst.* 11.3.91). It cannot have been any different in Menander's day; the use of direct speech without the use of quotatives (introductory words, such as "he said," that mark the quotation as such) is a distinctive feature of Menander's drama. Narratives with frequent and otherwise unmarked changes of voice would be unintelligible without mimicry of the voices quoted. Plato complained precisely about dramatic "imitation in voice and gesture" that required "every kind of pitch and rhythm if it is to be delivered properly" (*Rep.* 397a–c). Surely vocal mimesis is indicated by the admonition of "Euripides" to his kinsmen to "effeminize his voice" when he adopts a female disguise (*Women at the Thesmophoria* 267–268) and Praxagoras's command to the women in male disguise to speak "like men" (*Assemblywomen* 149).

But naturalism in New Comic acting is only part of the story. New Comic acting styles share the same dualism that permits New Comedy to juxtapose naturalistic costumes and masks for free leisure-class gentlemen to grotesque and residually Old Comic costumes and masks for slaves and working-class characters. Hunter (in Easterling and Hall 2002) identifies in Menander a "high" and a "low" acting style. In *Dyskolos,* for example, the low style is associated with the cook Sicon and the slave Getas, whose celebration in the play's final scene reproduces action previously negotiated by respectable characters earlier in the play, but through the distorted mirror of pure farce. After the more serious characters have withdrawn to celebrate the double betrothal of Sostratus and Gorgias to each other's sisters, the slaves begin their own celebration by ragging the misanthrope Cnemon. This happens through a series of door-knocking scenes, a comic shtick since Aristophanes, but in the case of Sostratus and Gorgias, Menander aborted the scenes as soon as the young men showed they had the gumption to call out the cranky old man. Having turned a hackneyed joke into serious drama, Menander now reproduces it, through the agency of the low characters, as violent farce. It is a reversion to full-scale Old Comic style, in which the slave and cook, for the only time ever in extant Menander, chant iambic tetrameters rhythmically to the accompaniment of the piper (metatheatrically addressed in 880 and 910), make obscene jokes, and engage in knockabout. It is also a planned and "staged" performance designed to infuriate Cnemon, although this time it is the comic mode that is framed within the naturalistic. In acting, as in everything else, Greek New Comedy seems an unresolved mixture of naturalism, adopted from tragedy, and Old Comic burlesque.

Further Reading

Green 1995 and Green 2008 offer a bibliographical survey of all literature relating to the production of ancient drama from 1987 to 2006. We lack a general work on the evolution of performance styles in the Greek theater. The best overviews are Wiles 2000 and the collection Easterling and Hall 2002, in particular the essays by Hall, Wilson, Valakas, Green, Csapo, Sifakis, Handley, Hunter, and Lada-Richards, though the emphasis in most of these essays is on tragedy. All aspects of Old Comic production are excellently served by Revermann 2006. Wiles 1991 contains much of interest on the performance of Menander.

The most important works on comic artifacts, though forbidding to the nonexpert, are Webster and Green 1978 for Old Comedy and Webster, Green, and Seeberg 1995 for New Comedy. Far more accessible introductions to the kinds of information that theater-related artifacts can yield are Green 1994, for a general overview; Taplin 1993, for West Greek vase painting; Nervegna 2013 for art illustrating scenes from Menander; and Csapo 2010, which also discusses the reception of theatre and actors in antiquity. Comic acting is a virgin field: Green 1997 and Green's essay in Easterling and Hall 2002 are pioneering studies in comic gestural language. while Csapo 1993 investigates the performance of the running slave shtick. Recent excavation and research have rendered obsolete all the standard discussions in English of theater topography. The most reliable and accessible general introductions are in French (Moretti 2001) and German (Goette 1995, Froning 2002). Roselli 2011 is a comprehensive study of the Athenian theater audience.

BIBLIOGRAPHY

Bakola, E. 2010. *Cratinus and the Art of Comedy*. Oxford: Oxford University Press.

Csapo, E. 1993. "A Case Study in the Use of Theatre Iconography as Evidence for Ancient Acting." *Antike Kunst* 36: 41–58.

——. 2010. *Actors and Icons of the Ancient Theater*. Malden, MA: Wiley-Blackwell.

Easterling, P. E. and E. Hall. 2002. *Greek and Roman Actors: Aspects of an Ancient Profession*. Cambridge, UK: Cambridge University Press.

Froning, H. 2002. "Bauformen—Vom Holzgerüst zum Theater vom Epidauros." In *Die Geburt des Theaters in der griechischen Antike,* edited by S. Moraw and E. Nölle, 31–59. Mainz: Von Zabern.

Goette, H. R. 1995. "Griechische Theaterbauten der Klassik—Forschungsstand und Fragestellungen." In *Studien zur Bühnendichtung und zum Theaterbau der Antike,* edited by E. Pöhlmann, 9–48. Frankfurt: Peter Lang.

Green, J. R. 1994. *Theatre in Ancient Greek Society*. London and New York: Routledge.

——. 1995. "Theatre Production: 1987–1995." *Lustrum* 37: 7–202.

——. 1997. "Deportment, Costume and Naturalism in Comedy." *Pallas* 47: 131–43.

——. 2008. "Theatre Production: 1996–2006." *Lustrum* 50: 7–391.

MacDowell, D. M. 1989. "Athenian Laws about Choruses." In *Symposion 1982. Vorträge zur griechischen und hellenistischen Rechtsgeschichte,* edited by F. J. Fernandez Nieto, 67–77. Akten der Gesellschaft für griechische und hellenistische Rechtsgeschichte 5. Cologne: Böhlau.

Marshall, C. W. 2006. *The Stagecraft and Performance of Roman Comedy*. Cambridge, UK: Cambridge University Press.

Moretti, J.-C. 2001. *Théâtre et société dans la Grèce antique: Une archéologie des pratiques théâtrales*. Paris: Librairie générale française.

Nervegna, S. 2013. *Menander in Antiquity: The Contexts of Reception*. Cambridge, UK: Cambridge University Press.

Pickard-Cambridge, A. 1968. *Dramatic Festivals of Athens*. 2nd ed., edited by J. Gould and D. M. Lewis. Oxford: Clarendon Press.

Revermann, M. 2006. *Comic Business: Theatricality, Dramatic Technique, and Performance Contexts of Aristophanic Comedy*. Oxford: Oxford University Press.

Roselli, D. K. 2011. *Theater of the People: Spectators and Society in Ancient Athens*. Austin: University of Texas Press.

Taplin, O. 1993. *Comic Angels*. Oxford: Clarendon Press.

Webster, T. B. L., and J. R. Green. 1978. *Monuments Illustrating Old and Middle Comedy*. BICS Suppl. 39. London: Institute of Classical Studies.

Webster, T. B. L., J. R. Green, and A. Seeberg. 1995. *Monuments Illustrating New Comedy*. BICS Suppl. 50. London: Institute of Classical Studies.

Wiles, D. 1991. *The Masks of Menander: Sign and Meaning in Greek and Roman Performance*. Cambridge: Cambridge University Press.

———. 2000. *Greek Theatre Performance: An Introduction*. Cambridge: Cambridge University Press.

Wilson, P. 2000. *The Athenian Institution of the Khoregia*. Cambridge: Cambridge University Press.

CHAPTER 3

DIONYSIAC FESTIVALS IN ATHENS AND THE FINANCING OF COMIC PERFORMANCES

ANDRONIKE MAKRES

THE institution of liturgies in Ancient Athens was a system whereby rich Athenians were assigned the task of providing funding for special public needs. There were two kinds of liturgy, military and festival. The major military one was the trierarchy, for which a rich funder (trierarch) equipped and commanded a trireme (warship) for a year; the main festival liturgy was the choregia (pl. choregiai), for which a rich funder (choregos, pl. choregoi) took charge of producing a dithyrambic, tragic, or comic chorus that performed at a public festival. Since the performances took place in a competitive context (the agon), the choregia was also termed an "agonistic liturgy." This chapter focuses on the latter type of liturgy, the choregia. It first offers some brief remarks on the ideological foundations of this institution, and then discusses the choregia for comedies performed in the dramatic contests at the two major city festivals, the City (or Great) Dionysia and the Lenaea, both in honor of the god Dionysus. Next, discussion turns to the duties and responsibilities of the choregos, and after that, to the monuments he dedicated when victorious in the festival contests. Theatrical performances, of course, were not events administered only at the central level of the polis; demes, too, had their own local theaters and festivals, and a subsequent section of this chapter is devoted to comedy at the Rural Dionysia in the demes of Attica. The end of the institution of the choregia in the last years of the fourth century BCE forms an appropriate—and controversial—subject for the conclusion.

IDEOLOGICAL FOUNDATIONS OF THE
INSTITUTION OF CHOREGIA

The introduction of the choregia raises questions regarding its ideological founda-tions; e.g., was it fundamentally a democratic or an aristocratic institution? From one perspective, the institution of liturgies exemplifies fundamental characteristics of the developing Athenian democracy. At the operational level, the institution manifests the expansion of state control into the economic, religious, and military spheres that was crucial to the entrenchment of democracy. The liturgical system formed an inte-gral part of the mechanism that managed the public affairs of the city; its organization and operation were based on the Cleisthenic civic order that was the foundation of the democratic system. On the ideological level, one could argue that the institution of litur-gies relied on a nonaristocratic principle of cooperation that imposed not only a moral but also a statutory obligation on privileged or qualified individuals to contribute to the common good (see the expression *ta prostattomena* "state orders," typically used when referring to liturgies in Isaeus 4. 27; 7. 36; Lysias 7. 30–1; 16. 171; 18. 18; 21. 23; Dem. 38. 26; 47. 48). Thus, by emphasizing an intrinsic relation between liturgies and democracy, one could argue—rightly, I think—that the institution of liturgies is more likely to have emerged under the democratic order, and so its introduction might be dated soon after the Cleisthenic reforms (508 BCE).

On the other hand, liturgies can also be viewed as an institutionalized version of aristocratic largess, thus representing a survival of an aristocratic past, since the per-formance of liturgies was proof of wealth and a source of prestige that might lead to prominent positions in society. In support of this view, one can adduce J. K. Davies's seminal work (1971) that shows that the Athenians who are known to have performed liturgies in ancient Athens were also those who constituted the dominant class in terms of public administration and political power.

Concerning the nature of the institution of choregia the following points can be made:

1. Under the democratic order, a high degree of organization is manifest in the public affairs of the city of Athens; specific religious and administrative tasks were precisely set for state authorities or citizens to carry out, and records of payments and accomplished duties were kept (Rhodes 2012: 57–77; Scafuro 2010 and Scafuro 2013, Sinclair 1988, Stockton 1990). The institution of choregia reflects the same degree of organization.

2. From a financial point of view, it was important that the liturgical financing of festivals functioned as a regular source of revenue for the state in the sense that expenses that would otherwise be incurred by the state were instead transferred to wealthy individuals. Although the Athenians did not have a formal budget until at least the end of the fifth century BCE (Rhodes 2006: 263 = Rhodes

2010: 299), they did have some idea of their likely expenditures and revenues, and the liturgical system was one basic mechanism that was meant to strike a balance between the two.

3. On the ideological level, both the conception and the operation of the liturgical system were governed by democratic principles and values: it provided a mechanism for "taxing" the wealthy class; it ensured that their resources were used for the advancement of the majority's interest; and it ensured that those propertied individuals were not only financially but also personally involved in those duties, thus forcing the wealthy to be involved in the affairs of the democratic polis and preventing the alienation of the upper class from the rest of society. Finally, the reliance of the institution of liturgies, of which choregia was a part, upon the principles of *philotimia* (the desire or eagerness of an individual to be the recipient of public honors), of *philonikia* (the desire or eagerness to be the winner in a contest), and of public *charis* (a sense of obligation or gratitude of the community towards individual contributors) offered an alternative to upper-class attitudes: instead of pursuing narrow-minded self-interest that was potentially disruptive to the well-being of society, wealthy individuals were consistently challenged to experience the gratification of having pursued and served common causes.

4. Finally, it should be noted that while democratic principles may have guided the legislation that made the choregia and other liturgies work, the cooperation of the wealthy, and especially the harmonious fit of their own goals and sociopolitical aspirations with the democratic community, were crucial factors in the successful operation of the institution.

The two major dramatic festivals were the City or Great Dionysia and the Lenaea, both held annually in the urban center of Athens. The City Dionysia took place during Elaphebolion (the ninth month of the archontic year, approximately equivalent to our March) and were administered by the principal magistrate of Ancient Athens, the eponymous archon, who was designated simply archon. The festival served many ends, and two important and interrelated ones were to reinforce the civic identity of the Athenians and to advertise the democracy as a successful system of government (see Goldhill 1987, Connor 1989, and Rhodes 2011: 73–74). The City Dionysia comprised both dramatic (tragic and comic) and dithyrambic competitions. The Lenaea were held in Gamelion (the seventh month, a winter month approximately equivalent to our January) and were administered by the member of the board of nine archons designated basileus (king), who was primarily a religious official. The Lenaea comprised only dramatic competitions, not dithyrambic ones.

The official participation of comedy in the City Dionysia began, according to the *Suda*, in 487/6 BCE with a contest in which the victory was won by Chionides. Aristotle reports the admission of comedy to the festival in this way: "it was at a later time when the archon granted a comic chorus; previously the performers were volunteers" (*Poetics* 1449b καὶ γὰρ χορὸν κωμῳδῶν ὀψέ ποτε ὁ ἄρχων ἔδωκεν, ἀλλ᾽ ἐθελονταὶ ἦσαν). The archon's grant was "late"; probably Aristotle means "late" in comparison to the archon's grants of choruses to tragedy and dithyramb, but the reasons for the delay are not specified. Probably performances of comedy had not been absent from the City Dionysia before 487/6 BCE but had been held in an unofficial manner (see Rusten chapter 1, pp. 36–39). In Aristotle's report, the *official* participation of comedy is harbingered by the archon's grant of the chorus for comedies; the state had now taken control of the festival contests (the agon) through its highest magistrate (the archon), who became the main figure involved in the choregic organization of the City Dionysia. Probably the act of the archon's granting the choruses to the comic poets implies that the choruses were financed by liturgies; the choregic system was thus probably operating at least as early as 487/6 BCE, when comedy officially entered the City Dionysia, as well as earlier in support of the tragic and dithyrambic contests.

The performances of comedy (and of tragedy and dithyramb) were held in a competitive (agonistic) context. The first epigraphically documented comic victory (though the inscription mentioning it was inscribed much later) is that of Magnes at the City Dionysia in 473/2 BCE, with Xenocleides as choregos. In the same year, the victorious choregos in tragedy was Pericles, with Aeschylus as the poet. The epigraphic document that supplies this evidence is a much-discussed inscription known as the *Fasti* (IG II^2 2318, *DFA*^{2}: 71–2 and Millis and Olson 2012: 5–58) which listed all the victories at the City Dionysia starting from the point when the contests were formally introduced (perhaps in 501 BCE—unfortunately, a few of its first entries are lost). For each year the *Fasti* recorded first the archon's name, then the victorious tribes and choregoi for the dithyrambic competitions, then the victorious choregos and poet in comedy, and finally the victorious choregos and poet in tragedy (see Millis and Olson 2012:6, and 10 for an example of the entries in the Greek text).

THE CITY DIONYSIA AND THE APPOINTMENT OF ITS CHOREGOI FOR COMEDY

The archon, as soon as he has entered on his office, first makes a proclamation that whatever each man possessed before his entry into office he shall possess and control until the end of it. Next he appoints *choregoi* [individuals who would be in charge of producing the choruses for the performances at the festivals] for the tragedies, the three richest of all the Athenians; formerly he also appointed five *choregoi* for the comedies, but these are now nominated by the tribes. The tribes nominate *choregoi* for the Dionysia (for men's choruses, boys' choruses, and comedies) [...] The archon receives the names of the choregoi who were nominated by the tribes. Then he holds challenges to an exchange [*antidoseis*], and introduces into court claims for exemption [*skepseis*] when a man claims that he has performed this liturgy before, or is exempt because he has performed another liturgy and his period of exemption is not yet over, or has not reached the required age (*choregoi* for boys' choruses must be over forty years old). (Arist. *Ath. Pol.* 56.2–3; translation based on P. J. Rhodes, 1984: 101–102.)

This passage from the Aristotelian *Athenian Constitution* is more or less the only available evidence on the procedure followed for the appointment of choregoi in comedy at the City Dionysia in Ancient Athens. At the time when the Aristotelian treatise was written, the second half of the fourth century BCE, the choregoi for comedy at the Dionysia were nominated by the ten Athenian tribes.[1]

We are not told how the nomination procedure itself was carried out. Nomination of choregoi by tribes, however, was a regular feature in contests that were tribally organized. A tribally organized festival contest meant that tribal authorities were involved both in the organization of the contests and in the procedure of appointing the choregoi; once appointed, the choregoi represented the tribe to which they belonged, they recruited the chorus among the members of their own tribes, and a victory was not considered an individual one, the choregos's, but a collective one—the victory belonged to the tribe. Dithyramb was tribally organized, but the tragic and comic contests were not, and this remained the case in spite of the change in the procedure of nominating choregoi for comedy from the tribes.

The distinction between nomination and appointment is noteworthy (see, e.g., Dem. 21.13, where speeches and recriminations were allegedly exchanged between archon and *epimeletai* when a choregos had not been appointed for the tribe Pandionis). The nomination of some choregoi seems always to have been the responsibility of tribal authorities (see, e.g., Dem. 20.130, referring to the exemption from liturgies of the descendants of Harmodius and Aristogeiton: unspecified choregoi nominated by tribes; 39.7: unspecified choregoi nominated by tribes since ca. at least 349 BCE, the approximate date of the speech) and was a less final act than the actual appointment made by the archon, which indicates that the archon was the authority with the last word in those arrangements. How did the ten Cleisthenic tribes nominate five choregoi for comedy at the City Dionysia? The tribal authorities responsible for their nomination in the fourth century are known as the *epimeletai* ("supervisors") of the tribes (see Dem. 21.13; also Traill 1986: 79–92 and MacDowell 1990: 237), with one coming from each *trittys* in each of the ten tribes, thereby producing a total of thirty (see n. 1 for "*trittys*"); the *epimeletai* were the most important tribal officials, whose range of duties included supervision of the tribe's funds. There is no evidence for the time of year when the nomination procedure for choregoi was held except for *Argument* II, 2 to Dem. 21 (a not particularly reliable document), namely that within the first month after the end of the festival, choregoi

---

[1] Since 508 BCE, when Cleisthenes introduced his reforms, the population of Athens had been divided into ten tribes, each tribe comprising members of local communities (demes) situated in each of the three geographical subdivisions (*trittyes*) of Attica, namely the city (*asty*), the inland (*mesogaia*), and the coast (*paralia*). The demes were the local communities of Athens; they were both autonomous sociopolitical entities and constituents of the polis (see the comprehensive study on the demes of Attica Whitehead 1986).

for the next festival were nominated; if this is true, nominations by the tribal authorities for the City Dionysia took place in the month Mounichion, the third month before the beginning of the new archontic year.

The same passage from the *Athenian Constitution* also tells us that earlier, at an unspecified time, the archon had appointed five choregoi for comedy. Unfortunately no explanation is given for the subsequent change to nomination by tribes (to be followed by appointment by the archon) nor for the odd consequence, namely that choregoi for comedy at the Dionysia were nominated by tribes even though comedy was not itself a tribally organized contest like that of dithyramb. Perhaps the change suggests a limitation on the archon's powers, since he would now no longer be able to choose freely among the men who were members of the liturgical class (Davies, 1971: xx); instead, he would have to draw on a restricted pool of men nominated by the tribes. The change could thus be viewed as a further step in the gradual democratization of the official procedures involved in the choregic system, since the former concentration of power in the hands of the archon enabled him, if he wished, to choose and combine poets with choregoi on the basis of political sympathies.[2]

The date for the change in procedure for appointing comic choregoi can only be conjectured. J. Keaney (1970: 128–134, 330, nn. 17, 19) suggested that it took place around the middle of the fourth century and associated it "with one of the main themes in the historical part of *AP*," which is "that the demos appropriated powers which had originally belonged to the archons and to the Areopagos" (see also Rhodes commentary ad. loc.). In any case, we can be certain that in the fifth century BCE, the archon was responsible for appointing both the three choregoi for tragedy and the five choregoi for comedy at the City Dionysia. He had to choose among the wealthiest Athenians who had to pay for the cost of the production of the dramatic choruses. This may have been an oral agreement concluded on the spot, and it seems that the archon's discretion during this process was not officially restricted or controlled in any way.

THE LENAEA AND ITS CHOREGOI

The basileus managed the contests at the Lenaea (Arist. *Ath. Pol.* 57.1) and appointed the choregoi for the tragic and comic performances. In Dem. 39. 9, the basileus is mentioned as being responsible for appointing liturgists; it follows that these liturgists were choregoi for the Lenaea. The sources do not provide any details on the procedure; probably it was similar to that carried out by the archon at the City Dionysia. Davies (1967: 34 and nn. 17, 21;

---

[2] It is also logical to assume that the *epimeletai* who were responsible for the nomination of the choregoi for comedy reflected a democratic development; see Theophr. *Char.* 26.ii, where the oligarchic man objects to the appointment of democratic *epimeletai* to help the archon with the organization of a procession; also Rhodes 1981: 627.

similarly *DFA*² 1988: 40) dated the liturgical financing of the comic contests at the Lenaea to the 440s, the years in which the first entries for the victorious comic poets appear on the didascalic inscription, IG II ² 2325 (Millis and Olson 2012: 178). Davies (ibid.) further suggested that the tragic contest as well as its liturgical financing at the Lenaea may have begun in 432 BCE, at least a decade after the comic contest had entered the competition.

The Lenaea was the only festival at which metics were allowed to perform choregiai and noncitizens were allowed to perform as chorus members (see schol. Arist. *Wealth* 953: οὐκ ἐξῆν δὲ ξένον χορεύειν ἐν τῷ ἀστικῷ χορῷ…ἐν δὲ τῷ Ληναίῳ ἐξῆν ἐπεὶ καὶ μέτοικοι ἐχορήγουν; 'It was not possible for a foreigner to become a chorus member in the civic chorus [i.e., the City Dionysia]; at the Lenaean one, however, this was possible because metics were also appointed choregoi'). There is also epigraphic evidence that may attest the choregia of metics at the Lenaea, namely, a fragmentary list of men and *phialai* (vessels) dedicated by individuals who had performed liturgies ([φιάλας λειτουργι]κάς; Lewis 1968; Meyer 2010: 126–129). The list, dated to 331/0, includes the choregoi at the Lenaea and thus ll. 46–47 of *fragment d* could be restored as the name of the resident deme of a metic who was one of the choregoi for comedy.³ The choregoi for comedy who had dedicated *phialai* in this list are named *before* the choregoi for tragedy; this order is consistent with that of the entries referring to the Lenaea in the didascalic inscription (see IG II² 2319–2323; *DFA*² 1988: 107 and Millis and Olson 2012: 59–118).

Another piece of epigraphic evidence that more certainly attests metic choregia at the Lenaea is an important dedicatory monument (Ag I 7168; SEG 32. 239, Camp 1986: 53, Milanezi 2004: 210–15), the marble base of a herm found in situ in front of the Royal Stoa (the seat of the basileus) in the Athenian agora that was dedicated by the basileus Onesippus (see Figure 3.1).

While he was holding office as basileus (ca. 400 BCE), Onesippus commemorated the victorious theater personnel at the Lenaea:⁴ in comedy, the metic choregos Sosicrates, a "copper dealer" (his status as metic is evident from the absence of a patronymic), together with the poet Nicochares, and in tragedy, the choregos Stratonicus son of Straton (his citizen status is evident from his patronymic), together with the poet Megacleides.⁵ Once again, the name of the victorious choregos for comedy was recorded before the one for tragedy. It is unclear whether this ordering suggests that the contest in comedy at the Lenaea was more important than that of tragedy or that it predated the admission of tragedy—or if it is simply an inexplicable habit.

---

³ A citizen is characteristically designated by his first name, then his father's name, followed by his demotic, i.e., the name of the deme in which he was registered (X the son of Y from the deme Z). A metic was not registered in any deme (thus showing he was not a citizen); he was designated by first name and name of the deme of residence (X, in [ἐν] deme Y residing [οἰκῶν]).

⁴ It should be noted that this is not a choregic monument (as Goette 2007: 124–125 has misleadingly stated) but a dedication of the basileus commemorating his service.

⁵ The Greek text runs as follows (see Figure 3.1):
˙ Ὀνήσιππος Αἰτίο Κηφισιεὺς βασιλεὺς ἀνέθηκε[ν].
ο[ἵδ]ε Ὀνησίππο βασιλεύοντος χορηγōντες ἐνίκων·

κωμωιδῶν·	τραγωιδῶν·
Σωσικράτης ἐχορήγε χαλκοπώλης,	Στρατόνικος ἐχορήγε Στράτωνος,
Νικοχάρης ἐδίδασκε.	Μεγακλείδης ἐδίδασκε.

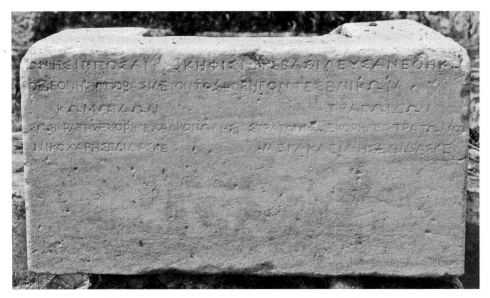

FIGURE 3.1 The dedication of basileus Onesippus (ca. 400 BCE) (Ag I 7168; SEG 32. 239). In line 3 (left) one can read κωμωιδῶν, and below it the name (Sosicrates) of the victorious metic choregos at the comic contest at the Lenaea. The name of the victorious poet Nicochares follows below. Photo by Craig Mauzy, American School of Classical Studies at Athens: Agora Excavations.

No tribally organized contests took place at the Lenaea, only contests of tragedy and comedy. This difference from the performances at the City Dionysia, together with the differences noted in the preceding paragraphs (namely that metics could serve as choregoi of comedy and that comedies may have been performed at the Lenaea before tragedies were performed there), is suggestive of another difference. It may be that the change that occurred at the City Dionysia before the middle of the fourth century, whereby choregoi for comedy were no longer appointed directly by the archon but were nominated first by the tribes, applied *only* to the City Dionysia (*pace* MacDowell 1989: 67): it is highly unlikely that tribal authorities would ever nominate metics, as they were not formal members of tribes. The wealthy metic choregos for comedy at the Lenaea will have been appointed by the basileus.

DUTIES AND RESPONSIBILITIES OF THE CHOREGOS

It seems that specific laws defined the duties of the choregos (see Dem. 4. 35–6) and that magistrates who were responsible for the contests at the festivals kept a close eye on the choregos's activities and the preparation of the chorus in general (see Xen. *Hiero*

9.4). Regarding the expenses involved, we have specific figures for the cost of the tragic and comic choregia toward the end of the fifth century BCE. From Lysias 21.1–5 we learn that the speaker spent 3,000 drachmas for his tragic chorus at the City Dionysia and 1,600 drachmas for a victorious comic chorus in 402 BCE, including the cost of the dedication of the *skeue* (see below); we also learn that the dithyrambic chorus was significantly more expensive. Unfortunately, we know nothing about the duties of the choregos in comedy or in tragedy. The evidence we possess concerns choregoi in dithyramb and comes primarily from two forensic speeches: Antiphon 6 (*On the Choreutes*) esp. 11–14, where the speaker gives a descriptive account of his conduct as choregos for a boys' chorus at the Thargelia at some point in the last quarter of the fifth century, and Dem. 21 (*Against Meidias*), in which Demosthenes gives an account of his own production of a men's chorus at the City Dionysia soon after the middle of the fourth century. How far it is possible to extrapolate from the evidence we have on dithyramb for the duties of the choregos in comedy is impossible to determine. The two types of performance (dithyramb and comedy) were different, and consequently the experience of being a choregos for one or the other would also have been different. The main differences are as follows:

1. Unlike dithyramb, as mentioned above, comedy was not a tribally organized contest, which means that (a) the choregos was not limited to recruiting chorus members from his fellow tribesmen but could recruit among all the Athenians; (b) during the contest of comedy the members of a particular tribe were not represented by a particular chorus, so that their desire for a particular comic play's victory had nothing to do with their tribal affiliation; (c) unlike dithyramb, the victory did not belong to the tribe but to the individual choregos, poet, etc.; and (d) unlike dithyramb, the victorious choregos in comedy did not receive a bronze tripod as a prize which he would then be (morally) obliged to return to the god by creating a dedicatory monument on which to display it.

2. Unlike comedy, dithyramb was fundamentally if not exclusively a musical performance, so that the choice of the piper was a matter of major concern and of utmost priority to the choregos; this meant that the individual choregoi and their tribes were eager to hire the most virtuoso piper to ensure victory.

3. The dithyrambic chorus was considerably bigger than the comic one; the former may have had as many as fifty members, whereas the latter had twenty-four (at least in the fifth century).

The liturgist's own experience as choregos for comedy may have changed over time. The comic chorus began to play a lesser role at the beginning of the fourth century BCE, and while there may have been some shifts and resurgences, comedy certainly, even if gradually, lost its vibrant political nature (for a recent comprehensive discussion of the matter see Konstantakos 2011, esp. 175–182). By the late 320s, the time of Menander's debut, comedy was largely dominated by domestic plots.

On the other hand, the "Panhellenization" or "internationalization" of comedy will have been antithetical to the part played by the chorus in fifth-century Attic political comedy; "Attic political topicality" was out (Konstantakos 2011). These developments meant the marginalization of the comic chorus: it was no longer an organic part of comic drama, so that fewer chorus members were necessary and less preparation was needed. The same developments may have looked to a diminished role for choregoi in comedy.

Some aspects of the choregos's duties must have been common for all genres, namely:

1. The choregos had to provide a space appropriate for the training and rehearsal of the chorus, either in his house or in a separate distinct building. This space was called *choregeion* or *didaskaleion,* and we have specific definitions in Bekker's *Anecdota Graeca* (1, p.72) and in Pollux's *Onomasticon* (iv, 106): it was the place where the choregos brought together the chorus members and the actors for their training and rehearsals.
2. The choregos had to recruit the members of his chorus.
3. The choregos was to be available during the whole period of training the chorus and was to provide whatever was needed. Personal involvement on the part of the choregos during "the preparation" of the chorus was expected.
4. The choregoi were involved in the procedure whereby the candidates for the judges at the contests were selected. First, the process of selection took place in the presence of choregoi (see Lysias 4.3). Furthermore, the choregoi together with the *prytaneis* sealed the ten urns that contained the names of the candidates from each tribe (see Isocr. 17. 34; on the selection procedures of the judges, see, DFA[2] 1988: 95–98 and Rhodes 1972:131).
5. The choregos provided the costumes.
6. The victorious choregos would normally commemorate the victory with a choregic monument.

COMMEMORATION OF CHOREGIC VICTORIES

As mentioned earlier, in the contests of dithyramb, the victorious tribe received as a prize a bronze tripod that the choregos was (morally) obliged to return to the god by creating a dedicatory monument. These monuments consisted of a stone base of varying size supporting the bronze tripod; an inscription on the base commemorated the name of the victorious tribe as well as the names of the choregos, *didaskalos,* and *auletes* (piper). Occasionally the name of the archon was included at the end of the inscription, allowing us to date exactly the dithyrambic victories commemorated there.

In the case of the *dramatic* victories, however, there was no durable prize awarded such as the bronze tripod for dithyramb so that the victorious choregoi in tragedy or comedy could make dedications of them that might survive to the present; consequently, we must rely on the scant literary references to such dedicatory victory monuments. From Aristotle (*Politics* 1341a) we learn about a *pinax* (probably a wooden tablet) that Thrasippus dedicated when he was choregos for the comic poet Ecphantides. From the speaker of Lysias 21 we learn that in 402 BCE he dedicated the *skeue* when he was victorious in comedy. The *skeue* may have been the costumes (see Ghiron-Bistagne 1976: 94) of the chorus (or the actors?) including the masks, or the masks only (see Webster 1972: 455–456 and Green 1982: 245). One must imagine that such dedications were common after comic victories and that they were made in the sanctuary of Dionysus with an inscription carved on perishable material such as wood mentioning the name of the victorious poet and choregos and the title of the dramatic play that had won the contest. Although the evidence for dedications of victorious choregoi in dramatic contests is meager, we do know that such dedications existed and that they included, in addition to the *skeue*, votive tablets with paintings and inscriptions, or reliefs showing comic performances.

The absence of substantial remains of monuments commemorating tragic and comic victories won at the City Dionysia and the Lenaea led many scholars in the past to believe that a few choregic dedicatory monuments (e.g., IG II² 3091, IG I³ 969, IG II² 3101), found not in the city center of Athens (the area surrounding the Acropolis) but in the outlying demes, commemorated victories won at the city festivals rather than at those celebrated locally in the demes (i.e., the Rural Dionysia; see below). The main reason for these ascriptions was the fact that some of these monuments recorded the tragic and comic victories of well-known poets such as Aristophanes, Cratinus, Sophocles, and Euripides, first-rate poets one would not expect to find as participants at the Rural Dionysia.

A well-known example illustrating this point is the much-disputed choregic inscription IG II² 3091, found by Papagiannopoulos-Palaios in 1929 in an area between modern Voula and Vari, a location corresponding with the ancient deme of Halae Aexonides (Eliot 1962: 20 and 29–30, Matthaiou 1992–1998: 168 note 55); it is now exhibited in the Epigraphical Museum of Athens (EM 12693). The base mentions tragic and comic victories of two choregoi (Epichares and Thrasybulus) with the comic poets Ecphantides (and the play *Peirai*) and Cratinus (the play being *Boukoloi*) and the tragic poets Timotheus and Sophocles. Did the monument celebrate city or local victories? Some scholars (e.g., Wilamowitz, Koerte, Pickard-Cambridge, Davies) have thought it rather likely that the victorious choregoi in dramatic competitions of *city* festivals would have dedicated choregic monuments in *demes*, thus advertising their city victories locally, especially when the poets were as famous as Sophocles and Cratinus. Others (e.g., Papagiannopoulos-Palaios, Guarducci, Kirchner, Makres, Csapo) have thought that these victories should be attributed to competitions held at the local level of the deme (in this case of Halae Aexonides), i.e., the Rural Dionysia, which seem to have been a flourishing institution in the fifth and fourth centuries BCE. Other scholars (e.g., Konstantakos 2011 and Scafuro, ch. 10) have pointed out the near impossibility for dramatists to have presented all their plays at only two city festivals.

CHOREGIA FOR COMEDY IN THE ATTIC DEMES

In addition to the contests of comedy administered at the central level of the city for the City Dionysia and the Lenaea, comic performances were also administered locally, in the demes of Attica (see note 1 and Whitehead 1986: 327–345). Every year during the winter in the month Poseideon (corresponding more or less to December), they celebrated the so called "Lesser" or "Rural" Dionysia (*DFA*²: 42–56, Whitehead 1986: 212–220). The Rural Dionysia were most likely celebrated in every deme (*contra* Jones 2004: 140–141, who believes that the Dionysia were celebrated only in the larger demes) but not necessarily on the same days; Pickard-Cambridge rightly points to a passage in the *Republic* where "Plato speaks of people going from one of the festivals to another to gratify their desire for entertainment, and at this time, when troupes of actors travelled from one to another with their repertoire of plays, time must have been allowed for their movements."[6] Although we have evidence (archaeological, epigraphic, and literary) of deme theaters for only a few Attic demes (less than 15 percent of the total number of demes),[7] still, the assumption can be defended that each had its own local theater (see Whitehead 1986: 219–222). Demes needed theaters for their local assembly meetings and for religious functions (Parker 2005: 64). A theater does not require a permanent material such as the marble structure of the theater of Dionysus on the southern slope of the Acropolis. As a minimum requirement, a few "front stone seats" located before a flat area would suffice for dignitaries; the rest of the audience could sit on wooden structures (see Csapo 2007: 103–108; and Paga 2010: 369–370). Modest theaters such as these are not likely to have survived, though future surveys and excavations may uncover more substantial ones.

The theatrical contests at the Rural Dionysia comprised performances of tragedy, comedy, and occasionally dithyramb. Performances of comedy are attested in several demes, for example, in Aexone, Eleusis, Rhamnus, Anagyrus, Thoricus, and Acharnae. The local festivals were particularly popular, manifesting the artistic and religious expression of the demes, not as detached local communities, but as organic subdivisions of the polis. The performances needed the support of choregoi. The evidence attesting the administration of the choregia in the demes is meager, but we can be certain that the demarch who was the head administrator of each deme was in charge of these arrangements (see for example IG I³ 254 with Makres 2004: 132–140). The choregos in a deme festival acted primarily

---

[6] *DFA*² 43, citing Plato *Rep.* v. 475: ὥσπερ δὲ ἀπομεμισθωκότες τὰ ὦτα ἐπακοῦσαι πάντων χορῶν περιθέουσι τοῖς Διονυσίοις οὔτε τῶν κατὰ πόλεις οὔτε τῶν κατὰ κώμας ἀπολειπόμενοι.

[7] According to the recent study Paga 2010: 352, fig. 1 and 353–354, there are nineteen deme theaters attested out of 139 demes. Paga 2010 suggests, on the basis of the geographical distribution of the theaters of Attica attested so far, that during the Classical period there was one theater area per *trittys* per *phyle*, i.e., a total of thirty theaters, and consequently that the Rural Dionysia took place on a *trittys* level rather than being celebrated as individual festivals in separate demes. However, the epigraphic evidence so far suggests that each theater was used exclusively by one deme and was not shared with other demes (S. Aliferi *per epistulam*).

as a "demesman" (i.e., he was a member of the deme of his birth and proud of this origin), and conversely, the demes had every reason to encourage their individual members to contribute eagerly and generously to these common causes, in other words to become choregoi for the performances held at the local festivals, in particular the Rural Dionysia.

An example of a deme decree that illustrates a deme's values regarding choregic performance comes from the deme of Aexone in 313/12 BCE during the archonship of Theophrastus (Whitehead 1986: 235–252; for confirmation of the date of the inscription to this archon, the later one of that name, see Tracy 1995: 39 n. 16, 73, n. 7). The decree is recorded on a stone stele (slab) and is now kept in the Epigraphical Museum of Athens (EM 13262= Lawton 1995: 49, 148 nr. 154, Pl. 81; SEG 36.186: see Figure 3.2). In

FIGURE 3.2 EM 13262 (SEG 36.187). Pedimental stele with relief showing Dionysus with satyr; above it are five comic masks, below it is the text of the deme decree from Aexone (313/12 BCE), and below the text are two crowns. Courtesy of the Epigraphical Museum of Athens, photo by V. Stamatopoulos.

this decree, two men, Auteas the son of Autocles and Philoxenides the son of Philippus, are honored by the demesmen of Aexone for having performed their choregic duty well (καλῶς) and with a sense of love for honor (φιλοτίμως). The adverb φιλοτίμως (see p. 72 above) reflects a particular social value of ancient Athens and ancient Greece in general whereby certain acts, motivated by the "love for honor," were performed with the expectation that the community would honor the individuals who had performed them.

The essential provisions of the decree are as follows: the two choregoi from Aexone are each awarded a golden crown worth 100 drachmas; the proclamation of the crowns is to take place at the theater when the competitions of comedy (see figure 3.3) take place and is to serve as an inspiration for others who will be choregoi in the future so that they will be motivated by a love for honor (ὅπως ἂν [φ]ιλοτιμῶνται καὶ οἱ ἄλλοι χορηγοὶ οἱ μέλλοντες [χ]ορηγεῖν); the demarch and treasurers are to give the honorands ten drachmas for carrying out a sacrifice; and the treasurers are to inscribe the decree on a stone stele and set it up *at the theater* so that the Aexonians can celebrate the Dionysia in the best possible way (στῆσαι (τὴν στήλην) ἐν τῶι θεάτρωι ὅπως ἂν Αἰξωνεῖς ἀεὶ ὡς κάλλιστα Διονύσια ποιῶσιν). It is thus certain that the deme of Aexone had a theater of its own and that comic performances were held locally. Significantly, the upper part of

FIGURE 3.3 Detail of EM 13262 showing the text of the decree. Lines 4 to the beginning of 6 announce that the proclamation of the crowns is to take place at the theater when the competitions of comedy take place: στεφανῶσαι αὐτοὺς χρυσῶι στεφάνωι ἑκάτε-/[ρ]ον ἀπὸ ἑκατὸν δραχμῶν ἐν τῶι θεάτρωι τοῖς κω-/μωιδοῖς. Courtesy of the Epigraphical Museum of Athens, photo by Z. Chroni.

the stele has a pedimental crowning decorated with five comic masks representing comedy of the later fourth century.

Several epigraphic monuments other than stelai are related to the performance of comedy at the Rural Dionysia. Among the dedications of victorious choregoi, two will be presented briefly. The first is worth mentioning here, not only because it belongs to the fifth century BCE (a period that is less well epigraphically documented than the fourth century BCE), but also because Aristophanes is mentioned in it (see Figure 3.4). This is a choregic dedication from Eleusis (IG I³ 970; Papangeli 2004: 308–309, no. 185; Clinton *Eleusis* vol. IA 2005: 70–71, no 53, vol. IB, Plate 25, and Vol. II 2008: 82–3), made by two men who were victorious choregoi in comedy with Aristophanes as the poet (lines 1–3). A victory for tragedy with Sophocles as poet (lines 4–5, "another victory, for tragedy") is also recorded; this victory may belong to a later year (so Clinton 2008: 83, with reference to fundamental discussions in *DFA²* 47–48, 87 n. 3, and Capps 1943). The Sophocles mentioned here may be the great tragedian's grandson.

FIGURE 3.4 The choregic dedication of Gnathis, the son of Timocides, and Anaxandrides, the son of Timagoras, from Eleusis, who were together victorious in two different occasions in the comic and the tragic contests of the Dionysia of Eleusis. Last quarter of the fifth c. BCE (IG I³ 970, E 946 and E 254; Papangeli *ΑΓΩΝ* 2004: 308–309, no. 185; Clinton *Eleusis* vol. IA 2005: 70–71, no 53, vol. IB, Plate 25 and Vol. II 2008: 82–83). The victory in the comic contest (line 2) and the name of Aristophanes (line 3) are recorded. The Greek text runs: [Γ]νάθις Τιμοκ[ήδ]ο[ς, Ἀ]ναξανδρίδης Τιμα[γ]όρο/ χορηγõντες κωμωιδοῖς ἐνίκων·/ Ἀριστοφάνης ἐ[δ]ίδασκεν./ ἑτέρα νίκη τραγωιδοῖς·/Σοφοκλῆς ἐδίδασκεν. Courtesy of the Archaeological Museum of Eleusis, 3rd Ephorate of Prehistoric and Classical Antiquities.

The dedication's inscription proves that great poets such as Aristophanes and Sophocles (grandfather or grandson) were participants in the Rural Dionysia early on and that the Rural Dionysia were a flourishing institution; thus:

> Gnathis son of Timocedes and Anaxandrides son of Timagoras
> having been choregoi in the contest of comedy were victorious
> with Aristophanes as the *didaskalos*
> and [the same pair of men] won a second victory in the contest of tragedy
> with Sophocles as the *didaskalos*.

Here, more than one individual has undertaken the choregia. This sharing, known as *synchoregia*, is not uncommon in local competitions; two or even three individuals might share the responsibility and the honor if they were victorious (IG II² 1198, 1200, 3092, 3095, 3096). *Synchoregia* on the city level, however, is attested only in the year 406/5 (see Capps 1943: 8 and Millis and Olson 2012: 17) and was probably due to the financial devastation that the Athenians suffered from the Peloponnesian War. Limited resources due to the war may likewise be the cause for *synchoregia* in the Eleusis inscription, but in later instances in the demes, a desire to share not only the cost but also the honor may have been the impulse.

The second monument mentioning a choregos for comedy is the impressive dedication of Megacles the son of Megacles from the deme of Rhamnus, situated at the northeast edge of Attica (see Figure 3.5). The monument is now displayed in the National Archaeological Museum of Athens (inv. no 231 (IG II² 3109), Petrakos 1999 Vol. I: 280–283, Vol. II 99–100, nr. 120; Kaltsas 2002:272–273, nr. 568).

The monument belongs to the second half of the fourth century BCE. It is an inscribed base bearing a spectacular statue of Themis, the goddess who was the personification of legal justice and who, together with Nemesis, had a prominent sanctuary and cult in the deme of Rhamnus (the monument itself was found at the left rear corner inside the little temple of the sanctuary of Nemesis; see Staes 1891: 45–53 [on the find spot, see p. 46] and Pl. 4). On the face of the base, the inscription states that Megacles dedicated the image of the goddess in order to commemorate three of his personal achievements (a) for being crowned by his fellow demesmen as having been a just man (στεφανωθείς ὑπὸ τῶν δημοτῶν δικαιοσύνης ἕνεκα)—and judging from the dedicatory object, the statue of Themis, this must have been the principal reason for his dedication; (b) for having won as a *gymnasiarchos* (a liturgist who sponsored torch races at festivals), for the divisions both of boys and men (καὶ νικήσας παισὶ καὶ ἀνδράσι γυμνασιαρχῶν); and (c) for having been victorious as a choregos for comedy (καὶ κωμωιδοῖς χορηγῶν); see Figure 3.6. That last victory was certainly won at the local Dionysia held in Rhamnus, but Megacles chose not to dedicate a separate choregic monument to Dionysus for that victory but rather to combine it with his victories as *gymnasiarchos* on the same monument that was dedicated to Themis. This is a truly impressive monument, unique of its kind.

FIGURE 3.5 The statue of Nemesis from Rhamnus dedicated by Megacles the son of Megacles. It stands on its original inscribed base. Late fourth c. BCE. National Archaeological Museum inv. no 231 (IG II² 3109, SEG 40. 148).

THE END OF THE CHOREGIA

The considerable expenses involved in the choregia and the mandatory aspect of the institution make it legitimate to wonder to what extent propertied Athenian citizens were willing to undertake liturgies. Regarding the fourth century, the Aristotelian passage (*Ath. Pol.* 56.2–3) quoted earlier in this chapter explicitly says that, after the archon received all the choregoi nominated by the tribes, he held the *antidoseis* (claims of relative poverty so that the liturgy should be passed on to another wealthier individual or,

FIGURE 3.6 Detail of the right side of the inscribed base. Below the molding one can read ΚΩΜΩΙΔΟΙΣ ΧΟΡΗΓΩΝ. National Archaeological Museum, Athens copyright © Hellenic Ministry of Education and Religious Affairs, Culture and Sports/Archaeological Receipts Fund. Photos by K. Kourtidis.

if the latter refused, that there should be an exchange of properties with that individual) and brought the *skepseis* (claim for exemption from the liturgy on the basis of specified legal grounds) to trial for those who had the right to be exempted. The *antidosis* and the *skepsis* were the two legal means available for those among the tribal nominees who wished to decline a liturgy (see Scafuro 2011: 106–109). The Aristotelian text implies that the ones who were liable to exemptions were only nominees of the tribal authorities and not yet appointed by the archon. It seems unlikely, however, that those who were appointed choregoi directly by the archon (for tragedy and comedy, and in Aristotle's time only for tragedy) could not claim exemption.

Some evidence (Isocr. 1. 128; Dem. 36. 39; Theophr. *Char.* 26. 6) has suggested that there may have been an increase in requests for exemptions and, in general, liturgy avoidance during the fourth century; the trend has been explained as due to crisis—first, the Corinthian War and later, the Social War (Christ 1990)—or else to a change in the valuation of the importance of choral performance by the wealthy. The hypothesized reduction of positive response to volunteer spending for agonistic liturgies is contradicted, however, in an interesting way: the choregic monuments dedicated by victorious choregoi in dithyrambic contests (i.e., inscribed stone bases supporting tripods)—which must have involved significant expense—had a tendency to grow larger and more costly in the second half of the fourth century BCE. Indeed, some resembled temple-like constructions; thus the monument of Lysicrates in 335/4 BCE, the monument of Nicias in 320/19 BCE, the monument of Thrasyllus in 320/19 BCE, and many other monuments whose foundations are preserved in the area surrounding the Theater of Dionysus and along the ancient course of the street of the Tripods (see Korres 1983 [1989]: 14–16 and Drawing 1 on p. 12; Choremi-Spetsieri 1994: 31–42; Kavvadias 2005: 167–190; Korres 2009: 76–8 and figs 4.1 and 4.2). But at the very moment when the choregic monuments become truly extravagant, they seem to disappear. The last of the series of surviving choregic dedications are the two large (extravagant) monuments both dated to 320/19, i.e., that of Nikias (IG II³ 3055), who was victorious with a boys' chorus, and that of Thrasyllus (IG II³ 3056), who was victorious with a men's chorus.

The choregia was abolished and replaced by the *agonothesia*, an office held by the *agonothetes*; he was a single elective magistrate who would use public funds to pay for the performances at festivals and who would also be prepared (and was expected) to contribute large sums from his own pocket during his term in office. No longer did the archon appoint or the tribe nominate wealthy individuals to carry out choregiai. At this time, monuments celebrating the office of the *agnothetes* began to be set up; the first extant agonothetic monument, that of Xenocles (or Androcles, see Lambert 2000–2003: 99–105) of Sphettus, is dated to 307/6 (IG II² 3073).[8] Traditionally, scholars (e.g. Köhler 1878, Ferguson 1911, Pickard-Cambridge (DFA²), Gherke 1978, Rhodes 1993, Habicht, 1997, Mikalson 1998, et al.) have viewed the end of the institution of choregia and its subsequent replacement by the *agonothesia* (an elective office) as parts of the legislative activity of Demetrius of Phalerum (318/7–308/7 BCE). The latter was a Peripatetic, a pupil of Theophrastus, and thus his thinking had a strong Aristotelian coloring (for Aristotle's criticism of the choregia, see *Pol.* 1309a11[9] and cf. 1320b4, and for Demetrius's own negative view of the choregic monuments of his time see Plutarch, *De Gloria Ath.* [*Mor.* 349 a–b] = Wehrli fr. 136, *FGrHist* 228 F25).[10] Scholars have also viewed the ending of the choregia and of the practice of dedicating choregic monuments as reflecting Demetrius's oligarchic aims, namely to protect private wealth by sparing propertied individuals from having or wanting to spend on public causes such as agonistic liturgies or on extravagances such as funerary or choregic monuments.

---

[8] Of this first extant agonothetic monument, three fragments are preserved. Two can be seen in the area of the Theater of Dionysus (fragments a and b), for which see Korres 1983 [1989], B 1, 10 c. phot. tab. 15a, and one (fr. c) is kept in the Epigraphical Museum of Athens (EM 8726). So far, it is the only monument of its kind commemorating a victory in comedy by mentioning the victorious poet and actor in the comic contest (IG II² 3073, ll. 5–6: ποιητὴς κωμω[δ]οῖς ἐνί[κα Φιλήμω]ν Δάμωνος Διομειεύς, ὑποκριτὴς κ[ωμωιδοῖς ἐνίκα Καλλιπ]πος Καλλίου Σουνιεύς).

[9] βέλτιον δὲ καὶ βουλομένους κωλύειν λειτουργεῖν τὰς δαπανηρὰς μὲν μὴ χρησίμους δὲ λειτουργίας, οἷον χορηγίας καὶ λαμπαδαρχίας καὶ ὅσαι ἄλλαι τοιαῦται; i.e., it is better to prevent men—even if they wish to—from undertaking costly but not useful liturgies, such as the choregiai and the sponsoring of torch races and other similar public services.

[10] τοῖς δὲ νικήσασιν ὁ τρίπους ὑπῆρχεν, οὐκ ἀνάθημα τῆς νίκης, ὡς Δημήτριος φησιν, ἀλλ᾽ἐπίσπεισμα τῶν ἐκκεχυμένων βίων καὶ τῶν ἐκλελοιπότων κενοτάφιον οἴκων; i.e., for those (choregoi) who were victorious there was the tripod, which was, as Demetrius says, not a dedication to commemorate a victory but a libation of their spilt livelihood and an empty grave of their bankrupt estates.

The traditional view briefly sketched here has recently been challenged (see, e.g., O'Sullivan 2009; Wilson and Csapo 2009, Wilson and Csapo 2010, and Wilson and Csapo 2012; Bayliss 2011): the institution of the *agonothesia* is now being attributed not to Demetrius but to the restored democracy immediately following Demetrius's flight from Athens in 307/6; this view is said to be corroborated by the fact, already mentioned, that our first extant agonothetic monument is dated to 307/6. The matter is controversial, but the traditional view remains the more probable. It is difficult to imagine how the restored democracy would have made this institutional change so quickly. Moreover, the *agonothetes* was a magistracy that replaced the choregoi in the same way and at approximately the same time that the *gymnasiarchos* ceased being a liturgist who was responsible for the organization and funding of the torch races and became a magistracy (the Director of the Gymnasium, who, apart from using public funds, was also expected to spend large sums from his own pocket not only for providing oil but also for constructing entire buildings for the Gymnasium); both changes, with their relief of burdens on the wealthy class, are developments of an oligarchic character. Moreover, that these magistrates were expected to spend from their own cash stores[11] when the public coffers were insufficient is also suggestive of their oligarchic character (see Aristotle *Pol.* 1321a 31–40). Finally, the phrase ὁ δῆμος ἐχορήγει ("the demos was choregos") used in the agonothetic inscriptions need not suggest, as the newer view iterates, a democratic origin for the institution of the *agonothesia,* but rather the democratic "appearance" of Demetrius's legislation.[12]

BIBLIOGRAPHY

This chapter draws extensively on the Oxford D. Phil. thesis of the author, *The Institution of Choregia in Classical Athens*, submitted in September 1994 (unpublished but available in the Bodleian Library). It also takes into account and uses selectively scholarship that has appeared since, as noted in the chapter and represented below.

Bayliss, A. J. 2011. *After Demosthenes: The Politics of Early Hellenistic Athens.* London: Continuum.

Camp, J. 1986. *The Athenian Agora: Excavations in the Heart of Athens.* London: Thames and Hudson.

Capps, E. 1943. "A New Fragment of the List of Victors at the City Dionysia." *Hesperia* 12: 1–11.

Choremi-Spetsieri, A. 1994. "Η οδός Τριπόδων και τα χορηγικά μνημεία στην αρχαία Αθήνα." In *The Archaeology of Athens and Attica under the Democracy: Proceedings of an International Conference Celebrating 2,500 years since the Birth of Democracy in Greece, Held at the*

---

[11] This phenomenon is described by Hakkarainen 1997: 21 as the "liturgisation of offices in the Athenian polis" which according to her was a gradual development which can be traced back already in the 340s.

[12] Regarding how careful Demetrius of Phalerum was in keeping the democratic modes in place and showing scruple with the appearance of democracy, see Tracy 1995: 36–38.

American School of Classical Studies at Athens, December 4–6, 1992, edited by W. Coulson, O. Palagia, T. Shear, H. Shapiro and F. Frost, 31–42. Oxford: Oxbow.

Christ, M. 1990. "Liturgy avoidance and Antidosis in Classical Athens," *TAPA* 120: 147–169.

Clinton, K. 2005–2008. *Eleusis, The Inscriptions on Stone: Documents of the Sanctuary of the Two Goddesses and Public Document of the Deme*. 2 vols (IA Text, IB Plates, II Commentary). Athens: Archaeological Society at Athens.

Connor, W. R. 1989. "City Dionysia and Athenian Democracy," *Classica et Mediaevalia* 40: 7–32.

Csapo, E. 2004. "The Rise of Acting: Some Social and Economic Conditions behind the Rise of the Acting Profession in the Fifth and Fourth Centuries B.C." In *Le statut de l'acteur dans l'Antiquité grecque et romaine: Actes du colloque qui s'est tenu à Tours les 3 et 4 mai 2002*, edited by Ch. Hugoniot, F. Hurlet and S. Milanezi, 53–76. Tours: Presses universitaires François Rabelais.

——. 2007. "The Men Who Built the Theatres: Theatropolai, Theatronai, and Arkhitektones." In *The Greek Theatre and Festivals*, edited by P. Wilson, 87–115. Oxford: Oxford University Press.

——. 2010. *Actors and Icons of the Ancient Theater*, Chichester, UK: Wiley-Blackwell.

Csapo, E. and P. Wilson. 2010. "Le passage de la chorégie à l'agonothésie à Athènes à la fin du IVe siècle." In *L'argent dans les concours du monde grec*, edited by B. Le Gruen, 83–105. Saint Denis: Presses Universitaires de Vincennes.

Davies, J. K. 1971. "Demosthenes on Liturgies: A Note." *JHS* 87: 33–40.

——. 1971. *Athenian Propertied Families 600–300 B.C.* Oxford: Clarendon Press.

Eliot, C. W. J. 1962. *Coastal Demes of Attika: A Study of the Policy of Kleisthenes*. Toronto: University of Toronto Press.

Ferguson, W. S. 1911. *Hellenistic Athens: An Historical Essay*, London: Macmillan.

Gherke, H. J. 1978. "Das Verhältnis von Politik und Philosophie im Wirkendes Demetrios von Phaleron." *Chiron* 8: 149–199.

Ghiron-Bistagne, P. 1976. *Recherches sur les acteurs dans la Grèce antique*. Paris: Les Belles Lettres.

Goette, H. R. "Choregic Monuments and the Athenian Democracy." In *The Greek Theatre and Festivals*, edited by P. Wilson, 122–149. Oxford: Oxford University Press.

Goldhill, S. 1987. "The Great Dionysia and Civic Ideology." *JHS* 107: 58–76.

Green, J. R. 1982. "Dedications of Masks." *Revue Archéologique* 2: 237–248.

Habicht, C. C. 1997. *Athens from Alexander to Antony*. Translated by D. L. Schneider. Cambridge, MA: Harvard University Press.

Hakkarainen, M. 1997. "Private Wealth in the Athenian Public Sphere during the Late Classical and the Early Hellenistic Period." In *Early Hellenistic Athens: Symptoms of a Change*, edited by J. Frösén, 1–32. Helsinki: Suomen Ateenan-instituutin säätiö.

Jones, N. F. 2004. *Rural Athens under the Democracy*. Philadelphia: University of Pennsylvania Press.

Kaltsas, N. 2002. *Sculpture in the National Archaeological Museum, Athens*. Los Angeles: The J. Paul Getty Museum.

Kavvadias, G. 2005. "Ειδήσεις από την οδό Τριπόδων." In *Teseo e Romolo: Le origini di Atene e Roma a confronto: Atti del Convegno Internazionale di Studi: Scuola archeologica italiana di Atene, Atene, 30 giugno–1 luglio 2003*, edited by E. Greco, 167–190. Athens: Scuola archeologica italiana di Atene.

Keaney, J. 1970. "The Date of Aristotle's Athenaion Politeia." *Historia* 19: 326–336.

Köhler, U. 1878. "Dokumente zur Geschichte des athenischen Theaters." *Att. Mit.* 3: 229–257.

Konstantakos, I. M. 2011. "Conditions of Playwriting and the Comic Dramatist's Craft in the Fourth Century." *Logeion: A Journal of Ancient Theatre*. 1: 145–183.

Korres, M. 1983 [1989]. "Α' Εφορεία Προϊστορικών και Κλασικών Αρχαιοτήτων Ακροπόλεως: Εργασίες στα μνημεία." *Arch. Delt.* 38: 9–21.

———. 2009. "Οδικό Δίκτυο γύρω από την Ακρόπολη." In ΑΤΤΙΚΗΣ ΟΔΟΙ: Αρχαίοι δρόμοι της Αττικής, edited by M. Korres, 74–95. Athens: Ekdotikos Oikos Melissa.

Lambert, S. 2000–2003. "The First Athenian Agonothetai." *Horos* 14–16: 99–105.

Lawton, C. L. 1995. *Attic Document Reliefs: Art and Politics in Ancient Athens*. Oxford: Clarendon Press.

Lewis, D. M. 1968. "Dedications of Phialai at Athens." *Hesperia* 37: 368–380, Pls. 111–112.

MacDowell, D. M. 1989. "Athenian Laws about Choruses." In *Symposion 1982: Vorträge zur griechischen und hellenistischen Rechtsgeschichte*, edited by F. J. Fernández Nieto, 65–77. Cologne: Böhlau.

———, ed. 1990. *Demosthenes Against Meidias: Oration 21*, Oxford.

Makres, A. 1994. "The Institution of Choregia in Classical Athens." PhD diss., University of Oxford.

———. 2004. "The Rediscovery of IG I³ 253–4." In *ΑΤΤΙΚΑΙ ΕΠΙΓΡΑΦΑΙ: Πρακτικὰ Συμποσίου εἰσ μνήμην Adolf Wilhelm (1864–1950)*, edited by A. Matthaiou, 123–140. Athens: Hellenike Epigraphike Hetaireia.

Matthaiou, A. P. 1992–1998. "Αἰξωνικά." *Horos* 10–12: 133–169.

Meyer, E.A. 2010. *Metics and the Athenian Phialai-Inscriptions: A Study in Athenian Epigraphy and Law*. Stuttgart: Franz Steiner.

Mikalson, J. D. 1998. *Religion in Hellenistic Athens*. Berkeley: University of California Press.

Milanezi, S. 2004. "Mémoire civique et mémoire comique des concours en l'honneur de Dionysos à Athènes (Ve–IIIe siècles av. J.-C)." Thèse d' habilitation, Université Panthéon-Sorbonne.

Millis, B., and S. D. Olson. 2012. *Inscriptional Records for the Dramatic Festivals in Athens: IG II² 2318–2325 and Related Texts*. Leiden and Boston: Brill.

O'Sullivan, L. 2009. *The Regime of Demetrius of Phalerum in Athens, 317-307 BCE: A Philosopher in Politics*. Mnem. Suppl. 318. Leiden and Boston: Brill.

Paga, J. 2010. "Deme Theaters in Attica and the Trittys System." *Hesperia* 79: 351–384.

Papangeli, K. 2004. "No. 185." In *Agon: National Archaeological Museum, 15 July–31 October 2004*, edited by N. Kaltsas, 308–309. Athens: Hellenic Ministry of Culture.

Parker, R. T. C. 2005. *Polytheism and Society at Athens*. Oxford: Oxford University Press.

Petrakos, B. C. 1999. *Ο δήμοσ του Ραμνούντοσ: Οι επιγραφέσ: Σύνοψη των ανασκαφών και των ερευνών (1813–1998)*. Athens: He en Athenais Archaiologike Hetaireia.

Pickard-Cambridge, A. 1968. *The Dramatic Festivals of Athens*. Sec. ed. Revised by J. Gould and D. M. Lewis. Reissued with supplement, 1988. Oxford (referred to as *DFA²*). [First edition 1953.]

Rhodes, P. J. 1972. *The Athenian Boule*. Oxford: Clarendon Press.

———. 1981 (Revised 1993). *A Commentary on the Aristotelian Athenaion᾿ Politeia*. Oxford: Clarendon Press.

———. 2006. *A History of the Classical Greek World 478-323 B.C.* Malden, MA: Blackwell.

———. 2011. "The Dionysia and Democracy Again." *CQ*, n.s., 61: 71–74.

———. 2012. "The Working of the Athenian Democracy in the Second Half of the Fifth Century B.C." In *Two Lectures on Athenian History*, by P. J. Rhodes, 57–77. Athens: Hellenike Epigraphike Hetaireia.

Scafuro, A. C. 2010. "Conservative Trends in Athenian Law: Documents Pertaining to the Mysteries." *Symposion 2009: Vorträge zur griechischen und hellenistischen Rechtsgeschichte (Seggau, 25.-30. August 2009),* edited by G. Thür, 23–46. Vienna: Verlag der Österreichischen Akademie der Wissenschaften.

——. 2011. *Demosthenes, Speeches 39–49.* Austin: University of Texas Press.

——. 2013. "Keeping Record, Making Public: The Epigraphy of Government." In *A Companion to Ancient Greek Government,* edited by H. Beck, 71–74. Oxford: Wiley-Blackwell.

Sinclair, R. K. 1988. *Democracy and Participation in Athens.* Cambridge: Cambridge University Press.

Staes, V. 1891. "Ἀγάλματα εκ Ραμνούντος." *Archaiologike Ephememeris:* 45–62, Tab. 4–7.

Stockton, D. L. 1990. *The Classical Athenian Democracy.* Oxford: Oxford University Press.

Tracy, S. V. 1995. *Athenian Democracy in Transition: Attic Letter Cutters of 340 to 290 B.C.,* Berkeley: University of California Press.

Traill, J. S. 1986. *Demos and Trittys: Epigraphical and Topographical Studies in the Organization of Attica.* Toronto: Athenians.

Webster, T. B. L. 1972. "Scenic Notes II." In *Antidosis, Festschrift fur Walther Kraus zum 70 Geburtstag,* edited by R. Hauslik, A. Lesky, and H. Schwabl, 454–457. Vienna: Hermann Böhlau.

Whitehead, D. 1986.*The Demes of Attica 508/7-ca 250 B.C.: A Political and Social Study.* Princeton, NJ: Princeton University Press.

Wilson, P. 2000. *The Athenian Institution of the Khoregia: The Chorus, the City and the Stage.* Cambridge, UK: Cambridge University Press.

Wilson, P., and E. Csapo. 2009. "The End of the Khorēgia in Athens: A Forgotten Document." In *La musa dimenticata: Aspetti dell'esperienza musicale greca in età ellenistica,* edited by M. Ch. Martinelli, F. Pelosi and C. Pernigotti, 47–74. Pisa: Edizioni della Normale.

——.2012. "From *Chorēgia* to *Agōnothesia*: Evidence for the Administration and Finance of the Athenian Theatre in the Late Fourth Century BC." In *Greek Drama IV: Texts, Contexts, Performance,* edited by D. Rosenbloom and J. Davidson, 300–321. Oxford: Aris & Phillips.

I I

The Greek Comedians and Their Plays

CHAPTER 4

THE FIRST POETS OF OLD COMEDY

IAN C. STOREY

THE EARLY PHASE OF OLD COMEDY

WHETHER it developed from prancing men costumed as animals or satyrs, from reveling padded dancers, or from the riotous exchange of insults at public festivals, Old Comedy became part of the dramatic competitions at the Dionysia early in the fifth century BCE. Two names are attached to the first years of Old Comedy: Susarion and Chionides. The one fragment attributed to Susarion is accompanied by stories about the personal circumstances behind his denunciation of women and attributed to a "performance" at the Dionysia. Some sources call him a Megarian, but this may just be an attempt to justify the claim by the mainland Megarians to be the originators of comedy (Aristotle *Poetics* 1448a30–32). There was certainly an early form of comedy known as "Megarian," dismissed by the Athenians as something crude and rustic (*Wasps* 57, Eupolis K-A fr. 261, Ecphantides K-A fr. 3), but whether it predated or had any influence upon Old Athenian Comedy is doubtful.

The *Suda* (χ 318), however, names Chionides as "the first competitor of Old Comedy," which implies that Chionides was the first name found on the victory-lists at the Dionysia. The *Suda* adds that "he produced eight years before the Persian Wars," and it is this statement that yields the traditional date of 487/6 for the debut of Old Comedy. Olson (2007: 382–388) has shown the evidence from the victory-lists could support a date as early as the late 490s and as late as the early 470s. The traditional date of 486 thus falls comfortably within these two termini. Susarion was perhaps a creator of "comedy" before its formal adoption or an early comic poet who never won the prize. For Chionides we have three titles and seven fragments, one of which (K-A fr. 4–*Beggars*) suspiciously mentions Gnesippus, a comic target of the 430s.

Edwards (1993) proposed that since a date for the introduction of comedy in the early 480s coincides with the first use of ostracism against the friends of the tyrants, comedy began as the voice of the new democracy, insulting and thus attacking the traditional rich who were seen as hostile to the democracy that had just survived the first Persian invasion. Then some decades later this essentially democratic art form was "hijacked" by the Right and made into a weapon against radical democracy (Seeberg 1995). But I find it unlikely that comedy possessed such a radical political element from its very beginning. The evidence for early comedy may be scant, but there is almost nothing to suggest a serious aspect at this stage. I prefer to regard the political and personally humorous element as entering Old Comedy in the 440s and 430s; the crucial figure here, I would argue, is Cratinus, acting in the tradition of iambic poetry and responding to the contentious political atmosphere of the 440s and 430s.

The first comic poet about whom we can say anything with confidence is Magnes. The anonymous writer *On Comedy* (Koster III.7) credits him with eleven victories,[1] the most of any Old Comic poet, and the sixth entry on the victors' list at the Dionysia (IG ii^2 2325.44) gives a partial name,.....] s, with eleven victories. This must be Magnes. IG ii^2 2318.8 gives him a victory at the Dionysia of 472, perhaps another at the Dionysia of 471. Did these victories come early or late in his career? The former would suggest career dates in the 480s and 470s, the latter a career from the late 470s into the 450s or later. Aristophanes (*Knights* 520–525) calls the spectators in 424 to remember the failure of Magnes in his old age. This is presumably an event of reasonably recent memory, more likely in the 430s than in the 460s; the other two comedians mentioned, Cratinus and Crates, belong to the 430s and 420s.

Much of what we know about Magnes comes from this passage from Aristophanes (*Knights* 520–525) and the accompanying scholia:

> Because I recognized long ago how changeable your nature is, how you betray the poets of the past when they reached old age, and because I was well aware of what happened to Magnes, when he grew old and grey. He had put up the most victory-trophies over his rivals, making every sort of sound for you, strumming the lyre, flapping his wings, playing the Lydian, buzzing like a fly, dyed green like a frog, but it wasn't enough, and in the end, in his old age, never when he was young, he was rejected because he failed in making jokes [*skoptein*].

The scholiast gives actual play-titles for Magnes—*Lyre-Players* [*Barbitistai*], *Birds*, *Lydians*, *Gall-Flies* [*Psenes*, or *Fruit Flies*], and *Frogs*—but only *Lydians* is attested elsewhere, and the scholiast may just be creating titles from Aristophanes's descriptions. Aristophanes alleges that Magnes's "rejection" in his old age was due to his failure in *skoptein*. Now while *skommata* and *skoptein* can just mean jokes and joking generally, the terms can also mean what we would call personal jokes (*to onomasti komoidein*),

---

[1] Koster (1975) collects the various testimonia to Old Comedy, many of these being anonymous writers of late antiquity, while others, although named (e.g., Platonius), provide no indication of their date. Of the writers cited in this essay, only Diomedes is known as a grammarian of the fourth century CE.

and I would suggest that Magnes, after an unmatched string of successes in his early career (say, 475–460), essayed a comeback in the 440s or early 430s at the time when Cratinus was pioneering personal and political comedy, and that his more primitive comedy paled spectacularly in comparison with the rougher stuff that audiences were now expecting.

According to Diomedes (*Ars Grammatica* 488.23 = Koster XXIV.46–51), Magnes created a sort of comedy that was "less polished and charming," while the *Glossary of Ansileubus* (Koster XXVII.8–13) asserts that Magnes's plays were "rather silly" and did not exceed 300 lines in length. When we add the evidence from *Knights*, we may see in the comedy of Magnes, and perhaps of the first generation of Attic comedy, a primitive sort of drama, based on slapstick, mummery, rude sounds and physical humor, and men dressed as animals. Nothing in the earliest testimony and fragments suggests anything like the personal humor of the last part of the century, apart from Chionides K-A fr. 4, which as I have mentioned suspiciously attacks a target from the 430s. Magnes's K-A fr. 1 ("and these are just the side-dishes to my problems") and K-A fr. 6 ("so tell me, just now you swore this hadn't happened, and now you say it did?") do suggest a linear plot with some complications and deceptions.

The anonymous writer (Koster III.18–19) records that "none of his works has survived, but nine plays are attributed to him." With a record of eleven victories, his original oeuvre must have been considerably greater. Two late sources (Hesychius λ 1352, *Suda* λ 784) describe *Lydians* as a "revised comedy." We do know that later comic poets reworked their plays (Aristophanes's unfinished *Clouds*, Eupolis's *Autolycus*), and if it was Magnes himself who revised *Lydians* for production in the 430s, this may be the comedy that was rejected by the fickle audience of the day.

The other poets of the earliest phase of Old Comedy are, with one exception, mere names: Myllus, Euetes, Euxenides, Alcimenes (victor in the 460s, if his is the fragmentary name at IG ii² 2325.46), and Euphronius (victor at the Dionysia of 458). We do know something about Ecphantides, whose name with four victories appears on the victors' list at the Dionysia after Euphronius (458) and before Cratinus, whose debut is traditionally put in 454/3. We have two titles (*Experiments* [*Peirai*], *Satyrs*) and six fragments. With Ecphantides we get the first hints of the combative relations between comic poets, since other comedians gave him the nickname "Smoky" either because that term was applied to wine that had gone bad or because "he had never written anything brilliant" (Σ *Wasps* 151b). Cratinus (K-A fr. 502) combines the names of a comic and older tragic poet into a bizarre compound "Choerilecphantides," suggesting perhaps that the resulting product was less than thrilling.

THE SECOND PHASE OF OLD COMEDY

We can say considerably more about the next phase of Old Comedy. Two things affected comedy between 453 (the traditional date for the debut of Cratinus) and the early 420s, when Eupolis, Aristophanes, Phrynichus, and Plato burst upon the scene. First, a second venue for the performance of drama was introduced, the Lenaea festival of Dionysus, held in the Athenian month of Gamelion (late January). Literary and epigraphic evidence attests that both tragedy and comedy competed at the Lenaea, but there is a suggestion that this was a lesser competition than that at the Dionysia. One inscription from the 410s (IG ii² 2319.70–84) records tragic poets presenting only two tragedies (without satyr-dramas?), while inscriptions from the 430s show five competitors for comedy. *POxy.* 2737 implies that for comedy a poor finish at the Dionysia in one year meant "relegation" to the Lenaea for the next, but this is by no means a secure interpretation of the text.

The second development is the rise of political themes and personal humor. Aristotle (*Poetics* 1449a1–6) sees comedy as the dramatic equivalent of iambus or "blame poetry," and ancient critics are almost unanimous in regarding personal humor as the quintessence of Old Comedy, finding in it the social value that redeemed this otherwise aggressive and shameful form of drama. Its relationship with the law is frequently the object of speculation, and its demise is often explained by a formal political act, e.g., Horace, *Art of Poetry* 283–285. Athenian festivals, such as the Lenaea and the Eleusinian Mysteries, featured as part of a procession personal insults either from or at those participating, and some have sought to find the origins of personal humor in comedy in such rituals. But a more plausible ancestor lies in the literary tradition of the iambic poems of Archilochus (early seventh century) and Hipponax (mid-sixth), and comedy has much in common with the iambus, not just in the poet abusing his personal targets, but in the crudity and imagination of its language. Platonius (Koster II.1–2) describes Cratinus as "an emulator of Archilochus," and his comedy, entitled *Archilochuses*, perhaps had a double chorus of contrasting poets and an agon involving poetic genres and styles. The poets of Old Comedy, not just Cratinus, do display a knowledge of, quotations from, and parody of Archilochus in their works.

It is one thing to make a one-off joke in the public atmosphere of a festival, but another to create sophisticated and repeated caricatures in a formal dramatic production. By the 420s, Old Comedy had become "political" in the modern sense of the word, engaging with personalities and issues of the Athenian state. *Acharnians* (425) and *Lysistrata* (411) both concern the matter of peace versus war, *Knights* and the other demagogue comedies the personality of the popular leaders of the late fifth century, and even before the arrival of Aristophanes Cratinus and Hermippus were making personal and political capital out of Pericles. Platonius (Koster I) rightly stressed the link between Old Comedy and the freedoms of the Athenian democracy—"so then in the time of the comedy of Aristophanes and Cratinus and Eupolis the poets were an irresistible force against wrong-doers." Politics were a contentious business in democratic Athens, and it was inevitable that comedy would reflect the controversial people and issues of the day. The crucial figure here is Cratinus, who in the 440s and 430s brought together the literary tradition of the poet attacking his favorite targets and the political themes of imperial Athens. I would, however, reserve full-blown political comedy for the 420s, especially in the plays of Aristophanes, who appears to have pioneered the demagogue-comedy in 424 with his prize-winning *Knights*, directed against Cleon.

CRATINUS

Cratinus was considered as one of the canonical three playwrights of Old Comedy. A late source cites 454/3 for Cratinus and Plato being "well known." This may be thirty years too early for Plato, but it fits well with Cratinus's position on the list of victors at the Dionysia (IG ii² 2325.50), where he comes two places after Euphronius, whose sole victory we can date to 458. The anonymous (Koster III.20) says that "he won after the 85th Olympiad" (440/439–437/436). This was emended by Meineke to "81st" Olympiad (456/5–453/2), but it is more likely that the anonymous is recording Cratinus's first victory at the Lenaea. On that victors' list, his name comes fourth (IG ii² 2325.121), indicating a victory in the early 430s.

At the lower end of his career, we know of productions at the Lenaea of 425 (*Tempest-Tossed* [*Cheimazomenoi*]), at the Lenaea of 424 (*Satyrs*), and then his brilliant victory with *Wine-Flask* [*Pytine*] at the Dionysia of 423. At *Peace* 700–703 (Dionysia of 421), Hermes, speaking for Peace, asks whether "the great Cratinus is still alive" and receives the answer that "he died, when the Spartans invaded…he just passed out, couldn't stand to see a full jar of wine smashed." As the Spartans had not invaded since 425, and since Cratinus was alive and producing *Wine-Flask* in 423, this is chronologically impossible. The simplest explanation is that Cratinus had in fact died by the Dionysia of 421, and that Aristophanes has made up this comic account of his death. When the anonymous writer (Koster III.23) cites *Peace* 700–703, he adds the phrase "<when the Spartans invaded> *for the first time*," thus dating Cratinus's death to 431, an even more improbable date.

The *Suda* (κ 2344) gives the number of his comedies at twenty-one and of his victories at nine. The latter figure is confirmed by the entries for Cratinus on the list of victors (IG ii² 2325.50, 121), six victories at the Dionysia and three at the Lenaea. We could have as many as twenty-nine titles, although the existence of some is doubtful. We have fragments assigned for twenty-two plays, plus two titles known only from the hypotheses to two comedies by Aristophanes. We can work with a total of twenty-four comedies in a career that lasted about thirty years.

The testimonia reveal Cratinus as the grand old man of Old Comedy. Several sources regard him as a brilliant and creative poet, the anonymous (Koster III.26) describing him as "composing in the style of Aeschylus," but others, while admitting his success, still see him as rough and uneven in his composition: "harsh," "lacking in *charis*," "inconsistent in the development of his plots" (Platonius 2 = Koster II.1–8), "old-fashioned and lacking in order" (Koster V). Cratinus was especially associated with personal jokes against his targets. Platonius 2 speaks of his "emulation of Archilochus," while the anonymous (Koster V.19) describes him as using comedy "as a sort of public whip." According to the

Life of Aristophanes (Koster XXVIII.4–5), both he and Eupolis "were saying bad things more than was necessary."

Of the twenty-four titles, at least one-third seem to have been burlesques of myth. These can take two forms in Old Comedy: a comic spoof of the myth in its original setting, or the intrusion of a mythical figure into a modern context. Cratinus appears to have written comedies of both kinds. The best-known example of the former is his *Dionysalexander*, of which we have a few fragments but most of the hypothesis (plot summary), published in 1904 as *POxy.* 663 and as K-A test. i:

> ...seek...all (?) ...judgment Hermes (5) leaves, while they say some things to the spectators about the poets. These joke and make fun of Dionysus when he appears (10). When <the goddesses and Hermes arrive> and <make promises> to him: from Hera unshaken tyranny, from Athena (15) success in war, and Aphrodite to make him as beautiful and attractive as possible, he judges her [Aphrodite] to be the winner. After this he sails off (20) to Sparta, takes Helen away, and returns to Ida. But he hears a little while later that the Greeks are ravaging the countryside (25) <and looking for> Alexander. He hides Helen very quickly in a basket (30), and changing himself into a ram awaits developments. Alexander appears and detects each of them (35), and orders them to be taken to the ships, meaning to give them back to the Greeks. When Helen refuses, he takes pity on her and retains possession of her, to keep her as his wife. Dionysus he sends off to be handed over (40). The satyrs go along with him, encouraging him and insisting that they will not betray him. In the play Pericles (45) is very skillfully and suggestively made fun of for having brought the war on the Athenians.

Cratinus takes the familiar story of the Judgment of Paris and substitutes Dionysus for Paris in both the Judgment and its consequences, including both Helen and the angry Greeks. The appearance of Paris later in the comedy allows the story of the Trojan War to continue in its traditional form. The chorus is composed of satyrs, the familiar attendants upon Dionysus more usually found in satyr-drama but not unknown in comedy. Dionysus appears in his familiar comic role as "anti-hero," the object of the satyrs' laughter, running for cover at the first sign of the Greeks and finally handed over to the Greeks for punishment.[2]

The hypothesis has raised a number of problems. First, after the departure of Hermes, presumably to fetch the goddesses, "they [the chorus] say some things to the spectators *about the making of sons*" (6–9). That is the traditional text, expanded from the papyrus π(ερὶ) ὑῶν ποί(σεως), but Körte's emendation π(ερὶ) τῶν ποιη(τῶν) ("about the poets") has often been accepted—see K-A test. i. Whatever the reading in line 8, the chorus is breaking the dramatic illusion by addressing the spectators directly on a matter outside the drama. In Aristophanes this usually happens in the *parabasis*, coming anywhere between lines 500 and 1000. For that reason, critics have concluded that this part of the

---

[2] Recent studies of this lost comedy include McGlew (2002: 25–56), Storey (2006; 2011: I.284–295), Wright (2007), and Bakola (2010).

hypothesis (6–9) marks the *parabasis* and that a great deal of earlier action is thus missing from the summary. But it is equally possible that not much occurred before the summary becomes intelligible; moreover, since the dramatic break at line 19 is where the
parabasis should naturally occur, the words, "they say some things to the spectators"
(6–9) may have been spoken in the *parodos*, the entry song of the chorus. Aristophanes
seems not to have broken the dramatic illusion in the *parodos* (apart perhaps from *Frogs*
364–371), but we can find a number of occasions in the fragments where Cratinus and
Eupolis appear to have done so.

The identity of the main chorus has been debated. In lines 6–12, "these (unidentified) say some things to the spectators and then make fun of Dionysus when he
appears," while at lines 42–44 "the satyrs go along with him, encouraging him and
insisting that they will not betray him." The natural inference is that the satyrs are
the "these" of line 6. Some object that the satyrs, Dionysus's traditional companions,
would not be presented as making fun of him, and postulate a principal chorus of
local shepherds on Mount Ida, but Dionysus can be impatient with the satyrs, as at
Aeschylus *TrGF* fr. 78 (*Isthmian Athletes*), where they have abandoned him for the
competition of the games, and the simplest course is to identify them as the main
chorus. Satyrs more properly form the chorus for satyr-drama, but at least five comedies of the late fifth century had satyr choruses, one of which was Callias's *Satyrs* of
437. Marshall (2000) has cleverly suggested that this was comedy's response to the
satyrs missing from Euripides's *Alcestis* of 438. On the assumption of an earlier date
for *Dionysalexander* (see below), these satyrs could also be part of a comic conversation with satyr-drama.

The final sentence of the hypothesis (44–48) unexpectedly reveals that the comedy
was not solely a burlesque of myth: "in the drama Pericles is very convincingly made
fun of by insinuation for bringing the war on the Athenians." Scholars, assuming that
"the war" is the Peloponnesian War, which broke out in 431 and that the comedy must
have been produced before Pericles died in 429, have widely accepted a date of 430 or
429.[3] The latter assumption is weakened by the fact that Aristophanes can blame Pericles
for his responsibility for the War in *Acharnians* (425) and again in *Peace* (421). Against
the former is that an equally possible candidate for "the war" is the conflict with Samos
(440/39). This war was taken seriously by the Athenians (Thucydides 1.115–117) and we
know that Pericles was blamed for it because of his Milesian mistress, Aspasia (Plutarch,
Pericles 25)—the war started when Athens sided against the Samians in a territorial dispute with Miletus. Thus in the public mind both the Trojan War and the Samian War
could be viewed as wars "fought because of a woman."

This last sentence has also suggested to many that the comedy was a thoroughgoing political allegory in which Dionysus stood for Pericles throughout the play. For

---

[3] Geissler (1969: 24–25) argues for a date in 430; see also K-A test. i for other scholars who accept the
traditional date. In favor of "the war" being the Samian War and thus of an earlier date are Mattingly
(1977) and Storey (2006), Storey (2011 I.285).

instance, the Greeks ravaging the countryside (lines 24–30) while Dionysus just hides away alludes to Pericles's policy of sitzkrieg in 431/0 (see Thucydides 2.21, Hermippus K-A fr. 47). But the last sentence may just mean that at some point in the comedy there was a skillful allusion to Pericles and the war. In view of the play's title, should we not be looking at Alexander (Paris) for the source of this comment? By keeping Helen, he brings the Trojan War on his people. The play is probably first and foremost a burlesque of myth, exploring the comic possibilities of Dionysus in yet another tight situation.

One final problem is a capital eta (H) in line 27 of the hypothesis, between the title *Dionys[alexandros* and the author *Krat[einou*. There appears to be a line over the eta, thus making it a numeric, "eighth." On either date for *Dionysalexander* (437 or 430/29), "eighth" seems chronologically unlikely, given Cratinus's debut in 453, while alphabetically *Dionysalexander* is the fifth or sixth of the titles we have. Edmonds proposed that the eta was not a numeric but stood for ἤ ("or") and that *Dionysalexander* had an alternative title,[4] for which Luppe (1966) proposed *Idaioi* ("Men of Ida"), arguing that these local shepherds formed the main chorus of the play. Bakola (2010) accepts *Idaioi* as an alternative title, but in the sense of "Satyrs from Ida," thus keeping the satyrs as the principal chorus. The obvious alternative title for *Dionysalexander* would be *Satyrs*, Cratinus's comedy at the Lenaea of 424, but that would entail abandoning both the traditional date of 430/29 and my preferred date of 437.

Other mythological burlesques of the first sort would include *Runaways* (*Drapetides*, or *Fugitive Women*), where in K-A fr. 53 Theseus speaks about his encounter with Cercyon and in K-A fr. 61 is addressed as "son of Pandion"; *Men of Seriphus* (*Seriphioi*), where in K-A fr. 222–3 Perseus receives directions for an aerial journey; and *Nemesis*, a burlesque of the myth by which Helen is born of an egg resulting from the union of Zeus and Nemesis and incubated by Leda. At K-A fr. 114, someone gives Zeus instructions "to become a big bird," at K-A fr. 116 a male figure (almost certainly Zeus) exclaims how much he is enjoying a diet of "rosebuds and apples and parsley and mint," and at K-A fr. 115 Hermes (?) assigns Leda her task to incubate this egg and "hatch for us a beautiful and wonderful chick."

Of considerable interest is Cratinus's burlesque of the encounter between Odysseus and the Cyclops in *Odyssey* 9, called *Odysseus and Company* (*Odysses*). Some of Homer's details are preserved: the marvelous wine (K-A fr. 145–146), the name of Odysseus (K-A fr. 145), the fleeing comrades (K-A fr. 148), the cheese and milk (K-A fr. 149), and the threatening Cyclops (K-A fr. 150) with one eye (K-A fr. 156). Platonius [Koster I.29–31, 51–52] writes that this comedy belonged to the "type of Middle Comedy," since it lacked "choral

---

[4] Alternative titles for Old Comedy are by no means rare, but they seem to have been the creation of ancient scholarship rather than the deliberate choice of the comic writers. We know from *Clouds* 554 and Eupolis K-A fr. 89 that Aristophanes's *Knights* (424) was known by that title in the early 410s, and we may conclude that the ancient poets did give their plays a title. But the double (or occasionally triple) titles may in part be the later scholars' attempt to distinguish two plays with the same title (e.g., Aristophanes's *Dramas* or *Centaur* and *Dramas* or *Niobus*) or (as in the case of *Dionysalexander*?) based on the assumption that plays should be named after their chorus. Σ *Lysistrata* 389 rejects the attempts of earlier scholars to give *Lysistrata* the alternative title of *Adoniazousai* ("Women celebrating the feast of Adonis").

parts and parabases" and also personal insult, the humor being directed at the Homeric original. But K-A fr. 151 shows that there was indeed a chorus, the comrades of Odysseus. The meter there is anapaestic dimeter, and it has been argued that what the play lacked was not a chorus per se, but choral songs and *parabaseis* in complicated lyric meters. See, however, K-A fr. 153, which K-A restore in glyconics. Platonius is not known for his accuracy in matters of detail—for example, he seems to think that *Odysseus and Company*, Eupolis's *Dyers* (*Baptai*), and Aristophanes's *Aeolosicon* all belong to the same period, whereas they are about fifty years apart. None of the fragments, however, has any personal jokes, and perhaps Platonius was correct on that point, but not about the chorus. This lack of personal humor has led many to the attractive conclusion that the plays belong to the years 439–436, when such jokes were subject to a legal ban (see Σ *Acharnians* 67).

For mythical intrusions into the present, we may cite *Chirons*, where K-A fr. 246 is spoken by the ghost of Solon and K-A fr. 251 refers to the court of the *nautodikai* at Athens, where trials for *xenia* were held. K-A fr. 258–259 are part of a song attacking Pericles and Aspasia, while K-A fr. 256–257 pick up the theme of the better life in the past. At K-A fr. 253, the chorus of Chirons (centaurs) explain that they have come (to Athens, presumably) for some purpose involving *hypothekai* (precepts or mortgages?). But more important is *Wealth-Gods* (*Ploutoi*), whose K-A fr. 171 contains the one major papyrus fragment that we have of Cratinus. From the book fragments we knew that the Golden Age theme was part of the play (K-A fr. 172, 176), but the papyrus has revealed that the chorus was made up of Titans released from their captivity, and "now that the rule of tyranny is over and the people rule" (K-A fr.171.22–3), they have come to Athens to seek out an old and decrepit relative (Prometheus?) and also to punish those who have acquired their wealth unjustly. Some have seen in the reference to the end of tyranny and the rule of the people an allusion to Pericles's removal from office in late 430 and thus dated the play to 429, but the point of the joke may just be that events on Olympus have followed the example at Athens, tyranny followed by democracy. Athenaeus (267e–270a) cites a number of comedies with the theme of the ideal society in chronological order, beginning with *Wealth-Gods*. As one of the later plays is the *Beasts* of Crates, a poet whose career belongs to the 440s and 430s, a date in the early 430s for *Wealth-Gods* seems preferable.

Of Cratinus's other plays we may mention *Archilochuses*, which may have had a double chorus of two sorts of poets and perhaps a contest over the proper type of poetry to follow; *Thracian Women* (the nature of the chorus is uncertain), which contains a famous joke against Pericles:

> Here comes Pericles, the onion-headed Zeus, with the Odeion on his head, now that ostracism has gone away. (K-A fr. 73)

and *Poofters* [*Malthakoi*], where the chorus of soft-living and effeminate males list the various flowers with which they deck their hair (K-A fr. 105)—one wonders how sympathetic a chorus these gender-challenged men would make before an audience that was largely male.

But perhaps Cratinus's greatest success lay with his *Wine-Flask*, which defeated Aristophanes's *Clouds* at the Dionysia of 423.[5] The previous year Aristophanes had included Cratinus among his former stars of comedy at *Knights* 526–536:

> Then with Cratinus in mind, who used to flow on a wave of praise, coursing through the open plains, sweeping headlong from their roots oaks and plane trees and enemies. Singing at a party had to include "Goddess of bribes with fig-wood shoes" and "Makers of clever hymns." He was great then. But now you look on and have no pity for him in his dotage—his frets have fallen out, his strings have lost their tuning, and his harmonies are full of holes. An old man, he stumbles about like Connas, "with withered crown and dying of thirst," when because of his previous victories he should be having a lifetime of free drinks in the Council House, and instead of spouting nonsense he should be sitting splendidly beside Dionysus.

The plot of the comedy is given by the scholiast to *Knights* 400. Cratinus makes himself the main character in his own play, married to Comedy, whom Cratinus has abandoned for drunkenness (some would capitalize Drunkenness and make her a rival personification and character in the play). Friends of Cratinus, very likely the chorus, arrive and learn that Comedy wishes to leave him and charge him formally with abuse (*kakosis*). Bakola (2010) points out that an heiress could bring a suit of *kakosis* for neglect by her husband, and finds other instances of artistic creation expressed in sexual terms (*Knights* 515–517, *Frogs* 92–97, and especially Pherecrates K-A fr. 155).

Thereafter we can only guess at the plotline. Was Cratinus "cured" of his addiction and did he return to his true wife, a sober man, and on what terms would Comedy agree to take him back? Or did he prevail by showing that drink is necessary to the creative process (K-A fr. 203)? Here we should compare the end of *Wasps* (422), where an irascible and uncontrollable old man resists the well-meaning attempts of a family member to change his behavior and ends the play triumphant and suffering the effects of strong drink. Biles (2002) and Sidwell (1995) argue that Philocleon in that comedy owes more than a little to Cratinus's self-parody in *Wine-Flask* eight months earlier. The drunken Philocleon leading in a flute girl may recall a scene where Cratinus enters with Drunkenness.

A trial or a contest requires an antagonist, and while Comedy or the chorus might well fulfil such a role (note the plural in K-A fr. 206), I wonder if Cratinus brought not only himself into his own play but also a rival poet, and who better than Aristophanes? A rival would be the ideal person to threaten his drinking paraphernalia (K-A fr. 199) and perhaps speak (K-A fr. 198) the reaction to something Cratinus has just said:

> Lord Apollo, the flood of his words, springs splashing, twelve spouts to his mouth, an Ilissus in his throat. What can I say? If somebody doesn't put a plug in his mouth, he will inundate everything here with his poetry.

---

[5] Recent studies of *Wine-Flask* include Luppe (2000), Rosen (2000), Bakola (2010: 59–64, 252–261), and Storey (2011 I.362–375).

It would be quite appropriate for a comic Aristophanes to repeat the river metaphor that he exploited in *Knights* 526–536. K-A fr. 208–209 suggest that there was a scene in which Cratinus is sketching out a comedy.

What of the "wine flask," which was important enough to give the comedy its name? K-A fr. 201 tells us that a *pytine* was a wicker wine container (often made by prisoners) and sealed with pitch. In some fashion it must have been the symbol of the action of the play. Was it the indestructible nature of the container—compare the threat to smash all his drinking vessels at K-A fr. 199? Or did it represent the level to which Cratinus would descend, reduced to drinking from a *pytine*? Was a mute actor brought on stage dressed like a wine flask, like Peace in that comedy or Diallage in *Lysistrata* or the kitchen utensils in *Wasps*?

But however we reconstruct the comedy, it is clear that Cratinus purposely presents himself in a negative light, as an unfaithful husband, an aging drunk and philanderer, and a poet who has abandoned his art. What Cratinus has done is to take the comic picture Aristophanes used in *Knights* and, rather than oppose it, reinforce it by agreeing to the points of caricature and recasting himself as the lovable drunk for whom alcohol is his comic inspiration. Biles makes the good point that we should not be ransacking *Clouds* seeking reasons why it finished third; rather we should be recognizing in *Wine-Flask* a brilliant comedy that simply outclassed Aristophanes.

We find also in Cratinus an intertextual engagement with other comic poets and with tragedy. His coinage "Choerilecphantides" (K-A fr. 502), combining the comedian Ecphantides with the early tragedian Choerilus, has already been mentioned. More famous is the astute juxtaposition of Euripides and Aristophanes (K-A fr. 342):

> "Who are you?" some clever spectator might ask, a quibbler of words, a maker of maxims, a Euripidaristophanizer.

Since Aristophanes's debut belongs in 427, this comes from a late play by Cratinus, most probably *Wine-Flask* (Dionysia 423). Bakola (2010) has made a strong case for Cratinus's engagement with tragedy, particularly that of Aeschylus—the anonymous (Koster III) describes him as "writing in the style of Aeschylus." In particular, she sees in *Runaways* a scene with Theseus welcoming the effeminate "runaways" as influenced by the arrival of the fugitive daughters of Danaus in Aeschylus's *Suppliants* or perhaps that of Adrastus in Aeschylus's *Men of Eleusis*. More probable is a link between the lost *Loosing of Prometheus* attributed to Aeschylus and *Wealth-Gods*, as both plays had a chorus of Titans released from their captivity coming in search of a lost relative. But we do not find Aristophanes's comic preoccupation (obsession?) with tragedy, to the point of creating a new word for comedy, *trygoidia*, a term meant to pair comedy off with tragedy.

HERMIPPUS

Hermippus was dismissed by Norwood (1931: 22) as "unimportant as a playwright," but his status was considerably rehabilitated by Gilula (2000). Firm dates are a victory at the Dionysia of 435 (IG ii² 2318) and his *Bakery-Women* (*Artopolides*) in 420 or 419, and K-A fr. 47, which refers to Pericles's conduct of the war, must belong to 430 or 429. Similarly if K-A fr. 63 belongs to *Basket-Bearers* (*Phormophoroi*, or *Stevedores*), then that comedy belongs between 431 and 425, since Sitalces, mentioned in line 7, was dead by 424. On the Dionysia victors' list (IG ii² 2325.57) his name appears after that of Pherecrates and before Aristophanes, while on the Lenaea list he is found with four victories after Cratinus and before Phrynichus (debut 429). A conservative dating of his career would be 435–415. The *Suda* (ε 3044) records a total of forty comedies, but as we have only ten secure titles, I suspect that the *Suda's* figure is in error rather than that we have lost any record of three-quarters of the output of an important comic poet.

Several play titles suggest comic burlesques of myth. His *Birth of Athena* anticipates by several decades the vogue of divine birth comedies in the early fourth century, and we know of his *Agamemnon*, *Europa*, and *Cercopes*, and quite likely *Fates*. K-A fr. 77 we know to have been put in the mouth of Dionysus. But a strong political theme can be detected as well. K-A fr. 47, plausibly assigned to *Fates* for its metrical and thematic similarities to K-A fr. 48, attacks Pericles for his lack of enthusiasm in prosecuting the war and records a political threat from the demagogue Cleon. Aristophanes complains at *Clouds* 557 that Hermippus followed Eupolis in launching a dramatic attack on Hyperbolus, for which the scholiast informs us that this comedy was *Bakery-Wives* but also that the play was not an attack on Hyperbolus from start to finish, in the manner that *Knights* attacked Cleon and Eupolis's *Marikas* caricatured Hyperbolus. Hermippus does make jokes at political figures, but he may not have written full-scale political comedy.

Plutarch (*Pericles* 32.1) makes the intriguing statement that "Aspasia was the defendant in a court case for impiety, launched by Hermippus the comic poet, in which he alleged that she entertained free women in a certain place for Pericles." While several critics accept the historicity of this prosecution, comparing similar actions in the 430s against Phidias and Anaxagoras, the whole thing sounds more like something from a comedy that Plutarch or his sources has interpreted as "fact." Plutarch (*Pericles* 13.14) mentions comic allegations against Pericles seducing the wife of a friend and against Pyrilampes for using his collection of peacocks to entice women for Pericles (see also K-A adespota fr. 702). The attack on Pericles in K-A fr. 47 belongs to 430 or 429; the late 430s would be a likely date for a comic attack on Aspasia.

Perhaps the most interesting fact about Hermippus is his activity in other poetic genres. He is explicitly credited with iambic poems (West fr. 1–8) and with the writing of "parodies." Both have clear links with comedy: iambus for the crude and violent language aimed at a target, and parody for the burlesque of a more serious poetic form, in this case epic. Thus K-A fr. 63 and 77, both in the epic hexameter (rare for comedy), may be from either a comedy or a parody.

TELECLEIDES

Teleclides was a comic poet of the 430s and perhaps 420s. K-A fr. 44 mentions Nicias, who does not come to prominence until the early 420s; this fragment may refer to his resigning the generalship in favor of Cleon in 425. Charicles, another target of K-A fr. 44, is a known politician of the 410s, which would push his career down into that decade. One ancient source (Koster VIII) assigns Teleclides seven plays. Athenaeus (*ap. Suda* τ 488) knows only of three titles (*Amphictyons*, *Magistrates* [*Prytaneis*], *Rigid Ones* [*Sterroi*]); we have fragments of these and also of *Truth-Tellers* (*Apseudeis*) and *Hesiods*, and the Roman inscription (IG *UrbRom* 215) adds two further partial titles. But on the list of victors he is credited with eight victories at the Lenaea and Dionysia. Clearly we have lost a great deal about and by this comic poet.

The most significant fragment (K-A fr. 1) comes from his *Amphictyons*, where an unidentified figure (Cronus?) describes "the way of life that I used to provide for mortals...men were fat then, the stuff of giants." The seventy-three fragments show us a poet much in the style of Aristophanes, titles implying significantly involved choruses and frequent personal and political jokes (K-A fr. 45 and 47 against Pericles). Of particular interest is Teleclides's engagement with poets and literary themes: the play-title *Hesiods* (e.g., poets like Hesiod?); K-A fr. 15, where a female speaker (Tragedy or a Muse?) disparages the tragic poet Philocles; the insults at Gnesippus (K-A fr. 36) and Nothippus (K-A fr. 17) and perhaps Aristophanes (K-A fr. 46); the link between Euripides and Socrates (K-A fr. 41–42); and perhaps another joke aimed at Euripides and his mother (K-A fr. 40).

CRATES

Crates represents an entirely different strand of Old Comedy. On the list of victors at the Dionysia (IG ii² 2325.52), he appears with three victories between Cratinus (debut in the mid-450s) and Callias (victory in 446). The anonymous (Koster III.26–8) places him between Cratinus and Pherecrates, Aristophanes at *Knights* 537–40 after Magnes and Cratinus. His career thus belongs to the 440s and 430s, and the reference to the "displeasure and angry insults that Crates had to put up with" at the hands of the spectators (*Knights* 537) suggests that this was a recent experience (late 430s) and that Crates is no longer on the scene by 424. The *Suda* (κ 2339) records seven plays and gives six titles. We have multiple fragments from six comedies.

We know about his comedy from three ancient sources: (1) Aristotle's well-known statement (*Poetics* 1449b5) that "of the Athenians Crates was the first to abandon the iambic mode and to write whole stories and plots"; (2) the anonymous writer (Koster III.27–8) who records that Crates was "very funny and entertaining, the first to bring drunken characters on stage" and that Pherecrates "followed the example of Crates and likewise refrained from personal insult" (III.29–30); and (3) Aristophanes's comments about this earlier poet (*Knights* 537–540):

> And the angry reception and the insults that Crates had to put up with. He used to send you home, serving a nice lunch on a small budget, kneading some witty concepts from his delicate palate. However, he did all right, sometimes crashing, sometimes not.

We do need to remember that compliments in comedy are often double-edged and condescending, and Aristophanes, while conceding some positive attributes to Crates, is also denigrating him and his comedy. In his K-A fr. 347 Aristophanes alludes to "the ivory salt-fish" of Crates (K-A fr. 32) as an instance of earlier "marvelous comic fare," but even here his jokes were just "giggled at."

The fragments bear out these judgments. No play title suggests a political theme, nor are there any personal jokes in the sixty fragments. The most significant remains are those from *Beasts* (*Theria*, K-A fr. 16–17), where the comic utopian theme (cf. Teleclides K-A fr. 1, Cratinus *Wealth-Gods*) is being debated by two speakers. Here it is not a past Golden Age being described but one proposed for the future, and the debate seems not to be over the desirability of the utopia but what its characteristics will be (food on demand or personal conveniences). The meters of the two fragments differ (iambic tetrameter catalectic and the more "prosaic" iambic trimeter), and Athenaeus (267e) may be misleading us when he claims that K-A fr. 17 comes "right after" K-A fr. 16. Was the "angry reception" to a late comedy by Crates, which perhaps paled before the newer and more political sort pioneered by Cratinus and Teleclides?

PHERECRATES

Finally there is Pherecrates, an important figure who enjoyed a career of several decades and who, like Crates, produced a different sort of Old Comedy. The anonymous (Koster III.29–31) connects him with Crates as his mentor and model in the avoidance of personal humor and then goes on to say that "his success lay in new themes and in inventing plots." Since on the list of victors at the Dionysia (IG ii² 2325.56) his name comes before Hermippus, the latest date for whose first victory is 435, Pherecrates's debut at that festival must belong at the latest to the early 430s or even the late 440s. On the list of victors at the Lenaea (IG ii² 2325.122) he comes fifth, immediately after Cratinus. His *Wild-Men* (*Agrioi*) is securely dated to the Lenaea of 420, while the reference in K-A fr. 64 to the house of Poulytion suggests a date in the 410s. If *Chiron* is in fact by Pherecrates (see below), the mention of Timotheus (K-A fr. 155.19–28) would date that comedy to the last years of the century. A safe span of dates would be 440–415, although his career may well have continued to the end of the century. He is credited with seventeen or eighteen comedies; we have nineteen titles, and if *Metics* is really by Plato and the two titles *Heracles the Mortal* and *False-Heracles* refer to the same comedy, that nineteen is nicely reduced to seventeen. There was some controversy in antiquity over the authorship of *Miners*, *Persians*, and *Chiron*—unfortunately so, since these are the best represented among the remains of Pherecrates.

The fragments do not tell us much about his plots. But as for personal humor, of the three hundred or so fragments of Pherecrates perhaps ten make jokes at people outside the drama, and apart from a shot at the gender confusion of Alcibiades (K-A fr. 164), none is aimed at a political figure. Most of the *komoidoumenoi* in Pherecrates are poets or musicians. Norwood (1931) may overstate the case by postulating "the school of Crates," but it is clear that Pherecrates wrote a different sort of comedy from the stereotypical topical and political comedy of Aristophanes.

Domestic comedy was a mainstay of Pherecrates. His comedy *Corianno* had a woman in the title role, perhaps a *hetaira*—Athenaeus (567c) tells us that several comedies were named after celebrated *hetairai*. K-A fr. 73–76 show a drinking scene involving several women that would not be out of place in later comedy of types and manners. K-A fr. 77–79 of the same comedy mention an old man in love (inappropriately, given his age, it seems). Titles such as *Old Women, Thalassa, Petale,* and *Pannychis* very probably bear the names of *hetairai,* and perhaps the anonymous writer on comedy means by "new plots" something like the romantic comedy of errors that would become the staple of New and Roman comedy.

There was some debate about the authorship of *Miners* and *Persians,* but both seem to have turned on the familiar theme of the Golden Age and the "automatic" utopian life. K-A fr. 113 (*Miners*) consists of a dialogue of thirty-three lines in which a woman details the ideal life that awaits one in the underworld, while K-A fr. 114 describes meadows and flowers that, if also part of the underworld, remind one of the home of the dead initiates in *Frogs* 323–459. This is a utopia to be found "out there" (or rather "down there"), while the speaker of the ideal society described in *Persians* (a people presented in art and literature as stereotypically wealthy and fortunate) asks:

> What need have we now of your [sing.] plows or your yoke-makers, of your sickle-makers or coppersmiths, of seed and stakes? For on their own [*automatoi*] through the crossroads shall flow rivers of black broth with shiny speckle cakes and Achilles-buns.

This appears to be a utopia realized in the future, although it could be the result of relocating elsewhere, e.g., Persia—compare Metagenes K-A fr. 6 [*Thurio-Persians*], where life in Thurii is described as a utopian ideal.

Pherecrates did write some burlesques of myth, notably *Ant-Men* (*Myrmekanthropoi*), which had as characters Deucalion and Pyrrha surviving the Flood. Whatever the correct title of the comedy about Heracles (*Heracles the Mortal* or *Heracles the Deserter*), it was likely an example of a mythical character intruding into modern reality (cf. Dionysus in Eupolis's *Officers* [*Taxiarchoi*]). The longest extant fragment of Pherecrates is K-A fr. 155 (*Chiron*), quoted by [Plutarch] 1141c, who records that "Pherecrates the comic poet brought Music on stage as a woman, her whole body mistreated, and had Justice ask the cause of her condition." Music is being presented as a high-class *hetaira* who takes one lover at a time, and the result is an extended series of double entendres that mix musical terms with suggestions of sexual and physical assault. For *Chiron* we have to recreate a play with scenes where Justice complains to Music (Poetry?) about her mistreatment by the new musicians (Melanippides, Cinesias, Phrynis, Timotheus), an old man reminisces about a carefree past (K-A fr. 156), Achilles seems to appear in a parody of *Iliad* 9 (K-A fr. 159), and Hesiod is parodied in dactylic hexameters (K-A fr.

162). Add the Chiron Vase (Taplin 1993: plate 12.6), which could well be illustrating this play, and we have some intriguing, if confusing, hints about this lost comedy.[6]

Two other comedies of Pherecrates deserve a mention. *Wild-Men* (Lenaea 420) is one of several comedies of the 410s which turn on the theme of civilization and the wild life—see also *Birds* (414) and Phrynichus's *Hermit* (*Monotropos,* 414). Plato (*Protagoras* 327cd) informs us that the chorus was made up of terrifying *misanthropoi,* "who have no system of education, no courts or laws, and no necessity to care about virtue at all." The comedy seems to have had one or two men (from Athens?) who go to the wilds seeking a better way of life, but we cannot determine whether their encounter with the *agrioi* of the title caused them to repent of their mission or whether, as in *Birds,* they were able to co-opt the inhabitants for their own advantage. Finally, there is *Tiddlers* (*Krapataloi*), named for an imaginary unit of coinage invented by Pherecrates and used in the under-world (see K-A fr. 86, where *krapataloi* are sub-divided into *psothia*). *Krapataloi* can mean also "small fish" (hence my translated title) or "worthless things," and perhaps this term was applied to the chorus, either by others or by themselves. K-A fr. 87 is spoken by a "toothless old man" in some distress, probably the familiar "hero" of Old Comedy. We are told K-A fr. 100 ("I who constructed and handed on to them a great craft") was spoken by Aeschylus, and K-A fr. 96 has by many been put in the mouth of Jocasta. K-A fr. 85 seems to be an instruction on how to die and thus get to the underworld (compare *Frogs* 117–164). This play, like *Frogs,* seems to have had a literary theme and been set in the underworld, and Pherecrates's comedy is almost certainly the earlier.

Pherecrates, then, was creating a different sort of comedy from what we usually understand by Old Comedy. His plays have less to do with politics and personal humor and more to do with social themes and domestic characters, and even in the occasional burlesque of myth. In *Ant-Men* Pyrrha complains to Deucalion (K-A fr. 125), "never serve me fish again, even if I ask for some." As many as five plays may bear the names of women, and we can see in Corianno and in Music (in *Chiron*) the figure of the high-class courtesan, who will become a familiar feature of later comedy. The fragments we have give us a glimpse of a poet whom we are sorry to have lost, who deserves a higher place of recognition in the study of comedy. A more representative triad for Old Comedy would perhaps have been Cratinus (myth + politics), Pherecrates (myth + domestic comedy), and Aristophanes (politics + tragedy).

Old Comedy began, I suspect, as something primitive and basic, an animal chorus, slapstick with crude and obvious jokes, and an emphasis on song and dance. Here we should compare tragedy, where Phrynichus, the earliest poet we know anything about, was remembered especially for his sweet songs and exciting dances (*Wasps* 219, 1490). But by the 440s and 430s we begin to detect sustained mythical burlesques, where comedy shares common ground with satyr-drama. We find also the repeated theme of the ideal society, comic utopias being sought in the past (paradise lost), in the future

---

[6] Recent studies of *Chiron* include: Dobrov and Urios-Aparisi (1995), Csapo (1999–2000), Henderson (2000), and Storey (2011 II.494–505).

(paradise regained), and somewhere out there (paradise found). Play-length plots of intrigue are attested for this period, perhaps taking place within the domestic world. But the most striking theme, for which Old Comedy would be best remembered, is the combination of political comedy and personal humor, as comedy responded to the flourishing and vigorous Athenian democracy. Here comedy was seen as having a redeeming social value, and Cratinus celebrated for wielding his "public whip."

FURTHER READING

Heath, M. 1990. "Aristophanes and his Rivals." *Greece & Rome* 37: 143–158.

Lowe, N. 2007. *Comedy*. Greece & Rome New Surveys in the Classics 37. Cambridge: Cambridge University Press.

Rosen, R. 1988. *Old Comedy and the Iambographic Tradition*. Atlanta: Scholars Press.

Rothwell, K. 2007. *Nature, Culture, and the Origins of Greek Comedy: A Study of the Animal Choruses*. Cambridge: Cambridge University Press.

Rusten, J., et al., ed. and tr. 2011. *The Birth of Comedy: Texts, Documents, and Art from Athenian Comic Competitions, 486–280*. Baltimore: Johns Hopkins University Press.

Schmid, W. 1946. *Geschichte der griechischen Literatur*, vol. I.4. Munich: Beck.

Sommerstein, A. H. 2009. "Old Comedians on Old Comedy." In *Talking about Laughter: And Other Studies in Greek Comedy*, by A. H. Sommerstein, 116–135. Oxford: Oxford University Press.

Storey, I. C.2010 "Origins and Fifth-Century Comedy." In *Brill's Companion to the Study of Greek Comedy*, edited by G. Dobrov, 179–225. Leiden: Brill.

——. 2011. *The Fragments of Old Comedy*, 3 vol. Loeb Classical Library 513–515. Cambridge, MA: Harvard University Press.

Storey, I. C., and A. L. Allan. 2005. *A Guide to Ancient Greek Drama*. Oxford: Blackwell, 2005. See 169–229.

BIBLIOGRAPHY

Bakola, E. 2010. *Cratinus and the Art of Comedy*. Oxford: Oxford University Press.

Biles, Z. 2002. "Intertextual Biography in the Rivalry of Cratinus and Aristophanes." *American Journal of Philology* 123: 169–204.

Csapo, E. 1999–2000. "Euripidean New Music." *Illinois Classical Studies* 24–25: 399–426.

Dobrov G., and E. Urios-Aparisi. 1995. "The Maculate Muse: Gender, Genre and the Chiron of Pherecrates." In *Beyond Aristophanes*, edited by G. Dobrov, 139–174. Atlanta: Scholars Press.

Edmonds, J. M. 1957. *The Fragments of Attic Comedy*. Vol. 1. Leiden: Brill.

Edwards, A. 1993. "Historicizing the Popular Grotesque: Bakhtin's *Rabelais* and Attic Old Comedy." In *Theater and Society in the Classical World*, edited by R. Scodel, 89–117. Ann Arbor: University of Michigan Press.

Geissler, P. 1969. *Chronologie der altattischen Komödie*. 2nd ed. Dublin and Zurich: Weidmann.

Gilula, D. 2000. "Hermippus and his Catalogue of Goods." In *The Rivals of Aristophanes*, edited by F. D. Harvey and J. Wilkins, 75–90. London/Swansea: Duckworth and the Classical Press of Wales.

Henderson, J. 2000. "Pherekrates and the Women of Old Comedy." In *The Rivals of Aristophanes*, edited by F. D. Harvey and J. Wilkins, 135–150. London/Swansea: Duckworth and the Classical Press of Wales.

Koster, W. J. W. 1975. *Scholia in Aristophanem*. Part I, Fasc. 1A: *Prolegomena de Comoedia*. Groningen: Bouma's Boekhuis.

Luppe, W. 1966. "Die Hypothese zu Kratinos' *Dionysalexandros*." *Philologus* 110: 169–193.

——. 2000. "The Rivalry between Aristophanes and Kratinos." In *The Rivals of Aristophanes*, edited by F. D. Harvey and J. Wilkins, 15–21. London/Swansea: Duckworth and the Classical Press of Wales.

Marshall, C. W. 2000. "*Alcestis* and the Problem of Prosatyric Drama." *Classical Journal* 95: 229–238.

Mattingly, H. 1977. "Poets and Politicians in Fifth-Century Greece." In *Greece and the Eastern Mediterranean in Ancient History and Philosophy*, edited by K. H. Kinzl, 231–245. Berlin/New York: de Gruyter.

McGlew, J. 2002. *Citizens on Stage: Comedy and Political Culture in the Athenian Democracy*. Ann Arbor: University of Michigan Press.

Norwood, G. 1931. *Greek Comedy*. London: Methuen.

Olson, D. 2007. *Broken Laughter*. Oxford: Oxford University Press.

Rosen, R. 2000. "Cratinus' Pytine and the Construction of the Comic Self." In *The Rivals of Aristophanes*, edited by F. D. Harvey and J. Wilkins, 23–39. London and Swansea: Duckworth and the Classical Press of Wales.

Seeberg. A. 1995. "From Padded Dancers to Comedy." In *Stage Directions: Essays in Ancient Drama in Honour of E. W. Handley*, edited by A. Griffiths, 1–12. London: Institute of Classical Studies.

Sidwell, K. 1995. "Poetic Rivalry and the Caricature of Comic Poets: Cratinus' *Pytine* and Aristophanes' *Wasps*." In *Stage Directions: Essays in Ancient Drama in Honour of E. W. Handley*, edited by A. Griffiths, 56–80. London: Institute of Classical Studies.

Storey, I. C. "On First Looking into Kratinos' *Dionysalexandros*." In *Playing Around Aristophanes*. Edited by L. Kozak and J. Rich. Oxford: Oxbow, 2006, 105–125.

——. 2011. *Fragments of Old Comedy*. 3 vols. Loeb Classical Library 513–515. Cambridge, MA: Harvard University Press.

Taplin, O. 1993. *Comic Angels*. Oxford: Oxford University Press.

Wright, M. 2007. "Comedy and the Trojan War." *Classical Quarterly* 57: 412–431.

CHAPTER 5

THE LAST LAUGH: EUPOLIS, STRATTIS, AND PLATO AGAINST ARISTOPHANES

MARIO TELÒ

BEGINNING AT THE END: ARISTOPHANES AS CONTROLLER OF THE CANON

From the moment Hyperbolus lowered his guard, they have been stomping [κολετρῶσ'] the wretch without letup, and his mother too. First of all Eupolis dragged [παρείλκυσεν] his *Marikas* before you, hacking over [ἐκστρέψας] our *Knights*, hack that he is, and tacking onto it a drunken crone for the sake of the *kordax*, the same crone that Phrynichus long ago put onstage, the one the sea monster wanted to eat. Then Hermippus again attacked [ἐποίησεν εἰς] Hyperbolus in a play, and now all the others are launching [ἐρείδουσιν] into Hyperbolus, copying [μιμούμενοι] my own similes about the eels.

(Aristophanes, *Clouds* 551–559; trans. Henderson)

The chapter of comic literary history shrewdly sketched out here, in the *parabasis* of *Clouds*, foreshadows and conditions the Aristophanocentric view of Old Comedy that Alexandrian scholarship handed down to posterity. The passage strikingly names two poets contemporary with Aristophanes—Eupolis and Phrynichus—while describing a group of anonymous others, among whom we can likely identify Plato, the author of a play named after the demagogue Hyperbolus. Aristophanes defines his relationship with his current rivals by reference to his originality and their imitation. While earlier in the same *parabasis* he had laid claim to supremacy in poetic sophistication and creativity ("I have the skill [σοφίζομαι] to present novel [καινάς] forms of comedy every time out, none of them like the others and all of them ingenious [δεξιάς]," 547–548, trans. Henderson), here he presents the dramatic output of his adversaries as either a violent distortion or a pedestrian replica of his own comedic practice.

In one text of the so-called *Comic Prolegomena*, which may preserve Alexandrian material, Aristophanes is presented as "by far the most skilled in words among the Athenians and surpassing all in natural talent" (μακρῷ λογιώτατος Ἀθηναίων καὶ εὐφυΐᾳ πάντας ὑπεραίρων, Koster III 9.36–37); another treatise of the same collection bestows praise upon him for "having practiced comedy more skillfully than his contemporaries" (μεθοδεύσας τεχνικώτερον τῶν μεθ' ἑαυτοῦ τὴν κωμῳδίαν, Koster V 14.21–22). Aristophanes's self-styled poetic hegemony has been converted into an "objective" critical judgment; his literary production is thereby elevated to the canonical position that it retained almost unchallenged in the following centuries.

In the same *parabasis*, Aristophanes sharply distances his judicious practice of ὀνομαστὶ κωμῳδεῖν ("lampooning by name") from the excessive and altogether ineffective vehemence of the attacks that his rivals, especially Eupolis, launched against the demagogue Hyperbolus.[1] After all, Aristophanes says, he refrained from "jumping on Cleon when he was down" (550). He also expresses contempt for forms of hackneyed obscenity such as the "drunken crone" venturing a lascivious dance (*kordax*), whom both Eupolis and Phrynichus had introduced into their plays. On the opposite end of the spectrum, he identifies his poetic self with a restrained, even chaste, model of comedy: "Look how naturally decent [σώφρων] she [= my comedy] is" (537, trans. Henderson). In two other *parabaseis* (*Wasps* 1023–1028; *Peace* 762–763), Aristophanes advertises this model in a direct polemic against Eupolis by claiming that, unlike his rival, he never wandered into the wrestling schools trying to pick up boys. Personal conduct and comic styles are inextricably connected. Aristophanes's self-constructed image as a restrained comedian, however ironical, subsequently informs the account of his contribution to the history of the genre in the *Vita* ("Life") that was transmitted along with his comedic corpus. The *Vita* depicts the poet as elevating an unsettled (πλανωμένη) κωμῳδία to modern σεμνότης ("dignity") above the archaic, "too shameless" (αἰσχρότερον) manner that was still pursued by Eupolis.

By building up his poetic identity through these and similar self-authorizing gestures, Aristophanes anticipated (and perhaps predetermined) the ancient reception of Old Comedy and sentenced his rivals' dramatic output to merely fragmentary survival. The charges that he levels against Eupolis in this *parabasis* thus silenced, as it were, his adversary's claim of an active role in the making of *Knights* as expressed in *Baptai* ("Dyers"): †κἀκεῖνος† τοὺς Ἱππέας / ξυνεποίησα τῷ φαλακρῷ <– x> κἀδωρησάμην ("I collaborated with the bald one on *Knights* and [...] made him a gift of it," K-A fr. 89). The Aristophanocentric image of Old Comedy that has come down to us from antiquity promotes to "truth" Aristophanes's self-serving depiction of his rival as a plagiarist and denies credibility to the model of authorial collaboration put forward by Eupolis. Our attempt to recapture the multifaceted nature of Old Comedy is, in other words, vitiated

---

[1] In the same treatise that celebrates Aristophanes's all-surpassing εὐφυΐα, Eupolis is chastised for his Cratinean display of exaggerated λοίδορον ("slander") and σκαιόν ("mischief"); a similar pattern underlies Persius's positioning of Aristophanes's "grandiosity" (*praegrandis*) above Cratinus' "boldness" (*audaci*) and Eupolis' "anger" (*iratum*) in *Satires* 1: 123–125. Cf. Nesselrath 2000; Hunter 2009: 79–80.

by the overpowering fascination exerted by Aristophanes's tendentious portrayals of his colleagues on ancient readers and critics.

In this chapter, I bring into focus three comic poets (Eupolis, Strattis, Plato) who interacted or directly competed with Aristophanes between the 420s and 380s;[2] I attempt to rescue their contributions to the development of Old Comedy from the distorted lens of the *parabasis* of *Clouds* and its legacy in later critical literature. I have chosen these three authors,[3] two of whom are suggested by the Aristophanic *parabasis*, because the extant textual evidence allows us to base conclusions on relatively firmer ground. As I hope to show, each led Old Comedy in directions that nuance, complicate, and even destabilize the picture handed down to ancient and modern readers by Aristophanic drama and Aristophanocentric critics. In what follows, I linger on select moments of the literary production of Eupolis, Plato, and Strattis in order to tease out the distinctive ways in which these other voices shaped the poetics and the generic configuration of Old Comedy.

1. EUPOLIS, CRATINUS, AND THE SUBLIME

A widespread anecdote dating back to the Hellenistic age depicts Eupolis as dying a violent death in retaliation for the fierceness of his political satire. While Eupolis was serving on military duty in the Sicilian expedition of 415, Alcibiades, the commander-in-chief of the Athenian fleet, threw the famous comic playwright into the sea. The couplet that Alcibiades supposedly delivered before condemning Eupolis to death—or, according to some versions of the story, sparing him in extremis—is symptomatic of the interpretive process that lies behind the fabrication of the episode: "so drown / dip (βάπτε) me in the theater and I will soak (κατακλύσω) you in very bitter (ἀλμυρωτάτοις) waters."[4] Alcibiades was probably featured as the main target of mockery in the play *Baptai* ("Dyers" or "Dippers"), in which Eupolis must have associated the controversial

---

[2] Eupolis put on *Noumeniai* ("New Moons") competing against *Acharnians* at the Lenaea of 425 and *Kolakes* ("Flatterers") against *Peace I* at the Dionysia of 421. For a survey of all the polemic allusions that Eupolis and Aristophanes make to each other in their plays, cf. Storey 2003: 281–307 and Kyriakidi 2007: 101–196. See also Bakola 2008: 20–26. The readings of Sidwell 2009 argue that Eupolis lurks behind many Aristophanic characters. Plato's *Cleophon* was defeated by *Frogs* in 405; a possible allusion to Plato's *Rhabdouchoi* ("Mace-Bearers") has been detected in Aristophanes's *Peace* 734–735 (cf. Rossi 1981: 84–85 and Hartwig 2010: 28); on the parody of *Peace* in Plato's *Nikai* ("Victories") and Eupolis's *Autolycus*, cf. Kyriakidi 2007: 150–154. Aristophanes refers to Strattis's *Callippides* in K-A fr. 490 from the play *Skenas Katalambanousai* ("Women Claiming Tent-Sites").

[3] For a detailed survey of the other most eminent comic poets having their floruit in the same years, Phrynichus (420s–410s), Archippus (410s–380s), and Theopompus (410s–380s), cf. Storey 2010: 200–211.

[4] Tzetzes, *Proem*. 1 (= Eupolis, *Baptai* K-A test. iv). The version of the couplet transmitted by the scholion to Aelius Aristides *Or*. 3. 8 (= K-A test. iii) is slightly different: "you dyed (βάπτες) me in the theater and, by drowning (βαπτίζων) you in the waves of the sea, I will make you die with very bitter inundations (νάμασι πικροτάτοις)." Following a suggestion of Handley, Furley 1996: 132 n. 5 observes that, according to this anecdote, "Eupolis would have baptised Alcibiades in the salty wit of comedy."

Athenian general with the effeminate worshippers of the goddess Cotyto, the chorus after whom the play was named. It is evident that the pseudobiographical story turns on the multiple meanings of the verb βάπτειν ("to dip," "to drown," "to dye"); the drowning of Eupolis is fashioned as a punitive reenactment of the mysterious ritual activity (corresponding either to "dipping" or "dying") that was practiced by his play's lascivious chorus. But Alcibiades's distich layers this anecdote with a further, hitherto unnoticed implication. The notions of "dipping," "drowning," and "soaking" evoke the metaphorical language deployed by Cratinus to align his impetuous and virulent techniques of abuse with Archilochean iambus. In his play *Archilochoi,* Cratinus likened Archilochus's and his own invective to a spicy dipping sauce (K-A fr. 6). Additionally, in the most metatheatrical of his comedies, *Pytine* ("Wineflask"), he assimilated his own unrestrained comic force to a verbal inundation arising from the depths of his throat:

> Lord Apollo, the flood of his words, springs splashing, twelve spouts to his mouth, an Ilissus in his throat. What can I say? If somebody doesn't put a plug in his mouth, he will inundate (κατακλύσει) everything here with his poetry

> (K-A fr. 198, trans. Storey)

A similar image of flooding vehemence appears in Aristophanes's portrait of his older rival as an embodiment of the comedy of the past in the *parabasis* (526–528) and throughout the plot of *Knights* (see Storey, chapter 4).

It is thus evident that the story of Eupolis's drowning stages the alleged Cratinean quality of his dramatic production by turning the figurative imagery of iambic violence against its practitioner. Eupolis is forced to undergo the same experience of being "dipped" and "soaked" in "bitter waters" that his invective metaphorically inflicted upon his victims. According to Platonius's treatise *On the Different Types of Comedy* (Koster I 3–4), the death of Eupolis paved the way for the transition—from political engagement to escapist detachment—that underpins the traditional model of Greek comedy's development from *Archaia* ("Old Comedy") to *Mese* ("Middle Comedy"). Old Comedy is thus identified with its most aggressively iambic expressions.

But does the extant evidence of Eupolis's output confirm the Cratinean image that this critical narrative carves out for him? And if so, shall we subscribe to the charges of lack of inventiveness and dearth of σεμνότης ("dignity") that Aristophanes and later critics have leveled against him?

Very few fragments survive of the piece named *Astrateutoi* ("Draft-Dodgers") or *Androgynoi* ("Effeminates" or "Girly Men"); the double title suggests, however, that Eupolis thematized military cowardice as gender inversion through a chorus of deserters dressed up in female clothing or even presented as women.[5] Cratinus's *Drapetides* ("Fugitive Women") encoded the same type of choral plot and capitalized upon the piquant effects of the physical assimilation of a group of Athenian service dodgers to the

---

[5] The plots of this and the other Eupolidean plays discussed here are analysed at length by Storey 2003.

Danaids who begged the king of Argos for refuge in Aeschylus's *Hiketides* ("Suppliant Women"). Not only in *Drapetides* but also in the play eloquently called *Malthakoi* ("Effeminate Men," or "Poofters" as translated by Storey), Cratinus inscribed comic invective within the framework of gender bending and sexual humor (cf. Bakola 2010: 141–158).

Eupolis seems to have drawn extensively upon this Cratinean plot model. The central scene of the play *Taxiarchoi* ("Commanders") staged the conversion of Dionysus from effeminate and cowardly god to brave warrior under the supervision of the famous Athenian commander Phormion. *Kolakes* ("Flatterers" or "Toadies") instantiated a kind of social satire in keeping with the derisive depiction of aristocratic soft living in Cratinus's *Malthakoi*; it presents itself as a comic tirade against the debauched lifestyle of the Athenian profligate Callias and his parasitic guests. In *Autolycus*, Callias figures again as a target of invective; the play's programmatic focus on his *eromenos* ("beloved"), which the title showcases, probably provided the same graphic obscenity that distinguished *Astrateutoi* and its Cratinean precedents. In all likelihood, *Philoi* ("Friends") featured a chorus of personal or political comrades of an unidentified public figure and treated them no differently from the crowd of spongers animating Callias's house in *Kolakes*. It is possible that the relationship of social and political subordination that bound these *philoi* to the chief character of the play was charged with sexual implications.[6]

The plot of *Baptai* deployed its chorus of effeminate worshippers, engaged in orgiastic rites, to tinge the mockery of Alcibiades with obscenity. The paucity of textual evidence makes it impossible to reconstruct the precise terms of *Baptai's* polemic against him, but presumably the association of the Athenian politician with the lascivious worshippers of Cotyto turned the agonistic structure of the plot into an ideological conflict between gender inversion and normative masculinity. The practitioners of satire in all its generic expressions (iambus, comedy, Roman satire) customarily turn altercations with their "enemies" into military campaigns and displays of *andreia* ("manliness, courage"). Aristophanes himself revels in situating his comic attacks against his favorite targets such as Cleon on the metaphorical terrain of the battlefield (see for example *Wasps* 1036–1037: "on seeing such a monster, he [= the comic poet] says, he didn't get cold feet and take bribes to betray you, but fought then as he fights [πολεμεῖ] now on your behalf", trans. Henderson). In Eupolis's *Astrateutoi* and *Taxiarchoi*, the figurative warfare of the comic poet merges with the celebration of martial bravery and the pro-war viewpoint that these plays more or less explicitly endorse. The emasculation of Alcibiades staged in *Baptai* probably included his transformation into an *astrateutos* ("cowardly man," "draft-dodger"). From this perspective, Alcibiades's acting as an imperious general in the fanciful story of Eupolis's drowning could serve to restore the politician to the role that the comedian had symbolically usurped in his play.

---

[6] In a fragment from the play *Demoi* (K-A fr. 99. 25–27), the political meaning of *philoi* is clearly collapsed into the erotic one. Cf. Telò 2007: 365–380.

Aristophanes thrives on representing male characters in drag (e.g., Agathon in *Women at the Thesmophoria*), but in his dramatic corpus there is no trace of a play comparable to Cratinus's *Drapetides* or Eupolis's *Astrateutoi* or *Baptai*. Conversely, Hermippus, a poet who is mentioned in the *parabasis* of *Clouds* but whose floruit overlapped with Cratinus's, produced the play *Stratiotai* ("Soldiers") or *Stratiotides* ("Female Soldiers"), which, as the double title suggests, may have resembled Eupolis's *Astrateutoi* or *Androgynoi*. The image of Eupolis as a Cratinean comedian, which the Alexandrian critical narrative reproduced in the Alcibiades anecdote, seems thus to be grounded in the extant evidence. Accepting the Aristophanic view of Cratinus as a poet of the past and at the same time applying the metaphor of comic invective as a military undertaking, we could say that in his "Cratinean plays" Eupolis takes on the overboldness and crude bellicosity of a primitive hero.

This is, however, a one-sided picture of Eupolis. The flooding streams and unrestrained flows—with which Cratinus associates his poetic self-presentation and through which the "Alcibiades anecdote" creates its Cratinean construction of Eupolis—preview the aesthetic imagery of the later sublime tradition. Nevertheless, in antiquity it is Eupolis, not Cratinus, who is categorized as a sublime comic poet, if only by two isolated critical sources. Both locate the sublime quality of Eupolidean comedy in *Demoi* ("Demes"), the best-known play of Aristophanes's contemporary, in which four central figures of the Athenian political past (Solon, Miltiades, Aristides, and Pericles) were brought back to life from the Underworld thanks to the utopian inventiveness of the comic hero Pyronides.

In his treatise *On the Different Styles of Comic Dramatists* (Koster II 6. 9–12), Platonius assigns the critical label of ὑψηλός ("sublime") to Eupolis; he holds up *Demoi* as an example of the poet's ability to create grand stagings (τὰς γὰρ εἰσηγήσεις μεγάλας τῶν δραμάτων ποιεῖται) and of the visionary power of his dramatic constructs (Εὔπολις δὲ εὐφάνταστος μὲν εἰς ὑπερβολήν ἐστι κατὰ τὰς ὑποθέσεις). Pseudo-Longinus borrows from the same play the only comic quotation in his work *On the Sublime* (Περὶ ὕψους). Discussing the use of oath as a rhetorical figure productive of sublime effects (§ 16), Pseudo-Longinus draws attention to the ὑπερβάλλον ὕψος ("transcendent sublimity") and πάθος ("emotion, pathos") achieved by Demosthenes's invocation of the fallen at Marathon in his speech *On the Crown* (208 οὐκ ἔστιν ὅπως ἡμάρτετε, μὰ τοὺς ἐν Μαραθῶνι προκινδυνεύσαντας, "it cannot be that you were wrong; no, by those who risked their lives at Marathon"). Pseudo-Longinus reports the commonly held view that the "seed" (σπέρμα) of this oath is to be sought in the following distich from Eupolis's *Demoi*:

> οὐ γὰρ μὰ τὴν Μαραθῶνι τὴν ἐμὴν μάχην
> χαίρων τις αὐτῶν τοὐμὸν ἀλγυνεῖ κέαρ
> No, not by my battle at Marathon, will anyone
> of them grieve my heart and get away with it.
> (K-A fr. 106, trans. Storey)

As Pseudo-Longinus explains, what transforms the solemn intonation of these two lines into the genuine moment of aesthetic sublimity in Demosthenes is the marked shifting of the oath's object from inanimate (μάχη) to animate (τοὺς ἐν Μαραθῶνι προκινδυνεύσαντας). In his view, the sublimity of Demosthenes's ὅρκος ("oath") consists precisely in its immortalizing power and in the symbolic apotheosis that it performs: φαίνεται δι' ἑνὸς τοῦ ὀμοτικοῦ σχήματος... τοὺς μὲν προγόνους ἀποθεώσας ("one has the impression that through the single figure of adjuration... he has deified the ancestors"). I suggest, however, that the characterization of the dead politicians who are resuscitated in *Demoi* partakes of the same poetics.

The speaker of the fragment quoted by Pseudo-Longinus is undoubtedly Miltiades. The grandiose aura of his oath stems from the tragic provenance of the distich, which is patterned upon the Euripidean Medea's invocation of Hecate when she determines to take revenge on Jason and his new family: οὐ γὰρ μὰ τὴν δέσποιναν ἣν ἐγὼ σέβω / μάλιστα πάντων καὶ ξυνεργὸν εἱλόμην, / Ἑκάτην, μυχοῖς ναίουσαν ἑστίας ἐμῆς, / χαίρων τις αὐτῶν τοὐμὸν ἀλγυνεῖ κέαρ ("By the goddess I worship most of all, my chosen helper Hecate, who dwells in the inner chamber of my house, none of them shall pain my heart and smile at it," 395–398, trans. Kovacs). The incorporation of Medea's tirade within the speech of Miltiades configures an intertextual dynamic that overturns the usual hierarchy of comic paratragedy. Miltiades's usurping of Medea's voice neither entails a bathetic deflation of tragic textuality nor engenders the expected collision of registers between a borrowed elevated diction and a low-brow comic context. Conversely, Medea's appropriation of the quintessentially heroic fear of enemies' laughter inevitably distorts (or even "parodies") a pivotal principle of masculine identity by importing that fear into the realm of feminine subjectivity. If the dramatic force of the Euripidean lines feeds upon the ideological discrepancy between heroic content and speaker, their intertextual reappearance in the speech of the much-celebrated hero of Marathon is repurposed to establish a harmonious convergence of form and *ethos*. Instead of playing on the potentially comic effects of Miltiades's assumption of a tragic female voice as he utters his oath, the significant replacement of Hecate with the battle of Marathon seems to be a corrective attempt to relocate the heroic code inappropriately taken over by Medea within the masculine domain of political struggle. The unidentified parties (αὐτῶν) against whom Miltiades promises to launch a Marathon-inspired attack are in all probability the "new" politicians whose unworthy conduct has elicited the comic hero's utopian journey to the Underworld (cf. Telò 2007: 259). Among the four resurrected politicians, Aristides too cites tragic verse deprived of the customary comic distortion. In one fragment, he reemploys a half-line of Euripides's *Phoenix* (fr. 810 K) to name φύσις ("nature") as decisive in shaping his proverbial δικαιοσύνη ("justice"): "Nature was the most important factor (ἡ μὲν φύσις τὸ μέγιστον <ἦν>), and then I enthusiastically helped nature along" (fr. 105.2–3 KA, trans. Storey). In another fragment, by earnestly embodying justice, Aristides ventures into a quasi-parabatic address to the city and thus aligns his authoritative warning with the poet's voice: ἐγὼ δὲ πάσῃ προαγορεύω τῇ πόλ[ει / εἶναι δικαίους ("To all the city I proclaim to be just," K-A fr. 99.118–119).

In *Demoi* tragic diction contributes to differentiating the political ancestors—or at least two of them—brought back to Athens from the other characters and transforming them into *spoudaioi* ("serious") figures. The contrast with Cratinus's characterization of another illustrious *progonos* ("ancestor") of Athens may be illuminating in this respect. *Drapetides*, which, as we have seen, provided Eupolis with a fertile plot model, presents itself as a comic distortion of a suppliant-tragedy, casting Theseus as a protector of Athenian draft dodgers. The paratragic framework of this play resulted in an unflattering image of Theseus and in a mocking critique of the patriotic ideology in which the fifth-century view of the mythical Athenian king was implicated. The following fragment, spoken by Theseus, eloquently reveals that not only was his glory "as a king and champion of suppliants rendered vulgar, but his labours were stripped of heroism" (Bakola 2010: 154):

> τὸν Κερκύονά θ' ἕωθεν ἀποπατοῦντ' <ἐγὼ>
> ἐπὶ τοῖς λαχάνοις εὑρὼν ἀπέπνιξα

> And I found Cercyon taking a crap at dawn among the cabbages and I throttled him.

> (K-A fr. 53, trans. Storey)

It is quite the opposite in the utopian fantasy of *Demoi*: the construction of Miltiades and Aristides through the language of tragedy heroizes them as in the finale of *Knights* (line 1325) where the two *progonoi* are evoked to recapture an idealized past. Pericles, the youngest among the four, is occasionally the target of jokes and irony, but the comic force of the play may well have resided in the "low" versus "high" contrast stemming from the interaction between the morally degraded politicians of the present and the larger-than-life heroes of the past. Eupolis's treatment of Miltiades and Aristides seems, thus, to evince the same memorializing and monumentalizing impetus that, according to Pseudo-Longinus, pervades Demosthenes's sublime invocation of the dead at Marathon. In fact, sublime aesthetics draw upon the epitaphic aspiration to transform "vanished events into memorials of themselves" and to transmute dead bodies into "live bodies rendered as things."[7] The plot of *Demoi* enacts this paradoxical process of revivification and monumental reification.

The heroic characters of *Demoi* bring it close to the myth-based plots of tragedy, which, more or less explicitly, invite the audience to juxtapose the figures of the epic past with the *hic et nunc* of fifth-century Athens. However, Alexandrian scholarship's identification of Eupolis's poetic personality with *Baptai* deliberately excludes the generic experimentalism of *Demoi*, placing the comic poet alongside the "old-fashioned"

---

[7] The quotations come from Porter 2010: 465, 474, to whom my discussion of the monumental sublime is indebted.

Cratinus and against Aristophanes. Though in a number of plays Eupolis appropri-
ates Cratinus's plot devices and thereby adheres to the sublime vehemence of his predecessor's inundating invective, in *Demoi*, on the contrary, he projects a new model of
the comic sublime that prompts comedy to explore and even assimilate itself to tragic
σεμνότης ("dignity").[8] It is the resulting exercise in epitaphic "invention of tradition"
that ensured this play great renown in antiquity as a historical and rhetorical source and,
at the same time, set it apart from the rest of Eupolis's dramatic output.

We will now consider how the same comic fascination with cross-generic inventiveness and subversion produces the opposite effects in the works of another contemporary
of Aristophanes: not the assimilation of comedy to tragedy, but a sustained incorporation of tragedy in comedy.

2. Compulsive Paratragedy in Strattis

As the famous Cratinean coinage Εὐριπιδαριστοφανίζειν testifies, Aristophanes's preoccupation with the generic worldview of tragedy attracted the attention and the criticism of his contemporaries. Modern scholars have long believed that the pervasive
paratragic dimension of Aristophanes's plays reflected this dramatist's idiosyncratic,
almost obsessive, interest in tragedy and have, at times, colored this conviction with
misleading biographical details. The scope and relevance of Aristophanic comedy's
self-positioning against the sister genre, especially in its Euripidean incarnations, are
undoubtedly exceptional, but if we take a quick look at the surviving titles of Strattis's
comic production, we discover that this is the comic poet who deserves the palm of the
most fully committed paratragedist.

In nearly all Strattis's plays, the creation of comic fiction is overtly predicated on
the manipulation of tragic materials and the systematic embedding of characters and
dramatic action within the intertextual framework of tragedy. Cratinus's *Eumenides*,
Hermippus's *Agamemnon,* and three fragmentary plays of Aristophanes (*Phoinissai*
["Phoenician Women"], *Lemniai* ["Lemnian Women"], *Polyidus*) supply isolated examples of the programmatic "comedification" of tragedy that Strattis's titles trumpet as
the all-embracing horizon of his poetic output. Even when the plot seems to veer into a
simple paramythical mode, preference is persistently accorded to subject matter and figures of recognizable tragic pedigree. This tendency emerges in the plays *Anthroporestes*
("Man-Orestes") and *Iphigeron* ("Iphi–Old man"), where the downgrading of classic
tragic characters (Orestes, Iphigenia) to extravagant hybrids of heroic and lowly traits
crafts a self-conscious convergence of thematics and poetics.

---

[8] Revermann 2006: 315–316 detects intriguing resemblances between the finale of the play and the
closing scene of *Eumenides*.

The intergeneric configuration of Strattis's plays can take different forms. His *Medea* and *Phoinissai* present themselves as palimpsestic rewritings of the corresponding plays; their diction and signature scenes are transplanted into the "real" world of contemporary Athens and subjected to burlesque debasement by actors probably dressed in a mix of tragic and comic costume. In other plays (*Chrysippus, Myrmidons, Philoctetes, Troilus*), the surviving textual evidence leaves uncertain the extent to which they conformed to the scripts and the verbal constructions of their subtexts and how they adapted the mythical apparatus of tragedy to comedy's fictionalized social topicality. The only extant fragment of *Myrmidons* (K-A fr. 37) defies any attempt at plot reconstruction; the possible historical reference in one line, however, has prompted the hypothesis that Strattis construed Achilles, the Myrmidons' leader and protagonist of the eponymous Aeschylean play, as a mythical equivalent of Alcibiades. If this hypothesis is correct, one could also speculate that the homoerotic theme of Aeschylus's *Myrmidons* may have allowed Strattis to pepper his representation of the relationship between Alcibiades and his army with piquant overtones. His *Myrmidons* could thus have amounted to a mythically disguised version of Eupolis's *Baptai* or *Astrateutoi*. In fictionalizing historical topicality through the distancing filter of tragic myth, Strattis pushes comedy's generic identity in directions that are characteristic of the representatives of the so-called *Mese* ("Middle Comedy").

The plots of Strattis's drama showcase not only a paratragic, but also a metaperformative—or "parathespian"—compulsion. The play *Callippides*, named after a much-maligned actor of the new generation, seems to have been a meditation upon the mimic excesses and the social dangers of modern (over)acting. In *Cinesias*, the conflict of temporalities, a staple of comic agonism, pitted Strattis's "old" comedy against the "new" music of the virtuosic dithyrambist Cinesias. How does the parathespian mode that these two plays emblematize interact with Strattis's practice of paratragedy? To answer this question, I wish to analyze a fragment from *Phoinissai* in which an essential device of the mechanics of dramatic performance functions as a figure of the agonistic dynamics in Strattis's transformation of the Euripidean tragedy.

These three lines from the beginning of the play feature Dionysus positioned on the *mechane* ("crane"), complaining about the discomfort that the playwright has inflicted upon him:[9]

> Διόνυσος ὃς θύρσοισιν † αὐληταὶ δει· λ
> κω[…] ἐνέχομαι δι' ἑτέρων μοχθ[ηρ]ίαν
> ἥκω κρεμάμενος ὥσπερ ἰσχὰς ἐπὶ κράδης

> I am Dionysus, involved with thyrsuses, *aulos* players, and revelries. Here I am, trapped by the wickedness of others, hanging on a branch like a fig.

> (K-A fr. 46, transl. Storey)

---

[9] The translation presupposes the supplements αὐληταῖ[ς] (l.1) and κώμ[οις] (l. 2) suggested by Webster 1972: 445 and Miles 2009: 189, 323–325. For δει· λ, read perhaps τε καὶ, as proposed by Miles 2009.

This spectacular epiphany of the god of the theater is laden with a number of *aprosdo-keta* ("surprise effects") which set the tone for the rest of the play. Dionysus's speech is unexpectedly patterned not upon the first lines of Euripides's *Phoinissai*, but upon the prologue of his *Hypsipyle*; there the eponymous character, Dionysus's granddaughter, sets the action in motion by evoking her kinship with the god: Διόνυσος, ὃς θύρσοισι καὶ νεβρῶν δοραῖς / καθαπτὸς ("Dionysus, who girded with thyrsuses and fawnskins…," fr. 752 K, trans. Collard-Cropp). Not only does Dionysus appropriate the words of the "wrong" Euripidean heroine (Hypsipyle instead of Jocasta), but he also violates the clo-sural function of *dei ex machina* ("gods from the machine") by appearing at the very outset of the play. It is certainly no coincidence that in *Hypsipyle* the god makes his appearance at the end and brings all the conflicts of the play to a resolution. Thus, in this prologue, Strattis's *Phoinissai* styles itself as an upside-down version of the Euripidean tragedy. But this prologic Dionysus evinces other layers of metapoetic signification.

The collision of divergent tragic narratives that Dionysus causes by bringing the voice of Hypsipyle into the plot of *Phoinissai* mimics the bold combination of mythical tradi-tions that Euripides placed at the core of the dramaturgical design of his *Hypsipyle*. In this play, the twin sons whom Hypsipyle had borne to Jason in Lemnos arrive at the sanc-tuary of Nemea; there the heroine serves as slave to the priest Lycurgus at the same time as the army of the Seven is on its march to Thebes, and with the help of Amphiaraus, she recognizes and reunites with her sons, redeems herself, and returns to Lemnos. While the connection between the foundation of the Nemean games, which *Hypsipyle* etiologi-cally reenacts, and the expedition of the Seven against Thebes predates Euripides's play, the involvement of the Lemnian heroine in this mythical cluster is his own invention. This process of mythological interweaving is dramatized in the *parodos*, where the con-trast between Hypsipyle's attachment to her Argonautic past and the Chorus's alignment with the present mission of the Seven adds up to a choice between mutually exclusive singing options:[10]

> Why are you here at the doorway, dear friend? Are you sweeping the house's entrance, or sprinkling water on the ground, as a slave woman will? Are you singing (ᾄδεις) now of Argo, that fifty-oared vessel that your voice is always celebrating (τὰν διὰ σοῦ στόματος αἰεὶ κληζομέναν), or the sacred golden fleece which the eye of the serpent, coiled round the boughs of the tree, keeps under guard? And does your memory dwell on Lemnos lying in the sea, which the Aegean encircles and beats with echoing waves? Come here †to the† Nemean meadow. All of the plain is flashing with the Argives' arms of bronze. Against the bastion, the work of Amphion's lyre (τᾶ[ς] κιθάρας… τᾶς Ἀμφιονίας ἔργον)… swift-footed Adrastus..
>
> (Eur. fr. 752f. 15–34 K, trans. Collard-Cropp)

The shift from Argonautic/Lemnian songs to Amphion's Theban lyre, which the Chorus recommends to Hypsipyle in these lines, is fashioned as a move from

---

[10] For this reading of the parodos of *Hypsipyle*, cf. Battezzato 2004.

solo to choral performance as well as a transition from a domestic to a public and martial space; the Euripidean play is continually suspended between these two opposed spaces, corresponding to two separate mythical traditions and different poetic modes.

In Strattis's paratragic opening, Dionysus's physical suspension (κρεμάμενος) on the *mechane* causes his incorporation of Hypsipyle's speech within the overarching Theban scenario of *Phoinissai* to evoke and gibingly comment on Euripides's hybrid play. The theater god's unresolved position illustrates Strattis's agonistic posturing. His techniques of plot-making are continuous with those of Euripides: in *Lemnomeda*, whose blending of unrelated tragic tales (those of Hypsipyle and Andromeda) is unparalleled in the extant corpus of Greek comedy, Strattis used the same procedure with which Euripides confronted (and surprised) the audience of *Hypsipyle*. Dionysus's hanging between "low" and "high," which the *mechane* puts on display, materializes Strattis's systematic conflation of comedy with tragedy and pits it against Euripides's mythological crossbreeding. The metatheatrical unveiling of the unsteadiness of the *mechane* thus figures a struggle between two forms of dramatic hybridism that engrossed tragedy and comedy between the fifth and fourth centuries, thus creating a thinner divide between the literary properties of the two genres. From this perspective, the "others" (ἑτέρων) whose wickedness, according to Dionysus's report, has undermined the "stability" grounded in his customary attributes ("thyrsuses, *aulos* players, and revelries") and exposed him to generic "dizziness" could be identified with comedians and tragedians vying in a turbulent contest of innovation and experimentalism. Within this contest, however, Strattis's distorting assimilation of tragedy into the thematic fabric of his plays allows his comedy to take on the hegemonic role in the exploration and merging of poetic boundaries.

A high degree of poetic self-reflexivity is built into Strattis's practice of paratragedy. Significantly, the first occurrence of the word *paratragedy* is in a badly preserved fragment of his *Phoinissai* (K-A fr. 50), where an unidentified character casts himself in the role of stage manager by announcing the intention to ask somebody else to παρατραγῳδῆσαι. This metatheatrical disclosure of the play's textual program recalls the line of Plautus's *Pseudolus* (707)—*ut paratragoedat carnufex!* ("How he parodies tragedy, the scoundrel!")—with which Charinus comments on the sophisticated poetic craft of the archetypal clever slave. We will now see how another contemporary of Aristophanes led Old Comedy's metafictional sensitivity in new directions that foreshadow Plautus's comic worldview.

3. PLATO AND THE FUTURE OF COMEDY

The remaining fragments of Plato's dramatic output confront us with the paradox of a playwright negotiating his comic identity between two opposed images: the committed practitioner of political invective on one side and the crafter of *désengagés* plots in the typical style of later fourth-century comedy on the other. In both these incarnations of his comic persona, Plato puts the generic possibilities of Old Comedy to innovative uses.

As we have seen at the beginning of this chapter, Plato is notably unnamed in the list of alleged imitators of *Knights* that Aristophanes compiled in the parabasis of *Clouds*. While, as far as we know, two of the comedians explicitly mentioned there (Eupolis and Hermippus) as well as Aristophanes himself produced, in the course of their careers, only one example of the so-called "demagogue comedy" (*Marikas, Artopolides* ["Bakery Girls"], and *Knights* respectively), Plato seems to have taken a special interest in this plot model, which recasts the head-on confrontations of archaic iambography into an all-encompassing political dimension. Three play titles (*Pisander, Hyperbolus, Cleophon*) display Plato's use of this form of dramatic invective at different times and against different demagogic targets. The titles also reveal the distinctive feature that unifies Plato's "demagogue comedies." Differently from his past and present colleagues, who, in their versions of the model, disguise their targets as made-up characters (Pericles as Dionysus in Cratinus's *Dionysalexander,* Cleon as Paphlagon in Aristophanes's *Knights,* Hyperbolus as Marikas in Eupolis's eponymous play), Plato deprives his political satire of any allegorical filter, feeding the illusion of bringing on stage the demagogues in the flesh. This choice must have complicated, nuanced, and even ironized the intricate game of disentangling reality from fiction and seriousness from humor into which the audience of political comedy is inevitably drawn.

The poetic personality that exudes from these plays is at odds with the core of Plato's dramatic output, namely, mythological plots that replace political topicality with domestic and bourgeois atmospheres. By revising the paradigm of diachronic transformation inherited from ancient critics, recent scholarship has made a strong case for viewing political engagement and mythological escapism as parallel or interconnecting strands throughout the entire arc of Greek comedy (cf. Csapo 2000). Not only Crates and Pherecrates but also Cratinus and Aristophanes practice mythological parody in forms that downplay or exclude political topicality. Among the representatives of Old Comedy, however, Plato's dramatic constructs bear the most striking resemblances, underscored by several overlapping titles, to the products of the so-called Middle Comedy of the fourth century and even to the subsequent developments of New Comedy. Three plays—*Europa, Io,* and *Nyx Makra* ("Long Night")—dramatize episodes of Zeus's adulterous career, anticipating later comedy's fascination with the opportunities for intrigue and role-playing that illegitimate romance and amorous deception afford. The relatively clear picture of *Nyx Makra* that emerges from the extant fragments shares significant details with the treatment of the same subject matter—the sexual encounter of Heracles's mother, Alcmena, with Zeus dressed up as her husband—in Plautus's *Amphitryo*. In *Zeus Kakoumenos* ("Zeus Harmed"), Plato maps the relationship of Zeus with Heracles onto the paternal-filial dynamics of Aristophanes's *Banqueters* and *Clouds*. The "harm" (κάκωσις) alluded to in the title probably refers to the consequences of Heracles's behavior as a debauched son that we see acted out in the metatheatrically charged scene of his initiation into the *kottabos* game (K-A fr. 46). But if we consider that the prize offered for the sympotic game are the kisses (l. 5 φιλημάτων) of *hetairai*, we can speculate that Plato may have spiced his representation of the Oedipal conflict between Heracles and his equally womanizing father with the tones of erotic competition that acquire special prominence in Plautus's *Asinaria* ("The Comedy of Asses"), *Casina*, and *Mercator* ("The Merchant").

A fragment from *Phaon* yields insights into the new forms that theatrical self-reflexivity takes in the domestic scenarios of Plato's comedy. This play, produced in 391, revolves around the mythical boatman of Lesbos; after ferrying for free Aphrodite in the guise of a poor old woman, he received from her a vase of rejuvenating ointment that drew to him all the female inhabitants of the island; like Adonis, however, he subsequently encountered a violent death. Plato's plot probably commingled ritual parody with graphic sexual humor by depicting Phaon as vexed both by the advances of a crowd of lustful women and by the abuses of Aphrodite cast in the comic part of the jealous and greedy procuress. In this fragment, Phaon, worn out by the sexual requests of the women of Lesbos, attempts to recuperate his lost vigor with the aid of a book of aphrodisiac recipes:

(A) I'd like to read this book to
myself sitting here in solitude.
(B) And what book is that, I ask you?
(A) It's the 'nouvelle cuisine' of Philoxenus.
(B) How 'bout a sample? (A) OK, then, listen: (*reads*)   5
'I'll start with bulbous vegetables, and I'll take it up to tuna fish.'
(B) To tuna fish?! Then surely it's by far the
best thing to be stationed in the last position.
(A) (*reading aloud*) 'Tame [δαμάσας] the bulbs [βολβούς] with ashes
[σποδιᾷ], douse [δεύσας] them in sauce [καταχύσματι]
and then consume as many as you can: this'll straighten up a man's cock.'   10
That's it for that part; now I'll move on to the 'children of the sea...'
                    (*Several verses appear to be missing*)
'...and the frying-pan isn't bad either, though the sauce-pan is better,
I think...'
                    (*Several verses appear to be missing*)
'Don't cut up the perch, the trout, the bream,
the saw-tooth, unless you want heaven's wrath to breathe down on you,   15
but cook and serve it up whole; that's much better.
If you tenderize the tentacle of the octopus at just the right moment
it is far better boiled than baked, at least if it's a large one.
But if two are baked, then to hell with the boiled one.
The red mullet doesn't usually help stiffen up the 'nerve,'   20
since that fish belongs to the virgin goddess Artemis, and hates a hard-on.
And now the scorpion...' (B) ... 'will sneak up and sting you right in the asshole!'

                                        (K-A fr. 189, trans. Rosen, adapted)

The elaborately crafted hexametric quotation that punctuates this passage with obscene innuendos is probably borrowed from a work of Philoxenus of Leucas[11] that was similar in content and style to the gastronomic poetry of the fourth-century authors Archestratus of Gela and Matro of Pytane. The flamboyant array of meticulous instructions dished out, with descriptive panache, in Philoxenus's excerpt performs a sophisticated collapsing of poetic textuality and culinary material. Reifying, as it were, Aeschylus's well-known assimilation of his plays to "slices from the banquet of Homer" (cf. Athenaeus 8. 347e), Philoxenus forges his therapeutic prescriptions out of Homeric language. For example, line 9 contains three words (σποδιᾷ, δαμάσας, δεύσας) that unmistakably smack of epic diction (cf., e.g., Homer, *Iliad* 13. 655; 18. 113; 21. 119; *Od.* 5. 488; 9.59). Each ingredient is thus literally merged into the textual substance of the epic morsel that supplies its verbal definition, and every Homeric snippet is similarly commodified and encoded with the *Sachlichkeit* of food. In this way, Philoxenus goes beyond the metaphorical mapping of poetry or rhetoric onto cooking and posits a complete identification between verse-making and culinary art. Along comparable lines, several plays of later fourth-century comedy present figures of boastful μάγειροι ("cooks") who showcase unrivaled mastery in deploying the verbal density and richness of New Dithyramb to turn the description of culinary delicacies into a parade of poetic virtuosity. For example, in the following fragment of Antiphanes a cook layers his definition of flat-cake with convoluted and baroque ornamentation:

> ...the creamy flood that flows from bleating she-goats, mingled with fountains from the tawny bee, and nested in a flat covering of the maiden daughter of chaste Demeter, luxuriating in countless delicately compounded wrappings

> (K-A fr. 55. 7–10, trans. Dobrov)

This and the other dithyrambic cooks of later fourth-century comedy look forward "to the *servus callidus* ['clever slave'], a stage figure that develops far beyond the μάγειρος to 'star' status in New Comedy and its Roman adaptations" (Dobrov 2002: 173). Pseudolus, the archetypal *servus callidus* whose actions put him in metatheatrical control of the plot, famously compares himself to a poet (395–405), but is also paired with the cooks of the play. The *dapsilia dicta* (l. 396 'a banquet of words') that Pseudolus offers to his young master captures well these overlapping identities (cf. Gowers 1993: 95).

Plato's Phaon too can be regarded as an ancestor of this distinctive character of Roman comedy. For the ancients, reading aloud entails the impersonation of the writer's voice and the symbolic appropriation of the contents of the written text. Therefore, by reading out the passage from Philoxenus's cookbook, Phaon performs and internalizes the persona of the gastro-epic poet or the poetic chef showing off his technical talent. But what makes Phaon's assumption of this role particularly close to Pseudolus's is its

[11] For the attribution to Philoxenus of Leucas, not to the better-known dithyrambic poet Philoxenus of Cythera, see Degani 1998. Cf. also Wilkins 2000: 341–350 and Olson 2007: 268–271.

connection with the ferryman's use of written textuality as a plot device. Plautine slaves often resort to texts (usually letters) to bring intricate situations to brilliant solutions. By drawing attention to the power of writing in the molding and altering of reality, they metatheatrically blur their manipulation of textuality into the processes of plot-building and script-making (cf. Jenkins 2005). Phaon's staged reading of Philoxenus's text similarly occurs at a critical juncture of the plot (the frozen moment occasioned by his sexual impotence) and figures as the inventive—and probably effective—response that a character of low standing, afflicted by a social superior (the goddess Aphrodite), devises to overcome an impasse.

Another element reinforces the analogy between the self-reflexive texture of Plato's fragment and the metatheatrical strategies of Plautine comedy. Exotic and refined spices for the concoction of soups and sauces are the culinary secrets on which the cooks of "Middle" and New Comedy most frequently pride themselves. In the play-within-the-play world of Plautus, the flavorings flaunted by his cooks figuratively correspond to the dramatic conceits through which the playwright and his alter egos within the fiction unfold the plot (cf. Gowers 1993: 93–107). For example, in this passage from *Pseudolus* the pimp Ballio equates the *condimenta* ("condiments") employed by the clever cook he has hired with *mendacia* ("lies, deceptions"), i.e., the essential ingredient of Plautus's dramatic constructs: *At te Iuppiter / dique omnes perdant cum condimentis tuis / cumque tuis istis omnibus mendaciis* (836–838, "May Iuppiter and all the gods destroy you with your seasonings and all these lies"). In a parallel fashion, within the fusion of gastronomic and textual layers that the hexametric quotation realizes, the dipping sauce recommended by Philoxenus at l. 9 is poised not only to restore Phaon to virility but also to mark a turning point in the thematic movement of the plot.

The instruction imparted in l. 9 is key to appreciating the intertwining of food, sex, and textuality that this fragment brings to the fore. It also provides an illuminating snapshot of Plato's peculiar position within the comic poets contemporary with Aristophanes. According to Philoxenus's cookbook, soaking (δεύσας) wild onions (βολβούς) in sauce (καταχύσματι) will produce miraculous effects on Phaon's health. As we have observed at the beginning of this chapter, the images of "dousing," "dipping," "drowning" in liquids (a spicy sauce, salty water, a flooding stream or the sea) are used to signal Cratinus's self-representation as the inheritor of the iambic tradition and Aristophanes's downgrading of his predecessor to old-fashioned poet. The same images are also used to signal the Alexandrian critics' view of Eupolis as an outmoded Cratinean comedian—a view that is largely indebted to the Aristophanic portrait of his contemporary, especially in the parabasis of *Clouds*. The shift in metaliterary meaning that the idea of "soaking in sauce" registers in Plato's fragment epitomizes the transformation of comedy's generic drive towards invective into a creative or "poietic" impulse manifesting itself in the resourceful and self-conscious resolution of the plot's knots. In the *parabasis* of *Clouds*, Plato is not mentioned, but, in all probability, he is silently positioned near Eupolis. Only one quality of Plato's comic "sauce" is accounted for. The subsequent history of ancient comedy proves that it is on the other that Plato's legacy will rest.

FURTHER READING

On Aristophanes's representation of his rivals in the parabasis of *Clouds,* see most recently Biles 2011: 181–187. On the rivalry between Aristophanes and Eupolis, see Halliwell 1989; Sidwell 1993, Sidwell 2009, esp. 48–56; Storey 2003, *passim*; Kyriakidi 2007; Bakola 2008. Eupolis's role in the periodization of comedy is discussed by Nesselrath 2000. Storey 2003 offers a thorough treatment of Eupolis's career and the contents of his plays; on *Demoi,* see Revermann 2006: 311–319, Telò 2007, Sidwell 2009: 278–283. Orth 2009 and Fiorentini 2009 provide full-scale commentaries on the surviving fragments of Strattis. On Strattis's use of paratragedy, see Lowe 2000: 323–324 and Miles 2009; his parathespian dimension is addressed by Meriani 1995 (on *Cinesias*) and Braund 2000 (on *Callippides*). On Plato's dramatic career, see most recently Hartwig 2010. Pirrotta 2009 is a detailed commentary on the extant fragments. On Plato's "demagogue comedies," see Sommerstein 2000; Rosen 1995 examines his mythological plays, including *Phaon.* On this play, see also Degani 1998 and Casolari 2003.

BIBLIOGRAPHY

Bakola, E. 2008. "The Drunk, the Reformer and the Teacher: Agonistic Poetics and the Construction of Persona in the Comic Poets of the Fifth Century." *Cambridge Classical Journal* 54: 1–29.

——. 2010. *Cratinus and the Art of Comedy.* Oxford: Oxford University Press.

Battezzato, L. 2005. "La parodo dell'*Ipsipile.*" In *Euripide e i papiri: Atti del Convegno internazionale di studi, Firenze, 10–11 giugno 2004,* edited by G. Bastianini and A. Casanova, 169–203. Florence: Istituto papirologico G. Vitelli.

Biles, Z. P. 2011. *Aristophanes and the Poetics of Competition.* Cambridge: UK Cambridge University Press.

Braund, D. 2000. "Strattis' *Callippides*: The Pompous Actor from Scythia?" In *The Rivals of Aristophanes: Studies in Athenian Old Comedy,* edited by D. Harvey and J. Wilkins, 151–158. London and Swansea: Duckworth and the Classical Press of Wales.

Casolari, F. 2000. "Platons *Phaon* als Beispiel einer Mythenparodie zwischen Alter und Mittlerer Komödie." In *Skenika: Beiträge zum antiken Theater und seiner Rezeption: Festschrift zum 65. Geburtstag von Horst-Dieter Blume,* edited by S. Gödde and Th. Heinze, 91–102. Darmstadt: Wissenschaftliche Buchgesellschaft.

Csapo, E. 2000. "From Aristophanes to Menander? Genre Transformation in Greek Comedy." In *Matrices of Genre: Authors, Canons, and Society,* edited by M. Depew and D. Obbink, 115–133. Cambridge, MA: Harvard University Press.

Degani, E. 1998. "Filosseno di Leucade e Platone comico (fr. 189 K.-A.)." *Eikasmos* 9: 81–99.

Dobrov, G. W. 2002. "Μάγειρος ποιητής: Language and Character in Antiphanes." In *The Language of Greek Comedy,* edited by A. Willi, 169–190. Oxford and New York: Oxford University Press.

Fiorentini, L. 2009. "Studi sul commediografo Strattide." PhD diss., University of Ferrara.

Furley, W. D. 1996. *Andocides and the Herms: A Study of Crisis in Fifth-Century Athenian Religion.* London: Institute of Classical Studies.

Gowers, E. 1993. *The Loaded Table: Representations of Food in Roman Literature.* Oxford: Clarendon Press.

Halliwell, S. 1989. "Authorial Collaboration in the Athenian Comic Theatre." *GRBS* 30: 515–528.

Hartwig, A. 2010. "The Date of the *Rhabdouchoi* and the Early Career of Plato Comicus." *ZPE* 174: 19–31.

Hunter, R. 2009. *Critical Moments in Classical Literature: Studies in the Ancient View of Literature and its Uses.* Cambridge, UK: Cambridge University Press.

Jenkins, T. E. 2005. "At Play with Writing: Letters and Readers in Plautus." *TAPA* 135: 359–392.

Kyriakidi, N. 2007. *Aristophanes und Eupolis: Zur Geschichte einer dichterischen Rivalität.* Berlin and New York: Walter de Gruyter.

Lowe, N. J. 2000. "Comic Plots and the Invention of Fiction." In *The Rivals of Aristophanes: Studies in Athenian Old Comedy*, edited by D. Harvey and J. Wilkins, 259–272. London and Swansea: Duckworth and Classical Press of Wales.

Meriani, A. 1995. "Il *Cinesia* di Strattis." In *Seconda miscellanea filologica*, by I. Gallo, 21–45. Naples: Arte tipografica.

Miles, S. 2009. "Strattis, Tragedy, and Comedy." PhD diss., University of Nottingham.

Nesselrath, H. G. 2000. "Eupolis and the Periodization of Athenian Comedy." In *The Rivals of Aristophanes: Studies in Athenian Old Comedy*, edited by D. Harvey and J. Wilkins, 233–246. London and Swansea: Duckworth and Classical Press of Wales.

Olson, S. D. 2007. *Broken Laughter: Select Fragments of Greek Comedy.* Oxford: Oxford University Press.

Orth, C. *Strattis: Die Fragmente: Ein Kommentar.* Berlin: Verlag Antike.

Pirrotta, S. 2009. *Plato Comicus: Die fragmentarischen Komödien: Ein Kommentar.* Berlin: Verlag Antike.

Porter, J. I. 2010. *The Origins of Aesthetic Thought in Ancient Greece: Matter, Sensation, and Experience.* Cambridge, UK: Cambridge University Press.

Revermann, M. 2006. *Comic Business: Theatricality, Dramatic Technique, and Performance Contexts of Aristophanic Comedy.* Oxford: Oxford University Press.

Rosen, R. M. 1995. "Plato Comicus and the Evolution of Greek Comedy." In *Beyond Aristophanes: Transition and Diversity in Greek Comedy*, edited by G. W. Dobrov, 119–137. Atlanta: Scholars Press.

Rossi, P. 1981. "Sull'esordio di Platone Comico." *Homonoia* 3: 81–90.

Sidwell, K. 1993. "Authorial Collaboration? Aristophanes' *Knights* and Eupolis." *GRBS* 34: 365–389.

——. 2009. *Aristophanes the Democrat: The Politics of Satirical Comedy during the Peloponnesian War.* Cambridge, UK: Cambridge University Press.

Sommerstein, A. H. 2000. "Platon, Eupolis and the Demagogue-Comedy." In *The Rivals of Aristophanes: Studies in Athenian Old Comedy*, edited by D. Harvey and J. Wilkins, 437–451. London and Swansea: Duckworth and Classical Press of Wales.

Storey, I. C. 2003. *Eupolis Poet of Old Comedy.* Oxford: Oxford University Press.

——. 2010. "Origins and Fifth-Century Comedy." In *Brill's Companion to the Study of Greek Comedy*, edited by G. W. Dobrov, 179–225. Leiden and Boston: Brill.

Svenbro, J. 1993. *Phrasikleia: An Anthropology of Reading in Ancient Greece.* Ithaca, NY: Cornell University Press.

Telò, M. 2007. *Eupolidis Demi.* Florence: F. Le Monnier.

Webster, T. B. L. 1972. "Scenic Notes II." In *Antidosis: Festschrift für Walther Kraus zum 70. Geburtstag*, edited by R. Hauslik, A. Lesky, and H. Schwabl, 454–457. Vienna: Hermann Böhlau.

Wilkins, J. 2000. *The Boastful Chef: The Discourse of Food in Ancient Greek Comedy*. Oxford: Oxford University Press.

CHAPTER 6

....

ARISTOPHANES[1]

....

BERNHARD ZIMMERMANN

1. LIFE

....

ARISTOPHANES, son of Philippus from the Attic deme Cydathenaeum of the tribe Pandionis (K-A test. 5), was probably born in the middle or, more likely, at the end of the forties of the fifth century BCE (K-A test. 13–18). The date of his birth is inferred from the statement at *Clouds* 530 that at the time of his first comedy, *Banqueters* (427 BCE), he was still "a virgin, incapable of giving birth," in other words very young. *Acharnians* 652–654 suggest a link to the island of Aegina (K-A test. 10). Near the end of his life he served as *prytanis* (K-A test. 9). He seems to have died around the middle of the eighties of the fourth century BCE. Araros, Philetaerus (or Nicostratus), and Philippus (K-A test. 7–8), who were active as comic poets in the fourth century, are identified as his sons.

On the basis of *Knights* 541–550 and *Wasps* 1018–1022 it is possible to reconstruct, albeit tentatively, three stages of Aristophanes's career as a comic poet. (1) At first, he assisted other poets who had already made a name for themselves in a kind of poetic apprenticeship, broadcasting his own comic inventions through the mouths of others in the manner of a ventriloquist. (2) Later he composed entire plays that came to be known as his, but still shrank from the difficult task of directing (*komoidodiskalia*), which he entrusted instead to somebody else, Callistratus (*Banqueters* in 427 BCE to *Acharnians* in 425 BCE). (3) Only after that, starting with *Knights* in 424 BCE, did he muster the confidence to take the helm and steer his poetic craft himself.

At the beginning of his career, Aristophanes may have received support from influential fellow demesmen, to whom he may refer obliquely at *Clouds* 528. The comic characters Amphitheus (*Acharnians* 46ff.) and Simon (*Knights* 242) were priests of Heracles and, along with Panaetius (*Knights* 242f.), Hipparchus, and Philonides—very likely a comic poet and Aristophanes's director (*didaskalos*)—are listed as members of a *thiasos*

---

[1] Translated by Carolin Hahnemann and Zachary P. Biles.

of Heracles in Cydathenaeum for 425/4 BCE (IG II² 2343). Viewed against this backdrop, the attacks of Aristophanes of Cydathenaeum against the demagogue Cleon, who hailed from the same deme, acquire a highly charged connotation: it is possible that besides matters of politics, private or local affairs played a role as well.

Acharnians (502–505, 630–632, 659–664) and Wasps (1284–1291) contain allusions to a legal dispute between Cleon and Aristophanes; whether this incident is historical or not is a subject of scholarly debate. Cleon is said to have dragged the poet into court for speaking ill of the city in Babylonians (426 BCE) in the presence of noncitizens. According to the testimony of Pseudo-Xenophon (2, 18), the demos did not permit anyone to malign it in toto. But whether Cleon in fact brought charges is doubtful; the poet may have agreed to a compromise with the politician that he later failed to abide by.

2. WORKS

We cannot determine the precise number of plays Aristophanes composed. The Vita (K-A test. 1. 59–61) ascribes forty-four comedies to him, of which four (Poetry [Poiesis], Shipwrecked [Nauagos; cf. Dionysus Shipwrecked K-A test. iii], Islands [Nesoi], and Niobus [Dramas K-A test. iii]) belonged to Archippus "in the opinion of some." The anonymous author of De comoedia (K-A test. 4. 10f.) attributes fifty-four comedies to Aristophanes, including the four of doubtful authenticity. The discrepancy may be due to a scribal error: if one counts the second, attested versions of Aeolosicon, Peace, Wealth, Women at the Thesmophoria, and Clouds, the number of preserved titles is forty-five. Eleven comedies have come down to us intact; to this must be added 924 fragments and fifty-one dubia.

Aristophanes's career as a comic poet began with a series of spectacular successes. His very first play, Banqueters (427 BCE), was awarded second place (festival unknown); only one year later, he seems to have been victorious at the Great Dionysia with Babylonians. In this way, the poet broke the phalanx of established comic poets at a very young age. After Hermippus's victory in 435 BCE, no new name appears in the records of the Dionysia. And Aristophanes's success continued: he took first place at the Lenaea with Acharnians (425 BCE) and Knights (424 BCE), in the latter case acting as the chorodidaskalos for the first time. After this streak of victories, the defeat of Clouds, which placed third at the Dionysia of 423 BCE, came as a blow. In 422 BCE, the poet entered two plays at the Lenaea, perhaps because the defeat at the Dionysia in 423 BCE prevented him from applying for a chorus for this more important festival. He took first place with Proagon, which was known to be by Aristophanes even though it was entered in the competition by Philonides, and second with Wasps, which he directed himself. At the Dionysia in 421 BCE, he came in second with Peace. Also from these early years date Farmers (Georgoi, 424–422 BCE) and Merchant Ships (Holkades, probably Lenaea 423 BCE). For 414 BCE, the records list two productions, Amphiaraus at the Lenaea and Birds at the Dionysia (second place). He produced two comedies again in 411 BCE, Lysistrata and *Women at the Thesmophoria*. The didascalic notice specifying the festival is missing; the *communis opinio* puts *Lysistrata* at the Lenaea and *Women at the Thesmophoria* at the Dionysia.

Some scholars date the second version of *Peace* shortly after the conclusion of the Peace of Nicias, when the city was still in a state of euphoria (420 BCE). Alternatively, it may belong to the years after the occupation of Deceleia by the Spartans in 413 BCE, since longing for peace must have been at a peak in this period. *Anagyrus*, *Seasons* (*Horai*), and *Heroes* belong to the years between 420 and 412 BCE. The vague allusion to the actor Callippides in fr. 480 of *Women Claiming Tent-Sites* (*Skenas Katalambanousai*) might be an indication that the play was performed after 418 BCE. *Triple Phallus* (*Triphales*) and probably also *Old Age* (*Geras*) were produced after 411 BCE. For *Phoenician Women*, the performance of Euripides's tragedy by the same name (411–409 BCE) serves as terminus post quem. *Polyidus* is dated to 415 BCE and *Lemnian Women* to ca. 410 BCE. The first version of *Wealth* was performed in 408 BCE, close to *Gerytades* and the second version of *Women at the Thesmophoria*, which was staged somewhere between 415/4 and 407/6 BCE. *Fry-Cooks* (*Tagenistai*), *Danaids*, and *Daedalus*, as well as *Dramas* or *Centaur* and *Tel(e)messians*, might also belong to this period.

In 405 BCE, Aristophanes celebrated the greatest triumph of his career with *Frogs*, with which he took first place at the Lenaea; according to the *Vita* (K-At test. 1,35–39), the citizens honored him with a wreath made from branches of the sacred olive tree for his plea for reconciliation in the *parabasis*. According to Dicaearchus (fr. 84 Wehrli = Hypothesis III end), the political message in the *parabasis* earned this play the special privilege of a second performance, a singular honor which otherwise in the fifth century was granted solely to Aeschylus, and only after his death.

In the fourth century, Aristophanes produced *Assemblywomen*, which has been assigned to the period between 393 and 391 BCE, with 391 BCE carrying the greatest probability. He staged the second (preserved) *Wealth* in 388 BCE. In 387 BCE, Aristophanes's son won first prize at the Dionysia with *Cocalus*, and he may also have put on his father's second *Aeolosicon* in 386 BCE before making his first public appearance with a play of his own. *Storks* (*Pelargoi*) probably dates from the time after 400 BCE as well.

The poet's productivity reached its peak during the Archidamian War, between 427 und 421 BCE: eleven or more plays in seven years. Between 414 BCE and the end of the century, he wrote fourteen or more comedies in fourteen years; in the period from 392/1 BCE until his death, five plays in about six years.

A survey of the comedies leads to the striking realization that time and again throughout his career Aristophanes would revise his plays (*Clouds, Peace, Women at the Thesmophoria, Wealth, Aeolosicon*, perhaps the *Dramata* comedies). But it is impossible to say whether he did so because he was dissatisfied with the outcome of the original production, as happened with *Clouds*, or in order to save himself additional labor, as is plausible in the case of the second *Wealth* and *Aeolosicon*, both of which count among his late works.

3. LANGUAGE AND STYLE

The language of comedy in the fifth century is an artificial language which makes use of a spectrum of different idioms. Admittedly, the language of Old Comedy tends to disguise its artificial nature and approximate colloquial Attic in a kind of "dramatic realism" (artificial language with a centripetal tendency), in contrast to the language of tragedy, which aims to distance itself from colloquial Attic (artificial language with a centrifugal tendency). Still, a thorough analysis of comic usage shows that the language of the comic poets, too, differs from spoken Attic, for example, in terms of morphology.[2]

Besides the spoken language, which then as now provides a frame of reference for all literary idioms, since the typical style of a genre or an author becomes apparent against this backdrop, an important point of comparison is furnished by the other "Dionysiac" languages that were in competition with comedy, namely the idiom and style of the other genres which were produced at the Great Dionysia, especially that of tragedy but also that of dithyramb. In addition to these, there is also the language of lyric and of epic and, occasionally, administrative jargon. Comedy makes use of the artificial languages of tragedy and of dithyramb primarily for the purpose of parody, but at times also incorporates them into its own comic language without parodic intent. Both functions are at work in the case of the mimicking of bird calls (*Birds* 227ff., 737ff., 769ff.), the croaking of frogs (*Frogs* 209ff.), or the vocal imitation of the sound of musical instruments (*Frogs* 1286ff., *Wealth* 290, 296). Here, Aristophanes's aim on the one hand is parody—ridiculing the musical mannerisms of the New Music—but on the other hand, he incorporates these sound effects into his own compositions in such a way that they retain their comic effect even if the parody goes unrecognized. Despite this dependence of comic language on other artificial languages, however, it should be noted that the poets of comedy took pains to develop an artificial language of their own that could measure up to that of its sister genre, tragedy. The concept of *trygoidia*, for which the young Aristophanes boldly claims a place on the same level with tragedy (*Acharnians* 500), pertains not only to matters of content but also of form and, above all, of language.

The autonomy of comic language becomes especially clear when we compare the use of compound words and neologisms, which comedy has in common with dithyramb and, to some degree, with tragedy.[3] The function of such neologisms in dithyramb and

---

[2] See Willi (2002): 115: while in Attic prose the ending for the first person plural middle is invariably -μεθα, in Aristophanes we find seventy-six instances of -μεσθα (as compared to 177 instances of -μεθα); in inscriptions, the endings -οισι(ν) and -αισι(ν) for the dative plural disappear around 420, but in comedy they persist.

[3] A few examples (in the translation of A. H. Sommerstein): *Wasps* 220 ἀρχαιομελισιδωνοφρυνιχήρατα ("lovely-old-honeyed-Sidonian-Phrynichus-songs"); *Wasps* 505 ὀρθροφοιτοσυκοφαντοδικοταλαιπόρων ("early-morning-going-out-and-judging-trumped-up-lawsuit-toil-and-troublous habits"), *Lysistrata* 457f. ὦ σπερμαγοραιολεκιθολαχανοπώλιδες, / ὦ σκοροδοπανδοκευτριαρτοπώλιδες ("you brood-of-the-porridge-and-vegetable-market, you garlic-landlady-breadsellers"). The longest neologism is the mega-dish at *Assemblywomen* 1169–1175, cf. Zimmermann 1985b: 85–90.

tragedy is exactly the opposite of their function in comedy: the former genres employ them to impart loftiness and pathos, while the latter uses them for comic objectives, often—in the case of comically coined names—in connection with personal attacks.[4]

As a polyphonic genre, comedy freely avails itself of other literary forms and their registers. Prayers and hymns provide a good example of this. While the language used in prayers tends to be more personal, the language of hymns—since these are intended for public occasions—is more conventional and polished. The linguistic register is specifically chosen in order to create a particular relationship between the person who is praying and the deity who is being prayed to. For instance, the *parabasis* of *Knights* contains both a democratic hymn addressed to Athena (581–594) and an aristocratic one addressed to Poseidon (531–564). The different characters of the two deities are reflected in differences of style: "The prosaic use of the article makes the language of the hymn to Athena more 'demotic' since it comes closer to everyday speech, whereas the article was customarily omitted in the lyric tradition of the élite" (Willi 2003: 36).

Aristophanes likes to use fashionable jargon, above all that of the sophists with its predilection for adjectives ending in *-ikos*,[5] verbal nouns ending in *-sis*,[6] and abstract nouns ending in *-ma*,[7] as an instrument of characterization, showing the influence of the sophists on the aristocratic youth of Athens. Technical terms, especially medical ones, often reinforce a scene's comic effect; for example, when the treatment of Lamachus after his accident is announced in paratragic language in *Acharnians* 1174–1189, or when Euripides describes putting Aeschylus's bloated tragedy on a purging diet in *Frogs* 939–944.

Although Aristophanes shrinks from thoroughgoing linguistic characterization—he often has his characters break role for the sake of a comic effect—he likes to construct linguistically marked antitheses that emphasize a difference in social background, attitude to life, or age. Compare, for example, the contrast between the uneducated country bumpkin Strepsiades and the sophistically inclined Socrates, or between Pheidippides (after he has been corrupted by Socrates) and his father (*Clouds* 1353ff.). Even this mode of characterization, however, is applied selectively rather than consistently by the playwright; in any case, as far as his depiction of Socrates is concerned: "*Clouds* stages a Socrates who holds Diogenean ideas, lives in a Pythagorean setting, and uses

---

[4]   Cf. *Acharnians* 603 Τεισαμενοφαινίππους Πανουργιππαρχίδας (Rogers 1910: 91: "a combination of noble birth and little worth"; regarding the denigrating, generalizing plural, cf. *Acharnians* 270 Λάμαχοι; Olson 2002: 149f., 229. There is also Cratinus's well-known description of Aristophanes: K-A fr. 342. 2 εὐριπιδαριστοφανίζων ("a euripidaristophanizer") implying that Aristophanes criticizes and at the same time imitates Euripides, as explained by the scholium to Plat. *Ap.* 19c; cf. Beta 2007: 16–21. Cf. below, p. 32.

[5]   Cf. especially *Knights* 1375–1381 for a cluster of adjectives of this type (συνερτικός, περαντικός, γνωμοτυπικός, κρουστικός, καταληπτικός, θορυβητικός, καταδακτυλικός, λαλητικός; "cohesive, penetrative, productive of original phrases, clear, incisive, repressive, vociferative," translations by Sommerstein); cf. Peppler 1910 und Willi 2003: 139–145.

[6]   E.g. *Clouds* 317f. (Socrates describes the benefactions of the cloud goddesses using διάλεξις, περίλεξις, κροῦσις, and κατάληψις; "intelligence, discourse, understanding, fantasy, circumlocution, incisive and repressive power"; translations by Sommerstein); cf. Willi 2003: 134f.

[7]   Cf. e.g. the neologism φρόντισμα ("idea," *Clouds* 155) or νόημα ("idea," *Clouds* 743); cf. Peppler 1916; Willi 2003: 136–139.

Empedoclean language" (Willi 2003: 116). Similarly, the poet uses typically feminine expressions, polite and cordial utterances, to mark women as a group. His jibes against Cleophon in *Frogs* 679–683 are based on a deviation from standard Attic usage, and in the prologue to *Wasps* (44f.) he exploits the comic potential of Alcibiades's speech defect. Euphemisms, too, in particular if they veil sexual and scatological expressions, often serve as a tool of characterization; for instance, Better Argument in *Clouds* consistently resorts to euphemistic circumlocutions to describe his pederastic inclinations.

This "linguistic realism," as one might call the characterization of an individual or group through deviations from standard Attic usage, is especially conspicuous in the portions composed in dialect. Studies by Dover (1987: 240), Colvin (1999), and Willi (2002: 125–127) have made the case that at least in Aristophanes's surviving comedies, in contrast to modern comedy, the use of dialect does not necessarily serve comic ends: "Probably Aristophanes simply made Megarians, Thebans and Spartans speak in ways which the audience recognized as genuine because if he had made them speak Attic that would have struck a wrong note with the audience" (Dover 1987: 240). Whether this rule applies generally, however, is not at all certain, since the differences between the Boeotian and the Attic dialect are used as a source of humor in a fragment of Strattis's *Phoenician Women* (K-A fr. 49), and Aristophanes's *Peace* (929f.) contains a pun based on differences of dialect as well.

The treatment of the "foreign speech" of non-Greek barbarians, such as the Triballian god in *Birds* (1565ff.) or the Scythian policeman in *Women at the Thesmophoria* (1001ff.), is another matter entirely; its purpose is to provoke laughter—especially in contrast to Poseidon's high diction and Euripides's tragic verses. In *Lysistrata*, Aristophanes uses Doric dialect not merely for reasons of dramatic realism, but first and foremost for reasons of content: in the *exodos*, the Spartans sing about the Athenians' as well as their own exploits during the Persian Wars in Doric dialect (1247–1270) and summon the Laconian muse to Athens (1296–1320). The fact that the conclusion of the peace is being celebrated in Attic as well as Doric serves as a linguistic signal for the success of Lysistrata's plan.

Another, and as yet insufficiently explored, aspect of Aristophanes's language is its acoustic dimension and the use of sound effects and rhetorical figures; the alliteration of p-sounds accompanying the chorus's pugnacious entrance song in *Knights* (246–251) constitutes a striking example. Rhymes, jingles, and deliberate sound effects appear to occur with some frequency, but it is necessary in each case to consider carefully whether the effect is indeed intentional.

4. METRICAL STYLE

The comic poets of the fifth century BCE had at their disposal a multitude of metrical forms that they could use in composing a play.[8] In comedy, the rules governing the construction of the verse used for conversation, the iambic trimeter, are much less rigid than

---

[8] The metrics of Aristophanes's comedies have been analyzed in depth, most recently by Zimmermann 1985a and Zimmermann 1985b as well as Parker 1997.

in tragedy, with the result that it resembles spoken language more closely; Porson's law (which prohibits a word break after a long syllable in anceps position except in the central caesura) is broken in approximately every fifth verse. Sequences of two shorts occur frequently, and sometimes there is no caesura. By contrast, in paratragic passages the rules of the tragic trimeter are observed. The recited segments contain long verses: iambic, trochaic, and anapaestic catalectic tetrameters. In the lyric portions, which were sung, we must differentiate between typically comic meters and meters that have been influenced by the serious genres, tragedy and choral lyric. Genuinely comic rhythms are marked by their simplicity, which points to their popular origin. They are based primarily on iambic and trochaic as well as aeolic rhythms, but are often interspersed with syncopes and catalectics. Whenever comedy makes use of the metrical forms of a serious genre, it can be taken to signal parody. In these cases, along with the shift in meter, the linguistic form changes to an excessively solemn idiom. This is especially clear in the case of dochmiacs, the most multiform of Greek meters, which are used in tragedy in scenes of extreme excitement. A similar explanation applies to dactylo-epitrite, which is familiar from tragedy and choral lyric, and ionic, which strikes an exotic, oriental note or evokes a Dionysiac ambience.

It is possible to distinguish between a characterizing and an evocative function in the use of the individual metrical forms. "Characterizing" means that the rhythm, which is also reflected in the choreography, contributes to the characterization of the speakers, whether in their role throughout the entire play or merely in the immediate context. "Evocative" means that the choice of meter, and of course of the accompanying melody and dance, evokes particular associations in the spectators, either with traditional types of song, such as hymns, *hymenaioi, enkomia, skolia,* and songs of mockery, or with modes of composition familiar from tragedy and choral lyric. In some cases, both functions may also overlap, as in the case of the ionic meter.

Metrical analysis of the entrance songs of the choruses reveals how Aristophanes uses certain metrical forms to characterize the chorus. For instance, catalectic iambic tetrameters suit the labored gait of older people (*Wasps, Lysistrata, Assemblywomen, Wealth*). Proof of this interpretation comes from the *parodos* of *Assemblywomen*, in which young women mimic old men in precisely this meter (278f.). *Wasps* constitutes a special case: here regular catalectic iambic tetrameters (230–247) are followed by syncopated catalectic iambic tetrameters (248–272: x - v - x - v - / - v - v - -), which convey rhythmically that the old men are stumbling on the wet street. Catalectic trochaic tetrameters express speed and aggression (*Acharnians, Knights, Peace, Birds*), an effect that can be reinforced by alliteration (*Acharnians* 204f.; *Knights* 247–250). Resolution constitutes yet another means of expressing affect (e.g. *Knights* 284–296). The connection between the role of the chorus, the plot, and the meter is especially clear in the case of *Wasps* and *Lysistrata*. In *Wasps,* the meter changes from catalectic iambic tetrameters at the beginning to irritated trochees as soon as the old men, provoked by Bdelycleon's impudence, discover their true, waspish nature (415ff.). The same is true in *Lysistrata*, where the two half-choruses in the quarrel scene switch from the iambics of their entrance song to trochees (614ff., 781ff., 1014ff.).

The sung portions of the *parodos* are metrical transformations of whatever meter has been used in the chanted entrance song: trochees turn into cretics (- v -) and paeons (vv v - or - v vv), recited iambics turn into sung ones, i.e. into metrical shapes which can be reduced to the basic metrical unit of the iamb (baccheus: v - -; molossus: - - -; cretic: - v -; choriamb: - vv -; spondee - -). Eloquent testimony for the interrelation between the chorus's role and the metrical form comes from the *parabasis* odes, in which it is customary for the chorus to invoke its deity and sing about itself. Both in *Acharnians* (665ff., 692ff.) and in *Wasps* (1060ff., 1091ff.), these odes are composed in paeonic-cretic rhythm, which had already been used in the lyric portions of the *parodos* to characterize the chorus.

As a comparison of the meters in the individual comedies shows, the characterizing function applies only to the trochaic and iambic meters, and to metrical forms that can be reduced to trochees or iambs. Moreover, Aristophanes keeps up the characterizing function only as long as he is using the chorus as an agent in the plot. In other portions of the drama—especially in the episodic scenes following the *parabasis*—both meters can also have other functions; for example, the catalectic iambic tetrameter in the *exodos* signals the departure of the chorus.

In the case of other types of meter, a more complex process seems to be at work: Aristophanes makes use of certain associations inherent in a given meter, which, in turn, can have a characterizing effect. A good example of this is the ionic meter (basic form: vv - -). The combination of ionic and dactylo-epitrite in the serenade sung by the chorus of wasps to their imprisoned peer Philocleon gives the impression of an old-fashioned melody (*Wasps* 273–289). This fits perfectly with the characterization of this chorus, whom Bdelycleon had already described as being fond of outmoded songs in the style of the long-dead tragedian Phrynichus (*Wasps* 219f.). The audience finds confirmation for this portrayal of the chorus in the tottering gait of the old men (expressed by syncopated catalectic iambic tetrameters) as well as their old-fashioned rhythms and songs. At *Women at the Thesmophoria* 101–129, the polymetrical form, with free ionic units in various shapes interspersed within it, lends a foreign air (cf. v. 120f.) to Agathon's monody. This serves to characterize not merely Agathon's compositions but, on a second level, also creates a negative portrayal of Agathon himself as abnormal and alien. In addition, the accompanying ionic rhythm and the Phrygian melody are connected with the East (cf. Aeschylus, *Persae* 65–125) and call up various associations relating to the Orient, such as lasciviousness and effeminacy. The reaction of Euripides's kinsman emphasizes this: he feels sexually aroused by Agathon's singing (*Women at the Thesmophoria* 130–133). Finally, in the *parodos* of *Frogs* a third application of ionic rhythm emerges. By delivering the entrance song in ionic rhythm, the chorus identify themselves as followers of Dionysus, because ionic rhythms with their emotional appeal have their proper place in the cult of Dionysus, which was introduced from the East (cf. Euripides, *Bacchae* 64–88).

In the episodic scenes following the parabasis, the acephalic (i.e., missing the first element) aeolic meters—telesilleia (o- vv - v -) and reiziana (o- v v - -)—evoke predominantly traditional types of song, which were familiar from daily life, such as *enkomia*, wedding songs, and *skolia* (*Assemblywomen* 938–941, 942–945). By means of rhythmical and musical signals, he invites the spectator to compare the song he has just heard with its conventional counterpart. In some instances, he also produces certain associations simply by means of short metrical signals, individual periods or striking breaches of responsion (the metrical symmetry of strophe and antistrophe). A significant breach of responsion occurs, for example, in *Peace* 951–953 and 1034–1036: to the iambs in the ode (951–953) correspond acephalic aeolic meters (telesilleia, reizianum) in the *antode* (1034–1036). While the iambs suit the mocking tone of the ode, the aeolic meters fit the praise of the protagonist in the *antode*.

The evocative function of the meter has its most pervasive application in parodies. By means of certain metrical forms, especially if these are rare in comedy, the poet alerts the spectator to the parodied model. Three types of this sort of metrical application can be distinguished:

(1) The parody extends to the language as well as the meter of the original (*Women at the Thesmophoria* 101–130, 1015–1054; *Frogs* 1264–1277, 1285–1295, 1309–1328, 1331–1363). The comic effect results from Aristophanes's exaggerating the linguistic and rhythmical peculiarities of the original, thereby exposing the latter's metrical and linguistic extravagance.

(2) The parody applies only to the language, while the meter is unexceptional for comedy. Typically comic meters, like paeonics and cretics, are paired with elevated diction to create stark incongruity (e.g., *Acharnians* 208–218, 223–233; *Birds* 1069f., 1099f.).

(3) The parody applies only to the rhythmic form, but not the language, which is colloquial throughout or turns colloquial after some high diction at the start. This can be seen in passages where typically tragic meters, such as dochmiac and dactylo-epitrite, are combined with colloquial diction (e.g., *Acharnians* 358ff., 385ff., 489ff., 566ff.; *Knights* 1264ff.). Aristophanes is especially fond of using this technique in mocking songs: in the first few verses he relies on meter and language to bring an elevated original to mind, only to switch unexpectedly, in an *aprosdoketon*, to mockery and colloquial language while retaining the metrical structure of the elevated original.[9]

Detailed metrical analysis confirms observations regarding the plays' structure and content. Just as a multitude of discourses contributes to the content and language of Aristophanic comedy and just as a multitude of texts—be they literary works, texts of daily use, or texts stemming from political discourse—are alluded to through acute references, so also does the metrical skeleton mirror this polyphony and multiformity.

---

[9] For a discussion of *aprosdoketa*, see p. 155 below.

5. STRUCTURE AND PLOT IN OLD COMEDY

While until recently scholars tended to analyze tragedy according to the structural elements described by Aristotle in the twelfth chapter of his *Poetics* (1452^{b}14–27), the disappearance of the relevant book of that work saved comedy from the fate of its sister genre. Unencumbered by any Aristotelian scheme of organization, scholars were free to explore the dramatic structure as a product of the plot and pay special attention to the formal characteristics of Aristophanic comedy.

The structure of an Aristophanic comedy results from the interaction of chorus and actors. While the chorus has the lyric portions, the actors express themselves in spoken verse, most often iambic trimeters, which are appropriate for the purpose. When chorus and actors converse with each other, they tend to switch to recitative in long verses. Monodies occur, other than in cultic songs (*Acharnians* 263–279, *Lysistrata* 1247–1272, 1279–1294, 1296–1315), in parodic contexts, above all in the two comedies in which Aristophanes deals extensively with tragedy (*Women at the Thesmophoria* 1015–1054, *Frogs* 1264–1277, 1309–1328, 1331–1363, cf. *Wasps* 317–323). Consequently, fifth-century comedy bears a much closer resemblance to an opera than to a modern piece of spoken drama, in terms of its modes of delivery. Its high percentage of recited verses sets it apart from the tragedies of Sophocles and Euripides, rendering it more akin to those of Aeschylus.

The most conspicuous formal element of Old Attic Comedy is purely choral: the *parabasis*, where the chorus addresses the audience directly (Sifakis 1971; Hubbard 1991). Although it interrupts the plot, it is not disconnected from the play's general sequence of events, but can be linked, in terms of content and language, to the plot. Aristophanes is wont to place the two great choral segments, *parodos* and *parabasis*, in close connection with each other through language, meter, and content, or to use the *parabasis* as a means of preparing the ground for further plot developments: for instance, in the *parabasis* of *Frogs* (686ff.) the chorus leader emphasizes the claim of the comic chorus that they are entitled to act as political advisers to the city of Athens, and in this way anticipates the theme of the polis's salvation, with which the play ends (1419, 1500f.).

In its complete form, the *parabasis* consists of seven parts, three simple elements and four that relate to each other in pairs. It begins with the *kommation* ("little part") in anapaests or lyric meters (*Clouds* 512–517, *Birds* 676–684), which forms a bridge between the events of the plot and the *parabasis*. Next follows the *parabasis* proper, which is also called "the anapaests" (*Knights* 504, *Birds* 684), after the meter that is most often used for it, the catalectic anapaestic tetrameter. (At *Clouds* 518ff. we find eupolideans: oo - x - vv - oo - x - v x). In this segment, the chorus leader speaks in the name of the chorus or on behalf of the poet, sometimes even as the poet himself, about the role of the poet in society, the special qualities of his compositions, or the poet's relationship to the audience. In *Knights*, for example, Aristophanes uses a remark about the Athenian public's relationship to the comic poets as a starting point for giving a history of Attic comedy and expressing his appreciation for his predecessors Magnes (520ff.), Cratinus (526ff.), and Crates (537ff.).[10] Attached to the long verses in anapaests is a concluding *pnigos* ("choker"), in which the chorus leader, without taking a breath, bursts forth in verbal fireworks.

The *parabasis*'s second, corresponding half, the epirrhematic syzygy, belongs entirely to the chorus. It consists of two lyric parts, an ode and an *antode* sharing the same metrical shape, which most often take the traditional form of hymnic invocations of a god (*hymnos kletikos*). After each of these comes a recited passage comprising either sixteen or twenty catalectic trochaic tetrameters, the *epirrhema* (the "afterwards speech", i.e. a speech following upon a sung portion) and its matching *antepirrhema*. In this portion, the chorus sings and speaks about itself and its role in the play, and explains its mask.

A sequence of sung and recited segments, as exists in the *parabasis*, is typical for fifth-century comedy and occurs also in other parts of the drama in a slightly modified form. The most important structural element composed in epirrhematic form is the epirrhematic agon, which, like the *parabasis*, has a regular structure (Gelzer 1960). In this part, the protagonist engages either the chorus or another *dramatis persona* in a debate, which can be quite heated, in order to persuade his adversary of the legitimacy of his plan. Such an agon can take place after the chorus's entrance or at various other junctures in the play. In the latter case, it amounts to a kind of arbitration and can be divided into four parts: quarrel, agreement to arbitration, debate, and judgment. Each of the two parts of the epirrhematic agon starts with a choral song (ode, *antode*) that corresponds metrically. In the ode, the chorus reflects on the significance of the imminent debate or already takes one of the two parties' sides. In the *antode*, it sums up the arguments that have been presented or gushes forth with admiration for them. Next, the chorus leader recites the *katakeleusmos* ("exhortation") and *antikatakeleusmos*, comprising two long verses each, with which he prompts discussion in the *epirrhema* or *antepirrhema*. (In *Birds* 336–338, the *katakeleusmos* takes up an exceptional two and a half verses). The fact that the *katakeleusmos* establishes the meter for the *epirrhema* and *antepirrhema* reinforces the chorus's or chorus leader's role as moderator in this segment. Sometimes *epirrhema* and *antepirrhema*, like the anapaests of the *parabasis*, are followed by a *pnigos* at the climax of the dispute, with a nonstop barrage of arguments. The entire epirrhematic agon may close with the so-called *sphragis* ("seal"), praising the character whose arguments have carried the day (e.g., *Wasps* 725ff.). The two-part form naturally lends itself to a clash of speech and counterspeech. Aristophanes, however, does not adhere strictly to this pattern; rather, in some of his comedies, like *Birds* (451ff.) or *Lysistrata* (476ff.), he gives the whole agon to the comic hero, who thus has an opportunity to set out a position in detail without having to deal with the opposing view. The epirrhematic structure occurs also in scenes of confrontation, which in some plays follow directly after the entrance of the chorus, the *parodos* (Zimmermann 1985a). It obviously constitutes the structural element of Old Comedy created to permit close interaction between chorus and actors, as well as interplay of stage and orchestra; consequently, its natural position

---

[10] For a more detailed discussion of this passage, see p. 157. below.

in a play's structural sequence is ahead of the *parabasis*, since after the *parabasis* the chorus ceases to influence events directly.

Since in Old Comedy the chorus plays a vital role in the plot, comedies are rich in *amoibaia*, songs of lyric exchange between chorus and actor(s), in which the chorus actively moves the action along and plays an important part in it, or interprets the action, or exhorts persons on stage to action (Zimmermann 1985a). The different roles played by the chorus in the *amoibaia* are reflected also in the different forms of composition. If the chorus is an agent of the plot, a segment in epirrhematic structure with recited long verses follows the *parodos*; by contrast, if the chorus's role is to interpret action, there follows—usually after the *parabasis*—an "iambic syzygy": the chorus's ode and *antode* are set apart by spoken verses (iambic trimeters) delivered by the actor(s). As was noted above, an indication of the importance of the chorus in the epirrhematic scenes is the *katakeleusmos*, with which the chorus leader initiates action or discussion. The iambic syzygies after the *parabasis*, on the other hand, contain no *katakeleusmos*. The plot evolves solely among the actors, without any direct participation by the chorus. In these scenes, the function of the chorus approximates that of a spectator, its reaction to the events ranging from envy to admiration to enthusiasm, depending on its attitude toward the comic hero and his plan.

The structure of a typical fifth-century comedy can be outlined as follows. In the prologue, the protagonist, out of dissatisfaction with the state of affairs in the city or in his household, conceives an idea for how the situation can be remedied (Koch 1968). Since at the beginning of a play it is especially important for the poet to grab the audience's attention, the introductory portion of the play tends to be extremely rich in novelties and involve a rapid series of events. The points of detail required to make sense of the plot are provided either right at the start in an expository monologue, as in *Acharnians* or *Clouds*, or—much more frequently—are delayed. In the latter case, the spectator is confronted with a situation he cannot understand at first, but which will be explained to him after the event (*Knights* 36ff.; *Wasps* 54ff., 87ff.; *Peace* 50ff.; *Birds* 30ff.). To put it another way, the opening action presents a sort of dramatic riddle that is solved as the plot unfolds (cf. *Peace* 47). By 411 BCE (*Lysistrata, Women at the Thesmophoria*), the exposition is no longer addressed to the spectators but emerges in dialogue. This development fits with the trend observable from *Lysistrata* onward, to furnish the drama with a continuous plot from beginning to end and to avoid elements that break the dramatic illusion. Next follows a series of scenes that begins with the *parodos*, or entrance of the chorus, which in contrast to tragic practice always takes place comparatively late, never before verse 200, and continues with a sequence of actions that relate directly to the entrance of the chorus. The late entrance of the chorus is due to the fact that comedy must always offer something new, so that a more detailed exposition is required in comedy than in its sister genre. As the fourth-century comic poet Antiphanes put it mockingly in his *Poetry* (*Poiesis*, K-A fr. 189, 5ff.), in a tragic performance the mere mention of Oedipus's name suffices to remind the audience of the entire plot.

This entire sequence of scenes can be called a "*parodos* complex," inasmuch as it constitutes a coherent structural element in relation to the plot. How this structural element is shaped depends fundamentally on the chorus's role in the play and especially on its attitude toward the protagonist's plan. In some plays, the chorus is summoned by the comic hero to help with his plan (*Knights* 242f., *Peace* 296–298). If, on the contrary, the chorus has a hostile attitude toward the protagonist, it appears of its own accord in order to thwart the protagonist's intentions (*Acharnians* 204ff., *Lysistrata* 254ff.). In *Lysistrata* (319ff.), to the surprise of the chorus of old men who obstruct the female protagonist, a second chorus appears, consisting of old women who support Lysistrata's plan. It stands to reason, however, that the spectators expected the appearance of another half-chorus because of the reduced number of chorus members in the male chorus. A third option is that the chorus has no knowledge of the plans of the characters when it enters (*Wasps* 230ff., *Women at the Thesmophoria* 295ff., *Frogs* 316ff.). In a play of this type, the chorus must first be let in on what is happening before it can react with approval or disapproval. In types 2 and 3, the stage is empty when the chorus enters; in *Frogs,* there is an "eaves-dropping" arrangement: the actors step aside and watch the chorus.

If the chorus's attitude toward the protagonist is hostile, its arrival is often accompanied by a scene of quarreling in epirrhematic form. The dramaturgical point of such quarreling scenes is to establish an agreement between the opponents and to forego brute force in favor of words and arguments. This, in turn, prepares the way for the round of discussion in the epirrhematic agon, in which the protagonist defeats his adversary by the force of his words. With that, the climax of the comedy is reached: the comic hero can put his plan into action. Accordingly, the protagonist's triumph is followed by the *parabasis,* which at the same time concludes the first portion of the play and marks the culmination of the comic plot. After this, there may be a series of scenes ("episodic scenes"), demonstrating the implications of the new state of affairs the protagonist has brought about. Most often, various persons appear who want to share in the hero's success, but they are almost always curtly rebuffed by him. The individual scenes are set apart by choral odes. Either the chorus, addressing the audience, sings the praises of the hero (*makarismos*), or they embark on a mocking song that may be inspired by events on stage but has little or nothing to do with the plot itself. Alternatively, it may begin an alternating song with the protagonist (*amoibaion*), usually as a means of expressing its admiration for the comic hero. Some plays (*Knights* 1264ff., *Clouds* 1115ff., *Wasps* 1265ff., *Peace* 1127ff., *Birds* 1058ff.) contain another *parabasis* ("second *parabasis*"), consisting of an ode, *epirrhema,* and *pnigos* together with their counterparts (Totaro 2000), to mark a strong turning point in the second half of the comedy.

In the period from *Acharnians* to *Birds,* the scenes after the *parabasis* do not necessarily have a strictly logical connection or compelling chronological sequence. In the second part of *Birds* (1337ff.), for example, the scenes in which the parricide Cinesias and the sycophant are rebuffed could be reordered without any loss to the comic tension. Some scenes, however, bear a clear relationship to each other, for instance, the two scenes involving sycophants in *Acharnians* (818ff., 909ff.).

The last segment of the play (*exodos*) often contains the celebration of a feast after the protagonist has successfully defended the newly established state of affairs against unwelcome intruders and parasites; chorus and actors exit in a joyful procession.

A comic plot takes its point of departure from the city's political problems at the time of production, which spark the comic hero's criticism and lead to the comic scheme. The starting point of the action is the polis of Athens. Even in comedies like *Birds* and *Frogs* where the action is not set in Athens, the city remains present in the background and its problems determine the plot. Aristophanes's comedies do not offer a faithful portrait of reality, however; rather, the poet depicts real life in a grotesque and unfamiliar manner, so that the fantastical world of comedy, embodied in the protagonist and the chorus, constantly clashes with everyday life in Athens, represented by figures like Socrates, Lamachus, Meton, and so forth. The result is a multilayered reality that, like a palimpsest, contains the past within itself, not in any abstract fashion but, as befits the technique of comedy, embodied in a chorus of the founders of democracy (*Lysistrata*), the men who fought at Marathon and Salamis (*Acharnians, Wasps, Lysistrata*), or representatives of the good old days like the rejuvenated Demos in *Knights* or Aeschylus in *Frogs*. But the layers of this comic palimpsest contain not just the past; as the multitude of choruses made up of animals shows, the natural landscape in which humans live is equally present, as is the world of the gods, whether celestial (as in *Peace*) or chthonic (as in *Frogs*).

While Aristophanes had at his disposal a standard repertoire of traditional forms and structures, he was in no way slavishly tied to these structural elements. On the contrary, the art of the comic poet consists precisely in his ability to play with the expectations of an audience that has been trained by regular attendance at theatrical events. Thus, Aristophanes can use a certain structural sequence to lead the spectators to anticipate a particular plot development (quarrel or discussion), only to disappoint them at the last moment by leaving out the expected component, for example the *pnigos*, and so create surprise. In *Wasps*, Aristophanes even plays with the basic plot structure itself: Bdelycleon, who conceived the comic scheme and prevailed in the epirrhematic agon, should therefore, according to the audience's expectation, turn out to be the comic hero who triumphs in the end. But he loses the role of the protagonist in the scenes after the *parabasis* to his adversary Philocleon, who triumphs in his place in the *exodos*.

6. The "Comic Hero," the Other *Dramatis Personae*, and the Location of the Plot

All attempts to distill a consistent pattern for the comic hero, even just for the eleven preserved comedies of Aristophanes, fail, due to the multiformity of the comic heroes and the deliberate inconsistencies in their design.[11] Some protagonists, like Dicaeopolis or Trygaeus, represent the wishes and desires of the audience; thus the spectators can easily identify with them and, in their laughter at all things high and mighty, forget the hardship

---

[11] Cf. Whitman (1964); Dover (1972) 31–41; Olson (1992); Silk (2000) 207–255.

of their daily lives. In other plays, identification with a protagonist is difficult or impossible, as in the case of Strepsiades in *Clouds* or Peisetaerus in *Birds*. Just hearing these characters' speaking names—"he who twists the law" and "he who persuades *hetairoi*" (i.e. the members of an aristocratic-oligarchic club)—could raise misgivings. In other plays, such as *Knights* or *Wasps*, the protagonist's fantastic transformation—by means of rejuvenation or a return to previous vitality—gives a positive twist to the audience's initial unease, enabling them to identify with the hero at the end of the play. In the plays dominated by female characters, it cannot have been easy for the predominantly male audience to accept the comic plan of the female protagonists, however justified it may have been in and of itself, but all the more so when the men in these plays cut a poor figure. In *Frogs*, identification is impossible because the protagonist is a god who in the second half of the play takes on the role of a clown (*bomolochos*). Aristophanes has fun with the audience's desire to identify with the protagonist by bringing on stage comic heroes whose multifaceted personalities are pieced together bit by bit, like a mosaic, in the course of the action. Thus Dicaeopolis starts out as a disappointed spectator (*Acharnians* 1–16) before turning into a disappointed Athenian citizen and a simple farmer (32) in the Assembly (17–42). In keeping with this mode of gradual characterization, comic heroes as a rule remain anonymous at first and reveal their name—often a speaking name that ties in directly with the play's themes—only late in the play. In *Knights* this revelation occurs shortly before the end (1257); *Lysistrata* (6) and *Frogs* (22), on the other hand, constitute exceptions to the rule. The comic hero's multiform personality comes to light especially in those comedies where behind the character on stage a different person emerges; in *Knights*, for instance, Cleon, Nicias, and Demosthenes become clearly visible behind Master Demos's three household slaves. One may also regard Dicaeopolis in *Acharnians* as a case in point: he takes on the role of the Euripidean Telephus and at the same time speaks in the voice of the poet without, however, completely merging identities with Aristophanes (496–556). The game of changing identities (A acts as B), which is typical of comedy, can be traced in the title of Aristophanes's play *Aeolosicon* as well as in the comic coinage of the name "Herakleioxanthias" (*Frogs* 499): Dionysus disguised as Heracles presses his slave Xanthias to pretend to be Heracles. The transgressive change of identity, which is typical for the cult of Dionysus, seems to manifest itself in the very nature of the comic hero, which is unstable and liable to undergo frequent role changes (Fisher 1993).

Like the comic hero, the location of the action oscillates. Usually the city of Athens is the setting, but just as the hero easily changes his character by taking on someone else's role as the action demands, so, too, the location of the action can be in continuous flux. The example par excellence is *Acharnians*, in which the location changes from the Pnyx to Dicaeopolis's native deme, thence back to the city in front of Euripides's house, then again to the houses of Dicaeopolis and Lamachus, and after the *parabasis* to the protagonist's free-trade market. And just as the poet gives his hero free rein to cross boundaries of space, he also allows him to jump around in time—in *Acharnians*, from the Assembly to the rural Dionysia and subsequently to the Choes feast at the Anthesteria.

The comic hero possesses superhuman powers. Effortlessly he transcends all boundaries of time and space, even forcing his way into the sky and the underworld. And just as effortlessly he triumphs over all the adversities of everyday life. Be it out of unbridled egotism or total omnipotence, he drives away all parasites who want to share in his success or grants them a share as he sees fit. Other figures surrounding the comic hero thus underscore the protagonist's eminent position. In contrast to the male comic heroes, the women, Lysistrata and Praxagora, act as representatives of a collective or even as the collective itself, for example in *Women at the Thesmophoria*.

In contrast to tragedy, in comedy the poet can himself be present, above all as a "backstage character." Aristophanes tends to depict himself as a comic hero of nearly superhuman powers, as a second Heracles, for taking on the monstrous Cleon (*Wasps* 1029–1037, *Peace* 752–760)—a benefactor to mankind on a par with the great mythical hero (*Wasps* 1037). Already in the *parabasis* of *Acharnians* (633–664), one can clearly see the poet's effort to take on the role of this hero who wards off evils: Aristophanes's poetry, he claims, benefits the Athenians by providing political education. He dissuades the Athenians from falling for every piece of flattery (634f.); instead, he proclaims what is right (645, 658). This appropriation of Heracles seems to have provoked the mockery of other comic poets, as the jibes by Ameipsias (K-A fr. 27), Plato (K-A fr. 107), Aristonymus (K-A fr. 3), and Sannyrion (K-A fr. 5) show.

The comic hero inevitably eclipses the other *dramatis personae*, with the exception of the chorus; especially in dramas where the chorus strives to thwart the protagonist's plan (*Acharnians, Wasps, Lysistrata* [semi-chorus of men]), it is given a strength of character that makes it a worthy opponent of the protagonist. In all three plays, it is characterized as an extremely vigorous representative of the good old days, the time of the foundation of democracy and the battles at Marathon and Salamis. Similarly to the comic hero's immunity to the laws of space and time, the chorus in these plays is, as it were, immortal: through the chorus the past bursts into the fantastically grotesque present of the comic action.

The rest of the protagonist's opponents—e.g., Lamachus in *Acharnians*, Hermes in *Peace*, or the Probulus in *Lysistrata*—appear now and again to oppose the comic hero, only to be overwhelmed by him. The same is true for the multitude of persons who, in the scenes following the *parabasis*, want to share in the comic hero's success and are unceremoniously dismissed.

Among the minor characters are numerous slaves. Aristophanes uses slaves as mute characters, some of whom remain anonymous, while others are addressed by name, most often in the vocative, and especially when called upon to perform some service or other. By contrast, slaves who participate actively in the plot tend to remain anonymous.[12] Slaves can certainly have a comic function in a play: the domestic servants of

---

[12] *Acharnians* 395–402, 432–434: Euripides's porter; *Acharnians* 958–968,1174–1189: Lamachus's slave; *Knights* 1–497: Demos's domestic slaves; *Peace* 1–113: Trygaius's domestic slaves; *Peace* 824–1126: slave who greets Trygaius and assists him in making the sacrifice and driving out Hierocles; *Clouds* 56–58 (cf. 18f): Strepsiades's domestic slave; *Clouds* 133–221: Socrates's domestic slave; *Birds* 60–84: bird slaves, porter; *Women at the Thesmophoria* 36–70: Agathon's domestic slave, porter; *Frogs* 464–478, 650–671, 738–813: Pluto's porter; *Frogs* 738–813: Persephone's female slave; *Assemblywomen* 1112–1143: female slaves who announce the meal.

intellectuals like Euripides, Socrates, and Agathon have adopted their masters' manners all too well (*Acharnians* 395–402, 432–434; *Clouds* 133–221; *Women at the Thesmophoria* 36–70). Dionysus's slave Xanthias in *Frogs* constitutes an interesting exception (Dover 1993: 43–50): Dionysus addresses his slave by name (271: "Xanthias"), and even uses a diminutive nickname (582: "Xanthidion"). In this manner, the master tries to curry favor with his slave (579) and begs Xanthias to play the part of Heracles in his stead. Evidently, Dionysus has lost his last shred of dignity: he would put up even with being beaten at his slave's behest (584–589). Just as in *Clouds* or *Wasps* the relationship between young and old, between father and son, is turned upside down, in *Frogs* the relation between master and slave has come unraveled. In this way, Dionysus is depicted as effeminate and ineffectual, but the exchange of roles also points beyond the hilarity of the immediate context to the central passage in the comedy's *parabasis* (693f.). The chorus of initiates here claims the right to act as advisors to the city (686f.) and offers blunt criticism: slaves who took part in a single sea battle—the battle at Arginusae (cf. 33)—were set free and awarded citizens' rights, thus turning from slaves into masters, while honest citizens who committed a single offence—meaning the oligarchic coup of 411 BCE—have been robbed of their status as citizens! The results of such politics are demonstrated prior to the *parabasis* by Dionysus and Xanthias, the joke being that Xanthias did not participate in the battle at Arginusae and therefore continues to be merely a slave, but nevertheless has the insolence of putting on airs as if he were the master.

Gods and heroes also appear in minor roles. They are either given short shrift by the comic hero (Iris, Prometheus, Heracles, Poseidon, and the Triballian god in *Birds*) or have a limited role in the action (Hermes in *Peace*; Heracles, Charon, and Pluto in *Frogs*). In *Frogs*, Dionysus appears in his function as god of theater.

In keeping with the tendency of Aristophanic comedy to translate abstracts into stage action, there are several characters who symbolize the new state of affairs attained by the protagonist: beautiful women like the Peace Treaties (*Spondai*) in *Knights* (1389); Harvest (*Opora*) and Festival Joy (*Theoria*), the female companions of the peace goddess, in *Peace* (523); the Queen (*Basileia*) as a manifestation of Peisetaerus's omnipotence in *Birds* (1708–1765); and Reconciliation (*Diallage*) in *Lysistrata* (1114). Besides these mute symbolic figures, which the poet employs to illustrate the action on stage, there are also personifications who actively take part in the proceedings. The most striking instances are Master Demos embodying the Athenian populace in *Knights* and Wealth and Poverty (*Ploutos* and *Penia*) in *Wealth*. Furthermore, there are War (*Polemos*) and Tumult (*Kydoimos*) in *Peace* (204ff.) and the two arguments (*Logoi*) in *Clouds* (889ff.).

Contemporary people can appear in minor roles, as do Amphitheus (*Acharnians* 45f.) or Theorus (*Acharnians* 134). They frequently represent an entire group or a current phenomenon, thus standing in for something abstract, similar to the symbolic figures. For example, Euripides and Agathon in *Acharnians*, *Women at the Thesmophoria*, and *Frogs* serve as stand-ins for New Poetry; Aeschylus in *Frogs* for traditional tragedy and, more generally, for the good old days; Cinesias for choral lyric of a modern stamp (*Birds* 1372–1409); Meton for mathematics and astronomy (*Birds* 992–1020); Socrates in *Clouds*

(180) for rhetoric and philosophy as a second Thales; and Lamachus in *Acharnians* for war and its attendant phenomena.

7. COMIC THEMES AND TECHNIQUES

While we cannot say very much about the comic poets whose works we possess only in fragments, we are in a position, as it were, to look over Aristophanes's shoulder as he develops his comic themes. This is especially true of the first phase of his career, during the Archidamian War. The theme of the poet's clash with the demagogue Cleon predominates. Closely tied to this is the criticism of the sovereign power, the Attic demos, and its magistrates, a theme that can be traced through *Babylonians, Acharnians, Knights,* and *Wasps.* In *Knights,* the motif of rejuvenation is central. Here Aristophanes borrows the myth of Medea when he has the sausage-seller restore Demos's youth by boiling him at the end of the play, and thereby softens his earlier criticism of Demos's behavior in favor of a more reconciliatory tone. As a result, the play has two endings: a critical one, which ends after the first strophe of the *amoibaion* between Demos and the knights (1120), and a second, reconciliatory one, in which the first critical ending nonetheless continues to resonate. The motif of rejuvenation is taken up again in connection with the antithesis of young and old in *Wasps,* and it is likely to have played a role in *Old Age* (*Geras*) and *Triple Phallos* (*Triphales*) as well. The problem of education, which was raised in Aristophanes's first play, *Banqueters* (427 BCE), reappears in the conflict between the generations in *Clouds* and *Wasps.*

The interplay of dominant and subdominant chords in themes and motifs is evident also in the various forms of Aristophanic comedy: Aristophanes uses the form of "transparent comedy," where a second layer can be made out behind the action on stage, as matrix for the whole plot of *Knights*; for one scene, namely the domestic court, in *Wasps* (764ff.); and again for the entire comedy in *Birds.*

We can trace similar developments also in the realm of metaphors and personifications. Aristophanes briefly conjures the vision of a world turned upside-down in *Acharnians* (688), while in *Knights* and *Peace* he makes it into a guiding idea. While the characters War (*Polemos*) and Reconciliation (*Diallage*) are merely mentioned in *Acharnians* (977 and 989), Polemos has a speaking part in *Knights* (236–288) and Diallage appears as a beautiful woman in *Lysistrata* (1114).

Even with neologisms we can see favorite expressions dominating certain periods of the poet's career: *taraxikardios* "churning up the heart" (*Acharnians* 315) returns as *taraxippostratos* ("pest of the knight troops") at *Knights* 247. We see from this that in addition to speaking of a "comic repertoire" belonging to the comic poets as a group (Heath 1990: 152, 156), we must also pay attention to a poet's individual repertoire, which he was constantly developing.

War and Peace: The way Aristophanes treats the topic of war and peace in three comedies from three different phases of the Peloponnesian War—*Acharnians, Peace I* and *II,* and *Lysistrata*—is clearly a response to the state of military affairs and domestic politics at each juncture. *Peace I* (421 BCE) occupies a special position in that it anticipates the celebration of a peace treaty, but at the same time also shows—above all in the comments on Greek politics during the recovery of the goddess of peace (459ff.)—the perils threatening this peace because of individuals like the general Lamachus and groups that stand to profit from the war's continuation. This comedy openly discusses the fragile transition from war to peace. In the end, it is the farmers who have suffered the most in the war and who, by a concerted effort, succeed in recovering the peace goddess (508–519). The symbolic wedding of the protagonist Trygaeus with Opora, the vintner with the harvest, and the exit of the bride and groom together with the chorus heading back to the country, underscore the inseparable connection between peace and agriculture in stark dramatic terms. (This connection must have played a considerable role also in *Peace II* in the personification of agriculture.) Comparison with *Acharnians* and *Lysistrata* is illuminating. In both cases, no conclusion of a peace treaty with Sparta was in sight at the time of performance (425 and 411 BCE); consequently, the peace treaty that comes to pass on stage bears utopian, fantastic features. The starting situation is comparable in both comedies. The conclusion of a peace treaty is nowhere in sight: society—the Attic demos and its magistrates (*Acharnians*) or the entire male population of Greece (*Lysistrata*)—is either unwilling or unable to end the war, since that objective is being thwarted by certain groups of people who are profiting from a state of constant war. In response, one individual opts out of society, creating a private realm of peace for himself and his family in *Acharnians*. In *Lysistrata*, the women coerce the stubborn males into making peace by refusing to have sex with their spouses—hence this peace is not based on rational considerations but brought about by the sexual plight of the Greek men. As the sequence of events in *Lysistrata* shows, it is a prerequisite for the conclusion of peace that a domestic reconciliation must precede the settlement of foreign affairs; onstage, this takes the form of the two semi-choruses uniting. A balancing of interests and concord (*homonoia*) must prevail against egotism and the interests of particular groups, as the chorus of initiates stresses in the parabasis of *Frogs* (686ff., 718ff.). The song of the Spartan (*Lysistrata* 1247ff.) expresses the conviction that all Greeks must turn their minds back to the exploits of the Athenians and the Spartans in the Persian Wars near Cape Artemisium and Thermopylae if there is to be a chance for a lasting peace.

Alternative Worlds, The Fantastic, and Utopia: From the basic structure of Aristophanic comedy—a critical idea leads to the protagonist's remedying a bad state of affairs by executing a fantastic scheme—results the creation of a comic counterworld in juxtaposition with grotesquely distorted reality. Alternative worlds, in particular inversion or even destruction of the normal order (old—young, man—woman, human—animal, individual—society, outside—inside) belong without a doubt to the Dionysiac elements at the root of comedy. The Aristophanic comedies permit us to fathom how this Dionysiac substratum connects to other kinds of discourse. As a rule, political discourse determines a comedy's alternative world first and foremost, but there are additional elements, such as literature, philosophy, education, and music, which are themselves political in so far as they concern matters of the polis. This is especially clear in *Assemblywomen*: here, the Dionysiac inversion of the relationship between the sexes and the role reversal of men and women is combined with thoughts about an ideal form of government current at the time of production, thus resulting in a fully fledged utopian alternative to the prevailing situation. The strenuous provocation inherent in the harsh criticism of male rule in the first part of the comedy is resolved ironically in the second part when the results of communistic female rule are presented on stage. Theory fails in practice; it is thwarted by the egotism of the very people for whose benefit it was invented. In translating a political program into comic action, Aristophanes proceeds in the same manner as when he translates abstract concepts into comic images: the program's results for those concerned are put to the test within the play itself. What remains is perhaps an irritation, one that could lead the spectator to reflect on the comparison of the ironic resolution and the well-intentioned program with its legitimate criticism.

Mockery (ὀνομαστὶ κωμῳδεῖν): An essential element that sets Old Comedy apart from comedy of later periods is the mockery by name of famous personages from the realms of politics and the arts, sciences, and literature. In the motley group of people thus ridiculed, we find the tragedians Euripides and Agathon, the mathematician Meton and the philosopher Socrates, the poet of dithyrambs Cinesias, and politicians like Pericles, Cleon, and Hyperbolus. Mockery can be restricted to a single verse, as a surprising jibe, or shape the plot and structure of an entire play: in *Knights*, the demagogue Cleon stands at the center of the action; in *Clouds*, the philosopher Socrates; in *Women at the Thesmophoria*, the tragic poet Euripides. But also in instances where no single person stands at the center, the poet wraps his play, as it were, in a net of mocking remarks that reinforce the critical idea and the comic subject; just as Aristophanes is fond of translating abstract concepts into images on stage, he ties general themes that shape the play to characters, thereby making them conspicuous and intelligible, as the prologue of *Acharnians* demonstrates.

The two spheres that are introduced at the beginning of *Acharnians* and within which the play moves—on the one hand, the theatrical and Dionysiac sphere, and on the other, politics—are represented from the start by, among other things, people. Some of these are only mentioned, while others appear onstage. By means of these figures, and above all by means of the ridicule to which they are exposed, the play's critical idea—no one is looking after the well-being of the polis and peace (26f.)—is clarified and shown to be legitimate. On the other hand, the poet also uses the people mentioned to open the comic theme up to other, closely connected areas. Personal mockery, especially the mocking songs addressed directly to the audience, therefore serves as a bridge between the fantastical action of the play and the real situation in the year of performance.

From the outset, Dicaeopolis sketches the central themes by means of the individuals mentioned and mocked: comedy and politics (Cleon), assuming verses 5–8 allude to a scene in *Babylonians*; old-fashioned tragedy (Aeschylus) as well as its contemporary form (Theognis); good and bad music (13–17: Moschus, Dexitheus, Chaeris). The poetological level is resumed in the extended scene with Euripides (392ff.): whereas in Dicaeopolis's monologue the contrast between old and modern tragedy was only hinted at in the names of Aeschylus and Theognis, in verses 392ff. Euripidean tragedy, as the main representative of the modern tragic form, is subjected to parodic scrutiny. The mention of Cleon paves the way for the "autobiographical" level, in the construction of the poetic "I." This is resumed in the speech on the butcher's block, in which the protagonist's persona merges with the poet's (502), and culminates in the chorus's praise of the poet in the *parabasis* (628–664). Dicaeopolis's reproach of the Athenian magistrates and the demos itself, that nobody is speaking up for peace (25f.), is immediately shown to be legitimate: Amphitheus, who alone has been authorized by the gods to conclude a peace treaty with the Spartans, is just as unable to get a hearing in the Assembly as is Dicaeopolis, who therefore sides with him (45–64). The reason why the peace effort is leading nowhere in the Assembly is then demonstrated in two scenes featuring embassies (65–125, Persian; 134–173, Thracian): the ambassadors are greedy frauds, who were living it up in foreign parts while the common man was barely getting by, doing military service as a rower for the benefit of the city (162f.). Thus Aristophanes sets up the contrast between egotistical magistrates and simple, patriotic citizens, which he later translates into stage action in the conflict between Dicaeopolis and the general Lamachus (594–619).

The two embassy scenes are constructed along the same lines as the sycophant scenes in the second part (817–835 and 908–958): first, an anonymous representative of each group makes his appearance, then two historical figures, Theorus and Nicarchus.[13] Theorus, however, like Lamachus later, is brought on stage for the sake of his speaking name (*theoros*, "leader of an embassy") and it makes no difference whether he in fact headed the Athenian delegation to Thrace. Thus, the deplorable state of affairs is first sketched in general terms and then brought into clearer focus by an identifiable character who serves as a representative of the whole group. The same holds true for the mocking remarks against Cleonymus (88), Cleisthenes (118), and Straton (122), which are uttered in passing in the scene with the Persian embassy. These are not merely disconnected jibes against famous Athenians without any relevance to the plot; rather, they pave the way for the central conflict between upright and able-bodied ordinary citizens and parasitic magistrates. Aristophanes depicts all three men as cowardly and effeminate in his comedies[14] —the exact opposite of good citizens like Dicaeopolis.

The treatment of Theorus, who is pilloried, on account of his speaking name, as a representative for a whole class of individuals who are abusing their privileges as ambassadors, is similar to that of Lamachus later in the play. The latter's speaking name, "the mighty warrior," makes him an ideal candidate to represent the faction that favors war and all those embarked on a military career. At the same time that Lamachus represents the group that supports the war (cf. v. 297, the plural Λάμαχοι) and profits from it, he

---

[13] Theorus serves as target of Aristophanes's jibes until *Wasps* (422 BCE). He is placed within Cleon's sphere of influence and reputed to have curried favor with the demos and the magistrates (Olson 2002: 114). Nothing is known about Nicarchus.

[14] Cleonymus is mocked as somebody who "threw away his shield," i.e., a cowardly deserter; Cleisthenes and Straton as beardless, i.e., effeminate; cf. Olson 2002: 100, 109, 111.

is also mocked as an individual, since he himself played a not inconsiderable part in the Athenian wars. Similar to the practice of tragic poets, who in choral lyric and *stasima* use mythical paradigms as well-known exempla to illustrate the current situation, comic poets provide an example of the abstract in the form of a historical personage.

In focusing his ridicule on the rich, the aristocrats, and the *dynamenoi*, which is to say those in power and those with certain faculties that set them apart from the general mass of the population, Aristophanes is in agreement with the Old Oligarch ([Xen.] *Ath.* 2. 18). Social status and occupation are the principal elements that elicit ridicule, as the ones for which a given person finds himself in the spotlight of public notice. Politicians, for example, are corrupt, avaricious, ambitious, ruthless, uneducated and so forth. As for any additional elements that might contribute to an impression of "individual" mockery—often, certain physical oddities or behavioral quirks or public transgressions—it is no longer possible to ascertain whether they are historically accurate or not; in providing explanations for such details, the scholiasts appear all too often to draw their knowledge from the comic texts themselves. Still, it is hard to imagine that these features were made up from whole cloth; rather, they must have had some basis *in persona* or *in re* that—in keeping with the technique of Old Comedy—was grotesquely enhanced for humorous effect. It stands to reason, for instance, that many Athenians did not always comport themselves in an exemplary heroic manner on the battlefield. But if a man happened to be named Cleonymus ("renowned for heroic glory") and his breach in behavior, even if it occurred only once, was diametrically opposed to the Homeric concept of *kleos*, he would inevitably become a target of comic ridicule.

The characters that are made fun of have a semantic function within the context of the play that is closely connected to the play's critical idea and comic theme. This semantic function, however, is in no way incompatible with a play's satiric promotion of a kind of social hygiene, since such mockery provides a harmless outlet to vent any latent aggression against all those who stand out from the crowd (as described by the Old Oligarch).

Parody: Mockery is not restricted to public figures or types within Athenian society; rather, anything that appears grand, or seeks to appear grand, can be targeted. Thus, Aristophanes pokes fun at prayers and hymns in the same way as he does at the grand literary genres, especially tragedy (Rau 1967) and choral lyric (Zimmermann 1997). Above all, the parodic-critical treatment of the sister genre tragedy—the term *paratragoidia* occurs in Strattis (K-A fr. 50)—pervades Aristophanes's oeuvre from *Acharnians* in 425 BCE to *Frogs* in 405 BCE. The poet approaches the subject from a variety of angles: on the one hand, he investigates tragedy from a political point of view, especially its didactic function in the Athenian community (thus in *Frogs*), and on the other from a poetological perspective. In the parody of Euripides in *Acharnians* (393ff.), for example, Aristophanes finds fault with the lack of decorum displayed by such "heroes in rags" as Telephus. In *Women at the Thesmophoria*, he subjects the tragic pattern involving *anagnorisis* and intrigue that is so prevalent in Euripides's late plays to a critical-parodic analysis. In particular, he ridicules Euripides's typical monodies. In *Women at the Thesmophoria* and *Frogs*, parody serves to expose the peculiar characteristics of Euripidean monody, such as its great metrical variety, its musical mannerisms like coloratura and falsetto arias, and its daring verbal imagery. Above all, however, Aristophanes points out the literary risk inherent in these bold compositions: because the grand lyrical form is often used to describe matters that are essentially banal, pathos can be turned into comedy with little effort.

Staged Metaphors: In *Clouds* as in *Wasps*, the chorus exemplifies a typical technique of Aristophanic comedy, the translation of abstract concepts into staged metaphors, turning complex ideas into action and thereby making them more prominent and directly intelligible (Newiger 1957). Thus the Clouds serve as a visible embodiment of the nebulous, unstable, intangible nature of rhetoric and philosophy, which one cannot get a firm hold of. Likewise, Socrates's suspended position in the floating basket (*Clouds* 218) symbolizes the philosophers' remove from the real world and the laziness of intellectuals (*Clouds* 316, 332, 334). The chorus's identity as wasps in that play gives physical form to the belligerent and irritable disposition of the Athenian Heliasts. In *Knights*, Aristophanes continually moves back and forth between the foreground meaning of the stage action—the unpleasant situation in the house of Master Demos, where a new domestic slave is asserting his dominance—and the background meaning that regularly shines through—the political organization of democracy in Athens, where demagogues are lording it over the demos. Private and political spheres are clearly brought into relation to each other by means of several clusters of metaphors. The interlacing of different semantic domains to create a stageable symbol of an abstract idea is especially clear in *Acharnians*; here, Dicaeopolis's private peace is distilled into the *spondai* of peace—the libations of wine that are offered at the conclusion of a peace treaty. Like wine, peace can have a certain age, meaning a certain duration, and the older it is, meaning the longer it lasts, the better.

Irony: Dramatic irony, the phenomenon whereby a character's utterances or behavior acquire an additional meaning that runs counter to the speaker's intentions in the ears of the spectators because they possess more information than the *dramatis personae*, is absent from Aristophanic comedy. But it is possible to speak of a special type of dramatic irony in the case of Aristophanes's comedies, which arises when the splendid result that has been reached at the end of the comedy, the triumphant execution of the protagonist's scheme, turns slightly bitter and becomes ambiguous because it is treated ironically or extended *ad absurdum*.

Birds of 415 BCE furnishes a good example. While the protagonist Peisetaerus succeeds in establishing an empire over gods and men, having dethroned Zeus and married Basileia, the divine guarantrix of his power, in the course of the play Aristophanes time and again intersperses quiet notes of doubt to call the hero's imminent triumph into question. For instance, at the end of the play he takes up again the aristocratic-oligarchic theme that he first raised at the beginning of the drama through the word *apragmon* (44), which encapsulates the detachment of the aristocrats who are keeping their distance from the city's bustle, and by calling his protagonist Peisetaerus ("he who persuades the *hetairoi*," the members of an aristocratic-oligarchic club). For in the *exodos* the comic hero sets himself up as tyrant of the birds—in front of an audience that in the year of production was consumed by a manic fear of an oligarchic coup or attempt at tyranny (Thuc. 6. 53). Above all, Peisetaerus's behavior in the final scene directly offends against the spectators' religious sensibilities. The aspiration to become like Zeus, not to mention the desire to marry a goddess, amounts to blasphemy, and mythology is full of examples of blasphemers who paid a high price for such hubris. Accordingly, Aristophanes leaves it up to the spectators to think beyond the conclusion of the comedy and to discover the darker layers of meaning behind the glittering surface.

Aristophanes was also familiar with the presentation of ironic actions, very much in keeping with the definition of later philosophical theories as we find them in Aristotle's *Nicomachean Ethics* and Theophrastus's *Characters* or in rhetorical works: "The *eiron*," according to Aristotle's definition (*Nicomachean Ethics* 1127ᵃ22f.), is a person who denies existing things or makes them seem less," while the *alazon* pretends to possess something that in fact he does not. In Latin terminology, the latter *simulat*, "pretends as if," while the former *dissimulat*, "pretends as if not." The character type of the *eiron* can be seen in *Knights*, when the old Master Demos, at what amounts to the play's reversal, reveals that his doltish behavior to this point has been a tactical deception: he was permitting his demagogical slaves to take advantage of him for the ultimate purpose of using the politicians to his own ends (1111–1150). Consequently, the old master simultaneously pulls the wool over the eyes of the chorus, the demagogues, and the spectators by pretending to be naive when he is not. In *Clouds*, the chorus puts on a similar act. Only after Strepsiades's scheme to rid himself of his creditors by means of dialectics and rhetoric has failed miserably does the chorus reveal its true nature (1458–1461). The old man, along with Socrates and the audience, was wrong about the nature of the Clouds.

Aprosdoketa: Another source of comedy is the frequent disappointment of the spectators' expectations in the form of an *aprosdoketon*, regarding word choice and musical form, plot structure and stagecraft. Verbal *aprosdoketa* often take the form of obscene disruptions of a grandly emotional context, e.g., in *Women at the Thesmophoria* 39–62, when Euripides's kinsman keeps dropping crude remarks that interrupt the domestic slave of the tragic poet Agathon while he is announcing his master's epiphany in tragic-bombastic style. Structural *aprosdoketa* occur when the poet deliberately breaks symmetries in comedy's typical structural elements or employs a stock element, but does not follow up with the consequences for the plot that this element leads one to expect. One can speak of dramaturgical *aprosdoketa* when a play's title elicits certain expectations in the audience that are subsequently disappointed, or poses a riddle that is resolved in the course of the action. The former is the case in *Frogs*. The title virtually compels the spectators to place the drama in the tradition of animal choruses, but that expectation is flatly disappointed, since in fact the play's main chorus is made up of initiates, while the secondary chorus of frogs (209–268) may not even have been visible. The second alternative can be observed in *Clouds*: although the title's plural form alerts the spectators to the chorus's identity, its function develops gradually until its true nature is revealed in the play's final stages (1454–1461).

Slapstick: Besides these rather intellectual sources of comedy, which spring from the dramaturgy and conception of the play, we must not forget slapstick and simple jokes. Aristophanes frequently alludes to his rivals' attempts to get a laugh out of his audience in this unsophisticated manner, a method he brands as unworthy of the art of comedy but then resorts to himself, perhaps with a wink of the eye, as in *Clouds*. In this play's *parabasis* (*Clouds* 537–543), he heaps scorn on vulgar costumes and obscene dances, trite jokes about physical ailments, old people beating somebody up, slapstick, and superfluous shouting, only to bring these very modes of entertainment on stage in the play's closing scene (1490, 1493). Through a sort of comic *praeteritio* in the prologue of *Frogs*, he has Dionysus and his slave Xanthias enumerate all the base jokes he rejects (1–11); in *Peace*, he sneers at his rivals' gluttonous Heracles (741), but in *Birds* he brings the hero on stage in precisely this role (1565–1693). Just like the Athenian audience, which was a mixture of people from all social strata, Aristophanes's comedies offer a variety of different types of humor corresponding to the taste of the individual groups.

8. THE POETICS OF ARISTOPHANIC COMEDY

Competitive dialogue, a typical feature of Old Comedy (Biles 2011), resulted in a need for the poets to define their art in ever new ways, by pointing out the merits of their own and the shortcomings of their rivals' comedies. Time and again Aristophanes uses a play's *parabasis* to reflect on what a comedy should look like if it is going to be of high quality and still please the audience, and what an audience must be like to be able to judge a play's quality. In brief, we can glean from the comedies the following poetics and model of interactions between poet and audience. While all comic poets are under constant pressure to offer their audience something new (*Clouds* 547, *Wasps* 1044), Aristophanes sets a specific target for himself in one stratum of the population: those of good taste (*Peace* 739–751, *Frogs* 1–34) and moderation (*Clouds* 537, *Wasps* 1023–1028). He exudes confidence in laying claim to the epithet "sophisticated" for his own comic art (*Peace* 750; *Frogs* 901, 906) and proudly emphasizes that a good comedy should rely exclusively on its literary quality (*Peace* 749f.). A play that conforms to such high standards can only be successful, however, if the spectators who receive it share the poet's criteria for quality and are themselves as intelligent (*sophos*) and clever (*dexios*) as the poet and his work (*Clouds* 518–532, *Wasps* 1051–1059). If this is not the case, even the very best poet producing the very best comedy might suffer catastrophe, as happened to Aristophanes with *Clouds*.

In addition to these literary qualities to which the poet lays claim, there is the didactic and enlightening function of his comedies, as the chorus points out already in the *parabasis* of *Acharnians* (628ff.). Aristophanes ennobles his comic art by claiming for it a function he takes for granted for tragedy: to know what is right (*Acharnians* 500, *Frogs* 1054f.). The neologism *trygoidia* (*Acharnians* 499f.) stresses the juxtaposition with the sister genre, and Aristophanes repeats this claim with ever new variations of the neologism (*Acharnians* 886; *Wasps* 650, 1537, fr. 347). In the parodos of *Frogs*, he puts into the mouth of the chorus of initiates a related definition for the function of comedy: mixing jokes and seriousness, humor and playfulness, with the goal of saying what is right in a humorous way (386–395, 399–410). The initiates honor this announcement in the *parabasis* with their mocking call to internal concord (686–705, 718–737). This motto of Aristophanic art was sounded already in the parabasis of *Peace* (764): "giving little offence and much joy and providing everything demanded by the situation."

The comparison and even rivalry with tragedy that is implied by the neologism *trygoidia* of necessity led to the paradox that Cratinus expressed in his bon mot, *euripidaristophanizon* (K-A fr. 342). With this coinage, Cratinus imagines a spectator asking how Aristophanes's criticism of Euripidean tragedy, and especially its sophistic tenor, can be reconciled with the fact that he simultaneously integrates elements of this kind into his own plays. How do the subtle jingling of words and delight in polished aphorisms fit with the harsh censure that Aristophanes directs at the tragedian? This is a paradox to which all authors who work in a polyphonous genre like comedy find themselves exposed, because they draw comic potential in no small measure from the parody of "serious" genres. With a perspicacity that would do credit to any literary critic, Aristophanes on the one hand recognizes the latent, albeit unwitting, comic potential of, for example, the musical mannerisms of a Euripides or Agathon, but on the other hand does not ignore the attractiveness of the musical achievements of his own period, which however, in terms of propriety, are out of place in the Dionysiac sister genres although they suit comedy.

By combining the descriptions of the three comic poets Magnes, Cratinus, and Crates that Aristophanes offers in his short history of Attic comedy (*Knights* 520–540), we can assemble the ideal form of comedy, against which Aristophanes hoped to be measured. This includes musical variety and boldly mimetic strokes in music and song, as well as rich imagination in the identity and costuming of the chorus, for which Magnes serves as paradigm (520–525). Paired with this ideal is a "Dionysiac elemental force" in the lyric sections (526–530), which was the mark of the young Cratinus. Most important, however, are the sophisticated ideas of a Crates (539), which were staged without much ado and with sober intelligence (537–540). Since none of the three poets remained a success throughout their careers in spite of the merits he could boast in a particular area, it follows that a good and successful poet must combine the characteristics of all three paradigms. Aristophanes obviously prizes most of all the qualities he ascribes to Crates again and again he comes back to the sophistication of his ideas, which set him apart from the inept jests of his rivals (*Clouds* 547ff., *Peace* 734ff., *Frogs* 1ff.)—ideas that well befit a city like Athens.

FURTHER READING

An online bibliography for Aristophanes, compiled by N. Holzberg, is available at http://www.klassphil.uni-muenchen.de/extras/downloads/index.html (accessed October 9, 2012).

Halliwell, S. 2008. *Greek Laughter: A Study of Cultural Psychology from Homer to Early Christianity*, Cambridge, UK: Cambridge University Press.

Henderson, J. 1991. *The Maculate Muse: Obscene Language in Attic Comedy*. 2nd ed. New York and Oxford: Oxford University Press.

Holzberg, N. 2010. *Aristophanes: Sex und Spott und Politik*. Munich: Beck.

Olson, S. D. 2007. *Broken Laughter: Select Fragments of Greek Comedy*. Oxford: Oxford University Press.

Robson, J. 2009. *Aristophanes: An Introduction*. London: Duckworth.

Sommerstein, A. H. 2009. *Talking about Laughter and Other Studies on Greek Comedy*. Oxford: Oxford University Press.

Zimmermann, B. 2006. *Die griechische Komödie*. Frankfurt: Verlag Antike.

——. 2011. *Handbuch der griechischen Literatur*. Vol. 1, *Die Literatur der archaischen und klassischen Zeit*. Munich: Beck. See 671–800.

Bibliography

Beta, S. 2007. "Giocare con le parole." In *Diafonie: Esercizi sul comico: Atti del seminario di studi, Venezia, 25 maggio 2006*, edited by A. Camerotto, 13–44. Padua: Sargon.

Biles, Z. 2011. *Aristophanes and the Poetics of Competition*. Cambridge: Cambridge University Press.

Colvin, S. 1999. *Dialect in Aristophanes: The Politics of Language in Ancient Greek Literature*. Oxford: Clarendon Press.

Dover, K. J. 1972. *Aristophanic Comedy*. Berkeley: University of California Press.

——. 1987. *Greek and the Greeks*. Vol. I, *Language, Poetry, Drama*. Oxford and New York: Blackwell.

——. 1993) *Aristophanes, Frogs*. Oxford: Clarendon Press.

Fisher, N. R. E. 1993. "Multiple Personalities and Dionysiac Festivals: Dicaeopolis in Aristophanes' *Acharnians*." *G&R* 40: 31–47.

Gelzer, T. 1960. *Der epirrhematische Agon bei Aristophanes: Untersuchungen zur Struktur der attischen Alten Komödie*. Munich: Beck.

Heath, M. 1990. "Aristophanes and His Rivals." *G&R* 37: 143–158.

Hubbard, T. K. 1991. *The Mask of Comedy: Aristophanes and the Intertextual Parabasis*. Ithaca: Cornell University Press.

Koch, K. D. 1968. *Kritische Idee und Komisches Thema: Untersuchungen zur Dramaturgie und zum Ethos der Aristophanischen Komödie*. 2nd ed. Bremen: Friedrich Röver.

Newiger, H.-J. 1957. *Metapher und Allegorie: Studien zu Aristophanes*. Munich: Beck.

Olson, S. D. 2002. *Aristophanes, Acharnians*. Oxford: Oxford University Press.

——. 1992. "Names and Naming in Aristophanic Comedy." *CQ* 42: 304–319.

Parker, L. P. E. 1997. *The Songs of Aristophanes*. Oxford: Clarendon Press.

Peppler, C. W. 1910. "The Termination -κός as Used by Aristophanes for Comic Effect." *AJPh* 31: 428–444.

——. 1916. "The Suffix -μα in Aristophanes." *AJPh* 37: 459–465.

Rau, P. 1967. *Paratragodia: Untersuchungen einer komischen Form des Aristophanes*. Munich: Beck.

Rogers, B. B. 1910. *The Acharnians of Aristophanes*. London: G. Bell.

Sifakis, G. M. 1971. *Parabasis and Animal Choruses: A Contribution to the History of Attic Comedy*. London: Athlone Press.

Silk, M. 2000. *Aristophanes and the Definition of Comedy*. Oxford: Oxford University Press.

Totaro, P. 2000. *Le seconde parabasi di Aristofane.* 2nd ed. Stuttgart: Metzler.

Whitman, C. H. 1964. *Aristophanes and the Comic Hero.* Cambridge, MA: Harvard University Press.

Willi, A. 2002. "Languages on Stage: Aristophanic Language, Cultural History, and the Athenian Identity." In *The Language of Greek Comedy*, edited by A. Willi, 111–168. Oxford and New York: Oxford University Press.

———. 2003. *The Languages of Aristophanes: Aspects of Linguistic Variation in Classical Attic Greek.* Oxford and New York: Oxford University Press.

Zimmermann, B. 1985a. *Untersuchungen zur Form und dramatischen Technik der Aristophanischen Komödien.* Vol. 1: *Parodos und Amoibaion.* 2nd ed. Königstein im Taunus, Germany: A. Hain. (2nd ed.);

———. 1985b. *Untersuchungen zur Form und dramatischen Technik der Aristophanischen Komödien.* Vol. 2: *Die anderen lyrischen Partien.* 2nd ed. Königstein im Taunus, Germany: A. Hain.

———. 1997. "Parodie dithyrambischer Dichtung in den Komödien des Aristophanes." In *Aristophane: La langue, la scène, la cité: Actes du Colloque de Toulouse, 17–19 mars 1994,* edited by P. Thiercy and M. Menu, 87–93. Bari: Levante.

CHAPTER 7

COMEDY IN THE FOURTH CENTURY I: MYTHOLOGICAL BURLESQUES

IOANNIS M. KONSTANTAKOS

Genre and Background

As Boileau once remarked (*Art poétique* 3.337), the Greeks were natural-born mockers. Even their own mythical tradition, the exalted world of their gods and heroes, could not escape their derisive attitude. Humorous tales about mythical figures are an exceedingly old phenomenon in Greek culture, occurring already in the Homeric poems. One of the best examples is Hera's deception of Zeus (*Iliad* 14.153–351), a domestic comedy of notably light tone, with Hera as a luscious hypocrite, full of cunning and pretended squeamishness, and Zeus as a gullible Don Juan, bragging about his erotic conquests. In other scenes of the *Iliad*, where the Olympian gods fight against each other in the battlefield ("theomachy": 21.385–433, 470–513, cf. 5.311–430), the divine figures are caricatured and their brawls involve slapstick and physical knockabout. Demodocus's delicious song in the *Odyssey* (8.266–366) narrates a saucy adultery novella involving a love triangle of divine characters: Aphrodite is the lubricious unfaithful wife, Ares the swashbuckling lover, and Hephaestus the embittered but crafty cuckolded husband. The Homeric *Hymn to Hermes* features the god as an infant trickster and includes scenes of amusing roguishness and broad humor.

This kind of comic mythical tale must have been inherited from pre-Homeric poetic traditions, perhaps from jesting songs performed for entertainment at merry banquets, or even from cult hymns destined for festive ceremonies. It seems to have deep roots in the human psyche and is probably a manifestation of a lively folk religiosity, that impulsive sense of familiarity with the godhead that characterized the common man of archaic times. For the early Greek, laughter and comic play were an integral part of his worldview, admissible even in connection to the loftiest matters. These elements also formed an essential constituent of popular religious festivals, which accommodated moments of merriment and ridicule. In the context of the festive occasion, laughing at the gods and their myths was not a sign of irreverence but contributed to the joy of the celebration and thus became itself, paradoxically, a form of offering to the gods (see Scullion, chapter 16, this volume). In the same spirit, comedies caricaturing gods and myths were performed as part of religious festivals in fifth-century Athens, in the sacred precinct of a god (Dionysus) and in the priests' presence. Analogous phenomena are also found in other ancient cultures. Hittite mythical narratives, such as the *Disappearance of Telipinu* and the songs of Kumarbi and Ullikummi, contain scenes of slapstick, grotesque humor, and sexual pranks. Sexual ribaldry and coarse jokes permeate the gods' adventures in the Egyptian *Contendings of Horus and Seth* (from a New Kingdom papyrus). Even in modern popular traditions, especially among Mediterranean peoples, there are comparable stories that present Christ or the Saints involved in funny incidents or tricked by crafty humans.[1]

In the Athenian comic theater, this age-old popular tendency fueled an entire subgenre of plays, usually termed "mythological burlesque" or "mythological travesty" and consisting in full-scale burlesque of traditional stories about gods or heroes. The heyday of this genre seems to have started around 400 BCE and lasted until the 340s (see Nesselrath 1990: 189–204; Hunter 1983: 23–24). This chronological frame is deduced from the distribution of mythological plays among the successive generations of comic poets that held the stage during the fourth century. Poets who were active from the early decades until about the middle of the century or not long afterwards (Araros, Philetaerus, Eubulus, Anaxandrides, Ephippus) produced a great number of mythological burlesques (amounting to a third or even half of their known output). For poets starting their career after the middle of the century (Amphis, Anaxilas, Timocles, Theophilus), the proportion of such plays is much smaller (a quarter or a sixth of their output). The poets of New Comedy (after ca. 330) presented few mythological dramas; apparently, the genre rapidly declined and became extinct in the last decades of the fourth century. Accordingly, dramatists with an exceptionally long career, such as Antiphanes and Alexis, whose activity began in the earlier part of the century but extended deep into the New Comedy period, have considerably lower ratios of mythological burlesques than their less long-lived contemporaries (a quarter of the total known plays for Antiphanes, active from the 380s to the 310s; a sixth or a seventh for Alexis, active ca. 350–270). It thus seems that these two dramatists gave up mythological plays in the later part of their careers. On the other hand, some of the contemporaries or younger contemporaries of Aristophanes (Plato Comicus, Alcaeus, Diocles, Nicochares,

---

[1] On the Homeric burlesques of gods, see Friedländer 1934; Reinhardt 1960: 23–27; Burkert 1960; Zervou 1990 with further bibliography; Muth 1992: 1–71. For the Hittite myths, see Riemschneider 1954: 114–121; Hoffner 1998: 14–20, 42–44, 55–61; for the Egyptian tale, Simpson 2003: 91–103; cf. the Old Norse *Loki's Quarrel* (from the *Poetic Edda*), which resembles the Homeric theomachies with its boisterous slapstick and colorful exchanges of insults. On medieval and modern traditions, see Moessner 1907: 157–166; Zervou 1990: 177, 205–206.

Nicophon, Philyllius, Strattis, Theopompus), whose activity spanned the first decades of the fourth century, also staged a significant number of mythological burlesques. It is plausible to suppose that the majority belong to the later part of those poets' careers, around or after ca. 400 BCE, when the mythological genre was coming into vogue. Aristophanes's own last plays (*Cocalus* and *Aeolosicon*, performed in the 380s) were also travesties of myth. The wide popularity of this kind of drama in the early fourth century is indicated by a didascalic notice, preserved in an ancient hypothesis of Aristophanes's *Wealth* and recording the program of the festival at which this latter play was performed in 388 BCE. Aristophanes's comedy competed with Nicochares's *Lacones*, Aristomenes's *Admetus*, Nicophon's *Adonis* and Alcaeus's *Pasiphaë*. To judge by the titles, three out of the five comedies of the festival were mythological burlesques. The grand era of mythological travesty was in full bloom, and the genre unfailingly entertained Athenian audiences for six decades.

Unfortunately, no Greek play of this kind has survived intact. Nonetheless, a large number of textual fragments (mostly from the indirect tradition) testify to the great inventiveness and verve of fourth-century myth burlesque. Plautus's *Amphitruo*, the only known specimen of mythological comedy in ancient Rome, is also usually considered as based on a Greek comic play of the fourth century (see Christenson 2000: 50–55; Konstantakos 2002: 158, with further bibliography); it shares with the Greek fragments a number of comic procedures for caricaturing myth (cf. Hunter 1987). The textual remains are supplemented by numerous vase paintings that depict scenes from comic plays on mythical themes. These vases originate chiefly from South Italy and were formerly thought to illustrate a local Italiote popular farce, the *phlyakes*. Recent research, however, has proved that they depict South Italian performances of Attic comedies, or at most, local dramas heavily influenced by the Attic theater.[2] They thus furnish useful information about Athenian comedy and its subject matter. With the help of these remnants, it is possible both to form a fair picture of mythological burlesque and to reconstruct its basic conventions and techniques.

COMIC ANTECEDENTS

The idea of making comic plays out of mythical material did not arise suddenly in early-fourth-century Athens. The immediate antecedents of the genre can be found in fifth-century "Old Comedy." Various plays of Aristophanes feature gods or mythical heroes involved in funny, undignified situations or characterized by low and ridiculous human failings. Dionysus appears cowardly and faint-hearted, to the point of soiling himself (*Frogs*); Heracles is an inveterate glutton and a thick-headed bully (*Birds*), and

---

[2] See Csapo 1986; Taplin 1993; Green 1994: 46–47, 65–67, 70–71; Green 1995: 143–146; and Csapo, chapter 2 in this volume.

Hermes a self-interested fawner and jack of all trades (*Wealth*). This kind of comic "degradation" is the essence of every mythical travesty through the ages, from the Homeric poems to the burlesques of Lucian. The world of myth is reduced to the level of ordinary life; the lofty gods and heroes are presented like common mortals, with all the base flaws familiar from everyday experience.

Another comic process of Aristophanic travesty is also of interest. The mythical figures are drawn into the life and society of fifth-century Athens, which provide the material of the plot. They associate with common Athenians or famous celebrities of the time that appear as characters, and display knowledge of the affairs of contemporary Athens. Dionysus in the *Frogs* is an expert on Athenian theater, consorts with its major dramatists, and reads their works; he has also embarked in an Athenian warship and discusses the political affairs of the city. Sometimes the gods and heroes themselves are fashioned in the likeness of known fifth-century character types. Poseidon in the *Birds* (1565–1692) is portrayed as a pompous Athenian aristocrat, with his distinctive snobbery and indignation against democratic procedures. Tereus, the mythical king of Thrace, who appears in the same play transformed into a hoopoe, as told in myth, retains certain habits of an Athenian petty bourgeois: he keeps a bird-slave for menial tasks and has a taste for small fry from Phalerum and pea-soup—the favorite fare of the Attic populace (70–79). Such traits foreshadow the technique of "Atticization," the assimilation of mythical figures to ordinary Athenian folk of the poet's own time, which becomes a staple constituent of fourth-century burlesques. While mythical travesty has not yet taken over the central themes of Aristophanic plays—the mythical figures are involved in an invented plot of fantasy and satire of contemporary society—nevertheless, it is a relatively short distance to the fourth-century genre: once the travestied gods and heroes dominate the entire plot and comically enact their own traditional stories, a full-scale mythological burlesque emerges.

Parody of tragedy, a seminal technique in fifth-century comic dramaturgy, may also have been a source of inspiration for the later mythical travesties (see Hanink chapter 12, this volume). Sizable episodes in Aristophanes's plays reproduce and ridicule scenes from tragic dramas (especially by Euripides), bringing them down to a domestic or trivial context. The comic poet takes over the solemn tragic situation, with its lofty tone and grave events, and transfers it to everyday or laughable circumstances. For example, in the parody of Euripides's *Helen* in the *Women at the Thesmophoria* (850–922), Euripides and his old kinsman act the parts of Menelaus and Helen, the mythical couple reuniting in Egypt, and make a collage from portions of various scenes of the Euripidean tragedy. But this tragic-mythical fiction collides with the Athenian reality of the surroundings. The tragic hero and heroine are incarnated in the persons of two elderly Athenians, one of them ludicrously disguised as a woman; the actual setting is not the exotic fairytale Egypt of Euripides's play but a shrine in contemporary Athens. Everyday comic realism invades the mythical world in the person of Critylla, a common Athenian lady left behind to guard Euripides's kinsman. She regularly interrupts the paratragic enunciations of the mock-heroic couple and interjects her own comments, in the low-brow parlance of comedy, by means of which she draws attention to the real, ordinary

circumstances of the scene. It is she who points out that the kinsman is not the mythical Helen, daughter of Tyndareus, but a nasty old villain; that the place of action is not
Proteus's palace but the Thesmophorion of Athens; and that she herself is not Theonoe,
the tragic prophetess, but a plain Athenian woman. The clash between the mythical and
the ordinary will be the core of later mythological burlesque and the main source of its
comic effect.

In the fourth century, mythological burlesques often draw inspiration from particular
tragedies, parodying their plots and episodes (e.g., Eubulus's *Antiope* and Antiphanes's
Aeolus, demonstrably based on Euripides's homonymous dramas). But even when no
tragic model is known and the comedy is evidently ridiculing the mythical story per se,
as generally known from oral tradition, the poet may again parody tragic motifs and
style in various sections of his play (see *adespota* K-A fr. 1062 below). Tragedy was par
excellence the dramatic genre based on myth; therefore, the comic playwright, when
treating a mythical story, felt an urge to imitate tragic conventions and modes, so as
to allude to the main literary receptacle of myth inter-generically and exploit its register of expression comically. In all these respects, fourth-century poets are the heirs of
fifth-century paratragedy.

In fact, full-scale mythological burlesque was already inaugurated in Old Comedy.
The towering figure in this field was Cratinus, who composed a series of mythological plays. Some of them (*Dionysalexander, Nemesis*) were political allegories, presenting
Athenian statesmen such as Pericles in the guise of mythical heroes and using the myths
to satirize contemporary political affairs (see Storey, chapter 4 pp. 100–103, this volume).
A more straightforward kind of comedy was the *Odysses* ("Odysseus and Company"), a
fairly close adaptation of the adventure with the Cyclops in *Odyssey* 9 that pokes fun at
epic diction and situations. A scene of this play displays in germ the comic method that
was subsequently to bloom in fourth-century mythological comedies. This is how the
Cyclops declares his intention to devour Odysseus and his sailors (K-A fr. 150):

> In return for this, I will seize all you trusty companions
> and fry you, stew you, broil you on the coals and roast you,
> and then dip you into pickle-sauce and vinegar-pickle and garlic-pickle
> moderately hot; and whoever of you seems to me
> nicely cooked, I shall nibble him up, dear soldiers.[3]   5

In the *Odyssey*, the Cyclops eats like a wild beast or a savage cannibal: he crushes
Odysseus's men on the ground, cuts them to pieces, and devours them raw (9.287–
298). In Cratinus, by contrast, he enumerates a variety of cooking methods and tasty
sauces, which he intends to apply to his victims. The sauces mentioned in v. 3 (ἅλμη,
ὀξάλμη and σκοροδάλμη, piquant dressings made of fish-broth and salt, with provisional addition of oil, vinegar, or garlic) were specially meant for fish (Olson and Sens
2000: 91, 185; Dalby 2003: 157, 291, 293–294). The cooking methods are also suitable to
fish courses: "broiling on the coals" (v. 2 κἀπανθρακίσας), for example, was a favorite

---

[3] All translations from the ancient Greek used in this chapter are mine.

method for preparing small fishes (called ἐπανθρακίδες, see, e.g., *Acharnians* 670, *Wasps* 1127). The Cyclops plans to cook and flavor Odysseus's companions like dainty courses of seafood. Significantly, fish was the favorite food of epicures and fine eaters in classical Attica. Polyphemus is depicted as a fifth-century Athenian gourmet, with a taste for seafood and detailed expertise in cuisine. This is not simply the debasement typical of every mythical travesty. The Homeric monster is not only degraded to the level of ordinary men, becoming a gourmand with all too human qualities; he is more specifically transformed into a figure from the poet's contemporary Athenian milieu. Similarly, in another fragment (146: "I have never yet drunk nor shall I drink such a Maronian wine") the Cyclops speaks like a connoisseur of wines: his words suggest that he has wide experience in wine-tasting and can thus appreciate Odysseus's Maronian drink in comparison with the other vintages he has savored.[4]

Other fifth-century burlesques may have employed the same technique. In Callias's *Cyclopes* (434 BCE), the mythical monsters held a symposium, observing characteristic rituals of Athenian drinking-parties (K-A fr. 9), consuming fish (K-A fr. 6, 10) and playing *kottabos*, a favorite sympotic game in Athens (K-A fr. 12). Aristophanes's *Dramas* or *The Centaur* (before 422), which dramatized Heracles's visit to Pholus and his quarrel with the Centaurs, may also have presented the heroes in an Athenian-style symposium with dancing-girls (K-A fr. 287) and other elements of the fifth-century demimonde (brothels and tavern-keepers, K-A fr. 283, 285).[5] The dramatists of the following generations will take over and fully exploit these comic devices.

ATTICIZATION AND ANACHRONISM

In the fourth century, writers of mythological burlesques developed a series of interrelated techniques for constructing their stage world and producing comic effect. The fundamental process, already delineated above, can be termed "Atticization" or "urbanization": the mythical world is refashioned according to the model of the poet's contemporary Athenian society. Gods and heroes assume the traits of recognizable professional types or private men of fourth-century Athens and operate in a milieu that copies contemporary urban and domestic life.[6] Consider K-A fr. 140 from Alexis's *Linus*; according

---

[4] On Cratinus's *Odysses* (*Odysseus and Company*) and its presentation of the Cyclops, see especially Tanner 1915: 175–180; Phillips 1959: 63–64; Rosen 1995: 127–131; Mastromarco 1998: 34–40; Casolari 2003: 61–77, 149–150; and Storey chapter 4 in this volume. Nesselrath 1990: 236–240 argues that Cratinus's play was radically different from the fourth-century type of mythical burlesque because it contains no trace of "Atticization" of the myth. The fragments discussed above disprove this claim.

[5] On these plays, see Mastromarco 1998: 34, 38; Imperio 1998: 204–217; Casolari 2003: 150–153, 254–258.

[6] See Nesselrath 1990: 205–240, with many examples.

to Athenaeus, who transmits the text (4.164b–d), the personages involved are Linus and
his pupil Heracles:

> (Linus) So, come close
> and pick up from here any papyrus scroll you like;
> then you will read it; examine them carefully
> according to the labels, quietly and at your leisure.
> Orphic poems are in here, Hesiod, Greek tragedies,   5
> Choerilus, Homer, Epicharmus, prose writings
> of every kind. In this way you will show me what subject
> you are most inclined to by nature. (Heracles) I am picking this one.
> (Lin.) Show me first what it is. (Her.) A cookery book,
> according to the label. (Lin.) It is obvious that you are   10
> quite a philosopher, since you passed over so much literature
> and chose Simus's trade. (Her.) Who is this Simus?
> (Lin.) A very ingenious fellow. He has now turned
> to tragedy, and he is far and away the best cook
> among actors, according to the people who employ him,   15
> and the best actor among cooks.
>
>   *   *   *
>
> (Lin.) This fellow is bulimia personified! (Her.) Say what you like.
> I am hungry, this is for sure!

In myth, Linus was a wise musician and lyre-player, who taught the lyre to many
heroes (Orpheus, Musaeus, Thamyras, etc.); he also undertook the musical coaching
of Heracles, who proved to be an extremely difficult pupil. In Alexis's comedy, however,
Linus is presented as a teacher of letters (*grammatistes*)—the typical schoolmaster of
classical Athens, whose task consisted in teaching children to read and write and subsequently introducing them to the great works of literature. Appropriately, he possesses
a collection of papyrus scrolls (the standard book format of the time), covering all the
works that a fourth-century teacher might be expected to have (from Homer, Hesiod,
and classical tragedies to Orphic poems, the sayings attributed to Epicharmus, and sundry prose works). The mythical citharist has been transformed into a familiar figure
from the playwright's contemporary Athens. Heracles, for his part, is portrayed as a gluttonous boy, totally indifferent to intellectual pursuits and interested only in food. This
was the standard image of Heracles in all comic drama (Galinsky 1972: 81–100; Casolari
2003: 249–295). In Alexis, however, his traditional gluttony is again placed within the
specific context of fourth-century urbanity. Heracles picks up from among Linus's
books a manual of cookery or compilation of recipes (ὀψαρτυσία); writings of this kind,
in prose or verse, came into vogue in the fourth century and apparently enjoyed some
notoriety in Athenian society, as they are often mentioned in comedy (see Olson and
Sens 2000: xxviii–xliii; Dalby 2003: 97–98; and Telò's discussion of Philoxenus's cookbook in chapter 5 of this volume. Philoxenus's cookbook in Plato's *Phaon*).

The Simus of vv. 12–16 must have been a real-life personage of Alexis's time, possibly an actor who took an interest in cuisine. This jest points to another effective comic tool of Atticization, anachronism. The mythical characters gossip about celebrities and affairs of contemporary Athens as though they were themselves ordinary fourth-century folk. Contemporary reality thus makes its way into the mythical world. Similarly, in Anaxandrides's *Protesilaus* a slave of the eponymous hero describes a famous event of 386 BCE, the wedding of the general Iphicrates with the sister of the Thracian ruler Cotys (K-A fr. 42); and a character in Eubulus's *Antiope* sarcastically comments on the sexual habits of the politician Callistratus of Aphidna (K-A fr. 10). Occasionally, minor figures of the myth may be given ordinary Attic names. Eubulus's *Antiope*, a burlesque of Euripides's homonymous tragedy, included a character called Chariades (K-A fr. 10); he is possibly the herdsman who found and brought up Antiope's exposed infants, a key figure in Euripides's play, here christened with a common Athenian name (cf. Nesselrath 1990: 225).

Another variant of the same process is to invest mythical heroes with distinctive habits or customs of Attic culture. In Plato Comicus's *Zeus in Trouble* (*Zeus Kakoumenos*), Heracles, having put up at an inn or brothel, engages in a game of *kottabos* with a young girl who has caught his fancy (K-A fr. 46). He also converses with another character ("A."), the girl's master (perhaps a pimp or procuress):[7]

> (A.) . . . to play *kottabos*, until I prepare dinner inside
> for the two of you. (Her.) I am quite willing.
> But is there a bowl? (A.) No, you have to play in a mortar instead.
> (Her.) Fetch the mortar, bring water, set cups
> beside us. Let's play for kisses.   5
> (A.) I shall not let you play in an unworthy manner.
> I set as *kottabos* prizes for the two of you
> these platform shoes here that she is wearing
> and your goblet. (Her.) Wow! This contest that is coming up
> is bigger than the one at the Isthmian games.   10

Heracles evidently hopes to enjoy the girl's erotic ministrations, and this is why he is lured to stay and play. But character "A." has his eyes on the large and presumably valuable vessel (κότυλος) that Heracles is carrying with him, and sets the game up in order to relieve the hero of his precious possession. As a subsequent fragment shows (K-A fr. 47), Heracles was a clumsy player (uncouthness and gauche manners are typical features of his comic figure) and presumably lost his belongings in the game. The precise identity of the other two characters is unknown. They may have been mythical figures comically degraded to the lowest human level, but they could also be fictional

---

[7] The date of *Zeus in Trouble* (*Zeus Kakoumenos*) is uncertain (Pirrotta 2009: 124–125), but the play presents strong similarities to the mythological burlesques of the fourth century (Rosen 1995: 124–126).

personages, a common innkeeper or pimp and a servant-girl or prostitute, invented by the playwright. In that case, Heracles would be absorbed into the demimonde of classical Athens, enjoying the dolce vita of the poet's own society; compare Aristophanes's *Frogs* 549–578, where Heracles, on his way to the underworld, puts up at a common inn and brawls with its landladies. Similarly, in Antiphanes's *Birth of Aphrodite* the gods practice playing the *kottabos* (K-A fr. 57), and in his *Ganymede* a slave of Laomedon, the king of Troy, is fond of riddles (K-A fr. 75)—another popular game during Athenian symposia.

TREATMENT OF MYTHICAL WONDERS

Greek myths abound in magical elements, fabulous beings, and miraculous incidents wrought by the gods' superhuman powers. Faced with such material, the playwrights developed various strategies to accommodate it in the comic world. One strategy is manifested in the following fragment (*adespota* K-A fr. 1062), which survives on a papyrus, unfortunately without the name of the poet or the title of the play:

> "What do I care about your troubles?" one of you
> might say. But I shall quote that verse of Sophocles:
> "Alas, the evils I have suffered!" Old Cronus
> drinks up and gobbles all my children
> but hands me over no share at all.   5
> Instead, he grabs them in his hands, takes them off to Megara,
> sells whatever I have given birth to and spends the money on eating.
> For he is afraid of the oracle like. . .
> For Apollo once lent Cronus one drachma
> and did not get it back. So, fuming with anger,   10
> he no longer lent him anything of any value,
> neither household items nor money, by Zeus, but gave an oracle
> that Cronus would be expelled from kingship by a child of his own.
> This is why he is afraid and swallows all his children.

The speaker is clearly Rhea, Cronus's wife and mother of his divine children, and her exposition of the background of her situation doubtless belongs to the prologue of the play. The speech is a comic imitation of the narrative prologues of tragedy (a typically Euripidean mannerism), and Rhea parodies tragic quotations or style at several points (vv. 3, 9, 10). Although this comedy does not seem to have been based on a particular tragic drama (no tragedy on Cronus and the birth of his children is known), the poet makes his personage talk like a tragic heroine, thus intertextually alluding to the primary mythical genre.

The play dramatized the old myth about Cronus eating his offspring, but the "eating" of the divine children takes an unexpected metaphorical form here. Cronus does not really swallow his children but sells them as slaves in the market at Megara and spends the profits on food and drink (compare the Megarian man in Aristophanes's *Acharnians,* who sells his own daughters to acquire a little food). This comic idea rests on the idiomatic sense of the verbs ἐσθίειν and πίνειν used in the Greek text. In ancient Greek a man could be said to "eat" and "drink" (ἐσθίει and πίνει) his money or belongings, meaning that he squanders them on food and drink (see Konstantakos 2000: 80–81 for examples). Thus, the terrible child-devouring god is transformed into a spendthrift glutton and drunkard who surrenders himself to culinary pleasures and even sells his offspring so as to have enough means for his eating and drinking bouts. The mother-goddess Rhea plays the role of the wretched wife complaining of her prodigal husband. And the supernatural theophagy is replaced by a simple metaphor or idiom referring to a mundane situation (cf. Nesselrath 1995: 22–26).

This is one of the comic methods developed for dealing with the marvels of myth: the poet rationalizes and euhemerizes the marvelous elements, turning them into normal actions and explaining away their wondrous parameters as mere metaphors. Similarly, in Anaxandrides's *Tereus* (K-A fr. 46) the hero is not actually transformed into a bird, as in myth, but simply acquires the appellation ὄρνις ("bird," but also more specifically "cock") as a derisive nickname, because he received rough treatment from the women of his household (just as a cock may be beaten by hens, a fact proverbially known among the Greeks). The miraculous metamorphosis is reduced to a linguistic pun. In Eubulus's *Amaltheia,* the eponymous heroine was perhaps presented as an innkeeper keeping her profits in a large horn until Heracles, who was lodging at her inn, stole them and made a high living off them (see Hunter 1983: 89–90 and Casolari 2003: 288 for the testimonies). The fabulous goat and her magic horn of plenty are thus euhemerized and acclimatized to the milieu of domestic comedy.

The same strategy appears in a comic scene illustrated on an Apulian bell-crater of ca. 380–370 BCE (British Museum F 151, *PhV*² 37; see Figure 7.1). An old man, who apparently moves with difficulty, is shown assisted by two slaves in order to ascend some steps leading up to the stage-platform. One of the slaves stands on the platform and drags the old man up while the other pushes him from behind, bending forward and pressing his chest and hands on the old man's buttocks. An inscription indicates that the old man is Chiron the Centaur, here ludicrously transformed into an arthritic old dotard. The Centaur's monstrous appearance has been rationalized in a visual manner that would have afforded great amusement in the performance. Chiron is not half-man, half-horse; he has an ordinary human waist and legs. But as he is being pushed from behind by his assistant, their two bodies almost merge and create an impression that the man is virtually four-legged.

Rationalization, however, was not the only available strategy. In other comedies, the mythical marvel is retained intact but placed within an urban, Atticized environment. It thus appears outrageously incongruous in its new surroundings and creates a comic contrast. An Apulian bell-crater of ca. 380–370 BCE (Bari, Museo Archeologico Provinciale 3899, *PhV*² 18) illustrates a scene from a comedy on the birth of Helen (see Figure 7.2). As in the myth, Helen emerges as a fully formed young girl from a giant egg.

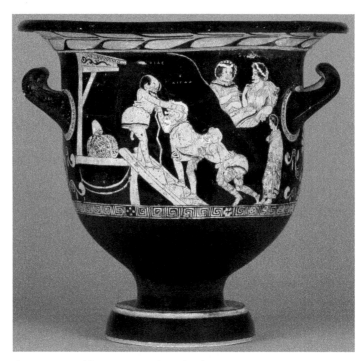

FIGURE 7.1 Chiron as an old man assisted to climb up steps. Apulian bell-crater, ca. 380–370 BCE. British Museum F 151. © Trustees of the British Museum.

But this miraculous incident is placed in a totally mundane milieu, conforming to the usual bourgeois setting of comedy. Tyndareus, the king of Sparta, is pictured as a comic *senex* most astonished with the huge egg that has landed in his household. He is preparing to split the egg open with a large axe, but a comic slave opposite him raises his hand to stop him, because at that very moment the egg hatches and young Helen appears. The egg itself is placed in a laundry basket, with pieces of cloth spread around in disarray. The entire scene takes place in front of an ordinary house door, at which an old woman is standing; this must be Leda, the beautiful princess who charmed Zeus, here transformed into an ugly hag. In the midst of this petty domestic milieu, the mythical egg looks preposterous and absurd, almost surreal.

A mythical marvel appears once again in K-A fr. 5 of Ephippus's *Geryones*: an enormous fish, larger than Crete, is described; an unnamed king cooks it in a correspondingly large vessel, around which entire populations are settled. A forest is cut down to light the cooking fire; a whole lake full of water is needed for the broth; and a hundred pairs of animals are incessantly employed for eight months to carry the salt required for the sauce. The king is presumably the eponymous hero, Geryones, who must be imagined as commensurate in size to the colossal creature he cooks and eats (cf. Konstantakos 2011: 231–238). In Ephippus's comedy, therefore, the mythical monster has retained something of his uncanny supernatural stature. While we do not know whether Geryones was portrayed as three-headed or triple-bodied, he was apparently a giant of

FIGURE 7.2 Comic birth of Helen from the egg. Apulian bell-crater, ca. 380–370 BCE. Bari, Museo Archeologico Provinciale 3899. By permission of the Servizio Biblioteca S. Teresa dei Maschi - de Gemmis, Provincia di Bari.

wondrous dimensions. The mixture of the fabulous and mundane once again produces a comic incongruity: the monstrous giant, instead of slaying strangers, is occupied with cooking seafood and seasoning it with pickle-sauce, like an expert Athenian cook.

ASSIMILATION TO COMIC PATTERNS

Another strategy that affects all aspects of dramaturgy—characters, plot, and performance—is the assimilation of mythical material to standard patterns of comedy. The mythical heroes are cast as stereotypical figures of the comic stage, i.e., well-known types that regularly appeared in comedies with contemporary setting. Apollo's portrayal in *adespota* K-A fr. 1062.9–12 is a good example. Punning on the double sense of the verb ἔχρησε ("gave an oracle"—par excellence the competence of oracular Apollo—but also "gave a loan"), the playwright presents the Delphic god lending Cronus the small sum of one drachma. When Cronus fails to pay it back, Apollo is filled with anger and bursts into damning prophecies. In this way, Apollo is caricatured as a petty money-lender, irascible and worried about the return of his money. The comic tradition offers many examples of this type, from the creditors in Aristophanes's *Clouds* to Misargyrides of *Mostellaria*, including several cases in fourth-century comedies (see Konstantakos 2000: 134–135 for examples): like Apollo, the comic moneylenders regularly appear on stage irritated and complaining against those who fail to pay their debts.

Another specimen comes from Eubulus's *Oedipus* (K-A fr. 72):

> The man who first discovered dining at someone else's expense
> was plainly a great democrat in disposition.
> But whoever invites a friend or foreigner to dinner
> and then exacts a contribution from him,
> may he flee the country without taking anything from home.   5

This passage is full of catchphrases typical of the comic parasite: "dining at someone else's expense" (v. 1 τἀλλότρια δειπνεῖν) and feasting in banquets without paying any "contribution" for his meal (v. 4 συμβολάς) are the parasite's trademarks and recur in a multitude of fragments spoken by parasites or describing them. It is an interesting possibility that Eubulus's passage was delivered by Oedipus himself; the curse in v. 5 recalls the Sophoclean Oedipus, who is fond of cursing (Soph. *OT* 236–275, *OC* 1383–1396; cf. Webster 1970: 85; Hunter 1983: 162–163). If so, Oedipus would have been portrayed as a comic parasite, going about in search of free meals and invitations from generous hosts—a humorous distortion of the mythical hero who wandered destitute in exile after his fall and expulsion from Thebes.

Finally, in Ephippus's *Busiris* Heracles boasts about his courage in battle (K-A fr. 2):

> (Her.) By God, don't you know that I am an Argive
> from Tiryns? These people are always drunk when they fight
> their battles. (B.) Yeah, this is why they run away every time.

Heracles's point is that his Tirynthian countrymen get drunk in order to become furious in battle and fight without heeding danger (like, e.g., ancient Iranian warriors, who drank the intoxicating *haoma* potion before battle to attain ecstatic fury). He presumably intends to intimidate his addressee, exalting his own and his people's superhuman valor. The other speaker, however, is not impressed: on the contrary, he regards Heracles's people as cowards who flee the battlefield. In this way, the comic type of the braggart soldier (known to Attic comedy since Aristophanes's Lamachus and popular on the fourth-century stage) is projected on Heracles's figure. Like a *miles gloriosus*, the hero brags about his military prowess, but his boasts are shown to be lies; his interlocutor does not believe him and sees him as a faint-hearted deserter.

On the level of plot, the traditional myths are adjusted to standard comic scenarios or reworked into well-known comic routines and situations. An elementary procedure is to provide happy endings for originally tragic myths. Aristotle reports a specimen of this in his *Poetics* (1453a30–39), when he describes the closure properly pertaining to comedy in the following manner: "Those who are the deadliest enemies in myth—like Orestes and Aegisthus—become friends and leave the stage at the end, and no one slays or is slain." It has been plausibly assumed that Aristotle has here in mind a burlesque of the Orestes myth that had recently been produced in the theater (Webster 1970: 57; Hunter 1983: 27). In that play, the traditional murderous outcome (which would have been impossible for a comedy) was replaced by conciliation and mutual contentment. A similar ending must be surmised for the comedy illustrated on an Apulian bell-crater (ca. 400–375): Priam, wearing a bizarre crown of Oriental style, is seated on an altar and makes a supplicatory gesture towards Neoptolemus, who threatens him with a sword (*PhV*² 21; illustrations in Trendall and Webster 1971: 139, fig. IV, 29; Taplin 1993, plate 18.19). Obviously, the murder of the old king, as known from mythical tradition, could not have occurred in the comedy. At the last moment, something must have deterred Neoptolemus from slaying him, and the situation would have developed in the way described by Aristotle, with the mythical enemies being finally reconciled. The repertoire of mythological burlesques includes many more myths concluding with killings or suicides (Antiphanes's *Aeolus*, Eubulus's *Medea*, etc.). In all these cases, the playwright must have devised some means (recognition, false death, or other turn of events) to avert evil and secure a happy ending.

Another distinctively comic adjustment was applied to happier myths containing a wedding or reunion. When such an occasion was present in the traditional story, the comic poets greatly emphasized and expanded it, providing a lavish banquet and a lengthy series of relevant scenes (descriptions of the feast and foodstuffs, the cook's arrival, and his speeches, etc.). Anaxandrides's *Protesilaus* included a splendid marriage feast (presumably for the nuptials of Protesilaus and Laodameia) which is exhaustively described by a household slave in a long tirade, listing every single item on the menu (K-A fr. 42). Eubulus's and Philyllius's plays with the title *Auge* also contained feasts, probably for the heroine's wedding with Heracles, which are described by cooks or attending servants (Eubulus K-A fr. 14, Philyllius K-A fr. 3, 5). In addition, Philyllius's play included a scene with a cook or slave arriving from the market and giving a lyrical account of his provisions (K-A fr. 4). In this way, the wedding, with its banquet, food descriptions, and cook scenes, occupies a much larger proportion of dramatic time than its place in the traditional myth would warrant. The mythical story material is remolded and reproportioned in accordance with the peculiar interests of comedy.

The course of events may be shaped according to comic plot patterns. An integral constituent of fourth-century comedy is the love affair, whose formation and evolution follow a basic model: A young man is in love with a woman, but certain obstacles, arising from circumstances or characters in the play, prevent him from being united with her. To overcome the obstacles, the lover implements a scheme or intrigue, often with the assistance of a helper. This elementary pattern, which admits of countless variations in its actual details, underlies most New Comedy plays and was already being developed from the earlier part of the fourth century. Aristophanes's *Assemblywomen* contains its seed (see 877–1111, the love affair between the young man and the girl, obstructed by the old hags), and it is traceable in the remains of several poets who flourished in the decades from 380 onwards (Philetaerus, Anaxandrides, Eubulus, Antiphanes, etc.; see Konstantakos 2002). A number of mythological burlesques treating Zeus's love adventures with various heroines (Danaë, Io, Europa, Leda, Alcmene, Callisto) seem to have based their plot on this "comic love pattern": they presented Zeus in the role of the comic lover, confronted with obstacles in fulfilling his desire and employing a scheme to get round them, often with the help of Hermes, who played the part of his servant or confidant. In Sannyrion's *Danaë* (K-A fr. 8), Zeus appears outside the room in which the eponymous heroine is imprisoned and wonders what kind of metamorphosis would enable him to sneak in through a narrow hole. In Plato Comicus's *Europa* (K-A fr. 43), one person contemplates raping a sleeping woman, but his interlocutor points out the superior attractions of a lady awake; these characters might be Zeus, searching for an opportunity to satisfy his desire for Europa, and his advisor. In a play of Amphis about Callisto (K-A fr. 46), the heroine, as a companion of Artemis, was sworn to virginity, so Zeus took on the guise of Artemis and went about hunting with Callisto, until he found occasion to seduce her. In a comedy illustrated on a Paestan bell-crater (ca. 350), Zeus is shown paying a nocturnal visit to a ladylove; the woman appears at a window, and Zeus prepares to climb up to her on a ladder while Hermes lights his way with a lamp (*PhV*² 65; Trendall and Webster 1971: 134–135, fig. IV, 19; Pickard-Cambridge 1968, fig. 106). Plato Comicus's *Long Night* (*Nyx Makra*) probably also contained a secret nocturnal visit of Zeus to Alcmene (K-A fr. 90–91). The traditional tales about Zeus's amorous encounters are thus adapted to the love intrigue typical of bourgeois comedy.

Other mythical love relationships were also tailored on typically comic patterns of action. In Nicochares's *Galateia,* the enamored Cyclops was presented as a coarse, ignorant boor; he tried to win Galateia's favor with his clumsy song, but the nymph scorned him for his lack of education and refinement (K-A fr. 3–5, cf. Casolari 2003: 134–136). The mismatch of an elegant, sophisticated lady with an uncouth boor is a familiar situation in ancient comedy, with obvious potential for entertainment: highlights include Strepsiades and his aristocratic wife in Aristophanes's *Clouds*, the rustic Strabax as lover of the polished urban *meretrix* in Plautus's *Truculentus*, and some fourth-century comedies that presented an *agroikos* involved in a love affair with a city *hetaira* (Konstantakos 2005). Polyphemus's ill-assorted love for the sea-nymph was ideally suited to this comic routine.

Finally, the conformation to the generic rules of comedy would have been evident in every aspect of the design and production of a mythical burlesque. As the South Italian comic vase paintings show, mythical personages were dressed up in the standard costumes and paraphernalia of Attic comedy, with the characteristic comic padding in the belly and buttocks and a large leather phallus. Although certain exceedingly popular heroes, such as Heracles, had their own special masks, most mythical figures wore one of the typical comic masks used for ordinary characters (old or young men, old and young women, slaves, etc.) in the plays with contemporary setting and domestic plot. In fact, their appearance would be indistinguishable from that of ordinary comic characters, save for the specific emblems that they occasionally wear or carry (a crown for Zeus, a broad-brimmed cap and herald's staff for Hermes, a large Oriental crown for Priam, etc.). Scenic space is also organized according to the conventions of comedy. Helen's birth, in the Apulian vase painting discussed above, takes place in front of a practicable stage door, identical to the doors of common houses depicted on other South Italian comic vases. In Antiphanes's *Ganymede*, the setting comprised two neighboring houses on a street in Troy, each one presumably represented by its own door (K-A fr. 74). This is a typical scenic arrangement of domestic comedy, traceable already in Aristophanes (*Clouds*, *Assemblywomen*) and standardized by the New Comedy period. One of the houses belongs to Laomedon, the king of the city, but is nonetheless styled οἰκία, as if it were the private residence of an ordinary householder. It would also have been pictured like a comic urban οἰκία on the scenic facade (see Nesselrath 1990: 210–212; Konstantakos 2000: 101–105).

OTHER TECHNIQUES

Much entertainment must have been derived from another artifice of mythological burlesques, the reversal of traditional mythical roles and situations. One form of reversal has already been discussed: the conciliation of personages that were bitter enemies in myth and the transformation of the traditional grievous outcome into a happy ending. Comic inversion may also affect the main incidents and storyline, the very core of the myth. A comic vase painting, from a fragmentary Paestan calyx-crater (ca. 340s), shows Cassandra (identified by an inscription) manhandling a fully armored warrior who clings to a statue of Athena, while Cassandra is grabbing his helmet and pushing her knee onto his back. The warrior is evidently Ajax of Locri, who, according to myth, raped Cassandra at the sack of Troy, dragging her from Athena's cult statue, where the Trojan prophetess had taken refuge. Here the mythical situation has been turned upside down: Ajax is the one seeking refuge at the statue, while Cassandra is the assaulter (*PhV*[2] 86; Trendall and Webster 1971: 139, fig. IV, 30; Taplin 1993, plate 17.17). We do not know exactly how the comic dramatist worked out his scenario. Perhaps Ajax attempted to violate Cassandra in the comedy as well, but she proved stronger and threatened to beat him down, so Ajax took refuge at the statue to save himself. Alternatively, Cassandra may have been portrayed as a nymphomaniac, furiously pursuing Ajax with sexual intentions, while he ran away to avoid her.

K-A fr. 15 from Eubulus's *Bellerophontes* clearly shows the hero in flight:

> Who will catch hold of my leg from below?
> For I am lifted aloft like a *kottabos* shaft!

According to myth, Bellerophontes tamed Pegasus, the winged horse, using a golden bridle provided by Athena, and then rode him, flying in the air, in order to accomplish various exploits. In the end, he attempted to fly to heaven, but the gods wrathfully cast him down to earth. In Eubulus's scene, Bellerophontes is rising in the air, presumably on the back of Pegasus. His ascent was doubtless accomplished by means of the *mechane* or stage-crane, the device commonly used for flying personages in Greek drama (see Hunter 1983: 108–109). But Bellerophontes is not flying by his own will. His reaction to his ascent is terror; he cries for help and calls for someone to hold him down. Once again, it is impossible to guess how exactly this comic scenario was developed. Perhaps Bellerophontes initially mistook Pegasus for an ordinary horse and so attempted to mount him; then the horse suddenly rose in the air, dragging the astonished hero up on his back. In any case, the comic effect ensues from the subversion of mythical data: Bellerophontes flies against his will; it is not he that tames Pegasus, in order to rise on his back, but the winged horse that drags him up by force. A comparable reversal of established mythical roles occurred perhaps in Alexis's *Odysseus at the Loom*. In Odyssean myth, weaving was traditionally Penelope's activity: she kept weaving a shroud for Laertes during the day and unstitching it at night, so as to delay her wedding to a suitor. In the comedy, Odysseus somehow undertook Penelope's rightful role in a topsy-turvy rendering of the story (Arnott 1996: 465–466).

Finally, some of the humor in mythological burlesques was generated from the mingling of the lofty myths with lowbrow jokes and farcical antics. The earlier fourth-century dramatists did not hesitate to exploit the resources of popular farce and unsophisticated laughter any more than had their boisterous Old Comedy predecessors. Alexis's *Linus* serves as an example. In the myth, Linus struck Heracles, exasperated with his ineptitude, and the hero furiously retaliated, killing Linus on the spot. K-A fr. 140 ominously closes with Linus scoffing at Heracles for his gluttony, a situation that would provide good grounds for a brawl. Obviously, the comedy could not lead up to Linus's killing. But Heracles probably gave Linus a sound thrashing, producing a hilarious scene of physical knockabout. In general, Heracles's standard comic portrayal as a gargantuan glutton afforded many opportunities for broad humor about food and the physical aspects of gobbling. Occasionally, there are even scatological jokes, like the "ridiculous spectacle" of "a man stuffed with food and pressed to shit, who has to walk a long way, biting his lips" in Eubulus's *Cercopes* (K-A fr. 52).

Decline and End

Literary genres often suffer the fate of biological species: they decline and gradually become extinct. It has happened to the choral ode and the fable, the exemplum and the miscellany, the chronography and the mystery play. Mythological burlesque followed the same path, rapidly growing out of fashion after about 340 BCE. The dramatists of the first generation of New Comedy, such as Philemon, Diphilus, and Philippides, produced very few mythological plays (one or two each, although Diphilus may have staged four or more). Menander, the star of the new age, did not try his hand at all at this decaying genre. It may be surmised that, after six decades of intensive cultivation, the genre had exhausted its comic potential and audiences were growing weary of it. The few specimens attested for the New Comedy period are probably to be dated to the early years of their playwrights' careers, the 330s or 320s, as final remnants of a type tending towards extinction. Alternatively, they may represent sporadic attempts to revive the outdated genre, made by dramatists who wished to experiment by rehashing earlier artistic forms. Diphilus in particular, who seems to have kept a tighter association with the earlier traditions of "Middle" Comedy, would be likely to indulge in such revivalist experiments. However, these attempts do not seem to have had enough appeal to lead to a large-scale revival of mythological burlesque. They remained solitary ventures without imitators and afterlife.[8]

FURTHER READING

Abbreviations of scholarly journals in the references listed below follow the *Année Philologique*.

The fullest discussions of fourth-century myth burlesques are Nesselrath 1990: 188–241 (the most perspicacious analysis to date) and Casolari 2003, especially 23–25, 127–183, 214–225, 249–295. Useful briefer discussions are Meineke 1839: 278–285, 439; Moessner 1907: 11–13, 66–81; Körte 1921: 1262–1263; Norwood 1931: 22–23, 38–39, 49–51, 173–175; Schiassi 1955; Lever 1956: 169–170; Oliva 1968: 61–73; Webster 1970: 6–7, 16–19, 57, 82–97, 115; Arnott 1972: 71–75; Hunter 1983: 22–30; Handley 1985: 368–373, 402–404; Mangidis 2003: 24–28; Konstantakos 2005–2006: 67–69, 73–75; Papachrysostomou 2008: 25–27. For examination of the mythological output of particular dramatists, see Hunter 1983 on Eubulus (under the headings of individual mythological plays); Arnott 1996 on Alexis (see Index s.v. myth travesty); Millis 2001 on Anaxandrides (9–10 and under individual plays); Mangidis 2003 on Antiphanes; Papachrysostomou 2008: 30–35, 84–88, 115–119, 236–242, 263–268 (on Amphis, Aristophon, Philetaerus, and Theophilus); Orth 2009 on Strattis (23, 26–27, and under individual plays); and Pirrotta 2009 on Plato Comicus (45–46, 55–56, and under individual plays). Commentary on sundry fragments from myth burlesques is offered by Carrière 1979: 306–309, and Olson 2007: 125–134, 265–271, 311–318, 369–371. Special aspects, themes, or characters of the genre are studied by Schmidt 1888: 385–400; Phillips 1959; Galinsky 1972: 85–100; Hunter 1981; Hunter 1987: 292–296; Nesselrath 1993; Nesselrath 1995; Rosen 1995: 123–136; Konstantakos 2000: 94–124; Konstantakos 2002: 156–167; and Konstantakos 2011. On the antecedents of myth burlesque in fifth-century theater (ridicule of gods and myths, paratragedy, etc.), see especially Moessner 1907: 14–23, 49–153; Hošek 1963; Rau 1967, especially 11–18, 56–63, 69–70, 85–89; Hofmann 1976, especially 72–137; Carrière 1979: 51–55; Dover 1972: 30–33, 73–75; Muth 1992: 84–133; Zimmermann 1998: 156–166; and Bowie 2000.

---

[8] Compare recent attempts to revive outdated genres, such as the western or the Roman or Biblical film, in present-day mainstream cinema: e.g., Clint Eastwood's *Unforgiven* (1992), Ridley Scott's *Gladiator* (2000), and Mel Gibson's *The Passion of the Christ* (2004). All these films, as individual works, were successful and popular with audiences. But none of them led to a full-scale resuscitation of its respective genre, inspiring other creations of the same kind.

BIBLIOGRAPHY

Arnott, W. G. 1972. "From Aristophanes to Menander." *G&R*, n.s., 19: 65–80.

——. 1996. *Alexis: The Fragments: A Commentary*. Cambridge, UK: Cambridge University Press.

Bieber, M. 1961. *The History of the Greek and Roman Theater*. 2nd ed. Princeton: Princeton University Press.

Bowie, A. 2000. "Myth and Ritual in the Rivals of Aristophanes." In *The Rivals of Aristophanes: Studies in Athenian Old Comedy*, edited by D. Harvey and J. Wilkins, 317–339. London and Swansea: Duckworth and The Classical Press of Wales.

Burkert, W. 1960. "Das Lied von Ares und Aphrodite: Zum Verhältnis von Odyssee und Ilias." *RhM* 103: 130–144.

Carrière, J. C. 1979. *Le carnaval et la politique: Une introduction à la comédie grecque suivie d'un choix de fragments*. Paris: Les Belles Lettres.

Casolari, F. 2003. *Die Mythentravestie in der griechischen Komödie*. Münster: Aschendorff Verlag.

Christenson, D. M. 2000. *Plautus, Amphitruo*. Cambridge, UK: Cambridge University Press.

Csapo, E. 1986. "A Note on the Würzburg Bell-Crater H5697 ('Telephus Travestitus')." *Phoenix* 40: 379–392.

Dalby, A. 2003. *Food in the Ancient World from A to Z*. London and New York: Routledge.

Dover, K. J. 1972. *Aristophanic Comedy*. Berkeley and Los Angeles: University of California Press.

Friedländer, P. 1934. "Lachende Götter." *Die Antike* 10: 209–226.

Galinsky, G. K. 1972. *The Herakles Theme: The Adaptations of the Hero in Literature from Homer to the Twentieth Century*. Oxford: Basil Blackwell.

Green, J. R. 1994. *Theatre in Ancient Greek Society*. London and New York: Routledge.

——. 1995. "Theatre Production: 1987–1995." *Lustrum* 37: 7–202.

Handley, E. W. 1985. "Comedy." In *The Cambridge History of Classical Literature*. Vol. 1, *Greek Literature*, edited by P. E. Easterling and B. M. W. Knox, 355–425. Cambridge, UK: Cambridge University Press.

Hoffner, H. A. 1998. *Hittite Myths*. 2nd ed. Atlanta: Scholars Press.

Hofmann, H. 1976. *Mythos und Komödie: Untersuchungen zu den Vögeln des Aristophanes*. Hildesheim and New York: Georg Olms Verlag.

Hošek, R. 1963. "Herakles auf der Bühne der alten attischen Komödie." In Γέρας: *Studies Presented to George Thomson on the Occasion of his 60th Birthday*, edited by L. Varcl and R. F. Willetts, 119–127. Prague: Charles University.

Hunter, R. L. 1981. "P.Lit.Lond. 77 and Tragic Burlesque in Attic Comedy." *ZPE* 41: 19–24.

——. 1983. *Eubulus: The Fragments*. Cambridge, UK: Cambridge University Press.

——. 1987. "Middle Comedy and the Amphitruo of Plautus." *Dioniso* 57: 281–298.

Imperio, O. 1998. "Callia." In A. M. Belardinelli, O. Imperio, G. Mastromarco, M. Pellegrino and P. Totaro, *Tessere: Frammenti della commedia greca: Studi e commenti*, 195–254. Bari: Adriatica Editrice.

Konstantakos, I. M. 2000. "A Commentary on the Fragments of Eight Plays of Antiphanes." PhD diss., University of Cambridge.

——. 2002. "Towards a Literary History of Comic Love." *C&M* 53: 141–171.

——. 2005. "Aspects of the Figure of the ἄγροικος in Ancient Comedy." *RhM* 148: 1–26.

——. 2005–2006. "Το κωμικό θέατρο από τον 4ο αιώνα στην ελληνιστική περίοδο: Εξελικτικές τάσεις και συνθήκες παραγωγής." *Epistemonike epeteris tes philosophikes Scholes tou Panepistemiou Athenon* 57: 47–101.

——. 2011. "Ephippos' *Geryones*: A Comedy between Myth and Folktale." *Acta Antiqua Academiae Scientarum Hungaricae* 51: 223–246.

Körte, A. 1921. "Komödie (griechische)." *RE* 11.1: 1207–1275.

Lever, K. 1956. *The Art of Greek Comedy*. London: Methuen.

Mangidis, T. 2003. *Antiphanes' Mythentravestien*. Frankfurt a. M.: Peter Lang.

Mastromarco, G. 1998. "La degradazione del mostro: La maschera del Ciclope nella commedia e nel dramma satiresco del quinto secolo a.C." In A. M. Belardinelli, O. Imperio, G. Mastromarco, M. Pellegrino and P. Totaro, *Tessere: Frammenti della commedia greca: Studi e commenti*, 9–42. Bari: Adriatica Editrice.

Meineke, A. 1839. *Fragmenta Comicorum Graecorum*. Vol. 1, *Historia Critica Comicorum Graecorum*. Berlin: G. Reimer.

Millis, B. W. 2001. "A Commentary on the Fragments of Anaxandrides." PhD diss., University of Illinois at Urbana-Champaign.

Moessner, O. 1907. *Die Mythologie in der dorischen und altattischen Komödie*. PhD diss., Friedrich-Alexanders-Universität zu Erlangen.

Muth, R. 1992. *Die Götterburleske in der griechischen Literatur*. Darmstadt: Wissenschaftliche Buchgesellschaft.

Nesselrath, H.-G. 1990. *Die attische Mittlere Komödie: Ihre Stellung in der antiken Literaturkritik und Literaturgeschichte*. Berlin and New York: Walter de Gruyter.

——. 1993. "Parody and Later Greek Comedy." *HSPh* 95: 181–195.

——. 1995. "Myth, Parody, and Comic Plots: The Birth of Gods and Middle Comedy." In *Beyond Aristophanes: Transition and Diversity in Greek Comedy*, edited by G. W. Dobrov, 1–27. Atlanta: Scholars Press.

Norwood, G. 1931. *Greek Comedy*. London: Methuen.

Oliva, C. 1968. "La parodia e la critica letteraria nella commedia post-aristofanea." *Dioniso* 42: 25–92.

Olson, S. D. 2007. *Broken Laughter: Select Fragments of Greek Comedy*. Oxford: Oxford University Press.

Olson, S. D., and A. Sens. 2000. *Archestratos of Gela: Greek Culture and Cuisine in the Fourth Century BCE*. Oxford: Oxford University Press.

Orth, C. 2009. *Strattis: Die Fragmente: Ein Kommentar*. Berlin: Verlag Antike.

Papachrysostomou, A. 2008. *Six Comic Poets: A Commentary on Selected Fragments of Middle Comedy*. Tübingen: Narr.

Phillips, E. D. 1959. "The Comic Odysseus." *G&R*, n.s., 6: 58–67.

Pickard-Cambridge, A. 1968. *The Dramatic Festivals of Athens*. 2nd ed., revised by J. Gould and D. M. Lewis. Oxford: Clarendon Press.

Pirrotta, S. 2009. *Plato Comicus: Die fragmentarischen Komödien: Ein Kommentar*. Berlin: Verlag Antike.

Rau, P. 1967. *Paratragodia: Untersuchung einer komischen Form des Aristophanes*. Munich: Beck.

Reinhardt, K. 1960. *Tradition und Geist: Gesammelte Essays zur Dichtung*. Göttingen: Vandenhoeck & Ruprecht.

Riemschneider, M. 1954. *Die Welt der Hethiter*. Stuttgart: Gustav Kilpper Verlag.

Rosen, R. M. 1995. "Plato Comicus and the Evolution of Greek Comedy." In *Beyond Aristophanes: Transition and Diversity in Greek Comedy*, edited by G. W. Dobrov, 119–137. Atlanta: Scholars Press.

Schiassi, G. 1955. "Parodia e travestimento mitico nella commedia attica di mezzo." *RIL* 88: 99–120.

Schmidt, I. O. 1888. "Ulixes Comicus." *Jahrbücher für classische Philologie*, supplement 16: 373–403.

Simpson, W. K., ed. 2003. *The Literature of Ancient Egypt: An Anthology of Stories, Instructions, Stelae, Autobiographies, and Poetry*. 3rd ed. New Haven and London: Yale University Press.

Tanner, R. H. 1915. "The Ὀδυσσῆς of Cratinus and the Cyclops of Euripides." *TAPhA* 46: 173–206.

Taplin, O. 1993. *Comic Angels and Other Approaches to Greek Drama through Vase-Paintings*. Oxford: Clarendon Press.

Trendall, A. D., and T. B. L. Webster. 1971. *Illustrations of Greek Drama*. London: Phaidon.

Webster, T. B. L. 1970. *Studies in Later Greek Comedy*. 2nd ed. Manchester: Manchester University Press.

Zervou, A. K. 1990. *Ironie et parodie: Le comique chez Homère*. Athens: Bibliopoleio tes Hestias.

Zimmermann, B. 1998. *Die griechische Komödie*. Düsseldorf and Zürich: Artemis & Winkler.

CHAPTER 8

....

COMEDY IN THE FOURTH CENTURY II: POLITICS AND DOMESTICITY

....

JEFFREY HENDERSON

THE ancient tripartition of comedy into Old, Middle, and New eras, an evolutionary model defined at either end by the paradigmatic status awarded to Aristophanes ("political") and Menander ("domestic"), has tended to focus attention on salient trends and change and to play down variety and continuity, but even in antiquity this model was at best a blunt heuristic tool. In recent decades, closer study of the fragments themselves has revealed a greater variety of themes and subjects in each era and no revolutionary breaks between the eras. Since Greek comedy in the fifth and fourth centuries mirrored and spoke to the world of spectators whose primary identity was rooted in household and polis, it is unsurprising that both domestic and political themes and subjects were already in the repertory when our attestation begins ca. 440 and continued to be fruitful as poets in successive generations broadened or refined them in a continuous process of experimenting, catering to current spectator interest, and responding to social and political change. The theatrical landscape was changing too: in the fourth century, comedy became professional and truly international, no longer the preserve primarily of Athenian poets and audiences; the focus of attention moved from choruses to actors; and poets and spectators alike grew more sophisticated and cosmopolitan as the genre matured—classic comedies circulated as texts and in 339 began to be revived at the Dionysia. As in the fifth century, there were fads and fashions but also variety, since no element in the repertory was ever entirely abandoned; some poets specialized, some were more versatile, and some changed focus at different points in their careers, which often overlap the putative eras; some novelties were dead ends, some caught on, some were ahead of their time; and while some plays belonged primarily to one of the major types—mythological, fantastic/escapist, political, or domestic—others were combinations.

COMIC POLITICS IN THE FIFTH CENTURY

Typical of all types of comedy in the "Old Comic" era, and traditionally its defining feature, was incidental mockery of individuals and groups, mostly Athenian, across a broad spectrum, from mere foibles, physical abnormalities, or character flaws (centered mainly on money, eating, drinking, and sex) to activity with political or civic (including artistic or intellectual) impact; ancient scholars noted as exceptional its avoidance by certain poets (Crates and Pherecrates) or particular plays (e.g., Cratinus's *Odysseus and Company*). The great majority of the targets (*komoidoumenoi*: Sommerstein 1996) were associated with politics and the courts, the rest mainly with the arts (especially theater) and the trades or professions. Also impressive in the eyes of posterity were political comedies proper: those that focused topically on public life, that engaged with individuals and/or civic and political issues in a sustained or thematic way, that could criticize or admonish the spectators, and that could involve the poet himself as a partisan, at least in the case of Aristophanes in his series of plays (from 426 to 422) attacking Cleon.

A striking feature of Old Comic mockery and political engagement is its consistent bias. Virtually all of the political targets are democrats in the populist mold of Pericles and his successors (the "demagogues" who emerged after his death in 429), while rightist figures like Nicias, Laches, Alcibiades, those implicated in the scandals of 415, and the oligarchs disenfranchised after the coup of 411—all having obvious potential for mockery—are almost entirely spared and occasionally even defended, and this bias persists even when rightists were ascendant. At the ideological and policy level too, the comic poets consistently espouse the social, moral, cultural, and political sentiments of elite conservatives; decry full popular sovereignty (a gullible majority intent on soaking the rich and empowering scoundrels) and the operation of the council, the assembly, and the courts; criticize the poor as a class but never the wealthy (at least in the fifth century: Sommerstein 1984); avoid the always-live issue of oligarchy while instead ridiculing the populist bogey of elite tyranny (Henderson 2003); and attack the prosecution of the Peloponnesian War when (and only when) it either exposed the Attic countryside, and thus the landowners, to enemy devastation or bolstered the authority of leaders like Cleon. Like Thucydides (2.65), the comic poets held that the democracy needed but tended not to choose the best as its leaders, except that comedy did not include Pericles in the latter category.

This ideological complexion of politically engaged comedy jibes with its pattern of production: clustered in periods when the elite were politically sidelined or came under populist attack. In the late 430s, during the run-up to the Peloponnesian War, Cratinus and Hermippus launched the subgenre by using myth-comedy to criticize Pericles's policies as well as his character and private life, especially his relationship with Aspasia. In Cratinus's *Dionysalexander*, where Dionysus impersonates Paris in the Judgment, Pericles was somehow attacked "very convincingly by implication [ἔμφασις] for bringing the war on the Athenians" (K-A test. i.44–48), and in *Nemesis*, produced at around the same time, where Zeus seduces Nemesis in Attica and the Helen-egg is hatched by Leda in Sparta, Zeus is assimilated to Pericles (K-A fr. 118; Henderson 2012). In Hermippus's *Moirai* (*Fates*), a "king of satyrs" (= Pericles: Plu. *Per.* 33.6) is chided for his pusillanimous conduct of the war (K-A fr. 47), and the tradition that Hermippus prosecuted Phidias for impiety and Aspasia for arranging liaisons for Pericles with free-born women (K-A test. 2) may well derive from his comedies of this period.

The ascendancy of Cleon and other untraditional (nonelite) political leaders after 429 inspired Aristophanes to move from mythological *emphasis* (still operative in *Babylonians* of 426) to open engagement (*Acharnians* in 425) and then to the "demagogue-comedy" (Sommerstein 2000) that focused on a single individual (the Paphlagonian slave = Cleon in *Knights* of 424). This type of play was abandoned by Aristophanes after the death of his favorite target in 422 but was pursued by rival poets: Eupolis in *Marikas* (421: Hyperbolus); Hermippus in *Breadwomen* (ca. 420: Hyperbolus); Plato in *Peisander* (ca. 421), *Hyperbolus* (418), and *Cleophon* (405); and likely Archippus in *Rhinon* and Theopompus in *Teisamenus*. Other plays, such as Aristophanes's *Clouds*, and mostly by these same poets, addressed political and civic issues more broadly, but they too seem to be clustered in periods of populist leadership: ca. 430 to ca. 417 (when Hyperbolus was ostracized), 413 to early 411 (the failure of the Sicilian expedition and renewed investment of Attica), 410–405 (after the oligarchy, when Cleophon was ascendant), and for a short time after 403, when the democracy was restored and the laws reformed.

In defining this period of civic and political comedy, a generational factor was also at work, for its main poets began their careers in the run-up to the Peloponnesian War or shortly thereafter. The young Aristophanes's novel style of sociopolitical engagement, capitalizing on stresses occasioned or aggravated by the war, won him the first Dionysian victory by a new poet in ten years (Storey 2003: 65) and a string of subsequent successes, and there is evident copycatting, competition for credit, and perhaps even collaboration (e.g. Eupolis K-A fr. 89) as the novel ideas caught on (Kyriakidi 2006). During this period, mythological comedy experienced a hiatus, but just afterward it picked up where it had left off (for example birth-comedies, inaugurated ca. 430 by Cratinus's *Nemesis* and Hermippus's *Birth of Athena*), and likewise domestic (mainly *hetaira*) comedy, though meanwhile some of its elements had been enlisted for plays with a primarily civic or political focus (for example Aristophanes's *Knights*, *Clouds*, *Wasps*, and *Lysistrata*; Cratinus's *Wine Flask*; and Eupolis's *Flatterers*: Hutchinson 2011). After 403, political comedy receded after its brief run as a dominant type, not only because times and theatrical tastes were changing but also because it had based itself so narrowly as to leave little scope for development either by veterans like Aristophanes or new generations of poets, who by and large chose to develop the traditional types of comedy as they adapted to increasingly diverse and less parochial audiences (Konstantakos 2011). Nevertheless, it would be many more decades before comedy turned away from political engagement altogether.

POLITICAL ELEMENTS IN
FOURTH-CENTURY COMEDY

Later tradition held that fifth-century political comedy died without issue, the victim of legal and/or political suppression as it abused its laudable freedom to denounce vice openly and was then allowed to do so only covertly and in more decent language. In reality, only the part about more decent language is accurate (e.g., Arist. *EN* 1128a22 ff), though sex itself remains alive and well even if more decently described: e.g., Amphis K-A fr. 20 (on the impotence-inducing effects of lettuce); frequent attention to the world of *hetairai* and prostitutes; the phallus still appearing on theatrical vases (it would disappear only in the time of Menander); plays like Plato's *Phaon*, Eubulus's *Orthannes* and *Impotent Men*, Xenarchus's *Priapus*, and Timocles's *Conisalus*; and for Diphilus, a contemporary of Menander, a sexual raciness (homosexual in *Pederasts*: K-A fr. 42, 49) that recalls Old Comedy and is reflected in Plautus's *Casina* and *Rudens*.

Otherwise, the basic elements of political comedy remained in play throughout the fourth century except for New Comedies, whose characters were fictitious (or dead, e.g., the famous courtesan Thais) and operated in cordon-sanitaire plots. We find not only incidental mockery (the touchstone for ancient scholars) but also actual contemporaries as title characters, suggesting sustained comic treatment; titles or fragments indicating prominent political themes or criticism of institutions; and incidental remarks that often help to date the plays (Webster 1952), all now embracing non-Athenians as well (Webster 1970: 10–56; Csapo 2000: 119–121; Arnott 2010: 300–308). And if there was suppression, it did not come at the end of the fifth century; well into the fourth, orators cited, and philosophers complained about, comic mockery and criticism of Athens: Aeschines 1.157 (345) cites "a certain anapaestic verse" addressed by the comic actor Parmenon to the chorus as evidence of Timarchus's sexual misbehavior (indeed, forensic and comic modes of abuse are strikingly similar: Henderson 1998); Plato would ban all forms of mockery (*Lg.* 935e), Aristotle would restrict it to mature audiences (*Pol.* 1336b), and Isocrates 8.14 (355) complains that *parrhesia* is only for "the most thoughtless speakers here [in the assembly] who care nothing for you and in the theater for comic producers: which is the most awful of all, to show as much favor to those who publicize Athenian failings to the rest of Greece as disfavor to those who benefit you, and to be just as ill-tempered toward those who criticize and admonish you as toward those whose actions damage the city," the sort of complaint about comedy that is rebutted by Aristophanes/Dicaeopolis in *Acharnians* 497 ff., 628 ff. (Michelini 1998).

Suppression is visible rather during the period beginning with the oligarchy of Antipater's henchman Phocion in 322/1, when the Greek revolt against Macedon was blamed on the democrats (whose leaders were purged), citizens whose property was worth less than 2,000 drachmas were exiled or disenfranchised (only 9,000 retained the franchise), and the *theorikon* was abolished; it continues during the subsequent garrisoning of Athens under Cassander's appointed regent, Demetrius of Phalerum

(317–307), when the purges resumed and the *choregia* was abolished; and is apparent during the "tyranny" of Lachares (ca. 299–295). During this period the apolitical, elite-oriented style of comedy perfected by Menander, who debuted in 321, became permanently dominant, though political comedies reminiscent of the fifth century reappear in the turbulent period after 307, when the Antigonid Demetrius I (Poliorcetes) "liberated" Athens, and again in 294, after the expulsion of Lachares.

Titles like *Kapelides* (Theopompus), *Gynaikokratia* (Amphis and Alexis), *Demosatyrs*, *Dionysiazousai* (Timocles), and *Adoniazousai* (Philippides) suggest criticism of (democratic) institutions. Theopompus (and possibly Eubulus too) wrote a *Peace* (380s). The target of Antiphanes's *Philothebaeus* was probably Aristophon, an important politician active from 403 to the late 340s, said (*adespota* K-A fr. 836) to have been ridiculed in comedy for taking money from the famous soldier Chares in return for his support, for often escaping indictment for illegal proposals, and for plundering the Ceans when he was a general (364). Sometimes title characters cannot be identified with any of the attested candidates, e.g., Heniochus's *Polyeuctus,* Anaxandrides's *Sosippus,* and Aristophon's *Callonides.* In the period before 322, Timocles (340s to ca. 317) seems particularly to keep the Old Comic style alive (*Aegyptians, Delos, Demosatyrs, Dionysiazousai, Icarians, Caunians, Conisalus, Marathonians, Neaira, Orestautocleides, Philodicastes,* and personal or political references in nearly half the fragments), as do Archedicus and Philippides after 307 (see below).

Many topical plays of this era concern non-Athenians, reflecting the importance of Athens' relations with other Greek cities and foreign potentates and the often contentious issues that they raised. Eubulus's *Dionysius* featured the Sicilian tyrant and tragic poet (bad plays: Ephippus K-A fr. 16), Mnesimachus's *Charinus* probably the pro-Macedonian politician active in the late 340s (D. 58.37), and Philemon's *Pyrrhus* probably the king of Epirus and brother-in-law of Demetrius Poliorcetes. Heniochus's *Cities* (presumably the title) K-A fr. 5 had a chorus of cities whom the prologue-speaker is about to introduce individually, as in Eupolis's play; they have gathered at Olympia to celebrate their imminent freedom from tribute, but Irresolution (*aboulia*) has afflicted them, together with "a pair of women, Democracy and Aristocracy, who now get them into drunken brawls." Philyllius's *Cities* K-A fr. 10 is in Doric. Anaxandrides's *Cities* contains discussion of relationships with other states (the Athenian speaker of K-A fr. 40 has rejected an alliance with Egypt, cf. *Protesilaus* K-A fr. 41 ridiculing Melanopus: D. 24.126–27); K-A fr. 66 (perhaps from this play) "the city, unconcerned with any of its laws, wanted it" adapts an infamous line of Euripides (K-A fr. 920) referring to Heracles's rape of Auge (quoted by Menander, *Epitrepontes* 1123, in that context), apparently assimilating the city in question to her. Alexis's *Olynthians* featured poor people, perhaps refugees after that city's destruction by Philip in 384, and Anaxandrides's *Thessalians* perhaps reflects the short-lived treaty with Athens of 361.

Meanwhile, every important politician and celebrity came in for the traditional incidental mockery about embarrassing moments or personal foibles (occasionally even in New Comedy). But the spotlight shifts from the political and legal shenanigans of (mostly) popular leaders to the extravagances of the wealthy: gourmanderie (especially as regards fish), drinking, lavish spending, partying and gambling, inheritance-squandering, and sexual (mis)behavior. The prominence of luxury—actual as distinct from the fantastic or utopian in Old Comedy—is due not solely to selective excerpting by Athenaeus but surely also to the reality of the times: the high life of the Persian courts, fabulous in fifth-century comedy (e.g. *Acharnians* 65–90, Pherecrates's *Persians*, Metagenes's *Thuriopersians*), now becomes the familiar reality of the Macedonian court(s) and of local elites who followed suit: in Antiphanes K-A fr. 172, Pelops compares Greek cuisine unfavorably to Persian. Extremely elaborate, even fetishistic, descriptions of ordinary objects (especially cooking and drinking utensils and food) abound, for example the many descriptions of "Thericlean cups" (Athen. 11.471d): Eubulus's *Dice Players* K-A fr. 56 is even more elaborate than Praxagora's address to her lamp at the opening of *Ecclesiazusae* and shows, inter alia, the increasing influence of dithyramb in this period (Nesselrath 1990: 241–266). Cookbooks and collections of banquet witticisms also become popular as early as Plato's *Phaon* (392/1), where someone consults the "newly published cookbook by Philoxenus" (K-A fr. 189), while the pompous cook in Dionysius's *Thesmophoros* K-A fr. 2 (320s) dismisses Archestratus and all other writers of cookbooks. But before New Comedy turned for its themes and settings to the private life and ideology of the wealthy classes, freshly empowered after 322, comedy writers still viewed their world from a demotic/democratic angle as an opportunity for mockery and satire (exemplifying vices), celebrity gossip, or sheer marvelousness.

In comedy, as in the law courts, the characteristic institution of the elite was the symposium (e.g. D. 36.45 on the undemocratic conduct of Apollodorus; 48.53–55; Lycurg. 1.17–22; similarly Pl. *R.* 373a3, 420a, 568e3). Symposia lower on the socioeconomic scale held little interest for comedy; the dining was unremarkable, and paid prostitutes stood in for the fascinating *hetairai* who inhabited the noncommercial world of friendship and gifts, seduction, and love (Glazebrook and Henry 2011). By law, a prostitute's fee was limited to two drachmas ([Arist.] *Ath.* 50.2) so that they would be widely available, and the law attributed to Solon by Philemon K-A fr. 3 for the provision of public prostitutes, whether genuine or not, had a similar purpose: to discourage adultery and the pursuit of *hetairai* by those who could not afford such adventures (Eubulus K-A fr. 67, 82, Xenarchus K-A fr. 4). Putting symposia and associated komastic behavior on an egalitarian basis is a revolutionary and utopian proposal in Aristophanes's *Assemblywomen* (391).

As a prominent comic focus, the symposium world belongs to the fourth century; in fifth-century comedy, there are descriptions of symposia and (more often) of banquets celebrating an everyman hero's success, and there are scenes of preparation and aftermath, but few certifiable stagings of symposia themselves (male dining societies such as the one depicted in Aristophanes's *Banqueters* were held outside the home and were not conducted as symposia): Pherecrates's *Corianno* and Theopompus's *Nemea* (women alone, as in Menander *Synaristosai* and frequently in vase-paintings: Peschel 1987:70–79, 110–112) and probably other early *hetaira*-comedies (see below), Eupolis's *Flatterers* and the two *Autolycus* plays, Ameipsias's *Kottabos Players*, and Plato's *Zeus Kakoumenos*

(K-A fr. 46). But such stagings (as in Roman adaptations) become increasingly frequent in the early fourth century, e.g., in Philyllius's and Eubulus's *Auge* and Anaxandrides's *Boors, Kitharistria*, and *Nereids* (Konstantakos 2005a), as do *hetaira*-comedies. Vase-painting and sympotic poetry show the same pattern: a heyday before ca. 440 and a resumption, in more restrained form, ca. the 380s.

Gourmands—only ten are mentioned in Old Comedy, only one (Callias in Eupolis *Flatterers*) a wastrel (Sommerstein 1996: 351)—are now listed in long catalogues (e.g., Antiphanes K-A fr. 27, 188, Euphanes K-A fr. 1), and their cooks (none in Old Comedy; in Aristophanes, the hero typically plays this role, e.g., *Acharnians, Peace, Birds*) and suppliers, especially fishmongers (rare in Old Comedy), gain new prominence, as do their companions in high living: *hetairai*, pimps (one in Old Comedy), and parasites (two in Old Comedy, though these seem to have been not parasites properly speaking but mere spongers). For the scenario, cf. Antiphanes's *Fisherwoman* K-A fr. 27 (early 330s), where actual *hetairai* and their lovers, gathered at a meeting of a famous dining club with sixty members (Alexis K-A fr. 102; Philip allegedly paid a talent for a book of their jokes: Athen. 13.614d–e), are metaphorically portrayed as fish (gluttons often had fish-nicknames) by a female speaker who seems as much bawd-impresario as fisher-woman (Nesselrath 1997: 279–281). One famous gourmand, Philonides of Melite (dead by 366), a patron of parasites and lover of the *hetaira* Nais, is even a title character in Aristophon. In Antiphanes's *Rich Men* K-A fr. 188, someone relates that the gourmands Phoenicides (in Euphanes K-A fr. 1, a Homeric hero at eating seafood) and Taureas (the two fight over an eel in Antiphanes's *Auletris or Twin Sisters* K-A fr. 50, ca. 350) were outraged when Euthynus the fishmonger ran short; they gather groups and make a speech: the few control the sea and spend massive sums but no fish sail in; why then administer the islands? why not have a law requiring the special import of fish? No, Mato (a greedy fish-eater: Anaxilas K-A fr. 20, Antiphanes K-A fr. 117) has monopolized the fishermen and Diogeiton has convinced them all to bring their catch to him—how undemocratic! Similarly, in Alexis's *Kettle* K-A fr. 130, 131 (early 320s), the wealthy politician Aristonicus (active 334–322) is applauded for a law forbidding special fish-pricing for insiders, while in *Dorcis or Poppyzousa* K-A fr. 57, fishmongers erect a monument to the oligarchic politician and famed gourmand Callimedon (active 345–318).

Lack of context makes it difficult to tell if high living is being remarked on to make a political point, but some fragments are suggestive: in Timocles's *Delos* K-A fr. 4 (a conversation naming bribe-takers in the Harpalus scandal of 323), Callisthenes at least had the excuse of poverty (because he had squandered his inheritance on fish and *hetairai*: Antiphanes K-A fr. 27); in Anaxandrides's *Protesilaus* (between 386 and 361), the extravagance of Iphicrates's wedding to the daughter of King Cotys of Thrace (386) reflects the current relationship between Athens, Sparta, and Thebes (K-A fr. 42); Mnesimachus's *Philip*, which portrayed Demosthenes at a banquet in Macedon (probably in 346, when he went there as an ambassador) to which Pharsalians are invited, refers (K-A fr. 8) to "eating an Achaean town roasted," i.e., Halus, reduced by Philip on behalf of the Pharsalians (for the idea compare *Peace* 242–252); Heraclides K-A fr. 1 praises Chares for his feasting of the Athenians on one big bird in celebration of their victory over Philip's mercenaries under Adaeus "the Rooster" (ca. 350); and Ephippus's *Geryon* K-A fr. 5 imagines a giant fish being cooked for the title character—naturalized in typical fourth-century fashion from mythic monster to petty Oriental king—with the assistance of various peoples, cities, and leaders. Of a *gynaikonomos*, a magistracy created under Demetrius of Phalerum that regulated the behavior of elite women and limited the number of guests at a symposium, someone in Timocles's *Philodikastes* K-A fr. 34 remarks, "he would do better to count the houses of those who have no dinner."

Intellectuals, only occasionally targeted in Old Comedy (Carey 2000), are now joined by philosophers and their schools for prominent attention—not only Plato, the most frequently attested *komoidoumenos* of the fourth century (Weiher 1913: 37–55; Arnott 1996: 6; Imperio 1998: 121–129), but also Peripatetics (Antiphanes's *Cleophanes*), Pythagoreans (Alexis and Cratinus Junior's *Pythagorizousa* and *Tarentines*, Aristophon's *Pythagoristes*), Stoics (Damoxenus K-A fr. 2.64–67, Philemon K-A fr. 88), Epicureans (Antiphanes K-A fr. 202, Bato K-A fr. 3, 5, Damoxenus K-A fr. 2, Hegesippus K-A fr. 2), and collective menageries (Plato's *Sophists*, Philemon's *Philosophers*). Caricature and egghead stereotypes continue: in Epicrates (K-A fr. 10, play unknown), someone tells of a herd of youths gathered at the gymnasium of the Academy to discuss with Plato, Speusippus, and Menedemus inter alia the classification of a pumpkin, and are briefly interrupted by a passing Sicilian doctor who "farted at them as fools"; in Aristophon's *Plato,* a speaker (probably Plato, apparently a character also in Amphis's *Dexidemides*: K-A fr. 13) promises to make an enrollee in the Academy as thin as a corpse, like Philippides (updating Chaerephon, *Clouds* 500–504), though elsewhere Academicians are portrayed as luxurious and effeminate (Antiphanes K-A fr. 35) and elegantly turned out, like the young man about to address the assembly in Ephippus's *Nauagos* K-A fr. 14.

By now, such intellectual pursuits, no longer a threatening novelty or a focus of generational conflict, evoke little alarm or hostility, and philosophical precepts and techniques had become familiar enough to enliven everyday comic conversations: in Theopompus's *Hedychares* K-A fr. 16, someone alludes to Socrates's dyad problem (*Phaedo* 96e) by observing "for one isn't even one, and in fact two are scarcely one, according to Plato," and in Amphis's *Amphicrates* K-A fr. 6, a slave says to his young master (probably involved with a *hetaira*), "about whatever good you expect to realize through her, I've less an idea than about Plato's Good." Philosophy had also begun to inform the ethical subtleties increasingly characteristic of fourth-century comedy: thoughts about the nature of love in Alexis's *Phaedrus*, which may owe its title to Plato's dialogue, are clearly informed by the *Symposium* (202–204 ~ K-A fr. 247), as is the definition of a lover in his *Wounded Man* (203b–d ~ K-A fr. 236), and Peripatetic thought suffuses the plays of Menander, a pupil of Theophrastus.

Nevertheless, philosophical institutions or communities were still to a degree suspect in the eyes of ordinary people, and when they were identified with oligarchy or monarchy, as was the Lyceum, they could come under attack in periods of democratic reaction, as in 399 (Socrates), 322 (Aristotle, tutor of Alexander), 318 (Theophrastus, tutor of Demetrius of Phalerum), and 307, when philosophers were required to register, fled in protest (an event applauded by a character in Alexis's *Knight* K-A fr. 99), and returned the following year when the requirement was repealed (Arnott 1996: 858–859). It is hard to say whether philosophical ideas themselves played a role in such reactions. In Menander (Major 1997), they harmonize with the lives and private dilemmas of the well-to-do main characters but are given no political context. Although plays in this style were at home in an oligarchic environment and frame civic ideals more often by the lights of an Aeschines than a Demosthenes, they do not seem overtly anti-democratic (or democratic either, *pace* Lape 2004) and remained popular during democratic res- torations. So Diogenes Laertius was probably correct to say (5.79 = Menander K-A test. 9) that when Menander was among those arraigned in 307 (the leading advocate was Demochares; see below), he "came close to standing trial for no other reason than because he was [Demetrius of Phalerum's] friend, but Demetrius's cousin Telesphorus appealed for his release." But it is still unclear what Telesphorus's motivation or connec- tion with Menander may have been: friend or friend of a friend? fan? opposed to these trials generally? (Potter 1987); in the event, none of those who stood trial were sentenced (Philochorus *FGrH* 328 F 66).

There is also the statement in a papyrus summary of Menander's plays that he put his *Imbrians* "into production for the Dionysia [of 302/1] but it did not take place on account of Lachares the tyrant [...] Callipus of Athens was the actor" (K-A test. 52).[1] It is unfortunately unclear whether it was the whole Dionysia or only Menander's play that "did not take place"; whether the author correctly attributes the action to Lachares, who was not yet tyrant, or has simply assumed that Lachares must have been respon- sible, perhaps mistaking Lachares for Stratocles; or whether the whole incident was a false inference from contemporary comedy (O'Sullivan 2009). If the statement is cor- rect, Lachares was still the popular leader he seems to have been before throwing in with Cassander after Ipsus, and "the tyrant" is due to chronological carelessness or simply asserted to flag the identity of the sparsely attested Lachares. In any case, such an action against Menander at this time would have been motivated on grounds similar to his arraignment in 307: associating with (anti-Antigonid) oligarchs or somehow espousing their interests in (a) play(s).

It was in this period of democratic revival after 307 that political comedy reappeared for a brief and final encore, notably in the plays of Archedicus and Philippides. Both were politically active oligarchs—Archedicus a partisan of Antipater and Demetrius of Phalerum and prominent (as *anagrapheus*, who replaced and expanded the authority

---

[1] ἐξ]-
ἔδωκεν εἰc ἐργαcίαν [εἰc]
Διονύcια, οὐκ ἐγένετο δ[ὲ διὰ]
Λαχάρην τὸν τυρανν.[
τα ὑπεκρίνετο Κάλ[λιπ]-
οc Ἀθηναῖοc
    τύραννν[ον. ἔπει]τα Wilamowitz: τυραννν[ῆσαν]τα· Groenewald:
    τυραννν[εύον]τα· Luppe: τυραννν[εύσον]τα?

of the traditional *grammateus*) in the regime of Phocion (Habicht 1993), Philippides a partisan of Lysimachus and a foe of Demetrius Poliorcetes (Philipp 1973)—and as in Old Comedy their targets were then-ascendant popular leaders.

Archedicus K-A fr. 4 attacked Demochares, nephew of Demosthenes and Stratocles's rival, for oral prostitution (so that he was "unfit to blow the sacrificial flame") and for "outdoing the practices described by such obscene writers as Botrys and Philaenis." The charge was accepted by the historian Timaeus, who lived and wrote in Athens and who attributed it also to Demochares's enemies ("Democleides and his circle"); Suda ω 263 further notes that Duris attributed the same charge to Pytheas against Demosthenes (*FGrH* 76 F 8). But Polybius rejected it on the grounds that it was in fact leveled only by the comic poet (12.13). The date of this attack is uncertain, but far likelier between 307 and 303 (when Demochares was exiled) than during the Antipatrid regime.

Philippides attacked Stratocles in a play that perhaps included him as a character (K-A fr. 26 with Plutarch's comment, *Amat.* 4.750e), claiming that it is impious flattery of Demetrius that "undoes [καταλύει] the demos, not a comedy" (K-A fr. 25), echoing a slogan of the day ([Plu.] *Mor.* 851e, f) and defending a prior comic criticism in a situation reminiscent of Aristophanes's defense against Cleon; Plutarch's comparison of Cleon and Stratocles as demagogues (*Demetr.* 11.2–3) was no doubt prompted by Aristophanic echoes in such comedies (O'Sullivan 2009: 72–75); *adespota* K-A fr. 698 = Plu. *Demetr.* 27.1–3 dubs Demetrius's extravagant lover, the *hetaira* Lamia, "the true city-taker" (Athens another Troy taken by another "besieger"), cf. Aspasia's alleged influence on Pericles in comedies of the 430s. Philippides also paid a price, going into exile after the stasis of 303. Demetrius II in *Areopagite* of ca. 294, after Poliorcetes had ousted Lachares, recalls the "tyrant" as having feasted during the famine of 295/4, when Poliorcetes was besieging the city, but thereafter real people retire from the comic stage. Their doings and memorable sayings are now the concern of collectors of anecdotes (*chreiai*), who drew on past comedy and were sometimes comic poets too, e.g., Lynceus of Samos, brother of the historian Duris (in his only preserved comic fragment, a Perinthian and his Rhodian dinner host belittle Attic cuisine; Lynceus was also a noted writer on food), and Machon (e.g., his anecdotes about Demetrius and Stratocles, K-A fr. 15, 16).

DOMESTICITY

Fifth-century comedies about typical people, households, personal relationships, and love affairs were rare—Crates (ca. 450–430) and Pherecrates (ca. 440–410) were singled out as exceptional by later critics—as were the requisite personnel: unmarried citizen boys (seldom) and girls (virtually never), citizen wives (first in Aristophanes's plays of 411 but in protected public spaces, before then only market-women and relatives of "demagogues"), prominent slaves (first in *Frogs* and *Wealth*), and characters representing trades, professions, or personality types (mainly in brief illustrative scenes). Comedies with a civic and political orientation, which include the fantastic/escapist varieties, naturally featured adult male citizens operating in public spaces, and house-holds were depicted (if at all) from a civic vantage point or with the women elided (e.g. *Knights, Clouds, Wasps*); the erotic fracas involving a citizen girl in Aristophanes *Assemblywomen* 877–1111 is hard to imagine in the fifth century. To some extent, this ori-entation was forced by social inhibitions that protected the private world of the house-hold and the respectability of its women (Sommerstein 1980, Sommerstein 2009), so that plots about family or love were the province of myth- and *hetaira*-comedy; in all eras, the great majority of nonmythical or legendary (e.g., Sappho, Cleobulina) women who are title characters or are named in comedies are living, dead, or fictitious *hetairai*. Even tragic intrigues that seemed "realistic" (as in Euripides) could be denounced as outrageous (*Women at the Thesmophoria, Frogs*). But by the turn of the century, myth- and *hetaira*-comedies had overtaken the fantastic/escapist and political types in popu-larity, and their domestic elements (now including symposia) began to coalesce in the sort of plays that paved the way for New Comedy, as they do also in vase-paintings and figurines (Green 2010: 75–93).

Comedies with fictional plots on domestic or erotic themes by Crates and Pherecrates and a few others were thus ahead of their time. Crates K-A fr. 46 (in Doric) is prob-ably spoken by a stereotypical doctor. Plato's *Phaon* starred an old man whose virility and desirability have been restored by Aphrodite. Pherecrates's *Slave-Trainer* suggests a domestic scenario. Cratinus's *Wine Flask* (323) featured Cratinus himself estranged from his wife (Comedy) and having an affair with Methe (Drunkenness). Philonides wrote a *Philetairos*, a title also for Antiphanes, Amphis, Heniochus, and Hegesippus. Phrynichus's *Monotropos*, Plato's *Man in Great Pain*, Crates II's *Money-Lover*,[2] and Theopompus's *Hedychares* anticipate the type-comedy of Antiphanes's *Misoponeros* and Menander's *Dyskolos*. Cratinus's *Kleoboulinai* featured riddles (very popular in the fourth century) propounded by the heroine, Thales's mother Cleobulina (a title char-acter also for Alexis), and Ameipsias's *Sappho*, though we have no fragments, may well have included erotic elements (including songs: Epicrates K-A fr. 4), as did some of the later comedies bearing her name by Amphis, Ephippus, Antiphanes, Epicrates, Timocles, and Diphilus (Dover 1978: 174).

Pherecrates seems to have pioneered the *hetaira*-comedy with *Corianno, The Forgetful Man or Thalatta, Petale*, and perhaps *Kitchen or Pannychis* and *Tyrannis*; in *Chiron*, Music is portrayed as a mature *hetaira* mistreated by abusive lovers (= contemporary composers; Henderson 2000, 2002). The title character of *Corianno* keeps a prosperous household where much eating and drinking take place; characters include a boastful soldier just returned from Asia (K-A fr. 73–74), a nurse (?) Glyke (K-A fr. 75–76), and a young man telling a love-struck old man (his father?) that "it is fitting for me to be in love, but your time is past" (K-A fr. 77–79, cf. *Wasps* 1326–86, where a son admonishes

---

[2] This Crates is classified as Old Comic by Suda κ 2340, which lists three titles; *Money-Lover* and *Treasure* sound so like later comedy that the Suda's classification has been doubted, but the third, *Birds*, does suggest Old Comedy.

his father, who has abducted the *auletris* Dardanis from a symposium). It is unknown whether Pherecrates's *hetairai* were actual or fictional, though Thalatta, an attested *hetaira* name (Athen. 567c), is also the title of a play by Diocles (fl. 410s to ca. 450), and Pannychis, a *hetaira* name in Petr. *Sat.* 25 and Luc. *Meretr.* 9, is also a title for Eubulus (370s to ca. 330). One actual *hetaira*, Myrrhine, lover of Leogoras, seems to have been a character in Eupolis's *Autolycus II* K-A fr. 50; this play (ca. 418), like *Flatterers* (421), portrayed the extravagance of the wealthy wastrel Callias.

Toward the end of the century *hetaira*-comedies become popular and often portray actual *hetairai* (Nesselrath 1990: 318–324), sometimes over a long career: Lais was born ca. 422, soon renowned (a *pais* in Strattis K-A fr. 27), and still active, though in sad decline, in the 360s (Epicrates K-A fr. 3). Such situations were an object lesson about life and time (Philetaerus's *Huntress* K-A fr. 9) as well as a source of humor: in Timocles's *Orestautocleides* K-A fr. 27, a group of old *hetairai* (actual) surround the pederast Autocleides as the Furies had surrounded Orestes in Aeschylus's *Eumenides*. Examples are Cephisodorus's *Rival of Lais* (also Epicrates), Diocles's *Thalatta* and *Melissai* (also Antiphanes's *Melissa*), Poliochus's *Corinthiast* (also Philetaerus), Theopompus's *Nemea*, *Pamphile* (also Alexis), and perhaps *Batyle* and *Sirens*, Alcaeus's *Callisto* and *Palaestra* (also Amphis: associated with Socrates by Aelian *VH* 13.12, as was Theodote by X. *Smp.* 3.11.4 ff.), Philyllius's (or Eunicus's) *Anteia* (also Antiphanes and Alexis). At least thirty-seven names of *hetairai* appear in comedies ca. 380–320 (from Lais to Pythionice), often in groups (e.g., Anaxandrides K-A fr. 9, where old men reminisce about grand *hetairai* of the past; Philetaerus K-A fr. 9; Theophilus K-A fr. 11; Diphilus K-A fr. 42.38–40), and their exploits or connection with famous men, sometimes over a long career, help to date the plays (Schiassi 1951, Webster 1952).

Hetairai offered well-to-do men, young and old, the showiness, companionship, wit, and entertainment that were unavailable from their own or others' wives and that were open to public view. We hear about the superiority of *hetairai* to wives (e.g., Philetaerus K-A fr. 5), but outside of myth-comedy, adultery scenarios are rare—Alcaeus's *Sisters Seduced*, Ameipsias's *Adulterers* (also Antiphanes), Philemon's *Adulterer*—and possibly involved not wives but free *hetairai* or mistresses; likewise, the seduction of maidens is rare (Moschion, apparently, in Menander's *Samia* is exceptional): the preference expressed in Timocles K-A fr. 24 for sleeping with a virgin instead of a streetwalker might refer to rape ("...despite having to struggle and be slapped by her delicate hands"). *Hetairai* thus afforded comic poets both a glamorous terrain to explore and an avenue for portraying either actual love affairs, which could have a political dimension, or inventing fictional ones (the rule in New Comedy) that offered free scope for excitement, intrigue, suspense, and ambiguity about (mostly female) identity or status.

By midcentury, many of the typical features are in place. Anteia is a model of the wealthy *hetaira* (Philyllius or Eunicus). Philetaerus's *Korinthiastes* had a young man, *Huntress* an old man, in love with a *hetaira*. In Eubulus's *Pamphilos*, someone gets a maiden's nurse drunk, probably in an intrigue, and in *Kampylion* a man encounters obstacles (a stern father, as in Anaxandrides K-A fr. 54?) in his love for a *hetaira* who is "well-behaved" (and so ultimately to be recognized as a citizen?); the title character, probably a slave, assists, as in Amphis's *Amphicrates*. Eubulus's *Neottis* certainly had a recognition-scene (K-A fr. 69). In Antiphanes's *Hydria* K-A fr. 210, a *hetaira* is already a citizen (cf. Is. 3.10–17), "without a guardian or kinfolk" but a "real girlfriend" (*hetaira*), unlike others who abuse that designation. In Anaxilas's *Neottis,* there is praise of a "nice" *hetaira* (K-A fr. 20) and also a general tirade against them (K-A fr. 21, a catalogue of examples comparing them to she-monsters of myth) by a disillusioned young man, a friend or slave, or a father or pedagogue. Antiphanes's *Hydria* had another nice *hetaira* (a "real girlfriend" K-A fr. 210), again perhaps anticipating a citizen recognition. Antiphanes was apparently known for *hetaira* plots that included fights over them (Athen. 13.555a), a frequent motif (Amphis K-A fr. 23, Alexis K-A fr. 103, Theophilus K-A fr. 11); *hetairai* also competed in love (Nicostratus's *Anterosa*). Alexis *Agonis* or *Hippiskos* had a young man in love (K-A fr. 3), a scheme to dupe a foreigner (soldier?) (K-A fr. 2), and probably a recognition (*hippiskos* is a garment or jewel), while *Demetrius or Philetaerus* (to judge from Turpilius's adaptation) had a young man who dupes his father out of a talent to pursue an affair with a *hetaira.*

Also involved in love plots in the semiprivate ambit of the symposium are prostitutes, musicians (Anaxandrides's *Kitharistria*, Antiphanes's *Auletris* [-*ides* Phoenicides], Alexis's *Poetria*, Theophilus's *Philaulos*, Dromo's *Psaltria*), and other slaves (e.g. Alexis's *Hairdresser*, where a father has two sons, one a partygoer and the other a "clod" [K-A fr. 113], one or both perhaps involved with the title character), often foreigners (Anaxandrides's *Amprakiotis* and *Samia*, Theophilus's *Boiotia*, Alexis's *Milesia* and *Olynthia*), in thrall to an unsavory figure like a pimp[3] or a boastful soldier and then recognized as citizens or otherwise rescued, as in Eubulus's *Stephanopolides, Pimp,* and *Pamphilus*; Anaxilas's *Neottis*; Antiphanes's *Neottis* and *Hydria*; and Alexis's *Agonis* and *Olynthia*. In Antiphanes's *Auletris,* the girl in a brothel is a lost twin, in Alexis's *Olynthia* a noble girl finds herself in a poor household. In Antiphanes *Neottis* K-A fr. 166, a girl and her sister have been taken by a merchant from their home in Syria and sold to a wicked and stingy moneylender. In Alexis's *She Drinks Mandrake,* a girl is drugged to prevent her capture by a rival, while in *Soldier* a dispute over ownership of a baby (K-A fr. 212) may anticipate Menander's *Epitrepontes.*

In the development of purely domestic plots, myth-comedy played an essential role (Konstantakos, chapter 7, in this volume), affording Old Comic poets a way around the social inhibitions that protected citizen households from public view and providing established plots that their successors gradually domesticated by identifying elements amenable to comic exploitation and translating them into contemporary settings. The earliest plays seem to have been more or less straight burlesque, not unlike

---

[3] The pimp (*pornoboskos*) as a character (always unsympathetic) or as a lead role is not attested in Old Comedy, but frequently thereafter, e.g., Anaxilas's and Axionicus's *Etruscan*, Dioxippus's *Rival Pimp*, Eubulus's *Hyacinthus or The Pimp*: Nesselrath 1990: 323–325, 329.

satyr drama, with which comedy seems to have intersected (Storey 2005, Bakola 2010: 81–117; for Middle Comedy, Shaw 2010), relying on implication (ἔμφασις) when they wanted to reflect contemporary life, e.g., Cratinus's *Nemesis*, suggesting Pericles in the story of the seduction of a maiden (the goddess Nemesis) by Zeus, with Hermes (as often) and Aphrodite assisting. In addition there was paratragedy (especially of Euripides), enabling comic characters to channel mythical figures and repurpose tragic plots, e.g., Euripides's *Telephus* in *Acharnians* and *Women at the Thesmophoria*; paratragedy became a specialty of poets in the period 410–380, notably of Strattis. Tragedy contributed as well, in particular the "romantic" dramas of adventure and intrigue that Euripides began to produce after 415 and that introduced more mundane characters and situations.[4] After its heyday from ca. 410 to the 340s, the popularity of myth-comedy rapidly recedes in favor of fully domestic comedy.

For love-plots, myth-comedy was the main vehicle (Konstantakos 2002), particularly the affairs of Zeus, already well developed in tragedy and satyr-drama by Aeschylus's *Alcmene*, *Callisto*, *Carians* or *Europa*, and *Semele*; Sophocles's *Amphitryo*, *Daedalus*, *Danae*, *Minos*, and *Tyro* (twice); Euripides's *Alcmene*, *Antiope*, *Cretans*, *Danae*, *Lamia*, *Melanippe the Wise*, and *Pasiphae*; Ion's *Alcmene*; Chaeremon's *Io*; and Dionysius II of Syracuse's *Leda*. It was explored in comedy to ca. 380 by Crates's *Lamia*; Hermippus's *Europa*; Aristophanes's *Daedalus*; Archippus's *Amphitryo* (twice); Plato's *Daedalus*, *Europa*, *Io*, and *Long Night*; Alcaeus's *Callisto*, *Ganymede*, and *Pasiphae*; Apollophanes's *Cretans* and *Danae*; Nicochares's *Cretans*; Polyzelus's *Demotyndareus* and *Birth of Dionysus*; and Sannyrio's *Danae* and *Io*, and then in the Middle Comic period by, e.g., Anaxandrides's *Helen* and Eubulus's *Auge* and *Ion*. A number of plays about homosexual affairs (Antiphanes's *Pederast*, Diphilus's *Pederasts*, Damoxenus K-A fr. 3), a type which Plutarch praises Menander for not writing (K-A test. 104), may have taken as their inspiration plays about Zeus and Ganymede by Alcaeus and Eubulus (Antiphanes composed one as well), and possibly Plato (*Laius*) and Strattis (*Chrysippus*) (Nesselrath 1990: 209–211).

Ancient scholars identified particular innovations; the *Life of Aristophanes* (K-A test. 1.50) informs us that his *Cocalus* (387), a myth-comedy about the killing of Minos by Cocalus's daughters (treated also by Sophocles in *Men of Camicus*), "introduced rape and recognition and the other themes that Menander imitated," while Suda α 1982 credits Anaxandrides (fl. 380s–340s) as "the first to introduce love affairs and the rape of maidens."[5] These statements are compatible if Aristophanes was the innovator in the myth-comic mode and Anaxandrides in the domestic mode, which was not pursued

---

[4] For example, the old female slave who menaces Menelaus in *Helen* 435–482 and the Phrygian slave who beseeches Orestes in broken Greek in *Orestes* 1369–1536. Euripides remains influential in the Middle (e.g., Axionicus's and Philippides's *Phileuripides*) and New Comic periods (e.g., Menander's repurposing of the long messenger speech in *Orestes* 866–956 to suit the contemporary situation in *Sicyonian(s)*, 176–271).

[5] Euripides's contribution was recognized as well; e.g., Satyrus *Life* (P. Oxy. 1176 F 39).

by Aristophanes; likely candidates are *Amprakiotis, Kanephoros, Kitharistria, Samia,* and *Phialephoros.* It is worth noting that Anaxandrides also composed paratragedy (*Helen*) and myth-comedy, in both mythic (*Birth of Dionysus*) and contemporary settings (*Protesilaus*), as well as *hetaira*-comedy (*Gerontomania*), character-comedy (*Farmers, Hoplomachos*), situation-comedy (*Twins, Treasure*), and even political comedy (*Cities*)—a range typical of the Middle Comic period and pointing forward to the New. That Anaxandrides was an innovator is also suggested by the revival of his *Treasure* in 311, when other plays of this type were in vogue. Innovations ahead of their time are nothing new in the history of comedy, so that we should not dismiss out of hand the dating of Euetes to the 380s (Suda ε 2766) simply because *Heiress* (his only attested title) should not be so early (it next appears as a title for Alexis, Antiphanes, Heniochus, Diphilus, and Menander).

Many other innovations and amplifications of earlier comic elements along the road to Menandrian domesticity are identifiable in the period after ca. 380. As comedy shed its topical and mythical grounding and became entirely fictional—actual contemporaries making only cameo appearances, the sense of particular place fading, and gods relegated to the role of prologue-speaker—characters acquired typical roles, names (or nicknames, especially for slaves and parasites, e.g., the catalogue in Anaxandrides K-A fr. 35), and personalities, and eventually type-masks. Characters identified by a (manual) profession or typical activity became prominent, especially cooks (Arnott 2010:319–322), parasites (the first full-play treatment perhaps Alexis's *Parasite* (350s), cf. Athen. 6.235e, Nesselrath 1990: 309–317), athletes,[6] musicians, pimps, soldiers,[7] and rustics (Konstantakos 2005b), their wide range suggesting "a conscious aim for novelty in this area" (Arnott 2010:314). Abstract themes attracted interest, e.g., Anaxandrides's *Anteros* and *Hybris,* Anaxilas's *Euandria,* Eubulus's *Olbia,* and Menander's *Orge.* Objects or incidents became central to the plot, especially recognition-plots—e.g., Alexis's *Ring* and *Kettle* (perhaps the original of Plautus's *Aulularia*)—as did cases of mistaken identity (as early as Ephippus's *Homoioi* in the 370s) and issues of identity generally. Above all, successful plots became plot-types that were freely shared among poets and were gradually winnowed into a narrow repertory that prized nuance and virtuosity over originality (as in Old Comedy) and versatility (as in Middle Comedy).

.

[6] Not identifiable in comedy before the mid-fourth century: Alexis, Philemon, Theophilus (K-A fr. 8 identifies gluttony as a typical trait) in *Pancratiast*; Alexis's *Apobates*; Eubulus's and Xenarchus's *Pentathlete.*

[7] The real-life counterparts of the comic soldier, a boastful mercenary who stands in the way of a civilian's love affair, began to appear in Athens in the 360s and in comedies in the 350s, e.g., Ephippus's *Peltast,* Alexis's *Man Moving In,* and Alexis's and Antiphanes's *Soldier* (the title of plays by six Middle Comic poets as well as Menander). In New Comedy, soldiers provide virtually the only contact of the plot with the wider world: Lape 2004: 32–33, 62–67, 199–201, 172–173, although her argument that they represent the oppressive Hellenistic kingdoms takes inadequate account of their long-standing stereotypical nature.

FURTHER READING

A comprehensive study of politics and domesticity in fourth-century comedy before Menander is yet to be written, but useful surveys are Arnott 1972 and 2010, Bellardinelli 1998, Handley 1985, and Webster 1970. Rusten et al. 2011 contains new translations of the major fragments and testimonia, and detailed information can be found in K-A and in the critical commentaries on Alexis (Arnott 1996), Anaxandrides (Millis 2001), Antiphanes (Konstantakos 2000), Eubulus (Hunter 1983), Plato (Pirrotta 2009), Strattis (Orth 2009), and the selections in Bellardinelli 1998, Olson 2007, and Papachrysostomou 2008.

BIBLIOGRAPHY

Arnott, W. G. 1972. "From Aristophanes to Menander." *G&R* 19: 65–80.
——. 1996. *Alexis: The Fragments: A Commentary*. Cambridge: Cambridge University Press.
——. 2010. "Middle Comedy." In *Brill's Companion to the Study of Greek Comedy*, edited by G. Dobrov, 279–331. Leiden and Boston: Brill.
Bakola, E. 2010. *Cratinus and the Art of Comedy*. Oxford: Oxford University Press.
Belardinelli, A. M., O. Imperio, G. Mastromarco, M. Pellegrino, and P. Totaro. 1998. *Tessere: Frammenti della commedia greca: Studi e commenti*. Bari: Adriatica.
Boedeker, D., and K. Raaflaub, eds. 1998. *Democracy, Empire, and the Arts in Fifth-Century Athens*. Cambridge, MA: Harvard University Press.
Carey, C. 2000. "Old Comedy and the Sophists." In *The Rivals of Aristophanes: Studies in Athenian Old Comedy*, edited by D. Harvey and J. Wilkins, 419–436. London: The Classical Press of Wales.
Csapo, E. 2000. "From Aristophanes to Menander? Genre Transformation in Greek Comedy." In *Matrices of Genre: Authors, Canons, and Society*, edited by M. Depew and D. Obbink, 115–133. Cambridge, MA: Harvard University Press.
Depew, M., and D. Obbink, eds. 2000. *Matrices of Genre: Authors, Canons, and Society*. Cambridge, MA: Harvard University Press.
Dobrov, G., ed. 1997. *The City as Comedy: Society and Representation in Athenian Drama*. Chapel Hill: University of North Carolina Press.
——, ed. 2010. *Brill's Companion to the Study of Greek Comedy*. Leiden and Boston: Brill.
Dover, K. J. 1978. *Greek Homosexuality*. London: Duckworth.
Easterling, P. E., and B. M. W. Knox. 1985. *The Cambridge History of Classical Literature*. Vol. 1, *Greek Literature*. Cambridge, UK: Cambridge University Press.
Glazebrook, A., and M. M. Henry, eds. 2011. *Greek Prostitutes in the Ancient Mediterranean, 800 BCE–200 CE*. Madison: University of Wisconsin Press.
Green, J. R. 2010. "The Material Evidence." In *Brill's Companion to the Study of Greek Comedy*, edited by G. Dobrov, 71–102. Leiden and Boston: Brill.
Habicht, C. 1993. "The Comic Poet Archedikos." *Hesp.*62: 253–256.
Handley, E. 1985. "Comedy." In *The Cambridge History of Classical Literature*. Vol. 1, *Greek Literature*, edited by P. E. Easterling and B. M. W. Knox, 355–425. Cambridge, UK: Cambridge University Press.
Harrison, W. M., ed. 2005. *Satyr Drama: Greek Tragedy at Play*. Swansea: The Classical Press of Wales.

Harvey, D., and J. Wilkins. 2000. *The Rivals of Aristophanes: Studies in Athenian Old Comedy.* London: The Classical Press of Wales.

Henderson, J. 1998. "Attic Old Comedy, Free Speech, and Democracy." In *Democracy, Empire, and the Arts in Fifth-Century Athens*, edited by D. Boedeker and K. Raaflaub, 255–273. Cambridge, MA: Harvard University Press.

———. 2000. "Pherekrates and the Women of old Comedy." In *The Rivals of Aristophanes: Studies in Athenian Old Comedy*, edited by D. Harvey and J. Wilkins, 135–150. London: The Classical Press of Wales.

———. 2002. "Strumpets on Stage: The Early Comic Hetaera." *Dioniso: Rivista Annuale* 1: 78–87.

———. 2003. "Demos, Demagogue, Tyrant in Attic Old Comedy." In *Popular Tyranny. Sovereignty and its Discontents in Ancient Greece*, edited by K. A. Morgan, 155–179. Austin: University of Texas Press.

———. 2012. "Pursuing Nemesis: Cratinus and Mythological Comedy." In *No Laughing Matter: Studies in Athenian Comedy*, edited by C. W. Marshall and G. A. Kovacs, 1–12. London: Bristol Classical Press.

Hunter, R. 1983. *Eubulus: The Fragments.* Cambridge: Cambridge University Press.

Hutchinson, G. O. 2011. "House Politics and City Politics in Aristophanes." *CQ* 61: 48–70.

Imperio, O. 1998. "La figura dell' intellettuale nella commedia greca." In *Tessere: Frammenti della commedia greca: Studie e commenti*, edited by A. M. Balardinelli et al., 43–110. Bari: Adriatica Editrice.

Konstantakos, I. M. 2000. "A Commentary on the Fragments of Eight Plays of Antiphanes." PhD diss., University of Cambridge.

———. 2002. "Towards a Literary History of Comic Love." *C&M* 53: 141–171.

———. 2005a. "The Drinking Theatre: Staged Symposia in Greek Comedy." *Mnem.* 58: 183–217.

———. 2005b. "Aspects of the Figure of the ἄγροικος in Ancient Comedy." *RhM* 148: 1–26.

———. 2011. "Conditions of Playwriting and the Comic Dramatist's Craft in the Fourth Century." *Logeion* 1: 145–183.

Kyriakidi, N. 2006. *Aristophanes und Eupolis: Zur Geschichte einer dichterischen Rivalität.* Berlin: De Gruyter.

Lape, Susan. 2004. *Reproducing Athens: Menander's Comedy, Democratic Culture, and the Hellenistic City.* Princeton: Princeton University Press.

Major, W. E. 1997. "Menander in a Macedonian World." *GRBS* 38: 41–73.

Marshall, C. W., and G. A. Kovacs. 2012. *No Laughing Matter: Studies in Athenian Comedy.* London: Bristol Classical Press.

Michelini, A. 1998. "Isocrates' Civic Invective: *Acharnians* and *On the Peace*." *AJP* 128: 115–133.

Millis, B. W. 2001. "A Commentary on the Fragments of Anaxandrides." PhD diss., University of Illinois at Urbana-Champaign.

Morgan, K. A. 2003. *Popular Tyranny: Sovereignty and its Discontents in Ancient Greece.* Austin: University of Texas Press.

Nesselrath, H.-G. 1990. *Die attische Mittlere Komödie: Ihre Stellung in der antiken Literaturkritik und Literaturgeschichte.* Berlin: De Gruyter.

———. 1997. "The Polis of Athens in Middle Comedy." In *Brill's Companion to the Study of Greek Comedy*, edited by G. Dobrov, 271–288. Leiden and Boston: Brill.

O'Sullivan, L. 2009. "History from Comic Hypotheses: Stratocles, Lachares, and *P.Oxy.* 1235." *GRBS* 49: 53–79.

Olson, S. D. 2007. *Broken Laughter: Select Fragments of Greek Comedy.* Oxford: Oxford University Press.

Orth, C. 2009. *Strattis: Die Fragmente: Ein Kommentar*. Berlin: Verlag Antike.

Traill, J., ed. 1994–2012. *Persons of Ancient Athens*. Toronto: Athenians.

Papachrysostomou, A. 2008. *Six Comic Poets: A Commentary on Selected Fragments of Middle Comedy*. Tübingen: Gunter Narr Verlag.

Peschel, I. 1987. *Die Hetära bei Symposion und Komos in der attisch-rotfigurigen Vasenmalerei des 6.–4. Jahrhundert v. Chr.* Frankfurt a/M: P. Lang.

Petrides, A. K., and S. Papaioannou, eds. 2010. *New Perspectives on Postclassical Comedy*. Newcastle upon Tyne: Cambridge Scholars Publishing.

Petrides, A. K. 2010. "New Performance." In *New Perspectives on Postclassical Comedy*, edited by A. K. Petrides and S. Papaioannou, 79–124. Newcastle upon Tyne: Cambridge Scholars Publishing.

Philipp, G. B. 1973. "Philippides, ein politischer Komiker in hellenistischer Zeit." *Gymnasium* 80: 493–509.

Pirrotta, S. 2009. *Plato Comicus: Die fragmentarischen Komödien: Ein Kommentar*. Berlin: Verlag Antike.

Potter, D. 1987. "Telesphoros, Cousin of Demetrius: A Note on the Trial of Menander." *Historia* 36: 491–495.

Rusten, J., et al., eds. 2011. *The Birth of Comedy: Texts, Documents, and Art from Athenian Comic Competitions, 486–280*. Baltimore: The Johns Hopkins University Press.

Schiassi, G. 1951. "De temporum quaestionibus ad Atticas IV saeculi meretrices et eiusdem comicas fabulas pertinentibus." *Rivista di filologia e di istruzione classica* 79: 217–245.

Shaw, C. A. 2010. "Middle Comedy and the 'Satyric' Style." *AJPh* 131: 1–22.

Sommerstein, A. H. 1980. "The Naming of Women in Greek and Roman Comedy." *Quaderni di storia* 11: 393–418, reprinted with additions in *Talking about Laughter and Other Studies in Greek Comedy*, by A. H. Sommerstein, 43–69. Oxford: Oxford University Press.

——. 1984. "Aristophanes and the Demon Poverty." *CQ* 34: 314–333.

——. 1996. "How to Avoid Being a *Komodoumenos*." *CQ* 46: 327–356.

——. 2000. "Platon, Eupolis and the 'Demagogue-Comedy.'" In *The Rivals of Aristophanes: Studies in Athenian Old Comedy*, edited by D. Harvey and J. Wilkins, 437–451. London: The Classical Press of Wales.

——. 2009. *Talking About Laughter and Other Studies in Greek Comedy*. Oxford: Oxford University Press.

Storey, I. C. 2003. *Eupolis: Poet of Old Comedy*. Oxford: Oxford University Press.

——. 2005. "But Comedy Has Satyrs Too." In *Satyr Drama: Greek Tragedy at Play*, edited by W. M. Harrison, 201–218. Swansea: The Classical Press of Wales.

Webster, T. B. L. 1952. "Chronological Notes on Middle Comedy." *CQ* 2: 13–26.

——. 1970. *Studies in Later Greek Comedy*. 2nd ed. Manchester: Manchester University Press.

Weiher, A. 1913. *Philosophen und Philosophenspott in der attischen Komödie*. Munich: Beck.

CHAPTER 9

....

COMEDY IN THE LATE FOURTH AND EARLY THIRD CENTURIES BCE

....

ADELE C. SCAFURO

As earlier authors in this volume have indicated, there are no clear or revolutionary breaks to mark the traditional division of Greek comedy into "Old" and "Middle," no cutting-edge playwright in the early to mid-fourth century to designate as the harbinger and catalyst of a brand new epoch. Athenian theater-goers in the last two decades of the fourth century, however, on the cusp of what later came to be called New Comedy (closely associated with the period extending from Menander's first production in 321 through the middle of the next century, though productions in this style continue into the third century CE), may have noticed some changes or trends regarding themselves and the productions they viewed. The first changes stem from the dissolution of their democracy after defeat by Antipater in the Lamian War: now, with a new oligarchic regime in place in 321–318, the poorest Athenians were deprived of citizen rights (9,000 remained on the citizen rolls: Diod. Sic. 18.18.5) and probably at that time, or at any rate before the end of the century, the *theorikon* (fund for free theater tickets) was eliminated.[1]

During the next decade (317–307), under the regime of Demetrius of Phalerum (perhaps in 316/15: *DFA*² 92 n. 4, possibly a few years later), the *choregia* was eliminated and

---

[1] The abolition of the "ticket entrance fund" and its date can only be surmised, since there is no explicit statement in the ancient sources; see Buchanan 1962. Ticket price is said to be two obols at Dem. 18.28, referring to the year 346 BCE (unheeded by Csapo 2007: 114 n. 61), but one drachma in Philoch. *FGrHist* 328 F 33; for references to these same amounts in scholia and lexicographers, see *DFA*² 265–268. A five-drachma sum is mentioned at Dein. 1.56 and Hyper. *Dem.* col. 26, but whether it covered one festival or several is disputed (*DFA*² 268; Roselli 2011: 108–109 sees a continuous rise in price from two obols to five drachmas). Ticket price has been associated with the sum required to pay for the setting up and removal of the wooden bleachers on which spectators sat during each festival (Rosivach 2000); such payments would become unnecessary once the stone theater of Lycurgus was completed (ca. 329: Goette 2007: 116). Lycurgus, however, may have retained an admission price as revenue for the city. Theater admission is mentioned in Theophr. *Char.* 9.5 and implied at 30.6 but cannot be dated.

subsequently replaced by an elected official, the *agonothetes* ("supervisor of competitions"); this official might often supplement public funds with his own (for the oligarchical appeal of this office, see Arist. *Pol.* 1321a31–42 and cf. IG II² 657.38–40).²

The new Lycurgan theater (completed ca. 329 BCE) was bigger than its predecessor, holding ca. 16,000 (this volume, pp. 55–56). The Athenian members of the audience that filled it during the oligarchic regimes may have been somewhat less variegated in terms of personal wealth, possibly even tilting toward an elite majority, but it is difficult to imagine that the less prosperous ceased coming altogether. The theater/festival habit seems to have been firmly ingrained among Athens' inhabitants; even Menander's "refined" plays had plenty of slapstick humor and lively characters to attract those with less highly evolved aesthetic sensibilities—and Menander was but one poet among a host of others. If their seats were no longer subsidized, some portion of the poorer Athenians may well have economized elsewhere and attended performances anyway (similarly, Rosivach 2000; Lape 2004: 10; contra: Roselli 2011: 105–117). Foreigners were not, of course, excluded (and their entrance fees would certainly have been appreciated). Numerous foreigners, moreover, contributed to the intellectual life of the city, not only as students and teachers in the philosophical schools but also as writers of plays (e.g., Anaxandrides, who may have been from Camirus in Rhodes or from Colophon; the remarkably prolific Antiphanes, who may have been from Chios, Smyrna, or Rhodes; the slightly less prolific Alexis of Thurii; Philemon of Syracuse; Diphilus of Sinope in the Pontus; and Apollodorus of Carystus). Still, Athens was not the imperial center of the universe it once had been. Athenian theater-goers will have taken notice.

Indeed, Athens would soon become (and to some degree, already was) one stop on the theater circuit, as plays—old (revivals) and new (freshly composed)—were more widely performed throughout the Greek world, as guilds of dramatic artists became more organized and powerful, and as actors won an international reputation and an *auctoritas* more potent than the imprimatur of star quality acquired from a "first place" prize for acting at Athenian festivals (for a grand example, see Plut. *Alex.* 29). Nonetheless, the acting competition was important in Athens; conferral on tragic actors at the Dionysia and Lenaea began early, ca. 450 and the 430s BCE, respectively, and on comic actors at the same festivals, later, at some point during the last three decades of the fourth century and possibly as late as 312 for the City Dionysia.³ The tardy arrival of the award for comic

---

² The dating of the elimination of the *choregia* is not secure, and motives for it and its replacement with an elected *agonothetes* are also controversial (see Mikalson 1998: 54–58 and Makres in this volume); some scholars have recently viewed these as reforms of the "restored democracy" of 307/6: thus, arguing in different ways, O'Sullivan 2009a: 168–185, Bayliss 2011: 105, and Csapo and Wilson 2012. Caution is advised.

³ First competition for tragic actors at the Dionysia, beginning ca. 451/0–448/7: IG II² 2318b2; at the Lenaea: IG II² 2325 fr. r; for comic actors at the Dionysia, a date between 328 and 312 BCE is an inference from IG II² 2318 (the text breaks off at 329/8 without mention of comic actors' competition) and IG II² 2323a, Col. I.4 (contest in place); for comic actors at the Lenaea, ca. the third quarter of the fourth century: IG² II 2322; for discussion of the dates given here, see Millis and Olson 2012: pp. 13, 208, 73, and 111 (respectively). All references in this essay (including column and line nos.) to IG II² 2318–25, inscriptional records of the dramatic festivals of Athens, are from Millis and Olson 2012.

actors is probably to be connected with the date for the first *revival* of a comedy: whereas revival of a tragedy first appears as a regular part of the City Dionysia in 387/6 (IG II² 2318.1010), the first revived comedy appears in 340/39 (IG II² 2318.1565). Revivals were plays for the actors; they both produced and performed them (Nervegna 2007: 17). It would not be surprising, then, if the "new" performances of revived comedies, beginning in 340/39 (though perhaps not immediately a regular annual event), by putting the spotlight on the actor rather than the poet, fired appreciation for comic skill and enthusiasm for an actor's prize in the "new" comedies during the last decades of the century. Our Athenian theater-goers in the last decades of the fourth century will definitely have noticed their comic actors.

Other changes that extend over the course of the last eighty years of the century might better be designated "trends." Mythical themes in comedy become less prevalent after 370/60, though they do appear now and again in the remainder of the century (see Konstantakos, this volume). Productions become less extravagant: choruses, over time, play a lesser and different role, even if they do not entirely disappear (Rothwell 1995); costumes become less spectacular (absent the grotesque masks earlier in the century and later, absent the *phalloi*—though a resurrection has been hypothesized in Diphilus: Green 1994: 193 n. 30); *mechanai* (stage machinery, esp. the "crane") are less resorted to for that last-minute rescue or a surprise visit from the ether (Pöhlmann 1995). These trends in production may be ascribed to a new pursuit of "illusionism and naturalism for their own sake" (Csapo, this volume), and so, too, other features: the gradual deployment of a new and more wide-ranging set of masks that corresponded to character (see p. 206 below),[4] and concomitantly, a more subtle and complex playing of character, even as "character-types" became firmly established (and perhaps because of that!): the soldier, young lover, strict father, rustic, *hetaira*, pimp, parasite, flatterer, cook, and cunning slave (Nesselrath 1990: with much refinement). Other trends include the almost exclusive turn to spoken delivery after the middle of the century (compare the nearly sixty lines of anapaestic dimeters without break and so possibly spoken in one breath by a virtuoso slave/cook at Anaxandrides *Protesilaus* K-A fr. 42, composed sometime between the mid-380s and 361, with the occasional appearance

---

[4] Pollux (*Onom.* 4.143–154) writing about theatrical paraphernalia in the second century CE but probably relying on an earlier source (possibly, directly or indirectly, *On Masks*, by Aristophanes of Byzantium, ca. 260–185: Nesselrath 1990: 183 n. 99; *MNC³* I: 6), had listed and briefly described forty-four masks of New Comedy, divisible into four genera according to gender, age, and status: old men, young men, women, and slaves. These are amplified and illustrated especially by the theatrical terracottas from the Lipari Islands (published by Bernabó-Brea 1981), including some tragic masks from the early fourth century as well as over 300 masked comic statuettes from the fourth century and over 300 comic masks from the early third century. Bernabó-Brea thought that a standard set of masks had been established by the time of Menander's death and that this set was reproduced throughout the Greek world, first at Lipari; moreover, he argued that Menander was responsible for establishing the collection (cf. Brown 1988: 184–185 and Poe 1996 for healthy skepticism). Bernabó-Brea 2001 (in collaboration with Cavalier) updates the main section of the 1981 work (third-century terracotta masks) and addresses their classification and identification (Parte IV); a briefer English version of the main text (trans. by S. Cullotta) appears at the end of the volume (pp. 273–302).

of anapaestic dimeters in Menander, at the opening of *Leukadia* and in *Kolax* fr. 7 S);[5] the toning down of diction from its high flown and colorful flights in earlier comedy, its riddance of a great deal of obscenity but not total eradication of vulgarity (e.g., ἱππόπορνε, "whoreslut!" in Menander *Theophoroumene* 19; see also *Perikeiromene* 394, 482–85; Handley 2009: 28; Bruzzese 2011: 79–80); the growing number of comedies as the century proceeds that narrated a story in consequential acts, so unlike the episodic disarray of scenes in older comedy and so much more like tragedy in construction and borrowed themes—indeed, its evolving relationship with classical tragedy: a diminution of paratragic episodes, an increase in sophisticated allusions especially to Euripides (Arnott 1996b: 63), and an extensive appropriation of structure tantamount to the embedding of the one genre in the other (Cusset 2003, Petrides 2010); finally, the gradual narrowing of repertoire to the repetitious domestic plots of impeded love and misconstrued identity and status.

1. An Athenian Septuagenarian Theater-Goer in 305 BCE Looks at Comedy

But would members of the Athenian audience themselves have observed any of these features as "epochal changes" rather than "trends," especially those last mentioned, during the last decades of the fourth century? Probably not, and not, at close range, an addicted spectator who had attended numerous performances, deme performances as well as the City Dionysia and Lenaea (cf. Plato *Rep.* 475D; Heraclides Criticus 1.4–5 Pfister).[6] Such a spectator, who was born in 380 and who in 305 may have been attending theater performances regularly for some sixty years and himself sung in dithyrambic choruses as a boy and young man, will not have seen Old Comedy—these comedies were not, so far as we know, ever "revived" in fourth-century Athens—but he will have seen Philemon's *Hypobolimaios* (*Suppositious Child*), reputed to have been a remake of Aristophanes's *Cocalus* that had probably been produced by his son in 387 (Philemon K-A test. 32 and *ad Hypobolimaios ante fr.* 85). He will also have enjoyed many comedies seasoned with political mockery—e.g., by Timocles (active in the 340s until ca. 317)—and taken some delight in his play *Delos* (ca. 323/2?), with its post-Harpalus dialogue on

---

[5] There may be more metrical variation in Menander as more fragments are firmly assigned: dactylic hexameters in Florentine papyrus assigned to *Theophoroumene*: Handley 2002: 174, Arnott 1996a, II: 57, 64–66 (vv. 36–41, 50?, 52, 56); Sandbach 1990: 146 "*fragmentum dubium*." See also Handley 1990: 141 with Arnott 2000: 372 on *POxy* 3966 (possible anapaests).

[6] See Petrides 2010: 79 for a stimulating depiction of an ideal spectator of the late fourth century sitting in the new Lycurgan Theater of Dionysus. E. Hall 2007: 269–271 resuscitates two Athenians, born ca. 450–440, to survey changes in the tragic theater ca. 380, testimony to the usefulness of septuagenarians.

bribery between two men who cynically discuss the takings of Demosthenes, Moericles, and (interestingly) Hyperides (K-A fr. 4). From 321 to 307, however, our spectator may have observed a brief hiatus of such mockery under the oligarchical regimes—but soon thereafter, with the restoration of democracy, he will have perceived a renewal in plays by Archedicus and Philippides (see Henderson, this volume; O'Sullivan 2009b: 64–73). So political mockery was alive in recent theater memory, even if not continuously produced onstage, year in and year out. Moreover, many components of the "new repertoire" had already appeared in earlier comedies of the fourth century: *hetaira* comedies were not new to the stage, love-plots flourished in the earlier mythical burlesques, the stock characters mentioned earlier had been established, and philosophical preoccupations were not unknown (Henderson and Konstan, this volume). Not much was "new," then, for our theater addict during the first decade and a half of the period designated New Comedy. On the other hand, there were some "disappearances"; e.g., our septuagenarian no longer witnessed those long virtuoso monologues in anapaestic dimeters such as the one mentioned earlier in Anaxandrides's *Protesilaus* (K-A fr. 42) and another (with sixty-five verses in anapaestic dimeters and monometers) in Mnesimachus's *Hippotrophos* (*Horseowner*) K-A fr. 4, both show-stopping, breath-choking "arias" with endless lists of gastronomic delights and descriptions of feasting—these and others like them had disappeared before the middle of the century (Nesselrath 1990: 272–276).

Our aging theater-goer will have had favorite comic poets. He may have followed closely the careers of Alexis of Thurii and Philemon of Syracuse over the course of his spectating life; in 305, Alexis may have been producing plays for nearly fifty years and Philemon for twenty-five. The first may have been born in the late 370s and died in the early 260s—at any rate, he is said to have lived 106 years and to have produced 245 comedies (K-A test. 1); 135 titles survive. While the figure of 245 plays may be inflated (Arnott 1996b: 13–14), there is no reason to doubt Alexis's longevity. Some thirty-seven of the plays can be dated, and these roughly span the years 354–270 (?), but only one can be dated after the year 300, and that probably in the 270s (Arnott 1996b: 10, 15–18 and 687–88). The fragments of an early play, *Trophonius*, suggest a link with Old Comedy (K-A fr. 239): an actor appears to have addressed the chorus with a command and in a meter (Eupolidean) suitable for introducing a *parabasis* (Arnott 1996b: 671–672). On the other hand, in a fragment of *Kouris* (*Hairdresser*: date unknown, so possibly coincident with Menander's lifetime or even later), one character announces the arrival of a chorus of comasts (K-A fr. 112) in the way Menander introduces his choruses at the end of the first act. Some thirteen to eighteen titles (a small percentage of those extant) suggest myth burlesque, but only one, *Minos*, can be even roughly dated, to ca. 350–330 ("early period": Arnott 1996b: 460). Comedies with evolving stock types abound, especially cooks and parasites. The makings of typical New Comedy scenes are also plentiful: e.g., in K-A fr. 212 of *Stratiotes* (*Soldier*), dating to the late 340s, one man carrying an infant tries to fob it off on another actor (playing a male? a female?); scholars have seen in this a precursor of the arbitration scene in Menander's *Epitrepontes* (Arnott 1996b: 606; Nesselrath 1990: 282 n. 1) or of a scene from Plautus's *Truculentus*

389ff. (Webster 1970: 64)—but a prefiguring of Menander's *Andria,* as suggested in Terence's homonymous play at 748ff., cannot be discounted. In *Lebes (Kettle),* a play of the mid-320s, Alexis mentions a *nomothetes* (lawmaker), Aristonicus, probably a contemporary politician from Marathon (Arnott 1996b: 98, 363–364), and commends him for drafting a law to control the price of fish (K-A fr. 130). In *Hippeus (Knight)* K-A fr. 99, a play apparently performed in 307 or 306 after Demetrius of Phalerum had fled Athens, someone applauds Demetrius Poliorcetes and the *nomothetai* (lawmakers) for passing a law requiring "those imparting the so-called powers of argument to the young to get out of Attica and go to the devil" (for the date, see Arnott 1996b: 260; 858–859; Habicht 1997: 73). A comedy referred to by two titles, *Crateia* and *Pharmakopoles (Pharmacist),* may represent an earlier and later (revised) production of the same play. Two fragments (K-A fr. 117, 118) of the play mention a pro-Macedonian politician Callimedon as if he were still active in Athens—but he left the city in 318. In another fragment (K-A fr. 116) of the play, a toast is proposed for the victory of King Antigonus, the "lad" Demetrius (Poliorcetes), and another for Phila Aphrodite (daughter of Antipater, wife of Demetrius, perhaps divorced from her at this time); the "toasting" must postdate the Macedonian defeat of the Ptolemaic fleet off Cyprian Salamis in spring or summer 306/5, when Antigonus had assumed the royal title and bestowed it on his son as well (Arnott 1996b: 308–311; Habicht 1997: 76 with n. 31). The first production, then, will have been produced before 318 and the "revised" one in 305. In the latter year, an inscribed text first appears with the names of father and son (restored), bearing the title *basileis,* "kings": IG II² 471. The public arena has been brought into the theater, and thus, squarely, into the "age of Menander."

Philemon, probably at least a few years younger than Alexis (born ca. 365, died ca. 265: guesswork), is said to have lived either 97, 99, or 101 years (K-A test. 1, 5, 4, 6) and to have produced 97 plays (test. 1, 2, 4); he is also said to have flourished "a little earlier than Menander" (test. 1), to have produced comedy before 328 (test. 2), and to have been victorious at the City Dionysia of 327 (test. 13). Plausible but not certain rough dates have been deduced for some of his plays on the basis of historical figures named or alluded to in them (Bruzzese 2011: 24–34): thus ca. 330 for *Lithoglyphos (Sculptor*: K-A fr. 41, Aristomedes), 320s for *Babylonios* (K-A fr. 15, Harpalus and his famous mistress Pythionice), 318–300 for *Metion/Zomion (Stalker/Little Soup* or *Little Fatso*: K-A fr. 43, Agyrrhius, son of Callimedon), 300–294 for *Neaira* (K-A fr. 49, Seleucus and his tiger) and a similar date for *Philosophoi* (K-A fr. 88, Zeno). The fragments of these plays are too exiguous for comment here, except that *Babylonios* may have been a *hetaira* comedy and *Lithoglyphos* and *Metion* included political jokes at the expense of contemporaries; the latter comedy also featured a lively conversation (K-A fr. 42) between a cook and a dissatisfied client—a traditional topos during the fourth century. Philemon's political jokes may have been sharp-edged; at any rate, Plutarch (*On Restraining Anger* 9.458A, K-A test. 9) tells us that Magas (a half-brother of Ptolemy II, governor of Cyrene and then king beginning ca. 300/275: Marquaille 2008: 44 n. 23), because he had been satirized by Philemon onstage, had him humiliated but not hurt when he was caught offshore in a storm. (A fragment from the "insulting comedy" may remain, K-A fr. 132, but is not informative.) Apparently, comic writers still took risks and reached out into the wider Hellenistic world for their targets.

While our aging theater-goer near the end of the fourth century will probably not have seen the "Magas comedy," he will have viewed, by that time, a wide range of plays, including Alexis's *Trophonius* and possibly his *Kouris* (date unknown), as well as his *Minos, Stratiotes, Lebes, Hippeus*, and two productions of *Crateia/Pharmakopoles*, one earlier and one later; he will have witnessed Philemon's early plays—along with a host of others: a speaker in Athenaeus *Deipnosophistai* claims to have "read more than 800 plays of the so-called Middle Comedy" (πλείονα τῆς μέσης καλουμένης κωμῳδίας ἀναγνοὺς δράματα τῶν ὀκτακοσίων, 336D8), and a late anonymous writer on comedy tells us "there have been sixty-four poets of New Comedy, and the most notable of these are Philemon, Menander, Diphilus, Philippides, Posidippus, and Apollodorus" (*Prolegomena on Comedy* III p. 10 Koster 1975). Our theater-goer will have attended Menander's first play, produced in 321 (festival unknown; the play is uncertain: Schröder 1996: 36 n. 9 argues for *Orge, Anger*; Iversen 2011 argues for *Thais*); he will have seen Menander win first prize for *Dyskolos* at the Lenaea in 317/16 and another first prize at the City Dionysia in 316/15. He will also have seen him take a lowly fifth place for *Heniochos* (*Charioteer*) at the same festival in 313/12 and possibly for *Paidion* (*Young Child*) in 312/11.[7] The septuagenarian may have preferred Philemon over Menander, as many apparently did (cf. Blanchard 2007: 91–98): ancient writers, usually with embarrassment, tell us that the former often defeated the latter (Quint. 10.1.69; Apuleius *Florida* 16); one writer, sympathetic to Menander, adds the anecdote that "When he met the man by chance, Menander said, 'Please Philemon, tell me frankly: when you defeat me, aren't you embarrassed?'" (Aulus Gellius 17.4.1). The competition between the two surfaces again in Alciphron; Menander has written a letter to Glycera (IV.18), informing her that Ptolemy has invited him, and also Philemon, to visit his court; Philemon, moreover, has sent his invitation to Menander for his perusal; but Philemon's letter appears to him rather silly in comparison to his own and written with less brilliance, as it was not, says Alciphron's comic poet, addressed to Menander.

At the City Dionysia in 312/11 (IG II² 2323a Col. I.5–6), our septuagenarian will have viewed the revival of an "old comedy," *Thesauros* (*Treasure*, IG II² 2323a Col. I.2)—its author Anaxandrides is known to have produced comedies from the early 370s to the early 340s, and so our septuagenarian will have seen the comedy's premiere as a young man. Would he have noticed differences? It's a pity that we do not know whether the "revival" would have been performed in an "old style," reusing or making anew costumes and masks from the earlier age; if our theater addict recalled the theatrical paraphernalia of the premiere of *Thesauros* as he watched its revival in 312/11 alongside the new plays

---

[7] Menander's name is restored in the didascalic notice at IG II² 2323a Col. I. 17 (Millis-Olson) by Webster 1952: 20.

being performed at the festival (Philippides, first place with *Mystis*; Nicostratus, second place with *Joskopos, Tunny?] watcher*; Aminias, third with *Apoleipousa, Deserteress*; Theophilus, fourth with *Pancratiast*; and possibly Menander, fifth with *Paidion, Young Child*), he may have noticed little change at all—except in the matter of song within the plays (those long runs of anapaestic dimeters), now absent for the most part and replaced with song during choral interludes, and also in the matter of mask and acting technique: the visual cuing of type by mask (and now, a far greater variety of them) along with the possibility of acting in conformance with the expectations created by a particular mask—or against them.[8]

Probably the appropriation of new masks (and "New Style" as opposed to "Old Style" masks: *MNC*³ 55–56) was a gradual process, sparked by those used in post-classical tragedy (Pollux 4.133–142, listing twenty-eight such masks; Wiles 1991:154). Green, who assessed material artifacts (terracotta figurines and masks) for their market popularity through the four quarters of the fourth century, found that Old Men and Slaves maintained the highest percentages throughout the century (with Slaves being the most popular), but that Young Women "increase their share of the market over time" (1994:73)—e.g., the mask of the *pseudokore* ("girl who will turn out to be a respectable young girl after all"), which is found at the beginning of the fourth century, increases in numerical appearances over time; moreover, in the third quarter of the century, *hetairai* become more varied in range, and likewise (though to a smaller extent) the *korai* (free-born virgins). Presumably, as Green suggests, the creation of new mask types on the market "must reflect a growing interest in young women in the new theater and they allowed a greater subtlety in plot and/or characterisation" (1994: 74–75).[9]

Whenever it was that the new masks came to be used in extenso and actors learned how to perform with them, comedy performance will have broken new ground and the harmony of written text with performance method, like orchestral piece and orchestral performance, acquired a new potential for perfection. Something important had happened on the Athenian stage and elsewhere in the Greek world—and it would last for centuries with little change; by 50 BCE, "New Comedy" had certainly lost its "newness": "The costume of the theatre must have looked more and more artificial and the masks at least seem to have been made deliberately so" (*MNC*³: 60). But in 305 BCE, contemporary theater-goers, especially those who, like our septuagenarian addict, had been attending for decades, while they may not have noticed a radical shift, will probably have

---

[8] MacCary 1969, MacCary 1970, MacCary 1972; Brown 1988 for judicious refinement; Wiles 1991; Petrides 2010: 111–123 and chapter 21 here; also Csapo in this volume, with illustrated examples.

[9] More recently, Petrides 2011 considers whether the reduced frequency of youth masks among Middle Comedy finds necessarily indicates that youths were less foregrounded in the plays themselves. Possibly this is so, but the evidence, he thinks, is insufficient to decide. On the other hand, for Menander's New Comedy, the increased number of finds of youth masks correlates with the significant roles that young men and women have in the plots of the plays.

come to anticipate and enjoy the creative nuancing and realism of character and script, performed with a range of mask types and acted by expert players.

Of course, not even our septuagenarian will have registered that a new "genre" had been born—that was left to a taxonomist-scholar in Alexandria, and his observation may not have been made for another sixty or seventy years. While Callimachus, Eratosthenes, and Aristophanes of Byzantium, successive heads of the library, had all pored over the thousands of comedy texts from those first available to those in their own age, the youngest of the trio may have been the first to make the tripartite division into Old, Middle, and New Comedy (Nesselrath 1990: 172–187). Aristophanes (ca. 260–185), author, inter alia, of separate treatises on masks, on *hetairai*, and on parallels between Menander and other authors, was certainly the first to single out Menander from the crowd of other comic poets as the best among them (Menander K-A test. 83). In doing so, of course, he laid the groundwork for the disappearance of his nearest competitors. "O Menander, O life/ which of you was imitating the other?" The encomium of Menander and realia may have nodded quite seriously now and again, but never fell into a final sleep.

2. Comic Topoi and Techniques of Menander's near Contemporaries: Making Sense of Fragments in the Twenty-first Century

Philemon of Syracuse, Diphilus of Sinope, and Apollodorus of Carystus are best known to us through the Roman playwrights who used their plays as models or springboards for their own. We have already met Philemon, Menander's older contemporary. Diphilus is another near contemporary, perhaps only slightly younger than Philemon; he may have been born ca. 360 and died ca. 295 (Webster 1970: 152). He is said to have written a hundred plays (K-A test. 1); fifty-nine titles are extant. In 237/6, his play *Misa?]nthropes* was revived, and at that time he will certainly have been dead for some decades.[10] Apollodorus may have belonged to the generation following Menander and is not to be confused with Apollodorus of Gela, another comic poet who was Menander's contemporary; twelve titles survive from the Carystian's oeuvre. Plautus used Philemon's *Emporos* for his *Mercator* (*Merchant*), his *Thesauros* for *Trinummus*, and perhaps his *Phasma* for *Mostellaria* (summary of arguments: de Melo 2011: 307–308).

---

[10] The revival is dated in the archonship of Alcibiades; Meritt 1938: 117 (no. 22) and 135 had put Alcibiades in 251/0, but Millis and Olsen 2012: 125–126 places him properly in 237, following Osborne 2009 (cf. IG II^2 776.16).

He used Diphilus's *Kleroumenoi* for *Casina*, an unknown Diphilan play for *Rudens* (*Rope*), and possibly his *Schedia* for the fragmentary *Vidularia*. He also used Diphilus's *Synapothneskontes* (*Dying Together*) for his *Commorientes*, which is not extant; Terence subsequently used a scene from the same Diphilan play (apparently *not* used by Plautus) to liven up his *Adelphoe* (Terence *Adelphoe* 6–11). Terence also used Apollodorus's *Epidikazomenos* (*Claimant*) as the model for *Phormio* and his *Hecyra* for his like-named play. Plautus famously tells us that the Greek comic poet Demophilus wrote a play called *Onagos* and that he has transformed this into *Asinaria* (*Demophilus scripsit, Maccus vortit barbare*, *Asinaria* 11); no fragments of the Greek author survive.

Rather than examining the Roman comedies to discover what the Greek "originals" may have been like, it will serve us better here to focus on some longer Greek fragments and identify topoi and characteristics of comic style. Apollodorus will be omitted—few fragments remain (though K-A fr. 5 is of great interest), and attribution is uncertain between him and Apollodorus of Gela. Philemon and Diphilus supply us with a fair number of long passages, and to these we may add now and again from other comic poets. In identifying topoi, sometimes the "lead-ins" to passages cited by Athenaeus are helpful, but often the repetition of ideas (so that the idea becomes a "topos") and modes of presentation (i.e., "technique") become evident over a range of passages. The speakers in fragments are usually not labeled unless a speaking partner provides a name, but their "type" is often identifiable from the contents of their speeches. For the most part, putative pimps and cooks are presented here—secondary characters. What stand out in these fragments are propensities to resort to what appear to be routine and traditional "stand-up topoi" (which may, to some extent, be a reflection of the interests of the book sources that cite them); to quote speeches of others with virtuoso effect; to create now and again a comic paratactic patter which significantly depends on voicing a dramatic punctuation for conditions or questions, imperatives, and explanations— a patter that extends throughout the life of Greek Comedy; and, last but not least, to "euripidize."

Philemon K-A fr. 3, a monologue from his *Adelphoi* and plausibly spoken by a *pornoboskos* (a pimp), has won notoriety among discussants of the poet; it ascribes a law to Solon by which public prostitutes were first established to keep young men from fulfilling natural impulses in errant ways (cf. the law Eutychus pronounces at the end of *Mercator*). Earlier poets (Eubulus K-A fr. 67, 82; Xenarchus K-A fr. 4) had similarly depicted prostitutes standing on display, naked or in diaphanous robes (a kind of democratic transparency?) in open doorways as remedies against sexual misconduct—a topos, therefore, of traditional if vulgar interest, especially in the specificity of detail, and all, including Philemon's, apparently outside of the plotline and so *extra comoediam*; what is different in Philemon K-A fr. 3, however, is not only the designation of Solon as inventor of the "democratic and life-saving enterprise" (δημοτικόν... πρᾶγμα καὶ σωτήριον)—possibly a parody of the way orators frequently ascribe any good law that serves the interest of the moment (cf. Bruzzese 2011: 86)—but the patter of the final verses:

οὐκ εὖ σεαυτοῦ τυγχάνεις ἔχων· ἔχεις
....† πως † ἡ θύρα 'στ' ἀνεῳγμένη.
εἷς ὀβολός· εἰσπήδησον· οὐκ ἔστ' οὐδὲ εἷς
ἀκκισμὸς οὐδὲ λῆρος, οὐδ' ὑφήρπασεν·
ἀλλ' εὐθύς, ἥν βούλει σὺ χῶν βούλει τρόπον.
ἐξῆλθες· οἰμώζειν λέγ', ἀλλοτρία 'στί σοι.

You happen not to be feeling well. You're
[ ] the door is open.
One obol: leap inside! There's not a bit of
coyness or nonsense—no teasing here!
But at once—the one you want and the way you want.
You leave; tell her go hang, she's nobody to you.

(vv. 11–16, trans. Konstan *BOC* 2011, modified)

The speaker draws in the audience—not only by prurient depiction of imminent delight, but also by smart-alecky abruptness: he addresses the audience directly in the second person, though he could easily present the opening verse, if "dull logic" ruled (Arnott 1996b: 275), as a general impersonal condition ("if someone happens to feel ill..."). The actor (or the *didaskalos,* "poet-director") might choose to present this "conditional" (and presumably the choice is his) as a question: "You happen to feel ill?" The interrogative/declarative condition—which involves an unfortunate situation—is then followed by an imperative (elsewhere, by a declarative assertion of a responsive action), the carrying out of which is a remedy for the crisis; oftentimes, an explanation is appended of the remedial action (as here, "There's not a bit of coyness or nonsense" explains the invitation to "leap inside"). The patter/pattern occurs frequently among comic poets and is often asyndetic;[11] it is also, so it seems, *extra comoediam*—for this is quintessentially the stuff of stand-up comedy. An earlier example appears in a monologue in trochaic tetrameters in Alexis's *Isostasion* (*Equivalent*) K-A fr. 103, 7–13, 16–20, where the speaker, probably a young lover, describes the artifices of the demimonde from a common stock of motifs, but the paratactic patter freshens it up, as a few verses will show (see Arnott 1996b: 277–279 for difficulties and 268–269 for interesting thoughts on whether the tetrameters were spoken by a character and integrated into the play, like Cnemon's speech in *Dyskolos* 708ff., or delivered "extra-dramatically, perhaps as an entr'acte, by the leader of the chorus"):

[11] The frequency of asyndeton in these passages among many comic poets gives the lie to Demetrius's oft-quoted observation from his treatise *On Style* contrasting "a loose style" that is also called "the actor's style, since lack of connectives stimulates one to act" with a "written style that is easier to read"; he continues: "this style is organized and one might say made foolproof by connectives. It is for this reason that people act out Menander, since he does not use connectives, but Philemon they read" (193). On Demetrius's "acting" and "reading" styles, cf. Bruzzese 2011: 223–231 and Nesselrath, chapter 34, in this volume. Strikingly similar patter to that in the Philemon fragment appears at Dem. 22.26–27 (including a reference to Solon) and Hyp. *Eux.* 5–6.

She's got a pot-belly?
They have the sort of breasts comic actors use;
by pushing them out like this, they swing the dress out
away from the stomach as if with barge poles.
One woman has red eyebrows? They paint them with lampblack.
She happens to be dark? She is plastered with white lead.
She's too light-skinned? She rubs on a little rouge.
Some part of her body has real beauty? She shows it naked.

(vv. 12–19, trans. Slater *BOC* 2011, slightly modified)

One source of humor in ancient comedy in general is the assignment of eating habits to different groups according to ethnicity, wealth, craft, and age; possibly this feature's prominence in the fragments is due to Athenaeus being so often their source (but see Henderson, this volume, for luxurious living in the fourth century). In *Deipnosophistai* 10.417B, he introduces a string of passages from different comic poets (fourth and third century) to illustrate their penchant for mocking "whole nations for overeating" (and yet the constant allusion to "whole nations" is also emblematic of the Hellenistic Weltanschauung that permeates later comedy) and offers the Boeotians as example (καὶ ἔθνη δὲ ὅλα εἰς πολυφαγίαν ἐκωμῳδεῖτο, ὡς τὸ Βοιωτόν). Diphilus's *Boeotian* K-A fr. 22 is his sixth instance: "the sort who begin to eat before daybreak or again at daybreak." It is of course the comic cooks who most frequently single out ethnic and other groups. In Diphilus's *Apolipousa* (*Deserteress*) K-A fr. 17, a cook is asking his client about the number of guests (itself a topos: cf. Menander, *Samia* 285–292, possibly parodic) and their homelands for an imminent wedding feast—are they all from Attica, or are some from the emporium? The client wonders why the cook must know this. He responds with a set of rules for preparing meals according to ethnicity; the patter pattern is evident here and there: "Suppose you have invited Rhodians; immediately upon their arrival, hand them a big [ladle] ... If Byzantines, soak whatever you serve in wormwood" (vv. 7–8, 11–12). The same topos is found in Menander's *Trophonius* K-A fr. 351: a cook expounds the dishes he makes for different groups of foreigners—islanders, Arcadians, and Ionians.

In Diphilus's *Zographos* (*Painter*) K-A fr. 42, the topos appears again, but this time with a dramatic twist. A cook addresses a forty-one-line uninterrupted speech to a man named Draco, probably a *trapezopoios* (table-setter) whom he is trying to hire for the day. Assuring him that he knows how to choose clients, the cook tells him he keeps a register of all the types (ἔστιν δ' ἀπάντων τῶν γενῶν μοι διαγραφή) and proceeds to list four in an expanded patter pattern. First: "For example, the crowd at the emporium, if you like..." (v. 9); this is followed by description of an unfortunate merchant (vv. 10–12) and then, "This kind I let go" (v. 13). Second: "But another has sailed from Byzantium..." (v. 18); this is followed by description of the merchant's success (vv. 19–22), and then, "This one I bow down to as soon as he disembarks" (v. 23). Third, briskly: "Again, a lad in love is devouring and squandering his patrimony—I march up" (v. 26–7). Fourth: "Other lads are joining together for a Dutch-treat dinner... shouting,

'Who wants to make the pasta puttanesca?' I let them holler" (vv. 28, 30–32). Next, an explanation for refusing to serve: "For, if you demand your pay, 'First bring me a chamber pot' they say. 'The lentil soup lacks vinegar.'(vv. 34–36). At speech's end, the cook reveals where he is leading Draco: to a brothel where a courtesan is lavishly celebrating the Adonia. A dramatic twist thus has come at the end of expanded patter (laced with lively "speech within speech"): the preceding catalogue of clients has been used as a foil for the prosperous *hetaira*, the best reserved for last, a priamel after the fact, and a persuasive strategy to entice the table-setter.

Comic cooks in the late fourth century are erudite, though less bombastic than their dithyrambizing, philologizing counterparts earlier in the century (Nesselrath 1990: 298–301). Anaxippus, a late-fourth-century (?) comic poet, presents a well-trained cook's advice to a potential client (?) in *Enkalyptomenos (Man Wrapped Up)* K-A fr. 1— the fragment consists of forty-nine verses, all but a line or two spoken by the cook. He first details his credentials: his culinary arts teacher was Sophon of Acarnania, who outlasted his rival Damoxenus of Rhodes—the two had been students of Labdacus of Sicily, vv. 1–20. The cook with teaching credentials is traditional, going back at least to Alexis K-A fr. 24 (Nesselrath 1990: 303). Anaxippus's cook is himself a *philosophos* and plans to leave behind a new treatise on cookery (vv. 21–22, with a possible parodic "learned" allusion to Alcidamas, *On the Sophists* 32); he offers the potential client a taste of his discoveries: he doesn't offer the same meals to all, but has arranged them according to his clients' lifestyles—there are different meals for lovers, philosophers, tax collectors, and old men (30–31). Again, the patter pattern is evident here and there, especially in this last (largely asyndetic) section on the different meals, e.g., "a lad with a girlfriend is devouring his patrimony: this fellow I serve cuttlefish and squid..." (31–33), followed by the reason for the small fare: "really, this type is not a serious diner—his mind is on loving" (36–37). The final lines of the fragment may be a parody of the "new" study of physiognomy, with perhaps a metatheatrical joke: "If I see your face, I'll know what each of you wants to eat." While this cook is a smart one, he is not quite in the same league as that most ethereal among cooks, that Agathonian Homerist of the culinary arts, presented in Straton's *Phoinikides* K-A fr. 1 (cf. Philemon K-A fr. 114); remarkably, the entire depiction is conveyed by the perplexed client, who reports in *oratio recta* the conversation he held with him—truly a virtuoso piece, and possibly the work of a poet of New Comedy (Nesselrath 1990: 62–63 and Nünlist 2002: 248, focusing on its lengthy quoted speech dialogue; the work of Philemon: Konstan *BOC* 2011: 618).

Cooks addressing students seem to have appeared later in the fourth century— Dionysius I K-A fr. 3 may be the first (Nesselrath 1990: 305)—and lessons in culinary theft become a topos. Euphron, a comic poet who may have flourished in the early third century, presents in *Adelphoi (Brothers)* K-A fr. 1 a culinary instructor who praises a current student, Lycus, who will be the youngest to have finished training with him, and for comparison, he names the cooking feats of modern culinary stars (*sophistai!*): Agis of Rhodes, Nereus of Chios, Chariades of Athens, and three others without ethnic; these (with Lycus) are the new seven sages (vv. 1–11, ἑπτὰ δεύτεροι σοφοί). As for himself, he was the inventor of a special kind of theft, and Lycus has followed in his footsteps and broken new ground (cf. Dionysius K-A fr. 3; Menander, *Aspis* 229–231, possibly parodic): he had filched goat parts during a sacrifice of the people of Tenos (?) four days ago, and just yesterday, while grilling pilfered intestines, he twittered to the accompaniment of a gut-stringed lyre while the cooking instructor himself had watched: the one was a serious play, but this was farce (ἐκεῖνο δρᾶμα, τοῦτο δ᾽ ἐστὶ παίγνιον, summary of vv. 13–35; consult K-A *App. Crit.* II on 34–35). In the cook's eyes, the latter is superior.

While not all these fragments exemplify the comic patter illustrated in the first examples, a Menandrian one will remind us of its form before we examine a "look-alike." In *Dyskolos,* Act III, first Geta has tried, unsuccessfully, to borrow a pot from Cnemon, and now Sico the cook, who berates the slave for his failure (he simply does not know how to ask properly), prepares to approach the grouchy old man: he has discovered a *techne* for such requests, he has helped tens of thousands in the city, he barges in on neighbors and borrows successfully from everyone—this is because the borrower needs to be flattering (489–93); he continues:

> πρεσβύτερός τις τ[ῆι] θύραι
> ὑπακήκο᾽· εὐθὺς πατέρα καὶ πάππα[ν λέγω.
> γραῦς· μητέρ᾽. ἂν τῶν διὰ μέσου τ[ις ἦι γυνή,
> ἐκάλεσ᾽ ἱερέαν. ἂν θεράπων [νεώτερος,
> βέλτιστον.

> Suppose an older man answers the door. [I call]
> [Him] 'Father' straight away, or 'Dad'. If it's
> A hag, then 'Mother'. If [a] middle-aged
> [Woman], I call her 'Madam'. If a [youngish (?)] slave,
> 'Good chap.'

> (493–497, trans. Arnott)

Menander's use of the topos—and the patter—fits right into the tradition (for similar patter used for "naming" people: Anaxandrides K-A. fr. 35); but the speech of Menander's cook, as we shall see in the next chapter has a pervasive thematic resonance in *Dyskolos.* A recurrent feature in the passages mentioned so far is the frequency with which the cook (like Sicon in *Dyskolos*) refers to his *techne.* In Diphilus fr. 17, the cook prefaced his presentation of meals suitable for different groups with reference to the important principle of his *techne* (4–5); in fr. 42, the cook refers to his *diagraphe* (7) before displaying his learning; and the long-winded cook in Anaxippus fr. 1 mentions not only the *techne* of his teacher and his eager yearning to leave behind a new treatment of it (21–22), but also provides a self-depiction: every morning he has books in hand as he searches for the principles of his *techne* (24–25)

The patter pattern sometimes has a deceptive likeness to a "quasi-legal formula"; this happens when the condition is explicit ("if an old man opens the door" rather than "suppose an old man answers the door") and answered by an imperatival apodosis that provides for or eases a *legal* remedy (basically, "if X does Y, then he must pay Z penalty; if X has not done Y, then there is no penalty"). An example, more formally contrived and less paratactic than patter pattern, appears in Diphilus's *Emporos* (*Merchant*) K-A fr. 31. One character, possibly a cook (but possibly a slave sent out on a shopping errand), in conversation with an unidentifiable partner (presumably a foreigner), begins by saying, "This is customary (νόμιμον τοῦτ' ἐστί) here, among the Corinthians":

> if we [the Corinthians] see anyone shopping conspicuously
> all the time, to examine [ἀνακρίνειν] this fellow: what does he live off
> and what does he do? And if he has property
> with income to cover his expenses,
> [it is customary] to let him enjoy his current lifestyle.
> But if he happens to be spending beyond his means,
> they [sc. the Corinthians] forbid him from doing this any longer,
> and if he disobeys, they impose a fine [ἐπέβαλον ζημίαν],
> and if he doesn't have anything at all but lives expensively,
> they hand him over to the executioner.

(2–11, trans. Konstan BOC 2011, modified)

Reformulated to "patter," this would read: "Someone is shopping conspicuously all the time? Examine the fellow! Does he have cash to cover his expenses? Let him go!...Does he have none at all? Hand him over to the executioner!" In the *Emporos* fragment, proximity of quasi-legal formula to patter may be part of the humor; additionally (as a remote possibility), the alleged Corinthian custom may be a parody of the Athenian law on lunatic spendthrifts, about which we admittedly know very little (Aristotle *Constitution of the Athenians* 56.6); but what is brilliantly contrived and humorous here is the precise articulation of the Corinthian "custom" to a person who at least pretends to have no idea why it concerns him (11). In the continuation of the fragment, the "cook" is relentless and provides an imaginative and teasingly suspenseful list of criminal activities, one after the other, that a man with no cash will engage in (12–17). When his respondent still claims ignorance (18), he drives home the point: the respondent has been spotted shopping prodigally, there's not a bit of fish left in the market, the inhabitants are fighting over celery in the vegetable stalls, he's the first to grab any rabbit, and the birds have flown away, he's driven the price of foreign wine way up! Of course we cannot know how this little episode fits into the play, and it may very well be extraneous to the plot (as is often the case with "cook scenes"); nonetheless, it is a fine example of Diphilus's skill in creating a comic dialogue that is for all intents and purposes an expansive patter monologue with a dramatic twist (cf. Diphilus, *Zographos* fr. 42 above).

A final example of comic patter will lead us to tragedy. *Dionysiazousai* (*Women at the Dionysia*) K-A fr. 6, by Timocles (active from the 340s to after 317), amounts to an encomium of schadenfreude. The unidentifiable speaker explains that "the mind, forgetting its own cares, and beguiled by contemplating [ψυχαγωηθείς] the sufferings of others, ends up pleasured and educated at the same time—for consider first, if you like, how the tragic poets benefit everyone." He continues with "patter" examples of tragic heroes and heroines, first Telephus and Alcmaeon, and then;

> Someone has eye-disease? Phineus's sons are blind
> Someone's child has died? Niobe can console him!
> Someone is a cripple? He can look at Philoctetes!

> (13–15, trans. Rosen *BOC* 2011, slightly modified)

While the benefits conferred by tragedy may belong to a contemporary debate on the educative value of tragedy (Pohlenz 1956: 73 n.1), the easy allusion to the tragic stage is part and parcel of comedy from the outset; from here it is an easy step to Demea offering Niceratus soothing advice upon learning of his daughter's out-of wedlock parturition in Menander's *Samia* (588–591): Niceratus should think of the tragic poets and their plays about Zeus ravishing Danae: that should help!

The characters of comedy, like their fifth century counterparts, are (timeless?) theater spectators themselves. A character in an unidentified play by Philemon (K-A fr. 160) says to another, "You're praising yourself, woman, like Astydamas." The latter was an extremely successful tragic poet of the fourth century who, after winning the prize for *Parthenopaeus* in 341/0 (IG II2 2320 Col II 22), had been awarded a statue; he himself had written the epigram. Euripides, however, was the all-time favorite for comedy writers in the fourth and third century. A character in Philemon *incerta* K-A fr. 118 says that if the dead have perception, he would hang himself to see Euripides. In Diphilus's *Synoris* fr. 74, a courtesan is speaking to a parasite, playing dice for small change; a pun is made on Euripides's name—it is also a dicing throw—and the courtesan appears to think that such a throw could help her, but it may be impossible ("How could I throw a Euripides?"); the parasite responds that Euripides would never help a woman, seeing that he hates them in his tragedies—but he loves parasites; then he quotes three verses, as if one follows the other, but the first and third are certainly from different plays (v. 7 from Eur. *fr.* 187.1 *Antiope* and v. 9 from *IT* 535). When the courtesan asks from what play the verses come, the parasite responds, "Why does it matter to you—for it's not the drama we're considering, but the sense." These of course, are explicitly flagged references to the poet. Scholars have also identified numerous "revised quotations" elsewhere: a cook, for example, opens a long monologue in Philemon *Stratiotes* (*Soldier*) K-A fr. 82, aping the opening of the nurse's speech at *Medea* 57–58. It is Euripides's *Orestes*, however, that wins the palm for the most often recollected: Menander *Aspis* 424–425, 432; *Samia* 326; *Sikyonioi* 176ff., 182. More subtle and extensive correspondences have been noted between *Samia* and *Hippolytus* (Katsouris 1975: 131–134; Omitowoju 2010), for example, and between *Dyskolos* and both *Bacchae* and *Electra* (Petrides 2010). It may be no coincidence that along the road from Piraeus to the city, the Athenians erected two monuments to its famous dramatists, Menander's tomb and Euripides's cenotaph (Pausanias 1.2.2).

FURTHER READING

For English translations of numerous fragments of Philemon, Diphilus, and other New Comic poets, see *BOC*. For readers who may want to sample the works of "analytic critics" who have tried to extract the "Diphilan" or "Philemonian" or "Apollodoran" originals from Plautine and Terentian comedies, see, e.g., Marx 1928, Lowe 1983, Ludwig 1968, Fantham 1968, MacCary 1973, Lefèvre 1978 and 1984, Webster 1970 (1953), Fraenkel 1922/1961/2007. Special studies of the individual comic writers: Damen 1995, Belardinelli et al. 1998, Olson 2007, Bruzzese, 2011.

Bibliography

Arnott, W. G. 1996a. *Alexis: The Fragments: A Commentary.* Cambridge, MA: Cambridge University Press.

——. 1979. *Menander.* Vol. 1. Loeb Classical Library 132. Cambridge, MA: Harvard University Press.

——. 1996b. *Menander.* Vol. 2. Loeb Classical Library 459. Cambridge, MA: Harvard University Press.

——. 2000. *Menander.* Vol. 3. Loeb Classical Library 460. Cambridge, MA: Harvard University Press.

Bayliss, A. J. 2011. *After Demosthenes: The Politics of Early Hellenistic Athens.* London: Bloomsbury Academic.

Belardinelli, A. M., O. Imperio, G. Mastromarco, M. Pellegrino, and P. Totaro. 1998. *Tessere: Frammenti della commedia greca: Studi e commenti.* Bari: Adriatica.

Blanchard, A. 2007. *La comédie de Ménandre: Politique, éthique, esthétique.* Paris: Presses de l'Université de Paris-Sorbonne.

Bernabó-Brea, L. B. 1981. *Menandro e il teatro greco nelle terracotte liparesi.* Genoa: Sagep.

——, with M. Cavalier. 2001. *Maschere e personaggi del teatro greco nelle terracotte liparesi.* Rome: "L'Erma" di Bretschneider.

Brown, P. McC. 1988. "Masks, Names and Characters in New Comedy." *Hermes* 115: 181–202.

Bruzzese, L. 2011. *Studi su Filemone comico.* Lecce: Pensa multimedia.

Buchanan, J. J. 1962. *Theorika: A Study of Monetary Distributions to the Athenian Citizenry during the Fifth and Fourth Centuries B.C.* New York: J. J. Augustin.

Csapo, E. 2007. "The Men Who Built the Theatres: *theatropolai, theatronai,* and *arkhitektones.*" In *The Greek Theatre and Festivals,* edited by P. Wilson, 87–115, with an archaeological appendix by H. R. Goette, 116–121. Oxford.

Cusset, Ch. 2003. *Ménandre ou la comedie tragique.* Paris: CNRS.

Damen, M. 1995. "The Comedy of Diphilos Sinopeus in Plautus, Terence and Athenaeus." PhD diss., University of Texas, Austin.

Fantham, E. 1968. "Terence, Diphilus and Menander." *Philologus* 112: 196–216.

Fraenkel, E. 1922. *Plautinisches im Plautus.* Philologische Untersuchungen 28. Berlin: Weidmann.

——. 1961. *Elementi Plautini in Plauto.* Translated by F. Munari. Florence: La Nuova Italia.

——. 2007. *Plautine Elements in Plautus.* Translated by T. Drevikovsky and F. Muecke. Oxford: Oxford University Press.

Goette, H. R. 2007. See Csapo 2007.

Green, J. R. 1994. *Theatre in Ancient Greek Society.* London: Routledge.

Habicht, C. C. 1997. *Athens from Alexander to Antony.* Translated by D. L. Schneider. Cambridge, MA: Harvard University Press.

Hall, E. 2007. "Greek Tragedy 430–380 BC." In *Debating the Cultural Revolution: Art, Literature, Philosophy, and Politics 430–380 BC,* edited by R. Osborne, 264– 287. Cambridge, UK: Cambridge University Press.

Handley, E. W. 1990. "The Bodmer Menander and the Comic Fragments." In *Relire Ménandre,* edited by E. Handley and A. Hurst, 123–148. Geneva: Droz.

——. 2002. "Acting, Action and Words in New Comedy." In *Greek and Roman Actors:Aspects of an Ancient Profession,* edited by P. Easterling and E. Hall, 165–188. Cambridge, UK: Cambridge University Press.

——. 2009. "Menander, *Epitrepontes.*" *POxy* 73: 25–36.

Iversen, P. 2011. "Menander's Thaïs: 'Hac primum iuvenum lascivos lusit amores.'" *CQ* 61: 186–191.

Katsouris, A. G. 1975. *Tragic Patterns in Menander.* Athens: Hellenic Society for Humanistic Studies.

Koster, W. J. W. 1975. (ed.) *Scholia in Aristophanem. Pars. I: Prolegomena de Comoedia. Scholia in Acharnenses, Equites, Nubes. Fasc. IA: Prolegomena de Comoedia.* Groningen: Bouma's Boekhuis B.V.

Lape, S. 2004. *Reproducing Athens: Menander's Comedy, Democratic Culture, and the Hellenistic City.* Princeton: Princeton University Press.

Lefèvre, E. 1978. *Der Phormio des Terenz und der Epidikazomenos des Apollodor von Karystos.* Zetemata 74. Munich: Beck.

——. 1984. *Diphilos und Plautus. Der* Rudens *und sein Original.* Abhandlungen der Geistes- und sozialwissenschaftlichen Klasse 10. Mainz: Akademie der Wissenschaften und der Literatur.

Lowe, J. C. B. 1983. "Terentian Originality in the 'Phormio' and 'Hecyra.'" *Hermes* 111: 431–452.

Ludwig, W. 1968. "The Originality of Terence and His Greek Models." *GRBS* 9: 169–182.

MacCary, W. T. 1969. "Menander's Slaves: Their Names, Roles, and Masks." *TAPA* 100: 277–294.

——. 1970. "Menander's Characters: Their Names, Roles, and Masks." *TAPA* 101: 277–290.

——. 1972. "Menander's Soldiers: Their Names, Roles, and Masks." *AJPh* 93: 279–298.

——. 1973. "The Comic Tradition and Comic Structure in Diphilos' *Kleroumene.*" *Hermes* 101: 195–208.

Marquaille, C. 2008. "The Foreign Policy of Ptolemy II." In *Ptolemy II Philadelphus and His World,* edited by Paul McKechnie and Philippe Guillaume, 39–64. Mnemosyne Supplements 300. Leiden and Boston: Brill.

Marx, F. 1928. *Plautus: Rudens.* Leipzig: Hirzel. (Reprinted 1959, Amsterdam: Hakkert.)

Meritt, B. D. 1938. "Greek Inscriptions." *Hesperia* 7: 77–166.

Mikalson, J. D. 1998. *Religion in Hellenistic Athens.* Berkeley: University of California Press.

Millis, B., and S. D. Olson. 2012. *Inscriptional Records for the Dramatic Festivals in Athens. IG II² 2318–2325 and Related Texts.* Leiden and Boston: Brill.

Nervegna, S. 2007. "Staging Scenes or Plays? Theatrical Revivals of 'Old' Greek Drama in Antiquity." *ZPE* 162: 14–42.

Nesselrath, H.-G. 1990. *Die attische Mittlere Komödie: Ihre Stellung in der antiken Literaturkritik und Literaturgeschichte.* Berlin: De Gruyter.

Nünlist, R. 2002. "Speech within Speech in Menander." In *The Language of Greek Comedy,* edited by A. Willi, 219–259. Oxford: Oxford University Press.

O'Sullivan, L. 2009a. *The Regime of Demetrius of Phalerum in Athens, 317–307 BCE: A Philosopher in Politics.* Leiden and Boston: Brill.

——. 2009b. "History from Comic Hypotheses: Stratocles, Lachares, and P. Oxy. 1235." *GRBS* 49: 53–79.

Olson, S.D. 2007. *Broken Laughter: Select Fragments of Greek Comedy*. Oxford: Oxford University Press.

Omitowoju, R. 2010. "Performing Traditions: Relations and Relationships in Menander and Tragedy." In *New Perspectives on Postclassical Comedy*, edited by A. K. Petrides and S. Papaioannou, 125–145. Newcastle upon Tyne: Cambridge Scholars.

Osborne, M. J. 2009. "The Archons at Athens 300/299–228/7." *ZPE* 171: 83–99.

Petrides, A. K. 2010. "New Performance." In *New Perspectives on Postclassical Comedy*, edited by A. K. Petrides and S. Papaioannou, 79–124. Newcastle upon Tyne: Cambridge Scholars.

——. 2012 (2009). "Masks in Greek Theatre." *The Literary Encyclopedia*, http://www.litencyc.com/php/stopics.php?rec=true&UID=7211.

Poe, J. P. 1996. "The Supposed Conventional Meanings of Dramatic Masks: A Re-examination of Pollux 4.133–54." *Philologus* 140: 306–328.

Pöhlmann, E. 1995. *Studien zur Bühnendichtung und zum Theaterbau der Antike*. Frankfurt am Main: Peter Lang.

Pohlenz, M. 1956. "Furcht und Mitleid?" *Hermes* 84: 49–74.

Roselli, D. K. 2011. *Theater of the People: Spectators and Society in Ancient Athens*. Austin: University of Texas Press.

Rosivach, V. 2000. "The Audiences of New Comedy." *Greece & Rome*, 2nd ser., 47: 169–171.

Rothwell, K. S. 1995. "The Continuity of the Chorus in Fourth-Century Attic Comedy." In *Beyond Aristophanes. Transition and Diversity in Greek Comedy*, edited by G. Dobrov, 99–118. Atlanta, GA: Scholars Press.

Sandbach, F. H. 1990. *Menandri reliquiae selectae*. Oxford: Oxford Classical Texts, Rev. ed.

Schröder, S. 1996. "Die Lebensdaten Menanders (Mit einem Anhang über die Aufführungszeit seines Ἑαυτὸν τιμωρούμενος)." *ZPE* 113: 35–48.

Webster, T. B. L. 1952. "Chronological Notes on Middle Comedy." *CQ*, n.s., 2: 13–26.

——. 1970. *Studies in Later Greek Comedy*. 2nd ed. Manchester: Manchester University Press. First published in 1953.

Wiles, D. 1991. *The Masks of Menander: Sign and Meaning in Greek and Roman Performance*. Cambridge, UK: Cambridge University Press.

Wilson, P., and E. Csapo. 2012. "From *Chorēgia* to *Agōnothesia*: Evidence for the Administration and Finance of the Athenian Theatre in the Late Fourth Century BC." In *Greek Drama IV: Texts, Contexts, Performance*, edited by D. Rosenbloom and J. Davidson, 300–321. Oxford: Aris & Phillips.

CHAPTER 10

MENANDER

ADELE C. SCAFURO

1. MENANDER'S LIFE AND OEUVRE

MENANDER son of Diopeithes of the deme Cephisia was born in 342/1 BCE (K-A test. 2) and died in 292/1 or in 291/0 (K-A test. 2, 3, and 46).[1] These and other testimonies about Menander's life and career are uncertain. The Athenian poet served as an ephebe (military cadet) along with Epicurus (K-A test. 7) and is reported to have produced his first play during that youthful military service (K-A test. 3). Alexis is said to have been his paternal uncle (K-A test. 1) and teacher (K-A test. 3; see Arnott 1996a: 11–13). Diogenes Laertius in his *Lives of the Philosophers* (5.36) reports that Theophrastus, Aristotle's successor as head of the Lyceum, taught Menander as well as Demetrius of Phalerum (5.75); the Macedonian Cassander had made the latter ruler of Athens in 317 BCE. That both Menander and Demetrius of Phalerum had a connection with the Peripatic school is likely enough.

Friendship between Demetrius and Menander is often surmised on the basis of another report from Diogenes (5.79), that Menander was "nearly" put on trial (Μένανδρος ὁ κωμικὸς παρ᾽ ὀλίγον ἦλθε κριθῆναι) for no other reason than that he was Demetrius's friend—but a kinsman (Telesphorus) of that same Demetrius interceded (Potter 1987); the "near-trial" apparently arose in the wake of Demetrius's flight from Athens in 307 after Demetrius Poliorcetes, son of Antigonus Monophthalmus, took Piraeus. The local historian Philochorus reports that many citizens had been denounced (by *eisangelia*) along with Demetrius of Phalerum; those who did not await trial were condemned to death, and those who underwent it were acquitted (*FGrHist* 328 F 66). If the two reports are to be connected, then Menander's name may have been proposed

---

[1] Contradictory testimonies on Menander's date of death (which have called his date of birth into contention as well) have not been finally resolved; recently, De Marcellus 1996 argues for the earlier date of death and Schröder 1996 for the later.

for trial, but rejected when voted upon. And he may have suffered political backlash of another kind a few years later—that is, if there is truth to the report that his production of *Imbrians* for the Dionysia of 301/0 was cancelled on account of the "tyrant" Lachares (*P. Oxy.* X 1235, col. iii, 105–112);[2] as Henderson (this volume) suggests, an association with anti-Antigonid oligarchs (i.e., anti-Demetrius Poliorcetes and his followers) may have motivated the action (or the tradition). In a city where politics and friendship were bound together in inexplicable ways, it is difficult to call Menander "apolitical," but Menander the "friend" and Menander the "poet" may not be precisely identical—the verdict is still out. While scholars have generally found Menander's plays disengaged from the political arena, some have argued that they show signs of his support for Macedon's first Athenian governor, Demetrius of Phalerum, and his policies (Major 1997; Owens 2011, unrealistically), or signs of changing support as times and regimes changed (Wiles 1984), or even signs that he was a promoter of democracy (Lape 2004). In the face of this complexity, one might consider the stele that carries a grand Athenian decree, IG II² 657 of 283/2 (now standing in the reception hall of the Epigraphical Museum in Athens), conferring *megistai timai* ("greatest honors") on Philippides. This comic poet, whose first attested work won first prize in 312/11 and who died in the late 280s, did not at all eschew political comment in his plays; yet in the long inscribed text, although there is mention of his service as *agonothetes*, there is not a single mention that he is Philippides the comic poet. The omission is intriguing: does it suggest an even more complicated and nuanced relationship between comedy and politics—or that the "political world" considered the comic arena of no account except for its elected officials?

Menander is said to have written 105 (K-A test. 1, 46), 108 (K-A test. 3, 46, 63), or 109 plays (K-A test. 46). Mention was made in the last chapter that his first play was performed in 321 (festival unknown; K-A test. 48, 49; Schröder 1996: 36 n. 9: the play was *Orge* [*Anger*]; Iversen 2011: the play was *Thais*),[3] that he won first prize for *Dyskolos* at the Lenaea in 317/16 (K-A test. 50, P. Bod. *hyp.*) and first prize again at the City Dionysia in 316/15 (K-A test. 48; the play is unnamed), but that he took fifth place at the same festival for *Heniochus* (*Charioteer*) in 313/12 and probably again for *Paidion* (*Young Child*) in 312/11 (K-A test. 51; see chapter 9 n. 7). Apollodorus, the Hellenistic chronicler (*FGrHist* 244) who ascribed 105 plays to Menander, is reported as saying that he won "only" eight victories; the "only" may be the addition of his reporter (Gellius, and cf. K-A test. 94, 98, 99)—surely eight victories was nothing to despise. Antiphanes, who is said to have begun producing plays in 388/4 (K-A test. 2) and may still have been producing plays at the end of the fourth century (K-A fr. 306), is credited with thirteen victories (K-A test. 1), eight at the Lenaea (K-A test. 4) and presumably the other five at the City Dionysia— yet he is ascribed with composing 365, 280, or 260 plays (K-A test. 1 and 2), and 138 titles survive! Moreover, neither Antiphanes nor Menander could have produced all these plays at competitive festivals—many will have been produced in the demes or

---

[2] For chronological difficulties, see Habicht 1997: 83 n. 58 and Osborne 2012: 22–36; for skepticism: O'Sullivan 2009.

[3] Menander's *Heauton Timoroumenos* had been an earlier contender (Bethe 1902).

elsewhere; e.g., if Menander produced two plays per year, one at the City Dionysia and the other at the Lenaea, for thirty consecutive years, that would leave around forty-five plays for noncompetitive production elsewhere (for similar thrust but more extensive argument, cf. Konstantakos 2008 and Konstantakos 2011: 158–162). Proportionally, Menander appears to have been a great success in his lifetime—even if Philemon may have been preferred on occasions when they competed against each other.

Menander's fame increased after his lifetime; the extant record of revivals attests to this (two of *Phasma*, in 237/6 and 168/7, and *Misogynes* in 198/7, IG II² 2323.172, 412; SEG 26.208 fr. A10), as does the number of extant papyri carrying his texts—only those of Homer and Euripides surpass him (Arnott 1979: xx). His popularity is further attested by the use of his comedies in schools and among teachers of rhetoric, the numerous statues and busts sculpted in his likeness, and the numerous representations of scenes from his plays on murals and paintings found in places as far distant as Pompeii and Mytilene; indeed, the recent publication of a stunning mosaic pavement of early-third-century CE Daphne (a suburb of Antioch-on-the-Orontes) is a reminder of the longevity of Menander's theater (Gutzwiller and Çelik 2012). His popularity makes it all the more surprising that no manuscript of a Menandrian comedy made its way into the Middle Ages (see Blanchard this volume). At the beginning of the twentieth century, only meager scraps of the playwright were available to readers. The only way to envision a complete comedy at that time was to try to reconstruct its skeleton on the basis of the Roman plays that had used Menander as a model: Plautus's *Bacchides* (Menander's *Dis Exapaton*), *Cistellaria* (*Synaristosai*), *Stichus* (*Adelphoi A*), and probably *Aulularia*; and Terence's *Andria* (Menander's *Andria* with additions from his *Perinthia*), *Heauton Timorumenos* (Menander's play of the same title), *Eunuchus* (Menander's play of the same title with additions from *Kolax*), *Adelphoe* (*Adelphoi B* with an additional scene from Diphilus' *Synapothneskontes*).

That picture changed dramatically with two major discoveries of papyri. The first came in 1905 and led to Lefebvre's publication of the Cairo codex two years later, with parts of *Epitrepontes, Heros, Perikeiromene, Samia*, and an unidentified play. The second major find came in the late 1950s, with a papyrus codex (known as the Bodmer Codex) containing parts of *Samia, Dyskolos* (complete), and *Aspis*; publication of *Dyskolos* followed in 1958/59, and of the other two plays in 1969. From other sources, fragments of a new play, *Sikyonios/oi* (*Sicyonian* or *Sicyonians*—the title is disputed; see Arnott 2000: 196–198; hereafter the plural will be used), were discovered and published in 1964, and numerous scrappy fragments also came to light, many of great interest, such as some forty lines of text from *Dis Exapaton* published in 1968 (Handley), with additions in 1972 (Sandbach OCT) and some altered readings and further additions in 1997 (Handley P.Oxy. 4407). New finds and identifications continued. Sandbach's revised edition (1990) of the 1972 Oxford Classical Text included eighteen plays from papyrus finds (all fragmentary except for *Dyskolos*); fifteen additional fragmentary plays with titles, together with many fragments of unidentifiable plays from the "indirect tradition"; and an Appendix of new papyrus fragments (notably *Epitrepontes* and *Misoumenos*). Arnott's three-volume edition for the Loeb series (1979, 1996, 2000) adds *Leukadia* and scraps of *Synaristosai* and *Encheiridion* (1979: 358–364). New papyrus fragments have continued to appear (see Blume 2010; also Blanchard and Bathrellou, this volume); recently, new fragments of *Epitrepontes* (Römer 2012a and b) and the mosaics from Daphne previously mentioned have increased our knowledge of the poet's work.

2. COMPOSITIONAL STRUCTURES

Since antiquity, Menander has been admired for the careful construction and variety of his plots. These are superficially similar: a young man is in love with a young woman, an obstacle to the romance obtrudes (a difference in status, a questionable pregnancy, a misunderstanding between the couple, or the parentage of one or the other may be unknown, or a death may be supposed to have occurred); in the end, the obstacle is overcome. While plot segments are fastidiously linked together (e.g., Nünlist 2004: 101–102), so that entrances and exits are well motivated and punctiliously timed (Frost 1988), the devil, as the saying goes, is in the detail, and the detail reveals not only the zig and zag of not-quite-repetitive Trollopian plot turns (compare, for instance, Demea's "take heart" monologue at *Samia* III 325–356, when he thinks his mistress has borne a child to his adoptive son, and Chaerestratus's similar monologue at *Epitrepontes* V 981–1006[?], when he thinks Habrotonon has borne a child to his best friend), but far more, Menander's evocative and nuanced language and his creation of lively scenes, intrepid characters, and overall, an imagistic web of realism.

With the new Menander available by the late 1960s, and especially with a complete play to study, scholars could at last assess the poet's art firsthand. The mechanics of plot construction were opened to new scrutiny (see, e.g., Blanchard 1983 and chapter 11 in this volume). Choral interludes divided *Dyskolos* into five acts (signaled by the appearance of XOPOY at the end of each of the first four), and that division could reasonably be inferred not only for his other plays (XOPOY appeared at the end of two acts of *Samia* and at the end of Act III of *Misoumenos*, and a papyrus published by Gronewald in 1986 added a third XOPOY to *Epitrepontes*), but also more widely for Menander's contemporaries and followers (Donatus *praef. ad Ad.* I.4; Euanthius *de Fab.* III.1). Moreover, the five-act division was established as Greek in origin (possibly Theophrastan: Webster 1960: 184; not Roman: Lowe 1983: 442); how early the practice began is not known.[4] The evidence of the plays suggests that an actor onstage signals the first entrance of the chorus (*Dyskolos* 246–249, *Epitrepontes* 169–171, *Perikeiromene* 261–262), whereas subsequent appearances are cued by the departure of the actors from the stage (Handley 1990: 130–131). No literary trace of their performance survives (song and dance, one or both?), but

---

[4] The fishermen in Plautus's *Rudens* 290ff. and the *advocati* in *Poenulus* 504ff. may have appeared in the Diphilan original of the one and in the likely Alexian original (Arnott 1996a: 285–287) of the other, but it is difficult to hypothesize that they were used as "true" choruses and not simply for interludes (Lowe 1990: 276–277).

apparently the choruses had no connection to the action onstage—or no more than the drunken "Pan-worshippers" (if Πανιστάς is what Menander wrote at v. 230: Handley 1965 and 1990: 129, Παιανιστάς) who are sighted at the end of *Dyskolos* Act I. The choral interludes between acts allowed for the passage of time, so that, for example, a character could make a long journey from one place in Attica to another (Hunter 1983:36–37).

The evidence of the extant plays so far suggests that the central dramatic climax is staged and resolved either in the fourth act (*Epitrepontes*, and seemingly in *Dyskolos* and *Samia*) or in the fifth (*Misoumenos*, *Sikyonioi*). A climax in the fourth act allows for surprises in the fifth. Thus, in the final scene of Act IV (690–783) of *Dyskolos*, Cnemon, now rescued from his fall in the well (one component of the crisis), is assisted onstage, probably by an *ekkyklema* (758: Pöhlmann 1995: 160–162; Sandbach 1973: 239–241). He then reflects on his life in a serious speech (711– 747) in trochaic tetrameters (a change from the preceding iambic trimeters) which continue to the end of the act, addressing Myrrhine his estranged wife, her son Gorgias, and their daughter: he has realized, to some degree, the error of solitary life; he will adopt Gorgias, leave him heir, and make him guardian of his daughter—he is to find her a husband. This provides a happy ending, for Sostratus, the girl's Pan-struck lover, is on hand for betrothal at the end of the scene (the second component of the crisis). The play is virtually over, the crisis has been resolved, yet another act follows (784–969): now Gorgias will be betrothed to Sostratus's sister (a surprise—there has been no preparation for this), and, in the major scene (880—958), delivered in lively catalectic iambic tetrameters to the accompaniment of a pipe (the effect of which will be considered shortly), the cook Sicon and the slave Geta take a farcical and cruel, but not undeserved, revenge on Cnemon before joining the celebration of the day's events in the cave of Pan.

A definition of scenes within acts has proven more difficult; sometimes they are demarcated by an "empty stage," when one set of characters leaves and another set enters, but scenes are not always so defined—there is only one "empty stage" (95–96) in the substantial remains of *Samia*. Hunter (1983: 44–45) describes different ways in which scenes are set off from one another: most often by variation of tempo and emotional intensity, and secondarily by metrical variations, for example by shifts from scenes in iambic trimeters to a scene in trochaic tetrameters or other meter. Two such shifts in Acts IV and V of *Dyskolos* were noted in the last paragraph. Furley (2009: 13) in his commentary on *Epitrepontes* observes a tendency for each act to have three distinct scenes, not always separated by an "empty stage" but linked together in different ways, sometimes by a character remaining onstage at the end of one scene and figuring in the next, or by the entrance of a new character who picks up a thread of the scene in progress but really begins a new scene. One major character is the focus of action in each scene, and when focus shifts to another actor, the "scene" has changed. Furley suggests a link of such scene construction to the "three-actor convention" of New Comedy (for division of *Epitrepontes* into scenes, see also Martina 1997 II 1: 39–49).[5]

---

[5] Green 2000 points out that it was difficult for actors in New Comedy to change roles, since "belly padding" was put beneath the actor's tights, and therefore "if an actor had to change from being a slim

This important and controversial convention (Horace, *Ars Poetica* 192; Diomedes, *Gramm. Lat.* 3.490–91) is explained in two ways: either no more than three actors speak in any scene even though a troupe may have more than three actors at its disposal (the term "actor" excludes silent walk-on parts or a "super" wearing the mask of a character who elsewhere has a speaking part), or, more strictly, no more than three actors speak in a play and the troupe is limited to three (Sandbach 1975). By either explanation, it is thought that a specific character in a comedy would have to be played by more than one actor; consequently, there would be no unity of voice (except by one actor imitating the voice of another), and character identification would be achieved by mask, costume, and idiosyncrasies of gesture, voicing, and possibly diction assigned to a particular character. Some scholars have been skeptical that Menander would heed such restrictions, given his propensity for realism (e.g., Blume 1998: 66–68). Yet records from the Delphic Soteria in the third century show that the comic troupe was usually composed of three actors (DFA[2]: 155); more relevant to our time period, the award of an actor's prize in comedy at both major festivals that began at some point during the last three decades of the fourth century (see chapter 9) recommends the view that individual character roles were *not* distributed among multiple actors—for how else could an actor be awarded a prize for a particular role, unless he was awarded instead for his capacity to carry out multiple roles and to mimic the voices of the other actors? And practically speaking, how, indeed, could another actor carry on the "voicing" of characters who have been given quite remarkable speeches—such as Demea's great monologue that opens *Samia* Act III or that miserable soldier's shorter but remarkable monologue that opens *Misoumenos*? Given the constraints of using only three actors per scene, one can see that the demarcation of a scene and the marking of exits and entrances of actors take on added importance. Furley's linking of a particular kind of scene construction to the "three-actor rule" therefore makes sense. He has been able to demonstrate that, with two exceptions in two scenes, the same actor can play the same character throughout *Epitrepontes*; similar attention to scene construction may show similar results in other plays.

In his prologues, Menander sometimes uses a god (e.g., Pan in *Dyskolos*) or abstract divinity (Agnoia, "Misconception," in *Perikeiromene* and Tyche, "Luck," in *Aspis*) to provide the expository information necessary for understanding the plot, and once (so far, with certainty) he uses a mortal (Moschio in *Samia*) to carry out the task.[6] In his use of a prologue speaker, Menander follows the tradition of tragedy. Probably his contemporaries did the same: Philemon K-A fr. 95, for example, introduces a divinity, Aer ("Air"), as prologue to a lost play that is sometimes thought to be *Philosophoi*, who proclaims both his omnipresence and omniscience (for discussion of possible parody of Diogenes of Apollonia and of philosophers more generally in this play, see Bruzzese 2011: 110–116).

young man to a fat-bellied slave, or vice versa, he needed quite a lot of time to change"; he suggests that this is "the sort of practical factor which must have affected the way that Menander and his colleagues structured their plays."

   [6] A mortal speaker addresses the audience twice as ἄνδρες in Pap. Didot II (= P.Louvre, Sandbach OCT p. 330, K-A fr. com. adesp. 1001, Arnott III [2000] Fab. Inc. 2) vv. 3 and 13. This may be a prologue, and it may be Menander; see Bain 1977: 186 n.3.

Scholars have often compared Philemon's *Aer* with the prologue speaker (Arcturus) of Plautus's *Rudens*, and so have posited the same practice for Diphilus, Plautus's model here. Sometimes the Menandrian prologue speaker delivers his exposition as prelude to the comedy (like Pan in *Dyskolos* and perhaps Persephone in *Sikyonioi*: Arnott 2000: 210), but sometimes he does so after an opening scene (the "delayed prologue"). There is no parallel for the delayed prologue in tragedy, but there appears to be a connection with Old Comedy technique. A delayed prologue (Tyche) is strikingly used in *Aspis*; she corrects the error of the slave who appears at play's opening, announcing that he has carried home the shield of his dead master, Cleostratus. Other delayed prologues have been inferred for *Epitrepontes* (Martina 1997 I: 29–41; Handley 2009: 28; Furley 2009 suggests *Diallage*, "Reconciliation"), *Heros* (a hero-god, possibly of the deme; for this and other suggestions see G-S 1973: 386), *Misoumenos*, and *Perikeiromene*. A portion of a divine prologue is preserved for *Phasma*, but its place in the comedy is uncertain (opening prologue in Sandbach 1990 text 1–25, delayed divine prologue in Arnott [2000] text 40–56 following Turner 1969). Fragments from some other plays might also be from prologues, e.g., *Xenologos* K-A fr. 255, 256, and *Pseudherakles* K-A fr. 411 (Webster 1960: x and 7).

3. METER

The shifts from one scene to another that are indicated by metrical variation are noticeable in the first instance because such variation in Menander is so rare a phenomenon (cf. chapter 9, n. 5). Indeed, the lengthy remnants of *Epitrepontes* and *Misoumenos* are composed entirely in iambic trimeters, the most common meter in Menander's oeuvre. Trochaic tetrameters are found in four of the longer plays (*Aspis* Act V 516–544; *Dyskolos* Act IV 711ff.; *Perikeiromene* Act II 267–353; *Sikyonioi* Act III (?) 110–149; *Samia* Acts IV and V 670ff.) and in numerous of the fragmentary ones (for a list, see Sandbach 1973: 36 n.1). While the meter often appears in scenes of high emotion and farce, it also appears in speeches of serious reflection, as in Cnemon's at *Dyskolos* 711ff.

Catalectic iambic tetrameters so far have appeared only at the end of *Dyskolos* (and these accompanied by a pipe: 880 and 910), where Cnemon meets his painful come-uppance at the hands of Getas and Sicon. Interpretations of the metrical effect vary. Some have viewed the play's conclusion as being in the "tradition of revelling endings to comic plays, which Menander exploits on this occasion by making his ending a reprise of the borrowing scenes with slave, cook and Knemon earlier in the play (456–521)" (Handley 2002: 174). Sandbach points out that catalectic iambic tetrameters are frequent in Old Comedy (in choral recitative and debate scenes) but seem gradually to have all but disappeared during the fourth century; accordingly, Menander was "perhaps a little old-fashioned" here, creating a lively scene at play's end and abandoning realism by virtue of its being acted to the rhythm of the *aulos* and adding "an element of fantasy" in the ragging of the old man (1973: 267). But there are further complexities: Cnemon has not really been shown to be reformed; he betrays hardly any interest in the betrothal of his daughter and refuses to attend the prenuptial feast (748–758; 852–870; Zagagi 1995: 111–112)—though in a comedy, he should be reformed and *voluntarily* reintegrated into society. There is thus an inconsistency between "the suggestion of a 'happy ending' and what might be foreseen from a realistic appreciation of Knemon's character"; that inconsistency, however, is obscured from the audience's view: such is the power of old-fashioned music and farce (Sandbach 1973: 269; cf. Wiles 1984: 177–178). Hunter (2002: 201–203) sees in the ending a contrast of two different performance cultures: the "high comedy" ends with the civilized departures of Gorgias and Sostratus to join the party inside the cave; the following scene provides "a 'low' or farcical reflection of the main action" and the "use of music, the extravagant gesture and dancing and the rare, perhaps old-fashioned metre seem something of a throwback to a livelier style of comedy, as though Menander was exploiting his awareness (and that of his audience?) of the general drift of comic history" (202).

Shifts in rhythm, however, are not only from one meter to another, but can intervene within a meter: iambic trimeters on occasion have a tragic scansion, notably in the long recognition scene in *Perikeiromene* (IV 768–827). Here, beginning at 779 and extending to 824 (and much of this is stichomythia, in tragic manner), long syllables are rarely resolved, caesura and Porson's Law are observed, anapaests are almost entirely excluded (except in 779 and 789). The tragic scansion accords with the seriousness of the scene— and yet it remains comic: Moschio eavesdropping and commenting on the side lowers the emotional tension, while tragic reminiscences are "over the top" (at 788, a nearly absurd reworking of a line from a well-known passage in Euripides's *Melanippe the Wise* fr. 484.3; at 785 and 805, the slow eliciting of details relevant to the recognition between father and daughter). The blend of comedy with tragic elements is subtle but nonetheless observable. In other plays, the tragic versification (often in combination with "high" poetic diction) is less extensive and may have different affects, just as in *Perikeiromene* IV: it may stress a serious moment or be absurdly inappropriate, or both at the same time (examples at *Misoumenos* 214, *Samia* 516–517, *Epitrepontes* 324; see Sandbach 1970: 125– 126). While perhaps few in the audience would catch the shift to tragic scansion or recognize a revised quotation from tragedy, no actor would be so obtuse: tragic quotation and scansion, and indeed, shifts of meter, were overt cues. They were indicators of delivery, of voicing, solicitations to interpret and run with the poet—if only he would!

4. Diction, Linguistic Characterization, and Thematic Expansion

The language of Menander's characters, at least of those playing citizen roles, is a mixture of (what we imagine to be) the everyday language of the educated man on the street—artificially turned into, for the most part, iambic trimeters—with shorter or longer flights into a higher poetic register (with overlay of tragic and sometimes epic borrowings), and every now and then a plunking down into the gutter (all of which is found, e.g., in Demea's monologue at *Samia* 325–356). Many literati of the Imperial Age (e.g., Quintilian, Plutarch, K-A test. 101, 103, 104) thought Menander a quintessential transmitter of pure Attic, an exemplar of persuasion for future orators, and a poet with the capacity to present a range of emotions and all sorts of characters. Not everyone, however, agreed on the first point; the Atticist Phrynichus (K-A test. 119) condemned Menander's language for numerous and ignorant "counterfeits." While his criticism has been interpreted as meaning that Menander admitted koine features into his scripts, his diagnosis was disputed in the early part of the twentieth century and also in the latter part, when scholars with larger chunks of the author at their disposal showed, for example, that Menander uses relatively few nouns in -μός or adjectives in -ώδης and -ικός, phenomena that are frequent in writers of koine (for references, see Willi 2002: 21–22). Menander, however, might use some such words to color certain characters; Onesimus in *Epitrepontes*, as Sandbach (1970: 134–136) has shown, "stands alone among Menander's persons in this tendency to use nouns in -μός and adjectives in -τικός." Yet Onesimus' particular -μός words are quite uncommon and seem to depict, together with his facility for quoting swatches of tragedy, a slave who is a bit out of the ordinary in his skillful appropriation of language rather than one who picks up what he hears without discernment.[7]

Menander's linguistic depictions of stage characters are sometimes subtle, sometimes not; characters, for example, may have penchants for using particular words (like Onesimus in *Epitrepontes*) or evince syntactical peculiarities that become associated with them (see Sandbach 1970 for numerous examples). The impostor doctor in *Aspis* with his false Doric dialect is the most sensational of Menander's linguistic characterizations, but Cnemon's penchant for vituperative name-calling, perhaps the most extensive for an Old Man in the corpus, is also remarkable. His maligned subjects and addressees are sinners and criminals; they are *anosioi* ("unholy": 108–109 "ἀνόσιε ἄνθρωπέ," 469, 595; used only once elsewhere), *toichoruchoi* (lit. "thieves who dig through walls": 588 and cf. 447; elsewhere only in fragments), *androphona theria* ("homicidal beasts": 481; not elsewhere). Others of Cnemon's vocative terms of abuse are more widely used in the corpus, though no one of the more fully preserved plays instances them as often as this one does: *mastigia* ("rogue in need of a whipping"), *athlie* ("wretch"), and *trisathlie* ("monstrously-wretched").[8] Cnemon also curses frequently (432, 442, 600–601, 927–928) and threatens to kill his serving woman (931).[9] The grouchy old man is certainly not

---

[7] Gomme and Sandbach 1973: 321 on στριφνός at *Epitrepontes* 385 is instructive regarding the difficulty of identifying and interpreting koine in Menander's texts.

[8] *Mastigia* 471, used also by Sostratus at 140 and once each in *Epitrepontes*, *Kolax*, *Perikeiromene*, and *Samia*. *Athlie/oi* 702 and 955, used also by Geta at 880 and once each in *Epitrepontes*, *Kolax*, and *Samia*. *Trisathlie*: 466, used also by Sicon at 423; elsewhere, by Smicrines in *Aspis* 414.

[9] Cnemon's name-calling is almost matched by the curmudgeonly Smicrines in *Epitrepontes* (1064, 1100, 1122; 1073; 366; 1080; 1113). Thrice his addressees are called *hierosyloi* (lit. "temple robber"

the only wielder of abusive speech in the play (see, e.g., Sicon at 487–488, below); none-theless, his particular brand of name-calling, with its clustering of sinners and criminals, is suggestive of his self-righteous stand-alone morality, more fully articulated elsewhere in the play (e.g., 442–455 and 742–747), and is his most distinctive linguistic trait. It is all the more prominent because a polite—though sometimes ironic—addressing of char-acters occurs extensively throughout the play; this in turn may be due to the particular situation of the comedy: the imminent celebration of Pan by a genteel Athenian family and their slaves and assistants who meet and mingle with the "locals" from Phyle.[10]

Cnemon's penchant for name-calling is given attention right at the start, before he even sets foot on stage. It is hinted at in the prologue, when Pan depicts him as δύσκολος πρὸς ἅπαντας, οὐ χαίρων τ' ὄχλωι ("peevish to everyone, never giving a friendly nod to the crowd," 7, expanded in 9–10) and made vivid in the first scene: Pyrrhia, whom Sostratus had bidden to meet the old man, reports the experience in a series of short speeches (87–144) to Sostratus and his friend Chaerea. The slave had gone to the farm, sighted the man, approached:

> I was still a good
> Way from him, but I wanted to be a
> Friendly and tactful sort of fellow [ἐπιδέξιός], so
> I greeted him. 'I've come,' I said, 'on business,
> To see you, sir, on business, it's to your
> Advantage.' Right away, 'Damned heathen [ἀνόσιε
> ἄνθρωπε],' he Said, 'trespassing on my land? What's your game?'
> He picked a lump of earth up, which he threw
> Smack in my face! (104–111, trans. Arnott 1979)

A small but vivid portion of the speech is delivered through quoted speech (107–110 and 112–115). Cnemon's first response has been to call his uninvited visitor "ἀνόσιε ἄνθρωπε"—and this after the slave's concern to present himself as ἐπιδέξιος, a "tactful sort of fellow." Pyrrhia continues his narrative: the man beat him with a stake, shouting,

---

but apparently any kind of "crook": 1064, 1100, 1122). In the first and third instance, Smicrines uses "*hierosyle grau*" of Sophrone, whom he later threatens to drown and kill at night (1073); *hierosyle* as an abusive address appears twice elsewhere in *Epitrepontes* (935, 952; see Martina 1997 I2: 521 on 952), but only four times in other plays (*Aspis* 227, *Dyskolos* 640, *Samia* 678, *Perikeiromene* 366). For linguistic characterizations of other old men, especially in *Samia*, see Grasso 1995: 235–239.

[10] Among the polite addresses in *Dyskolos*, we find βέλτιστε used six times (144, 319, 338, 342, 476, 503); μειράκιον six times, sometimes coresponsive with βέλτιστε (269, 299, 311, 342, 539, 729; Cnemon himself uses μειράκιον once to address his son, and this occurs in the course of his "speech of redemption"); ὦ τᾶν "good sir" is used twice (247 and 359); μακάριε twice (103 and 701); πάτερ as a term of respect for an older man, twice (107 and 171)—and this list excludes the terms for the members of a household (*pais, graus, pater, meter, thugatrion*) who are also frequently addressed by different characters in the play. The explicit attention to language in the play suggests that Sostratus' remark (201–202) on the girl's use of a predominantly "male oath" is just as much a critical comment on her inappropriate language as it is a compliment on her open manner (cf. Bain 1984: 40–41); on the girl's language, see Traill 2008: 54–55. See Dickey 1995.

at the top of his lungs, "Don't you know the public road?" (115); Cnemon pursued him for fifteen stades, slinging clods of earth, stones, even pears when nothing else remained. He sums up the old man's character and offers advice to Sostratus: "What a savage brute, an absolutely damnable/ Old heathen (ἀνόσιος γέρων)! Get out of here, *please!*" (122–123, trans. Arnott, mod.). Pyrrhia has picked up Cnemon's language (ἀνόσιος γέρων), iterates the message to leave this neck of the woods, but adds his own endearing "*please!*" (ἱκετεύω σ').

Indeed, courteous versus abusive address and its reception play into a pervasive theme: hospitality (that great Greek virtue), and especially now, on the occasion of a sacrifice, hospitality that is tested in this play by knocking on a neighbor's door to borrow pots for the sacrifice to Pan and finding a welcome (or not), and by invitations to join in celebrating a wedding feast. Sicon, the cook who accompanies Sostratus's mother to Pan's shrine, makes the case for the utility of courteous address later in the play. Geta, another slave in Sostratus's family, had tried to borrow a pot from Cnemon, had miserably failed, and generated a great deal of annoyance by asking—Cnemon had left the stage, complaining of "homicidal beasts" who come knocking on one's doors "as if to a friend's house" (III 481–486). Sicon now reacts as he comes onstage, obviously having watched the preceding scene:

> Be damned to you! He told
> You off? Perhaps you asked with the finesse
> Of a pig! Some folk don't know how to do a thing
> Like that. There's a technique to it that I've
> Discovered. I help millions in the town,
> Pestering their neighbors, borrowing pans from all
> Of them. A borrower must use soft soap.
> Suppose an older man answers the door. [I call]
> [Him] 'Father' [πατέρα] straight away, or 'Dad' [πάππα[ν]. If it's
> A hag, then 'Mother' [μητέρ']. If [a] middle-aged
> [Woman], I call her 'Madam' [ἱερέαν]. If a [youngish(?)] slave,
> 'Good chap' [βέλτιστον]. You people though—[be (?)] hanged!
> O what stupidity! [Claptrap like (?)] 'Boy! Slave!' *My* approach
> Is, 'Come on, dad [πατρίδιον], [I want (?)] you!

(487–499, trans. Arnott)

Sicon addresses lines 497–499 to Geta, and, as he concludes his speech, knocks on Cnemon's door to provide the proof of his technique (Arnott 1979: 261, 263). But the poor cook is hardly given a chance: Cnemon calls for a leather strap to beat the man; Sicon asks to be released and (desperately) adds a "βέλτιστε" ("good chap") at 503, to no avail and apparently in violation of his own script—he has used the address that *he* reserves for slaves as part of "soft soap delivery." Left alone onstage, Sicon sizes up the situation: "Yes, he's ploughed me nicely! The importance of the tactful appeal [οἷόν ἐστ' ἐπιδεξίως / αἰτεῖν]—by Zeus, how that does matter!" 514–516. The cook has fared no better than Pyrrhia had in the opening scene, "wanting to be a friendly and tactful sort of fellow [ἐπιδέξιος]", 105–106. Sicon, shown here as a man who thinks about the way he uses language, and who elsewhere appears as "a man of metaphors and colourful language" (Sandbach 1973: 282; also Sandbach 1970: 119–120), is given a "linguistic climax" in the last act when he describes (whether as enticement or torment for Cnemon), in poetically tinged language and metrically strict rhythm, the feasting that is taking place inside Pan's shrine (946–953).

Menander's linguistic characterizations are carefully constructed and, in the instances discussed here, play into the larger themes of the comedy. Cnemon's abusive name-calling is part of the "address system" of (in)hospitality, hinted at in the prologue, made explicit by Pyrrhia in the first act and theorized by Sicon in the third. Its "courteous side" is shown elsewhere in the play, especially in the first dialogue between Sostratus and Gorgias in Act II. Here are two men, from disparate backgrounds, and certainly one of them at odds with the other, who achieve a balance of courtesy, marked by a frequent exchange of personal address (μειράκιον and βέλτιστε: 269, 299, 311, 319, 338, and 342, perhaps the most intimate moment, where the two terms are exchanged in one antilabic line; see Dickey 1995 and Dickey 1996: 73–74 and 119–120).[11]

5. THE MONOLOGUE

Menandrian plays abound with monologues—characterizing monologues, emotional monologues, expository monologues (including prologues), entrance monologues, "link monologues" (which, as the tag suggests, "link" scenes to one another), quasi-monologues (lengthy uninterrupted speeches by one character before an internal audience of cast members who remain silent, as in the case of Cnemon's "speech of redemption" in *Dyskolos* Act IV, or who may interrupt now and again with a line or two, as in the case of Davus's speech before Smicrines in *Epitrepontes* Act II). Often these are moments in the comedy that are essentially unrealistic—for (a) who in real life walks down a street explaining where he is coming from and why he appears alone, and (b) who stands before his house bemoaning to the world at large and to no one in particular that his mistress despises him or that she has been intimate with his son? Traditionally, monologists who provide expository information (as in "a") have been interpreted as directing their speeches toward the audience, while those who reflect

---

[11] Polite addresses cluster in *Epitrepontes* in the arbitration scene and especially in Act IV, where Habrotonon (H.) engages Pamphila (P.) in a dialogue marked by sensitive and meaningful exchange of address: γύναι (858 H.), γύναι (859 P.), φιλτάτη (860 H.), γλυκεῖα (862 H.), γύναι (864 P.), φιλτάτη (865 H.), γύναι (866 H.), φιλτάτη (871 P.), μακαρία γύναι (873 H.). Pamphila's adoption of affectionate address at 871 is a significant moment. See Sandbach 1973: 359 for the addresses in the latter scene; Martina 1997 II2 on 860; Turner 1980 for Menander's technique of questioning and answering; Scafuro 1990: 150–151 for the curious questioning here.

on the dramatic situation ἐν ἤθει ("in the persona of the dramatic character," as in "b") have been interpreted as engaging in an interior discussion, having a conversation with themselves, a soliloquy; but surely in many instances no clear line demarcates the one kind from the other (Bain 1977:185–207; Blundell 1980: 63).

Theatrical tradition fully embraced the convention of monologue. Even so, Menander turned it into a new art form that enlivens the ongoing drama; as Leo pithily put it in 1908 (and thus with a limited corpus at hand): "The characters of Demeas and Moschion in *Samia*, of Onesimus and Charisius in *Epitrepontes*, of Moschio in *Perikeiromene* are no more lively during the most excited dialogues than when they address themselves alone" (89). Menandrian monologists certainly know how to take the audience into their confidence, to draw them into their dramas, not only because the events they report can be so crucial to the plot of the play, but also because they speak so vividly—they demand attention. Examples abound: (1) Onesimus, in remarkable language (*Epitrepontes* Act IV 878–907), relates Charisius's response to overhearing Pamphila's defense of her loyalty to her husband, quotes the words of his master in deep distress (see G-S 361 on 891), and thus prepares the audience for his manic entrance and delivery of his own redemptive monologue in the next scene. (2) There Charisius records the *daemonion*'s rebuke to him, quotes Pamphila's response to her father's request to leave him, and rehearses his own retort to Smicrines (908–932?). (3) The soldier Thrasonides, at the very opening of *Misoumenos*, stands outside his house and, bizarrely apostrophizing Night and distressed that his mistress's feelings have changed, sets the stage for the crisis in his house. (4) In Act IV of the same play, the soldier's slave Geta enters (685), ambulates here and there in deep conversation with himself, trying to figure out how in the world both the father of Thrasonides's mistress and she herself could refuse the soldier's request for marriage, and along the way, in fact, from the start, a neighbor follows him about (697: σ]υμπεριπατήσω καὐτός), trying to get his attention with questions and exasperated interjections until he finally succeeds (724)—but this only happens after Geta has provided a verbatim account: what Crateia's father said, what Thrasonides said, what Crateia did not say, what Geta would have done; all this is economically accomplished in fifty lines in one of the most comical scenes in the oeuvre. (5) This coup de théâtre is followed by the entrance of Thrasonides in the next scene (cf. Charisius' entrance after Onesimus's monologue in *Epitrepontes* IV): he now delivers what appears to be a melancholic monologue (757–815, text from Arnott 1996b, with many partial verses—the scene is rather mutilated), delivered without interruption but as if he were questioning and responding to answers about his situation to another character onstage (potentially quite comical), and possibly ending with a plot to pretend suicide. Among other monologue highlights, it is difficult to omit (6) Demea's address at the opening of *Samia* Act III when he comes onstage like a shipwrecked man (his metaphor) and invites the audience to judge whether he's sane or mad, whether he's misconstrued the situation entirely, and then reports the busy scene of his son's wedding preparation and finally the conversation he overheard between Moschio's old nurse and maid by which he has

deduced that the crying infant is Moschio's son by his mistress (206–282); and difficult to omit (7) his follow-up monologue, when later in the same act he is thoroughly
convinced of his mistress's treachery and displays a remarkable range of emotions,
lamenting his tragic universe (quoting Eur. *Oedipus*) and apostrophizing himself as an
idiot: he must buck up, his son was not to blame, it was his mistress's fault—that Helen
(324–356). And finally, a quick mention must be made of (8) the "messenger"s speech'
in *Sikyonioi* Act IV (176–271), where, in the course of narrating the unfolding drama of
a deme gathering where the fate of Philumena is being determined, the speaker, with
overarching allusions to the famous messenger speech in Euripedes *Orestes* (866–956,
reporting the Argive Assembly that determined the fates of Orestes and Electra), brilliantly recreates the crowded scene, quoting numerous speakers: now the soldier's
slave Dromo, now the collective crowd, then the soldier's rival for the girl's affection,
then an anonymous individual, the rival again, the collective crowd, the soldier, and so
on (while speakers and change of speaker are sometimes difficult to identify, in 264–
269, possibly seven different voices are heard); the role of this messenger was surely a
demanding one to play.

These Menandrian monologists hardly *appear* as lone speakers who only address
themselves; and while they sometimes do that (i.e., explicitly address themselves), they
might also address the audience, apostrophize personifications (as in no. 3 above), report
the speech of a personification (as in no. 2), and report conversations with others (for a
complete catalogue and discussion of quoted speech in Menander, see Nünlist 2002).
"Speech within speech" is perhaps the stylistic device that most enlivens monologue—
though the range of linguistic register (from tragic to comic) and the occasional stricter
scansion (as in the messenger's speech in *Sikyonioi*) also invite attention. Quoted speech
is not limited to monologue; in the last section, for example, we saw Pyrrhia using it as
he narrated his meeting with Cnemon in the opening scene of *Dyskolos*, and among the
instances cited in this section, the "messenger's speech" is "quasi-monologue"—an uninterrupted long speech addressed to a character onstage. While its capacity to enliven
(depending, of course, on the delivery of a good comic actor—not Quintilian's "over the
top" comic actor: 11.3.91) is perhaps obvious, and likewise its capacity to present scenes
that could not be presented onstage for technical restrictions (three-actor rule, unity of
place, masks), quoted speech served other functions as well, it served to introduce and
characterize both the quoting character and the characters who were absent from the
stage (Nünlist 2002: 253). Indeed, many of the "quoted speeches" occur in *expository*
monologues, and these defy the traditional view that such monologues can be easily
distinguished from reflective or "character-typifying" monologues. This is especially so
in monologue no. 2, where Charisius not only gives information about what happened
offstage but also deeply characterizes himself in the process; similarly, in monologue
4, we are given a fine idea of Geta's loyalty as he strolls back and forth onstage telling us
what happened offstage just a few moments ago; and in monologue no. 6, Demea, while
ostensibly informing the audience of how he discovered his son's alleged affair with his
mistress, also gives us a very good idea of just what kind of man he is.

CONCLUSION: MENANDER AND HIS AUDIENCE

Not only Menandrian monologists but most Menandrian characters know how to take the audience into their confidence. In concluding this chapter, it will be useful to consider this capacity a bit more in conjunction with the community of Menander's theater. In the introduction to their commentary on Menander, Gomme and Sandbach drew attention to the proximity of the Greek audience to the actors; in contrast to much modern drama, "the spectators were more immediately present at the events going forward in front of them, and the actor…draws them in to participate. He informs them of what has happened off-stage, he confides in them, may even put questions to them, although he gives no opportunity for an answer. This link between actor and audience is an inheritance from Old Comedy, and from Old Comedy is inherited, too, the traditional vocative used in addressing the spectators: ἄνδρες." (p. 14 with n. 1). The vocative is the most explicit indication of audience address; it can reveal itself by the use of second person plural verbs and pronouns (e.g., *Dyskolos* 484, Cnemon speaking, and often in parts "outside the play," in prologues and endings: see Bain 1977: 186–187 for examples). And sometimes, as Gomme and Sandbach point out (ibid.), in monologues where neither vocatives nor second person plurals appear, the audience is nonetheless addressed. These observations raise many questions about the way monologues functioned in New Comedy. Here, only two interrelated questions can be posed: where spectators are explicitly addressed as ἄνδρες, who is this audience and what are these addresses all about?

The monologists of the last section addressed the audience as ἄνδρες ("men") six times (*Epitrepontes* 887, *Samia* 269 and 329, *Sikyonioi* 225, 240 [supplemented] and 269); the address appears on ten occasions elsewhere among the longer preserved plays (*Dyskolos* 194, 659, 666, 921, 967; *Misoumenos* 994; *Samia* 447, 683, 734; *Sikyonioi* 405; additionally, see n. 6 for ἄνδρες in Did. Pap. II). These addresses can be categorized by a brief description of the speeches in which they appear: three are outside the play (at play's end, calling on the audience for applause: *Dyskolos* 967, *Misoumenos* 994, *Samia* 734),[12] four have internal addressees (the three addresses in the messenger's speech in *Sikyonioi* and one at *Dyskolos* 921), and four occur in expository speeches that also vividly portray the character and reflections of the speakers (*Dyskolos* 659; and 666; *Epitrepontes* 887; *Samia* 269). The remaining five occur in reflective speeches (*Dyskolos* 194; *Samia* 329, 447, 683; *Sikyonioi* 405). Explicit addresses to the audience are not plentiful; nonetheless,

---

[12] Agnoia ("Misapprehension") addresses the audience as θεαταί as she says her farewell to the spectators upon finishing her prologue speech in *Perikeiromene*; no one else, as the corpus now stands, addresses the audience thus, but cf. ἄνδρες in Did. Pap. II, n. 6 above.

it is important to consider how to understand them, especially those embedded in the last two groups (that is, in the expository/characterizing speeches and in the reflective characterizing speeches). These are all monologues, including Sostratus's one-liner at *Dyskolos* 194, and their speakers all take the audience into their confidence on rather serious matters—for these are speeches that go beyond the mere conveyance of information to the audience. Who do these speakers imagine themselves addressing? Is it, as Gomme and Sandbach thought, the ἄνδρες inherited from Old Comedy?

Comparison with Aristophanes's comedies is telling. While a great deal could be said here, I conclude with one observation and expand on that. The observation: Aristophanic addresses to the audience *are* different; they occur in speeches that are less personal than Menander's, and while their speakers certainly "take the audience in," they hardly take the audience into their confidence. There are twenty-eight explicit allusions to current spectators (to θεαταί and θεώμενοι) and six vocative addresses to them; in almost all instances, the "spectators" are treated in their capacity as that, as "men at a show," who are often flattered as being smart, or simply cajoled, or occasionally insulted or treated to information (i.e., expository passages); sometimes they are mentioned neutrally, almost like bystanders (cf. Revermann 2006: 101–102). The lion's share of Aristophanes's addresses to ἄνδρες, on the other hand, are "internal," to members of the chorus (e.g., the knights, the wasps as judges) and to others onstage at the moment (thirty-nine out of forty-nine instances in the extant plays); there are two addresses to ἄνδρες in *parabaseis* (*Acharnians* 496, *Birds* 685; cf. λεῴ at *Wasps* 1015, *parabasis*: νῦν αὖτε, λεῴ, προσέχετε τὸν νοῦν), another of similar tenor in a song (*Lysistrata* 1043–1044), and two in expository and play-ending passages (*Birds* 30 and 1357).[13] There is an occasional soliciting of the audience for assistance or acquiescence in an opinion (ἄνδρες κοπρολόγοι at *Peace* 9 and ἄνδρες ἥλικες at *Clouds* 1437). Only rarely does the speaker address the audience a bit more personally, as at *Peace* 13, 244, and 276; the first two are jokes (the second spoken aside), and the third is a melodramatic rhetorical question. These, of course, are only the most explicit addresses—and important enough in themselves; there is no space here for discussion of second person plurals and implicit addresses, or a more convoluted discussion of the possible identification of internal audience with the one sitting in the theater, but even if these were added to the mix, the conclusions as drawn in the next paragraph might be very much the same.

Aristophanic addresses to the audience, whether as "spectators" (θεαταί and θεώμενοι) or "men" (ἄνδρες), overlap but little with the audience addresses of Menandrian characters. The intimacy of confidences offered to the audience by Demea in *Samia*, by Onesimus and Charisius in *Epitrepontes*, by Moschio in *Sikyonioi* are nowhere to be found in Aristophanes. It is a different world. While it is perilous to point to an absence in the Menandrian syntactical lexicon, no human character ever addresses the audience

---

[13] "Public tenor" also attaches to the vocative address to βροτοί ("men") at *Peace* 236 (thrice), 286, and *Birds* 687; also to the address to λεῴ at *Acharnians* 1000, *Wasps* 1015 (*parabasis*), *Peace* 298 and 551. Neither βροτοί nor λεῴ appear in Menander.

as θεαταί and none (so far) modifies ἄνδρες, so that only a portion of the population is being called upon, such as the "dung collectors" and "gentlemen of my own age" in *Peace* and *Clouds* respectively. And while it is also perilous to end an essay with conjecture, I hazard that the Menandrian "men" who are addressed explicitly (and also implicitly: Bain 1977: 195–207) in both reflective and expository monologues (wherever the line is drawn) are addressed in their larger human capacity, not in their more prescribed roles as theater-goers, but as men with hearts and brains and souls, who may need to know, since the scene could not be staged (*Dyskolos* 666–690), that Cnemon fell into a well and that Gorgias jumped down and rescued him, but who are also immensely rewarded by knowing just exactly how Sostratus felt as he stood at the lip of the well with Cnemon's daughter as lone companion. Sostratus has taken the audience into his confidence.

Menander's audience, the one that can be constructed from his characters' speech, appears to be a far more intimate one than that of Aristophanes, even if universalized— or perhaps *because* its members are universalized—as men with hearts and brains and souls. Talking to such men is perhaps not so very different from talking to oneself— or better, no different from talking to one's best friends. One's most personal observations are to be shared with friends. While the older comic poet certainly passed on his tricks of the trade, and while the actors of both poets were playing to the audience from the beginning of the performance straight through to the end, those audiences were quite different. The contemporary schools of philosophy (especially the Lyceum) and the symposia of elite intellectuals, by providing opportunities for dialogue on art, life, and love, may have had an equal if not greater role in the composition of Menander's plays, to say nothing of the composition of his audience. That audience, at least while sitting in Athens in the Lycurgan theatre, will have been larger than it had been in the late fifth century; a larger component of these spectators may now have been wealthy (see chapter 9), and some, specially schooled, may have been particularly sparked by Menander's portrayal of character and emotions (see Konstan, chapter 13, this volume) and by philosophically tinged jokes such as the play on a vitiated syllogism in *Samia* (see Scafuro 2003). It may be, in many cases, that this last group felt themselves to be the particular ἄνδρες addressed by Menander's characters, but there is no reason to exclude any (male) member of the audience at all: each is invited into the circle of friendship. As for women, if they were in the audience: surely they will have been pleased by the intimate admissions of the men—and if not really pleased, then content that they knew better.

FURTHER READING

I have foregrounded linguistic characterization (including personal and audience address) in its interaction with dramatic technique in the latter part of this chapter, seeing it as a promising pathway for further study, especially as the number of published Menandrian papyri increases, and keeping in mind that the assignment of verses to characters can be a tricky and fluctuating business (cf. Sandbach 1973: 554 on 98–101a and Arnott 2000: 32 on 96–105) and that a second person plural addressee can be interestingly ambiguous (internal or external audience?).

Menander's linguistic characterizations, sometimes involving a distinction between men's and women's speech, are highlighted by Sandbach 1970 (brilliant), Katsouris 1975, Turner 1980 (on questions and answers), Bain 1984 (female speech), Brenk 1987 (young men, comparison with Euripides), and Grasso 1997 (on old people); catalogued by Arnott 1995 (who suggests that Alexis may have been a precursor); acutely analyzed by Sommerstein 2009 (contrasting male and female speech in Aristophanes and Menander; see now Willi 2003: 157–197 on female speech in Aristophanes); given a big boost by Dickey in 1995 and 1996 (in which later work she uses Aristophanes and Menander and an assortment of poets as comparanda to a long list of prose writers: see Sommerstein 2009: 39, *addendum* to p. 29) as well as by Krieter-Spiro 1997: 201–53 (slaves, cooks, and hetaerae); and broadly sketched by Willi 2002: 29–30. Nünlist 2002, the important study "Speech within Speech in Menander," follows in the wake of Osmun 1952, Bers 1997, and Handley 1969: 93 and 1990: 135–138 and at the same time as Handley 2002: 178–182. Studies of the topics articulated here could be enriched by considerations of mask, costume, gesture, voicing, and staging.

Other topics: Konstan's recent bibliography (*Menander of Athens: Oxford Bibliographies Online Research Guide*) provides a list of earlier annotated bibliographies and surveys of scholarship from 1968–2007, as well as a briefly annotated list of recent texts, lexica, and commentaries, and other works listed under various rubrics (e.g., "Menander and Social Life"). (Blanchard this volume) appends a list of important editions of Menander since the sixteenth century. (Bathrellou this volume) provides a survey of papyrus finds from 1973 to the near present. Petrides and Papaioannou 2010 is a collection of essays surveying recent trends, especially in cultural, gender, and performance studies of postclassical comedy. References to specialized studies of Menander regarding the place of tragedy (especially Euripides), philosophy, politics, law, and religion in his work may be found in the essays, respectively, of Hanink, Konstan, Henderson and Rosenbloom, Buis, and Scullion in this volume.

BIBLIOGRAPHY

Arnott, W. G. 1996a. *Alexis: The Fragments: A Commentary*. Cambridge, MA: Cambridge University Press.

——. 1979. Menander. Vol. 1. Loeb Classical Library 132. Cambridge, MA: Cambridge University Press.

——. 1995. "Menander's Manipulation of Language for the Individualisation of Character." In *Lo spettacolo delle voci*, edited by F. De Martino and A. H. Sommerstein, 147–164. Bari: Levante.

——. 1996b. *Menander*. Vol. 2. Loeb Classical Library 459. Cambridge, MA: Harvard University Press.

——. 2000. *Menander*. Vol. 3. Loeb Classical Library 460. Cambridge, MA: Harvard University Press.

Bain, D. 1977. *Actors & Audience: A Study of Asides and Related Conventions in Greek Drama*. Oxford: Oxford University Press.

——. 1984. "Female Speech in Menander." *Antichthon* 18: 24–42.

Bers, V. 1997. *Speech in Speech: Studies in Incorporated* Oratio Recta *in Attic Drama and Oratory*. Lanham, MD: Rowman & Littlefield.

Bethe, E. 1902. "Die Zeit des Heauton Timorumenos und des Kolax Menanders." *Hermes* 37: 278–282.

Blanchard, A. 1983. *Essai sur la composition des comédies de Ménandre*. Paris: Les Belles Lettres.

Blume, H.-D. 1998. *Menander*. Darmstadt: Wissenschaftliche Buchgesellschaft.

——. 2010. "Menander: The Text and its Restoration." In *New Perspectives on Postclassical Comedy*, edited by A. K. Petrides and S. Papaioannou, 14–30. Newcastle upon Tyne: Cambridge Scholars.

Blundell, J. 1980. *Menander and the Monologue*. Göttingen: Vandenhoeck und Ruprecht.

Brenk, F. E. 1987. "*Heteros tis eimi*: On the language of Menander's young lovers." *ICS* 12: 31–66.

Bruzzese, L. 2011. *Studi su Filemone comico*. Lecce: Pensa multimedia.

De Marcellus, H. 1996. "*IG* XIV 1184 and the Ephebic Service of Menander." *ZPE* 110: 69–76.

De Martino, F., and A. H. Sommerstein, eds. 1995. *Lo spettacolo delle voci*. Bari: Levante.

Dickey, E. 1995. "Forms of Address and Conversational Language in Aristophanes and Menander." *Mnem.*, 4th ser., 48: 257–271.

——. 1996. *Greek Forms of Address: From Herodotus to Lucian*. Oxford: Oxford University Press.

Easterling, P., and E. Hall, eds. 2002. *Greek and Roman Actors: Aspects of an Ancient Profession*. Cambridge, UK: Cambridge University Press.

Frost, K. B. 1988. *Exits and Entrances in Menander*. Oxford: Clarendon Press.

Furley, W. D. 2009. *Menander*: Epitrepontes. London: Institute of Classical Studies.

Gomme, A. W., and F. H. Sandbach. 1973. *Menander: A Commentary*. Oxford: Oxford University Press.

Grasso, L. 1997. "Il linguaggio dei vecchi nelle commedie di Menandro (imprecazioni ed esclamazioni)." *Rudiae* 9: 231–243.

Green, J. R. 2000. "Forty Years of Theatre Research and Its Future Directions." In *Theatre: Ancient and Modern: Selected Proceedings of a Two-Day International Research Conference Hosted by the Department of Classical Studies, Faculty of Arts, the Open University, Milton Keynes, 5th and 6th January 1999*, edited by L. Hardwick, P. Easterling, S. Ireland, N. Lowe, and F. MacIntosh, 1–20. Milton Keynes, UK: The Open University, and www2.open.ac.uk/ClassicalStudies/GreekPlays/Conf99/index.htm. (last accessed Dec. 12, 2012).

Gronewald, M. 1986. "Menander, *Epitrepontes*: Neue Fragmente aus Akt III und IV." *ZPE* 66: 1–13.

Gutzwiller, K., and Ö. Çelik. 2012. "New Menander Mosaics from Antioch." *AJA* 116: 573–623.

Habicht, C. 1997. *Athens from Alexander to Antony*. Translated by D. L. Schneider. Cambridge, MA: Harvard University Press.

Handley, E. W. 1965. *The* Dyskolos *of Menander*. London: Methuen.

——. 1968. *Menander and Plautus: A Study in Comparison: An Inaugural Lecture Delivered at University College, London 5 February 1968*. London: H. K. Lewis.

——. 1969. "Notes on the *Theophoroumene* of Menander." *Bulletin Institute of Classical Studies* 16: 88–101.

——. 1990. "The Bodmer Menander and the Comic Fragments." In *Relire Ménandre*, edited by E. W. Handley and A. Hurst, 123–148. Geneva: Droz.

——. 1997. "Menander, *Dis Exapaton*." *POxy* 64: 14–42.

——. 2002. "Acting, Action and Words in New Comedy." In *Greek and Roman Actors: Aspects of an Ancient Profession*, edited by P. Easterling and E. Hall, 165–188. Cambridge, UK: Cambridge University Press.

——. 2009. "Menander, *Epitrepontes*." *POxy* 73: 25–36.

Hunter, R. L. 1985. *The New Comedy of Greece and Rome*. Cambridge: Cambridge University Press.

——. 2002. "'Acting Down,': The Ideology of Hellenistic Performance." In *Greek and Roman Actors: Aspects of an Ancient Profession*, edited by P. Easterling and E. Hall, 189–206. Cambridge, UK: Cambridge University Press.

Iversen, P. 2011. "Menander's Thaïs: 'Hac primum iuvenum lascivos lusit amores.'" *CQ* 61: 186–191

Katsouris, A. G. 1975. *Linguistic and stylistic characterization: Tragedy and Menander.* Ioannina, Greece: University of Ioannina.

Konstantakos. I. 2008. "Rara coronato plausere theatra Menandro? Menander's Success in His Lifetime." Quaderni urbinati di cultura classica, n.s., 88: 79– 106.

——. 2011. "Conditions of Playwriting and the Comic Dramatist's Craft in the Fourth Century." *Logeion: A Journal of Ancient Theatre.* 1: 145–183.

Krieter-Spiro, M. 1997. *Sklaven, Köche und Hetären: Das Dienstpersonal bei Menander: Stellung, Rolle, Komik und Sprache.* Stuttgart: Teubner.

Lape, S. 2004. *Reproducing Athens: Menander's Comedy, Democratic Culture, and the Hellenistic City.* Princeton: Princeton University Press.

Leo, F. 1908. *Der Monolog im Drama: Ein Beitrag zur griechisch-römanischen Poetik.* Berlin: Weidmann. Reprinted 1970, Nendeln, Liechtenstein: Kraus.

Lowe, J. C. B. 1983. "Terentian Originality in the 'Phormio' and 'Hecyra.'" *Hermes* 111: 431–452.

——. 1990. "Plautus' Choruses." *RhM* 133: 274–297.

Major, W. E. 1997. "Menander in a Macedonian World." *GRBS* 38: 41–73.

Martina, A. 1997. *Menandri* Epitrepontes: *Accedunt tabulae phototypae.* Rome: Kepos.

Nünlist, R. 2002. "Speech within Speech in Menander." In *The Language of Greek Comedy*, edited by A. Willi, 219–259. Oxford: Oxford University Press.

——2004. "The Beginning of *Epitrepontes* Act II." In *Menandro—Cent'anni di papiri: Atti del convegno internazionale di studi, Firenze, 12–13 giugno 2003*, edited by G. Bastianini, and A. Casanova. Florence: Istituto papirologico G. Vitelli.

O'Sullivan, L. 2009. "History from Comic Hypotheses: Stratocles, Lachares, and *P.Oxy. 1235.*" *GRBS* 49: 53–79.

Osborne, M. J. 2012. *Athens in the Third Century B.C.* Athens: Hellenike Epigraphike Hetaireia.

Osmun, G. F. 1952. "Dialogue in the Menandrean Monologue." *TAPA* 83: 156–163.

Owens. W. M. 2011. "The Political Topicality of Menander's *Dyskolos.*" *AJPh* 132: 349–378.

Petrides, A., and S. Papaioannou, eds. 2010. *New Perspectives on Postclassical Comedy.* Newcastle upon Tyne: Cambridge Scholars.

Pöhlmann, E. 1995. *Studien zur Bühnendichtung und zum Theaterbau der Antike.* Frankfurt am Main: Peter Lang.

Potter, D. 1987. "Telesphoros, Cousin of Demetrius: A Note on the Trial of Menander." *Historia* 36: 491–495.

Revermann, M. 2006. "The Competence of Theatre Audiences in Fifth- and Fourth-Century Athens." *JHS* 126: 99–124.

Römer, C. 2012a. "New Fragments of Act IV, *Epitrepontes* 786–823 Sandbach (P. Mich. 4752 a, b and c)." *ZPE* 182: 112–120.

——. 2012b. "A New Fragment of the End of Act III, *Epitrepontes* 690-701 Sandbach (P. Mich. 4805)." *ZPE* 183: 32–36.

Sandbach, F. H. 1970. "Menander's Manipulation of Language for Dramatic Purposes." In *Ménandre: Sept exposés suivis de discussions,* edited by E. G. Turner, 113–136. eneva: Fondation Hardt.

——. 1973. See Gomme, A.W. and Sandbach, F. H. 1973.

——. 1975. "Menander and the Three Actor Rule." 197–204 in J. Bingen, G. Cambier and G. Nachtergael eds., Le monde grec: Pensée, littérature, histoire, documents: Hommages à Claire Préaux. Brussels: Editions de l'Université de Bruxelles.

——. 1990. *Menandri Reliquiae selectae.* Rev. ed. Oxford: Oxford University Press. First published 1972.

Scafuro, A. C. 1990. "Discourses of Sexual Violation in Mythic Accounts and Dramatic Versions of 'The Girl's Tragedy.'" *differences: A Journal of Feminist Cultural Studies* 2: 126–159.

—— 2003. "When a Gesture was Misinterpreted: διδόναι τιτθίον in Menander's *Samia.*" In *Gestures: Essays in Ancient History, Literature, and Philosophy Presented to Alan L. Boegehold,* edited by J. Bakewell and J. Sickinger, 113–135. Oxford: Oxbow.

Schröder, S. 1996. "Die Lebensdaten Menanders (Mit einem Anhang über die Aufführungszeit seines Ἑαυτὸν τιμωρούμενος)." *ZPE* 113: 35–48.

Sommerstein, A. H. 2009. "The Language of Athenian Women." In *Talking about Laughter and Other Studies in Greek Comedy,* by A. H. Sommerstein, 15–42, with "Addenda." Oxford: Oxford University Press. First published in 1995.

Traill, A. 2008. *Women and the Comic Plot in Menander.* Cambridge: Cambridge University Press.

Turner, E. G. 1980. "The Rhetoric of Question and Answer in Menander." *Themes in Drama 2: Drama and Mimesis*: 1–23.

Webster, T. B. L. 1960. *Studies in Menander.* 2nd ed. Manchester: Manchester University Press.

——. 1970. *Studies in Later Greek Comedy.* Manchester: Manchester University Press.

Wiles, D. 1984. "Menander's *Dyskolos* and Demetrius of Phaleron's Dilemma." *G&R* 31: 170–180.

Willi, A., ed. 2002. *The Language of Greek Comedy.* Oxford: Oxford University Press.

——. 2003. *The Languages of Aristophanes: Aspects of Linguistic Variation in Classical Attic Greek.* Oxford: Oxford University Press.

Zagagi, N. 1995. *The Comedy of Menander.* Indiana: Indiana University Press.

CHAPTER 11

··

RECONSTRUCTING MENANDER

··

ALAIN BLANCHARD[1]

I. Before the Modern Discovery of the Papyri

1. The Disappearance of Menander

Date

During the whole of antiquity, Menander was immensely popular. Already in Alexandria in the second century BCE, the learned grammarian and librarian Aristophanes of Byzantium ranked Menander immediately after Homer (IG XIV 1183 = K-A test. 170c). Plutarch (end of the first century CE) writes that "he has made his poetry, of all the beautiful works Greece has produced, the most generally accepted subject" (*Mor.* 854 B, Fowler transl.). Menander's popularity showed itself in three different ways: his plays were often produced in the theaters (K-A test. 53–55); at dinner parties, passages of his plays were often read (see Plutarch, *Mor.* 712 B-D); and finally, in the schools, from an elementary level (as can be seen from the *Menandri Sententiae*) to the higher level of rhetorical education, Menander was used. We know from Dionysius of Halicarnassus, *Opusc.* IX 2, 14 (Aujac), Dio Chrysostom 18, 6–7, and Quintilian X 1, 69–72, that reading Menander played an important role in the formation of orators.

Though it seems incredible, we do not have a single manuscript from the Middle Ages or the Renaissance which contains any part of the plays of Menander. According to the *Vind. hist.* 98 (*olim* 49) of the sixteenth century, the Patriarchal Library in

---

[1] Translated by Adam Bülow-Jacobsen.

Constantinople should have possessed all twenty-four plays by the poet with a commentary by Michael Psellus (1018–1078), and another library, in Thrace, was also reputed to have possessed the comedies of Menander, but now no one believes this (see the edition Koerte-Thierfelder 1959, 13). As far as Psellus is concerned, it is probable that his teaching of Menander, which he mentions in his *Encomium of His Mother* 30 (= K-A test. 160), was based on indirect evidence, like the course on Archilochus on which he prided himself. As a matter of fact, we lose trace of Menander perhaps already with Choricius of Gaza at the beginning of the sixth century, or at least with Theophylactus Simocatta, who seems to have read plays by Menander at first hand a century later. If we want more precision, we must explore the cause of this surprising disappearance.

Causes

A reason was first proposed around 1490 by Demetrius Chalcondyles, according to what Pietro Alcionio reports in his *Medices Legatus de exilio*, first published in Venice in 1522 and often reprinted since: the Church disliked the alluring picture of love which we see in Menander's theater (as in other poets such as Sappho and Anacreon), and had made these dangerous authors disappear. The first editor of the Cairo Menander Codex, Gustave Lefebvre, was still of this opinion in 1907. This is, in fact, not what the manuscript tradition tells us, at least not where Anacreon is concerned, and as for the alluring picture of love, one might wonder why the Church had not also made the Greek novels disappear. If we do not want to attribute everything to chance, the best current explanation is to be found in a combination of political and cultural factors. In Constantinople, Photius (ca. 810–after 893) was in harmony with the view of Phrynichus, the Atticist grammarian from the time of Marcus Aurelius and Commodus and writer of a *Sophistic Preparation* summarized in Photius *Bibliotheca* (codex 158)—namely, that the literary history of glorious Athens, in other words *History itself*, stops at Demosthenes and excludes Menander, the symbol of Macedonian domination. Menander had been a pupil of Theophrastus (D.L. V 36), the successor of Aristotle (who had been the tutor of Alexander), and friend of the pro-Macedonian "tyrant" Demetrius of Phalerum (D.L. V 79), another pupil of Theophrastus (Str. IX 1, 20; D.L. V 75, and cf. Cic. *de off.* I 1, 3; *de fin.* V 19, 54); like every good pro-Macedonian, Menander was represented beardless in his statue in the theater of Dionysus in Athens (Zanker 1995: 80). The fifth-century comic poet of a free and glorious Athens, Aristophanes, because he lived so long and because his latest pieces were said to foreshadow the *Nea*, became the only representative of Attic comedy, eliminating not only Menander but also Eupolis in the realm of the *Archaia* (Nesselrath 2000). The substantial medieval transmission of the so-called *Menandri Sententiae* (little of which may now be positively identified as Menandrian) cannot then be seen as the final result of a process which caused the disappearance of the real Menander; these innocuous *Sententiae*, intended for schoolchildren, contributed only to the concealment of this disappearance (Blanchard 2007: 18–26). The Vatican palimpsest (*Vaticanus sir.* 623), a recent discovery (D'Aiuto 2003), shows that the fourth-century codex, whose surviving portions contain parts of Menander's *Dyskolos* and (according to a plausible suggestion made by C. Austin and E. G. Handley in a workshop of the

British Academy in December 2007) *Titthe*, was reused for a text of Nemesius in the seventh or eighth century: the comic poet was no longer interesting. Egypt, so favorable to Menander, was separated from Constantinople in the seventh century by the Arab conquest and hence was no longer in a position to copy his comedies (or any other Greek texts).

Under these conditions (and *pace* Lowe 2007: vi: 72), it is probable that Menander was not included in the second campaign of transcription into minuscule script which took place toward the end of the tenth century and assured the transmission to us of Greek poetry, such as we know it.

2. The Durability of Terence

Knowledge of Menander through the Latin Adaptations

In the Middle Ages, the Occident presents a scene very different from the Orient as far as the knowledge of Menander is concerned. We do not know by what mysterious means the theme of Menander's *Androgynos* came to the mind of Guillaume de Blois when he wrote his *Alda* (cf. vv. 9–20). But it seems of great importance that during this entire period there was much reading of Terence, a poet who does not hide that the model for his *Andria* (cf. vv. 10–20) and his *Eunuchus* (cf. v. 20) can be found in the comedies of Menander of the same names. If Terence is less explicit concerning his models for *Adelphoe* and his *Heauton Timorumenos*, the grammarians Donatus (*Ad. Praef.* I 1 and III 8 Wessner) and Eugraphius (beginning of commentary on the *Ht.*) provide the information. From 1470, the printing press produced a multitude of editions of Terence, and thanks to editions of Donatus and Eugraphius, a whole doctrine of comedy was formed, in which Menander has his place. The early high repute of Menander is corroborated by Gellius's comparison (*NA* II 23) of Caecilius's *Plocium* with Menander's, to the disadvantage of the former. Note that the theater of Plautus is not involved at this time. Only fairly recently has it been possible to draw a parallel between Plautus's *Stichus* and Menander's *Adelphoi I* (thanks to Angelo Mai's reading of the Ambrosian palimpsest in May 1815), or between *Bacchides* and *Dis Exapaton* (F. Ritschl, *Parerga*, in 1845), or *Cistellaria* and *Synaristosai* (E. Fraenkel in his paper from 1932). In spite of strenuous efforts, no firm link has yet been found between the *Aulularia* and a play by Menander.

Difficulties

While the limited knowledge of Menander in the West was reasonably accurate thanks to Terence, nevertheless the beginnings of critical thought in the Renaissance brought several difficulties to the surface. These stem first of all from what has become known as "contamination" in Terence. In *Andria*, vv. 9–14, Terence announces that he has used not only the *Andria* of Menander but also elements from his *Perinthia*, a comedy of different style but similar plot. Similarly, in *Eunuchus* Terence announces that he has used characters from the *Kolax* by Menander. In the *Adelphoe* (cf. vv. 6–11), external elements have been borrowed from a comedy by another poet, Diphilus's *Synapothneskontes.* Hence came the modern (wrong) idea that the comedy of Menander supplied only a couple in love, and that Terence had doubled them and each time merged two comedies by Menander (so Norwood 1932: 47). This view, criticized by Duckworth (1952: 189 and 203, about *contaminatio*), gave rise to an essential misunderstanding of both Menander and Terence. A second misunderstanding arose from considering Terence simply as a faithful translator of the plays of Menander which he staged in Latin, and from setting this faithfulness against the freedom that, by comparison, Plautus is thought to have taken in his plays (so Jachmann 1934). But how could scholars estimate this Plautine freedom as well as this Terentian faithfulness? Here we need to have a better knowledge of Menander's original Greek text, but we must also resist the temptation to ascribe to Menander everything we know from the Latin adaptors. An initial access to the Greek text itself, insufficient but necessary, could only be had by collecting fragments of the indirect tradition.

3. The Indirect Tradition

Collecting the Fragments

The initiative toward producing a collection of the indirect tradition of Menander did not come from the editions of Donatus and Gellius, in spite of the fragmentary parallels they offered between Terence (or Caecilius) and Menander. It came rather from the editions of Greek texts, especially from the *Florilegium* of Stobaeus by Conrad Gesner (Zürich 1543, first edition and Basel 1549, second edition). With these began a series of collections of short, mainly ethical, quotations from comic poets, among whom Menander was just one; completing Stobaeus was the primary aim. Such editions of Menander were made by Guillaume Morel in 1553 (the edition by which the French playwright Jean Racine had access to Menander), by Jacob Hertel in 1560, and by Hugo Groot in 1626. This last edition did not even give a full text of Stobaeus, but only references; nevertheless, Groot's edition began the classification of Menander's plays, no longer by theme but in alphabetical order. The enlargement of this corpus continued with editions of Menander and Philemon by Jean Leclerc (1709, an edition severely criticized by Richard Bentley) and by August Meineke (1823, an edition from which Goethe acquired his admiration for Menander and which was reproduced by Friedrich Dübner in 1839). The later works, like the large edition by the same Meineke of the Greek comic poets, vol. IV, in 1841, or that of Theodor Koch in 1888, built on what had already been established. But amplification of the indirect tradition of Menander is always a work in progress (cf., for instance, the new discoveries in the Photius manuscripts) and the papyri will offer new fragments (as, for instance, in *P.Oxy.* 42.3005, *P. Gissen* 152 or *PSI* 15.1476) or at least the possibility of identifying *adespota* of Menander and even the *Nea.* Examples of such new discoveries are found in the editions by Alfred Koerte from 1910 to 1959, by John Maxwell Edmonds in 1961 (vol. III B of his *Fragments of Attic Comedy*—which marked a step backward in textual criticism), by Rudolph Kassel and Colin Austin in their *Poetae Comici Graeci* (only the second volume of the part devoted to Menander, the *Testimonia et Fragmenta*, has appeared, in 1998), and by W. Geoffrey Arnott (incomplete for the indirect tradition) in 1979–2000.

Parallel to this, collections were also made of fragments of lost Latin comic poets who, like Plautus and Terence, had adapted plays by Menander (editions by O. Ribbeck in 1873 and E. H. Warmington in 1935–1938). These provide a welcome aid to the reconstruction of the plot in the Greek originals.

A New Approach: the Iconographic Tradition with Inscriptions

The iconography of Menander's comedies is now both very rich and very useful because of the inscriptions that normally accompany the pictures. Among the mosaics, the most important example is that of Mytilene (beginning of the fourth century CE), where for *Plokion, Samia, Synaristosai, Epitrepontes, Theophoroumene, Encheiridion,* and the *Messenia,* the title of the play, the number of the act, and the names of the three characters onstage are indicated; for *Kybernetai, Leukadia, Misoumenos,* and *Phasma,* only the title and the number of the act are written (Charitonidis et al., 1970). Another series with title and number of act, recently discovered in Turkey at Antakya, the ancient Antiochia on the Orontes, concerns *Perikeiromene, Philadelphoi, Synaristosai,* and *Theophoroumene* (Gutzwiller-Çelik 2012). Only the title of the play is given in Bulgaria for *Achaioi* (Ivanov 1954); in Crete for *Plokion* (Markoulaki 1990), *Sikyonios,* and *Theophoroumene* (Markoulaki 2012); and at Zeugma in Turkey for *Synaristosai* (Abadie-Reynal et al., 2003). The same is true about paintings: those from Ephesus of the second century CE (Strocka 1977) illustrate *Sikyonioi* and *Perikeiromene* (pictures of three more comedies by Menander are now illegible) with the name of the play, but no indication of act or names of characters.

A First Result: The Titles of the Comedies

Tradition (Gellius XVII 4, 4) attributes to Menander 105 (the most certain number) or 108 or even 109 plays. From our various sources, we now know 106 titles of plays, but at least eight of them are alternative titles. Abbreviations in the list are fr. = fragment(s)

Ἀδελφοί α '	The Brothers I	Plautus *Stichus*, test., fr.
(ἢ Φιλάδελφοι)	or The Loving Wives	
	of Two Brothers	test., fr., mos.
Ἀδελφοί β '	The Brothers II	Terence *Adelphoe*, test., fr.
Ἁλαεῖς	The Men of Halae	test.
Ἁλιεύς (Ἁλιεῖς)	The Fisherman(-men)	test., fr.

Ἀνατιθεμένη	*The Girl Who Revoked*	fr.
Ἀνδρία	*The Girl from Andros*	Terence *Andria*, test., fr.
Ἀνδρόγυνος	*The Man-Woman*	
ἢ Κρής	or *The Cretan*	Guillaume de Blois *Alda*, test., fr.
? Ἀνεχόμενος	? *Thwarted*	? test.
Ἀνεψιοί	*The Cousins*	test., fr.
Ἄπιστος	*The Distrustful Man*	test., fr.
Ἀρρηφόρος	*The Arrhephore*	
ἢ Αὐλητρίς (-ίδες)	or *The Aulos-Girl(s)*	test., fr.
Ἀσπίς	*The Shield*	test., fr., pap.
Αὐτὸν πενθῶν	*The Self-Mourner*	test., fr.
Αὐτὸν τιμωρούμενος	*The Self-Punisher*	Terence *Ht.*, test., fr.
Ἀφροδίσιον	*Aphrodision*	test., fr.
Ἀχαιοί	*The Achaeans*	mos.
ἢ Πελοποννήσιοι	or *The Peloponnesians*	test., fr.
Βοιωτία	*The Girl from Boeotia*	test., fr.
Γεωργός	*The Farmer*	test., fr., pap.
? Γλυκέρα	? *Glycera*	? test.,? fr.
Δακτύλιος	*The Ring*	test., fr.
Δάρδανος	*The Man from Dardania*	test., fr.
Δεισιδαίμων	*The Superstitious Man*	test., fr.
Δημιουργός	*The Bridal Manager*	test., fr.
Δίδυμαι	*The Twin-Sisters*	test., fr.
Δὶς ἐξαπατῶν	*Twice a Swindler*	Plautus *Bacch.*, test., fr., pap.
Δύσκολος	*The Bad-Tempered Man*	
ἢ Μισάνθρωπος	or *The Misanthrope*	test., fr., pap., palimpsest
Ἐγχειρίδιον	*The Dagger*	test., fr., pap., mos.
Ἐμπιπραμένη	*The Girl Set Afire*	test., fr.
Ἐπαγγελλόμενος	*The Promise*	fr.
Ἐπίκληρος αʹ	*The Heiress I*	test., fr.
Ἐπίκληρος βʹ	*The Heiress II*	test., fr.
Ἐπιτρέποντες	*The Arbitration*	test., fr., pap., mos.
Εὐνοῦχος	*The Eunuch*	Terence *Eunuchus*, test., fr.
Ἐφέσιος	*The Man from Ephesus*	fr.
Ἡνίοχος	*The Chariot-Driver*	test., fr.
Ἥρως	*The Hero*	test., fr., pap.

Θαΐς	Thaïs	test., fr.
Θεοφορουμένη	The Girl Possessed	test., fr., pap., mos., fresc.
Θετταλη	Thettale	test., fr.
Θησαυρός	The Treasure	test., fr.
Θρασυλέων	Thrasyleon	test., fr., pap.
Θυρωρός	The Doorkeeper	? test., fr.
Ἱέρεια	The Priestess	test., fr.
Ἴμβριοι	The Men from Imbros	test., fr.
Ἱπποκόμος	The Groom	fr.
Κανηφόρος	The Canephore	test., fr.
Καρίνη	The Girl from Caria	test., fr.
Καρχηδόνιος	The Man from Carthage	test., fr., pap.
Καταψευδόμενος	The False Accuser	fr.
Κεκρύφαλος	The Hair-Net	fr.
Κιθαριστής	The Cithara-Player	test., fr., pap.
Κόλαξ	The Flatterer	test., fr., pap.
Κυβερνῆται	The Pilots	fr., mos.
Κωνειαζόμεναι	The Women drinking Hemlock	test., fr., pap.
Λευκαδία	The Woman from Leucas	test., fr., pap., mos.
Λοκροί	The Locrians	test., fr.
Μέθη	Drunkenness	fr.
Μεσσηνία	The Girl from Messene	test., fr., mos.
? Μηλία	? The Girl from Melos	? test.
Μηναγύρτης	The Begging Priest	test., fr.
Μισογύνης	The Misogynist	test., fr.
Μισούμενος (ἢ Θρασωνίδης)	The Man she Hated (or Thrasonides)	test. fr. pap. mos.
Ναύκληρος	The Ship's Captain	test., fr.
? Νέμεσις	? Nemesis	? test.
Νομοθέτης (-αι)	The Lawgiver(s)	test., fr.
Ξενολόγος	The Recruiting-Sergeant	test., fr.
Ὀλυνθία	The Girl from Olynthus	fr.
Ὁμοπάτριοι	The Half-Brothers	fr.
Ὀργή	Anger	test., fr.
Παιδίον	Baby	? test., fr.
Παλλακή	The Concubine	fr.

Παρακαταθήκη	The Deposit-in-Trust	fr.
Περικειρομένη	The Girl with the Shaven Head	test., fr., pap., mos., fresc.
Περινθία	The Lady from Perinthos	cf. Ter. Andria, test., fr., pap.
Πλόκιον	The Necklace	Caecilius Plocium, fr., mos.
Προγαμῶν	Bedded Before Wedded	fr.
Προεγκαλῶν	The Counter-Accusation	fr.
Πωλούμενοι	Put Up For Sale	fr.
Ῥαπιζομένη	The Girl Who Was Slapped	test., fr.
Σαμία	The Girl from Samos	test., fr., pap., mos.
(ἢ Κηδεία)	(or The Alliance)	fr.
Σικυώνιοι	The Men from Sicyon	test., fr., pap., mos., fresc.
Στρατιῶται	The Soldiers	fr.
Συναριστῶσαι	Women Lunching Together	Plautus Cist., test., fr., mos.
Συνερῶσα	She Loved Him Back	fr.
Συνέφηβοι	Youths Together	test., fr.
Τίτθη	The Wet-Nurse	test. fr., palimpsest
Τροφώνιος	Trophonius	fr.
Ὑδρία	The Water-Pot	fr.,? pap.
Ὑμνίς	Hymnis	fr.,? pap.
Ὑποβολιμαῖος	The Changeling	test., fr;
ἢ Ἄγροικος	or The Boor	test., fr.
Φάνιον	Phanion	test., fr.,? pap.
Φάσμα	The Apparition	test., fr., pap., mos.
Χαλκεῖα	The Feasts of Smiths	test., fr.
Χαλκίς	Chalcis	fr.
Χήρα	The Widow	test., fr.
? Χρηστή	? The Good Girl	? test.
Ψευδηρακλῆς	The False Hercules	fr.
Ψοφοδεής	Noise-Shy	test., fr.

from the Greek indirect tradition; fresc. = fresco(s); mos. = mosaic(s); pap. = papyrus(-i); test. = *testimonium(-a)*.

Collecting the indirect tradition is an important factor in the reconstruction of Menander. Thanks to the preservation of titles, numerous papyrus fragments have been identified, and names of characters, both in the indirect tradition and in the identified papyrus fragments, often permit, if not an outright identification of the plays (since several names are found in more than one play), at least a useful verification that identification is not possible. Thus, as an example, the name Pheidias occurs both in *Heros* and in *Kolax* and thus the name alone cannot be used to attribute *P.Oxy.* 6.862 to *Phasma* as has been attempted; on the other hand, the names Dromon and Kle[that appear in *P.Oxy.* 22.2329 exclude its identification as a fragment of *Phasma*. Conversely, the papyri often help to put the fragments of the indirect tradition in order and, not least, to identify numerous *adespota* of Menander or of the *Nea* in general, the most famous case being that of the beginning of the *Misoumenos*.

II. The Papyri and the Direct Tradition

1. The Modern Discovery of Menander Papyri[2]

Chronology

The first modern contact with the direct tradition of Menander goes back to 1844, when Konstantin von Tischendorf visited the library of St. Catherine's Monastery on Mt. Sinai. There he found, as support for a book-binding, fragments of three pages of a parchment codex from the fourth century. Later, Porphyry Uspensky detached them and brought them to St. Petersburg. Two of them identified as belonging to *Epitrepontes* and one to *Phasma* (the order of the plays remaining unknown), these fragments were partially published by Gabriel Cobet in 1876 on the basis of Tischendorf's transcription, and completely, from the original, by Victor Jernstedt in 1891.

Actual papyrological discoveries (i.e., papyri found not in libraries but in the Egyptian *chora* by accident or during excavations), whether fragments of rolls or codices, began with the voyage to Egypt in 1896 of the Genevan scholar Jules Nicole, during which he bought, among others, a sheet with eighty-seven lines of *Georgos,* which he published in 1897–1898. But the so-called rebirth of Menander (Arnott 1979: XXVI–XXX) really began in 1905, when the French archaeologist Gustave Lefebvre found a large number of sheets in random order from a big papyrus codex in quires from the fifth century CE. These fragments of *Heros, Epitrepontes, Perikeiromene, Samia,* and one more as yet unidentified comedy had been used in antiquity to make a stopper for a jar that contained the archive of one Dioscorus, an official in the village of Aphrodite (now *Kom Ishqâw*) in the sixth century.

Sixty years were to pass before the discovery of the second important witness to Menander, an almost complete single-quire codex, a schoolbook containing three

---
[2] For more details, see Handley 2011.

comedies by the poet, in the order *Samia, Dyskolos, Aspis*, and the learned world had to wait a few more years before most of this codex arrived, by mysterious means, in the collection of the Swiss collector Martin Bodmer. *Dyskolos*, the central and complete play, was published in 1958 by Victor Martin, *Samia* and *Aspis* (with identification of the so-called *Comoedia Florentina – PSI* II 126) eleven years later by Rudolphe Kassel and Colin Austin. In 1964, the excitement created by the arrival of *Dyskolos* was renewed by the publication in Paris of important and difficult fragments of *Sikyonioi* from a roll of the third century BCE (for details, see the new edition by the discoverer of the papyrus, Alain Blanchard, in 2009). Then the Oxyrhynchus collection also gave us important and difficult pieces of *Misoumenos* (published by Eric G. Turner in 1965), and several fragments of the beginning of this play appeared after 1970. In 1968, from the same Oxyrhynchus collection, Eric W. Handley produced a sensational publication of fragments from *Dis Exapaton,* the first example of a Greek original for which a Latin adaptation was already known, namely Plautus's *Bacchides.* More recently, we must note the increasing number of minor *Epitrepontes* papyri as a lucky complement to our knowledge of this famous play. The latest important discovery is not papyrological but comes from a parchment codex (*Vat. sir.* 623), a double palimpsest: in the first script (from the beginning of the fourth century), two bifolia contain the *Dyskolos* (196 lines announced by D'Aiuto 2003: 270–278) and the *Titthe* (of which 100 lines were presented in a workshop at the British Academy on December 10, 2007); unfortunately, the difficulties of reading may considerably delay the final publication.

Geography

We must not forget that manuscripts (and papyri are manuscripts) may travel, but, apart from the two cases we have already mentioned, one from Mt. Sinai and the other (the palimpsest) from Syriac surroundings, everything we have of Menander comes from Egypt. The provenance of our oldest papyri is the Fayum; the *Sikyonioi* comes from the cemetery of Ghoran, the *Hydria* fragments from Gurob and from Hibeh. Later fragments of *Epitrepontes* and perhaps *Georgos* come from the Fayum without further specificity. Further south, Oxyrhynchus has delivered a great variety of texts: *Aspis, Dis Exapaton, Dyskolos, Encheiridion, Epitrepontes, Theophoroumene, Perinthia, Samia, Synaristosai, Phasma*, and also several *hypotheseis.* Oxyrhynchus was a second home to many scholars and provides some consolation for the total lack of texts from Alexandria. Another large town, Hermoupolis, has contributed modestly with a fragment of *Dyskolos*. Opposite Hermoupolis, on the other side of the Nile, Antinoopolis has given us fragments of *Samia* and perhaps of *Perikeiromene.* Further south, at Aphrodite in Wadi Sarga, the Cairo codex (with *Heros, Epitrepontes, Perikeiromene, and Samia*) was found, and further south still, perhaps at or near Panopolis, the Bodmer codex (with *Samia, Dyskolos* and *Aspis*). A fragment of *Georgos* is said to come from Upper Egypt without further specificity. Finally many fragments are without provenance, because they were acquired through the antiquities trade, which always covers its tracks.

2. The Rolls

The papyrological discoveries show us the two forms of books that were current in antiquity, the roll and the codex. The transmission of Menander, as of other authors, depends on both these media, which demand different approaches.

Places of Discovery of the Rolls

Papyrus rolls are essentially found in two kinds of environment. First there are the Ptolemaic cemeteries where mummy-cartonnage is found. Cartonnage can be made of worn and torn papyrus rolls and was used as a substitute for wooden coffins to protect the mummies. In this process, the worn papyrus is further cut into the necessary shapes and the unused portions are definitively lost. Further deterioration is incurred by the more or less brutal treatment used in modern times to dissolve the cartonnage. The gesso and paint on the surface is removed with acid, and it is often difficult to separate the layers of papyrus that form the cartonnage. This becomes even more difficult when the object is not flat (like, for example, a breastplate) but shaped to make the face or feet. The order of the fragments thus obtained can only be established by their contexts or by stichometric indications if any are present.

The second type of papyrus find comes from the ancient rubbish-dumps, like the Oxyrhynchus papyri. The best preserved are found at mid-height, where they have not been crushed by the upper layers but have been protected against wind, sand, and moisture on the surface. The rubbish dumps thus contain both well-preserved pieces and some in a lace-like condition.

Other find spots are possible, for example secret hollows in the walls of houses, but for papyri acquired through the trade, such details are always veiled in mystery.

Precious Relics of Complete Works

The fragments of rolls bring us back to the time when the complete works of Menander still circulated. This explains both why they are difficult to use and why they are interesting. The difficulty is best shown by the great number of *adespota* of the *Nea* from papyri, since one may estimate that all these *adespota* are probably by Menander—at least, it has so far been impossible to demonstrate with certainty that any papyrus fragment was by any other poet of the *Nea*. An optimist will say that there is a good stock of texts for the future, and optimism is permitted, for sometimes apparently minor discoveries have great consequences. A small, and in itself paltry, fragment from Cairo (*P.IFAO inv* 89 v°) has served as spinal column for several fragments of the indirect tradition and enabled the reconstruction of the better part of the beginning of *Misoumenos*, which in its turn has been completed by other papyrus fragments. *P.Oxy.* 60. 4020, a small fragment of a *hypothesis*, has served to identify the first three verses of *Epitrepontes*, which were known and identified from elsewhere. It is probable that the indirect tradition is particularly rich where the beginnings of plays are concerned. But caution is called for, and successes must not lead to rashness, especially not in the field of identification and restoration. Hasty identifications may seem irresistible, as we saw in 1977 with *Hydria*. In the same way, the difficult art of restoring mutilated texts is a risky business, and whoever practices it must always fear being proven wrong by the appearance of new papyri, which are very numerous when they are fragments of rolls (see Turner 1977 for the beginning of *Misoumenos*, and Furley 2009: 84–89 for *Epitrepontes* Acts III and IV; a striking instance recently appeared with the edition of new fragments of the Michigan papyrus in Römer 2012a and b, and cf. Furley 2013). Practiced with caution and restraint, however, the art of restoration does help to advance our knowledge.

The interest of the fragments of rolls amply compensates for the difficulty in using them. Thus fragments of *Dis Exapaton* show how Plautus went about adapting a Greek play into Latin. Fragments of *Perinthia* and *Kolax* give us direct access to comedies that were "contaminated" by Terence. If, for a moment, we disregard the Latin adaptations of Menander and also the plays transmitted in codex form, we are left with a diversity that is otherwise difficult to imagine. In *Sikyonioi,* the relationship between Menander and Euripides is vividly illuminated, as are the problems of Athenian democracy as Plato and Aristotle analyzed them. In *Theophoroumene* we discover that staging, like the musical element, is important in a comedy by Menander. This is also true of the surprising beginning of the *Leukadia* (*P.Oxy.* 60.4024): the spectator can see the Temple of Apollo perched on Cape Leucatas and hear the temple servant sing a long monody in anapaestic dimeters.

3. The Codices

The Finds and their Use

As with the rolls, codex fragments have also been found in ancient rubbish dumps. But the predominant sources of codex fragments are jars, which protected the sheets for centuries, even if the sheets sometimes only served as stoppers. But sheets that had been well protected during long centuries were at risk as soon as they were discovered in modern times. This is very clear in the case of the Cairo papyrus and even more so with the Bodmer codex. But still, what is left represents by far the longest pieces of continuous text.

In spite of their present state, reduced to loose sheets many of which are fragmentary, these codices give possibilities beyond those of the roll. Sometimes pages are numbered. Sometimes the very structure of the papyrus book, whether it is a single- or a multiple-quire codex, allows us to reconstruct *bifolia* when fiber patterns can be followed from one sheet to another, or, equally important, in other cases prevents us from joining sheets. Great advances can be made at once, while "grey areas" may be reduced by new finds. For instance, the publication in 2009 of *P.Oxy.* 73.4936 led to a rearrangement of the Cairo codex, so that two pages were taken from *Heros* and added to *Epitrepontes.* Finally, the texts of the codices more often contain *notae personae* and punctuation.

The Byzantine Choice

The codices have considerably extended our knowledge of Menander, but the price has been a narrowing of our field of vision. With the codices—apart from the Vatican palimpsest, whose nature is unknown, but we cannot rule out the possibility of an edition of the complete works—we have access to only a dozen plays (three of which, the Cairo *fabula incerta* and *P. Antinoopolis* 15 and 55, are not identified with certainty). In the two most important witnesses to Menander, the Cairo codex and the Bodmer codex (which have at least the *Samia* in common), the order of the plays is neither alphabetical nor chronological, which excludes the possibility that they were parts of a complete edition of Menander; rather, one may think of them as the remains of what might be called the Byzantine choice of Menander. This choice was undoubtedly first made on scholarly grounds (probably at a high level) and does not necessarily reflect the popularity of the plays, but was the answer to a specific policy.

That policy seems to be based on a triadic structure that, in turn, is based on the Aristotelian principle of two extremes surrounding a middle. Thus, in the Bodmer triad (*Samia, Dyskolos, Aspis*), the boorish Cnemon, awkward for his family but an enemy of evil, is in the middle between the too-well-behaved Moschion and Smicrines, the inhuman miser. It is immediately clear that this principle suggests a dramatic progression and at the same time shows the art of Menander in its various manners.

From this perspective, the Cairo codex probably contained four triads (Blanchard 2012), following a new principle of Roman origin, double parallelism. In the first triad, at the beginning of the codex, there was a lost play which was almost certainly *Phasma*, as can be deduced from the parchment fragment in St. Petersburg (*P.Petrop.* inv. G. 388); this play was followed by *Heros* and *Epitrepontes*. The common theme is the suffering woman: a woman has been raped, and her relation to the resulting child is threatened before the happy ending that is required in a comedy. The summit is reached in *Epitrepontes*, Menander's most famous play both in antiquity and today: the woman must expose the infant at birth, but her marriage is nevertheless threatened. The second triad begins in the Cairo codex with *Perikeiromene*; it may continue with *Misoumenos*, as suggested by *P.Oxy.* 33.2656, but the third play is unknown (*Thrasyleon?*). The common theme here is the suffering man: a soldier is abandoned by his mistress, whom he has maltreated in a fit of jealousy or, on the contrary, has always treated with the utmost kindness. Here again, the dramatic progression is clear. After these triads that treat pathos (with often important legal background, see Scafuro 1997) comes the Bodmer triad, which is concerned with ethics. It is probable that a fourth triad of the ethical type concluded the selection, but nothing can be said about it. The most important element of triadic arrangement is the organization according to ethos and pathos that goes back to Aristotle's *Rhetoric*, and it is not surprising, as has been mentioned already, that the reading of Menander was recommended in the schools of rhetoric.

III. RETURN TO THE LATIN MENANDER

1. Introduction: the Greek Practice of Five Acts

The Example of Dyskolos

It is remarkable that the Byzantine choice does not include any of the plays that we know through Latin adaptations, and one wonders whether this was by design (Blanchard 2004). Accordingly, so as to have a more complete view of Menander, we should return to the Latin branch, but with knowledge that was not available to readers in the Middle Ages or Renaissance. For, thanks to the *Dyskolos*, the only complete comedy, today we have an accurate idea of the structure of a Menandrian play, and this is essential if we want to discern what is due to the Greek original in the plays of Plautus and Terence.

In the structure of *Dyskolos* we immediately see a close link between the first half of Act III (427–521, before an empty stage) and the second half of Act V (874–969, after an empty stage). In the first case, the boorish Cnemon rebuffs the slave Geta and beats the cook Sico when they come to ask him for a cooking pot. In the second case, Geta and Sicon take their revenge on Cnemon. The end of Act V is thus a vigorous reversal of the beginning of Act III. One soon discovers that this first half of Act III and this second half of Act V are final parts of a triple series of first and second halves of acts. In the first half of Act I (50–188, the prologue 1–49 being separate), as in the first halves of Acts II (233–320) and III, the problem is for various characters to meet Cnemon to ask him for something. In the first two cases, the attempt is delayed because the young lover, Sostratus, is at first dissuaded from asking for the girl in marriage. In the third case, the attempt is carried out, but is unsuccessful when Geta and Sicon are rebuffed and beaten for their audacity in asking the irascible old man for a cooking pot. So we find a classical sequence of A A' B, where B symbolizes the realization (actually, the reversal) of a form of action that has been attempted twice in A and A'. In the same way, the second halves of Acts III (522–619), IV (691–783), and V are dominated by a refusal by Cnemon: refusal to accept help in Act III, refusal to have anything to do with the marriage of his daughter in Act IV, and refusal to participate in the banquet that unites the families in Act V. The first two refusals are respected by the others: Geta simply pities Cnemon, who insists on descending into the well in dangerous conditions, and Gorgias agrees to give away his sister, but the third refusal is countered by Geta and Sicon, who drag the old man off to the banquet. We thus have, once again, A A' B. If we look at the remaining parts, the second halves of Act I (198–232) and Act II (321–426) and the first halves of Act IV (620–690) and Act V (784–873), we see that they correspond, in a minor way and in the framework of a concentric structure, to the first halves of Acts V and IV and to the second halves of Acts II and I. To give an example, in the first half of Act V (784–873) it seems that Cnemon has not really changed his character, even if, in Act IV, he became conscious of his errors, and everything seems ready to start over again as if nothing had happened, as in the beginning of Act I, where we are shown the *dyskolia* of the old man in full force. But in point of fact, at the end of the play Cnemon is no longer in a position to obstruct the happiness of the young leading couple, and the first part of Act V plays out as a faint echo of the first part of Act I (Blanchard 2008: 67–73).

The Theory

It is useful to keep in mind the overall themes which give the structure of *Dyskolos* a concrete character; nevertheless, the diversity of Menander's plays is such that it is necessary to have a more abstract, and thus more generally valid, idea of this structure. There are two important texts that may help us, one being Aristotle's *Poetics* 18, 1455 b 26–29 on the division of the tragic action into knot (δέσις) and solution (λύσις), the other being that of Evanthius, *De fab.* 4, 5 (Wessner, ed. of Donatus) on the division of comic action into πρότασις (initial tension), ἐπίτασις (mounting tension), and καταστροφή (reversal of the situation). If we take into account the division into five acts, we can make the following table (see Figure 11.1):

This table does not in any way allow us to reconstruct a play by Menander if the textual basis is insufficient, any more than one can reconstruct the text of overly mutilated passages; not everyone can play at being Menander! But it gives at least an overview of the critical requirements that must be satisfied if we really want to find Menander in the Latin plays.

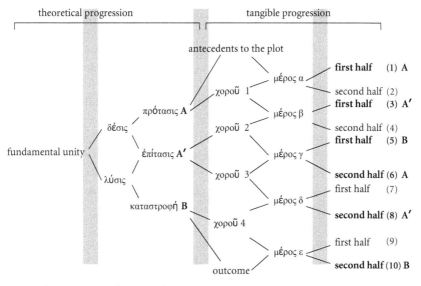

FIGURE 11.1 The structure of Menandrian comedy

2. Obstacles, Cleared and Remaining

There is no lack of obstacles on the way to recovering Menander in the Latin poets. The first is the Latin practice of continued action, which Donatus recognizes even if he tries to divide the plays of Terence into five acts. Experience shows that this grammarian of the fourth century did not have access to the original plays of Menander; instead, he transmits scraps of older erudition, for example some fragments of Menander and some elements of doctrine such as—correctly—the division into five acts, but sometimes he does this badly; in particular, his definition of an entracte as an empty stage will not do. We now know that there were, in the plays of Menander, instances of an empty stage that did not correspond to an entracte (e.g., after *Dyskolos* 521, in the middle of Act III). It is better to consider the relative distance (from afar or nearby) that a character who appears several times must travel: from afar supposes an entracte since his previous appearance. The movements of actors, therefore, are better guides to the delimitation of the acts. Another considerable obstacle is the disappearance of the prologue in the Latin plays, at least in the form Menander understood it, either at the beginning of the play or after the first scene. A look at the differences among modern attempts at dividing the original Greek plays into five acts on the basis of the extant Latin plays should suffice to suggest the difficulties involved.

It will not come as a surprise that these formal disagreements have also had an influence on the recognition of the topics of the originals and that the specifically Roman moral concepts of the adaptors have also added to the confusion. The best example of this is no doubt the difficulty in interpreting the end of Terence's *Adelphoe* (Blanchard 1983: 235–243). The last entracte has been variously placed after v. 712, 762, 775 (Donatus), 787, or 854! In fact, the whole understanding of the comedy is at stake: who is the principal character in Menander's play, the one whose faults make the play comical? In other words, what is the moral of the play? We know that Terence's plot opposed two brothers, one mild (Micio), the other severe (Demea), on the question of how to exert parental responsibility over adolescents, and that the outcome turns out (at the end of Act IV) in favor of the mild approach: it leads to the prospect of a good marriage for the adoptive son of the mild brother and to the immediate joy of a great banquet. But then, in v. 855, the plot seems to be reversed: the severe father appears on stage, visibly moved by the banquet. Here arises one of the knottiest problems of literary criticism in the whole of Terence's production. Demea appears suddenly to change character: from being a severe father he becomes an indulgent one. At the same time, Micio seems to become ridiculous, and his brother induces him to commit all kinds of eccentricities, not least to marry—he who has always seemed a confirmed bachelor. This is disconcerting for the audience.

In 1758, in his *Discours sur la poésie dramatique*, Diderot quoted *Adelphoe* as an example of the uncertainty in which great writers leave us. He does not refer to the relation between Terence and Menander, but the indirect tradition shows that this ending of the play is not a pure invention by the Latin poet, and whether they mention Menander or not, the most recent scholars are divided as to the interpretation of the play (see Blanchard 1983: 235–243). Some think that Menander wrote first of all to create laughter, with an ending worthy of the *Archaia*, and without being too fussy about the resulting inconsistencies in his play. Others have thought that Menander refused to take a position in favor of one or the other of the fathers. This, in their view, would be proof of his inability to choose between two systems of education and hence a sign of decadence, or a sign that he condemns all extremism, whether on the side of severity or of indulgence. Or they have considered that Menander did support one of the characters: some think Demea, others Micio. These latter are perhaps the more likely to be right, for Terence has perhaps exaggerated here, so as not to appear too lax to a Roman audience. But he has respected the general plot of the Greek original, which is clearly in favor of the liberal father and against the severe one. There can be no doubt as to this for anyone who has read the Greek Menander. Cnemon does not change character in Act V of *Dyskolos*, in spite of what he has learned in Act IV, and neither does Demea after v. 855 of *Adelphoe* in spite of what he has learned in the previous act. He still tries to get the upper hand over his brother, but he can do nothing to change a situation which proves that he was wrong and which he finally has to accept. Never mind, then, that Micio is exposed to a little ridicule. In Menander, all characters are more or less ridiculous, except the leading young woman (Blanchard 2007: 76). Once again, a better knowledge of the Greek poet has helped to eliminate a false problem and so to advance this same knowledge.

EDITIONS OF MENANDER: A SELECTION

Τὰ ἐκ τῶν Μενάνδρου σωζόμενα. *Ex comoediis Menandri quae supersunt, Colligebat Guil. Morelius.* Paris: Morel, 1553.

Τὰ ἐκ τῶν παλαιῶν καὶ πάντων σοφῶν κωμικῶν ν' γνωμικὰ σωζόμενα, ἑλληνιστὶ καὶ ῥωμαϊστὶ καλῶς κατὰ στοιχεῖον εἰς τόπους τινὰς συντεταγμένα. *Vetustissimorum sapientissimorum comicorum quinquaginta, quorum opera integra non extant, sententiae, quae supersunt: Graece et Latine collectae et secundum literas Graecorum in certos locos dispositae.* Basel: Jacob Hertel, 1560.

Excerpta ex Tragoediis et Comoediis Graecis tum quae extant, tum quae perierunt: Emendata et latinis versibus reddita ab Hugone Grotio, cum notis et indice auctorum et rerum. Paris: Nicolas Bron, 1626.

Menandri et Philemonis reliquiae, quotquot reperiri potuerunt: Graece et Latine, cum notis Hugonis Grotii et Joannis Clerici, qui etiam novam omnium versionem adornavit, Indicesque adiecit. Amsterdam: Thomas Lombrail, 1709.

Menandri et Philemonis Reliquiae. Edited by August Meineke.*Accedunt R. Bentleii in Menandrum et Philemonem Emendationes Integrae.* Berlin: A. Mylius, 1823.

Fr. Dübner, *Menandri et Philemonis Fragmenta*, in Ἀριστοφάνους κωμῳδίαι καὶ κωμῳδιῶν ἀποσπασμάτια. *Aristophanis Comoediae et Perditarum Fragmenta ex nova recensione Guilelmi Dindorf.* Paris: Firmin-Didot, 1838.

Fragmenta Comicorum Graecorum. Edited by August Meineke. Vol. 4, *Fragmenta Poetarum Comoediae Novae.* Berlin: G. Reimer, 1841.

Comicorum Atticorum Fragmenta. Edited by Theodor Kock. Vol. 2, *Novae Comoediae Fragmenta. Pars 2.* Leipzig: Teubner, 1888.

Menandri Quae supersunt. Edited by Alfred Koerte. Leipzig: Teubner. Vol. 1 *Reliquiae in papyris et membranis vetustissimis servatae,* 1938. Vol. 2, *Reliquiae apud veteres scriptores servatae,* 1953; 2nd rev. ed., 1959.

The Fragments of Attic Comedy. Edited and translated by John Maxwell Edmonds. Vol. 3 B, *Menander.* Leiden: E. J. Brill, 1961.

Menandri reliquiae selectae. Edited by Francis Henry Sandbach. Oxford: Oxford Classical Texts, 1972, 2nd ed. 1990.

Menander. Edited and translated by W. Geoffrey Arnott. Cambridge, MA, and London: Harvard University Press. Vol. I, *Aspis to Epitrepontes,* Loeb Classical Library 132, 1979; vol. II, *Heros to Perinthia,* Loeb Classical Library 459, 1996; vol. 3, Loeb Classical Library 460, 2000.

Poetae Comici Graeci (PCG). Edited by Rudolf Kassel and Colin Austin. Berlin: W. de Gruyter. Vol. 6, 2, *Menander: Testimonia et fragmenta,* 1998.

Menandri reliquiae selectae. Edited by Colin Austin. Oxford: Oxford Classical Texts, forthcoming.

A searchable database of editions of Menander may be found on the website of the Centre de Documentation de Papyrologie Littéraire: http://promethee.philo.ulg.ac.be/cedopal/indexsimple.asp, accessed March 15, 2012. To retrieve the list of editions, select Menander from the drop-down menu titled "Auteurs disponibles."

BIBLIOGRAPHY

Arnott, W. G., ed. 1979. *Menander.* Vol. 1, *Aspis to Epitrepontes.* Loeb Classical Library 132. Cambridge, MA, and London: Harvard University Press.

Abadie-Reynal, C., J.-P. Darmon, and A.-M. Lévêque. 2003. "La maison et la mosaïque des *Synaristôsai* de Zeugma." *JRA* Suppl. 51, *Zeugma Interim Reports*: 79–99.

Blanchard, A. 1983. *Essai sur la composition des comédies de Ménandre.* Paris: Les Belles Lettres.

——. 2004. "Les *Synaristosai* et la constitution du Choix de Ménandre." In *Studien zu Plautus' Cistellaria,* edited by R. Hartkamp and F. Hurka, 11–19. Tübingen: Gunter Narr Verlag.

——. 2007. *La comédie de Ménandre: Politique, éthique, esthétique.* Paris: PUPS.

——. 2008. *Dans l'ouvroir du poète: Structures et nombres de la poésie grecque antique.* Paris: PUPS.

——. 2012. "Le papyrus Bodmer et la réception de Ménandre à l'époque byzantine." In *Actes du 26ᵉ Congrès international de papyrologie (Genève, 16–21 août 2010),* edited by P. Schubert, 77–82. Geneva: Droz.

Charitonidis, S.[cross] L. Kahil, and R. Ginouvès. 1970. *Les mosaïques de la Maison du Ménandre à Mytilène.* Bern: Francke.

D'Aiuto, F. 2003. "*Graeca* in codici orientali della Biblioteca Vaticana (con i resti di un manoscritto tardoantico delle commedie di Menandro)." In *Tra Oriente e Occidente: Scritture e libri greci fra le regioni orientali di Bisanzio e l'Italia,* edited by L. Perria, 227–296. Rome: Pubblicazioni del Dipartimento di Filologia Greca e Latina, Università di Roma La Sapienza.

Duckworth, G. E. 1952. *The Nature of Roman Comedy: A Study in Popular Entertainment*. Princeton: Princeton University Press.

Furley, W. D. 2009. *Menander:* Epitrepontes. London: *BICS* Suppl. 106.

—— 2013, "Pamphile Regains Her Voice: on the Newly Published Fragments Of Menander's *Epitrepontes*". *ZPE* 185: 82–90.

Gutzwiller, K., Çelik, Ö. 2012. "New Menander Mosaics from Antioch," *AJA* 116: 573–623.

Handley, E. 2011. "The Rediscovery of Menander." In *Culture in Pieces: Essays on Ancient Texts in Honour of Peter Parsons*, edited by D. Obbink and R. Rutherford, 138–159. Oxford: Oxford University Press.

Ivanov, T. 1954. *Une Mosaïque romaine de Ulpia Oescus*. Sofia: Édition de l'Académie bulgare des Sciences.

Jachmann, G. 1934. "P. Terentius Afer." In *Paulys Real-Encyclopedie der classischen Altertumswissenschaft*, V A, Vol. 1, edited by A. Pauly, G. Wissowa, and K. Ziegler, col. 598–650. Stuttgart: J. B. Metzler.

Koerte, A., and A. Thierfelder, eds. 1959. *Menandri quae supersunt: Pars altera, Reliquiae apud veteres scriptores servatae*. 2nd rev. ed. Leipzig: B. G. Teubner.

Lowe, N. J. 2007. *Comedy*. New Surveys in the Classics 37. Cambridge: Cambridge University Press.

Markoulaki, St. 1990. "Ψηφιδωτά 'Οικίας Διονύσου' στο Μουσείο Χανίων." In *Πεπραγμένα του ΣΤ´ Διεθνούς Κρητολογικού Συνεδρίου 24–30 Αυγ.1986*, edited by B. Niniou-Kindeli, 449–463. Chania, Greece: Philologikos Syllogos Chanion "O Chrysostomos."

——. 2012. "Dining with Menander in West Crete (Greece): A New Mosaic Pavement in Kissamos." In *Actes du XIIᵉ Colloque de l'AIEMA (Venise,11–15 septembre 2012)*, forthcoming.

Nesselrath, H.-G. 2000. "Eupolis and the Periodization of Athenian Comedy", in Harvey D., Wilkins J. (eds.), *The Rivals of Aristophanes. Studies in Athenian Old Comedy*. 233–246. London, Duckworth and The Classical Press of Wales.

Norwood, G. 1932. *Plautus and Terence*. New York: Longmans, Green.

Römer, C. E. 2012a. "New Fragments of Act IV, *Epitrepontes* 786–823 Sandbach (P. Mich. 4752 a, b and c)." *ZPE* 182: 112–120.

—— 2012b "A New Fragment of End of Act III, *Epitrepontes* 690–701 Sandbach (P. Mich. 4805)", *ZPE* 183: 33–36.

Scafuro, A. C. 1997. *The Forensic Stage: Settling Disputes in Graeco-Roman New Comedy*. Cambridge: Cambridge University Press.

Strocka, V. M. 1977. *Die Wandmalerei der Hanghäuser in Ephesos*. Vienna: Verlag der Österreichischen Akademie der Wissenschaften.

Turner, E. G. 1977. "The Lost Beginning of Menander, *Misoumenos*." *PBA* 63: 315–331.

Zanker, P. 1995. *The Mask of Socrates: The Image of the Intellectual in Antiquity*. Berkeley: University of California Press, 77–85.

CHAPTER 12

··

CROSSING GENRES: COMEDY, TRAGEDY, AND SATYR PLAY

··

JOHANNA HANINK

THE anonymous speaker in a fragment of Timocles's fourth-century comedy *Dionysiazousai* (*Women at the Dionysia* K-A fr. 6) offers a consolation for the sufferings of human life. He opens by praising the distraction, as well as instruction, granted by the arts:

> Consider first, if you will, the benefits the tragedians
> bestow on everyone. One guy, who's a pauper,
> finds out that Telephus was poorer than he is
> and immediately he has an easier time putting up with his own poverty.
> The man who's a bit unstable thinks of Alcmaeon.
> Someone has an infected eye; Phineus's sons are *blind*.
> Someone's child has died; Niobe cheers him up.
> [...]
> Because when a person considers all the bad luck
> even worse than his own that's hit other people,
> he complains less about his troubles. (trans. Olson)

Tragedy and comedy were two entirely distinct dramatic genres in classical antiquity, and yet the surviving Greek comic texts talk about tragedy—and not just about vaguely tragic events or in loosely tragic terms, but about tragic plays and the experience of watching them—to a startling degree. Greek comic playwrights satirized their tragic counterparts and cast the tragic genre as a rival of their own, and the comic fragment of Timocles quoted here even goes so far as to shower high praise on tragedy and the relief from sorrows that it can bring.[1]

But despite the strong presence of tragedy in ancient comic discourses, from the perspective of actual dramatic production a great and strange—at least to modern

---

[1] Timocles was active from roughly the mid-340s to c. 317; on the fragment see also Scafuro chapter 9, pp. 213–14 in this volume.

sensibilities—divide separated the two forms. At the end of Plato's *Symposium,* the last symposiasts nod off as Socrates supposedly argues that a playwright should be equally skilled at composing tragedy and comedy (223d). Such an argument would be curious, particularly in the light of the text's dramatic setting (the celebration of Agathon's first victory in tragedy in 416): no giant of the Athenian theater ever entered, let alone took the prize in, both tragic and comic competitions. In Athenaeus's much later *Deipnosophistae* (third century CE), Timocles himself is singled out for having written both comedies and tragedies (9.407d; modern scholars are doubtful), but Athenaeus's choice to highlight this talent only serves to affirm the general rule: comic plays were the province of the comic playwrights, and only tragedians wrote tragedies.

The peculiarity of the argument reported in the *Symposium* is further underscored by an observation that Socrates makes in the *Republic.* There he remarks that the same people are never proficient in even the most closely related types of mimesis, the prime example being the writing of comedy and tragedy (3.394e–395a). Although a modern reader might offer numerous contrary examples (Shakespeare and Oscar Wilde, to name but two), Socrates's statement does refract an important reality of the ancient theater. Only in Rome, and not until the end of the third century BCE, did successful poets such as Livius and Ennius attempt both dramatic genres (see Manuwald, chapter 29 in this volume). In classical Athens, comic and tragic playwriting always remained wholly distinct arts. Not only did individual actors and playwrights specialize in one genre or the other, but so too did the city's sometimes multigenerational "theatrical families" (Sutton 1987).

Although the vocations of tragic and comic playwrights were remarkably distinct in Greek antiquity, the surviving plays do nevertheless reveal that each group took inspiration from and engaged with the other's work; for example, comic poets frequently parodied tragedy, and tragic poets used satyr play as an arena to experiment with humorous language and comical plotlines. In the course of this chapter I explore points of contact such as these between the dramatic forms of classical Athens: comedy and tragedy, as well as satyr drama. I do not attempt to discuss or to reconstruct these genres within a framework of modern genre theory, although others have arrived at important insights in doing so; instead, I focus on how Greek comedy was defined both against and in relation to the other contemporary dramatic genres. While the earliest origins and first evolutionary phases of Greek drama remain relatively obscure (though see Csapo and Miller 2007; Rusten, chapter 1 in this volume), it is clear that by the early fifth century BCE Athenian comedy and tragedy had evolved alongside and with mutual awareness of each other as more or less parallel, yet absolutely separate, forms. During that same period, the Greek terms *tragoidia* and *komoidia* also came to signify clearly defined and distinct manners of performance.[2]

I focus the following discussion primarily on texts from the last quarter of the fifth century, the period in which tragedy and comedy engaged in especially dynamic

[2] The word *trugoidia,* or "comedy [as opposed to tragedy]," first occurs in Aristophanes's *Acharnians* (499 and 886) as a term that highlights comedy's oppositional relationship with the similar-sounding *tragoidia;* see Taplin 1983 and Zanetto 2006.

cross-genre dialogue. Some scholars have seen the two dramatic modes in these decades as characterized by a tendency "to define each other by their opposition and their reluctance to overlap" (Taplin 1986: 164), while others have argued that "a loosening of generic boundaries occurred in late fifth-century Athens" (Foley 2008: 17; cf. Zimmermann 1989). I take for granted that the emergence of clearer parameters for the dramatic genres did not preclude a coincident increase in genre-bending experimentation. The variety of highly self-conscious cross-genre borrowing, allusion, and "transgression" that distinguishes dramatic production in this period points rather to a combination of the two tendencies, as well as to a heightened awareness on the part of the playwrights as to the genres' special qualities. Here I begin by outlining parallels and contrasts between the conventions and "performance grammars" of late fifth-century comedy and tragedy (section i). Next, I discuss ways in which *komoidia* and *tragoidia* (including satyr play) actively gestured to and appropriated elements of each other in the same period (sections ii and iii). I then conclude with a brief overview of comedy's interaction with tragedy in the fourth century, when modes of comic interaction with tragedy developed new complexities, but comedy's explicit allusions to tragedies also became largely restricted to works by the "canonical" fifth-century tragic poets (section iv).

I. PERFORMANCE CONTEXTS AND CONVENTIONS OF GENRE

Despite the strict division between the playwrights and personnel of comic and tragic productions, both types of play were performed on the same occasions and shared a number of formal dramatic features. Comic and tragic poets alike applied to an archon for the right to exhibit at the major dramatic festivals (Aristotle, *Constitution of the Athenians* 56.3; *Poetics* 1149a), and both types of plays required a *choregos* ("producer"), a chorus of males who danced in the theater's *orchestra*, and a set of masked and costumed actors. In the city of Athens, as elsewhere in the Greek world, comedy and tragedy were performed in the same space (the Theater of Dionysus) and at the same annual festivals. The largest of these were the City or "Great" Dionysia and the Lenaea. In the second half of the fifth century, a comic chorus was about twice as large as a tragic one (with twenty-four members as opposed to twelve or fifteen), and tragic and comic masks and costume differed radically. Despite such distinctions, however, the "family resemblances" between comedy and tragedy do suggest that they were, as Socrates remarks in the *Republic*, two of the most closely related types of mimesis.

At the dramatic festivals, however, comic and tragic playwrights always competed in separate competitions, and a playwright made a firm declaration of genre in applying to the archon for either a comic or a tragic chorus. In the fifth century and part of the fourth, each entrant in the tragic competitions at the Great Dionysia exhibited his slate of plays (three tragedies and a satyr play) during a single day, for a total of three days of tragedy. Comic playwrights, who first competed at the festival in 486 BCE, entered a single play. During the fifth century, each celebration of the Great Dionysia featured five comedies performed on the same day, though it is possible that during part of the Peloponnesian War only three comedies were staged, one at the conclusion of each day of tragedy (cf. Csapo and Slater 1995: 107). The Lenaea was a smaller-scale dramatic festival celebrated from about 440; it had the same number of comic performances as the Dionysia, five or three, but featured only two tragedians, who submitted two tragedies each but no satyr play. Victory records suggest that the Lenaea was on roughly equal footing with the Dionysia as a venue for comic premieres (Aristophanes often competed and won there), but that the tragedians saw the Dionysia as the more prestigious of the contests.

The close performative proximity of comedy and tragedy at festivals is illustrated in a passage from Aristophanes's *Birds* in which the avian chorus taunts the audience with the idea that if they too had wings, they could fly up to join the birds when they tired of watching the tragedies, then swoop back down to the theater to rejoin "us" (i.e., the comic performers) after lunch (786–789; Csapo and Slater 1995, III.39). This passage not only highlights tragedy's and comedy's shared performance spaces and occasions, but also sheds light upon Attic comedy's apparent preoccupation with parodying tragedy and mocking the tragic playwrights (see section ii below). Because tragedies and comedies were performed at the same festivals, and likely sometimes on the same day, tragic plays and spectatorship constituted shared points of reference and topical objects of satire.

Aside from the position of a play within the festival's program, a wide range of linguistic, visual, and performative features would also have enabled ancient audiences to distinguish a comedy from a tragedy. A spectator might recognize a comic production at first sight of its lavish (and often animal-themed) choral costumes, and the commonplace "stage-nakedness" of comic actors, represented by body tights and appended comic phalluses (on costuming and other aspects of comic performance, see 'Csapo, chapter 2 in this volume). On the whole, comedies were more colorful and crowded productions, generally "busier" than tragedy (see especially Revermann 2006a); this was partially due to Old Comedy's less rigid adherence to the "three-actor" rule that was observed by tragedy and also by comedy in subsequent periods (on the number of actors in Old Comedy see Pickard-Cambridge 1988: 149–153 and MacDowell 1994).

Tragic and comic plays also differed in the nature of their plots, though such an axiomatic statement has its complications. Our vision of typical dramatic content is somewhat distorted by the surviving plays of Aristophanes, which are set in contemporary Athens and are largely concerned with current events; nonetheless, their plots do not necessarily represent "typical" Old Comedy (cf. Revermann 2006a: 95–106). Between the fifth and fourth centuries, a large portion of comedies drew their plots—as tragedy nearly always did, but Aristophanes generally did not—from the epic and other mythological cycles (see especially Guidorizzi 2006 and Konstantakos, chapter 7 in this volume). Classical tragedies also did not always end with "tragedy" (the deus ex machina, for example, might be used to avert disaster), nor did comedies always end on an unequivocally joyous note. Some critics in antiquity even lamented that the endings of certain fifth-century tragedies were too "comic" for their tastes: the ancient summaries of Euripides's *Orestes* and *Alcestis* comment on each play's "rather more comic" (*sc.* than tragic) outcome. In *Poetics* ch. 13, Aristotle would find fault with tragedies that employ the "double endings" more appropriate to comedy, i.e., endings with good outcomes for the good characters and bad for the bad. Modern scholars have also identified overarching comic patterns in later Euripidean plays such as *Ion* and *Helen*. Satyrus, a Hellenistic biographer of Euripides, even credited the tragedian with developing "to perfection" the New Comic plot devices par excellence, such as the recovery of lost children and recognition by tokens (Satyrus F 6 fr. 39.7 Schorn), both of which occur in, for example, Euripides's *Ion*. On the other hand, for some scholars the transmitted version of Aristophanes's *Clouds*, which ends with the frenzied Strepsiades burning down Socrates's "Thinkery" and calling for the philosopher's violent death, is a tragedy "in fact, if not in name" (Sommerstein 1973: 14; cf. Zimmermann 2006). Even, then, if there is some truth to a generalization such as "Old Comedy tends towards closed, wrapped-up, reassuring endings, while tragedies tend to reach open, disturbing, unsettled endings" (Taplin 1996: 196), it would be difficult to classify the surviving tragedies and comedies as such solely on the basis of their resolutions.

Nevertheless, other strong indicators of genre, such as performance conventions and—most important by far—poetic register (that is, the use of markedly "high" versus "low" language), meant that an ancient audience would never have had trouble distinguishing an instance of *komoidia* from one of *tragoidia*. The performance conventions that clearly distinguish comedy and tragedy may be viewed as aspects of each genre's different "performance grammar," that is, the particular set of formal principles, patterns, and rules that defines a given performance tradition. Poetic meter was one area in which the performance grammars of comedy and tragedy differed: although the poetry of both kinds of plays used the same metrical building blocks (iambs, trochees, anapaests, etc.), the grammar of comedy allowed for more frequent resolution (two short syllables in place of a long) and substitution (two short syllables in place of one short).

Dramatic structure is also a critical element of any tradition's performance grammar, and here, too, fifth-century comedy and tragedy display fundamental similarities and differences. An expositional prologue, for example, typically occurred towards the beginning of both types of plays. Similarly, tragic and comic audiences alike would have anticipated the chorus's processional entrance (*parodos*) towards the beginning of the play and expected its exit (*exodos*) near the end, although the *parodos* tended to occur later in a comedy. In between the *parodos* and *exodos*, tragedy used a simple structure of episodes (the structural predecessors of dramatic "acts") followed by choral songs ("odes" or *stasima*). The architecture of Old Comedy, on the other hand, was both more flexible and more complex (Zimmermann, chapter 6 this volume; Sifakis 1992; see section iv below on comic structure in the fourth century). Old Comedy did employ episodes, but it also made heavy use of two other distinctive elements, the *parabasis* and *agon*. At the heart of both was a repeated pattern of recitative sung by the chorus leader and followed by full choral song (epirrhematic syzygy). The comic *agon* was framed as a rhetorical competition between two characters of strongly opposed views, such as between "Euripides" and "Aeschylus" at *Frogs* 895–1098 or the "Just" and the "Unjust" arguments at *Clouds* 949–1104. A number of fifth-century tragedies also featured an *agon*, but the comic versions display more complex structures and more elaborate choral involvement.

The choral *parabasis*, on the other hand, was unique to Old Comedy, and is already absent from Aristophanes's fourth-century plays. As part of a *parabasis,* the comic chorus would often shed its dramatic character (and even part of its costumes: cf. *Acharnians* 627) so as to address the spectators on behalf of the poet. This structure afforded the comedian an unparalleled opportunity to "say what he wants to the audience [*theatron*]" (Pollux, *Onomasticon* 4.111, second century CE). In the first *parabasis* of *Wasps* (1015–1121), for example, the chorus step out of their role as juror-wasps and reproach the audience for their past treatment of Aristophanes (the chorus leader begins: "the poet now wishes to censure you spectators"). Similar defenses of the playwright appear in the *parabaseis* of *Acharnians* and *Knights*. In tragedy, by contrast, when actors addressed the audience (as in tragic prologues) they did so more strictly in character.[3]

Aristophanic protagonists also sometimes assumed the voice of their creator in offering commentary on contemporary affairs or even upon the nature of comic drama itself, as when Dicaeopolis delivers his pseudo-defense of Sparta in *Acharnians* in the blended voice of playwright and character: "Do not begrudge me, spectators," he begins, "if, though a beggar, I speak to Athens about the state in a comedy [*trugoidia*]: comedy too knows a thing or two about justice" (497–500). Such moments of direct audience engagement marked an occasion for comic reflection upon the comic genre, a device which the decorum of tragedy (and the conventions of later comedy) generally did not permit. The *parabasis* itself was just one such device that granted comedy space for open political and social commentary. Tragedy, too, commented upon and engaged deeply with social issues, political problems, and "current events" (see e.g. Goldhill 1987 with Shear 2011: 154–165), but because of its distinctive grammar and conventions comedy was able to do so more frankly, without the disguise of mythology. When Aristophanes wanted to lampoon Cleon he could do so by name or through thinly veiled parody; when he wanted to caricature Euripides, he could bring the tragedian—or at least a version of him—onto the stage.

---

[3] See Bain 1977 and Roselli 2011: 38–39 on dramatic "asides" and other forms of audience address. Scholars have identified a number of instances of choral "self-referentiality" in passages of tragic choral lyric (i.e., moments when the chorus speaks as an Athenian citizen chorus rather than as a body of tragic characters: Henrichs 1994–1995). Unlike their comic counterparts, however, tragic choruses do not treat the audience as an imagined interlocutor (Taplin 1986; cf. Taplin 1996).

11. COMIC PARATRAGEDY

In the fifth century, comic plays could serve as a site for reflection upon the very nature of comic drama, but the comedians' extensive critical engagement with tragedy was also a distinctive quality of the Athenian theater. Comedy had experimented with tragedy even before a relatively clear dramatic mode of *komoidia* entered the Athenian festival programs. A play called *Komoidotragoidia* is attested for Dinolochus (K-A 3), who was active in the first decades of the fifth century and whom the *Suda* (entry δ.338) places in the Sicilian comic tradition as a younger contemporary of Epicharmus. Word of Dinolochus's play must eventually have reached Athens, where two early fourth-century poets of Middle Comedy, Alcaeus and Anaxandrides, each composed a *Komoidotragoidia* (19–21 and 26 K-A, respectively). The stock comic title may also have inspired a Latin coinage by the Roman playwright Plautus. In the prologue of his *Amphitruo* (c. 190 BCE), the god Mercury hails the play as a *tragicocomoedia* (lines 59 and 63), in that its dramatis personae will be drawn from the two different worlds of the two dramatic genres: kings and gods as in a tragedy, and the types of slaves familiar from the comic stage (see again Manuwald, chapter 29 in this volume).

The comic playwrights' interaction with their tragic counterparts was, however, broadest and deepest in Athens, especially during the last quarter of the fifth century. Although only comedies by Aristophanes survive intact from that period, the combination of his corpus with fragments of plays by contemporaries indicates that a large repertory of comic devices took tragedy as a point of reference.[4] Comedy could, for example, appropriate tragic language and costume, allude to and parody the plots of well-known tragic plays, and make jokes at the expense of specific tragic playwrights. These kinds of explicit comic references to tragic drama and its conventions mark instances of "paratragedy." As a comic device, paratragedy presumed an audience that was familiar with tragic drama and au courant with recent productions (see Revermann 2006b on the "competence" of the Athenian audiences in this respect). Comedy also spoofed the very milieu of the dramatic festivals. For example, the plot of Aristophanes's (lost) *Proagon* likely centered on the "pre-contest" (*proagon*) held before the Dionysia at which the competing poets announced the titles of their plays. No informative fragment of the *Proagon* survives, but a scholium to line 61 of Aristophanes's *Wasps* offers the tantalizing notice that in the play Euripides was "brought onstage," that is, was portrayed as a comic character.

Aristophanes was particularly fond of turning the city's tragedians into comic characters (cf. Tammaro 2006), and in this regard Euripides was by far his favorite target.

---

[4] Recent studies have demonstrated the importance of paratragedy in fragments of Aristophanes's contemporaries: on Cratinus, see Bakola 2010, ch. 3: "Cratinus and Tragedy"; on Eupolis's *Demes*, see Telò 2007: 68 and 106–121; on Strattis, see Miles 2009 and in Telò, chapter 5 this volume. Miles 2009: 17–117 provides an overview of paratragedy in non-Aristophanic fifth-century comedy.

Euripides was "brought onstage" in three of Aristophanes's surviving plays: *Acharnians*, *Women at the Thesmophoria*, and *Frogs*. In the *Acharnians* (the prize-winning comedy at the Lenaea of 425), the physical presence of "Euripides" would have cued the audience to recognize that much of the plot was adapted from Euripides's own *Telephus* (438 BCE). *Telephus* has not survived, but was well known and influential in antiquity (its "hostage scene" is parodied in *Women at the Thesmophoria*; in the *Frogs*, "Aeschylus" criticizes Euripides's unheroic characterization of the title character). In *Acharnians*, a comedy set against the background of the Peloponnesian War, Dicaeopolis plays the Telephus role and delivers a speech in defense of the Spartans (a basket of charcoal replaces the baby Orestes as his hostage; on the parody see especially Foley 1988). But before making his speech, Dicaeopolis goes to the house of Euripides in the hopes that he will outfit him with appropriately tragic clothing for his disguise. Euripides finally agrees to lend him the costume from the actual production of *Telephus*, but as Dicaeopolis goes on to demand prop after prop as accessories, an exasperated Euripides exclaims: "You'd rob me of the whole tragedy!" (464). It is difficult to resist reading this line metatheatrically, as an imagined reaction on the part of "Euripides" to more than just Dicaeopolis's demands: by appropriating so much of the *Telephus* in the *Acharnians*, Aristophanes himself nearly "robs" Euripides of his entire tragedy.

Euripides plays an even larger role in Aristophanes's *Women at the Thesmophoria* (411 BCE). There the women of Athens decide to take action against the slander that Euripides has committed against them by so often writing unfaithful and duplicitous female leading roles (such as Stheneboea in the lost *Stheneboea* and Phaedra in *Hippolytus*). "Euripides," therefore, plots to send his elderly kinsman to spy on the women as they debate how best to take their revenge. But because the occasion of the women's discussion is the female-only festival of the Thesmophoria, the kinsman must disguise himself as a woman to gain entrance; the play accordingly contains an extended "cross-dressing" scene in which Euripides and his fellow tragic poet Agathon help the man into his costume (see Zeitlin 1981). With Euripides as protagonist, the play unsurprisingly features a wide variety of paratragic moments and gags, including the appearance of "Euripides" himself on the stage-crane that was typically used for the arrival of a deus ex machina— a type of ending that Euripides particularly favored (Rau 1967: 42–89 and Austin and Olson 1994 *passim*).

Euripides may even have acknowledged his own comic portrayal in *Women at the Thesmophoria* by rewriting its cross-dressing scene in one of his own plays. In the highly metatheatrical *Bacchae* (which premiered in 405 BCE, after Euripides's death), the character Pentheus, like Euripides's kinsman in *Women at the Thesmophoria*, cross-dresses in an attempt to infiltrate female rites. The two cross-dressing scenes have much in common. In both, the cross-dressers begin their toilette with reluctance, but show increasing enthusiasm as their female appearances take shape: "Come on now, arrange the folds [of the dress] around my thighs," Euripides's kinsman orders him (256), while in the *Bacchae* the god Dionysus helps to style Pentheus's female hairdo and comments on the draping of his *peplos* (928–938). Some critics have read the Euripidean scene as marked by dark and ominous humor (see especially

Seidensticker 1978 and Seidensticker 1982: 123–129). Perhaps its most provocative aspect, however, is the implication that Euripides was willing to engage in two-way dialogue with a comic counterpart. It is certainly tempting to see a wryness in Euripides's own (re-)casting of the scene: in *Bacchae*, the role of cross-dressing helper that "Euripides" had played in Aristophanes's play is assigned to Dionysus, the god of theater himself.

The character of Euripides dominates *Women at the Thesmophoria*, but *Frogs* (Lenaea, 405 BCE) marks Aristophanes's most extensive engagement with Athenian tragedy; it is also the only play in which all three of the great Athenian tragedians (each by then deceased) appear as characters. The premise of *Frogs* is that the god Dionysus, who is convinced that the wayward city of Athens needs a tragedian to guide it back onto the right course but also that no worthy candidates are left alive, makes a descent to Hades in order to bring back a revered poet of the past. There he presides over a contest in which Aeschylus and Euripides, the two contenders for resurrection, each presents the case that he is the better poet and of greater value to the city. Throughout the play, both tragedians are assimilated by way of caricature to the poetry that they produced in life: the character of Aeschylus is full of highfalutin martial bombast (he boasts of bellicose moments in his *Persians* and *Seven Against Thebes*), and his over-wrought speech serves to evoke the highly complex poetic language of his plays. On the other hand, "Euripides" prays to newfangled gods before the great *agon* begins (compare *Frogs* 889–894 with Euripides, *Trojan Women* 884–889); we also hear that upon his arrival in Hades he had "performed" with great success for the resident lowlifes, who presumably identified with Euripides's sordid dramatic characters (771–778; cf. Hunter 2009: 10–16).

Frogs is an important witness to early debates about the purpose of tragic poetry and the effects of its performance upon spectators. In some cases, it also marks the first appearance of terms and concepts which would become staples of literary-critical agendas for much of antiquity (Hunter 2009: 10–52). It is, however, important to remember that the arguments that "Aeschylus" and "Euripides" make in the play about the civic responsibilities of tragedy are filtered through Aristophanic principles regarding the purpose of drama. When "Aeschylus" argues that his tragedies encouraged martial valor and "Euripides" retorts that he achieved more by teaching Athenians to think, these positions correspond to a vision of tragedy that is cast in Aristophanes's own terms—according to which all poetry should aim to better the citizens—and do not necessarily reflect any real agendas actively pursued by the tragedians. Nevertheless, *Frogs* does mark a complex comic statement of appreciation for tragedy; it also proposes one provocative articulation of the civic functions of both dramatic genres: Athens needed good tragedians to guide it, but it also needed incisive comedians who would ensure that audiences applied a critical lens to what they saw and heard on the tragic stage.

III. Tragic Play and Satyr Drama

Paratragedy marked one of the most explicit modes of intersection between Athenian dramatic genres in the fifth century, but in their own understated ways the tragedians also borrowed from and made reference to comic plays and conceits. Certain tragic lines, scenes, characters (particularly low-status ones, such as the guard in Sophocles's *Antigone*), and even more comic-type plot structures (as in, e.g., Euripides's *Ion, Helen,* and *Iphigenia in Tauris*) could mark departures from high tragic style. In rare instances, a tragedy might even contain what appears to be an outright joke, as when in Euripides's *Trojan Women* Hecuba entreats Menelaus not to allow Helen to board his ship and Menelaus retorts "Why is that? Has she put on weight?" (1050, the scholiast calls this *geloion,* "laughable" or "ridiculous"). Scholars still disagree about the interpretation of the verse (is it truly a joke, and if so, why is it uttered and how funny is it?), but this disagreement may be revealing in itself, if the play's first audiences were also divided about whether to laugh (Goldhill 2006).

Tragic poets could also turn to the "low-register" diction of comedy—the language of bodily functions and nauseating sights and smells—not to elicit laughter, but to lay jarring emphasis on the repulsiveness of tragic events. In a study of comic language in Aeschylus's *Oresteia,* Sommerstein discusses the low-register language that erupts in the trilogy (some thirty times) after the death of Agamemnon, language which is nearly always uttered by or about the Erinyes. Within the dramatic world, the uncontainable horror that the Erinyes represent creates what Sommerstein calls "ugly deeds that can only be described in an ugly way" (Sommerstein 2002: 165). Other aspects of the *Eumenides*—such as the nonhuman chorus of the Erinyes themselves, the play's topical references to the reform of the Areopagus, and the torch-lit final procession—also suggest that Aeschylus was experimenting with appropriation of comic conventions and structures (Herington 1963).

Cases of "paracomedy," or allusion to comic conventions, devices, and plays, also occur in tragedy; these attest to the existence of a real two-way dialogue between the tragic and comic playwrights. In antiquity, Euripides was the tragedian most associated with comedy, and modern discussions of the relationship between tragedy and comedy also center on his works (see, e.g., Knox 1979, Seidensticker 1982, Gregory 2000). Euripides's *Orestes,* which the comic poet Strattis called his "cleverest play" (*dexiotaton drama,* K-A 1), is often viewed as an important predecessor of "domestic" comedy (Lazarus 2005; cf. Zeitlin 1980 and Dunn 1996, ch. 10). Scholars have also detected echoes of comic conventions within individual tragic scenes and passages. In Euripides's *Heracles,* for example, Heracles's fantasy that his weapons are rebuking him (1380–1381) has been read as a gesture to the more traditionally comic conceit of talking objects.[5]

---

[5] Kirkpatrick and Dunn 2002; see also Scharffenberger 1995 and Scharffenberger 1996 on "paracomic" scenes in Euripides's *Phoenissae* and *Antiope,* respectively.

The surviving tragic plays also contain references to other tragic texts; this suggests that, like the comedians, the tragedians entered into dialogue with their predecessors and competitors. At Eur. *Phoenissae* 751–752, for example, Eteocles tells Creon that to bother naming the invaders of Thebes would only waste time better spent defending the city. Since antiquity, critics have seen this as an allusion to the lengthy descriptions of the Argive leaders in Aeschylus's *Seven Against Thebes* (Mastronarde 1994 *ad loc.*; scholars debate whether the allusion is made in the spirit of satire or homage). Similarly, in Euripides's *Electra*, the heroine remarks that it would be unfeasible (*amechanon*) for Orestes's hair and footprints—the tokens by which she recognizes him in Aeschylus's *Libation Bearers*—to match her own, given that Orestes is larger than she is and has a different sort of hair (524–537; for a recent interpretation see Torrance 2011). Among spectators familiar with the Aeschylean "originals," Euripides's emulous allusions may have elicited knowing smiles, if not audible laughter.

The tragedians also enjoyed a unique and separate space for experimental genre-crossing in the form of the satyr play. In the *Republic*, Socrates claims that comic and tragic mimesis are necessarily the domains of different people, yet the tragic playwrights (and actors, choreuts, and *choregoi*) of Socrates's own day were also responsible for producing the more lighthearted—though still "tragoidic"—genre of satyr play. Satyr plays concluded a tragedian's entry at the Dionysia and typically ended "happily."[6] They were not performed at the Lenaea, but scholars have seen satyr performances as an important and particularly Dionysian vehicle for the formation and performance of male Athenian citizen-identity at the Great Dionysia, in the context of that festival's many civic rituals and ideological displays (Hall 1998 and Hall 2006; Griffith 2002 and Griffith 2005b).

Satyr plays were shorter than tragedies and followed the exploits and misadventures of satyrs (ithyphallic woodland companions of Dionysus) as set against the background of mythological tales and events from the epic cycle. Whereas the human and divine characters of satyr play spoke and behaved with the decorum of tragic personae, the chorus of typically obscene and hypersexual satyrs tumbled about alongside their father Papposilenus, drinking and making jokes about bodily functions (on satyr-play choruses, see especially Seidensticker 2003). Unlike tragedies, satyr plays also chronicled happy love matches between their main characters and often ended in scenes of celebratory revelry. Aeschylus was especially renowned in antiquity for his satyr dramas (see especially Podlecki 2005). Although no complete satyr play of his survives, the fragmentary *Diktyoulkoi* (*Netfishers*) stands as one witness to his success in the genre: *Diktyoulkoi* appears to have influenced the plot of Diphilus's *Epitrope* (late third century BCE), which in turn was the model for Plautus's *Rudens* (Sutton 1978; cf. Petrides 2010: 114).

Euripides's *Cyclops* is the only full (but perhaps not entirely typical) representative of the satyric genre. *Cyclops* rewrites Odysseus's encounter with Polyphemus in *Odyssey*

---

[6] Euripides's tragedy *Alcestis* was performed in 438 BC in place of a satyr play; see Slater 2005. Despite the lack of satyrs, elements of *Alcestis* recall other typical satyric *topoi* and stylistic features (cf. esp. Sutton 1973).

9 to include a band of rambunctious satyrs enslaved in the Cyclops's cave (the same Homeric scene was also the subject of Cratinus's comedy *Odysseus and Company*: see Storey, chapter 4 in this volume). Satyr plays sometimes alluded to and parodied tragedy; *Cyclops* itself contains many verbal echoes of the scene of Polymestor's blinding in Euripides's *Hecuba* (Gregory 1999: 170). Satyr play was, however, a discrete constituent of fifth-century *tragoidia*, and not parasitic or otherwise "dependent" upon tragedy (Griffith 2010: 51–52). The best-preserved fragmentary satyr play, Sophocles's *Ichneutai* (*Trackers*), for example, covers much the same mythical ground as the *Homeric Hymn to Hermes* (i.e., the birth of Hermes and his theft of Apollo's cattle) and is a good illustration of both satyr drama's autonomy and its interaction with forms other than tragedy, in particular comedy (for Old Comedy's interplay with satyr drama, see Bakola 2005). Many motifs appear in *Ichneutai* that either evoke Old Comedy or look forward to certain type-scenes in New Comedy (Zagagi 1999); these include a "negotiation" scene between Apollo and Silenus (with typical comic inversion of the master-slave relationship), Silenus's portrayal as a "braggart slave," and an attempted forced entry of a cave on the part of the satyrs that anticipates later comic "knocking scenes." In Plautus's *Cistellaria*, the speech delivered by Halisca as she looks for the lost casket (671–703) recalls the "tracking scene" of *Ichneutai* so vividly that a direct line has been argued to connect the two plays via Menander's *Synaristosai*, Plautus's Greek model (Süss 1935: 134–135; cf. Zagagi 1999: 196–197).

Nevertheless, *Ichneutai*, *Cyclops* and other satyric fragments have more in common with tragedy than might perhaps have been expected, given the nature of the satyrs and the presence of satyr choruses in a number of fifth-century comedies (Storey 2005). The shape of the iambic trimeters in satyr play more closely resembles tragic than comic metrical practice, and other linguistic markers (such as incidence of compound adjectives: see especially Griffith 2005a) clearly align satyr play with tragedy rather than comedy. The speech of non-satyr satyr-play personae and tragic characters can even be so indistinguishable as to prevent firm assignment of dramatic fragments to one or the other genre. The material record also suggests that, with the exception of the choruses, satyric and tragic characters wore the same costumes (Wyles 2010). Thus although critics have often viewed satyr play as occupying a kind of middle ground between the two other dramatic genres (on the history of this classification see Griffith 2008: 73–79), the famous ancient description of satyr drama as "tragedy at play" (*tragoidia paizousa*, pseudo-Demetrius, *de Elocutione* 169), serves as a reminder that, at least in the fifth century, satyr play belonged squarely to *tragoidia*—a taxonomy that would be colorfully reaffirmed four centuries later by Horace in *Ars Poetica* (lines 220–233).

IV. Beyond the Fifth Century

In the last quarter of the fifth century, Athenian drama was characterized by vigorous allusion, parody, and experimentation; the innovative plots of Euripidean plays such as

Ion and *Helen* also signaled expanded conceptions of tragic drama. In the fourth century, new views about the dramatic genres become partially reflected in the modifications made to the program of the Great Dionysia. By 340 BCE, the festival only showcased a single satyr play (IG II² 2320), which stood at the head of the dramatic performances and served to whet the audience's appetite for the tragedies and comedies to come. Over the course of the century, theatrical revivals also became part of the Dionysia: in 386, tragic "old drama" (*palaion drama*) joined the program, and in 339 a category was added for productions of "old" comedy (IG II² 2318; the plays revived under this rubric belonged to what later became known as "Middle" and "New Comedy"). The introduction of these categories is further evidence for an impulse, evident as early as *Frogs* in 405, to define the dramatic genres by constructing historical narratives accounting for their development (cf. Aristotle, *Poetics* ch. 4, from about 330 BCE; on the "theorization" of the theater in the fourth century and its effects on dramatic production, see Hall 2007: 272–274 and Petrides 2010: 86–92).

No fourth-century tragedy survives, nor does any full comedy from the period between Aristophanes's *Wealth* (388 BCE) and Menander's *Dyskolos* (316 BCE). Aristophanes's last surviving plays (*Assemblywomen* in c. 393 and *Wealth* in 388) already suggest his abandoning of the *parabasis* and *agon* so central to his earlier works. Another of Aristophanes's last plays, *Aeolosicon* (produced posthumously by his son), is singled out by the grammarian Platonius as particularly representative of Middle Comedy (Kaibel *CGF* 1.7; date unknown). Middle Comedy was not characterized by the same level of Atheno-specific political topicality as Old Comedy had been (though see Csapo 2000 on the hazards of schematic periodization, and Henderson, chapter 12 in this volume). Parodies and adaptations of tragic plays and plots again constituted especially popular material; the title of Aristophanes's *Aeolosicon*, for example, may point to a parody or comic reworking of Euripides's lost *Aeolus*. In the first half of the fourth century, the emergent category of "classical" tragedy became a particularly important reference point for the comedians, who were no doubt inspired by the tragic revivals now being staged at the Great Dionysia and elsewhere.

On the other hand, when later fourth-century comic fragments allude to *contemporary* tragic production they tend not to engage explicitly with specific plays or playwrights (on theatrical allusion in Middle Comedy, see Cusset 2003: 31–52; cf. Slater 2005). For example, the speaker in K-A fr. 6 of Timocles's *Dionysiazousai* (quoted at the beginning of this chapter) discusses the benefits that people derive from "the tragedians" by illustrating his point with examples of standard tragic plots and not of particular plays. In a fragment of Antiphanes's *Poetry* (K-A fr. 189), another anonymous speaker declares that "tragic poetry [*tragoidia poiema*] is lucky in every way," since tragedians have their plots readymade by mythology, whereas comic poets must invent novel material. To prove his point, this speaker cites the fame of the stories about Oedipus and Alcmaeon, both of whom were stock tragic protagonists: all three of the great tragedians had treated Oedipus, both Sophocles and Euripides produced versions of an *Alcmaeon*, and fourth-century tragedies also often reworked such "classical" plots (Astydamas was victor at the Great Dionysia of 341 with a slate that included *Antigone*; he also wrote an

Alcmaeon). The short catalogues of tragic characters in Timocles and Antiphanes (and Aristotle's *Poetics*: 1453a17–22) thus appear to stand for tragic drama as a whole rather than to evoke particular plays and productions.

Comedy may have begun to avoid topical references to recently premiered plays in part so as not to alienate spectators—whether infrequent visitors at the Dionysia or audiences outside of Athens—unfamiliar with the latest productions. This hardly means, however, that the comic poets had lost interest in the fifth-century tragedians and their works. The "classical" plays now served as shared reference points for audiences across Greece, and comic playwrights took advantage precisely of the enormous popularity of earlier Athenian (and especially Euripidean) tragedy. Alexis, who first won at the Dionysia in 347, wrote a play called the *Tragedy Lover* (*Philotragoidos*), while a *Euripides Lover* (*Phileuripides*) is attested for Alexis's contemporary Axionicus as well as for Philippides, a poet of New Comedy. K-A fr. 3 of Axionicus's play describes two lovers so mad for Euripidean songs (*mele*) that all other music has become unbearable. Other plays from this period mock the pretensions of low-status characters who cite and adapt tragic verse to their own ends, such as the drunkard in a play by Antiphanes (uncertain title, K-A fr. 228) who adopts verses from Haemon's monologue in Sophocles's *Antigone* for a speech in praise of drinking.

Episodes of tragic (pseudo-)citation and references to the figure of Euripides also occur in New Comedy,[7] but Menander's plays engaged with classical tragedy on a remarkable variety of other levels. By Menander's era, the external structures of comedy and tragedy had nearly converged, with both genres now employing a simple structure of alternating episodes and choral pieces. Menander's plays also abided by tragedy's longstanding "three-actor rule" (Sandbach 1975), more closely resembled fifth-century tragedy on points of staging (Petrides 2010: 105–106), and no longer made use of the Old Comic forms of audience apostrophe. The gradual diminishment of the chorus's role in fourth-century comedy (Hunter 1979 and Rothwell 1995) is also paralleled in tragedy, where the chorus came to have less to do with the dramatic action (Xanthakis-Karmanos 1980: 10–11; cf. Aristotle, *Poetics* 1456a29–32). The clear influences of Old Comedy and classical tragedy alike have led scholars to write of Menandrian New Comedy as having a "dual parentage" (Arnott 1986: 1) or even as a "hybrid genre" (Petrides 2010, 107).

Ancient critics, too, saw precursors of New Comedy in both Euripides and Aristophanes (see especially Nesselrath 1993). The ancient *Life* of Aristophanes claims that "Menander and Philemon took their starting points" from Aristophanes's *Cocalus* (lines 5–7), the play which first "introduced seduction and recognition and all the other sorts of things on which Menander was keen" (54–55); Satyrus, on the other hand, credited Euripides with developing New Comic devices "to perfection" (F6 fr. 39.7 Schorn; cf. section ii above). In Menander's *Epitrepontes*, a coal-maker involved in a dispute about the "recognition tokens" left with a baby foregrounds the "tragic" nature

---

[7] The former are surveyed by Cusset 2003: 133–162; examples of the latter occur at Diphilus, *Synoris* K-A fr. 74; *Parasite* K-A fr. 6; and Philemon (uncertain play) K-A fr. 118.

of his own plotline: he enjoins Smicrines to decide the dispute on the basis of tragic precedent ("You've seen tragedies, I know, and you understand all of this," 325–326; cf. Gutzwiller 2000: 111–112; on the scene—which may have Euripides's lost *Alope* as a model—see Katsouris 1975: 143–156; Scafuro 1997: 154–161; Cusset 2003: 168–187). The combination in Menander of tragic influences and storylines ending in marriage and celebration also implies debt to satyr play, which is further suggested by the echoes of Aeschylus's *Diktyoulkoi* and Sophocles's *Ichneutai* in Diphilus's *Epitrope* and Menander's *Synaristosae*, respectively (cf. section iii above).

Menander's comedies thus actively alluded to tragedy by appropriating tragic plots, characterization, and devices, as well as by engaging in extended intertextual reference. For example, the messenger scene in *Sikyonios* owes much to the Eleusinian messenger's speech in Euripides's *Orestes*. In both plays, the messenger reports an assembly's decision about the fate of important characters (a sentence of death for Orestes and Electra and a declaration of citizenship for Philumene), and the Menandrian speech contains a number of verbal and structural echoes of the tragic messenger's lines (see especially Katsouris 1975: 28–54 and Cusset 2003: 201–210). On the other hand, in the *Samia* a series of events leads Demeas to suspect that a kind of *Hippolytus* plot is unfolding within his own household (a "*malentendu tragique*": so Cusset 2003: 165): Demeas mistakenly thinks that his mistress has given birth to a child by his own son. The scene of confrontation between Demeas and Moschion (*Samia* 452–538) closely resembles the Euripidean exchange between Theseus and Hippolytus (*Hipp.* 902–1101; on the tragic parallels see especially West 1991 and Sommerstein forthcoming). Both *Sikyonios* and *Samia* may thus gesture to well-known tragic plots so as to enhance the suspense that precedes the averted crises: in the alternate world of tragedy, these plays would hardly have ended on notes of celebration. Recently, Petrides has also emphasized that Menander's allusions to classical tragedy would also have had a visual dimension. The opening scene of *Perikeiromene*, for example, in which a mournful Glycera appears onstage with her (newly shorn) hair concealed, may have activated a "funereal" atmosphere for the spectator who recalled the similar tableau in Aeschylus's *Niobe* (2010, 79–82).

In Aristophanes, pseudo-tragic structures and diction did not always signal a particular tragic reference; likewise, Menander's "tragic" borrowings and allusions do not in every instance point to a specific play. And although such "domestic" tragedies as *Helen* and *Ion* do seem to presage the rapes, childbirths, and recognition scenes that became foundational New Comic plots, it is difficult to say to what extent these kinds of devices were regarded as "Euripidean" (on developments and trends in fourth-century tragedy, see especially Xanthakis-Karamanos 1980: 6–18; cf. Easterling 1993). Webster observed that "Menander's recognition scenes make such a good commentary on Aristotle's chapter in the *Poetics* [i.e., ch. 16] that the conclusion is inevitable that Menander knew the Aristotelian classification" (Webster 1974: 59), and it is certainly possible that by Menander's era "recognition" had come to be regarded as a characteristically dramatic, rather than specifically comic or tragic, plot type. Nevertheless, Menander's comedies reveal great variety and creativity in their engagement with classical plays, and his inspiration on this score likely derived both from his spectatorship at tragic revivals and his personal study of earlier dramatic texts. Certainly, admiration for those texts motivates many of the allusions to them within Menander's works: by the close of the fourth century, Euripides was a revered classical author and dramatic predecessor rather than a fellow citizen whose eccentric habits and avant-garde drama all but invited satire.

FURTHER READING

On the ancient genre-markers of comedy, see especially Csapo 2000, Silk 2002 (especially ch. 2: "Comedy and Tragedy"), Platter 2007, and Konstan forthcoming; on genre and classical tragedy, see Most 2000 and Mastronarde 2000 and Mastronarde 2010, ch. 2: "Problems of Genre." Recent overviews of the interaction between the fifth-century Athenian dramatic genres include Taplin 1986 and Taplin 1996, Rosen 2005, Seidensticker 2005 (which also discusses dithyramb), Lowe 2007: 23–29, and Foley 2008. The only full-length study of Aristophanic paratragedy is Rau 1967 (Silk 1993 makes a programmatic distinction between paratragedy and tragic parody). Seidensticker 1982 remains the most extensive single study of comic elements in tragedy; along similar lines, there is also the collection Medda et al. 2006. For the genre of satyr play, see the edited volume Harrison 2005 and recent work by Griffith (e.g. Griffith 2005a, Griffith 2005b, Griffith 2008, Griffith 2010); Krumeich et al. 1999 is the most comprehensive edition of satyr fragments and also contains an extensive introduction to the genre. The influence of classical tragedy (and particularly Euripides) on Menander has been one of the dominant threads of scholarship on New Comedy; the most extensive treatments are Cusset 2003 (which also discusses tragic and theatrical allusion in Middle Comedy) and Katsouris 1975.

BIBLIOGRAPHY

Arnott, W. G. 1986. "Menander and Earlier Drama." In *Studies in Honour of T. B. L. Webster, Volume 1*, edited by J. H. Betts, J. T. Hooker, and J. R. Green, 1–9. Bristol: Bristol Classical Press.

Austin, C., and S. D. Olson, eds. 1994. *Aristophanes: Thesmophoriazusae*. Oxford; New York: Oxford University Press.

Bain, D. 1977. *Actors and Audience: A Study of Asides and Related Conventions in Greek Drama*. Oxford: Oxford University Press.

Bakola, E. 2005. "Old Comedy Disguised as Satyr Play: A New Reading of Cratinus' *Dionysalexandros* (P.Oxy 663)." *Zeitschrift für Papyrologie und Epigraphik* 154: 46–58.

———. 2010. *Cratinus and the Art of Comedy*. Oxford and New York: Oxford University Press.

Collard, C., M. Cropp, and K. H. Lee, eds. 2005. *Euripides: Selected Fragmentary Plays, Volume 1*. Warminster, UK: Aris and Phillips.

Csapo, E. 2000. "From Aristophanes to Menander? Genre Transformation in Greek Comedy." In *Matrices of Genre: Authors, Canons, and Society*, edited by M. Depew and D. Obbink, 115–133. Cambridge, MA: Harvard University Press.

Csapo, E., and M. C. Miller, eds. 2007. *The Origins of the Theater in Ancient Greece and Beyond: From Ritual to Drama*. Cambridge, UK: Cambridge University Press.

Csapo, E., and W. J. Slater, eds. 1995. *The Context of Ancient Drama*. Ann Arbor: University of Michigan Press.

Cusset, C. 2003. *Ménandre ou la Comédie Tragique*. Paris: CNRS Editions.

Dover, K. J. 1993. "The Contest in Aristophanes' *Frogs*: The Points at Issue." In *Tragedy, Comedy, and the Polis*, edited by A. H. Sommerstein, et al., 445–460. Bari: Levante Editori.

Dunn, F. M. 1996. *Tragedy's End: Closure and Innovation in Euripidean Drama*. New York: Oxford University Press.

Easterling, P. E. 1993. "The end of an Era? Tragedy in the Early Fourth Century." In *Tragedy, comedy, and the polis*, Papers from the Greek Drama Conference, Nottingham, 18–20 July 1990, edited by A. H. Sommerstein [et al.], 559–569. Bari: Levante ed.

Foley, H. P. 1993. "Tragedy and Politics in Aristophanes' *Acharnians*." In *Theater and Society in the Classical World*, edited by R, Scodel, 119–138. Ann Arbor: University of Michigan Press.

——. 2008. "Generic Boundaries in Late Fifth-Century Athens." In *Performance, Iconography, Reception: Studies in Honour of Oliver Taplin*, edited by M. Revermann and P. Wilson, 15–36. Oxford: Oxford University Press.

Goldhill, S. 1987. "The Great Dionysia and Civic Ideology." *The Journal of Hellenic Studies* 107: 58–76.

——. 2006. "The Thrill of Misplaced Laughter." In *Κωμῳδοτραγῳδία: Intersezioni del tragico e del comico nel teatro del V secolo a.C.*, edited by E. Medda, M. S. Mirto, and M. P. Pattoni, 83–102. Pisa: Edizioni della Normale.

Gregory, J. 1999. *Euripides, Hecuba: Introduction, Text, and Commentary*. Atlanta: Scholars Press.

——. 2000. "Comic Elements in Euripides." In *Euripides and Tragic Theatre in the Late Fifth Century*, edited by M. Cropp, K. Lee, and D. Sansone, 59–74 [= *Illinois Classical Studies* 24–25 (1999–2000)]. Champaign, IL: Stipes.

Griffith, M. 2002. "Slaves of Dionysos: Satyrs, Audience, and the Ends of the *Oresteia*." *Classical Antiquity* 21: 195–258.

——. 2005a. "Sophocles' Satyr-Plays and the Language of Romance." In *Sophocles and the Greek Language*, edited by I. J. F. De Jong and A. Rijksbaron, 51–72. Leiden and Boston: Brill.

——. 2005b. "Satyrs, Citizens, and Self-Representation." In *Satyr Drama: Tragedy at Play*, edited by G. W. M. Harrison, 161–199. Swansea: Classical Press of Wales.

——. 2008. "Greek Middlebrow Drama: Something to Do with Aphrodite?" In *Performance, Iconography, Reception: Studies in Honour of Oliver Taplin*, edited by M. Revermann and P. Wilson, 59–87. Oxford: Oxford University Press.

——. 2010. "Satyr Play and Tragedy, Face to Face." In *The Pronomos Vase and Its Context*, edited by O. Taplin and R. Wyles, 47–64. Oxford, Oxford University Press.

Guidorizzi, G. 2006. "Mito e commedia: Il caso di Cratino." In *Κωμῳδοτραγῳδία: Intersezioni del tragico e del comico nel teatro del V secolo a.C.*, edited by E. Medda, M. S. Mirto, and M. P. Pattoni, 119–135. Pisa: Edizioni della Normale.

Gutzwiller, K. 2000. "The Mask of Comedy: Metatheatricality in Menander." *Classical Antiquity* 19: 102–137.

Hall, E. 1998. "Ithyphallic Males Behaving Badly; or, Satyr Drama as Gendered Tragic Ending." In *Parchments of Gender: Deciphering the Body in Antiquity*, edited by M. Wyke, 13–37. Oxford: Clarendon Press.

——. 2006. "Horny Satyrs and Tragic Tetralogies." In *The Theatrical Cast of Athens: Interactions between Greek Drama and Society*, by E. Hall, 142–169. Oxford: Oxford University Press.

——. 2007. "Greek Tragedy 430–380 BC." In *Debating the Athenian Cultural Revolution*, edited by R, Osborne, 264–287. Cambridge, UK: Cambridge University Press.

Handley, E. W. 1969. "The Conventions of the Comic Stage and Their Exploitation by Menander." In *Ménandre: Sept exposés suivis de discussions*, edited by E. G. Turner, 1–42. Vandoeuvres-Geneva: Fondation Hardt.

Harrison, G. W. M., ed. 2005. *Satyr Drama: Tragedy at Play*. Swansea: Classical Press of Wales.

Heath, M. 1987. "Euripides' *Telephus*." *Classical Quarterly* 37: 272–280.

Henrichs, A. 1994–1995. "Why Should I Dance? Choral Self-Referentiality in Greek Tragedy." *Arion* 3: 56–111.

Herington, C. J. 1963. "The Influence of Comedy on Aeschylus' Later Trilogies." *Transactions of the American Philological Association* 94: 113–125.

Hunter, R. 1979. "The Comic Chorus in the Fourth Century." *Zeitschrift für Papyrologie und Epigraphik* 36: 23–38.

——. 2009. *Critical Moments in Classical Literature: Studies in the Ancient View of Literature and its Uses*. Cambridge, UK: Cambridge University Press.

Kaibel, G. 1899. *Comicorum Graecorum Fragmenta*. Berlin: Weidmann.

Katsouris, A. G. 1975. *Tragic Patterns in Menander*. Athens: Hellenistic Society for Humanistic Studies.

Kirkpatrick, J., and F. M. Dunn. 2002. "Heracles, Cercopes, and Paracomedy." *Transactions of the American Philological Association* 132: 29–61.

Knox, B. 1979. "Euripidean Comedy." In *Word and Action: Essays on the Ancient Theater*, by B. Knox, 250–274. Baltimore: Johns Hopkins University Press.

Konstan, D. Forthcoming. "Defining the Genre." In *The Cambridge Companion to Greek Comedy*, edited by M. Revermann. Cambridge, UK: Cambridge University Press.

Krumeich, R., N. Pechstein, and B. Seidensticker, eds. 1999. *Das griechische Satyrspiel*. Darmstadt: Wissenschaftliche Buchgesellschaft.

Lazarus, B. M. 2005. "Parodies and Breakdowns in Euripides' 'More Comic' Orestes." *Iris* 18: 2–12. Available online at http://classics-archaeology.unimelb.edu.au/CAV/iris/volume18/lazarus.pdf.

Lowe, N. J. 2007. *Comedy*. New Surveys in the Classics 37. Cambridge, UK: Cambridge University Press.

MacDowell, D. M. 1994. "The Number of Speaking Actors in Old Comedy." *The Classical Quarterly* 44: 325–335.

Mastronarde, D. J. 1994. *Euripides: Phoenissae*. Cambridge, UK: Cambridge University Press.

——. 2000. "Euripidean Tragedy and Genre: The Terminology and Its Problems." In *Euripides and Tragic Theatre in the Late Fifth Century*, edited by M. Cropp, K. Lee, and D. Sansone, 17–39. Champaign, IL: Stipes.

——. 2010. *The Art of Euripides*. Cambridge, UK: Cambridge University Press.

Medda, E., M. S. Mirto, and M. P. Pattoni, eds. 2006. Κωμωιδοτραγωιδία: *Intersezioni del tragico e del comico nel teatro del V secolo a.C.* Pisa: Edizioni della Normale.

Miles, S. 2009. "Strattis, Comedy, and Tragedy." PhD diss., University of Nottingham. Available online at http://etheses.nottingham.ac.uk/887/1/Miles-phd-ethesis-Strattis.pdf.

Most, G. W. 2000. "Generating Genres: The Idea of the Tragic." In *Matrices of Genre: Authors, Canons, and Society*, edited by M. Depew and D. Obbink, 15–35. Cambridge, MA: Harvard University Press.

Nesselrath, H.-G. 1993. "Parody and Later Greek Comedy." *Harvard Studies in Classical Philology* 95: 181–195.

Olson, S. D., ed. and trans. 2006–2011. *Athenaeus: The Learned Banqueters*. 7 vols. Cambridge, MA: Harvard University Press.

Petrides, A. K. 2010. "New Performance." In *New Perspectives on Postclassical Comedy*, edited by A. K. Petrides and S. Papaioannou, 79–124. Newcastle upon Tyne: Cambridge Scholars Press.

Pickard-Cambridge, A. 1988. *The Dramatic Festivals of Athens*. 2nd ed. Revised by J. Gould and D. M. Lewis. Oxford: Clarendon Press (referred to as *DFA*²).

Platter, C. 2007. *Aristophanes and the Carnival of Genres*. Baltimore: Johns Hopkins University Press.

Podlecki, A. J. 2005. "Aiskhylos Satyrikos." In *Satyr Drama: Tragedy at Play*, edited by G. W. M. Harrison, 1–20. Swansea: Classical Press of Wales.

Rau, P. 1967. *Paratragodia: Untersuchung einer komischen Form des Aristophanes (Zetemata 45)*. Munich: Beck.

Revermann, M. 2006a. *Comic Business: Theatricality, Dramatic Technique, and Performance Contexts of Aristophanic Comedy*. Oxford: Oxford University Press.

——. 2006b. "The Competence of Theatre Audiences in Fifth- and Fourth-Century Athens." *The Journal of Hellenic Studies* 126: 99–124.

Roselli, D. K. 2011. *Theater of the People: Spectator and Society in Athens*. Austin: University of Texas Press.

Rosen, R. 2006. "Aristophanes, Old Comedy and Greek Tragedy." In *The Blackwell Companion to Tragedy*, edited by R, Bushnell, 251–268. Oxford: Blackwell.

Rothwell, K.S. 1992. 'The Continuity of the Chorus in Fourth-Century Attic Comedy,' pp. 99-118 in G.W. Dobrov, ed., *Beyond Aristophanes. Transition and Diversity in Greek Comedy*, Atlanta, Georgia.

Sandbach, F. H. 1975. "Menander and the Three-Actor Rule." In *Le monde grec: Pensée, littérature, histoire, documents: Hommages à Claire Préaux*, edited by J. Bingen, G. Cambier, and G. Nachtergael, 197–204. Brussels: Éditions de l'Université de Bruxelles.

Scafuro, A, C. 1997. *The Forensic Stage: Settling Disputes in Graeco-Roman New Comedy*. Cambridge, UK: Cambridge University Press.

Scharffenberger, E. W. 1995. "A Tragic Lysistrata? Jocasta in the 'Reconciliation Scene' of the *Phoenician Women*." *Rheinisches Museum* 138: 312–336.

——. 1996. "Euripidean 'Paracomedy': A Re-consideration of the *Antiope*." *Text and Presentation* 17: 65–72.

Seidensticker, B. 1978. "Comic Elements in Euripides' *Bacchae*." *The American Journal of Philology* 99: 303–320.

——. 1982. *Palintonos Harmonia: Studien zu komischen Elementen in der griechischen Tragödie*. Göttingen: Vandenhoeck & Ruprecht.

——. 2003. "The Chorus of Greek Satyr Play." In *Poetry, Theory, Praxis: The Social Life of Myth, Word and Image in Ancient Greece: Essays in Honour of William J. Slater*, edited by E. Csapo and M. C. Miller, 100–121. Cambridge, UK: Cambridge University Press.

——. 2005. "Dithyramb, Comedy, and Satyr-Play." In *A Companion to Greek Tragedy*, edited by J. Gregory, 38–54. Oxford: Blackwell.

Shear, J. 2011. *Polis and Revolution: Responding to Oligarchy in Classical Athens*. Cambridge, UK: Cambridge University Press.

Sifakis, G. M. 1992. "The Structure of Aristophanic Comedy." *The Journal of Hellenic Studies* 112: 123–142.

Silk, M. S. 1993. "Aristophanic Paratragedy." In *Tragedy, Comedy, and the Polis*, edited by Alan H. Sommerstein et al., 477–504. Bari: Levante Editori.

——. 2002. *Aristophanes and the Definition of Comedy*. Oxford and New York: Oxford University Press.

Slater, N. W. 1985. "Play and Playwright References in Middle Comedy." *Liverpool Classical Monthly* 10: 103–105.

——. 2005. "Nothing to Do with Satyrs? *Alcestis* and the Concept of Prosatyric Drama." In *Satyr Drama: Tragedy at Play*, edited by G. W. M. Harrison, 83–101. Swansea: Classical Press of Wales.

Sommerstein, A. H., ed. and trans. 1973. *Aristophanes: Lysistrata; The Acharnians; The Clouds.* London: Penguin.

——. 2002. "Comic Elements in Tragic Language: The Case of Aeschylus' *Oresteia*." In *The Language of Greek Comedy*, edited by A. Willi, 151–168. Oxford: Oxford University Press.

——.2014. "Menander's *Samia* and the Phaedra Theme." In *Ancient Comedy and Reception: Essays in Honor of Jeffrey Henderson*, edited by S. D. Olson. Berlin and Boston: de Gruyter.

Storey, I. C. 2005. "But Comedy Has Satyrs Too." In *Satyr Drama: Tragedy at Play*, edited by G. W. M. Harrison, 201–218. Swansea: Classical Press of Wales.

Süss, W. 1935. "Nochmals zur *Cistellaria* des Plautus." *Rheinisches Museum* 87: 97–141.

Sutton, D. F. 1973. "Satyric Elements in the *Alcestis*." *Rivista di Studi Classici* 21: 384–391.

——. 1978. "Aeschylus' *Dictyulci* and Diphilus' *Epitrope*." *The Classical Journal* 74: 22–25.

——. 1987. "The Theatrical Families of Athens." *The American Journal of Philology* 108: 9–26.

Tammaro, V. 2006. "Poeti tragici come personaggi comici in Aristofane." In *Κωμωιδοτραγωιδία: Intersezioni del tragico e del comico nel teatro del V secolo a.C.*, edited by E. Medda, M. S. Mirto, and M. P. Pattoni, 249–262. Pisa: Edizioni della Normale.

Taplin, O. 1983. "Tragedy and Trugedy." *Classical Quarterly* 33: 331–333.

——. 1986. "Fifth-Century Tragedy and Comedy: A *Synkrisis*." *The Journal of Hellenic Studies* 106: 163–174.

——. 1996. "Comedy and the Tragic." In *Tragedy and the Tragic: Greek Theatre and Beyond*, edited by M. S. Silk, 188–202. Oxford: Clarendon Press.

Teló, M. 2007. *Eupolidis Demi.* Florence: F. Le Monnier.

Torrance, I. 2011. "In the Footprints of Aeschylus: Recognition, Allusion, and Metapoetics in Euripides." *The American Journal of Philology* 132: 177–204.

Webster, T. B. L. 1974. *An Introduction to Menander.* Manchester: Manchester University Press.

West, S. 1991. "Notes on the *Samia*." *Zeitschrift für Papyrologie und Epigraphik* 88: 11–23.

Wyles, R. 2010. "The Tragic Costumes." In *The Pronomos Vase and Its Context*, edited by O. Taplin and R. Wyles, 231–253. Oxford, Oxford University Press.

Xanthakis-Karamanos, G. 1980. *Studies in Fourth-Century Tragedy.* Athens: Akademia Athenon.

Zagagi, N. 1999. "Comic Patterns in Sophocles' *Ichneutae*." In *Sophocles Revisited: Essays Presented to Sir Hugh Lloyd-Jones*, edited by J. Griffin, 177–218. Oxford: Oxford University Press.

Zanetto, G. 2006. "*Tragodìa* versus *Trugodìa*: La rivalità letteraria." In *Κωμωιδοτραγωιδία: Intersezioni del tragico e del comico nel teatro del V secolo a.C.*, edited by E. Medda, M. S. Mirto, and M. P. Pattoni, 307–326. Pisa: Edizioni della Normale.

Zeitlin, F. I. 1980. "The Closet of Masks: Role-Playing and Myth-Making in the *Orestes* of Euripides." *Ramus* 9: 51–77.

——. 1981. "Travesties of Gender and Genre in Aristophanes' *Thesmophoriazusae*." *Critical Inquiry* 8: 301–327.

Zimmermann, B. 1989. "Gattungmischung, Manierismus, Archaismus." *Lexis* 3: 25–36.

——. 2006. "*Pathei mathos*: Strutture tragiche nelle *Nuvole* di Aristofane." In *Κωμωιδοτραγωιδία: Intersezioni del tragico e del comico nel teatro del V secolo a.C.*, edited by E. Medda, M. S. Mirto, and M. P. Pattoni, 327–336. Pisa: Edizioni della Normale.

CHAPTER 13

CROSSING CONCEPTUAL WORLDS: GREEK COMEDY AND PHILOSOPHY

DAVID KONSTAN

"That the comedy of those like Cratinus, Aristophanes and Eupolis is politics and philosophy in the form of dramas, who can dispute? This kind of comedy engages in philosophy on the pretext of laughter." ([Dionysius of Halicarnassus], *Rhetoric* 8.11)

THERE is something naturally funny about philosophy, or at least about philosophers, and this makes them an especially fit subject for satire and comedy. Classical philosophy in particular was susceptible to such caricature, since it did not limit itself to abstract questions of logic or metaphysics but purported to serve as a guide to life and investigated such areas as psychology, ethics, politics, and religion. In this respect, it was as vulnerable to send-up as psychoanalysis is in our day, and contradictions between the ostensible comportment of philosophers and the doctrines they preached were fair game for comedians, along with ridicule of pretentiousness, wild utopian schemes, and scientific gobbledygook. Nevertheless, characters in comedy often assume a philosophical pose and pronounce lofty opinions on morals, education, and the human condition that have their source, sometimes explicitly mentioned, in the doctrines of one or another philosophical school. Philosophers, for their part, tended to be suspicious of comic frivolity, and yet they also had an indirect and subtly positive influence on comedy, since their reflections on human nature and the trajectory of our lives helped to shape the way comic poets portrayed character and fashioned their plots. A case can be made, for example, for parallels between the evolution of comedy from Old to New and the innovations in philosophy inaugurated by Aristotle and the Hellenistic schools.

Among the thousands of Greek and Roman comedies that have been wholly lost or are known to us only through indirect mentions or occasional quotations, a great many touched on philosophical themes. It is inevitable to begin with the one surviving comedy in this genre—Aristophanes's parody of Socrates's teachings in the *Clouds*, which, according to Plato (*Apology* 19C), contributed to the prejudice that led to his execution almost twenty years later—but it is salutary to recall that at the same festival at which this play was produced (in 423), Ameipsias, one of Aristophanes's rivals, staged a comedy entitled *Connus* (K-A fr. 7-11) in which he too made fun of Socrates, who must have done something to attract attention around that time (Athenaeus 5.218C reports that this play had a chorus of thinkers that did not include Protagoras, though he did figure in Eupolis's *Toadies*, produced two years later in 421). What is more, Eupolis, an older contemporary of Aristophanes, wrote a comedy in which a character declares: "I hate Socrates, the babbling beggar, who theorizes about everything else but neglects to think where he can get a meal," and either he or someone else (presumably in this same play) says: "But teach him to babble, you sophist you" (K-A fr. 386, 388). It is likely that Plato's *Phaedo* (70C), in which Socrates says, "I do not think that anyone who hears me now— even if he should be a comic poet—will claim that I am babbling and making speeches about irrelevant matters," refers to this play.[1]

Aristophanes's *Clouds* provides abundant examples of ridicule. Socrates is represented as running a school (called the *phrontisterion*, "Theory-House" or, in local Attic parlance, more like "Worry-Joint"), where his disciples carry on ostensibly secret research on how far a flea can jump in proportion to its size and whether gnats make noise with their mouths or anuses, along with investigations into the nether earth, the heavens (Socrates appears suspended in a swing, to get a better view), and geometry, so as to map and measure the world. It is unlikely that Socrates himself indulged in this kind of speculation, but he is a convenient figure on which to pin and lampoon the explorations into natural science that were pursued by some of his contemporaries (sometimes paradoxically referred to as "pre-Socratics"), such as Diogenes of Apollonia, who was especially interested in meteorology (fragments 3-5 Diels-Kranz); Hippo of Elis; the geometer Meton; Anaxagoras, who argued that the sun was really a stone about the size of the Peloponnesus; and Diagoras of Melos, who was widely regarded as an atheist. Socrates is also represented as interested in exotic questions about grammar (what's the masculine for "chicken"?), reminiscent of Protagoras's pursuits. These are the kind of abstruse and useless topics that lend themselves readily to spoof and even derision, since they were not seen as entirely harmless: scientific cosmology might appear to conflict with traditional religious beliefs (see Konstan 2011).

Aristophanes was not alone in mocking such inquiries. The scholia on Aristophanes *Clouds* (96) inform us that Cratinus, in his comedy *All-Seers* (*Panoptai*, K-A fr. 167), had ridiculed Hippo of Elis for comparing the sky to the lid of a pot. Diogenes Laertius (3.26)

---

[1] Two fourth-century dialogues, Plato's *Protagoras* and Xenophon's *Symposium*, are said to have taken their respective historical frames from the *Toadies* and *Autolycus* of Eupolis (Athenaeus 5.216C–D, 218B). All translations of the fragments of Greek comedy, and testimonies relating to the fragments, are taken from Rusten 2011. Other translations of Menander are my own.

reports that the comic poet Theopompus (late fifth–early fourth century), in *Pleasure Seeker* (*Hedychares*, K-A fr. 16), satirized Plato as follows: "For one is not even one, and in fact two are scarcely one, as Plato says." The reference is no doubt to Plato's *Phaedo* (96E), where Socrates says: "Since I don't accept that when someone adds one to one anything becomes two, neither the one to which it was added, nor the one which was added to it, not the one added and the one to which it was added because of the addition of one to the other." This sounds just enough like double-talk to invite parody. The comic exploitation of such conundrums goes back to the Sicilian Epicharmus, one of the earliest comic poets of whom we have any knowledge, who toyed with them enough to have inspired a collection of philosophical adages that circulated under his name (compare the "Sentences" attributed to Menander, and partly culled from his plays). An example is his use of the paradox that was sometimes labeled "Theseus's Ship" (first described in Plutarch's *Life of Theseus* 22–23): that is, if all the constituents of a thing have been replaced over time, then it is no longer the same object. A fragment of a papyrus commentary on Plato's *Theaetetus* (152E; P. Berlin 9782, second c. CE = Epicharmus K-A fr. 136) reports: "He also made it into a joke about a man who was asked to make a payment and claimed he wasn't the same man, because some parts were subsequent arrivals, and some had departed, and when the collector beat him and was charged with it, the other in turn claimed that the man who had done the beating and the defendant were different people." Strepsiades in Aristophanes's *Clouds* employs much the same kind of sophistry in attempting to evade his debts. The comic poet Alexis (fourth–third c. BCE) particularly enjoyed poking fun at the obscurantism of the philosophers, as in his *Ancylion* (fr. 1, cited in Diogenes Laertius 3.27): "You're talking about things you don't understand. Run off to Plato and learn about carbonate of soda and onions"; so too Amphis, in his *Amphicrates* (K-A fr. 6, quoted in Diogenes Laertius 3.27), writes: "As to the good that you say you are going to enjoy because of her, master, I'm not any more sure about it than I am about the Platonic good"; and in Philemon's *Pyrrhus* (quoted in Stobaeus 4.14.5), someone proclaims: "Philosophers investigate it, so I've heard, and they spend a lot of time on it—what 'good' is; but no one has yet discovered what it is. They say it's virtue and wisdom, and they spin out everything except what the good is. I, busy in my field and digging the earth, have now discovered it: it's peace"). In another fragment of Alexis (*Himilco*, K-A fr. 98, quoted in Athenaeus 8.354D), a character defends his willingness to dine on cold food by affirming: "Plato says that the good is good everywhere, see? And the sweet is just as sweet both here and there." A rather lengthy passage from the poet Epicrates (K-A fr. 10; fourth c.) has been preserved by Athenaeus (epitome) 2.59D:

> (A) What about Plato and Speusippus and Menedemus?
> What are they spending time on now?
> What thought, what discourse undergoes their scrutiny?
> Explain these things wisely to me,
> by the Earth, if you know anything. []
> (B) Well, I know how to talk clearly of these things,
> for at the Panathenaea, when I saw a herd
> [] of youths

at the gymnasium of the Academy,
I heard ineffable, extraordinary talk.
For in making definitions about nature
they differentiated the life of animals
and the nature of trees and the genuses of vegetables.
And at this point they enquired into
the genus of the pumpkin.
(A)However did they define it and the genus
of the plant? Reveal it, if you know anything.
(B)Well, first of all they all stood speechless
and, bowing their heads,
they cogitated for some time.
Then suddenly while the lads
were still nodding and thinking,
one said it was a round vegetable,
another a grass, and another a tree.
A Sicilian doctor,
when he heard these things,
farted at them as fools.
(A)Were they terribly angry?
Did they complain about being mocked?
†That's the fitting thing to do in such discussions.
(B)It didn't bother these boys.
Plato was there and, not at all upset, quite gently
instructed them again []
to define the genus,
and they determined it.

The same sort of take-off on the fussy overprecision of philosophers is evident in the following excerpt too, from Damoxenus's *The Foster Brothers* (K-A fr. 2, quoted by Athenaeus 3.101F; fourth–third c.), although there are new features at work here as well; I take the liberty of quoting it at length (with a few omissions):

(A)You see in me a student
of the intellectual Epicurus, with whom
in less than two years and ten months
I consolidated four talents.
(B)What does that mean? Tell me. (A) Holy offerings.
He was a cook too — although perhaps he didn't know it.
(B)What do you mean, a cook? (A) Nature is
the chief conceiver of every art...
(B)"chief conceiver," eh? You criminal!
(A)Nothing is more intellectual than labor,
and the task was easy for one who was practiced
in this field: much is done by deduction.
That is why whenever you see a cook
who hasn't read all of Democritus,

and the *Canon* of Epicurus, tell him
"Beat it, shit-face." He's not part of the school.
You have to know first, my good man, how a baby shark
differs from summer to winter; then recognize
when the Pleiad sets, or at the solstice,
what sort of seafood is appropriate....
But who follows these precepts? The indigestion
and flatulence that result may cause the guest
considerable embarrassment. But the edibles served by me
are nourishing and digestible, and he does his exhaling
out the right end. The result is that the humors are mixed
homogeneously into the arteries.
(B)Humors? (A) Democritus says so; and blockages
don't occur to induce gout in the customer.
(B)You seem to have some medical training also.
(A)So does everyone who is involved with Nature!
As for today's cooks, just observe how ignorant they are:
When you see them making a combined stock
from fish that are at odds with each other —
even rubbing sesame into it! Then you should take
every last one of them and fart in their faces. (B) I should?
You're putting me on! (A) What good can come
when the individuality of one is mingled with another
and weaves into it touches of discord?
It's not washing plates or stinking of soot
that is the goal of our innate art, but understanding this.
You see, I never work at the oven.
(B)But why not? (A) I sit nearby and observe;
others perform the labor. (B) What do *you* do? (A) I expound
causes and effect: "Ease up, the base is sharp."
(B)He's a maestro, not a cook! (A) "Get moving, the flame needs
a more even tempo. The first casserole
isn't cooking in tune with the next ones." You see
what I mean? (B) Good God! (A) And it looks like an art?
Besides, I serve no food without due deliberation, you see,
but all in a harmonious blend.
(B)How does that work? (A) Some of them
are major combinations, some minor, some diminished.
I distribute them at the right intervals,
interweave them right into different courses....
That is how Epicurus consolidated pleasure:
he masticated carefully—he alone realized
what "the highest good" is. The boys in the Stoa are still
looking, but they don't have a clue. Therefore, what
they don't possess, and don't apprehend, they couldn't
communicate to another. (B) I agree with you.
So let's skip the rest; it's long been obvious....

The *Canon* of Epicurus was his work on logic, or more precisely, on inference; the mixing of humors recalls Hippocratic medicine, but is here ascribed to Democritus; the language of musical harmony reflects Pythagorean ideas, among others.[2] That it is a cook who expounds these ideas makes the dialogue all the more amusing, since his is a relatively humble profession (though not without a certain social esteem); the pseudo-philosophical patter is exploited to make fun of his pretentions to high art. There is one further point to notice: by invoking Epicurus (and Democritus, who was in large measure the inspiration for Epicureanism), the cook is aligning himself not just with any philosophical school, but with the one that preached pleasure as the goal of human life. This is a new wrinkle, one which entered comedy only in the Hellenistic period, when Epicurus and some other thinkers turned their backs on the Socratic preoccupation with virtue, inherited by both Plato and Aristotle and after them by the Stoics, and openly proclaimed pleasure as the end (though not necessarily in the way the comic poets travestied their views). It chimed perfectly with the rise to prominence of the figure of the cook in Middle and New Comedy. Thus, in Hegesippus's *Loyal Comrades* (K-A fr. 2, quoted in Athenaeus 7.279D), someone remarks that "Epicurus the wise was once asked by someone to tell him what was the good, that people constantly seek: his reply was, 'pleasure.' Well done, you wisest and best of men! You see, there is no greater good than eating; and the good is an attribute of pleasure." Even Plato, with a bit of sophistry, could be roped into expressing a comparable ideal; thus, in Philippides's *Rejuvenatrix* (K-A fr. 6, quoted in Stobaeus 4.22), a character affirms: "I told you not to marry, but rather live in pleasure. This is the Platonic good, Pheidylus: not to take a wife, nor to expose oneself to fortune amid countless dangers."

Comedy went with the times, as comedy must, and changed its targets as new currents of thought emerged. The Epicurean emphasis on pleasure was naturally congenial to the spirit of comedy, with its delight in the bodily functions (as Bakhtin has observed). The comic poet Baton (middle of the third century), known for his put-downs of philosophers, writes in his play *Man-Killer* (K-A fr. 3, quoted by Athenaeus 7.279C):

> . . . when he could have been at dinner with a beautiful woman
> and taken two potfuls of wine from Lesbos.
> Now *this* is your man of sense, *this* is "the good."
> Everything I'm saying to you is what Epicurus said:
> if everyone lived the kind of life I do,
> there wouldn't be a single bad man or adulterer.[3]

---

[2] On this passage, see Belardinelli 2008: 77–79, 82–86, 89–92; for the art of cooking as a kind of science, see pp. 77–81, with a discussion of related treatments of cooks in New Comedy (continued on pp. 87–89). Contrary to Dohm 1964, Belardinelli sees in Damoxenus's treatment a critique of philosophy alone, and not of related *tekhnai* such as music and medicine; in this, New Comedy is said to differ from Old (on which, see pp. 92–102).

[3] Plutarch, *How to Tell a Flatterer from a Friend* (55C) reports: "When Baton had composed a line against Cleanthes [successor to Zeno as head of the Stoic school] in a comedy, Arcesilaus forbade him entry to his school, but once Baton had repented and made up with Cleanthes, Arcesilaus was reconciled."

Contrast the self-defense of the misanthrope Cnemon in Menander's *Grouch* (*Dyskolos*), who argues rather that the world would be a better place if everyone practiced his kind of austerity. Alexis, in his play, *PhD in Profligacy* (*Asotodidaskalos*, K-A fr. 25, quoted in Athenaeus 8.336B; possibly not by Alexis), has a slave named Xanthias speak to his fellow slaves as follows:

> You idiot, why are you blithering back and forth
> about the Lyceum, the Academy, the gates of the Odeon,
> all philosophers' drivel? There's not one good thing in them.
> Let's drink, drink deep, Sicon, my friend,
> let's enjoy ourselves, as long as there's breath in us.
> Raise a ruckus, Manes: there's no sweeter pleasure than the belly.
> That alone's your father and your mother too.
> Accomplishments like embassies and generalships
> ring like hollow boasts, like dreams.
> Fate will chill you out at the destined time.
> All you'll take with you is what you eat and drink:
> the rest is dust, including Pericles, Codrus, and Cimon.

But even if the association between philosophy and pleasure received a particular impetus with the emergence of Epicureanism, Socrates himself could be seen as advocating selfish pleasures, since his critical cross-examinations of his contemporaries and his conviction that he knew nothing tended to act corrosively on received values, or could be taken in this sense. In the *Clouds*, Aristophanes has Socrates's students boast that he has discovered a clever means of stealing cloaks to pay for dinner (177–179; cf. 497, 856), and the reason why Strepsiades, the protagonist of the play, seeks out Socrates's help is to learn enough rhetoric and logic-chopping to fend off his creditors. True, the image of Socrates and his retinue is not precisely one of luxury: they are poor, have threadbare cloaks, go barefoot (as Socrates himself usually did), and eke out a living despite the fees that Socrates is alleged to charge for his services as a sophist. But in the *agon* of the play, which takes the form of a debate between the so-called Weaker and Stronger Arguments (the Stronger representing traditional values, only to be discomfited by the Weaker), the subversive Weaker Argument, which stands for the new antinomian principles of the philosophers, defends precisely a life of pleasure—eating, drinking, sex of the most demeaning sort, games, and other nefarious activities (1071–1082). Despite his sober habits, Socrates is implicitly associated with a life of ease and diversion.

Still, Socrates himself is not all bad in the *Clouds*—or at least, some scholars have sought to insert a wedge between the representation of the master, a head-in-the-clouds visionary but not particularly avaricious or dishonest, and some of his followers. If comedy has an affinity for sensual gratification, it is equally given to exposing the hypocritical posturing of pretenders to virtue, and hence to upholding, however inconsistently, the ideals of the more sober philosophers. It is possible to see, even in the *Clouds*, a certain sympathy for Socrates. The fourth-century comic playwright Posidippus, in his play, *Men Transformed* (*Metapheromenoi*, K-A fr. 16, quoted in Diogenes Laertius 7.27), has a character say of another: "so that in ten days he'll seem to be more self-controlled

than Zeno," the founder of the Stoic school. Epicurus, in turn, could be seen as a cor-
rupter of the youth. Thus Baton, again, in his play *Partner in Deception* (K-A fr. 5, quoted
by Athenaeus 3.103B), has a father protest at his son's dissipated way of life, under the
influence of the slave appointed to care for him:

> (A)You have taken my son and destroyed him,
> you villain, and persuaded him to take up
> a life that is wrong for him. Now he drinks
> in the morning because of you, which he never used to do.
> (B)Then you are critical, master, because he has learned how to live?
> (A)That's living? (B) The philosophers say so.
> Epicurus, you know, says that the good
> is, of course, pleasure; and you can't get that
> any other way, but from living really finely
> †so all could succeed, † you'll have to agree.
> (A)Tell me, have you ever seen a philosopher
> drunk, or seduced by the arguments you are using?
> (B)All of them! Those men with brows raised high
> in seriousness, searching for a man of intelligence in the Stoa
> and gathering places, as if he were a runaway slave,
> if you ever serve them a grayfish, that's when
> they can dig into the topic at hand with no delay,
> and locate the matter's salient points in a way
> that leaves everyone stunned.

Baton is among the latest of the known Greek comic poets, and the above excerpt suggests a plot type that is common in New Comedy: a young man falls in love with a
woman not suitable for marriage (a foreigner, a courtesan, or a poor parentless girl), and
is assisted in his amours by a clever slave, while his father opposes the liaison and tries
to compel him to marry properly. It is not certain that Baton's play developed along precisely these lines, but the scene is reminiscent of several in Terence, which are modeled
in turn on Menander. Alexis and Epicrates belong to an earlier generation, whose plays
are sometimes classified as Middle Comedy, and the context for their send-ups of philosophers may have been different. The Old Comedy of Aristophanes and his contemporaries, in turn, had its own characteristic plots and structure. The opposition of virtue
and pleasure was a perennial theme, but the comic poets adapted it to their purposes.
Likewise, the major philosophical issues and debates altered over the course of the fifth,
fourth, and third centuries, and provided new material and new inspiration.

We have noted that the philosophers had their suspicions of comedy, and among
these, Plato was perhaps the most critical voice, finding comedy (like most poetry) to be
contrary to the high seriousness he valued. Thus, in the *Laws* (7.816), he affirms:

> It is impossible to understand the serious without the ridiculous (or to understand
> anything without its opposite), but it is also impossible to perform them both,
> if we are going to possess even a modicum of virtue; for this very reason we must

understand it, to avoid inadvertently doing or saying what is ridiculous when it is not required, but we must order the imitation of it upon slaves and hired foreigners and order that absolutely no serious study be devoted to it, that no free man or woman openly be discovered to be studying it, and that there always seem something novel about the ridiculous in imitations. As for the laughable plays, then, which of course we all call comedy, let our legislation and our discussion be sufficient with this.

With particular reference to the tendency in Old Comedy to ridicule living people who might have been in the audience, Plato is clear (*Laws* 11.935): "To the poet of comedy or any music, iambic or lyric, it shall never be allowed in any way, in either word or picture, with anger or without it, to mock any of the citizens." The comic poets took their revenge after Demetrius Poliorcetes, who had driven the philosophically minded Demetrius of Phalerum out of Athens, issued a decree (in the year 307 or 306) that required all philosophers in Athens to be registered, which caused many to leave the city; a character in Alexis's *The Knight* (*Hippeus*, K-A fr. 99, quoted in Athenaeus 13.610E) celebrates the event: "This is the Academy, this is Xenocrates? May the gods grant much good to Demetrius and the lawgivers, because they decreed that those who impart the so-called powers of argument to the young should get out of Attica and go to the devil." Amphis, in his *Dexidemides* (K-A fr. 13, quoted in Diogenes Laertius 3.28), has a character exclaim: "O Plato, the only thing you know how to do is scowl, pushing your eyebrows together like two snails." Aristotle was more tolerant of drama, perhaps because he lived after the decline of the more scurrilous vilification of public figures associated with Old Comedy and was content to restrict the enjoyment of comedy to those who had reached the age of discretion (*Politics* 7.17.1336b12ff.): "It must also be decreed that youths may witness neither iambic performances nor comedy, until they attain the age at which they will also have occasion to share in reclining at parties and drinking, by which time their education will have made them immune to the harm that can occur from such things." It may be for this reason, along with his relatively pragmatic attitude in contrast to the radical programs of Plato, Epicurus, and the Stoics, that Aristotle seems to be less in evidence as the butt of comedy (but see the reference to the Lyceum in Alexis's play, cited above).

If philosophers could be derided as pedants, hypocrites, or preachers of hedonism, they were also vulnerable to the critique of constructing utopian dream-worlds that were impossible to realize and would be awful if they could be. Exhibit A is surely Aristophanes's *Assemblywomen*, in which he stages a takeover of the Athenian government by women, who proceed, despite their protestations of conservatism, to transform the city entirely, abolishing private property and sexual exclusiveness: from now on, everything will be provided by the state, there will be common dining halls, and men and women will have free choice of partners, with the proviso that first dibs go to the oldest and ugliest, so that no one is deprived of a fair share. The scheme bears a rough resemblance to the social arrangements that Plato proposed for the governing class in the ideal state that he imagined in the *Republic*, in which property will be communal and the family will be eliminated; instead, children will be taught that all elders are their parents, all agemates their siblings. Of course, Plato did not endorse indiscriminate sex, as Aristophanes's women do; on the contrary, intercourse was to be regulated by a complex calendrical system designed to select the best unions for the production of superior offspring. When comedy takes hold of such a scheme, it naturally emphasizes the hedonistic side. Nowhere in the play is there a reference to a particular philosophical model, but it is conceivable that Plato's ideas were already in circulation at the time of its production (390), or that other thinkers had concocted similar programs. Behind both Aristophanes and Plato there lay myths of a bygone golden age, when the social institutions characteristic of contemporary Athens were not required to ensure a world of plenty.

Athenaeus, the author of the *Deipnosophistai,* or "Educated Conversation over Dinner," mentions (267–268) in chronological order of production several comedies in connection with the topic of work and slavery, beginning with Cratinus's *Wealths* (*Ploutoi,* 420s), who describe themselves as Titans from the age of Cronus (K-A fr. 171), that is, the golden age before the reign of Zeus, who is here characterized as a tyrant and apparently stands for Pericles, whom Cratinus was known for lambasting. In those days, people played dice with loaves of bread, since food was so plentiful (K-A fr. 176; Teleclides's *Amphictyons,* mentioned third in Athenaeus's list, also depicts a bygone age of luxury, K-A fr. 1; cf. also Pherecrates's *Mineworkers* K-A fr. 113, cited fourth, on the abundance of rich foods). Next comes Crates's *Wild Beasts* (*Theria*), in which two men discuss conditions in what is evidently an ideal regime, something like that imagined by Aristophanes (K-A fr. 16–17):

> (A) Then absolutely no one will get a slave man or woman,
> but an old man will have to be his own servant?
> (B) No! I'll make everything able to walk.
> (A) But what good is that to them? (B) Each of the utensils
> will come to you by itself, when you call it. "Appear beside me, table!"
> Set yourself! Grain-sack, knead the dough!
> Ladle, pour! Where is the wine cup? Go and wash yourself!
> Up here, bread-dough! The pot should spit out those beets!
> Come here, fish." "But I'm done only on one side yet."
> "Then turn yourself over, and baste yourself—with a little salt."
> (C) Well, try this on! To counter you, first
> I'll bring hot baths for my people
> on top of pillars like in the Paionion,
> to flow from the sea into everyone's tub;
> the water will say "you can turn me off now";
> then the perfume-bottle will march right up
> followed by the moving sponge and sandals.

It is not clear whether this fantasy derives from traditional images of the golden age or from some philosophical scheme that Crates is sending up. Aristotle, in the *Politics* (1253b33–38), defends the need for slaves on the grounds that, without them, citizens would not have the leisure to achieve the kind of cultivation required for civic participation: "if it were possible that every utensil accomplished its task when summoned or on its own initiative, and, like the objects made by Daedalus, as they say, or the tripods of Hephaestus, which the poet says, 'on their own enter the divine assembly' [Homer, *Iliad* 18.376], and if shuttles could weave and plectrums pluck the lyre this way, then build-ers would have no need of workers or masters of slaves" (it is notable that, by contrast, in Aristophanes's *Assemblywomen* it is the slaves who will work so that the citizen class may enjoy the communal bounty, 651). Aristotle may, of course, have Crates's comedy in mind, or another like it, but it is plausible that the idea was in the air, and that Crates bears witness to contemporary utopian schemes. The reference to plumbing in the Paionion (whatever its exact significance) suggests that this idea, at least, was not utterly far-fetched. An animal elsewhere in the play—very likely a member of the chorus—tells a human being to eat fish and to refrain from meat (K-A fr. 19); that human beings were vegetarians in the golden age, or at all events limited themselves to fish, was again a com-monplace, but vegetarianism of one sort or another was also preached by some of the early philosophers such as Pythagoras and Empedocles, and had made enough of an impact for Theseus to mock his son—an expert hunter—for this oddity in Euripides's *Hippolytus* (952–953).

Comedy's image of an ideal society was thus two-sided, simultaneously fantasiz-ing a complete liberation from toil and revealing the absurdity of such utopias by showing their limitations (for instance, competition for sexual favors, as at the end of the *Assemblywomen*) or by exaggeration to the point of the bizarre, like having fish protest that they were not yet fried on both sides. So too, comedy had a complex relationship to philosophical ideals of virtue, both endorsing them and teasingly undermining them in an antinomian spirit of carnivalesque profligacy. The comic poets were all too happy to poke fun at rigorous abstemiousness, and Pythagoras, well known for his fetishistic taboos, was an easy target. Antiphanes, in his comedy *Baby Chick* (K-A fr. 166, quoted in Athenaeus 3.108E), has a girl—evidently brought up as a *hetaira*—explain: "As a child, I was taken with my sister by some merchant, and came here to Athens. My family was from Syria. When we were for sale, we were found and bought here by this moneylender, a character unsurpassable in wicked-ness, the sort to bring inside his house nothing, not even what the great Pythagoras used to eat, except some thyme." Aristophon, in *The Pythagoreanist* (K-A fr. 12, quoted in Diogenes Laertius 8.37 on comic poets who mocked Pythagoras), has a character report:

> (A)He said that he descended to where they lived below
> and saw them all; the Pythagoreans
> were very different from the corpses. They alone
> had dined at Pluto's table, so he said,
> because of their piety. (B) He must be a laid-back god
> to enjoy the company of people who are so filthy
> ...and they eat
> greens washed down with water.
> Their fleas and their rags and their lack of baths
> are such as no one today could stand.

To the Pythagoreans' fastidiousness about foods, the poets readily joined their poor sanitation as an object of satire: though their poverty could be seen as a sign of virtue, any kind of excess was fair game for abuse (cf. also Aristophon K-A fr. 10). A dialogue from Alexis's *Tarentines* (K-A fr. 223, quoted in Athenaeus 4.161B) runs:

> (A) In fact the Pythagoreans, so we hear,
> eat neither fish nor a single other thing
> that's animate, and they alone don't drink wine.
> (B) Epicharides eats dogs, however—
> he's one of the Pythagoreans. (A) Once he's killed one —
> then it's no longer animate. Pythagoreanisms and
> subtle arguments and refined thoughts
> are their nourishment, but their daily diet's this:
> one loaf of white bread each, one cup
> of water—that's it. (B) You're talking
> prison diet. Do all wise men carry on
> thus and suffer such privations? (A) No.
> These guys live in luxury compared to others. Don't you know
> that Melanippides is a follower and Phaon
> and Phyromachus and Phanus, who every
> four days feast on half a pint of barley meal?

Not that the Pythagoreans' pretensions to asceticism were taken at face value. Aristophon, in *The Pythagoreanist* (K-A fr. 9, quoted in Athenaeus 4.161E), has a character declare: "By the gods, do we think that the old-time Pythagoreans really wanted to be filthy or enjoyed wearing rags? In my opinion, absolutely not. But it was inescapable, since they had nothing, to invent a fine excuse for the simple life, by decreeing that being poor was good. You can test it by serving them fish or meat; if they don't gobble it up and their own fingers too, you can hang me ten times over" (cf. Theognetus, in *Ghost or Greedy Man* [*Phasma* or *Philargyros*] K-A fr. 1, quoted in Athenaeus 3.104B). And in Antiphanes (K-A fr. 225 [play's title unknown], quoted in Athenaeus epitome 2.60B) someone—perhaps a peasant—lauds the benefits of moderation but concludes with a comic twist: "The dinner is dough palisaded with chaff, prepared with thrift in mind, and a grape-hyacinth bulb and some garnishes, some sow-thistle or a mushroom or the sort of thing that this poor countryside offers its equally poor people. Living this way we have no fevers or phlegm. But no one eats his heart out when meat's for dinner, not even those who pretend to be Pythagoreans" (on the philosophers' penchant for fine dining, cf. Alexis's *Linus*, K-A fr. 140, quoted in Athenaeus 4.164A–D, and Alexis's *Galatea* K-A fr. 37, cited in Athenaeus 12.544E). Athenaeus reports too (11.509B) that "Ephippus the comedy writer in his play *Ship Captain* [*Nauagos*, K-A fr. 14] has ridiculed Plato himself and some of his cronies as money-grubbing, showing that they dressed very expensively and paid more attention to their appearance than our present-day wastrels." Indeed, a clever playwright could turn the argument for poverty against the philosophers, as Baton does in *Man-Killer* (K-A fr. 2, quoted in Athenaeus 4.163B): "I summon here the prudent philosophers who never allow themselves the slightest enjoyment, searching for a man of intelligence in the Stoa and gathering places, as if he were a runaway slave. You sinner, why, if you can pay your share of the bar bill, do you refuse to drink? Why commit such a crime against the gods? Why, man, have you decided that money is more valuable than it really is? By drinking water, you harm the city economically: you harm the farmer and the merchant, whereas I get drunk and keep their incomes high. And then you carry around your oil-bottle checking the oil level from morning on, so that you'd think you didn't have an oil bottle, but a water clock." Consumerism is good for the economy. The double-edged attitude toward parsimony, already evident in Aristophanes's *Wealth*, in which Poverty personified defends the frugal way of life, was noted by Clement of Alexandria (2nd c. CE), who remarked of Philemon's comedy *The Philosophers* (K-A fr. 88, quoted in Clement of Alexandria, *Miscellanies* 2.121.2): "Even as they tear it apart, the comic poets bear witness to the teaching of the Stoic Zeno somewhat as follows: 'For this man philosophizes a novel philosophy: he teaches going hungry and gets disciples. One loaf, a dried fig for relish, drink water after.'"

It is time now to consider the more subtle kinds of exchange between comedy and philosophy, and more particularly the way philosophical investigations of character may be reflected in comic representations. Sometimes, characters in plays simply speak like philosophers, as in this fragment from a comedy by Philemon (K-A fr. 97, quoted in Stobaeus 3.9.21): "The just man's not the one who does no injustice, but the one who, able to do an injustice, doesn't wish to; nor is he the one who's refrained from taking little, but the one who persists in not taking much though able to have and conquer with impunity; nor is he the one indeed who only observes all this, but the one who has a guileless and genuine nature and wishes to be just, not just seem to be." The attribution may well be explicit; Alexis, in his *Olympiodorus* (K-A fr. 163, quoted in Diogenes Laertius 3.28), has this snatch of dialogue, doubtless uttered tongue in cheek:

> (A) My mortal body became withered,
> but the immortal part rose up into the air.
> (B) Isn't this Plato's teaching?

Clement of Alexandria (*Miscellanies* 6.23.4–5) went so far as to charge the comic poets with plagiarism: "Didn't Plato say, 'we could perhaps affirm this without absurdity: that sight is the commencement of love, hope [augments] the passion, memory nourishes it, and habit guards it?" and doesn't the comic poet Philemon [K-A fr. 126] write: 'First all men see, then admire, next examine, then plunge into hope; and so from these arises love?'" But it is not just opinions that cross over from philosophy to comedy, but ways of behaving in the world. In Menander's *Woman from Samos* (*Samia*), Demea, the *senex* in the play, falsely concludes that his concubine and his son Moschio have had an affair during his absence. At this juncture, Demea meets and cross-examines the slave Parmeno, whom he suspects of complicity in the affair, and Parmeno is obliged to confess, under threats of torture, that the child is indeed Moschio's (320). In his rage, however, Demea assumes, wrongly, that Chrysis, his concubine, is the mother (in fact, it is the girl next door). Demea begins to bellow in rage, but then takes himself in hand: "Why are you shouting, you fool? Control yourself, bear up. Moschio has not wronged you" (327–328). Turning to the audience, which he casts in the position of jurors (*andres*, 329), he announces in good rhetorical fashion: "The argument is risky, perhaps, but true" (328–329), and he proceeds to come up with reasons to exonerate the boy. First, he infers that if Moschio had acted deliberately, or out of real passion for Chrysis, or again out of hatred toward his father, he would have opposed the idea of marrying the neighbor's daughter (whom he got with child), but in fact he consented at once when Demea proposed the idea to him. Demea's reasoning is sound enough, but since he believes that Moschio slept with Chrysis, he concludes further, and errone-ously, that Moschio is eager to marry the neighbor's daughter in part because he desires to escape Chrysis's charms, to which he has succumbed. Hence, he concludes, it is she who is "responsible for what happened" (338). Demea argues further that Moschio was doubtless drunk and not in control of himself (340) when Chrysis seduced him; besides, he is still young. All of these are mitigating factors in regard to anger. He repeats that it is not at all plausible (*pithanon*, 343) that a youth who was always well behaved and modest toward everyone else should treat his own father badly, "even if he was ten times over adopted, and not my own son by birth: for I look not to this, but to his character [*tropos*]" (346–347). Having convinced himself of Moschio's good intentions, Demea turns violently against Chrysis, whom he now regards as the sole culprit: "You must be a man," he admonishes himself: "forget your desire [*pothos*], stop being in love" (349–350). He resolves to expel Chrysis from his house, while keeping the real cause concealed for his son's sake.

Throughout the play, Demea has been shown to be prone to anger, consistent with the portrayal of older men in comedy. But if he is irascible by temperament, he is not so in an unreflecting or indiscriminate way. He seeks reasons to justify his rage, and is prepared to forego it if he finds a plausible reason for pardon. In the *Rhetoric*, Aristotle defines anger (*orge*) as "a desire, accompanied by pain, for a perceived revenge, on account of a perceived slight on the part of people who are not fit to slight one or one's own" (2.2, 1378a31–33). As Aristotle observes in his discussion of calming down, which he treats as the opposite of anger, a slight must be voluntary, and people therefore react mildly toward unintentional offenses (2.3, 1380a8–12). He adds that anger is reduced toward those who admit that they were wrong and show that they regret it (1380a14). In the *Nicomachean Ethics*, Aristotle briefly mentions that *sungnome* (pardon) is appropriate when people act either under external compulsion, or else in excusable ignorance of the facts or circumstances (1109b18–1111a2). In addition, "*sungnome* may be granted when someone does things one ought not to do on account of circumstances that are beyond human nature and which no one could endure" (3.1, 1110a23–26). Demea is employing reasoning in respect to the question of Moschio's guilt that is consistent with Aristotle's understanding of how anger is caused and appeased, and this allows him to exonerate his son, unfortunately at the expense, here, of his concubine (he will later discover her innocence, and at once renounce his anger toward her). Whatever his natural dispo-sition, he has acquired the kind of character or ethos that permits him to subject his impulses to rational evaluation and to guide his emotional responses accordingly.

Tradition has it that Menander was acquainted (or studied) with Theophrastus, Aristotle's successor as head of the Lyceum and the author of a famous set of sketches called *The Characters* (he is also said to have served in the military as an ephebe along with Epicurus), and this experience may have influenced his character portraits in his comedies, which indeed offer numerous scenes of apparently philosophical deliberation (see Fortenbaugh 1974). A case can be made that the plots of New Comedy generally, based as they so often are on the tension between youthful passion and paternal authority, are designed to exhibit qualities of character in action. Plutarch, in his *Comparison of Aristophanes and Menander* (854 A–C), praised Menander in particular at the expense of Aristophanes: "Some of those who produce comedies write for the mob and the commons, others for the few.... Aristophanes, however, is neither pleasing to the many nor endurable to the wise.... But for philosophers and lovers of literature, just as when painters' eyes grow weary they turn to the colors of grass and flowers, so too Menander is a resting place from their unremitting intensity, figuratively welcoming their thoughts in a flowery, shaded, and breeze-filled meadow." Plutarch would appear to have in mind a passage in Aristotle's *Nicomachean Ethics* (4.1128a16–25) where he observes: "A sense of good taste is also proper to a moderate character; good taste consists of saying and listening to the sort of things that befit a liberal and reasonable man. There are in fact certain things that are fitting for such a man to say and hear in jest, and the jokes of a liberal man will be different from those of a slavish one, and those of the educated from the uneducated. One can observe this difference in past comedy and contemporary: the one considered obscene talk to be funny, whereas the other merely hints at such things for humor. They are very different in their respectability." Before the age of Menander and his more refined peers, then, was comic characterization untouched by philosophy? Surely not.

We have seen that Aristophanes's *Clouds* is directed principally at the sophists of his day, with sideswipes at theorists of the natural world, all rolled up in the person of Socrates. Old Strepsiades wants some of the skills that the sophists purported to teach, though he proves incapable of mastering them (his son does so, and demonstrates that it is legitimate for sons to beat their fathers). In frustration, Strepsiades burns down Socrates's think tank (at least in the revised version of the play that survives), but other comic heroes are far more resourceful when it comes to argument: Dicaeopolis in the *Acharnians* is prepared to lay his head on the chopping block while proving to the chorus that Athens should strike a truce with Sparta in the Peloponnesian War, and Praxagora, the heroine of the *Assemblywomen*, not only devises a scheme so that the women may take over the state but concocts a whole new social order, much in the way Protagoras and others drew up constitutions for cities (one may compare also the newly created avian empire in the *Birds*). It is possible that the bold, creative protagonists of Old Comedy, at least in its Aristophanic form, were exhibiting in their very temperaments the Protagorean dictum that man is the measure of all things.

If the plot of Old Comedy was, at least in many cases, dominated by a wily character who bent the world to his or her will, and thus gave a special shape to the story as a whole—one of the little guy triumphing over all obstacles, natural, human, and even divine—New Comedy might seem to work in just the opposite way, with the characters subject to forces beyond their control, represented, for example, by the role of Chance (*Tyche*) who speaks the prologue in Menander's *Shield* (*Aspis*). But here too, the trajectory of events is more the product of human character and decisions, and the happy outcome depends on the wits, calculations, and integrity of the principals rather than on the mysterious hand of fortune (Cinaglia 2011). The order of events in New Comedy, more than in any other genre, would seem to follow Aristotle's prescription in the *Poetics* (1454a33–b2) that "as in the structure of the plot, so too in the portraiture of character, the poet should always aim either at the necessary or the probable. Thus a person of a given character should speak or act in a given way, by the rule either of necessity or of probability; just as this event should follow that by necessary or probable sequence. It is therefore evident that the unraveling of the plot, no less than the complication, must arise out of the plot itself, it must not be brought about by the *deus ex machina*, as in the *Medea*." The agents' responses to events must be intelligible and consistent with their character, and it is this that leads to the denouement.

The quarrel between comedy and philosophy is a kind of sibling rivalry, for the two are more alike than may strike the eye (see Nightingale 1995; Freydberg 2008; Hanink, chapter 12, this volume). Both are engaged in critiques of conventional wisdom, and both look to uncover truths about human nature and relationships. Comedy makes its points lightly, but the laughter it evokes often involves an element of self-recognition in the audience. I may leave the last word to Alexis, in whose *Phaedrus* (K-A fr. 247, quoted in Athenaeus 13.562A), a character muses, with a deft allusion to the opening of Plato's *Republic*: "As I was coming from the Peiraeus, it occurred to me to philosophize about my troubles and confusion. They seem ignorant to me, in short, these artists of Eros, when they make images of this god. It's neither female nor male, nor again god or human, neither stupid nor wise, but put together from everywhere, supporting many forms in one shape. It has the courage of a man, but a woman's timidity, the confusion of madness, but the logic of sense, a beast's violence, but the endurance of steel, and a divine pride. And these things—by Athena and the gods! I don't know exactly what it is, but nonetheless it's something like this, and I'm close to naming it."

FURTHER READING

Although the topic would seem to be attractive, there are in fact few studies of the interaction between comedy and philosophy, especially from the perspective of comedy, apart from the obvious case of Aristophanes's *Clouds*. Because Menander is believed to have had some connection with the school of Aristotle, a number of studies explore possible influences of peripatetic thought in his comedies. But a vast number of ancient Greek comedies (in the thousands) have been lost, or survive only in excerpts. In this chapter, I have attempted to give these their due, but while specialized articles touch on one or another of these fragments, there is no full survey of them in relation to philosophy. In this connection, the reader can hardly do better than to consult the English translation of all the important fragments edited by Jeffrey Rusten.

The list of references below includes all works mentioned in the text, with the addition of a few other studies that are relevant to the topic.

BIBLIOGRAPHY

Belardinelli, A. M. 2008. "Filosofia e scienza nella commedia nuova." *Seminari Romani* 11: 77–106.

Brock, R. 1990. "Plato and Comedy." In *Owls to Athens: Essays on Classical Subjects Presented to Sir Kenneth Dover*, edited by E. M. Craik, 39–49. Oxford: Oxford University Press.

Cinaglia, V. 2011. "Aristotle and Menander on the Ethics of Understanding." PhD diss., University of Exeter.

Dohm, H. 1964. *Mageiros: Die Rolle des Kochs in der griechisch-römischen Komödie.* Munich: Beck.

Fortenbaugh, W. W. 1974. "Menander's *Perikeiromene*: Misfortune, Vehemence, and Polemon." *Phoenix* 28: 430–443.

Freydberg, B. 2008. *Philosophy and Comedy: Aristophanes, Logos, and Eros.* Bloomington: Indiana University Press.

Gaiser, K. 1967. "Menander und der Peripatos." *Antike und Abendland,* 13: 8–40.

Halliwell, S. 2008. *Greek Laughter.* Cambridge, UK: Cambridge University Press.

Hosek, R. 1991. "Die Gestalt des Philosophen auf die Bühne der mittleren attischen Komödie." *Graecolatina Pragensia* 13: 23–51.

Imperio, O. 1998. "La figura dell'intellettuale nella commedia greca." In A. M. Belardinelli, O. Imperio, G. Mastromarco, M. Pellegrino, M. Totaro, *Tessere: Frammenti della commedia greca, studi e commenti,* 43–130. Bari: Adriatica Editrice.

Konstan, D. 2011. "Aristophanes." In *The Cambridge Companion to Socrates,* edited by Donald Morrison, 75–90. Cambridge, UK: Cambridge University Press.

Munteanu, D. 2002. "Types of *Anagnorisis*: Aristotle and Menander, A Self-Defining Comedy." *Wiener Studien* 115: 111–126.

Nightingale, A. 1995. "Philosophy and Comedy." In *Genres in Dialogue: Plato and the Construct of Philosophy,* edited by A. Nightingale, 172–193. Cambridge, UK: Cambridge University Press.

Pellegrino, M. 2000. *Utopie e immagini gastronomiche nei frammenti dell'* Archaia. Bologna: Pàtron.

Rusten, J., ed. 2011. *The Birth of Comedy: Texts, Documents, and Art from Athenian Comic Competitions, 486–280.* Translations by J. Henderson, D. Konstan, R. Rosen, J. Rusten, and N. W. Slater. Baltimore: The Johns Hopkins University Press (referred to as *BOC*).

Steinmetz, P. 1960. "Menander und Theophrast: Folgerungen aus dem *Dyskolos*." *Rheinisches Museum* 103: 185–191.

Tylawsky, E. I. 2002. *Saturio's Inheritance: The Greek Ancestry of the Roman Comic Parasite.* New York: Peter Lang.

III

Attic Comedy and Society

CHAPTER 14

THE POLITICS OF COMIC ATHENS

DAVID ROSENBLOOM

ATHENS AS THE COMIC SCENE

ATHENS is the comic city par excellence. Unlike tragedy, in which the city features rarely (Knox 1979: 9), mainly as an object of praise, Old Comedy stages present-day Athens as an object of blame, often against the backdrop of the city's praiseworthy Persian War past (Rosenbloom 2002: 326–329). Nine of Aristophanes's eleven surviving plays transpire at least in part at Athens. The two outliers are thoroughly Athenocentric. Though set mainly in the underworld, *Frogs* (Lenaea 405) remains fixated on the city and its putative salvation; *Birds* (Dionysia 414), located in a far-off fantasyland of birds, founds Nephelococcygia, a polis analogous but antithetical to Athens (Arrowsmith 1973; Rosenbloom 2006: 265–271). The Old Comic universe revolves around Athens and Athenians—actual citizens such as Socrates, Euripides, and Hyperbolus (Sommerstein 1996; Storey 2003: 384–386 for Eupolis); allegorized citizens such as Paphlagon and Maricas, and fictionalized citizens such as Dicaeopolis, Trygaeus, Peisetaerus, and Chremylus. Citizens in the last group often plot to transform the politics, society, religion, or economy of Athens.

Although no complete comedies survive from the period 387–317, extant titles (Arnott 2008: 311–319) and fragments indicate that Athens continues to be the comic scene. Even the mythical burlesques considered essential during this period transpire in contemporary Athens.[1] Comedy remained Athenocentric in the fourth century despite both the expansion of performance opportunities at festivals in theaters that burgeoned

---

[1] Mythical burlesque: Platonius I 28–31, 46–56 (Koster 1975); Nesselrath 1990: 204–241; Bowie 2008: 153–157; Arnott 2008: 294–300. Athenian setting: e.g. Alexis *Linus* K-A fr. 140; *adespota* K-A fr. 1062=Philiscus fr. 215 *CGFP*; Nesselrath 1995: 22–27.

throughout the Mediterranean in the period ca. 400 to ca. 340 (Csapo 2010: 95–103) and the increasing internationalization of the personnel of the Athenian theater. Important fourth-century comedians hailed from outside of Athens (Csapo 2010: 86; Konstantakos 2011): Alexis (Thurii), Anaxandrides (Camirus, Colophon), Antiphanes (various origins), Diphilus (Sinope), Philemon (Syracuse), to name a few. Fictionalized Athenian types remain focal points of the plot, but actual and allegorized citizens almost entirely disappear from comedy in the course of the fourth century. The transformation of the politics, economics, religion, and society of Athens and of the world ceases to be an objective of fourth-century comedy after Aristophanes.

By 321 BCE, the date of Menander's debut, the tradition of locating comic plots in Athens and Attica was entrenched. Of Menander's sixty-one plays for which we have more than titles, only three certainly take place outside of Athens: *Perikeiromene* (Corinth; cf. Diphilus, *Overseas Trader* K-A fr. 31), *Leukadia* (Leucas), and *Imbrians* (Imbros). Two others, *Man from Ephesus* and *Fisherman*, are probably set abroad. The vast majority of Menander's comedies whose locales are known take place at Athens; some are set in demes of Attica (*Dyskolos* at Phyle, *Sikyonioi* at Eleusis, *Hero* at Ptelea, *Epitrepontes* at Halae Araphenides, *Heauton Timoroumenos* at Halae Aexonides, Webster 1974: 80, 144; cf. Lape 2004: 37–38 with n.112). All six of Terence's surviving comedies and twelve of Plautus's twenty are set at Athens. The center of the comic universe in Old Comedy, Athens remained the location of comic plots at the time of Menander.

1. From Old to New Comedy: Democracy the Key Variable?

We possess complete comedies that span over a century, from Aristophanes's *Acharnians* (Lenaea 425) to Menander's *Dyskolos* (Lenaea 316). Because comedy is an Athenocentric genre set in the contemporary city, scholars from antiquity to the present have been tempted to interpret the evolution of comic styles as a function of political, social, and economic change at Athens during the period. These styles, conventionally termed "Old" (440s? to 380?), "Middle" (380–322), and "New Comedy" (322–ca. 250), are best viewed as synchronic descriptions of plot elements (Csapo 2000), which assume dominant and recessive forms as the genre evolves. The fantastic and political dominate in Old Comedy, the mythological and sympotic in Middle Comedy, and tales of "rape and recognition," already a part of the comic repertoire at the time of Aristophanes (e.g. Aristophanes *Cocalus*; Aristophanes K-A test. 1.4–6, 41–46), in New Comedy. But recessive forms remain potentially active.

Theories of the evolution of comedy that developed in antiquity employ democracy as the decisive variable. In Platonius's account, Old Comedy is an institution of Athenian democracy that features choregic expenditure, choral songs, and *parabasis*, and aims at "censuring generals, jurors who give the wrong verdicts, and those who amass fortunes unjustly and choose a morally deficient life" (Platonius I 44–46; cf. 3–10, 13–20,

25–27, 32–41, 49–51 [Koster 1975]). The sociopolitical context of Old Comedy is the antagonism of rich and poor, who delight in the foibles of the wealthy (Platonius I 10–11 [Koster 1975]).

Platonius understands Middle Comedy as a response to oligarchy shaped by poets' fears of reprisal from powerful individuals after the breakdown of democracy and its institutions. The apocryphal story that Alcibiades drowned or attempted to drown Eupolis for ridiculing him in *Dyers* (*Baptai*), as well as Cratinus's *Odysseus and Company* (*Odysses*) and Aristophanes's *Aeolosicon*, which allegedly lacked choral parts and ridicule of named individuals, are prominent examples.[2] This style of comedy ridicules poetry or disguises mockery of wealthy and powerful citizens in riddling language (Platonius I 13–31, 42–63; Anon. *On Comedy* IV 11–17; *Anon. Kram.* XIc 37–42, "symbolic mockery" [Koster 1975]; cf. Arist. *EN* 1128a22–24).

New Comedy allegedly feared offending Macedonians and their representatives (who dominated Athens to varying degrees from 322 to 167) to such an extent that it used grotesque masks to avoid identification with them (Platonius I 42–165 [Koster 1975]) and ceased to ridicule the wealthy and magistrates even in cryptic language (Anon. *On Comedy* IV 13–17 [Koster 1975]), mocking slaves and foreigners instead (*Anon. Kram.* XIc 41–43 [Koster 1975]). Shifts in the balance of political power at Athens drove the evolution of comedy: the wealthy and powerful exerted control over comedians and audiences in conformity to their interests, transforming the genre from a "democratic" spectacle, in which the poor enjoyed mockery of the wealthy, to an "oligarchic" spectacle, in which comedians were afraid to ridicule the wealthy and powerful and vented their impulses to lampoon on outsiders.

This picture of comedy's evolution is riddled with inaccuracies (Nesselrath 1990: 28–36; 2000). Platonius misconstrues the nature of the *choregia* and chorus in fourth-century comedy. To be sure, Aristophanes's last two plays, *Assemblywomen* (? 392) and *Wealth* (? 388), both lack a *parabasis*. Manuscripts of *Assemblywomen* mark an absent ode with "of the chorus" (*CHOROU*) at 876, while those of *Wealth* mark absent choral songs in the same way at 322, 626, 802, 958, and 1097 (Handley 1953); the chorus plays an attenuated role in the play. Nevertheless, fourth-century comedy continued to feature a chorus,[3] perhaps even as a collective character interacting with actors and playing a role in the plot (e.g. Eubulus, *Garland Sellers*; Hunter 1979: 36–37; Hunter 1983: 191–199). Menander's revelers enter after the first act (Zagagi 1995: 72–82; Lape 2006) and may sing songs unrelated to the plot of the drama between acts. But we cannot be certain that contemporary playwrights employed choruses in the same way (Rothwell 1995: 116).

---

[2] Platonius I 18–23, 29–31; *Anon. Kram.* XIc 19–43 (Koster 1975). See Nesselrath 2000: 234–235; *Aeolosicon* K-A fr. 9 indicates that the play had a chorus of women; *Odysseus and Company* featured a chorus of Odysseus's companions (K-A fr. 151).

[3] Hunter 1979; Taplin 1993: esp. 55–63; Rothwell 1995: 110–118.

Similarly, the Archon eponymous (not the demos) appointed comic *choregoi* and *synchoregoi* throughout the fifth and into the fourth century. It seems that the tribes appointed comic *choregoi* at some time before the composition of the Aristotelian *Constitution of the Athenians* ([Arist.] *Ath.Pol.* 56.3; Pickard-Cambridge 1988: 86–87; Rhodes 1993: 622 624; Wilson 2000: 50–57; but cf. Makres, chapter 3, this volume). The change from Archon-appointed *choregoi* to a magisterial *agonothetes* is often considered an oligarchic reform of Demetrius of Phalerum, a pupil of Aristotle, who was critical of the institution (Plut. *Mor.* 349A; Arist. *Pol.* 1309a13–20, 1320a35–b4); supposedly the reform occurred when he was Nomothetes in 316/5 (Pickard-Cambridge 1988: 91–93) or Archon in 309/8 (Köhler 1878), but it may rather have been a reform of the democracy instituted in 307/6 (Wilson and Csapo 2012; but see Makres, chapter 3, this volume). In any case, there is little justification for interpreting the diminished role of the chorus in the fourth century as a symptom of a faltering democratic ethos. The change is better understood as a result of the professionalization of the fourth-century theater and the growing sophistication of theater audiences, which found the interaction of amateur *choreutai* and professional actors unappealing (Csapo and Slater 1994: 349–354, esp. 351; cf. Wallace 1995: 207–210). Moreover, the heightened realism of the comic plot limited the role of music and the chorus.

Oligarchy left no lasting imprint on the culture of democratic Athens, though the desire to avoid oligarchy became an element of fourth-century Athenian culture. The oligarchic takeover of the Four Hundred in 411 and the regime of the Five Thousand in 411/10 together lasted only thirteen months (Buck 1998: 125). The tyranny of the Thirty (404/3; cf. Platonius I 13–116 [Koster 1975]) ended after eight months (Krentz 1982: 152). Democracy flourished at Athens from its restoration in 403/2 until the imposition of Macedonian rule in 322 (Ober 1989; Hansen 1991). Comedy exercised the privilege of free speech into the fourth century (Isoc. 8.14; Pl. *Laws* 935d–936a), continuing to ridicule politicians unnamed (e.g., Antiphanes, *Sappho* K-A fr. 194; cf. Nicostratus, *Rhetor*) and named (see Webster 1970: 23–50; Nesselrath 1997; Arnott 2008: 300–305 and below). The tenor of political mockery changes in the course of the fourth century, but a weakened democratic ethos, oligarchy, and fear of reprisal do not explain the change.

After Athens's defeat in the Lamian War in 322 BCE, the Macedonian general Antipater imposed a 2,000-drachma requirement for citizenship, disfranchising either 12,000 (Plut. *Phoc.* 28.7; Jones 1957: 57–98) or 22,000 citizens (D.S. 18.18.5; Hansen 1986: 36). Demetrius of Phalerum, who took control of Athens in 318/7 under the patronage of the Macedonian general Cassander, reduced the property qualification for citizenship to 1,000 drachmae (Habicht 1997: 42–53). Seizing control of Athens, Demetrius Poliorcetes declared the restoration of democracy in 307/6 (Plut. *Demetr.* 10.1–2; cf. 24.12; Habicht 1997: 67–81), doing away with the 1,000-drachma threshold for citizenship. Democratic impulses found institutional expression again in 295, when Demetrius regained control of the city (Ferguson 1911: esp. 136–141; Chaniotis for the "illusion of democracy" in the Hellenistic polis). The political context of comedy until 322 is securely democratic. The fragments of comedy after this indicate neither a large nor an oppressive Macedonian presence in the genre.

The tradition of comic license prevailed to some extent even after Athens lost its political independence. Demetrius of Phalerum probably introduced officials called *gynaikonomoi* ("regulators of women"), who limited the number of people allowed to assemble at private feasts to thirty (Athen. 245a–c), and may have also enforced restrictions on the conduct of women (Pollux 8.112; Arist. *Politics* 1300a5–8, 1323a3–6, O'Sullivan 2009: esp. 66–72). Characters in comedy raised a voice against these officials. In Timocles's *Juror Lover*, a speaker grudgingly orders the doors of the house opened so that *gynaikonomoi* can count the guests "in accordance with the new law" (4), but insists that these officials should scrutinize the homes of those who go without supper (cf. Rosivach 1991). Menander also took a swipe at this "new law" in his *Hairnet*: so greedy are *gynaikonomoi* for information about guests at private feasts that they have enrolled chefs in the city to act as informants (K-A fr. 208).

During interludes of democratic rule under Macedonian hegemony, comedians ridiculed democratic politicians by name (similarly, Henderson, chapter 8, this volume). It is perhaps no coincidence that two surviving examples of such invective were composed by politically active comedians. Philippides, a comic poet and politician friendly to the Diadoch Lysimachus, excoriated Demetrius's mouthpiece Stratocles for corrupting Athenian rituals to please Demetrius, bringing disaster to the polis (K-A fr. 25, ca. 301; Philipp 1973). Archedicus, a comic poet and political agent of Antipater, slandered Demosthenes's nephew, Demochares, as performing oral sex for money and hence unfit to blow on sacred flames (K-A fr. 4 =Plb. 12.13.1–7; Timae. *FGrHist* 566 F35a–b; Habicht 1993). This is conservative ridicule directed at more democratic opponents: Stratocles appeared to be imitating Cleon (Plut. *Demetr.* 11.2), while Demochares was the true heir of his democratic uncle Demosthenes (Tracy 2000: 228; [Plut.] *Lives of the Ten Orators* 850F1–851C10).

In sum, the understanding of the evolution of comedy found in Platonius and other ancient writers is deficient. The notion that democracy, oligarchy, and Macedonian hegemony functioned as matrices of the evolving phases of comedy is too simplistic to be useful when it is not simply wrong. Other important historical factors, such as the Peloponnesian War (and concomitant demographic and political shifts) and the Athenian Empire and the Second Naval Confederacy, play no role in models like Platonius's; his and other such explanations neglect sociocultural changes at Athens over the course of the fifth and fourth centuries relevant to the evolution of comedy: increased specialization, professionalization, and monetization of public, private, and intellectual roles; internationalization of comic playwrights, audiences, and theater practitioners; and competition and antagonism among art forms and discourses. Ancient scholars, however, were correct to identify democracy as a variable basic to the development of Athenian comedy. The next section examines precisely how this was the case.

Comic *Parrhesia*: From Democracy to Oligarchic Revolution

Democracy and its characteristic social structures played a central role in comedy's genesis and evolution. Comedy was institutionalized at the City Dionysia in 487/6 during an era of rapid democratization that witnessed the first four ostracisms (488/7–485/4 BCE), selection of archons by lot (487/6 BCE; [Arist.] *Ath.Pol.* 22.4–5; Henderson 2007), and creation of a navy, typically rowed by a community's poorest citizens (483/2 BCE). Comedy's entailment of democracy featured in debates about the Megarian origins of the genre "when there was democracy among them" (Arist. *Poet.* 1448a32). Old Comedy exemplifies the values of "free speech" (*parrhesia,* literally "saying everything") and "equality" (*isegoria*) essential to Athenian democracy.[4] As performed at Athens, Old Comedy is a function not merely of polis life, as Rhodes (2003) has argued, but of life in a democratic polis.

The nexus between comedy, democracy, and democratic social structures was recognized in the fifth century BCE. Pseudo-Xenophon situated comedy at the heart of Athenian democratic political culture, treating it as an instrument in the class war that maintained the rule of the poor majority over the wealthy minority. The demos, he insists, does not authorize itself as the target of comic abuse in order to protect its reputation, but permits "a rich, noble, or powerful man" to be mocked (2.18; cf. Platonius I 8–10 [Koster 1975]). According to him, some of "the poor and demotic" can be ridiculed "for meddling in others' affairs" or "for seeking to get the better of the demos" (ibid.). The polemicist exaggerates his claim: the Athenian demos was in fact the target of comic mockery (Gomme 1940: 218–219, 222). Some scholars question when this became so. Olson (2008: 37), following Roscher (1842: 528–29) in dating the tract to 424 BCE, suggests that *Knights* was the first play to ridicule the demos and hence was outside Pseudo-Xenophon's purview. It is difficult to specify an exact date for the tract, but Gomme (1940: esp. 244–245) and Mattingly (1997) present cogent arguments for a later range (420–415 BCE; Rosenbloom 2004a: 87–90). As many have realized, this text has scant claim to objective truth. Dating the text to 424 BCE in order to salvage its illusory veracity also ignores the likelihood that *Babylonians,* performed at the Dionysia of 426 BCE, had already ridiculed the demos.

In *Babylonians,* Aristophanes skewered "allotted and elected magistrates and Cleon" (Schol. Ar. *Ach.* 378 = *Babylonians* K-A test. iv). Cleon indicted Aristophanes before the Council for "defaming the polis when strangers were present" (*Ach.* 502–503) and for "mock[ing] our polis and dishonor[ing] the demos" (630–631; cf. 377–382, 659–664;

---

[4] For *parrhesia,* see Halliwell 1991; 2004; Goldhill 1991: esp. 188–200; Carey 1994: esp. 69; Henderson 1998; Sommerstein 2004a; cf. Raaflaub 2004: 223–225; for *isegoria,* see Nakategawa 1988; Raaflaub 2004: esp. 95–97.

Sommerstein 2004a: 145–154; Wallace 2005: 364–366; cf. *Wasps* 1284–1291). Cleon hoped to incite the demos's anger over mockery of it and its representatives—most notably Cleon himself—before strangers at the City Dionysia. But the demos never considered the case; it ended in the Council with an unknown outcome (cf. Sommerstein 2004a: 159–160). Moreover, *adespota* K-A fr. 700, which criticizes the demos for "no longer tolerating obedience to authority, taking a bite out of Euboea, and pouncing on the islands," probably dates from the early 440s: comedians criticized the demos before *Babylonians*. Comedy originated and flourished in a democratic polis, but it was not a tool of democratic control as Pseudo-Xenophon imagined it.

Nor did Old Comedy employ speech that conformed to the statutes of the polis on slander, as modern scholars imagine it (e.g., Sommerstein 2004). It was illegal to accuse falsely a citizen of throwing away his shield in battle (Lys. 10.1–12, esp. 9, 385/4 BCE; Aeschin. 1.28–32, 346/5 BCE; Wallace 1994: 115). Comedians repeatedly mocked the politician Cleonymus for this offense, both openly (e.g., Aristophanes, *Clouds* 353–354) and by innuendo (Aristophanes, *Knights* 1372). Alan Sommerstein (2004: 214) argues that because Cleonymus was guilty of this offense, ridicule of him did not breach the law. In the competitive world of Athenian democratic politics, however, Cleonymus would have faced career-ending prosecution and conviction if the charge were true or could be convincingly represented as true (the penalty was disfranchisement: Aeschin. 1.29; 3.175–176). Since Cleonymus exercised political leadership throughout the period of ridicule (IG I³ 61, 68–70, 1454, ca. 430–423 BCE; And. 1.27, 415 BCE), the charge was unsubstantiated. Old Comedy likewise broke a law that prohibited defaming the dead (D. 20.104; Wallace 1994: 110–112). Aristophanes slandered a dead Cleon in *Peace* as "eating shit in Hades" (47–48). Using the insulting monikers "hide-seller" and "pestle," he blamed internecine war among the Greeks on Cleon's extortions (268–270, 618–647; cf. 313–315, 748–760; cf. *Acharnians* 524–538 for dead Pericles). If *Women at the Thesmophoria* was produced in 410 BCE, as some argue (e.g., Tsamakis 2012), Hyperbolus would have been insulted after his death as a "vile, base, and incompetent" (*poneros*) public figure (830–845). Statutes did not constrain the speech employed in Old Comedy.

One way to avoid this conclusion is to characterize Old Comic *parrhesia* as a festive license for ritual laughter (Halliwell 1991a: esp. 292–296; 2008: esp. 206–214) devoid of political consequences and immune to legal action (e.g., Halliwell 1991: 54). If comedy were such a performance, why would Cleon have prosecuted Aristophanes, and why would Lysias's client Phanus adduce "annual" comic ridicule of Cinesias for "committing such crimes against the gods" as relevant to his conviction (fr. 195 Carey)? Likewise, in his prosecution of Timarchus in 346 BCE, Aeschines alleges that the audience of a comedy performed at the rural Dionysia in Collytus looked at Timarchus when the actor Parmenon used the phrase "big Timarchan prostitutes"—this, according to Aeschines, demonstrated public knowledge that Timarchus was a prostitute (Aeschin. 1.157). Plato's Socrates insists that *Clouds* shaped public opinion and informed the charges that his accusers used to prosecute him nearly a quarter century later (Pl. *Ap.* 18b4–e4, 19a8–d7). The effect of comic ridicule was not limited to the theater and festival occasion of its performance. Political and legal actors used it to advantage themselves and to disadvantage their adversaries in competitive democratic institutions; it had both direct and indirect influence on public perception. If we deny this, then Pseudo-Xenophon's view that comedy is an instrument of demotic rule (2.18) and Isocrates's complaint that comedians but not politicians have *parrhesia* (8.14) become inexplicable. Rather, the incorporation of Old Comic political invective into fourth-century forensic oratory (Harding 1994; cf. Heath 1997) and the development of politician/comedians such as Archedicus and Philippides at the end of the fourth century underscore the kinship between comic and political speech.

Old Comedy consistently employed *parrhesia* to ridicule and criticize the democratic regime and its chief agents. The report in a scholium to Aristophanes (Schol. Ar. *Ach.* 67) that the demos passed a law banning comic "ridicule" (*me komoidein*) from 440/39 to 437/6 BCE suggests tension between comic *parrhesia* and democracy as the rule of the demos. Many believe the law was passed in turbulent times after the quelling of the Samian revolt (Halliwell 1991: 57–58, 63; Sommerstein 2004: 208–209; Sommerstein 2004a: 156–157; Wallace 2005: 362–365). The substance of the law is ambiguous: *komoidein* can mean "compose a comedy" and "ridicule." That Aristomenes presented a comedy at the City Dionysia of 439 and Callias probably at the Lenaea of 437 rules out the former. Perhaps the scholiast meant "ridicule by name" (*onomasti komoidein*). The phrase *onomasti komoidein* and obsession with its illegality are not attested until the Second Sophistic (e.g. Aristid. 3.117–118 Jebb; Sopat. Rh. *Peri Staseon* 11.8–30 Rabe). One ancient theory holds that comedy was the institutionalization of farmers' nocturnal, anonymous charges of wrongdoing against individuals in the city—these proto-comedians were not allowed to name the perpetrators, as if this were the natural condition of comic speech (Anon. *On Comedy* IXa; cf. Anon. *On Comedy* IV). Rejection of this "law" is justified (Gomme 1945: 387; Podlecki 1998: 127; Rusten 2010: 22). Scholia to Aristophanes are not trustworthy sources for otherwise unattested fifth-century laws.

In recent scholarship, the relationship between democracy and Old Comedy has been the subject of debate in which no clear consensus has emerged (see Olson 2008). The best-known fifth-century comedian, Aristophanes, occupies every position on the sociopolitical spectrum. He is a radical democrat and follower of Hyperbolus (Sidwell 2009), one of the "constituent intellectuals of the democracy" (Henderson 1990: 272; cf. Carey 1994), an internal social and political critic who sought to prevent popular self-deception (Ober 1998: 125), a conservative poet working in a genre that manifests a "right-wing bias,"[5] and a Cimonian aristocrat disgruntled with the exercise of mass power at Athens (Ste. Croix 1972: 357).

Aristophanes's extant comedies seek to solidify bonds between small and large landowners, peasants and aristocrats, around the humiliation and expulsion of a new

---

[5] Sommerstein 1996: 366; cf. Storey 1994: 107–108 for Eupolis; Storey 2003: 338–348 offers a virtual denial that Eupolis was a political comedian. See Edwards 1993 for an attempt to sketch the historical basis for the genre's political conservatism. Sommerstein 2010, esp. 120–132, argues that the theater audience exhibited an increased "right-wing bias" (cf. n.35, 125–126) after an increase in the fee for admission in the 430s.

political elite ("demagogues," *prostatai tou demou*, "leaders/representatives/protectors of the demos"), whose exemplary members derived from households that produced commodities or services—Cleon the "hide-seller," Hyperbolus the "lamp-seller," Androcles the "prostitute" and "day-laborer," and Cleophon the "lyre-maker" (Rosenbloom 2002: 318–329). *Knights* ridicules such leaders as a class of hucksters who succeed one another like kings (125–145; cf. *Peace* 679–691; *Frogs* 725–733). Comedy depicts these wealthy politicians as low-class scoundrels of the marketplace who lack the education and moral excellence to lead (Aristophanes, *Knights* 178–181; Eupolis, *Maricas* K-A fr. 208), treating them as neither citizens nor Greeks, but as slaves and barbarians (Rosenbloom 2002: 308–309 n.102). The demos serves as their attack dogs as paid jurors (*Wasps* 704–705; cf. *Knights* 255, 946), achieving the interests of the demagogues to the detriment of the polis. These leaders represent themselves as the "watchdogs" of the masses' interests and the democracy against those of the wealthy and well-born (Connor 1971; Ostwald 1986). Old Comedy blames them for democratic misrule.

After the death of Pericles in 429, these politicians featured as the quintessential villains of Old Comedy, both in the subgenre of "demagogue comedy" (Lind 1991: esp. 235–252; Sommerstein 2000) devoted specifically to ridicule of them—Aristophanes's *Knights* (Lind 1991), Eupolis's *Maricas* (Cassio 1985; Sommerstein 2000: 441; Storey 2003: 197–214), Hermippus's *Bread Sellers* [*Artopolides*], Plato's *Hyperbolus, Peisander*, and *Cleophon*—and in comedies whose plots do not revolve around them. Achieving the aim of an Aristophanic comedy is often tantamount to expelling, excluding, humiliating, or even advocating the death of a politician, most commonly Hyperbolus or Cleonymus (*Acharnians* 836–847; *Knights* 1274–1315, 1357–1364; *Wasps* 1003–1007; *Peace* 916–921, 1316–1331). The conservatism of Old Comedy is a reaction to sociopolitical changes after the death of Pericles, as an elite of the marketplace joined the established landed and military elite as political leaders.

In the *Symposium*, Plato attributes to Aristophanes a myth in which he defines human desire (*eros*) as a yearning for the restoration of the original wholeness and unity of individuals severed from their other halves (189c1–193c5). Aristophanic comedy often enacts a return to origins, a reunion with a lost object of desire that makes individuals and the polis vigorous and whole again. *Acharnians, Peace,* and *Lysistrata* restore the peace and pleasure of pre–Peloponnesian War Athens. *Knights* returns Demos to the youthful vigor of the Persian Wars; *Frogs* fantasizes the restoration of Persian War greatness, returning Aeschylus to Athens "to save the city" (1500–1503). *Birds* and *Wealth* enact the return to a pre-Jovian, primordial time: the rule of the birds in the cosmos and the restoration of Plutus's sight, enabling moral worth to be the precondition for wealth, hence making all men (except the sycophant) rich. The ideological aim of Old Comedy accords with the wider aims of its fantasy: the restoration of a pre-demagogic polis, in which large and small landholders hold hegemony in the interests of peace, pleasure, and sociopolitical harmony.

From 424 to 405 BCE, the comic stage relished the prospect of the deaths of leaders whose litigiousness and bellicosity seemed to prevent such harmony. A reformed Demos swears he will tie a stone around Hyperbolus's neck and cast him into the pit where traitors were thrown (*Knights* 973–976). *Frogs* threatens Cleophon with extralegal murder and forced suicide a year before oligarchs executed him (674–685, 1510–1514; cf. Schol. E. *Orestes* 772; Rosenbloom 2012: 433–435). A character in Plato sums up Old Comic attitudes toward this political elite: he laments the lack of an Ioleos to cauterize the heads of the Hydra that the "vile" (*poneroi*) democratic orators had become in the city—when one dies, two spring up to take his place (K-A fr. 202; cf. Aristophanes *Wasps* 1029–1043).

The extent of the humiliation Old Comedy inflicted on these leaders appears in the degrading mockery it inflicted on Hyperbolus's and Cleophon's mothers (Aristophanes, *Clouds* 551–562). Eupolis may have put Hyperbolus's mother on stage as a drunken hag dancing the vulgar comic dance (*kordax*) in *Maricas* (Aristophanes, *Clouds* 553–556). In *Bread-Sellers*, Hermippus apparently insulted her as a fat, old prostitute (*sapra kai pasiporne kai kapraina*, K-A fr. 9). Perhaps a year after Hyperbolus's death, the chorus of *Women at the Thesmophoria* advocates forcing his mother to attend women's festivals with a shorn head and to sit behind mothers of respected public figures, such as Lamachus. The chorus goes further: if Hyperbolus's mother lends money at interest, people should not pay it, "but should take her money by force, saying this: 'here's the interest [*tokou*] you deserve, having born such a child [*tokon*]'" (844–845). Plato depicted Cleophon's mother speaking to him in "native" Thracian (Schol. Ar. *Frogs* 681).

The late-fifth-century comic stage transformed these leaders into ritual scapegoats (*katharmata, pharmakoi*).[6] So did the oligarchs who overthrew democracy in 411 and 404 BCE: they murdered Hyperbolus (Th. 8.73.3, on Samos), Androcles (Th. 8.65.2), and Cleophon (Lys. 13.7–12; 30.10–14) as a precondition of their rise to power. The oligarchic takeover and bloodbath of 404/3—some 1,500 were killed—started when political actors branded *poneroi* were murdered with the tacit support of the society at large (Lys. 25.19; [Arist.] *Ath.Pol.* 35.3; cf. X. *HG* 2.3.12; D.S. 14.4.2–3; Rosenbloom 2004b: 339–341). The actual violence of oligarchic revolution realized the symbolic violence of scapegoating *prostatai tou demou* in fifth-century comedy (*pace* Carriere 1979: 47). Whatever the comedians' intentions and views, their plays were virtually scripts for revolution (Rosenbloom 2002, Rosenbloom 2003, Rosenbloom 2004a, Rosenbloom 2004b, Rosenbloom 2012). Fifth-century comedy's invention of the "demagogue" determined the entire tradition of thought and writing about the figure (Rosenbloom 2012: 408–416). And no voices arose to contradict it.

Severed from its roots in Ionian *pharmakos* ritual, post-Aristophanic comedy tempered its ridicule of democratic political leaders. The tyranny, slaughter, and civil war of 404/3 demonstrated that there were no viable alternatives to democracy and the rule of law at Athens. The expression of fierce contempt for such politician-sellers as Cleon, Hyperbolus, and Cleophon in fifth-century comedy expressed and fed the rage

---

[6] *Pharmakoi*: *Knights* 1121–1130 with Schol., 1404–1405; *Frogs* 730–733 with Schol.; Eupolis K-A fr. 384 for generals; Rosenbloom 2002: 329–337. For *pharmakos* ritual, see Bremmer 1983; Huber 2005, esp. 115–130.

of disgruntled citizens against democracy. That political leaders came from households producing goods and services for the market was itself a scandal (e.g., Aristophanes, *Knights* 128–143, 178–194, 1300–1315; Cratinus, *Pytine* K-A fr. 209). Politicians deriving from such households gained greater acceptance in the next generation, particularly since some, such as Anytus, Cephalus, and perhaps Archinus and Thrasybulus, were instrumental in returning the demos to power in 403/2 and handling the delicate process of democratic restoration and normalization (Strauss 1986; Rosenbloom 2004b: 341–349).

Old Comedy exploited *parrhesia* and the democratic context of its performance to ridicule democracy. The terms of its ridicule—democracy as a socioeconomic order in which villains of the marketplace turn the polis and its institutions into commodities and transform citizens into hired labor, profiting from their leadership—articulated and fed the rage of those who demanded a ruling elite of the well-born, aristocratically educated, militarily trained, and landed wealthy (e.g., Aristophanes, *Frogs* 721–737). The scapegoating of *prostatai tou demou* who rose to leadership as litigators and defenders of the demos anticipated the violence of oligarchic revolution in 411 and 404. This factor catalyzed the development of different forms of comedy and of political comedy in the fourth century (cf. Sommerstein 2000: 444).

Philippides responded to a long tradition of ambivalence toward comic *parrhesia* when he excoriated Stratocles's flattery of Demetrius Poliorcetes: changing the sacred calendar and turning the Acropolis into an inn and the Parthenon into a brothel, as Philippides alleges Stratocles did on behalf of his Macedonian patron, not only cause divine disfavor, but "this subverts democracy (*kataluei demon*), not comedy" (K-A fr. 25). Philippides's denial that comedy "subverts democracy" implies accusations to this effect against the genre.

AFTER ARISTOPHANES: FROM *PROSTATAI TOU DEMOU* TO COMIC TYPES

Scholars are divided on the social and political tenor of comedy after the death of Aristophanes. For some, "fourth-century Athenians were much less public-spirited, more caught up in private affairs, more hedonistic" (Sutton 1990: 88; cf. Arnott 1989: 24). Others, such as Nesselrath (1997: 272), find a "reflection of political life...on a level still comparable...with Old Comedy." There is some truth to both positions. Ad hominem political invective persists, but the seller-politician-barbarian-slave-scapegoat vanishes from the comic stage, and with it the potential of comic ridicule to inflame revolutionary sentiment. Rather than central figures whose humiliation and expulsion are central to comic plots, politicians for the most part became peripheral to the plots of comedies after Aristophanes's death. Fourth-century comedy continues the tradition of the fifth century to this extent: it ridicules politicians of avowed loyalty to the demos and democracy with greater vehemence than those whose allegiance to the demos was dubious.

Timocles's *Demosatyrs* ("Satyrs of the People"; cf. Hermippus, *Fates* K-A fr. 47, for Pericles as "King of the Satyrs") and *Icarian Satyrs* may have been exceptional in that they focused on politicians (Constantinides 1969). The five extant fragments of *Icarian Satyrs* ridicule Hyperides (*APF* 517–20), Thudippus (*APF* 229), Telemachus of Acharnae (*PA* 13562), Cephisodorus (*PA* 8351), and Aristomedes (*APF* 65–66). The most distinguished orator of the group, Hyperides, receives the harshest treatment. Timocles's ridicule of him recalls Aristophanes's mockery of Cleon as Paphlagon (= "Paphlagonian" and "splutterer, blusterer"): he compares Hyperides to a fish-filled river that splutters (*paphlazon*) loud boasts and calls him "a hireling who waters the plain of one who gives [bribes]" (K-A fr. 17).

The most fiercely ridiculed politician in comedy of the period, Callistratus of Aphidna (*PA* 8157; *APF* 277–282; Sealey 1956; Antiphanes K-A fr. 293; Anaxandrides *Protesilaus* K-A fr. 41 with Scholtz 1996), was a popular politician, general, and imperialist who held his wealth primarily in liquid form. In *Mede*, Theopompus belittles his efforts to refound Athenian naval hegemony (IG II² 43; Cargill 1981) as doling out "small change" (K-A fr. 31). After his interlocutor comments on the size and beauty of his buttocks, Chariades declares that Callistratus should be enrolled as a street-walking "butt-boy" (Eubulus *Antiope* K-A fr. 10; cf. Cratinus *Pytine* K-A fr. 209). Eubulus indulges his fixation on Callistratus's bottom again in *Sphingokarion* when a character offering a riddle whose solution is "asshole" (*proktos*) has his interlocutor answer "Callistratus": they speak though tongueless; have the same name though male and female; are sometimes smooth, sometimes hairy; violate law after law (or melody after melody); are one and many; and if penetrated, remain unwounded (K-A fr. 106). The equivalence of democratic orator and passive homosexual or male prostitute persists from Old Comedy (e.g. Aristophanes *Knights* 417–425, 1241–1242; *Clouds* 1093; *Assemblywomen* 112–113; Plato K-A fr. 202).

Comedians ridicule Demosthenes, the premier democratic orator of his time, for insisting that Philip "give back" Halonnesus to the Athenians rather than "give" it to them (e.g., Antiphanes *Neottis* K-A fr. 167) and for swearing "by earth" (Antiphanes K-A fr. 288; Timocles K-A fr. 41). Timocles sarcastically mocks him as a blustering monster, a Briareus, who devours catapults and spears, despises discourse and counterproposals, and has the look of war in his eyes—but is too much a coward to fight (*Heroes* K-A fr. 12). Insulting references to Demosthenes as a "knife-seller," essential to Old Comic political ridicule, do not appear in the remains of fourth-century comedy, which represent politicians as consumers rather than hucksters. Aeschines includes such material in his ridicule of Demosthenes (3.93). The Old Comic demagogue-seller is more at home in the fourth-century law court than in the theater (Rosenbloom 2003).

Comedians mock Aristogeiton and Telemachus of Acharnae for low social origins: Telemachus carries a pot in his arms "like a newly bought Syrian slave" (Timocles, *Dionysus* K-A fr. 7); a character in Alexis's *Libation Bearer* claims to have seen Aristogeiton wearing a charcoal basket, implying servile status (Arnott 1996: 604–605).

Such ridicule is a far cry from Aristophanes's depiction of Cleon as the newly bought slave Paphlagon (*Knights* 43–45); Eupolis's representation of Hyperbolus as Maricas, a Persian menial; or Plato's slander of Hyperbolus as a Lydian slave, unable to speak Attic Greek, who wins the lottery for the Council ahead of his master, his alternate (Plato, *Hyperbolus* K-A frs. 182–183, 185). It is far milder than the character assassinations of Aristogeiton in contemporary forensic oratory (D. 25; [D.] 26; Din. 2; Rosenbloom 2003).

The treatment of Callimedon, nicknamed "the crayfish" (*ho karabos*; *PA* 8032; *APF* 279), demonstrates that comedians mocked anti-democratic politicians with a lighter touch than their democratic counterparts. Plutarch calls Callimedon "insolent and hostile to the demos [*misodemos*]" (*Phoc.* 27.9). He joined the Macedonian Antipater after Leosthenes besieged him at Lamia in 323 (Plut. *Dem.* 27.1–3), and his fortunes rose and fell with those of Phocion (Plut. *Phoc.* 33.4, 35). Extant fragments do not ridicule him for his politics. Perhaps comedians feared his Macedonian backers, but it is more likely that they neglected anti-democratic figures much as did fifth-century comedians did. Callimedon's hostility to the demos did not merit ridicule per se.

The majority of references to Callimedon mock his walleyes, his gluttony, and his nickname.[7] Theophilus ridicules him as an insipid orator, reducing him to his nickname by staging a son serving his father seafood: "The squid is excellent, Dad. How do you like the crayfish?" His father answers, "It's insipid [*psychros*]. I've got no taste for orators" (*Doctor* K-A fr. 4; cf. Philemon, *Metion* K-A fr. 43: by eating crayfish, Callimedon's son Agyrrhius ate his father). Another speaker hopes that his interlocutor will become a magistrate of the market (*agoranomos*) and prevent Callimedon from wreaking havoc in the fish market. The interlocutor replies: "You're talking about the work of tyrants, not of *agoranomoi*. Yes, the man's a handful [*machimos*], but he is useful [*chresimos*] to the city" (K-A fr. 249). Post-Aristophanic comedy favors the rule of law: an *agoranomos* upholds the law, and Callimedon's actions in the fish market are not illegal. Clearly, this character does not use love for the demos as a criterion for Callimedon's worth to the city. But why would he be "*chresimos* to the city?" Perhaps he was useful as a pro-Macedonian agent, whether as a member of the sixty diners whose fame reached Philip of Macedon and won the gift of a talent from him (Athen. 14.3 Kaibel) or as an opponent of Demosthenes (cf. Din. 4.94; Plut. *Dem.* 27.1–3; Athen. 3.57 Kaibel), or as a big spender in a city obsessed with economic value (see, e.g., Engen 2010).

Certainly fish-sellers valued his presence in the city for this last reason. In terms mirroring official decrees, a character in Alexis announces that fish-sellers have voted to erect a statue of Callimedon in the fish market during the Panathenaea, "since he is singled-handedly the savior of their trade, but all the rest are a liability" (*Dorcis* or *Girl*

---

[7] Wall-eyed: Alexis, *Crateia* or *Drug Seller* K-A fr. 117; Timocleides, *Busybody* K-A fr. 29; love of eel: Alexis, *Woman Who Drinks Mandrake* K-A fr. 149; Menander, *Drunkenness* K-A fr. 224; love of gray fish: Antiphanes, *Gorythus* K-A fr. 7; love of sow's belly: Alexis, *Man of Pontos* K-A fr. 198; Euphron, *A Girl Betrayed* K-A fr. 8; love of salt fish: Eubulus, *Men Trying to Return Safely* K-A fr. 8; nickname and/or love of crayfish: Alexis, *Isostasion* K-A fr. 102, *Pancratiast* K-A fr. 173; Antiphanes, *Fisherwoman* K-A fr. 27.5–8; Euphron, *A Girl Betrayed* K-A fr. 8; Philemon, *Metion* K-A fr. 43.

who Smacks Her Lips K-A fr. 57). Callimedon is mocked for spending a fortune on fish and for being honored by a despised segment of the city. Timocles mocks Thudippus, who embraced oligarchy with Phocion and died with him (Plut. *Phoc.* 35.1, 36.3), for disgusting flatulence (*Icarian Satyrs* K-A fr. 18.2–3). The others Plutarch names as sentenced to death with Phocion—Nicocles, Hegemon, Pythocles, and Charicles—are unmentioned in extant comedy. Unlike Callimedon and Thudippus, politicians serving the demos's interests are accused of spending ill-gotten gains on expensive seafood.

Misreading a riddle, a character in Antiphanes's *Sappho* sees *rhetores* as screeching profiteers who feed themselves and ridicule one another beside the demos, which is blind and deaf to their activities (K-A fr. 194; cf. Eubulus, *Sphingokarion* K-A fr. 106). In *Delos*, Timocles ridicules democratic politicians for taking bribes. One speaker reports blameworthy and illegal bribe-taking, while his interlocutor's ridiculous attempts to deflect culpability emphasize it. The speaker reports that Demosthenes possesses fifty talents, and the interlocutor replies: "and blessed he will be, if he shares it with nobody" (K-A fr. 4). This same speaker responds to the notice that Moerocles has a ton of money with the maxim "the giver is a nitwit, but the recipient fortunate" (ibid.). He forgives Demon and Callisthenes for taking bribes because "they were poor" (ibid.). Hyperides, "terribly clever at speaking," again receives harsher ridicule: the glutton will use bribe money to enrich greedy fishmongers (ibid.).

The fourth-century comic politician is less a monster that needs to be destroyed than a nuisance. Antiphanes's Callistratus is a gluttonous pest who can be gotten rid of with a chef (K-A fr. 293). The unitary seller-politician-villain of Old Comedy becomes differentiated to form the types of Middle and New Comedy; the scapegoat figure vanishes from comedy, kept alive in forensic rhetoric (Rosenbloom 2003). Old Comedy represented the *prostates tou demou* as a clever slave, boastful chef, parasite (e.g., Aristophanes, *Knights* 103, 213–216, 280–283, 1290–1299) slanderer, sycophant (40–72), the demos's *erastes* ("lover," 730–740, 1340–1345), and prostitute (Wohl 2002: 73–123). In fourth-century comedy, these roles become differentiated to form stock characters. A character in Diphilus equates the oath of an orator and of a prostitute (K-A fr. 101; cf. Callistratus above), but fourth-century comedy focuses on celebrated courtesans such as Neaera, Nannio, and Phryne (Webster 1970: esp. 22–23, 63–64; Henry 1985; Davidson 1997). A commonplace of the time is Solon's supposed institution of cheap prostitutes in Athens as "democratic" (*demotikon*, "on the side of the demos," Philemon, *Brothers* K-A fr. 3).[8]

Differentiated from the comic demagogue—for whom politics is like making sausages and who is adjured to "always win over the demos with a cook's rhetoric" (Aristophanes *Knights* 213–216)—the boastful chef, a contemptible, pompous hireling, becomes a fixture of post-Aristophanic comedy (Scodel 1993a; Wilkins 2000). The comic demagogue,

---

[8] Reading *nomon* rather than Kaibel's *monon* with K-A. See further Eubulus, *Nannion* K-A fr. 67; *All Night Revel* K-A fr. 87; Xenarchus, *Porphyra* K-A fr. 4. Rosivach (1995) and Frost (2002) rightly doubt the historicity of this tradition; see Scafuro, chapter 9, this volume.

a parasite and flatterer of the demos (Rosenbloom 2002: 306–307 with n.93), yields in fourth-century comedy to the stock character of the flattering parasite (Ribbeck 1883; Nesselrath 1990: 309–317; Arnott 1968; 2008: 322–324). The inventor of the parasite's art—eating other people's food—was "democratic in his ways" (*demotikos...tous tropous*, Eubulus, *Oedipus* K-A fr. 72; contrast, e.g., Diodorus, *Heiress* K-A fr. 4). A character in Diphilus's *Marriage* rants about the effects of the flatterer: such short-term pleasure overturns general, dynast, friends, and cities and has corrupted the masses and skewed their judgments (K-A fr. 23). Fourth-century comedy depicts democracy in an ironic and undermining way, as a locus for cheap sex and flattery for free meals, while suggesting the ethical implications of such an order.

Fishmongers replace democratic politicians as villains of the marketplace whose "vileness" (*poneria*) parallels that of the fifth-century politicians (Rosenbloom 2003; Paulas 2010 attributes their negative portrayal to the bazaar market, where communication and expectations about price were minimal). Characters in comedies rejoice not in their violation and/or extralegal death but in their being subjected to laws, real or imagined. Alexis offers two such laws allegedly introduced by Aristonicus: that any fishmonger who sells for less than his stated price can be dragged to jail (*Cauldron* K-A fr. 130, possibly genuine) and that all fishmongers must sell standing, a preliminary to next year's law that they must sell suspended like *dei ex machina* (*Cauldron* K-A fr. 131, fictional; Arnott 1996: 363–365, 377–383; for fishmongers breaking the law that forbids watering their fish, see Xenarchus, *Porphyra* K-A fr. 7). Nor do fishmongers steal from the public treasury; they impose tributes and tithes on consumers and destroy entire fortunes in a single day (Alexis, *Pylaea* K-A fr. 204). The focus of fourth-century comedy shifts to high-end consumption, and fishmongers, depicted as low-class scoundrels putting on airs (Amphis, *Vagabond* K-A fr. 30; Diphilus, *Busybody* K-A fr. 67) and selling expensive and often putrid food (Antiphanes, *Cnoethideus* or *Potbelly* K-A fr. 123; *Seducers* K-A fr. 159), are targets for the ire of the wealthy because of their deceptive, greedy, and vile character and practices (e.g., Diphilus, *Busybody* K-A fr. 67; cf. Antiphanes, *Hater of Bad Character* K-A fr. 157: bankers win the title "most abominable class" over fishmongers).

Fourth-century comedy after Aristophanes offers continuities with its fifth-century counterpart: democratic politicians take bribes, boast and splutter, are akin to prostitutes and slaves, and eat expensive seafood. Likewise, politicians devoted to the interests of the demos receive harsher treatment than those whose fidelity to the demos was suspect. Politicians are no longer the focus of comic plots or the arch-villains of the genre who need to be eradicated from the polis. Rather, the elements that went into the figure of the comic demagogue in the fifth century become differentiated into stock characters: villains of the marketplace, such as fishmongers, replace demagogue-sellers; "the rhetoric of cooks" becomes the discourse of the boastful chef rather than of the orator; parasites and flatterers are not *prostatai tou demou*, but those who flatter stupid, wealthy men to win a place at their table, though their art might still be depicted as "democratic"; the sycophant, though mentioned in later comedy (Diphilus, *Overseas Trader* K-A fr. 31; Alexis, *Poets* K-A fr. 187), is no longer the democratic politician (e.g., Aristophanes,

Knights 437; *Peace* 651–56). The demagogue as huckster and *"pornos* of the people" (Wohl 2002), whose worth is measured in terms of famous prostitutes (e.g., Aristophanes, *Women at the Thesmophoria* 805), and whose speech is nothing more than billingsgate (e.g., Aristophanes *Knights* 284–299), for the most part disappears from comedy, though it persists in the rhetoric of the law courts. The high-priced *hetairai* of the fourth century eclipse the politician-prostitutes of the fifth.

CONCLUSION: THE EVOLUTION OF COMEDY

Comedy and the Athens depicted in it evolve in the direction of conformity to the rule of law. Old Comic plots subvert or alter laws and policies of the demos and polis (Buis, chapter 15, this volume) and are overtly hostile toward democratic law courts (e.g., Telecleides, *Amphictyons* K-A fr. 2), where democratic power was concentrated (Aristophanes, *Wasps* 518–600; *Ath.Pol.* 9.1; Hansen 1974: 15–18). Old Comedy harshly ridiculed prosecutors who represented the demos in the prosecution of public crimes (Christ 1998: 118–159; Rosenbloom 2002: 292–300) and paid jurors who delivered verdicts (Rosenbloom 2002: 318–329). *Knights* concludes with the festive closing of the courts (1316–1318); *Assemblywomen* converts the courts into common messes (676). Evading the Athenian courts is the starting point of *Birds* (30–48; cf. 108–111, 1410–1469); ending Philocleon's jury service is the objective of the first half of *Wasps*. Litigiousness is a defining feature of Athens (Aristophanes, *Clouds* 207–208) and cause of comic mockery (*Birds* 39–42; *Assemblywomen* 439).

By contrast, "New comedy is...the most rule-bound and programmed of all classical narrative genres" (Lowe 2000: 190). The conduct of characters in New Comedy "is influenced by the pervasive effect of Athenian law and its sanctions upon their daily lives" (Scafuro 1997: 9–10). The telos of Menandrian comedy, marriage between two Athenian citizens, conforms to the laws of Athens (Lape 2004: 15–16). Respect for the rule of law is a feature of post-Aristophanic comedy; its features mirror the sentiments of Demosthenes, who declared that even if he were the vilest and most shamefully profiteering orator, he would deserve a trial and not extralegal violence (21.189). This attitude was foreign to Old Comedy.

In the early fourth century, comic plots evolve toward the enactment of equality between rich and poor. Aristophanes's *Assemblywomen* and *Wealth* realize such equality as the outcome of the plot. The former decrees communal ownership of property; the latter makes all honest and decent people (*chrestoi*) rich. Aristophanes's treatment of the theme involves the entire polis. New Comedy limits the fantasy to rich and poor families, which combine in marriage sealed by transfers of wealth (e.g., *Dyskolos, Samia*); the deserving poor become rich at the end of the play. At the same time, Menandrian comedy virtually institutionalizes asymmetry between rich and poor: love is the luxury of a rich youth, who either falls in love with or violates a less-well-off Athenian girl. The path to wealth is the largess of the wealthy (Rosivach 1998).

In general, comedy evolves from sympathy with the rich as victims of a democratic system that provides incentives for confiscating their wealth (e.g., Aristophanes, *Knights* 264–265, 324–327, 923–926, 1357–1361) to pity for the plight of poverty. Menander's *Farmer* expresses poverty with a realism and poignancy alien to extant fifth-century comedy. A character complains that contempt for the words of a poor man comes easy: people assume he speaks only for the sake of financial gain. Wearing a threadbare cloak (*tribon*), he is dubbed a "sycophant, even if he happens to be a victim of injustice" (fr. 1 Gomme/Sandbach; see further, e.g., Alexis, *Woman of Olynthus* K-A fr. 167, with Arnott 1996: 485–486). Niceratus, however, praises Athens as offering "plain and simple goods of poor folk" (Menander, *Samia* 100–101).

Comedy grows increasingly urban, free comic characters wealthier, and plots more *oikos*-centered. In particular, the Attic farmer-citizen-hoplite, the distinctive hero of Old Comedy, who plots to transform the cosmos, his society, or his place in that society, becomes obsolete. The sociopolitical view of the world he represents, which emphasizes the identity of the democratic citizen and the farmer, the self-sufficient life of the Attic countryside, and the nexus of small and large landowners, dies with Old Comedy; the fourth century develops away from this figure, depicting him as an ill-mannered country bumpkin (Konstantakos 2005). Rather, fourth-century comedy foregrounds economic identities marginalized in Old Comedy, as plays with titles such as *Cobbler, Plasterer, Fuller, Gardener, Ass Driver, Brick Carrier, Stone Mason, Porter, Miller, Well Digger, Wool Carders, Wool Workers, Seamstress* attest (see further Arnott 2008: 311–315). Urban commerce and urbanity play a larger role in fourth-century comedy (Rosenbloom 2004b), which explores the mutual dependence of urban consumers and the retailers who provide them with the goods and services required for the good life. Menandrian comedy retreats somewhat from the public space of the agora, but the families at the center of his comedy are exceptionally wealthy: they dower their daughters with two (*Shield* 135–136, 269, 321), three (*Dyskolos* 842–844) and four talents (*Epitrepontes* 134–135), magnitudes infrequently attested in actual dowries (Schaps 1979: 99; Casson 1976: 59 for the wealth of new comic characters).

The political tendency of Menander's comedy has been interpreted in a variety of ways. Scholars used to read Menander as apolitical and escapist (Tarn and Griffith 1952: 273; Gomme and Sandbach 1973: 23–24; Webster 1974: 4). More recently, scholars have differed over whether his drama supported Macedonian-imposed oligarchy (Owens 2011; Major 1997), or whether it "not only depicts and champions fundamental precepts of democratic ideology but... also...offers reaction to and commentaries on immediate political events" (Lape 2004: 10). Like Theophrastus (*Characters* 26), Menander mocks the "oligarchic man" defined by greed for power and profit, as Smicrines in *Sikyonioi* shows. Smicrines's a priori rejection of a claimant's appeal in favor of the finding of a committee (150–155) wins him the epithets "oligarchic" and "vile" (*poneros*, 156), a combination first made possible by the oligarchy of the Thirty (Rosenbloom 2003). The narrative of the democrat Blepes, reporting how members of the Eleusinian deme favored the appeals of Stratophanes over Moschion, reinforces the virtue of the democratic sensibility (176–271). Yet Smicrines will turn out to be Moschion's and Stratophanes's father, reducing the significance of political differences between them. And the model for Blepes's narrative, Euripides's *Orestes* 864–956, seems chosen precisely because it presents the dark side of the democratic process. In it, Tyndareus and a demagogue in his hire exploit the anger of a demos incapable of rationality, sympathy, and respect for nobility—the very qualities the crowd hearing Stratophanes's case in *Sikyonioi* displays. *Sikyonioi* represents mass decision-making in a positive light, but the passage from *Orestes* that it evokes diminishes the appeal of democratic decision-making (cf. Hofmeister 1997: 303–316).

Comedians preserved a conservative outlook from the democracy of the 420s through Macedonian hegemony a century later. Perhaps at the heart of comedy are principles similar to those Aristotle espouses in the *Politics*. Democracies, he maintains, have to spare the wealthy, and oligarchies have to show concern for the poor and reduce inequality (1309a14–32). Comedians consistently valued both principles.

BIBLIOGRAPHY

Arnott, P. D. 1989. *Public and Performance in the Greek Theatre*. London: Routledge.
Arnott, W. G. 1968. "Studies in Comedy I: Alexis and the Parasite's Name." *GRBS* 9: 161–168.
——. 1996. *Alexis: The Fragments: A Commentary*. Cambridge, UK: Cambridge University Press.
——. 2008. "Middle Comedy." In *Brill's Companion to the Study of Greek Comedy*, edited by G. Dobrov, 279–331. Leiden: E. J. Brill.
Arrowsmith, W. 1973. "Aristophanes' Birds: The Fantasy Politics of Eros." *Arion* 1: 119–167.
Boedeker, D., and K. Raaflaub, eds. 1998. *Democracy, Empire, and the Arts in Fifth-Century Athens*. Center for Hellenic Studies Colloquia 2. Cambridge, MA: Harvard University Press.
Bowie, E. 2008. "Myth and Ritual in Comedy." In *Brill's Companion to the Study of Greek Comedy*, edited by G. Dobrov, 143–176. Leiden: E. J. Brill.
Bremmer, J. 1983. "Scapegoat Rituals in Ancient Greece." *HSCP* 87: 299–320.
Buck, R. 1998. *Thrasybulus and the Athenian Democracy: The Life of an Athenian Statesman*. Historia Einzelschriften Heft 120. Stuttgart: Franz Steiner.
Cairns, D. L., and R. A. Knox, eds. 2004. *Law, Rhetoric, and Comedy in Classical Athens: Essays in Honour of Douglas M. MacDowell*. Swansea: The Classical Press of Wales.
Carey, C. 1994. "Comic Ridicule and Democracy." In *Ritual, Finance and Politics: Athenian Democratic Accounts Presented to David M. Lewis*, edited by R. Osborne and S. Hornblower, 69–83. Oxford: Clarendon Press.
Cargill, J. 1981. *The Second Athenian Sea League: Empire or Free Alliance?* Berkeley: University of California Press.
Carriere, J.-C. 1979. *Le carnaval et la politique: Une introduction à la comédie grecque, suivie d'un choix de fragments*. Annales Litteraires de l' Université de Besançon 212. Paris: Les Belles Lettres.
Cassio, A. 1985. "Old Persian *Marika-*, Eupolis' *Marikas*, and Aristophanes' *Knights*." *CQ* 35: 38–42.
Casson, L. 1976. The Athenian Upper Class and New Comedy. *TAPA* 106: 29–59.
Chaniotis, A. "The Illusions of Democracy in the Hellenistic World." Available at http://athensdialogues.chs.harvard.edu/cgi-bin/WebObjects/athensdialogues.woa/wa/dist?dis=43. Last accessed September 3, 2013.

Christ, M. 1998. *The Litigious Athenian*. Baltimore: Johns Hopkins University Press.

Connor, W. R. 1971. *The New Politicians of Fifth-Century Athens*. Princeton: Princeton University Press.

Constantinides, E. 1969. "Timocles' *Ikarioi Satyroi*: A Reconsideration." *TAPA* 100: 49–61.

Csapo, E. 2000. "From Aristophanes to Menander? Genre Transformation in Greek Comedy." In *Matrices of Genre: Authors, Canons, and Society*, edited by M. Depew and D. Obbink, 115–133. Center for Hellenic Studies Colloquia 4. Cambridge, MA: Harvard University Press.

——. 2010. *Actors and Icons of the Ancient Theater*. Malden, MA: Blackwell.

Csapo, E., and W. J. Slater. 1994. *The Context of Ancient Drama*. Ann Arbor: University of Michigan Press.

Davidson, J. 1997. *Courtesans and Fishcakes: The Consuming Passions of Classical Athens*. London: Fontana.

Davidson, J., F. Muecke, and P. Wilson, eds. 2006. *Greek Drama III: Essays in Honour of Kevin Lee*. BICS Supplement 87. London: Institute of Classical Studies.

Davidson, J., and A. Pomeroy, eds. 2003. *Theatres of Action: Papers for Chris Dearden*. Auckland: Polygraphia.

Depew, M., and D. Obbink, eds. 2000. *Matrices of Genre: Authors, Canons, and Society*. Center for Hellenic Studies Colloquia 4. Cambridge, MA: Harvard University Press.

Dobrov, G., ed., 1995. *Beyond Aristophanes: Tradition and Diversity in Greek Comedy*. Atlanta: Scholars Press.

——, ed. 1997. *The City as Comedy: Society and Representation in Athenian Drama*. Chapel Hill: University of North Carolina Press.

——, ed. 2008. *Brill's Companion to the Study of Greek Comedy*. Leiden: E. J. Brill.

Eder, W., ed. 1995. *Die athenische Demokratie im 4 Jahrhundert v. Chr.* Stuttgart: Franz Steiner.

Engen, D. 2010. *Honor and Profit: Athenian Trade Policy and the Economy and Society of Greece, 415–307 B.C.E.* Ann Arbor: University of Michigan Press.

Edwards, A. T. 1993. "Historicizing the Popular Grotesque: Bakhtin's *Rabelais* and Attic Old Comedy." In *Theater and Society in the Classical World*, edited by R. Scodel, 89–117. Ann Arbor: University of Michigan Press.

Ferguson, W. S. 1911. *Hellenistic Athens*. London: Macmillan. Reprinted 1969, New York: Howard Fertig.

Frost, F. 2002. "Solon *Pornoboskos* and Aphrodite Pandemos." *Syllecta Classica* 13: 34–36.

Gagarin, M., and D. Cohen, eds. 2005. *The Cambridge Companion to Ancient Greek Law*. Cambridge, UK: Cambridge University Press.

Goldhill, S. 1991. *The Poet's Voice: Essays on Poetics and Greek Literature*. Cambridge, UK: Cambridge University Press.

Gomme, A. W. 1940. "The Old Oligarch." In *Athenian Studies Presented to W. S. Ferguson, HSCP* Supplement 1, 211–245. Cambridge, MA: Harvard University Press.

——. 1945. *A Historical Commentary on Thucydides*. Vol. 1. Oxford: Clarendon Press.

——, and F. H. Sandbach. 1973. *Menander: A Commentary*. Oxford: Oxford University Press.

Habicht, Chr. 1993. "The Comic Poet Archedikos." *Hesperia* 62: 253–256.

——. 1997. *Athens from Alexander to Antony*. Translated by D. L. Schneider. Cambridge, MA: Harvard University Press. Orig. pub. as *Athen: Die Geschichte der Stadt in hellenistischer Zeit*. Munich: Beck, 1995.

Halliwell, S. 1991. "Comic Satire and Freedom of Speech in Classical Athens." *JHS* 111: 48–70.

——. 1991a. "The Uses of Laughter in Greek Culture." *CQ* 41: 279–296.

——. 2004. "Aischrology, Shame, and Comedy." In *Free Speech in Classical Antiquity*, edited by I. Sluiter and R. Rosen, 115–144. Leiden: Brill.

——. 2008. *Greek Laughter: A Study of Cultural Psychology from Homer to Early Christianity.* Cambridge, UK: Cambridge University Press.

Handley, E. 1953. "XOPOY in the *Plutus*." *CQ* 3: 55–61.

Hansen, M. H. 1974. *The Sovereignty of the People's Court in Athens in the Fourth Century B.C. and the Public Action against Unconstitutional Proposals.* Odense University Classical Studies 4. Translated by J. Raphaelsen and S. Holbøll. Odense, Denmark: Odense University Press.

——. 1986. *Demography and Democracy: The Number of Athenian Citizens in the Fourth Century B.C.* Herning, Denmark: Systime.

——. 1991. *The Athenian Democracy in the Age of Demosthenes: Structure, Principles, and Ideology.* Translated by J. A. Crook. Oxford: Blackwell.

Harding, P. 1994. "Comedy and Rhetoric." In *Persuasion: Greek Rhetoric in Action,* edited by I. Worthington, 196–221. London: Routledge.

Harvey, D., and J. Wilkins, eds. 2000. *The Rivals of Aristophanes: Studies in Athenian Old Comedy.* London: Classical Press of Wales.

Heath, M. 1997. "Aristophanes and the Discourse of Politics." In *The City as Comedy: Society and Representation in Athenian Comedy,* edited by G. Dobrov, 230–249. Chapel Hill: University of North Carolina Press.

Henderson, J. 1990. "The Demos and Comic Competition." In *Nothing to Do with Dionysos? Athenian Drama in its Social Context,* edited by J. J. Winkler and F. I. Zeitlin. 271-314. Princeton: Princeton University Press

Henderson, J. 1998. "Attic Old Comedy, Frank Speech, and Democracy. In *Democracy, Empire, and the Arts in Fifth-Century Athens,* edited by D. Boedeker and K. A. Raaflaub, 255-273. Cambridge, MA: Harvard University Press.

Henderson, J. 2007. "Drama and Democracy." In *The Cambridge Companion to the Age of Pericles,* edited by L. Samons II, 79–95. Cambridge: Cambridge University Press.

Henry, M. 1985. *Menander's Courtesans and the Greek Comic Tradition.* Frankfurt am Main: Peter Lang.

Hofmeister, T. 1997. "αἱ πᾶσαι πόλεις: Polis and *oikoumenê* in Menander." In *The City as Comedy: Society and Representation in Athenian Drama,* edited by G. Dobrov, 289-342. Chapel Hill: University of North Carolina Press.

Huber, I. 2005. *Rituale der Seuchen- und Schadensabwehr im Vorderen Orient und Griechenland: Formen kollektiver Krisenbewältigung in der Antike.* Stuttgart: F. Steiner Verlag.

Hunter, R. L. 1979. "The Comic Chorus in the Fourth Century." *ZPE* 36: 26–38.

——, ed. 1983. *Eubulus: The Fragments.* Cambridge, UK: Cambridge University Press.

Jones, A. M. H. 1957. *Athenian Democracy.* Oxford: Basil Blackwell.

Knox, B. M. W. 1979. "Myth and Attic Tragedy." In *Word and Action: Essays on the Ancient Theater,* by B. M. W. Knox, 3–24. Baltimore: Johns Hopkins University Press.

Köhler, U. 1878. "Dokumente zur Geschichte des athenischen Theaters." *MDAI(A)* 3: 229–258.

Konstantakos, I. 2005. "Aspects of the Figure of the ἄγροικος in Ancient Comedy." *RhM* 148: 1–26.

——. 2011. "The Conditions of Playwriting and the Comic Dramatist's Craft in the Fourth Century." *Logeion* 1: 145–184.

Koster, W. J. W. 1975. *Prolegomena de comoedia: Scholia in Archarnenses, Equites, Nubes.* Groningen: Bouma.

Krentz, P. 1982. *The Thirty at Athens*. Ithaca: Cornell University Press.

Lape, S. 2004. *Reproducing Athens: Menander's Comedy, Democratic Culture, and the Hellenistic City*. Princeton: Princeton University Press.

——. 2006. "The Poetics of the *Kōmos*-Chorus in Menander's Comedy." *AJP* 127: 89–109.

Lind, H. 1991. *Der Gerber Kleon in den Rittern des Aristophanes: Studien zur Demagogenkomödie*. Frankfurt am Main: Peter Lang.

Lowe, N. 2000. *The Classical Plot and the Invention of Western Fiction*. Cambridge, UK: Cambridge University Press.

Major, W. 1997. "Menander in a Macedonian World." *GRBS* 38: 41–78.

Markantonatos, A., and B. Zimmermann, eds. 2012. *Crisis on Stage: Tragedy and Comedy in Late Fifth-Century Athens*. Berlin: Walter de Gruyter.

Mattingly, H. B. 1997. "The Date and Purpose of the Pseudo-Xenophon Constitution of Athens." *CQ* 47: 352–357.

Nakategawa, Y. 1988. "Isegoria in Herodotus." *Historia* 38: 257–275.

Nesselrath, H.-G. 1990. *Die attische mittlere Komödie: Ihre Stellung in der antiken Literaturkritik und Literaturgeschichte*. Berlin: Walter de Gruyter.

——. 1995. "Myth, Parody, and Comic Plots: The Birth of the Gods and Middle Comedy." In *After Aristophanes: Tradition and Diversity in Greek Comedy*. Atlanta: Scholars Press, edited by G. Dobrov, 1–27.

——. 1997. "The City of Athens in Middle Comedy." In *The City as Comedy: Society and Representation in Athenian Comedy. Chapel Hill: University of North Carolina Press*, edited by G. Dobrov, 272–288.

——. 2000. "Eupolis and the Periodization of Athenian Comedy." In *The Rivals of Aristophanes: Studies in Athenian Old Comedy*, edited by D. Harvey and J. Wilkins, 233–246. London: Classical Press of Wales.

Ober, J. 1989. *Mass and Elite in Democratic Athens: Rhetoric, Ideology, and the Power of the People*. Princeton: Princeton University Press.

——. 1998. *Political Dissent in Democratic Athens: Intellectual Critics of Popular Rule*. Princeton: Princeton University Press.

Olson, S. D. 2008. "Comedy, Politics, and Society." In *Brill's Companion to the Study of Greek Comedy*, edited by G. Dobrov, 35–69. Leiden: E. J. Brill.

Osborne, R., and S. Hornblower, eds. 1994. *Ritual, Finance and Politics: Athenian Democratic Accounts Presented to David M. Lewis*. Oxford: Clarendon Press.

Ostwald, M. 1986. *From Popular Sovereignty to the Sovereignty of Law*. Berkeley: University of California Press.

O'Sullivan, L. 2009. *The Regime of Demetrius of Phalerum in Athens, 317–307 BCE*. Leiden: Brill.

Owens, W. 2011. "The Political Topicality of Menander's *Dyskolos*." *CP* 132: 349–378.

Paulas, J. 2010. "The Bazaar Fish Market in Fourth-Century Greek Comedy." *Arethusa* 43: 403–428.

Philipp, G. 1973. "Philippides, ein politischer Komiker in hellenistischer Zeit." *Gymnasium* 80: 492–509.

Pickard-Cambridge, A. 1988. *The Dramatic Festivals of Athens*. 2nd ed. Revised by J. Gould and D. M. Lewis. Oxford: Clarendon Press.

Podlecki, A. J. 1998. *Pericles and His Circle*. London: Routledge.

Raaflaub, K. 2004. *The Discovery of Freedom in Ancient Greece*. Translated by R. Franciscono. Chicago: University of Chicago Press.

Rhodes, P. J. 1993. *A Commentary on the Aristotelian* Athenaion Politeia. Oxford: Clarendon Press.

——. 2003. "Nothing to Do with Democracy: Athenian Drama and the *Polis*." *JHS* 123: 104–119.

Ribbeck, O. 1883. *Kolax: Eine ethnologische Studie.* Leipzig: S. Hirzel.

Roscher, W. 1842. *Leben, Werk und Zeitalter des Thukydides, mit einer Einleitung zur Aesthetik der historische Kunst überhaupt.* Göttingen: Vanderhoeck und Ruprecht.

Rosenbloom, D. 2002. "From *Ponêros* to *Pharmakos*: Theater, Social Drama, and Revolution in Athens, 428–404 BCE." *ClasAnt* 21: 283–346.

——. 2003. "Aristogeiton Son of Cydimachus and the Scoundrel's Drama." In *Theatres of Action: Papers for Chris Dearden,* edited by J. Davidson and A. Pomeroy, 88–117. Auckland: Polygraphia.

——. 2004a. "*Chrêstoi* vs. *Ponêroi*: The Ostracism of Hyperbolos and the Struggle for Hegemony in Athens after the Death of Perikles, Part I." *TAPA* 134: 55–105.

——. 2004b. "*Chrêstoi* vs. *Ponêroi*: The Ostracism of Hyperbolos and the Struggle for Hegemony in Athens after the Death of Perikles, Part II." *TAPA* 134: 323–358.

——. 2006. "Empire and its Discontents: *Trojan Women, Birds,* and the Symbolic Economy of Athenian Imperialism." In *Greek Drama III: Essays in Honour of Kevin Lee,* edited by J. Davidson, F. Muecke, and P. Wilson, 245–271. London: Institute of Classical Studies.

——. 2011. "The Panhellenism of Athenian Tragedy." In *Why Athens? A Reappraisal of Tragic Politics,* edited by D. Carter, 353–381. Oxford: Oxford University Press.

——. 2012. "Scripting Revolution: Democracy and its Discontents in Late Fifth-Century Drama." In *Crisis on Stage: Tragedy and Comedy in Late Fifth-Century Athens,* edited by A. Markantonatos and B. Zimmermann, 405–441. Berlin: Walter de Gruyter.

——, and J. Davidson, eds. 2012. *Greek Drama IV: Texts, Contexts, Performance.* Oxford: Aris & Phillips.

Rosivach, V. 1991. "Some Athenian Presuppositions about the Poor." *G&R* 38: 189–198.

——. 1995. "Solon's Brothels." *LCM* 20: 2–3.

——. 1998. *When a Young Man Falls in Love: The Sexual Exploitation of Women in New Comedy.* London: Routledge.

Rothwell, K. S., Jr. 1995. "The Continuity of the Chorus in Fourth-Century Attic Comedy." In *After Aristophanes: Tradition and Diversity in Greek Comedy.* Atlanta: Scholars Press, edited by G. Dobrov, 99–118.

Rusten, J., ed. 2010. *The Birth of Comedy: Texts, Documents, and Art from Athenian Comic Competitions, 486–280.* Baltimore: Johns Hopkins University Press.

Samons, L., II. 2007. *The Cambridge Companion to the Age of Pericles.* Cambridge, UK: Cambridge University Press.

Scafuro, A. 1997. *The Forensic Stage: Settling Disputes in Greco-Roman New Comedy.* Cambridge, UK: Cambridge University Press.

Schaps, D. M. 1979. *The Economic Rights of Women in Ancient Greece.* Edinburgh: University of Edinburgh Press.

Scholtz, A. 1996. "Perfume from Peron's: The Politics of Pedicure in Anaxandrides Fragment 41 Kassel-Austin." *ICS* 21: 69–86.

Scodel, R. ed. 1993. *Theater and Society in the Classical World.* Ann Arbor: University of Michigan Press.

——. 1993a. "Tragic Sacrifice and Menandrian Cooking." In *Theater and Society in the Classical World,* edited by R. Scodel, 161–176. Ann Arbor: University of Michigan Press.

Sealey, R. 1956. "Callistratos of Aphidna and his Contemporaries." *Historia* 5: 178–203.

Sidwell, K. 2009. *Aristophanes the Democrat: The Politics of Satire during the Peloponnesian War.* Cambridge, UK: Cambridge University Press.

Sluiter, I., and R. Rosen, eds. 2004. *Free Speech in Classical Antiquity*. Leiden: Brill.

Sommerstein, A. 1996. "How to Avoid Being a *Komodoumenos*." *CQ* 46: 327–356.

——. 2000. "Platon, Eupolis and the 'Demagogue Comedy.'" In *The Rivals of Aristophanes: Studies in Athenian Old Comedy*, edited by D. Harvey and J. Wilkins, 437–451. London: Classical Press of Wales.

——. 2004. "Comedy and the Unspeakable." In *Law, Rhetoric, and Comedy in Classical Athens: Essays in Honour of Douglas M. MacDowell*, edited by D. L. Cairns and R. A. Knox, 205–222. Swansea: The Classical Press of Wales.

——. 2004a. "Harassing the Satirist: the Alleged Attempts to Prosecute Aristophanes." In *Free Speech in Classical Antiquity*, edited by I. Sluiter and R. Rosen, 145–174. Leiden: Brill.

——. 2010. "The Theatre Audience, the *Demos*, and the *Suppliants* of Aeschylus." In *The Tangled Ways of Zeus: And Other Studies in and around Greek Tragedy*, by A. Sommerstein, 118–142. Oxford: Oxford University Press. First published in C. Pelling ed., *Greek Tragedy and the Historian*. Oxford: Oxford University Press, 1997, 63–79.

Ste. Croix, G. E. M. de. 1972. *The Origins of the Peloponnesian War*. London: Duckworth.

Storey, I. 1994. "The Politics of 'Angry Eupolis.'" *Ancient History Bulletin* 8: 107–120.

——. 2003. *Eupolis: Poet of Old Comedy*. Oxford: Oxford University Press.

Strauss, B. S. 1986. *Athens after the Peloponnesian War: Class, Faction, and Policy 403–386 BC*. Ithaca: Cornell University Press.

Sutton, D. F. 1990. "Aristophanes and the Transition to Middle Comedy." *LCM* 15: 81–95.

Taplin, O. 1993. *Comic Angels and Other Approaches to Greek Drama through Vase Painting*. Oxford: Oxford University Press.

Tarn, W. W., and G. T. Griffith. 1952. *Hellenistic Civilization*. 3rd ed. London: Arnold.

Thür, G. 1994. *Symposion 1993: Vorträge zur Griechischen und Hellenistischen Rechtsgeschichte*. Cologne: Böhlau.

Tracy, S. 2000. "Athenian Politicians and Inscriptions of the Years 307 to 302." *Hesperia* 69: 227–233.

Tsamakis, A. 2012. "Persians, Oligarchs, and Festivals: The Date of *Lysistrata* and *Thesmophoriazusae*." In *Crisis on Stage: Tragedy and Comedy in Late Fifth-Century Athens*, edited by A. Markantonatos and B. Zimmermann, 291–302. Berlin: Walter de Gruyter.

Wallace, R. W. 1994. "The Athenian Laws against Slander." In *Symposion 1993: Vorträge zur Griechischen und Hellenistischen Rechtsgeschichte*, edited by G. Thür, 109–124. Cologne: Böhlau.

——. 1995. "Speech, Song, and Text, Public and Private: Evolutions in Communications Media and Fora in Fourth-Century Athens." In *Die athenische Demokratie im 4 Jahrhundert v. Chr.*, edited by W. Eder, 199–217. Stuttgart: Franz Steiner.

——. 2005. "Law, Attic Comedy, and the Regulation of Comic Speech." In *The Cambridge Companion to Ancient Greek Law*, edited by M. Gagarin and D. Cohen, 357–373. Cambridge, UK: Cambridge University Press.

Webster, T. B. L. 1970. *Studies in Later Greek Comedy*. 2nd ed. Manchester: Manchester University Press.

——. 1974. *An Introduction to Menander*. Manchester: Manchester University Press.

Wilkins, J. 2000. *The Boastful Chef: The Discourse of Food in Ancient Greek Comedy*. Oxford: Oxford University Press.

Wilson, P. 2000. *The Athenian Institution of the* Khoregia: *The Chorus, the City and the Stage*. Cambridge, UK: Cambridge University Press.

——, and E. Csapo. 2012. "From *Chorêgia* to *Agônothesia*: Evidence for the Administration and Finance of the Athenian Theatre in the Late Fourth Century BC." In *Greek Drama IV: Texts, Contexts, Performance,* edited by D. Rosenbloom and J. Davidson, 300–321. Oxford: Aris & Phillips.

Winkler, J. J., and F. I. Zeitlin, eds. 1990. *Nothing to Do with Dionysos? Athenian Drama in its Social Context.* Princeton: Princeton University Press.

Wohl, V. 2002. *Love Among the Ruins: The Erotics of Athenian Democracy.* Princeton: Princeton University Press.

Zagagi, N. 1995. *The Comedy of Menander.* Bloomington: University of Indiana Press.

CHAPTER 15

....

LAW AND GREEK COMEDY

....

EMILIANO J. BUIS

τί ὦγαθ' ἀντιδικοῦμεν ἀλλήλοις ἔτι;
Why do we still go back and forth at law, my friend?

Thugenides, *Jurors* (K-A fr.1)

INTRODUCTION: ADDRESSING LAUGHS AND LAWS

....

WHILE many questions about the spectators of Athenian drama are still far from being fully answered, it is certain that the comic audience was mainly composed of adult citizens who were familiar if not intimate with Athenian law. We know from numerous sources that during the fifth and fourth centuries BCE the Athenians spent much time in court or dealing with all sorts of legal business (e.g., contracts, leases, inheritance). Large numbers served as *dikastai* ("judges," "jurors") for a year at a time or appeared in court as litigants or witnesses; all fifty-nine-year-olds served as public arbitrators who would hear most private cases for claims worth more than ten drachmas before they were sent to court. Moreover, Athenian citizens were used to listening to speakers proposing laws in the Assembly; they may also have listened to legal business in the Council for an entire year at a time and sometimes may have served a second term. If we take into account this firsthand experience of law, it is not surprising that comedy frequently refers to law and legal matters in order to accomplish its main mission, to elicit laughter and entertain the audience.

The general relationship between comedy and law, nevertheless, is not straightforward. Profound differences between the comedies of Aristophanes and those of Menander, as far as their legal background is concerned, suggest that Old and New Comedy should be discussed separately. I therefore begin with Aristophanes, first by surveying the terminology of Athenian law that is widespread in his plays and considering its use as a source for Athenian law. From there I turn to examining the different ways in which Aristophanes criticizes the courts and how his audience may have understood this critique. I follow this with a brief consideration of the legal apparatus of Aristophanes's rivals. I then focus on Menander; whereas Aristophanes's deployment of legal scenarios may be viewed as a kind of political overlay to his comic plots, Menander's deployment of the law is more fully embedded in the *oikos* ("household")-related themes of his plays.

1. Old Comedy and Athenian Law: Poetics and Politics of Justice

Despite the considerable number of studies on ancient Greek law published over the last century and their resurgence in the last two decades, Old Comedy seems to be underestimated as a source of law by a considerable number of legal historians.[1] Viewing the comic genre as a burlesque spectacle, many have disregarded its legal references, suspecting them of subjectivity, hyperbole, and unreliability; however, since puns and pranks always have an immediacy—as jokes are necessarily contextual—references to legal language in ancient comic drama are useful as a source for law and its reception. In this sense, comedy can supplement inscribed texts and the extant forensic speeches of Antiphon, Andocides, Lysias, and Isocrates (16–21) in the late fifth and early fourth centuries BCE.

i. Legal Vocabulary: Going to Court...

Scholars over the past decade and more have acknowledged the importance of technical languages in Old Comedy (e.g., Kloss 2001; Willi 2003; Beta 2004).[2] By granting at least a few pages to describing the specificity of a legal vocabulary in Aristophanes, they have

---

[1] Even if they did not reject comic drama as a source for understanding Athenian Law, earlier scholars, when touching upon or referring to poets of Old Comedy (e.g., Swoboda 1893; Lipsius 1905–1915; Harrison 1968), did not deal specifically with more fundamental problems arising from legal reference in Greek Comedy. Exceptional are MacDowell 1971, MacDowell 1978, MacDowell 1995, MacDowell 2010; Todd 1993: 40–42.

[2] Willi 2003 (73–76, Table 3.1) provides a list of "legal terms in *Wasps* and other plays." While he concludes that "large proportions of the legal vocabulary even in such a topical play as *Wasps* did not belong to a specialist discourse" (p. 79), nevertheless, he designates the list as "legal vocabulary." This is, I think, essentially right, especially as he sets his conclusions in the broader context as follows: "This appears to be a consequence of the Athenian legal system, in which a large part of the citizens over thirty could and did serve as jurors. As a consequence, advanced mastery of legal vocabulary was recognized as the cultural standard" (p. 79).

opened the door to the further study of juridical references in comic testimonies. If we agree that the Athenians developed a legal vocabulary that can be traced and examined in inscriptions and forensic speeches, we shall see that comedy uses much of this same terminology when referring to the performance of law-court trials and procedures. This can be perceived throughout the extant complete plays of Aristophanes (eleven out of more than forty) that were performed at the dramatic festivals in Athens (the Dionysia or the Lenaea) between 427 and 388 BCE.

Legal terms frequently appear in the plays, as a short and nonexhaustive survey can demonstrate. There is a constant appeal to specific lexical items and expressions to indicate decrees and legal statutes. While θεσμός ("ordinance," with reference to archaic legislation) occurs only once (*Birds* 331), the word νόμος (in its meaning "statute") appears ubiquitously, e.g.: "Ah, but *we* birds have an ancient *law* written on the Tablets [*kyrbeis*] of the Storks" (*Birds* 1353–1354); "our *laws* have to be obeyed" (*Assemblywomen* 1022). Occasionally, νόμος appears with forms of τίθεμαι in idiomatic expressions to mean "to propose a law" or "to lay down the law": "Well, wasn't it a man who *made that law* [ὁ τὸν νόμον θείς] in the first place?" (*Clouds* 1421) and sometimes as a reference to the "established laws," as in: "How pleasant it is to be intimate with what is new and clever, and to be able to look with scorn on *the established laws* [τῶν καθεστώτων νόμων]" (*Clouds* 1399–1400). Ψήφισμα ("decree") also appears frequently: "I'll compel them to give up moving *decrees* and go hunting instead" (*Knights* 1382–1383); "but he was born earlier, before the *decree* was passed" (*Assemblywomen* 649–650). As in other fifth-century writers, the distinction between law and decree is not especially rigid; in *Birds* 1037, the "decree seller" produces "new laws" for sale, while in *Women at the Thesmophoria* 361 both terms are set together (on νόμος and ψήφισμα see Quass 1972 and Hansen 1978).

The word δίκη ("justice," "trial," "lawsuit," "private legal action") and its cognates are also omnipresent, e.g.: "Suppose that when there was still one *case* pending before mine was called, I were to run off and hang myself?" (*Clouds* 779–780); "but there won't *be* any *lawsuits* in the first place" (*Assemblywomen* 657). *Dike* is also found personified as "Justice" in high-flown Aeschylean manner at *Birds* 1240. The diminutive δικίδιον, on the other hand, is a comic formulation and is used to denigrate a lawsuit in *Knights* ("Oh, you'd do a fine job if a *little case* fell to you and you had to take it all torn and raw," 347–350) or to trivialize them elsewhere (cf. *Clouds* 1109 and *Wasps* 511).

Several terms are used to indicate a summons before the court. Καλέω is used when a magistrate summons a case before a court, e.g., *"Call a case*, then" (*Wasps* 851) or "Go on, be insolent, until the magistrate *calls your case*" (*Wasps* 1441; cf. Dem. 21.56). Καλέομαι, in the middle voice, is employed as a technical term when the plaintiff wants to bring someone to justice, as when the inspector in *Birds* 1046 says "I summon [καλοῦμαι] Peisetaerus in the month of Munichion on a charge of wanton outrage"; the noun κλῆσις ("summons") appears in *Clouds* 875 and 1189. Προσκαλέομαι ("to summon into court") is also employed: "Old man, I *summon* you on a charge of wanton outrage" (*Wasps* 1417–1418); the noun πρόσκλησις appears at *Wasps* 1041. Other verbs that refer more generally to the action of initiating a legal procedure or litigating include εἰσάγω ("bring into court," *Clouds* 782, *Wasps* 826), δικάζομαι ("sue," *Clouds* 496, 1141–1142), and εἰσέρχομαι ("prosecute," *Wasps* 579). The action of prosecuting (διώκω) is mentioned frequently: "now wicked men hotly *prosecute* and cast us in lawsuits" (*Acharnians* 700); "I'll *prosecute* you for cowardice" (*Knights* 368). Specific mentions of accusing (κατηγορέω, *Women at the Thesmophoria* 444), replying to a charge (ἐλέγχομαι, *Wealth* 932; ἀποκρίνομαι, *Acharnians* 632, *Clouds* 1244–1245; ἀντιδικέω, *Clouds* 776), and witnessing (μαρτύρομαι, *Acharnians* 926; *Clouds* 494–496; *Birds* 1031) indicate trial activities. "Assessing a penalty" (τιμάω) is mentioned at *Wasps* 106 and 847 (cf. τίμημα at *Wasps* 897, *Wealth* 480). The expression δίκην δίδωμι ("impose a sanction") appears, as in "I'll haul you before the people and *get justice from you*" (*Knights* 710) and "I'll make someone *pay a penalty* today for what they've done to me" (*Clouds* 1491–1492). In several plays there are explicit references to being convicted (ἁλίσκομαι: *Acharnians* 662; *Peace* 1234) and being acquitted (ἀπολύω: *Wasps* 571, *Peace* 13; ἀποφεύγω / ἐκφεύγω: *Clouds* 1151; ἀφίημι *Wasps* 922).

Private actions are sometimes indicated without using the term *dike* but with the charge in the genitive, fully consonant with the idiom of the orators as in the "summons": "I summon you before the market-inspectors [in a suit] for damage (βλάβης) to my stock" (*Wasps* 1406–1407). The legal term γραφή ("public indictment": e.g., *Acharnians* 679) and its cognate verb γράφομαι (e.g., *Clouds* 758 and 1481–1482) are rarely found in conjunction with a specific charge as in *Wasps* 894–897 and *Peace* 107–108, and only in the latter case does it clearly match a public charge known from other sources. There are also frequent references to specific judicial actions and charges, such as the denunciation of someone who is illegally withholding state property (φάσις: e.g., *Acharnians* 542) or of an offender made before a public official capable of arresting him (ἔνδειξις: *Knights* 278). We hear of the decree of the Council or Assembly to hand over the doers of serious crimes to the lawcourts (εἰσαγγελία: *Wasps* 590–591) and explicit allusions to procedural examinations such as the δοκιμασία (*Wasps* 578) or εὔθυνα (*Knights* 825, *Wasps* 571).

As litigants or as collaborators to the parties, we find the defendant (φεύγω): "You'll *be the defendant in* four prosecutions" (*Knights* 442–443); the witness to the delivery of the legal summons (κλητήρ, *Wasps* 1408, 1416); the sycophant or blackmailer (συκοφάντης): "Let no *informer* enter here" (*Acharnians* 725), "This god will really be doing an invaluable service to the whole Greek people if he brings evil destruction to these evil *informers*" (*Wealth* 877–879); and the supporting speaker (ξυνήγορος), who may also be an appointed advocate (*Knights* 1358, 1361; *Wasps* 482) or an allotted one (*Wasps* 687–691). In regard to the allotted advocate, we also learn he received a drachma as a fee (τὸ συνηγορικόν, *Wasps* 691), a detail that appears nowhere else in our ancient sources and is probably authentic (MacDowell 1971 ad loc.). And of course, as part of the functioning of the tribunals, we find the judge (δικαστής, *Wasps* 563; ἡλιαστής, *Knights* 255) and numerous magistrates (archons) or court officers, such as the πολέμαρχος (*Wasps* 1042), the θεσμοθέτης (*Wasps* 775; *Assemblywomen* 443), the δήμαρχος (*Clouds* 37), the ἀγορανόμος ("market inspector": *Acharnians*

723, 824), the γραμματεύς ("court clerk": *Clouds* 770), the κῆρυξ ("herald": *Wasps* 752, 905) and the ὑπογραφεύς δικῶν ("signer of accusations," *Knights* 1256) All but the last of these legal players can be paralleled in the orators: the reference to ὑπογραφεύς δικῶν, a term that is appropriate for indicating those accusers who submitted the written statement of charges and who would thus accept the risk for bringing the case, might represent an example of comedy providing information not available elsewhere. Moreover, the single κλητήρ at *Clouds* 1218 and *Wasps* 1408 and 1416 provides us with our only evidence that in the 420s a single witness to a summons was sufficient; an additional witness was required in the late fifth and fourth centuries (MacDowell 1978: 238).

In *Wasps* (422 BCE), the play most heavily imbued with law in the Aristophanic corpus, the plot is structured so as to provide a harsh critique of the Athenian judicial system. The main character, Philocleon, is an old man addicted to court proceedings, suffering from a dangerous illness that compels him to spend every day acting as a juror. As a remedy, his son Bdelycleon manages to lock him up at home and sets up a mock-court there. He proposes that a household dog be tried because he has stolen and eaten a cheese. The description of the domestic court as well as details added elsewhere in the play are rich in the vocabulary of the material components of legal space (see Boegehold 1967 and Boegehold 1995): the physical furniture of the tribunal includes the railing of the court (δρύφακτος: *Wasps* 386, 552, 830), the access barrier (κιγκλίς: *Wasps* 124, 775), the front bench (ξύλον: *Wasps* 90), the pillar on which legal cases were posted (κίων: *Wasps* 105), the water-clock for timing the speeches (κλεψύδρα: *Wasps* 857–858; *Acharnians* 693), the boards where the notices of forthcoming trials were hung (σανίδες: *Wasps* 349, 848) and all the necessary objects for voting: the urns (καδίσκοι: *Wasps* 321–322; τὼ κάδω: *Birds* 1032; κημός: *Wasps* 756; ἐκ κιθαρίου: *Wasps* 674), the penalty tablet (πινάκιον, *Wasps* 167) and the stone used to count votes (λίθος: *Wasps* 332–333; cf. *Acharnians* 683). At the same time, ample evidence appears for the multiple courtrooms established in Athens: from the popular courts (δικαστήρια: e.g. *Knights* 308; *Wasps* 304, with a comic diminutive in *Wasps* 803) to other specific tribunals, such as the New Court (τὸ Καινόν: *Wasps* 120), Lycus's Court (τὸ ἐπὶ Λύκου: *Wasps* 819) or the archon's court, the Eleven, and the Odeon (οἱ μὲν ἡμῶν οὗπερ ἄρχων, οἱ δὲ παρὰ τοὺς ἕνδεκα, / οἱ δ' ἐν Ὠιδείῳ δικάζουσ', *Wasps* 1108–1109).[3]

Aristophanes, then, provides a wealth of legal vocabulary that is used with accuracy and paralleled by the orators; occasionally, he uses a term in a legal context or a procedure not found elsewhere—and we have seen no reason to discredit these as true representations of legal procedure. But how does Old Comedy really use this legal armature? It is not rare to find passages in which Aristophanes relies on the legal knowledge of the audience (i.e., its juridical encyclopedia) to understand a joke. But if humor requires a

---

[3] For courts and court paraphernalia, see Boegehold 1995.

distance between the comic reference and everyday experience, how is this gap achieved in Old Comedy?

ii. Textual Parody as a *Modus Comicus*: Mocking Justice

First, Aristophanes manipulates law as a source of laughter by frequent parodies of laws, decrees, and legislative proposals. For modern readers of Athenian drama, understanding the legal background is essential for discerning the jokes.

A clear example occurs in *Wasps*, when Bdelycleon reads the indictment against the dog (*Wasps* 894–897):

> Now hear the indictment [ἀκούετ' ἤδη τῆς γραφῆς] [*Reading*]: "The Hound of Cydathenaeum indicts Labes of Aexone for the crime [ἀδικεῖν] of having eaten up the Sicilian cheese all by himself. Proposed penalty [τίμημα]: a figwood collar [κλῳὸς σύκινος].[4]

The indictment is a parody of a legal instrument (cf. the indictment against Socrates quoted in DL 2.40.3.7):[5] while the crime itself is analogous to embezzlement (κλοπή, literally, "theft"), the charge is flagrantly ridiculous, for it is not the consumption of the cheese (the theft itself) but the *modus operandi* of the cheese consumer—eating it by himself and not sharing—that constitutes the humor (and the injustice from the prosecutor's point of view). The final allusion to the figwood (σύκινος) collar as punishment puns on the Greek term to designate *sykophantai*—i.e., professional blackmailers. The political dimension should also be considered: behind the allegations against Labes, the mock-court satirizes the situation of the Athenian general Laches, accused by Cleon for accepting bribes in Southern Italy (cf. MacDowell 1971: 249 and MacDowell 1995: 167–168; Mastromarco 1974: 61–64).

Two old men, Peisetaerus and Euelpides, enter the stage at the opening of *Birds* (414 BCE); both, tired of Athenian litigiousness, have decided to flee and travel in search of Tereus, the ancient king now transformed into a hoopoe. They have plans for a new polis that will host a society ruled by the ancient laws (*thesmoi*) of nature and not by Attic legislation. Subsequently, the protagonist disputes with an Athenian decree-seller who appears on stage to offer new *nomoi* for the polis. The latter quotes a couple of statutes (*Birds* 1035–1045), with clauses similar to some in fifth-century decrees (cf. IG I³ 19, 2–7, IG I³ 34, 31–32; IG I³ 40, 29–31). By the end of the play, Peisetaerus will even cite

---

[4] Here and elsewhere, I rely on translations of Aristophanes by A. Sommerstein.

[5] "Meletus son of Meletus of Pithus indicts and takes an oath against Socrates son of Sophroniscus of Alopece. Socrates has committed the offence of not recognizing the gods whom the state recognizes and introducing other new divinities; he has also committed the offence of corrupting the youth. Proposed penalty: death." Indictments were generally read by the court attendant at the beginning of the trial; cf. Rubinstein 2000: 36.

a "Solonian *nomos*" on bastardy (1660–1666) as a strategy to convince Heracles that he would not inherit Zeus's property because he is an illegitimate son (*nothos*):

> I'll actually quote you the law of Solon [ἐρῶ δὲ δὴ καὶ τὸν Σόλωνός σοι νόμον]: "A bastard shall not have the rights of a near kinsman, if there are legitimate children. Should there be no legitimate children the next of kin shall share in the estate."

The text differs from the possibly Solonian law that is quoted in [Dem.] 43.51 ("A bastard, whether male or female, shall not have the rights of a near kinsman either of sacred or of profane things, as from the archonship of Eucleides [403/02]"; and cf. the partial paraphrase at Is. 6.47); the Aristophanic text could be a purposeful misquotation (Humphreys 1974: 89 n.5; for a different view, see Harrison 1968: 66–68). The joke in the "Peisetaerean text" is that Heracles remains completely deprived of any right to the inheritance, whether there are legitimate offspring or not.

The so-called feminine comedies also exhibit (through male actors explicitly disguised as women) a parodic use of legal texts. In *Women at the Thesmophoria* (411 BCE), women accuse Euripides of misogyny and put him on trial. In 372–379, a female herald informs the audience about the decision the women have taken during their official meeting:

> Hear ye all! [reading] "The following was resolved by the Council of the women [ἔδοξε τῇ βουλῇ τάδε τῇ τῶν γυναικῶν], chairwoman [ἐπεστάτει], Timocleia; secretary [ἐγραμμάτευεν], Lysilla; proposer of motion [εἶπε], Sostrate: to hold an assembly at sunrise on the middle day of the Thesmophoria, being the day on which we have most free time, and to consider as first business the subject of Euripides, namely what penalty he shall suffer, since we are unanimously of opinion that he committed unjust acts [ἀδικεῖν]" Who wishes to speak? [τίς ἀγορεύειν βούλεται;]

The formal aspects of the motion will remind the spectators of well-known formulae (here, the obligatory prescript with the enactment formula ἔδοξε τῇ βουλῇ leading to an open *probouleuma* as in IG II² 330.ii; see Rhodes 1972: 82–84; Swoboda 1893: 570). The context is once again comic, not only because the members of the Council are women, traditionally excluded from political activities, but also because the charge is so wonderfully "misandrous."

Similarly, in *Assemblywomen* (393 or 391 BCE) another decree is presented onstage, this one voted by the women after they have assumed power in the polis (1014–1020):

> All right, I'm reading it to you. [*Reads*] "Resolved by the women [ἔδοξε ταῖς γυναιξίν]: if [ἦν] a young man desires a young woman, he shall not shag her until he has first screwed her elderly neighbour; and if [ἦν] he refuses to perform such pre-screwing and continues to lust after the young woman, the older woman shall be permitted [ἔστω], without penalty [ἀνατεί], to drag the young man away, taking hold of him by the peg."

The parody is evident: in a public (and male) context, the decree is quoted by an old woman who reads it with the purpose of convincing a young man to have sex with her. The comic device combines an elevated discourse with a low register of diction: to regulate sexual matters, the legal provisions are vulgarized and merged with obscene terminology.

It is worth noting that Bdelycleon's indictment, and the decrees and laws—including those carried about by the Decree Seller in *Birds*—that have been mentioned here, are all read from written documents (and some of them in *prose*). The characters who pronounce legal formulae thus indicate that the rules are not improvised but have been agreed upon and set down in advance. The comic effect is enhanced by the drastic collision between the apparent authority of the written laws and their comic application.

These are instances of what we might call "legal intertextuality": the dramatic script alludes in a more or less precise way to well-known written rules and provisions; other instances do not reproduce so accurately the structure of juridical or public documents but are suggestive of the oral, grassroots aspect of the law-making process. In the *parabasis* of *Acharnians* (425 BCE), the chorus of elderly charcoal-burning demesmen complain about the way trials are being carried out: young prosecutors take advantage of their weakness and age and bring them into court under false pretenses. As a remedy, they recommend a decree to end this particular maltreatment: the unequal positions of accusers and defendants in judicial claims must be balanced. The decree (*Acharnians* 713–718) uses a "prospective" formula (τὸ λοιπόν, "henceforth") that is typical of contemporary decrees (cf. IG I³ 32, 18–20; 28–30):

> But since [ἐπειδὴ] you refuse to let the old get any sleep, at least decree [ψηφίσασθε] that the indictments [τὰς γραφάς] should be segregated, so that an old defendant can have an old and toothless prosecutor [ξυνήγορος], and the young can have a wide-arsed fast talker, the son of Cleinias. In future [τὸ λοιπόν] you should [χρὴ] banish and fine the old, if they're charged by the old, and the young, if by the young.

Similarly, in *Clouds* (first written by 423 BCE, although the preserved text corresponds to a revised version from 418 or 417 BCE), the protagonist Strepsiades is worried that he will be taken to trial by creditors because of the unpaid debts of his son Phidippides. In order to train the latter to use appropriate legal arguments and to twist decrees and evade lawsuits, Strepsiades sends him to Socrates's Phrontisterion, where he acquires a sophistic knowledge of judicial chicanery. As soon as the young man leaves the school, he shows off some interesting subterfuges, e.g., he composes a new law allowing children to beat their fathers (1405). He then rationalizes his own creation by looking to the law-making process: the law imposing respect for parents was manmade, for it was a man who managed to persuade others about the convenience of its provisions (1421–1422); accordingly, statutes (even those supported by custom, 1416!) can be amended or modified whenever it is necessary. In the end, he proposes the passage of a new law employing the same "prospective formula" (*Clouds*, 1423–1426; see Harris 2002) we saw earlier, but this time with a protective and comical "grandfather clause" as well:[6]

> Is it then any less open to me in my turn to make a new law [καινὸν ... θεῖναι νόμον] for sons in the future [τὸ λοιπὸν], that they should beat their parents in return? All the blows we received before the law was made [πρὶν τὸν νόμον τεθῆναι] we wipe from the record, and we make it a concession to them that our having been thrashed hitherto shall remain without compensation.

By reproducing lawmaking protocols and distorting and parodying them on stage, Aristophanes draws the attention of Athenians to contemporary discussions of their legal system (see *Frogs* 686–692). Such parodies suggest a critical reception of the contemporary sophistic interpretation of positive and conventional justice. Sophists had pointed out that every city has its own laws, and these can be different from those in force elsewhere (cf. Protagoras according to Plato, *Theaetetus* 172a); Sophists were also skeptical of laws that could easily be amended and modified by those impelled by a mere change of mind (cf. Hippias according to Xenophon, *Memorabilia* 4.4.14).

If these phenomena—the manipulation of the formulaic phraseology of Attic laws and the exploitation of relativism in law-making (*Birds* 1421–1422) that have suggested a critical reception of contemporary sophistic thinking—occur in comedy, how serious, then, can this "critical reception" be? Aristophanes frequently distinguishes between vulgar spectators (who just laugh at silly jokes; e.g., *Wasps* 66, 1045, 1048) and smart spectators (who enjoy the intellectual depth of his plays; e.g., *Wasps* 65, 1049), and even appeals to both groups in *Assemblywomen* 1155–1157. While there is no reason to think that only the vulgar laughed, smart spectators surely saw these reflections as part of a political agenda that was critical of the demagogic and sophistic manipulation of the legal apparatus.[7]

iii. Trans-contextualization as a *Modus Comicus*: Athenian Law in Abnormal Situations

Like Strepsiades in *Clouds*, Peisetaerus in *Birds* flouts the law and gets away with it, questioning its authority, origin, and binding force when convenient, but endorsing its content when advantageous. Having fled Athens, he nevertheless will make use of Athenian

---

[6] Cf. Nicomenes's decree of 403/02 BCE that re-instated the "old" Periclean citizenship law, with the proviso that it should not be enforced against individuals born before that year (Σ Aeschin. 1.39 = Eumelus *FGrHist* 77 F 2). The decree is prospective but also "grandfathers" those born before Eucleides.

[7] The playwright, of course, also considers himself to be smart (*Clouds* 520, *Acharnians* 629) and a promoter of justice (e.g., *Acharnians* 500).

legal culture, and—having turned into a true specialist in the arts of sophistry—will dare to address the birds and convince them to make a claim to the gods for their ancestral power. He will reject a number of representatives of Athenian justice who come to his new city and will even apply a "bird law" to a human outsider who comes asking for wings and aspiring to live among the birds as a *metoikos* ("resident alien," 1345). Far from being frivolously invented, this ancient bird law is written on *kyrbeis* (the triangular tablets on which early laws were inscribed: Stroud 1979) and is probably a parody of a Solonian law according to which children are to support their parents; cf. Ruschenbusch F 55a–c).

Comic heroes cite and apply, fantastically, Attic law and procedure as they impose their wills on others or promote ingenious plans. But when these rules are transposed in their application to absurd situations we may identify a specific kind of parody, namely "trans-contextualization": this appears, for example, when noncitizens—slaves and women, who were unable in "real life" to conduct procedures on their own—cite Athenian law in Aristophanes's plays.

In *Frogs* (405 BCE), Dionysus, disguised as Heracles, descends to Hades with his slave Xanthias. Identified as Heracles, Dionysus is accused by two women of plundering their guesthouse during his previous visit. Soon afterwards, when Xanthias has now exchanged garb with "Heracles," he is charged with the theft of the dog Cerberus; at this point (615–622), a comic inversion of the Athenian procedure of *basanos* allows the slave (Xanthias as "Heracles") to invite the complainant Aeacus to torture his master (Dionysus, posing as Heracles's slave). While in Athens the testimony of unfree servants was permitted under torture to prove the innocence (or guilt) of their masters, the comic stage shows an example of a slave providing the instructions. Dead people also benefit by Athenian law in this play: there is a provision in Hades (νόμος τις...κείμενος, 761) similar to decrees that grant the privilege of dining in the Prytaneion to honored guests (cf. Plato, *Apologia* 36d) here it allows the best practitioner of each art to get free meals and a seat of honor next to Pluto.

Women are also given in comedy an unusual legal personality. In the "real Athens," an Athenian woman could only take part in a trial through the agency of her closest male relative or *kyrios* (in general, her father if unmarried, husband if married, or son if widowed). In the "feminine" comedies, women assume power in environments traditionally controlled by men. In *Wasps*, a citizen bread-seller named Myrtia comes with a witness and indicts Philocleon before the market-inspectors, as if she were an experienced male litigant. Myrtia is able to challenge the comic hero without further preamble, presenting the alleged charge in juridical language (1406–1408):

I summon you [προσκαλοῦμαι], whoever you are, before the market inspectors [πρὸς τοὺς ἀγορανόμους] [in a suit] for damage to my stock [βλάβης τῶν φορτίων]. I have Chaerephon here as a witness [κλητῆρ].

Young boys, too, are offered the opportunity of exercising an active legal personality in Old Comedy. Being only a *meirakion* (*Clouds* 990, 1000, 1270), Phidippides can think of the possibility of prosecuting his father for insanity (844–846):

> Heavens, what am I to do—for my father is out of his mind! Shall I take him to court and get him adjudged insane [παρανοίας αὐτὸν εἰσαγαγὼν ἕλω] or shall I tell the coffin-makers of his affliction?

Phidippides's musing here is ironic: prosecutions for insanity, on the grounds that a person is wasting his property, are brought before the archon (*Ath. Pol.* 56.6); the son is therefore considering a charge that his father might bring against him for squandering his property on horses!

What did the Athenian spectators make of this fantastic application of Athenian justice, acted out in the framework of the comic genre? For instance, how did they respond to *Assemblywomen* when the new revolutionary regime created by Praxagora changed the constitutional basis of the polis, endorsing sexual freedom, eliminating private property, and replacing the courtrooms with dining rooms? What did an Athenian citizen think watching *Peace*, when Trygaeus flew to Olympus and established an ideal landscape and a global Panhellenism, where Athenian law was replaced, in a new utopian Greece, by the rules of nature? Were the spectators sympathetic to Peisetaerus in *Birds* when he ends up being called a *tyrannos* among the avian creatures and replacing Zeus by marrying Basileia? Were they sympathetic to Strepsiades in *Clouds* after he burns Socrates's Phrontisterion in an unexpected comic ending? Surely some must have heard a political message when the constitutional order was affected and criticized or when a comic hero acquired superior individual power with the success of his plan. The didactic dimension of the comic content of the plays suggests that Aristophanes was well aware of the possible influence of his plots on deliberations surrounding the democratic system.

In *Acharnians* (425 BCE), Aristophanes explains that, as a consequence of the staging of his previous play, the demagogue Cleon had dragged him into the Council and slandered him (378–382).[8] The presentation of an elaborated juridical argument against Cleon by the comic hero Dicaeopolis—an alter ego for Aristophanes—shows how the stage could in fact become a forum for defense: comedy is undoubtedly a fictional space for discussing Athenian politics.[9]

---

[8] The alleged squabble between Aristophanes and Cleon might provide some clue to the political character of comedy. Cf. Rosenbloom in this volume. On the legal nature of this conflict, see Sommerstein 2004a and Sommerstein 2004b.

[9] Whether Old Comedy was granted a specific license or not, there appears to have been no general provision against personal invective or defamation (cf. Halliwell 1991). Wallace (2005) identifies three exceptional episodes in times of war in which some restrictions were established for political reasons.

iv. Exaggeration as a *Modus Comicus*: The Athenian Vice of Litigiousness

Aristophanes constantly refers to the Athenian legal universe. Litigiousness is so pervasive in the city that his plays easily reproduce its characteristics and implications in extenso. In *Clouds*, Strepsiades finds it hard to accept the location of Athens in a map of the world, since he is unable to identify the judges sitting in session (206–208). In *Birds*, whereas the cicadas are said to sing on tree branches for a month or two, Athenians are said to sing at trials all their life long (39–41). With evident exaggeration, Philocleon in *Wasps* is described as a "jurormaniac" (φιληλιαστής, 88): according to him, being a juror is equal to being a king (549), since there is no creature happier and more privileged (and no one more feared) than a juror (550–551).

Hyperbole extends beyond a craze for jury service to a craze for bringing suits. In *Knights* (424 BCE), both Paphlagon (an alter ego for the demagogue Cleon) and Agoracritus (the Sausage-seller) exchange an impossible number of accusations: the former charges his enemy with *four* public actions, perhaps for corruption (442–443), whereas the latter responds immediately by threatening Paphlagon with *twenty* indictments for evading the military service and with *more than a thousand* for theft (444–445).

Sycophants may be the greatest lovers of lawsuits on the Aristophanic stage: they were informers who misused the legal system by introducing or threatening public allegations and withholding them upon payment, thus making a living out of the work of the tribunals (see Osborne 1990, and the reply in Harvey 1990). Aristophanes puts them onstage frequently, exploiting them to dramatize abuse of the legal system and to provide a bittersweet excuse for laughter. In all their appearances as speaking characters (*Acharnians* 818–828, 908–958; *Birds* 1410–1469, *Wealth* 850–958), sycophants are mistreated, attacked, and even expelled from the stage by the comic hero who opposes them and makes fun of their forensic activity (Doganis 2001, Pellegrino 2010). The negative image of these blackmailers is so strong that some characters insist that they should not be mistaken for informers. In *Peace*, for example, Trygaeus quickly identifies himself to Hermes by personal name, deme, and occupation, and in the same breath denies he is either sycophant or lover of public troubles (οὐ συκοφάντης οὐδ' ἐραστὴς πραγμάτων, 191). The old hag in *Wealth*, who complains about the loss of her young gigolo, denies being an "informeress" (συκοφάντρια, 970–971). In a similar vein, Peisetaerus must tell Tereus in *Birds* that he not a juror (ἡλιαστά, 109)—he is a "jurorphobiac" (ἀπηλιαστά, 110).

The Aristophanic hero treads on the borderline between lawful and unlawful conduct, attacking the judicial system and using extralegal means to solve his problems, or profiting from the legal system to his own personal advantage. Excessive litigation is clearly comic, but when denounced or embodied by the protagonist, it draws the public's attention to a weakness of the Athenian legal system. Once again, the comic resort to *philopragmosyne* ("fondness for busying about other people's business") is complex: legal abuse is mentioned to draw laughs, but at the same time, it generates some awareness of the dangers of uncontrolled litigiousness. Disguised in humor, comic heroes instruct the public to get rid of corrupt politicians and demagogues who work through their underlings in the courts.

v. A "Broken" Justice: Athenian Law in Aristophanes's Rivals

The use of juridical allusions also constituted for Aristophanes's rivals an efficient humorous device. Titles of some lost plays (Cratinus's *Laws*, Eupolis's *Vigilantes* [*Hybristodikai*], Thugenides's *Jurors*), for example, suggest a common interest in the staging of litigiousness. Of course, the evidence we possess is exiguous; nonetheless, the importance of law and justice is indicated in some of the fragmentary remains.

The legal vocabulary of procedures, tribunals, and litigants is manifest: a character in Cratinus's *Chirons* (436/432?) mentions the maritime jurisdiction of the *nautodikai* (K-A fr. 251), and another one in Eupolis's *Cities* (422?) describes the island of Tenos as a natural habitat for scorpions and *sykophantai* (K-A fr. 245). Sycophancy is widely perceived as an evil: in Eupolis's best-known play, *Demes* [*Demoi*] (412/410?), the description of a demagogue and the encounter between Aristides and a sycophant on stage (K-A fr. 99, 79–120) display the rhetoric of denunciations and judicial defense pleas, as suggested by the informer's irate words: "Witnesses! [μαρτύρομαι] Shall we not go to trial? You summon me [καλέσας] and then beat me and tie me up!" (103–104, trans. Storey). This protest is related to the plot of the play, in which four politicians are sent back from Hades to fight against the *alazones* or "charlatans" (K-A fr. 104). Similarly, in *Marikas* (421) the protagonist (representing Hyperbolus, the successor of Cleon) behaves like a sycophant when he pushes his adversary to acknowledge that he has collaborated in Nicias's treason (K-A fr. 193: see Pellegrino 2010: 112–115).[10] The chorus of poor men immediately responds that the politician has been discovered: "Did you hear that, friends, Nikias caught in the act [ἐπ' αὐτοφώρῳ]?." Other legal and political scenarios involving demagogues appear—with lesser emphasis—in Cratinus's comedy *Wealth-Gods* [*Ploutoi*] (429?), where the chorus listens to charges against the politician Hagnon for ill-gotten wealth (K-A fr. 171, 57–76) or in Eupolis's *Spongers* (421?), where the reckless Callias is pilloried.

Not even the playwrights themselves can escape from the pervasiveness of lawsuits: a scholium to Aristophanes describing Cratinus's *Wine-Flask* [*Pytine*] (423) informs us that in the play, Cratinus's wife, Comedy, wanted a divorce because he was a drunkard

---

[10] Other late fifth-century comedies drawing on political issues centering on Hyperbolus include Hermippus's *Breadwomen* [*Artopolides*] (420?) and Plato's *Hyberbolus* (418).

and filed a lawsuit against him for maltreatment (Σ *Eq.* 400a, K-A test. ii; see Bakola 2010 and Storey, chapter four, this volume).

Laws are verbally and materially abused, and litigiousness is amply present. According to Plato Comicus (*Greece* or *Islands*), laws (*nomoi*) are like the thin cobwebs that the spider spins along the walls (K-A fr. 21). Cratinus makes us believe that ancient texts of laws have lost their value: in an unassigned fragment (perhaps belonging to *Laws*), a character swears by Solon and Dracon "on whose *kyrbeis* people now parch barley corns" (K-A fr. 300). In *Amphictyons* (late 430s), Teleclides calls on the citizens who are best "at shakedowns and lawsuits" to stop legal actions that devour one another (δικῶν ἀλληλοφάγων, K-A fr. 2).

These few examples suggest that the study of the legal background of Aristophanes's dramatic rivals complements our reading of Aristophanes's appeals to law.

2. NEW COMEDY AND ATHENIAN LAW: DOING JUSTICE TO FAMILY TIES

Politics is not absent in New Comedy during the last third of the fifth century, as the titles of some plays by Theopompus or Timocles –and later by Archedippus and Philippides—may suggest (Henderson and Scafuro, chapters 8 and 9 this volume). It has been widely acknowledged, however, that Menander (the only New Comedy poet for whom we have a complete drama) avoided dealing directly with politics or the city's administration of justice in his comedies. This does not mean, of course, that Menander or his contemporaries disregarded law. On the contrary, legal questions are of decisive importance for most of the plots. The manipulation of the juridical background, however, is different from the kind found in Aristophanes. In general, the public organization of the city is abandoned as a source of laughter. It is not startling, then, to find a significant absence of sycophants, jurors, and demagogues.

Whereas in Old Comedy the regulation of private relationships was not more—and probably less—important than other areas of law, in New Comedy it is nearly always family law that matters. Menander's plays all crucially involve marriage and family relationships, often quite complex ones. This accords with the general trajectory of some contemporary provisions in Athens that were enacted to regulate private behavior, first by Lycurgus and later by Demetrius of Phalerum. An example of this new legislation, reflected in comic texts as well, is the institution of γυναικονόμοι (supervisors of women), who were apparently in charge of scrutinizing private households. Menander mentions these inspectors in *Kekryphalos*, K-A fr. 208, and so does Timocles in K-A fr. 34, where it is indicated that their functions were laid down in a recent law (κατὰ τὸν νόμον τὸν καινόν).

Private law seems embedded in every comedy, even when its background seems obscure. In the beginning of *Dyskolos* (317/6 BCE), for instance, little information is given about the legal situation of Cnemon's family: we are told that he married a widow some years before (14), but we hear nothing about her current status. We know that she left him and went to live with Gorgias, her son from a previous marriage (22), but we (and the audience of the play) do not know whether he divorced her, nor who was legally entitled to represent the woman as her *kyrios*. What about this missing information, then? Should we infer that Menander expected spectators to recall and apply legal rules that were not explicitly mentioned? Or should we consider that the law is relevant only insofar as the playwright chooses to make it so? We can only say that Menander did not find it necessary to include specific information on every last little detail—which does not mean that he disregarded the importance of law or its effects. On the contrary, the law so eccentrically permeates *Dyskolos*, for example, that Cnemon will inform the audience that, if everyone lived as he did, there would be no law courts, people would not drag each other off to jail, and there would be no wars (743–745)—i.e., he rejects the importance of law—but he does this only moments after revising the terms of his estate and adopting Gorgias as his son (731–739)!

In *Aspis*, Menander focuses on the law of marriage and inheritance. After the supposed death of Cleostratus in war, his sister is apparently left as an heiress (*epikleros*); in accordance with Attic law, she was required to marry the father's nearest male relative if he claimed her as a legitimate wife—and this play provides the detail that the eldest brother of the father had priority (MacDowell 1982). Marrying an *epikleros* was a strategy to transfer inheritance in the absence of male children. When Smicrines, the greedy protagonist and eldest next-of-kin, finds out that Cleostratus left a rich cache of booty, he decides to claim the young girl as a wife by referring to the applicable law. While the play offers many details relevant to the laws of inheritance[11] it also shows its main character, the mean Smicrines, behaving not unlike the typical comic hero: against Chaerestratus (who wants to marry the *epikleros* to his step-son Chaeres), Smicrines will quote Athenian law as long as it suits his own selfish interests. The comic character, as so often, at one time highly values the law and so exploits it, and at other times, ignores it.

A similar pattern is found in *Epitrepontes*, when the old Smicrines verbalizes his wish to dissolve his daughter's marriage against her will. Pamphila, the wife of Charisius, argues with her father: instead of forcing her, he should persuade her to put an end to her marriage and not treat her as if she were a slave and he were her master (ἀλλ εἴ με σῴζων τοῦτο μὴ πείσαις ἐμέ / οὐκέτι πατὴρ κρίνοι ἂν ἀλλὰ δεσπότης, 714–715). The passage plays with the delicate issue of the right of a wife's premarital *kyrios* (usually her father) to terminate her marriage. Certainly the audience was expected to be aware of this problem and thus able to understand the logic of the plot. But from a dramatic perspective, an Athenian spectator would also see the importance of the legal reference

---

[11]   A dispute between MacDowell 1982 and Brown 1983 over details pertaining to the *epikleros* paves the way to a deeper discussion of the relationship between law and comedy during the fourth century BCE. Can it be said that all references to Athenian law are always correct in the mouth of the comic characters, as MacDowell implies? Or, on the contrary, should we consider it impossible to rely on New Comedy as a valid source to understand Attic law, as contended by Brown?

as showing that Smicrines (just like the other Smicrines in *Aspis!*) is trying to exercise a legal right without regard to the wishes or feelings of members of his *family*.

As in Old Comedy, the characters are able to quote the relevant law and use a specific vocabulary, but the interest that New Comedy has in law cannot be described as having a political dimension. Far from triggering a political attack on the contemporary abuse of the legal system, law in Menander seems to foster a rhetorical interaction that does not surpass the limits of the dramatic scene. Perhaps this is the reason why New Comedy exploits the staging of private settlements, where disputes are solved before going to trial. The small arbitral agon that comedy can reproduce serves better its comic purpose than the whole machinery of the Athenian *dikasteria*: unlike trial verdicts, which perpetuate enmity, agreed settlements end it; the latter accords far better with the spirit of comedy. *Epitrepontes*, for instance, dramatizes a successful scene of arbitration (thus its title) that includes perhaps the best forensic speech in all surviving comedy (218–375). Syriscus claims that Davus (who had given him a foundling) must hand over the ornaments with which the infant had been discovered. They agree to submit the controversy to Smicrines, a "fair judge" (κριτὴν...ἴσον, 226–227), who will listen to both parties and finally decide in favor of Syriscus (353–357).[12]

Compared to its treatment in Old Comedy, law in New Comedy does not seem to be radically subject to textual parody or exaggeration. Athenian *nomoi* are not explicitly taken as a source of humor, and the institutions of the polis are not criticized (but see MacDowell 1982). Of course, this does not mean that the Athenian audience—or, for that matter, an audience elsewhere in Greece—was not in control of legal details regarding inheritance and *epikleroi* and other *oikos*-related issues that are prominent in these comedies. Rather, literary representations of law in Menander's theater, where public affairs on stage are replaced by domesticity (Henderson and Scafuro, chapters 8 and 9, this volume), seem more generally inspired by a forensic practice whose rhetoric has been appropriated for dramatic purposes. Legal humor is grounded in the staging of conflicting positions about resorting to the judicial system, or in manipulating justice for private purposes. In general terms, law is no longer comic material in itself, but has become a contextual element (not a minor one) that contributes to the presentation of plots focused on family misunderstandings.

3. CONCLUSION: BETWEEN POLITICS AND POETICS

In democratic times, civic action was mainly exercised through the staging of public speeches in open spaces of participation. As has been frequently stated, theater,

---

[12] Scafuro (1997) deals carefully with comic passages where pre-trial dispute settlements are presented by means of threats of litigation, threats of legal summons, or self-help.

courtrooms, and the Assembly constituted areas that could be clearly connected within the large territory of political activity (cf. Pl. *Leg.* 876b). As formal spaces where every citizen could have his place, where actors and audience had discernible scripts, legislative procedures, legal trials, and drama were basically performative activities organized around the centrality of a competition (Garner 1987; Ober and Strauss 1990; Hall 1995; Todd 2005). The proximity of juridical to dramatic experiences should be taken into account in order to understand their interaction. Spectators attending comedies were used to listening to legal expressions and seeing "law in action" in the streets, marketplaces, courtrooms, and assemblies of Athens. Dramatic texts in Athens and elsewhere naturally exploited this shared knowledge as a functional dramatic device. But to what end? Despite obvious continuities, Aristophanes and Menander are fundamentally different in their presentation of citizens and the law: the older comic writer presents the language of tribunals and procedure in the course of instructing the audience on the perils of demagoguery, self-interest, and the misuse of the public arena, whereas Menander employs law to create arguments in which justice and fairness are required to reestablish the family balance.

Were Aristophanes and Menander *philheliasts* like Philocleon in *Wasps* (88) or *antiheliasts* like Peisetaerus in *Birds* (110)? Perhaps they were neither the one nor the other—or maybe both. What we do know is that law is an essential part of Greek comedy and that the comic poetics/politics of law stands right in the middle of contemporary discussions, such as those concerning the threats created by democracy versus the benefits it conferred or the interplay between the public and the private spheres of life.

FURTHER READING

Since the groundbreaking edition of *Wasps* by MacDowell (1971), only isolated articles—such as those by Carey (2000) and Cuniberti (2011)—have provided a specific overview of the importance of legal language in Aristophanic comedy. In spite of its title, MacDowell (2010) focuses basically on *Clouds*. On judicial and extrajudicial allusions in Menander, see Scafuro (1997). Wallace (2005) has worked on both Old and New Comedy, but has focused mainly on legal issues arising from comic freedom of expression. More recently, Fletcher (2012) has worked on oath-swearing in drama and has occasionally dealt with law. The collective volumes edited by Cantarella and Gagliardi (2007) and Harris, Leão, and Rhodes (2010) present a number of interesting essays on specific issues concerning the relationship between law and Greek theater (both tragedy and comedy). In more general terms, the isomorphism between dramatic spectacles and judicial procedures in Athens has been studied by Garner (1987), Ober and Strauss (1990), Hall (1995) and Todd (2005). A more comprehensive bibliographical survey on Greek law and comedy can be found in Sundahl, Mirhady and Arnaoutoglou (2011: 72–76) or online at www.sfu.ca/nomoi.

BIBLIOGRAPHY

Beta, S. 2004. *Il linguaggio nelle commedie di Aristofane: Parola positiva e parola negativa nella commedia antica*, Roma: Accademia nazionale dei Lincei.

Boegehold, A. L. 1967. "Philokleon's Court." *Hesperia* 36: 111–120.

——. 1995. *The Lawcourts at Athens: Sites, Buildings, Equipment, Procedure, and Testimonia*. The Athenian Agora 28, Princeton: American School of Classical Studies at Athens.

Brown, P. G. McC. 1983. "Menander's Dramatic Technique and the Law of Athens." *CQ* 33: 412–420.

Buis, E. J. 2002. "Labores propias, ¿litigios ajenos?: La mujer frente a las controversias mercantiles en la comedia aristofánica." Quaderni urbinati di cultura classica n. s. 72: 41–62.

——. 2007. "Del lecho al juzgado, del sexo al derecho: Un juego de palabras significativo en *Asambleístas* de Aristófanes." *Dike* 10: 85–112.

Cantarella, E., and L. Gagliardi, eds. 2007. *Diritto e teatro in Grecia e a Roma*. Milan: LED.

Carey, C. 2000. "Comic Law." *Annali dell' Università di Ferrara* 1: 65–86.

Cuniberti, G. 2011. "Aristofane *misodikos* e *philonomos*: Istituzioni democratiche, procedure giudiziarie e norme del diritto nella commedia attica antica." *Rivista di diritto ellenico* 1: 83–126.

Doganis, C. K. 2001. "La sycophantie dans la démocratie athénienne d'après les comédies d'Aristophane." *Journal des Savants* 2: 225–248.

Fletcher, J. 2012. *Performing Oaths in Classical Greek Drama*. Cambridge, UK: Cambridge University Press.

Garner, R. 1987. *Law and Society in Classical Athens*. London and Sydney: Croom Helm.

Hall, E. M. 1995. "Lawcourt Dramas: The Power of Performance in Greek Forensic Oratory." *BICS* 40: 39–58.

Halliwell, S. 1991. "Comic Satire and Freedom of Speech in Classical Athens." *JHS* 111: 48–70.

Hansen, M. H. 1978. "Nomos and Psephisma in Fourth-Century Athens." *GRBS* 19: 315–330.

Harris, E. 2002. "Pheidippides the Legislator: A Note on Aristophanes' *Clouds*." *ZPE* 140: 3–5.

Harris, E. M., D. F. Leão, and P. J. Rhodes, eds. 2010. *Law and Drama in Ancient Greece*. London: Duckworth.

Harrison, A. R. W. 1968. *The Law of Athens*. Vol. 1, *The Family and Property*. Oxford: Clarendon Press.

Harvey, R. 1990. "The Sykophant and Sykophancy: Vexatious Redefinition." In *Nomos: Essays in Athenian Law, Politics and Society*, edited by P. Cartledge, P. Millett, and S. Todd, 103–121. Cambridge, UK: Cambridge University Press.

Humphreys, S. C. 1974. "The Nothoi of Kynosarges." *JHS* 94: 88–95.

Kloss, G. 2001. *Erscheinungsformen komischen Sprechens bei Aristophanes*. Berlin: de Gruyter.

Lipsius, J. H. 1905–1915. *Das attische Recht und Rechtsverfahren*. Leipzig: O. R. Reisland.

MacDowell, D. M., ed. 1971. *Aristophanes' Wasps*. Oxford: Clarendon Press.

——. 1978. *The Law in Classical Athens*. Ithaca: Cornell University Press.

——. 1982. "Love versus the Law: An Essay on Menander's *Aspis*." *G&R* 29: 42–52.

——. 1995. *Aristophanes and Athens: An Introduction to the Plays*. Oxford: Oxford University Press.

——. 2010. "Aristophanes and Athenian Law." In *Law and Drama in Ancient Greece*, edited by P. J. Rhodes, E. M. Harris, and D. Ferreira Leão, 147–157. London: Duckworth.

Mastromarco, G. 1974. *Storia di una commedia di Atene*. Florence: La Nuova Italia.

Ober, J., and S. Strauss. 1990. "Drama, Political Rhetoric and the Discourse of Athenian Democracy." In *Nothing to Do with Dionysos? Athenian Drama in its Social Context*, edited by J. J. Winkler and F. I. Zeitlin, 237–270. Princeton: Princeton University Press.

Osborne, R. 1990. "Vexatious Litigation in Classical Athens: Sykophancy and the Sykophant." In *Nomos: Essays in Athenian Law, Politics and Society*, edited by P. Cartledge, P. Millett, and S. Todd, 83–102. Cambridge, UK: Cambridge University Press.

Pellegrino, M. 2010. *La maschera comica del Sicofante*. Lecce: Pensa Multimedia.

Quass, F. 1972. Nomos *und* Psephisma: *Untersuchung zur griechischen Staatsrecht*. Munich: Beck.

Rhodes, P. J. 1972. *The Athenian Boule*. Oxford: Clarendon Press.

Rubinstein, L. 2000. Litigation and Cooperation: Supporting Speakers in the Courts of Classical Athens. Stuttgart: Franz Steiner Verlag.

Ruschenbusch, E., ed. (with K. Bringmann) 2010. *Solon: Das Gesetzeswerk-Fragmente: Ubersetzung und Kommentar*. Wiesbaden: Franz Steiner Verlag.

Scafuro, A. C. 1997. *The Forensic Stage: Settling Disputes in Graeco-Roman New Comedy*. Cambridge, UK: Cambridge University Press.

Sommerstein, A. H. 2004a. "Comedy and the Unspeakable." In *Law, Rhetoric and Comedy in Classical Athens: Essays in Honour of Douglas M. MacDowell*, edited by D. L. Cairns and R. A. Knox, 205–222. Swansea: Classical Press of Wales.

———. 2004b. "Harassing the Satirist: The Alleged Attempts to Prosecute Aristophanes." In *Free Speech in Classical Antiquity*, edited by I. Sluiter and R. M. Rosen, 145–174. Leiden and Boston: Brill.

Stroud, R. S. 1979. *The Axones and Kyrbeis of Drakon and Solon*. Berkeley: University of California Press.

Sundahl, M., D. Mirhady, and I. Arnaoutoglou, eds. 2011. *A New Working Bibliography of Ancient Greek Law (7th–4th Centuries BC)*. Athens: Academy of Athens.

Swoboda, H. 1893. "Ueber den Process des Perikles." *Hermes* 28: 536–598.

Todd, S. C. 1993. *The Shape of Athenian Law*. Oxford: Clarendon Press.

———. 2005. "Law, Theatre, Rhetoric and Democracy in Classical Athens." *European Review of History* 12: 63–79.

Wallace, R. 2005. "Law, Attic Comedy, and the Regulation of Comic Speech." In *The Cambridge Companion to Ancient Greek Law*, edited by M. Gagarin and D. Cohen, 357–373. Cambridge, UK: Cambridge University Press.

Willi, A. 2003. *The Languages of Aristophanes: Aspects of Linguistic Variation in Classical Attic Greek*. Oxford: Oxford University Press.

CHAPTER 16

....

RELIGION AND THE GODS IN GREEK COMEDY

....

SCOTT SCULLION

REMARKABLY little has been published on religion and the gods in Greek comedy. This no doubt has partly to do with the difficulty of the most interesting questions about the role of religion in comic drama, and especially in Old Comedy: Are its often undignified portrayal of the gods and predominantly lighthearted approach to cultic matters evidence, as was generally supposed in the first half of the twentieth century, that contemporary Athenians did not take the gods wholly seriously, or that belief in the gods was waning in the later fifth century (e.g., Keller 1931; Kleinknecht 1937, esp. 116–122; Nilsson 1967: 779–783)? Or is it rather evidence—taken alongside, for example, the many hymns in Aristophanes which clearly owe a good deal to cultic congeners—that traditional piety thrived on, or even required, the outlet of comic license (e.g., Dover 1972: 31–33; Parker 2005: 147–152)? Or, as Keller 1931 suggested, is there perhaps a clear distinction between reduced seriousness about the mythology of the gods and routine cult on the one hand, and on the other, marked restraint and respect toward the Eleusinian mysteries?

Then there are the difficult questions about the relationship between comedy and real life, questions which we now rightly see as prior to those posed above, but which were often not adequately faced in earlier scholarship and remain underdiscussed in connection with religion and the gods (but see Given 2009 and above all Parker 2005: 147–152). No one has ever doubted that religion and the gods are put to poetic employment in comedy, that—whatever else they may be—they can certainly function as what Parker calls "enabling fictions" (Parker 2005: 145), but to what extent, if any, can we see beyond such employment and confidently detect predominant or common religious assumptions of an "Athenian audience?" Is, for example, the traditional view that comedians must rely on common assumptions to get laughs, just as orators must rely on them to be persuasive, really a safe criterion? Most importantly, perhaps, is it possible to avoid petitio principii in this matter, that is, to discover criteria allowing conclusions that are not simply based on prior assumptions about Athenian religiosity?

The questions about Old Comedy are interesting and difficult. New Comedy's treatment of religion and the gods, by contrast, can be described in a more straightforward manner, and can to some extent serve as a check on our ideas about Old Comedy.

CULT IN OLD COMEDY: FESTIVALS, SACRIFICE, AND ORACLES

Aristophanes is arguably our richest source from the classical period, alongside the inscriptional record, for the realities of fifth-century Athenian cult and the gods who were its recipients. The inscriptions give us a far wider range of evidence for the names, epithets, and sanctuaries of recipients of cult, the names and dates of festivals, ritual procedures, and sacrificial victims, but they generally tell us little or nothing about the attitudes of those participating in the cults—although texts that are "sacred laws" of course require and assume a high standard of seriousness and piety. Aristophanes, by contrast, does give us rare and precious glimpses of such attitudes, indications of how (some) participants in (some) rituals felt about them.

An instructive example of what Aristophanes (and inscriptions) have to tell us about cult is Strepsiades's account in *Clouds* of experiences at the festival Diasia. "By Zeus," he says, "exactly that happened to me once at the Diasia. I was roasting a haggis for my relatives and forgot to make a slit in it. So it puffed up and then suddenly exploded, spattered my eyes, and burnt my face" (408–411). He later mentions having bought a toy cart for Phidippides at the same festival (864). Strepsiades's haggis apparently contradicts the testimony of Thucydides (1.126.4), who mentions Diasia as a festival for Zeus Meilichios that does not involve sacrifices of "ordinary sacrificial victims" (1.126.6), i.e., the standard animal sacrifice with banqueting. Scholars of Greek religion, associating this with Xenophon's attestation of holocaust (wholly burnt) sacrifice to Zeus Meilichios (*Anab.* 7.8.4), used to conclude that animals were sacrificed at Diasia as holocaust offerings involving no banquet (e.g., Deubner 1932: 155–156). Zeus Meilichios, often portrayed in the form of a snake, seems to be the sort of underworld or chthonian god to whom holocaust can be appropriate, and all this seemed to square with much later evidence that the festival Diasia was conducted "with a certain grimness" (Σ Luc.107.15,110.27 Rabe; Hesych. δ 1312 Latte). The picture was, however, completely altered—and the evidence of *Clouds* strikingly confirmed—with the publication in 1963 and 1983 of two new Attic inscriptions (of the late fifth and mid-fourth centuries), both of which clearly attest standard animal sacrifice rather than holocaust at the Diasia (Sokolowski 1969, no. 18 A 37–42; *SEG* 33 [1983] 147.35). It turns out, therefore, that Aristophanes's evidence is more reliable than that of Thucydides, and surely also more reliable than the later evidence on the mood of the festival. The slapstick of the exploding haggis might just be squeezed into a picture of a "grim" Diasia, but taken together with Strepsiades's recollection of buying the toy cart—and Demosthenes (10.50) tells us that "the abundance and cheapness of the things for sale" was the mark of a well-organized festival—it seems safe enough to conclude that Strepsiades's barbecuing and toy-buying, like the sacrificial banqueting now securely attested, are evidence that for most participants Diasia was rather a jolly than a grim festival (see further Scullion 2007: 190–193).

Broadening our scope a little, we find that Aristophanes provides a good deal of suggestive evidence about the mood in which his contemporaries attended festivals. At *Peace* 815–816, the chorus ask the goddess-Muse to "play with me in this festival" (μετ' ἐμοῦ ξύμπαιζε τὴν ἑορτήν, cf. *Frogs* 319, 333, 375, 388, 392, 407b, 411, 415, 442, 452 with Dover 1993: 57–59; Menander, *Epitrepontes [Arbitrators]* 478), and in the vast majority of references to festivals in the plays the predominant mood is pleasure— relaxation, family, food and drink, entertainment—and above all the delights of peace in contrast to the horrors of war. There are sometimes hymns (and happy dancing to them), but little in the way of theology or demonstrative piety on the part of ordinary people, and there are often sacrifices, but it is their aspect as a meal that engrosses the ordinary participant's attention. The spirit of holiday is much more obviously invoked than that of holy day.

Chronologically the first, and one of the most famous, of the festival scenes in extant Aristophanes is Dicaeopolis's celebration in *Acharnians* (202, 241–279) of his own Rural Dionysia when he acquires a thirty-year peace treaty—a treaty in the shape of a libation-bowl or wineskin (with a pun on *spondai* = both "treaty" and "libation"). In this case, there are a number of marked cultic elements: Dicaeopolis begins by calling for ritual silence (241), musters a phallus procession with his daughter as basket-bearer, prays to Dionysus "that I may conduct this procession and sacrifice pleasingly to you, and that I and my household may hold the Rural Dionysia with good fortune now that I'm released from war-service, and that the thirty years' peace may be beneficial for me" (247–252), and sings a hymn to Phales—a personification of the large ritual phallus carried in the procession—which perhaps owes something to phallic hymns in cult but focuses on sexual antics and drinking as preferable alternatives to war in a way that cultic hymns will not have done (263–279). The choice of Dionysus and the Rural Dionysia, rather than any other god or festival, for the celebration of Dicaeopolis's separate peace is perhaps driven primarily by the representation of the treaties on offer as libation-bowls or wineskins and secondarily by a jolly rural festival—and one with sexual associations—being the natural choice of Dicaeopolis as a pleasure-loving rustic of the deme Cholleidae (406). There is no reason to think of the Dionysiac festival context of the performance of the play as relevant; Aristophanes makes such associations clear when they are relevant, as in *Frogs*. More importantly, we should notice that—as has often been observed of Old Comedy (recently, for example, by Given 2009)—the business of putting the world to rights, here of making the peace, is the task of human agents rather than of the gods. Dicaeopolis turns to the Rural Dionysia to celebrate something he has brought about himself, not—as would be normal in cult—to invoke the god's help beforehand in the hope of obtaining it, nor to thank the god afterward for having granted it. There is a touch of those standard modes of approach to the god in the phrase "that the thirty years' peace may be beneficial for me" (252), but Dicaeopolis's

Rural Dionysia is clearly much more a "celebration" in our secular sense than a festival whose professed cultic function is paramount.

The obvious question is whether this predominance of celebration and pleasure over cultic function is purely a product of the comic context or might rather tell us something important about how ordinary Greeks felt about festivals. It is difficult to feel confident drawing a conclusion, but the vast majority of references to festivals elsewhere in Aristophanes points in the same direction as the passage in *Acharnians*, and surely justifies us in assuming that priority of festival fun over cultic functionality was a familiar attitude to Aristophanes's audience. Just as most comic references to sacrifice center on eating and drinking, so too do many references to festivals—meat from the Apaturia festival for erotic go-betweens (*Women at the Thesmophoria* 558); thrushes (a favorite food, cf. *Clouds* 339) for Choes ("Jugs"), the second day of Anthesteria (*Acharnians* 961); and in the telling catalogue of pleasures associated with personified Peace by Trygaeus at *Peace* 530–532: "she smells of harvest, parties, Dionysia, pipes, tragic performances, Sophocles's songs, thrushes, little lines by Euripides." The drinking contest that was a feature of Choes (but not the fact of the day being apparently "unclean," possibly because the souls of the dead were thought to come up during it: Parker 2005: 294–295), also figures prominently in *Ach.* (1000–1002, 1085–1086, 1211, 1228–1229), which is our most important source for the events of this day of the festival (cf. *Women at the Thesmophoria* 745–747 and *Frogs* 215–219 for the third day of Anthesteria, Chytroi, "Pots").

Peace is a particularly rich source for attitudes to festivals. When Trygaeus frees Peace, she is accompanied by two attractive attendants, Opora, personified Harvest, whom Trygaeus will marry, and Theoria, personified "Junket" (see Scullion 2005: 126), whom he restores to the Athenian Council (in their reserved seats in the theater) and who represents the Council's jolly privilege of sending delegates to enjoy themselves at international festivals, which the coming of peace will allow them to do again. Theoria is exclusively associated with light-hearted references to the festival pleasures of food and above all of sex (341–342, 715–717, 872–874, 876, 879–880, 881–908; see Scullion 2005: 119–121). The motif of the festival as a place where men meet and sometimes impregnate women is familiar in the fifth century (e.g., *Wealth* 1013–1014, in tragedy Euripides *Ion* 545–554), and recurs in New Comedy (Menander, *Epitrepontes* 450–454, 472–480; *Samia* 31–49; also probably *Phasma* 194–207), and there is therefore no reason to conclude that in *Peace* comic exaggeration has lost touch with reality. Comic exaggeration there no doubt is, but still it is difficult not to see this most spectacular example of the "fun and games" model of the festival as telling us something important about Athenian attitudes, or at any rate about an available—and not a strange—attitude, even among official state delegates to the most prominent international festivals.

Festivals can also be treated quite disrespectfully. In *Clouds*, beyond the references to Diasia, there are references to two festivals marked as especially old-fashioned: Socrates calls Strepsiades a "moron smelling of the Cronia" (398), and Worse Argument employs Dipolieia (a festival of Zeus Polieus) and its ritual Bouphonia ("Ox-slaying") as marks of what is "antiquated" (984–985). It is remarkable that it should be divine festivals that Aristophanes makes spring to the lips of his characters as indicative of what is stale and fusty—but Cronia and Dipolieia are precisely the festivals a poet would choose who wanted his audience to find imputations of fustiness plausible. The Cronia was dedicated to Cronus and thus harked back to the divine ancien régime, and the Bouphonia ritual of Dipolieia, with its focus both on sacrifice as a guilty act and on trial of the sacrificial knife or axe, was strikingly distinctive and will have seemed to many fifth-century Athenians, as to many modern scholars, redolent of the remote origins of animal sacrifice.

Is the festival of the Eleusinian Mysteries, as Keller 1931: 54–61 suggested, treated by Aristophanes with exceptional respect? There is the difficulty here that, unlike most festivals, the Mysteries were subject to a strict requirement of secrecy, but even so there is nothing in *Frogs* resembling Sophocles's "How thrice-blessed are those of mortals who go to Hades having seen these rites, for to them alone is life given there, to the others all ills" (fr. 837 Radt *TrGF*; cf. *Hymn. Hom. Cer.* 480–482; Pindar, fr. 137 Snell-Maehler). The closest we come are Heracles's references to "fair sunlight" and "blessed bands of men and women" in Hades (154–157, cf. 327) and the chorus's final lines in the scene: "For us alone is there sun and sacred daylight, all of us who are initiated and behaved righteously toward strangers and ordinary people" (454–459). There are occasional references to Demeter, but she is invoked rather to protect the chorus so it can "safely play and dance all day" (387–388) than as goddess of mystic initiation. The chorus pray to her: "...and may I say many funny things, and many serious things, and frolicking and jesting worthily of your festival may I be garlanded as victor" (389–393); the prayer shifts us away from the mysteries to the comic contest at Dionysus's festival by blurring the chorus's plot-internal and -external identities. Otherwise, the emphasis throughout is on the pleasures of the dancing led by Iacchus, on "our uninhibited, fun-loving worship" (332–333—nor does Aristophanes eschew the scene's potential for sexual humor at 408–415). Thus there seems no reason to regard Aristophanes's treatment of the mysteries as especially restrained by contrast with his handling of other festivals.

What can we conclude? It seems safe to say that when they sat down to watch a comedy, an Athenian audience was not expecting to learn important things about the meaning and purpose of the festival of Dionysus during which the play was performed, or of any other festival. Rather, festivals are primarily events at which ordinary participants enjoy themselves, eat and drink too much, buy things, watch processions and athletic contests and shows, and perhaps misbehave sexually. That, we must assume—given the overwhelming predominance of the same set of attitudes throughout the plays—was, if not a universal, at any rate a very common attitude.

The two other staple elements of Greek religious practice which recur in Aristophanic comedy are sacrifice and oracles. Far more often than not, oracles come in for mockery as absurdly obfuscatory or as self-serving invention (or both), especially those cited by oracle-mongers (such as Hierocles the seer at the end of *Peace*) or those connected with the low-grade oracles of Bacis or Glanis. The oracle predicting the advent of the Sausage-Seller in *Knights* (128–147) turns out to be true, but unlike most comic oracles it also obviously serves an essential plot-function, elevating a most unlikely candidate to the status of savior of the city. Several Aristophanic sacrifices likewise play a role in organizing the plot—the establishment of the cult of Peace (*Peace* 922–1126), the sacrifice-blocking siege of the gods in *Birds* (190–193, 563–569, 809–811, 848–903), the setting of the scene of the Thesmophoria festival (*Women at the Thesmophoria* 284–288), and a sacrifice that loses its point when Wealth gains his sight and so can reward the good on his own initiative (*Wealth* 137–143, 1113–1116, 1171–1184). These more extended scenes do not focus on sacrifice primarily as a source of meat in the same way as passing references elsewhere do, but still involve plenty of humor of that kind. A fragment of the old comic poet Pherecrates (K-A fr. 28) reflects, as no extant passage of Aristophanes does, men's uncomfortable awareness that they rather than the gods enjoy the meat of standard sacrificial procedure —an oddity for which Hesiod's story of the tricking of Zeus by Prometheus is already an attempt to account (*Theogony* 535–557).

The importance of all this for our study of Aristophanic technique is obvious enough: even the realia of ritual and cult are grist to the poet's comic mill, and earn their place in his work either as useful premises of the plot or by their capacity to raise laughs, to be mocked, or to invoke nostalgia for the pleasurable pursuits of peace.

The Gods in Old Comedy

Let us explore further the question of Aristophanes's dramatic employment of the stuff of Greek religion by considering his depiction of the gods and their roles in the plays. His technique at the level of general plot-construction can be very subtle indeed. Perhaps the best example is his personification of the Clouds; he gives the impression at first that they are newfangled, appropriately vaporous deities of the sophists, but in the *parabasis* (518ff.) they take on a new guise as neglected divinities of traditional type, and by the end of the play they become stern defenders of belief in and respect for the traditional gods (1454–1455, 1458–1461 with 1470–1480, 1506–1509). The comic technique is striking: with minor exceptions, the full chorus manages to maintain from its opening words—one of the loveliest of many lovely hymns in Aristophanic comedy, in praise of holy Athens (299–313)—the identity of novel divinities who are nevertheless traditional both in their values and in their hymnic idiom. The audience's initial impression that they are sophistical divinities is created almost entirely by what Socrates, the Chorus Leader, and Strepsiades say in the opening scene (252–253, 258–259, 264–266, 316–318, 319–322, 331–334, 365–411, 412–419, 423–424, 427–428, 431–432, 435–436, 457–475 [whole chorus]). The comic technique here hardly promotes "coherent characterization," but it is highly effective and thematically important, both as manifestation of how much turns on how one looks at things, and—if only retrospectively for many in the audience— as a "ticking time bomb" of traditional good sense lying half-hidden until in the end it explodes sophistry.

One of the important effects of this kind of use of divinities or divine personifications is to keep the divine realm in the background while the human agents of the comedy work out their schemes—successfully or unsuccessfully, for good or ill—on their own. It has often been observed that though the gods are very frequently mentioned in

Aristophanes, they rarely play a very prominent or essential role in the working out of the comic plot, even in the few plays in which gods are characters (Hermes and silent Peace in *Peace*; Iris, Prometheus, Poseidon, Heracles, and the Triballian god in *Birds*; Dionysus, Heracles, and Pluto in *Frogs*; Wealth and Hermes in *Wealth*). In general, the driving force of an Aristophanic plot is someone's attempt to reshape the world in the form of human desire—or sometimes merely to sort out his own world to relieve his anxieties. Thus war must give way to peace (*Acharnians*, *Peace*, *Lysistrata*), political corruption (and war) to honesty (*Knights*), the generally wretched state of society to a new regime (*Birds*), bad new poetry to good old poetry (*Frogs*), the political incompetence of men to women's good sense (*Assemblywomen*), unjust distribution of wealth to reward of the good (*Wealth*)—or a man must escape his debts (*Clouds*), his father's jury-mania (*Wasps*), or his bad reputation with women (*Women at the Thesmophoria*).

If one reflects on these particular themes, the general sort of role the gods might play suggests itself readily enough. In Aristophanes, the Peloponnesian war is always an entirely manmade stupidity. Trygaeus is tempted to blame it on Zeus (*Peace* 57–71, 103–108), but soon learns from Hermes that the gods have decamped in disgust at mortal rejection of their attempts to arrange truces (204–226), and so Trygaeus must counteract vaguely personified Polemos ("War") to free the goddess Peace. *Lysistrata* is gender-inflected, so that the opponent there is men (with personified Reconciliation resembling Peace, and Lysistrata herself associated, through the real-world priestess Lysimache [Henderson 1987: xxxviii–xl], with Athena as savior of Athens). In *Acharnians*, the opponent is the belligerent Cleon and his ilk, and so again in *Knights*. The theme of a new regime of the world in *Birds* entails displacement of the gods as its traditional rulers and so brings scenes of a sacrificial blockade of the gods and a negotiated settlement (of sorts, through bribery of minor divinities), but the focus is very much on human rather than divine sources of the world's troubles, including a series of types of Athenian pest—poet, oracle-expounder, informer, and so on. The role of Dionysus (and likewise of Heracles and Pluto in *Frogs*) is obvious enough, and it is centrally important that Dionysus acts here primarily as a bereft lover of Athenian tragic drama rather than as the daunting god of myth and cult. *Assemblywomen*, like *Lysistrata*, is focused on the shortcomings of men, politics, and social mores. One can imagine a play about the injustices of wealth in which distorted human values were the problem, but not perhaps an old comedy. Aristophanes wants a vivid opponent, which the social causes of unfair distribution of wealth are too various and diffuse to provide (unlike the Athenian social pests who can appear as types in *Birds*): hence only in *Wealth* is a god (Zeus) vigorously accused of injustice toward those who honor him (*Wealth* 87–98, 123–126, 1117), and moreover, the regime he runs is overthrown when Chremylus succeeds in having Wealth cured of his blindness (1112–1119). The gods are bound to be less prominent in *Wasps*, with its focus not only on an individual's problems but also on manmade aspects of Athenian political culture. The Clouds come into their play because of the theme of sophistry, and the modest role of the *Thesmophoroi*, Demeter and Kore, naturally suits the setting of *Women at the Thesmophoria*. Looked at in this way—even with the ready concession that in any given case Aristophanes might have made quite other choices—it is clear how far the role of the gods depends on prior considerations of theme and plot, and how unsafe it therefore is to look for any consistent Aristophanic theology.

There is, however, evidence in the comedies that atheistic ideas, skeptical attitudes to the gods and cult, and quite remarkable acts of impiety were familiar to poet and audience. Such passages are not terribly common, but Euripides is taxed with disbelieving in the gods (*Women at the Thesmophoria* 450–452, cf. *Ran.* 889–893, 936); the chorus of *Women at the Thesmophoria* say that any man caught among them will be punished and "will say that the gods manifestly exist" (668–675); and in *Knights,* one slave asks another whether he really believes that gods exist (30–34). Socrates's powerful arguments against traditional accounts of Zeus's control of the weather are an example of the sort of thinking that might produce doubt of the gods' existence (*Clouds* 369–402). Carion's robustly satirical account of the goings-on in the Asclepieum during Wealth's incubation-cure is not quite skeptical—the cure, after all, succeeds—but with its priest "sanctifying the offerings into his sack" and so on, it certainly expresses a rather jaundiced view of healing cult (*Wealth* 653–747). Perhaps most startling among the acts of impiety mentioned is the Priest of Zeus Savior's complaint at the end of *Wealth* that no one now sacrifices or even enters a sanctuary, "except the thousands who come to relieve themselves" (1183–1184)—which sounds, though one cannot of course be certain, like the sort of joke that suggests such behavior was not uncommon.

All discussion of the gods in Aristophanes inevitably comes round to the indignities he visits upon them. A scholium on *Peace* speaks of the prevalence in Old Comedy of "Heracles the hungry, Dionysus the coward, and adulterer Zeus" (Schol. vet. Ar. *Pax* 741e; on Zeus as adulterer in comedy, see Parker 2005: 151 with n. 67). In his appearances in *Peace* and *Wealth*, Hermes cuts a rather poor figure, initial bluster giving way to greedy submission to bribery, and so too the trio of Poseidon, Heracles, and the Triballian who come to negotiate for the gods in *Birds*. But debate centers specially on Dionysus in *Frogs*, who soils himself in fear—twice (308, 479–493), envisages himself masturbating while watching his slave enjoy congress with a girl (541–547), and is generally craven and dim throughout. There are essentially two lines on this: the older view that it indicates that Aristophanes's contemporaries no longer took the gods very seriously, and the more up-to-date assumption that, as Parker puts it, "Greeks felt able to cheek the gods precisely because they did not doubt their power," and "reality itself provided the necessary corrective" (Parker 2005: 149, 150).[1]

This may be right, but the first suggestion is certainly rather paradoxical, and the second is an attempt to account for the absence of any corrective in the plays themselves, so that there is some risk here of reading in a prior assumption about the quality of Athenian religiosity, a problem to which we will revert. If we were right to suggest that

---

[1] An even more popular line of explanation has been festival license or the spirit of carnival, but Parker 2005: 149 with n. 61 speaks of the "easy victory" of this view, rightly noting the absence of "a comparative study which locates the Greek material clearly and firmly. It is not enough to know that in various religious traditions (e.g. medieval Christianity) laughter is permitted about sacred subjects: one needs a clear view of what may and may not be laughed at."

the average Athenian's sense of a festival had little strictly "religious" about it, might it not be reasonable to wonder whether in his notions of the gods he likewise operated with a minimal (or merely residual) attachment to the validity of myths and theological propositions, and a correspondingly active capacity (or even propensity) to enjoy seeing them sent up?

We cannot draw conclusions about Aristophanes's own religious views, but can we— as in the case of festivals—make safe inferences about the range of attitudes to the gods familiar to his audience? If so, we must begin by noting that the overwhelming impression his work gives is of a wide range both of "mythical" gods and of recipients of cult (particular forms of gods identified by epithets, such as Zeus Soter and so on) whose existence is taken very much for granted and who are regarded with affection rather than anxiety or fear. This last may also tell us something important in the sense that such an attitude can naturally slip over into not taking the gods very seriously. But clearly it was not *inconceivable* to think of Zeus or the generality of gods as operating a rather poor regime, and the question is therefore how far Aristophanic comedy suggests that such attitudes were confined to a small, generally despised minority of eggheads. Put another way, the central question is surely this: Is the comic marginalization of certain attitudes about the gods evidence that such attitudes were repugnant or scarcely conceivable to most Athenians, or should we conclude rather that their extreme marginalization in the plays is a reflex of comedy's clear tendency to create objects of (sometimes genial) contempt, and that, since we have no safe means of measuring the presence among and appeal to common people of such attitudes, it would be arbitrary to make the extreme assumption that their appeal was confined to a tiny and marginalized minority? The latter seems to me the more prudent conclusion, but a clear and still generally accepted statement of the other conclusion was given by Dover:

> Fifth-century Greece produced some individuals of extraordinary intellectual penetration, who speculated on the structure and history of the universe in terms of natural, intelligible processes from which the acts of personal gods were excluded; but in the same city as such an individual, often perhaps in the same household, we should find a majority for whom a strong wind was a person who decided when he would blow, a blight on the crops the manifestation of a god's anger for a sacrifice promised but not performed, and a sudden bright idea the intervention of an unseen being in the mental processes of an individual human. The average Greek, in short, felt himself to be living in a world populated by superhuman agents (the term 'supernatural' would beg the question), and although he might exhibit a cheerful agnosticism if pressed to discuss the precise character and operation of any one such agent, he would not so cheerfully omit the inherited system of festivals, rituals, sacrifices and observances which in his view had for so long ensured the survival of his family and city. (Dover 1972: 31–32)

Perhaps we can confine ourselves to two observations about this. First, it is a curiously polarized society Dover envisages, a kind of Pietyville that yet produced, as so many sports of nature rather than by organic processes, the individuals of extraordinary penetration—and there were very many of them indeed—who escaped the radical fundamentalism of the majority; it was a Pietyville, moreover, to which sophists from all over the Greek world were drawn. Secondly, how does Dover know that "the average Greek" held quite such fundamentalist attitudes, or that a "cheerful agnosticism" would only emerge when such a person was pressed, or that it was not primarily *delight* in festivals, rituals, and sacrifices, in combination with cheerful uncertainty or doubt about their metaphysical efficacy, that made omission of them unthinkable? The usual answer to this is that the appeals to conventional piety common in comedy itself and in oratory guarantee that conventional piety was widespread, but we have found reasons to be cautious about comedy in this respect and, as *Wasps* suggests, the context of a law court, as in a different but analogous way that of the comic theater, is conducive to the encouragement and adoption of more rigidly disapproving and judgmental attitudes than most other contexts. Dover may not be wrong, but the application of prior assumption is surely playing a bigger role here than it ought.

Before turning to New Comedy, we should notice finally a controversial line on religion in Old Comedy that appeals strongly to some scholars but seems quite unpersuasive to others. This is the notion that the plots of old comedies tend to be based on an underlying ritual matrix or model—the aetiological myth(s) of a rite, or its ritual elements, or both. Thus, for example, Lada-Richards 1999 argues that in the course of *Frogs* Dionysus goes through the stages of a mystic initiation. The most comprehensive—and most learned and circumspect—study on these lines is Bowie 1993 (with Bowie 2000 on the fragmentary plays). Stimulating as such studies—those on comedy no less than those on tragedy—can be, the references, allusions, or analogues to ritual that they posit tend to be so cryptic and/or so vague and approximate that they seem persuasive only to those inclined to assume a priori that Athenian dramatic poets somehow ought to have based their plots on ritual, but unpersuasive to those not inclined to make such an assumption, even though—indeed partly because—neither the assumption nor the interpretations to which it gives rise are conclusively falsifiable.

New Comedy: Menander

There is little to say about religion and cultic gods in the "Middle Comedy" of the first three quarters of the fourth century. We have many fragments of middle comedies, but no complete or nearly complete play has survived, and it is correspondingly difficult to speak with any confidence about the role of the gods in them, except to say that myths about gods, especially about the births of gods, figured among the mythological burlesques that seem to have been very popular in the first half of the fourth century (see Nesselrath 1990: 188–240, Nesselrath 1995, and Konstantakos in this volume). New Comedy, from its beginnings in the last quarter of the fourth century BC, completes a transition from fantastical Old Comedy with its coherent polytheism to thoroughly bourgeois plots and assumptions and to a combination of cultic "local color" with a big picture dominated rather by Tyche—Fortune or Chance personified or deified—than by the traditional pantheon or by any one god.

Greek cult in its traditional forms persisted throughout the great period of New Comedy and beyond, as is clearly reflected in the plays of its most famous practitioner Menander and in the fragments of such other new comedians as Philemon and Diphilus. Thus, for example, Habrotonon says that, having been celibate for two days, she is qualified to carry Athena's basket in the Panathenaea procession (*Epitrepontes* 438–439), and Moschion in *Kitharistes* (*Lyre-Player*) relates how he saw and fell in love with Phanias's daughter at a δειπνοφορία τις παρθένων, "a maidens' meal-carrying" in honor of Ephesian Artemis (*Kitharistes* 93–97). There are a number of passages in Menander useful to the student of Greek cult for their mention of ritual detail, for example the separate treatment of the tongue of sacrificial victims (*Kolax* [*Flatterer*] fr. 1.4–5 Sandbach), the gods' desire for a victim with good bones and a large spleen (*Samia* 399–404), and many details of the ritual of weddings (including the cutting of a sesame cake) in *Samia* (73–75, 122–125, 157–159, 190–191, 673–674, 730–731, cf. K-A fr. 340). There are similarly useful passages in *Theophoroumene* (*Demoniac Girl*) about ecstatic cult and the gods associated with it (25–28, 31–57).

A very common new comic type-role is the *mageiros*—butcher, sacrificer, cook— whose characteristically sardonic approach to his trade is splendidly exemplified in a long fragment of Diphilus in which a *mageiros* expounds the pros and cons of various kinds of customer, noting for example that the merchant sailor sacrificing to fulfill a vow after his ship was damaged or his cargo had to be thrown overboard is to be avoided because "he doesn't do it with any pleasure, but purely for the sake of *nomos* (convention)" (Diphilus K-A 42.13–14, cf., e.g., Menander *Aspis* 216–233, *Dyskolos* 393–424, *Perikeiromene* 995–1000, *Samia* 286–294, fr. 409 K-A). Among Menander's plays, sacrifice looms largest in *Dyskolos* (*Bad-Tempered Man*), where Sostratus's mother, who sends Getas to fetch a *mageiros*, is keenly indiscriminate in her offerings to gods (259–264), a superstitious attitude that generally comes in for disdain in Menander, as it does here in the scene between Getas and the *mageiros* Sicon at 393–414 (other references to sacrifice at *Dyskolos* 198, 400–401, 417–418, 430, 439–441 [sacrificial requisites mentioned], 474).

The bad-tempered man himself, Cnemon, who regards the shrine of Pan and the Nymphs next to his house as a mere nuisance, expounds an even more sardonic view of sacrifice than Diphilus's *mageiros*: "How they sacrifice, the thieves! They bring hampers and wine-jars, not for the sake of the gods but of themselves. The incense and the cake are piously dealt with—all of it put on the fire and the god gets that. But having dedicated the tail-bone and the gall bladder—because they're inedible—to the gods, they wolf down everything else themselves" (*Dyskolos* 447–453). Of course, Cnemon is grumpy and jaded, but there can be no doubt that the dubious status of traditional modes of sacrifice as "gifts for the gods" was clear enough—noticed, as we have seen, by the old comedian Pherecrates, and also by the middle comedian Eubulus (K-A fr. 127)—and that Cnemon's vigorous denunciation is therefore telling. His allowance that offerings of incense and cake are pious chimes with and perhaps reflects the views of Menander's older contemporary Theophrastus, who in *On Piety* recommends such simple offerings and condemns animal sacrifice. There is an even more sharply satirical treatment of the theme in a fragment of Menander's *Methe* (*Drunkenness*), whose speaker notes that he is bringing the gods a little ten-drachma sheep but has spent a talent (a huge sum) on such other provisions for the feast as dancing-girls, perfume, wine, eels, cheese, and honey. If we had to expend as much on the gods as on ourselves, he says, "wouldn't the bother of sacrifices be doubled?" (πῶς οὐχὶ τὸ κακὸν τῶν ἱερῶν διπλάζεται; Menander K-A fr. 224.10). It again seems safe to conclude that this attitude must have been familiar—or at any rate recognizable—to Menander's audience, and it is a natural enough development of the primary focus on sacrifice as a source of meat that is exemplified in Old Comedy; there would of course be (for example) a gently rueful way of holding and expressing the same essential idea. As Nilsson put it many years ago when speaking of sacrifice in New Comedy, "As had already been the case earlier, the feast was the main thing, the sacrifice only a form" (Nilsson 1974: 194). There is no doubt at all that this sort of attitude was countered by advocates of traditional piety or, as in the case of Theophrastus, of reformed piety, but beyond the existence of a debate about the nature of piety there are no demographic facts or statistical trends available to us now for the reconstruction of "standard" and "nonstandard" contemporary attitudes (but see e.g. Mikalson 1998: 68–74 for an argument in favor of piety as predominant).

A range of divine recipients of cult finds mention in New Comedy, but nothing like as wide a range as in Old Comedy. Such gods typically enter the picture because their sanctuary is in or near the stage setting, and seldom for any other reason. They are far more marginal than their congeners in Old Comedy, and indeed in most cases provide little more than pleasant local color. Menander's *Sikyonioi* is set at Eleusis, for example, and an Eleusinian goddess spoke its prologue, and his *Leukadia* was set at a temple of Apollo on the island of Leucas, whose holy spring is mentioned (*Leukadia* 7). Some local divinities of this type—the Eleusinian goddess just mentioned; the *heros theos* or hero-god of Menander's *Heros*, who was a local divinity of the deme Ptelea; or, the best-known example, Pan in *Dyskolos*—can conveniently deliver the prologue speech which is a standard component of Menandrian comedy, providing background information necessary for comprehension of the plot. Some prologues are, however, spoken not by traditional divinities but by personified abstractions such as Agnoia ("Misconception") in *Perikeiromene* (*Girl with Her Hair Cut Short*) and Tyche in *Aspis* (*Shield*).

With Tyche, we come to the "big picture" and the question of how New Comedy's characters perceive the universe as operating. This figure, "Fortune" or "Chance"—originally a simple personification, but in time a goddess of cult—plays the central, controlling role in the Menandrian world, largely displacing Zeus and the gods and little associated with the cultic modes of converse traditional with them, so that a divide seems to appear in the coherent system of cultic practice and divine governance. Menander K-A fr. 681 says that Tyche is the only divinity, the others empty names. In some respects, therefore, we move here beyond what students of Greek religion regard as their proper domain and into the realm of popular philosophy. A very inconsistent philosophy it is too, and not only, one suspects, because of the varying views, temperaments, and situations of the characters who talk about Tyche in the plays, but also because there was simply no standard or predominant line on the matter in contemporary society.

In *Aspis* (*Shield*), Tyche describes herself as "in charge of all this [the plot situation], to judge and control it" (*Aspis* 147–148), but human perception of her—and the very fact that Tyche can equally well be translated "Chance" as "Fortune"—suggests rather that her operations are highly unpredictable and sometimes hostile or indifferent to human desire. The Tyche of *Aspis* tells us that she is a god, but "fortune" also occurs often as a common noun. Daos in *Aspis* opines that "*tyche* is uncertain" (248–249) and quotes from the fourth-century tragedian Chaeremon the line "human affairs are a matter of *tyche*, not good counsel" (411); a fragment of *Kitharistes* (*Lyre-Player*) describes *tyche* as "various and deceptive" (fr. 8 Sandbach), as the personified goddess is "blind and wretched" at K-A fr. 682. A character of Philemon's says that there exists no divinity Tyche, but that τὸ αὐτόματον, "mere chance" or "the accidental" which happens to each person, is called *tyche*—with a pun on *tyche* and the verb τυγχάνω, "happen" (Philemon K-A fr. 125), but Demeas in *Samia* says that τὸ αὐτόματον is a sort of god (*Samia* 163–164).

Many of the most interesting passages about Tyche / *tyche* are found among the fragments of the new comedians excerpted precisely for their sententiousness by anthologists. The old idea that one's character is one's *daimon* or presiding divinity occurs frequently—for example, in the form "νοῦς ["mind"] is the god in each of us" (Menander fr. K-A 889)—and is now often associated with Tyche. Thus a Menandrian character says that a man who does not cope well with his own affairs calls his own character *tyche* (K-A fr. 687), and we encounter the related ideas that we would not need Tyche if we all helped one another (Menander K-A fr. 686) and that *tyche* works best when one helps it oneself (Philemon K-A fr. 56). On the other hand, some character argues rather that "it is divinity that gives bad fortune or otherwise, not a flaw of character" (Menander K-A fr. 321.3–4).

In two passages, the relation between character and fortune or divinity is developed at some length. A character in Philemon says that there is not a single *tyche*, but that each person gets his own inborn *tyche* when he is born, and that one cannot get *tyche* from another (K-A fr. 9). A fragment of Menander develops similar ideas in more traditional terminology: everyone has a good *daimon*, as *mystagogos* ("mystic guide") of his life, from birth, for we must not believe that there exist evil *daimones*, nor that god possesses evil, but rather that he is in all respects good. "Those who themselves become evil," it continues, "through their own character, making a mess of their lives, hold a *daimon* responsible and call him evil, having become evil themselves" (Menander K-A fr. 500). This is of course a good, traditional Greek view, going back to Homer (*Odyssey* 1.32–43).

Tyche and *tyche* tend to predominate in general reflection, but such traditional talk of the gods or *daimones* as we have just seen is not uncommon. Sometimes such god-talk is positive, as when Misconception in the prologue of *Kolax* (*Flatterer*) holds that "through divinity even evil turns to good" (*Kolax* 169) or someone claims that "the poor are always regarded as the gods' care" (*Leukadia* fr. 5 Sandbach) or that "god, if you consider the matter, is fair to all, to free and slaves alike" (Menander K-A fr. 451). More often, though, talk of the gods is negative: "But where are such just gods to be found, Getas?" (*Misoumenos* [*The Hated Man*] fr. 7 Sandbach); "the gods [are inclined to favor?] the bad people" (*Kolax* 27); "there is unjust judgment, as it seems, even among the gods" (Menander K-A fr. 291); "I sacrificed to gods who give me nothing" (Menander K-A fr. 612). Onesimos in *Epitrepontes* (*Arbitrators*) offers an account of how things work that nicely sums up the range of views we have been surveying. "Do you think, Smicrines," he asks, "that the gods have so much leisure as to distribute ill and good day by day to each person?" There are one thousand towns in the world, he goes on, and thirty thousand people in each town—can the gods ruin or save every single one of them? Rather, the gods have put character in us, and this is each man's god, "the cause of success and of failure for each" (*Epitrepontes* 1084–1099).

Students of Menandrian comedy have long seen that the gods and religious motifs, including the gods and abstractions who speak prologues, are thoroughly embedded in the internal literary economy of the plays (e.g., Zagagi 1994: 142–168), and it is clear in the case of the many passages from (more or less) extant comedies quoted above, and can be safely inferred in the case of the fragments, that they are serving specific purposes of theme or plot. As in the case of Old Comedy, then, we can get no purchase on a Menandrian theology. As with the motifs of cult, however, we are entitled to conclude that a very wide range of ideas about the (divine) governance of the world was in circulation in contemporary society. Recent scholarship has tended to conclude of New Comedy that its moralizing tendency is on the whole consistent with traditional piety (e.g., Mikalson 1998: 68–74, Parker 2005: 147–147), but as in the case of Old Comedy we ought perhaps to proceed more cautiously and not attempt to "reconcile" the range of views expressed in the plays, nor too readily marginalize the skeptical, cynical, and grim views, which are very common indeed. No doubt, traditional piety did remain strong in the sense that traditional religious practice was carried on with little outward change, but that is eminently compatible with considerable change at the level of "belief." It may be, though, that there wasn't a radical change in the fourth century, and that New Comedy rather confirms our emphasis on the relaxed attitudes to cult and the gods, focused on practice rather than belief, in Old Comedy—attitudes of which the range of views about religion and the gods reflected in New Comedy can be seen as a not unnatural development. Perhaps comedy after all suggests that what characterized the "ordinary Greek" of both periods was a profound emotional attachment to what Gilbert Murray (1946: 66–67) called the "inherited conglomerate" of myths, practices, and (possible) beliefs, an attachment that was ethnic, nostalgic, traditionalist, sometimes perhaps antiquarian, as well as based on the simple pleasures of feast and festival—but all of this salted with an equally profound capacity for wit and irony, which can be and often are species of skepticism, and which find natural expression in comedy.

FURTHER READING

The best recent discussion of religion and the gods in comedy—brief but pithy— is Parker 2005: 147–152, an important alternative to the general line taken here. Also helpful or important on various aspects are Marianetti 1992, Bowie 1993 and Bowie 2000, Given 2009, and

Jay-Robert 2002. Keller 1931 is still worth reading, if rather superficial methodologically, and Kleinknecht 1937 and Horn 1970 are useful studies of parodies of prayer and hymns. Anderson 1995 is a detailed study of epithets of Athena in Aristophanes, perhaps useful primarily for students of Greek religion. I have, alas, not seen Gellar 2008, a dissertation on sacrifice and ritual imagery in Menander and the Roman comedians. Zagagi 1994 contains perhaps the best chapter on the gods in a literary study of Menander.

Bibliography

Anderson, C. 1995. *Athena's Epithets: Their Structural Significance in Plays of Aristophanes.* Stuttgart and Leipzig: Teubner.

Bowie, A. 1993. *Aristophanes: Myth, Ritual and Comedy.* Cambridge, UK: Cambridge University Press.

——. 2000. "Myth and Ritual in the Rivals of Aristophanes", in D. Harvey and J. Wilkins, eds., *The Rivals of Aristophanes: Studies in Athenian Old Comedy,* edited by D. Harvey and J. Wilkins, 317–339. Swansea: The Classical Press of Wales.

Deubner, L. 1932. *Attische Feste.* Berlin: H. Keller.

Dover, K. 1972. *Aristophanic Comedy.* Berkeley: University of California Press.

——. 1993. *Aristophanes: Frogs.* Oxford: Clarendon Press.

Gellar, T. 2008. "Sacrifice and Ritual Imagery in Menander, Plautus, and Terence." PhD diss., University of North Carolina at Chapel Hill, 2008. *Non vidi.*

Given, J. 2009. "When Gods Don't Appear: Divine Absence and Human Agency in Aristophanes." *CW* 102: 107–127.

Henderson, J. 1987. *Aristophanes: Lysistrata.* Oxford: Clarendon Press.

Horn, W. 1970. *Gebet und Gebetsparodie in den Komödien des Aristophanes.* Nuremberg: Carl.

Jay-Robert, G. 2002. "Fonction des dieux chez Aristophane: Exemple de Zeus, d'Hermès et de Dionysos." *Revue des Études anciennes* 104: 11–24.

Keller, G. 1931. *Die Komödien des Aristophanes und die athenische Volksreligion seiner Zeit.* Tubingen: Laupp.

Kleinknecht, H. 1937. *Die Gebetsparodie in der Antike.* Stuttgart: W. Kohlhammer.

Lada-Richards, I. 1999. *Initiating Dionysus: Ritual and Theatre in Aristophanes'* Frogs. Oxford: Clarendon Press.

Marianetti, M. 1992. *Religion and Politics in Aristophanes'* Clouds. Hildesheim: Olms-Weidmann.

Mikalson, J. 1998. *Religion in Hellenistic Athens.* Berkeley: University of California Press.

Murray, G. 1946. *Greek Studies.* Oxford: Clarendon Press.

Nesselrath, H.-G. 1990. *Die attische mittlere Komödie: Ihre Stellung in der antiken Literaturkritik und Literaturgeschichte.* Berlin: De Gruyter.

——. 1995. "Myth, Parody, and Comic Plots: The Birth of Gods and Middle Comedy." In *Beyond Aristophanes: Transition and Diversity in Greek Comedy,* edited by G. Dobrov, 1–27. Atlanta: Scholars Press.

Nilsson, M. P. 1967. *Geschichte der griechischen Religion.* Vol. 1. 3rd ed. Munich: Beck.

——. 1974. *Geschichte der griechischen Religion.* Vol. 2. 3rd ed. Munich: Beck.

Parker, R. 2005. *Polytheism and Society at Athens.* Oxford: Oxford University Press.

Scullion, S. 2005. "'Pilgrimage' and Greek Religion: Sacred and Secular in the Pagan Polis." In *Pilgrimage in Graeco-Roman and Early Christian Antiquity: Seeing the Gods*, edited by J. Elsner and I. Rutherford, 111–130. Oxford: Oxford University Press.

Scullion, S. 2007. "Festivals." In *A Companion to Greek Religion*, edited by D. Ogden, 190–203. Oxford and Malden, MA: Wiley-Blackwell.

Segal, C. 1961. "The Character and Cults of Dionysus and the Unity of the *Frogs*." *HSCPh* 66: 207–242.

Sokolowski, F. 1969. *Lois sacrées des cités grecques*. Paris: E. de Boccard.

Zagagi, N. 1994. *The Comedy of Menander: Convention, Variation and Originality*. London: Duckworth.

I V

The Diffusion of Comedy in the Hellenistic World

....

THE DIFFUSION OF COMEDY FROM THE AGE OF ALEXANDER TO THE BEGINNING OF THE ROMAN EMPIRE[1]

....

BRIGITTE LE GUEN

IN antiquity, professional comic poets and actors lived an itinerant existence. Authors and performers made their living by participating in various theatrical competitions organized by the political powers of the age that included contests in comedy. In the fifth century BCE, most of these professionals were drawn to Athens. The city offered them the chance to win the victory palm at the Lenaea and the Great (or City) Dionysia, which were celebrated in the city itself in honor of the god of the theater, and also in particular Attic demes on the occasion of the rural Dionysia (Csapo 2004). This was still true in the 350s, even if by then the artists began to have new opportunities to perform, as we can infer from the roughly ninety-five theaters whose construction at the end of the fourth century is attested by archaeological, epigraphic, and literary evidence (Frederiksen 2002). Most of the time, however, we do not know the specialization of the artists who were hosted at these new theaters or even the form of the spectacles that they took part in. But what about the period that followed, from the conquests of Alexander the Great to the beginning of the Roman Empire? What can be said about the place that comedy occupies thereafter and the manner of its diffusion throughout the eastern Mediterranean and also in Sicily and Magna Graecia—the western Mediterranean— whose Hellenization dates back to the archaic period?

---

[1] Translated by Christopher Welser.

COMEDY AT THE TIME OF ALEXANDER'S EXPEDITION

With Alexander, the limits of the performance world were completely changed. In his wake, the extent of artists' travels no longer bore any relation to the distances that their counterparts in earlier centuries had regularly covered.

Unless I am mistaken, Alexander organized in the course of his expedition some twenty competitions of various kinds to celebrate his military victories (Le Guen forthcoming). In some cases, the celebrations were athletic (sometimes including torch races), in other cases athletic and equestrian, and in still other cases athletic and musical. Despite the ambiguity of the adjective *mousikos*, which Arrian, one of our main sources, uses exclusively to describe non-sporting competitions (*Anabasis* 1.11.1, 2.5.8, 3.1.4, 3.5.2, 3.6.1, 7.14.1, 7.14.10; *Indika* 8.36.3) and which applies both to musical contests sensu stricto and to dramatic contests and contests that are both musical and dramatic, our available evidence reveals that theatrical performances took place on at least four occasions. After conquering Egypt and returning to Phoenicia in 331, Alexander held magnificent celebrations in Tyre that in some respects resembled Athens's Great (City) Dionysia (Arrian, *Anabasis* 3.6.1; Plutarch, *Life of Alexander* 29.5 and *On the Fortune or the Virtue of Alexander the Great* II, 334e; Quintus Curtius 4.8.16).

The place of honor at these celebrations was no doubt held by dithyrambs and tragedies performed by the theatrical stars of the era. Nevertheless, comedy was not altogether forgotten: in the passage from the *Life of Alexander* in which Plutarch recalls the festivities, the presence of Lycon of Scarpheia, a celebrated comic actor (Stephanis, no. 1567), is also mentioned. This allows us to suppose that he performed on this occasion, whether alone or with his troupe, even if he did not participate officially in the competition (these apparently included only two contests). We cannot, however, specify how long he remained at Alexander's court (and thus reconstruct his travels), because we do not know when he arrived. Perhaps he had joined in with the expedition immediately, or perhaps in Memphis, where the king invited the most renowned artists of Greece (Arrian, *Anabasis* 3.1.4; unfortunately, neither their specialities nor their names appear in our sources). Or perhaps he came much later, arriving by sea with the embassy that had come seeking the Athenians imprisoned by Alexander, since they doubtless formed part of the audience at Tyre (Arrian, *Anabasis* 3.6.1; Quintus Curtius 4.8.16).

A fragment of the *History of Alexander* of Chares of Mytilene, preserved by Athenaeus (*Deipnosophists* 538–539), attests that Lycon also participated in the famous marriage ceremonies at Susa in 324. With him were two other comic actors, Phormion—possibly the victor at the Athenian Lenaea not long before (Stephanis, no. 2578)—and one Ariston, otherwise unknown (Stephanis, no. 377). Also present were three tragic actors, including Athenodorus and Thessalus, two stars of the Athenian stage who had themselves previously been invited to Tyre. These artists were very likely still there a short time later at Ecbatana (Arrian, *Anabasis* 7.14.1) and then at Babylon, where, during the funeral rites of his friend Hephaestion, "Alexander also planned athletic and musical games far more splendid than any before in the number of competitions"—3,000 *ago-nistai* in all—"and the cost of production" (Arrian, *Anabasis* 7.14.10, tr. Brunt 1976). Unfortunately, we cannot say anything about the exact nature of these "musical" competitions. A description of them by Plutarch assures us that they included a theatrical element, but he associates them with the competitions that took place at Ecbatana and ended with Hephaestion's death (Plutarch, *Life of Alexander* 72.1); these are specifically qualified as "thymelic" (i.e., musical sensu stricto) by Diodorus (17.110.4).

These examples demonstrate exceptionally well the principal difficulties we face in trying to reconstruct the spread of dramatic genres (particularly comedy) from the places where artists gathered, and thus on the journeys we infer they must have made. And these difficulties are compounded by our almost complete ignorance of the plays they performed—all that reaches us (via Athenaeus, 586d) is the name of one "little satyr play," the *Agen*, that was probably composed by Python of Catana (or Byzantium) and staged in a location whose identity is disputed (Krumeich et al. 1999).

The examples also show that dramatic competitions continued to be held within a religious context, primarily following thanksgiving sacrifices by the king for military victories. This was the case at Tyre as well as at Salmous in Carmania (Arrian, *Indika* 8.36.3; Diodorus 17.106.4), where we know there were theatrical *agones* but do not know whether contests in comedy formed part of the program. The same is true for Ecbatana (if Plutarch's testimony can be preferred to that of our other sources) and Babylon, as it was essentially in a hero-cult context that the athletic and musical competitions (perhaps with a theatrical element) were organized in Hephaestion's memory. At Susa, on the other hand, none of our sources describes any competition. Thus, the tragic and comic actors, whose names we know, were very likely there to display their art in the absence of any agonistic rivalry; that practice is characteristic of an offering to a divinity. But in what fashion was this done? One cannot assert that they appeared along with their troupes by supposing our sources would name only the leading actors, who were also the leaders of their companies, because this observation applies only within the official context of a competition (DFA²: 126–135). Accordingly, we do not know whether they gave solo performances of selected parts of prizewinning plays—in which case their services would be similar to those of performers of every sort in the context of symposia— or whether, together with the actors who accompanied them, they performed revivals of comedies and tragedies in their entirety and outside of any agonistic context, according to the custom that emerged in Athens at the Great Dionysia from 387/6 BC on for tragedy and from 340/339 on for comedy.

The available evidence for comedy shows that, beginning with the Great Dionysia of 339 BCE (IG II² 2318, l. 317–318), comic actors would stage on their own initiative and as a prelude to the official competition plays already presented to the public. These revival plays were identified as "old" (*palaiai*) in contrast to new creations (*kainai*), but the labels did not signal any association with Old, Middle, or New Comedy (cf. Csapo 2000: 115–121 on the relevance of these distinctions). These revivals became regular from 311/10 on and they were undoubtedly already contributing to the formation of a comic repertoire (IG II/III² 2323a, l. 39–40). They were later introduced into competitions; the date is disputed, but I concur with Daniela Summa in identifying it as 279/8 (Summa 2003 and Summa 2008, where the author argues for the creation at this date of a new agon with performances of new and ancient plays, in order to celebrate the Greek victory over the barbarian Celts).

Whatever may be the form in which comedy was performed at Susa, it certainly *was* performed there. This goes to show how far away *komoidia* would henceforth find herself from the lands of her birth, and these circumstances help us better understand the construction of theatrical buildings, shortly after Alexander's death, in lands as distant as present-day Afghanistan and Iraq, at Aï Khanoum, Babylon, and Seleucia on the Tigris (Le Guen 2003: 331–341).

THE DIFFUSION OF COMEDY IN THE HELLENISTIC ERA

In the Eastern Mediterranean

The new realm created by Alexander's conquests stretched from the Balkans to the first cataract of the Nile and from the shores of the Adriatic to the Indus. In it cities were founded or refounded in the same fashion that they had been before his death, while at the same time a number of native towns rose to the rank of poleis. As in the oldest Greek communities, so too within these cities many festivals, whether newly established or newly transformed from older ones, would include a theatrical element. Time and again, we find comic competitions among them. Some were dedicated to Dionysus and were called *Dionysia* in the traditional fashion. Others bore double names that attested different associations of Dionysus with various deified Hellenistic rulers: thus in 295 BCE *Dionysia-Demetrieia* are attested at Athens, while at Cyme in Aeolis we find *Dionysia-Antiocheia* around 280–270, followed around 200 or soon thereafter by *Dionysia-Attaleia*, and so on (Le Guen 2010a: 501–504). Still others, such as the *Heraia* at Argos or the *Rhomaia* at Magnesia-on-Maeander, involved the worship of divinities without any immediately obvious connection to the god of the theater.

This was one of the era's major innovations, with profound consequences for the religious and cultural life of the Greeks. The new festivals offered many theatrical performers the chance to practice their craft and participate in the spread of the genre that they represented. Meanwhile, another new but related trend appeared: the creation of religious and professional associations known as *synodoi* or *koina ton peri ton Dionyson tekhniton* (Sifakis 1967: 136–146; DFA²: 279–321; *CAD*: 239–255; Le Guen 2001a; Lightfoot 2002; Aneziri 2003 with Le Guen 2004b). Placed under the protection of Dionysus, and sometimes of a Hellenistic monarch as well (Aneziri 1994; Le Guen 2003: 353–355 and Le

Guen 2007a: 275–278), they brought into a union stage specialists who were experts in various crafts (*tekhne*), hence their name of "Dionysiac *tekhnitai*."

According to our sources, at least four such groups were created in the Eastern Mediterranean in the course of the third century BCE: (1) the association of Athenian *tekhnitai*—perhaps the oldest and certainly the first to be attested (Le Guen 2001a II, general index, s.v.; Aneziri 2003: 25–51; Le Guen 2007b); (2) the association of Egyptian *tekhnitai*, under the patronage of Dionysus and the Lagid monarchs—that is, first designated as being under the patronage of "Dionysus and the Fraternal Gods (*Theoi Adelphoi*)," and then later as under "Dionysus and the Gods Made Manifest (*Theoi Epiphaneis*)" ; it may have preceded the Athenian guild, and had its seats at Ptolemais and perhaps Alexandria, as well as an affiliate active on Cyprus between the middle of the second century and the beginning of the first century BCE (Aneziri 1994; Le Guen 2001a II, 5–9 and general index, s.v.); (3) the association of the Artists of Dionysus who travel together (or contribute towards) Isthmus and Nemea, with branches established over time at Argos, Thebes, Thespiae, Opus, Chalcis, and perhaps also at Sicyon and at Dion in Macedonia (Le Guen 2001a II, general index, s.v.; Aneziri 2003: 51–70); and (4) the association of the Artists of Dionysus (who are active) in or (who travel) to Ionia and the Hellespontine region," which then became "the association of the Artists of Dionysus (who are active) in or (who travel) to Ionia and the Hellespontine region and those who are devoted to Dionysus Kathegemon, one of whose centers was at Teos and the other at Pergamum (Le Guen 2001: II, general index, s.v.; Aneziri 2003: 71–109; Le Guen 2007a: 260–268).

The designation of this last group is particularly interesting, because it highlights the territory in which its members work, rather than—I emphasize—the context in which the performers were recruited; in fact, all four associations welcomed performers from anywhere in the Greek world. As extensive as its territory already was, the Anatolian association nevertheless could not confine itself within it, for a decree published by the association ca. 171 declares that the Dionysiac *tekhnitai* took part in competitions in honor of Pythian Apollo, the Heliconian Muses, and Dionysus at Delphi during the *Pythia* and *Soteria*, at Thespiae during the *Mouseia*, and at Thebes during the *Agrionia* (IG XI, 4, 1061, l. 14–16)—i.e., at competitions which were held in mainland Greece. The text implies that participation in these festivals was a regular occurrence.

The only list that we possess, which is incomplete, shows that at the end of the reign of Ptolemy II (*reg.* 285–246) the association established at Ptolemais counted among its members working in tragedy not only one *auletes* and two poets but also five actors, one of whom is called *tragoidos* and the rest classified as synagonists, who perform alongside the protagonist but are not entitled to claim the victor's crown (Aneziri 1997a: 59–60). Also appearing are three epic poets and various musicians (a citharodist, a citharist, a trumpeter) as well as a chorus leader (*chorodidaskalos*), a dancer, and—to use a modern expression— various associated VIPs (in this case, five *proxenoi* and six patrons or *philotekhnitai*). Comedy is represented by two poets and six actors (*komoidoi*) (Le Guen 2001a I, 296–299, TE 61). Other documents attest to comic synagonists and to chorus members for both tragedy and comedy among the ranks of the Dionysiac guilds, an indication that dramatic works could sometimes be performed with choruses. We have, for example, evidence for comic choruses—sometimes containing as many as nine members—at the contest at Delphi during the amphictyonic *Soteria*; these choruses were shared among the participating troupes (between two and four in number) and undoubtedly had but little connection to the action of the plays (Sifakis 1967: 73–80). By contrast, we find nothing like this in the case of tragedy, at least for these festivals.

Such was the professionalism of the *tekhnitai* belonging to an association that some among them were proficient in multiple specialities, often closely interrelated (Chaniotis 1995; Le Guen 2001a II.105–130). Thus numerous *komoidoi* are also described as "singers." One member of the association at Athens, Thymoteles, son of Philocles (Stephanis, no. 1236), was simultaneously a dramatic poet (we do not know whether in comedy or tragedy) and a comic actor, while another, Praxiteles, son of Theogenes, was a singer (*oidos*), comic synagonist, *tragoidos*, and herald (Stephanis, no. 2137).

Organized as cities in miniature, situated in the heart of other states, and furnished with officials whose roles were essentially religious, financial, and administrative, these associations passed decrees, negotiated their members' terms of employment, dispatched ambassadors, and received those who had been sent by various contemporary political authorities. Because of their elaborate structure and the diversity of their members' skills, they were the main negotiating partners of the festival's organizers, whose task was complicated by overlapping schedules of games in different locales and increasing distances between two *agones* that competitors sometimes had to traverse.

Through the timely dispatch of requisite specialists, the associations of Artists of Dionysus allowed an effective response to the growing demand for artistic displays in general and theatrical performances in particular. They also offered their own members a desirable status, one associated with many vital privileges for the practice of their art. It was indeed for their collective benefit that they demanded of the authorities in any particular locale (Amphictyons administering the sanctuary at Delphi, a Cappadocian monarch, or Roman generals such as L. Mummius and Sulla) the grant, confirmation, or extension of some of these privileges, which had formerly been conceded only grudgingly and on an individual basis. Most important among these privileges were *asphaleia*, the guarantee of safety that prevented the *tekhnitai* from being arrested, and *asylia* (inviolability), which shielded them from legal seizures and reprisals except in the case of private debts. Thanks to these privileges, the Artists of Dionysus could move about with security in a world perpetually at war and could thus hone their profession (Le Guen 2001a II, 69–71). Other equally valuable advantages for the performers' nomadic condition included exemptions from military service and from the obligation to provide soldiers with lodging—obligations that were normally very onerous for those on whom they were imposed.

We lack sources that would allow us to compile a comprehensive list of the cities that organized *Dionysia* and that thus attracted performers belonging to these associations or who practiced their profession independently (on the existence of this latter category, see Le Guen 2004a: 94–104), but such a list would certainly be quite long. If we consider only the Aegean basin (Le Guen 2001b: 267–277; Moretti 2001: 93–97), we find that in the Hellenistic Era almost no island of the Aegean Sea failed to celebrate festivals at which comedy must have occupied a prominent place. We should not forget, however, that the festivals called *Dionysia* did not systematically reproduce the agonistic program that we know existed at Athens so as to incorporate precisely the same number of contests. Ultimately, everything depended on the funds that were available.

Let us now consider the festivals that hosted theatrical competitions under various names other than *Dionysia* and the role that comedy played in them. Several lists of competitors and some victor lists clearly show that a number of Hellenistic cities and leagues imitated the Athenian model by instituting such competitions: in fact, they organized as many competitions in comedy as in tragedy, and the programs for these competitions included new creations as well as revivals of older works. This was true, notably, of the *Mouseia* at Thespiae, which dates to before 230–225 or to the middle of the third century (Mette 1977: 58–61, II C a–f); the *Serapeia* at Tanagra, which is assigned a date between 100–90 and 85 BCE (Mette 1977: 53–4, II C 2); and the *Charitesia* at Orchomenus (Mette 1977: 54–5, II C 3) as well as the *Amphiaraia-Rhomaia* at Oropus, ca. 85–84 or after 73 BCE (Mette 1977: 56–8, II C 4a–d). It is also true of the annual musical agon of the Athenian *tekhnitai*, created shortly before 130 BCE in honor of the king and queen of Cappadocia, Ariarathes V and his wife Nysa, assuming one adopts Dittenberger's restorations (as do Le Guen 2001a I, 67–74, TE 5 and Aneziri 2003: 44–45, 198; *contra*, BOC 709, n.2), which suggest the existence of an annual gathering with a prize offered for actors in comic and tragic performances both old and new (Le Guen 2001a II, 71). We can add to this list the biannual (trieteric) *Soteria* at Acraephia, where poets competed in three genres (dithyramb, tragedy, and comedy) in the first century BCE, but where it seems actors were only rewarded if they performed plays already in the standard repertoire (IG VII, 2727). The fact that they are designated *tragoidos* or *komoidos*, however, by no means entitles us to conclude that during the last three centuries BCE these were the designations for performers who only put on revivals. As we have seen, at least until the first century BCE these two nouns are generic labels for *tekhnitai*-actors who performed in both new plays and revivals and were the only ones entitled to be rewarded with a prize. Nevertheless, it is true that in a number of victory lists an actor performing in revivals (*komoidos ho ten palaian*, IG VII 540, l. 41 or *hypocrites palaias komoidias*, IG VII 1760, l.30) is distinguished from one who performs in newly composed pieces (*hypokrites kaines komoidias, ibid.*). As time passed, on certain occasions the term *komoidos* came to designate only the actor performing in revivals—all the more easily since it refers to the protagonist (the other actors being identified as synagonists), who was alone qualified to restage a play referred to as "*palaia*" (see Nervegna 2007: 20, n. 42 and 21).

We must not forget the second century BCE *Heraia* of Samos. No competition in ancient comedy is thought to have taken place at it—but this is only an inference; perhaps it was a more frequent venue for comedy and was only exceptionally excluded in the particular year documented by our single victor list (IG XII 6, 1, 173) because it was impossible to organize on that occasion. Finally, we note the *Asklepia* and *Apollonia* at Epidaurus (IG IV 2, 1, 99, III, l. 25), for which a list of performers subjected to fines informs us that the comic actor Dionysius, son of Dionysius, of Rhodes (Stephanis, no. 731) was condemned to pay four minas for breach of contract. Still, we do not know whether he had been hired to perform in an old or new play or what the exact program for the competitions was. We are similarly uncertain about the programs for the Theban *Agrionia* (Le Guen 2001a I, 134–141, TE 20 and 21), the Euboean *Demetrieia*, and the Karystian *Aristonikeia*, inaugurated between 297 and 288 (Le Guen 2010a: 515–520), although we do know that comic and tragic actors were recruited for these different occasions.

The *Soteria* of the Delphic amphictyony, whose first lists go back to around 265 BCE (Nachtergael 1977: 299–328, with *Actes* 2–11; cf. Sifakis 1967: 71–83, 156–165 and Le Guen 2001a I, 166–172, T 24), is unique in displaying among its programs only contests involving "old" plays, comic as well as tragic; as in classical Athens, both types were performed by three actors. At the same time, they were produced not by the protagonists themselves, according to the usual practice, but by a person whose particular job it was to do this: the *didaskalos*.

In none of these cases does comedy seem to have been less popular than tragedy, and this same conclusion can be reached on the basis of other sources. Stephanis's prosopography includes around 240 known specialists in comedy and 210 in tragedy (Le Guen 2007b: 88–91; cf. Chaniotis 1995), while lists of competitors, as well as our surviving victory lists, indicate that when no agon in Old Comedy is attested for a given festival—like the *Rhomaia* in Magnesia-on-Maeander ca. 150–100 (*Syll.*[3] 1079)—there was generally no agon in Old Tragedy either. Nevertheless, there is nothing to prove that revivals of comedies and tragedies did not occur; it may simply be that the relevant lists were inscribed on stones that were separate from the rest of the program and that these have not survived.

Comedy also had a place outside the official context of competitions. Thanks to the lists of the Delian archons, we know of many actors and a number of comic poets who offered free performances (*epideixeis*) in honor of the island's preeminent god, Apollo, very likely before the inauguration of the *Dionysia* or after the conclusion of the contest (Sifakis 1967: 148–152, Table 1). Among other actors we find, in the year 282 (mentioned on the Delian *tabulae archontum*, IG XI 2, 106), Cephisius of Histiaea, who had performed Diodorus's *Mainomenos* at Athens in 285/4 (IG II[2] 2319, 1.64). We also find, in 280, Telesis of Paros and, in 279, Aristophanes of Soloi (Stephanis, nos. 1392, 2391, 373). The situation was similar, though not identical, in the city of Iasus (*IK* 28-*Iasos*, 160–217; Crowther 2007): to cite only one example, the contributions of four former *choregoi* and one former *agonothetes* ca. 190–180 allowed the hiring for five days of a comedian named Athenodorus, son of Heracleides, about whom we have no other information (Stephanis, no. 78). Athenodorus, together with two *auletai* recruited in the same manner, did not contribute to the *Dionysia* with a performance outside the competition, as is generally asserted (Migeotte 1993 and Migeotte 2010: 134); rather, he participated in festivities which in that year did not necessarily include actual contests in comedy or music. Likewise, there was no proper competition during the winter *Soteria* at Delphi. It seems to me that the city of Iasus, in the throes of serious financial difficulties at the beginning of the second century BCE, continued to celebrate its *Dionysia*, but in a somewhat peculiar way. Unlike Migeotte (1993), I do not think the city supplemented the actual competitions through artistic exhibitions, which were financed outside normal channels, with the goal of increasing the prestige of the festivities. In my opinion, Iasus rather invited only a number of specialists varying from year to year who, unusually, would not have rivals to compete against. As evidence of this, we see that the term *thea*, "spectacle," replaces *agon* in the documents dated to ca. 190–180, as it does in a regulation of Scepsis in the Troad recording the community's decision to organize choruses in honor of the god on the occasion of the *Dionysia* without establishing a formal agon (A. Wilhelm, *Jahreshefte* 3, 1900, 54–57 and *Jahreshefte* 32, 1940, Beiblatt, 61 for the restoration of lines 26–28). If we reject this hypothesis, it is very difficult to understand how, during such a troubled period, the political authorities of the Carian city could have devised an unusual system of financing with the sole objective of extending the traditional competitions (for which funds must already have been running short) with performances that sometimes lasted more than a week, even if they did not themselves take on the expense. Over time (other documents date to ca. 185–180 and 120–115), the system was simplified and became more rational: the inscriptions no longer record either the performers hired or their specialities, and the word *thea* has disappeared. Instead there appear only the amounts of money, rigorously identical from year to year, that were paid by the current *agonothetes* and some former *choregoi*. Employed according to the needs and wishes of Iasus, these payments thus served, I believe, to supplement public funds in the conduct of the *Dionysia* with its lyric and/or dramatic *agones*, or as a substitute for public funds (when these were lacking) for exhibitions outside the official competition, or else to finance in whole or in part performances that were not part of the competitions in order to enhance the competitions' appeal.

Sources and Problems

For comic poets and actors, the opportunities for competition in the last three centuries BCE were considerable. They were found in regions as diverse as mainland Greece, the Peloponnese, the Aegean region, Anatolia, Egypt, and Cyprus, to which we should also add Babylon, Armenia, Central Asia, and probably Syria (Le Guen 2003: 337–341); Boeotia, long known for hosting musical *agones*, had a marked preeminence. The festivals held across this huge territorial expanse involved performers of every sort of national origin, which suggests that they had been able to organize themselves in their homelands, and indeed within their families (as in the past), before they joined, when necessary, an association of *tekhnitai*. This is further proof that the genre in which they specialized had been widely diffused.

The nature of our sources unfortunately makes it impossible to reconstruct the spread of comedy chronologically and geographically. For example, we cannot rely on the journeys undertaken by the actors and poets who participated in the competitions discussed above. The lists of competitors and victors that document these journeys never actually record the artists' possible affiliation with a Dionysiac guild, and do not always indicate their patronymics and ethnicities along with their names. It is for this reason that, unless we can correlate these lists of performers with information provided in decrees published in their honor by the associations of the Artists of Dionysus themselves, we do not know, in most cases, where competitors came from: it might be from their native countries, from the headquarters of their associations, or even from the last cities in which they had competed. Emblematic of such difficulties is the case of the comedian Philonides, son of Aristomachus, of Zacynthus (Stephanis, no. 2568; Le Guen 2001b: 287). He was a member of the Isthmian and Nemean guild, which had subsidiary companies in Argos, Thebes, Chalcis, Opus, and perhaps Corinth. So we are unable to say where he came from when he appeared as *komoidos* in Delphi for the amphictyonic *Soteria* (260/259–257/256 or 256/255–253/252 BCE). It might have been from one of those cities as well as from the last country in which he took part in a competition. Philonides of Zacynthus could also be identified with the comedian named Philonides (without patronymic and ethnic: Stephanis, no. 2567) who won the Great Dionysia at Athens ca. 285–265 and the Lenaea once, and who offered a free performance for the god Apollo in Delos (263 BCE).

Moreover, even when we know for certain that an association co-organized a particular festival (for example, the Isthmian-Nemean guild collaborated with the cities of Delphi, Thebes, and Thespiae in the organization of the amphictyonic *Soteria*, *Agrionia*, and *Mouseia*, respectively), the situation is no easier: we cannot actually conclude ipso facto that all the competitors attested are members of the same corporation, because some performers belonging to another corporation or practicing their profession outside the framework of the associations could have entered the competition as well (Le Guen 2004a: 86–104). Specialists too often fail to take this into consideration when they compile lists of the ethnicities of competitors for a particular festival (cf. Sifakis 1967: 166–167, Table 4, where the caption "*Provenances* [my italics] of participants in the Amphictyonic *Soteria*" is ambiguous; likewise in Aneziri 2003: 448, Table 8). The only festivals that create no difficulty are the Delphic *Soteria*, since the inscriptions for these specify that they were celebrated entirely by the Isthmian-Nemean guild, to the exclusion of any other association, contrary to the usual practice (Le Guen 2001a I.126, TE 24).

Furthermore, we cannot find in our Hellenistic documents—nor, a fortiori, can we construct from them—some sort of "comic circuit" comparable to the *periodos* of archaic times composed of four major festivals (the *Olympia* at Pisa, the *Isthmia* at Corinth, the *Pythia* at Delphi, and the *Nemeia* at Nemea). In fact, with the exception of one tragic actor's victor lists (*Syll.*[3] 1080), we have no similar document to help us identify a particularly prestigious or preeminent competition at which comic poets and actors (whether they specialized in revivals or in new plays) had to appear if they wanted a successful career. Indeed, we must remember that victory lists for performers and athletes present the victories of contestants not in chronological order of their successes, but according to the status of the competitions in which they had been victorious (Panhellenic—the ancient texts say "sacred" and/or stephanitic—regional, local; see Robert 1984: 36–39 on these essential distinctions, with the remarks of Slater 2010: 263–281).

Our sources are limited in another way as well: they do not allow us to form any very definite idea of the plays presented to the public at comic *agones*, with the exception of those organized at Athens. In that city, thanks to the meager fragments of the *Didaskalia* preserved until around the middle of the second century BCE, we actually do know the names of many of the new comedies that were performed and of their authors as well. Thus we know, for example, that the *Mystis* (*Initiatrix*) of Philippides won at the Great Dionysia of 311 (IG II² 2323 fr. a, l. 41) and that in 183 the entrants were the *Ephesioi* (*Ephesians*) of Crito (I), the *Nauagos* (*Shipwrecked*) of Paramonus, the *Philokleios* (*Family Man*) of Timostratus, the *Philodespotes* (*Loyal to His Master*) of Sogenes, and the *Milesia* (*Woman from Miletus*) of Philemon III (IG II² 2323 fr. b, col. III, l. 151–159). With respect to revivals, the oldest of the two lists unearthed in the Athenian agora that formally attest to their existence in the city's competitions in the middle of the second century (*SEG* 26.208; the text is dated to 262 or 258 in *BOC* 121, 96.E but to 255/4 by Summa 2003 and Summa 2008), reveals that the *Misanthropoi* (*Misanthropes*) of Diphilus placed first, the *Phasma* (*Apparition*) of Menander second, and the *Ptokhe* (*Beggar*) of Philemon third. Thanks to the *Didaskalia*, we know that in 312/11 the *Thesauros* (*Treasure*) of Anaxandrides, a poet associated with Middle Comedy, was the play presented outside the competition in the "*palaia*" category (IG II² 2323 fr. a, l. 39–40). The same source also furnishes the following information about revivals: at an uncertain date in the first half of the second century, the winning entry was the *Phokeueis* (*Phocians*) of Philemon II (IG II² 2323 fr. f, col. I, l. 101); ca. 195–193, it was the *Misogynes* (*Misogynist*) of Menander (IG II² 2323 fr. b, col. II, l. 130); then, in 185, the *Megarike* (*Megarian Woman*) of Simylos (IG II² 2323 fr. a, col. III, l. 147); and, in two revivals in 183 and 181, the *Apokleiomene* (*Woman Locked Out*) of Posidippos (*Horos* 6, 1988, 13–4 and IG II² 2323 fr. b, col. III, l. 164); in 167, Menander's *Phasma* won again (IG II² 2323 fr. c, col. IV, l. 207), whereas in 154 the *Philathenaios* (*Lover of Athens*) of Philippides was victorious (IG II² 2323 fr. d, col. V, l. 33).

Here we find mainly the authors who constitute the comic canon of the *Nea*, even if this varies noticeably depending on the source. But one would like to know more about the comedies that were preferred outside Athens both by the actors who performed them and by the public that gathered in the theater seats to watch their performances. We would especially like to be able to say whether a play belonging to Old Comedy (*arkhaia*) was ever produced again (and where) and what happened to the works associated with Middle Comedy. It may be that the choices of theater professionals with respect to "old" (*palaiai*) comedies will have been different from those of the philologists and other grammarians who contributed to the selection, and thus the survival, of past works. Outside Athens, we do not have information concerning revivals but only concerning some new compositions performed during individual *Rhomaia* festivals at Magnesia-on-Maeander. Thus, at some date no earlier than 150 BCE, a certain Metrodorus, son of Apollonius, was victorious there in the newer comedies category with a play titled *Homoioi* (*Lookalikes*). He was certainly a native of the city, since his national origin is not specified. A later winner was Diomedes, son of Athenodorus, of Pergamum, with a play whose name is lost as a result of breaks in the stone. Agathenor, son of Aristonax, of Ephesus, won with the *Milesia(i)* (*Milesian Woman* or *Women*) in the first half of the first century BCE.

Thus, although we know the names of more than a hundred comic poets active between the end of the fourth century and the end of the first (as suggested by K-A, though the names of twenty-six of these are incomplete and some may have been counted twice; according to the anonymous author of the treatise *On Comedy*, there were only sixty-four representatives of the *Nea*), and although we even know some of the titles of their plays and have a decent number of fragments connected with them, we do not normally know the locations where the comedies were first produced or where they were eventually returned to the stage; we are likewise ignorant as to the number of their revivals. The means by which the comedies might acquire widespread approbation, away from the Athenian stage if necessary, are unknown to us and perhaps will never be known, though, in view of their tremendous significance in the artistic life of their time, we can be sure that the role played in this process by the associations of *tekhnitai* was a crucial one.

In the Western Mediterranean

It is also very difficult for us to know precisely how Greek comedies that were performed in the eastern part of the Mediterranean gained popularity in the west, most notably in the city of Rome.

In light of the abundant archaeological evidence (theater buildings, vase paintings depicting scenes from the stage, statuettes of actors, masks, etc.), it is clear that there was, from the classical era onward, intense dramatic activity in the Greek cities of Sicily and Southern Italy, mainly in Apulia, Calabria, and Campania. This was not only the result of purely local practice, embodied for example in the fifth century by the comic theater of Epicharmus (K-A I, 8–137; *BOC* 59–78) and in the 300s by the *phlyax* comedies or "hilarotragedies" of one Rhinthon of Tarentum (K-A I, 260–270; cf. Gigante 1971 and Gigante 1988; Le Guen 2001a II, 113 and n. 540; Aneziri 2001–2002: 51–53). It also reflects Athenian influences, whether direct (connected with the performance in Magna Graecia and Sicily of plays from the Attic repertoire of Old and Middle Comedy) or indirect (via circulation of the texts of certain Attic comedies or certain iconographic themes). Maffre (2000: 308) raises, for example, the question of whether there were in fourth-century Apulia (i.e., Taranto) writers of comedy who, somewhat like Plautus and Terence in later times, created pieces in the Athenian manner on the basis of Athenian plays.

For the Hellenistic Era, the literary sources (e.g., Aulus Gellius, *Noctes Atticae*, 2.23.1), including several plays, show without the least room for doubt that certain writers for the Latin stage translated and adapted the comedies of their Greek counterparts, chiefly those of the poets forming the canon of the *Nea*. Thus, three plays of Plautus and four of Terence were composed on the basis of comedies by Menander, and two other plays of Terence derive from two works of Apollodorus of Carystus, while Diphilus too served as a source for Plautus and Menander for Caecilius. But how did these plays arrive in Sicily and Italy, and how did they then became popular at Rome, where we see them produced, beginning in the second century BCE, on the occasion of various *ludi* which included a theatrical element (Bernstein 1998; Polverini 2003)?

No doubt the diffusion of the Greek repertoire was rapid, since less than fifty years elapsed between the death of Menander (292/1) and the first Roman adaptation. According to the tradition, Livius Andronicus was the first poet "who gave Rome plays for the stage" (Cicero, *Brutus* 18) and the first work translated from Greek in 240 (Dumont 1997: 42) or perhaps in the 240s (*CAD* 207 and 213). It is hard to see how the Hellenistic Greek comedies could have spread to Rome except from Sicily (Dearden 2006), Campania, and Calabria—i.e., from regions whose natives included not only Livius Andronicus (he left the Greek milieu of Tarentum for Rome; Dumont 1997: 42 stresses, however, that he could equally well have come from Syracuse, Naples, or any city of the Greek world) and Naevius (who likewise translated Greek plays) but Ennius as well. The transmission of the Greek repertoire took place more easily insofar as the links between the Italian capital and Sicily and the southern part of the peninsula had increased in the wake of the first two Punic Wars.

Scholars' accounts nevertheless differ as to how Greek drama had previously been introduced into these regions. Some cite as intermediaries itinerant troupes of Greek actors and indeed of *tekhnitai* who came from the Dionysiac associations of the Eastern Mediterranean but who occasionally appeared in the West (Beacham 1991: 29). Others, based on a highly controversial passage of Varro (*apud* Gellius 3.3.14), propose the hypothesis that such associations had had headquarters there since the third century and that Plautus was in fact one of their members. For example, Webster (1963: 541) assumes the existence of an association at Tarentum in this period, and Rusten (*BOC*, 726) asserts, without being more precise, that there must have been associations in Sicily and Southern Italy before the first century. Sifakis (1967: 79), for his part, says of Plautus that he began his career "in the ranks" of the Dionysian *tekhnitai*.

Can we choose between these diverse views? Although we know that writers and actors from Sicily and Magna Graecia participated in competitions organized in the eastern part of the Mediterranean (Leppin 1992: 158, n. 111) and were admitted to one of the associations that had appeared there—Callias, son of Archetimus (Stephanis, no. 1325), and Philostratus, son of Sosistratus (Stephanis, no. 2551), were both Syracusans and affiliated in the third century BCE with the *koinon* of the Isthmus and Nemea— we have no document that mentions travels on the part of any association of *tekhnitai* to the western areas. Clearly this does not exclude the arrival of performers from the Greek east, whether or not they were affiliated with an association. It also certainly does not exclude the presence of small troupes of Greek performers in the colony cities of southern Italy and Sicily. The available sources refer to their members in Greek as *hoi dionysiakoi tekhnitai* or even *hoi peri ton Dionyson tekhnitai* and in Latin as *artifices scaenici*. It cannot be overemphasized that these expressions do not by themselves indicate a formally constituted organization; in a passage from his *Rhetoric* (III.2.1505a.23), Aristotle in fact explains quite clearly that the formula *hoi dionysiakoi tekhnitai*, which is attested there for the first time—and which occurs again in *Problemata* XXXIII.209 and then again in *Noctes Atticae* 20.4.2, where Aulus Gellius establishes terminological equivalences between Greek and Latin—is only a figure of speech. It also does not necessarily refer to an official status. The addition of the qualifier "Dionysiac" in these expressions enables us only to distinguish stage artists from other specialists who also possessed a *tekhne*, such as (for example) potters, physicians, and rhetoricians (Le Guen 2001a I, 26–27). We must believe that these troupes had available, if not the totality of the *Nea*'s productions, then at least certain plays from the Attic repertoire, works that circulated freely during the Hellenistic era. Is it not reported that Terence personally went to Athens to procure those of Menander's plays that he did not possess? If this anecdote is true, it tells us that he must already have obtained in Italy a number of the Athenian poet's comedies. If it is false, it only reminds us of the great number of Athenian comedies already present on Italian soil at this time.

In any event, it is not until the first century BCE that we find six epigraphic documents, for the most part badly damaged, that formally attest the existence of three associations of Dionysiac performers on Italian and Sicilian soil (Le Guen 2001a II, 36–38, Index 167). One of these was established at Rhegium and, like the fraternity in Egypt, included *proxenoi* among its ranks (IG XIV, 615; cf. Le Guen 2001a I, 317–319, TE 72). The other two were headquartered at Syracuse. The first, placed under the aegis of Dionysus and associated with Apollo and the Muses in one of the preserved inscriptions (if the restoration is correct), was supposed to have been created by Hiero II, the great admirer of the Athenian and Lagid originals (De Sensi Sestito 1985: 190). The patron of the second was Aphrodite "*Hilara*," an unfamiliar cultural epithet. Louis Robert was the first to suggest that we should see her as the protectress of those *tekhnitai* called "hilarodes" or "hilarotragedians" (*Bull. ép.* 64, 622; subsequently Le Guen 2001a I, 323–326 and II, 37; Fountoulakis 2000; Aneziri 2001–2002; and Aneziri 2003). Literary texts indicate the presence of *tekhnitai* at Naples (Plutarch, *Brutus* 21.2), and a fraternity established there is attested for the imperial period (it was there in 133 that Hadrian met *tekhnitai*, athletes, and delegations from various cities, as the document mentioned below indicates), but there is nevertheless nothing that tells us that the same was true at any time during the Hellenistic era. Nor do we have the least evidence for Tarentum (*pace* Webster 1963: 541), although the city was furnished with a theater at the beginning of the third century BCE (Dio Cassius, Frg. 39.5; Dionysius of Halicarnassus, 19.5.3).

In fact, the existence of one or more associations of *tekhnitai* before the beginning of the first century BCE does not seem to me at all plausible, for the simple reason that in the western Mediterranean there were no festivals (famous or less renowned) that were sufficiently numerous and held with sufficient regularity (Polverini 2003: 386–387), and where the Greek dramatic works could be staged either in Greek or in the form of Latin adaptations. Even if many Greek artists are certain to have come to Rome from the 180s BCE onward (Livy 39.22.2 and 39.22.10), Tacitus (*Ann.* 14.21.1) makes L. Mummius (consul in 146) the first to present stage spectacles (and not merely athletic spectacles) at Rome in the Greek manner. Other munificent Romans then imitated him: Marius, Sulla, and perhaps Pompey—all later than the third century BCE (Robert 1984: 38; Leppin

1992: 169 with notes). The fact is that Sicily, like Southern Italy, had previously been the scene of a long series of wars, and this was hardly favorable to instituting festivals of this sort (Leppin 1992: 169–176; Bernstein 1998). Now, in the increase of competitions and the elevation of many of them to the rank, beginning in the first half of the third century, of "sacred and/or stephanitic" *agones* (*hieroi kai stephanitai*), we should see one of the main reasons for the development of associations of Dionysiac *tekhnitai* in Greece, Anatolia, and Egypt. In fact, the epigraphic evidence clearly indicates that, even though these new types of organization were obliged to serve the gods (particularly Dionysus) in competitions whose significance was local (like the *Dionysia* in most cities), their primary mission was to provide participants for, and occasionally to assist in the organization of, the newly founded or upgraded *agones* whose status was equal to that of the four major competitions of the archaic and classical era (Robert 1984: 36–39). This explains their presence at the *Pythia* along with the Delphic *Soteria* (which were organized by the Aetolians as a stephanitic competition), the Thespian *Mouseia*, and also the *Agrionia* at Thebes.

In these circumstances, we cannot connect the spread of Greek theater to Rome with the presence of any Dionysiac *koinon* (or, a fortiori, with multiple *koina*) that would have been active from the early Hellenistic era. Instead, it makes sense to attribute this process to troupes of Greek performers that operated in Magna Graecia and Sicily and whose strength was on occasion augmented by performers who came from the eastern Mediterranean. Their success alone was responsible for the transmission of the Greeks' theatrical heritage to the West, even before the associations of the Artists of Dionysus were created there.

A "COMEDIC CIRCUIT" IN THE ROMAN EMPIRE?

We have seen how Greek comedy spread very widely across the whole Mediterranean during the three centuries of the Hellenistic era and to a lesser extent during Alexander's expedition, but we remain unable to reconstruct any formally designated itinerary that poets and actors might have followed in their quest for glory and recognition and that would correspond to the progressive expansion of comedy itself.

The situation changes under the empire, which in the words of Louis Robert is characterized by a veritable "agonistic explosion" ("explosion agonistique": Robert 1984: 38). Now for the first time an emperor can complete the systematic harmonization and rationalization of the Greek festivals (not only athletic but also musical and dramatic) throughout the *oikoumene* ("inhabited world")—coordinating, that is, the dates and duration of the various *agones* and thus facilitating attendance at them. Bearing witness to this is an extraordinary document recently discovered at Alexandria in the Troad (Petzl and Schwertheim 2006; cf. Jones 2007; Slater 2008; AE 2006 (B. Puech):1403a–c; Guerber 2009: 224–233; Strasser 2010; Le Guen 2010b). It consists of three letters written by Hadrian in 133/4 to a guild of artists designated as "the itinerant and thymelic association of *tekhnitai* under the patronage of Dionysus, winners in the sacred com-petitions and recipients of crowns" (l. 5–7); in fact, it concerns athletes as well as stage professionals (Aneziri 2009: 217–236 and Le Guen 2010b). Here one sees the emperor establishing an agonistic circuit, over the course of an Olympiad and accompanied by a timetable. The circuit offers individuals the chance to participate in a certain num-ber of contests of their own choosing, now without fear of overlapping dates or inter-vals between contests too short to allow for the completion of long journeys by land and sea. Through more or less drastic reorganizations of the normal schedule, the emperor creates a new *periodos*. Among those who might have taken part in it are the *komoidoi* Quintus Marcius Straton (Stephanis, no. 2312) and Quintus Marcius Titianus (Stephanis, no. 2313), who are designated at an uncertain date as *periodoneikai* in IG II^2 12644; they participated in the *periodos* that (since the time of Augustus) included the *Aktia* at Nicopolis (Robert 1984: 38; Bonnamente 2003) as well as the four traditional *agones* of the archaic period (the *Olympia* at Pisa, the *Isthmia* at Corinth, the *Pythia* at Delphi, and the *Nemeia* at Nemea).

Hadrian's decisions thereafter allowed the linking together of a great many *agones* across the whole Mediterranean, *agones* that were entirely Greek—those constituting the archaic *periodos*, to which were added, notably, the contests that Hadrian himself had established or reestablished (the *Hadrianeia*, the *Olympeia*, and the *Panhellenia*, which were assigned, respectively, to the first, third, and fourth years of the Olympiad)—and also *agones* "à la grecque" like Rome's *Capitolia* and the Nicopolitan *Aktia*. In addition, the emperor required that cities be scrupulously respectful of their contractual arrange-ments with the performers who participated in the artistic and athletic life of his age.

Even if theater generally and comedy more particularly were not part of the program at all these festivals, what Hadrian had in mind was the perpetuation and diffusion of Greek culture, and this alone. Hadrian was a devotee of Hellenism, and he was not con-cerned with Roman *ludi* or *spectacula*. In the new circuit fashioned by his imperial will, the eastern and western halves of the Mediterranean were intimately linked and Athens once again occupied a central place.

BIBLIOGRAPHY

Aneziri, S. 1994. "Zwischen Musen und Hof: Die dionysischen Techniten auf Zypern." *ZPE* 104: 179–198.

——.1997a. "Les synagonistes du théâtre grec." In *De la scène aux gradins: Théâtre et représentations dramatiques après Alexandre le Grand (Pallas 47)*, edited by B. Le Guen, 53–71. Toulouse: Presses universitaires du Mirail.

——. 2001–2002. "A Different Guild of Artists: τὸ Κοινὸν τῶν περὶ τὴν Ἱλαρὰν Ἀφροδίτην τεχνιτῶν." *Archaiognosia* 11: 47–56.

——. 2003. *Die Vereine der dionysischen Techniten im Kontext der hellenistischen Gesellschaft: Untersuchungen zur Geschichte, Organisation und Wirkung der hellenistischen Gesellschaft*. Stuttgart: F. Steiner.

———. 2009. "World Travellers: The Associations of Artists of Dionysus." In *Wandering Poets in Ancient Greek Culture*, edited by R. Hunter and I. Rutherford, 217–236. Cambridge, UK: Cambridge University Press.

Beacham, R. C. 1991. *The Roman Theatre and Its Audience*. London: Routledge.

Bernstein, F. 1998. *Ludi publici: Untersuchungen zur Entstehung und Entwicklung der öffentlichen Spiele im republikanischen Rom*. Stuttgart: F. Steiner.

Bonnamente, M. 2003. "I ludi scaenici in età imperiale." In *Teatro postclassico e teatro latino: Teorie e prassi drammatica: Atti del convegno internazionale, Roma, 16–18 ottobre 2001*, edited by A. Martina, 397–410. Rome: Università degli Studi Roma Tre.

Brunt, P. A. 1976. *Arrian: Anabasis of Alexander*. Vol. 1, *Books I–IV*. The Loeb Classical Library 236. Cambridge, MA: Harvard University Press.

Chaniotis, A. 1995. "Sich selbst feiern? Städische Feste des Hellenismus im Spannungsfeld von Religion und Politik." In *Stadtbild und Bürgerbild im Hellenismus: Kolloquium, München, 24. bis 26. Juni 1993*, edited by M. Wörrle and P. Zanker, 147–172. Munich: Beck.

Crowther, C. 2007. "The Dionysia at Iasos: Its Artists, Patrons and Audience." In *Greek Theatre and Festivals*, edited by P. Wilson, 294–334. Oxford: Oxford University Press.

Csapo, E. 2000. "From Aristophanes to Menander? Genre Transformation in Greek Comedy." In *Matrices of Genre: Authors, Canons and Society*, edited by M. Depew and D. Obbink, 115–151. Cambridge, MA: Harvard University Press.

———. 2004. "Some Social and Economic Conditions behind the Rise of the Acting Profession in the Fifth and Fourth Centuries BC." In *Le Statut de l'acteur dans l'antiquité grecque et romaine: Actes du colloque qui s'est tenu à Tours les 3 et 4 mai 2002*, edited by C. Hugoniot, F. Hurlet and S. Milanezi, 53–76. Tours: Presses universitaires François Rabelais.

———. 2010. *Actors and Icons of the Ancient Theater*. Malden, MA: Wiley-Blackwell.

De Sensi Sestito, G. 1985. *La Calabria in età arcaica e classica: Storia, economia, società*. Rome: Gangemi.

Dearden, C. 2006. "Sicily and Rome: The Greek Context for Roman Drama." *MeditArch* 17: 121–130.

Dumont, J. C. 1997. "*Cantica* et espace de représentation dans le théâtre latin." In *De la scène aux gradins: Théâtre et représentations dramatiques après Alexandre le Grand (Pallas 47)*, edited by B. Le Guen, 41–50. Toulouse: Presses universitaires du Mirail.

Fountoulakis, A. 2000. "The Artists of Aphrodite." *AntClass* 69: 133–147.

Frederiksen, R. 2002. "The Greek Theatre: A Typical Building in the Urban Centre of the Polis?" In *Even More Studies in the Ancient Greek Polis*, edited by T. H. Nielsen, 65–124. Stuttgart: F. Steiner.

Gigante, M. 1971. *Rintone e il teatro in Magna Grecia*. Naples: Guida.

———. 1971. "Civiltà teatrale e epigrammatica a Tarento in età ellenistica." *Taras* 8: 7–33.

Guerber, E. 2009. *Les Cités grecques dans l'Empire romain: Les privilèges et les titres des cités de l'Orient hellénophone d'Octave Auguste à Dioclétien*. Rennes: Presses universitaires de Rennes.

Jones, C. P. 2007. "Three New Letters of the Emperor Hadrian." *ZPE* 161: 145–156.

Konstantakos, I. 2011. "Conditions of Playwriting and the Comic Dramatist's Craft in the Fourth Century." *Logeion* 1: 145–183.

Krumeich, R., N. Pechstein, and B. Seidensticker, eds. 1999. *Das griechische Satyrspiel*. Darmstadt: Wissenschaftliche Buchgesellschaft.

Le Guen, B. 2001a. *Les Associations de Technites dionysiaques à l'époque hellénistique*. 2 vols. Nancy: A.D.R.A.

——. 2001b. "L'activité dramatique dans les îles grecques à l'époque hellénistique." In *Les Îles de l'Égée dans l'Antiquité,* edited by P. Brun, 261–298. Pessac: Revue des Études anciennes.

——. 2003. "Théâtre, cités et royaumes en Anatolie et au Proche-Orient de la mort d'Alexandre le Grand aux conquêtes de Pompée." In *L'Orient méditerranéen de la mort d'Alexandre aux campagnes de Pompée,* edited by F. Prost, 329–355. Rennes: Presses universitaires de Rennes.

——. 2004a. "Le statut professionnel des acteurs grecs à l'époque hellénistique." In *Le Statut de l'acteur dans l'Antiquité grecque et romaine: Actes du colloque qui s'est tenu à Tours les 3 et 4 mai 2002,* edited by C. Hugoniot, F. Hurlet and S. Milanezi, 77–106. Tours: Presses universitaires François Rabelais.

——. 2004b. "Remarques sur les associations de Technites dionysiaques de l'époque hellénistique (à propos de l'ouvrage de Sophia Aneziri, *Die Vereine der dionysischen Techniten im Kontext der hellenistischen Gesellschaft,* Stuttgart, 2003)." *Nikephoros* 17: 279–299.

——. 2007a. "Kraton, Son of Zotichos: Artist's Associations and Monarchic Power in the Hellenistic Period." In *Greek Theatre and Festivals,* edited by P. Wilson, 246–278. Oxford: Oxford University Press.

——. 2007b. "L'association des Technites d'Athènes ou les ressorts d'une cohabitation réussie." In *Individus, groupes et politique à Athènes de Solon à Mithridate,* edited by J. Ch. Couvenhes and S. Milanezi, 339–364. Tours: Presses universitaires François Rabelais.

——. 2010a. "Les fêtes du théâtre grec à l'époque hellénistique." *Revue des Études grecques* 123: 495–520.

——. 2010b [2012]. "Hadrien, l'Empereur philhellène, et la vie agonistique de son temps: À propos d'un livre récent: *Hadrian und die dionysischen Künstler. Drei in Alexandreia Troas neugefundene Briefe des Kaisers an die Künstler-Vereinigung.*" *Nikephoros* 23: 205–239.

——. Forthcoming. "Theatre, Religion, and Politics at Alexander's Travelling Royal Court." In *Death of Drama or Birth of an Industry? The Greek Theatre in the Fourth Century B.C.,* edited by E. Csapo and P. Wilson.

Leppin, H. 1992. *Histrionen: Untersuchungen zur sozialen Stellung von Bühnenkünstlern im Westen des Römischen Reiches zur Zeit der Republik und des Principats.* Bonn: Habelt.

Lightfoot, J. L. 2002. "Nothing to Do with the Artists of Dionysus?" In *Greek and Roman Actors: Aspects of an Ancient Profession,* edited by P. Easterling and E. Hall, 209–224. Cambridge, UK: Cambridge University Press.

Maffre, J.-J. 2000. "Comédie et iconographie: Les grands problèmes." In *Le Théâtre grec antique: La comédie,* edited by J. Leclant and J. Jouanna, 269–315. Paris: Académie des Inscriptions et Belles-Lettres.

Mette, H. J. 1977. *Urkunden dramatischer Aufführungen in Griechenland.* Berlin and New York: De Gruyter.

Migeotte, L. 1993. "De la liturgie à la contribution obligatoire: Le financement des Dionysies et des travaux du théâtre à Iasos au IIe siècle avant J.-C." *Chiron* 23: 267–294.

——. 2010. "Le financement des concours dans les cités hellénistiques: Essai de typologie." In *L'Argent dans les concours du monde grec: Actes du colloque international Saint-Denis et Paris, 5–6 décembre 2008,* edited by B. Le Guen, 127–143. Saint-Denis: Presses universitaires de Vincennes.

Moretti, J.-Ch. 2001. *Théâtre et société dans la Grèce antique: Une archéologie des pratiques théâtrales.* Paris: LGF.

Nachtergael, G. 1977. *Les Galates en Grèce et les Sôteria de Delphes: Recherches d'histoire et d'épigraphie hellénistiques.* Brussels: Palais des Académies.

Nervegna, S. 2007. "Staging Scenes or Plays? Theatrical Revivals of 'Old' Greek Drama in Antiquity." *ZPE* 162: 14–42.

Petzl, G., and Schwertheim, E. 2006. *Hadrian und die dionysischen Künstler: Drei in Alexandreia Troas neugefundene Briefe des Kaisers an die Künstler-Vereinigung.* Bonn: Habelt.

Polverini, L. 2003. "Tempi e luoghi delle rappresentazioni teatrali a Roma." In *Teatro postclassico e teatro latino: Teorie e prassi drammatica: Atti del convegno internazionale, Roma, 16–18 ottobre 2001,* edited by A. Martina, 385–395. Rome: Università degli studi Roma Tre.

Robert, L. 1984. "Discours d'ouverture." In *Praktika tou 8. Diethnous Synedriou Hellēnikēs kai Latinikēs Epigraphikēs, Athēna, 3–9 Oktōvriou 1982.* Vol. 1, edited by Kalogeropoulou, A. G., 35–45. Athens: Hypourgeio Politismou kai Epistemon. (=*Opera Minora Selecta 6,* by L. Robert, 709–719. Amsterdam: Hakkert).

Sifakis, G. M. 1967. *Studies in the History of Hellenistic Drama.* London: The Athlone Press.

Slater, W. 2008. "Hadrian's Letter to the Athletes and Dionysiac Artists Concerning Arrangements for the Circuit of Games." *Journal of Roman Archaeology* 21: 610–620.

——. 2010. "Paying the Pipers." In *L'Argent dans les concours du monde grec: Actes du colloque international Saint-Denis et Paris, 5–6 décembre 2008,* edited by B. Le Guen, 249–281. Saint-Denis: Presses universitaires de Vincennes.

Strasser, J.-Y. 2010. " 'Qu'on fouette les concurrents...': À propos des lettres d'Hadrien retrouvées à Alexandrie de Troade." *Revue des Études grecques* 123: 585–622.

Summa, D. 2003. "Le Didascalie e il teatro postclassico." In *Teatro greco postclassico e teatro latino: Teorie e prassi drammatica: Atti del convegno internazionale, Roma, 16–18 ottobre 2001,* edited by A. Martina, 293–304. Rome: Università degli studi Roma Tre.

——. 2008. "Un concours de drames 'anciens' à Athènes." *Revue des Études grecques* 121: 479–496.

Webster, T. B. L. 1963. "Alexandrian Epigrams and the Theatre." *Miscellanea di studi alessandrini in memoria di Augusto Rostagni,* 531–543. Turin: Bottega d'Erasmo.

CHAPTER 18

HELLENISTIC MIME AND ITS RECEPTION IN ROME*

COSTAS PANAYOTAKIS

THE Hellenistic period was in all probability a turning point in the history of the long-lasting but elusive theatrical form of entertainment known as mime. Its origins as a type of popular drama are perhaps best linked not with Athens but with provincial cities, such as Megara, Corinth, Sicyon, and Sparta in the Peloponnese, and a good indication of the material which popular farce may have exploited during the preclassical period of Greek drama is probably given through representations in vases of comic episodes involving Dionysus, or through ancient scholarly accounts concerning unsophisticated depictions of ordinary scenes from everyday life, such as fruit-stealing, the advice of foreign doctors, or the punishment of wine thieves.[1]

The noun μῖμος, unattested in the *Iliad* and the *Odyssey*, occurs for the first time in extant Greek literature in Aeschylus (*TrGF* 57.9 Nauck), but its meaning is "an imitator," not "an actor." It is not until the fourth century BCE, in Demosthenes (2.19), that we find the word in the sense of "an actor," or, in Aristotle (*Po.* 1447b10), as "a form of drama." Likewise, the denominative verb μιμέομαι and its derivatives—meaning "to represent," "to portray"—are first attested in the *Homeric Hymn to Apollo* (163) and in the satirical late Hellenistic epic *Batrachomyomachia* (7), while the use of the verb as a technical term in the sense of "acting" with reference to mime-players is not found before the 380s

* A draft version of this chapter was read out on November 5, 2011, at the Langford Seminar on Bucolic and Mime in Antiquity, held at Florida State University, Tallahassee. I am greatly indebted to F. Cairns, who invited me to the Seminar and offered me generous hospitality and—along with P. Bing, R. Höschele, and K. Kapparis—constructive feedback and bibliographical help with my paper.
[1] Illustrations in Corinthian vases of the sixth century BCE of scenes linked with popular farce are in Bieber (1961): 38. The important connection (in a quasi-dramatic context) between, on the one hand, Sparta and Sicyon and, on the other, δικηλισταί or δεικηλισταί, namely "fabricators" (σκευοποιούς) and "mimes" (μιμητάς), is made by the late Hellenistic chronographer Sosibius (cited by Athenaeus 14.621d–f).

BCE, the terminus post quem for Xenophon's *Symposium* (2.21). This, then, is the period during which mime as a form of high literature with staging potential acquires poetic form and substance as a genre; it focuses on the depiction of realistic scenes from everyday life and is interested in subtle character portrayal, and the desired effect is achieved through carefully crafted poetry on a small scale. The elevation of mime compositions to high levels of sophistication is chiefly due both to the erudite "urban mimes" of the Syracusan Theocritus (2 "ΦΑΡΜΑΚΕΥΤΡΙΑ" "The Sorceress," 3 "ΚΩΜΟΣ" "The Revel," 14 "ΑΙΣΧΙΝΑΣ ΚΑΙ ΘΥΩΝΙΧΟΣ" "Aeschinas and Thyonichus," and 15 "ΣΥΡΑΚΟΣΙΑΙ Η ΑΔΩΝΙΑΖΟΥΣΑΙ" "Syracusan Women or Women keeping the Adonia")[2] and to the "Alexandrian" poems of Herodas, who took the initiative to dress the low subject matter of the nonliterary mime with the meter and the language of the old Ionic iambic poetry.

The situation about mime in the Hellenistic period is made more complex, however, when we take into account what may be termed the "popular" or "performative" strand of mime tradition, as exemplified through the lively presence of mime-actors, jesters, and other such entertainers in the courts of Macedonian and Eastern royal palaces (Dem. 2.19; Diod. Sic. 31.16.3), a phenomenon that continued to take place in the private banquets of wealthy Roman patrons in the first century BCE (Plut. *Sull.* 2.3–6, 33.3, 36.1). The performance of these popular entertainers, often accompanied by music, may or may not have been based on a script, and the technical term by which they were defined professionally seems to have varied. To what extent these musical spectacles shared the literary qualities of Herodas's works cannot now be ascertained; some may well have done so, but (on the basis of the—admittedly meager—evidence) I doubt that this was the case for all of them. However, the dual nature of the Hellenistic mime, combining "bookishness" and dramatic performance or—at least—performability, has passed into the Roman literary mime and into other forms of Latin literature, but not unproblematically or simply: there existed a strong native Italian theatrical tradition (for instance, unscripted farce which, in the first century BCE, came to be known as "Atellan comedy"), with which the mime from the East was blended to form what should be more correctly termed as the Greco-Roman mime. My aim in this chapter, then, is to consider whether and how the Hellenistic mime, both in its literary variety and in its lower, sensationalized version, was exploited selectively not only in Roman nondramatic literature but also in Latin mime compositions, namely mime scripts destined for the stage, or Latin mimiambs, which were probably meant only for the appreciation of the educated reader.

What is our evidence for mime spectacles in the Hellenistic period? In the second Olynthiac, dated to 349/8 BCE, Demosthenes (2.19) rebukes Philip for welcoming at the royal court low comedians and composers of indecent songs (μίμους γελοίων καὶ ποιητὰς αἰσχρῶν ἀισμάτων)—a tradition followed by Philip's son Alexander, according to Athenaeus (1.20a), who mentions by name three θαυματοποιοί ("magicians"),

---

[2] Some of Theocritus's poems (2 and 15) were, according to the ancient scholiast (Σ Arg. (2), Σ 2.69, and Σ Arg. (15)), explicitly modeled on the mimes of the fifth-century BCE Sicilian playwright Sophron.

two πλάνοι ("itinerant showmen"), and one γελωτοποιός ("comedian"). The Sicilian tyrant Agathocles, who ruled from 316 BCE to his assassination in 289/8 BCE, is said to have been "by nature both a comedian and a mimic" (καὶ φύσει γελωτοποιὸς καὶ μῖμος) (Diod. Sic. 20.63.2). More importantly, an Athenian terracotta lamp, dated to the late third century BCE, preserves our earliest representation of a mime drama (ὑπόθεσις; see *LSJ* s.v. II.5); a clear reproduction of it is in Bieber (1961) fig. 415. It is entitled "The Mother-in-Law" (Ἑκυρά), and could have required at least four characters in its cast (the three unmasked and beardless male figures represented on the lamp, one of them clearly being the stereotypical bald mime-fool, and an actress playing the mother-in-law of the title); presumably they worked as members of an official mime troupe. The inscription on the back of the lamp, which may have been baked to commemorate the successful performance of the play, reads ΜΙΜΟΛΩΓΟΙ Η ΥΠΟΘΕΣΙΣ ΕΙΚΥΡΑ "Mime-actors: *play*, 'The Mother-in-law.'"

Similar to this group of mime-actors were the solo performers who are referred to mainly in the text of Athenaeus (14.620d–621d). His sources are Aristoxenus from Tarentum, the famous scholar of music (fourth century BCE; see Villari (2000)), and Aristocles the musicologist (end of second century BCE; see *RE* 2 (1896) 936–937). Each of the terms used for the performers mentioned by Athenaeus is a compound substantive, one of whose parts points to the use of music in their (presumably solo) performance (whatever that was): μίμαυλος, μιμωιδός, ἱλαρωιδός, μαγωιδός, σιμωιδός and λυσιωιδός. It is very difficult to tell the difference among these artists, both because some of the terms used for them appear to have been synonyms and because Athenaeus's text is convoluted and textually problematic. However, it gives valuable information regarding the subject matter of some of these spectacles, and I cite it here (almost) in full, according to Olson's new translation of Athenaeus in the Loeb series (I have put my own brief explanatory comments within square brackets):

> The so-called hilarodes [ἱλαρωιδοί]—some people today refer to them as *simôidoi*, according to Aristocles in Book I of *On Choruses* [*FHG* IV.331 M], because Simus of Magnesia was the best-known hilarodic poet—likewise appeared constantly at our parties. Aristocles also includes them in the catalogue in his *On Music*, writing as follows: *Magôidos*: this individual is the same as a *lusiôidos*. But Aristoxenus [fr. 111 W] claims that a man who plays male and female parts is referred to as a *magôidos*, whereas a man who plays female parts dressed in male clothing is a *lusiôidos*; but they perform the same songs, and everything else about them is identical. An *Ionikologos* performs the so-called Ionian poems of Sotades and his predecessors...This type of performer is also known as a *kinaidologos*. Sotades of Maroneia excelled in this genre...The so-called *hilarôidoi* are more respectable than poets of this sort; for they do not *schinizomai* [meaning unknown; *LSJ* s.v. has "of certain movements in a dance"], and they wear white, male clothing and have a gold garland on their head, and in the old days they wore sandals, according to Aristocles [*FHG* IV.331 M], although nowadays they wear high boots; a man or a woman plays the harp to accompany them, as also in the case of *aulôidoi*. Hilarôidoi and *aulôidoi* are allowed to wear garlands, whereas harp-players and pipe-players are not. The so-called *magôidoi* have drums and cymbals, and wear only female clothing;

they *schinizomai* [see above] and behave in all the ways no one should, *sometimes pretending to be women who are having affairs or arranging liaisons for others, at other times playing a man who is drunk or who appears at his girlfriend's house with a group of troublemakers* [my emphasis]. Aristoxenus [fr. 110 W] claims that because *hilarôidia* is respectable, it is connected with tragedy [παρὰ τὴν τραγωιδίαν εἶναι], whereas *magôidia* is connected with comedy [τὴν δὲ μαγωιδίαν παρὰ τὴν κωμωιδίαν].[3] *Magôidoi* frequently took over comic plots [Is Athenaeus here referring to plots derived from New Comedy? This interpretation seems to be supported by the papyrus mime fragments in *P.Lit.Lond.* 52 and *P.Lit.Lond.* 97: see Rusten and Cunningham (2002): 360–361] and acted them out in their own fashion and style. *Magôidia* got its name from the fact that they pronounced *magika* ("magic spells"), as it were, and displayed unnatural powers.

I emphasized the information about the subject matter which *magôidoi* sometimes portrayed in their performances ("the adulteress," "the bawd," "the drunkard," "the revel"), because we find instances of it both in Herodas's mimiambs (for instance, 1 "ΠΡΟΚΥΚΛΙ[Σ] Η ΜΑΣΤΡΟΠΟΣ" "A Matchmaker or Procuress") and in the popular mime-pieces of unidentified authorship, which survive in Greek papyri (and to which I will return later in this chapter).

But mime flourished also in the Hellenistic kingdoms of the Eastern Mediterranean, and it is from cultural centers such as Antioch in Syria and Alexandria in Egypt that mime-actors are reported to have travelled to Italy and Rome (see Macr. *Sat.* 2.7.6–7; *HA*, *Verus*, 8.11), either individually or as members of traveling troupes and as associates of an official theatrical guild (the *Parasiti Apollinis* or a *commune mimorum*). Already in the third century BCE, mime-jesters, such as Herodotus ὁ λογόμιμος ("writer or actor of spoken mimes," *LSJ* s.v.) and Archelaus ὁ ὀρχηστὴς ("the dancer"), entertained the court of Antiochus II Theos (261–246 BCE; Athen. 1.19c) and of Antiochus IV Epiphanes (175–164 BCE), who is said to have participated naked along with mime-actors in licentious dancing spectacles during a banquet (Ath. 5.195f; Diod. Sic. 31.1.6.3). What did these entertainers do at a banquet? Presumably they performed a variety of entertainments, each according to his own specialism. It would be interesting to speculate what Herodotus would have done: would he have acted or recited mime pieces which would have involved even more than one character in the story? The contribution of symposia to the emergence of mime as a distinct kind of theater has perhaps been underestimated. It may well be that some mimes found their way to the stage after they had been successfully performed in the houses of wealthy and influential patrons; Cameron (1995: 89–90) and Hordern (2004: 9 n. 22) do not rule out the possibility that even the works

---

[3] An obscure phrase, but Olson translates it successfully. Gulick, the previous translator of Athenaeus in the Loeb series, took παρὰ + accusative = "as a parody of" (*LSJ* s.v. C I 6a); Hunter (1995): 219 renders the meaning more accurately, translating παρὰ τὴν τραγωιδίαν as "derives from tragedy" and παρὰ τὴν κωμωιδίαν as "derives from comedy." Fraenkel (1960): 317 n. 1 (= [2007] ch. 10, n. 26) had put it even more clearly: " 'The mood and attitude in hilarodia correspond to tragedy, and in magodia to comedy' is really all that the pointed dictum expresses" [transl. by Drevikovsky and Muecke].

of Herodas (writing probably in the mid-third century BCE) and Theocritus (working at the Alexandrian court in the 270s BCE) were performed at a banquet (see also the important contributions of Mastromarco (1984) and Hunter (1993) to the debate).

The abovementioned types of solo public performers in the Hellenistic world who combined song or recitation with role playing contribute to the fluidity of the term "mime," which becomes difficult to pin down, because it may have signified not only unscripted spectacles by solo performers of music and role playing but also scripted poems of high sophistication. The most notable representative of the latter category is Herodas, an author of Doric origin. He composed short "mimetic" poems ("mimi-ambs") in the choliambic meter (iambic trimeters which have a long penultimate), and his extraordinary style comprises realistic subject matter presented in a stylized fashion (e.g., in mimiamb 2, a brothel keeper complains in front of a jury about his mistreat-ment by a sea captain; but the low-life brothel keeper appears to be implausibly familiar with all the tools of the rhetorical trade). He also combines the portrayal of trivial situa-tions with an intertextually complex layer and a very learned (even artificial) language, which may have been addressed to a coterie of educated readers rather than to the cul-turally varied audience of a live performance. For example, in mimiamb 1, an old match-maker visits a woman, whose male companion has been away for some time, and tries to persuade her to yield to the sexual advances of another man; the younger woman may be viewed as a Penelope figure of the Hellenistic age waiting faithfully for the return of her Odysseus (for the relationship between the mimiambs and epic, see Esposito 2010: 272–276).

In addition to the "urban mimes" of Theocritus and the mimiambs of Herodas, there are fragments of Greek works found in papyri, which, although they have no generic label attached to them, have been—more or less plausibly—called mimes by modern editors. This is what Esposito (2010: 279–280) recently wrote about them:

> a series of papyrus texts and documents...bear witness to the dissemination in Greco-Roman Egypt of what is customarily called "popular" mime. These texts, all of which have come down to us anonymously, are less sophisticated than the mimiambs or the *Idylls* from a stylistic and structural point of view, suggesting that they served an audience less exacting than the one targeted by the two *docti poetae* [i.e.,Theocritus and Herodas]. In any event, literary and "popular" mimes should not be viewed as separate spheres but as interdependent and engaged in an intense and dynamic exchange....

The so-called "popular" mimes include the following pieces: (a) the extract from a girl's speech in which a drunkard is apparently mentioned (dated about 100 BCE; *P.Tebt.* 2dv [Berkleiae, Bibl.Univ.Calif. n. 2471 = 2 Cunningham]); (b) the dialogue between two characters, one of them a drunk man in love who wishes to set out on a κῶμος "a revel," the other restraining him (dated to the second or first century BCE; *O.Rein.* 1 [Parisiis, Inst.papyrol.Sorbonn. inv. n. 2223 = 3 Cunningham]); and, most importantly, (c) the so-called Alexandrian Erotic Fragment, which was edited for the first time in 1896 by Bernard Grenfell, and was thus subsequently known as the *Fragmentum Grenfellianum*

(= *FG*; dated to the period between 173 and the end of the second century BCE: *P.Grenf.* 1v [= *P.Lit.Lond.* 50; Londini, Bibl. Brit. inv. n. 605 = 1 Cunningham]).

The *FG* is a lyric monody, whose tense atmosphere and emotional variations resemble in complexity Simaetha's incantations in Theocritus 2 (Φαρμακεύτρια), the threats of the anonymous adulteress (Μοιχεύτρια) in *P.Oxy.* 413, the frustration of Manon in her aria "Sola perduta abbandonata" in Puccini's *Manon Lescaut*, the pleas of Medea in her aria "Dei tuoi figli la madre tu vedi vinta e afflitta" in Cherubini's *Medea*, and the suffering of Norma in her opening aria in Bellini's *Norma*. Although the piece starts off with dactyls and iambs, its largest part consists mostly of lyric meters (anapests, cretics, and—especially—tragic dochmiacs), whose arrangement and unusual combination recall late Euripidean tragedy. The piece is written in κοινή in a very simple style, which is juxtaposed with the complex emotional stages of the speaker and initially gives the impression that the work was intended for popular entertainment. It contains recurring motifs (the pain felt by the unnamed female speaker, the military force of Eros, the madness brought by unreciprocated love) which give unity to the various sections of the song. Its subject matter is the lament of a distraught woman who has been abandoned by her man, a second Ariadne or Medea who has come in the night outside the door of her Theseus or her Jason to address him while he is inside, enjoying himself at a drinking party (perhaps in the company of another woman). There would presumably have been *aulos* accompaniment, and the arrangement of the text on the papyrus signifies it was destined for oral delivery (for instance, the vowels are elided whenever meter requires it). The text may be an instance of what was known as μαγῳδία, a "mimetic song" (see the passage of Athenaeus cited above), and (if this hypothesis is correct) the abandoned female lover (an *exclusa amatrix*) would have been played by a man dressed as a woman. I now give my own translation of the first column of the papyrus (forty lines), which is more complete and legible than the second. The text I used is from Cunningham 2004: 36–38.

> Each of us chose the other;
> we were joined. Cypris is the surety
> of our love. Pain seizes me
> when I recall
> how he used to kiss me while treacherously about   5
> to abandon me,
> that inventor of instability
> and founder of love.
> Desire took hold of me,
> I do not deny it, having him in my thoughts.   10
> Dear stars and you, Lady Night, who love together with me,
> bring me yet to the man to whom Cypris
> is leading me as a captive,
> Cypris and the mighty Desire who has captured me.
> I have as my guide the mighty flame,   15
> which is blazing in my soul.

But these are the things that wrong me, these that hurt me.
The mind-deceiver,
he who until recently used to be proud and would deny
that Cypris was an accessory to my desire,   20
he did not tolerate
a chance offense on my part.
I am about to go crazy; jealousy has me in its grip
and I am utterly blazing, having been abandoned.
Just for this reason, throw away from me these garlands,   25
with which I, the deserted woman, will crown myself.
Master, do not let me be shut out;
receive me; I am ready to serve as a slave to jealousy.
†...† causes great pain.
For it is necessary to feel jealousy, to bear up, to be patient.   30
And if you devote yourself to only one man, you will be foolish.
For love for only one man causes madness.
Know that I have a spirit that is unconquerable
when strife gets hold of me; I go mad when I recall
that I will sleep alone,   35
but you run off to lie with another.
Now, if we get angry, we must soon
also reconcile.
Is it not for this that we have friends,
who will judge who is being unjust?   40

As typical elements of the "popular" strand of the mime of the Hellenistic period,
I would single out in this piece the vividly portrayed personality of the protagonist
(a vengeful Medea-type heroine), the unreciprocated love theme, and the rhythmical variety. These features will recur in Greek mime-pieces found in papyri of the
Imperial period (second and third centuries CE), which are not directly relevant to
the scope of the current discussion (see Rusten and Cunningham 2002: 390–415). But
it would be misleading to perceive the song under discussion as unsophisticated or
inferior to other literary portrayals of scorned women. The anonymous composer of
this metrically complex piece has been viewed as fully knowing and deliberately sub-
verting the conventions of the literary *paraklausithyron* (a verse composition which
a lover addresses to his beloved after she has shut him out), and this song has been
regarded as his response to the compositions of poets such as Rufinus and Asclepiades,
who exploited the images of the address to the Night and of the "excluded" female
lover (*exclusa amatrix*) in their amatory epigrams (see *AP* 5.43 and 5.164; likewise,
Propertius finishes Book 3 of his elegies with the imagined vision of the "excluded"
Cynthia: 3.25.15–16). But the debt to earlier literary tradition may extend beyond the
level of thematic resemblances to the field of linguistic borrowings, and a good case
has been made for the influence of Sappho, Hellenistic prose, and legal discourse on
the portrayal of the female narrator (Bing 2002: 384; Esposito 2005: 35–39). We do not
know how the piece ended, and we cannot be sure that the unusual combination of

stylistic registers mentioned above permeated its whole structure. But there is perhaps enough evidence here to prevent us from thinking that, at least in the Hellenistic
period, there were clearly defined and easily recognizable boundaries between erudite mime-pieces and supposedly unsophisticated works belonging to the popular
theater.

Emotionally and prosodically complex pieces such as the *FG* may have contributed
not only to the origin of Plautine *cantica* (in spite of the lengthy objections of Fraenkel
1960: 311–320 on the matter) but also to the prominence of the *exclusus amator* motif
in Roman comedy (e.g., Pl. *Menaechmi* 698–700, *Curculio* 1.164, Ter. *Eunuchus* 46–55),
Latin elegy and lyric (e.g., Prop. 1.8.21–24, 1.16.17–48, Tib. 2.6.11–20, Hor. *Carm.* 1.25,
2.8.17–20), Roman satire (e.g., Hor. *S.* 1.2.64–67, 2.3.259–264), and the Roman novel (e.g.,
Petr. *Sat.* 26.4–5, 94.7–8). But how likely is it that the Romans would have known Greek
mimes and would have made the connection between Hellenistic Egypt and the theater
of the mime in all its manifestations?

We do not know exactly when a mime-actor or actress appeared for the first time on
the stage of a Roman theater during a festival or at an event which formed part of the
entertainment at a private dinner party. However, on the basis of literary and documentary sources it is possible to infer that the mime profession was clearly associated in the
Roman mind with Greek-speaking lands, especially Sicily. This assumption was fruitfully exploited in Roman rhetoric and historiography as part of a political, satirical, and
moral agenda regarding the influence of foreign cultures. The connection the Romans
made between mime and Greek culture is not unjustified, because a large amount of the
terminology employed for the specializations attributed to mime-actors and actresses
(for example, *archaeologus, archimimus / archimima, biologus, ethologus, mimologus,
mimographus, mimus / mima*), and the stage names borne by many mimes (for instance,
Protogenes, who had died by the early third century BCE, and Eucharis, who, according
to her epitaph (*CIL* 6.10096 = *ILS* 5213), performed *Graeca in scaena*, or Ecloga, Cytheris,
and Thalassia) are Greek in origin, while some mime plays produced at Rome may even
have been performed in Greek (Suet. *Iul.* 39.1; *Aug.* 43.1). Furthermore, in the mid-fifties
BCE Cicero made a disparaging statement about the *mimicae fallaciae* ("mime-tricks")
of Alexandria; this can be found in his speech in defense of Rabirius (35). Wishing to
denigrate the reputation of the Alexandrian opponents of his client, Cicero presents
Alexandria as a den of cultural debauchery, where mime and trickery reign supreme.
So the link between mime and Greece in the theatrical culture of (at least) the republic
seems to be strong.

However, it is far from certain that Herodas's Greek *mimiamboi* in choliambics influenced *in any substantial way* the style and language of the so-called literary mimes of
the Latin mimographers Decimus Laberius, Publilius, and their colleagues. It is true
that the Roman mimes, like the work of the Sicilian Sophron and of Herodas, seem
to draw their material from everyday life, and exploit colloquialisms, vulgarisms, and
sententious moral statements. In addition to them, there are in Laberius's extant corpus many instances of proverbial expressions, technical terms, rare and archaic words,
and phrases whose formation is clearly influenced by Greek syntax and grammar. The

imagery he employs to create comic effect comes from the spheres of agriculture, medicine, philosophy, cooking, chariot racing, and the kingdom of animals and birds. The
multilayered and wide-ranging style of Laberius has been compared to the style of
the erudite Herodas, the compositions of the *novi poetae*, and the *Menippean Satires*
of Varro, and has been interpreted as Laberius's artistic response to the growing intellectual demands and sophistication of the Roman theatrical audience of the mid-first
century BCE in linguistic innovation and playwriting skills. But, while there is no doubt
that Laberius's language is complex, it is important to note that the verbal humor of his
mimes would also have been recognized and enjoyed by spectators whose erudition
was not as impressive as that of the members of the Roman upper classes. His neologisms are not aimed exclusively at the entertainment of a small group of educated people, because many of the suffixes, prefixes, and verbal stems which Laberius employs
in a witty fashion would have been known to the average Roman spectator, who would
have been amused at the realization that parts of ordinary speech have been used in an
original way.

Therefore, the extant fragments of the mimes of Laberius do not seem to me to have
reached the high literary standards required for the appreciation of their Hellenistic
counterparts. In my opinion Laberius was playing with mime as a literary genre, which
in his hands acquired the elevated status that the improvised and unscripted "Atellan
farces" had acquired in the nineties and eighties BCE in the hands of the playwrights
Pomponius and Novius. Could it also be that some of Laberius's mimes (not necessarily those which have a Greek word as their title) are direct translations or adaptations
of now lost Greek plays (perhaps Hellenistic mimes) along the lines of Plautus's and
Terence's Latin reworkings of Hellenistic comedies? This is possible but unlikely. There
is no extract that I know of in a surviving Greek comedy or mime that looks remotely
similar to a fragment of Laberius. Although some of the titles attributed to plays by
Laberius point to characters exercising a low profession (for example, *Belonistria* "The
Seamstress," *Centonarius* "The Fireman," *Staminariae* "The Weavers"), and consequently
may have resembled the mimes of Herodas in which the character portrayal of a lowlife
character dominates the plot (e.g., ΜΑΣΤΡΟΠΟΣ "The Procuress," ΠΟΡΝΟΒΟΣΚΟΣ
"The Brothel keeper," ΣΚΥΤΕΥΣ "The Cobbler"), many Laberian titles refer to stock
characters and motifs of comic drama (for instance, *Augur* "The Soothsayer," *Gemelli*
"The Twins," *Sorores* "The Sisters") rather than to Laberius's direct debt to specific Greek
originals. On the whole, then, there is not enough evidence to argue persuasively that
Laberius based his mimes on the works of Sophron or Herodas or one of the Hellenistic
New Comedy playwrights.

Nor is it possible to see whether Herodas's mimiambs exerted any influence on the
mimiambi of Mattius or Matius (who wrote possibly before Varro) and of Vergilius
Romanus (a contemporary of the Younger Pliny), about whose mime careers we know
next to nothing; "it is possible," writes Courtney (1993: 106), "that Matius (whose choliambics are the first at Rome) was translating parts of the oeuvre of Herodas which we no
longer possess, and the calques may favour this view, but he may also have been creating
independently, as later in this genre Pliny's friends Vergilius Romanus (*Ep.* 6.21.4) and

(in Greek) Arrius Antoninus (4.3.3)." The testimony of the Younger Pliny on the style of these two poets is cited below in Walsh's translation for the Oxford World's Classics series [but the brief comments within square brackets are mine]:

(A) Pliny, *Ep.* 6.21.2–5: Indeed, I recently listened to Vergilius Romanus reading to a small group a work modelled on the Old Comedy. It was so good that it can at some time serve as a model for others. I am not sure if you know him, but you ought to. He is the epitome of honest manners, refined talent, and literary versatility. He has written graceful, sharp [*argute*; the adverb is repeated in passage (B) below and has been associated mostly with rhetorical style: *OLD* s.v.], and charming [*venuste*; this adverb too is repeated in passage (B) below and occurs mostly with reference to the style of Catullus and the orators: *OLD* s.v.] iambic mimes, and is supremely eloquent in this genre (for there is no category of writing which when perfected cannot be pronounced supremely eloquent). He has written comedies rivalling Menander and others of that age; you can regard these as on a par with those of Plautus and Terence.

(B) Pliny, *Ep.* 4.3.3–4: For when you [Pliny is writing to Arrius Antoninus] speak, that honey of Homer's fabled ancient seems to issue forth, and as for your writings, the bees seem to fill and to entwine them with the sweetness of the blossoms. Such at any rate was the effect on me in my recent reading of your Greek epigrams and your iambic mimes [*mimiambos* is the reading of the manuscript family γ and has been favored by Skutsch (1892); *iambos* is the reading of the manuscript families αβ]. What culture, what charm they embody, how agreeable and affecting they are! What clarity, what propriety lie in them! I thought that I was handling Callimachus or Herodas, or such as is better than these—yet neither of these poets wrote, or sought to write, poetry in both genres.

Fantuzzi and Hunter (2004: 463) agree with Courtney's assessment:

The *Mimiambi* of Cn. Matius (date uncertain) may have been inspired by Herodas, but the extant fragments show no obvious point of contact with our text of the Greek mimiambist.

What observations may be made about Cnaeus Matius as an author of Latin mimiambs in comparison to, say, Laberius as an author of Latin mimes? Matius's mimiambs have not survived complete, but the extant remains may not be unrepresentative of his general style of writing. On the basis of Courtney's text, I give below my own translation for all but two of the fragments, and I put in parenthesis the words that are worthy of linguistic or metrical comment:

(a) Gellius 15.25.1–2: Cnaeus Matius, a learned man, in his *Mimiambs* neither inappropriately nor unpleasantly coined the word *recentatur* for the notion which the Greeks express with ἀνανεοῦται, that is "it is born again and it again becomes new." The lines of verse in which the word occurs are as follows:

At any time now Phoebus grows bright (*albicascit*) and becomes new again
(*recentatur*)
The common light of pleasure for mortals.

Matius also, in the same *Mimiambs*, uses *edulcare*, which means "to make sweeter," in
the following lines:

Therefore, it befits to make life sweeter (*edulcare*),
And to govern bitter worries with the senses.

(b) Gellius 20.9: Antonius Julianus [Gellius's teacher of rhetoric] used to say that his
    ears were charmed and soothed by the neologisms of Cnaeus Matius, a learned
    man; they include the following, which he [i.e., Antonius Julianus] used to say
    had been written by Matius in his *Mimiambs*:

Revive your cold love in your hot embrace,
by pressing together lip (*labra*) to lip (*labris*) like little doves (*columbulatim*).

And this also he [i.e., Antonius Julianus] was habitually saying had been devised
pleasantly and delightfully:

The close-shorn rugs (*tapetes*) are now drunk with the dye
With which the purple-fish has drenched and imbued them.

(c) Gellius 10.24.10: Cnaeus Matius, an immoderately learned man, in his *Mimiambs*,
    instead of our expression *nudius quartus*, or "four days ago," uses *die quarto*, in
    the following lines:

Recently, four days ago, as I recall (yes, I am sure about it),
He broke the only water jug in the house.

(d) Macrobius, *Sat.* 3.20.5 [*Kaster's translation in the Loeb series*]: Figs that do not
    ripen are called *grossi* . . . Mattius [*sic*] says:

in so many thousands you'll not see not one unripe (*grossus*), and a little later,
you could get from another unripe figs (*grossi*) dripping (*diffluos*) with milky
juice.

(e) Priscian 1.274 [Courtney 1993: 105]: I bestow more manure on my garden than
    I derive vegetables from it (*meos hortulos plus stercŏrō quam hŏlĕrō*).

Of the thirteen choliambics that have been attributed to Matius, twelve are metrically complete. As far as Matius's lexicon is concerned, in the tiny corpus that survives

I counted six hapax legomena (*albicascit* [however, I am suspicious of the fact that Gellius does not comment on the form of the verb; did he know more instances of it, or did he perhaps confuse it with *albesco* "to become white," which is frequently attested in high poetry?], *recentatur, edulcare, columbulatim, diffluos*, and *holero*), as well as one accusative plural according to the Greek declension (*tapetes* has a short final syllable and a long penultimate). Morphologically, the coinages are effective and charming but rather predictable and conservative. For instance, the adverb *columbulatim* is coined by the affectionate diminutive *columbula* "little dove" (elsewhere attested once in Pliny's letters: 9.25.3) and the ending *-atim*, which is normally employed to signify that something is happening either "gradually, one at a time" (for instance, *guttatim* "drop by drop," *ostiatim* "door by door," *paul(l)atim* "bit by bit," *pauxillatim* "little by little"; *OLD* s.v.) or "in the manner of" (for example, *muricatim* "in the manner of shellfish"; *OLD* s.v.). Now, Laberius had used the same suffix to coin the adverb *Mauricatim* "in the Moorish language," but his approach to word formation is much more unpredictable, unorthodox, and amusing (see Panayotakis 2010: 154–156). To return to Matius's neologisms, *edulco* is a compound verb, whose prefix *ex-* has *not* privative force (so *edulcare* does not mean "to take the sweetness out") *but* intensifying meaning (*edulcare* = "to sweeten completely"). *Recentor* is a denominative deponent verb morphologically and semantically analogous with the Greek middle verb ἀνανεόομαι, while Courtney, in his discussion of Matius's fragments (1993: 105), rightly compares *holero* with the Greek denominative verb λαχανεύω "to plant vegetables." Has Matius been translating from Greek? This possibility occurred to me not only in relation to Matius's fragment (e), but also when I read in Courtney's notes (1993: 104) that Friedrich Leo had compared Matius's fragment (c) above with a fragment of Hipponax, the sixth-century BCE iambic poet who, according to the late antique author Terentianus Maurus, was the metrical model for Matius's mimiambs. The passage of Hipponax (4 Knox), to be compared with Matius's lines above, says

she had no tumbler; her slave had fallen on it and smashed it,

while the relevant passage of Terentianus Maurus (6.397–399 Keil), which has appropriately been composed in choliambics, states:

Mattius produced mimiambs in this meter:
for he followed with similar wit and meter the example of the same bard
[i.e., Hipponax] who was tinged with Attic thyme.

So far, then, there is nothing striking or unusual in terms of lexicon, syntax, and morphology that links Matius specifically with Herodas or makes Matius more innovative when compared with the mimographer Laberius. Metrically, the thirteen extant choliambics of Matius present few surprises. In line 2 of the first fragment cited by Gellius 20.9 (see (b) above), the nouns *labra* and *labris* seem to have a long penultimate, but normally *labrum* (= "lip") has a short *a* to distinguish it from *lābrum* (= "bowl," "large basin"). The passage of Matius cited by Priscian (see (e) above), however, presents a much more interesting peculiarity: all the other extant choliambics of Matius end with the sequence short-long-long-anceps. This pattern, according to Courtney (1993: 105), was favored by Herodas, Callimachus, and Catullus, although it is also possible to find in Herodas's mimiambs the favorite Hipponactean sequence long-long-long-anceps at the end of a choliambic line. But if one scans Matius's line cited by Priscian, counting *meos* as a single long syllable with synizesis, it becomes obvious not only that the sixth and final foot (the sequence long-anceps) is missing from Priscian's citation but also that the fifth foot, beginning with the elided *quam*, is neither a spondee nor an iamb, but an anapest: *qu(am) hŏlĕrō*. Courtney (1993: 105) notes that this variation may be accidental, but adds that fifth-foot anapests occur once in Hipponax and twice in Herodas (but two out of these three instances are doubtful). Courtney also has an alternative suggestion:

> the second half of the line is missing after *stercoro* and ... *quam holero* begins a new line; there are nine lines beginning with an anapaest in Herodas. No anapaests appear in what we have of the *Iambi* of Callimachus.

If, therefore, we assume that the scribe of Priscian's text was careless in copying accurately and lacked training in the area of prosody (that is, he did not know how to divide a citation into metrically coherent units), then we have here a deliberate nod of Matius back to Herodas and an invitation from the playwright to the reader of the Latin *Mimiambi* to recognize the rare metrical appearance of the anapest and to make the connection with the Greek source of inspiration. This hypothesis requires an educated Roman reader who understood Greek and Latin meter to pay careful attention to Herodas's prosody. How plausible would this have been? That Herodas's volume would have been available to at least some readers of Matius's time (but when was this?) is not a hypothesis that should be easily dismissed.

Pliny's reference to Herodas in his letter to Arrius Antoninus (*Ep.* 4.3.3–4) stresses the qualities which a reader, as opposed to a viewer, would find in Herodas, and this is confirmed by the infinitive Pliny uses in relation to Callimachus's and Herodas's works: *tenere credebam* "I thought that I was handling." For Pliny, his circle, and his readers, Herodas was primarily (if not exclusively) a reading volume, not a collection of short sketches that could usefully be put on the stage either in a public location or at the banquet of a wealthy and erudite host. This is also Esposito's view, when she concludes (2010: 277) that "Herodas was a household name to Pliny's friends and the quality and status of his work a matter of agreement, even if we cannot tell if and how much they actually *read* him" [my emphasis]. Such a conclusion, however, should not mean that the Roman authors who knew Herodas's text did not appreciate and exploit both the dramatic character and theatrical potential of his compositions and the low-life atmosphere and humorous subject matter which he was presenting in a high linguistic register. But although there is some evidence to suggest that Greek mime-plays were performed in Rome at the time of Julius Caesar and of Augustus (Suet. *Iul.* 39.1; *Aug.* 43.1), I am inclined to think that certain aspects of Herodas's text, including his fondness for realism and metaliterary self-awareness as exemplified through (for instance) the use of proverbs and colloquialisms, rendered the Greek mimiambs more easily adaptable and suited to Roman literary creations *other than drama*, namely Latin satire and Latin fiction, both of which, however, are literary categories that display a close generic affiliation with Latin comedy. Many modern scholarly views have been put forth to argue that various Latin prose and verse authors present intertextual affinities with, and intentional echoes of, Herodas. Of these views I am persuaded most by the arguments made in relation to the author of the satirical *Apocolocyntosis* (was this Seneca the Younger?) and to Petronius, who penned the low *Satyrica*. Below I list the passages of Herodas, Seneca, and Petronius which Di Gregorio (1997: 49, 63–64) singles out, apparently for their unmistakable similarity. Most of these so-called parallels are too general and too vague to be persuasive echoes and deliberate intertexts, but some of them (for example, the passages cited under (c) in the section *Herodas and Seneca* and, again, under (c) in the section *Herodas and Petronius*) make a more attractive case than the rest because of the linguistic similarities they present and because of the irony that permeates the contexts of both the Greek and the Latin passages, even though there may be no resemblance whatsoever between the pair of speakers in each text.

Herodas and Seneca

a) Her. 1.9 (Cunningham) (Metriche to Gyllis) τί σὺ θεὸς πρὸς ἀνθρώπους; ≈ Sen. *Apocol.* 13.2 (Eden) (Narcissus to Claudius) *'quid di ad homines?'*
b) Her. 1.15 (Cunningham) (Gyllis speaking) ἐγὼ δὲ δραίνω μυῖ' ὅσον˙ ≈ Sen. *Apocol.* 10.3 (Eden) (Augustus is referring to Claudius) *hic, p.c., qui vobis non posse videtur muscam excitare, …*
c) Her. 3.74–76 (Cunningham) (Lampriskos to Kottalos) ἀλλ' εἰς πονηρός, Κότταλ', ὤ<σ>τε καὶ περνάς | οὐδείς σ' ἐπαινέσειεν, οὐδ' ὅκου χώρης | οἱ μῦς ὁμοίως τὸν σίδηρον τρώγουσιν ≈ Sen. *Apocol.* 7.1 (Eden) (Hercules to Claudius) *tu desine fatuari. venisti huc, ubi mures ferrum rodunt.*

Herodas and Petronius

a) Her. 1.15 (Cunningham) (Gyllis speaking) ἐγὼ δὲ δραίνω μυῖ' ὅσον˙ ≈ Petr. *Sat.* 42.4 (Müller) (Seleucus speaking) *utres inflati ambulamus. minoris quam muscae sumus, <muscae>* [add. Heinsius] *tamen aliquam virtutem habent.*
b) Her. 5.14–15 (Cunningham) (Bitinna to Gastron) ἐγὼ αἰτίη τούτων, | ἐγῶιμι, Γάστρων, ἤ σε θεῖσ' ἐν ἀνθρώποις ≈ Petr. *Sat.* 39.4 (Müller) (Trimalchio speaking) *patrono meo ossa bene quiescant, qui me hominem inter homines voluit esse.*
c) Her. 5.26–27 (Cunningham) (Gastron to Bitinna) Βίτινν', ἄφες μοι τὴν ἁμαρτίην ταύτην. | ἄνθρωπός εἰμ', ἥμαρτον˙ ≈ Petr. *Sat.* 75.1 (Müller) (Habinnas speaking) *post hoc fulmen Habinnas rogare coepit ut iam desineret irasci et 'nemo' inquit 'nostrum non peccat. homines sumus. non dei.'* ≈ Petr. *Sat.* 130.1 (Müller)

(Encolpius to Circe) *Polyaenos Circae salutem. fateor me, domina, saepe peccasse. nam et homo sum et adhuc iuvenis.*

d) Her. 5.77–79 (Cunningham) (Bitinna speaking) οὐ τὴν Τύραννον, ἀλλ᾽ ἐπείπερ οὐκ οἶδεν, | ἄνθρωπος ὤν, ἑωυτόν, αὐτίκ᾽ εἰδήσει | ἐν τῶι μετώπωι τὸ ἐπίγραμμα ἔχων τοῦτο. ≈ Petr. *Sat.* 103.4 (Müller) *implevit Eumolpus frontes utriusque ingentibus litteris et notum fugitivorum epigramma per totam faciem liberali manu duxit.*

Moving away from lists of linguistic parallels, and concentrating on thematic correspondences, McKeown (1979) believes that a fairly strong case can be made for the influence on Propertius, especially poems 2.29 and 4.9, of the type of mime-play conventionally known as "adultery mime" and of what he (McKeown) calls "komastic mime." Likewise, in Hunter's view both Herodas and Plautus

> play upon their audience's knowledge of other modes to produce a complex representation in which we enjoy not merely the scenes presented to us 'for their own sakes', but also because we recognise (and laugh at) distortions of other, perhaps more 'serious', modes. As Herodas assimilates comic material to the 'lower' milieu of mime and *iambos*, so Plautus often assimilates the plots and characters of his Greek originals to the 'lower' milieu of Italian farce. (Hunter 1995: 163 = Hunter 2008: 220)

Hunter does not go on to discuss whether or not the process of assimilation he describes is equally complete and the outcome is equally satisfactory both in Herodas and in Plautus. Other instances of literary cross-pollination seem less convincing; I have in mind the view of Ellis (1891) that Virgil employs phrases from the conversation between Gyllis and Metriche in Herodas 1 to construct the scene between Dido and Anna in *Aeneid* 4.[4]

In the light of this rich tradition of mime, a term which by the Hellenistic period could signify (at least) two cultural products, a poem of dramatic nature and superior literary qualities and an artless spectacle of an actor or an actress or a group of actors performing tricks, dancing lasciviously, and making improvised, obscene jokes, it is frustrating to be unable to point with certainty to the means by which (and the form in which) mime was transferred from Greek-speaking lands into Italy and Rome. Perhaps this happened, as I mentioned above, through the performances of traveling troupes of mimes or the presentations of mime-pieces at banquets. There is little doubt, however, that the Romans primarily got to appreciate Herodas and Theocritus as highly sophisticated nondramatic literature which, certainly in Theocritus's case and possibly also in Herodas's case, they sought to emulate and compete with. The performance in the Roman theater of pieces such as Virgil's *Eclogues* (if such an event ever took place: see Highet 1974, Quinn 1982, and Panayotakis 2008) is yet another manifestation of the Roman upper classes'

---

[4] Herodas and Plautus: Hunter 1995. Herodas and Virgil: Ellis 1891. Herodas and Cicero: Ellis 1900. Herodas and Persius: Marcantoni 1938, Bo 1967, and Tartari Chersoni 2003.

appreciation and acknowledgment of the literary genius and achievement of Virgil and Theocritus in the field of pastoral poetry, but literature of such high sophistication was normally transplanted into Rome as *reading material*, not through the channel of full-scale stage performance.

FURTHER READING

Many important contributions to the study of ancient Greek mime are in German and in Italian, so a good knowledge of these languages is necessary to students embarking on research related to the Hellenistic mime. The best account of mime in antiquity is still Wüst 1932 (the Hellenistic period is covered on pp. 1738–1739), to which Panayotakis 2010: 1–32 is indebted. Reich's massive and incomplete project (1903), often referred to in handbooks of ancient drama as the most authoritative introduction to ancient mime, is confusing and verbose. Nicoll (1931) writes in a very accessible style, discusses all periods in the develop- ment of mime as a form of entertainment, and is wonderfully illustrated, but he does not go deep enough. He needs to be supplemented by, among others, Swiderek 1954, Breitholz 1960, Wiemken 1972, and Mastromarco 1991. Wiemken 1972 deserves to be singled out because of its sharp focus on papyrus fragments containing pieces in Greek that have been labeled mimes (but some of his views, especially those related to the Imperial Greek mimes, have been recently challenged by Tsitsiridis 2011). On individual mime-actors, mime troupes, and docu- ments related to mime productions, see the invaluable Leppin 1992 and Maxwell 1993, along with Fountoulakis 2000 and Tedeschi 2002. Excellent accounts of the influence of Sophron's mimes on Theocritus's *Idylls* are in Burton 1995 and Hunter 1996a, Hunter 1996b: 116–123, and Hunter 1999: 10–11. The affinities between Theocritus's *Idylls* and Herodas are presented well in Simon 1991: 19–82 and Ypsilanti 2006. Herodas's short poems are now the topic of an exhaustive and bibliographically exhausting commentary published in two large volumes written in Italian: Di Gregorio 1997 and Di Gregorio 2004. Students interested in any aspect of Herodas as author and/or dramatist, including his ancient reception, would need to consult Di Gregorio, although there is still excellent value in the commentary of Cunningham 1971; Esposito 2010, which covers also Herodas's ancient and modern reception (on pp. 277–279), and the new commentary Zanker 2009 in the Aris & Phillips Classical Texts series are fine additions to the existing scholarship on Herodas. The fragments of the so-called "popular" Greek mime have been edited in Cunningham (2004) and have been translated into English also by Cunningham in the Loeb series (Rusten and Cunningham 2002: 362–367). But new Greek fragments which may be mimes have been found after the publication of Cunningham's work: see Elliott 2003 and West 2010. The *Fragmentum Grenfellianum* has recently received considerable scholarly attention. There are important contributions in Hunter 1996b: 7–10, Esposito 2002, Bing 2002, Esposito 2005 (an excellent monograph), and Battezzato 2009 towards the appreciation of the literary texture and significance of the piece. Nonetheless, the turning point for our better understanding of the literary qualities of the *Fragmentum* remain Crusius 1896 and Wilamowitz-Moellendorff 1896, and they should still be consulted. The bib- liography on the *paraklausithyron* and on its various manifestations in Latin literature is very rich; to give the reader an impression of how scholarship on this topic started and where it is going, I single out Canter 1920, Copley 1956, Schmeling 1971, Cairns 1972, Henderson 1973, and Johnson 2003–2004. The language and style of Decimus Laberius have been discussed by Panayotakis 2010: 57–67. My discussion, in this chapter, of Matius's fragments owes much to Kroll 1930 and to the comments of Courtney 1993: 102–106; Courtney also edited the extant corpus of Matius.

BIBLIOGRAPHY

Battezzato, L. 2009. "The *Fragmentum Grenfellianum*: Metrical Analysis, Ancient Punctuation, and the Sense of an Ending." In *The Play of Texts and Fragments: Essays in Honor of Martin Cropp*, edited by J. R. C. Cousland and J. R. Hume, 403–420. Leiden and Boston: Brill.

Bieber, M. 1961. *The History of the Greek and Roman Theater*. Princeton: Princeton University Press.

Bing, P. 2002. "The 'Alexandrian Erotic Fragment' or 'Maedchens Klage.'" In *The Bilingual Family Archive of Dryton, His Wife Apollonia and Their Daughter Senmouthis (P.Dryton)*, edited by K. Vandorpe, 381–390. Brussels: Koninklijke Academie voor wetenschappen letteren en schone kunsten van België.

Bo, D. 1967. "Note a Persio." *Rendiconti dell' Istituto Lombardo, Classe di Lettere, Scienze morali e storiche* 101: 150–155.

Breitholz, L. 1960. *Die dorische Farce im griechischen Mutterland vor dem 5. Jahrhundert: Hypothese oder Realität?* Stockholm: Almqvist & Wiksell.

Burton, J. B. 1995. *Theocritus' Urban Mimes: Mobility, Gender, and Patronage*. Berkeley: University of California Press.

Cairns, F. 1972. *Generic Composition in Greek and Roman Poetry*. Edinburgh: Edinburgh University Press.

Cameron, A. 1995. *Callimachus and his Critics*. Princeton: Princeton University Press.

Canter, H. W. 1920. "The Paraclausithyron as a Literary Theme." *AJPh* 41: 355–368.

Copley, F. O. 1956. *Exclusus Amator: A Study in Latin Love Poetry*. Madison, WI: American Philological Association.

Courtney, E. ed. 1993. *The Fragmentary Latin Poets*. Oxford: Clarendon Press.

Crusius, O. 1896. "Grenfells Erotic Fragment und seine litterarische Stellung." *Philologus* 55: 353–384.

Cunningham, I. C., ed. 1971. *Herodas: Mimiambi*. Oxford: Clarendon Press.

——. 2004. *Herodas: Mimiambi: Cum appendice fragmentorum mimorum papyraceorum* Munich: K.G. Saur. First published 1987, Leipzig: Teubner.

Di Gregorio, L., ed. 1997. *Eronda: Mimiambi (I–IV)*. Milan: Vita e Pensiero.

——, ed. 2004. *Eronda: Mimiambi (V–XIII)*. Milan: Vita e Pensiero.

Elliott, J. M. 2003. "A New Mime-Fragment (P.Col. inv. 546A)." *ZPE* 145: 60–66.

Ellis, R. 1891. "Note on the Epoch of Herodas." *CR* 5: 457.

——. 1900. "Ad Ciceronis epistulas." *Philologus* 13: 473.

Esposito, E. 2002. "Il pubblico del mimo popolare nell' Egitto tolemaico: Dryton e il *Grenfellianum*." *Eikasmos* 13: 199–214.

——. 2005. *Il Fragmentum Grenfellianum (P. Dryton 50): Introduzione, testo critico, traduzione e commento*. Bologna: Pàtron.

——. 2010. "Herodas and the Mime." In *A Companion to Hellenistic Literature*, edited by J. J. Clauss and M. Cuypers, 267–281. Chichester, UK, and Malden, MA: Wiley-Blackwell.

Fantuzzi, M., and R. Hunter. 2004. *Tradition and Innovation in Hellenistic Poetry*. Cambridge, UK: Cambridge University Press.

Fountoulakis, A. 2000. "The Artists of Aphrodite." *L'Antiquité Classique* 69: 133–147.

Fraenkel, E. 1960. *Elementi Plautini in Plauto*. Translated by F. Munari. Florence: La Nuova Italia. Originally published as *Plautinisches im Plautus* (Berlin, 1922).

——. 2007. *Plautine Elements in Plautus*. Translated by T. Drevikovsky and F. Muecke. Oxford: Oxford University Press.

Henderson, W. J. 1973. "The Paraklausithyron Motif in Horace's *Odes*." *Acta classica: proceedings of the Classical Association of South Africa* 16: 51–67.

Highet, G. 1974. "Performances of Vergil's *Bucolics*." *Vergilius* 20: 24–25.

Hordern, J. 2004. *Sophron's Mimes: Text, Translation, and Commentary*. Oxford: Oxford University Press.

Hunter, R. 1993. "The Presentation of Herodas' *Mimiamboi*." *Antichthon* 27: 31–44. Reprinted in R. Hunter, *On Coming After*. Part 1: *Hellenistic Poetry and Its Reception* (Berlin and New York, 2008), 189–205.

——. 1995. "Plautus and Herodas." In *Plautus und die Tradition des Stegreifspiels: Festgabe für Eckard Lefèvre zum 60. Geburtstag*, edited by L. Benz, E. Stärk, and G. Vogt-Spira, 155–169. Tubingen: Gunter Narr. Reprinted in R. Hunter, *On Coming After*. Part 1: *Hellenistic Poetry and Its Reception* (Berlin and New York, 2008), 212–228.

——. 1996a. "Mime and Mimesis: Theocritus, Idyll 15." In *Theocritus*, edited by M. A. Harder, R. F. Regtuit, and G. C. Wakker, 149–169. Groningen: E. Forsten. Reprinted in R. Hunter, *On Coming After*. Part 1: *Hellenistic Poetry and Its Reception* (Berlin and New York, 2008), 233–256.

——. 1996b. *Theocritus and the Archaeology of Greek Poetry*. Cambridge: Cambridge University Press.

——. 1999. *Theocritus: A Selection*. Cambridge: Cambridge University Press.

Johnson, T. S. 2003–2004. "Locking-in and Locking-out Lydia: Lyric Form and Power in Horace's C. I.25 and III.9." *CJ* 99: 113–134.

Kroll, W. 1930. "Cn. Matius." *RE* 14.2: 2211–2212.

Leppin, H. 1992. *Histrionen: Untersuchungen zur sozialen Stellung von Bühnenkünstlern im Westen des Römischen Reiches zur Zeit der Republik und des Principats*. Bonn: Habelt.

Marcantoni, J. D. 1938. "A Note on the Third Satire of Persius." *Mnemosyne* 6: 152.

Mastromarco, G. 1984. *The Public of Herondas*. Amsterdam: Gieben.

——. 1991. "Il mimo greco letterario." *Dioniso* 61: 169–192.

Maxwell, R. L. 1993. "The Documentary Evidence for Ancient Mime." PhD diss., University of Toronto.

McKeown, J. 1979. "Augustan Elegy and Mime." *PCPhS* 25: 71–84.

Nicoll, A. 1931. *Masks, Mimes and Miracles: Studies in the Popular Theatre*. London, Sydney, and Bombay: Harrap.

Panayotakis, C. 2008. "Virgil on the Popular Stage." In *New Directions in Ancient Pantomime*, edited by E. Hall and R. Wyles, 185–197. Oxford: Oxford University Press.

——, ed. 2010. *Decimus Laberius: The Fragments*. Cambridge: Cambridge University Press.

Quinn, K. 1982. "The Poet and His Audience in the Augustan Age." *ANRW* II.30.1: 76–180.

Reich, H. 1903. *Der Mimus: Ein litterar-entwickelungsgeschichtlicher Versuch*. Berlin: Weidmann.

Rusten, J., and I. C. Cunningham, eds. 2002. *Theophrastus, Characters; Herodas, Mimes; Sophron and Other Mime Fragments.* Cambridge, MA, and London: Harvard University Press.

Schmeling, G. 1971. "The *Exclusus Amator* Motif in Petronius." In *Fons perennis: Saggi critici di filologia classica raccolti in onore del Prof. Vittorio D'Agostino*, 333–357. Turin: Amministrazione della Rivista di studi classici.

Simon, F. J. 1991. *Tὰ κύλλ' ἀείδειν: Interpretationen zu den Mimiamben des Herodas.* Frankfurt am Main and New York: P. Lang.

Skutsch, F. 1892. "Der jüngere Plinius über Herodas." *Hermes* 27: 317–318.

Swiderek, A. 1954. "Le mime grec en Égypte." *Eos* 47: 63–74.

Tartari Chersoni, M. 2003. "I *Choliambi* di Persio: Osservazioni metrico-stilistiche." *Philologus* 147: 270–288.

Tedeschi, G. 2002. "Lo spettacolo in età ellenistica e tardo antica nella documentazione epigrafica e papiracea." *Papyrologica Lupiensia* 11: 89–187.

Tsitsiridis, S. 2011. "Mimic Drama in the Roman Empire (*P.Oxy.* 413: *Charition* and *Moicheutria*)." *Logeion* 1: 184–232. Available online at www.logeion.upatras.gr.

Villari, E. 2000. "Aristoxenus in Athenaeus." In *Athenaeus and His World: Reading Greek Culture in the Roman Empire*, edited by D. Braund and J. Wilkins, 445–454. Exeter, UK: University of Exeter Press.

West, M. L. 2010. "The Way of a Maid with a Moke: P. Oxy. 4762." *ZPE* 175: 33–40.

Wiemken, H. 1972. *Der griechische Mimus: Dokumente zur Geschichte des antiken Volkstheaters.* Bremen: Schünemann.

Wilamowitz-Moellendorff, U. von. 1896. "Des Mädchens Klage." *Nachrichten von der königlichen Gesellschaft der Wissenschaften zu Göttingen: Philologisch-historische Klasse aus dem Jahre 1896*: 209–232. Reprinted in U. von Wilamowitz-Moellendorff, *Kleine Schriften* 2 (Berlin, 1941), 95–120.

Wüst, E. 1932. "Mimos." *RE* 15.2: 1727–1764.

Ypsilanti, M. 2006. "Mime in Verse: Strategic Affinities in Theocritus and Herodas." *Maia* 58: 411–431.

Zanker, G. 2009. *Herodas: Mimiambs.* Oxford: Oxbow.

PART TWO

ROMAN COMEDY

I

....

Beginnings

....

CHAPTER 19

THE BEGINNINGS OF ROMAN COMEDY

PETER G. MCC. BROWN

For us, Roman comedy (and indeed Latin literature) begins with Plautus, since plays by him are the earliest Latin works to have survived complete; Livius Andronicus and Naevius are known to have written comedies before him, but we have only meager fragments of those plays, totaling about six lines by Livius and 135 by Naevius. All three authors wrote what came to be called *fabulae palliatae*, plays based on preexisting Greek comedies and set in Greece; they themselves called them simply *fabulae* ("plays") or *comoediae* ("comedies," transliterating the Greek word). According to the generally accepted chronology, Livius's first dramatic production was in 240 BCE (see Cicero's discussion at *Brutus* 72–73), Naevius's in 235 (Gell. 17.21.44–45); in other words, they began writing plays a generation before Plautus did. Since (unlike Plautus) both wrote tragedies as well as comedies, we cannot be sure that these were the dates of their first comedies rather than their first tragedies; Cassiodorus in his *Chronica* (under the year 239, as it happens) says that Livius gave the first performances of both tragedy and comedy at the *Ludi Romani* in that year, but Cicero regularly refers to one play only (at *Brutus* 72 and 73, *de Sen.* 50, *Tusc.* 1.3), and Gellius is inexplicit about Livius at 17.21.42 and about Naevius at 17.21.45, speaking in both cases of their "putting on plays." In any case, for both types of drama their seminal innovation was the adaptation of Greek plays for performance in Latin. (The evidence for this in the case of Livius's comedies is not strong, but it is consistent with what is known of the rest of his output, and there is no reason to doubt it.) The ancient sources for their activity make very little of this; Cicero, for instance, says only that Livius "was the first to put on a play" (*primus fabulam ... docuit*, *Brutus* 72), though there were surely dramatic performances of some kind at Rome before 240 (see below). But not the least remarkable aspect of the innovation is that Livius is said to have been a Greek from Tarentum: Latin literature as we understand the term (and as the Romans themselves understood it) was invented by a nonnative speaker, and the plays were written in meters imported from Greek drama that required to be adapted to the different nature of the Latin language. We do not know whether

Livius was the first to use these meters in Latin, but we have no strong reason to doubt it, and as Gratwick (1982: 93) says, "The origin of the Roman brand of iambo-trochaic verse remains a mystery, but whoever did invent the form ... was a genius."

We do not know, either, why Livius was selected for the honor of having his play (or plays) put on in 240, or what sort of evidence he had provided of his competence to write such works. It is possible that he had already written his translation of the *Odyssey* into Latin in the Saturnian meter, and perhaps he had been experimenting with this sort of activity for some years before he received the commission for 240. In any case, it was surely no accident that this first formal presentation of a Greek play in Latin came so hard on the heels of the end of the First Punic War in 241: "The games of which it formed part plainly served to celebrate that national victory ... Victory in the First Punic War not only confirmed Roman ascendancy in Hellenic south Italy but extended it to Hellenic Sicily. The accomplishment would be marked by elevation of the ludi to a cultural event that announced Rome's participation in the intellectual world of the Greeks" (Gruen 1990: 82, 84). There is abundant evidence for Roman contact with Greek culture well before this time, but the games of 240 marked a significant new development. Manuwald (2011: 36) stresses that "although the availability of a qualified poet such as Livius Andronicus probably contributed to the introduction of proper drama to Rome, the transplantation was presumably the result of a decision by the authorities rather than an organic process carried out by actors and/or writers who sought new areas for activity."

Feeney (2005) has rightly emphasized the peculiarity of Latin literature: "on the available evidence, no society in the ancient world other than the Romans took over the prototypical forms of Greek literature as the basis for a corresponding institution in their own vernacular" (Feeney 2005: 230, following Fantham and Mayer, as referred to there). On the other hand, it does not seem strange that there was a market for Latin versions or adaptations of acknowledged masterpieces of Greek drama, and perhaps no one at the time felt that Livius Andronicus was doing anything quite as grand as laying the foundations of Latin literature.

There were vigorous dramatic traditions of Greek origin in south Italy and Sicily from at least the early fifth century onwards, and Livius will have been familiar with them from his upbringing in Tarentum. Many Romans must also have been familiar with them to some extent, though the extent is hard to gauge. We have no evidence for visits of Greek theater companies to Rome until late in Plautus's career (Livy 39.22.2 and 10, 186 BCE—but it is not certain that the *artifices* mentioned there performed Greek texts), though Fraenkel (2007: 423) found it "not at all unlikely that they also occasionally appeared in Rome as early as the third century." In terms of political and military intervention, Rome had become progressively more involved in the affairs of the Greek cities of south Italy during the first quarter of the third century, and with the capture of Tarentum in 272 her control over these cities on the mainland was complete (Cornell 1995: 363–364). The First Punic War (264–241) added Sicily to her sphere of influence, and it has often been suggested that it was precisely while fighting in Sicily during this war that many Romans had become acquainted with the Greek theater, and that this stimulated a demand which Livius satisfied. Their campaigning in that area may indeed have heightened their awareness of the importance of the theater in Greek life, but how much time did Roman soldiers spend actually sitting through performances of Greek plays, and with what pleasure? We need not doubt that the theatrical traditions of south Italy and Sicily were crucial to the development of drama at Rome, but it is hard to assess the impact of Livius's innovation at the level of his audience's appreciation of the plays as plays: was he presenting versions of Greek plays to an audience already acquainted with productions of such plays in Greek, or was he introducing his audience for the first time to performances of this kind of material?

By the time of Plautus, the *palliata* took its Greek models almost exclusively from New Comedy, the plays of Menander and his contemporaries and successors. We cannot judge whether this was true already of Livius Andronicus and Naevius, but New Comedy certainly established itself before long as the dominant type of comedy all over the Greek-speaking world, and it is not hard to see why. The family-based romantic plots have a universal and timeless appeal, and references to contemporary events and personalities are rare, making the plays easy to export outside the confines of their first performance. (On the spread of New Comedy from the early third century BCE onwards, see Nervegna (2013). The catalogue of Webster, Green and Seeberg (1995), vol. 1, pp. 1-96 suggests that it had spread quite far already by the end of the First Punic War (for more on this, see Le Guen, this volume)).

Gruen (1990: 87), following Jory (1970), suggests that Livius imported his performers and other theatrical personnel from the south and that acting companies at Rome remained predominantly Greek at this time. It is an attractive idea that Livius turned to experienced practitioners from home for help with his pioneering work in an alien environment, though we may wonder how many Greek *actors* would happily have adapted to performing scripts in Latin; other members of the company would not have had the same difficulty, but there is no positive evidence that Greeks were regularly imported to form the nucleus of theatrical companies at Rome. Livius could perhaps have found experienced practitioners closer to hand if he wanted to, though it is always possible that his plays required more elaborate production resources than any entertainments previously seen at Rome. Plautus is said to have made money "in the service of performing artists" (*in operis artificum scaenicorum*, Gell. 3.3.14), and Greek theatrical practitioners can be referred to in Latin as *artifices*; but the word was used not only with reference to Greeks, and we cannot conclude that Plautus had worked with Greek artists (even if we believe the story). He clearly managed to get texts of Greek comedies from somewhere, and it is not at all unlikely that he had contacts with Greek companies, but we can only guess at the nature of his contacts.

In addition to keeping alive the dramatic traditions of mainland Greece, south Italy produced at least one local playwright in the early third century, Rhinthon, perhaps also from Tarentum. Rhinthon wrote what appear to have been mythological burlesques, known either as *phlyakes* or as *hilarotragoidiai*; Steph. Byz. p.603.1 (Rhinton—the editors' preferred spelling—K-A test. 2) speaks of him "transforming the tragic into the comic." We cannot say quite how his plays differed in ethos from the mythological burlesques of Athenian comedy, but they were written in Doric and there is no sign that they included a chorus (Taplin 1993: 48–52). A number of south Italian vases used to be thought to illustrate Rhinthon's plays, but Taplin (1993) has argued a powerful case for regarding them as illustrations of Athenian comedy, and in any case they are earlier than Rhinthon (now see also Csapo [2010: 52-67] and Rusten [2011: 434-454]). It is possible that Rhinthon had some influence on the Oscan "Atellan farces" (see below), but the only *fabula palliata* to which he seems conceivably relevant is Plautus's *Amphitruo*, the one mythological burlesque in that genre. Some later authors, quoted at Rhinton K-A test. 5, include *Rhinthonicae* among dramatic genres in *Latin*, and Schmidt (1989) suggests that this was the label given to the *saturae* mentioned by Livy in his account of the development of theatrical entertainments at Rome (see next paragraph). But there is no reason to believe this other than the desire to justify the claims of these later authors.

According to Livy 7.2.3–4, officially organized theatrical entertainments (*ludi scaenici*) had been instituted at Rome in 364 BCE, though he says that the type of entertainment then introduced, dancing to the accompaniment of a reed pipe (an importation from Etruria), was essentially undramatic. His account of how the theater developed at Rome between 364 and 240 is far from clear, but in outline his story is that the young men of Rome began to imitate the Etruscan dancers, "at the same time pouring forth jokes at one another in rough verses, their voices being accompanied by appropriate movements"; this became an established practice, and it had something in common with the tradition of "Fescennine verses," songs of ribald abuse sung at weddings. In this case, according to Livy, what were performed were rough, improvised exchanges of abuse. But "native artisans" (*vernaculi artifices*) somehow took over and performed "satires filled with rhythms [*impletae modis saturae*], their singing arranged for pipe accompaniment, and with appropriate movements"; it was Livius who "first dared to move away from satires" and who was the first Latin author to compose a play with a plot (7.2.8). The nature of these "satires" has been much debated, but Livy suggests they did not have much by way of a story line. It is not at all clear from his account how greatly the performances of the "native artisans" differed from those of the "young men" which they replaced, but for our purposes that does not matter very much. At some later stage (after Livius had introduced scripted plays with plots), Livy says that the young men left the acting of plays to professionals but maintained their own amateur tradition of exchanges of jokey abuse in verse; this became the source of what were later called *exodia* ("end pieces") and were above all mixed in with Atellan farces. Livy explains that Atellan farces were a kind of performance acquired from the Oscans (the original inhabitants of southern Italy, including Atella in Campania), and that the young men at Rome maintained a tradition of acting in them as amateurs "and did not allow them to be polluted by professional actors"; but he does not otherwise discuss the nature of the performance. It is generally believed that Atellan farces came into existence in Campania well before Livius's innovation of 240 and that they were an unscripted, improvised form of entertainment showing a small number of stock characters in a variety of situations; they must have had rudimentary plots, but the general view is that the plots were simply an excuse for a succession of comic routines. Their influence can be detected with some plausibility here and there in Plautus (e.g., in the exchanges between Labrax and Charmides at *Rudens* 494–552), and according to one school of thought (that above all of Lefèvre and his students, e.g., in Lefèvre et al. 1991) it is rather more thoroughgoing than that; but in most of his plays Plautus maintains a plot directed towards a happy ending. In any case, his comedies are scripted, based on Greek models, and highly sophisticated in their use of language and meter; if Livius Andronicus pointed Latin drama in this direction, that surely represented a significant departure from the ethos of Atellan farces.

Livy's account says nothing about the fact that Livius was a Greek, producing versions of Greek plays, nor does he mention any possible link with the Greek dramatic traditions of southern Italy and Sicily. Also, though he regards the importation of Etruscan dancers as significant, he says nothing about the fact that Etruria was a possible channel for Greek influence: there are strong reasons for believing that drama had developed under Greek influence in Etruria before the third century, and it is generally accepted that key terms of Roman theatrical language came into Latin from Greek via Etruscan, e.g., *persona* ("mask," "character") and *scaena* ("stage") (see Oakley 1998: 52). Campania too, the home of Atellan farce, was a region by now under Roman control and much influenced by Greek culture. It is surprising (if true) that Greek drama had not made more of an impact at Rome itself before the end of the First Punic War.

We find a very similar account of the origins of drama at Rome at Valerius Maximus 2.4.4, and a rather more general account at Horace, *Epistles* 2.1.139–176. It is probable that much in all these accounts goes back to Varro, who published several works on the theater and who to some extent seems to have assimilated the development of drama at Rome to what he believed to have been the case at Athens. Not all the details in Livy's account can be explained away as deriving from such assimilation, and Varro (if it was Varro) presumably had some reason for tracing *ludi scaenici* back to 364 BCE; but the surviving accounts of what happened between then and 240 do not help us greatly to understand the background to the plays and fragments that we possess. Horace, like Livy, mentions Fescennine verses as an element in the prehistory of Roman drama (2.1.145); unlike Livy, he is explicit (at 2.1.156–167) that there came a stage when the Romans tried their hand at imitating Greek drama (tragedy, to be precise). His dating of this "after the Punic Wars" (162) has been much discussed: perhaps Horace ignored the achievements of Livius Andronicus and Naevius and preferred to date the origins of Roman tragedy to the end of the *Second* Punic War in 201 BCE, when Ennius was writing (so Manuwald 2011: 38–39, among others).

One type of entertainment which is hard to define but was at least sometimes theatrical (and at least to some extent derived from Greek traditions) was the mime. This came to be associated particularly with the Floralia, the festival in honor of Flora, which was instituted in either 241 or 238; *ludi scaenici* were officially added to the festival in 173, when it became established as an annual fixture, but this was perhaps simply the formalization of what had already become customary, and there is some evidence to suggest that mimes were being performed at Rome before the end of the third century. However, we cannot trace the performance of mimes at Rome any further back than the end of the

First Punic War at the earliest. We thus cannot regard mime as a precursor of the *palliata* at Rome, though both may perhaps have begun to flourish there at about the same time. (On all this see Panayotakis 2010: 22–25 and Panayotakis, this volume) Much the same must be said about Atellan farces: they were clearly familiar to Plautus's audiences (see *Bacchides* 1088 and perhaps also *Rudens* 535), but we cannot pinpoint more precisely when they moved from Campania to Rome.

As far as our evidence goes, it was in the late third century that Rome witnessed an explosion of interest in dramatic performances of various kinds, and this is reflected in the increasing number of opportunities for the performance of drama at official festivals. It is generally thought that the only festival that regularly included *ludi scaenici* in 240 was the *Ludi Romani* in September. But other such festivals were quick to be added, in addition to the Floralia: the *Ludi Plebeii* (Bernstein 1998: 162–163) and perhaps also the *Ludi Ceriales* (Bernstein 1998: 169–171), both in or about 220, the *Ludi Apollinares* in 208 (Bernstein 1998: 183–185), the *Ludi Megalenses* in 191 (Bernstein 1998: 201–203; Plautus's *Pseudolus* was commissioned for performance on this occasion). By 200, at least eleven days every year may regularly have been given over to performances of plays, in addition to the occasional extra games that were put on for various reasons (Taylor 1937: 291); although we cannot be sure, it is quite possible that in 240 only one day at the *Ludi Romani* had been devoted to *ludi scaenici* (we know only that in 214 it was an innovation to devote four days to them: Livy 24.43.7). By the mid-first century BCE, the number had grown to forty-nine days a year (Wiseman 2008: 175, arguing that a great variety of types of drama must have been put on to keep audiences entertained on so many days), but the increase between the ends of the First and Second Punic Wars is striking.

Admittedly, Bernstein's account of the *Ludi Plebeii* and *Ceriales* has been queried by Wiseman (2008: 167–174), who has also argued that we should accept the evidence of Naevius fr. 113R; Ovid, *Fasti* 3.785–786; and Ps.-Cyprian, *De spect.* 4.1 that the Liberalia on March 17 originally included *ludi scaenici* (Wiseman 1998: 35–39, Wiseman 2008: 85); others have suggested in particular that when Naevius refers to the *Ludi Liberales* he means either the *Ludi Ceriales* or the Athenian Dionysia (see, e.g., Schur 1927: 82). Even if Wiseman is right, however, we can only guess at what sort of performances were put on at the Liberalia before the late third century.

More importantly for our purposes, Wiseman has suggested in a number of publications that Romans were at least acquainted well before 240 BCE with Greek-influenced satyr plays of some kind that included an element of mythological burlesque (see Wiseman 1988, Wiseman 2004: 87–118, Wiseman 2008: 84–139); if plays were performed at the Liberalia, satyr plays would be appropriate for a festival in honor of Liber, who was identified with Dionysus. The evidence for these plays are the scenes depicted on a number of engraved bronze caskets and mirrors dating from the late fourth and early third centuries BCE, one of them certainly made in Rome and all of them argued by Wiseman to be evidence for "the story-world of Latium in general" (Wiseman 2008: 85). He suggests that the scenes "may imply a kind of Dionysiac dramatic performance … in which one feature was the participation of *mimae* [mime-actresses]" (ibid. 119), and he takes them to indicate "a common fourth-century culture of mimetic representation extending far beyond the Greek cities of southern Italy into Latium and Etruria" (123). If we can take the engravings to represent performances with which the artists were familiar from real life, Wiseman is clearly right, and these illustrations could be relevant to the *impletae modis saturae* of Livy 7.2.7 (see Oakley 1998: 55–58). Unfortunately, we cannot rule out the possibility that iconographic traditions had a more tangential relationship to everyday experience, but there is no reason in principle to reject Wiseman's conclusions. It will remain true that Livius Andronicus's Latinization of masterpieces of Greek drama was a new development, and the plays of Plautus and Terence have little in common with satyr drama; but Livy may have exaggerated considerably in suggesting that earlier dramatic performances at Rome had no plot.

We have seen that a great deal of guesswork is involved in reconstructing the background to the beginnings of Roman comedy. The theatrical traditions of south Italy (certainly Greek comedies, and perhaps also Atellan farces) must have played an important part, but we cannot confidently trace all the routes that Greek comedy took on its way to Rome. Even if Etruria was one of the conduits for some types of Greek drama, it may not be very relevant to *fabulae palliatae*. One striking feature of these is that they have a much larger musical element and (particularly in the case of Plautus) far more metrical variety than we find in Greek New Comedy; Livy's talk of the *impletae modis saturae* that preceded Livius Andronicus may point us to the evolution of a local performing style that had a strong influence in this respect on the early authors of *palliatae* (for this and other theories of the sources of Plautus's metrical variety, see the excellent discussion of Duckworth 1952: 375–380). Ritual exchanges of abuse may also have exerted some influence (see Wallochny 1992). But all the evidence suggests that what Livius Andronicus and his successors did was radically different from what had gone before at Rome.

Further Reading

Manuwald (2011) is now the obvious starting point for further consideration of the issues raised in this chapter; she gives further bibliographical references. On the popularity of Greek drama in south Italy and Sicily, see Csapo 2010, ch. 2 (and Le Guen in this volume).

Bibliography

Bernstein, F. 1998. Ludi Publici: *Untersuchungen zur Entstehung und Entwicklung der Öffentlichen Spiele im Republikanischen Rom.* Stuttgart: F. Steiner.

Cornell, T. J. 1995. *The Beginnings of Rome: Italy and Rome from the Bronze Age to the Punic Wars (c. 1000–264 BC).* London and New York: Routledge.

Csapo, E. 2010. *Actors and Icons of the Ancient Theater.* Malden, MA: Wiley-Blackwell.

Duckworth, G. E. 1952. *The Nature of Roman Comedy: A Study in Popular Entertainment.* Princeton: Princeton University Press. Reprinted with additional bibliography, Bristol, 1994.

Feeney, D. 2005. "The Beginnings of a Literature in Latin." *JRS* 95: 226–240.

Fraenkel, E. 2007. *Plautine Elements in Plautus.* Translated by T. Drevikovsky and F. Muecke. Oxford: Oxford University Press. Originally published as *Plautinisches im Plautus* (Berlin, 1922).

Gratwick, A. S. 1982. "The Origins of Roman Drama." In *The Cambridge History of Classical Literature.* Vol. 2, *Latin Literature,* edited by E. J. Kenney and W. V. Clausen, 77–93. Cambridge, UK: Cambridge University Press. Available in paperback reprint of Vol. 2, part 1, *The Early Republic,* 1983.

Gruen, E. S. 1990. *Studies in Greek Culture and Roman Policy.* Leiden and New York: Brill.

Jory, E. J. 1970. "Associations of Actors in Rome." *Hermes* 98: 224–253.

Lefèvre, E., E. Stärk, and G. Vogt-Spira. 1991. *Plautus barbarus: Sechs Kapitel zur Originalität des Plautus.* Tübingen: Narr.

Manuwald, G. 2011. *Roman Republican Theatre.* Cambridge: Cambridge University Press.

Nervegna, S. 2013. *Menander in Antiquity: The Contexts of Reception.* Cambridge, UK: Cambridge University Press.

Oakley, S. P. 1998. *A Commentary on Livy Books VI–X.* Vol. 2, *Books VII–VIII.* Oxford: Clarendon Press.

Panayotakis, C. 2010. *Decimus Laberius: The Fragments.* Cambridge: Cambridge University Press.

Rusten, J., et al., ed. and tr. 2011. *The Birth of Comedy: Texts, Documents, and Art from Athenian Comic Competitions, 486–280.* Baltimore: Johns Hopkins University Press.

Schmidt, P. L. 1989. "Postquam ludus in artem paulatim verterat: Varro und die Frühgeschichte des römischen Theaters." In *Studien zur vorliterarischen Periode im frühen Rom,* edited by G. Vogt-Spira, 77–134. Tübingen: Gunter Narr.

Schur, W. 1927. "Liberalia." In *Paulys Real-Encyclopedie der classischen Altertumswissenschaft: Neue Bearbeitung.* Vol. 13, fascicle 25, *Libanos–Lokris,* edited by A. Pauly, G. Wissowa, and K. Ziegler, 69–70. Stuttgart: J. B. Metzler.

Taplin, O. 1993. *Comic Angels and other Approaches to Greek Drama through Vase-Paintings.* Oxford: Clarendon Press.

Taylor, L. R. 1937. "The Opportunities for Dramatic Performances in the Time of Plautus and Terence." *TAPA* 68: 284–304.

Wallochny, B. 1992. *Streitszenen in der griechischen und römischen Komödie.* Tübingen: Narr.

Webster, T. B. L., J. R. Green, and A. Seeberg. 1995. *Monuments Illustrating New Comedy.* BICS Suppl. 50. London: Institute of Classical Studies.

Wiseman, T. P. 1988. "Satyrs in Rome? The Background to Horace's *Ars poetica.*" *JRS* 78: 1–13. Reprinted in T. P. Wiseman, *Historiography and Imagination: Eight Essays on Roman Culture,* Exeter, 1994: 68–85.

——. 1998. *Roman Drama and Roman History.* Exeter: University of Exeter Press.

——. 2004. *The Myths of Rome.* Exeter: University of Exeter Press.

——. 2008. *Unwritten Rome.* Exeter: University of Exeter Press.

CHAPTER 20

FESTIVALS, PRODUCERS, THEATRICAL SPACES, AND RECORDS

GEORGE FREDRIC FRANKO

WHO and what was involved in taking Roman New Comedy from page to stage? This chapter considers how festivals, producers, and theatrical spaces influenced the plays seen by Roman spectators in the half century covering the original staging of the comedies of Plautus and Terence (ca. 210–160 BCE). The task daunts because the ephemeral festivals, obscure producers, and temporary theaters of the republic have left only vestigial records. Although the archaeological and epigraphic record for theatrical activity is much fuller for the empire, that evidence is of limited value because it stands generations removed from the conditions that shaped our only surviving scripts of publicly performed Roman comedy. Despite some continuities, the *comparanda* of Roman imperial theatrical traditions, like the precedents of Greek New Comedy, can mislead as well as illuminate.

The evolution of the theater in the middle republic reflects Rome's dynamic, selective, and often ambivalent conflation of native traditions with foreign—especially Hellenistic Greek—cultural influences. The scripts and fragments of the *comoedia palliata* (Roman New Comedy) do exhibit an enduring stylistic unity in their formulaic plots, stock characters, and—Terence excepted—linguistic texture. But their theatrical context was not constrained by rigid, atavistic structures and procedures. Experimentation and growth trumped permanency and consistency. What might hold true for the production of Plautus's *Pseudolus* in 191 BCE probably would not apply to Terence's *Andria* only twenty-five years later, even though both premiered at the same festival. Thus C. W. Marshall's fine account of *The Stagecraft and Performance of Roman Comedy* (2006) largely focuses on Plautus and appends only a few circumspect comments about Terence. Plautus's pervasive use of *hodie* ("right here, right now") proclaims and encapsulates an underlying spirit of transitory immediacy. Roman drama claimed no fixed public venue such as the Theater of Dionysus did in Athens, but rather it temporarily appropriated spaces designed for other purposes. Plays were not devoted to a single divinity such as Dionysus, nor restricted to a single festival, and thus new opportunities emerged, especially with the inauguration of cults and temples. While Athenian drama divides rather cleanly into tragedy, comedy, and satyr play, Roman drama resists the generic classifications imposed by later Roman scholars.[1] Since the genre of the *palliata* lends itself to improvisation and the expansion or contraction of scenes, the scripts— especially those of Plautus—most likely underwent significant modifications in the hands of producers, actors, and copiers before becoming fixed decades later. And while we isolate scripted drama for study today, an inhabitant of Rome probably viewed plays as part of a spectrum that seamlessly merged into unscripted drama and such parathe-atrical ceremonies as aristocratic funerals with their masked impersonations of ances-tors, triumphal celebrations, gladiatorial combats, and executions, and even courtroom proceedings. Unlike classical Athenian drama with its citizen actors, Roman actors were a mix of free and slave, and most authors were freedmen or foreigners with tenuous, newfound relations to the Roman citizen body. In short, a history of early festivals, pro-ducers, and theatrical spaces resists summaries or generalizations because evanescence and a lack of stable boundaries characterize Roman New Comedy in the era of Plautus and Terence.

FESTIVALS

With no permanent playhouse or theater in Rome until that of Pompey in 55 BCE, there existed no public venue for a continuous run of offerings. Nevertheless, audiences, performers, and other individuals associated with theatrical productions could rely upon the city of Rome to support an annual cycle of dramatic performances, supple-mented by occasional additions to the cycle. The Roman calendar regularly prescribed *ludi solemnes*, "sacred games" or celebrations in honor of divinities. These *ludi* included both shows on stage (*ludi scaenici*) and such varied entertainments as chariot races (*ludi circenses*), boxing exhibitions, animal hunts, and tightrope walking. Festivals spanned several days, all free of charge. Although the *scaenici* and the *circenses* occurred on dif-ferent days, the prologue to Terence's *Hecyra* (33–41) asserts that anticipation of boxers and a tightrope walker disrupted one performance of the play and a rumor of gladia-tors scheduled in the same venue terminated another. This assertion should be taken less as a condemnation of Terence's dramaturgy or the audience's boorish taste than as a reminder that plays, though an important component of *ludi*, did not constitute the only

---

[1] Distinction is fairly clear for *comoedia palliata* (Roman New Comedy set in Greece and adapted from Greek New Comedy) and *comoedia togata* (comedy set in Italy); more nebulous are *fabula praetexta* (Roman historical themes), *crepidata* (based on Greek tragedy), and *tabernaria* (probably a synonym for *togata*). Moreover, unscripted Atellan farce and mime eventually became scripted. See Manuwald (2011) and, on Atellan farce, Petrides in this volume.

or even the main attraction for many Romans. The truly spectacular shows were the blood sports and the *circenses*. In terms of capacity, many thousands more could view a chariot race in the Circus Maximus than could see and hear a play on a stage. While spectators might hope to catch a repeat performance of a play because of *instauratio* (see below) or possibly an encore, the slaughters of lions, panthers, bears, elephants, or African animals were one-time-only events (Livy 39.22.2; 44.18.8). In terms of financial outlay, blood sports were the expensive shows.[2] The state funded the *ludi*, but individual magistrates might supplement shows from their own purses to enhance their reputation and political profile.

By the end of Plautus's career, at least a dozen regularly scheduled days in the cycle of festivals offered plays, perhaps two dozen in Terence's time (forty-two days in 44 BCE, 100 days by 325 CE; see Taylor 1937). The total is much higher and more evenly spread throughout the year than the roughly six days at two festivals for classical Athens. In order of presentation, the *ludi* that included drama were:[3]

Name	Roman month; when inaugurated; when scenic	Honored deity	Supervising magistrates	Number of days for drama	Key references; known productions
Ludi Megalenses	early April; 204; annual and scenic from 194	Magna Mater	curule aediles	2 (6 in empire)	Livy 34.54.3; Cicero *de Haruspicum Responsis* 22ff.; *Pseudolus* 191; *Andria* 166; *Hecyra* 165 (aborted); *Heauton Timorumenos* 163; *Eunuchus* 161
Ludi Cereales	mid April; by 201; scenic by Augustus	Ceres (and Liber)	plebeian aediles	2 (7 in empire)	Livy 30.39.8
Ludi Florales	late April–early May; 241 or 238; annual and scenic 173	Flora	plebeian aediles	2 (5 in empire)	mimes rather than scripted comedies
Ludi Apollinares	mid July; 212; annual from 208; scenic from origin?	Apollo	urban praetor	2 (7 in empire)	Livy 25.12.11-15
Ludi Romani	September; 364; scenic after 240	Jupiter, Juno, and Minerva	curule aediles	4-6 (9-15 in empire)	Livy 24.43.7; *Phormio* 161; *Hecyra* 160
Ludi Plebeii	November; 220; scenic by 200	Jupiter	plebeian aediles	3? (9-13 in empire)	*Stichus* 200

figure 20.1 *Ludi* that included drama

---

[2] Suetonius (*Life of Terence* 2) records that Terence's *Eunuchus* was performed twice in one day and earned him a record 8,000 *nummi* (= sesterces?). That figure represents a small fraction of the expenses required for the total entertainment package, whose scale we can envision from the thirty talents (=720,000 sesterces) reportedly needed for a respectable gladiatorial exhibition (Polybius 31.28.6).

[3] In the era of Plautus and Terence, the Roman calendar was out of joint with the seasons. An eclipse on March 14, 190 BCE (our time), was recorded as July 11, and another on June 21, 168 (our time), was recorded as September 3. Consequently, many of those April shows would have occurred in chilly winter rather than pleasant spring.

The four known *ludi* for scripted Roman comedy were the *Megalenses, Apollinares, Romani,* and *Plebeii.* Probably these festivals also included unscripted mimes, the main attraction of the *Ludi Florales.* It is unknown when the *Cereales* became *scaenici,* but given the tenuous nature of our evidence, it would be precipitous to omit them from the list of possible venues for Plautus and Terence. Indeed, were it not for a production notice preserved with *Stichus,* we would have no evidence for drama at the *Ludi Plebeii* in Plautus's day.

The chart lists only the regularly occurring opportunities for public performances at Rome. To this we must add four types of occasional *ludi* that at least sometimes included plays:

(1) to honor Jupiter Optimus Maximus (firmly attested in 217, 207, 203, 194 BCE);
(2) to accompany temple dedications;
(3) to celebrate funeral games for aristocrats (Terence's *Hecyra* and *Adelphoe* were presented for L. Aemilius Paullus in 160; four days were devoted to *ludi scaenici* at the games for T. Quinctius Flamininus in 174);
(4) to fulfill a vow to a god made by a victorious general (M. Fulvius Nobilior in 186, L. Scipio in 186, and L. Anicius Gallus in 167, all of whom imported Greek performers for their *ludi*). Plays are not attested as part of a triumph proper until that of L. Mummius in 145 BCE (Tacitus, *Annales* 14.21, a vexed passage).

Two absences deserve comment. First, given the attractive interpretation that Roman comedy owed much of its appeal to the Saturnalian inversion of the normative Roman value system, it is perhaps surprising that the Saturnalia did not offer formal public *ludi scaenici.* In a sense, during the Saturnalia all Rome was a stage, and all its inhabitants comic players. Second, unlike the situation at Athens, Dionysus had no monopoly on theater. Varro's assimilation of Roman theater history to Athenian theater history may have led him to attribute the origin of *ludi* to rustic celebrations of Liber, the Roman Dionysus (Tertullian, *de Spectaculis* 5). Possibly dramas used to be staged on the Liberalia, a March festival in honor of Liber, and Ovid notes the conflation of Liberalia and the *Ludi Cereales* (*Fasti* 3.783–786). Nevertheless, Roman drama in this era apparently had nothing to do with Dionysus. The earliest association of actors in Rome, despite having some affinities with the *technitai peri ton Dionyson* (see Le Guen in this volume), took Minerva as its patron. Perhaps the choice of Minerva was simply prudent avoidance of the Roman aristocracy's discomfort with Dionysus/Liber, which reached a crisis with the senate's harsh suppression of Bacchanalian cult in 186 BCE.

We should not underestimate the influence of religion on the *ludi* in the middle republic. Claims that religious elements were subordinated to the political are at best unprovable and at worst reify a modern dichotomy foreign to the Roman mind. Divine directives to repulse the invading army of Hannibal led to the institution of the *Megalenses* and *Apollinares.* Plays were staged beside temples in part to impress and amuse the deities, as indicated by the custom of the *sellisternium,* the placing of a chair for the god to view and hear the production. The need to stage plays at various divine precincts contributed to Rome's reluctance to establish a single permanent theater.

Roman punctiliousness about the correct performance of religious ritual generated the phenomenon of *instauratio*, the repetition of a ritual from its beginning because of an interruption or irregularity. *Instaurationes* are specifically attested only for the *Ludi Romani* and *Plebeii*, but their frequency and potential duration is startling. Between 214 and 200 BCE, the *Ludi Romani* experienced *instaurationes* in eleven years, the *Plebeii* in nine. Livy (35.38.6) claims that the *Ludi Plebeii* in 189 BCE were repeated in their entirety five times; if they contained three days of *ludi scaenici*, that would have added fifteen days of performance. Some have speculated that a particularly good show could have induced intentional *instaurationes* to force encores, a possible but unprovable notion. Certainly repeated performances benefited audiences, supervising magistrates, hawkers, and so on, but we have no evidence of additional revenues for performers.

Ludi generated a holiday atmosphere by beginning with a colorful, noisy, and ribald parade followed by sacrifices, which meant consumption of meat likely washed down with wine (Dionysius of Halicarnassus 7.72.1–73.4, drawing on Fabius Pictor, a Roman source from ca. 200 BCE). The environment of joyous feasting perhaps inspires Plautine parasites to wax poetic on Italian pork products, and one might wonder if some plays were wreathed in the savory smoke of sacrificial victims. It is impossible to gauge the consumption of alcohol, or to what extent the symposiastic finales of Plautine plays reflect or encourage such celebration. The prologue of Plautus's *Poenulus* (41–43) advises raiding the cook shops before the play begins, and later a character pleads: "hurry up, the audience is thirsty" (1224). The prologues of Plautus and Terence beg noisy throngs for silence, and the speaker of *Hecyra*'s prologue claims that sometimes rowdy crowds drove him from the stage.

Since Roman *ludi* were not structured competitions as at Athens, the duration and sequence of events may have been fluid. We do not know how many plays were staged on a given day, or if there was ever a fixed number. Tragedies were not performed on separate days from comedies, and an indeterminate schedule could allow playwrights to explore generic tensions for comic opportunities. For example, the god Mercury, a figure appropriate to tragedy rather than a stock character for the *palliata*, declares in the prologue to Plautus's *Amphitruo*: "I shall divulge the plot of this tragedy. Huh? You frown because I said that this would be a tragedy? I'm a god; I'll transmogrify it. If you wish, I'll transform the same play from tragedy to comedy…I shall adulterate it. Presto: a tragicomedy" (51–55, 59). The joke exploits the audience's underlying uncertainty about the genre of the play about to be performed, even if it knew Plautus was the scheduled author.

Special *ludi* probably included productions of serious dramas on relevant themes, such as Ennius's historical *Ambracia* to celebrate M. Fulvius Nobilior's successful campaign there. But precious little connects comedies with specific festivals. Like Greek New Comedy, Roman New Comedy reveals none of the precise topicality of Aristophanic Old Comedy. Thus *Amphitruo*'s pervasive allusions to a triumphant general's homecoming cannot be connected with a particular commander. Were it not for the production notices in our manuscripts, we would have no basis for assigning any play to a specific festival. Terence's *Eunuchus* perhaps befits Magna Mater and her castrated priests, but how does *Pseudolus* befit the dedication of her temple? A joke about new aediles at *Trinummus* 990 suggests a staging in April, but no thematic connections emerge. Themes of adoption and the proper raising of sons make Terence's *Adelphoe* relevant to the life of Aemilius Paullus, but how did Terence and the actors have it written and rehearsed in time for his funeral? The case of Terence's *Hecyra* is more instructive: fully performed only in 160 at the *Ludi Romani* after aborted performances at the funeral games of Paullus and the *Ludi Megalenses*, the play suits all three contexts. Since Roman comedies exhibit a general carnivalesque and ludic atmosphere, they are portable with respect to occasion and performance space. An impresario might take his show on the road to other cities in Italy with longstanding, vibrant theatrical communities, such as those in Magna Graecia. After Rome's heavy dramatic schedule in April–May and the subsequent bimonthly opportunities for performance in July, September, and November, one-third of the year stood open for touring and making money in other Italian towns.

Producers

At the head of a company of performers (*grex*, "group") stood an *actor*, a term difficult to render precisely because his functions correspond to those of a producer, manager, or impresario, in addition to that of being the lead actor (see Brown 2002). He was not a director in a modern sense. Two *actores* stand out in our records. First is the shadowy T. Publilius Pellio, listed as *actor* in the production notice to Plautus's *Stichus*. In *Bacchides*, thought to be one of Plautus's later plays, the clever slave Chrysalus scoffs: "It's not the play but the *actor* that pains my heart. Indeed *Epidicus*, the play I love like my very self, I can't stand watching if Pellio's the *actor*" (213–215). Perhaps this is a metatheatrical joke to rib Pellio, who stands onstage. Perhaps the clever slave, a character who sometimes speaks as the mouthpiece of the poet, condemns the impresario Pellio for ruining a good script. If so, Pellio as *actor* apparently retains possession of the script, not to say exclusive rights, to produce *Epidicus*.

Second is L. Ambivius Turpio, speaker of at least two of Terence's prologues (*Heauton Timorumenos, Hecyra*) and identified by Donatus as portraying the title character in *Phormio*. In *Heauton Timorumenos* (35–47), Turpio claims that he grows weary of portraying running slaves, angry old men, hungry parasites, impudent tricksters, and greedy pimps at the top of his voice and with great effort. He declares that authors bring him plays full of action but take milder plays to another company, though he boasts of his ability to handle both styles. Clearly producers have no exclusive relationship with any one playwright. Both *actor* and author have the freedom to choose collaborations, quite unlike the Athenian system with state-appointed actors and producers for competitions. In *Hecyra* (11–27), Turpio describes his previous collaboration with the comic playwright Caecilius Statius, in which at first he was driven from the stage or barely held his place, but later his persistence and talent brought success. Restaging after initial setbacks implies a producer's retention of unsuccessful scripts, but we cannot know if a play's subsequent success involved any alteration of the script itself, a producer's change in the staging, or simply a friendlier audience. *Phormio*'s prologue clearly promotes the talent of the *actor* above that of the author for garnering popular success: "if [a rival poet] realized that when one of his new plays succeeded, it succeeded more because of the *actor*'s efforts than his own" (9–10).[4]

Since Roman magistrates entered office on March 15, one of the aediles' first duties likely was to prepare for a spate of *ludi* in April, including the selection of plays and letting of contracts for the construction of theatrical spaces. Aediles were neither professional bureaucrats nor CEOs of arts foundations—they were rising politicians for whom aesthetic considerations were not a priority, and many likely had no interest in the theater business beyond a few weeks in their annual magistracy. Terence's prologues offer perplexing glimpses of the process. *Eunuchus* 20–22 claims: "after the aediles purchased it [the *fabula*], a rival poet contrived for himself an opportunity to examine it and, when the official arrived, the play began." It remains unclear whether the *fabula* purchased by the aediles was the physical script from Terence or a promised performance from Ambivius Turpio. Remarks in the *Hecyra* prologue are similarly obscure. Turpio claims that the play is brand new rather than an attempt by the author to sell an old script for a second fee (5–7), which suggests Terence's control of the script. Turpio also boasts of putting on new plays bought at his own expense (*novas... pretio emptas meo*, 57), which suggests that he purchased scripts from authors and then sold productions by his troupe to magistrates. For what it is worth, Donatus construes the line to mean "bought at a price suggested by me," as if Turpio was a broker. We cannot determine if there existed a single, unchanging procedure for the period under discussion, and possibly different arrangements evolved for public *ludi* versus privately funded votive or funeral games.

The number and legal status of members in a producer's company is unknown, and no rule can be posited. Likely some were free men, likely some were slaves, with compositions changing over time. Claims that players were slaves and the *actor* was the *dominus gregis* ("owner of the group," *Asinaria* 2) extrapolate too much from jokes such as the conclusion of *Cistellaria* (782–785), which promises a drink for whoever performed well and a beating for whoever bungled his lines. There is no reason to assume that troupes performed exclusively tragedies or comedies, and prologue speakers in *Amphitruo* and *Captivi* toy with the possibility of the troupe staging a tragedy. Masks allowed a single actor to assume multiple roles and, perhaps, even different actors to play a single role; Turpio's boast of playing the various stock characters exemplifies the required range. Unlike Greek comedy and tragedy, Roman comedy clearly did not acknowledge a rule of three speaking actors, for many scenes have four or five concurrent speakers. Assuming role doubling, the extant comedies require anywhere from four to nine performers, excluding the musician. If economic considerations were primary, then we should posit a smaller troupe with jacks-of-all-trades. While we do not know who built

---

[4] Cicero (*De Senectute* 14.48) and Tacitus (*De Oratoribus* 20) praise Turpio as a model of excellent acting, and Symmachus (*Epistle* 10.2; 4th century CE) ranks both Pellio and Turpio among Rome's greatest.

the temporary wooden stages, *Menaechmi* 404 likens a ship's construction to "Pellio's equipment" (*supellex Pellionis*), which suggests that Pellio controlled wooden stage paraphernalia. That said, the company needed no stagehands for a crane or *ekkyklema*. Production notices for Terence's plays record the name of the *tibicen* (the musician playing the oboe-like instrument) as "Flaccus, slave of Claudius." Although actors had to rehearse with Flaccus, we cannot say whether he or Claudius was a permanent member of Turpio's troupe or a subcontracted performer.

Unlike the imperial era, for which inscriptions confirm a complex bureaucracy of specialists and middlemen, little evidence exists for early theater professionals unaffiliated with the *actor*. Two metatheatrical jokes in Plautus about a "*choragus*" provide an important exception. At *Persa* 159–160, we hear: "Whence the costume?" "Take them from the *choragus*, he must give them; he was contracted by the aediles to provide them." This metatheatrical joke suggests that the *choragus* operated independently of the troupe and that the producers did not retain control of costumes. *Trinummus* 857–860 supports this interpretation, for there a swindler claims that he obtained *ornamenta* (costumes) from a *choragus* at the latter's risk, implying rental. Editors assign the great extradramatic speech in *Curculio* to the *choragus* based on his allusion to "costumes I rented" (464). Donatus's claim (*ad Eunuchum* 967) that the *choragus* somehow supervised staging may refer to later practice, for apparently the Roman republican *choragus* was not the producer of a chorus as at Athens, but more the equivalent of the Hellenistic costumer (*himatiomisthes*). Whether the control of the *choragus* extended to other theatrical "software" such as masks, props, or backdrops is uncertain. The prologue in *Captivi* (61–62) declares that it is not right for the troupe to perform a tragedy with a comic *choragium*, a term the ancient grammarian Festus glosses as "*instrumentum scaenarum*" ("stage apparatus"). The domain of the *choragus* might thus extend to the some of the "hardware" of the stage construction itself.

How the *actor* rehearsed with his company remains unclear. He had a complete script, but we do not know if the other actors received only their speaking parts as in Elizabethan practice (and suggested by a first-century CE papyrus of Euripides's *Alcestis*), or excerpts, or if they learned orally from a prompter without a physical script. Literacy throughout a troupe cannot be assumed. With no permanent stage, rehearsals must have occurred off-site. *Eunuchus* proves that an aedile witnessed a rehearsal, and the ability of Terence's rival to preview a script or performance suggests that the process was not entirely behind closed doors. Playwrights may have modified their scripts in rehearsal, especially if they acted in their own plays. There is no reason to reject claims in the ancient sources that Livius Andronicus performed on stage and that Plautus made a living in the theatrical process (*in operis artificum scaenicorum*, Gellius 3.3.14). Terence apparently did not, but he likely had opportunity for interaction with the *actor*, as implied by the following (possibly apocryphal) anecdote. Donatus (on *Phormio* 315) records that during a rehearsal Turpio delivered Phormio's lines while drunk and picking his ear with his pinky, and Terence exclaimed that Turpio portrayed the parasite just as he had envisioned him while writing the script.

How many plays did a producer rehearse for staging at a given festival? For the funeral games of Aemilius Paullus, Turpio evidently had both *Adelphoe* and *Hecyra* ready— one brand new play and one retained by the company for five years. Since *Eunuchus* was staged twice in one day to meet demand, we must wonder about the conclusion of *Pseudolus*: "if you wish to applaud and approve this troupe and play, I'll invite you to tomorrow's" (1334–1335). Does "tomorrow's" allude simply to the cliché of closing with a joking invitation to dinner? Or does the speaker promise another performance of *Pseudolus* (whether an encore or a repetition precipitated by *instauratio*), another new play by Plautus or someone else, or a revived old favorite? And who decided? Although there was no formal contest for best play, the mention of claqueurs (*Amphitruo* 67) and exclamations at *Trinummus* 705–706 might suggest competition ("Excellent! Excellent, Lysiteles! Encore! You've easily won the palm; he's defeated; your comedy has triumphed!"). If there were no bonus for an additional performance, there would be no advantage for a company to give away its product, making encores and *instaurationes* more problematic. The stable organization of the Athenian dramatic festivals allowed finite preparations for the producers, and for us it enables precise calculations of the numbers of tragedies or comedies staged annually. For Rome, we cannot conjecture whether the demand for productions in a given year was for a handful or over a dozen, for new plays or revivals or a mixture, nor how many authors or companies met those needs, nor what percentage of tragedies or comedies might be desirable.[5] Since the joke about Pellio in *Bacchides* and Turpio's repeated restaging of *Hecyra* implies that producers retained the scripts, we should consider the possible emergence of a repertory system to meet Rome's hunger for comedies. The formulaic plots, stereotyped staging, stock characters with their routines resembling the *lazzi* of the commedia dell'arte, and strong Italian traditions of improvisatory drama make it feasible to envision quick refreshment of old scripts. For comparison, we learn from *Henslowe's Diary* that the Admiral's Men at the Rose in May 1595 CE, working Monday through Saturday, mounted twenty-seven performances of fifteen different plays, some of which were not new plays that season.

The demand for plays and the competition or collaboration among producers, companies, and authors influenced script formation, circulation, and preservation. Producers (and actors) were fully capable of reworking scenes and parts, as evidenced by the textual doublets that abound in Plautus and the alternate endings preserved for both his *Poenulus* and Terence's *Andria*. Companies clearly revised scripts in response to performance conditions changing over time and space, which means that our extant scripts could derive not from the author's manuscript but from recomposition from incomplete actors' copies or memories. The wildly incompatible versions of *Hamlet* in Quarto 1, Quarto 2, and the Folio offer an instructive parallel. The *Casina* prologue

---

[5] We have twenty-one scripts of Plautus, plus quotations from another thirty-two named plays. His oeuvre likely exceeded that total of fifty-three known titles, and Gellius claims that over 130 scripts were attributed to Plautus. We know forty-two titles for comedies by Caecilius Statius and thirty-four by Naevius. Ribbeck's 1898 collection of comic fragments lists twenty authors of the *palliata* from Livius Andronicus (ca. 240 BCE) to Turpilius (ca. 104 BCE); their output cannot be quantified.

states: "Nowadays the new comedies they produce are even more debased than the new coins. So after we heard the rampant rumor that you fervidly fancy Plautine plays, we dusted off an old-fashioned comedy of his that you greybeards liked...This play, when it premiered, topped them all!" (9–17). Our extant script derives from a later staging still within living memory of the premiere, and the producer sets his production squarely against newer, inferior examples of the genre. Terence's prologues repeatedly emphasize that the plays are new, perhaps to tout their novelty against revival productions. Terence declares that "*Colax* was an old play of Naevius and Plautus" (*Eunuchus* 25), which might suggest a single Greek original turned into two Roman plays, a play with joint authorship, or a Plautine redaction of an existing Naevian script. Ancient scholars disagreed on the attribution of several titles to Plautus or Naevius, and thus we should not immediately dismiss the claim of Aulus Gellius (3.3.13) that Plautus redacted some plays by older poets and thereby imbued many scripts with a uniform Plautine style. The 130 scripts that circulated under Plautus's name make not an impossibly large total for an individual when compared with the output of Menander, to say nothing of Sophocles, Euripides, and Aeschylus. If Plautus flourished for three decades, he would need to churn out four scripts per year. Certainly the *ludi* provided enough opportunities for performance, and the almost mechanical features of his dramaturgy—Greek models, stock characters, formulaic plots—make individual authorship plausible. But the improbably comic name Titus Maccius Plautus ("Dick McClown the Mime Guy") could proclaim the identity of a corporate body, a comedic troupe not unlike Monty Python, rather than an individual. We shall never know, but we should perhaps liken the poetic output of "Plautus" to that of "Homer": a masterful stylization of traditional yet mutable scripts, refined by several hands through performance before a live audience, only crystallized at a later date by readers and actors operating under different performance conditions.

THEATRICAL SPACES

To speak of Roman "theaters" rather than "theatrical spaces" assimilates the Roman experience to the Greek and thereby sets up inappropriate expectations and parallels. The salient feature of Roman theatrical spaces during the time of Plautus and Terence is the lack of a singular permanent venue devoted to drama. The stone and concrete theaters that impress modern visitors to so many ancient Mediterranean sites date from centuries later. Plautus and Terence did not compose scripts either for the Greek-style theaters nestled into the hillsides of Ephesus, Epidaurus, and Delphi or for the Roman-style freestanding concrete theaters, as at Pompeii. Their plays could, of course, be adapted to a theater with a raised concrete stage, an orchestra, permanent doorways, and a *scaenae frons*, such as we might see today at Merida or Hierapolis, but such settings alter the original staging. Stone theaters existed in Magna Graecia from the fourth century BCE, and in other Italian towns by the end of the second, but no physical space permanently devoted to theater existed in Rome until the end of the republic.

The despair of vacuum must not lead us to posit a steady evolutionary development of theater architecture from Hellenistic Greece to imperial Rome, still less reify some sort of theatrical "missing link" in the era of Plautus and Terence based on earlier and later visual evidence. We cannot project forward from the stages depicted on the so-called *phlyax* vases from Southern Italy in the fourth century BCE. Even if we assume accuracy in representation within the conventions of vase painting, those stages accommodated a different genre (Attic Old Comedy) for a culture with a different theatrical heritage (Greeks nurtured on classical and Hellenistic Greek plays rather than Romans fusing Greek scripts with their native Roman/Oscan/Etruscan performative traditions). Nor can we project backward from theatrical scenes in first-century CE wall paintings from Pompeii and Herculaneum. Those fanciful, trompe-l'oeil images are not replicas: they address aesthetic priorities other than architecturally accurate commemoration. Again, the prescriptive rather than descriptive designs of the architect Vitruvius, writing in the age of Augustus, are seldom found in imperial theaters and do not even attempt to inform us about the ephemeral Plautine and Terentian theatrical spaces.

Plautus and Terence wrote for a variety of spaces temporarily repurposed for theater. Only two precise venues can be asserted with confidence: the heart of the *Forum Romanum*, a frequent site of funeral games, and the open area before the steps of the temple of the Magna Mater on the Palatine. In the middle of *Curculio* (462–484), the *choragus* abandons the fictive setting of Epidaurus to give his audience a guided tour of the contemporary Roman Forum. The physical stage must have been very near the *comitium* in the Forum for the speech to work (Moore 1991). By cruel irony, we cannot generalize from the most site-specific passage in Roman comedy. Though brilliant, the speech is entirely detachable; *Curculio* may be performed elsewhere with the speech omitted or revised for a new venue. We cannot even know that the extant speech pertained to the original performance. As to the Palatine, Cicero tells us that the *Ludi Megalenses* were celebrated in front of the temple of Magna Mater in the very sight of the goddess (*de Haruspicum Responsis* 24). Sander Goldberg's "Plautus on the Palatine" (Goldberg 1998) assembles the scant evidence to corroborate Cicero's claim and to demonstrate how *Pseudolus*, whose premiere honored the dedication of the temple, fits into that space. For example, when the two-line prologue advised the spectators to stretch their legs, the listeners sat on newly laid temple steps. The location makes perfect sense if we recall the religious nature of the *ludi* and allow that a play's most important spectator—the deity—determined a temporary theater's location.

Among other venues, temple precincts offered an obvious choice both for religious reasons and for the availability of tiered steps for seating (or performing) adjacent to an open space. While part of the *Ludi Apollinares* occurred in the circus, its *ludi scaenici* likely were staged hard by the Temple of Apollo, and thus magistrates attempted to construct a permanent theater in 179 adjacent to that temple (Livy 40.51), near the site of the later Theater of Marcellus. Once we grasp that the term "Roman theater-temples" is more accurate than "Roman theaters" for the republic, we can appreciate Pompey's quip that his theater—Rome's first permanent stone theater—really was a temple of Venus with adjacent seating for spectacles (Tertullian, *De Spectaculis* 10; see Hanson

1959). To what degree staging incorporated the architecture of nearby temples is unclear. References to Apollo's shrine acquire metatheatrical immediacy if performed next to his temple, but one can still use a stage altar, and so it remains hard to distinguish imaginary sacred space from real. No one assumes that Euclio in *Aulularia* grabbed a shovel and began digging at the shrine of Fides on the Capitoline. But if Plautus's *Amphitruo*, which celebrates the birth of Hercules, accompanied the dedication of the Temple of Hercules Musarum in 187 BCE, then we might fruitfully speculate how the unique reference to Mercury climbing *in tecto* ("onto the roof," 1008) and the unique appearance of Jupiter as *deus ex machina* could allude not simply to a two-story stage building but to the temple facade.

The Circus Maximus and Circus Flaminius also may have offered venues. A passage in the Greek historian Polybius (30.22) proves that at least one special theatrical show occurred in the Circus Maximus in 167 BCE. Within the scripts themselves, a remark such as "Now I must perform my tricks (*ludi*) in the Circus in front of my house" (*Miles Gloriosus* 991) tantalizes us by momentarily dissolving the boundary between the play's Greek geography and Roman topography and allows us to envision the actor standing in the Circus Maximus. Temporary structures built for actors and spectators during the *ludi* need not have been exclusively or primarily for drama. The aforementioned chapter in Polybius reveals that the show included (and intermingled) musicians, dancers, and boxers, as well as tragic actors. To Terence, the spectators who disrupted his *Hecyra* looking for gladiators were the crass intruders; but to those spectators, Terence's listeners were the snooty squatters depriving them of prime and limited seating for the main event.

Wherever the venue, the arrangement and small size of the temporary theatrical spaces encouraged intimacy and permeability in dramaturgy and staging; there is no sense of "the fourth wall." Roman comedy had no orchestral space, and thus spectators sat or stood in close proximity to the actors, with only a thin and porous boundary between them. The *Poenulus* prologue celebrates an intimacy between actors and audience absent from Greek New Comedy and its context of huge theaters: "let no stinking whore sit on the stage, nor lictor mutter, nor his rods, nor usher scuttle around in front or assign a seat while an actor is on stage" (17–21). The clever schemers in Roman New Comedy exploit this closeness by treating their audiences as confidants, whereas audiences of Greek New Comedy sit as observers. The nature of the performance space encourages Plautus's frequent direct address to spectators during the play via second person verbs and appeals to *spectatores*, and it intensifies his metatheatrical jokes that dissolve the imaginary barrier between the world of the play and the world of the audience. The configuration of the stage within the theatrical space remains unknown and perhaps variable, and the terms *scaena* and *proscenium* appear interchangeable in our sources. The sense of intimacy and permeability makes it fair to question the assumption that early Roman comedy always used a proscenic rather than a thrust stage, and it allows us to speculate that running slave routines might pass through and interact with spectators. The smaller capacity of temple precincts also fostered the sense of close familiarity. Based upon the topography of the playing space and area for the audience,

Goldberg (1998) calculates that at most a couple thousand could have witnessed the premiere of *Pseudolus*. While this total represents only a small fraction of the classical, Hellenistic, or imperial theater capacities, it is comparable to Shakespeare's Globe (1,500–3,000). Small spaces could create the demand for encore performances. Was the staging of *Eunuchus* twice in one day at the *Ludi Megalenses* a spontaneous encore for the same satisfied crowd or a second showing for those who could not squeeze in for the premiere? Even the very fact that some Roman spectators stood must have generated a tension or energy different from that of an audience entirely seated as in a Greek theater.

Though the lack of topographic specificity in Roman comedy may frustrate our inquiries, it allows plays to adapt to the realities of shifting venues having different acoustics, sight lines, and spatial relationships with the audience. For example, rather than posit a convention that the forum must stand stage left and the port stage right, we should allow that the forum is on the right when a play was performed on the Palatine, left when performed on the Aventine, and so on, as demanded by a particular site. The convention of one to three doors on stage proved more powerful than the variety of venues for dramaturgy; that is, Roman playwrights did not compose one way for Palatine and another for Forum, in contrast with (e.g.) the later Shakespearean romances, which befit the intimate, candlelit indoor Blackfriars rather than the grander, open-skied Globe.

Records

Since Roman dramatic performances were not part of a competition as at the Dionysia or Lenaea in Athens, details of productions almost never survived into the permanent epigraphic or literary record. Bankrolling a dramatic show was not like a liturgy at Athens, where a private individual would seek the permanent and publicly enshrined honor of funding a chorus. Scattered references to a prize for best actor or company (*Amphitruo* 69–74, *Poenulus* 37–39) generated no impetus to compile lists of competitors and winners for public display. If Roman magistrates kept such records, they were housed out of sight and out of mind. This absence hampers not only us but also those Roman scholars in the later republic, such as Accius and Varro, who sought to reconstruct histories of their national drama along Athenian lines. Worse still, the findings of those republican scholars have not survived except in anecdotes and truncated excerpts in later imperial antiquarians and grammarians, such as Aulus Gellius or Donatus. The scattered observations on drama among the Roman historians present confused and confusing data because they invoke drama to suit the narrative purposes of military and political history. Livy, for example, makes a hash out of the introduction of drama, Livius Andronicus, and the Etruscans (see Brown in this volume). The orators offer useful comments, but their observations derive from reading scripts and seeing performances under theatrical conditions far different from the original practices.

Our manuscripts preserve *didascaliae,* brief production notices preceding Plautus's *Stichus* and *Pseudolus* and all the plays of Terence. These *didascaliae,* which date from decades after the play's initial production, provide valuable but minimal information. Generally they list the author and title of the Greek original; year, festival, and supervising magistrates; producers; composer of music; and type of pipes. We must resist the temptation to standardize and appear definitive, for these seemingly factual notices still contain riddles that undermine confidence and generate scholarly controversy. For example, the *didascaliae* list two *actores* for Terence's plays: alongside L. Ambivius Turpio we find L. Atilius Praenestinus named for four plays and L. Sergius Turpio for another. Were Atilius and Sergius assistant *actores* for the aging Ambivius Turpio? Supporting actors? Producers of later revivals or touring troupes? In one manuscript of *Adelphoe,* a certain Minucius Prothymnus, identified by Donatus as an actor in tragedies, appears in place of Turpio as *actor* alongside Atilius. The *didascalia* for *Phormio* in our oldest manuscript assigns the play not to the *Ludi Romani* but to the *Megalenses,* and Donatus concurs. Additionally, the garbled names of the consuls in that manuscript appear to refer to 141 BCE, which might reveal a revival production rather than confusion or scribal error. While the prominence given to musicians rather than actors provides a salutary reminder of music's importance to Roman comedy, commemoration of the type of pipe in the script (rather than the musical score) represents a strange bit of trivia likely of interest only to performers.

As noted in the discussion of theatrical spaces, iconography provides very limited help because we have no contemporary Roman theaters, vase paintings, or wall paintings. Presumption of continuity is unwarranted, for just as we cannot retroject Hellenistic Athenian practices onto classical, so we cannot apply images of later Roman republican or imperial practices onto Plautus and Terence.

FURTHER READING

Although Manuwald (2011) supersedes previous comprehensive surveys, chapters in the sane overviews of Beare and Duckworth remain useful. Csapo and Slater conveniently provide the essential literary and epigraphic primary sources; Garton provides a prosopography of actors. Beacham's survey, while good on the empire, too uncritically accepts ancient evidence and facile interpretations for the republic.

Beacham, R. 1991. *The Roman Theatre and Its Audience.* Cambridge, MA: Harvard University Press.

Beare, W. 1964. *The Roman Stage.* 3rd ed. London: Methuen.

Bieber, M. 1961. *A History of the Greek and Roman Theater.* 2nd ed. Princeton: Princeton University Press.

Csapo, E., and W. Slater. 1995. *The Context of Ancient Drama.* Ann Arbor: University of Michigan Press.

Duckworth, G. 1994. *The Nature of Roman Comedy.* 2nd ed. Norman: University of Oklahoma Press.

Garton, C. 1972. *Personal Aspects of the Roman Theater*. Toronto: Hakkert.

Goldberg, S. M. 2005. *Constructing Literature in the Roman Republic*. Cambridge, UK: Cambridge University Press.

Gruen, E. 1992. "The Theater and Aristocratic Culture." In *Culture and National Identity in Republican Rome*, by E. Gruen, 183–222. Ithaca: Cornell University Press.

Jory, E. 1986. "Continuity and Change in the Roman Theatre." In *Studies in Honour of T.B.L. Webster*, edited by J. Betts, J. Hooker, and J. Green, 143–152. Bristol, UK: Bristol Classical Press.

Moore, T. 1994. "Seats and Social Status in the Plautine Theatre." *Classical Journal* 90: 113–123.

Rawson, E. 1985. "Theatrical Life in Republican Rome and Italy." *Papers of the British School at Rome* 53:97–113.

Sear, F. 2006. *Roman Theatres: An Architectural Study*. Oxford: Oxford University Press.

Bibliography

Brown, P. G. McC. 2002. "Actors and Actor-Managers at Rome in the Time of Plautus and Terence." In *Greek and Roman Actors: Aspects of an Ancient Profession*, edited by P. Easterling and E. Hall, 225–237. Cambridge, UK: Cambridge University Press.

Goldberg, S. M. 1998. "Plautus on the Palatine." *JRS* 88: 1–20.

Hanson, J. A. 1959. *Roman Theater-Temples*. Princeton: Princeton University Press.

Manuwald, G. 2011. *Roman Republican Theatre*. Cambridge, UK: Cambridge University Press.

Marshall, C. W. 2006. *The Stagecraft and Performance of Roman Comedy*. Cambridge, UK: Cambridge University Press.

Moore, T. 1991. "*Palliata Togata*: Plautus,*Curculio 462–86*." *AJPh* 112: 343–362.

Taylor, L. R. 1937. "The Opportunities for Dramatic Performances in the Time of Plautus and Terence." *TAPA* 68: 284–304.

CHAPTER 21

....

PLAUTUS BETWEEN GREEK COMEDY AND ATELLAN FARCE: ASSESSMENTS AND REASSESSMENTS

....

ANTONIS K. PETRIDES[*]

BROACHING the question of Plautus's relationship with the various forms of Italian "popular" theater, and thus with his public's horizon of theatrical expectations, seems nowadays obvious and indispensable. However, when this discussion first emerged in the first decades of the twentieth century, and as it flared up mostly from the 1960s onwards, it represented a major breakthrough in Plautine scholarship. Investigating the formative stimuli of non-Greek or "nonliterary" traditions in the theater of Plautus was tantamount to emancipating Plautine studies from the despotic grip of Greek New Comedy; it was a decisive swing away from earlier attempts, earnest but desperate, to disinter the Greek originals from under piles of corrupting "plautinisms" (in German, *Plautinisches*).

This chapter critiques some of the most significant trends, advancements, and possible overstatements of twentieth- and twenty-first-century Plautine scholarship with respect to the competing influences of (Greek) "literary" and (Italian) "popular" theater on Plautus's comedy. By "popular theater," of course, one means the native traditions of Italy, primarily the *fabula Atellana*, and the Greek *phlyax*, as well as various Greek and Latin forms of mime and other such forms of performance with which the playwright himself and his public were deeply imbued and which necessarily conditioned their response to his work. The predominant characteristics of these theatrical traditions were silly buffoonery and uninhibited scurrility; wordplay, verbal skirmishes (*velitationes*),

[*] Warm thanks are due to David Konstan, Vayos Liapis, and Sophia Papaioannou for their very useful suggestions.

and other self-indulgent linguistic mechanisms (for instance, hyperbolic mythological exempla); lively physical action, slapstick, and situation comedy developed gratuitously to the detriment of verisimilitude; extemporaneity, and hence correspondingly loose and inconsistent dramatic plots; and stock characters (stupid and lascivious old men, hapless young lovers, crafty slaves, greedy parasites, cooks, pimps, professional soldiers, etc.), associated with traditional comic routines (conventionally called *lazzi* after the commedia dell'arte) and lacking coherent, realistic characterization. Finally, this kind of "popular" theater generally refrains from any manifest moral or sociopolitical agendas to the benefit of unadulterated farce. After all, the *malitia* or "heroic badness" of the quintessential Plautine hero, the scheming slave, consists in a sweeping and wanton schadenfreude and an unabashedly carnal self-interest. The divergence of this theatrical mode from the moralizing Menander and his logically crafted plots is striking.

This chapter comprises two sections. In the first, in an inevitably selective survey, whose reach, I hope, can be extended by the Further Readings section appended to the end of the chapter, I consider how the study of Plautus in juxtaposition with the native theatrical traditions of south Italy has been impacting Plautine studies, most momentously since 1922, the year Eduard Fraenkel published his epoch-making *Plautinisches im Plautus*. It goes without saying, of course, that this review is not by any means a "history of Plautine scholarship"; its goal is to show how the study of the intricate interplay between the two traditions that shaped Plautus's legacy, Greek New Comedy and the native performance traditions of Italy, paved many new avenues of critical insight, inaccessible as long as Plautus was considered, at best, a semiskilled usurper of Menander, Diphilus, and Philemon. Briefly put, the "Italian connection" provided a strong stimulus for scholars eventually to look at Plautus *for Plautus*, to understand in depth and in detail his techniques of *composition* (rather than merely of "adaptation"), and to position his Roman New Comedy in the context of the culture that produced and nourished it. This was a monumental journey for Plautine scholarship (find in Further Readings under the rubric "Review articles on Plautine scholarship" a number of general summaries of the work done on Plautus, mainly from the 1930s onwards).

Nevertheless, amidst all the understandable scholarly enthusiasm that the discovery of this brave new world of Plautine originality and distinctiveness has caused, at least in some aspects of Plautus's theater his divergence from the Greek code may have been exaggerated. I illustrate this possibility in the second part of this chapter by way of a relevant case study—namely, the question of masked performance on the Plautine stage. The nature of the Plautine mask, indeed whether Plautus used masks at all, is a puzzling open question, and the conviction that Plautus's comedy cross-pollinates with Italian culture and Italian "popular theater" plays a significant part in it: both schools of thought, those who believe that Plautus's actors did not perform in masks as much as those who hypothesize a hybrid *palliata* mask system generated by Atellan "interferences," base their theories, logically, on the premise that Plautus functioned in a cultural context different from the Greek. Nonetheless, coming full circle, the scale is nowadays liable to tilt too sweepingly in favor of the Italian element.

"POPULAR THEATER" AND THE HISTORY OF PLAUTINE STUDIES

As with many other fine things in Plautine studies, momentum for change in the way scholars assessed how Plautus handled the constituents of his art was generated chiefly by Eduard Fraenkel's *Plautinisches im Plautus* (1922; Italian translation 1960 with addenda). Fraenkel, to be sure, still worked under the paradigm of Plautus as an adapter, but no longer in order to recover the precious but regrettably lost Greek models. Rather he attempted to pinpoint, as an end in itself, Plautus's originality and playwriting craft. As the preface to the belated (2007) English translation puts it (Fraenkel 2007: xi): "by refocussing attention onto Plautus himself (primarily his characteristic modes of expression, but also the comic stage-action drawn from the non-literary traditions of Italy) Fraenkel attempted to transcend his origins." Those origins lay in the German analytical school and particularly in Leo's *Plautinische Forschungen* (1912), whose project, tellingly, had been "aus Plautus und Terenz die Technik der attischen Dichter entnehmen" ("to learn the technique of the Attic poets from Plautus and Terence," Leo 1908: 46). Fraenkel did not just rise above this reductive approach to Roman theater; his book sparked a veritable revolution in Plautine studies with very wide ramifications. He truly "pointed the study of Plautus in directions that are still being explored" (Fraenkel 2007: xi).

Naturally, over the course of the years many have found that Fraenkel's groundbreaking work could benefit from supplementation, adjustment, and refinement. It has been remarked, for instance, that many of Fraenkel's "Plautine" elements may indeed have been Plautus's additions to the specific originals he was adapting, but they were not necessarily alien to the Greek theatrical tradition; i.e., they are neither Plautine inventions nor features inescapably to be thought of as derived from Italian "popular" drama (see Further Readings under the rubric "On the doubtful 'Plautinity' of some 'Plautine' elements"). Furthermore, in his influential *Roman Comedy* (1983), David Konstan argued that even the sociopolitical conditions evoked by Plautine comedy are not altogether dissimilar from what we know from Menander, inasmuch as, at least on some level, they continue to affirm the idea of the polis. We need to keep this caveat in mind. Exaggerating Plautus's divergence from the Greek New Comedy tradition may not be fairly said of Fraenkel (the man himself provided answers to such criticisms in an addendum to the Italian translation of his work; see Fraenkel 2007: xii). However, it was not unknown in post-Fraenkelian scholarship.

For all the necessary fine-tunings, Fraenkel's overall methodology is still considered generally applicable today. Even the impressive textual discoveries of the second half of the twentieth century did not disqualify his approach in any fundamental manner. The comparisons of the corresponding scenes from Plautus's *Bacchides* and Menander's *Dis Exapaton,* for example by Eric Handley in his 1968 inaugural lecture and by W. S. Anderson in his *Barbarian Play* (Anderson 1983: especially 1–29), are a case in point. Both scholars eloquently show how Plautus's comic technique leans towards a "de-construction" (no reference to Derrida here) of the serious, tense, sentimental Menander along the parameters of farcical absurdity, insouciance, verbosity, and musical animation; that is, along the lines of "popular" theater—even if Anderson's underlying thesis that Plautus's intent was to "criticize" Menander and "implicitly enact the conquest and defeat of decadent Greece" (Anderson 1993: 140) may not be generally accepted.

Nevertheless, there can be little doubt that in the wake of Fraenkel, scholars no longer treat Plautus as a second-order phenomenon. They look at him as an autonomous, self-sufficient and ultimately original unity, as "the sum of his parts" (Segal 1968: 6). The farcical or "popular" elements of Plautus's art are now being reassessed as the organic constituents of a new whole, not as opportunistic instruments for enhancing the comicality of flat, intellectualist Greek models and thus for augmenting the plays' appeal to a notoriously fickle Roman audience that could be easily distracted by rival entertainments at the *ludi*. Even the perceived "stylistic unity" of the *palliata* before and after Plautus was ascribed by one scholar, albeit tentatively, to the influence of Greek and Latin south Italian theater, which stretched as far back in time as Epicharmus (Wright 1974: 187–196).

As Plautine studies grew ever more sophisticated, the importance of the Greek original as an interpretive factor petered out; Niall Slater (1985: 6) even makes a point of confining any discussion of it to the endnotes of his book. Correspondingly, modern discussions of the Greek playwrights whose plays Plautus adapted (such as that lately of Philemon in Bruzzese 2011) study the Greek fragments closely but pay only scant attention to Plautus. At long last, Plautus and Roman comedy have ceased being adduced simply as an appendage to the study of Menander and his colleagues, and can eventually be reincorporated into their rightful cultural and historical framework. The theater of Plautus can now be seen even as a polemically "national theater," which integrates native forms "to distinguish itself proudly from alien and (often) culturally threatening or dominating" forms and theories of drama (Castellani 1995). Plautus's "barbarian plays" have been believed to play ironically with "the ideological clash between Greece and Rome, the hate-love, inferiority-superiority ambivalence that characterizes this long and complicated relation" (Anderson 1993: 139). The latest tweaks of this theory, more redolent of neo-Marxist theories of culture, abandon the notion of nationalistic antagonism and instead ascribe a more introverted, Rome-oriented function to Plautus; he is seen as a polyphonic enunciator of social discourse, one who articulates (noncommittally and impartially) social "perspectives which assimilate uneasily to those propounded by the senate and the Roman ruling class" (Leigh 2004: 1; cf. also the views of Kathleen McCarthy analyzed below). Matthew Leigh's Plautus does not necessarily "confirm the Romans in their superiority" (Anderson 1993: 139–140) over the disdainful *Graeculi*, but evokes "the necessary negotiations attendant on rapid political and economic change" in Rome after the first Punic War. The progress from the old image of Plautus as a derivative shadow of Menander and other Greeks is tremendous.

Plautine studies have finally reached a stage in which the (one would think) self-evident premise that "Greek drama and Roman drama are distinctively different forms" (Wiles 1988: 261) is not only paid lip service but actively assimilated into scholarly discourse, sometimes even to a fault. The opposition between "Plautinisches" and "Attisches" (Jachmann 1931) no longer suffices to interpret the distinguishing features of Plautus; on the contrary, this conventional opposition is expanded by a third element, the Italian extempore tradition, which had informed both the taste of Plautus's audience and, as is commonly assumed, Plautus's own professional experience prior to taking up the art of the playwright. It is standard lore nowadays that what makes up the uniqueness of Plautus's achievement is the interplay of Greek, Roman, and native Italian elements. Hence, scholars now construct Plautus's distinctive *Romanitas* around a "triadic model" (Vogt-Spira 1997). "In Plautus," writes Slater (1985: 8), "the Greek, South Italian and Roman theatrical traditions collide with explosively creative results." Most importantly, Plautus is now believed to *supersede* the very traditions that are at the same time formative of and antagonistic to his own drama. The whole is finally acknowledged to be more important than the parts.

It can be argued, therefore, that in the history of Plautine studies, acknowledging the significance of the motley theatrical practices associated with "popular theater" was pivotal to, perhaps even the main impetus toward, a beneficial renegotiation of Plautine originality altogether, as well as to the reassessment of his engagement with the history, culture, and society of his time. In order to conceptualize how Plautus amalgamates the Greek and Roman ingredients of his art into a new irreducible theatrical product, i.e., in an attempt to develop a positively "triadic" reading of Plautus, two overarching theories and methodologies prevailed in Plautine studies of the late twentieth century: (a) the "saturnalian inversion" theory, first proposed by Erich Segal's *Roman Laughter* (1968); and (b) a set of approaches focusing on metatheater, "orality," and improvisation, thus touching on Plautus's compositional techniques, performance practices, or, in the best of cases, both, as in Niall Slater's *Plautus in Performance* (1985), T. J. Moore's *The Theater of Plautus* (1998), and C. W. Marshall's *Stagecraft and Performance in Roman Comedy* (2006).

There have been at least three varieties of the "saturnalian" approach, each with a number of advocates. First was E. Segal's aforementioned take, hailed by many as a trailblazer and criticized by others (for instance by Wiles 1988) as too schematic in his Freudianism and too saturated with the spirit of the 1960s. Segal observed the "humble" beginnings of Roman drama in "the 'rustic banter' that delighted farmers during the September holidays of a bygone age" (Segal 1968: 8). The occasions for comedy and holiday license continued to coincide throughout Plautus's career. In the spirit of the holiday and by manipulating farcical (i.e., "popular") elements alien to his Greek raw material, Segal's Plautus offered his audience, in the controlled and circumscribed environment of the *ludi*, an inverted image of their stern moral universe and the impossible exemplum of the *mos maiorum* in the age of Cato the Elder. This topsy-turvy world, however, in which cunning slaves reign supreme and authority is trampled on by plebeian vigor and self-justifying buffoonery, represents only a temporary reordering of the world, and one that barely elicits social revolution.

Many have doubted how historical Segal's image of this puritanical Rome that briefly lets go actually is. Yet the general notion that Plautine comedy tackled the "serious" issues of morality and authority as it negotiated the various dichotomies that constituted its universe (Greece/Rome, slave/free, father/son, duty/pleasure, etc.) took root. In 1977, Gianna Petrone gave Segal's theory a better-received turn toward audience response theory (Petrone 1977): her Plautine audience could juggle "moral" and "antimoral" impulses in the plays. Petrone refuses to linger on distinguishing the Greek and Roman elements exactly, and her argument is exclusively anchored to the *Stichus*, but as a refinement of Segal's thesis its value is wider—although whether or not the play's end does reflect popular jubilation springing from Rome's defeat of Hannibal, and exactly how it does so, should remain an open question (see Owens 2000). Audience response is never monolithic, after all.

Finally, a more recent trend is inspired by Mikhail Bakhtin's musings on dialogism and the carnival, by neo-Marxist studies of ideology, and by Michel Foucault's notion of discourse. An example of the approach is Kathleen McCarthy's *Slaves, Masters and the Art of Authority in Plautine Comedy* (2000). McCarthy considers Plautus's plays part of the so-called "public transcript," and she probes "the investment socially dominant Romans had in Plautine comedy" (McCarthy 2000: x, as all quotations in this paragraph). However, she is far from conceiving of the terms "Plautine comedy" or "socially dominant" as stable, univocal concepts. Injecting Petrone's contradistinction between "moral" and "antimoral" tendencies in Plautus with a dose of Bakhtin, McCarthy understands Plautine comedy "as the dialogic interaction of two very different modes of comedy, a naturalistic mode and a farcical mode," each with its distinctive dramatic devices but also its unique way of "envisioning the functioning of authority in the world." For the "naturalistic" mode hierarchies are transcendent; for the "farcical," arbitrary. Unlike Petrone, however, McCarthy notes most importantly that audience members necessarily occupy shifting positions toward the role of domination in their everyday life, so their investment in the one mode or the other must be shifting, too. Audience members have "a stake in both the clever slave's rebellion and the master's reassertion of control in the finale," hence the play's "liberatory potential" is only relative and transitory (cf. Segal's analogous position mentioned above).

This much suffices to show how fruitful the "saturnalian inversion" theory proved in the sequel; also exceptionally fertile have been metatheatrical approaches to Plautus interested in the oral and improvisational techniques he inherited from "popular theater." By "improvisation" one refers to an impromptu method of creating theater, one relying not on a full-fledged written script but on roughly sketched plot lines, stock roles, and traditional routines. In improvisatory theater, that is, the composition and performance of a play are simultaneous processes. According to this theory, improvisation also often coincides with "metatheater," a moment of theatrical self-consciousness, in which the dramatic illusion is ruptured and the performance allows the spectator to perceive its artificiality.

Again, the theory has been variegated and polymorphous. Here I would like to spotlight three different ramifications of it that I consider most suggestive. In answering the question of how Plautus exploited native Italian improvisational traditions, scholars have variously contended that: (a) he exploits extempore techniques only to assert his superiority over the popular tradition (Vogt-Spira); (b) he produces only a literary imitation of improvisation as a means to render transparent the theatricality of his work (Slater); or finally, (c) that Plautus's texts as transmitted to us are not the scripts created for the performance *ante eventum* but transcripts of the largely ad-libbed real event (Marshall).

Vogt-Spira developed his theory in two seminal articles (Vogt-Spira 1995, Vogt-Spira 1997).[1] In his view, the real competition for the early Roman dramatists was not their *exemplaria Graeca* but the other forms of drama flourishing in contemporary Italy. Hence Plautine procedures of adaptation can only be truly appreciated if seen from the perspective of orality, i.e., according to the principles of *ad libitum* acting, which, through the *Atellana*, the mime, and similar forms of "popular" theater, fostered the theatrical *Erwartungshorizont* of Plautus's audience. Plautus "transfers to the written medium" elements of extemporaneity in language and style, such as conducting the dialogue in accordance with the catchword technique of *par pari respondere* (taking a cue from the previous speaker's words without really answering him with any logical consistency: see, e.g., *Asinaria* 591–597) or the *verbivelitatio* (an indulgent duel of exchanging insults). Improvisational elements are detected in Plautus's scene structure and composition, too, for instance in scenes that do not advance the action but merely mark time, breaking down the "goal-directed" plot of New Comedy, or in which characters seemingly devise the plot as they go along (the most famous but by no means the only relevant example is the *Pseudolus*). However, as Vogt-Spira notes, Plautus reminds his audiences constantly that his plays are *not* extempore compositions but written plays derived from written models. Writing and literacy are constantly emphasized as preconditions of Plautine drama; they even acquire thematic significance in many plays (via circulating letters, for example, or by reminding the audience, in sardonic self-deprecation, that what they are watching is the result of an artless "barbarophone twist" of a Greek play; cf. *Asinaria* 11, *Maccius vortit barbare*). Vogt-Spira's Plautus distinguishes himself emphatically from and elevates himself above the *Atellana*; he supersedes both popular theater by taking over its comic qualities and, by logical extension, New Comedy by "funny-ing up" its scripts.

Vogt-Spira positions improvisation in the field of generic antagonism between Plautus and the rival native forms still flourishing in his time: Plautus absorbs in order to surpass. For Slater, Plautus *imitates* in order to refresh and to renew. Slater's fundamental position, developed most fully in his influential *Plautus in Performance* (1985) and later in a series of papers (e.g., Slater 1994, Slater 2004), is that improvisation in Plautus is but a literary imitation of the actual practices Plautus had encountered in the native traditions in which he was trained. Such contrivance is part of Plautus's agenda to incorporate both illusory and nonillusory theatrical elements in his plays and to "open up" his

---

[1] English translation of the former in Vogt-Spira 2001.

performance to metatheatrical transparency. Paradoxically, Slater infers, through a variety of nonillusory techniques Plautus creates *the illusion of un-scriptedness* in his performance. The figure of the cunning and roguish slave, people like Leonida, Chrysalus, Epidicus, Simia, and of course Pseudolus, who so often, seemingly on the spot, generate intrigues couched as play-within-the-play, are paramount in Plautine literary "improvisation" and have become, to a large extent thanks to Slater's own work, an emblem of Plautine theater. "Plautus' remarkable achievement," Slater notes, "is to include self-conscious awareness of theatrical convention in a new concept of comic heroism" (Slater 1985: 16). Because of their ability to improvise, the clever slaves acquire the awesome faculty of theatrical transformation, of "changing skins" (*versipellis*). Like puppeteers, or indeed like playwrights, they have the sheer mind and willpower to control all the characters that surround them, be they masters, pimps, or other slaves. They also possess the creative intelligence to conjure up unlikely solutions to impossible problems. To be sure, this kind of *servus callidus* has precedents in the Greek tradition, but unless the surviving evidence deceives us completely, the character rises to a wholly different status in the hands of Plautus.

Finally, C. W. Marshall's theories of Plautine improvisation (Marshall 2006, mainly 245–279) could be perceived as an Anglo-American response to the so-called Freiburg School of Plautine studies, a group of mostly German scholars influenced chiefly by the work of Eckard Lefèvre and Ekkehard Stärk. The Freiburg School has provided the staunchest (and, in the eyes of British and American academics at least, the most extreme) advocacy of Plautine originality to date (see Further Readings under the rubric "On the work of the Freiburg School"). This group of scholars, which considers itself the "Neoanalytical" equivalent to Fraenkel's "Analysis" (see Brown 1995: 677), has suggested that some Plautine plays (like the *Asinaria* or the *Menaechmi*) are entirely original creations independent of specific Greek models, while some others are so radically reworked that the original "instigation" wanes into a distant echo. In a book that can be seen as a manifesto of sorts for the Freiburg School, *Plautus Barbarus* (1991), Plautus is envisaged as constructing his plays afresh with a mind to the improvisatory techniques of the *Atellana,* that is, designing or redesigning whole scenes according to the logic and the requirements of extempore performance. Suggestively, Vogt-Spira co-authored this book with Lefèvre and Stärk, but the positions expounded here do not posit the balance between the components to be found later in Vogt-Spira's "triadic model"; rather, the Freiburg School's Plautus is *(re)working within* the native Italian theatrical tradition. He does not antagonize it, and he does not imitate its traits in a literary fashion; instead, he recasts New Comedy in an original Roman style, one in which the constituent Greek parts are inextricably fused with the more weighty, original Plautine elements, or, even more strongly put, whose influences were never anything more than a mere creative spur. Peter Brown described this tenet succinctly, in a long and important review of *Plautus Barbarus*, which can stand as an encapsulation of Anglo-American skepticism towards the Freiburg School: "Traditionally, 'Atellan' passages have been seen as Plautine incrustations on a Greek skeleton; now it is suggested that Plautus regularly composed whole scenes in a style so thoroughly characteristic of impromptu performance traditions that there is practically no scene left if you try to remove the elements which display that style—*it is the skeleton that is 'Atellan'*" (Brown 1995: 677, my emphasis).

Marshall echoes the Freiburg School when he allows a much wider scope for improvisation in the conception and execution of Plautus's plays than Slater or Vogt-Spira; yet contrary to both these scholars and to the Freiburg School, who still postulate improvisation or the literary imitation thereof as an *authorial* technique, Marshall is speaking of *actual* improvisation by the *actors* in the real time of Plautine performance. Vogt-Spira and Slater both regarded Plautine "improvisation" as a phenomenon of the written medium. Marshall, although clarifying that Plautus does not practice "pure" extempore theater, believes that his performance still "contained moments of improvisation" (Marshall 2006: 261). The "improviser," for Marshall, is not the playwright, as for Vogt-Spira, or the character, as for Slater, but the actor himself during the real event. Marshall believes that Plautus gave his actors only "a skeletal outline" of the scenario, and that the rest was the product of collective inventiveness on the spot. He even ventures the guess that the Plautine text as transmitted is not in fact the script of the performance, which may never have existed as a text prepared prior to the event, but a *transcript* created later as a record of the performance by *both* Plautus *and* the troupe.

Marshall assembles three classes of evidence in support of this theory. The first is the presence of "doublets" in the text. By these he refers to lines containing the same information with only slightly different vocabulary and structure. Such doublets, which Otto Zwierlein had regarded as interpolations (see Zwierlein 1990, Zwierlein 1991a, Zwierlein 1991b, Zwierlein 1992), are better seen, according to Marshall, as variants resulting from different performances (he points, by way of example, to *Pseudolus* 209–224 and *Poenulus* 123–128). The second class of evidence includes what Marshall terms "elastic gags" or "modular units." These are basically expandable comic routines developed and kept by actors in order to fit into different performances, where they are more or less applicable (for instance in *Mercator* 120–188). Marshall's third class of evidence has to do with the economics and the logistics of theatrical production. "The strongest reason," he writes, "to accept an element of improvisation in the performance of the plays of Plautus is that, when social context is also considered, the alternative is much more unthinkable." *Palliata* troupes, he maintains, had every reason to be cost-effective, but "scribal copying and verbatim memorisation [of a prewritten text] represent a wasteful use of both preparation time (both must precede useful rehearsals) and financial resources" (Marshall 2006: 273). The greatest weight of responsibility for fleshing out the performance, Marshall hypothesizes, must have been shouldered by two or three actors, who were not illiterate as the rest of the troupe are supposed to have been (Marshall 2006: 274). At least these individuals could have received their parts beforehand.

Marshall's theories push the *palliata* closer to the mime and the *Atellana*, in fact closer to the commedia dell'arte, than any other form of comedy we know. Taking his cue from the Freiburg School, Marshall denies Otto Zwierlein's attempts to ascribe sweepingly to a reviser any instances in Plautus's text where logic and consistency are breached, and thus to understand the "real" Plautus as falling in closely with his Greek models. Significantly, however, Marshall also thwarts the Freiburg School's intent to associate the plays exclusively with improvisatory theater, and thus to establish as proofs of Plautine originality and independence every suspicion of a *Stegreifspiel*: such "improvisations," Marshall warns, can exist either in an unscripted or in a scripted environment (for instance, the play-within-a-play). To a large extent, such elements have also been found to exist in the Greek tradition, too, contrary to earlier beliefs (e.g., the *servus currens*).

Some readers, of course, may still find that to move from "performance variants" (which can still be interpolations or insertions from a defective copy of the text)[2] and "elastic gags" (which can still be literary imitations) to the notion of a full-blown improvised performance does take a certain leap of faith. It may also be objected that the theory of the Plautine text as a collectively produced transcript of the ad-libbed event, for which there is admittedly little independent support anyway, may be contradicted by the accompanying assumption that for the leading actors there was in fact some kind of prepared written script that needed copying and memorizing: if Marshall's three actors were indeed the "pillars" of the whole show, this prepared script would be considerably more sizable (and costly) than a mere "skeletal outline."

We can be fairly certain, nonetheless, that Plautus took advantage of the comic possibilities of improvisation and that he produced at least a literary imitation of extempore theater, infusing ad-libbing techniques into the written script to create a semblance of unscriptedness. We can also rely on the finding that Plautus's performances resonated with his audiences on an ideological level and were not just pyrotechnics of inconsequential fun and farce. Such a refreshed understanding of Plautus as a playwright who juggles creatively his competing influences and moves with virtuosity between Greek New Comedy and Atellan Farce is the invaluable legacy of ninety years' worth of scholarly revisionism sparked by Eduard Fraenkel.

A CASE OF OVERCOMPENSATION? "POPULAR" THEATER AND THE NATURE OF PLAUTUS'S MASKS

As I have suggested, however, symptoms of the excessive dissociation of Plautus from his Greek points of departure can be found. Such may be the case of recent theories concerning the supposed influence of the *Atellana* on the nature of the *palliata* mask system before Terence, particularly on the physical appearance of the mask. Regarding Plautus's masks and popular theater, two hypotheses have been proposed by scholars in

---

[2] Jonathan Bates in his edition of Shakespeare's *Titus Andronicus* (3rd Arden Series, 1995, repr. 2004) discusses a number of possible false starts, doublets, and other inconsistencies in the text as evidence that the First Quarto of the play was set from the author's defective papers (I thank Professor V. Liapis for this reference). On doublets in Terence, see Benjamin Victor's chapter in this volume.

the past one hundred years: first, that Plautus used no masks at all, mainly because his actors were not the upper-class gentlemen of the *Atellana*; second, that he developed and employed a "syncretic" system of his own which conflated the Greek types with those of the Oscan farce.

The "no mask theory" used to be prevalent primarily among continental philologists, who approached Plautus as literature, largely disregarding (or misapprehending) the realities of performance. The arguments of this theory are no longer considered very strong. The ancient evidence has been exhaustively sifted (see Further Readings in this chapter) and need not be detailed again here.[3] By no means do these garbled, ambiguous, and late testimonies provide conclusive proof that the Romans, whether for reasons of religion, actors' social class, or otherwise, eschewed the use of masks in the time of Plautus, although they accepted it in the time of Terence. We would need much stronger and more explicit confirmation to adopt such a counterintuitive view, especially since the archaeological data show that the mask was everywhere in both the Hellenistic and the Roman world: proliferating as an object of dedication and decoration, a souvenir or a generic reference to the theater, the mask was the most visible and recognizable piece of theatrical σκευή in postclassical performance (see Green 1994: 105–141). Wiles's commonsensical position in this matter remains the most valid: the Romans could not have borrowed everything else from Greek theater except from the masks. "It is reasonable to assume," Wiles writes, "that the external ritual forms of the Great Dionysia—its masks, costumes, and music—were seen as more important than the aesthetic principles of poets. From a practical point of view, moreover, it is hard to see what could be gained by an abandonment of the mask, since the actor needed to be seen at a distance" (Wiles 1991: 132).

The "no mask theory" is thus fast losing momentum and credibility. The "syncretic mask" hypothesis, on the other hand, thrives among Anglophone classicists and theater scholars and is still influential. It comes in at least two varieties. The first, which we could brand "the subverted mask theory," builds on Cesare Questa's premise that Plautus employed a simplified version of the Greek taxonomy along the lines of Atellan farce (Questa 1982). It suggests that Plautus "uses his fixed repertory of masks to subvert the narrative and aesthetic codes of Hellenistic theatre" (Wiles 1991: 134), with or without changing the physical outlook of the mask. The second version of this theory hypothesizes proper visual syncretism: the masks of Plautus were hybrids that conflated the mask of Greek New Comedy with the mask of the *Atellana*.

The "subverted mask" theory maintains that Plautus deconstructed the semiosis of the Greek mask through "ever-new variations upon the relationship of actor and actant" (Wiles 1991: 135). Time and again in Plautus, the same mask indeed subsumes the traits of different Greek mask genera (or subgenera). For instance, the *mulier* in

---

[3] The main exhibits are Diomedes, *Gramm. Lat.* I, 489 Keil; Cicero, *De Orat.* 2.193, 3.221; *De Div.* 1.80; *De Nat. Deor.* 1.79; Evanthius, *De Com.* VI. 3; Donatus, *Praef. ad Ter. Eun.,* 6; *Praef. ad Ter. Adelph.* 6; *ad Ter. And.* IV.3.1; Festus, p. 217 Mueller. For a synoptic overview of the evidence, see Wiles 1991: 132–133.

Curculio is first introduced as an *ancilla*; then she acts as a professional *meretrix*, only to be recast in the end as a *virgo* (Wiles 1991: 137). This is not simply behaving contrary to type, but usurping the functions normally performed by other types; hence in this play "the *leno* is sick, the lover acts the slave, the *miles* acts the *adulescens* [and] the parasite takes over the conventional narrative functions of the slave, and is the resourceful schemer who allows the *adulescens* to obtain the heroine" (Wiles 1991: 135–136).

As a general pattern this is certainly correct. We can exemplify this further with a play like *Epidicus*. Here the case is not of a single mask performing three different actants, as with *Curculio*'s *mulier,* but the exact opposite, of a single actant, the "soldier," divvied up in three "actors." In *Epidicus,* all three major male characters are somewhat connected to professional military service: the *miles* himself is still on active duty; the lover is a soldier who has just retired but still bears a suggestive "military" name (Stratippocles); and Periphanes, Stratippocles's father, is an old man who used to be a soldier in his youth. The connection of these characters to soldiery affords an extra layer of meaning, an added value of absurdity, as it were, to the way they embody the major paradigms of arrogant *stultitia* in New Comedy. The bamboozled father, the *senatus columen* with the "illustrious" past (περιφανής), does not even have the legal expertise to protect his own interests. The hapless young spendthrift bears a resounding, haughty name, but unlike his peers in other plays, he does not even get his girl. In *Epidicus,* the soldier mask plays against itself, as it were, in various guises. The Miles-Periphanes scene in 437–492 is the finest illustration of this pregnant juxtaposition: two soldiers, one of the past and one of the present, measure up their supposed military deeds against each other. The *senex* castigates the soldier for his desperate need to tell tall tales to anyone who would listen, but in an aside admits that this is exactly what he himself had done in his youth—and what he threatens to do in retaliation right now: *immo si audias/ meas pugnas, fugias manibus demissis domum* (451–452). This is commonly thought to mean "like a sprinter" (with one arm before, one behind), but the image may just as well insinuate the way *monkeys* accelerate using their front legs. The monkey is a Plautine metaphor commonly associated with soldiers and the way they are bamboozled (cf. the character Simia, "The Ape," in the *Pseudolus* and the many references to "monkey business" in *Miles Gloriosus*).[4] Ironically enough, of all three "soldiers" in the *Epidicus,* humiliated least is the one who must actually wear the ἐπίσειστος ("wavy-haired") mask (Pollux, Comic mask no. 15).

The "subverted mask theory" can go very convincingly so far. David Wiles allows also for the possibility that Plautus may have invested his masks in some cases with an animalistic countenance, to abet the subversion of the Greek narrative and aesthetic codes. The aforementioned *mulier* in *Curculio,* for example, must have had, Wiles believes, visibly owlish traits (the inference is based on *Curculio* 191: *tun etiam cum noctuinis*

---

4 See Connors 2004.

oculis odium me vocas?). "The Plautine mask," he writes, "is not an imitation of observed human features, but a symbol" (Wiles 1991: 141). Its "infernal attributes" enhance its symbolic function and help the playwright shake off any embarrassing associations with the hallowed *imago*.

Wiles certainly flirts with the idea that Plautus's masks had a different physical look than Menander's. But, although his suggestion that Plautus drew on Italian culture to give his masks "a visual interpretation meaningful to his audience" (Wiles 1991: 141) is rather ambiguous, overall he seems to incline more strongly towards a metaphorical "metamorphosis," an undercutting of the mask's signification—or at least not to speculate any wide-scale visual *retouche* of the inherited Greek masks. This, however, is the contention of the second variety of "syncretic mask theory," which hypothesizes a fully hybrid Plautine mask system, on which the *Atellana* exerted formative influence not only regarding "meaning," but also with reference to the visual aspect of the mask (see Marshall 2006: 126–158). Marshall supports this theory with a number of case studies, which merit detailed examination: the slaves Pseudolus and Leonida (the latter of *Asinaria*), three of Plautus's pimps (Ballio of *Pseudolus*, Cappadox of *Curculio*, and Labrax of *Rudens*), and several other "individualized" masks.

Marshall notes that the three pimps are: (a) very different from each other in external appearance, and (b) incompatible with Pollux's description of the Greek Pimp mask (πορνοβοσκός: Pollux Comic Mask 8). Ballio, for instance, has a *hirquina barba*, a goat's beard, while the Greek πορνοβοσκός, on the contrary, is μακρογένειος ("with a long beard") like the previously-listed λυκομήδειος mask ("the Lycomedean," Pollux Comic Mask no. 7). Cappadox also contradicts Pollux's πορνοβοσκός, according to Marshall, because he is a sickly person with a greenish gaze and suffers from acute pains in his spleen that make him "disgustingly bloated" (Marshall 2006: 142). Finally, Marshall suggests that Labrax must look like a beggar, because his clothes are sea-washed, and that his beard is not as distinctive as the μακρογένειος attribute would require. What is more, Marshall is led to the conclusion that Labrax's mask "comprises elements evoking both the Atellan Manducus and the Hellenistic *pornoboskos*," as the greedy Manducus's distinguishing trait are his notable teeth (Marshall 2006: 144), by the exchange at *Rudens* 535–536 (LABR. *Quid si aliquo ad ludos me pro manduco locem?* CHARM. *Quapropter?* LABR. *Quia pol clare crepito dentibus*).[5]

All in all, Marshall concludes that the differences in the physical appearance among Ballio, Cappadox, and Labrax, as well as their perceived deviation from the Greek πορνοβοσκός, can be explained by the hypothesis that in these three cases Plautus devised masks which visually resembled different Atellan types each time. In particular, Ballio is tied to Pappus, Labrax to Manducus, and Cappadox to Dossennus, the latter because of the belly. Similarly, Marshall suggests, the details added to the descriptions of the slaves Pseudolus (*Pseudolus* 1218–1220) and Leonida (*Asinaria* 400–401), especially Pseudolus's flat feet, point to the Atellan character Maccus, a clown and a

---

[5] "LABR: How about hiring myself out at some fair as a... Manducus? CHARM: Why that? LABR: Gad! Because of the grand way I... gnash my teeth!" (transl. P. Nixon, adapted).

fool: "the Roman version" of the Leading Slave mask (Pollux 22, ἡγεμὼν θεράπων), it is surmised, which the slaves' Greek prototypes must have worn, was somehow fused with the Atellan figure, "since Maccus constitutes an element in the 'cultural literacy' of the average Roman theatregoer" (Marshall 2006: 139). Marshall's Plautus "did not simply import his masking tradition. There were innovations, and any description of Roman masks cannot be directly transposed from a Greek model" (Marshall 2006: 146). Plautus "could create a character that, through a combination of acting style, costume, and mask, could be identified to some degree with a figure from the *Atellanae*" (Marshall 2006: 145).

To these arguments, however, objections may be raised. For example, some might disagree that the three pimps are indeed all that dissimilar from Pollux's πορνοβοσκός mask. If somebody can pull Labrax's beard (see *Rudens* 769), then it is fairly long, like that of the πορνοβοσκός. Labrax is also *crispus* (curly-haired), as the πορνοβοσκός is οὐλοκόμος; he is *incanus* (white-haired), *recalvus* (balding, cf. ἀναφαλαντίας), sturdy, pot-bellied, and of a furrowed and frowned forehead — exactly like the πορνοβοσκός. In Ballio's case, too, a *hirquina barba* is not necessarily an indication of a different kind of beard and consequently of a mask that is not the πορνοβοσκός. A goat's beard may be shaped like a wedge, but is not necessarily short. Qualifying Ballio's beard as *hirquina*, while not contradicting his being long-bearded, all the while adduces the sexual implications of the *hirquus* imagery.

Furthermore, the association of these figures with the particular types of the *Atellana* is also open to doubt. Cappadox, for instance, is associated with Dossenus because of his belly, but Dossenus is paunchy because of gluttony, whereas Cappadox is bloated because of disease. As for Labrax, *Rudens* 543–544 and 558 are used as evidence that this pimp has a distinguished jaw and a wagging tongue like a real sea bass (λάβραξ). This, along with lines 535–536, where Manducus is mentioned explicitly, leads to a hypothesis of a fusion between the πορνοβοσκός and the Atellan type. However, it is Labrax's voraciousness in general, not his jaw — i.e., a character trait, not a physical feature — that is highlighted in lines 543–544 (*iam postulabas te, impurata belua,/ totam Siciliam devoraturum insulam?*). Labrax is an insatiable beast; these lines need not hint at the appearance of the mask. Furthermore, the reference to Labrax's gnashing teeth in *Rudens* 536 (quoted above) is an illustration not of gluttony but of his being wet and cold: again, not of a distinctive trait of appearance but of a transient state. There are limits, therefore, to how much one can invest in the face value of such statements to support the theory of a hybrid Plautine mask. Nevertheless, the mention alone of Manducus, which adds to the semantics of other verbal signs such as the character's speaking name and the overall imagery associated with him, *can perform its intertextual task without the need of a mask that cites the Atellan type visually.*

Apart from the suggestion that Plautus's masks adopt some of the physical features of the *Atellana* mask system, it has also been theorized that Plautus may individualize his masks by touching up some of their original features. Evidence is sought in such jokes as *Pseudolus* 636–639 (Marshall 2006: 147–149). Why does Harpax hesitate to accept that Pseudolus's name is Syrus, and what could be funny in this exchange? An ethnic joke must lurk here:[6] "When a character on the Hellenistic or Roman stage identified himself as 'Syrus' he was assuming a name associated with a particular place of origin, and, by extension, with certain genetic characteristics" (Marshall 2006: 148). Hence it has been inferred that the slave name Syrus must here be associated with a particular type of slave mask, unattested in Pollux: "one with dark features, almost certainly dark hair, against which the red-headed Thracian [Pseudolus] would stand out in contrast" (Marshall 2006: 148). However, no such dark-looking mask is really needed for the joke in *Pseudolus* 636–639 to work; only the ethnic stereotype is required, the expectations associated with one's Syriac origins. Pseudolus professes a name which suggests "black" while looking anything but that.

Equally debatable is whether Plautus invented a special mask for the character Philocrates in *Captivi* (Marshall 2006: 149–151). This supposition is based on the description of the character in lines 647–648: *macilento ore, naso acuto, corpore albo, oculis nigris, / subrufus aliquantum, crispus, cincinnatus.*[7] Most scholars take *subrufus* to refer to the character's hair, which creates a problem, as only slaves are redheads in Greek New Comedy. Nonetheless, *rufus*, "ruddy," is just as likely (perhaps more likely) to refer to complexion rather than hair color here. The description of Philocrates, especially the adjectives *crispus cincinnatus*, is generally compatible with Pollux's οὖλος νεανίσκος (Mask 12), who is precisely *subrufus aliquantum*: ὁ δ' οὖλος νεανίσκος μᾶλλον νέος, ὑπέρυθρος τὸ χρῶμα· αἱ δὲ τρίχες κατὰ τοὔνομα.[8] A possible objection, of course, is that if *subrufus* refers to complexion, then *corpore albo* is a contradiction. Not necessarily; *subrufus* may in fact qualify *corpore albo*: Philocrates is generally of a fair complexion, but with a slightly reddish tint or a flushed face. Nevertheless, even if we concede that the mask of this character for the particular needs of this play is given the anomalous trait of reddish hair, this would simply amount to a *hapax* variation of an established type. This is neither unheard of nor particular to Plautus: Glycera's shorn mask in Menander's *Perikeiromene* must also have been one such extraordinary variation. Certainly, such a *hapax* cannot prove that Plautus's mask system was altogether devised afresh, in disharmony with its Greek prototype and under the influence of the *fabula Atellana*.

We must concede that there is no incontrovertible proof that there was any differentiation *on the visual level* between Plautus's masks and their Greek prototypes, no explicit, independent confirmation that Plautus tampered with the surface constituents of New Comedy ὄψις by incorporating elements from the *Atellana*. On the contrary, as Wiles admits, the fact that we have "no definite iconographic evidence for Plautine performance, despite the fact that Plautus' plays remained in repertory for over a century [is] a lack which suggests that the Roman version of New Comedy had no completely

---

[6] Augoustakis 2007, however, interprets the joke entirely differently. He argues that the name Syrus evokes Surus, the name of Hannibal's favorite elephant.

[7] "He has a narrow face, a sharp nose, fair complexion, dark eyes, and his hair is somewhat reddish, wavy and curly" (transl. W. de Melo).

[8] "The curly-haired youth is still younger, with a ruddy complexion and hair in conformity with his name" (transl. Csapo & Slater).

independent visual style" (Wiles 1991: 133). But even if it is accidental that such an independent style for Plautus's masks is archaeologically unattested, it still seems risky to suppose that a hybrid Greco-Italian mask would have surfaced in Plautus's times for the needs of an otherwise Greek-looking genre and then would have lingered for less than a century, only to give way eventually to a purely Greek system again when Terence came along.

It is one thing to suppose that Plautus "contaminates" the Greek mask with Roman references, and another to speculate that this contamination also had visual, representational consequences. If we are looking for the deconstructive intent of Plautus on the Greek mask system he inherited, we would probably do better to look at the *dramatic discourse* and not at the visual aspect of his performance. The manner in which such masks as those of Pseudolus or Leonidas are described in Plautus's text, or the overt parallelism of Plautus's pimps with characters such as Manducus, indeed creates connotations which can inevitably and decisively *inform* the audience's response to the mask. For this associative function to be fulfilled, however, Plautus did not need the mask maker to effect an actual physical change on the mask; deconstruction of the Greek mask can be accomplished, perhaps even more effectively, on the level of discourse. The Greek mask Plautus inherits and most probably presents to his audience, a mask conducive to ἤθη of psychological subtlety, is by definition undermined when dislocated to a different performance context, where it is fused with a tradition of unadulterated farce. The New Comedy mask is singularly intertextual, as it resonates with various systems of literary and cultural reference (see Petrides 2010). To readjust those systems of reference is to create *a totally restructured version of the mask without having to lay hands on its surface appearance*. Referential, pregnant language jumbles the cultural associations of the Greek πρόσωπον, and in so doing creates a novel discursive space for the Roman theatrical *persona*. Therefore, if Plautus used masks at all (and there is little reason to believe that he did not), these masks are more likely to have retained the Greek style than otherwise. By recontextualizing his masks, Plautus changes their semiosis considerably. Indeed, Plautus's deconstructive project would arguably be done much greater service if *visual continuity* underscored the *essential discontinuity* between Plautus's and Menander's comic worlds. This was certainly the case in all other aspects of *palliata*'s ὄψις. Why not in the case of the mask, too?

The theory that the formative pressures of Italian "popular" drama on Plautus's Roman New Comedy were so great that they impinged even on the visual dimension of his performance, and for that matter selectively so (affecting the mask alone), seems to overcompensate for the earlier skewed view of Plautus as a derivative phenomenon, one whose usefulness was well-nigh exhausted in the clues he could yield for the vanished Greek masterpieces he adapted. The salutary potential afforded by rehabilitating the local context and theatrical traditions of Italy as a significant factor for understanding Plautus has been immense and illuminating. Caution is needed, however, in order to strike the right balance between Greek and Italian. At the end of the day, Plautus, a master in the poetics of incongruity, must have had better use of a *palliata* that looked Greek as it behaved distinctively Roman.

FURTHER READING

Review articles on Plautine scholarship: J. A. Hanson, "Scholarship on Plautus since 1950," *CW* 59 (1965–1966): 103–107, 126–129, 141–148; F. Bertini, "Vent'anni di studi plautini in Italia (1950–1970)," *BSL* 1 (1971): 23–41; J. D. Hughes, *A Bibliography of Scholarship on Plautus*, Amsterdam: Hakkert, 1975; D. Fogazza, "Plauto 1935–1975," *Lustrum* 19 (1976): 79–295; E. Segal, "Scholarship on Plautus, 1965–1976," *CW* 74.7 (1981): 353–433; D. Wiles, "Taking Farce Seriously: Recent Critical Approaches to Plautus," *Themes in Drama* 10 (1988): 261–271; F. Bubel, *Bibliographie zu Plautus, 1976–1989*, Bonn: Habelt, 1992.

On Plautus and "popular drama": W. Beare, "Plautus and the *Fabula Atellana*," *CR* 44 (1930): 165–168; A. McN. G. Little, "Plautus and Popular Drama," *HSCPh* 49 (1938): 205–228; A. S. Gratwick, "Titus Maccius Plautus," *CQ* 23 (1973): 78–84; D. Bain, "*Plautus vortit barbare*," in D. West and T. Woodman (eds.), *Creative Imitation and Latin Literature*, Cambridge: Cambridge University Press, 1979, 17–34; J.-C. Dumont, "Plaute, barbare et hereux de l'être," *Ktéma* 9 (1984): 69–77; V. Castellani, "Plautus versus *Komoidia*: Popular Farce at Rome," *Themes in Drama* 10 (1988): 53–82; E. Lefèvre, "Saturnalien und Palliata," *Poetica* 20 (1988): 32–46; H. Petersmann, "Mündlichkeit und Schriftlichkeit in der Atellane," in G. Vogt-Spira (ed.), *Studien zur vorliterarischen Periode im frühen Rom*, Tübingen: Narr, 1989, 135–159.

On Plautus and his Roman public: W. R. Chalmers, "Plautus and His Audience," in T. A. Dorley and D. R. Dudley (eds.), *Roman Drama*, London: Routledge & Kegan Paul, 1965, 21–50; E. Fantham, "The *Curculio* of Plautus: An Illustration of Plautine Methods in Adaptation," *CQ* 15 (1965): 84–100; E. W. Handley, "Plautus and His Public: Some Thoughts on New Comedy in Latin," *Dioniso* 46 (1975): 117–132; E. W. Leach, "The Soldier and Society: Plautus' *Miles gloriosus* as Popular Drama," *RSC* 27 (1979): 185–209; R. C. Beacham, *The Roman Theater and Its Audience*, Cambridge, MA: Harvard University Press, 1991; H. N. Parker, "Plautus vs. Terence: Audience And Popularity Re-examined," *AJPh* 117 (1996): 585–617; E. Gruen, "Plautus and the Public Stage," in E. Segal (ed.), *Oxford Readings in Menander, Plautus and Terence*, Oxford: Oxford University Press, 2001, 83–94.

On Plautus, metatheater and improvisation: M. Barchiesi, "Plauto e il metateatro antico," *Il Verri* 31 (1970): 113–130; F. Muecke, "Plautus and the Theater of Disguise," *CA* 5 (1986): 216–229; J. Blänsdorf, "Die Komödienintrige als Spiel im Spiel," *A&A* 28 (1986): 131–154; F. Muecke, "Plautus and the Theater of Disguise," *CA* 5 (1986): 216–229; B. Williams, "Games People Play: Metatheater as Performance Criticism in Plautus' *Casina*," *Ramus* 22 (1993): 33–59; L. Benz, E. Stärk, and G. Vogt-Spira (eds.), *Plautus und die Tradition des Stegreifspiels: Festgabe für Eckard Lefèvre zum 60. Geburtstag*, Tübingen: Narr, 1995; S. A. Frangoulidis, *Handlung und Nebenhandlung: Theater, Metatheater und Gattungsbewusstsein in der römischen Komödie*, Stuttgart: M & P Verlag für Wissenschaft und Forschung, 1997; J. Barsby, "Improvvisazione, metateatro, decostruzione: Approcci alle *Bacchidi* di Plauto," in R. Rafaelli and A. Tontini (eds.), *Bacchides,* Urbino: QuattroVenti, 2001, 51–70; W. W. Batstone, "Plautine Farce and Plautine Freedom: An Essay on the Value of Metatheater," in W. W. Batstone and G. Tissol (eds.), *Defining Genre and Gender in Latin Literature: Essays Presented to W.S. Anderson on his Seventy-Fifth Birthday*, New York: Lang, 2005, 13–46; C.

S. Hardy, "The Parasite's Daughter: Metatheatrical Costuming in Plautus' *Persa*," *CW* 99 (2005-2006): 25-33; L. Maurice, "Structure and Stagecraft in Plautus' *Miles Gloriosus*," *Mnemosyne* 60 (2007): 407-426.

On the work of the Freiburg School: E. Lefèvre, *Maccus vortit barbare: Vom tragischen Amphitryon zum tragikomischen Amphitruo*, Wiesbaden: F. Steiner, 1982; E. Stärk, *Die Menaechmi des Plautus und kein griechisches Original*, Tübingen: Narr, 1989; E. Lefèvre, E. Stärk and G. Vogt-Spira, *Plautus barbarus: Sechs Kapitel zur Originalität des Plautus*, Tübingen: Narr, 1991; E. Lefèvre, *Plautus und Philemon*, Tübingen: Narr, 1995; E. Lefèvre, *Plautus' Pseudolus*, Tübingen: Narr, 1997; L. Benz and E. Lefèvre (eds.), *Maccus barbarus: Sechs Kapitel zur Originalität der Captivi des Plautus*, Tübingen: Narr, 1998; T. Baier (ed.), *Studien zu Plautus' «Amphitruo»*, Tübingen: Narr, 1999; E. Lefèvre, *Plautus' Aulularia*, Tübingen: Narr, 2001; U. Auhagen (ed.), *Studien zu Plautus' «Epidicus»*, Tübingen: Narr, 2001; S. Faller (ed.), *Studien zu Plautus' «Persa»*, Tübingen: Narr, 2001; W. Hofmann, *Plautus: Truculentus*, Darmstadt: Wissenschaftliche Buchgesellschaft, 2001; R. Hartkamp and F. Hurka (eds.), *Studien zu Plautus' «Cistellaria»*, Tübingen: Narr, 2004; T. Baier (ed.), *Studien zu Plautus' «Poenulus»*, Tübingen: Narr, 2004.

On the doubtful "Plautinity" of some "Plautine" elements: W. G. Arnott, "Targets, Techniques, and Tradition in Plautus' *Stichus*," *BICS* 19 (1972): 54-79; N. Zagagi, *Tradition and Originality in Plautus: Studies of the Amatory Motifs in Plautine Comedy*, Göttingen: Vandenhoeck & Ruprecht, 1980; E. Csapo, "Plautine Elements in the Running-Slave Entrance Monologues?" *CQ* 39 (1989): 148-163; N. Zagagi, "The Impromptu Element in Plautus in the Light of the Evidence of New Comedy," in L. Benz, E. Stärk, and G. Vogt-Spira (eds.), *Plautus und die Tradition des Stegreifspiels*, Tübingen: Narr, 1995, 71-86; G. Guastella, "I monologhi di ingresso dei parassiti: Plauto e i modelli," in C. Questa and R. Rafaelli (eds.), *Due seminari plautini*, Urbino: Quattro venti, 2002, 155-198; W. G. Arnott, "Plautus' Epidicus and Greek Comedy," in U. Auhagen (ed.), *Studien zu Plautus' «Epidicus»*, Tübingen: Narr, 2001, 71-90.

On the issue of the mask in Plautus: C. Saunders, "The Introduction of Masks on the Roman Stage," *AJPh* 32 (1911): 58-73; A. S. F. Gow, "On the Use of Masks in Roman Comedy," *JRS* 11 (1912): 65-77; W. Beare, "Masks on the Roman Stage," *CQ* 33 (1939): 139-146; S. Magistrini, "Le descrizioni fisiche dei personaggi in Menandro, Plauto e Terenzio," *Dioniso* 44 (1970): 79-114; F. della Corte, "La tipologia del personaggio della *palliata*," in *Actes du IXe Congrès Association Guillaume Budé, Rome, 13-18 Avril 1973*, Paris: Les Belles Lettres, 1973, 354-394; F. Della Corte, "Maschere e personaggi in Plauto," *Dioniso* 46 (1975): 163-93; F. I. Harriet, *Ancestor Masks and Aristocratic Power in Roman Culture*, Oxford and New York: Oxford University Press, 1996.

BIBLIOGRAPHY

Anderson, W. S. 1993. *Barbarian Play: Plautus' Roman Comedy*. Toronto: University of Toronto Press.

Augoustakis, A, 2007. "*Surus cor perfrigefacit*: Elephants in Plautus' *Pseudolus*." *Philologus* 151.1: 177-182.

Brown, P. G. McC. 1995. Review of *Plautus barbarus: Sechs Kapitel zur Originalität des Plautus*, by E. Lefèvre, E. Stärk, and G. Vogt-Spira. *Gnomon* 67.8: 676-683.

Bruzzese, L. 2011. *Studi su Filemone comico.* Lecce and Brescia: Pensa Multimedia.

Castellani, V. 1995. "Captive Captor Freed: The National Theater of Greece and Rome." In *Griechisch-römische Komödie und Tragödie*, edited by B. Zimmermann, 51–69. Stuttgart: M & P Verlag für Wissenschaft und Forschung.

Connors, C. 2004. "Monkey Business: Imitation, Authenticity, and Identity from Pithekoussai to Plautus." *CA* 23.2: 179–207.

Fraenkel, E. 2007. *Plautine Elements in Plautus*. Translated by T. Drevikovsky and F. Muecke. Oxford and New York: Oxford University Press. Originally published as *Plautinisches im Plautus* (Berlin, 1922).

Green, J. R. 1994. *Theatre in Ancient Greek Society*. London and New York: Routledge.

Handley, E. 1968. *Menander and Plautus: A Study in Comparison*. London: Lewis.

Jachmann, G. 1931. *Plautinisches und Attisches*. Berlin: Weidmann.

Konstan, D. 1983. *Roman Comedy*. Ithaca, NY: Cornell University Press.

Leigh, M. 2004. *Comedy and the Rise of Rome*. Oxford: Oxford University Press.

Leo, F. 1908. "Der Monolog im Drama: Ein Beitrag zur griechisch-römischen Poetik." *Abhandlungen der königlichen Gesellschaft der Wissenschaften zu Göttingen* 10: 1–119.

———. 1912. *Plautinische Forschungen zur Kritik und Geschichte der Komödie*. 2nd ed. Berlin: Weidmann.

Marshall, C. W. 2006. *The Stagecraft and Performance of Roman Comedy*. Cambridge, UK: Cambridge University Press.

McCarthy, K. 2000. *Slaves, Masters and the Art of Authority in Plautine Comedy*. Princeton: Princeton University Press.Moore, T. J. 1998. *The Theater of Plautus: Playing to the Audience*. Austin: University of Texas Press.

Owens, W. M. 2000. "Plautus' *Stichus* and the Political Crisis of 200 B.C." *AJPh* 121.3: 385–407.

Petrides, A. K. 2010. "New Performance." In *New Perspectives on Postclassical Comedy*, edited by A. K. Petrides and S. Papaioannou, 79–124. Newcastle upon Tyne: Cambridge Scholars.

Petrone, G. 1977. *Morale e antimorale nelle commedie di Plauto: Ricerche sullo Stichus*. Palermo: Palumbo.

Questa, C. 1982. "Maschere e funzioni nelle commedie di Plauto." *MD* 8: 9–64.

Segal, E. 1968. *Roman Laughter: The Comedy of Plautus*. Cambridge, MA: Harvard University Press. 2nd ed. Oxford University Press, 1987.

Slater, N. 1985. *Plautus in Performance: The Theater of the Mind*. Princeton: Princeton University Press.

———. 1993. "Improvisation in Plautus." In *Beiträge zur mündlichen Kultur der Römer*, edited by G. Vogt-Spira, 113–124, Tübingen: Narr.

———. 2004. "Staging Literacy in Plautus." In *Oral Performance and its Context*, edited by C. J. Mackie, 163–177. Leiden: Brill.

Vogt-Spira, G. 1995. "Traditionen improvisierten Theaters bei Plautus." In *Griechisch-römische Komödie und Tragödie*, edited by B. Zimmermann, 70–93. Stuttgart: M & P Verlag für Wissenschaft und Forschung.

———. 1997. "Plauto fra teatro greco e superamento della farsa italica: Proposta di un modello triadico." *QUCC*, n.s., 58.1: 111–135.

———. 2001. "Traditions of Theatrical Improvisation in Plautus: Some Considerations." In *Oxford Readings in Menander, Plautus, and Terence*, edited by E. Segal, 95–106. Oxford: Oxford University Press.

Wiles, D. 1988. "Taking Farce Seriously: Recent Critical Approaches to Plautus." *Themes in Drama* 10: 261–271.

———. 1991. *The Masks of Menander: Sign and Meaning in Greek and Roman Performance.* Cambridge: Cambridge University Press.

Wright, J. 1974. *Dancing in Chains: The Stylistic Unity of the Comoedia Palliata.* Rome: American Academy.

Zwierlein, O. 1990. *Zur Kritik und Exegese des Plautus I: Poenulus und Curculio.* Stuttgart: F. Steiner.

———. 1991a. *Zur Kritik und Exegese des Plautus II: Miles gloriosus.* Stuttgart: F. Steiner.

———. 1991b. *Zur Kritik und Exegese des Plautus III: Pseudolus.* Stuttgart: F. Steiner.

———. 1992. *Zur Kritik und Exegese des Plautus IV: Bacchides.* Stuttgart: F. Steiner.

II

The Roman Comedians and their Plays

CHAPTER 22

···

PLAUTUS'S DRAMATIC PREDECESSORS AND CONTEMPORARIES IN ROME

···

WOLFGANG DAVID CIRILO DE MELO

AUTHORS OF ROMAN COMEDY
···

ROMAN comedy is traditionally divided into four distinct genres: the *fabula palliata* or "comedy in Greek dress," based on Greek New Comedy (and in some instances perhaps Middle Comedy) and set in Greek surroundings, though with many Roman elements; the *fabula togata* or "comedy in Roman dress," an offshoot of the *fabula palliata* and set in Roman surroundings; the *fabula Atellana* or "Atellan farce," a genre named after the Oscan town Atella and less dependent on Greek material, despite the Greek names of some plays; and the *mimus* or "mime," the only theatrical genre that was staged unmasked and had actresses as well as actors.

The *fabula palliata* is the best known type of comedy. In addition to the twenty-one plays by Plautus that belonged to the Varronian canon[1] and were transmitted via the direct manuscript tradition, and the six plays by Terence, we have a number of fragments ascribed to Plautus and others. The genre was invented by Lucius Livius Andronicus, a Greek by birth and freedman of the Livii, who produced both a comedy and a tragedy for the *ludi Romani* ("Roman Games") of 240. Livius Andronicus is better known for his translation of the Odyssey; of his comedies, only three titles and a total of six fragments survive, among them only one not quoted for grammatical peculiarities:[2]

---

[1] According to Gell. 3. 3, around 130 plays were ascribed to Plautus. Varro (as quoted in Gellius's essay) tells us that twenty-one of these were accepted as genuine by everyone, which is why they came to be known as "Varronian plays," despite the fact that Varro did not write them and actually believed other plays to be genuine as well.

[2] All quotations from Roman dramatists are taken from Ribbeck 1898.

(1)Lepus tute es: pulpamentum quaeris. (Liv. Andr. *com.* 8)

> You're a hare, and yet you look for a meat dish.

Donatus (fourth century CE) quotes this passage from Andronicus because the joke was borrowed verbatim by Terence (*Eunuchus* 426). Gnaeus Naevius, a Campanian by birth, followed the tradition established by Andronicus and wrote epic, tragedy, and comedy. His stage career began around 235, which makes him an older contemporary of Plautus. The number of fragments is large enough to allow linguistic and literary analysis. Another renowned writer of tragedy and epic was Quintus Ennius (239–169), who also tried his hand at comedy. Although little can be said about his comic work, since only two titles and four fragments have come down to us, two of the fragments belong to stock scenes: in Enn. *com.* 2 we have a response to violent knocking on a door and in Enn. *com.* 4 the mill is mentioned, the typical punishment for slaves. Caecilius Statius, an Insubrian Gaul by origin, is the only other early writer of *fabulae palliatae* of whom we have substantial fragments; among these is a lengthy papyrus fragment from Herculaneum, examined by Knut Kleve, which unfortunately is in such a bad state that most lines remain uncertain. Since Caecilius died in 168, he is a younger contemporary of Plautus. The other authors of whom we have fragments are Trabea (two fragments), possibly a contemporary of Plautus; Atilius (three fragments), possibly a contemporary of Plautus as well; Aquilius, of unknown date, listed with two fragments of the *Boeotia* in Ribbeck, even though in the first century BC Varro believed the author to be Plautus (Gell. 3. 3. 4); Licinius Imbrex (one fragment), who can be dated to around 200 if he is identical with P. Licinius Tegula; Iuventius (six fragments), of unknown date; Luscius Lanuvinus (two fragments), Terence's older rival, who, like Terence, seems to have favored greater adherence to the Greek originals than Plautus and his contemporaries; and finally, Sextus Turpilius (218 lines or half-lines), possibly a contemporary of Terence, but stylistically closer to Plautus than to Terence.

The three main authors of *fabulae togatae* are Titinius (188 lines and half-lines), perhaps an older contemporary of Terence[3] ; Lucius Afranius (439 lines and half-lines), who lived in the late second century BC; and T. Quinctius Atta (24 lines and half-lines), who died in 77 BCE. If Daviault (1981: 18) is correct in stating that the *togata* existed before Titinius, it is not unlikely that it partly influenced Plautus, though such influence will have gone in both directions; there are clear linguistic similarities, and the themes resemble those of the *palliata*. Based on Quint. *inst.* 10. 1. 100, it is often said that Afranius liked pederastic topics, something practically excluded from the *palliata*, but Welsh (2010a) rightly argues that the passage in Quintilian must be interpreted differently; his claim that the famous rhetorician probably had not read much of Afranius is less convincing.

Atellan farce existed long before Plautus. However, the genre will not be treated here, because the first scripted versions we know of date from the first two decades of the

---

[3] Titinius is dated to the early second century by Guardì (1985: 19) and to the second half of the third century by Daviault (1981: 18).

first century BCE, a hundred years after Plautus died and not far removed in time from the early works of Cicero. We have almost two hundred lines by Lucius Pomponius Bononiensis and a little more than one hundred lines by Novius. All we have in addition are a few lines from Mummius, one from Aprissius, and a handful of unassigned fragments, some from the early empire.

Mime, too, is an old genre, having had its first official presentation at the *Floralia* ("Games in honor of Flora") of 239. Like Atellan farce, it remained subliterary until the late republic. The remains we have are largely restricted to ninety-six fragments of Decimus Laberius, a Roman knight contemporary with Caesar, and the *Sententiae* of his rival Publilius Syrus; yet the *Sententiae*, though originally excerpts from his mimes, have to be treated with caution because it is impossible to distinguish between the work of Publilius and later accretions. The few other fragments of mime go back to Valerius, a certain Catullus, Lentulus, Marullus, and a certain Lucilius, none of them earlier than Laberius and Publilius.

In this chapter, I shall concentrate on the three predecessors or contemporaries of Plautus of whom we have relatively much material. After discussing why work with fragments is inherently problematic, I wish to show what the language and literary motifs of Naevian comedy were like and how Caecilius adapted Menander. Next to these two writers of *fabulae palliatae*, I shall also examine one representative of the *togata*, Titinius; here I shall concentrate on one play, his *Setina* "The Woman from Setia," and problems of plot reconstruction.

PROBLEMS IN DEALING WITH FRAGMENTS

As Plautus and Terence are the only dramatists of the republic of whom we have complete plays, studying Plautus's dramatic predecessors and contemporaries in Rome means studying fragments, with all the problems and pitfalls inherent in any such undertaking. The difficult question that nobody with an interest in fragmentary authors can avoid is to what extent the remains that we have are representative of a work or an author as a whole. For practical purposes, it is best to divide this question into two: first, do the fragments give us a reliable picture of an author's language? And second, do they allow us to reconstruct the plots of his plays? With regard to the second question, the scholar working on the fragments of Roman tragedy is in a better position than the one working on comedy: the plots of Roman tragedy are mostly based on Greek tragedy, and that is known partly through the Greek originals and partly through Greek and Roman mythographers, which means that plot reconstruction is in principle, if not always in practice, much more straightforward. By contrast, our remains of Greek New Comedy, the basis of much of Roman comedy, are scanty, and plot reconstruction is often only possible by comparing similar plays by Plautus and Terence; such a procedure is not ideal, but allowable because both Greek New Comedy and its Roman derivatives rely on stock characters, stock scenes, and stock plots.

As I have tried to show in de Melo 2010 (91–93), the extent to which we can reconstruct plots and language depends not only on the amount of fragments we have, but also on who the sources of these fragments are. Paradoxically, fragments quoted by grammarians are generally not very helpful for reconstructing linguistic features, while fragments quoted by men of letters are often of little use for broad literary questions. This can be seen very clearly when we look at the remains of two plays by Caecilius Statius, the *Titthe* ("The Nurse") and the *Synephebi* ("The Young Comrades"). Of the former play, we have six fragments, all quoted by the lexicographer Nonius (fourth century CE). Nonius has little interest in common usages, so it comes as no surprise that he only quotes what he considers to be linguistic oddities: the nominative / accusative *lacte* instead of *lac* "milk," *contendere* in the meaning "compare," the rare *grauidare* "make pregnant," the adverbial genitive *utrasque* "on both occasions," *compitus* instead of the more common *compitum* "crossroads," and *concedere* in the meaning "step aside." Not all of these usages are remarkable: Plautus has only *lacte*, never *lac*, and he also uses *contendere* in the meaning "compare" and *concedere* in the meaning "step aside"; *grauidare* has a classical parallel in Cicero (*nat. deor.* 2. 83), and in the passage in which Nonius quotes the masculine *compitus* (288 L.) he also quotes an example from Varro; finally, *utrasque*, while highly archaic and unusual, also occurs in Cassius Hemina (second century BCE) according to the passage in Nonius (269 L.) where the usage is cited for Caecilius. But while all these usages in Caecilius can be paralleled, not all of them are common; at least the adverbial *utrasque* is extremely unusual. If we were to reconstruct the language of Caecilius on the basis of these fragments, we would get the almost certainly wrong impression that it was remarkably odd. Nonius also quotes many passages from the Plautine plays outside the Varronian canon, and if this were all we had of Plautus, we would get an entirely false picture of this author.

By contrast, of the four fragments of the *Synephebi*, three come from Cicero, and these show much more clearly what the regular linguistic usage of Caecilius was like. The fourth fragment (Caecil. 215) is quoted by Nonius on account of the masculine *collus* "neck" instead of the neuter *collum*. But let us return to the three fragments in Cicero. With its eleven lines, the first fragment is rather long, in fact longer than all fragments of the *Titthe* added together. In it we find features like alliteration (199, 204, 209), the somewhat unusual combination of *studere* "devote oneself" with the genitive (201), and iambic shortening (206, 208). In the second fragment (210), the older form *saeclum* "generation" is used instead of the later *saeculum*, but this is not a marked archaism, as the two forms coexisted for a long time. The third fragment contains the genitive *deum* "of the gods" (211) instead of the later form *deorum*, the remarkable asyndetic combination of synonyms in 212, and the light syllable at the end of *facinora* "(mis)deeds" where the meter demands a heavy one. This license at the eleventh element of the trochaic septenarius, the *locus Jacobsohnianus*, is still found in Plautus, but no longer in Terence; yet as Questa (2007: 291–293) now prefers to scan cases like ours with a divided eleventh element and a subsequent violation of the law of Bentley and Luchs, we need not even invoke the *locus Jacobsohnianus* here. Real linguistic peculiarities are absent in all three fragments, as the highly archaic *noenu uolt* "she does not want" in 214 is only Ribbeck's conjecture; his earlier emendation (*nunc neuolt* "now she does not want") is more probable in the light of the other Caecilian fragments. The general impression one gets from these quotations is that the language of Caecilius was very similar to that of Plautus.

We can now turn to the literary side of the quotations. Even though the fragments of the *Titthe* quoted by Nonius are all exceedingly short, the longest amounting to no more than one and a half lines, we can find some typical motifs recurring in Plautus and Terence. Thus in Caecil. 221–222 we find a comparison between life in the city and life in the country, paralleled by Terence *Adelphoe* 94–95, though admittedly it is not clear from the Caecilius passage whether here too life in the country is regarded as preferable. Similarly, Caecil. 223 presents a man who raped a girl during a festival at night and made her pregnant, reminiscent of Lyconides in the *Aulularia* by Plautus. And Caecil. 227 is presumably spoken by someone trying to listen to a conversation secretly, a very common comedy motif. Of course similar motifs can be found in citations by literary authors, but in citations by grammarians we can be certain that the passages were not selected for content, and this means that they are more likely to be representative of themes and motifs used regularly by a specific writer of comedy.

How does this compare with the three fragments of the *Synephebi* quoted by Cicero? Here we have to ask ourselves why they are quoted. The first (Caecil. 199–209) is cited in *nat. deor.* 3. 72, where Cicero discusses argumentative strategies rather than any particular literary motif. For this reason we have a fairly long quotation, and it is a priori likely that standard literary motifs come up in such a piece, as is indeed the case: the speaker can be identified as an impecunious young man in love, the type so aptly described by Calidorus when he says of himself in the passive *amatur atque egetur acriter* "one is in love and dire financial need" (Plautus, *Pseudolus* 273); he also talks of stingy fathers and deceptions by clever slaves, both stock topics in Roman comedy. The fact that he then goes on to say that his father is so mild that he has hardly any justification for deceiving him does not necessarily mean a deviation from common patterns: there are also mild fathers in comedy, like Micio in Terence's *Adelphoe*, or seemingly mild and kind ones, like Demaenetus in Plautus's *Asinaria*, who later turns out to be a crook.

The second quotation comes from both *Cato* 7. 24 and *Tusc.* 1. 31:

(2)Serit arbores quae saeclo prosint alteri. (Caecil. 210)

"He plants trees that are to benefit the next generation."

In both instances, Cicero cites Caecilius as literary confirmation of what he himself believes to be true on philosophical grounds. Neither the motif of planting trees nor that of working for future generations is standard in comedy. Similarly, the third fragment (Caecil. 211–214), quoted in *nat. deor.* 1. 13, merely provides literary support for something Cicero wants to say anyway. It is cited as an instance of a *quiritatio*, the act of calling one's fellow-citizens to show them that a wrong has been done. Being a typically Roman (and originally Indo-European) institution, the *quiritatio* also recurs in Plautus *Menaechmi* 1004–1006 (in an Epidamnian setting) and *Rudens* 615–626 (in Cyrene), but it is not a frequent motif of comedy. In this third fragment, a prostitute, one of the stock characters of comedy, is mentioned, but this is not the reason why Cicero cites the fragment. Thus we can see that quotations by Cicero have to be treated with caution when we want to reconstruct themes or plots: while comic motifs may sometimes appear (as in the first and third fragment cited above), that is not always the case.

In conclusion, my initial claim seems to be borne out by the data: quotations by grammarians are useful for establishing literary themes, quotations by literary authors are useful for establishing linguistic usage. This means that for every fragmentary author we first need to check where our snippets come from. I shall now adopt this procedure when looking at Naevius.

LANGUAGE AND LITERARY MOTIFS IN GNAEUS NAEVIUS

We have 110 fragments of Naevius. Eighty of these belong to the thirty-two plays whose names we know. The remaining thirty fragments are transmitted only under the author's name, which means that some of them may actually belong to one or other of the thirty-two named plays. The amount of text we have for each of the thirty-two plays varies immensely. At one extreme we find the *Commotria*, of which we only know one word (*cārĕre* "card wool," Naev. *com.* 35ᵃ); at the other extreme, there are the *Tarentilla* with fifteen short fragments and the *Corollaria* with eleven. All of the fragments of the thirty-two named plays come from grammarians or lexicographers, and all but four of the remaining fragments come from nonliterary sources as well. The four fragments transmitted for literary reasons deserve to be quoted in full:

(3) Animum amore capitali compleuerint. (Naev. 136)

They have filled my heart with life-threateningly huge love.

(4)   Regum filiis
linguis faueant atque adnutent, nec <animis> subseruiant. (Naev. 111–112)

They would hold their tongues for the kings' sons and nod to them in assent, but they would not serve them with their hearts.

(5) Pati necesse est multa mortales mala. (Naev. 106)

Mortals must needs suffer many bad things.

(6) Etiam qui res magnas manu saepe gessit gloriose,
cuius facta uiua nunc uigent, qui apud gentes solus praestat,
eum suus pater cum pallio uno<d> ab amica abduxit. (Naev. 108–110)

Even the man who has often done great deeds gloriously, whose actions are alive and strong now, and who alone stands out among the peoples, even him his own father dragged away from his girl-friend with a single cloak.

The first two of these fragments are quoted by Fronto (ca. CE 95–167). Fragment (3) has a letter of Fronto's correspondent as subject; it is uncertain if the sentence also had a letter as subject in Naevius's play, and this uncertainty means that the fragment cannot tell us anything about the play at all. Much the same can be said of (4): we do not learn anything about the comedy as such because it remains unclear whether we are dealing with a general statement about a type of person or with a concrete condemnation of characters in the comedy. However, in the absence of any Plautine or Terentian parallel of kings appearing on stage I am inclined towards the first interpretation.[4] Fragment (5), cited in a letter by Jerome (CE 347–420), is equally unhelpful for reconstructing the comedy of Naevius; the gnomic statement could be applied to all sorts of situations. Fragment (6), quoted in Gell. 7. 8. 5, is the only of our four fragments that is given some context. Gellius (second century CE) tells us that they constitute an invective against Publius Scipio Africanus the Elder. Here we actually have an important difference between the theatrical practices of Naevius on the one hand and Plautus and Terence on the other. Naevius is said not to have been afraid of mocking the nobility, which ultimately led to his imprisonment (alluded to in Plautus, *Miles Gloriosus* 210–212), while Plautine allusions to contemporary events are never directed against individuals and Terence prefers to stay in the Greek world altogether.

From a linguistic perspective, these four fragments are interesting because they contain no deviations from Plautine usage and barely any from classical practices. In fact, only the fourth fragment, in iambic septenarii, contains nonclassical elements: in the first line there is iambic shortening in *manu*, in the second line *cuius* is monosyllabic, and in the third line we have to restore an ablative *unod* if we scan it like Ribbeck (in which case we also have the common hiatus after the eighth element); however, as the ablative *-d* in Plautus is restricted to the monosyllables *med* and *ted*, both of which only occur before vowel, alternative emendations of the line in Naevius may be preferable, for instance Bergk's *pallio uno <saepe>*.

Similar to these four fragments is the one quotation we have from the *Tribacelus* ("The Super-Faggot"):

(7) Deos quaeso ut adimant et patrem et matrem meos. (Naev. 95)

I ask the gods that they may take away my father and mother.

This quotation comes from Donatus (*in Ter. Ad.* 521). Though Donatus is mostly concerned with grammar, this passage from Naevius is quoted for the literary motif: in Terence, a slave wishes death on his young master's father so that the inheritance can be used for setting free some girl of easy virtue, and the young master agrees; in Naevius, the situation is more extreme because the young man himself wishes death on his father and adds his mother. In Plautus, too, both father and mother may be regarded as no

---

[4] In the prologue to the *Amphitruo,* it is said that *reges* will appear on stage (61); but since no real kings take part in the action, Christenson is right to interpret this word as "regal personages" (Christenson 2000: 149).

more than a source for money (*Pseudolus* 120–122), even though in this passage it is not a matter of life and death.

We can now turn to the fragments quoted by grammarians and lexicographers. Here our main sources are Charisius (fourth century CE) (thirty-three fragments), Festus (second century CE) / Paulus (eighth century CE) (twenty-one fragments), Nonius (nineteen fragments), and Varro (fourteen fragments). The fragments are not a uniform collection of oddities; especially Charisius is interested in illustrating regular usages with material from Naevius. Thus many of the words quoted by grammarians and lexicographers are not unusual from a Plautine or Terentian perspective, for instance, *admodum* "quite" (Naev. 27), *apluda* "chaff" (Naev. 117), or *guttur* "throat" as a masculine rather than a neuter noun (Naev. 135). Altogether, there are fifty-two such items.

Other usages are not attested in Plautus, sometimes undoubtedly merely due to chance, but have parallels elsewhere, for instance *aleo* "gambler" (Naev. 118; Catull. 29. 2) or *conspondere* "exchange pledges" (133ᵃ; *CIL* I² 581. 13). In total, there are twenty-one such words.

Of course, a number of hapax legomena occur as well: *ai* imperative of *aio* "say" (125), *amascere* "begin to love" (138), *bilbit* "sound made by a vessel" (probably verbal, though this could also be an indeclinable onomatopoeic word) (124), *buttubatta* "nonsense" (132⁵), *cassabundus* "stumbling" (120), *clucidatus* "sweet" (62), *defricate* "keenly (of speech)" (80), *dispuluerare* "turn something to dust" (57), *exbolus* "thrown out, discarded" (103), *herem* as accusative of *heres* "heir" (58), *lustro* "visitor of brothels" (119), *nauco* ablative⁶ of *naucum* "thing of little value" (105), *oppidum* "barriers at the beginning of the race course" (107), *parcui* as perfect of *parcere* "spare" (69), *patias* as active present subjunctive of *pati* "suffer" (67), *pēnītus* "furnished with a tail" (122ᵃ), *Pisatilis* "inhabitant of Pisae" (113ᵃ), *praebia* "charms" (71), *praemiator* "collector of rewards" (17), *promicare* "cause to spring forward" (16⁷), *prospicus* "looking ahead" and *despicus* "looking down" (25), *rutabulum* as metaphor for the penis⁸ (127), *sanderacinus* "red (from realgar)" (123), *socrus* masculine⁹ "father-in-law" (66), *sonticus* "genuine"¹⁰ (128), *trit* interjection imitating farting (48ᶜ), *tux pax* as exclamation of thanks (7¹¹). Of these *hapax legomena*, only four are distinctly archaic (*ai, nauco, socrus, sonticus*); most others

---

⁵ Also in Plautus fr. dub. 30 Monda, but listed here because the word does not occur elsewhere and is of somewhat uncertain meaning (it could conceivably be an interjection).

⁶ The genitive of this noun is common in fixed phrases in Plautus and still used by Cicero (*div.* 1. 132), but cases other than the genitive were no longer used, and the precise meaning of the noun was already unclear in Plautus's day (cf. *Mostellaria* 1042).

⁷ Apuleius also uses the verb (e.g., *Met.* 3. 10), but without the causative meaning; he may well have learned the word by reading Naevius.

⁸ Normally the word refers to some kind of shovel for turning coals.

⁹ Hofmann and Szantyr (1965: 6–7) believe that the noun was originally a *nomen commune* like *sacerdos* "priest / priestess," whose gender depended on the sex of the referent; the restriction of *socrus* to the feminine gender (and female referents) is a later phenomenon.

¹⁰ In the phrase *morbus sonticus* "serious disease (preventing someone from going to court)" the word remained in legal usage; the meaning of *senium sonticum* (Nov. Com. 37) is unclear.

¹¹ Plautus has *tuxtax* (*Persa* 264), but this imitates the sound of blows.

follow productive word-formation patterns, like *amascere* or *cassabundus*, or show morphological variation that we find in similar words in Plautus, for instance *patias* instead of *patiare* (cf. *opino* instead of *opinor* in Plautus). What is remarkable is the use of certain interjections not attested elsewhere. But given that the ancient grammarians could not find greater oddities than the ones listed here, one gets the impression that the language of Naevius was no more problematic than the language of Plautus, as is confirmed by a comparison with the quotes from literary authors.

In the Naevian fragments preserved by grammarians, all major literary motifs of Plautine comedy occur already. We find an alluring prostitute (75–79), the beginning of love (137–138), a young man wanting to borrow money to pay for a prostitute (96–98), the hiring of a prostitute (105), a pregnant girl of good family (125), references to slave punishments (13, 114, 115), a bombastic cook (121–123), a hanger-on (60), a list of delicacies (65), gluttony (135), and someone listening in on a conversation (32–34). The question whether it is better to marry a virgin or a widow (53–54) is reminiscent of Antipho's words in Plautus *Stichus* 118–119. Naevius praises his own plays (1) just as Plautus does (*Bacchides* 214, *Captivi* 1033–1034). In the same way as Plautus routinely refers to King Agathocles, Naevius mentions Pantaleon of Pisa (113ᵃ). Both authors mock the inhabitants of Praeneste (Naev. 21–24, Plautus *Truculentus* 690–691). And finally, the biting off of someone's nose could refer to passionate kissing, as the similar phrase in Plautus *Menaechmi* 194–195 shows, or to madness (*Captivi* 604–605). Thus these fragments show that Naevius was not only Plautus's predecessor in time, but also one of his major models; direct imitation can probably be observed in Naev. 75–79 and *Asinaria* 775–780: what the girl of easy virtue does in Naevius corresponds well with what the prostitute is forbidden in the hanger-on's contract in Plautus. We can now turn to Caecilius and see that this author adapted Greek plays in a way that is very similar to Plautus.

Caecilian Elements in Caecilius

The scholar trying to compare Roman comedies with their Greek models always faces the problem that we have very few remains of Greek New Comedy. Terence is generally assumed to remain relatively faithful to the plots and tone of his originals, even though he himself admits taking liberties and acknowledges following Plautus, Naevius, and Ennius in this (*Andria* 9–14, 18–20). Plautus, by contrast, is known to have adapted more freely: we have a papyrus fragment containing some sixty lines of Menander's *Dis exapaton* ("The Double Deceiver"; text and discussion in Handley 1968), which is the Greek original of Plautus's *Bacchides*. It shows that Plautus cut out an entire scene, expanded other elements, turned simple spoken language into elaborate song, and did not even leave the names of the characters unchanged (details in Bain 1979). The fact that Plautus was more of an adapter than a translator was widely accepted before our fragment of the *Dis exapaton* was published, and even before Menander's *Dyskolos* ("The Grumpy Man") became available to scholarship in 1959; the reason is that as early as 1922 Fraenkel published his important study on Plautine originality, *Plautinisches im Plautus* (now updated as Fraenkel 2007). Relying on internal evidence, such as allusions to Roman institutions and Latin puns, Fraenkel showed what types of expression were Plautine rather than Greek. He reached remarkable conclusions: for example, many references to Greek myths, customs, and places cannot have been in the Greek originals, but were inserted by Plautus; certain types of jokes and puns are also Plautine rather than Greek; and above all, Plautus typically expanded the role of the clever slave, who did exist in Greek comedy, but never had the prominence he has in Plautus.

Caecilius is usually considered to be closer to Plautus than to Terence. Gellius (2. 23) gives us three passages of Menander's *Plokion* ("The Necklace") and Caecilius's adaptation. All three of the Greek passages are in iambic trimeters and relatively neutral language. Caecilius has turned the first passage into a song, but left the others in iambic senarii, the Latin equivalent of the trimeter. More importantly, Caecilius has changed the content considerably. The first passage is full of Roman ritual terminology; the second contains some slapstick humor about the speaker's wife's bad breath, absent in the Greek original; and the third passage has been shortened and given a tragic ring.

The verdict reached by Gellius is unequivocal:

(8) Itaque, ut supra dixi, cum haec Caecilii seorsum lego, neutiquam uidentur ingrata ignauaque, cum autem Graeca comparo et contendo, non puto Caecilium sequi debuisse quod assequi nequiret. (Gell. 2. 23. 22)

Thus, as I said above, when I read these passages of Caecilius on their own, they do not seem devoid of grace and spirit at all, but when I compare and match them with the Greek passages, I do not believe that Caecilius should have followed a model he could not reach.

This judgment is certainly unfair. Let us compare the second passage from Menander and Caecilius:

(9) Α· ἔχω δ' ἐπίκληρον Λάμιαν· οὐκ εἴρηκά σοι
τοῦτ'; εἶτ' ἄρ' οὐχί; κυρίαν τῆς οἰκίας
καὶ τῶν ἀγρῶν καὶ τῶν ἁπάντων ἄντικρυς[12]
ἔχομεν, Ἄπολλον, ὡς χαλεπῶν χαλεπώτατον·
ἅπασι δ' ἀργαλέα 'στίν, οὐκ ἐμοί μόνῳ,
υἱῷ, πολὺ μᾶλλον θυγατρί—Β· πρᾶγμ' ἄμαχον λέγεις.
Α· εὖ οἶδα. (Menander K-A fr. 297)

A: I have an heiress-witch; haven't I told you this? I really haven't? We have her outright as ruler of the house, the fields, and everything, by Apollo, the most tiresome thing of all. She's troublesome to all, not just to me, but also to her son and much more so to her daughter—

---

[12] Kock's conjecture; the manuscript reading is παντωναντεκεινες.

B: You're telling me about something you can't fight against.
A: I know that well.

(10) A: Sed tua morosane uxor, quaeso, est? B: Vah![13] Rogas?
A: Qui tandem? B: Taedet mentionis, quae mihi,
      ubi domum adueni, adsedi, extemplo sauium
      dat ieiuna anima. A: Nil peccat de sauio.
      Vt deuomas uolt, quod foris potaueris. (Caecil. 158–162)

A: But tell me, is your wife difficult?
B: Bah! You ask?
A: Well then, how about it?
B: It upsets me to tell; when I come home and sit down, she immediately gives me a kiss with fasting breath.
A: She's not making any mistake about the kiss. She wants you to throw up what you drank outside.

In Menander the married man calls his wife an heiress, in reference to her dowry, and a witch; she is said to be domineering and to control both husband and children. Thus the main complaint the man has is that his wife, because of her dowry, has assumed too much power in the relationship. In Caecilius this complaint has completely fallen under the table. Instead, the husband complains about his wife's bad breath, which turns her kisses into an unpleasant experience, and his friend provides a malicious *para prosdokian* response— instead of sympathizing with him, he suggests that his friend deserves this treatment.

It would be too easy to be dismissive of Caecilius's adaptation and to say like Gellius that he did not achieve what Menander had been able to. However, such a statement would be unfair, because it would ignore the fact that Caecilius has aims vastly different from those of Menander. Menander makes us smile, but rarely laugh. Individual scenes are not independently important, but gain their significance from their function in the play as a whole. By contrast, Caecilius adapts his models in the same way as Plautus. The farcical jokes he inserted are a truly Caecilian element in Caecilius. Like Plautus, he takes such liberties because for him the unit that matters is not the comedy as a whole but the individual scene (for Plautus, see Lefèvre 1991: 81). If for Menander the sum is more than the whole of its parts, then for Caecilius and Plautus it is the individual scene that is emphasized, even if the coherence of the whole suffers. I shall now turn to Titinius and show why little can be reconstructed beyond individual scenes.

THE *SETINA* BY TITINIUS

There are six plays by Titinius of which we have ten fragments or more. Among these, the *Setina* ("The Woman from Setia") with its eighteen fragments is the longest, which is

---

[13] Thus Ribbeck in the apparatus; in the text he prints the peculiar *quam rogas.*

the reason I discuss it here. All of the fragments are transmitted by grammarians: eight by Nonius, six by Charisius, three by Festus, and one by Servius (fourth century CE).

Linguistically, most of the fragments are unremarkable. Nonius cites his eight fragments for the following reasons: *neuolt* "he does not want" for *non uolt*, a Plautine usage; *neuter tale* "such" for *talis*, where in reality we are dealing with either loss of final –*s* before consonant (*est tali' Setiae*) or prodelision (*talest Setiae*); *factio* "wealth, nobility," a frequent word; masculine *frons* "forehead," a common usage in older Latin; *cumatilis* "sea-colored," as in Plaut. *Epid.* 233; *itus* "gait," a relatively rare word, but also attested in the classical period; *catapulta* "missile," again a regular usage in early Latin; and *trua* "cook's ladle," a rare word also attested in Pompon. 96. The quotations in the other grammarians are also made for rather trivial reasons; the only usage that cannot be paralleled in other writers of comedy or in classical prose is *Tiberis* "Tiber" as a feminine noun (Titin. 120, cited in Serv. *Aen.* 11. 457). The only interesting lexical item in these fragments which is not cited by grammarians is the word *hermaphroditus*. In Latin literature, the noun is mostly employed as a proper name referring to a divinity with both male and female characteristics. As a common noun referring to a nonmythological being, the word occurs only here, in a pejorative sense, and in the scientific discussions in Pliny the Elder (*nat.* 7. 34 and 11. 262), where the word is stylistically neutral.

To what extent can we reconstruct the plot of the play? If we had a heavily damaged manuscript of Titinius with the same number of fragments, the situation would probably be easier than it is at present; for in manuscripts, the speakers are normally indicated, and the fragments would be in the correct order. As our grammarians are only interested in linguistic problems, we do not know which fragment belongs to which stock character or if there is a change of speaker within the fragment. And while grammarians like Nonius, as a result of their work methods, tend to put fragments later in their lists if they occur later in the plays, this fact is not very helpful, because our fragments occur in different parts of the grammatical treatises and in different grammarians.

Both Ribbeck and Guardì order the fragments thematically. Since the first nine fragments fall into clear thematic groups, the two editors differ here only in the ordering of fragments vii and viii. The order of the other fragments does not correspond in the two editions.

Fragments i–iii deal with the wedding between a man and a woman from Setia, presumably the one the play is named after. In fr. i, the man is said to be unwilling to marry, in fr. ii an engagement has already taken place, and in fr. iii someone, presumably the man from fr. i and ii, tells a certain Caeso that he may have acted imprudently by approaching a girl from such a wealthy and powerful family. Given that three fragments discuss a wedding, that the play is named after a woman, and that marriage plays such a central role in the *fabula palliata*, this may well be the central theme of the play.

Charisius is the source of the following two fragments, which are cited because of interjections. In fr. iv, a certain Paula, who may or may not be identical with the woman after whom the play is named, is asked to say *praefiscini* "touch wood" after some praise in order to prevent bad luck. We may guess that it is Paula who praised someone, and that this someone is Paula herself, as *praefiscini* is most common in such contexts, but neither of these assumptions can be verified. If Paula is the woman from a great family mentioned earlier and not a prostitute, her appearance on stage is somewhat unusual by the standards we are used to from the *palliata*. The interjection *edi medi* "so help me Dius Fidius" in fr. v is, according to Charisius, one of those used only by men, so the line must be spoken by a man, though probably not by the *magister* "teacher" that Ribbeck conjectured out of *magis* "more" (see Welsh 2010b). The addressee is, as Charisius tells us, an effeminate young man, probably the one we will encounter in the following fragments; he had said *pol edepol* "by Pollux," which Charisius claims is a women's oath and helps to characterize him as soft, but as this interjection is used gender-neutrally in all Roman playwrights, the joke need not be about the man's looks and behavior.

Fragments vi–ix have physical appearance as their unifying theme. In fr. vi, a man's hairstyle is ridiculed as if it belonged to a hermaphrodite; in fr. vii, it is also a man who is wearing the color blue; and in fr. viii, the person wearing *mullei*, a type of red shoes worn by patricians, is presumably also a man, as these were men's shoes. It seems, then, we are dealing with one and the same man, an extravagantly dressed character, and in all likelihood the mention of gait, bearing, and dress in fr. ix refers to the same person. Who this man is we cannot say, but as such detailed characterization would be odd for a minor figure, it must be a central character, probably the one from fr. v, who is perhaps even identical with the young man we have encountered in fr. i–iii.

In fr. x, the mouthpiece of a bridle, *oreae*, is mentioned, but the reference is unclear. Fr. xi must come from a dialogue; someone asks another person if he has seen the Tiber, and the reply is positive: it would be a good river to provide water for Setia. It seems that a character from rural Setia has recently been to Rome. In fr. xii, the erection of a statue with public money is talked about, but the context is unclear; could the speaker be a boastful slave? In Plautus, *Bacchides* 640, the slave Chrysalus says that he deserves a statue made of gold. Fr. xiii was tentatively regarded as part of a running-slave scene by Guardì (1985: 151), but this is doubtful at best, as running slaves only stop when they finally meet the person they are keen to meet; here, however, the person turns around when seeing someone else and runs away. Fr. xiv presents us with a cock flying off a roof, a good omen for Romans; again the context is impossible to determine. Fr. xv mentions a cook, but need not come from a cook scene: first we are told that a helmsman directs a ship with intelligence rather than strength, then we are told that a cook stirs a big pot with a tiny ladle; probably, then, the reference to the cook is merely meant to create a funny juxtaposition of a highly appreciated profession and one generally scorned. Fr. xvi is too short to be of any use. Fr. xvii comes from a house-cleaning scene that could be compared with Plautus, *Stichus* 62. Finally, fr. xviii appears to consist of insults against a slave, who needs beating; this is one of the most common motifs in Plautus.

As can be seen, many motifs of the *palliata* recur in this genre of comedy. If we did not know that the play was written by Titinius and called *Setina* (with a subsequent reference to the *ager Setinus*), the only clear indication that we are dealing with a *fabula togata* rather than a *palliata* would be the Roman names Caeso and Paula. The mention of visiting the Tiber means little in this context, as Plautus also mentions stealing the crown of the statue of *Iupiter Capitolinus* in Rome (*Trinummus* 83–85).

But while typical motifs are very much in evidence here, the plot itself remains elusive. It seems to be about the difficulties in securing a marriage between a woman from Setia, possibly called Paula, and a man, possibly the effeminate character we have encountered. Anything beyond this is mere speculation.

Conclusions

Working on Plautus's predecessors and contemporaries means working on fragments. Paradoxically, fragments preserved by grammarians are more helpful for learning about literary motifs than fragments preserved by men of letters, and fragments preserved by men of letters give a clearer picture of the regular linguistic usage of fragmentary authors than fragments preserved by grammarians. Most fragments of Naevius come from grammarians; they reveal that his literary motifs were very similar to Plautus. Linguistically speaking, Naevius seems not to have deviated much from classical and Plautine usages, although there are a number of hapax legomena. Just as Plautus was influenced by Naevius, Caecilius was influenced by Plautus; his working methods strike us as remarkably "Plautine," as a comparison of Menander's *Plocion* with Caecilius's adaptation shows. If the *Setina* is anything to go by, Titinius's *togatae* do not differ much in language and motifs from the *palliatae* we know, but the plots of his plays remain difficult to reconstruct.

FURTHER READING

Detailed discussions of Roman dramatists can be found in Suerbaum's monumental *Handbuch* (2002). For the student concentrating on comedy, Duckworth (1952) may be more useful because, unlike Suerbaum, he excludes other genres. Deufert (2002) is indispensable for questions of textual transmission. Wright (1974: 1–13) uses Plautus's *Mostellaria* to argue that the type of fragments we have does not allow us to reconstruct much. For the fragments of Atellan farce and a commentary see Frassinetti (1953 and 1967); further discussion can be found in Raffaelli and Tontini (2010). For an excellent overview of mime and an edition of the Laberian fragments with commentary, see Panayotakis (2010).

BIBLIOGRAPHY

Bain, D. 1979. "*PLAVTVS VORTIT BARBARE*: Plautus, *Bacchides* 526–61 and Menander, *Dis exapaton* 102–12." In *Creative Imitation and Latin Literature,* edited by D. West and A. Woodman, 17–34. Cambridge, UK: Cambridge University Press.
Christenson, D. M. 2000. *Plautus: Amphitruo.* Cambridge: Cambridge University Press.
Daviault, A. 1981. *Comoedia togata: Fragments.* Paris: Belles Lettres.

de Melo, W. D. C. 2010. "The Language of Atellan Farce." In *L'Atellana letteraria: Atti della prima giornata di studi sull'Atellana: Succivo (Ce) 30 ottobre 2009,* edited by R. Raffaelli and A. Tontini, 89–123. Urbino: Quattro Venti.

Deufert, M. 2002. *Textgeschichte und Rezeption der plautinischen Komödien im Altertum.* Berlin: De Gruyter.

Duckworth, G. E. 1952. *The Nature of Roman Comedy: A Study in Popular Entertainment.* Princeton: Princeton University Press.

Fraenkel, E. 2007. *Plautine Elements in Plautus.* Translated by T. Drevikovsky and F. Muecke. Oxford: Oxford University Press. Originally published as *Plautinisches im Plautus* (Berlin, 1922).

Frassinetti, P. 1953. *Fabula Atellana: Saggio sul teatro popolare latino.* Genoa: Istituto di filologia classica.

——. 1967. *Atellanae fabulae* Rome: Ateneo.

Guardì, T. 1985. *Fabula togata 1: Titinio e Atta.* Milan: Jaca Book.

Handley, E. W. 1968. *Menander and Plautus: A Study in Comparison: An Inaugural Lecture Delivered at University College London 5 February 1968.* London: Lewis.

Hofmann, J. B., and Szantyr, A. 1965. *Lateinische Syntax und Stilistik.* Munich: C. H. Beck.

Lefèvre, E. 1991. "Curculio oder Der Triumph der Edazität." In *Plautus barbarus: Sechs Kapitel zur Originalität des Plautus,* edited by E. Lefèvre, E. Stärk, and G. Vogt-Spira, 71–105. Tübingen: Narr.

Monda, S., ed. 2004. *Vidularia et deperditarum fabularum fragmenta.* Urbino: Quattro Venti.

Panayotakis, C. 2010. *Decimus Laberius: The Fragments.* Cambridge: Cambridge University Press.

Questa, C. 2007. *La metrica di Plauto e di Terenzio.* Urbino: Quattro Venti.

Raffaelli, R., and Tontini, A., eds. 2010. *L'Atellana letteraria: Atti della prima giornata di studi sull'Atellana: Succivo (Ce) 30 ottobre 2009.* Urbino: Quattro Venti.

Ribbeck, O., ed. 1898. *Comicorum Romanorum praeter Plautum et Syri quae feruntur sententias fragmenta.* 3rd ed. Leipzig: Teubner.

Suerbaum, W., ed. 2002. *Handbuch der lateinischen Literatur der Antike.* Vol. 1, *Die archaische Literatur: Von den Anfängen bis Sullas Tod: Die vorliterarische Periode und die Zeit von 240 bis 78 v. Chr.* Munich: C. H. Beck.

Welsh, J. T. 2010a. "Quintilian's Judgement of Afranius." *Classical Quarterly* 60: 118–126.

——. 2010b. "A *magister* in the *togata*: C. Iulius Romanus on *edio fidio* (Char. p. 258. 1–7)." *Mnemosyne,* n.s., 63: 276–279.

Wright, J. 1974. *Dancing in Chains: The Stylistic Unity of the Comoedia Palliata.* Rome: American Academy.

CHAPTER 23

···

PLAUTUS AND TERENCE IN PERFORMANCE

···

ERICA M. BEXLEY

PERFORMANCE is a crucial element of drama. The appearance of the set, the audience's mood, how an actor chooses to deliver a particular line: each of these factors will affect not just a play's success but its very meaning. Studying theater in textual form often leaves us with a false impression of its stability, as if every enactment rendered characters and dialogue in precisely the same way. Of course this is never the case, but it is also difficult—some would say impossible—to recapture that fleeting moment in which a dramatic script is presented, live, before a group of spectators.

The last forty years of scholarship on Plautus and Terence have seen a growth in performance criticism. Plautine drama has proved especially fruitful, with many scholars analyzing its theatrically self-conscious style ("metatheater": Slater 1985; Moore 1998), or addressing issues of stagecraft and production (Beacham 1991; Marshall 2006; Manuwald 2011). The latter approach is as fraught with problems as it is important: scant and/or ambiguous evidence, combined with any performance's ephemeral nature, means that scholars of Roman stagecraft must engage in a degree of speculation and deductive reasoning accompanied, in some instances, by analogies drawn from practical experience. This essay faces the same limitations and addresses them in much the same way. Part 1 ("Production") examines whether and how performances of *comoedia palliata* were affected by the conditions of theater production prevailing ca. 210–160 BCE. Part 2 ("Performance") interprets the specific dramatic qualities of four individual scenes and describes aspects of their enactment by combining textual evidence with the author's own empirical knowledge of staging ancient drama.

PART 1: PRODUCTION

···

More than most other artistic media, drama depends on and is shaped by the very real, physical components of its presentation. Each aspect of the production process and setting will influence a play's appearance, so that *Hamlet* staged in a black-box studio is quite distinct from *Hamlet* at the reconstructed Globe. For the theater of Plautus and Terence, however, we have much less evidence than we do for Shakespeare. Even though towns in central and southern Italy had built permanent stone theaters as early as the third century BCE, Rome itself relied on temporary structures until 55 BCE, when Pompey unveiled a temple-theater in honor of Venus.[1] Nothing therefore remains of the stages that supported Plautus's and Terence's plays, and any attempt to understand what these performances looked like must employ vestigial and sometimes questionable evidence.

To begin with, some basic facts may be gleaned from the plays themselves. *Palliata* plots always take place in front of one, two, or three dwellings; it is therefore assumed that a typical *scaenae frons* consisted of three doors, any one of which could represent the house of a citizen, the house of a courtesan, or a temple (see Vitruvius 5.6.8 and Pollux 4.19.125–127). Further, *Bacchides* 832 implies that these doors were separated by a distance of three adult paces. On either side of this simple backdrop were the wings, which dramatic convention imagined as two roads, one leading to a rural area and the other to a civic location (Beare 1964: 248–255; Duckworth 1952: 85–88). Usually, performers used the same route for any given sequence of entry and exit, and for rare instances in which this did not occur, *palliata* employed the further convention of the *angiportum*, an alleyway invisible to the audience and supposed to connect the back doors of all three houses (e.g., *Persa* 678–679). That the *scaenae frons* also supported some kind of basic roof is suggested by *Amphitruo* (1021–1034 and *frag.* 1–6), where Mercury ascends to the house's gables with the intention of emptying pots on Amphitryon's head.

The texts themselves also give the impression of a crowded and noisy performance space. Plautus's prologues call on a herald to make the audience pay attention (*Asinaria* 4; *Poenulus* 11), and the prologue to *Poenulus* (17–18) expressly forbids spectators to sit on the stage. Similarly, Plautus's and Terence's habit of addressing the audience directly implies a degree of proximity and intimacy probably not experienced in permanent theater buildings, especially those of Greek design (see Manuwald 2011: 66–68).

More detailed description is virtually unattainable, and we must be wary of extrapolations from illustrated scenes on Southern Italian vases (fourth century BCE), or from Pompeian wall paintings (first century CE). Recent work by Goldberg (1998, see also Franko in this volume) has demonstrated how temporary Roman theaters were adapted to the urban space around them, for instance using preexisting structures such as temple steps in place of a separate, purpose-built *cavea*. Taken further, Goldberg's argument could imply that Rome's theaters had no one, uniform shape; that they changed according to whether a performance was held on the Palatine (*Pseudolus*), or in the forum (*Curculio*), or at an aristocratic funeral (*Hecyra*). These adjustments most likely affected

---

[1] Combining theaters with temples was not Pompey's innovation but an established Italic custom; see Hanson 1959 and Goldberg 1998. Following this custom enabled Pompey to sidestep senatorial criticism regarding permanent theaters in Rome: he claimed he had built merely a temple (cf. Gellius *NA* 10.1.7 and Tertullian *De Spec.* 10.5).

the audience's space more than they affected the actual stage, which needed a consistent layout in order to accommodate plays of the same genre.

Another potential source of evidence is the remains of stone theaters used in southern Italy during Plautus's and Terence's lifetime. Although the fact of their permanence resulted in a more uniform style and imposing *scaenae frons*, their stage dimensions needed to approximate those of Roman theaters if they were to host similar performances or even repeat performances of plays that had premiered at major Roman festivals.[2] These structures are characterized by deep stages that could hold a potentially large group of actors. Such an arrangement makes sense for performances of *palliata*, which allowed up to ten performers to appear on stage simultaneously (see section 2.1, below). Plautus and Terence frequently script conversations between four or five individuals (Franko 2004), and many of their scenes require mute extras as well. Rome's temporary stages must therefore have been deep enough to contain these crowded scenes, and to provide room for the frenetic movement that typifies Plautine comedy in particular.

Our knowledge regarding stage decoration is equally speculative. As Beacham (2007: 216) points out, the provisional nature of early Roman theater buildings need not preclude their having had sumptuous decor. In 58 BCE, for instance, L. Aemilius Scaurus erected an elaborate temporary theater comprising three stories (the first was marble!), 360 columns, and more than a thousand bronze statues (Pliny *N.H.* 36.11–15). Forty years earlier, Claudius Pulcher is said to have commissioned lavishly realistic scene-painting (*skenographia*) for the backdrop of a temporary stage (Pliny *N.H.* 35.23). We should not, however, place undue emphasis on these examples, since they pertain to the first century BCE, an era in which ambitious Roman aristocrats wooed the populace via increasingly competitive demonstrations of conspicuous consumption. Theaters of the late third and early second centuries BCE were much smaller by comparison, and the sponsorship of public shows in this period was not as likely to influence the outcome of elections (Goldberg 1998: 13–14). With less impetus and less space for splendid decoration, it is probable that the theaters used by Plautus and Terence were also less lavish than their counterparts in the late republic.

Likewise, dramatic sets were relatively simple. Beare (1964: 275–278) argues convincingly that *palliata* employed neither naturalistic scenery nor scene changes, both of which modern theater audiences accept as givens. The prologue to Plautus's *Menaechmi* implies that the specific elements of any set were left to the audience's imagination, so that nothing material distinguished the location of one story from that of another: *haec urbs Epidamnus est, dum agitur fabula / quando alia agetur, aliud fiet oppidum* ("this city is Epidamnus—while this play is being performed; / when another is performed, it will become a different town," 72–73). Since the stories of most *palliata* are set on an

---

[2] What happened to plays after they had premiered in Rome is, unfortunately, a mystery. Presumably, the troupes of actors that performed at festivals in Rome then toured regional Italy, giving repeat performances. This is the most reasonable hypothesis, but even it depends on yet another unknowable fact: whether playwrights sold or retained the rights to their compositions. Lebek 1996: 33–34 and Marshall 2006: 22 discuss the issue.

urban street, few if any changes would have been required from play to play. Though Plautus's *Rudens* furnishes a notable exception to this trend by opening with a description of rocks and rugged coastline (72–78), it is unlikely that even its stage setting tried to replicate the story's physical location in more than a rudimentary manner. Instead, the geographic detail in Arcturus's prologue suggests that the audience had to conceptualize what the backdrop did not depict.

A further argument for *palliata* being staged in relatively plain theaters is the fact that these structures appear to have hosted other kinds of entertainment as well. The prologue to Terence's *Hecyra* complains that the play's second performance, which occurred at the funeral games of L. Aemilius Paullus (160 BCE), had to be aborted because of a raucous mob that surged in, expecting to see a display of gladiators (*Hecyra* 39–42). The passage implies that these two events were scheduled either back-to-back or on subsequent days, and that spectators for the second show arrived early owing to a misunderstanding in the program (Parker 1996: 597). In the imperial period, when theaters and amphitheaters were distinct structures designed for specific purposes, this would have been a difficult mistake to make, but in second-century BCE Rome, gladiatorial duels, like plays, were generally held in makeshift venues. That a rival group of spectators could invade Terence's performance and not hesitate to assume that gladiators were about to be presented (*datum iri gladiatores*, *Hecyra* 40) suggests that both events used similar, and similarly neutral, settings.

Lack of permanent performance spaces also meant that troupes had few if any opportunities to rehearse on-site. Crucial to the modern production process, rehearsals "in the space" enable actors to adjust their performance so that it fits their physical surroundings. Since actors of *palliata* had little chance to make such adjustments, they presumably developed a flexible style and were capable of modifying a play's blocking at a moment's notice. Rehearsal time frames likewise demanded flexibility; Marshall (2006: 22–23) estimates a mere three weeks of preparation time between the *aediles* entering office on March 15 and the *ludi Megalenses* taking place in early April. Other festivals may have had a longer lead-up, and evidence in Terence (*Eunuchus* 20–22) suggests that playwrights were allowed to stage preliminary performances, perhaps with a view to testing audience reactions. Overall, though, the troupes that were performing *palliata* appear to have rehearsed to a tight schedule, with hardly any time spent in the actual theater prior to the play's first showing.

How, if at all, did these various conditions affect Plautus's and Terence's dramaturgy? Scholars writing about *palliata* tend to draw a sharp distinction between the two playwrights, and to argue that Plautus enjoyed greater success because he tailored his dramatic style to the circumstances of theater production prevailing in his era.[3] According to this reasoning, Rome's temporary stage buildings and variable performance spaces,

---

[3] The view comes in many forms, and its proponents are many. To cite a few: Marshall 2006 regards Plautus's dramatic style as a direct result of production conditions ca. 210–160 BCE; Gratwick 1982: 121, Goldberg 1986: 97–105, and Segal 1987: 1 assume that Terence was less successful because he did not follow Plautus in playing to popular tastes. Parker 1996: 608–613 summarizes the various versions of this hypothesis, and refutes them convincingly.

coupled with brief rehearsal times and sparse sets, encouraged the kind of improvisa-tory, slapstick comedy of which Plautus was the master (a major premise in Marshall 2006; see also Goldberg 1998). Yet, as Parker (1996) has shown, Plautus's reputation for unalloyed success is just as erroneous as is Terence's supposed reputation for failing to win his audience's attention, let alone its love: *both* playwrights were popular, and the difference between their styles probably owes more to individual choice than to pro-duction processes per se. Although scholars are right to emphasize that the nature and dimensions of any theatrical space will affect what audiences expect and how they react, we should refrain from enshrining this observation as the sole explanation for dra-matic form. If Terence's plays are less physical and less raucous than Plautus's, this need not mean they failed to fit contemporary theatrical conditions. After all, it is easier to rehearse dialogue in a variety of spaces than it is to rehearse movement; and in a small theater, Terence's restrained, Menandrian style could well generate just as much audi-ence rapport as Plautus's ribaldry is supposed to have done.

PART 2: PERFORMANCE

Reading a play and watching a play are two very different experiences. Enactment uncovers elements latent within a dramatic text, rendering them more noticeable, sig-nificant, or emotive. What is more, every performance is itself a fresh act of interpreta-tion that brings new meaning to a dramatic script or alters how an audience regards the work. To illustrate these potential effects of performance, the following section consid-ers four scenes—two from Plautus, two from Terence—and discusses what they could look like when staged. It is of course difficult to reconstruct Plautus's or Terence's origi-nal manner of staging, and while my analysis attempts this task on occasions, the bulk of it is ex hypothesi, focusing less on how these scenes *were* performed than on how they *could be.*

Plautus

2.1 *Pseudolus 129–229 ("Act 1 Scene 2")*

Plautus's *Pseudolus* premiered at the *Ludi Megalenses* in 191 BCE. Held to celebrate the dedication of a new temple to the Magna Mater on the Palatine Hill, the games on this occasion were particularly lavish (Fraenkel 2007: 101)—a fact that may explain why *Pseudolus* 129–229 is one of the most spectacular scenes in extant Roman comedy. On paper, it is impressive mainly because of its elaborate verbosity. The pimp, Ballio, enters at 133 and delivers a show-stopping *canticum* of polysyllabic abuse. When we think about this scene as a performance, however, we realize that Plautus's stagecraft creates an effect equally as impressive as Ballio's lyrics. Using a full cast, numerous props, rapid movement, and self-consciously theatrical style, the dramaturgy of *Pseudolus* 129–229 helps to focus the audience's attention on Ballio and to present him as the ultimate performer.

From its outset, *Pseudolus* 129–229 displays the sort of striking visual quality that marks it out as a showpiece. It is a physically crowded scene. Pseudolus and Calidorus are already on stage prior to Ballio's entrance; when the pimp's door creaks in warning of his approach (130), they stay to eavesdrop. There are three actors visible to the audience at this point and, given that Ballio will sing, a flute-player (*tibicen*) is probably present as well. From four individuals on stage, the number quickly rises to ten, possibly eleven, as Ballio calls out from his house a group of slaves, to each of whom he delivers a beating and assigns a specific task. Ballio's direct addresses (157–162) name five individuals, and his further command at 166 may indicate a sixth. Besides these, there must be one more slave who remains with Ballio (170) once all of the others have returned indoors. With so many bodies, the scene gives the impression of busyness and speed.

After dismissing his domestic chattel (168), Ballio turns to matters of finance (173–229). His second harangue names four courtesans—Hedylium (188), Aeschrodora (196), Xystilis (210), and Phoenicium (227)—which leads us to assume one of two performance options: either the prostitutes are played by four additional actors (so Fraenkel 2007: 99), or four of the performers recently appearing as slaves must reemerge on stage following a rapid costume change (so Marshall 2006: 103–104). Either option is practicable, though acting troupes in Plautus's day probably chose the latter because it made fewer demands on their resources. Performance groups in second-century BCE Rome generally comprised four to six members, with additional roles filled by hired extras (Manuwald 2011: 85–86). The logical result is that crowd scenes were more costly than those featuring only one or two actors. At a minimum, *Pseudolus* 129–229 requires nine or ten performers, more than any other scene in extant Plautine comedy (Marshall 2006: 109–111, with comparisons). Adding another four might well have broken the budget, and it is likely that the courtesans' roles were doubled in an effort to minimize expense.

Such doubling has the further effect of increasing the scene's pace. Five lines is a very brief space of time, even for the simplest of costume changes: Ballio's slaves will have to exit briskly and his courtesans may arrive out of breath. This rapid movement, which takes place around Ballio and on his orders, serves to emphasize the pimp's pivotal role as both impresario and director.

If we shift our attention from actors to props, it is clear that *Pseudolus* 129–229 requires many of these as well: Ballio wields a whip (*lorum*, 145), which he employs with vicious liberality (135; 154–155); one slave carries an urn (*tu qui urnam habes*, 156); another, an axe (*te cum securi*, 157); and when Ballio warns a third slave about cutpurses (170), we are probably safe in assuming the *puer* is holding a purse (*crumina*). Like performers, these objects crowd the stage and so increase the scene's visual density. On a separate plane, they also function as complex symbols of the kind that Robert Ketterer analyses in his series of articles about Plautine stage properties (Ketterer 1986a; Ketterer 1986b; Ketterer 1986c). Ballio's whip indicates the pimp's power and violent irascibility; it designates him as the main performer in this scene. In contrast to Ballio's dominant prop, the slaves carry domestic instruments, physical symbols of their inferiority. Whenever Ballio uses his whip, he reinforces this dynamic, as, for instance, in the curious exchange at *Pseudolus* 158–159:

> **Ballio:**   te cum securi caudicali praeficio provinciae.
> **Servus:**   at haec retunsast. **Ballio:** Sine siet; itidem vos plagis omnes.

> **Ballio:**   You with the axe, I appoint you to the duty of wood-splitting.
> **Slave:**   But the axe is blunt. **Ballio:** So what? You're all blunt too, from the lash.

As a text, this banter is unremarkable, even superfluous. But in performance, stage prop-erties enhance the exchange's meaning. Significantly, the only slave who dares to talk back to Ballio is the one holding an axe. His implement of domestic servitude therefore acquires a momentarily aggressive aspect: the axe rivals Ballio's whip just as the slave's response challenges his master's orders. The irony is that the slave complains about a blunt axe; in other words, the instrument really *does* symbolize the slave's impotence. And in reply, Ballio draws attention to his lash, which is in perfect working order. The scene's properties therefore affirm Ballio's power and ensure that he is the focal point of the audience's gaze.

As a final touch, Plautus makes the scene self-consciously dramatic or "metatheat-rical." By eavesdropping on the pimp's performance, Pseudolus and Calidorus take up the position of spectators and become an internal audience for Ballio's bravura display (Slater 1985: 122–123; Moore 1998: 34). They even evaluate his acting style: an arch-performer himself, Pseudolus admires the pimp as "grand" (*magnificus*, 194); Calidorus demurs: *atque etiam malificus* ("and he's a rascal, too," 195).[4] As Moore (1998: 98) points out, Ballio can be both *magnificus* and *malificus*: a really good pimp *is* a rascal. Pseudolus's and Calidorus's comments therefore confirm Ballio in his role. At the same time, they remind the play's real audience that this scene is something special. By drawing attention to Ballio's performance, Pseudolus and Calidorus (and behind them, Plautus) make sure that spectators recognize and appreciate its spectacular quality.

2.2 *Menaechmi 1050–1162 ("Act 5, Scenes 8–9")*

Having examined several different aspects of staging Plautus, let us now focus on one: role division. Though rarely necessary in contemporary performances, dividing roles was fundamental for much of ancient Greek drama, and probably persisted in *comoedia palliata*, though to a lesser degree. We have seen, for example, how *Pseudolus* 133–229 may require four actors to double as slaves and courtesans. Plautus's *Menaechmi* does not face the same restraints: role doubling here is optional rather than necessary,

---

[4] There is some confusion about the attribution of these lines: Willcock 1987 gives 194 to Pseudolus and 195 to Calidorus, while Moore 1998: 97–98 reverses Willcock's arrangement. I have used the former option because it seems to fit the characters' personalities better.

and the point to be stressed is that Plautus's dramaturgy *allows for* a doubled role in this play, regardless of how the work was staged originally. My suggestion, therefore, is purely hypothetical: one actor can play both Menaechmus brothers right up until the final scene, when the twin's reunion naturally calls for a second performer. As the result of such staging, the final two scenes of Plautus's *Menaechmi* will encourage the audience to participate more fully in the characters' confusion.

Since misidentification easily gives rise to farcical situations, stories featuring twins, doubles, or simply two people who share the same name are stock material in Greek New Comedy (e.g., Menander's *Dis Exapaton*); *palliata* (e.g., *Menaechmi*; *Bacchides*; *Amphitruo*); and Atellan farce (*Duo Dosseni*; *Macci Gemini*). In his *Miles Gloriosus*, Plautus takes this motif a step further and creates two identities from one character by having Philocomasium appear as both herself and her make-believe twin sister (*Miles* 150–152). Damen (1989) and Marshall (2006: 105–106) suggest that the same technique could apply in Plautus's *Menaechmi*, where it would increase the play's level of farce by augmenting the audience's perplexity: if the role is doubled, both Menaechmi will have the same voice, be the same height and, in the case of performance without masks, exhibit the same facial features.[5] The upshot is a self-consciously theatrical final scene in which Messenio and Menaechmus of Epidamnus struggle to recognize a familiar character precisely because he is represented by a new actor.

At *Menaechmi* 1049, the actor who has until now played both roles (henceforth M) exits into Erotium's house. While he is inside, a different performer (henceforth S) enters as Menaechmus of Syracuse (1050). S engages in a brief dialogue with Messenio, in which he assures his confused servant that he has certainly not granted any manumission (1050–1059). The audience may well share Messenio's confusion at this point, since it is the first time that Menaechmus of Syracuse has been represented by a separate actor and, as a result, he really is *not the same person* whom Messenio has performed alongside for most of the narrative. When M returns to the stage at 1060, he too is slow to comprehend S's identity. Cleverly, this casting method will conspire with the play's storyline, so that M, the familiar actor, embodies the genuine Menaechmus (of Epidamnus), while S, the new performer, represents the "impostor" Menaechmus whose name is actually Sosicles.

The bewilderment that ensues therefore takes place at both an intra- and extra-dramatic level. For instance, when Messenio tries to work out which of the two individuals is his master (1070–1077), he draws ironic attention to the recent role division and demonstrates that there are real, performance-based reasons for his perplexity. He even alludes to the staged nature of Menaechmus's double identity by remarking to S: *illic homo aut sycophanta aut geminus est frater tuos!* ("that man is either a fraud/

---

[5] A performance without masks would necessarily be a modern interpretation, because actors in Plautus and Terence's era probably wore them. This, at least, is the current scholarly consensus after decades of debate about whether *comoedia palliata* used masks at all. For a summary of this debate, its permutations, strengths, and weaknesses, see Wiles 1991: 132–133 and, more substantially, Petrides's chapter in this volume.

actor or he's your twin brother!" 1087). Role doubling also compels audience members to participate in the process of recognition. Uncovering a character's true identity is a common motif in *palliata* and Greek New Comedy, where physical tokens often prompt fortuitous revelations (as, for instance, in Menander's *Epitrepontes* or Terence's *Hecyra*). If Plautus's *Menaechmi* is staged with one actor in two roles, recognition becomes a crucial issue not just within the plot, but also for the people watching its performance: audience members will need some means of distinguishing between two characters that are literally identical. In *Amphitruo*, another Plautine doubles comedy, Mercury assures spectators that a feather in his hat will differentiate him from Sosia, while Jupiter will identify himself by means of a gold knot (*Amphitruo*, 142–147). *Menaechmi* achieves a similar effect by using one entirely separate piece of apparel: the mantle (*palla*) that Menaechmus of Epidamnus steals from his wife at the beginning of the play. For the drama's first half, this mantle signifies Menaechmus of Epidamnus; for the second half, it identifies Menaechmus of Syracuse, who takes it from Erotium's house at 466 and keeps it in his possession until the play's last lines. The upshot is that the audience must pay careful attention to this prop. Like characters in one of New Comedy's recognition scenes, they must use a significant object to aid their judgment of an individual's true identity.

Further, delaying the division of Menaechmus's role lends the play's final recognition scene an ironic twist. Although the *palla* has constituted a kind of "recognition token" *for the audience* throughout most of the performance, it is personal information, not physical objects, that defines the brothers' identity at the play's end. This change from material to immaterial methods of recognition makes sense at an extra-dramatic level: once Menaechmus's role has been split between two actors, the audience can see the difference and thus no longer needs to rely on stage properties. One simple casting decision therefore affects the entire tenor of *Menaechmi*'s final scene, enhancing its playful self-consciousness and encouraging audience members to make up their own minds regarding the twins' identities.

Terence

2.3 *Eunuchus 46–206* ("Act 1, Scenes 1–2")

Ancient posterity valued Terence for his rhetoric. Caesar praised his "pure diction" (*purus sermo*, Suet. *Vita Ter.* 7), Cicero quoted him frequently (e.g., *De Or.* 2.172 and 326), and Quintilian used passages from his plays to illustrate points of rhetorical technique (e.g., *I.O.* 9.2.58). Though in essence complimentary, such opinions have helped generate the erroneous yet dominant modern hypothesis that, in the words of Goldberg (1986: 169): "Terence won his lasting fame as a stylist, not a playwright, and his dramatic tradition did not long survive so bookish an achievement." Not necessarily so: Terence's plays seem to have been restaged at various points in both the late republic and the early empire. Apart from ambiguous hints in literary authors (Horace *Epist.* 2.1.56–61; Quint.

I.O. 11.3.178–82; Varro *RR* 2.11.11?), the *didascaliae* on manuscripts of Terence sometimes mention revival productions (*relata est*; see also Tansey 2001). The reason we typically regard these plays as predominantly literary creations instead may be simply because Terence, unlike Plautus, was canonized as a school text (Parker 1996: 590). Since these plays were written to be performed and since it is in performance that many of their most distinctive qualities emerge, contemporary scholarship will benefit from lending greater weight to understanding Terence's stagecraft.

For example, in the second scene of *Eunuchus* (81–206), the courtesan Thais explains at length why on the preceding day she locked her young paramour, Phaedria, out of her house: the soldier who is also one of her clients has bought her a present, a young girl who Thais suspects is her own long-lost adoptive sister; in order to get her hands on the girl, Thais must indulge the soldier for a few days, so she asks Phaedria to let his rival "play the leading role" (*sine illum priores partis hosce aliquot dies / apud me habere*, 151–152). Phaedria responds angrily:

> aut ego nescibam quorsum tu ires? "parvola
> hinc est abrepta; eduxit mater pro sua;
> soror dictast; cupio abducere, ut reddam suis."
> nempe omnia haec nunc verba huc redeunt denique:
> ego excludor, ille recipitur.
>
> Did you think I didn't know where you were going?
> "A tiny little girl was abducted from this place;
> Mother raised her as her own; people call her my sister;
> I want to get hold of her, so that I can return her to her own family."
> To be sure, all of these words come down to one thing in the end:
> *I* am shut out; *he* is let in.
> (*Eunuchus* 155–159)

When Phaedria summarizes Thais's narrative (155–157), he employs the dramatic technique of "speech within speech," a style that Terence favors and appears to have inherited from Menander (Handley 2002: 179–186; see also Scafuro on Menander and Fontaine on Plautus in this volume). Its effect is *ethopoiia* or "character study" (cf. Quint. *I.O.* 9.2.58), which gives actors the opportunity to impersonate each other's performances. Menander uses it primarily to provide expository material (e.g., *Epitrepontes* 878–900) and to introduce a character prior to his or her actual appearance on stage (e.g., *Dyskolos* 103–116; see also Nünlist 2002). Moreover, if it is possible to generalize from such fragmentary remains, Menandrian "speech within speech" occurs most frequently in monologues (e.g., Demea in *Samia* 236–261), or at least in situations where the quoted individuals are not present (e.g., Geta in *Misoumenos* 297–322). In Terence, however, Phaedria imitates Thais while she is standing right beside him. The result is a harsher kind of *ethopoiia*, not gentle imitation as much as mockery and sarcasm; Phaedria's speech recapitulates the expository material that Thais has already provided (107–143) and as a consequence, it invites the audience to reassess the courtesan's veracity. At the same time, the actor playing Phaedria can jeer at Thais by mimicking her tone of voice

and physical mannerisms. We know from Quintilian (*I.O.* 11.3.91) that those performing first-century CE revivals of Menander would often alter their voices when reporting
another character's words. It seems reasonable to suppose that the same was happening
in Terence's day, and that passages like *Eunuchus* 155–157 were composed with a view to
such playful impersonation.

In fact, "speech within speech" is Terence's way of focusing our attention on how
characters represent themselves and how they expect others to behave. When Phaedria
mimics Thais's narrative, he implies that she is lying. He does so again at *Eunuchus* 176,
this time quoting Thais directly (*"potius quam te inimicum habeam"*). Ironically enough,
the more faithfully Phaedria repeats the courtesan's words, the more he manages to
insinuate that she is *not* speaking the truth. This effect becomes even more apparent on
stage: if another actor replicates Thais's role, albeit for just one line, he can quite literally expose it as a performance. Of course, the play's events will prove that Thais is not
lying and further, that she does not fit the comic stereotype of the wicked prostitute (cf.
Eunuchus 37). But Terence wants to keep his audience guessing at this early point in the
drama, and *ethopoiia* enables him to stereotype characters while also encouraging spectators to concentrate on issues of identity.

Nor is Thais's character the only one subject to mimetic mockery. In the play's first
scene, the slave Parmeno imitates his master, Phaedria, in a teasing attempt to make the
lovesick *adulescens* see sense. *Eunuchus* opens with Phaedria pacing up and down, ago-
nizing over how he should respond to Thais's recent behavior; Parmeno points out that
in matters of the heart deliberation is futile:

> et quod nunc tute tecum iratus cogitas
> "egon illam, quae illum, quae me, quae non . . . ! sine modo
> mori me malim, sentiet qui vir siem":
> haec verba una mehercle falsa lacrimula,
> quam oculos terendo misere vix vi expresserit
> restinguet.

> And whatever you now think to yourself in anger:
> "Shall I? When she—him—me—and she didn't . . . ! Just wait. . .
> I'd rather die: then she'll know what kind of man I am"
> One tiny false tear will quench all these words,
> One she's scarcely squeezed out by rubbing her eyes.

Parmeno exaggerates his impersonation and so invites the audience to laugh at
Phaedria's despair. The slave's elliptical sequence of pronouns (*egon illam, quae illum,
quae me, quae non*) not only reproduces Phaedria's staccato anger, but also parodies the
play's famous opening lines, where Terence employs a choppy style to evoke Phaedria's
distress (46–56). At the same time, Parmeno's "speech within speech" insinuates that
Phaedria is merely playing a role, and that his "Wretched Lover" act will dissolve as
quickly as Thais's tears.

Lastly, Parmeno's *ethopoiia* puts him in a momentary position of power, and not
just because it lets him jest at his master's expense. In performance, the actor playing

Parmeno may choose to appropriate Phaedria's voice and therefore, to usurp his master's role. The result is the sort of subversive, "Saturnalian" behavior generally regarded as typical of Plautus, not Terence (Segal 1987; see also Fontaine on Plautus and Petrides in this volume), and it is tempting to think that we might find more examples of the same if only we manage to treat Terence as drama rather than simply text.

2.4 Hecyra 623–726 ("Act 4, Scene 4")

This scene from Terence's *Hecyra* marks the climax of the play's multiple misunderstandings. The final act will unravel each of the plot's complex threads, but at this point neither the audience nor any of the characters on stage know the full story. Moreover, the characters who appear at 623–726 are unaware of their own ignorance; each makes assumptions from the evidence available to him: Phidippus thinks that his wife has behaved like a hostile mother-in-law; Laches thinks that *his* wife has done the same; both old men assume that Pamphilus is the father of Philumena's child; Pamphilus believes he is *not* the father. Because spectators share Pamphilus's knowledge, they will assume throughout the course of the scene that his version is the correct one. To reinforce allegiance between Pamphilus and the audience, Terence scripts a series of asides, which evoke feelings of secretive complicity (on asides, see Slater 1985: 158–160). The asides also characterize Pamphilus—incorrectly, it turns out—as someone in possession of superior knowledge. Subsequent scenes will, of course, reveal that Pamphilus is wrong and the old men right: the child *is* his. But, for this scene, Terence's dramaturgy tricks the audience into adopting a view that is just as misguided as Pamphilus's.

Like a split screen in a movie, a dramatic aside provides two (roughly) simultaneous views. Unlike a split screen, it tends to privilege one view over the other, since the character making asides generally does so from an informed position that enables him or her to comment on the situation at hand. *Hecyra* 623–726 illustrates this inequality via the characters' contrasting reactions: Laches is overjoyed to know he has a grandson (642–643, 651–653), but the news only makes Pamphilus despair (653); when Laches encourages his son not to worry, all the *adulescens* can do is worry more (650–651). Each of Pamphilus's asides separates him from the conversation, emphasizing his emotional isolation and inviting audience members to regard him differently from the way they view the others. Since an aside is essentially a means of analyzing concurrent onstage action, Pamphilus's comments place him momentarily above and beyond the drama's events.

His isolation is, however, merely figurative. On stage, Pamphilus stands beside Laches and Phidippus, who nonetheless cannot hear the young man's desperate exclamations. Such physical proximity makes the asides challenging to perform, and of the three main options available for staging *Hecyra* 623–726, each will affect how the audience perceives both Pamphilus's character and the nature of his dilemma.

The simplest way for any actor to perform Pamphilus's asides is to cup his hand around the side of his mouth and pretend to whisper, all the while projecting his voice at regular volume. This method will not only separate him from the other characters' conversation, but also create an immediate and close rapport with the play's audience. Spectators will feel that Pamphilus is addressing his problems directly to them, and they will identify with him as a result. Further, the more spectators identify with Pamphilus, the more they will be tricked into believing his version of events.

The second and slightly more complex performance method involves all three actors. For each of Pamphilus's asides, the two old men can freeze their movements in a stylized tableau, a technique that places Pamphilus momentarily beyond the story's temporality. While Laches and Phidippus maintain a state of suspended animation, the actor playing Pamphilus can voice his asides in any way he pleases. With this kind of staging, however, his comments will seem more like thoughts than utterances; they will appear even more private and removed than the "whispered" asides, and as such, they will not involve the audience to the same degree.

The third option takes this isolation a step further. Impossible on the Roman stage but standard in modern theaters, lighting can be used to focus spectators' attention on particular characters. In *Hecyra* 623–726, Pamphilus can speak his asides underneath a spotlight while the rest of the stage is dimmed or even darkened. Like the second performance method, this arrangement suspends the play's action and makes Pamphilus's asides resemble thoughts. Since a darkened stage also tends to cut ties between actors and audience, this kind of performance leaves Pamphilus very much on his own. The performer in this role need not, therefore, direct his comments towards those watching, but can speak them to himself instead. As a result, spectators will feel no particular allegiance to Pamphilus, though they may still regard his knowledge as superior to that of other characters.

All three scenarios can generate laughter easily. In the first, the actor's behavior is un-naturalistic to the point of being ludicrous. The second and third performance options differ slightly in that they make Pamphilus's comments seem more serious. But the manner in which they achieve this effect will rapidly become a source of laughter, as eight asides in fewer than 100 lines will cause tableaux or lighting changes to occur with ridiculous frequency.

*   *   *

The most basic tenet of performance criticism is that we need to think about drama as both textual and physical, as something that is done (δράω) as well as read. Since performance is fleeting, this approach is always a challenge, more so for anyone studying *comoedia palliata*, where textual evidence far outweighs anything else. Nevertheless, the task is not completely impossible. We may never know *exactly* what Plautus's and Terence's plays looked like in performance, but with a little imagination, a little deduction, and some careful sifting of evidence, we can at least begin to move these works off the page and onto the stage.

FURTHER READING

For general information on the stagecraft and production of Roman comedy, Duckworth (1952) and Beare (1964) remain valuable and reliable resources. Recent work on the topic includes

Manuwald (2011), a comprehensive survey of republican drama, and the performance-based studies Beacham (1991) and Marshall (2006), both of which focus primarily on Plautus.

Scholarship about more specific elements of performance can be found in Kurrelmeyer (1932: roles and role division); Ketterer (1986a, 1986b, 1986c: stage properties); Saunders (1909: costume); and Wiles (1991: masks). Again, Plautine drama is by far the preferred topic; Terence's stagecraft awaits fuller study. Another way of discussing performance is to analyze it at the internal level of "metatheater," for which approach Slater (1985) and Moore (1998) constitute the two fundamental examples.

On the whole, Terence has received less scholarly attention than Plautus. Büchner (1974) and Goldberg (1986) are standard book-length treatments, while chapters in Manuwald (2011) and Lowe (2007) provide useful overviews of the playwright's life and work. Parker (1996) takes a refreshingly positive view of Terence, and questions scholars' willingness to rank him as a second-rate playwright. Though Büchner (1974) touches on issues of performance, most studies approach Terence's plays as literary rather than dramatic pieces.

BIBLIOGRAPHY

Arnott, P. D. 1959. *An Introduction to the Greek Theatre*. Bloomington: Indiana University Press.

Auhagen, U. 2009. *Die Hetäre in der griechischen und römischen Komödie*. Munich: Beck.

Barsby, J. A. 1982. "Actors and Act-Divisions: Some Questions of Adaptation in Roman Comedy." *Antichthon* 16: 77–87.

——. 1999. *Terence: Eunuchus*. Cambridge, UK: Cambridge University Press.

Beacham, R. C. 1991. *The Roman Theatre and its Audience*. London: Routledge.

——. 2007. "Playing Spaces: The Temporary and the Permanent." In *The Cambridge Companion to Greek and Roman Theatre*, edited by M. McDonald and J. M. Walton, 202–226. Cambridge, UK: Cambridge University Press.

Beare, W. 1964. *The Roman Stage: A Short History of Latin Drama in the Time of the Republic*. 3rd ed. London: Methuen.

Bertini, F. 1983. "Les resources comiques du double dans le théâtre de Plaute." *LEC* 51: 308–318.

——. 1995. "Sosia e Gemelli in Plauto." In *Atti dei Convegni "Il mondo scenico di Plauto" e "Seneca e i volti del potere": (Bocca di Magra, 26–27 ottobre 1992; 10–11 dicembre 1993)*, 7–15. Genoa: Università di Genova, Facoltà di Lettere.

Bieber, M. 1961. *The History of the Greek and Roman Theater*. Princeton: Princeton University Press.

Büchner, K. 1974. *Das Theater des Terenz*. Heidelberg: C. Winter.

Christenson, D. M. 2000. *Plautus: Amphitruo*. Cambridge, UK: Cambridge University Press.

Csapo, E., and W. Slater. 1994. *The Context of Ancient Drama*. Ann Arbor: University of Michigan Press.

Damen, M. 1989. "Actors and Act-Divisions in the Greek Original of Plautus' *Menaechmi*." *CW* 82: 409–420.

Denzler, B. 1968. *Der Monolog bei Terenz*. Zürich: P. G. Keller.

Duckworth, G. E. 1952. *The Nature of Roman Comedy: A Study in Popular Entertainment*. Princeton: Princeton University Press.

Fantham, E. 1973. "Towards a Dramatic Reconstruction of the Fourth Act of Plautus' *Ampitruo*." *Philologus* 117: 197–214.

Fraenkel, E. 2007. *Plautine Elements in Plautus*. Translated by T. Drevikovsky and F. Muecke. Oxford: Oxford University Press.

Franko, G. F. 2004. "Ensemble Scenes in Plautus." *AJPh* 53: 243–251.

Fontaine, M. 2010. *Funny Words in Plautine Comedy*. Oxford and New York: Oxford University Press.

Garton, C. 1972. *Personal Aspects of the Roman Theatre*. Toronto: Hakkert.

Goldberg, S. 1986. *Understanding Terence*. Princeton: Princeton University Press.

———. 1998. "Plautus on the Palatine." *JRS* 88: 1–20.

Gratwick, A. S. 1982. "Drama." In *Cambridge History of Classical Literature*. Vol. 2, *Latin Literature,* edited by E. J. Kenney and W. V. Clausen, 77–137. Cambridge, UK: Cambridge University Press.

———. 1993. *Plautus Menaechmi*. Cambridge, UK: Cambridge University Press.

Handley, E. 2002. "Acting, Action and Words in New Comedy." In *Greek and Roman Actors: Aspects of an Ancient Profession,* edited by P. Easterling and E. Hall, 165–188. Cambridge, UK: Cambridge University Press.

Hanson, J. A. 1959. *Roman Theatre Temples*. Princeton: Princeton University Press.

Ketterer, R. C. 1986a. "Stage Properties in Plautine Comedy. Part I: Introductory Analysis (*Curculio*)." *Semiotica* 58: 193–216.

———. 1986b. "Stage Properties in Plautine Comedy. Part II: Props in Four Plays of Exchange." *Semiotica* 59: 93–135.

———. 1986c. "Stage Properties in Plautine Comedy. Part III: Props in Four Plays of Identity." *Semiotica* 60: 29–72.

Kurrelmeyer, C. M. 1932. *The Economy of Actors in Plautus*. Graz: Deutsche Vereins-Druckerei.

Lebek, W. D. 1996. "Moneymaking on the Roman Stage." In *Roman Theater and Society: E. Togo Salmon Papers 1,* edited by W. J. Slater, 29–48. Ann Arbor: University of Michigan Press.

Lowe, N. J. 2007. *Comedy*. Greece & Rome New Surveys in the Classics 37. Cambridge, UK: Cambridge University Press.

Manuwald, G. 2011. *Roman Republican Theatre*. Cambridge, UK: Cambridge University Press.

Marshall, C. W. 2006. *The Stagecraft and Performance of Roman Comedy*. Cambridge, UK: Cambridge University Press.

Moore, T. 1998. *The Theatre of Plautus: Playing to the Audience*. Austin: University of Texas Press.

Moorehead, P. G. 1953. "The Distribution of Roles in Plautus' *Menaechmi*." *CJ* 49.3: 123–127.

Nünlist, R. 2002. "Speech within Speech in Menander." In *The Language of Greek Comedy,* edited by A. Willi, 219–259. Oxford: Oxford University Press.

Parker, H. 1996. "Plautus vs. Terence: Audience and Popularity Re-examined." *AJPh* 117: 585–617.

Sandbach, F. H. 1977. *The Comic Theatre of Greece and Rome*. London: Chatto & Windus.

Saunders, C. 1909. *Costume in Roman Comedy*. New York: Columbia University Press.

Segal, E. 1987. *Roman Laughter: The Comedy of Plautus*. 2nd ed. Oxford and New York: Oxford University Press.

Slater, N. W. 1985. *Plautus in Performance: The Theatre of the Mind*. Princeton: Princeton University Press.

Tansey, P. 2001. "New Light on the Roman Stage: A Revival of Terence's *Phormio* Rediscovered." *RhM* 144: 22–43.

Wiles, D. 1991. *The Masks of Menander*. Cambridge, UK: Cambridge University Press.

Willcock, M. M. 1987. *Plautus Pseudolus*. Bristol: Bristol Classical Press.

CHAPTER 24

METRICS AND MUSIC

MARCUS DEUFERT

1. INTRODUCTION

ROMAN comedy was musical entertainment. A large proportion of its verses (on average, more than 60% in a play of Plautus and almost 50% in a play of Terence) was accompanied by the music of *tibiae* (pipes). In the rare instances where we can directly compare verses of Roman comedies with their Greek originals, the adaptations are more musical and metrically more diverse than their models: We find unaccompanied iambic trimeters of Menander and Apollodorus of Karystos changed to accompanied trochaic septenarii by Plautus (Menander *Dis Exapaton* 91–112 ~ *Bacchides* 530–562; Menander *Synaristosai* K-A fr. 337 ~ *Cistellaria* 89–93) and Terence (Apollodorus K-A fr. 10 ~ *Hecyra* 286–287; Apollodorus K-A fr. 11 ~ *Hecyra* 380) and to accompanied iambic octonarii by Terence (Menander K-A fr. 11 ~ *Adelphoe* 605–607; probably also Apollodorus K-A fr. 9 ~ *Hecyra* 214). The polymetric *canticum* of Caecilius com. 142–157 is based on iambic trimeters of Menander's *Plokion* (K-A fr. 296), and the same is likely to be true of the polymetric *canticum* that opened Plautus's *Cistellaria* (see Kassel-Austin on Menander K-A fr. 335). Similar observations can be made on Roman tragedy, so that the generalization of the grammarian Diomedes (gramm. I p. 490, 22–23) that *in Latinis...fabulis plura sunt cantica quae canuntur* ("in Latin plays there are more songs that are sung") seems justified.[1]

It is therefore not surprising that the Roman audience admired Plautus particularly for the great variety of his meters, as the tears of the *Numeri innumeri* in his alleged epitaph indicate.[2] Such appraisal, however, shifted to dismissal and even contempt by the end of the republic, when the prosody of the early Latin comedies was no longer

---

[1] See Fraenkel (1922): 352 n. 1; Jocelyn (1967): 29–30.

[2] It is quoted by Aulus Gellius 1. 24. 3 from Varro's *de poetis: et Numeri innumeri simul omnes conlacrimarunt* ("and the countless Rhythms all cried together simultaneously"). On the date of the epigram (late second century BC?) and the pun on *Numeri innumeri,* see Deufert (2002): 74–75.

understood and its metrical art no longer appreciated. Horace despises earlier generations for their admiration of Plautus and condemns the roughness of his rhythms.[3] Quintilian (inst. 10. 1. 99) complains that the comedies of Terence would have been more appealing if the poet had limited himself to iambic trimeters, the unaccompanied verses of his Greek originals. More than one and a half millennia of darkness follow. During this period, the Terence commentary of Donatus,[4] the grammatical and metrical writings from late antiquity to the Renaissance,[5] the Renaissance supplements of Plautus,[6] and the editions of Plautus and Terence from the fifteenth to the seventeenth centuries[7] all lack any real understanding of the comic meters.

Light slowly returned when Richard Bentley, in an impromptu reaction to a provocation, edited Terence in 1726. He was the first to disengage himself from the superficial schematism of the ancient metrical theories and to learn Terentian meter from his own painstaking reading of the verses. This approach, which led Bentley to the first discoveries of fundamental metrical and prosodic rules, was further advanced by Gottfried Hermann and has become the rule today. It was the critical study of the corpus of dramatic verses in the nineteenth century, particularly in its second half, to which we first and foremost owe our knowledge of the peculiarities of archaic prosody and the basic rules and licenses of its iambo-trochaic verses,[8] and it was the careful interpretation of Plautus's polymetric *cantica* in their transmitted layout which has enabled scholars since the late nineteenth century to grasp the full dimension of their metrical diversity.[9]

Therefore in 1861 Lucian Müller wrote his seven monumental books "de re metrica poetarum Latinorum *praeter Plautum et Terentium*," because he had to concede "that very much in these poets remains doubtful and a large part of this, I am afraid, can never be sufficiently illuminated."[10] Cesare Questa, however, was able to finish his *Metrica di Plauto e di Terenzio* in 2007, a full and systematic treatment of its subject which, in spite of all remaining uncertainties,[11] will prove a standard account for a very long time.[12]

---

[3] Hor. *epist*. 2. 3. 270–274 with Brink (1971): 307–309 and Deufert (2002): 78–79.

[4] See Jakobi (1996): 47–51. Donatus's notes on *Adelphoe* 60 and 559 show that he had no notion of the law of Hermann-Lachmann (see below) and the law of Bentley-Luchs (see below).

[5] See De Nonno (1990), Deufert (2002): 271–273, Leonhardt (1989a).

[6] See Braun (1980): 74–82.

[7] See Prete (1978).

[8] On the modern studies of the meters of the archaic Roman dramatic poets from Bentley until the end of the nineteenth century, see Deufert (2010). The place of honor belongs to Carl Friedrich Wilhelm Müller (1869), who discovered the legality of iambic shortening, which is the most fundamental principle of the prosody of the early Roman dramatic poets.

[9] The study of the Plautine *cantica* begins with Hermann (1796) and Hermann (1816); seminal for the progress in the twentieth century were Leo (1897), Questa (1984), and Questa (1995).

[10] Müller (1861): 6: "permulta in illis superesse dubia, e quibus bona pars vereor ut umquam satis possit absolvi." Compare his slightly less pessimistic remark in the second edition (1894), p. 2.

[11] For a fresh look on important laws of Plautus's iambo-trochaic meters, with a strong tendency to defend anomalies and exceptions for linguistic reasons, see Fortson (2008).

[12] Questa (2007); also his concise *Introduzione alla metrica di Plauto* (Questa 1967) remains useful. Gratwick (1993): 40–63 and Soubiran (1995): 1–74 offer valuable introductions into Plautine, Gratwick

Particularly fruitful fields for further research are the "métrique verbale" (the rhythmical shape of the individual word and its position in the verse) and comparative studies on all aspects of iambo-trochaic versification of the Greek and Roman poets, which one day might lead to a full historical account of the development of these Greek and Latin verses.[13]

2. Unaccompanied and Accompanied Verse. Performance and Delivery

The scene headings in the Palatine tradition of Plautus reveal the activity of an ancient grammarian who marked scenes in iambic senarii with the letters *DV* and all other scenes with *C*. His distinction between *deuerbia*[14] (the spoken parts of a play) and *cantica* (songs) in Plautus matches the evidence of the festive final scene of *Stichus*, where the meter changes from trochaic septenarius to iambic senarius at *Stichus* 762, when the flute player takes a drink. The senarius continues until the flute player has finished his drink; in 769, when he starts to play again, the meter changes from the senarius to a short polymetric canticum, which concludes the play. This passage, as well as much additional evidence, proves a basic dichotomy between the delivery of iambic senarii, which were unaccompanied, and the delivery of all other verses, which were accompanied by the music of the flute player.[15] This music, as we learn from the *didascaliae*, the ancient production records, of Roman comedy, was not composed by the comic poet himself but by a musical specialist who probably belonged to the troupe and played the flute on stage.[16] The *didascaliae* also mention that the *tibiae* used in the comedies of Plautus and Terence differed in size and pitch.[17]

There is little evidence concerning the actual performance of musically accompanied scenes in Roman comedy. Whereas in Greek drama the *auletes* led the chorus into the

---

(1999): 209–237 into Terentian metric. Harsh (1958) and Ceccarelli (1991—an excellent piece of work) review much of the research on early Latin meter and prosody in the twentieth century.

[13] The starting point for such research is the outstanding analysis of Soubiran (1988). A data bank of the metrically annotated iambo-trochaic lines of Plautus, as a tool for systematic researches in the field of "métrique verbale," is being prepared under my supervision and has been financed, as part of the eAQUA project, by the German Federal Ministry of Education and Research (see www.eaqua.net).

[14] On the formation and meaning of *deuerbium*, see Ribbeck (1875): 633 n. 2 and Moore (2008): 20 n. 34. There is little ancient evidence for *diuerbium*, and it is unreliable, but many modern scholars use that form instead.

[15] See Moore (2008), who carefully collects and discusses the evidence and acknowledges some rare exceptions.

[16] Wille (1967): 169; Wilson (2002): 66. On the *didascaliae* of Plautus and Terence, see Deufert (2002): 88–96 and 224–226.

[17] On the Roman *tibiae*, see Wille (1967): 169–175 and Wilson (2002): 66–67; on the Greek *auloi*, see West (1992): 81–109.

orchestra in the *parodos* and stayed there until the end of the play,[18] we do not know how and when the Roman *tibicen* appeared on stage. During the musically accompanied scenes, he was visible there and approached the actor whose chant he had to accompany.[19] Livy argues in his notoriously unreliable report on the early history of Roman drama that Roman actors merely mimed when the *tibicen* played, whereas the text was sung by expert singers.[20] Since such a practice, however, would impose almost grotesque problems of staging, Livy's account has been rejected by most modern scholars and plausibly regarded as an etiological fiction to explain the origin of pantomime.[21] Another question of dispute is how the Roman actors actually delivered their verses to the music of the *tibicen*. In Greek drama, the evidence points to a triple mode of delivery: unaccompanied iambic trimeters were spoken, accompanied iambo-trochaic tetrameters were recited, and accompanied choral songs and polymetric monodies were sung.[22] The same division is regularly assumed for the Roman stage as well. This assumption seems to be based principally on two observations. First, a number of prosodic and metric features (e.g., the handling of iambic shortening and the resolution of *elementa longa* and *ancipitia*, the laws of Bentley-Luchs and Meyer, and the license of Jacobsohn) closely unite the iambo-trochaic septenarii and octonarii with the iambic senarius against the meters of the polymetric *cantica*. It is therefore probable that the stichic iambo-trochaic long verses, despite being accompanied by the *tibicen*, were delivered in a manner nearer to the spoken senarii than the polymetric *cantica*.[23] Second, some ancient editions of Terence[24] distinguished between *deuerbia* (spoken senarii), *cantica* (the stichic passages in septenarii and octonarii), and *cantica mutatis modis* (i.e., passages that combine longer and shorter trochaic and iambic lines: the Terentian equivalent to the polymetric *cantica* of Plautus). This tripartition of the verses may well correspond to a triple mode of delivery as known from Greek drama.[25]

A final problem that concerns delivery has been particularly prominent in metrical research since the days of Bentley. In the *Schediasma de metris Terentianis* which opens his edition of Terence, Bentley observed that in iambo-trochaic verse, particularly in its middle, the word accent falls with great regularity on the elementa longa (i.e., the even elements in iambic and the uneven elements in trochaic verse). Therefore he concluded that these verses were composed with regard to an "ictus": a regularly recurring stress on *all* elementa longa.[26] Later scholars who followed Bentley aimed for an almost

---

[18] See Wilson (2002): 60–61; for Greek New Comedy, see Handley (1965): 286.

[19] See Wille (1967): 172 and 510 on the basis of Cic. *Mur.* 26.

[20] Liv. 7.2.8–10; on the textual problem in 7.2.10, see Oakley (1998): 65–66.

[21] See, e.g., Oakley (1998): 66, Hall (2002): 25, Moore (2008): 27–28.

[22] See Pickard-Cambridge (1968): 156–158, 257–262.

[23] See Hall (2002): 33.

[24] See Moore (2008): 21–26: The evidence comes from Donatus's prefaces to the comedies of Terence and from a passage in the anonymous "excerpta de comoedia" at the beginning of Donatus's commentary (p. 30, 11–16 Wessner). The latter text is difficult to understand and probably corrupt.

[25] See Jocelyn (1967): 29, n. 1.

[26] See Kapp (1941).

complete coincidence of word accent and metrical ictus, which they tried to achieve either by emending[27] or by explaining away as many of the alleged cases of clash between accent and ictus as possible. The most ambitious attempts were undertaken by Fraenkel (1928) and Drexler (1932–1933). The former argued that, where accent and ictus clashed, the accent was modified for syntactical and stylistic reasons. The latter postulated a secondary accent on the last syllable of cretic words or word groups. However, the very nature of the Latin word accent and the structure of iambo-trochaic verse with its fixed caesurae must automatically result in "a positive correlation between word accents and the onsets of the longa,"[28] particularly in the middle of the verse. In addition, no convincing explanation has been found for the many thousands of cases where the word accent does not fall upon an elementum longum and the elementum longum consists of an unaccentuated syllable.[29] The assumption of a verse ictus, which is not attested in the ancient sources,[30] has therefore been generally dismissed in recent times, and indeed it seems no less absurd to pronounce, e.g., Plautus, *Asinaria* 16 *sicút tuúm uis únicúm gnatúm tuáe* than to read Vergil *Aeneid* 1, 2 *Ítaliám fató profugús Lavínaque vénit*, on which Bentley poured scorn in his *Schediasma*.[31] To deny the existence of a verse ictus and to regard Roman comedy as purely quantitative poetry[32] does not mean, however, that the comic poets did not pay attention to the word accent in their versification. The great regularity with which the word accent appears on the elementa longa raised certain rhythmical expectations in the audience[33] which the poet could fulfill or frustrate for certain effects; he surely aimed to avoid rhythmical monotony,[34] but he was also able to emphasize or downplay the artistic or poetic nature of his verse as something distinct from the cadence of prose. It is certainly no coincidence that in the so called *versus quadratus*,[35] a special type of the trochaic septenarius marked by its clear rhythmical structure and many figures of speech, the elementa longa regularly coincide with the word accent. Verses like Plautus, *Mercator* 832–833

> *usus fructus uictus cultus iam mihi harunc aedium*
> *interemptust interfectust alienatust. occidi.*

sound significantly different from verses like Terence, *Adelphoe* 631–632

> *cessatum usque adhuc est: iam porro, Aeschine, expergiscere!*
> *nunc hoc primumst: ad illas ibo ut purgem me: accedam ad fores,*

---

[27] Deufert (2010): 289 discusses as an example a conjecture of Gottfried Hermann at Trin. 977.
[28] Gratwick (1993): 59, a point already made by Maas (1929) in his important review of Fraenkel (1928).
[29] See Maas (1929): 589–590; Soubiran (1988): 307–336.
[30] See the important study Stroh (1990).
[31] See Kapp (1941): 313–314.
[32] This is the sound basis of the standard works of Questa: See Questa (1967): x ff., Questa (2007): 10–12.
[33] This important point is made by Soubiran (1988): 311.
[34] Gratwick (1993): 60. On the rhythmical variety in the stichic iambo-trochaic verses of Roman comedy, see Gratwick and Lightley (1982).
[35] See Fraenkel (1927), Gerick (1996).

although they are based on the same metrical scheme. In the first instance, both style and rhythm, to which the uniformly accented elementa longa largely contribute, emphasize the poetic character of the verse, whereas the lack of these elements in the second instance makes the verse resemble the sound and diction of educated everyday speech.

3. THE METERS OF ROMAN COMEDY

a) The Iambic Senarius

In its broadest form, the iambic senarius (ia⁶) can be described as a quantitative verse consisting of twelve elements. Each uneven element is anceps (x: consisting of either a short or a long syllable or resolved in two short syllables) except the eleventh, which must be short (v); each even element is long (–) except the last, which is indifferent ($\frown$). All long elements can be resolved in two shorts.

```
 1  2  3  4  5  6  7  8  9  10  11  12
 x  –  x  –  x  –  x  –  x   –   v   ⌒
```

The word "senarius" is already attested in Cicero (*Or.* 184. 189) and Varro fr. 288 Funaioli (= Rufinus, *Gramm.* VI 556, 14–15)[36]. As the name indicates, the verse was regarded as a succession of six iambic "feet,"[37] in which only the sixth foot must be a pure iamb (v –), whereas in all other feet the iamb could be replaced by a tribrach (v v v), a spondee (– –), a dactyl (– v v), an anapaest (v v –), or a proceleusmatic (v v v v). We find such podic descriptions in the metrical treatises of late antiquity as well as in many modern accounts,[38] but the podic analysis is misleading because it gives the impression that the senarius is a quantitative verse of almost bare arbitrariness. In fact, of the elementa ancipitia the first, fifth, and ninth elements are significantly more often long (or resolved) than the third and seventh elements.[39] By contrast, the third and seventh elements are regularly short if a polysyllabic word ends after the fourth or the eighth element.[40] This observation shows that the Roman senarius is distinguished only in degree from the dipodic iambic trimeter of the Greeks, in which the third and seventh elements

---

[36] See Questa (2007): 328 n. 2.

[37] For the history of podic analysis of Greek and Latin verse in antiquity, see Gratwick (1993): 45 n. 57.

[38] See Rufinus, *Gramm.* VI 562, 11–18 (excerpting the influential metrical treatise of Iuba) and, from modern times, e.g., Duckworth (1952): 365–366; MacCary-Willcock (1976): 220–221; Barsby (1999): 293–295.

[39] For this observation, see Soubiran (1988): 7–62, Gratwick (1993): 44–45.

[40] On this observation, the law of Meyer, see Ceccarelli (1988), with the important review Gratwick (1991); Questa (2007): 383–413.

must be short in tragedy but are allowed to be resolved into two shorts in comedy.[41] The Latin poets varied and extended this license of the comic Greek trimeter. Like the Greek trimeter, the Roman senarius is therefore better described as a succession of three dipodies. In each dipody a preference can be observed to realize its first anceps with a long (or two shorts) and its second anceps with a short syllable. This preference is most obvious in the last dipody, where the second anceps is always short, and the first anceps must be long (or resolved), according to the law of Bentley and Luchs, if a polysyllabic word ends in the tenth element.[42]

The principally dipodic nature of the iambic senarius (and the other iambo-trochaic verses) is taken into account in the so-called alphabetic notation of these meters, which Adrian Gratwick has developed more recently.[43] He describes the senarius as three sequences of A B C D, each letter representing a single element:

A B C D A B C D A B C D

This notation allows a clear and easy description of an actual line, in which an element realized by a long syllable is represented by a capital (A, B, C, D), an element realized by a short syllable is represented by a lowercase (a, c), and a resolved element by two lowercases (aa, bb, cc, dd).[44] In an appendix to this chapter, I scan several sample lines in both the traditional (symbolic) and the alphabetic notation.

In addition to the law of Bentley and Luchs, there are other rules and observations that contradict the alleged arbitrariness which the bare quantitative scheme of the verse with all its substitutions suggests. Word-end after the fifth element occurs, at least in Plautus, with such regularity that the senarius can almost be regarded as a bipartite verse consisting of two cola of five and seven elements.[45] Although the resolution of elementa longa and ancipitia is more often permitted in the Roman senarii than in the Greek trimeters, these resolutions follow very rigid rules.[46] Most important are the laws of Ritschl and Hermann-Lachmann, which stipulate that the two shorts of a resolved longum or anceps must not be divided between two words (unless the former word is

---

[41] See West (1982a): 81–90. In tragedy, resolution of the third and seventh element is only possible if a proper name with the sequence v v— has to be accommodated to the verse.

[42] On the law of Bentley-Luchs, see Questa (2007): 371–383; cf. also Soubiran (1988): 383–389 and Gratwick (1993): 56–57. The latter acutely observes that, as a consequence of the laws of Meyer and Bentley-Luchs, a cretic sequence (– v –) is generally placed in such a way that the short syllable constitutes the third, seventh, or eleventh element rather than the fifth or ninth.

[43] See Gratwick (1993): 52–59 and Gratwick (1999): 211–218. Gratwick modifies the description of the corresponding Greek verses in Handley (1965): 56–62.

[44] Note that what can be realised, e.g., by A, a, or aa in an actual line is all subsumed under A in the abstract scheme of the verse. Gratwick (1999: 212) is aware of this problem: he uses roman font for the general verse schemes and italic font when he scans actual lines.

[45] See Jocelyn (1990): 212 and below, 486. See also West (1982a): 40), who interprets the Greek iambic trimeter as a compound verse of two cola split by a penthemimeral caesura.

[46] See Soubiran (1988): 175–303.

a monosyllabic or an elided disyllabic word) and must not be the final syllables of a tri-syllabic or longer word.[47] The same bias for the penthemimeral caesura and the same strictness in the handling of the resolutions can be observed in the trimeters of Seneca's tragedies. This shows that the tradition of dramatic verse in Rome is basically uniform and fundamentally Greek in nature.

In Menander's comedies, iambic trimeter is the predominant meter. Almost 85% of the *Dyskolos*, his only play that survives complete, is composed in this meter, and no other meter is discernible in the largely preserved *Epitrepontes*.[48] In Roman comedy, due to its more musical nature, the iambic senarius is much less dominant; only about 38% of Plautus's and 52% of Terence's total verses are senarii.[49] As the only unaccompanied meter, it appears regularly when documents are read on stage and when the audience learns important pieces of information (as in the prologues and, in Terence, the subsequent expository scenes).[50] A Roman comedy never ends in iambic senarii; the only exceptions are the interpolated alternative endings of Plautus's *Poenulus* and Terence's *Andria*.[51]

b) Accompanied Stichic Long Verses

Of the iambo-trochaic long verses, the iambic septenarius (ia⁷), the iambic octonarius (ia⁸), and the trochaic septenarius (tr⁷) are used stichically by Plautus and Terence in nonpolymetric contexts. Their quantitative schemes can be described in their broadest form as follows:

	1	2	3	4	5	6	7	8	9	10	11	12	13	14	15	16
ia⁷:	x	–	x	–	x	–	x	–	x	–	x	–	x	–	⌒	
ia⁸:	x	–	x	–	x	–	x	–	x	–	x	–	x	–	v	⌒
tr⁷:	–	x	–	x	–	x	–	x	–	x	–	x	–	v	⌒	

In the alphabetic notation, the same verses can be represented as follows[52]:

```
ia⁷: A B C D A B C D A B C D A B D
ia⁸: A B C D A B C D A B C D A B C D
tr⁷: B C D A B C D A B C D A B C D
```

---

[47] On these two laws see Questa (2007: 207–244), who aptly labels them as "constanti di primo grado." For exceptions to the law of Hermann-Lachmann, see Deufert (2012).
[48] See Barsby (1999): 27.
[49] The statistics are taken from Duckworth (1952): 362–363 with n. 5.
[50] See Moore (1998): 248, Moore (1999): 133–136.
[51] See Zwierlein (1990): 49–50, 56–101.
[52] See Gratwick (1999): 212.

These verses have their counterparts in the Greek catalectic and acatalectic iambic tetrameter and the catalectic trochaic tetrameter. The relationship between the Greek models and the Roman adaptations is similar to that between the iambic trimeter and the senarius (see above), and the same prosodic and metrical rules apply.

In Greek and Roman versification, an iambic long line, whether catalectic or acatalectic, a septenarius or an octonarius, is normally structured either by a median diaeresis after the eighth or a caesura after the ninth element. These two types of verse are approximately equal in frequency in Greek drama,[53] whereas in Roman comedy Plautus prefers the type with median diaeresis, Terence the type with caesura after the ninth element.[54] This marks an important difference. If there is diaeresis in a Roman iambic long verse, the seventh element has to be a short syllable and the eighth element can be realized either by a long or a short syllable (syllaba brevis in longo), but it must not be resolved. In addition, Plautus also allows hiatus in the diaeresis. All these peculiarities emphasize the asynartetic nature of the Roman iambic long verse: the diaeresis splits it into two half lines; therefore the two elements before the diaeresis are equally treated as the two elements before the end of an acatalectic iambic verse. Such an asynartetic structure of the verse matches the Roman practice of dividing longer verses into fixed cola of equal or almost equal length, a technique which appears most clearly in Saturnian verse.[55] The Plautine technique of the iambic long verse is rooted in traditional Roman versification, whereas Terence, by preferring to structure the line with a caesura after the ninth element and avoiding hiatus after the diaeresis, approaches the technique of his Greek models.

Menander composed the turbulent finale of *Dyskolos* (880–958) in catalectic iambic tetrameters; its Roman equivalent is used with similar frequency in Plautus (about 6% of his total verse) and Terence (about 7%). The acatalectic iambic tetrameter is securely attested only in Greek satyr play.[56] The corresponding iambic octonarius is also rare in Plautus (about 2%), who largely reserves it for soliloquies (e.g., Mercury's entrance speech in the manner of a *servus currens* in *Amphitruo* 984–1005). Terence, however, makes more extensive use of it (about 15%) and composes lively dialogue scenes in this meter.

Plautus's favorite stichic meter is the trochaic septenarius. He uses it almost twice as often as Terence (about 40% versus 22%). Apart from *Persa, Pseudolus,* and *Stichus* with their polymetric *finali*, all comedies of Plautus and Terence end with a scene in this meter. Its Greek equivalent, the catalectic trochaic tetrameter, is the only long verse which regularly occurs in Menander: more than 30% of *Samia* is composed in it, and further long passages survive in *Dyskolos, Phasma, Perikeiromene,* and *Sikyonios.* In all

---

[53] See Handley (1965): 61, West (1982a): 92–93.

[54] See Questa (2007): 341–348 for the iambic septenarius and 348–354 for the iambic octonarius. The discussions of Lindsay (1922): 274–277 and Laidlaw (1938): 104–108 are still useful for some stylistic details.

[55] See Leo (1905), Kloss (1993), Deufert (2002): 367–377.

[56] Soph., *Ichneutai* 298–328 (dialogue between the chorus and Cylene), and, probably, Ion, *Omphale TrGF* 19 F 20; see West (1982a): 93.

three poets, the meter is used in a wide variety of emotional contexts, including serious discourse and rapidly alternating dialogue.

An ancient metrical theory explains the catalectic trochaic tetrameter as an iambic trimeter to which a cretic sequence (– v –) is added at its beginning[57] ; and indeed the rhythm of both verses is fundamentally the same.[58] The same holds for their Roman equivalents. Plautus certainly felt the intrinsic affinity of the iambic senarius and the trochaic septenarius, as his treatment of the third element in the septenarius shows. There, brevis in longo and hiatus are allowed[59] : the initial cretic colon is regarded as a fixed entity which can be added or removed in order to change a senarius to a septenarius and vice versa:

```
tr⁷  –   x   ⌢  |   x   –   x   –   x   |   –   x   –   x   –   v   ⌢
ia⁶               |   x   –   x   –   x   |   –   x   –   x   –   v   ⌢
```

The section between the initial cretic colon and the median diaeresis (i.e., elements four to eight of the septenarius) is then identical to the first half of the senarius until the penthemimeral caesura; the second halves of both verses are also identical. Therefore, Plautus fills the corresponding sections in both verses with equal or almost equal phrases[60] :

Plaut. *Epidicus* 443 (ia⁶)   *omnis mortalis | agere deceat gratias*
Plaut. *Captivi* 798 (tr⁷)   *dentilegos | omnes mortales | faciam quemque offendero.*
Plaut. *Captivi* 373 (ia⁶)   *sequere. em tibi hominem. | # gratiam*[61] *habeo tibi.*
Plaut. *Miles Gloriosus* 1425 (tr⁷) *obsecro uos. # soluite istunc. | # gratiam habeo tibi.*

The obvious identity of the senarius and the septenarius after its initial cretic colon helps us to accept a number of metrical irregularities such as the penthemimeral hiatus in the senarius, which has often raised suspicion. As in all iambo-trochaic long lines, hiatus is permissible in the trochaic septenarius after its diaeresis; it should therefore be equally accepted at the corresponding position in the senarius, where it is well attested in the comedies of Plautus.[62] The admission of hiatus at the corresponding positions in the senarius and septentarius shows that the modern distinction between caesura and

---

[57] On the so-called theory of derivation and its history in Greece and Rome, see Leonhardt (1989b).
[58] See West (1982a): 40.
[59] This licence was discovered by Jacobsohn (1904: 4–5 and 7–8); see now Questa (2007): 279–299 (especially 282–283).
[60] See Marx (1922): 55; Deufert (2002): 373.
[61] On the identical hiatus between *gratiam* and *habeo,* see again Jacobsohn (1904): 1–8 and Questa (2007): 279–299 (especially 279–282 and 283–285). As Jacobsohn discovered, the eighth element of the senarius and the corresponding eleventh element of the trochaic septenarius allows brevis in longo and hiatus.
[62] See Soubiran (1988): 123–126; Deufert (2002): 373–374.

diaeresis is arbitrary and misleading[63] : Both are defined by word-end at a fixed position in the verse; both are purely rhythmical features analogous to the end of line; both often do, but neither must, coincide with a syntactic break.[64]

There is only one nonpolymetric scene in Plautus that is not composed in iambo-trochaic verse: the lively dialogue of Milphidippa, Palaestrio, and Pyrgopolynices in *Miles* 1011–1093 consists entirely of anapaestic septenarii.[65] The Greek equivalent of this verse, the catalectic anapaestic tetrameter, is common in the Old Comedy of Aristophanes (particularly in the *parabaseis*),[66] but so far is not attested in the extant remains of Menander, although he did compose a song in anapaestic dimeters for a temple custodian in his *Leukadia*.[67] The stichic anapaestic septenarii in *Miles* differ remarkably from Plautus's usual habit of combining different anapaestic meters as well as other meters in polymetric *cantica*. Compared to the anapaests in polymetric cantica, the stichic anapaestic septenarii in *Miles* contain significantly more long syllables and are more regular. Iambic shortening and proceleusmatic sequences are avoided. Some lines (*Mil.* 1051, 1052, 1072) consist exclusively of long syllables. The metrical difference most likely reflects a difference in delivery: the anapaests in the polymetric *cantica* were sung, whereas the stichic anapaestic septenarii in *Miles*, which lacks polymetric *cantica*, were recited.[68] Caecilius's anapaests in the polymetric *canticum* of his *Plocium* (frg. 142–157 Ribbeck) display the Plautine technique of anapaests in polymetric contexts.[69] Terence avoids anapaestic meters altogether.

c) Polymetric *Cantica*

The remaining 15% of an average Plautine comedy consists of polymetric *cantica*. On average, there are three *cantica* per play. However, there are considerable differences between the individual plays: *Miles*, at one end of the spectrum, contains no *canticum* at all; at the opposite end, *Amphitruo, Captivi, Menaechmi, Mostellaria, Persa, Pseudolus*, and *Truculentus* have five sung passages each. The most polymetric play, however, is *Casina*, in which four polymetric passages (144–251, 621–758, 798–846, 855–962) amount to almost

---

[63] The distinction is not supported by ancient sources: see West (1982b): 292; West avoids the term "diaeresis" and uses the term "caesura" for a rhythmical, not a syntactic, break.

[64] See the fundamental account of Soubiran (1988: 63–174). The opposite view that a caesura must involve a syntactic break is expressed by, among others, Drexler (1950), who still has his adherents, for instance Korzeniowski (2000: 681–682).

[65] On Plautine anapaests, see Boldrini (1984), on the anapaestic septenarii in *Mil.* 1011–1093 Boldrini (1984): 43–93.

[66] See White (1912): 121–122, Parker (1997): 58–59.

[67] See the Loeb edition of Arnott, Vol. II, 230–231; Handley (2002): 174. Anapaestic dimeters are especially characteristic of Greek Middle Comedy; see Nesselrath (1990): 267–280.

[68] See Boldrini (1984): 92–93 and Boldrini (1999): 121.

[69] For a metrical interpretation of Caecilius's *canticum*, see Questa (1984): 381–397. Some details remain controversial: see Ceccarelli (1991): 297–298.

40% of the whole play.[70] Plautine *cantica*, almost without exception, open a new scene and are sung by the entering characters. As a rule, the *canticum* is preceded by a scene in spoken senarii and followed by stichic long verses (most often trochaic septenarii).[71]

The principle meters of the *cantica* are the bacchius (x – –) and cretic (– x –).[72] Bacchiac and cretic lines normally appear as quaternarii, but there are also shorter and syncopated bacchiac and cretic verses,[73] which editors since Leo have learned to accept rather than emend and supplement. In addition to bacchiac and cretic verses, we most often find iambic, trochaic, and anapaestic verses (varying in length from dipodies to octonarii and continuous systems), but also aeolic verses (marked by at least one choriambic sequence: – v v –), ionic verses (marked by the sequence – – v v or v v – –), and versus Reiziani (marked by the colon Reizianum x – x – ⌒). In many *cantica*, there is a predominant meter that suits the mood of the speaker. Charinus, for instance, utters his trembling uncertainty about the future of his love in a *canticum* that largely consists of bacchiacs (*Mercator* 335–363), a meter that Plautus prefers for laments or other forms of serious or dignified speech.[74] Many polymetric *cantica* contain large sections that are composed of stichic verses. A famous example is *Aulularia* 406–448, where a panic-stricken cook escapes from old Euclio's house with a short soliloquy in a mixture of iambic, trochaic, and anapaestic verses. When Euclio catches up with him, the *canticum* continues as a dialogue which consists of more than thirty stichic versus Reiziani that have puzzled commentators since antiquity.[75] However, in the metrically most complex *cantica*, such as the final triumph of the drunken Pseudolus over his master (*Pseudolus* 1246–1335), all kinds of verses are combined and the meter changes again and again.

The metrical interpretation of Plautus's polymetric *cantica* remains a difficult enterprise because of the prosodic ambiguity of many words and word groups and the manifold possibilities of the quantitative realization of most of his verses.[76] However, a number of important principles have proven valuable in dealing with Plautine cantica.[77] First, the colometry of the archetype of the Plautine tradition, normally preserved or only superficially obscured in our oldest extant manuscripts, should be preserved wherever possible, because it ultimately goes back to a metrically competent editor of the late second century BCE.[78] Second, metrical unit and syntactical unit tend to coincide

---

[70] See Duckworth (1952): 369–370.

[71] See Law (1922).

[72] For the realization of the elementa ancipitia in bacchiacs and cretics, see Kloss (1993): 92–93.

[73] See Questa (2007): 415–441. A rule for syncopated cretic and bacchiac quaternarii has been discovered by Schaps (1979): when syncope (the omission of an elementum longum) occurs, there is normally a word break at that point of the verse, the schemes being – x – – x – – x – | v ⌒ and x – – x – – x – | x – ⌒.

[74] See Duckworth (1952): 370–371 for further examples.

[75] See Questa (1984): 65–66; on the versus Reiziani of Plautus in general, see Questa (1982).

[76] The starting point for future investigation is Questa (1995).

[77] A catalogue of four principles is assembled in Willcock (1986): 479 and Willcock (1987): 152. Willcock's fourth principle (regard for coincidence of word accent and metrical ictus) has to be dismissed.

[78] See Leo (1897): 5–8, Questa (1984): 75–79, Deufert (2002): 59–61.

in Plautine verse[79]; line divisions at syntactical breaks should therefore be preferred to divisions which cause enjambment. Third, the context of the *canticum* can help to interpret the meter of a given line.[80] As in all polymetric and astrophic poetry, units of content tend to be metrical units; therefore, breaks in subject matter are emphasized by a change of meter, and correspondences of content are highlighted by the use of similar metrical patterns. Moreover, there is also a link between the meter and the mood or ethos of the person singing the *canticum*. Drunken slaves, for instance, seem to brim over with metrical diversity, whereas a serious and reflective character is emphasized by the metrical continuity of his utterance. This aspect of Plautine meter has received little attention,[81] and may warrant a full-scale investigation.

Caecilius, as the monody from his *Plocium* (142–157) clearly indicates, composed his *cantica* in the same fashion as Plautus. Terence largely abandoned the use of polymetric *cantica*.[82] An exception is Aeschinus's lyric lament in *Adelphoe* 610–617, which is dominated by aeolic verses and constitutes a true, though short, polymetric *canticum*.[83]

The meters of the Plautine cantica also appear in Roman tragedy from its very beginnings. The meager fragments include cretics (Liv. Andr. trag. 20–22), bacchiacs (e.g., Enn. trag. 81–83. 300; Naev. trag. 6 is uncertain), and anapaests (e.g., Enn. trag. 24–30. 87–94 Jocelyn), as well as iambic (Naev. trag. 8) and trochaic (Enn. trag. 185–186 Jocelyn) octonarii.[84] In addition, in adapting their Greek models the Roman tragedians, just as Plautus and Caecilius did in adapting plays of New Comedy, changed spoken iambic trimeters to polymetric cantica.[85] In tragedy, however, there is an obvious reason for such changes: the nature of the Roman stage and other pragmatic conditions forced the Roman tragedians to discard or prune the choral songs of their Greek originals or transform them into spoken or recitative verse.[86] This loss of music was compensated for by changing the spoken verse of the original to song. The way to such a change was paved by the Hellenistic acting companies, who set to music scenes of Greek tragedy composed in spoken verse. Such Greek theatrical representations must have been familiar to the early Roman tragedians Livius Andronicus, Naevius, and Ennius, who all came from Magna Graecia.[87] The metrical forms that the Roman poets gave to the spoken verse of the Greek originals—nonchoral, astrophic, and polymetric song—have their models in the astrophic

---

[79] See Leo (1905): 14–15, Maurach (1964), Jocelyn (1967): 370, Deufert (2007).

[80] See Braun (1970). More research needs to be done on the important "Prinzip der Einheit von Inhalt und metrischer Gestaltung" (p. 5).

[81] I have not seen the unpublished thesis of Tobias (1970) on Plautus's metrical characterization.

[82] See above, 480.

[83] On its interpretation, see Questa (1984): 399–415 and Questa (2007): 486. On two further short cantica in his earliest play—*Andria* 481–486 (largely in bacchiacs) and 625–638 (largely in cretics)—see Questa (2007) 438–441.

[84] See Jocelyn (1967): 34, n. 4.

[85] See Fraenkel (1922): 336–341.

[86] See Fraenkel (1922): 336–337, Hose (1999).

[87] On the evidence for converting spoken scenes to song and the influence of the practice on early Roman tragedy, see Gentili (1979): 15–41.

monodies of the last plays of Sophocles and, particularly, Euripides[88] and in the dramatic lyric of the Hellenistic period, such as the "Grenfell Fragment," which contains the lament of an abandoned woman (CA 177–180): Its manifold and complex metrical structure (predominating dochmiacs combined with dactyls, iambics, cretics, anapaests, and other meters), as well as its highly emotional language, have much in common with a Plautine monody.[89]

Given the infrequent use of bacchiac and cretic passages in Greek drama,[90] the predominance of these meters in the polymetric *cantica* of Roman tragedy and comedy seems startling at first glance. It is, however, a characteristic feature of verse making in the Hellenistic period that meters which appeared only sporadically in the classical period are suddenly used stichically; in so doing, the Hellenistic poets wanted to "widen the repertory of stichic and distichic meters."[91] With their polymetric *cantica*, the Roman playwrights continued with and contributed to this distinctive feature of Hellenistic versification.

All this shows the principally Greek nature of the polymetric *cantica* of early Roman drama. They consist entirely of Greek meters, and the frequent stichic use of meters that are rare in the Greek drama of the classical period is a regular Hellenistic practice. Hence it would be only natural if the Roman editors of the early Latin theatrical scripts used the same general type of metrical description which had been applied at Alexandria and Pergamum to the Greek tragedies and comedies.[92]

When Plautus composed his polymetric *cantica*, he did not work as an original genius who added to his Greek models "the features of song and dance which he had found in the earlier Italian popular farces."[93] Instead, he followed a technique inherited from the earliest generation of Roman playwrights, who composed both tragedies and comedies without significant differences in their metrical structure.[94] The practice of replacing spoken passages in the Greek originals with astrophic polymetric *cantica* in the Roman adaptations originated in the genre of Roman tragedy; the poets did so in order to counterbalance the suppression of choral music. After the tragic poets had accepted the practice, it was probably transferred immediately to the genre of comedy, in which

---

[88] See West (1982a): 135–137. Aristophanes's Aeschylus parodies this kind of song in *Frogs*, 1329–1363; see Dover (1993): 358–362 and Parker (1997): 508–519.

[89] See Gentili (1979): 37–38 and 82–86; for a metrical interpretation of the Grenfell Fragment and an analysis of its language and style, see the commentary of Esposito (2005), particularly 27–39.

[90] For a collection, see Jocelyn (1967): 34 n. 4. Particularly close to the Roman technique are the cretic and bacchiac passages in the aria of the Phrygian slave in Eur. *Orest.* 1419–1424 and 1437–1440; see Wilamowitz-Moellendorff (1921): 333 ("Von hier aus führt der Weg unmittelbar zu der Praxis der plautinischen Cantica") and 335.

[91] West (1982a): 149. For this aspect of Hellenistic versification, see particularly Leo (1897): 62–70 and Wilamowitz-Moellendorff (1921): 124–129.

[92] See Jocelyn (1967): 32 and Deufert (2002): 59–61.

[93] Duckworth (1952): 380. There is no evidence for an indigenous tradition as assumed by Duckworth.

[94] On this explanation of the origin of the Plautine *cantica*, see Fraenkel (1922): 321–373; Fraenkel's assumption is endorsed by Gentili (1979): 15–41. On metrical differences in Roman tragic and comic verse, see Jocelyn (1967): 36–37; they are much less significant than those between Greek tragic and comic verse.

the Greek originals (at least those from Menander) exhibit only a very small amount of lyric passages.[95]

d) Change of Meter and its Dramatic Significance

The change of meter fulfills similar functions in Plautus and Terence, but with different frequency. In Plautus metrical switches most often occur at entrances or exits of characters and therefore frame scenes, whereas Terence regularly changes the meter within a single scene, when the course or the atmosphere of the conversation takes a turn.[96] The dramatic significance of the selection of a meter has recently been illuminated in a number of articles by Timothy Moore, who concentrates on the distinction between unaccompanied senarii on the one hand and the accompanied meters on the other hand (see above).[97] Although each comedy has its own distinctive pattern of metrical changes and musical accompaniment, some general patterns can be discerned: passages of particular importance for the progress of the plot tend to be in iambic senarii, and passages in which a new major unit of action begins are regularly highlighted by musical accompaniment. Likeable characters such as the young lovers and their supporters much more often chant accompanied verses than unsympathetic antagonists such as pimps or soldiers. Particularly refined is Terence's handling of accompanied verse[98] : In *Heauton Timorumenos, Eunuchus,* and *Phormio,* he contrasts the two pairs of lovers by associating one male lover with iambic octonarii and the other with trochaic septenarii. The iambic septenarius is a meter that Terence particularly connects with the lady love, just as Plautus had done already in *Mercator*.

4. CHARACTERISTIC DIFFERENCES BETWEEN PLAUTUS'S AND TERENCE'S VERSIFICATION

The versification of Plautus shows two features which characterize archaic Latin verse as a whole. First, his units of verse tend to coincide with units of sense and syntax. Second, his verses are structured by a rigid system of fixed caesurae and consist of smaller units. This colometric structure is emphasized by metrical licenses: hiatus and syllaba brevis in longo are allowed in the elements before a caesura, which is treated like a verse end. Terence, on the contrary, no longer accepts these licenses. He abandons hiatus and

---

[95] On the evidence for song in Menander's *Theophoroumene, Leukadia,* and *Phasma,* see Handley (2002): 174; on the evidence for songs in Greek Middle and New Comedy, see Marx (1928): 254–263, and in the Mese Nesselrath (1990): 267–280.

[96] See Braun (1969) and Bruder (1970).

[97] Moore (1998) and Moore (1999).

[98] Moore (2007).

brevis in longo in the loci Jacobsohniani, and hiatus in the penthemimeral caesura of the senarius, in the diaeresis of the trochaic septenarius and probably also in the diaeresis of the iambic long-verses, where he occasionally admits brevis in longo.[99] Terence also attaches less weight to the principal caesurae; in Plautus (just as in Livius Andronicus, Naevius, and Ennius), word-end after the fifth element (= penthemimeral caesura) occurs in 92% of the senarii, in Terence only in 80%,[100] while median diaeresis occurs in 96% of the Plautine but only 91% of the Terentian trochaic septenarii.[101] With the abolition of hiatus and the slackening of the rigid system of caesurae, the verse of Terence comes closer to the technique of Menander[102] and approaches the cadence of prose.

The last observation is corroborated also by the slightly higher frequency of synaloephe and resolutions in Terence[103] and by Terence's handling of the line-end. Particularly in his iambic prologues and his expository scenes, which are entirely or largely monological, Terence often abandons the unity of verse and sentence and introduces strong forms of enjambment.[104] Like Menander and other Greek dramatic poets,[105] Terence does not hesitate to place a conjunction (*Adelphoe* 38–39: *instituere aut / parare*) or preposition (*Eunuchus* 859–860: *inuolem in / capillum*) at the end of a verse. By obscuring the line-end, Terence further blurs the metrical nature of his plays and steers away from the traditional symmetry of meter and syntax that characterizes early Roman verse. Hence, whereas the verses of Plautus and Terence fit the same metrical schemes, there is a clearly audible difference: Plautus emphasizes the metrical character of his comic speech, while Terence conceals it and aims for a speech which is truer to life.

5. APPENDIX: SCANNING PLAUTINE AND TERENTIAN VERSES: SOME EXAMPLES

a) Plautus, *Mercator* 229–233 (iambic senarii):

mercari visus mĭhĭ sum formosam capram;
1 2 3 4 5   6 7 8 9 10 11 12
– – – – – / – – – – – ᴗ –
A B C D A / B C D A B c D

---

[99] See Laidlaw (1938): 84–86; his material must be used with caution.
[100] See Soubiran (1988): 79 and 121–122, Deufert (2007): 54–55.
[101] See Soubiran (1988): 92.
[102] Hiatus is not allowed in Menander; penthemimeral caesura occurs only in 68% of the trimeters (Soubiran [1988]: 79), whereas median diaeresis is observed to a very high degree. See Handley (1965) 60.
[103] For synaloephe, see Soubiran (1966): 565–567: 138 synaloephes occur in 100 senarii of Plautus (143 in Terence), 182 synaloephes occur in 100 septenarii of Plautus (203 in Terence). For resolutions, see Soubiran (1988): 185 and 260–261: 100 senarii of Plautus display 119 resolutions (Terence: 127), 100 septenarii 174 (Terence: 195).
[104] See Deufert (2007): 58–66 for detailed statistical data from Terence, Plautus, and Menander.
[105] See Deufert (2007): 57.

ēi ne noceret quam dom(i) ant(e) habui capram

1	2	3	4	5	6	7	8	9	10	11	12
–	–	v	–	– /	–	v	–	vv	–	v	–

A B c D A / B c D aa B c D

neu discordarent, s(i) amb(ae) in un(o) essent loco,

1	2	3	4	5	6	7	8	9	10	11	12
–	–	–	–	– /	–	v	–	–	–	v	–

A B C D A / B c D A B c D

posteriu(s) quam mercatus fueram, visus sum

1	2	3	4	5	6	7	8	9	10	11	12
–	vv	v	–	–	–	–	vv	–	–	v	–

A bb c D A B C dd A B c D

in custodelam simiae concredere.

1	2	3	4	5	6	7	8	9	10	11	12
–	–	–	–	– /	–	v	–	–	–	v	v

A B C D A / B c D A B c d

b) Plautus, *Mercator* 834–837 (trochaic septenarii)

di penates meūm parentum, familiai Lar pater,

1	2	3	4	5	6	7	8	9	10	11	12	13	14	15
–	v	–	–	–	v	–	– /	vv	v	–	–	–	v	–

B c D A B c D A / bb c D A B c D

vobis mando, meūm parentum rem ben(e) ut tutemini.

1	2	3	4	5	6	7	8	9	10	11	12	13	14	15
–	–	–	–	–	v	–	– /	–	v	–	–	–	v	–

B C D A B c D A / B c D A B c D

ego mi(hi) alios deōs penatis persequar, alium Larem,

1	2	3	4	5	6	7	8	9	10	11	12	13	14	15
vv	v	vv	–	–	v	–	– /	–	v	–	vv	–	v	–

bb c dd A B c D A / B c D aa B c D

ali(am) urb(em), aliam civitat(em): ab Atticis abhorreo.

1	2	3	4	5	6	7	8	9	10	11	12	13	14	15
vv	–	vv	–	–	v	–	v /	–	v	–	v	–	v	–

bb C dd A B c D a / B c D a B c D

BIBLIOGRAPHY

Barsby, J. 1999. *Terence: Eunuchus.* Cambridge, UK: Cambridge University Press.
Boldrini, S. 1984. *Gli anapesti di Plauto: Metro e ritmo.* Urbino: QuattroVenti.
——. 1999. *Prosodie und Metrik der Römer.* Stuttgart and Leipzig: Teubner.

Braun, L. 1969. "Polymetrie bei Terenz und Plautus." *Wiener Studien* 82: 66–83.

——. 1970. *Die Cantica des Plautus*. Göttingen: Vandenhoeck and Ruprecht.

——. 1980. *Scenae suppositiciae, oder Der falsche Plautus*. Göttingen: Vandenhoeck and Ruprecht.

Brink, C. O. 1971. *Horace on Poetry: The "Ars poetica."* Cambridge, UK: Cambridge University Press.

Bruder, H. W. 1970. *"Bedeutung und Funktion des Verswechsels bei Terenz."* Zürich: Juris Druck und Verlag.

Ceccarelli, L. 1988. *La norma di Meyer nei versi giambici e trocaici di Plauto e Terenzio*. Rome: Ediun Coopergion.

——. 1991. "Prosodia e metrica latina arcaica 1956–1990." *Lustrum* 33: 227–400, 411–415.

Deufert, M. 2002. *Textgeschichte und Rezeption der plautinischen Komödien im Altertum*. Berlin: de Gruyter.

——. 2007. "Terenz und die altlateinische Verskunst: Ein Beitrag zur Technik des Enjambements in der Neuen Komödie." In: *Terentius Poeta*, by P. Kruschwitz, W. Ehlers, and F. Felgentreu, 51–71. Munich: C. H. Beck.

——. 2010. "'Quid aliud est Plautina emendare quam ludere?': Gottfried Hermanns Bedeutung für die Plautusphilologie des 19. Jahrhunderts." In *Gottfried Hermann (1772–1848): Internationales Symposium in Leipzig 11.–13. Oktober 2007*, edited by K. Sier and E. Wöckener-Gade, 277–297. Tübingen: Narr.

——. 2012. "*Maccus vortit barbare*? Eine übersehene Lizenzstelle im iambischen Senar." *Philologus* 156: 78–100.

De Nonno, M. 1990. "Ruolo e funzione della metrica nei grammatici latini." In *Metrica classica e linguistica: Atti del colloquio: Urbino 3–6 ottobre 1988*, edited by R. Danese, F. Gori, and C. Questa, 453–494. Urbino: QuattroVenti.

Dover, K. 1993. *Aristophanes: Frogs*. Oxford: Oxford University Press.

Drexler, H. 1932–1933. *Plautinische Akzentstudien*. 3 vols. Breslau: Marcus. Reprinted Hildesheim: G. Olms, 1967.

——. 1950. "Caesur und Diaerese." *Aevum* 24: 332–366.

Duckworth, G. E. 1952. *The Nature of Roman Comedy: A Study in Popular Entertainment*. Princeton: Princeton University Press. 2nd ed. Norman: University of Oklahoma Press, 1994.

Easterling, P., and E. Hall. 2002, eds. *Greek and Roman Actors: Aspects of an Ancient Profession*. Cambridge, UK: Cambridge University Press.

Esposito, E. 2005. *Il fragmentum Grenfellianum (P. Dryton 50)*. Bologna: Pàtron.

Fortson IV, B. W. 2008. *Language and Rhythm in Plautus: Synchronic and Diachronic Studies*. Berlin and New York: de Gruyter.

Fraenkel, E. 1922. *Plautinisches im Plautus*. Berlin: Weidmann.

——. 1927. "Die Vorgeschichte des Versus quadratus." *Hermes* 62: 357–370. Reprinted in E. Fraenkel, *Kleine Beiträge zur klassischen Philologie*, vol. 2, Rome: Edizioni di storia e letteratura, 1964, 11–24.

——. 1928. *Iktus und Akzent im lateinischen Sprechvers*. Berlin: Weidmann.

Gentili, B. 1979. *Theatrical Performances in the Ancient World: Hellenistic and Early Roman Theatre*. Amsterdam: Gieben.

Gerick, T. 1996. *Der versus quadratus bei Plautus und seine volkstümliche Tradition*. Tübingen: Narr.

Gratwick, A. S. 1991. Review of *La norma di Meyer nei versi giambici e trocaici di Plauto e Terenzio*, by L. Ceccarelli. *Classical Review* 41: 281–284.

——. 1993. *Plautus: Menaechmi*. Cambridge, UK: Cambridge University Press.

——. 1999. *Terence: The Brothers*. 2nd ed. Warminster, UK: Aris & Phillips.

——, and S. J. Lightley. 1982. "Light and Heavy Syllables as Dramatic Colouring in Plautus and Others." *Classical Quarterly* 32: 124–133.

Hall, E. 2002. "The Singing Actors of Antiquity." In *Greek and Roman Actors: Aspects of an Ancient Profession,* edited by P. Easterling and E. Hall, 3–38. Cambridge, UK: Cambridge University Press.

Handley, E. 1965. *The Dyskolos of Menander*. London: Methuen.

——. 2002. "Acting, Action and Words in New Comedy." In *Greek and Roman Actors: Aspects of an Ancient Profession,* edited by P. Easterling and E. Hall, 165–188. Cambridge, UK: Cambridge University Press.

Harsh, P. W. 1958. "Early Latin Meter and Prosody 1935–1955." *Lustrum* 3: 215–250, 279–280.

Hermann, G. 1796. *De metris poetarum Graecorum et Romanorum libri tres*. Leipzig: Fleischer.

——. 1816. *Elementa doctrinae metricae*. Leipzig: Fleischer.

Hose, M. 1999. "Anmerkungen zur Verwendung des Chores in der römischen Tragödie der Republik." In *Der Chor im antiken Drama*, edited by P. Riemer and B. Zimmermann, 113–138. Stuttgart: J. B. Metzler.

Jacobsohn, H. 1904. "Quaestiones Plautinae metricae et Grammaticae." PhD diss., University of Göttingen.

Jakobi, R. 1996. *Die Kunst der Exegese im Terenzkommentar des Donat*. Berlin and NewYork: de Gruyter.

Jocelyn, H. D. 1967. *The Tragedies of Ennius*. Cambridge, UK: Cambridge University Press.

——. 1990. Review of Soubiran (1988). *Gnomon* 62: 212–218.

Kapp, E., 1941. "Bentley's Schediasma 'De metris Terentianis' and the Modern Doctrine of Ictus in Classical Verse," *Mnemosyne* III 9: 187–194 (= Kapp, E., *Ausgewählte Schriften*, Berlin 1968, 311-317).

Kloss, G. 1993. "Zum Problem des römischen Saturniers." *Glotta* 71: 81–107.

Kruschwitz, P., W.-W. Ehlers, and F. Felgentreu, eds. 2007. *Terentius Poeta*. Munich: C. H. Beck.

Korzeniowski, G. 2000. Review of *Essai sur la versification dramatique des Romains,* by J. Soubiran. *Gnomon* 72: 674–686.

Laidlaw, W. A. 1938. *The Prosody of Terence: A Relational Study*. Oxford: Oxford University Press.

Law, H. H. 1922. *Studies in the Songs of Plautine Comedy*. Menasha, WI: George Banta.

Leo, F. 1897. *Die plautinischen Cantica und die hellenistische Lyrik*. Berlin: Weidmann.

——. 1905. *Der Saturnische Vers*. Berlin: Weidmann.

Leonhardt, J. 1989a. *Dimensio syllabarum: Studien zur Prosodie- und Verslehre von der Spätantike bis zur frühen Renaissance*. Göttingen: Vandenhoeck & Ruprecht.

——. 1989b. "Die beiden metrischen Systeme des Altertums." *Hermes* 117: 43–61.

Lindsay, W. M. 1922. *Early Latin Verse*. Oxford: Clarendon Press. Reprinted 1968.

Maas, P. 1929. Review of *Iktus und Akzent im lateinischen Sprechvers*, by E. Fraenkel. *Deutsche Literaturzeitung für Kritik der internationalen Wissenschaft* 50: 2244–2247. Reprinted in P. Maas, *Kleine Schriften*, Munich: Beck, 1973, 588–591.

MacCarey, W. T., and M. M. Willcock. 1976. *Plautus: Casina*. Cambridge, UK: Cambridge University Press.

Marx, F. 1922. *Molossische und bakcheische Wortformen in der Verskunst der Griechen und Römer*. Leipzig: Teubner.

——. 1928. *Plautus Rudens: Text und Kommentar*. Leipzig: SAW. Reprinted Amsterdam: Hakkert, 1959.

Maurach, G. 1964. *Untersuchungen zum Aufbau plautinischer Lieder*. Göttingen: Vandenhoeck & Ruprecht.

Moore, T. J. 1998. "Music and Structure in Roman Comedy." *American Journal of Philology* 119: 245–273.

——. 1999. "Facing the Music: Character and Musical Accompaniment in Roman Comedy." *Syllecta Classica* 10: 130–153.

——. 2007. "Terence as Musical Innovator." In *Terentius Poeta,* edited by P. Kruschwitz, W.-W. Ehlers, and F. Felgentreu, 93–109. Munich: C. H. Beck.

——. 2008. "When did the *Tibicen* Play? Meter and Musical Accompaniment in Roman Comedy." *Transactions and Proceedings of the American Philological Association* 138: 3–46.

Müller, C. F. W. 1869. *Plautinische Prosodie*. Berlin: Weidmann. Reprinted Hildesheim: G. Olms, 1971.

Müller, L. 1861. *De re metrica poetarum Latinorum praeter Plautum et Terentium libri septem*. Leipzig: Teubner. 2nd rev. ed. 1894, reprinted Hildesheim: G. Olms, 1967.

Nesselrath, H.-G. 1990. *Die attische Mittlere Komödie: Ihre Stellung in der antiken Literaturkritik und Literaturgeschichte*. Berlin: de Gruyter.

Oakley, S. P. 1998. *A Commentary on Livy Books VI–X. Vol. 2, Books VII–VIII*. Oxford: Clarendon Press.

Parker, L. P. E. 1997. *The Songs of Aristophanes*. Oxford: Clarendon Press.

Pickard-Cambridge, A. W. 1968. *The Dramatic Festivals of Athens*. 2nd ed. Oxford: Oxford University Press, Reprinted 2003.

Prete, S. 1978. "Camerarius on Plautus." In *Joachim Camerarius (1500–1574): Essays on the History of Humanism during the Reformation*, edited by F. Baron, 223–230. Munich: Fink.

Questa, C. 1967. *Introduzione alla metrica di Plauto*. Bologna: Pàtron.

——. 1982. *Il reiziano ritrovato*. Genoa: Università di Genova, Facoltà di lettere.

——. 1984. *Numeri innumeri: Ricerche sui cantica e la tradizione manoscritta di Plauto*. Rome: Edizioni dell'Ateneo.

——. 1995. *Titi Macci Plauti Cantica*. Urbino: QuattroVenti.

——. 2007. *La metrica di Plauto e di Terenzio*. Urbino: QuattroVenti.

Ribbeck, O. 1875. *Die römische Tragödie im Zeitalter der Republik*. Leipzig: Teubner. Reprinted Hildesheim: G. Olms, 1968.

Schaps, D. 1979. "An Unnoticed Rule of Plautine Meter." *Classical Philology* 74: 152–154.

Soubiran, J. 1966. *L'élision dans la poésie latine*. Paris: Klincksieck.

——. 1988. *Essai sur la versification dramatique des Romains: Sénaire iambique et septénaire trochaique*. Paris: Editions du Centre national de la recherche scientifique.

——. 1995. *Prosodie et métrique du Miles gloriosus de Plaute: Introduction et commentaire*. Paris: Peeters.

Stroh, W. 1990. "Arsis und Thesis oder: Wie hat man lateinische Verse gesprochen?" In *Musik und Dichtung: Neue Forschungsbeiträge, Viktor Pöschl zum 80. Geburtstag gewidmet*, edited by M. von Albrecht and W. Schubert, 87–116. Frankfurt: P. Lang. Reprinted in *Apocrypha: Entlegene Schriften*, by W. Stroh, Stuttgart: Franz Steiner Verlag, 2000, 193–216.

Tobias, A. J. 1970. "Plautus' Metrical Charaterization." PhD diss., Stanford University.

West, M. L. 1982a. *Greek Metre*. Oxford: Clarendon Press.

——. 1982b. "Three Topics in Greek Metre." *Classical Quarterly* 32: 281–297.

——. 1992. *Ancient Greek Music*. Oxford: Clarendon Press.

White, J. W. 1912. *The Verse of Greek Comedy*. London: Macmillan.

Wilamowitz-Moellendorff, U. von. 1921. *Griechische Verskunst.* Berlin: Weidmann. Reprinted Darmstadt: Wissenschaftliche Buchgesellschaft, 1984.

——. 1925. *Menander: Das Schiedsgericht.* Berlin: Weidmann. Reprinted 1958.

Willcock, M. M. 1986. Review of *Numeri innumeri: Ricerche sui cantica e la tradizione manoscritta di Plauto,* by C. Questa. *RFIC* 114: 473–480.

——. 1987. *Plautus: Pseudolus.* Bristol: Bristol Classical Press.

Wille, G. 1967. *Musica Romana: Die Bedeutung der Musik im Leben der Römer.* Amsterdam: P. Schippers.

Wilson, P. 2002. "The Musicians among the Actors." In *Greek and Roman Actors: Aspects of an Ancient Profession,* edited by P. Easterling and E. Hall, 39–68. Cambridge, UK: Cambridge University Press.

Zwierlein, O. 1990. *Zur Kritik und Exegese des Plautus. Vol. 1, Poenulus und Curculio.* Mainz: Akademie der Wissenschaften und der Literatur.

....

CHAPTER 25

PROLOGUE(S) AND *PROLOGI*

....

BORIS DUNSCH

SURELY the worst helmsman is the one who runs his ship aground while leaving harbor, says Quintilian in his treatment of the proem (*I.O.* 4.1.61). The rhetorician is right. Beginnings must be handled deftly and with care. The beginning of any literary text, not least of a drama, can be regarded as a threshold leading to another dimension and introducing an imaginary world, the relative order of which must be kept apart from the chaos of the real world. To see how Roman comedians repeatedly succeeded in transporting us to the imaginary one, it is helpful first to examine what exactly a "prologue" is.

DEFINITION AND FUNCTION(S): THE MODERN VIEW

....

If we define the simplest form of drama as an interaction between actor (B) and spectator (C), in which B pretends by some kind of mimesis to be A while C is watching, it is evident that any dramatic performance is set in two worlds at the same time, the real one and an imaginary one. While B and C, as people, are physical entities in the real world, the dramatic character (A) belongs to the illusionary world of enacted representation. Such an arrangement can only work if C is given the cognitive means to distinguish between what is real and what is illusory, that is, "the ability to recognize the performance *as such*" (Elam 1980: 87). This is achieved by a method that could be called "double framing," as usually two layers of framing are needed, an outer and an inner frame,[1] to separate actions that are performed by inhabitants of the play's imaginary world from actions performed by inhabitants of the real world (Pfister 1988: 11). The outer frame is nonverbal. It is constituted by the physical structure of the theater itself

---

[1] At the beginning of any text, its recipients encounter the frames within which their authors create their textual worlds; cf. Elam (1980) 87: "Frames are conceptual or cognitive structures [...] applied by participants and observers to make sense of a given 'strip' of behaviour."

(whether improvised or permanent), with its ordered space separating playing area from auditorium and with all its theatrical paraphernalia, such as stage props and costumes. The inner frame is verbal. It is constituted by conventionalized speech acts that are performed by members of the troupe, demarcating the points in time when the dramatic enactment commences and when it ends, i.e., some kind of introduction ("prologue") and some kind of valediction ("epilogue"). However phrased or staged in detail, the declaration that the play has begun creates and establishes the beginning of the play itself (and thus, at the same time, of the play *as* a play) and secures the initial attention of the audience (cf. Wessels 2012: 59).

One of the most important functions of a prologue is, therefore, to provide a cognitive demarcation of the actual point in time at which the conventions of the real world are temporarily suspended and superseded by those of the ludic cosmos, i.e., the transition from the outer (theatrical) to the inner (dramatic) frame. This requisite suspension enables the actors to behave in ways that an audience would otherwise neither accept nor believe.

At the same time, the inner frame serves as a bridge. In crossing over it, the dramatic text's recipients—whether spectators or readers—become empowered to encounter and interact with the setting, situation, inhabitants, and actions of the fictional world. This stage will prove crucial for everything that follows, since the remainder of their interaction with the text is likely to hinge on the impressions they gain at this important threshold.[2]

This is particularly true in the case of performance. It is during these crucial first moments of a play that experienced spectators decide whether they like what they see. From an established playwright, they anticipate satisfaction of their already high expectations; from a novice, they hope to see a show of at least the same quality or, even better, something unusual or extraordinary.[3]

A further prerequisite for a successful performance is the willingness of C to suspend normal beliefs or expectations about the real world and to accept that "an alternative and fictional reality is to be presented by individuals designated as the performers, and that his own role with respect to that represented reality is to be that of a privileged 'onlooker'" (Elam 1980: 88). By the same token, it is necessary that performers on stage act in apparent oblivion of the spectators. Actors and audience must enter into a kind of mutual contract that defines with some precision what is to be excluded from and what included in the outer and inner frames of the performance.

---

[2] Psychological studies have shown the crucial influence that initial information exerts on the process of perception ("primacy effect"), cf. Rimmon-Kenan 1983: 120.

[3] Plautus's Pseudolus refers to this requirement in a metatheatrical remark at *Pseudolus* 568–570, where the clever slave declares to the audience that one who enters the stage ought to bring something newly thought up in a new fashion, and that one who can't ought to yield the stage to the one who can. Terence offers a separate reflection on the same requirement at *Eunuchus* 35–43. For the topical old/new antithesis in Plautus and Terence, especially in the prologues, see Dunsch 2013: 253–268.

The request "please suspend your conventional expectations now" can be put to the audience in two basic ways. It can be put abruptly, without further ado; or it can arrive piecemeal, by coaxing them further and further into the play, gently edging them on, easing their way into believing (and liking) what they see. In any case, at some point the world of the play must be established as the default state by mutual consent and cooperation between players and spectators. And since spectators are more likely to cooperate with players who succeed in engaging their emotions, this affective function of the prologue is of the utmost importance. If the players do not connect with their audience on an affective level, if they fail to establish a close emotional rapport, a successful performance will be difficult (cf. Moore 1998: 12–17). Conversely, for agelasts in the audience who fail to shift into an adequately festive mood, the play will never really begin, for they will show little readiness to play along with the troupe's efforts to draw them into the world of their performance.

Apart from the cognitive aspect, addressing the spectators' emotions is at least equally important. Their willing collaboration is needed for the performance to succeed. Yet this is not all. Even if the spectators' attention and affection are secured, the play is bound to fail if they do not understand what is going on during the action. They need to be told the main facts that will enable them to follow what is said and done onstage, so that they are ready to *learn*. This second cognitive function is important, for—at least according to some ancient theorists of drama—we attend a play to learn something from it, to help or encourage us to examine and perhaps even modify our own views and values. At any rate, this kind of dramatic entertainment is regarded as far superior to baser forms that simply impress us with visual or verbal fireworks, or in some other sensational manner.

DEFINITION AND FUNCTION(S): ANCIENT VIEWS

As we have seen, in modern thinking the purpose of the prologue is to prepare the audience for what is to follow by rendering them attentive, benevolent, and informed. These are the main functions of any prologue (and indeed, of all kinds of proems), and our summary corresponds to what we are told by ancient authorities (Quint. *I.O.* 4.1.5, with reference to forensic speeches):

> *Causa principii nulla alia est, quam ut auditorem, quo sit nobis in ceteris partibus accommodatior, praeparemus. id fieri tribus maxime rebus inter auctores plurimos constat, si benivolum attentum docilem fecerimus, non quia ista non per totam actionem sint custodienda, sed quia initiis praecipue necessaria, per quae in animum iudicis ut procedere ultra possimus admittimur.*

> The reason for a proem is none other than to prepare the hearer to be more favorably disposed towards us during the rest of the proceedings. Most experts agree that there

are three main ways of achieving this: by making the hearer well disposed, attentive, and ready to learn, not because these aims would not have to be observed through the entire speech, but because they are most crucial in its initial stages, through which we gain admission to the judge's mind, so that later on we may progress further.

Greek and Roman playwrights had several ways of beginning their plays. The various opening gambits can be grouped according to different criteria. The most elementary difference is perhaps the degree to which the spectators' presence is acknowledged by whoever delivers the first words on stage. In Roman comedy, the opening words can be spoken either by human or divine characters; they can form either a monologue or a dialogue; and they can be spoken either plainly, in iambic senarii, or to musical accompaniment (whether "chanted," as in trochaic septenarii, or actually sung, as in a polymetric *canticum*). Of these, it is only the first of each pair—the monologue spoken to an audience in direct address—that we, usually and formally, call a "prologue" (Sharrock 2009: 28f.).[4] As we shall see below, this narrow view imposes limitations on our understanding of the comedians' practice, but in adopting it we are following ancient authorities even more venerable than Quintilian.

Ancient lore holds that the spoken prologue was an innovation first introduced to tragedy by Thespis.[5] The Greek word *prologos* is first attested in Aristophanes's *Frogs*, but the way in which it is employed suggests it was already current at that time. It appears several times in *Frogs* 1119–1250, where, in the presence of Dionysus as arbiter, Aeschylus and Euripides criticize the opening lines of a number of each other's tragedies. There have been doubts as to whether *prologos* is actually used here to mean "prologue" as we (and Aristotle) would understand it or just "opening lines" (Dover 1993: 331), but certainty is unattainable.

Be that as it may, according to a traditional view traceable at least to Aristotle,[6] the primary function of the prologue is preliminary exposition (Arist. *Rhet.* 3.14, 1414b19–21):

---

[4] Rufinus in his *Commentarium in metra Terentiana* (p. 19, 6–9 d'Alessandro) actually says that the Roman playwrights (*nostri*), following the practice of the writers of Greek *comoedia vetus*, composed prologues and the first scenes (*prologos . . . et primarum scaenarum actiones*) in iambic senarii (*trimetris comprehenderunt*).

[5] Cf. Themistius's account of Aristotle's report (*Or.* 26, 316d). Yet, in view of the absence of any reference to Thespis at Ar. *Poet.* 4, 1449a16, the quote is somewhat suspect and, even if authentic, the attempt at a historical reconstruction, whether Aristotelian or otherwise, remains speculative; see Taplin (1977): 62.

[6] At *Rhet.* 3.14, 1415a11–19, Aristotle states that epic as well as dramatic poetry has proems to indicate what the piece is about, so that the spectators would not be left in suspense. His quantitative definition of the tragic prologue as the "entire portion of the play that precedes the entry of the chorus" (*Poet.* 12, 1452b19–20, discussed below) is not contradictory but supplementary to this observation, and also implies that "monologue delivered by one character before any others appear" would be too narrow a definition. Rather than securing coherence in the opening section physically by simply putting one single person on stage, a text's inner unity must be generated by what is said in the text itself, regardless of whether it is staged as a monologue or a dialogue.

The introduction [*prooimion*] is the beginning of a speech, just like the prologue [*prologos*] in poetry and the prelude [*proaulion*] in flute-play, for they all are beginnings, a paving of the way [*hodopoiesis*], so to speak, for what is to follow.

According to Aristotle, prologues are used to indicate what the drama is actually about. The spectators are not left in suspense, but are given the information necessary to form an opinion about the purpose of the play (Arist. *Rhet.* 3.14, 1415a7–25):

It must be understood that the introductions to forensic speeches have the same potential as the prologues of dramas and the introductions to epic poems. [...] In prologues[7] and in epic poetry an outline of the plot [*deigma...tou logou*] is given, so that the audience may know in advance what the plot is about and their understanding [*dianoia*] is not left hanging in the air. For the undefined [*to aoriston*] causes error. So anyone who gives (the spectators) some kind of grasp of the beginning, achieves that, by holding on to it, they can follow the plot. [...] The tragedians, too, clarify the central idea of their play [*delousi peri hou to drama*], if not immediately in the prologue, like Euripides, at least somewhere else, like Sophocles [...]. And comedy does the same. So the most necessary and actually unique function [*ergon*] of the introduction [*prooimion*] is to clarify what is the end for the sake of which [*to telos hou heneka*] the speech [*logos*] is composed (therefore no introduction should be used where the action is clear and brief).

Aristotle's definition of the prologue focuses on its cognitive function. The prologue is used to ensure an adequate understanding of the play. It provides the cognitive framework within which the play is to be watched in order to prevent errors of judgment about the action presented on stage, errors that would make it difficult for a drama to exert its positive, potentially salubrious influence on the spectators. From this point of view, prologues fulfill a function of great importance. If it is not made clear right from the beginning what an action is actually about, what is dealt with onstage, what the topic of a play is, it becomes exceedingly difficult to draw any conclusions from it, since the spectators cannot distinguish between the important and the unimportant—everything seems to be of the same importance, and confusion ensues. An insufficient prologue will interfere with the playwright's didactic intentions. If, however, the playwright provides information where it is not needed because the action is easily comprehensible, he risks boring his audience.

Much the same is said in a fragmentary passage of Antiphanes's *Poiesis*, probably its prologue (cf. Bain 1977: 189 n.1) and perhaps with Poetry personified taking the role of speaker (fr. 189 K-A). In it, she says that tragedy is a fortunate genre (1–16), since the poet need only remind the spectators of the plot, which is well known to them beforehand. And should they not know how to go on with the action, they merely "raise the crane

---

[7] I adopt Ross's *en de prologois* here, following the old Latin translation of *Rhetoric*, instead of *en de tois logois*, an expression that would be rather pointless in this context.

[*mechane*] like a finger and the spectators are satisfied" (15f.). For comedy, the situation is quite the opposite (17–23; the end may be lost), since everything, including new names (*onomata kaina*), has to be invented from scratch. A coherent plot must be presented, including past events, the present situation, an ending (*katastrophe*), and a prologue (*eisbole*—facetiously placed at the end of the list). Should a Chremes or a Pheidon leave any of this out, he will be hissed off the stage; i.e., incoherence will meet with spectators' protests.

While the stress that Antiphanes's speaker lays on the cognitive function of the comic prologue is remarkably reminiscent of Aristotle (cf. Konstantakos 2003–2004: 27), the passage also bears some similarities in tone and outlook to some of Plautus's and all of Terence's self-advertising prologues. Thus this fragment may well be a lonely specimen of a once much larger group of Middle and New Comedy prologues that on the one hand looked back to the practice of Old Comedy, and on the other explored "new concepts, which will become crucial for the self-definition of comedy in the late 4th century" (Konstantakos 2003–2004: 13). Such prologues may have inspired Terence and others when they devised their own comic openings, though they did not provide a model for the impersonal prologue speaker (cf. Bain 1977: 188f.; Hunter 1985: 32).

Elsewhere, Aristotle (*Poet.* 12, 1452b19f.) defines the *prologos* structurally as the whole portion of a play that comes before the entry song of the chorus: "The *prologos* is the entire portion [*meros holon*] of a tragedy that precedes the entry of the chorus." With a view to the Aristotelian usage of *holos* (cf. *Metaph.* 4.26f., 1023b12–37), it would appear that in this passage he refers to the prologue as some kind of coherent "organic" unity. This would suit what Aristotle says about it in the *Rhetoric*, for a speech that is used to clarify something should itself be clear and well constructed, since otherwise it might not achieve its purpose. Nevertheless, it seems that both before and usually after Aristotle, the use of the term *prologos* was narrower, referring only to the first speech of exposition in a play, not to the entire portion of text extending to the choral entry.[8]

TESTING THE THEORY: HOW TO MAKE UP A PROLOGUE

In view of the ancient definitions, the prologue could be regarded as an address to the audience designed to inform the spectators of the situation at the time when the action begins. Still, the ancient definitions do not give the whole picture. This is mainly because, from another perspective, such a prologue is quite unnecessary. Any information provided in a prologue could just as well be given to the audience piecemeal by the stage characters in the course of the action proper through monologues and dialogues;

---

[8] Cf. Taplin (1977): 471f. Despite the serious doubts that have been raised about the Aristotelian authorship of ch. 12, the case still stands; cf. Schmitt (2008): 433–435.

the same holds true for "grabbing the attention" of the audience (Sharrock 2009: 23). In part, this is because people about to attend a theatrical performance usually know a great deal about it beforehand. As mentioned earlier, all spectators (excepting the incorrigibly naive and the absolutely inexperienced) will know that what they are going to see is not real in the same sense that the everyday world around them is real, but that it rather belongs to a different ontological category, the world of the play. They also know that the actors know that they know this. To ease their audience into the requisite collaboration, the troupe must constantly work to establish and maintain a close rapport with them right from the beginning, constantly bidding for their attention. And spectators know that their collaboration is required; to adapt Umberto Eco's term for readers of prose narratives, they know that they are *spectatores in fabula* (cf. Raffaelli 2009: 277–286), and often enough, the actors *themselves* remind the audience of this fact during the play.[9]

The spectators' sympathetic attention is the currency of dramatic success. Consequently, all efforts of the actors and, by implication, the playwright also, are governed by certain principles of an economy of attention.

Making up a prologue ourselves may help to illustrate this point. The shortest conceivable version of a Roman comic prologue might run as follows (bracketed sentences refer to what is not spelled out but implied by what is said):

> "Greetings! This is a play (and you are the audience). This is not Rome, but Greece (so relax, it's not about you). This is the problem and how it came about (and you are privileged to know about it). Don't worry, this is going to end well (and you'll enjoy it). Farewell."

The prologue-speaker does not of course usually utter such a message verbatim, nor are the implications put on the table so bluntly. Rather, the prologue is the first rhetorical set piece of the play, affording an actor a prime opportunity to display his professional skills. Fleshed out to more customary proportions, our prologue *in nuce* would in fact appear more like this:

> "Greetings, I am Mercury, and also the speaker of this prologue. Thank you for choosing to attend this play, which proves your superior taste—well, at least as long as you

---

[9] It is therefore hard to see how such reminders can constitute ruptures of the so-called "dramatic illusion." Though much used, the term is unhelpful for describing the complex and essentially conspiratorial interaction between audience and actors. Dover (1972: 56) defines dramatic illusion as "the uninterrupted concentration of the fictitious personages of the play on their fictitious situation." One can, however, ask whether there had ever been any drama in Greece or Rome where this ideal kind of illusion is carried through for the entire duration of the play. At the least, one should be careful not to assume that the keeping up of the dramatic illusion is the default state from which its "rupture" deviates. Is it not rather the other way around, in that the acknowledgement of the audience's presence and a strong rapport with the spectators is the default state, which is further reinforced by interspersing passages of "dramatic illusion?" For Plautine comedy as nonillusory drama, see Wessels (2012): 74 and cf. Slater (1985): 151 (on the *prologus* prologues): "The audience is thus drawn not into illusion but into participation in the creation and functioning of the play."

choose to stay seated and pay attention. This comedy is called *Capella*. It was turned into Latin by Titius Bucco. Its model is *Aigidion* by Antiphanes.[10] Now I will reveal to you the details of the plot. A merchant bought a slave-girl on a business trip to Lemnos and has brought her to Sicyon, the city where this comedy is set. Here, he tries to have an affair with her behind the back of his wife, who is away on their country estate. The girl, however, had been stolen by pirates when she was still a baby. She had a twin sister, who has been the consolation of their devastated parents ever since. The twins' father is a wealthy merchant dealing in livestock. He happens to be the old man's next-door neighbor, here, in this house behind me. His firstborn son is married to his neighbor's remaining daughter. As you will see, there is plenty of opportunity to mistake one twin for the other. However, since both merchants, unlike so many others, have always done more than their due when they sacrificed to me, I am resolved to help. I will arrange to have the girl recognized by her old nurse and married to the neighbor's younger son. Farewell now, and be fair and square judges of our performance. Then I promise to see to it that all of you make some profit."

From Theory to Praxis: Plautus's Prologues and *Prologi*

This make-believe text contains all the elements that may be found in a Plautine prologue: (a) introduction, (b) information about the Greek author and/or title of the model, (c) indication of the play's setting, (d) narration of the plot (*argumentum*), (e) prediction of how the play will end, (f) valediction (cf. Gratwick 1993: 31). The introductory part usually includes an appeal to the goodwill of the audience (*captatio benevolentiae*), the name of the Roman playwright, and some metatheatrical references. Yet such is Plautus's variety of treatment that none of the six elements enumerated above seems to be absolutely obligatory, and there are only two prologues that employ them all (*Poenulus, Rudens*).

Prologues are commonly delivered by a divinity, by characters from the play, or by a fixed "*prologus*" who neither has any part in the play nor pretends to be a deity or a human character. This last is the case in some (probably post-Plautine) prologues of the Plautine corpus and in all of Terence's comedies.[11] *Amphitruo, Aulularia, Cistellaria, Rudens,* and *Trinummus* have a divine prologue (preceded in *Cistellaria* by an opening scene and an expository monologue spoken by a human character; see Hurka 2004). In

---

[10] We do not know of a play called *Aigidion* by Antiphanes, but considering that Eupolis wrote *Aiges* and that *aix* ("she-goat") could be used as a nickname for courtesans (Davidson 1997: 205), there could well have been a New Comedy play of that title. At any rate, the name is invented here simply *exempli gratia*.

[11] For details, see, e.g., Duckworth (1952): 211–218, Hunter (1985): 24–35, and especially Raffaelli (2009): 13–31 (divine prologues), 33–52 (prologues spoken by dramatis personae), and 53–67 (prologues spoken by a *prologus*). Still important for Plautus in particular is Abel (1955).

Asinaria, Captivi, Casina, Menaechmi, Poenulus, Pseudolus, Truculentus, and *Vidularia,* the prologue is spoken by a member of the troupe, in most cases probably a younger one (cf. Terence, *Heauton Timorumenos* 1–3) who was specially dressed for the part (cf. Terence, *Hecyra* 9). In *Miles Gloriosus* (deferred prologue: *Miles Gloriosus* 79–153) and in *Mercator,* as we shall see below, the prologue is spoken by a character of the play, while the situation in the lost opening of *Bacchides* remains unclear (cf. Barsby 1991: 93-97). *Curculio, Epidicus, Mostellaria, Persa,* and *Stichus* have no formal prologue (and probably never had one, cf. Marshall 2006: 194f.), instead providing exposition in the course of the action, mostly the first scenes.

In Menander, divine prologues are either found at the start of the play, in a manner comparable to Euripidean practice, or occasionally after the spectators' initial interest has been aroused by some other kind of opening scene (cf. Bain 1977: 187–189; Scafuro, chapter 10, this volume). In either case, the divine prologists have the stage to themselves. When we turn to Plautus, we find a greater variety of treatment. His divine prologues are sometimes Menandrian-like (*Aulularia, Rudens,* and, delayed, *Cistellaria*), but sometimes different. The god might share the stage with another character (*Trinummus*), or go on to participate in the play as a character himself (Mercury in *Amphitruo*).

In this last respect, *Amphitruo* resembles *Mercator.* In the latter play, the prologue (1–110), "forse il prologo piú complesso" (Questa 1984: 12), is delivered by a character of the play, Charinus, who makes his intermediary, metatheatrical status explicit right from the outset (1–8; see also Dunsch on religion, this volume), and by the same token immediately makes clear "that he wants the audience's attention and sympathy" (Moore 1998: 31):

> Duas res simul nunc agere decretumst mihi:
> et argumentum et meos amores eloquar.
> non ego item facio ut alios in comoediis
> \<vi\> vidi Amoris facere, qui aut Nocti aut Dii
> aut Soli aut Lunae miserias narrant suas: 5
> quos pol ego credo humanas querimonias
> non tanti facere, quid velint quid non velint;
> vobis narrabo potius meas nunc miserias.

> For me, it's been decided to act out two things now at once:
> Expound both the plot and my loves.
> *I* don't just do what I've seen others in comedies
> do under the power of Love, who tell either the Night or the Day
> or the Sun or the Moon their miseries.
> These, I think, by Pollux, don't care *that* much [*gesturing with his hand*]
> about the complaints of mortals—what they want, what they don't.
> Rather, I'll now tell my miseries to *you.*

It is an "innovative and unusually effective" feature (Slater 2010: 5) of this prologue that Charinus is simultaneously both a *prologus* and a character taking part in the action of the play he announces. In the course of his prologue, he "changes," almost imperceptibly, from a *prologus* to a character involved in the action. The transition from exposition to action is thus quite smooth. Like *Amphitruo*'s Mercury, who has already assumed the likeness of the slave Sosia before entering the stage, and unlike the *prologus* of Terence's *Hecyra* prol. II, Charinus is from the very beginning dressed as an *adulescens*, wearing the costume and mask of the part he is to play (on costumes and masks in Roman comedy, see Questa 1984 and Manuwald 2011: 75–80, and on masks in particular, Petrides in this volume). Charinus's double function offers the playwright the advantage of presenting the main facts of the exposition[12] while simultaneously characterizing the two people who will prove most important: the merchants, father and son. This is important because *Mercator* as a play is chiefly concerned with character (*ethos*), and several character traits emphasized in this prologue turn out to be keynotes later on (lines 42, 46–78, 103).[13] The audience certainly appreciated, for instance, how the unsuspecting Charinus here presents his father's humorously inconsistent self-stylization (Dunsch 2008: 26–31).

This prologue-monologue is longer than others in Plautus, but the playwright has taken careful measures to prevent it from becoming tedious. Rather than simply stating the bare facts, Charinus presents the spectators with a lengthy list of *vitia amoris* (18–36) and tells them briefly about his previous expensive love affair (40–45) and his father's reaction (46–60). This in turn allows him to speak of his father's disposition and to share with us some of his father's stories about his own youth (61–78), enriching them with a lively prosopopoeia (70–72). This leads to the narration of Charinus's own two-year business trip to Rhodes (12, 85–106), inspired by his father's exhortations (11, 79–84), where he met a stunningly beautiful slave-girl, fell instantly in love with her (13, 100–103), bought her, and brought her back "here" to "Athens" (104–106). The events narrated in the prologue are tightly and conclusively concatenated. What is more, Plautus embroiders this tightly stitched web with numerous rhetorical devices (contrived alliteration, hyperbaton, irony, prosopopoeia, and variations in the pacing of the narrative; cf. Goldberg 1986: 183).

How original is Plautus's contribution to his prologues? *Mercator*'s prologue contains an assortment of allusions and terms that sound Greek and remind the audience of the supposedly "Greek" setting of the play (3 *comoediis*, 9 *Emporos*, 11 and 93 *Rhodum*, 40 and 61 *ex ephebis*, 67 *peplum*, 75 *metretas*, 87 *cercurum*, 89 *talentum*, 91 *paedagogus*, 99 *hilare*). Such "markers of Greekness" could at first sight be attributed to the original, assuming that Plautus is here simply Philemon's translator. However, as Fraenkel (2007 [= 1922]: 365n. 78) long ago pointed out, "it is unacceptable to interpret Greek or

---

[12] Of the two characters familiar with the situation and thus in theory available as *prologi* (apart from an omniscient deity), only Charinus is actually available, as his trusted slave Acanthio will soon be needed as a messenger of crucial information (*servus currens*, cf. 117, 180f., 182, 203, 333f.; Fields 1938: 102f.).

[13] Wilner (1938): 22 compares *Aulularia* 21f., 37–39, *Miles Gloriosus* 88–92, *Rudens* 33–38, and *Truculentus* 12–16, and also points out that in some plays, as here, the description of the *ethos* of one or more characters is "a short-cut method of explaining the opening situation" (cf. lines 42, 103–105; she compares *Amphitruo* 104–139, *Captivi* 27–34, *Miles Gloriosus* 138–153, *Poenulus* 98–101, and *Rudens* 47–56).

half-Greek words in Plautus as 'word-for-word reminiscences of the model.'" Many such markers may actually be indicative of Plautus's having consciously amplified the Greek "flavor" of a passage, as Terence demonstrably did on occasion (cf. Williams 1968: 290f.). Recognized long ago (Leo 1912: 106f.; Fraenkel 2007 [= 1922]: 88–95), this artistic strategy has recently been given the apt label "hyper-Hellenization" (Moore 1998: 61). We cannot establish whether every marker of Greekness is a sign of deliberate hyper-Hellenization or not, but we should not assume that Plautus cannot sound Greek when he wants to, cannot spin out a shorter passage of the original while contriving at the same time to sound Greek, and cannot conjure up the atmosphere of a *civitas Graeca* when he so chooses.[14]

Akin to this difficulty of interpretation is the question of authenticity. The Plautine prologues as transmitted to us pose several grave problems of authorship (cf. Fantham 1965; Gratwick 1993: 30f.). At least in part, some prologues are manifestly post-Plautine, as are parts of the *Casina* and *Menaechmi* prologues, and, depending on how much (or little) we are willing to credit to Plautus's daring and innovative spirit, probably also the two-liner opening of *Pseudolus* (cf. Willcock 1987: 96). The status of other prologues remains subject to debate; hardly any mentions a contemporary event that must be due to Plautus himself (Beare 1968: 159). Whatever modifications were made, they all probably date to the decades after Plautus's death (ca. 180 BCE), when his plays were still being performed and the text had not yet been standardized for a reading public (Beare 1968: 159; cf. Deufert 2002: 25–31). The most plausible theory is that producers and stage managers made the changes when adapting the prologues to the particular circumstances and exigencies of revival performances.

TERENCE: *PROLOGI* AND PROLOGUES

One important role of the comic prologue is exposition. Plautus seems to have dispensed with an expository prologue on occasion (cf. *Trinummus* 16f., *sed de argumento ne expectetis fabulae: / senes qui huc veniunt, i rem vobis aperient.*), but only rarely. Terence explicitly eschews this function (cf. especially the prologues of *Andria* and *Adelphoe*) and prefers to let the plot emerge from the play proper. In so doing, he eliminated the expository prologues that were probably prefixed to each of his Greek models (though occasionally failing to make adequate dramaturgical compensation: Gratwick 1999: 15 and 27f.; Damen 1987). The Terentian prologue neither establishes the initial situation *ad spectatores* nor sets the action going (cf. Gratwick 1982: 121); its purpose is metatheatrical; that is, just as Plautus does in his prologues, but in a much more systematic and regular fashion, the Terentian *prologus* makes the prologue itself and Terence's work as

---

[14] Prime examples are the *parasitus currens* monologue in *Curculio* (280–298), which contains a high proportion of markers of Greekness but is probably Plautine, and the inimitable line *Miles Gloriosus* 213 *euge euscheme hercle astitit dulice et comoedice* which was probably not in the Greek play. For more on this theme, see Gaertner in this volume.

a playwright the central theme, often taking the opportunity to defend the playwright against criticism from literary opponents. *Adelphoe* is representative of his approach and interests.

Adelphoe's formal prologue falls into four parts of decreasing length. The first (1–14) contains literary polemic. The prologue speaker reports how the poet is concerned about the attacks of his literary critics, especially their objections to his use of scenes that other Roman poets had previously turned into Latin, a practice they seem to have called *furtum*, "theft." This technique of adaptation is called *contaminare* in other prologues (on "*contaminatio*," see Fontaine on Plautus in this volume and cf. Dunsch 1999: 104f.).

These criticisms are rejected. Using the speaker as mouthpiece, the poet invites the spectators to act as judges: *vos eritis iudices* (4). And as he proceeds to defend himself in detail, he simultaneously extends this preliminary bid to arrest his audience's interest, for the speaker now mentions a scene in which a courtesan is forcefully taken away from a pimp (6–11). The nonillusory details about this *contaminatio* are, however, simultaneously part of the exposition of the (illusory) action; and what is more, they contain an element of surprise, for most members of the audience will probably expect that it is her lover who abducts the *meretrix*, not a third party, as proves to be the case (cf. Martin 1976: 99).

The next section (15–21) deals with a potentially more damaging allegation leveled against Terence. While in the first section the poet had to face charges regarding his dramatic technique, the second charge is *ad personam*. It is claimed that the play is not his own work, but some "noble people" had helped him write it (15). Commentators have speculated about the identity of these *homines nobiles* since antiquity, and although the likeliest candidate is Scipio Aemilianus (who fought at Pydna in 168 BCE), it is impossible to be certain; the reference is more safely understood as an allusion to aristocratic patronage and a kind of "name dropping" (Martin 1976: 100) that does not actually identify anyone in particular and so remains discreet and unassailable. The play's first performance context (the funeral games for L. Aemilius Paullus) will have left the audience enough possibilities to fill in the gaps. As Martin (1976: 99f.) notes, "Terence is engaging in a *captatio beneuolentiae* for himself" and this "passage [. . .] is not designed to refute a serious accusation from Terence's opponents."

At first glance, the two allegations raised in sections 1 and 2 do not add up. If we take both at face value, Luscius Lanuvinus—for Donatus tells us that is the name of Terence's opponent (cf. Garton 1972: 41–72)—would at the very least be a foolhardy critic. For if allegation 2 is correct, it should be the *homines nobiles* who must face the charge of *furtum* (or at least of endorsing it) that is hurled against Terence in section 1. This bit of chicanery is one hint that Terence is not being entirely straightforward in his presentation of "the facts."

Sections 3 and 4 of the prologue are much shorter. In the third (22–24a), the audience is told not to expect the plot to be disclosed by the *prologus*. Rather, that will be accomplished by the two *senes* who are about to appear, partly in words, partly in action (the passage bears a striking resemblance to Plautus, *Trinummus* 16f., quoted above). The prologue concludes with a final appeal to the audience's sense of fairness (24b–25).

This quality is characteristic of good judges, the sort the audience was asked to be in the first few lines (cf. 4, above). The prologue has come full circle—and ends with an implicit threat, as the last two lines may imply that should the playwright find his latest creation does not get a fair hearing, he may just stop writing new plays (cf. Gratwick 1999: 52f., 179).

Before investing these prologues with too much authorial meaning, we must—as with Plautus's prologues—face a question of authenticity. It is by no means clear that Terence himself wrote the prologues. It is equally possible that their author is Ambivius Turpio, Terence's actor/stage manager, at least of those believed to be spoken by him (cf. Marouzeau 1947: 28; Garton 1972: 60f.; Gratwick 1999: 3).

This risk does not apply, however, to a second prologic function in *Adelphoe*. In ignoring exposition in the prologue proper, Terence transforms the entirety of the backstory and plot to a series of inferences the spectators must draw out from the play. The particular function of the first scene, a soliloquy spoken by Micio, is *argumentum fabulae aperire* (23). It provides the informational background to the action. The other part of the opening scene (80b–140) serves to *ostendere argumentum in agendo* (24), or, in the terms favored by modern drama theory, as "exposition proper" and "dramatic introduction" (Pfister 1988: 86). The form of this soliloquy is determined by its purpose. The overall impression provided by 26–80 is of a tranquil dramatic movement (*in statario charactere*; cf. Don. *Ad.* 24, 2, p. 12, 5 Wessner), and in sum and function, therefore, this first scene acts as a prologue as well. (It may indeed even have had that function in the Greek model as well, rather than merely incorporating material taken from the original prologue, as has been argued: cf., e.g., Lefèvre 1969: 45–47).

Micio's soliloquy is thus akin to Charinus's prologue in *Mercator*, with the important difference that Charinus's soliloquy is explicitly and overtly a prologue, whereas Micio's performs this function only implicitly and ironically. Its procedure and, in particular, its rhetoric therefore merit close analysis as a prologue.[15] As the text is too long to quote in full, in what follows readers are asked to have a text of verses 26–78 before themselves.

The soliloquy is realistic in that Micio addresses himself rather than the audience. He is "alone," there is no abusive language, his speech is controlled and his style elaborate. The situation is established economically. At first, Micio calls out for an absent slave (26) on a cold (36), still dark (37f.) morning (26). Without further ado, he begins a series of four antitheses that lead to the skillfully prepared (60–67), sudden appearance of Demea (78–80). The first antithesis appears at 28–34 (*uxor—parentes propitii*). The misogynist caricature of an upset wife makes him seem like the epitome of a caring father. His self-portrait (35–38a) is then, of course, modeled on the ideal of the *parens propitius*. Despite his rhetoric, however, the analogies are inadequate: being a child is

---

[15] On the rhetorical character of Terence's (and Plautus's) prologues in general, see, e.g., Barsby (2007): 39–43; on Terence's in particular, see Lefèvre (1969), Gelhaus (1972), Büchner (1974): 484–497, and Goldberg (1986): 31–60. On Micio's monologue, see also Schmude (1990), whose findings partly differ from the ones presented here.

not like being a husband, and being a wife is not like being a parent. Thus he alters the level of reflection and wrecks the logic of his argument, while at the same time smugly suggesting that his way of indulgent parenting has something divine about it (*propitius* is stronger than "indulgent" or "doting" and is often used of the benevolent attitude of gods in Roman prayer language; cf. *Mercator* 678 and 680; see also Dunsch on religion, this volume).

However, in 38f. Micio comments drastically on the irrationality of his choice (*vah, quemquamne hominem in animum instituere / parare quod sit carius quam ipse est sibi!*). This exclamation introduces the second antithesis (38b–41): altruism—selfishness (*carius quam ipsest sibi*: 39). In 40f., the effect of this antagonism is clarified. The passage is closely connected to the previous lines: Micio's abstract idea is illustrated by reference to Aeschinus's two identities as adopted and genuine son, and to the different methods of education for him and Ctesipho.

The contrast between *ex me* and *ex fratre* prepares for the third antithesis (42–58): *ego* (42–44a, 47b–49)—*ille* (44b–47a), his brother Demea. The picture that Micio draws of Demea is efficient. The audience is made to believe that his brother is a representative of the *senex durus* type (45; cf. 64). Demea's harshness is even evoked audibly through Micio's growling *r*-sounds (*contra, ruri, agere, semper, parce, duriter*, etc.), a sound that Persius aptly called the *canina littera* (*Sat.* 1, 109). Micio's self-portrait, by contrast, is full of soft *m*- and *n*-alliterations (*hanc clementem vitam urbanam...otium*, etc.) and *o*-assonances (47b–49). The diction is deliberately rhetorical, as can be seen in the enumeration of synonymous verbs emphasizing his paternal love. Yet, as far as Micio's adoption of one of Demea's sons and his generosity are concerned, he seems to congratulate himself just that annoying little bit too often (cf. 38–40, 48f., 50–52; esp. 51f.: *non necesse habeo omnia / pro meo iure agere*). In 49, Micio switches from the masculine gender (referring to Aeschinus) to the neuter. This phenomenon as such is not uncommon in Latin, but the contrast is underlined by the fact that the previous lines convey an air of sentimental, doting love. This change and the inadequacy of the verb *habui* (48) probably point to an essential emotional shortcoming in Micio which is not outweighed but rather emphasized in the following verses ("me and my son"), in which Micio briefly defines how he expects his paternal love to be repaid and how he thinks he achieves his educational aims (50–52a). Micio exposes his concept of being a father to common ridicule, as his "arguments are potentially [...] disturbing to traditional Roman ways of thinking" (cf. Gratwick 1999: 181). In the last part of the third antithesis (52b–58), Micio sums up his principles (*postremo*, "in short": 52b), claiming a strong contrast between his obedient and honest son, Aeschinus (54), and the *alii*, naughty impudent liars and good-for-nothings (52f.). A clichéd reason for liberal education (55f.) is appended to this bold claim. Micio's concept finds its most emphatic expression in the pathos-laden paronomasia *liberalitate liberos* (57).

The fourth antithesis (59–80a) continues the previously introduced binary Micio—Demea opposition (*senex lepidus* versus *pater durus*), but now with a closer focus on Demea. The figure of Micio's antagonist becomes clear-cut, and the audience will laugh at Demea in 81ff., as his personality actually seems to bear a striking resemblance to the ludicrous caricature previously drawn by his brother. Micio characterizes him as *increpitans* (60), and identifies *iurgare* as Demea's habitual pastime (79f.).

Mentioning his own principles (59), Micio thinks of his brother and acts his part in a vivid and dramatically effective passage (60–63). The part devoted to Demea is shorter and again somewhat unfairly embedded between the descriptions of Micio's own ideas. Demea is caricatured as a rustic would-be rhetorician. He cannot open his mouth without uttering expletives or petulant questions (serialized interrogatives, triadic anaphora of *quor* [cf. the actual Demea at 799f.]), short asyndetic sentences, ethical dative: 61, anaphora of *nimium*: 63f.). Surprisingly, it is Micio who continues the anaphora and completes the triadic structure: the formulaic expression *praeter aequomque et bonum*, used to reprimand Demea's behavior, would be more consonant with the *senex durus*—thus, Demea's idiolect is ironically inverted and turned against him.

In 65–67, Micio states that Demea's educational principles are essentially based on the faulty ideas he has already attacked (55f.). Consequently, with brilliant rhetoric he sets his own policy in opposition to his brother's (67–77), merely inflating his previously stated ideas (57f.). His style may be characterized as verbose, elevated, rhetorical, tinged with emotion (indicated by more than two metrical resolutions per line: 66, 68, 72, 74; two resolutions: 71, 75, 76), and even paratragic in tone and style (clichés and metaphors, e.g., in 70b; pathetic exaggerations, e.g., 76f.; jussive *fateatur*: 77). From 64 onwards, Micio uses words with legal and political connotations (*bonum, imperium, amicitia, officium, beneficium, par referre, dominus, imperare*) and expressions carrying legal undertones (e.g. *praesens absensque*: 73). This generic intertextuality makes him sound almost as if pleading his cause at court, or, with equal didactic enthusiasm, "on a soapbox" (Gratwick 1999: 182). In spite of his pomposity, however, Micio cannot save his intrinsically faulty argument. Micio's shallowness is thus revealed at the very beginning of a play that will end with the derision of this *senex lepidus* and would-be educator.

In sum, Terence's use of this "prologic" soliloquy thus gives us not quite "suspense"—a quality that he is usually credited with—but on the contrary, something rather akin to active misdirection. He leads the audience to expect a rather run-of-the-mill, double-plot intrigue play wherein the old and the young are conventionally paired off. However, what we finally get at the end of *Adelphoe*—a transformation of *pater durus* into *senex lepidus*, thus exposing the artificiality of the dramatic convention—is a wholesale send-up of the entire conventional duality method (cf. Damen 1990: 99f.). In this regard, Terence's use of the *Adelphoe* prologue, taking the word in its Aristotelian sense, is very different from anything found in Plautus and from much found elsewhere in Terence.

CONCLUSION

To sum up, the most important functions of the prologue as the opening of a play are cognitive *and* emotional, consisting in exposition proper and in dramatic introduction. In a way, this comes quite close to the system of four distinct functions or prologue-types drawn up by Donatus (*Excerpta de comoedia* 7.2, p. 27, 5–11 Wessner; cf. Goldberg 1986: 59f.): *commendativus*, "praising the poet or his work"; *relativus*, "attacking rivals or winning the audience's favor"; *argumentativus*, "giving the plot"; and *mixtus*, a combination of the previous three. Insofar as the prologue-speakers, regardless of who they are, employ rhetorical strategies that have cognitive as well as emotional aims, almost all prologues in Plautus and Terence belong to the *mixtus* type. The prologue is there to remind the audience of its task, of its "job" as an audience. As Beacham says (1995: 38), "The festive frame of mind, as well as the aesthetic conditions in which it can be indulged—the rules of the game—are the object of careful preparation by Plautus, principally in his prologues." By contrast, Terence's use of the prologue can sometimes be more experimental and demanding on the audience—Plautus focusing more on the spectators and their expectations, Terence striving to challenge exactly those expectations and exploring the outer rim of the *palliata* genre. Both Plautus and Terence use their prologues to interact with their audience, prepare its cognitive appreciation of the action, and at the same time establish the emotional rapport necessary for drawing up the mutual player-spectator "contract" by which alone theatricality as such becomes possible. Simply put, certain things can best be said and done in prologues. Although dramatic economy suggests they are perhaps not strictly necessary, they do remain an indispensable tool in the dramatist's workbox.

Bibliography

Abel, K. 1955. "Die Plautusprologe." PhD diss., Johann Wolfgang Goethe-Universität Frankfurt.

Bain, D. 1977. *Actors and Audience: A Study of Asides and Related Conventions in Greek Drama.* Oxford: Clarendon Press. Repr. 1987.

Barsby, J. 1991. *Plautus: Bacchides.* 3rd corr. impr. Warminster: Aris & Phillips.

———. 1999. *Terence: Eunuchus.* Cambridge, UK: Cambridge University Press.

———. 2007. "Native Roman Rhetoric: Plautus and Terence." In *A Companion to Roman Rhetoric*, edited by W. Dominik and J. Hall, 38–53. Malden, MA: Blackwell.

Beacham, R. C. 1995. *The Roman Theatre and its Audience.* London: Routledge.

Beare, W. 1968. *The Roman Stage: A Short History of Latin Drama in the Time of the Republic.* London: Methuen.

Büchner, K. 1974. *Das Theater des Terenz.* Heidelberg: Carl Winter Universitätsverlag.

Damen, M. 1987. "Reconstructing the Beginning of Menander's *Adelphoi* (B)." *Illinois Classical Studies* 12: 67–84.

———. 1990. "Structure and Symmetry in Terence's *Adelphoe.*" *Illinois Classical Studies* 15: 85–106.

Davidson, J. N. 1997. *Courtesans and Fishcakes: The Consuming Passions of Classical Athens.* London: HarperCollins.

Deufert, M. 2002. *Textgeschichte und Rezeption der plautinischen Komödien im Altertum.* Berlin and New York: de Gruyter.

Dover, K. J. 1972. *Aristophanic Comedy.* Berkeley and Los Angeles: University of California Press.

———. 1993. *Aristophanes: Frogs.* Oxford: Clarendon Press.

Duckworth, G. E. 1952. *The Nature of Roman Comedy: A Study in Popular Entertainment.* Princeton: Princeton University Press. Repr. 1994.

Dunsch, B. 1999. "Some Notes on the Understanding of Terence, *Heauton timorumenos* 6: *Comoedia duplex, argumentum simplex*, and Hellenistic Scholarship." *Classica & Mediaevalia* 50: 97–131.

——. 2008. "Il commerciante in scena: Temi e motivi mercantili nel *Mercator* plautino e nell'*Emporos* filemoniano." In *Lecturae Plautinae Sarsinates XI, Mercator (Sarsina, 29 settembre 2007)*, edited by R. Raffaelli and A. Tontini, 11–41. Urbino: QuattroVenti.

——. 2013. "Die plautinische Komödie in republikanischer und kaiserzeitlicher Literaturkritik." In *Epos, Lyrik, Drama: Genese und Ausformung der literarischen Gattungen: Festschrift für Ernst-Richard Schwinge zum 75. Geburtstag*, edited by B. Dunsch, A. Schmitt, and T. Schmitz, 237–300. Heidelberg: Carl Winter Universitätsverlag.

Elam, K. 1980. *The Semiotics of Theatre and Drama*. London: Routledge. Repr. 2001.

Fantham, E. 1965. "The *Curculio* of Plautus: An Illustration of Plautine Methods in Adaptation." *Classical Quarterly* 15: 84–100.

Fields, D. E. 1938. "The Technique of Exposition in Roman Comedy." PhD diss., University of Chicago.

Fraenkel, E. 1922. *Plautinisches im Plautus*. Berlin: Weidmann.

——. 2007. *Plautine Elements in Plautus*. Translated by T. Drevikovsky and F. Muecke. Oxford: Oxford University Press.

Garton, C. 1972. *Personal Aspects of the Roman Theatre*. Toronto: Hakkert.

Gelhaus, H. 1972. *Die Prologe des Terenz: Eine Erklärung nach den Lehren von der* inventio *und* dispositio. Heidelberg: Carl Winter Universitätsverlag.

Goldberg, S. M. 1986. *Understanding Terence*. Princeton: Princeton University Press.

Gratwick, A. S. 1982. "Drama." In *Cambridge History of Classical Literature*. Vol. 2. Part 1, *The Early Republic*, edited by E. J. Kenney and W. V. Clausen, 77–137. Cambridge, UK: Cambridge University Press. Repr. 1995.

——. 1993. *Plautus: Menaechmi*. Cambridge, UK: Cambridge University Press.

——. 1999. *Terence: The Brothers*. Warminster: Aris & Phillips.

Hunter, R. 1985. *The New Comedy of Greece and Rome*. Cambridge, UK: Cambridge University Press.

Hurka, F. 2004. "Die beiden προλογίζοντες der *Cistellaria*." In: *Studien zu Plautus' Cistellaria*, edited by R. Hartkamp and F. Hurka, 29–49. Tübingen: Gunter Narr Verlag.

Klose, D. 1966. "Die Didaskalien und Prologe des Terenz." PhD diss., Albert-Ludwigs-Universität zu Freiburg i. Br.

Konstantakos, I. M. 2003–2004. "This Craft of Comic Verse: Greek Comic Poets on Comedy." *Archaiognosia* 12: 11–53.

Lefèvre, E. 1969. *Die Expositionstechnik in den Komödien des Terenz*. Darmstadt: Wissenschaftliche Buchgesellschaft.

Leo, F. 1912. *Plautinische Forschungen zur Kritik und Geschichte der Komödie*. 2nd ed. Berlin: Weidmann. Repr. 1973.

Manuwald, G. 2011. *Roman Republican Theatre*. Cambridge, UK: Cambridge University Press.

Marouzeau, J. 1947. *Térence: Comédies*. Vol. 1. 2nd ed. Paris.

Marshall, C. W. 2006. *The Stagecraft and Performance of Roman Comedy*. Cambridge, UK: Cambridge University Press.

Martin, R. H. 1976. *Terence: Adelphoe*. Cambridge, UK: Cambridge University Press.

Moore, T. J. 1998. *The Theater of Plautus. Playing to the Audience*. Austin: University of Texas Press.

Pfister, M. 1988. *The Theory and Analysis of Drama*. Cambridge, UK: Cambridge University Press Repr. 1993.

Questa, C. 1984. "Maschere e funzioni nelle commedie di Plauto." In *Maschere, prologhi, naufragi nella commedia plautina*, edited by C. Questa and R. Raffaelli, 9–65. Bari: Adriatica Editrice.

Raffaelli, R. 2009. *Esercizi plautini*. Urbino: QuattroVenti.

Rimmon-Kenan, S. 1983. *Narrative Fiction: Contemporary Poetics*. London: Routledge. Repr. 1994.

Schmitt, A. 2008. *Aristoteles: Poetik*. Berlin: Akademie Verlag.

Schmude, M. P. 1990. "Micios Erziehungsprogramm: Zur rhetorischen Form von Terenz, Adelphoe I 1 (26–81a)." *Rheinisches Museum* 133: 298–310.

Sharrock, A. 2009. *Reading Roman Comedy. Poetics and Playfulness in Plautus and Terence*. Cambridge, UK: Cambridge University Press.

Slater, N. W. 1985. *Plautus in Performance: The Theatre of the Mind*. Princeton: Princeton University Press. Repr. 1987.

——. 2010. "Opening Negotiations: The Work of the Prologue to Plautus's *Mercator*." *New England Classical Journal* 37: 5–13.

Taplin, O. 1977. *The Stagecraft of Aeschylus: The Dramatic Use of Exits and Entrances in Greek Tragedy*. Oxford: Clarendon Press. Repr. 1999.

Wessels, A. 2012. "Zur Exposition bei Plautus." In *Der Einsatz des Dramas: Dramenanfänge, Wissenschaftspoetik und Gattungspolitik*, edited by C. Haas and A. Polaschegg, 59–74. Freiburg: Rombach.

Willcock, M. M. 1987. *Plautus: Pseudolus*. Bristol: Bristol Classical Press. Repr. 2001.

Williams, G. 1968. *Tradition and Originality in Roman Poetry*. Oxford: Clarendon Press.

Wilner, O. L. 1938. "The Technical Device of Direct Description of Character in Roman Comedy." *Classical Philology* 33: 20–36.

CHAPTER 26

....

BETWEEN TWO
PARADIGMS: PLAUTUS

....

MICHAEL FONTAINE

Two centuries before Horace demanded Melpomene's laurels (*Odes* 3.30), Plautus might well have claimed her garland. Alongside Horace, Catullus, and Statius, he reigns as Rome's fourth great lyric poet—with the critical difference, however, that his lyrics were set to music.

The W. S. Gilbert of his age, T. Maccius Plautus (apocryphally born 254 in Sarsina, Italy, *fl.* ca. 210–184) penned at least twenty-one of the extant Latin *comoediae*, "libretti adapted from Greek κωμῳδίαι," that grammarians in later ages would come to call *fabulae palliatae*, "plays starring characters in Greek cloak." Assembled in the 1st century BCE by the republican scholar M. Terentius Varro (116–27 BCE) as works of unquestioned authenticity, the conventional list of Plautus's extant libretti and, where known, their dates of first performance and the Greek plays from which they are adapted, appears on the next page. Beyond them survive several hundred short and scattered fragments of noncanonical plays. Among these are the further nineteen that Varro (probably) personally considered authentic: *Addictus, Artemo, Astraba, Boeotia, Cacistio, Commorientes* (from Diphilus's *Synapothneskontes*), *Condalium, Faeneratrix, Fretum, Frivolaria, Fugitivi, Gemini lenones, Hortulus, Nervolaria, Parasitus medicus, Parasitus piger, Saturio, Sitellitergus,* and *Trigemini.*[1]

---

[1] On the "Varronian" canon, see Ritschl (1845): 126–154; for Ritschl's calculation 40–21 = 19, see Suerbaum (2002): 222 §127 T. Maccius Plautus T 66 and T 70. Varro's impressionistic criteria included *filum atque facetia sermonis* (Gellius, *NA* 3.3.3), *iocorum venustas,* and *iocorum copia* (Macrobius, *Sat.* 2.1.10–11, with Deufert [2002]: 104 n. 278). The remaining fragments come from some ninety plays later fathered on Plautus (Gellius, *NA* 3.3.11; in general, Deufert 2002).—Except for *Stichus* and *Pseudolus,* all dates given on the next page are conjectural; suggestions are those of the introductory notes of de Melo 2011–2013 (but on *Amphitruo* at the Megalesian Games, see Hannah 1993: 71 n. 10). *Faute de mieux,* the traditional axiom is that Plautus increased the proportion of polymetric song in his plays as he matured—not a criterion that inspires much confidence. Otherwise, *Bacchides* mentions *Epidicus, Trinummus* seemingly mentions *Curculio, Menaechmi* quotes from *Mostellaria,* and *Rudens* from *Mercator* or vice versa; all these references are debated.

BETWEEN TWO PARADIGMS: PLAUTUS 517

Title	Date	Greek source text and/or author
1. *Amphitruo*	ca. 190–185, Megalesian Games?	
2. *Asinaria* (The Jackass Affair)	ca. 212 or 211?	*Onag(r?)os* of Demophilus
3. *Aulularia* (The Pot Affair)	ca. 190	Menander or Alexis?
4. *Bacchides* (Bacchises)	189?	*Dis Exapaton* of Menander
5. *Captivi* (The POWs)	189?	
6. *Casina*	after 186?	*Kleroumenoi* of Diphilus
7. *Cistellaria* (The Casket Affair)	209–207?	*Synaristosai* of Menander
8. *Curculio*	ca. 193?	
9. *Epidicus*	ca. 195?	
10. *Menaechmi* (Menaechmuses)	after *Mostellaria*	Posidippus?
11. *Mercator* (The Merchant)	no indication	*Emporos* of Philemon
12. *Miles Gloriosus* (The Braggart Soldier)	206–205?	*Alazon*
13. *Mostellaria* (The Apparition Affair)	190s?	*Phasma*; Philemon?
14. *Persa* (The Persian)	after 191?	
15. *Poenulus* (The Little Carthaginian)	189–7?	*Karchedonios* of Alexis?
16. *Pseudolus*	191, Megalesian Games	Menander? (see §4 below)
17. *Rudens* (The Rope)	after *Stichus*?	Diphilus
18. *Stichus*	200, Plebeian Games	first *Adelphoi* of Menander
19. *Trinummus* (The Three-Dollar Day)	188–7?	*Thesauros* of Philemon
20. *Truculentus* (The Grouch)	186?	
21. *Vidularia* (The Knapsack Affair)	after 201?	*Schedia*; Diphilus?

1. PLAUTUS AS COMIC LIBRETTIST

Conventional as it is, in setting Plautus's plays alongside their "models," this list is gravely misleading. Although the Roman comedians did call their creations *comoediae*, as the Greek comedians had, the Roman species was an entirely different animal. Greek New Comedy was written as a series of five acts predominately in mimetic, spoken iambic trimeters, with musical interludes performed by a chorus between acts. Roman *comoediae*, by contrast, were so thoroughly musical that a more accurate rendering in English than "comedies" would be "comic operas" or "Broadway musicals." (As will be discussed in the next chapter, Terence, a reformer rather than conformist, is excluded from this generalization.) The difference derives from two related structural changes.

First, the Roman comedians eliminated the chorus entirely in favor of continuous performance from start to finish. More importantly, they then transformed more than half of their models' simple spoken iambic verses into longer verses that were chanted or sung to musical accompaniment performed on reed pipes (*tibiae*). This musicalized verse (*cantica*) includes not only the sophisticated lyrical songs in constantly changing meters (*cantica mixtis modis*) that correspond to what we would call arias and duets. It also includes the fairly regularized trochaic *septenarii*. The Roman poets, in other words, first massively increased the proportion of these musical verses relative to that of spoken verse (*deverbia*), and then *integrated* this song into the continuous mimesis, presenting these songs in scenes alternating at unpredictable intervals with the spoken iambic *senarii*. Though it self-avowedly took much of its material for plot and character from a Greek play, then, many a Roman comedy was essentially a musical, not a "drama" as we conceive of it, and in performance the two plays would have created a very different impression.

In other words, Plautus, like his peer comedians, drew on the great New Comedies of Athens and transformed their spoken, mimetic scripts into wildly imaginative libretti for a new form of musical entertainment resembling our comic opera.

This musical dimension must be emphasized from the outset because one still encounters the half-conscious notion that Greek New κωμῳδία and Latin *comoedia* were functional equivalents, just in different languages, and that they therefore bear rational comparison on aesthetic grounds. This notion is of venerable pedigree, but the misguided premise underlying such "fidelity criticism" can be detected because it is directly traceable not to the living theater but to the grammar school, the study, and the symposium—to private contexts, that is, in which the tremendous and fundamental structural changes just mentioned are apt to be overshadowed by the far more salient difference between Greek and Roman comedy—namely, the change of language.[2]

Because Roman comedy is written in Latin instead of Greek, it invites us to inquire about *translation* (including cultural translation) rather than *adaptation*. (It also means that Plautus tends to get studied by Latinists rather than Hellenists, whereas he really should be of equal interest to both.) Moreover, with every passing year our knowledge of Plautine song increases (see Deufert in this volume and now Moore 2012, the flower of this research), but because the music has long since disappeared and because all of Plautus's meters are rather complex, students, novices, and nonspecialists reading alone are least apt to recognize songs or other musicalized verse as such—they are least apt to appreciate, that is, the very feature that in recent years Plautine scholars have

---

[2] Grammar school context: Caesar and Cicero in Courtney (1993): 153 = Suetonius, *Vita Terenti* 6–7; Quintilian, *Inst. Orat.* 10.1.99. The study: Cicero, *Fin.* 1.4 (note *legam*). The symposium: Gellius, *N.A.* 2.23.1–22 (a novelty entertainment). Men wiser or earlier compared Roman comedians only to one another (Sedigitus in Gellius, *N.A.* 15.24 = Courtney (1993) 93–4; Varro, *Menippeans* fr. 399 Astbury = Courtney (1993): 96).

become increasingly interested in. Our growing appreciation of the musical dimension of Roman Comedy promises to shed new light on some familiar questions of Plautine criticism as well as suggest new ones.[3]

This is not to say, however, that the comparison of Plautus's texts to his models is not illuminating on other grounds. It is, for several reasons. In particular, if one wants to understand the two competing paradigms into which the comedian is slotted and how we arrived at them (see §5 below), we must begin by comparing Plautus to his models.

2. *VORSIO*, "ADAPTATION": *DIS EXAPATON* AND *BACCHIDES*

The central text for scholarly study of Plautus's relationship to his source material is a 110-line papyrus fragment from the middle of Menander's *Dis Exapaton* (Δὶς Ἐξαπατῶν, "*The Double Deceiver*"), edited definitively in 1997 by Eric Handley (*POxy.* 64, 4407). It parallels lines 494–561 of Plautus's *Bacchides* (*Bacchises*), a comedy of courtesans, mistaken identity, and deceptions engineered by a crafty slave named Chrysalus. First identified only in 1968 (and thus qualifying the claims of all scholarship written before that date), it has naturally attracted attention from many quarters (see Further Reading). Most impressively, perhaps, the fragment validated many arguments and the methodology that on intuitive and stylistic grounds Eduard Fraenkel had first developed forty-six years before in his *Plautinisches im Plautus* (Fraenkel 1922 = Fraenkel 2007).[4] Along with Fraenkel's book as heuristic guide, then, the papyrus has now become the starting point for assessing Plautine methods of adaptation. Before we examine some longer extracts, its principal lessons can be briefly summarized here.

The papyrus proves that Plautus changed or retained character names at will. Menander's Sostratus, Moschus, Syrus, and Lydus—all conventional names—become, respectively, Mnesilochus, Pistoclerus, Chrysalus, and Lydus. Plautus adds puns on these names (Lydus/*ludus*, 129; Chrysalus/*crux*, 362, 687, 1183; cf. Archidemides/*dempturum*, 285)—and he does so not only in Latin, but even in Greek (Chrysalus/χρυσῷ, 704, an example of code switching). Because Menander's slave was named Syrus, an irreverent allusion that Chrysalus makes to typical comic slaves named Syrus in 649 had always seemed a Plautine addition to his model. The papyrus raises the possibility, however,

---

[3] *Epidicus* and *Persa*, for example, both begin with expository *cantica*. Since the words must be heard over and understood *despite* the music, anyone momentarily distracted by it might not immediately apprehend the plot or miss critical information. A study of when plot points are revealed in song is therefore a desideratum.

[4] Fraenkel's principal observations (and updates to them) are succinctly summarized by de Melo (2011–2013) Vol. 1, xxiv–xxix, and are briefly discussed by Petrides in this volume.

that the comment (or an analogous one) appeared already as such in Menander's play (compare Demosthenes 45 86). Even if it did, however, the papyrus also tells us that for any cognoscenti in Plautus's audience familiar with Menander's play, the allusion reads as an ironic joke about Plautus's source text. Unsurprisingly, too, the fragment demonstrates that Plautus changed the meters of his source text and musicalized them extensively.

Yet the papyrus reveals other surprises, some unexpected and startling. Among these is comparative length. As we will see, the first ten lines of each text correspond closely, but thereafter Plautus makes more radical changes. He deletes two scenes of dialogue (*Dis Exapaton* 31–63/64–90, cf. *Bacchides* 521–525), thus altering the sequence of entrances and eliminating an act break, and he cuts another monologue entirely (91–102, cf. *Bacchides* 530–531). Yet Plautus also extends favored scenes and completely alters their tone. Let us have a look at some of these changes.

3. SAMPLE TEXTS

1. *Dis Exapaton* 18–30, *Bacchides* 500–525. A revealing example of Plautine expansion and alteration of source material is his treatment of the soliloquy spoken by Menander's lovelorn young man, Sostratus (= Plautus's Mnesilochus).

As his friend's father departs, Sostratus here reflects on the dire straits in which he believes another young man, Moschus, now finds himself. Moschus has met a courtesan, possibly named Chrysis, and that is bad news. Yet in the course of his soliloquy Sostratus is soon overtaken by a flurry of emotions. He imagines himself speaking now to "Chrysis," now her to him, then snapping out of it, and back again (18–30, iambic trimeters)[5]:

> ἤδη 'στὶν οὗτος φροῦδ[ο]ς· ἐν πληγῆι μιᾶ[ι]
> τούτου καθέξει. Σώστρα[τ]ον προήρπασας.
> 20   ἀρνήσεται μέν, οὐκ [ἄ]δηλόν ἐστί μοι—
> ἰταμὴ γάρ—εἰς μέσον τε π[ά]ντες οἱ θεοὶ
> ἥξουσι. "μὴ τοίνυν ὀνα[ί]μην"· νὴ Δία·
> "κακὴ κακῶς τοίνυν"—ἐ[πάν]αγ[ε, Σ]ώστρατε·
> ἴσως σε πείσει. "δοῦλο[ς ἥκ]ε[ις ἄ]ρα πατρός".
> 25   ἐγὼ μάλισθ', ἡ δ' ὡ[ς κενὸν συ]μπεισάτω,
> ἔχοντα μηδ[έν· πᾶν ἀποδώσω τ]ῷ πατρὶ
> τὸ χρυσίον· π[ι]θαν[ευομέν]η γὰρ παύσεται
> ὅταν] ποτ' αἴσθητα[ι, τὸ τῆς πα]ροιμίας,
> νεκρῷ] λέγουσα [μῦθον. ἀλλ'] ἤδη [με] δεῖ
> 30   χωρεῖν ἐπ'] ἐκεῖνον[.

---

[5] I cite Handley's 1997 text for *Dis Exapaton* and Questa 2008 for *Bacchides* but follow Gratwick 1995 for *Bacchides* 500–511, adopting his *rego* (for *gero*) in 509 and adding a dash of my own in 507a. Unless marked otherwise, translations here and elsewhere are my own.

So he now he's gone, gone—in one fell swoop she'll get him!
 (*suddenly, as if to "Chrysis"*) Got your talons in Sostratus first, didn't you?
(*himself again*) Oh, she'll deny it—that's obvious. She's unstoppable—and in will
 come a stack of bibles for her to—
 (*in a flirty female voice, imagining himself as "Chrysis" vowing to behave*)
"Why, in that case may it do me no good at all!"—
(*interjecting himself, with angry malice*)—Oh God, *yes!*—
 (*courtesan-voice again*) "Why, in that case may I die a terrible death!"
(*his own voice again, but to himself*) [Hold on,] Sostratus: Maybe she'll persuade
 you that—
 (*courtesan-voice*) "So, [you're here as] your father's slave, then?"
(*Sostratus-voice, as if to her*) Yes, definitely!
(*Sostratus-voice, himself again*) And let her try persuading me—me,
 empty-handed and penniless! (*resolving triumphantly*) I'll give dad back all the
 gold. She'll stop her "reasoning" the moment she sees, as the saying goes, she's
 telling a tale to a dead man!
 (*calming down*) Oh—I've got to go get him now.

Menander gives us a remarkable monologue filled with examples of the "speech within speech" for which he is famous. The actor playing Sostratus needs virtuoso skills to convey the various turns and breaks of thought and their addressees, possibly even availing himself (as suggested above) of an effeminate voice for the parts of "Chrysis" (cf. Quintilian, *I.O.* 11.3.91).[6]

Here is the corresponding monologue in Plautus, spoken by Sostratus's Plautine counterpart, Mnesilochus (500–522, iambic *senarii*):

500	inimiciorem nunc utrum credam magis
	sodalemne esse an Bacchidem—incertum admodumst.
	illum exoptavit potius?—habeat, optumest.
	ne illa illud hercle cum malo fecit—meo;
	nam mi divini numquam quisquam creduat,
505	ni ego illam exemplis plurumis planeque—amo.
	ego faxo hau dicet nactam—quem derideat.
	nam iam domum ibo atque—aliquid surrupiam patri.
507a	id—isti dabo. ego istanc multis ulciscar modis.
	adeo ego illam cogam—usque ut mendicet—meus pater.
	sed satine ego animum mente sincera rego,
510	qui ad hunc modum haec hic quae futura fabulor?
	amo hercle opino, ut pote quod pro certo sciam.
	verum quam illa unquam de mea pecunia
	ramenta fiat plumea propensior,
	mendicum malim mendicando vincere.
515	numquam edepol viva me inridebit. nam mihi
	decretumst renumerare iam omne aurum patri.

---

[6] On "speech in speech" in Menander, see Nünlist 2002 and Handley 2002: 178–185, esp. 183–185 (but note that his paper cited as "Handley forthcoming" there never appeared), as well as Csapo and Scafuro in this volume.

igitur mi inani atque inopi subblandibitur
tum quom mihi <illud> nihilo pluris referet
quam si ad sepulcrum mortuo narret logos.
520   profecto stabilest me patri aurum reddere.
eadem exorabo, Chrysalo causa mea
pater ne noceat...

500   (*rationally, reflectively*) Who should I now think is my greater enemy—my good friend, or Bacchis? It's really not certain. She chose him instead? Fine, let her have him! (*flaring up in anger*) But good lord!, she's certainly made sure there'll be hell to pay—
         (*suddenly meek*)...by me.
(*angrily*) Yes, let no one believe my solemn word if I don't manifestly prove that I absolutely—
         (*meekly*)...love her.
(*angrily*) I'll make sure she won't go around saying she found in me—
         (*meekly*)...some laughingstock.
(*angrily*) Yes, I'll go home right now and—
         (*meekly*)...steal something from dad! I'll give it to—
(*angrily*) *that* bastard [*sc. Pistoclerus*]. I'll get my revenge on *her* in all sorts of ways! I'll force her!—to put beggar's rags on!—
         (*meekly*)...my father.
   (*snapping out of it, rationally once more*) But do I really have control over my heart, using sound judgment, when I've been saying like this what's going to happen here today? Good lord! I think I'm in love, as far as I do know anything for certain.
   (*Resolutely*) But sooner than let any money of mine make her a feather's weight heavier, I'd rather outbeggar a beggar. By god, so long as she lives she'll never mock me! My mind's made up—I'll count out all the gold back out to my father right now. Then she can ply her flattery on me when I'm empty-handed and penniless, when it won't make any more difference than if she were to tell a dead man tales at his tomb. Yes, it's final: I'll give dad back the gold. At the same time I'll persuade him to let Chrysalus off for my sake...

"Translation," we see, was clearly not the aim of Plautus's art—let that be said once and for all. The few lexical equivalents in these two passages cluster heavily in *Dis Exapaton* 25–29 and *Bacchides* 515–519 ([κενὸν], [συ]μπεισάτω, 25 ~ *inani, subblandibitur*, 517; [πᾶν ἀποδώσω τ]ῷ πατρὶ τὸ χρῡσίον, 26–27 ~ *decretumst renumerare iam omne aurum patri*, 516; [νεκρῶι] λέγουσα [μῦθον], 29 ~ *mortuo narret logos*, 519), and, though plausible, are mainly conjectural (restored, of course, from Plautus's play).

Beyond lexicon, comparison of content offers numerous lessons as well. Like Menander's, Plautus's young man here makes the critical decision to return the gold to his father. Meter, too, remains the same, but far more striking than these two similarities are the great many *differences* between the two passages; length and minor details (verbal tense and mood, enjambment, and reordering of one line, *Dis Exapaton* 26/7, to follow 25/6 in Plautus's 516 and 517) are only the most obvious ones.

More salient departures combine to alter psychology and characterization. The soliloquies begin with different ideas and end with different intentions, and Plautus's continues on for several more lines. More significantly, Plautus's monologue, like Menander's, is marked by distracted and broken speech, but of a strikingly different kind. Menander's young man imagines himself speaking to "Chrysis," and his mental distraction is implicit and ironic. Plautus's young man is also of two minds, but explicitly and extensively so; he is at war with *himself*. As A. S. Gratwick (1995: 103) explains, the soliloquy portrays his conflicting emotions on an *odi et amo* pattern—now angry at Bacchis (Plautus's "Chrysis"), now in love with her, and back again.[7] Mnesilochus's vacillations even conclude with a characteristically self-conscious or "metatheatrical" touch in 509–510—an ironic aside within the soliloquy, as it were (*ad hunc modum fabulor*). Parallels for such asides-within-monologue can be found in Menander (*Samia* 269), but in Plautus the aside here seems ironic, self-reflexive, and farcical (cf. *Rudens* 526). And though Mnesilochus's speech is marked by *para prosdokian* turns, the surprise endings are only "jokes" to the extent we enjoy laughing *at* the vacillating young man rather than pitying him.

Plautus's monologue is therefore only thematically reminiscent of Menander's. He has retained the general idea of a vacillating young lover as a starting point, but his treatment is entirely different. This is the hallmark of *adaptation* from one medium to another, much as (for example) Giorgio Venturini's 1962 film adaptation of *Aeneid* 6–12, *La leggenda di Enea*, borrows the athletic games that Virgil had set in Sicily and moves them to the court of Latinus, with necessary adjustments made accordingly.[8]

In fact, the many differences between the two plays might lead one to doubt that they are really related—and yet other passages on the papyrus show, as we will now see, that they definitely are.

2. *Dis Exapaton* 11–17 ~ *Bacchides* 494–499. In the lines immediately preceding the soliloquy, Moschus's father begs Sostratus to help him save his reckless son (iambic trimeters; the speakers are respectively the father, Lydos, and Sostratus (*Dis Exapaton* 11–17):

> σ]ὺ δ' ἐκεῖνον ἐκκάλε[ι
>]ν, νουθέτει δ' ἐναν[τίον
> αὐτόν τε σῶσον οἰκίαν θ' ὅλην φίλων.
> Λυδέ, προάγωμεν. (ΛΥ.) εἰ δὲ κἀμὲ καταλίποις—
> 15 Α. προάγωμεν· ἱκανὸς ο[ὗ]τος. ΛΥ. αὐτῶι, Σώστρα[τε,
> χρῆσαι πικρῶς, ἔλαυν' ἐκεῖνον τὸ[ν] ἀκρα[τῆ·
> ἄπαντας αἰσχύνει γὰρ ἡμᾶς τοὺ[ς] φίλους.—

> <*Father to Sostratus?*>] You should call him out
>] and rebuke him face to face,
> And save him, and his whole household of loved ones.
> Lydos, let's go. LY. But if you left me, too...
> 15 *Father* Let's go. He's enough. LY. Sostratus,
> Treat him harshly, assail that libertine:
> He's disgracing all of us, who're his friends.—

---

[7] The monologue's closest extant parallel is Catullus 8, a poem that, like Catullus 13 (a parasite's monologue), is probably a "fragment" of a Greek comedy (probably Menander). In *Bacchides*, however, it is as if Plautus had chopped off the poem's last six verses and shuffled them back through the earlier lines of the poem.

[8] On such adjustments and other features of adaptations, see Hutcheon 2006.

The corresponding passage is *Bacchides* 494–499, a scene featuring Philoxenus (= the father), Mnesilochus (= Sostratus), and Lydus (trochaic septenarii):

> PH. Mnesiloche, hoc tecum oro ut illius animum atque ingenium regas;
> 495   serva tibi sodalem | et mi filium. MN. factum volo.
> PH. in te ego hoc onus omne impono. Lyde, sequere hac me. LY. sequor.
> melius multo, me quoque una si cum | hoc reliqueris.
> PH. adfatim est. LY. Mnesiloche, cura, ei, concastiga hominem probe,
> qui dedecorat te, me amicosque alios flagitiis suis.—

> PH. Mnesilochus, I beg you, try to get control of his heart and mind.
> 495   Save a friend for yourself, and a son for me. MN. I want that to happen.
> PH. I'm putting the whole onus on you. Lydus, follow me. LY. Very well.
> It'll be much better if you leave me together with him, too.
> PH. He's enough. LY. Mnesilochus, go, take charge, castigate him well:
> He's disgracing you, me, and his other friends with his scandalous behaviors.—

This time, correspondences both verbal and thematic are easily picked out, but along with differences of tone and rhetoric, what stands out now is Plautus's change of meter. He has recast Menander's spoken iambics as musically accompanied trochaics—a kind of song.

3. *Dis Exapaton* 102–113 ~ *Bacchides* 534–561 The same change of meter and similar correspondences are found later in Plautus's adaptation in *Bacchides* 534–561 of a dialogue between Sostratus and Moschus (*Dis Exapaton* 102–113). In this scene, the central confusion of identity over the two girls—and just who exactly it is that's been involved with whom—is resolved. At this point Moschus enters from the house in which he has found Sostratus's girl and begun an affair with her sister:

> MO.   εἶτ' ἀκούσας ἐνθάδε
> εἶναί με, ποῦ γῆς ἐστι; χαῖρε, Σώστρατε.
> ΣΩ. καὶ σύ. <ΜΟ.> τί κατηφὴς καὶ σκυθρωπός, εἰπέ μοι,
> 105   καὶ βλέμμα τοῦθ' ὑπόδακρυ; μὴ νεώτερον
> κακὸν κατείληφάς τι τῶν [γ'] ἐνταῦθα; (ΣΩ.) ναί.
> (ΜΟ.) εἶτ' οὐ [λ]έγεις; (ΣΩ.) ἔνδον γὰρ ἀμέλει, Μόσχε. (ΜΟ.) πῶς;
> (ΣΩ.) τόν μ' ἐ[κτόπως] φιλοῦντα τὸν πρὸ τοῦ χρόνου
>   [-]τα· τοῦτο πρῶτον ὧν ἐρῶ·
> 110   δεινότατά μ' ἠδίκηκας. (ΜΟ.) ἠδίκηκα δὲ
> ἐγώ σε; μὴ γένοιτο τοῦτο, Σώστρατε.
> (ΣΩ.) οὐκ ἠξίουν γοῦν οὐδ' ἐγώ. (ΜΟ.) λέγεις δὲ τί;
> (ΣΩ.) ἐμὲ γάρ, τὸν ἔρωτα· τἄλλα δ' ἠνία μ' ἄγ[αν.

> MO. (*entering*) Humph! He heard I'm here—
> so where on earth is he? (*spotting him*) Hi, Sostratus.
> SO. (*scowling*) Hello. <MO.> Why are you so glum, so upset? Tell me;
> 105   You look like you're about to cry. You didn't get into some
> new local trouble, did you? (SO.) Yes, I did.
> (MO.) Will you tell me, then? (SO.) It's indoors, actually, Moschus.
> (MO.) (*puzzled*) How?

(SO.) The one who's always been my [very best] friend
[is deceiving me (?)]. I'll say this first:
110 You've wronged me terribly. (MO.) (*incredulous*) Huh? I—*I've*
hurt you? Say it isn't so, Sostratus.
(SO.) I'd hardly have expected it myself. (MO.) What are you saying?
(SO.) I mean it—me and my love. And the rest of it was unbearable, too.

Plautus's adaptation is as follows (*Bacchides* 534–539, 559–561):

PI. estne hic meus sodalis? MN. estne hic hostis quem aspicio meus?
535 PI. certe is est. MN. is est. PI. adibo contra. MN. [et] contollam gradum.
PI. salvus sis, Mnesiloche. MN. salve. PI. salvus quom peregre advenis,
cena detur. MN. non placet mi cena quae bilem movet.
PI. numquae advenienti aegritudo obiecta est? MN. atque acerruma.
539 PI. unde? MN. ab homine quem mi amicum esse arbitratus sum antidhac. [...]
559 video non potesse quin tibi eius nomen eloquar.
560 Pistoclere, perdidisti me sodalem funditus.
PI. quid istuc est?

PI. (*spotting Mnesilochus*) Is that my friend? MN. (*spotting him in turn*) Is that
my enemy I see?
535 PI. (*aside*) It's definitely him. MN. (*aside*) It *is* him. PI. (*aside*) I'll go talk to him.
MN. (*aside*) I'll go confront him.
PI. Hello, Mnesilochus. MN. Hi. PI. Since you're back safe and sound from your
travels,
a dinner's in order! MN. I don't like dinners that churn my bile.
PI. (*puzzled*) Did something bother you on your way back here? MN. Yes, and it
cut to the core.
539 PI. Where'd it come from? MN. From a man I'd always thought was my friend.
[...]
559 I can see I can't help telling you his name. (*pauses*)
560 Pistoclerus, you've destroyed me, your friend—completely destroyed.
PI. What's that you're saying?

Tenor and treatment are again notably different, beginning already with the very different entrances of the characters (532–533 are Plautus's own invention) and the insertion of the *cena adventicia*, "welcome-home dinner," a Roman custom. What we do not see in the extract above, however, is that Plautus has inserted a massive expansion of Menander's eleven-line dialogue between 539 and 559. Plautus's lines 540–558 have no correspondence at all in the Greek play. In them, the two young men moralize extensively on untrue friends in general terms, terms that we in the audience, with suspenseful and superb irony, understand to apply to Pistoclerus.

To complicate matters, however, there is some doubt whether all of the lines in the expansion are authentically Plautine. Because verses 540–551 are not transmitted in the Ambrosianus manuscript, we face a startling anomaly: although in sentiment the moralizing lines seem consummately Menandrian, the papyrus shows they cannot be from *Dis Exapaton*—thereby humbling such pre-papyrus intuitions as that once offered by

Friedrich Leo in 1912 (131): "Although it is missing in the Ambrosianus, the description of false friends in *Bacchides* 540–551 certainly comes from Menander."[9]

As commonly understood, the papyrus shows Leo was wrong; and yet in a different sense, his intuition might be correct. It is quite possible that Plautus (or an interpolator) took them from a different Menandrian source entirely. This brings us to the topic of "*contaminatio.*"

4. *Contaminatio* and the Original of *Pseudolus*

Plautus's wholesale deletion of two scenes in *Dis Exapaton* (as the papyrus confirms) validates what Terence had claimed was his practice on other occasions (*Adelphoe* 6–11, deletion of a scene from *Synapothneskontes*) and thus lends weight to Terence's analogous claim about what scholars call "*contaminatio.*" According to Terence (*Eunuchus* 25–34), Plautus was known to have spliced whole scenes from other plays into the adaptation of his main source model, making such adjustments as were necessary for continuity. (As some detractors saw it, this practice "contaminated" or spoiled the plays.) The hopes of validating Terence's claim through analytic scrutiny of Plautus's comedies once elicited a great deal of imaginative effort from scholars. None has carried universal conviction, but among scores of proposals that this or that scene has been "contaminated" into the main play, several likelier suggestions should be mentioned here. A. S. Gratwick has plausibly suggested that a passage of Menander's *Sikyonioi* (343–360) lies behind vv. 1099–1110 of Plautus's *Poenulus*, itself almost certainly adapted from Alexis's *Karchedonios*. A papyrus fragment (P.Köln 203 = Menander fr. 8 Arnott (*incert*) = *adespota* K-A fr. 1147) has also been plausibly claimed as a source for the opening scene, but no more, of *Curculio*. There are many thematic resemblances, but no verbal echoes to confirm the connection. Still, if the model was not this particular passage, then something very like it was (and, incidentally, as a papyrus of the third century BC it reveals the kind of text of Greek comedy Plautus himself probably read and worked from—a sobering reminder of the haphazard state of speaker division as he would have known it).

Along similar lines, several scholars have thought the opening scene of Plautus's *Miles Gloriosus* (1–78) is an unrecognized, "contaminated" fragment of Menander's *Kolax*—perhaps even a Plautine version of the same scene that Terence adapted as *Eunuchus* 391–453. The passages share interesting links among their parasites, who employ identical fawning tactics, and their soldiers in coincidences of

[9] "Gewiß stammt die Schilderung der falschen Freunde Bacch. 540–551, obwohl sie im Ambrosianus fehlt, von Menander her." Arguing for authenticity (with some reallocation of parts), Weisweiler and Riedweg (2004) offer a full review of the question.

detail—Cappadocia (*Kolax* fr. 2.2 ~ *Miles Gloriosus* 52), Alexander comparisons (*Kolax* fr. 2 ~ *Miles Gloriosus* 777), great professional responsibilities (*Miles Gloriosus* 75–76, 947–952 ~ *Eunuchus* 397–398, 402–405), and Indian elephants (*Eunuchus* 413 ~ *Miles Gloriosus* 25–30, 235).[10]

The realization that single scenes may be grafted onto other plays hinders the hunt for source texts, but only if one is concerned to identify a specific model by name. By contrast, the practices of expansion, elimination, and reorientation—in short, of *adaptation* rather than translation—as seen above suggest that we also possess on papyrus the source of another Plautine scene. Although we cannot *name* the play it comes from, the accretion of comic papyri over the last century and the massively improved understanding of them we now enjoy suggest that a relationship that in 1955 seemed "unmistakable" to Fraenkel on intuitive grounds should now (it is here argued) be seen as the certain source for the famous beginning of Plautus's *Pseudolus*. So too, moreover, should Menander's authorship of the fragment, the circumstantial evidence for which is as strong as it is for the *Dis Exapaton* papyrus itself.[11]

P.Freiburg 12 preserves the beginning of a comedy evidently so famous that Lucian could later quote it without attribution in his satirical pastiche *Zeus Rants*. In it, a loyal slave approaches and addresses his despondent master (Menander fr. 4 *incert.* Arnott = *adespota* K-A fr. 1027; tr. Arnott):

> ὦ Ζεῦ, τί σύννους κατὰ μόνας σαυτῷ λαλεῖς,
> δοκεῖς τε παρέχειν ἔμφασιν λυπουμένου;
> ἐμοὶ προσανάθου· λαβέ με σύμβουλον πόνων·

---

[10] *Sikyonioi*/*Poenulus*: Gratwick 1982: 98–103; PKöln 203/*Curculio*: Laplace 1997 (*contra*, Danese 2002)—pictures of the papyrus in Nünlist 1993; *Kolax*/*Miles Gloriosus*/*Eunuchus*: Fontaine 2010a, augmenting Becker 1837: 82–83.—Apart from the *Dis Exapaton* papyrus, the only other definite opportunities to compare Plautus with a model of more than a few words are *Cistellaria* 89–93 ~ Menander *Synaristosai* fr. 1 Arnott (= K-A fr. 337) and *Poenulus* 522–555 ~ Alexis *incert.* K-A 265 (probably *Karchedonios*). Both are short book fragments that, unhelpfully, are recognized as Plautus's models only by their obvious similarity to Plautus's text. His treatment there cannot therefore be taken as exemplary of his practice elsewhere. This is also true of all the fragmentary comedians, except for Terence (thanks to Donatus) and once for Caecilius Statius (*Plocium*, from Menander's *Plokion*, thanks to Gellius 2.23). Obvious similarity alone identifies Turpilius fr. 21–22 Ribbeck³ (*Demetrius*) with Alexis *Demetrios* fr. 47.1–3 and fr. 50–53 Ribbeck³ with Menander K-A fr. 129. The student new to Roman comedy should, however, study all these cases closely.

[11] Fraenkel 1955 (a paper oddly neglected by Plautine scholarship), Arnott 1999: 78–79 (add to his arguments that *Dis Exapaton* began with a similar oath). A further fragment of the play may lie behind the opening words of Alciphron *Epist.* 4.9 [1.36], Ἐβουλόμην μὲν ὑπὸ δακρύων οἰκίαν ἑταίρας τρέφεσθαι, "I wish that a courtesan's house were maintained on tears," which closely parallel *Pseudolus* 274 *misereat, si familiam alere possim misericordia*. Meanwhile, the rhetoric of *Pseudolus* 790–793 closely parallels Anaxandrides *incert.* K-A fr. 53.1–3 and so illustrates the kind of language Menander's play probably used at the corresponding part, while Syrus in Terence's (Menandrian) *Heauton Timorumenos* resembles Pseudolus in both his florid wordplay (-*ver*-, 372 and 356; *dom(i)na* ~ *damno*, 628) and brazen equivocation (*Heauton Timorumenos* 709–712 ~ *Pseudolus* 453–489 with Fontaine 2010b: 128–136).

μὴ καταφρονήσῃς οἰκέτου συμβουλίας.
5   πολλάκις ὁ δοῦλος τοὺς τρόπους χρηστοὺς ἔχων
τῶν δεσποτῶν ἐγένετο σωφρονέστερος.
εἰ δ' ἡ τύχη τὸ σῶμα κατεδουλώσατο,
ὅ γε νοῦς ὑπάρχει τοῖς τρόποις ἐλεύθερος.

God! Why gripe to yourself, alone and ill
At ease? The impression that you give, it seems,
Is one of anguish. Talk to *me*, and take
Me as your trouble-shooter! Don't despise
A servant's counsel. With integrity
5   Slaves can prove wiser than their masters.
If destiny's enslaved their bodies, still
The mind that serves their characters is free.

Compare *Pseudolus* 9–12 and 16–17, in which Pseudolus approaches his master, Calidorus (9–12, 16–17):

quid est quod tu exanimatus iam hos multos dies
10   gestas tabellas tecum, eas lacrumis lavis,
neque tui participem consili quemquam facis?
12   eloquere, ut quod ego nescio id tecum sciam. . . .
16   licet me id scire quid sit? nam tu me antidhac
supremum habuisti comitem consiliis tuis.

Why is it you've been carrying a tablet around
all these days, listless and washing it with your tears,
and you haven't made anyone partner to your plans?
Out with it, so that what I don't know, I will, like you . . . .
May I know what it's about? I mean, in the past you've
regarded me as your closest confidant.

The scenario and gambit are identical (1–2 ~ *Pseudolus* 9–11, 2–4 ~ *Pseudolus* 12 + 16–17), and there is a verbal reflex (σύμβουλον ~ *comitem consiliis*). As we might expect, however, Plautus omits Menander's philosophical sentiment in 5–8, but he compensates by adding a frivolous prelude to stimulate interest (*Psedolus* 1–8, not quoted here). Plautus probably also adds the bit of farce in which the young master interprets Pseudolus's oath literally (13–15):

CAL. Misere miser sum, Pseudole. PS. Id te Iuppiter
prohibessit. CAL. Nihil hoc Iovis ad iudicium attinet:
15   sub Veneris regno vapulo, non sub Iovis.

CAL. Oh, I'm miserable, Pseudolus, miserably so. PS. Jupiter
forbid! CAL. This case isn't with Jupiter's jurisdiction:
15   It was Venus who sentenced me to suffer, not Jupiter.

Although the fragment ends before we can confirm the suggestion, it seems likely that Calidorus's facetious twist of Pseudolus's oath *Iuppiter!* is inspired by the ὦ Ζεῦ oath that began Menander's play and that was apparently a characterizing tic or leitmotif (reflexes appear at *Pseudolus* 443, 574, and 934, and Questa (1970: 202) has suggested that analogous "contamination at a distance" may explain a reworking of *Dis Exapaton* 104–105 in *Bacchides* 668–669). And while Menander's slave might have played on σύμβουλος, "trouble-shooter" (3, cf. 4), and σύμβολον, "contract," to promote the importance of his role in the play (*symbolum*, a catchword, appears early at *Pseudolus* 55 and 57)—and this is no more than a guess—it is very unlikely that Menander's play continued on with the extraordinary string of corny jokes that dominate the scene in Plautus's play.

Writ small, the expansion of the crafty slave's role as envisioned here is exactly what Fraenkel had predicted in general (2007: 159–172) and that comparisons of the *Dis Exapaton* papyrus with *Bacchides* have subsequently proven. Although the recurrence of commonplace themes in New Comedy make such propositions impossible to verify, the comparative study of Greek fragments and Plautine comedy does help us better see the sort of material the Roman comedian was working from and how he adapted his source texts. The Greek material also helps us understand something of his originality and achievement, and especially about the nature of his dramatic illusion, of which sharply divergent and competing views can be found in recent scholarship. This brings us to what might be called the "war of the paradigms."

5. The War of the Paradigms

Roman Comedy scholarship of the last forty-five years tends to presuppose one of two competing paradigms. Because each paradigm seems right by its own logic, the two come to startlingly different and mutually incompatible conclusions about the nature of Plautus's comedy and the dramatic illusion his characters populate. I call the two paradigms "Saturnalian" and "Hellenistic" respectively, and I trace the split between them to 1968.

While in 1967 Eric Handley was busy deciphering and preparing publication of Menander's *Dis Exapaton* papyrus in England, a continent away, and entirely unaware of Handley's efforts, the American scholar Erich Segal was pioneering a very different approach to Plautine comedy. Published the same year as Handley's work, Segal's 1968 monograph, *Roman Laughter*, offered readers an entirely different take on Plautus, a take derived largely from the close study of Plautus's texts without reference to the Greek material. Over time, the gradual acceptance of Segal's claims in greater or lesser forms has given rise to the Saturnalian paradigm.

Named for Rome's winter festival as the spirit in which Plautine comedy was performed, the Saturnalian paradigm emphasizes "freedom" in a number of respects. It emphasizes Plautus's independence from or subversion of his model, it emphasizes the temporary freedom from Roman social mores that his audience enjoys while watching the plays, and within the dramatic illusion of the plays it emphasizes a "topsy-turvy" world free from mimetic reality itself. Accordingly, this view also emphasizes Plautus's "Romanism," and often looks to native Italian traditions of Atellan farce for the chief inspiration for these innovations (on this last development, see Petrides in this volume).

Against this view stands the Hellenistic paradigm. Beginning from the Greek material, it emphasizes Plautus's continuity with the Greek tradition. It acknowledges that Plautus necessarily wrote in a different language, but rather sees Roman comedy as primarily on a continuum with New Comedy rather than subversive of or indifferent to it. It does not deny that many "topsy-turvy" elements exist but sees them as minor rather than major elements, and is chary of attributing their origin to ideology. It prefers to attribute many of these elements to Plautus's writing in a different, adapted genre—the musical versus a play with four intermezzi. The paradigm therefore stresses continuity with the Greek tradition, though in updated form, much as with the Artists of Dionysus traversing the Hellenistic world in Plautus's time. A few scholars presupposing this paradigm also believe that later interpolations can best explain many farcical or inconsistent elements in Plautus.

These two paradigms do not rest merely on scholars' private presuppositions. They arise from and are reinforced by genuine ambiguities in Plautus's text, ambiguities whose resolution in one fashion rather than the other leads the reader to resolve similar ambiguities elsewhere in the text in similar fashion. Four brief examples, each showcasing the respective chain reactions of self-consistent assumptions and interpretations, will help illustrate the dilemma.

6. Some Examples

1.In the prologue of *Trinummus*, the neologism *trinummus* is offered, with some apology, as a translation or replacement of Philemon's title Θησαυρός "Treasure" (18–21):

> huic Graece nomen est Thensauro fabulae:
> Philemo scripsit, Plautus vortit barbare,
> 20   nomen Trinummo fecit, nunc hoc vos rogat
> ut liceat possidere hanc nomen fabulam.

> In Greek this play's name is Θησαυρός.
> Philemon wrote it, Plautus adapted it into barbarian-speak.
> 20   He's named it *Trinummus*, and now asks you
> that it be allowed to keep this name.

Since we cannot decide from this passage whether Plautus's title is meant as a *translation* or as a *replacement*, scholars usually interpret *Trinummus* to mean "The Three-Coin Day" on the basis of the Impostor's announcement at 843–844 (cf. 847–850):

> Huic ego die nomen Trinummo faciam: nam ego operam meam
> tribus nummis hodie locavi ad artis nugatorias.
>
> I'm going to call this day Three-Coin, because I've rented out
> my services in rascality for three coins.

Since this explanation seems straightforward, it is usually accepted at face value. Our acceptance of it as the meaning of the title, too, implies three corollaries, all of which are easily explained on the Saturnalian paradigm.

First, it suggests that Plautus deliberately debased the scale of Philemon's title from a "treasure" to a paltry sum. He did so, it appears, because *Plautus vortit barbare*—which must mean Plautus "barbarized," or freely altered, Philemon's play. Second, since both passages define *trinummus* identically, the Impostor's own definition so late in the play now seems redundant. Yet because the Roman audience was probably unruly and easily distracted amid the holiday cheer, they would appreciate the reminder—the word is, after all, unfamiliar. Third, since no character would make so redundant an announcement in a realistic drama, the Imposter must be speaking metatheatrically. On this view, the Imposter is speaking self-consciously not as a proper character but as the actor behind his mask or even as Plautus himself, and his announcement heralds not only the day but the play as well. All of the independence from and inversion or subversion of Philemon's play that these interpretations imply suits the celebratory spirit of freedom championed by the Saturnalian paradigm. And parallels for most points can be readily found elsewhere in Plautus's oeuvre.

The Hellenistic paradigm offers a different approach. It notices that the expository form of the etymology in 843–844 resembles that of a pun in *Menaechmi* 263–264:

> propterea huic urbi nomen Epidamno inditumst,
> quia nemo ferme huc sine damno devortitur.
>
> This city got its name of Epidamnus for just this reason—
> because practically everyone that stops here incurs damages.

It therefore suspects a pun here, too, and finds in the Greek comic material a use of the prefix τρι- meaning not literally "three" but simply "very, super," as in Greek τριγέρων, "superold." This usage explains Aristophanes's title Τριφάλης, "superphallus," as well as Naevius's titles *Triphallus*, "superphallus," and *Tribacelus*, "superfaggot." It notes that Plautus adapts this Greek usage for such hybrid words of his own coinage as *trifur* (i.e., τρι-*fur*), "*über*scoundrel" (*Aulularia* 633) and *triparcus* (i.e., τρι-*parcus*), "*über*cheap" (*Persa* 265), and, returning to the Greek material, it finds that Aristophanes punned repeatedly on the number three in his Τριφάλης (K-A fr. 561, 563, 566, and 569, and see Kassel-Austin on K-A fr. 561). It therefore concludes that *Trinummus*, "Megacoin, *Über*-Coin," is an excellent rendering of Θησαυρός, "Treasure," and that in similar fashion, Plautus's Impostor is in fact making a pun on this meaning in his entrance announcement at 843–844:

> (*Triumphantly*) I'm going to call this day *"Über*-Coin," because—(*face suddenly falling*) it's for three coins that I've rented out my services in rascality.

On this Hellenistic view, Plautus's coinage is suddenly revealed as a *para prosdokian* joke that simultaneously deflates both value and our expectations, akin to a sudden reanalysis in English of foreman as four men or forefathers as four fathers. And the corollaries that follow from it are very different from those of the Saturnalian view.

First, it suggests that Plautus did not change the scale of Philemon's title at all but in fact sought to capture it well. The apology in 20–21 for translating it with a coinage, *Trinummus*, instead of the loanword *Thensaurus* was merely to prepare the pun later in the play. Second, it suggests that *Plautus vortit barbare* is simply what a prologue speaking in Greek persona *would* say to mean "Plautus adapted it in that barbarian *language* of his," i.e., Ῥωμαικῶς, Latin. Third, it suggests that the Roman audience was not unruly and distracted but alert and attentive, and—because jokes ideally require 100% efficiency in communication—familiar indeed, somehow, with the Greek usage.[12]

2. Viewpoints similarly diverge in *Persa*, where disagreement over the interpretation of several characters' names has given rise to completely different interpretations of the play. The play is set in Athens and features a parasite whose name is spelled *Saturio*.

On the Hellenistic paradigm, that is simply Plautus's transliteration of *Satyrion* (Σατυρίων—*y* was only used in Latin after Plautus's death). The name is conventional and common in Greek comedy and society. It is therefore etymologically meaningless in Plautus's play, though it may be relevant to note that it is shared by a γελωτοποιός, "jester," in Lucian's *Symposium*, as well as by a third-century Greek comedian. The Hellenistic view objects to finding a Latin-named character in Athens, and so interprets a quip in 103 as a pun on his name (appropriately so, since the character is a parasite).

On the Saturnalian paradigm, by contrast, *Saturio* is better interpreted as a Latin name derived from *satur*, "full," and so means "Mr. Fatso"—whether appropriately or incongruously and therefore humorously so. It, too, interprets the quip in 103 as a pun on his name, but in a different way. And on the Saturnalian view there is no objection to finding a Latin-named character resident in Athens, because Plautus's dramatic illusion is not really a representation of Athens proper, but rather a hybrid Graeco-Roman world—a "Plautinopolis."

---

[12] For the Saturnalian view, see Segal 1987: 216–217; for the metatheatrical, Moore 1998: 12. For the Hellenistic view, see Stein 1966: 66–69 and Fontaine 2010b: 141 n. 84 (independently and with further parallels).

3.Similarly, in *Persa* 624 the parasite's daughter declares she was once known as *Lucris*. On the Hellenistic view she means people called her Λοκρίς, "Locrian (maiden)," and her declaration is merely a bitter, sarcastic quip that suits the immediate context. (Latin *u* often transliterates Greek omicron.) Her father, the parasite, is pretending to sell her to pay a debt. Her quip therefore succinctly captures her indignation—much as if she were to call herself an Iphigenia or an Electra. Two attested comedies titled Λοκρίδες, "Locrian Maidens" (Anaxandrides, Posidippus) probably treated the theme of fathers sacrificing their daughters, and to those inclined to the Hellenistic view it appears that Plautus's audience was somehow familiar with them.

On the Saturnalian view, by contrast, the girl means her name actually is Lucris, a hybrid name in -ίς derived from Latin *lucrum*—a word used repeatedly in the play. As we have just seen, the Latin interpretation of Saturio ("Mr. Fatso") demonstrates that Plautus gave his characters such cartoonish Latin names in Plautinopolis. And it is scarcely credible that a Roman audience was sufficiently familiar with the Λοκρίδες plays or the rituals of the Locrian Maidens to understand so sophisticated a quip without further elaboration.

4.Finally, among Plautus's shorter plays is one titled *Curculio*. Set in Epidaurus, its title refers to the main character, a parasite. On the Saturnalian view, his name is simply the Latin word for "weevil" (*curculio*) treated as a proper name. This fantastic name is eminently suitable for a parasite, not only because he lives off the σῖτος ("food," literally "grain") of another, but also because his counterpart in another play is named "Mr. Fatso" in Latin.

On the Hellenistic view, however, the man is really named Gorgylio (Γοργυλίων, "Furioso"). Like many characters in New Comedy, his name derives from γοργός ("fierce, vigorous, swift"), and it alludes to his violent running entrance midway through the play. As a speaking name it bears comparison with one Coecylion, "Mr. Gaga," so called because he gaped about while counting waves (*adespota* K-A fr. 71 = Aelian *VH* 13.15; Κοικυλίων from κοικύλλειν), and as a title *Gorgylio* resembles Greek comedies titled *Ankylion* (Alexis, Eubulus; cf. Aristophanes, *Wasps* 1397), *Botrylion* (Anaxilas), and *Kampylion* (Araros, Eubulus), all named for their principal characters. The odds against the name *not* being Greek, on this view, are simply incredible.

Analogous assumptions on either paradigm extend beyond beliefs about the composition and character of Plautus's Roman audience to beliefs about Plautus's own biography. A century and a half after his death, Varro wrote that the Italian-born Plautus had begun his career *in operis artificum scaenicorum*, evidently working somewhere outside of Rome. Varro's statement is preserved by Gellius (*N.A.* 3.3.14), who elsewhere tells us (*N.A.* 20.4.2) that *artifices scaenici* is the Latin translation of οἱ περὶ τὸν Διόνυσον τεχνῖται, the itinerant Artists of Dionysus that traversed the Hellenistic world performing Greek New Comedy (see LeGuen in this volume.)

On the Hellenistic paradigm, Varro's explanation is not only reasonable but likely, even if it is untrue. It would explain where Plautus became so familiar with Greek comedy and particularly with the works of its three canonical authors—Menander, Diphilus, and Philemon—that dominate both his and the Artists' repertoires. And on this view,

Varro's words *in operis*, conventionally translated "in the service of," probably mean "in the gang" or "in the ranks of," perhaps as a rendering of ἐν τῇ συνόδῳ or ἐν τῷ κοινῷ, "in the guild." On the Saturnalian paradigm, by contrast, Varro's explanation is so improbable that his statement has been reinterpreted to mean that Plautus began his career in comedy working in Atellan farce. (That of course may ultimately be true, but it is not what Varro says.) Yet Plautus's middle name, Maccius, does seem to pay homage to the clown of Atellan farce, Maccus, and it seems likelier than not that a farceur who generated the festive Saturnalian world must have drawn deeply from its influence.

On such tiny ambiguities of detail, resolved and reinforced according to our personal confirmation biases, rests much of our sense of Plautine comedy, and such are some of the fruits that they produce in the "war of the paradigms." Books and articles are now proliferating on Plautus as a cultural critic. Before many of their conclusions can be accepted wholesale, it is hoped that this chapter will stimulate a reexamination of the premises on which they rely.

FURTHER READING

Secondary literature on Plautus is vast, but as most early work was heavily philological, it has since been silently incorporated into later work. Many technical contributions to text and meter have been consolidated in the new *Editio Plautina Sarsinatis* texts of Plautus emanating from the scholars in Urbino, Italy. Suggestions here highlight recent work of interpretation, where more extensive bibliography can invariably be found.

On music, see Moore (2012) and, for a suggestive context, Flores (2011), who independently argues that Livius Andronicus's *Odyssey* was a musical adaptation rather than translation of Homer. The introductory essays in de Melo (2011–2013) on chronology are basic; Schutter (1952) remains the standard monograph. For the *Dis Exapaton* papyrus, see principally Handley (1997) and (1968), Anderson (1993), Bain (1979), Gaiser (1970), and Questa (1970). Goldberg (1998) has recently caused scholars to reassess the composition of Plautus's audience; Fontaine (2010b) offers one view, critiqued among other trends by Goldberg (2011).

Segal (1987) is the starting point for the Saturnalian paradigm, which he promoted in similar fashion in subsequent papers and translations. For examples of other interpretations the paradigm can produce, see the widely divergent overviews of Plautus in Gratwick (1982; excellent) and Lefèvre in *Der neue Pauly* s.v. Plautus. Lefèvre and his colleagues in Freiburg have argued extensively for the influence of Atellan farce on Plautus in numerous volumes of the *ScriptOralia* series. The best of these are Lefèvre, Stärk, and Vogt-Spira (1991) and Benz, Stärk, and Vogt-Spira (1995). Danese (2002) and Petrides in this volume offer helpful critiques.

I expand on many issues relevant to the Hellenistic paradigm in Fontaine (2010b) and (2014), offering in the latter revisions to the titles of the Varronian canon. Fontaine (2011) is a sample application of the Hellenistic paradigm to *Persa*. Despite their age, with their remarkable knowledge of Plautus's Greek background Leo (1912) and Fraenkel (2007) remain important starting points of Plautine research. J. C. B. Lowe has continued Fraenkel's analytical approach in numerous articles; Lowe (1992) is representative of his work and begins with a helpful contextualization of Fraenkel's method. Envisioning a hyper-Hellenistic Plautus, Zwierlein (1990–1992) argues for massive interpolation of the texts in antiquity. His conclusions are not credible (see Danese 2002, who surveys other recent trends), but Zwierlein's exhaustive analyses often do pinpoint problems that warrant further inquiry. Moreover, since an *index locorum plautinorum* to the Kassel-Austin edition of Greek comic fragments still does not exist, Zwierlein's monographs help direct attention to important parallels between Plautus and the Greek material.

Several recent trends in Plautus criticism not explicitly discussed here merit brief mention. One is "metatheater," a term that refers to Plautus's ironic allusions to the performance itself; Slater (2000) and Moore (1998) are the fundamental studies. Agostiniani and Desideri (2002), Leigh (2004), and Stewart (2012) are recent readings of Plautus in his Roman context. Dutsch (2008) breaks fresh ground by exploring "gendered speech" in Plautus.

BIBLIOGRAPHY

Agostiniani, L., and P. Desideri, eds. 2002. *Plauto testimone della società del suo tempo*. Naples: Edizioni scientifiche italiane.

Anderson, W. S. 1993. *Barbarian Play: Plautus' Roman Comedy*. Toronto: University of Toronto Press.

Arnott, W. G. 1999. "Notes on Some Comic Papyri." *ZPE* 126: 77–80.

——. ed. 1979–2000. *Menander*. 3 vols. Loeb Classical Library 132, 459, 460. Cambridge, MA: Harvard University Press.

Bain, D. 1979. "*Plautus vortit barbare*: Plautus *Bacchides* 526–61 and Menander *Dis exapaton* 102–12." In *Creative Imitation and Latin Literature*, edited by D. West and T. Woodman, 17–34. Cambridge, UK: Cambridge University Press,

Becker, G.A. 1837. *De comicis Romanorum fabulis maxime Plautinis quaestiones*. Leipzig: Fleischer.

Benz, L., E. Stärk, and G. Vogt-Spira, eds. 1995. *Plautus und die Tradition des Stegreifspiels*. Tübingen: Narr.

Courtney, E., ed. 1993. *The Fragmentary Latin Poets*. Oxford: Clarendon Press.

Danese, R. 2002. "Modelli letterari e modelli culturali del teatro plautino." In *Due seminari plautini: La tradizione del testo, i modelli*, edited by C. Questa and R. Raffaelli, 133–153. Urbino: QuattroVenti.

de Melo, W., ed. 2011–2013. *Plautus*. 5 vols. Loeb Classical Library 60–61, 163, 260, 328. Cambridge, MA: Harvard University Press.

Deufert, M. 2002. *Textgeschichte und Rezeption der plautinischen Komödien im Altertum*. Berlin: de Gruyter.

Dutsch, D. 2008. *Feminine Discourse in Roman Comedy: On Echoes and Voices*. Oxford: Oxford University Press.

Flores, E., ed. 2011. *Livi Andronici Odusia*. Naples: Liguori.

Fontaine, M. 2010a. "*Colax Menandrist…*": Review of *Menanders Kolax*, by M. J. Pernerstorfer. *CR* 60: 379–380.

——. 2010b. *Funny Words in Plautine Comedy*. New York and Oxford: Oxford University Press.

——. 2011. "Tale padre, tale figlia? Alcune ambiguità nel *Persa*." In *Lecturae Plautinae Sarsinates XIV: Persa (Sarsina, 18 settembre 2010)*, edited by R. Raffaelli and A. Tontini, 13–35. Urbino: QuattroVenti.

——. 2014. "The Reception of Greek Comedy in Rome." In *The Cambridge Companion to Greek Comedy*, edited by M. Revermann. Cambridge, UK: Cambridge University Press.

Fraenkel, E. 1922. *Plautinisches im Plautus*. Berlin: Weidmann.

——. 1955. "Ein Motiv aus Euripides in einer Szene der neuen Komödie." In *Studi in onore di Ugo Enrico Paoli*, edited by L. Banti, 293–304. Florence: F. Le Monnier. Reprinted in *Kleine Beiträge zur klassischen Philologie*, vol. 1 (Rome 1964), 487–493.

——. 1960. *Elementi plautini in Plauto*. Translated by F. Munari. Florence: La Nuova Italia. (Italian translation of Fraenkel 1922, with extensive addenda.)

——. 2007. *Plautine Elements in Plautus*. Translated by T. Drevikovsky and F. Muecke. Oxford and New York: Oxford University Press. (English translation of Fraenkel 1922, with addenda in Fraenkel 1960.)

Gaiser K. 1970. "Die plautinische *Bacchides* und Menanders *Dis exapaton*." *Philologus* 114: 51–87.

Goldberg, S. M. 1998. "Plautus on the Palatine." *JRS* 88: 1–20.

——. 2011. "Roman Comedy Gets Back to Basics." *JRS* 101: 206–221.

Gratwick, A. S. 1982. "Drama." In *The Cambridge History of Classical Literature*. Vol. 1, *Latin Literature*, edited by E. J. Kenney and W. Clausen, 77–137. Cambridge, UK: Cambridge University Press.

Handley, E. 1968. *Menander and Plautus: A Study in Comparison*. London: Lewis.

——. 1997. "Menander: Dis exapaton," *The Oxyrhynchus Papyri* 64: 14–42.

——. 2002. "Acting, Action and Words in New Comedy." In *Greek and Roman Actors: Aspects of an Ancient Profession*, edited by P. Easterling and E. Hall, 165–188. Cambridge, UK: Cambridge University Press.

Hannah, R. 1993. "Alcumena's Long Night: Plautus, *Amphitruo* 273–276." *Latomus* 52: 65–74.

Hutcheon, L. 2006. *A Theory of Adaptation*. New York and Oxford: Routledge.

Laplace, M. M. J. 1997. "P. Köln V 203: Un modèle de l'Acte I du *Curculio* de Plaute. Amour aveugle, amour stupéfié: un esclave et son maître devant les deux aspects de la personnalité d'une jeune fille." In *Akten des 21. Internationalen Papyrologenkongresses: Berlin, 13.–19. 8. 1995*. Vol. 1, edited by B. Kramer et al., 570–577. Stuttgart: Teubner.

Lefèvre, E., E. Stärk, and G. Vogt-Spira, eds. 1991. *Plautus barbarus: Sechs Kapitel zur Originalität des Plautus*. Tübingen: Narr.

Leigh, M. 2004. *Comedy and the Rise of Rome*. Oxford: Oxford University Press.

Leo, F. 1912. *Plautinische Forschungen zur Kritik und Geschichte der Komödie*. 2nd ed. Berlin: Weidmann.

Lowe, J. C. B. 1992. "Aspects of Plautus' Originality in the *Asinaria*." *CQ* 42: 152–175.

Moore, T. 1998. *The Theater of Plautus*. Austin: University of Texas Press.

——. 2012. *Music in Roman Comedy*. Cambridge, UK: Cambridge University Press.

Nünlist, R. 1993. "P. Mich. inv. 6950 (unpubliziert), *P.Köln* 203 und 243: Szenen aus Menanders *Dis Exapaton*?" *ZPE* 99: 245–278.

——. 2002. "Speech within Speech in Menander." In *The Language of Greek Comedy*, edited by A. Willi, 219–259. Oxford: Oxford University Press.

Questa, C. 1970. "Alcune strutture sceniche di Plauto e Menandro." In *Ménandre: Sept exposés suivis de discussions*, edited by Eric G. Turner, 181–215. Vandoeuvres-Geneva: Fondation Hardt.

——, ed. 2008. *Titus Maccius Plautus: Bacchides*. Urbino: QuattroVenti.

Questa, C., and R. Raffaelli, eds. 2002. *Due seminari plautini: La tradizione del testo, i modelli*. Urbino: QuattroVenti.

Ritschl, F. 1845. *Parerga zu Plautus und Terenz*. Leipzig: Weidmann.

Schutter, K. 1952. *Quibus annis comoediae Plautinae primum actae sint quaeritur*. Groningen: de Waal.

Segal, E. 1987. *Roman Laughter: The Comedy of Plautus*. 2nd ed. London: Oxford University Press.

Slater, N. W. 2000. *Plautus in Performance: The Theatre of the Mind*. 2nd ed. Amsterdam: Harwood Academic.

Stewart, R. 2012. *Plautus and Roman Slavery*. Malden, MA, and Oxford: Wiley-Blackwell.

Suerbaum, W., ed. 2002. *Handbuch der lateinischen Literatur der Antike*. Vol. 1, *Die archaische Literatur*. Munich: C. H. Beck.

Stein, J. 1966. "Trinummus." *American Numismatic Society Museum Notes* 12: 65–69.

Weisweiler, J. and C. Riedweg. 2004. "Gute Freunde, schlechte Freunde: Nochmals zu Plaut. *Bacch.* 540–51." *Hermes* 132: 141–151.

Zagagi, N. 1980. *Tradition and Originality in Plautus: Studies of the Amatory Motifs in Plautine Comedy*. Göttingen: Vandenhoeck & Ruprecht.

Zwierlein, O. 1990–1992. *Zur Kritik und Exegese des Plautus*. 4 vols. (1 *Poenulus und Curculio* [1990], 2 *Miles gloriosus* [1991], 3 *Pseudolus* [1991], 4 *Bacchides* [1992]). Stuttgart: Steiner.

CHAPTER 27

··

THE TERENTIAN
REFORMATION: FROM
MENANDER TO ALEXANDRIA

··

MICHAEL FONTAINE

RECENT decades have seen the emergence of a consensus about Terence's achievement but little agreement about what particular factors explain it. Although we still
cannot directly compare substantial portions of his plays to his source texts, as we can
with Plautus (see previous chapter), three important interventions have done much to
shake older orthodoxies and throw new light on his art and originality. First, in 1974
John Wright demonstrated that Terence deliberately avoided the verbal "stylistic unity"
that characterized the plays of Plautus, Naevius, Caecilius, and the other fragmentary
Roman comedians (Wright 1974: 127–151, 183 and *passim*). As Wright showed, the colorful, alliterative language of Plautine comedy was in fact conventional, widespread,
and traditional for comedy in Rome (see de Melo in this volume), and unlike the other
comedians of whom we know (including Turpilius, the last major writer of *palliatae*),
Terence alone seems to have eschewed the tradition for a more realistic idiom. Despite
occasional challenges (e.g., Manuwald 2011: 257), Wright's view withstands scrutiny well,
especially as augmented by supporting studies (principally Karakasis 2005). Second,
in 1982 Gratwick (1982: 122–123) exploded the longstanding misapprehension that
Terence was personally responsible for inventing a particular kind of *humanitas*. This
perceived commitment on his part to cosmopolitan human reason and relationships
had been repeatedly emphasized in older scholarship, but it rested on shaky foundations
and thus distorted the nature of Terence's artistic program. Gratwick's was an important ground-clearing operation, but its very success left us unsure what causes impelled
Terence to pursue the program that he did. Finally, in 1996 Parker (1996) demonstrated
that Terence was not the aesthetic failure that he long seemed to be. Such problems as
Terence did experience with his immediate public were due, Parker showed, not to artistic failings on his part but rather to external conditions beyond his control.

The convergence of these interventions has put Terence's comedy in a new light. We
now see more clearly than before that Terence boldly reformed Rome's rich tradition

of *comoedia*. Although he did musicalize his source texts extensively, he all but eliminated its polymetric musical showpieces and its other perceived excesses—the varied singsong meters, rollicking jokes, general buffoonery, and above all its exuberant verbal style. His comedies are more subdued and artistically coherent, they do not break the fourth wall unexpectedly, and their verse approaches the cadences of prose (on meter, see Deufert in this volume). The result is greater realism in speech, ethics, psychology, and sentiment, heightened suspense, and thus—in a word—drama as we know it. Collectively these choices read as a fundamentalist turn, a shift away from the bastard operatic form in which Rome had adopted Athenian comedy in the Hellenistic period, and an attempt to return instead to the genre's original, mimetic roots. What remains now is largely the question of influence and inspiration.

It is usually thought that Terence was interested in returning to Menander as New Comedy's greatest representative, and bringing a more faithful version of his comedy to the Roman stage. This view is correct, but it scarcely explains *why* Terence sought to do so. Moreover, the traditional scholarly focus on Terence's perceived Menandrianism tends to draw attention away from some very un-Menandrian traits of his art, traits that have less in common with other comedians (whether Greek or Roman) than they do with the sophisticated poets of Neoteric and Augustan Latin literature. Before turning to these, therefore, it will be helpful to begin by tracing the genesis of the association of Terence and Menander.

1.

The notion that Terence is himself a "Roman Menander" is of venerable pedigree. It first appears in fragmentary poems of Cicero and Julius Caesar (Menander K-A test. 64):

> Cicero fr. 2 Courtney (*Limon*):
> tu quoque qui solus lecto sermone, Terenti,
> conversum expressumque Latina voce Menandrum
> in medium nobis sedatis †vocibus† effers,
> quiddam come loquens atque omnia dulcia dicens.

> You as well, Terence, who alone in elegant speech
> bring us Menander converted and expressed
> in Latin voice, with sedate †words†,
> speaking neatly and saying all things sweetly.

> Caesar fr. 1 Courtney, 1–2:
> tu quoque, tu in summis, o dimidiate Menander,
> poneris, et merito, puri sermonis amator.

> You as well, you, o halved Menander, are placed among the
> greats, and deservedly so, you lover of pure speech.

There is no knowing what the original context of these verses was. They probably represent little more than schoolroom exercises composed after a reading of *Andria* and perhaps *Eunuchus*, but Caesar's sobriquet *dimidiatus Menander* has dogged Terence ever since. The tradition is easy to trace. Suetonius reproduced both fragments at the end of his *Life of Terence* (§7), thereby elevating them to the prestigious status of what Renaissance commentators would come to call *judicia veterum*, "judgments of the ancients (about the quality of a poet)." Donatus then reproduced the *Life* at the front of his commentary on Terence, thereby canonizing the claim, bequeathing it to us, and thus setting the terms of most modern discussion ever since.

On what grounds do broad claims of Terence's Menandrianism rest? Persistent as it is, on examination the idea proves surprisingly difficult to pin down. Terence did turn to Menander more than his predecessors, but only if his output is considered as a whole. Four of his six plays take Menandrian originals as their sources, but in absolute terms that is about on par with Plautus where known (*Bacchides*, *Cistellaria*, *Stichus*, and probably *Pseudolus* and *Aulularia*) and far fewer than Caecilius, who took at least thirteen of his approximately fifty plays, and probably more, from Menander.[1] We do not know what Terence might have done had he lived beyond 159 BCE, when premature death, mid-career, put a bookend on his output and thus proportionately and retroactively augmented his Menandrianism. Each successive play would have changed his reputation substantially. What is more, though he did base these four plays on Menandrian models, Terence's reputation cannot accurately rest on faithful replication of Menander's plots. Although he does not put the matter so strongly, Terence himself acknowledges that he has altered the plots of three of Menander's plays by adding alien material (*Andria* 8–16, *Heauton Timorumenos* 16–18, *Eunuchus* 30–33). Such distortion stands in sharp contrast with the practice of Luscius of Lanuvium, Terence's rival, who evidently did replicate Menander's plots faithfully, but in the stylistically unified language of traditional Roman comedy.

Caesar and Cicero themselves attribute Terence's Menandrianism to his verbal style (what they call *purus* and *lectus sermo*, "pure" and "choice" language). Terence's surface style is indeed largely uniform and unlike that of Plautus; Luscius—his Menandrianizing rival—criticized it as "thin and light" (*Phormio* 5). But for several reasons their idea is ill considered. First, Terence himself says that Menander's own style was not uniform but heterogeneous (*Andria* 12, *dissimili oratione...ac stilo*, referring to his *Andria* and *Perinthia*). Second, Terence's one play that is most "Plautine" and stylistically least like his others, *Eunuchus*, is actually a combination of *two* Menandrian originals (it draws heavily on his *Kolax*). And third, Terence's uniform style makes *Andria*, *Heauton Timorumenos*, and *Adelphoe* indistinguishable from *Hecyra* and *Phormio*—yet these

---

[1] These absolute figures are lost on Jerome, Donatus's pupil, who in a letter remarks (*Epist.* 57) *Terentius Menandrum, Plautus et Caecilius veteres comicos interpretati sunt*, "Terence translated Menander, Plautus and Caecilius the old comedians." For the argument that Plautus's *Pseudolus* is based on a Menandrian play, see previous chapter.

latter two are based on plays not of Menander but Apollodorus of Carystus, a comedian of the second generation (fl. third century). And although it is commonly claimed that Apollodorus was a close follower, admirer, acolyte, or disciple of Menander, there is no independent evidence for the view. That is no more than a back-inference from Terence's own texts, and a remarkably illegitimate one—no one would make the analogous claim about Plautus's models.[2]

Since our impression that Apollodorus was like Menander at all is probably best considered a testament to Terence's own artistry, it is time to turn to it directly.

2.

P. Terentius Afer (195/185–159) is the first Latin author whose total output and absolute chronology of production survives. Despite problems of detail, the usually accepted list reveals a remarkably compressed career:

- *Andria* in 166, Megalesian Games
- *Hecyra* in 165, Megalesian Games
  - restaged in 160, Funeral Games for Aemilius Paullus
  - restaged in 160, Roman Games
- *Heauton Timorumenos* in 163, Megalesian Games
- *Eunuchus* in 161, Megalesian Games
- *Phormio* in 161, Roman Games
- *Adelphoe* in 160, Funeral Games for Aemilius Paullus

This precise information not only enables us to trace artistic development from play to play, it also allows us to see that at times Terence reaches beyond the fourth wall in some subtle,

---

[2] Few fragments of Apollodorus's plays exist apart from what Donatus quotes from his *Hekyra* and *Phormio*, and while verbal parallels are apparent in some, so too are significant differences. Terence converts action to narrative (*Hekyra* K-A fr. 14 = Donatus on *Hecyra* 824), reassigns speaking parts (*Phormio* K-A fr. 18 = Donatus on *Phormio* 81), and adds foreign material (see below on *Phormio* 339). Other changes are likely. — Since none of Terence's models survives complete, opportunities to actually match up Terence and Menander are surprisingly scant. Some, but not KA, attribute a mutilated papyrus (*adesp*. K-A fr. 1129) to Menander's *Heauton Timoroumenos*; see Bathrellou's appendix in this volume. Randomly preserved parallels of equal length of Menander and Plautus (*Synaristosai* fr. 1 Arnott ~ *Cistellaria* 89–93) and Terence (*Heauton Timoroumenos* K-A fr. 77 ~ *Heauton Timorumenos* 61–64, quoted not by Donatus but in grammatical literature) show about equal verbal fidelity in translation, and both greater than the passages of Caecilius and Menander quoted by Gellius (*N.A.* 2.23), which, however, are quoted specifically to illustrate Caecilius's freedom in adaptation. Otherwise we must depend on Donatus, who may not be a reliable guide to Terence's alterations (Barsby 2002).

wry, and peculiar ways. It allows us to see, for instance, that by creatively positioning his plays and their characters, Terence makes his comedies allude both to the occasion of presentation (and thus reflect life) as well as to older Roman comedies (and thus reflect art). It also allows us to see that by repeatedly using the same names for the characters of the dramatis personae from one play to the next, Terence makes his characters self-consciously reflect earlier incarnations of themselves in a manner reminiscent of mythologically based poetry. In so doing, he manages to combine a quality associated above all with Menandrian drama with a quality associated primarily with the irony-rich, scholastic poetry of Alexandria.

These sophisticated dynamics are most succinctly illustrated by examining the occasion of presentation. Terence stages Menander's *Eunuchus* at a Roman festival honoring Magna Mater, "The Great Mother"—whose priests were eunuchs. At the same festival he exhibits *Hecyra*, "The Mother-in-Law"—a play about a surrogate "mother." More impressively, when the two sons of Aemilius Paullus commissioned him to compose a comedy for their father's funeral games, Terence finds among Greek Comedy a *Brothers* (*Adelphoi*) by Menander, a play that seemingly evokes the Roman brothers' actual situation in surreal ways. For just as Paullus had famously supervised the systematic education in Greek *paideia* of his two sons, who had been given up for adoption into other families, so Terence's play centers around two fathers' diverging philosophies of how best to educate two brothers, one of them adopted. What is more, Terence seems to seal the nod to reality by naming one father Micio (from μικρός, "small"), an apparent pun on Paul(l)us. Although the parallels are neither entirely straightforward nor exact (see Gratwick 1999: 19–21 and Leigh 2004: 158–191), they are certainly there, and amid the retrospective context of Paullus's Roman funeral the superficial similarities must have aroused attention.

With *Adelphoe*, then, Terence accordingly makes life imitate art, but he does so in a strikingly novel and erudite way. The Alexandrian librarian Aristophanes of Byzantium (ca. 265/257–ca. 190/180 BCE) had famously posed a rhetorical question meant to compliment Menander's art as the consummate imitation of life (Menander K-A test. 83 = Syranius's Hermogenes 2.23 Rabe): Ὦ Μένανδρε καὶ βίε, πότερος ἄρ' ὑμῶν πότερον ἐμιμήσατο; ("O Menander and Life! Which of you imitated which?"). As if in reply, Terence manages to exploit both the gap between third-century Athens and second-century Rome and the inherently secondary nature of Roman comedy to complicate Aristophanes's question. In his creative adaptation of details and in presenting the play on this particular occasion, Terence positions Menander's imitation of third-century Greek life as a prophetic, hyper-real imitation, or reflection, of second-century Roman life—and he stages it in the context of a Roman funeral, which was itself a retrospective imitation of a particular life.[3] Life or Menander? Who *is* imitating who, and how?

---

[3] On the retrospective character of aristocratic Roman funerals, see Polybius 6.53–54; on the mimetic character, Diodorus Siculus 31.25.2; both accounts are based largely on Paullus's famous funeral itself.

This creative positioning of plays to reflect the festival occasion is something new in Roman comedy, and it extends to Terence's treatment of characters within the play. Terence returns to the traditional names of New Comedy and repeats them from one drama to the next. Since Menander had similarly employed generic names for his *personae* but Plautus had not, his decision seems at first glance retrograde, as the consummate fundamentalist turn and a retreat from originality. In Gilbert Norwood's view (Norwood 1923: 4), "his [Terence's] writings show far more similarity of topic and even of treatment than can be found in any other poet of his eminence. It is, therefore, not surprising if casual readers regard them as more or less the same play, with 'Chremes' and his like passing palely though volubly through them." Actually, this very quality makes Terence's characters approach something like the situation of Greek mythology—and thus offers an opportunity for originality of a different sort. As S. Hinds says of Roman epic (Hinds 1998: 115), "For poets who handle mythological themes, occasions for negotiation between the time-frames of the narrated world and the time-frames of their own poetic traditions will tend to arise again and again."

Terence realized this and, though his intent has often been mistaken, apparently sought to explore the resulting dynamics. A conspicuous example appears in his "Plautine" *Eunuchus*, which features an *adulescens* incongruously named Chremes. Since the name elsewhere is regularly that of a *senex*, A. S. Gratwick notes, "In naming a *young* man 'Chremes' (*Eun.*), Terence was committing a striking solecism by the original principle."[4] A second mystery related to this one appears late in the play, when this Chremes boldly threatens a soldier not to delay him, or else... (801):

> faciam ut huius loci dieique meique semper memineris.
>
> I'll make you remember this place and this day and me forever.

Almost verbatim, Chremes's threat channels a threat made by the parasite Ergasilus in Plautus's *Captivi*. Amid a furious running entrance in *Captivi* 768–826, Plautus's parasite blusters—to no one in particular—that if anyone gets in *his* way (800),

> faciam ut huius diei locique meique semper meminerit.
>
> I'll make him remember this day and this place and me forever.

In the event, Ergasilus will meet with only a single person—a *senex* who is here eavesdropping on the parasite and who, impressed with the parasite's brazen threat, turns

---

[4] Gratwick 1993: 11 n. 21, emphasis original. Gratwick's remarks on the relation of names, masks, and tragedy on pp. 10–11 are illuminating. Terence meditates on the nature of his "second mythology" explicitly in closing the prologue to *Eunuchus*, plaintively wondering how to carve out an original space for himself at so late a point in his crowded literary tradition (35–41; discussed below). Terence's complaint sounds very much like that of the mid-career Virgil (*Georgics* 3.8–10)—a sobering parallel when one realizes that Virgil probably read Terence in school. For more on the literary dynamics in *Eunuchus*, see Fontaine 2014.

aside to ask us directly, "What giant undertaking is this guy up to, with such giant threats as these?" (801). Readers familiar with the poetry of Catullus or Ovid—and it seems likely that Terence's near-quotation of *Captivi* can only be intended for readers, not spectators—will easily recognize the ploy. Terence has tendentiously positioned Plautus's *senex* as a prophetic reflection on his own character, an *adulescens* with the generically mismatched name Chremes. Indeed, if we allow for the vagaries of transmission, it seems that Terence even sought to underline the allusion via a case of "stichometric intertextuality," i.e., by having the line numbers match.[5] Nor is this the only instance in *Eunuchus* where Terence is experimenting with textual memory in the world of Roman comedy. Elsewhere we find all the usual markers of competitive allusion familiar from Neoteric and Augustan Latin poetry: paradoxical claims of primacy and reflexive self-annotation (246–249; cf. 429), an "Alexandrian footnote" (419–429, alluding to Livius Andronicus fr. 6 Warmington [8 Ribbeck³] [*incert.*]), the rhetoric of literary appropriation (429), and other experiments with poetic memory (497–498). All look back not to Greek authors but to Latin ones, and most are concentrated in the play's parasite and soldier, the two characters that (as the prologue announces) Terence's rival playwright had believed were "plagiarized."

The theory underlying these moves is remarkable. Whereas Menander held a mirror up to life, Alexandrian poets alluded to each other's works. Realizing that *reflexivity* is the common element that could unite these two disparate types of poetry, Terence deserves credit for pioneering tensions that would prove extraordinarily productive in Latin poetry.

Realizing, too, that creative positioning is what makes reflexivity possible, Terence makes *Hecyra*, his second play, read as an intertextual response to *Andria*, his first (Penwill 2004). The young lovers in both comedies are named Pamphilus and Philumena, but the ethos of each Pamphilus is entirely different. In *Andria* he is conventional; in *Hecyra*, savage. Before the play begins, *Hecyra*'s Pamphilus has brutally raped a girl in a drunken struggle, gratuitously stolen her ring and given it to his mistress, and even so—though neither knows it—ends up married to Philumena. Yet he resents and refrains from sexual intimacy with her, and, upon discovering her pregnancy, makes plans to divorce her. Pamphilus is only dissuaded when, in a scene of supreme pathos, her poor mother, Myrrina, begs him on her knees not to abandon her daughter. She even offers to get rid of her daughter's baby (378–401).

By repeating the proper names but varying the ethos, Terence creates intertextual dynamism—as if in his hands Pamphilus and Philumena had become an Oedipus and Jocasta or a Jason and Medea. The play ends shockingly, not with divorce, but with the continued marriage of Pamphilus and Philumena and with the horror of forced silence. In a rare acknowledgment of the dramatic illusion, Pamphilus even conspires with

---

[5] On stichometric intertextuality, see Hinds 1998: 92 n. 80 (also discussing a one-number misalignment) and Lowe 2013; a clear example is Ovid's irreverent reworking of Virgil's *Aeneid* 10.475 at *Metamorphoses* 10.475. Kruschwitz (2001) documents Terence's close attention to making internal line numbers correspond.

his former mistress, the courtesan Bacchis, to cover up his violent rape (865–868, tr. Brown):

> PAM. dic mi, harum rerum numquid dixti iam patri?
> BA. nil.
> PAM. neque opus est.
> adeo muttito. placet non fieri hoc itidem ut in comoediis
> omnia omnes ubi resciscunt. hic quos par fuerat resciscere
> sciunt. quos non autem aequomst scire neque resciscent neque scient.

> PAM. Tell me, you haven't already said anything to my dad about any of this, have you?
> BAC. No.
> PAM. There's no need to breathe a word about it, either. I think it's best if this doesn't turn out the way things do in comedies, where everyone finds out about everything. In this case, those who needed to find out do know; but those who ought not to know won't find out and won't know about it.

Thus neither father will learn the truth of the rape, nor will anyone else, including evidently Philumena herself (the play takes pains to emphasize that the ring was recognized by Myrrina: 811–812, 830–832, 845–846). As the only person beside Pamphilus and Bacchis to know the truth, Myrrina becomes an object of our pity—a mother-in-law forced to live with the secret knowledge that her daughter is married to a monster. This arrangement is less like a comedy than a nightmare or a tragedy—as if Terence were smuggling into the comic theater Ovid's tale of Tereus, Procne, and Philomela under the conventional names of comedy. As we see in the extract above, he does call attention to the paradox, but in language that does not quite (or necessarily) break the dramatic illusion. In Plautus the conceit implied by *non . . . ut in comoediis* would be either "in tragedy" (*Amphitruo* 987, with 53–63) or "in reality, in real life" (*Captivi* 52), but in either event it would be played for laughs. Here the two oppositions are blurred, implying that "in tragedies" and "in real life" may well be the same thing—true horror, and especially for a woman, Terence suggests, can be found in contemporary domestic life. The ambiguous title underlines this perspective: is "The Mother-in-Law" Sostrata, who appears onstage in an earlier and larger role, or Myrrina, the most pitiable character in extant comedy?

Like the tendentious positioning, irony, and reflexivity described above, Terence's interest in female psychology and caddish men seems to be eminently characteristic of Alexandrian Greek and Augustan Latin poetry, and thus generates a challenge to conventional paradigms. To a traditional school of thought, the attempt to interpret these seemingly "Alexandrian" qualities in Alexandrian terms is misguided, *tout court*: "Terence's literary world was not the world that Vergil, Horace, Ovid, and Statius knew. Critical methods (and attendant presumptions) devised to explicate that later world may require modification to work effectively in this earlier one." Yet this simply begs the question, and it is therefore important not only to emphasize in response that Alexandrian influence on Roman literature demonstrably predates Terence, but also to localize it. This brings us to Ennius.[6]

---

[6] Quote: Goldberg 2011: 210 (similarly Goldberg 2005: 81). Alexandrian influence on Ennius: Gratwick 1982: 60–76 and Hinds 1998 *passim*.

3.

Rome's greatest poet before Virgil, Q. Ennius died in 169, three years before Terence staged his first play. It is easy to overlook that Terence is our first opportunity to explore Latin poetics in a post-Ennian Rome, and the oversight is all the stranger, since at the start of his first play, *Andria,* Terence himself announces that he wants "to emulate Naevius, Plautus, and Ennius, men he considers his authorities" (18–20). On the traditional view, the name of Ennius is a surprise in this list—we might have rather expected the great name Caecilius—and it has seemed natural to suppose that in it Terence is referring to Ennius in his role as a comedian. But Ennius's comedies seem to have been few and poor, and recent scholarship on allusion in other genres of Latin poetry has exposed the limitations of assuming that literary imitation extends in only one dimension or is always of the most obvious kind. Just as Ovid's literary parrot "imitates" in two dimensions—both humans with its voice, and Catullus's sparrow by dying—Terence may well have meant for his audience to reflect on what it would mean for *any* poet in Rome, in any genre, to find himself writing after Ennius.

A few indications in his comedy suggest that the impact of Ennius on Terence was greater than has been traditionally appreciated. For example, in 161 Terence staged two plays, *Eunuchus* at the Megalesian Games in April and *Phormio* at the Roman Games in September. Both plays contain points of contact with Ennius's poetry, but in different ways.

> (1) In *Eunuchus* 590, Chaerea recounts his rape in jubilation and, in describing a painting of Jupiter that he had seen inside the house, exclaims:
>
> at quem deum, qui templa caeli summa sonitu concutit!
> And what a god! The one who shakes the lofty vaults of heaven with his thunder!
> (tr. Barsby)

In his commentary on the line, Donatus tells us the phrase *templa caeli summa* is "tragic" and that *sonitu concuit* "parodies" something from Ennius. The parody is usually assumed to extend from *at* or *qui* to *concutit* and the source text to be one of Ennius's tragedies (fr. *incert.* 161 Jocelyn), although the parallel at Lucretius *DRN* 6.387–388 *divi* | *terrifico quatiunt sonitu caelestia templa* suggests the *Annals* is at least as likely a source.

> (2) In *Phormio* 338–343, the parasite elaborately prepares a piece of wordplay on the riddling phrase *cena dubia,* a "dubious dinner," i.e., a "dinner of doubtful quality." A glance at the historical record allows us to guess why. Early in 161, the Roman assembly had passed the *Lex Fannia,* a sumptuary law that severely restricted expenditure on dinner parties (*cenae*) at the Megalesian Games that the *principes civitatis* (civic leaders) hosted for their peers.[7] Since the law was

---

[7] Gellius, *NA* 2.24.2. On the meaning of *cena dubia,* see Tyrrell 1883: 2, rightly against recent translations.

extended later that year to limit expenditure on dinners at the Roman Games as well—the very occasion, that is, at which *Phormio* debuted—some aristocrats in the audience probably suspected that Terence had elaborated the verbal preparation precisely in order to twit their now-meager *cenae*, which might be justly called *dubiae*—dubious.

Chanting the trochaic septenarii, Phormio leads up to the phrase in question by explaining his contention that patrons aren't shown sufficient appreciation by their parasites for all they do (338–343):

> PHO. immo enim nemo satis pro merito gratiam regi refert.
> ten asymbolum venire unctum atque lautum e balineis,
> otiosum ab animo, quom ille et cura et sumptu absumitur!
> dum tibi fit quod placeat, ille ringitur. tu rideas,
> prior bibas, prior decumbas; cena dubia apponitur.
> GETA quid istuc verbist?
> PHO. ubi tu dubites quid sumas potissumum.

> PHO. No, no, it's the *patron* who isn't thanked enough for his services.
> Ha! *You* show up ἀσύμβολος [freeloading], oiled and washed at the baths,
> totally relaxed, while *he's* consumed by the worry and cost of it.
> While *you're* enjoying everything, *he's* gritting his teeth. *You* get to laugh,
> to drink sooner, sit down sooner. A doubtful dinner's put out.
> GETA What's that mean?
> PHO. It's where you're in doubt about what you most want to take!

Donatus reveals that lines 339–341 are modeled not on Apollodorus's original but on a six-line iambic passage of Ennius's *Satires* (Ennius's name is not clearly recorded, but the ascription is usually accepted). In it, a speaker, probably a parasite, explains (fr. 15 Blänsdorf = *ROL* Ennius *Sat.* incert. 14–19):

> quippe sine cura laetus lautus cum advenis,
> infestis malis, expedito bracchio
> alacer celsus, lupino expectans impetu,
> mox alterius abligurris cum bona,
> quid censes domino esse animi? pro divum fidem
> ille tristis est dum cibum servat, tu ridens voras.

> It's true: when you show up, carefree, cheerful, and spick and span,
> jaws hostile, your arm bared and ready,
> giddy, on cloud nine, waiting tautly, like a wolf —
> when moments later you're nibbling up another's goods,
> how do you think your host feels? For gods' sake
> he's *upset*, while *he's* been storing food up, and *you're* devouring it with a grin!

The two Ennian passages in Terence are very different. A contemporary audience might well recognize that the line in *Eunuchus* is a parody in performance; even without

Donatus, its stately tone and rhythm tell us it draws on weightier literature (cf. Plautus, *Rudens* 1). But the expansion in *Phormio* is hardly an allusion in the conventional sense that it could be readily recognized in performance. A reader in his study might notice it, but no spectator could: there are hardly any verbal repetitions (*lautus* ~ *lautum, venire* ~ *advenire*), and the meter is different. In either event, Ennius had died eight years before *Eunuchus* and *Phormio* were staged; his source texts are conceivably much older. Who then were the target audiences for the allusions? Because we do not know to what extent Ennius's works were circulating in 161 BCE, we cannot answer that question.[8] But if we redirect our attention from the audience to their author, we can ask a different question: why would Terence himself want to associate his comedy with Ennius—even if he could not count on anyone in the audience noticing it at the time of its original production? Putting the question this way leads in a different direction, for with artistic positioning goes *self*-positioning, or pose.

4.

In the present writer's view, artistic pose helps indicate that Ennius's intervention on the Roman literary scene is an unappreciated but decisive precondition of Terence's unusual career and dramatic art. More simply put: no Ennius, no Terentian comedy, at least in the form that we know it. This becomes evident when their artistic outputs are considered whole. Both authors pose as poetic fundamentalists, and in analogous fashions. Just as Ennius set his sights beyond Rome's existing tradition of saturnian-based epic— beyond Naevius's *Punic War* and beyond Livius Andronicus's *Odyssey*, which was probably a musical pastiche of Homer's (Flores 2011)—and sought his form and inspiration in Homer himself, so did Terence reject traditional Roman *comoedia* for a more "original" and (speciously) metrically pure style of κωμῳδία. And though both do pay some homage to their predecessors, the two authors seemingly force the entirety of previous efforts in their respective Latin genres into a narrow box of old-fashioned, outmoded, or unrefined native primitivism. The contours of these efforts are clear (on Ennius's, see Hinds 1998: 52–98).

---

[8] Macrobius does preserve a fragment of a speech from 161 in favor of the Lex Fannia that seemingly alludes to Ennius's *Alexander* fr. 72 Jocelyn, *nam maximo saltu superabit gravidus armatis equus,* "for with a mighty bound a horse pregnant with armed men will clear the way" (*Sat.* 3.13.3): *Nam Titius in suasione legis Fanniae obicit seculo suo quod porcum Troianum mensis inferant, quem illi ideo sic vocabant, quasi aliis inclusis animalibus gravidum, ut ille Troianus equus gravidus armatis fuit.* ("Indeed, Titius, in his speech supporting the law of Fannius, reproaches his contemporaries for serving Trojan pig, so-called because it is 'pregnant' with other animals enclosed within, just as the famous Trojan horse was 'pregnant with armed men'"; tr. Kaster.) Yet the indicative verbs *vocabant* and *fuit* show that the allusion is not Titius's but Macrobius's (contrast *inferant*), and thus they tell us nothing about the circulation of Ennius's works. (For what it is worth, Titius probably picked up the phrase itself from comedy: cf. Diphilus *incert.* K-A fr. 90.)

At the beginning of the *Annals*, the masterpiece that he probably finished late in life, Ennius claimed that Homer himself had appeared in a dream and revealed that he, Homer, had been reincarnated as Ennius. Although the immediate public may have viewed it skeptically, the bizarre and amazing claim is endorsed already by Lucilius, who later enjoyed the patronage of the same Scipionic Circle that had fostered Terence's career (fr. 1189 Marx = 413 Warmington): *Homerus alter ut Lucilius de Ennio suspicatur*, "a second Homer, as Lucilius believes of Ennius." For his part, in the *Eunuchus* prologue (35–43) Terence reveals himself as overtly anxious about his epigonal position as a poet of Roman comedy (the genre was now eighty years old). In a specific context, then, Ennius's flamboyant pose as (literally) the *alter Homerus* suddenly opened up for him an unprecedented opportunity to pose as the *alter Menander*, much as in the wake of World War Two Harold MacMillan used to hope for his Britain to play the Athens to America's Rome.

It is worth emphasizing that *any* comedian in Rome might have been considered the Roman Menander. An otherwise unknown Fundanius sought the title (Horace, *Sat.* 1.10.40–42), while in later times some thought that Afranius, whose *togata* comedies were set not in Greece but Rome, merited it (Horace *Epist.* 2.1.57, *dicitur Afrani toga convenisse Menandro*; cf. Cicero *Fin.* 1.7, *ut ab Homero Ennius, Afranius a Menandro solet*). What allowed Terence to succeed was the particular context—which was, however, not theatrical but academic. In Hellenistic times, Homer and Menander were the twin pillars of Greek education (Pini 2006: 447–456; Citroni 2006: 9–14; Nervegna 2013). Several double herms of Homer and Menander, such as seen in figure 27.1 here, offer salient reminders of their paired canonical status.

One inscribed herm credits Aristophanes of Byzantium with the judgment that of all Greek authors, Homer ranks first and Menander second (Menander K-A test. 170c = IG 14.1183). If Terence was indeed posing as the new Menander to Ennius's new Homer, his claim and career are extraordinarily ambitious. They imply he was not merely the reincarnation of Greece's greatest comedian, but of its second greatest author of all time.

It bears emphasizing that the particular analogy (Homer: Menander :: Ennius: Terence) is only intelligible in an academic context, outside of which Homer and Menander had nothing to do with one another. It is therefore unsurprising that it is precisely in Rome's own academic context that the analogy was most successfully received. Terence soon took a prominent and lasting place on its Latin syllabus alongside first Ennius, then Virgil, so that even many centuries later Jerome would write (*Epist.* 58.5) that "poets should emulate Homer, Virgil, Menander, and Terence" (*Poetae aemulantur Homerum, Vergilium, Menandrum, Terentium*). The only question is where and why the analogy originates.

It is usually assumed that cultural nationalists (such as in Horace *Epist.* 2.1.50–58) or Latin grammarians in Rome first made the association and then deliberately projected it back to ennoble their past or standardize their syllabi, and it is of course true that biographers would later reinforce the idea that Menander and Terence had lived parallel lives. Both comedians did stage their first play at or around age nineteen and did reportedly associate with political elites, though the more cartoonish incidents recounted in

FIGURE 27.1 Double herm of Homer and Menander. Pentelic marble. From the Barbuta area in Rome. / Rome, Museo Nazionale Romano Terme, inv. 124490. 1st century CE (Neronian/ Flavian), from a Hellenistic original.

Suetonius's *Life* (and in some modern reference literature) are undoubtedly fictions. The pretty story, for instance, that during a dinner party the fledgling Terence read *Andria* to Caecilius, then advanced in age, who greeted it "with enthusiastic approval," cannot be; the elder comedian had died two years before, and the sentiment of "passing the torch" is easily paralleled in fiction (compare *Aeneid* 2.293). Equally implausible is the idiosyncratic view of a first-century BCE grammarian named Cosconius, according to which Terence met his death in a shipwreck "on his way back from Greece . . . with translated adaptations he had made of Menander's plays" (*redeuntem e Graecia perisse in mari dicit cum fabulis conversis a Menandro*). Suetonius himself tells us no one else believed this story, which suspiciously parallels the legends that sprang up around the death of Percy Shelley. The twenty-nine-year-old author of *Prometheus Unbound* drowned in a shipwreck with a volume of Keats in his pocket; before long a volume of Aeschylus, too, was said to have been in another.[9]

---

[9] Donatus's text of Suetonius actually says "with 108 translated adaptations' (*cum C. et VIII. fabulis conversis a Menandro*), implying that Terence had reworked *every* comedy Menander had ever written (variously reported at 105 or 109). This incredible absurdity is occasionally still repeated in secondary literature, but is simply a mistake. In fact, an early copyist misinterpreted CVM, "with," as CVIII, "108".— The tradition that Menander himself had drowned is not ancient (Menander K-A test. 23 = Callimachus fr. 396 [dub.] Pfeiffer), but even so the implicit parallel need not be so exact (as if by his death Terence were an extreme Silius Italicus, who purchased, restored, and performed an annual devotion to Virgil's tomb (Pliny *Epist*. 3.7)).

But to credit these later groups for devising rather than merely strengthening an existing analogy is to underestimate just how old and deeply engrained in Roman culture
were the notions of exemplarity in general and of "Greek incarnation" in particular—the
idea that a Roman author of our times is the new Greek so-and-so. According to Plutarch,
in his youth (thus ca. 200 BCE, early in Plautus's career), the Elder Cato (234–149, consul 195) was commonly called the *Demosthenes Romanus* (Ῥωμαῖον αὐτὸν οἱ πολλοὶ
Δημοσθένη προσηγόρευον, "the masses were calling him a Roman Demosthenes," *Cato
Maior* 4.1). Furthermore, the obviously romantic episodes in Suetonius's *Life* are all the
statements of biographers, not of an autobiographer. If we turn instead to Terence's own
portrayal of his life, certain details cumulatively suggest that his public association with
Menander was at root a pose of his own.

5.

Terence's prologues are autobiographical. That does not mean they are true, though it is
usually assumed they are, but unlike the statements of later biographers, they show us
Terence as he wished to portray himself. They are occupied largely with literary polem-
ics, and collectively they depict a man constantly dogged by rival comedians' accusations: of "contaminating" plays, of plagiarism, of accepting help in writing, and of stylistic
incompetence (*Phormio* 5). They also suggest that Terence repeatedly failed to win a
crowd (*Hecyra* 10–27), even though other sources reveal that each of his plays was in fact
a success that and *Eunuchus* itself was an unprecedented success (Parker 1996: 591–592).
What is remarkable is that most of these elements have direct parallels with Menander's
life. The ongoing quarrel with an older rival mirrors Menander's well-attested rivalry
with Philemon, a comic poet twenty years his elder (Menander K-A test. 71, 101, and
114). This rivalry stemmed from the perceived difficulty Menander had in winning
victories—only eight times in his career (Menander K-A test. 46, cf. K-A test. 98; see
Scafuro on Menander in this volume)—such that, by Martial's time, Menander's failure
to please his public had become proverbial (Menander K-A test. 98 = Martial 5.10.9).
Above all, as Boris Dunsch emphasizes (Dunsch 1999: 129), Terence's self-presentation
is dominated by the charge of "literary *furtum*, plagiarism, which is, along with *contaminare*, the catchword of Terence's adversaries (cf. Ter. *Eun.* 23, 28, *Ad.* 13)." *Pace* recent
statements to the contrary, no other Roman comedian was accused of this crime—but
Menander himself was. The details are preserved in a discussion of *klope*, "theft, plagiarism," in Eusebius's *Praeparatio Evangelica* (10.3.12–13 = Menander K-A test. 76, 81, and
Δεισιδαίμων K-A test. 3):

... καὶ Μένανδρος τῆς ἀρρωστίας ταύτης ἐπλήσθη, ὃν ἠρέμα μὲν ἤλεγξε διὰ τὸ ἄγαν
αὐτὸν φιλεῖν Ἀριστοφάνης ὁ γραμματικὸς ἐν ταῖς *Παραλλήλοις* αὐτοῦ τε καὶ ἀφ' ὧν
ἔκλεψεν ἐκλογαῖς· Λατῖνος δ' ἐξ βιβλίοις, ἃ ἐπέγραψε *Περὶ τῶν οὐκ ἰδίων Μενάνδρου*,
τὸ πλῆθος αὐτοῦ τῶν κλοπῶν ἐξέφηνε·...Κεκίλιος δέ, ὥς τι μέγα πεφωρακώς,

ὅλον δρᾶμα ἐξ ἀρχῆς εἰς τέλος Ἀντιφάνους, τὸν Οἰωνιστήν, μεταγράψαι φησὶ τὸν Μένανδρον εἰς τὸν Δεισιδαίμονα.

This affliction metastasized even in the great Menander. While Aristophanes of Byzantium exposed him gently in his *Parallel Extracts from Him and Those he Plagiarized [eklepsen]* because he was overly fond of him, Latinus devoted six books he titled *Un-Menandrian Elements in Menander* to parading the extent of his plagiarism [*klopai*].... Moreover, it is with the air of one who has detected a massive heist that Caecilius [of Calacte] declares that in his *Superstitious Man* Menander copied [*metagrapsai*] an entire play—Antiphanes's *Augur*—from beginning to end.

Aristophanes's two books were probably collections of parallel diction (not necessarily of comic texts) rather than accusations of plagiarism (see Nesselrath in this volume; the title is surely Porphyry's). But a malicious interpretation of them, like that of Caecilius here (whose reaction resembles that of Luscius in *Eunuchus* 23–24), probably arose almost immediately.[10] This possibility puts Terence's famous quarrel in a new light. If Roman comedians really did "steal" and "contaminate" as a matter of course, as Terence says and as we suspect they did, then his decision to foreground charges of plagiarism and *contaminatio* could serve as a clever means of instantiating what had been, according to contemporary rumor, an aspect of Menander's own artistry.

Did Romans know Aristophanes's books or other parts of Menander's biography? Maybe; Aristophanes was an older contemporary of Plautus (they died within five years of each other), so his works were potentially available, as were the two volumes of "Memories" or "Sayings" (Ἀπομνημονεύματα, Ἀποφθέγματα) "On Menander" (Περὶ Μενάνδρου) written by Lynceus, Menander's younger contemporary (Menander K-A test. 75). And as Boris Dunsch has again aptly put it (Dunsch 1999: 199), our knowledge of the state of ancient literary criticism between the time of Aristotle in the fourth century and the first century in Rome is like a black box: "we cannot see what is going on during that time, but we can see what goes in and what comes out of it."

According to one school of thought, Rome would have had scant knowledge or interest in any of these materials. According to another and perhaps more plausible school, Rome in Terence's time was consciously Hellenizing and would naturally be interested in this kind of material—which (to mention a possible avenue of transmission), along with other Greek cultural treasures, may have flowed into Rome upon Aemilius Paullus's sack of Pella's Royal Library in 168, just two years before the commencement of Terence's career. Dunsch's "black box" metaphor helps us weigh the probabilities. Before Terence, we find Aristophanes's opinions that Menander's comedies had been a nearly perfect mirror of life and were matched in quality only by Homer—opinions that

---

[10]   Nothing is known of this Latinus (1st c. CE?), but Caecilius of Calacte (born c. 50 BCE) was a Greek rhetor of some standing in Augustan Rome; neither he nor this fragment (164 Ofenloch) is to be confused with Caecilius Statius, as in Goldberg 2005: 49 (delete the paragraph) and Manuwald 2011: 249.—It is unsettling to consider that what Lanuvinus and others called plagiarism may be no more than what in §2 above is called Terence's innovative use of literary allusion.

become universal after Terence's death. Before Terence, we find unflattering biographical lore about Menander (professional rivalry, trouble winning crowds, and plagiarism) and, in Rome, a traditional, stylistically unified kind of singsong comedy that continues on beyond Terence's death. In Terence's own comedies, we find a more realistic type of comedy and, in his prologues, rumors analogous to Menander's biography. Finally, before Terence we have in Ennius's *Annals* a bold pose of ignoring recent Latin epic in favor of a return to Homer, who was himself literally reincarnated in Ennius; in Terence, we have a type of comedy that superficially turns away from the Latin tradition and gets back to the basic, mimetic form—as well as (especially in *Eunuchus*) gestures toward Ennian poetics and Alexandrian aesthetics.

Since we simply do not know, the matter must rest there. Yet apart from providing a plausible context for explaining the remarkable originality of Terence, the possibility that the comedian kept one eye on Alexandrian literature may prove a fruitful avenue of future research.

FURTHER READING

Like a stalactite, scholarship on Terence tends to accrete slowly. Despite his long preeminence in the Latin curriculum, modern work remains comparatively scant and it tends to focus on matters external or incidental to his plays as artistic wholes. All six comedies could benefit from the kind of collective scholarly attention that Plautus's plays enjoy; A. S. Gratwick's edition of *Adelphoe* (1999^2) is a monument to the kind of interest his plays will generate if the right questions are asked. J. Barsby's edition of *Eunuchus* (Barsby 1999) is informative on many aspects of Terence's art, and readers new to Terence are particularly advised to begin there.

Beyond works cited in the footnotes above, among recent efforts Kruschwitz (2004) is a helpful introduction to all the plays, while the essays in Boyle (2004) are singularly stimulating. Barsby (2002) explores Terence's relationship to his models, Parker (1996) his audience, Wright (1974) and Karakasis (2005) his language and style, and Moore (2012) his music. As one of the most comprehensive specialist bibliographies in existence, Cupaiuolo (1984) with Cupaiuolo (1992) is an invaluable guide to older work. Auhagen (2001) briefly explores Lucilius's interests in (New) comedy and personal connections with Terence.

BIBLIOGRAPHY

Auhagen, U. 2001. "Lucilius und die Komödie." In *Der Satiriker Lucilius und seine Zeit,* edited by G. Manuwald, 9–23. Munich: C.H. Beck.

Barsby, J., ed. 1999. *Terence Eunuchus*. Cambridge, UK: Cambridge University Press.

——. 2002. "Terence and his Greek Models." In *Due seminari plautini: La tradizione del testo, i modelli,* edited by C. Questa and R. Raffaelli, 249–275. Urbino: QuattroVenti.

Boyle, A. J., ed. 2004. "Rethinking Terence." Special issue, *Ramus* 33, no. 1–2.

Citroni, M. 2006. "Quintilian and the Perception of the System of Poetic Genres in the Flavian Age." In *Flavian Poetry,* edited by R. Nauta, H.-J. van Dam, and J. Smolenaars, 1–19. Leiden: Brill.

Cupaiuolo, G. 1984. *Bibliografia terenziana (1470–1983)*. Naples: Società editrice napoletana.

——. 1992. "Supplementum Terentianum." *BStudLat* 22: 32–57.

Dunsch, B. 1999. "Some Notes on the Understanding of Terence, *Heauton Timorumenos* 6: *Comoedia duplex, argumentum simplex,* and Hellenistic Scholarship." *C&M* 50: 97–131.

Flores, E., ed. 2011. *Livi Andronici Odusia*. Naples: Liguori.

Fontaine, M. 2014. "Dynamics of Appropriation in Roman Comedy: Menander's *Kolax* in Three Roman Receptions (Naevius, Plautus, and Terence's *Eunuchus*)." In *Ancient Comedy and Reception. Essays in Honor of Jeffrey Henderson,* edited by S. D. Olson. Berlin and Boston: de Gruyter.

Goldberg, S. 2005. *Constructing Literature in the Roman Republic: Poetry and its Reception*. Cambridge, UK: Cambridge University Press.

——. 2011. "Roman Comedy Gets Back to Basics." *JRS* 101: 206–221.

Gratwick, A.S. 1982. "Ennius' *Annales*" and "Drama." In *Cambridge History of Classical Literature*. Vol. 2, *Latin Literature*, edited by E. J. Kenney and W. V. Clausen, 60–72 and 77–137. Cambridge, UK: Cambridge University Press.

——, ed. 1993. *Plautus Menaechmi*. Cambridge, UK: Cambridge University Press.

——, ed. 1999. *Terence: The Brothers*. 2nd ed. Warminster, UK: Aris & Phillips.

Hinds, S. 1998. *Allusion and Intertext: Dynamics of Appropriation in Roman Poetry*. Cambridge, UK: Cambridge University Press.

Karakasis, E. 2005. *Terence and the Language of Roman Comedy*. Cambridge, UK: Cambridge University Press.

Kruschwitz, P. 2001. "Verszahlresponsionen bei Terenz." *Philologus* 145: 312–323.

——. 2004. *Terenz*. Hildesheim: Olms.

Leigh, M. 2004. *Comedy and the Rise of Rome*. Oxford: Oxford University Press.

Lowe, D. 2013. "Women Scorned: A New Stichometric Allusion in the *Aeneid*," *CQ* 63: 442–445.

Manuwald, G. 2011. *Roman Republican Theatre*. Cambridge, UK: Cambridge University Press.

Moore, T. J. 2012. *Music in Roman Comedy*. Cambridge, UK: Cambridge University Press.

Nervegna, S. 2013. *Menander in Antiquity: The Contexts of Reception*. Cambridge, UK: Cambridge University Press.

Norwood, G. 1923. *The Art of Terence*. Oxford: Oxford University Press.

Parker, H. 1996. "Plautus vs. Terence: Audience and Popularity Re-examined." *AJPh* 117: 585–617.

Penwill, J. 2004. "The Unlovely Lover of Terence's *Hecyra*." In "Rethinking Terence," edited by A. J. Boyle, special issue, *Ramus* 33.1–2: 130–149.

Pini, L. 2006. "Omero, Menandro e i 'classici' latini negli *Apophoreta* di Marziale: Criteri di selezione e ordinamento." *RFIC* 134: 443–478.

Tyrrell, R. Y. 1883. "Vindiciae Latinae." *Hermathena* 4: 1–17.

Wright, J. 1974. *Dancing in Chains: The Stylistic Unity of the Comoedia Palliata*. Rome: American Academy.

CHAPTER 28

THE LANGUAGE OF THE *PALLIATA*

EVANGELOS KARAKASIS

THE present chapter aims to examine the language of the *fabula palliata*, that is, of Roman comedy in Greek dress, as represented mainly by Plautus and Terence and also by the fragments of various other comic poets, such as Naevius, Caecilius Statius, and Turpilius. Roman comedy exhibits considerable stylistic (Wright 1974) and linguistic unity, with Plautus as its prime stylistic/linguistic model and representative (Karakasis 2005: 145–203) and Terence as a major exception in many respects. In the following pages I elaborate on the linguistic affinity of Plautine language and style with the diction of the other comic poets of the *fabula palliata*, namely Naevius, Caecilius, and Turpilius, and I examine the linguistic behavior of Terence. The evidence from the *palliata* poets not mentioned above (Livius Andronicus, Ennius, Juventius, Trabea, Aquilius, and Atilius) is too scanty to allow concrete conclusions, although the few surviving lines from their comic oeuvre also create the impression of a Plautine linguistic coloring (Karakasis 2005: 197–203). This chapter further aims to examine how the diction of Roman comedy differs from Classical Latin, to appraise its colloquial and literary elements, and, finally, to show how Plautus and Terence use language as a means of linguistic characterization and differentiation.

Before embarking on the linguistic analysis proper, some initial methodological remarks are in order.

From a chronological point of view, Latin is here divided into three periods: Early Latin (EL hereafter), covering the years from the beginnings of the language up to 87 BCE; Classical Latin (CL hereafter), referring to the literary and epigraphic evidence from 87 BCE up to Livy (CE 17), when a tendency for a linguistic standardization and elimination of various linguistic variants is observable; and Post-Classical Latin (PC hereafter), designating the period from CE 17 until the sixth century CE, a long phase during which the linguistic purity and regularity of CL gradually recedes. This category covers both the so-called Silver Latin period (roughly until CE 200) and the Late Latin period (from 200 CE to the sixth century CE).

The second linguistic designation is more qualitative. Colloquial Latin is a linguistic term with a wide semantic range, denoting either the everyday conversational idiom of the upper classes or the speech of the uneducated. However, the term "colloquial" is used in the present chapter in a narrower sense, referring to linguistic elements of a lower sociolectal[1] register, i.e., features that appear in the lower literary genres of EL (comedy, satire), but are avoided by the higher generic formations of the period (epic, tragedy), disappear from the purist language of CL with the exception of lighter genres such as epistolography or satire, but reappear in the PC period, especially in sources of popular Latin such as the language of the freedmen in the *Cena Trimalchionis* of Petronius's *Satyricon* or the authors of the first period of Christian literature. Technical treatises and late grammarians are further sources of popular Latin, while additional evidence is provided by the later evolution of Latin as represented by the Romance languages, which derive from the vernacular and not from CL (Karakasis 2005: 26–28; see also Wahrmann 1908).

Last but not least, it should be understood that many lines cited in this paper are simply *exempli gratia*; examples could be greatly multiplied.

PLAUTUS AND THE COMIC POETS
OF THE *PALLIATA*

First, the linguistic unity of Roman comic language will be examined on the basis of the following linguistic categories: archaism (EL features), colloquialism, and PC linguistic favorites. Stylistic choices marking comic diction will also form a significant part of the following discussion. One should, of course, take into account that the corpus of the *palliata* authors (with the exception of Plautus and Terence) consists of fragments, mainly quoted by ancient grammarians for specific linguistic reasons. Therefore, one cannot achieve certainty as to the total picture of their linguistic tastes. However, despite the reservations one may be justified to express, I believe that the amount of the linguistic information drawn from the fragments is such as to allow us some general remarks regarding the linguistic trends of the *palliata*.

NAEVIUS

The first plays of Naevius (ca. 270–201 BCE) were staged soon after those of Livius Andronicus. The presence of several Romanisms (that is, allusions to Rome), as well

---

[1] This and similar technical terms are glossed at the end of the paper.

as Naevius's preference for titles coined by means of the Latin affix *-aria* (*Carbonaria*, *Testicularia*), bring him close to Plautine style (Fraenkel 1935: 622–640, Wright 1974: 33–59, Karakasis 2005: 187–197).

From a purely linguistic point as well, Naevius is part of the comic linguistic unity. As far as archaisms are concerned, for example, in Naevius one still finds, as in both Caecilius and Plautus, instances of original postvocalic final *-d* after a final long *-e* in pronominal forms, as in *med* (v. 10), although one cannot exclude the possibility that this EL feature may represent the normal stage of the historical evolution of Latin at the time and, accordingly, need not be viewed as a conscious linguistic mannerism. More conscious linguistic unity is attested, on the other hand, by various colloquial choices, common in the language of Naevius and other comic dramatists but avoided in Terence, as, for example, the use of the temporal *quando* in v. 27: *tibi servi multi apud mensam astant; ille ipse astat quando edit.* Second, numerous linguistic choices, without particular EL or colloquial flavor, are found in both Naevius and Plautus and further testify to a comic linguistic unity. Examples include *prime* in the function of a reinforcing particle in v. 1, *habere* used instead of *habitare* in v. 50, and *tam* with the meaning of *tamen* in *ex.inc.* 13–14.

Both Naevius and Plautus are fond of linguistic options that do not have the sanction of later CL speech but instead belong to the EL register, are avoided by the purism of CL, and may crop up in literature again in the PC period. This is the case, for example, in terms of morphology, with non-classical substantives in *-bulum*, for example *rutabulum* in *ex.inc.* 8 (cf. in Plautus *dentifrangibulum, mendicabulum, nucifrangibulum*); adjectives in *-bundus*, such as *cassabundus* in *ex.inc.* 22 (cf. in Plautus *deplorabundus, lixabundus, verberabundus*); and, on the level of lexicon, with the EL/archaizing use of *subservire* in *ex.inc.* 26 in the sense "to behave like a servant" (Plaut. *Men.* 766–767),[2] *efflictim* in place of *vehementer*, and *impense* in vv. 37–38.

CAECILIUS STATIUS

Caecilius (ca. 230/220–168 BCE), exclusively devoted to the *fabula palliata*, is dated in the period between Plautus and Terence. He is considered a forerunner of Terentian comedy, mainly due to his avoidance of distinct Romanisms, as opposed to Plautine comedy and its characteristic Roman flavor, as well as because of his extensive reworking of Menandrian material; as far as diction is concerned, however, Caecilius is demonstrably closer to the Plautine linguistic tradition.

In particular, Caecilius, unlike Terence, is fond of formations that lie outside later CL diction. On the morphological level, in the Caecilian comic corpus one finds several non-classical formations: for example, nouns in *-mentum* for *-men*, as *commemoramentum*

---

[2] A key to abbreviations for the titles of plays of Plautus and Terence cited herein may be found at the end of this paper.

in v. 162, or nouns in -*tas* for CL -*tudo*, -*tia,* and -*edo* synonyms, as *pulchritas* in v. 50 for *pulchritudo*; formations in -*tas* seem, in addition, to constitute a conspicuous idiolectal feature of Caecilian diction. The consonant stem genitive plural -*um* for CL -*ium*, v. 245 *amantum*, also brings Caecilius closer to Plautine linguistic habits. In terms of lexicon, this is further attested by the use of nonclassical forms as *publicitus* in v. 175: *publicitus defendendum est* in place of the CL *publice* in the sense of "publicly."

As far as EL features are concerned, one should distinguish again two main categories of archaisms in the Caecilian corpus: (a) EL features possibly attributable to the historical development of Latin, i.e., linguistic options that were common in the literature before Caecilius but become obsolete after his time and may occur randomly only as intentional archaisms, e.g. *eumpse* for *ipsum* in v. 26, and (b) EL features that Caecilius shares with Plautus as part of their common archaizing register, as attested by the placement of such forms in the middle of the line or at the end of the verse for metrical reasons, e.g., the third plural present indicative *danunt* for *dant* in v. 170, and nonperiphrastic forms of *nolo*, like *noltis* in v. 4.

Caecilius's colloquial register is also in many respects similar to that of Plautus. For instance, on the morphological level, in both Plautus and Caecilius one finds colloquial adjectives in -*tus* fashioned after participles of denominative verbs belonging to the first conjugation, like *atratus* in v. 248; and on the syntactic level, both authors construe the verb *currere* with the supine (Plaut. *Merc.* 857, Caec. *com.* 12; see also Petr. 71.9), while, on the lexical level, several Plautine colloquial lexemes turn up in the Caecilian lines, e.g., the frequentative *mantare* for the simple *manere* in v. 31, and *subpilare* for *rapere* in v. 110. Plautine linguistic favorites that do not have any particular archaic or colloquial character bring Caecilian language closer to Plautine diction; this is the case with *machaera* as equivalent to *ensis* and *gladius* in vv. 69–70, *arguere* for *accusare* in v. 142, and the imprecation formula *ut te di omnes infelicent!* in v. 109, where *infelicere* is used in the sense of *perdere*. Such stylistic choices as the *figura etymologica* (e.g., *sermonem serere* in v. 145) and the Caecilian penchant, in the vein of Plautus, for alliterative combinations of [k] and [m] (Boscherini 1999: 114–115) further demonstrate the stylistic/linguistic Plautine coloring of Caecilius's diction.

TURPILIUS

Sextus Turpilius, whose *floruit* is dated to the second half of the second century BCE, is considered by critics either contemporary or posterior to Terence. As in the case of Caecilius, Turpilius has been thought rather Terentian in his dramatic outlook, because of his penchant for Greek titles, his avoidance of Plautine Romanisms, and his emphasis on the erotic element of his dramas. Be that as it may, from a linguistic point of view Turpilius is also close to Plautine habits.

Thus in several instances, again in contrast to Terence, Turpilius opts for an EL or nonclassical linguistic equivalent. This is attested, e.g., on the morphological level by

EL *-tudo* derivatives (*suavitudo* in vv. 110–111, as a word of the *sermo amatorius*), and in terms of syntax by the accusative object-complement of a periphrasis consisting of an adjective + *esse*, as in v. 67: *scies ea, quae fuisti inscius.* This tendency is evident on the level of lexicon as well, e.g., the form *itiner* for *iter* in v. 208 or the use of *nec* for *non* in v. 25: *nec recte dici.*

The linguistic affinity of Turpilius's diction with Plautine language is also manifested by colloquialisms which are avoided by Terentian speech; both Turpilius and Plautus share, for instance, the colloquial syntax of *utor* with the accusative instead of the ablative (v. 166: *amicos utor primoris viros*), as well as *tuburcinari* in the sense of *raptim manducare, vorare* (v. 2). In the matter of linguistic equivalents without particular EL or colloquial flavor, Turpilius again opts for the Plautine alternative, e.g., the construction of *expars* with the ablative in place of the genitive case (v. 159: *expars malitiis*), *icere* for *percutere* in v. 27, periphrastic syntagms of *iurare* consisting of the past participle of the verb + forms of *esse* (v. 34: *non sum iurata*), and *numero* for *cito* in v. 35.

Terence and his *Eunuchus*—Reworking Comic Material in a Plautine Way

Terence stands closer to CL speech in avoiding most of the nonclassical linguistic options examined above. This tendency seems to account for the commendation that both Cicero and Caesar later expressed for the grace and purity of his diction (Suet. *Vita Ter.* 7; see also Cic. *Att.* 7.3.10: *elegantiam sermonis,* Hor. *Epist.* 2.1.59, and Quint. *I.O.* 10.1.99), which may be viewed as an effort, as opposed to Plautine linguistic verve, to suggest in Roman terms the charm of Menandrian language (cf. also Clackson and Horrocks 2007: 177). This linguistic refinement on the part of Terence is occasionally linked to his adherence to the sophisticated so-called Scipionic circle (see especially Comerci 1994 and Beacham 1991: 46–48 vs. Strasburger 1966, Astin 1967: 294–306, Zetzel 1972, and Parker 1996: 604–607). Caecilius, on the other hand, evidently in the linguistic shadow of Plautus, is censured by Cicero as a *malus auctor Latinitatis* (*Att.* 7.3.10).

Several EL and colloquial formations are not found in free usage within the Terentian corpus but are used instead chiefly as a means of linguistic characterization, i.e., as linguistic markers in the speech of old people and of characters of a lower social status (slaves, pimps, soldiers, courtesans). A significant exception is *Eunuchus.* After the failure of *Hecyra,* Terence seems here to have turned to old and tried comic tricks, including linguistic ones, and to a greater extent than in all his other dramas. Thus in the language of *Eunuchus* one finds the following linguistic features, favored by various comic poets but significantly avoided elsewhere by Terence (Karakasis 2005: 121–143).

In terms of syntax, for example, whereas Terence normally construes *careo* with the ablative case, as commonly in CL (e.g., *Haut.* 137), at *Eun.* 223: *ego illam caream* he opts for an accusative complement, as in both Plautus (*Curc.* 136, *Poen.* 820) and Turpilius (*com.* 33). The same also holds true for the construction of *equidem* with grammatical persons other than the first person singular at *Eun.* 956: *atque equidem* (the reading of the manuscripts) *orante ut ne id faceret Thaide*, a syntactical option also shared by Plautus and Turpilius (Plaut. *Aul.* 138, Turp. *com.* 160). Yet another common Plautine construction, the so-called appositional or epexegetic genitive (*genetivus definitivus*, Plaut. *Pers.* 204), also found in Caec. *com.* 246, appears in Terence at *Eun.* 696: *monstrum hominis*.

This rather traditional linguistic behavior of the *Eunuchus* is also discernible on the level of the lexicon. The common Plautine term of abuse *pessimus* (Plaut. *Cas.* 645 etc., Naev. *com.ex.inc.* 20, Turp. *com.* 26) occurs at *Eun.* 152–153 and 1017, and *tangere* in the usual comic sense "to trick" (= *circumvenire*) in a typical comic deception also occurs at *Eun.* 420–421 (also Plaut. *Pseud.* 120, Turp. *com.* 37). Similarly the common comic phrase *turbam / turbas dare / facere* "to create turmoil" is found at Plaut. *Bacch.* 357, Caec. *com.* 98, Turp. *com.* 200–201, Ter. *Eun.* 653, 744, and the periphrasis *se dare* with erotic connotations appears at *Eun.* 515–516: *ipsa accumbere mecum, mihi sese dare, sermonem quaerere* (cf. also Plaut. *Pseud.* 1277a, Naev. *com.* 75, Trabea *com.* 5R³). Finally, a further typical comic turn, consisting of interrogative syntagms of the type *quid + tibi +* abstract noun in *-tio + est* (either present or implied: Plaut. *Amph.* 519, Caec. *com.* 57–58) appears at *Eun.* 671: *quid huc tibi reditiost? quid vestis mutatio?* Morphological choices further add to the linguistic affinity of *Eunuchus* with the comic tradition of the *palliata*. For example, alternative non-classical ablative endings in *-i* in place of *-e* for third declension nouns, common in the comic tradition (Plaut. *Cas.* 428, Naev. *com.* 100), appear only in *Eunuchus* (*parti* for *parte*, *Eun.* 579).

It is not only through a comparison with the fragments of Naevius, Caecilius, and Turpilius that the traditional comic linguistic character of *Eunuchus* becomes clear. By means of a parallel reading of Plautine drama, we can find several Plautine linguistic and stylistic favorites in *Eunuchus* that Terence normally avoids elsewhere. Examples include:

(a.) terms of abuse: their frequency, wealth of variation, and accumulation is, in many passages, reminiscent of Plautine techniques, e.g., v. 1079: *fatuos est, insulsus tardus*.

(b.) Greek interjections (*papae, apage*) common in Plautus, but not in Terence, who usually prefers primary interjectional forms (*au, eho,* Barsby 1999: 21–22); similarly, the frequency in *Eunuchus* of Greek words in general approximates the percentage of their occurrence in Plautine drama (Maltby 1985: 120).

(c.) the higher proportion of non-CL forms (e.g., *famelicus* in v. 260, *culpare* in the sense of "to blame" in v. 387, *percipere* "to take hold of" in v. 972, *praeut* "in comparison to" in v. 301), which cannot be explained away in terms of the historical evolution of Latin, since in that case a greater number of non-CL forms would have been regular in Terence's earlier dramas (Maltby 1976: 213). Thus this effect should be explained in terms of Terence's artistic/poetic choices.

(d.) common Plautine syntactical choices, elsewhere avoided in the Terentian corpus (e.g., the infinitive of purpose and, what is more, outside the common *it...visere* type, e.g., v. 528: *misit...orare*; temporal *ubi* + the imperfective indicative with an iterative force in v. 405; the construction of verbs of waiting with a complement clause introduced by *si* instead of *dum* in v. 594, *nisi* for *nisi quia* in v. 735.).

(e.) Plautine stylistic markers, i.e., specific words like *mancupium* used of a slave (v. 274) or *occidi* as an interjection of despair (v. 827); formulaic imprecations (*di inmortales* in v. 232); etymological figures, such as *facinus facere* (v. 644); metonymic use of gods for things with which they are associated (v. 732: *sine Cerere et Libero friget Venus*); specific forms of address, such as syntagms consisting of a noun in the vocative case accompanied by a possessive pronoun, in the diction of a slave (v. 834: *era mea*); various formulaic combinations, such as *quid* + the partitive genitive *rerum* + *gero* in v. 923, the conversational greeting formula *unde is?* in v. 305, and the door-knocking formula *heus heus, ecquis hic?* in v. 530; asyndetic lists of synonyms or parallel items (v. 373); and extended use of alliteration and assonance (vv. 297, 556, 613–614, 687–688, 1047); see Barsby 1999: 23–24.

(f.) Plautine imagery, i.e., exuberant and vivid figurative usage, e.g., vv. 712–713: *possumne ego hodie ex te exsculpere verum?* (also Plaut. *Cist.* 541) and the use of *crux* in regard to a prostitute at vv. 383–384 (also Plaut. *Aul.* 522); agricultural imagery (v. 79: *nostri fundi calamitas*, vv. 236, 381); lengthy images, e.g., vv. 103–105, 121 (also, e.g., Plaut. *Aul.* 229–235); and the identification technique in v. 426: *lepus tute's, pulpamentum quaeris?*, consisting, as in Plautus (e.g., *Merc.* 361; also Caec. *com.* 34–35), of the animal object of the identification (*lepus*) (as commonly in Plautus, where persons are often identified with both animals and mythic figures), its subject (*tute*), and the explanation, i.e., the point that the subject and the object of the identification have in common (*pulpamentum quaeris*).

Plautine imagery is comparatively absent from Terence's first plays (*Andria, Hecyra*), where for the most part one finds conventional Greek imagery (teaching similes, sailing and hunting metaphors, the depiction of love as fire or disease, medical descriptions, "burning" with resentment), but makes its presence felt from the *Heauton Timorumenos* onwards, i.e., after the first failure of *Hecyra* in 165 BCE (especially military imagery mostly associated with slaves, cf. Barsby 1999: 24, Karakasis 2005: 131–134, Maltby 2007). The Plautine linguistic coloring of *Eunuchus* suits the Plautine character of the play's context and structure (e.g., farcical humor, long inorganic speeches, incongruous Romanisms, concentration of mythological references), as is regularly assumed for *Eunuchus* in the relevant scholarship.

Terence seems to approximate Plautus and the comic tradition in general in a few other instances as well, namely in some individual scenes where he demonstrably deviates from his original. This supposition has been compellingly suggested by Maltby 1983 for the last scene of Terence's *Heauton Timorumenos* (cf. also, e.g., in terms of derivation/

morphology, the nonclassical and vulgar Plautine *nomen personale* in *-o, -onis, gerro* in v. 1033: Wahrmann 1908: 78–79, and, on the lexical level, the use of *conciere* in the sense "stir up, provoke" in v. 970). Such "Plautine" usage appears mainly in the so-called Sannio scene in the *Adelphoe* (vv. 155–208), where the poet incorporates material from Diphilus's *Synapothneskontes* into a narrative primarily fashioned after Menander's *Adelphoi II*. Here one finds several lexical choices common in Plautus, such as the distinctively Plautine terms of abuse *periurus* (v. 189) and *scelestus* (v. 159, also found in *Eunuchus* [v. 71, etc.] and in the last scene of *Heauton Timorumenos* [v. 970]). We also find syntactical preferences reminiscent of Plautus, such as *quamquam* introducing an adversative clause without a preceding or following correlative (vv. 159, 205; also Plaut. *Asin.* 710, Caec. *com.* 21).

TERENCE AND LINGUISTIC COLLOQUIALISM

From the data reported above, it is evident that Terence keeps his distance from the language of the rest of the *palliata* playwrights. He does not always adopt their EL register; he generally avoids linguistic features not having the sanction of CL, thus foreshadowing later CL linguistic developments; in several instances he shuns idiolectal and stylistic options of a Plautine character; and last but not least, he does not incorporate in his diction several of the colloquial features that other comic authors of the *palliata* share with Plautus.

As far as colloquialism is concerned, Terence is quite reserved in comparison to Plautus (Baldi 2002: 228–231), and this, along with his avoidance of nonclassical doublets (see above), may also account for his characterization as *puri sermonis amator*.[3] Thus in the Terentian corpus very few colloquial linguistic options are to be found, in the sense described in the methodological introduction (Karakasis 2005: 21–43); colloquialism is evident chiefly on the level of production/derivation (substantives in *-arius* (*palmarium, cetarius, Eun.* 930, 257), *-tor / -trix* (*extortor, advorsatrix, Phorm.* 374, *Haut.* 1007), adjectives in *-inus* (*mustelinus, Eun.* 689) and *-osus* (*cadaverosus, Hec.* 441), verbs in *-issare* (*patrissare, Ad.* 564), verbs compounded with *ad-* and *cum-* (*adposcere, conmitigari, Haut.* 838, *Eun.* 1028), adverbs in *-im* (*unciatim, Phorm.* 43), and various diminutive and frequentative formations (*tardiusculus, commetare, Haut.* 515, *Haut.* 444)). Colloquialisms appear on the level of the lexicon as well, such as the use of *quidam* as a contemptuous reference to a person (*Eun.* 483) or *emungere* in the sense "to cheat" (*Phorm.* 682). Colloquial, too, is the syntax of the autonomous genitive at *Phorm.* 709–710: *ante brumam autem novi negoti incipere* (Löfstedt 1911: 108–109). These relatively limited colloquial features do not occur in the Terentian corpus in free use, but

---

[3] See also Müller 2007, which, however, argues that *purus sermo* refers to Terence's avoidance of Hellenisms and neologisms.

are instead employed with the particular stylistic aim of imparting a colloquial touch to the speech of low characters or to the rustic *senes* of Terentian comedy, namely Chremes and Demea of *Heauton Timorumenos* and *Adelphoe* respectively.

EL FEATURES

As already intimated, the language of Plautus (ca. 254–184 BCE) and Terence (ca. 195–159 BCE), to focus now on the two most important representatives of Roman comedy, represents an early stage of the historical evolution of Latin. As a result, both authors employ EL features, although the latter in several aspects foreshadows later CL linguistic trends and is accordingly more reserved in the use, e.g., of various archaic metaplastic forms, perfects of the *tetuli* type, and optative remainders (Palmer 1954: 89). Apart from those already observed above, in the comic texts one thus finds the following characteristic archaic linguistic options:

(a) Phonology

1) *-u* has not yet replaced *-o* in many inflectional endings; thus one finds, for instance, *-os / -om* endings instead of the common CL *-us / -um* equivalents, when another *u* (either vocalic or consonantal) precedes the *u* of the suffix (*mortuos*, Plaut. *Most.* 233, *servos*, Ter. *Eun.* 571); this is also the case with the verbal termination *-unt* when preceded by *v* or *u* (*ruont*, Plaut. *Truc.* 305, *proruont*, Ter. *Eun.* 599). *U* is also found instead of *i* before or after labials (*pessumus*, Plaut. *Most.* 192, Ter. *Haut.* 437); *vo* appears instead of *ve* (*vostram*, Plaut. *Most.* 77, Ter. *Andr.* 716). *E* has not taken over from *u* in the case of gerunds and gerundives (*faciundum*, Plaut. *Amph.* 891, Ter. *Eun.* 97).

2) The spelling of various words is different from CL; *c*, for example, is spelled as *qu*; thus *quor = cur, quoius = cuius, quoi = cui, quom = cum* (e.g., Plaut. *Amph.* 581, Ter. *Eun.* 87).

(b) Morphology

1) Noun, adjective, and pronoun declension: first declension singular genitive by-forms in *-ai* (*familiai*, Plaut. *Amph.* 359; *Cliniai*, Ter. *Haut.* 515); second plural genitive of the second declension in *-um* instead of *-orum* (*liberum*, Plaut. *Most.* 120; *amicum*, Ter. *Haut.* 24); vocative in *-e* for syncopated nouns of the second declension (*puere*, Plaut. *Asin.* 382, Ter. *Hec.* 719); *-uis* or *-i* singular genitive for fourth declension nouns (*tumulti*, Plaut. *Cas.* 649; *anuis*, Ter. *Haut.* 287); first declension endings in the genitive and dative singular for pronouns normally ending in *-ius*; *-i* in CL (*solae*, feminine dative at Plaut. *Mil.* 356, Ter. *Eun.* 1004); change of declension (*gnaruris* for *gnarus*, Plaut. *Most.* 100; *gracilae* for *graciles*,

Ter. *Eun.* 314); archaic pronoun forms (*tis* for *tui*, Plaut. *Mil.* 1033; *nostrorum* for *nostri*, Plaut. *Poen.* 540; *vostrarum* for *vestri*, Plaut. *Stich.* 141; *ipsus* for *ipse*, Plaut. *Men.* 100, Ter. *Eun.* 546; "internally inflected forms" of the pronoun *ipse* (*eumpse, eampse*, Plaut. *Truc.* 133; *ibus* for *eis*, Plaut. *Mil.* 74; the dative *eae* for *ei*, Plaut. *Mil.* 348); an ablative form *qui* of the relative and the interrogative pronoun (Plaut. *Stich.* 61, Ter. *Ad.* 179; the ablative form *aliqui* for the indefinite pronoun, Plaut. *Aul.* 24), addition of the affix *-ce / -c* at the end of several demonstrative pronouns (*hosce* vs. *hos*, Plaut. *Asin.* 737; *istuc* vs. *istud*, Ter. *Ad.* 133).

2) Verbal morphology: future and subjunctive sigmatic forms (*faxo*, Plaut. *Most.* 68, Ter. *Andr.* 854; *intrassis*, Plaut. *Men.* 416); change of conjugation (*emoriri* for *emori*, Plaut. *Pseud.* 1222, Ter. *Eun.* 432); *-ibam, -ibo* imperfect and future forms respectively, for verbs of the fourth conjugation (*scibat* for *sciebat*, Plaut. *Amph.* 22; *scibo* for *sciam*, Ter. *Ad.* 361[4]); perfect passive forms of impersonal verbs (*miseritum est*, Plaut. *Trin.* 430, Ter. *Phorm.* 99); archaic subjunctive forms (*creduas* for *credas*, Plaut. *Bacch.* 476; *fuat*, Ter. *Hec.* 610 with Foucher 2005; *foret*, Plaut. *Amph.* 21; *siet*, Ter. *Andr.* 234); optative forms (*duim, perduim*, Plaut. *Aul.* 672, Ter. *Phorm.* 713); archaic stems (the present stem *coepio*, Plaut. *Men.* 960; *coeperet*, Ter. *Ad.* 397); perfect reduplicated forms (*tetuli*, Plaut. *Amph.* 716, Ter. *Andr.* 832); imperative forms of *facere, ducere, dicere*, and *ferre* without deletion of the final *-e* (e.g., *face*, Plaut. *Asin.* 605); unsyncopated forms (*mavolo* for *malo*, Plaut. *Asin.* 835, Ter. *Hec.* 540); active forms for CL deponent formations (*venero*, Plaut. *Bacch.* 173); present passive or deponent infinitives in *-ier* (*utier*, Plaut. *Cas.* 220; *suspicarier*, Ter. *Hec.* 827).

(c) Syntax

Loose usage of the oblique cases (*careo* + accusative complements, Plaut. *Curc.* 136; dative of the gerundive in final function, Ter. *Hec.* 821); extensive use of the partitive genitive (Plaut. *Most.* 904: *quid...mercimoni*, Ter. *Eun.* 200); free use of the indicative (causal *nunc cum* clauses with the indicative, Ter. *Ad.* 737–738); archaic clause / infinitive complement syntagms (*usus est* + *ut* subject clause, Plaut. *Epid.* 167; *scilicet* + infinitive, Ter. *Haut.* 358–359); *ne* + present imperative combinations, used in comedy with inhibitive force (Ter. *Haut.* 83–84, de Melo 2011a: 330–331), *quisque* as the introductory pronoun of generalizing relative sentences (Plaut. *Capt.* 796–798, de Melo 2011a: 332–333).

(d) Lexicon

Various EL words or phrases, like *occipere* in the sense "to begin," *incipere* (Plaut. *Pseud.* 919, Ter. *Eun.* 22), the syntagm *minime gentium* (Plaut. *Poen.* 690, Ter. *Phorm.*

---

[4] Although not particularly productive with verbs of the third and fourth conjugation, the innovative future form in *-ibo* is very common with *scio* in both Plautus and Terence (de Melo 2009).

1033), and syntagms of *ecce* + pronoun (*eccillam*, Plaut. *Aul.* 781). Also found is *indaudio* for *inaudio* in Plautus (*Capt.* 30, *Mil.* 211).

(e) Meter

EL often retains a long final closed syllable where in CL a vowel would be scanned short, especially with (a) the third person singular when the second person singular ends in a long vowel (*amāt*, Plaut. *Cas.* 49), (b) instances of the third singular perfect indicative (*adiīt*, Plaut. *Cas.* 696), (c) various forms ending in -*s*, -*ēs* (Plaut. *Cas.* 615), and (d) endings in -*ar*, -*er*, -*or*, -*al* (Questa 1967: 9–11, MacCary and Willcock 1976: 213).

Not all of the features listed above are necessarily to be attributed to the historic evolution of Latin; as noted above, some were apparently considered obsolete already in the time of Plautus or Terence. Their productivity, the contextual settings in which the features in question appear, or their position within the line confirm their old-fashioned linguistic character. For example, lexical items bearing the archaic *d* (e.g., *antidhac*, Plaut. *Amph.* 711), subjunctive forms such as *fuam* or *siem*, optative formations, etymologically transitional forms such as *mavolo* for *malo* (from *magis volo*), perfect endings in -*ere* for -*erunt* (*pertulere*, Plaut. *Amph.* 216), and medio-passive infinitives in -*ier* tend to occur chiefly at the end of the line or half-line and, therefore, evidently have an archaic ring already in the Plautine corpus. On the other hand, old genitive forms in -*ai* found in portions of Plautine comedy that suggest parody (*Aul.* 295, *Mil.* 103, Coleman 1999: 42, Meiser 2002: 130) and restricted in Terence to the archaizing diction of *senes* (Ter. *Andr.* 439, *Haut.* 515) also seem to have acquired an archaic coloring already from the early second century BCE. The same holds true for the genitive plural -*um* for -*orum*, sigmatic infinitives like *impetrassere* at Plaut. *Aul.* 687, the form *tis* for the genitive of the second person personal pronoun, coupling by means of *que...que* (Plaut. *Men.* 590, Gratwick 1993: 196–197), and prevocalic pronoun forms of the type *med*, *ted* (Gerschner 2002, de Melo 2007, de Melo 2011: lxx–lxxi, Fraenkel 2007: 281).

It is also quite clear that several EL features in free use in Plautus begin to have an old-fashioned ring in Terence. In the Terentian corpus, they appear randomly, chiefly either in his first plays, where his linguistic purism seems to be less strict than in his later dramas (*medicor* for *medeor* at Ter. *Andr.* 831; Maltby 1976: 235–236 and Maltby 1979: 139 and n. 30, Karakasis 2005: 45 and n. 1), or are used to invest older characters with a linguistic antiquarianism. Examples on the level of morphology include the locative singular *luci* for *luce* (Ter. *Ad.* 841); on the level of syntax, syntagms consisting of *eo* + accusative supine functioning as a periphrastic future with a weak final function (*percontatum ibo*, Ter. *Phorm.* 462); the construction of temporal *ut* with the perfect tense with the meaning "since" (Ter. *Hec.* 751–752); of lexicon: *salvos si(e)s* for *salve* as a greeting formula (Ter. *Andr.* 906; Karakasis 2005: 44–61). In Terentian comedy, archaizing second singular passive forms in -*re* are found more frequently than their -*ris* equivalents (*irascere*, Ter. *Ad.* 136; Barsby 1999: 122). Several Plautine EL linguistic features, however, such as EL forms of the pronoun *is, ea, id*, and sigmatic infinitives, disappear in the Terentian comic corpus entirely (see above).

ROMAN COMEDY—A LITERARY LANGUAGE

Although the language of Roman comedy does reflect the spoken Latin of the period to a point, comic diction should never be considered a simple transcription of spoken Latin. All comic poets construct a literary language, a *Kunstsprache* (Happ 1967; Bagordo 2001a; Foucher 2003: 28), and thus frequently make use of various registers quite distant from everyday language, chiefly epic and tragic diction (often in paratragic settings, e.g., the "running slave" monologues in Plaut. *Curc.* 280–298; de Melo 2011: lxxxv), the standardized diction of the official and ritual language, and legalistic allusions. In Plautus, these features are mostly observable in recitative verse and polymetric cantica (Haffter 1934; Happ 1967).

Plautus and Terence both make free use of various linguistic options whose elevated register is attested by their frequency in highly stylized legalistic and administrative diction or in the *genus grande* of the period. *Quadrupes* "steed," for example, is found in Roman tragedy (Naev. *trag.* 25, Enn. *trag.* 157) but occurs in Plautus only in a parodic context (the paratragic praetor's edict at *Capt.* 814) and beside the equally elevated future imperative verb *constringito* in Ter. *Andr.* 865. Various composite expressions are also of a linguistically dignified character; *extra aedis* vs. *extra portam* is found in tragedy (Enn. *trag.* 238) and paratragic comic scenarios (Pompon. *atel.* 33). When the syntagm appears at Ter. *Hec.* 563 beside the equally archaic and elevated combination of *volo* with the perfect for the present infinitive (Allardice 1929: 85), *interdico ne extulisse extra aedis puerum usquam velis*, it enhances the dignified coloring of the passage. This sense of "linguistic dignity" is supported on the morphological level by the use of various elevated compounds, mainly of the type *damni-ficus, falsi-dicus* (Plaut. *Cist.* 728; see also a mock official/tragic setting at Plaut. *Asin.* 33–35; Maltby 1976: 207), and by such stylistic options as the collocation *dicam* + accusative + infinitive syntagms, which are also found in tragedy (Enn. *trag.* 300), in paratragic or mock official settings (Plaut. *Curc.* 1), and in the speech of high characters of Terentian comedy (the *matrona* Myrrina at *Hec.* 519–520; Collart 1979: 25, Jocelyn 1967: 423).

Further significant elevated linguistic features employed in the diction of Roman comedy, often drawn from legal, official, and sacral language (see especially Jocelyn 1967: 166, 172, 175, 195, 199, 215–216, 220, 226, 246, 249, 268, 278, 287, 298, 312–313, 378, 401), include:

a. In terms of morphology: adjectives in *-icus*, especially at the end of the line (*civicus*, Plaut. *Bacch.* 24); abstract substantives in *-tus* (*aspectus*, Plaut. *Epid.* 572); compounds in *-potens*, more frequently in prayers and in paratragic settings (Plaut. *Poen.* 275).
b. In terms of syntax: abstract nouns governing transitive verbs (Plaut. *Amph.* 1079); *si quis / qui velit / volet* + imperative forms of the third person (Plaut. *Poen.* 210–211); accumulation of *si* clauses securing a legal stylistic *abundantia* (Plaut. *Amph.* 67–74); various syntagms imitating official diction (e.g., *temperare* + infinitive at

Plaut. *Poen.* 22, patterned after the magistrates' diction); a disproportionately high use of the ablative absolute, especially in a primarily temporal syntactic function, in parody of a general's account of his accomplishments and in battle reports, (Plaut. *Amph.* 188–189).

c. In terms of lexicon: *quo* forms used with regard to persons (*era quo me misit, ad patrem, non est domi,* Plaut. *Merc.* 803); *quis* employed in a relative function (*supplici sibi sumat quid volt ipse ob hanc iniuriam,* Plaut. *Merc.* 991); various legal and administrative formulas such as *facessere* (Plaut. *Rud.* 1061–1062, Ter. *Phorm.* 635), the senatorial *hic ordo* (Plaut. *Cist.* 22–24), *ferre opem* in place of *ferre auxilium* (Plaut. *Rud.* 617, Ter. *Andr.* 473, *Ad.* 487); *paucis* in the sense of "in a few words" instead of semantically equivalent *pauca / ad pauca* syntagms (Ter. *Eun.* 1067–1068, Maltby 1976: 242–243), *pedem efferre* for *domo abire* (Plaut. *Bacch.* 423, Ter. *Andr.* 808, beside the archaic and elevated reduplicated perfect *tetulissem*).

d. In terms of style in general: relative clauses repeating the preceding noun (Plaut. *Aul.* 561, Ter. *Hec.* 10–11); the disjunction of *per* from its object in forms of supplication (*per hanc te dexteram [oro],* Ter. *Andr.* 289); abundant use of military language, especially by the *servus callidus* (e.g., Plaut. *Bacch.* 709–713); syntagms consisting of the perfect or the present along with the future of the same verb in parataxis within a line (*quiquomque ubi sunt, qui fuerunt quique futuri sunt,* Plaut. *Bacch.* 1087); anaphora of *o* combined with appeals in the vocative (Plaut. *Bacch.* 933); *-ve* linking questions (*quid pollent quidve possunt?,* Plaut. *Asin.* 636); phrases where a second part reiterates the first in a longer form (*tuae superesse vitae sospitem et superstitem,* Plaut. *Asin.* 16–17); instances of "asyndeton bimembre" (*propere celeriter,* Plaut. *Rud.* 1323).

This literary style is also achieved through various sound effects, especially alliteration and assonance, which are native to the Italic dialects and EL in particular (e.g., Plaut. *Cas.* 621–626, *Pseud.* 70, Ter. *Eun.* 1–45; Palmer 1954: 86); wordplay (see, for example, the pun on *ventum* at Plaut. *Curc.* 314–317, used in 314 as the past participle of *venire,* whereas in 317 the form is the accusative of the noun *ventus,* Duckworth 1952: 353); *figura etymologica* (*donis donatus,* Plaut. *Amph.* 137; *solide solum gavisurum gaudia,* Ter. *Andr.* 964), other figures of speech, such as hyperbaton (Plaut. *Amph.* 728, Ter. *Ad.* 170), polyptoton (Plaut. *Amph.* 221), and anaphora (*nil ornati, nil tumulti,* Ter. *Andr.* 365), rhetorical embellishment of other types (e.g., the *reprehensio* at Plaut. *Amph.* 384 and the forensic oratorical style of the Terentian prologues in particular; see, e.g., Goldberg 1986: 31–60); alliterative triplets (*retines, revocas, rogitas,* Plaut. *Men.* 114; *Pseud.* 64). Inflated style and stylized diction through parallel cola or phrases, congeries, and synonyms (*vos amo, vos volo, vos peto atque opsecro,* Plaut. *Curc.* 148) are usually found in Plautus in the longer lines rather than the senarii, which approximate everyday language.[5] Plautus's

---

[5] Bagordo 2007, however, argues that the longer and shorter lines of the Terentian comic corpus are not substantially different.

literary and stylistic aspirations can be seen in various comic formations; these include Greco-Latin hybrids (*plagipatidas*, Plaut. *Capt.* 472), noun and pronoun superlative forms (*patruissume*, Plaut. *Poen.* 1197, *ipsissumus*, Plaut. *Trin.* 988), and monstrously unnatural compounds (*turpilucricupidum*, Plaut. *Trin.* 100); see Duckworth 1952: 345–346. What is more, as part of his comic linguistic arsenal, Plautus not only coins words but also attributes new semantic content to extant ones, as is the case, for example, with *oppugnare* at *Cas.* 412, where the verb occurs in the sense of "to hit with the fist" (de Melo 2011: l). Imitation of Greek syntax, as in *daturus dixit* (Plaut. *Asin.* 633–634; de Melo 2011: lxxx–lxxxi, de Melo 2011a, 335–336), where the nominative complement is found for the regular accusative, is a further conscious artistic choice, lending authenticity to the Greek characters who use it.

ROMAN COMEDY AND SPOKEN LATIN

Despite being a *Kunstsprache* in the sense described above, Roman comedy is full of markers of everyday diction, although Terentian comedy is, from this aspect as well, more reserved than Plautine drama. Everyday linguistic features include various interjections and interjectional expressions, repetition (Plaut. *Cas.* 326–328, Ter. *Eun.* 193–195), redundancy (free and loose usage of the personal and the demonstrative pronouns (Ter. *Andr.* 113), double comparatives and negatives (Plaut. *Capt.* 644, Ter. *Eun.* 147–148), extensive pleonasm (*amplius…plus*, Plaut. *Aul.* 420; *ante oculos coram*, Ter. *Eun.* 794), high frequency of terms of abuse or slang in general (Plaut. *Bacch.* 1088, *Pseud.* 360–366, Ter. *Eun.* 643–648), various standardized wish and curse formulas (*ita vivam, ne vivam*), frequent set questions, often preceding other interrogative phrases in order to catch the attention of the listener, and answers (e.g., *quid?, quid ais?, quid istic?, ita, non*), as well as set words and phrases; these include a range of polite modifiers such as *obsecro* and *sis*, syntagms such as *sex septem* and *nil supra*, and various imperative forms such as *abi* at Ter. *Eun.* 221 (Barsby 1999: 123). A preference for lengthened forms (often through suffixation) or a more emphatic equivalent (often in a figurative sense) is a further marker of the spoken language; examples include *nullus* for *non* (Plaut. *Asin.* 408, Ter. *Eun.* 216), *fabulor* for *dico* (Plaut. *Truc.* 830, Ter. *Phorm.* 654), compounded forms in lieu of their single equivalents, especially with the prefix *con-* (*comedo*, Plaut. *Men.* 521, Ter. *Haut.* 255), frequentatives instead of simple verbs (*fugitare*, Plaut. *Asin.* 485, Ter. *Phorm.* 835), diminutives for simplex nondiminutive formations, either in an affectionate function or to denote contempt (Plaut. *Pseud.* 64–68; *mi animule*, Plaut. *Cas.* 134; *servolo*, Plaut. *Amph.* 987; de Melo 2011 : lxxiii), and periphrastic formations (*audiens sum*, Plaut. *Amph.* 989).

One frequently finds morphological contraction (*sis* for *si vis*, Plaut. *Amph.* 286, Ter. *Eun.* 311; *dixis* for *dixeris*, Plaut. *Aul.* 744) as well as "allegro," i.e., phonetically reduced formations, in general (*sicin*, Plaut. *Epid.* 627; Clackson and Horrocks 2007: 176, 179). Various features within the realm of syntax convey the impression of spontaneous conversational diction. These include parataxis; coordination or asyndeton instead of subordination (*vir ab[i]erit faxo domo*, Plaut. *Cas.* 484; *interea fiet aliquid, spero*, Ter. *Andr.* 314: *accepi: acceptam servabo*, 298; Blänsdorf 1967: 6–41); anacoluthon (Plaut. *Cas.* 39–41, Ter. *Hec.* 286); contamination and loose syntax in general, resulting from the spontaneity of conversational diction (Plaut. *Bacch.* 461, Ter. *Andr.* 258–259); informal word order, especially regarding verb position (Clackson and Horrocks 2007: 176); proleptic syntagms (accusative, Plaut. *Amph.* 398: *tu me vivos hodie numquam facies quin sim Sosia*, Ter. *Andr.* 169–170); exclamations (accusative and nominative forms, Plaut. *Cas.* 842–843: *o corpusculum malacum!*; exclamatory infinitive, Plaut. *Cas.* 89: *non mihi licere*); elliptical expressions (Plaut. *Rud.* 849: *vicinus Veneris = vicinus fani Veneris*; Ter. *Andr.* 29: *paucis te volo*), abbreviated, broken, and disconnected phrases (Ter. *Andr.* 344: *quis homost, qui me…?*); and parenthetical expressions (Plaut. *Amph.* 94: *hanc fabulam, inquam, hic Iuppiter hodie ipse aget*, Ter. *Ad.* 190); all are thoroughly examined by J. B. Hofmann in his seminal *Lateinische Umgangssprache* (Hofmann 1951). A further characteristic of an informal everyday idiom is interruption, as speakers are not allowed to complete their utterances, broken by various comments of their interlocutors; in terms of a lively repartee with short phrases and ellipsis, however, it is Terence who excels (Ter. *Andr.* 359–366), whereas Plautus makes use of this stylistic device less often (Barsby 2001: 20, de Melo 2011: lxxii).

LINGUISTIC CHARACTERIZATION

In both Plautus and Terence, language differs according to the gender and social status of the speaker. It has long been compellingly argued that female diction differs from male language (cf. especially Adams 1984). Characteristic markers include (a) interjections and oaths; for example, *ecastor* and *au* appear only in female speech, whereas (*me*) *hercle* and *ei* are favored by men, while oaths that Plautus's women swear by Hercules suggest their assertiveness (*Cist.* 52; Stockert 2004: 367–368). Other markers characteristic of female speech include (b) polite modifiers, such as *amabo, amo* in formulaic expressions denoting gratitude vs. the parenthetic *quaeso* and intensive modifiers such as *sis, sodes, age* occurring in male language; (c) diminutive formations; (d) addressing of other characters by a title (*vir, gnatus*) in conjunction with the vocative of *meus*; (e) self-pitying formulations (e.g., *misera*); and (f) language of affection, compliments, and forms of address consisting in *mi/mea* + vocative. All of these markers occur either exclusively or with disproportionate frequency in female diction. What is more, they often appear in clusters (e.g., Ter. *Eun.* 663–667).

A second well-established linguistic distinction has to do with the way language is used by characters belonging to different social registers. In both Plautus and Terence, low characters (slaves, parasites, soldiers, pimps) use Greek words (often of a technical character) more frequently than other comic characters do (see especially Maltby 1985, Maltby 1995). The large number of Greek and Grecizing words and expressions (e.g., verbs based on the common Greek verbal affix -ίζω, -*issare*, such as *patrissare* and *graecissare*) indicates that Greek was largely understood by the contemporary Roman audience. Moreover, Plautus's Greek has occasionally a Doric dialectal ring, probably reflecting the kind of Greek that was spoken in parts of Italy (de Melo 2011: lxix–lxx, lxxvi–lxxxiii; de Melo 2011a: 337). Finally, in both Plautus and Terence language patently depends on the emotional state of a comic character; as Donatus rightly observes (ad *Eun.* 65) for example, animated characters may have recourse to the figure of aposiopesis.

Various studies have demonstrated Plautus's ability to differentiate characters or character types by assigning linguistic idiolectal habits to them. In *Menaechmi*, for example, the twin brothers are distinguished by contrasting vocabulary (Leach 1969); in *Bacchides*, the trickster slave Chrysalus stands out by means of his colorful and colloquial diction (Karakasis 2003); in *Stichus*, the leading sister is prominent for her moral diction (Arnott 1972); in *Poenulus*, Punic (or perhaps pseudo-Punic) aims to characterize Hanno's speech (Petersmann 1995: 132). In *Aulularia*, Euclio likes asyndetic combinations, while Staphyla frequently avails herself of periphrasis (Stockert 1982; see also Hofmann 1977 on greetings as a means of linguistic characterization in *Aulularia*). Rustic spellings or misspellings may also constitute Plautine means of linguistic characterization; for example, *billam* (for *villam*) in the Palatine manuscripts at *Truc.* 648 may reflect the speech of the rustic Strabax (Petersmann 1996–1997, Danese 2006, Fontaine 2010: 29–30), while the misspellings of *b* as *v* at Plaut. *Mil.* 832–860 may suggest the slurred speech of an inebriated slave (Stadter 1968). The vulgar formation *pappo* "to eat" is used by the slave Epidicus (Plaut. *Epid.* 727; Petersmann and Petersmann 2003: 114). Low characters also display a preference for construing an accusative of direction with verbs not denoting motion (*in mentem fuit* for *in mente fuit* or *in mentem venit*; Petersmann 2002–2003: 99–100), while in the speech of old men and women of a higher social status we occasionally find archaizing features (Euclio in *Aulularia*, Panegyris and Pamphila in *Stichus*; Petersmann and Petersmann 2003: 110–111). Parasites are fond of animal comparisons and plays on proper names (Maltby 1999); Plautine soldiers are characterized by pompous words, hyperboles, neologisms, and verbal aggression, such as insults (Filoche 2007); Plautus's *uxores pudicae* are linguistically marked by a restrained use of the imperative (Schauwecker 2002).

However, evidence has now accumulated that linguistic differentiation is more subtle and systematic within the Terentian comic corpus than in Plautus. Apart from female linguistic markers and the penchant of lower characters for Greek words, in Terentian diction one may also point out the following regularities:

1. EL features regularly occur in the speech of old characters, i.e., *senes* and *matronae* as well as aged slaves, such as Syrus in *Adelphoe*.
2. The speech of old characters is also characterized by long-windedness, as manifested by pleonastic expressions and accumulated synonyms.
3. Colloquialisms mark the speech of the "lower" characters as well as of the rustic *senes*, i.e., the ones living in the countryside, such as Chremes in *Heauton Timorumenos*.

4. Syntactic Hellenisms also concentrate in the language of low and rustic characters.

5. Elevated linguistic features, drawn from the legal, ritual, or administrative register as well as from epic and tragedy, are normally found in the speech of "higher" characters, i.e., *senes, matronae*, and *adulescentes*.

6. Idiolectal features characterize the speech of specific characters or character types; thus old characters, for instance, use *repente*, the expression *infitias ire*, and *si* in an adversative function, and the old man Chremes of *Heauton Timorumenos* frequently uses *pati* in the sense of *sinere, permittere*, as well as *etsi* + indicative syntagms.

7. A binary linguistic opposition is developed between the rustic *senex* Demea and his urban brother Micio in *Adelphoe* and similarly between Chremes, living in the countryside, and Menedemus, recently having moved to the *rus* as part of his self-punishment, in *Heauton Timorumenos*. Demea and Chremes intersperse their diction with several EL and colloquial features, whereas Micio in *Adelphoe* (but not Menedemus in *Heauton Timorumenos*) resorts to elevated linguistic options.

8. Figurative language may also occasionally function as a means of linguistic characterization (Maltby 2007). With the exception of *Andria*, it is normally "low" characters who make greatest use of figurative speech. Imagery may also be used in instances of binary linguistic differentiation, i.e., between two characters belonging to the same character type. Thus Laches in *Hecyra* makes use of metaphorical diction more often than Phidippus, Demea is more colorful than his counterpart Micio in *Adelphoe*, and this is also the case with pairs of comic *adulescentes*; for example, Aeschinus resorts to imagery more frequently than Ctesipho in *Adelphoe*, whereas Chaerea is more colorful than his foil, Phaedria, in *Eunuchus*.

9. There is a gradual development in Terentian techniques of linguistic characterization, with *Adelphoe* standing supreme. Linguistic differentiation by means of EL features and long-winded expressions is absent from both *Andria* and *Eunuchus*. Pleonasm and accumulated synonyms function as stylistic means of differentiation chiefly in the senarii; however, in other metrical forms pleonasms and synonyms are again commoner in the language of old people in *Hecyra, Phormio*, and *Adelphoe*.

10. It is not only the speaker but also the addressee who regulates the distribution of various linguistic features. This means that linguistic and stylistic options associated with the diction of a particular character or character type, as attested by the higher ratios that these features display in their speech, may occasionally occur as random instances in the speech of other characters, but only when they engage in a dialogue with those characters showing a particular penchant for the linguistic option in question. Furthermore, several characters respond, from a linguistic point of view as well, according to the identity of their interlocutor. Thais, for example, the *meretrix* of *Eunuchus*, addresses

Phaedria, her "official" lover, by means of *mi* + vocative syntagms (86, 95, 144, 190), whereas other *adulescentes* are invoked by her through a plain vocative (751, 765, 880, 893).

Although occasionally misinterpreted, several of these patterns were already observed by Terence's scholiast, Donatus (Reich 1933). The ancient grammarian points out the linguistic idiosyncrasy of female speech (ad *Hec.* 824, ad *Ad.* 291), the long-windedness of senile diction (ad *Ad.* 959), the *vitiosa locutio* of some low characters (ad *Phorm.* 249), the penchant of some comic figures for a particular linguistic usage (ad *Eun.* 95), as well as the linguistic differentiation according to both the demands of the contextual setting (ad *Eun.* 65) and the status of the addressee (ad *Hec.* 753). Similar linguistic techniques have been traced by recent scholarship in the language of Menander as well (namely, male vs. female speech; idiolectal options associated with the diction of specific characters; binary linguistic opposition, such as the one developed between the slaves Davus and Syrus in *Epitrepontes*; and the dependence of language upon the contextual setting, cf. Arnott 1995); and this Menandrian linguistic usage may also account to some extent for the patterns of linguistic characterization encountered within the Terentian comic corpus, since Menandrian comedies function as the main model for four of the six comedies of Terence.

FURTHER READING

Palmer 1954 is a fine introduction to the language of both Plautus and Terence; it focuses on the colloquial and EL character of the comic diction, but also elaborates on its artificial linguistic character. For a discussion of spoken Latin in Terentian comedy in particular, one should consult Bagordo 2001 and for the EL verbal forms, see recently de Melo 2007, whereas Karakasis 2005 gives the relevant information for the linguistic unity of Roman comedy, the patterns of linguistic characterization in Terence, and the linguistic affinity that Terence occasionally shows with Plautine diction. For the Plautine linguistic character of the last act of Terence's *Heauton Timorumenos*, Maltby 1983 is the standard work, whereas Maltby 1995 and Maltby 1985 cover the distribution of Greek words in Plautus and Terence respectively. Wright 1974 is still the primary reference work regarding the stylistic unity of Roman comedy, and Fantham 1972 and Maltby 2007 are two further excellent accounts of comic imagery, while the best discussions of female comic speech are Adams 1984 and Dutsch 2008. Gerschner 2002 is a comprehensive account of nominal declension in Plautus. Fontaine 2010 successfully employs rigid philological tools and brings to the fore various heretofore unnoticed aspects of Plautus's verbal play. For a convincing look at Plautine metrics through the lens of Latin linguistics, see Fortson 2008. De Melo 2011 is a recent, theoretically informed account of the language of Roman comedy, where issues of spelling, phonology, and meter as well as of morphology, syntax, and lexicon are thoroughly and systematically discussed. Zagagi 2012 brings to the fore the way Plautine usage of Greek, in scenes of madness, symposium, deception, and effeminacy, reflects Roman prejudices against negative Greek stereotypes that oppose the *mos maiorum*.

For the language of individual Roman comedy playwrights, see especially Fraenkel 1935, Vereecke 1971, Pasquazi Bagnolini 1977, Guardì 1981, Molinelli 1983, Molinelli 2006, Mandolfo 2004, Livan 2005, and de Melo 2010.

For an account of linguistic and stylistic differences between Plautus and Terence (seemingly dispensed with in *Eunuchus*), see Hofmann 1951: 9–39, Duckworth 1952: 331–360, Miniconi 1958, Palmer 1954: 74–94, Lilja 1965: 78–85, 90–94, Fantham 1972, Barsby 1999: 19–27.

On Early Latin features, see especially Smith 1890, Neue and Wagener 1892–1905, Lindsay 1907, Bennett 1910–1914, Allardice 1929, Harsh 1940, Bléry 1965, Hofmann and Szantyr 1965, Ernout and Thomas 1972, Raios 1998: 120–126, Barsby 1999, Rosèn 1999, Karakasis 2005: 44–61, and de Melo 2007.

On the use of epic, tragic, official, ritual, and legal diction in Roman comedy, see especially Ploen 1882, Kroll 1910–1912: 8–10, Thierfelder 1939, Palmer 1954: 85–88, 91–94, Hoffmann 1980–1981, Danese 1985, Hunter 1985: 114–136, Piccaluga 1991, Gratwick 1993: 139, Blänsdorf 1996, Christenson 2000: 151, Karakasis 2005: 90–100, and de Melo 2011: lxxii. On the comic use of sound effects, especially alliteration and assonance, see especially De Vivo 1994, Oniga 1994, Traina 1999, Sharrock 2009: 167–171, and Molinelli 1983.

On Roman comedy and spoken Latin, see especially Palmer 1954: 74–94, Papadimitriou 1998; see also Hofmann 1951, Shipp 1960: 44–55, Barsby 1999: 20–23, and Bagordo 2001.

On linguistic characterization in Roman comedy, apart from Karakasis 2005, see especially Nicolson 1893, Tcherniaef 1900, Hough 1947, Shipp 1953, Carney 1964, Salat 1967, Arnott 1970, Maltby 1976, Maltby 1979, Maltby 1985, Maltby 1995, Gilleland 1979, Gilleland 1980, Adams 1984, Nuñez 1995, Martin 1995, Müller 1997, Petersmann 1995, Petersmann 1996–1997, Papadimitriou 1998, Petersmann and Petersmann 2003, Barsby 2004, Dutsch 2008, and Lech 2010.

On linguistic characterization in Menander, see especially Zini 1938, Arnott 1964, Arnott 1995, Sandbach 1970, Webster 1974: 99–110, Del Corno 1975, Katsouris 1975: 101–183, Bain 1984, Brenk 1987, and Krieter Spiro 1997: 201–253.

Text acknowledgement: For Caecilius and Naevius (comic fragments), the edition of E. H. Warmington, *Remains of Old Latin* (London, 1935–1940), is followed, while for Turpilius that of L. Rychlewska, *Turpilii comici fragmenta* (Leipzig, 1971) is preferred. Unless otherwise stated, for both Plautus and Terence the OCT texts are followed.

BIBLIOGRAPHY

Adams, J. N. 1984. "Female Speech in Latin Comedy." *Antichthon* 18: 43–77.

Allardice, J. T. 1929. *Syntax of Terence*. London: Oxford University Press.

Arnott, W. G. 1964. "The Confrontation of Sostratos and Gorgias." *Phoenix* 18: 110–123.

——. 1970. "*Phormio parasitus*: A Study in Dramatic Methods of Characterization." *G&R* 17: 32–57.

——. 1972. "Targets, Techniques and Traditions in Plautus' *Stichus*." *BICS* 19: 54–79.

——. 1995. "Menander's Manipulation of Language for the Individualisation of Character." In *Lo spettacolo delle voci*, edited by F. De Martino and A. H. Sommerstein, 147–164. Bari: Levante.

Astin, A. E. 1967. *Scipio Aemilianus*. Oxford: Clarendon Press.

Bagordo, A. 2001. *Beobachtungen zur Sprache des Terenz: Mit besonderer Berücksichtigung der umgangssprachlichen Elemente*. Göttingen: Vandenhoeck & Ruprecht.

——. 2001a. "Lingua e stile in Plauto (note all' *Epidicus*)." In *Studien zu Plautus' Epidicus,* edited by U. Auhagen, 297–312. Tübingen: Narr.

——. 2007. "Langversstil und Senarstil bei Terenz." In *Terentius Poeta*, edited by P. Kruschwitz, W.W. Ehlers, and F. Felgentreu, 127–142. Munich: C. H. Beck.

Bain, D. 1984. "Female Speech in Menander." *Antichthon* 18: 24–42.

Baldi, P. 2002. *The Foundations of Latin*. Berlin and New York: Mouton de Gruyter.

Barsby, J. 1999. *Terence: Eunuchus*. Cambridge, UK: Cambridge University Press.

——. 2001. *Terence: The Woman of Andros; The Self-Tormentor; The Eunuch*. Cambridge, MA: Harvard University Press.

——. 2004. "Some Aspects of the Language of *Cistellaria*." In *Studien zu Plautus' Cistellaria,* edited by R. Hartkamp and F. Hurka, 335–345. Tübingen: Narr.

Beacham, R. C. 1991. *The Roman Theatre and Its Audience*. London: Routledge.

Bennett, C. E. 1910–1914. *Syntax of Early Latin*. Boston: Allyn & Bacon.

Blänsdorf, J. 1967. *Archaische Gedankengänge in den Komödien des Plautus*. Wiesbaden: Steiner.

——. 1996. "Un trait original de la comédie de Plaute: Le goût de la parodie." *CGITA* 9: 133–151.

Bléry, H. 1965. *Syntaxe de la subordination dans Térence*. Rome: "L'Erma" di Bretschneider.

Boscherini, S. 1999. "Norma e parola nelle commedie di Cecilio Stazio." *SIFC* 27: 99–115.

Brenk, F. E. 1987. "*Heteros tis eimi*: On the Language of Menander's Young Lovers." *ICS* 12: 31–66.

Carney, T. F. 1964. "The Words *sodes* and *quaeso* in Terentian Usage." *AClass* 7: 57–63.

Christenson, D. 2000. *Plautus: Amphitruo*. Cambridge, UK: Cambridge University Press.

Clackson, J., and G. Horrocks. 2007. *The Blackwell History of the Latin Language*. Malden, MA: Wiley-Blackwell.

Coleman, R. G. G. 1999. "Poetic Diction, Poetic Discourse and the Poetic Register." In *Aspects of the Language of Latin Poetry*, edited by J. N. Adams and R. G. Mayer, 21–93. Oxford: Oxford University Press.

Collart, J. 1979. *Plaute: Curculio*. Paris: Presses universitaires de France.

Comerci, G. 1994. "*Humanitas, liberalitas, aequitas*: Nuova paideia e mediazione sociale negli *Adelphoe* di Terenzio." *BStudLat.* 24: 3–44.

Corno, D. del. 1975. "Alcuni aspetti del linguaggio di Menandro." *SCO* 23: 13–48.

Danese, R. 1985. "Plauto, *Pseud.*702–705a: La 'costruzione stilistica' di un eroe perfetto." *MD* 14: 101–112.

——. 2006. "Plauto e l'*urbanitas* del dialetto." *Linguistica e Letteratura* 31: 37–66.

De Melo, W. D. C. 2007. *The Early Latin Verb System: Archaic Forms in Plautus, Terence, and Beyond*. Oxford: Oxford University Press.

——. 2009. "*Scies* (*Mil.* 520) e *scibis* (*Mil.* 1365): Variazione accidentale?" In *Lecturae Plautinae Sarsinates XII: Miles gloriosus (Sarsina, 27 settembre 2008)*, edited by R. Raffaelli and A. Tontini, 41–52. Urbino: QuattroVenti.

——. 2010. "The Language of Atellan Farce." In *L'Atellana letteraria: Atti della prima giornata di studi sull'Atellana: Succivo (Ce) 30 Ottobre 2009*, edited by R. Raffaelli and A. Tontini, 121–155. Urbino: QuattroVenti.

——. 2011. *Plautus: Amphitryon; The Comedy of Asses; The Pot of Gold; The Two Bacchises; The Captives*. Cambridge, MA: Harvard University Press.

——. 2011a. "The Language of Roman Comedy." In *A Companion to the Latin Language*, edited by J. Clackson, 321–343. Malden, MA: Wiley-Blackwell.

De Vivo, A. 1994. "Lingua e comico in Plauto." *BStudLat.*24: 417–431.

Duckworth, G. E. 1952. *The Nature of Roman Comedy: A Study in Popular Entertainment.* Princeton: Princeton University Press. Repr. with bibliographical appendix by R. L. Hunter (1994), London: Bristol Classical Press.

Dutsch, D. M. 2008. *Feminine Discourse in Roman Comedy: On Echoes and Voices.* Oxford: Oxford University Press.

Ernout, A., and F. Thomas. 1972. *Syntaxe latine.* Paris: C. Klincksieck.

Fantham, E. 1972. *Comparative Studies in Republican Latin Imagery.* Toronto: University of Toronto Press.

Filoche, C. 2007. "Le miles plautinien, ou le langage comique d'un anti-héros." *REL* 85: 46–65.

Fontaine, M. 2010. *Funny Words in Plautine Comedy.* New York and Oxford: Oxford University Press.

Fortson, B. W., IV. 2008. *Language and Rhythm in Plautus.* Berlin: de Gruyter.

Foucher, A. 2003. "*Siem, sies, siet,* dans les vers de Plaute et de Térence: Quelques remarques de prosodie, de métrique et de stylistique." *REL* 3: 11–28.

——. 2005. "Un aspect formulaire de la langue et de la métrique plautiniennes: Les formes de subjonctif *fuam, fuas, fuat, fuant.*" *REL* 5: 97–115.

Fraenkel, E. 1935. "Naevius." *RE* Suppl. 6: 622–640.

——. 2007. *Plautine Elements in Plautus.* Translated by T. Drevikovsky and F. Muecke. Oxford: Oxford University Press. Originally published as *Plautinisches im Plautus* (Berlin, 1922).

Gerschner, R. 2002. *Die Deklination der Nomina bei Plautus.* Heidelberg: Winter.

Gilleland, M. E. 1979. "Linguistic Differentiation of Character Type and Sex in the Comedies of Plautus and Terence." PhD diss., University of Virginia.

——. 1980. "Female Speech in Greek and Latin." *AJPh* 101: 180–183.

Goldberg, S. M. 1986. *Understanding Terence.* Princeton: Princeton University Press.

Gratwick, A. S. 1993. *Plautus: Menaechmi.* Cambridge, UK: Cambridge University Press.

Guardì, T. 1981. "Note sulla lingua di Titinio." *Pan* 7: 145–165.

Haffter, H. 1934. *Untersuchungen zur altlateinischen Dichtersprache.* Berlin: Weidmann.

Happ, H. 1967. "Die lateinische Umgangssprache und die Kunstsprache des Plautus." *Glotta* 45: 60–104.

Harsh, P. W. 1940. "The Position of Archaic Forms in the Verse of Plautus." *CPh* 35: 126–142.

Hoffmann, Z. 1980–1981. "Gebetsparodien in Plautus' Komödien." *Helikon* 20–21: 207–218.

Hofmann, J. B. 1951. *Lateinische Umgangssprache.* Heidelberg: Winter.

Hofmann, J. B., and A. Szantyr. 1965. *Lateinische Syntax und Stilistik.* Munich: C.H. Beck.

Hofmann, W. 1977. "Zur Charaktergestaltung in der *Aulularia* des Plautus." *Klio* 59: 349–358.

Hough, J. N. 1947. "Terence's Use of Greek Words." *CW* 41: 18–21.

Hunter, R. L. 1985. *The New Comedy of Greece and Rome.* Cambridge, UK: Cambridge University Press.

Jocelyn, H. D. 1967. *The Tragedies of Ennius: The Fragments.* Cambridge, UK: Cambridge University Press.

Karakasis, E. 2003. "Language and Plot in Plautus' *Bacchides.*" *RCCM* 45: 47–67.

——. 2005. *Terence and the Language of Roman Comedy.* Cambridge, UK: Cambridge University Press.

Katsouris, A. G. 1975. *Linguistic and Stylistic Characterization: Tragedy and Menander.* Ioannina, Greece: University of Ioannina.

Krieter Spiro, M. 1997. *Sklaven, Köche und Hetären: Das Dienstpersonal bei Menander: Stellung, Rolle, Komik und Sprache.* Stuttgart: Teubner.

Kroll, W. 1910–1912. "Der lateinische Relativsatz." *Glotta* 3: 1–18.

Leach, E. W. 1969. "*Meam quom formam noscito*: Language and Characterization in *Menaechmi*." *Arethusa* 2: 30–45.

Lech, P. G. 2010. "Gender, Social Status, and Discourse in Roman Comedy." PhD diss., Brown University.

Lilja, S. 1965. *Terms of Abuse in Roman Comedy*. Helsinki: Suomalainen tiedeakatemia.

Lindsay, W. M. 1907. *The Syntax of Plautus*. Oxford: Oxford University Press.

Livan, G. 2005. *Appunti sulla lingua e lo stile di Cecilio Stazio*. Bologna: Pàtron.

Löfstedt, E. 1911. *Philologischer Kommentar zur Peregrinatio Aetheriae: Untersuchungen zur Geschichte der lateinischen Sprache*. Uppsala: Almqvist & Wiksell.

MacCary, W. T., and M. M. Willcock. 1976. *Plautus: Casina*. Cambridge, UK: Cambridge University Press.

Maltby, R. 1976. "A Comparative Study of the Language of Plautus and Terence." PhD diss., Cambridge University.

——. 1979. "Linguistic Characterisation of Old Men in Terence." *CPh* 74: 136–147.

——. 1983. "The Last Act of Terence's *Heautontimorumenos*." *Papers of the Liverpool Latin Seminar* 4: 27–41.

——. 1985. "The Distribution of Greek Loan-Words in Terence." *CQ* 35: 110–123.

——. 1995. "The Distribution of Greek Loan-Words in Plautus." *Papers of the Leeds International Latin Seminar* 8: 31–69.

——. 1999. "The Language of Plautus's Parasites." In *Theatre: Ancient & Modern: Selected Proceedings of a Two-Day International Research Conference Hosted by the Department of Classical Studies, Faculty of Arts, the Open University, Milton Keynes, 5th and 6th January 1999*, edited by L. Hardwick, 32–44. Milton Keynes: Open University. Available online at http://www2.open.ac.uk/ClassicalStudies/GreekPlays/Conf99/Maltby.htm

——. 2007. "The Distribution of Imagery by Plays and Characters in Terence." In *Terentius Poeta*, edited by P. Kruschwitz, W. W. Ehlers, F. Felgentreu, 143–165. Munich: C. H. Beck.

Mandolfo, C. 2004. "La lingua di Nevio comico." *Sileno* 30: 143–62.

Martin, R. H. 1995. "A Not-So-Minor Character in Terence's *Eunuchus*." *CPh* 90: 139–151.

Meiser, G. 2002. *Historische Laut- und Formenlehre der lateinischen Sprache*. Darmstadt: Wissenschaftliche Buchgesellschaft.

Miniconi, P. J. 1958. "Les termes d' injure dans le théâtre comique." *REL* 36: 159–175.

Molinelli, M. 1983. "Allitterazione e hapax legomena in Nevio (Nota a *Com.* 57 e 76 R.)." *AFLM* 16: 513–520.

——. 2006. "Lingua e stile in Nevio: Il caso di '*exanimabiliter*' (Nevio, com. 35R.[3])." *Orpheus* 27: 92–100.

Müller, R. 1997. *Sprechen und Sprache: Dialoglinguistische Studien zu Terenz*. Heidelberg: Winter.

——. 2007. "*Pura oratio und puri sermonis amator*: Zu zwei Begriffsklippen der Terenz-Forschung." In *Terentius Poeta*, edited by P. Kruschwitz, W. W. Ehlers, F. Felgentreu, 111–125. Munich: C. H. Beck.

Neue, F., and K. Wagener. 1892–1905. *Formenlehre der lateinischen Sprache*. Leipzig: O. R. Reisland.

Nicolson, F. W. 1893. "The Use of *hercle* (*mehercle*), *edepol* (*pol*) and *ecastor* (*mecastor*) by Plautus and Terence." *HSCPh* 4: 99–103.

Nuñez, S. 1995. "Materiales para una sociología de la lengua latina: Terencio y los modificadores de imperativo." *FlorIlib* 6: 347–366.

Oniga, R. 1994. "L' allitterazione in Plauto e Terenzio: Un esperimento di analisi quantitativa." *Lexis* 12: 117–134.

Palmer, L. R. 1954. *The Latin Language*. London: Faber and Faber.

Papadimitriou, M. 1998. *Στοιχεία της ομιλούμενης Λατινικής στον Τερέντιο και η χρήση τους στη διαφοροποίηση του λόγου των χαρακτήρων του*. Ioannina, Greece: University of Ioannina.

Parker, H. N. 1996. "Plautus vs. Terence: Audience and Popularity Re-examined." *AJPh* 117: 585–617.

Pasquazi Bagnolini, A. 1977. *Note sulla lingua di Afranio*. Florence: F. Le Monnier.

Petersmann, H. 1995. "Zur mündlichen Charakterisierung des Fremden in der Komödie des Plautus." In *Plautus und die Tradition des Stegreifspiels*, edited by L. Benz, E. Stärk, and G. Vogt-Spira, 123–136. Tübingen: Narr.

———. 1996–1997. "Die Nachahmung des *sermo rusticus* auf der Bühne des Plautus und Terenz." *AAntHung* 37: 199–211.

———. 2002–2003. "Bedeutung und Gebrauch von lateinisch *fui*: Eine soziolinguistische Analyse." *Die Sprache* 43: 94–103.

Petersmann, H., and A. Petersmann. 2003. "Sprach und Stil als ein Mittel des Personencharakterisierung in den Komödien des Plautus." In *Altera Ratio: Klassische Philologie zwischen Subjektivität und Wissenschaft: Festschrift für Werner Suerbaum zum 70. Geburtstag*, edited by M. Schauer and G. Thome, 108–119. Stuttgart: Steiner.

Piccaluga, G. 1991. "*At ego aiio id fieri in Graecia et Carthagini / Et hic…* (Plaut. *Cas.* 71 sg.): il linguaggio 'religioso' in Plauto." *RSA* 21: 9–22.

Ploen, H. 1882. *De copiae verborum differentiis inter varia poesis Romanae antiquioris genera intercedentibus*. Strasbourg: Truebner.

Questa, C. 1967. *Introduzione alla metrica di Plauto*. Bologna: Pàtron.

Raios, D. 1998. *Ρωμαϊκή κωμωδία: Πλαύτου Μέναιχμοι*. Ioannina, Greece: University of Ioannina.

Reich, V. 1933. "Sprachliche Characteristik bei Terenz (Studien zum Kommentar des Donat)." *WS* 51: 72–94.

Rósèn, H. 1999. *Latine loqui: Trends and Directions in the Crystallization of Classical Latin*. Munich: W. Fink.

Salat, P. 1967. "L' adjectif *miser*, ses synonymes et ses antonymes chez Plaute et chez Térence." *REL* 45: 252–275.

Sandbach, F. H. 1970. "Menander's Manipulation of Language for Dramatic Purposes." *Fondation Hardt* 26: 113–136.

Schauwecker, Y. 2002. "Zum Sprechverhalten der Frauentypen bei Plautus." *Gymnasium* 109: 191–211.

Sharrock, A. 2009. *Reading Roman Comedy: Poetics and Playfulness in Plautus and Terence*. Cambridge, UK: Cambridge University Press.

Shipp, G. P. 1953. "Greek in Plautus." *WS* 66: 105–112.

———. 1960. *P. Terenti Afri Andria*. Melbourne: Oxford University Press.

Smith, K. W. 1890. *Archaisms of Terence Mentioned in the Commentary of Donatus*. Baltimore: Friedenwald.

Stadter, P. 1968. "Special Effects in Plautine Dialogue: *Miles Gloriosus*, III, ii." *CPh* 63: 146–147.

Stockert, W. 1982. "Zur sprachlichen Characterisierung der Personen in Plautus' *Aulularia*." *Gymnasium* 89: 4–14.

———. 2004. "Schwören auch Frauen bei Herkules? Bemerkungen zu *Cist.* 52 und anderen Plautus-Stellen." In *Studien zu Plautus' Cistellaria*, edited by R. Hartkamp and F. Hurka, 363–369. Tübingen: Narr.

Strasburger, H. 1966. "Der 'Scipionenkreis.'" *Hermes* 94: 60–72.

Thierfelder, A. 1939. "Plautus und römische Tragödie." *Hermes* 74: 155–166.

Traina, A. 1999. *Forma e suono: Da Plauto a Pascoli*. Bologna: Pàtron.

Tcherniaef [i.e., Chernyaev], P. 1900. *Terentiana: Des traces de Térence dans Ovide, Horace et Tite Live*. Kazan, Russia: Kidalinsky.

Vereecke, E. 1971. "Titinius, Plaute et les origines de la fabula togata." *AC* 40: 156–185.

Wahrmann, P. 1908. "Vulgärlateinisches bei Terenz." *WS* 30: 75–103.

Webster, T. B. L. 1974. *An Introduction to Menander*. Manchester, UK: Manchester University Press.

Wright, J. 1974. *Dancing in Chains: The Stylistic Unity of the Comoedia Palliata*. Rome: American Academy.

Zagagi, N. 2012. "What Do Greek Words Do in Plautus?" In *Greek into Latin from Antiquity until the Nineteenth Century*, edited by J. Glucker and Ch. Burnett, 19–36. London: Warburg Institute.

Zini, S. 1938. *Il linguaggio dei personaggi nelle commedie di Menandro*. Florence: Le Monnier.

Zetzel, J. E. G. 1972. "Cicero and the Scipionic Circle." *HSCPh* 76: 173–180.

GLOSSARY

The following linguistic terms as used in this paper are defined as follows (the definitions are largely based on and informed by D. Crystal, *A Dictionary of Linguistics and Phonetics*, Singapore, 2008):

denominative verbs: verbs derived from nouns

idiolect: linguistic or speech habits associated with a particular person

lexeme: the smallest distinctive element in terms of the semantics of a language

morphology: the division of grammar that deals with the form of words, namely inflections and word-formation

phonology: the sector of linguistics that deals with the sound systems of a language

postvocalic: a term of phonology denoting a sound that comes after a vowel

prevocalic: a term of phonology denoting a sound that precedes a vowel

sociolect: a term of sociolinguistics denoting a linguistic variety associated with a specific social or professional class

suffix: an affix added to a word stem

syntagm: collocation, syntactical construction

vernacular: a term of sociolinguistics denoting the native, natural, i.e., not standardized and artificial, language of a linguistic community

ABBREVIATED TITLES

Plautus: *Amph.* = *Amphitruo, Asin.* = *Asinaria, Aul.* = *Aulularia, Bacch.* = *Bacchides, Capt.* = *Captivi, Cas.* = *Casina, Cist.* = *Cistellaria, Curc.* = *Curculio, Epid.* = *Epidicus,*

Men. = Menaechmi, Merc. = Mercator, Mil. = Miles Gloriosus, Most. = Mostellaria, Pers. = Persa, Poen. = Poenulus, Pseud. = Pseudolus, Rud. = Rudens, Stich. = Stichus, Trin. = Trinummus, Truc. = Truculentus, Vid. = Vidularia

Terence: *Ad. = Adelphoe, Andr. = Andria, Eun. = Eunuchus, Haut. = Heauton Timorumenos, Hec. = Hecyra, Phorm. = Phormio*

CHAPTER 29

TRAGEDY, PARATRAGEDY, AND ROMAN COMEDY

GESINE MANUWALD

INTRODUCTION

BOTH Greek-style tragedy and Greek-style comedy were introduced to Rome by the same person, Rome's first poet, Livius Andronicus (ca. 280/70–200 BCE), at about the same time (ca. 240 BCE). His immediate successors, Naevius (ca. 280/60–200 BCE) and Ennius (239–169 BCE), also wrote tragedies and comedies (besides works in other literary genres). Hence the transition from Greece and the emergence of these two dramatic genres in Rome operated within the same time frame and on the same basis; formal elements such as metrical patterns or use of musical accompaniment seem to have been shared. Nevertheless, differences between tragedy and comedy in tone and subject matter can be observed in the earliest surviving Latin remains; there is an obvious contrast between the verse "Fleas or bugs or lice? Come, answer me," transmitted for Livius Andronicus's *Gladiolus*, regarded as a comedy, and the lines "You must endure the duty of obedience to what my majesty demands. Lead you this woman from the temple!" attested for his *Aegisthus*, which must be a tragedy.[1]

Since both dramatic genres in Rome were taken over from the Greeks in highly developed form, they displayed typical generic characteristics from the start. The

---

[1] Cf. Liv. Andr. *Com.* 1 R.³ = 1 W.: *pulicesne an cimices an pedes? responde mihi.*; *Trag.* 13–14 R.³ = 12–13 W.: *quin quod parere <mihi> vos maiestas mea / procat, toleratis temploque hanc deducitis?* [trans. E. H. Warmington]. Fragmentary dramatic texts are quoted from Ribbeck's third editions of the tragic and the comic fragments (Ribbeck 1897, Ribbeck 1898), along with Warmington's numbering (Warmington 1935, Warmington 1936) and those of more recent special editions where applicable; editions are identified by editors' initials. Quotations from Plautus and Terence follow the respective OCTs.—For full details see the bibliography, and for an overview of some introductory works and important studies on this topic see the section on "Further reading."

specifics of the evolution of Roman drama, along with the fact that later there was a greater range of dramatic genres (dramatic genres adapted from Greece as well as locally developed ones), seem to have led to an increased generic awareness: soon poets (and audiences) were familiar with the characteristics of the various dramatic genres and able to engage with those across genres. Although in Greece Aristophanes (ca. 445–385 BCE) had already provided a prime example of a comic poet reacting to tragedy, interactions between dramatic genres seem to have been more distinctive in the Roman world, partly because there are not only comments by "comedy" on "tragedy," but, beyond that, various combinations of "comic" and "tragic" elements can be observed.[2]

This essay will highlight different types of intertextual and intergeneric connections between Greek-style comedy and serious dramatic genres, particularly Greek-style tragedy, in the republican period. Although the identification of uses of "tragic" material in republican comedy and distinctions between the different dramatic forms are not always clear-cut, this contribution will make an attempt at outlining types of relationships and their likely functions and effects; it will focus on significant examples rather than give comprehensive lists of all possible allusions. Among what is extant, Plautus appears as the most creative poet as regards engaging with other dramatic genres, and the character of allusions can be determined more easily in complete texts; therefore a large number of examples will be taken from Plautus's comedies. However, brief consideration of other comic playwrights will provide a broader basis. So, at the end, the article will suggest some conclusions on the relation of Greek-style comedy to serious dramatic genres in republican times.

DEFINITIONS

No full-scale set of definitions for individual dramatic genres survives from the productive period of republican drama; there are only treatments by late-antique grammarians and commentators, which go back to earlier sources.[3] According to writers such as Diomedes, Evanthius, or Donatus (fourth–fifth centuries CE), whose works provide tidy systems, Greek and Roman dramatic genres are distinguished mainly by setting, social status of the protagonists, tone, and atmosphere: dramatic genres differ by their Greek or Roman context; the various dramatic forms on each side (serious or light) differ by tone, the social and ethical level of the protagonists, and the character of the plots, while Greek and Roman versions in the same position correspond in type. Other possible distinctive features such as dramatic structure, metrical form, or language are not applied.

---

[2] In this chapter the terms "comedy" / "tragedy" and "comic" / "tragic" will be used in a neutral sense denoting the dramatic genre; they do not imply that the features referred to are particularly "funny" or "sad."

[3] Cf., e.g., Diom. *Ars* 3, Gramm. Lat. 1, pp. 482–91; Evanth. *Fab.* 4.1–3; Donat. *Com.* 6.1–2; on Ter. *Ad.* 7; Lydus, *Mag.* 1.40; *Lib. gloss.* 1.2–8; 2.9–11.—On the criteria used to distinguish between tragedy and comedy in ancient dramatic theory, cf. Seidensticker 1982, esp. 17, 249–260.

These writers describe a fully developed system with terminology covering all dramatic forms (*crepidata, praetexta, palliata, togata, mimus / planipes, Atellana*). However, the terms *fabula, tragoedia, comoedia* (and on one occasion *tragicomoedia* and also *paratragoedo*) are the only ones to be attested for the main creative period of republican drama, as they are found in the works of the playwrights themselves. By late republican and early Augustan times, further descriptions such as *praetexta, palliata, togata, mimus,* and *Atellana* had emerged; the first attestations of these technical terms tend to be later than the earliest surviving texts assigned to the respective dramatic genres.

The fact that republican playwrights used several terms defining dramatic genres indicates that they were aware of the status of their own pieces within the generic framework. This becomes obvious in prologues to extant Roman comedies by Plautus (ca. 250–184 BCE) and Terence (ca. 195/4–159 BCE), when these include comments about the play's dramatic genre. Such remarks occur most frequently when there is anything unusual, in that a piece does not comply exactly with the standard form of a stock comedy. Conversely, this practice reveals the playwrights' views on the comic genre and its limitations as well as on its potential relationship to other dramatic genres, and it shows that poets expected audiences to know what a standard comedy looked like.

That republican dramatic poets talked about the generic identity of plays in nonstandard cases agrees with the fact that later Roman writers insisted on distinctions between dramatic genres and the need to maintain them, particularly between tragedy and comedy, so that a mixture of tragic subject matter and comic diction was avoided (cf. Cic. *Opt. gen.* 1; Hor. *Ars P.* 89–93; Quint. *Inst.* 10.2.21–2). The late-antique commentator Evanthius regarded it as one of Terence's virtues that he stuck to a true comic style and did not include elements reminiscent of tragedy or mime into his comedies as other comic poets did (Evanth. *Fab.* 3.5), while Gellius accused Caecilius of doing precisely that and thereby worsening Menander's text (Gell. *NA* 2.23.12; 2.23.21).

Irrespective of definitions and assessments, playwrights experimented with deviations from the standard setup and stretched the limits of their dramatic genre. The prologue to Plautus's *Captivi*, for instance, suggests that comedies (though not this one) typically feature pimps, courtesans, and braggart soldiers (Plautus, *Captivi* 55–62), which some Terentian prologues confirm (cf. Terence, *Heauton Timorumenos* 35–42; *Eunuchus* 35–41). In a fragment from the comedies of Caecilius (ca. 230/20–168/7 BCE), *comici stulti senes* ('stupid old fools to be found in comedies') are mentioned (Caec. *Pall.* 243–244 R.³ = 236–237 W. = 256–257 G. [trans. E. H. Warmington]). In his comedy *Synephebi*, there is ironic play with the generic type of the strict and fooled father: a father in this play is so mild and lenient that his son in love complains, since the father does not offer him the opportunity of cheating him out of money (Cic. *Nat. D.* 3.72: Caec. *Pall.* 199–209 R.³ = 189–199 W. = 196–206 G.). The common behavior of a *meretrix* is also reversed, as she does not want to take money from her lover (Caec. *Pall.* 213–214 R.³ = 203–204 W. = 211–212 G.).

These passages show that across the three most prominent *palliata* poets in the republican period there was a consistent view of what constituted a stock comedy and also the tendency to play with these standards. This practice can extend to drawing on material from other dramatic genres. This can happen on a micro-level concerning individual phrases or scenes and on a macro-level affecting the setup and atmosphere of a play. As for the combination of "comic" and "tragic" elements, there seems to be a scale from smooth and seamless integration of "tragic" themes and structures into comedies to "tragic" features standing out as incongruous.

Under the premise that individual instances may be assigned to any of those categories, the question of how to label them arises. For clarity's sake, "tragicomedy" or "combination of comedy with tragedy" will be used for a fusion of "comic" and "tragic" elements throughout an entire play, which need not be inhomogeneous and have a comic effect. "Paratragedy" and "allusion" will be used for single references to works of serious dramatic genres; these are more likely to be incongruous and thus "parody of tragedy." Although no comprehensive definition of "parody" survives from antiquity, it seems that it came to denote ridicule of existing material and to include comic twisting of tragedy, which was also called "paratragedy"; this is why in modern scholarship "paratragedy" is normally applied to comedy's reaction to tragedy.[4]

TRAGICOMEDY

The most famous example of a Roman dramatic poet explicitly talking about the characteristics of several dramatic genres and exploiting them to create his own blend is found in the prologue to Plautus's *Amphitruo*. After the play has been introduced by the unspecific term *fabula* (*Amphitruo* 15), Plautus has the prologue speaker Mercury define it as *tragoedia* when it comes to characterizing it more precisely. When this description allegedly meets with the disapproval of the audience, who are portrayed as preferring comedies, the god promises to turn the *tragoedia* into a *comoedia* without any changes, on account of his divine powers. In fact, he then declares this play to belong to the mixed form of *tragicomoedia*, since, as he says, it is a play in which kings and gods as well as servants appear and which therefore cannot be assigned to a single dramatic genre (*Amphitruo* 50–63).

What is at issue is not changing any elements of the drama, but rather finding the right label. The term *tragicomoedia* in this passage was apparently coined as a generic term for the occasion; in antiquity it is only attested here and in a later comment referring back to this passage (Lactant. on Stat. *Theb.* 4.146–147). An expression describing a mixture of "tragedy" and "comedy" has possible Greek forerunners such as *hilarotragoedia*;[5] yet the

---

[4] For ancient definitions of parody, cf. *Suda*, s.v.; Schol. on Ar. *Ach.* 8; Hsch. 1026 (on this issue cf. Lelièvre 1954).—For a discussion of the terms "parody" and "paratragedy," cf. Rau 1967: 7–18, which distinguishes them from "tragicomedy," where "comic" and "tragic" elements are combined on equal footing; for a discussion of "tragicomedy" and "paratragedy," cf. Bianco 2006: 53–54.—For a definition of ancient "parody" and an overview of major examples, cf. Glei 2000; on parody in the ancient world, cf. Cèbe 1966.

[5] *Suda* defines Rhinthon's dramas (s.v.) as κωμικὰ τραγικά. Dramas entitled Κωμῳδοτραγῳδία are attested for Alcaeus (K-A II p. 9), Anaxandrides (K-A II p. 249) and perhaps Dinolochus (cf. K-A II p. 9).

inversion of the order of the two parts of the determinative compound presents Plautus's play as a special type of "comedy," including "tragic" elements. This weighting is confirmed by the fact that the play is referred to as *comoedia* (*Amphitruo* 88; 96; 868) or (without specification) as *fabula* (*Amphitruo* 94) elsewhere in the script. Social status as a criterion to distinguish between serious and light drama recurs in late-antique definitions (and beyond). This explanation of the generic status of Plautus's play does not include further information, e.g., on the character of the resulting piece.

Therefore, and because there is no comparative evidence for "Roman tragicomedy," there is some discussion on what characterizes Plautus's *Amphitruo* as a "tragicomedy" or whether there is rather parody of tragedy. The prologue does not suggest that either dramatic genre is to be ridiculed; a combination is apparently intended, for it seems that on other levels too, beyond the social status of the protagonists, there is a genuine mix of "tragic" and "comic" features. For instance, the motifs of deception, mistaken identity, and characters thrown into doubt about themselves or the slave pretending to be brave and rehearsing a report about a battle he had fled out of cowardice are comic elements; the messenger's report as such (*Amphitruo* 203–261a) or the figure of Alcumena, unknowingly deceived and made guilty, and her reflections on the relative shares of joy and distress in life (*Amphitruo* 633–653) would be appropriate in a tragedy (both including similarities in wording: e.g., *Amphitruo* 216–218 vs. Enn. *Trag.* 139–140 R.^{3} = 164–165 W. = 153–154 J.; *Amphitruo* 636 vs. Enn. *Trag.* 354 R.^{3} = 212 W. = 335 J.). It is only by the overall context into which these "tragic" elements are inserted that they acquire a comic twist. Such a mixture presumably is the essence of Plautus's "tragicomedy," in which comic elements predominate.

The events concerning Amphitruo have the potential for tragic presentation, as Accius's tragedy *Amphitruo* suggests, although this play seems to have dramatized Hercules's return from the underworld, rather like Euripides's *Heracles*. Indeed, it has been assumed that Plautus's comic version of the Amphitruo story was inspired by a tragedy on the subject, perhaps a Latin version of Euripides's *Alcmene*;[6] Euripides's *Protesilaus* has also been suggested as a source for the motif of the husband returning to his wife (Pelliccia 2011). It may be inferred from Plautus's prologue that a dramatic treatment of this story would most naturally be described as "tragedy" and that the active involvement of Jupiter in a comedy is unusual. If Plautus had reworked a tragedy by adding comic elements such as the figure of the slave, there would be an organic reason for the fusion of characteristics of the two dramatic genres,[7] and this could be regarded as the basis for the prologue's claim that "old" subject matter is presented in "new" form (Plautus, *Amphitruo* 118–119).

---

[6] Cf. Lefèvre 1982, Lefèvre 1998b, Lefèvre 1999: 11–15 (with a review of the discussion in the meantime), supported by Stärk 1982 (with an overview of earlier treatments of the story); contra Braun 1991 and Oniga 2002: 205; cf. also Flores 1998: 145 and Christenson 2000: 53–55.

[7] It has been assumed that the way in which Mercury describes the genesis of the "tragicomedy," changing the initial description of "tragedy" to "tragicomedy," reflected the process carried out by the comic poet in adapting a tragedy as a comedy (cf. Schmidt 2003: 89). Such a metaliterary reading would not be alien to Plautine comedy, but the particular structure of the argument could also have been determined by the intended effect on the audience.

Taking the idea of a tragic model into another direction, scholars have thought that Plautus's comic version of a story involving gods as proper characters was inspired by the model of Euripides's *Bacchae* (or a Roman version thereof). It has been suggested that, irrespective of differences in plot and a limited number of verbal similarities, both dramas are plays about the nature of theatre and conscious of their own theatricality.[8] With respect to a drama like *Amphitruo* that is self-conscious and constantly plays with conventions, a metatheatrical reading is not implausible. However, differences in plot structure are considerable, and metatheater (to different degrees) is a general feature of Plautine drama; therefore this theory must remain an unproven hypothesis.

At any rate, the creation of a tragicomedy suggests a profound engagement with tragedy and a close familiarity with its main characteristics on the poet's part; it also presupposes a high level of generic awareness among the audience. Although the explicit description of this generic mixture is restricted to formal categories, an analysis of the play can detect a fusion also on deeper levels of the resulting construct; irrespective of the play's actual source, which perhaps was rather a combination of sources (Oniga 2002: 207–208), one might describe this "tragicomedy" as a "tragedy in comic dress," since the gods enjoy the comedy they play with the human characters, and the humans are pushed into difficult situations as in tragedy (Schmidt 2003).

OTHER (UNNAMED) COMBINATIONS OF "COMEDY" WITH "TRAGEDY"

It is only in *Amphitruo* that Plautus explicitly goes beyond the confines of comedy and takes the step of assigning a play to another (newly created) dramatic genre. Elsewhere, he sticks to the expected generic assignment of comedy, although further pieces may equally be regarded as containing features of "tragedy."

In *Captivi*, for instance, Plautus provokes the audience's interest and attention by introducing the drama as something special in having the prologue speaker promise that it is not composed in the hackneyed fashion nor like others, that it will not feature some of the typical comedy figures, particularly morally problematic ones, or have strong language; at the same time, the audience is assured that battles mentioned in this context will not feature in the play but will take place "offstage," since it would be unreasonable to suddenly start acting a tragedy with comic equipment (*Captivi* 55–62). The actors' epilogue confirms the special nature of the play and explains that it belongs to a rare type of comedy in which the usual immoral actions are not included, but which

---

[8] Cf. Stewart 1958 (for suggesting a possible connection) and Slater 1990 (for adding a metatheatrical interpretation and arguing for a direct relationship); contra Christenson 2000: 54–55 and Oniga 2002: 204–205.

is designed to make good people better with its presentation of high moral standards (*Captivi* 1029–1036).

In *Captivi*, deviations from the stock setup (i.e., lack of certain characters and structures) are thought to deserve pointing out, but they are apparently not regarded as so significant as to require or allow a generic renaming. Even if some typical comic figures are missing, there are no gods or individuals of high social status, which would point to "tragedy" according to formal criteria. There is only a rejection of elements associated with other dramatic genres, and it is thus suggested that there will not be an incongruous combination of "comic" equipment and "tragic" features. In fact, the plot of *Captivi* is almost as much a fusion of "comic" and "tragic" features as that of *Amphitruo*: elements such as the recognition between a parent and a long-lost son, the use of deception and mistaken identity, and the important function of slaves recall common structures of comedies, but other items such as the lack of a love affair, the motif of sacrificing oneself for one's friend, the portrayed loyalty of slaves, the need of a character to deal with the demands of two masters, and the ill success of good intentions, as well as allusions and narratives instead of bawdy scenes, are reminiscent of themes and motifs found in tragedy. Hence, in effect, "comic" and "tragic" elements are mixed in this "comedy," which Plautus describes as a comedy of particular character.

Some scholars have warned against interpreting the prologue to *Captivi* too literally, since references to generic conventions were used to tease the audience (Segal 1987). It is true that the play includes trickery, farce, wordplay, and other comic elements. However, such features have not been excluded by prologue and epilogue; only certain actions and characters have been denied for this drama, and the stock characters mentioned in the prologue have no part in it. Moreover, the piece contains a moving scene of loyalty and moral reflections. Hence the prologue is correct in describing the play as atypical in some aspects of cast and plot.[9] Although these comments refer to this particular play and have an immediate function in their context, they again reveal the playwright's engagement with generic characteristics.

Others scholars have described *Captivi* as a "tragicomedy" like *Amphitruo* or *Rudens* (Köhler 1930: 3–4, 19). Such a classification may be applied if used as a description of a mixture of "tragic" and "comic" elements according to modern terminology; however, it does not agree with Plautus's own comments on the play's dramatic genre. The impression of a generic mixture only arises when one surveys themes and motifs in the play as a whole, but there is no room for reclassification if one applies formal criteria as in Plautus's *Amphitruo*; accordingly, the play can only be defined as a particular form of comedy on that basis.

There are more examples of Plautine plays exhibiting a mixture of "comic" and "tragic" elements, albeit with less signposting. Plautus's *Rudens*, for instance, could be

---

[9] This special character, however, and the fact that the play addresses an issue of warfare do not make this play comparable to a *fabula praetexta* (so Lefèvre 1998a, esp. 36–37, 46): there are no references to an actual war fought by the Romans, it is not the heroic aspects of the war that are being portrayed, and it is true for all Greek-style plays that the issues presented are relevant to Roman society in a general way.

seen as at least as "tragic" as *Amphitruo* and *Captivi* in terms of its plot, but in this drama's script there are no explicit comments on dramatic genre. A possible reason might be that *Rudens* does not present a generic problem to Plautus, as it fulfills some of the criteria for comedies mentioned elsewhere by both himself and Terence in terms of cast and plot: it presents a fictitious story of everyday people; there is the standard personnel (Greek citizens, old men, young men in love, girls, slaves, pimps—but no gods or heroes as participants of the action); a young man is in love with a girl in possession of an evil pimp, but eventually she is released and recognized as freeborn and the lost child of another character, which enables a recognition scene between parents and children as well as a happy marriage between this girl and the young man; there are arguments between masters and their slaves who are threatened with punishment and an additional love affair between servants, as well as differences between husband and wife.

At the same time, the piece contains elements that deviate from the standard comedy setup and that seem to be more frequent in contemporary tragedies than in comedies, but none that are closely associated with tragedy or that Plautus seems to have regarded as typically "tragic": the play is set not in Athens but in Cyrene, and not in a street in the town but on the coast between a farm and a temple of Venus; there is no conflict between a young man in love and his father; although slaves play an important role, there is not really an intriguing slave; the values of justice and appreciation of honesty are presented as important principles; there is a dream narrative; people in danger take refuge at an altar; the prologue is spoken by a divinity, who has supported the girls and opposed the pimp; the marriage between a young Athenian and the girl who is proved to be freeborn is announced but not acted out; there is no scene of punishment and revenge on the pimp.

Apparently it was not regarded as necessary to indicate a modification of scene structures if there was no violation of formal criteria. In this case, the combination of "comic" and "tragic" leads to a smooth synthesis of the two dramatic genres: the play preserves a number of elements that constitute a comic plot and make it interesting and funny, and this is supplemented by a considerable amount of morally relevant content. Despite all variation and the addition of "tragic" elements, the basic plot of *Rudens* remains closer to a standard comedy setup than do those of *Amphitruo* or *Captivi* and therefore does not require justification. The mixture in a drama classified as comedy does not result in incongruity, and there is no obvious ridicule. Still, scholars have noted that *Rudens* should be classified as "tragicomedy" in the same manner that *Amphitruo* and *Captivi* are (Marx 1928: 274–278; Köhler 1930: 3–4, 19); this may be a possible description according to modern definitions of "tragicomedy," but it contradicts what can be inferred about Plautus's views on dramatic genres and on the status of this particular piece.

Plautus seems to have exploited generic conventions and unusual combinations of elements taken from the two dramatic genres of comedy and tragedy so as to create a greater range of possible plots and styles, to heighten the tension for the audience, and to increase the attractiveness of his plays. His dramas display a wide variety of combinations of "comic" and "tragic" elements; they differ not only in the ways in which typical characters, themes, and structures of tragedies are integrated in comic plots, but also in the ways in which Plautus presents these mixtures. In one instance only, where the fusion is obvious on a formal level, has he created a new term for the resulting construct (*tragicomoedia*). Elsewhere, tragic elements are added to the basic comic structure, with or without comment in prologues and/or epilogues. In all cases, tragic elements are not ridiculed but smoothly integrated. Audiences were apparently deemed sophisticated enough to appreciate such a treatment of dramatic genres.

INTERTEXTUAL REFERENCES TO SPECIFIC TRAGEDIES

Crossing of generic boundaries can be seen not only in clever combinations of "comedy" with "tragedy" but also in references to particular plays. In line with their metatheatrical character, Plautus's plays frequently mention other dramas, the most common instance being the identification in the prologue of title and/or writer of the Greek model (e.g., Plautus, *Asinaria* 10–12; *Mercator* 9–10; *Miles Gloriosus* 86–87; *Poenulus* 50–55a; *Trinummus* 18–21). Besides, Plautus has a reference to a performance of one of his own plays: in *Bacchides*, Chrysalus says that he loves *Epidicus*, but watches with great displeasure when Pellio is doing it (*Bacchides* 214–215). Yet such references are not limited to the comic genre; they can extend to tragedies.

In Plautus's *Rudens*, the prologue speaker, the god Arcturus, explains that he had aroused a great tempest (to save the girl from the pimp) the night before (*Rudens* 67–71). Consequently, the first utterance after the prologue refers to this storm; the character compares it with Euripides's *Alcmene* to illustrate its force (*Rudens* 86). If such a comparison is employed to replace a description of the storm, it must refer to a well-known tragedy (perhaps in a Latin adaptation, although no republican tragedy of this title is attested). Recalling the thunderstorm in this particular tragedy seems more important than a comment on the dramatic genre. The reference point could be a scene full of thunder and lightning similar to the conditions described for the time when Alcumena was giving birth in Plautus's *Amphitruo* (*Amphitruo* 1053–1081); yet Euripides's *Alcmene* seems to have included a scene in which Jupiter sent a thunderstorm to rescue Alcumena when Amphitruo, enraged at the apparent adultery, was about to light a fire.[10] Then there would also be a structural parallel between the two plays (indicated for the audience), as in both cases the storm would have been sent on divine orders to rescue a woman.

The prologue to Plautus's *Poenulus* starts by insinuating that a tragedy is about to be performed, as the first two words mention Aristarchus's *Achilles* and this play is defined as a *tragoedia* in the second line; the contemporary audience would presumably relate this to Ennius's adaptation of this tragedy. When the prologue speaker goes on to say

---

[10] Cf. Kannicht, *TrGF* V.1, p. 219 (with further references; reconstruction based on vase paintings).

that he will take the beginning of the current play from this tragedy, it might seem that a remake is about to follow. But at the end of the fourth line, it is revealed that this was a joke and the play is going to be a comedy (*Poenulus* 1–4). This was probably what the audience expected, and to have this confirmed after getting confused and unsettled would create a sense of relief and happy anticipation (Slater 1992).

In contrast to these precise references, there is an unspecific mention of "an old poet" who writes tragedies in *Curculio*; he is reported to have said that two women were worse than one (Plautus *Curculio* 591–592). Presumably such a statement had assumed proverbial character and therefore was no longer associated with a specific playwright or play. In this case, as for the reference to Euripides's *Alcmene*, there is no distancing from the dramatic genre of tragedy as there is in the opening lines of *Poenulus*, where this is used to win the audience's attention.

PARATRAGEDY

While in the instances discussed so far, references to tragedies and the use of "tragic" elements have been integrated into comedies, in other Plautine plays allusions to "tragic" features are made to stand out and to create an immediate incongruous effect.

One of the most obvious examples, which also defines this type of reaction to tragedy, is found in Plautus's *Pseudolus*. After the eponymous slave has resolved to address the young man he is about to meet "in the grand manner" (*Pseudolus* 702: *magnufice*) and has uttered a few lines in high-flown language with an abundance of alliteration, anaphora, and wordplay on the number "three," Plautus has the young man comment: "How he is trying to be tragic, the rapscallion!" (*Pseudolus* 708: *ut paratragoedat carnufex!*). This remark points to the fact that the slave's speech was unexpected and inappropriate. It makes clear that tension arises because speaking "in the grand manner" belongs to another dramatic genre, and in its exaggeration and misappropriation the tragic style is ridiculed. The comment also reaffirms for the audience that they are watching a comedy and that there will not be a complete change in dramatic genre or tone.[11]

According to the late-antique commentator Donatus, Terence uses an Ennian phrase (likely to come from one of his tragedies) in *Eunuchus* (*Eunuchus* 590, with Donatus on Terence, *Eunuchus* 590[2]–[3]: Enn. *Trag.* 372 R.³ = 386 W. = CLXI J.). As it is employed in a description of Jupiter, the elaborate language is not immediately incongruous; it rather enhances the status of the god and increases the contrast to the

---

[11] Sharrock (2009: 204 n. 93) suggests that "by means of the poetological role of Pseudolus…the *carnufex* who *paratragoedit* in this case is actually Plautus—or could it be also Euripides or Ennius?" Obviously, on the level of the plot it is the slave who uses tragic words and it is to him that the young man's comment refers, but it is the poet Plautus who has made the slave use these words and create an allusion to tragic language.

human character, called *homuncio* ("a mere mortal") in the following line (*Eunuchus* 591), who still argues that he is allowed to do what Jupiter has done. But as the point of comparison is finding ways of entering the chamber of a beloved girl (*Eunuchus* 584–591), the grand description of Jupiter as the all-powerful god in tragic manner creates some tension. This is perhaps what Donatus means when he describes the passage as "parody of Ennius" (*parodia de Ennio*). Donatus also realizes that the poet aimed at such an effect, since he notes that tragic material has been inserted "on purpose, not out of error" (*de industria non errore*).

Elsewhere Donatus comments on the generic character of entire plays: he describes Terence's *Andria* as having an "almost tragic *catastrophe* (i.e., ending)" (Donatus on Terence, *Andria, praef.* 1.5), while he notes for *Phormio* that Terence kept the appropriate comic framework throughout, for instance by balancing the intensity of sad events by comic serenity (e.g., Donatus on Terence, *Phormio, praef.* 1.5; cf. also Evanth. *Fab.* 3.5). It is true that Terence's comic plots tend to have a more serious outlook and a more sober atmosphere than those of Plautus and thus invite comparisons with tragedy on this account, but he makes sure (also by means of "contamination") that the plays include true comic scenes and characters as well as formally happy endings.

Terence's mock battle in *Eunuchus* (IV 7) could be interpreted as an instance where he left comedy proper and included parody of tragedy, since, according to Plautus, battles were rather a feature of tragedy (Plautus, *Casina* 58b–62), which is supported by the character of the slave's battle narrative in *Amphitruo* (*Amphitruo* 203–261a). Yet the section in Terence is shaped as a purely comic scene, which gains its effect from the discrepancy between the reason for the attack and the inappropriate manner and ridiculous equipment of the fighting on the one hand and the attitude to this enterprise and the language used by the people involved on the other.

Another classic tragedy scene is the description of a character's madness, best known from Euripides's *Heracles*. There is double play with this feature associated with tragedy in Plautus's *Menaechmi* (*Menaechmi* 831–875; cf. also Plautus, *Captivi* 592–608): it is not "real" madness but feigned madness, and the character creates the impression of "madness" by using high-flown language that is out of context but typical of characters out of their minds in tragedies. This signals "madness" to audiences and the other characters, while the exaggeration shows that in this play it is feigned, on the level both of the plot and of its generic character in metatheatrical terms.

Plautus frequently creates effects by using language, themes, or structures that display typical "tragic" characteristics and thus differ from the comic environment. In *Mercator*, for instance, the young man, having returned safely from a sea voyage and about to get into trouble with his father, addresses the sea in elaborate language and compares the two situations metaphorically (Plautus, *Mercator* 195–197). A pathetic address to the sea is incongruous, and the description of himself as "having escaped tempests" contrasts with the apparently trouble-free voyage; above all, the potential storm arising from a conflict with the father is incommensurate with a real danger during a tempest at sea. Like an earlier attempt at describing the situation philosophically, which is brushed away by the slave (*Mercator* 145–148), this passage shows that the young man tries to find ways to express his predicament. Yet these elaborate comparisons are inappropriate to the basic human problems that confront him.

Beyond specific forms of speaking, there is parody of tragedy's typically elevated and exaggerated language in Plautus. A good example is what seems to have been a famous description of the title character in Pacuvius's tragedy *Antiopa*: like other noble protagonists in Pacuvius (ca. 220–130 BCE) and Accius (170–ca. 80 BCE), she was brought on stage in rags, disheveled and dirty, and her appearance was described in high-flown, complicated language (e.g., Pac. *Trag.* 20^{a-b}; 9 R.^{3} = 13–14; 24 W. = 8; 9 S.). A combination of passages using complex, rare vocabulary, explicitly connected with *Antiopa* in one case, suggests that the scene with its unnatural language was ridiculed by the contemporary satirist Lucilius (ca. 180–103/2 BCE), parodied by Plautus in no less than three comedies, and commented upon by the Neronian satirist Persius.[12] It was apparently the highly refined language describing a situation typical in early Roman tragedy that caught the comic playwright's attention.

Allusions to tragedy can extend to themes and subject matter typical of tragedy. For instance, a subject frequently presented in republican tragedies, events connected with the Trojan War, is comically referred to in *Bacchides*, when Plautus has the scheming slave deliver a *canticum* in which he compares his attack against his master to trick him out of money with the attack of the Greeks against Troy by means of the Trojan Horse (*Bacchides* 925–978). This comparison between an action within the comedy and an event typically narrated in other literary genres, enhanced by the use of tragic language and the slave's alleged superiority over the Trojan heroes, gains its comic effect from the incompatibility of the two items, in addition to possible parody of individual well-known lines from Ennian tragedy.[13]

The relationship to tragedy might even have influenced the presentation of characters on stage: it has been suggested that the maiden in Plautus's *Persa*, who appears in disguise, not only hides her identity, as required by the scheming, but even wears a costume associated with tragedy (esp. *Persa* 154–161; 464; 465–466), in line with her moral and sententious pronouncements, which stand out from the utterances of other characters (Shaw Hardy 2005). In that case, there would be a visual juxtaposition of dramatic genres, enhancing the comic plot: the "tragic" character stands out in various ways, while at the same time it is essential for the intrigue and conveys a metatheatrical and deeper layer of meaning.

While references to tragedy can be identified and assessed most easily in complete comedies, the practice of "paratragedy" seems not to have been restricted to playwrights

---

[12] Cf. Lucilius 597–598, 599–600 M. = 729–730, 727–728 W.; Plautus, *Casina* 759–762; *Persa* 11–12; 712–713; *Pseudolus* 771–772; Perius, *Satires* 1.77–78 (and scholium ad loc.).—On these passages cf. Thierfelder 1939; Cèbe 1966: 108.

[13] Cf. Plautus, *Bacchides* 933–934 vs. Ennius *Trag.* 81–88 R.^{3} = 101–108 W. = 87–94 J.—On this passage, cf. Sedgwick 1921, Cèbe 1966: 107, Swoboda 1972: 65–66, Sheets 1983: 200–201, and Prinzen 1998: 23–25.—Although Zwierlein (Zwierlein 1992: 13–20) deletes substantial parts of the Troy *canticum*, he does retain this line with the possible Ennian allusion as Plautine.

whose works survive in their entirety; fragments remaining from the dramas of other poets suggest that this phenomenon was more widespread. One of the frequent sententious phrases in Caecilius concerns bearing injustice if it is free from insult; this thought occurs in similar form both in his *Fallacia* and in Pacuvius's *Periboea* (Pac. *Trag.* 279/80 R.³ = 304 W. = 209 S.; Caec. *Pall.* 47–48 R.³ = 43–44 W. = 43–44 G.). Since the notion is a factual description of a character's situation in Pacuvius and an elaborate and pathetic general phrase, which starts with trouble and moves on to injustice, in Caecilius, the comic poet is likely to be the one who refers to the other playwright. Because of its starting point, the comment might refer to a minor inconvenience, so that the exaggerated descriptions and distinctions seem ridiculous.

Turpilius, the last *palliata* poet of the Roman Republic (d. 104/3 BCE), wrote a play *Leucadia*, which is likely to have been based on Menander (cf. Serv. on Verg. *Aen.* 3.279). It included the story of Sappho and Phaon, though it was probably not told directly. Nevertheless, the setting and the fact that information about Phaon as the founder of the local temple was included suggest that similarities between the situation of a helpless lover described in the play and the mythical characters were hinted at. According to Cicero's report (Cic. *Tusc.* 4.72–73: Turp. *Pall.* 115–120 R.³ = 117–122 Ry.), the desperate lover appealed to all gods for help except Venus. Cicero agrees with the characterization of this character as "insane," apparently voiced by other figures in the play, and mocks his emotional exclamations and his expectation that the whole divine realm should care for his amatory difficulties. He comments "Note what a tragic air of passion he puts on!" (*at quas tragoedias efficit!* [trans. J. E. King]). As the term *tragoedia* is used in the plural, this does not necessarily imply that Cicero regarded this behavior as reminiscent of the dramatic genre of tragedy in the strict sense, but he obviously saw this as an exaggerated emotional scene, which he found unusual in its context. Irrespective of Cicero's assessment, such a play might imply that Turpilius, like Terence, integrated themes and plot structures typical of tragedy in his plays, although he seems to have maintained a comic atmosphere overall.

EXCURSUS: *FABULA TOGATA* AND *FABULA ATELLANA*

Although, due to the fragmentary transmission, details are more difficult to ascertain for *palliata*'s Roman counterpart, for *fabula togata* there is enough evidence to indicate that poets writing comedies set in Rome also reacted to other dramatic genres by commenting on them or adapting their characteristic features.

Afranius (fl. ca. 160–120 BCE), the most famous representative of this dramatic genre, referred to Terence as a model (cf. Suet. / Donat. *Vita Ter.* 7: Afr. *Tog.* 29 R.³) and freely admitted that he borrowed from Menander what suited him, as he did from any Greek or Latin writer (cf. Macrob. *Sat.* 6.1.4: Afr. *Tog.* 25–28 R.³). One of the remaining fragments includes a "quotation" from Pacuvius with explicit attribution: "it is not easy, as Pacuvius says, to find just one good woman" (Afr. *Tog.* 7 R.³ = 9 Dav.: *haut facul, ut ait Pacuvius, femina <una> invenitur bona*).[14] Seneca claims for *togatae* that they were midway between *tragoedia* and *comoedia* and contained some seriousness; he implies that they talked about philosophical questions (Sen. *Ep.* 8.8; 89.7). In the text of Fronto's letters, *sententiae* in *togatae* are described as "elegant" (*urbanae*), in contrast to those in other light dramatic genres (Fronto, *Ep. ad Ant.* 4.2, *m² in margine*[d)] [p. 106 v.d.H.]).

At least in its literary form, *fabula Atellana*, the originally Oscan genre of light drama, included a mythical subtype: titles of such plays refer to mythical figures or incidents and can be identical with those of tragedies (cf. Pomponius's *Armorum iudicium* or Novius's *Andromacha*), yet they seem to have presented humorous versions of myths; for instance, in Novius's *Phoenissae* a character threatens to kill another with a "club made from bulrushes" (Nov. *Atell.* 79 R.³: *clava scirpea*).

These observations underline that all varieties of light drama in Rome make use of intertextual references within and beyond their dramatic framework and create special effects by means of references to "tragedy." The engagement with other pieces across dramatic genres was apparently not just taken over from Greece, but actively pursued by Roman playwrights.

CONCLUSIONS

Although this survey could only discuss a selection of examples, it should have become clear that reactions to serious dramatic genres on the Roman stage, particularly Greek-style tragedy, are relatively frequent in Roman *fabulae palliatae* throughout the republican period and can take a variety of forms. Plautus's oeuvre provides a prime example, and his inclusion of "tragic" elements in his comedies covers the entire range of possible relationships, from parody and pastiche via imitation for comic effect to smooth integration of tragic elements to give a plot another dimension. *Palliata* comedy, created by poets active in different literary genres and being an experimental and mixed dramatic genre, as it combines elements from indigenous dramatic traditions and conventions adapted from Greece, seems to have been particularly ready to engage with features of other dramatic genres.

The playwrights' own metaliterary statements reveal that they knew the key characteristics of each dramatic genre and were able to play with them. This is partly supported by Horace in the Augustan period; although he argues for strict generic distinctions, he

---

[14] Cf. Pac. *Trag. inc.* LIV R.³ = 35 W. = 261 S.—On the text, cf. Daviault 1981 and Schierl 2006 ad loc. Interestingly, the statement is attributed to the poet Pacuvius rather than to a character in his tragedies; either the poet is seen as the person who has put it into the mouth of a character, or this implies that the line comes from a prologue detached from the plot.

allows comedy and tragedy to use the other dramatic genre's mode of expression in certain contexts where it is appropriate (Hor. *Ars P.* 89–98).

Obviously, comedy in Greece had already reacted to tragic motifs and structures in various ways, and it cannot always be determined clearly whether Roman comedy's engagement with tragedy has been stimulated by or adapted from Greek comedy or whether it is the work of Roman playwrights. However, generic awareness can be observed for Roman playwrights across the board from the start, and it comes to the fore in prologues, which must have been composed by Roman poets; reactions to other dramatic genres are also found in genuinely Roman dramatic genres. Furthermore, at least some of the references to tragedies in *palliatae* must have been introduced by Roman comic poets (rather than taken over from the underlying Greek comedies), as they consist of comments on plays that were shown on the Roman stage or allusions to specific phrases in Roman tragedy. The picture would be clearer if the transmission of early Roman drama and Hellenistic Greek drama were less patchy.

Only in a few cases are references to tragedy signaled by mention of the title and/or author of a tragedy or by discussion of a play's generic status. Since numerous other references are unmarked (see above), playwrights were apparently addressing a literary and sophisticated audience. In this context, one has to bear in mind that the earliest evidence comes from Plautus; by his day, Latin plays had been shown in Rome for a generation and Greek plays in Italy for even longer, so that audiences could have become familiar with the conventions. Explicit discussion of a piece's generic status only happens in prologues and epilogues, and it is designed to catch the audience's attention by highlighting a play's special character.

The evidence demonstrates that there was productive and creative engagement among the different dramatic genres in Rome throughout the republican period. If one considers just the two *palliata* poets of whom complete plays survive, it seems that Terence's comedies have a more serious outlook overall, approaching tragedies in some respects, while Plautus adds individual tragic elements to comic plots to create a peculiar coherent mixture or an effect by contrast. This may be due partly to the poetic personalities of the two playwrights, but the meager evidence from other writers as well as the increase in entertaining features in tragedies suggest that the relationship between dramatic genres was developing during the republican period, leading both to generic diversification and to individual dramatic genres assimilating features of other dramatic forms.[15]

---

[15] Sheets (1983: 204–209) has suggested that *palliata* comedy as produced by Plautus could take on so many different shapes because it was still in the process of acquiring its own characteristic form distinct from tragedy, as both went back to a common origin. This hypothesis might explain the ease of switches in diction or meter. But as Plautus mentions key characteristics of comedies and apparently feels obliged to offer an explanation when a play differs too widely from the standard setup, the basic structure of a Roman *palliata* seems to have been established by his time.

Identifying reactions to tragedy in Roman comedy is therefore not a mere scholarly pursuit; because of the intricate relationship between dramatic genres in Rome, it makes an essential contribution to understanding early republican drama.

FURTHER READING

There are several comprehensive treatments of Roman republican drama as well as of tragedy and comedy, which provide good starting points for an understanding of the characteristics of each dramatic genre, although the specific issue of intergeneric relationships tends to be dealt with rather briefly. For overviews of Roman republican theatre, cf. Beare 1964 and Manuwald 2011; for overviews of Roman (republican) tragedy cf. Erasmo 2004, Fantham 2005, and Boyle 2006 (for bibliography cf. Manuwald 2004); for overviews of Roman (republican) comedy, cf. Duckworth 1952 and Hunter 1985.

For a long time, it has been well known that Plautus's comedies include references to other dramatic genres as well as to a number of other forms of speaking (e.g., laws, oaths, and prayers); this may have been facilitated by the fact that *palliata* can be seen as a "mixed genre" (cf. especially Chiarini 1980: 94–99, 123–124; also Oniga 1985: 206–208). For a summary of parodied genres, cf. Blänsdorf 1993: 59–60, 66; on parody in comedy, cf. Cèbe 1966: 37–117; on parody in Plautus, cf. Swoboda 1972 and Blänsdorf 1996; on parody of Ennius in Plautus and Terence, cf. Prinzen 1998: 21–27.

The relationship of comedy to tragedy has always met with special interest, albeit more with reference to individual examples than to the question as such. However, Leo (1912: 132–137) and, more recently, Sheets (1983) and Blänsdorf (1993) have pointed out that there is parodic imitation of tragic style or particular passages from tragedy in Plautus, but that not every allusion to or imitation of tragedy in Plautus is meant to be humorous or ridiculing (on paratragedy in Plautus, under the aspect of *"paratragedia 'al femminile,'"* cf. also Bianco 2007). For definitions of tragedy and comedy in ancient dramatic theory, cf. Seidensticker 1982.

Scholars mainly have collected passages in comedies that are likely to be allusions to tragedy and have discussed the generic relationship with reference to specific plays in which mixtures of dramatic genres of various kinds are prominent; for lists of passages that may be regarded as "paratragedy" and brief discussions of them, cf. Sedgwick 1927, Thierfelder 1939, and Cèbe 1966: 103–115. On "tragicomedy" in *Amphitruo*, cf. Lefèvre 1982, Lefèvre 1998b, Lefèvre 1999, Blänsdorf 1993, Moore 1995, Flores 1998, Bond 1999, Manuwald 1999, Christenson 2000 passim, and Schmidt 2003 (with further bibliography); cf. also Segal (1975), who argues that *Amphitruo* is not an atypical but a very Plautine and Roman comedy.—On *Captivi* as a "commedia anomala," cf. Raffaelli 2006.—On paratragedy in *Pseudolus*, cf. Leo 1912: 134, Sedgwick 1927, Cèbe 1966: 109–110, Sheets 1983: 198–200, and Sharrock 2009: 204.—On the mixture of "comedy" and "tragedy" in *Rudens,* cf. Blänsdorf 1993 and Sharrock 2009: 204–219.

Bibliography

Beare, W. 1964. *The Roman Stage: A Short History of Latin Drama in the Time of the Republic.* 3rd ed. London: Methuen.

Bianco, M. M. 2006. "*Ut Medea Peliam concoxit... item ego te faciam*: La Medea di Plauto." In *La commedia di Plauto e la parodia: Il lato comico dei paradigmi tragici*, edited by G. Petrone and M. M. Bianco, 53–79. Palermo: Flaccovio.

——. 2007. *Interdum vocem comoedia tollit: Paratragedia "al femminile" nella commedia plautina.* Bologna: Pàtron.

Blänsdorf, J. 1993. "Plautus, Amphitruo und Rudens—oder wieviel literarische Parodie verträgt eine populäre Komödie?" In *Literaturparodie in Antike und Mittelalter*, edited by W. Ax and R. F. Glei, 57–74. Trier: Wissenschaftlicher Verlag.

——. 1996. "Un trait original de la comédie de Plaute: Le goût de la parodie." In *Panorama du théâtre antique: D'Eschyle aux dramaturges d'Amérique latine*, edited by A. Moreau, 133–151. Montpellier: Groupe interdisciplinaire du théâtre antique.

Bond, R. P. 1999. "Plautus' *Amphitryo* as Tragi-Comedy." *G&R* 46: 203–220.

Boyle, A. J. 2006. *An Introduction to Roman Tragedy.* London and New York: Routledge.

Braun, L. 1991. "Keine griechischen Originale für Amphitruo und Menaechmi?" *WJA* 17: 193–215.

Cèbe, J.-P. 1966. *La caricature et la parodie, dans le monde romain antique des origines à Juvénal.* Paris: E. de Boccard.

Chiarini, G. 1980. "Compresenza e conflittualità dei generi nel teatro latino arcaico (per una rilettura dell'Amphitruo)." *MD* 5: 87–124.

Christenson, D. M., ed. 2000. *Plautus: Amphitruo.* Cambridge, UK: Cambridge University Press.

Daviault, A., ed. [Dav.] 1981. *Comoedia togata: Fragments.* Paris: Belles Lettres.

Duckworth, G. E. 1952. *The Nature of Roman Comedy: A Study in Popular Entertainment.* Princeton: Princeton University Press. (2nd ed. Norman: University of Oklahoma Press, 1994.)

Erasmo, M. 2004. *Roman Tragedy: Theatre to Theatricality.* Austin: University of Texas Press.

Fantham, E. 2005. "Roman Tragedy." In *A Companion to Latin Literature*, edited by S. Harrison, 116–129. Oxford: Blackwell.

Flores, E. 1998. "Il comico (*Pseudolus*) e il tragicomico (*Amphitruo*) in Plauto." *Lexis* 16: 139–147.

Glei, R. F. 2000. "Parodie." In *Der Neue Pauly*, Vol. 9, edited by H. Cancik and H. Schneider, 345–349. Stuttgart and Weimar: J. B. Metzler.

Guardì, T., ed. [G.] 1974. *Cecilio Stazio: I frammenti.* Palermo: Palumbo.

Hunter, R. L. 1985. *The New Comedy of Greece and Rome.* Cambridge, UK: Cambridge University Press.

Jocelyn, H. D., ed. [J.] 1967. *The Tragedies of Ennius: The Fragments.* Cambridge, UK: Cambridge University Press (repr. with corr. 1969).

Kauer, R., and W. M. Lindsay, eds. 1958. *P. Terenti Afri comoediae*, supplements by O. Skutsch. Oxford: Clarendon.

Köhler, O., ed. 1930. *Ausgewählte Komödien des T. Maccius Plautus.* Vol. 2, *Captivi.* Leipzig and Berlin: Teubner.

Lefèvre, E. 1982. *Maccus vortit barbare: Vom tragischen Amphitryon zum tragikomischen Amphitruo.* Wiesbaden: F. Steiner.

——. 1998a. "Plautus' *Captivi* oder Die Palliata als Prätexta." In *Maccus barbarus: Sechs Kapitel zur Originalität der Captivi des Plautus*, edited by L. Benz and E. Lefèvre, 9–50. Tübingen: Narr.

——. 1998b. "L' Anfitrione di Plauto e la tragedia." In *Amphitruo*, edited by R. Raffaelli and A. Tontini, 13–30. Urbino: QuattroVenti.

——. 1999. "Plautus' *Amphitruo* zwischen Tragödie und Stegreifspiel." In *Studien zu Plautus' Amphitruo*, edited by T. Baier, 11–50. Tübingen: Narr.

Lelièvre, F. J. 1954. "The Basis of Ancient Parody." *G&R* 23, n.s., 1: 66–81.

Leo, F. 1912. *Plautinische Forschungen: Zur Kritik und Geschichte der Komödie*. 2nd ed. Berlin: Weidmann.

Lindsay, W. M., ed. 1904–1905. *T. Macci Plauti comoediae*. 2 vols. Oxford: Clarendon.

Manuwald, G. 1999. "Tragödienelemente in Plautus' *Amphitruo*—Zeichen von Tragödienparodie oder Tragikomödie?" In *Studien zu Plautus' Amphitruo*, edited by T. Baier, 177–202. Tübingen: Narr.

——. 2004. "Römische Tragödien und Praetexten republikanischer Zeit: 1964–2002." *Lustrum* 43: 11–237.

——. 2011. *Roman Republican Theatre*. Cambridge, UK: Cambridge University Press.

Marx, F., ed. [M.] 1904–1905. *C. Lucilii carminum reliquiae*. 2 vols. Leipzig: Teubner (repr. Amsterdam: Hakkert, 1963).

——. ed. 1928. *Plautus, Rudens: Text und Kommentar*. Leipzig: Teubner (repr. Amsterdam: Hakkert, 1959).

Moore, T. J. 1995. "How Is It Played? Tragicomedy as a Running Joke: Plautus' Amphitruo in Performance." *Didaskalia* Suppl. 1. Available online at www.didaskalia.net/issues/supplement1/moore.html.

Oniga, R. 1985. "Il canticum di Sosia: Forme stilistiche e modelli culturali." *MD* 14: 113–208.

——. 2002. "I modelli dell'*Anfitrione* di Plauto." In *Due seminari plautini: La tradizione del testo; I modelli*, edited by C. Questa and R. Raffelli, 199–225. Urbino: QuattroVenti.

Pelliccia, H. 2011. "Unlocking *Aeneid* 6.460: Plautus' *Amphitryon*, Euripides' *Protesilaus* and the Referents of Callimachus' *Coma*." *CJ* 106.2: 149–219.

Prinzen, H. 1998. *Ennius im Urteil der Antike*. Stuttgart and Weimar: J. B. Metzler.

Raffaelli, R. 2006. "Una commedia anomala: I *Captivi*." In *La commedia di Plauto e la parodia: Il lato comico dei paradigmi tragici*, edited by G. Petrone and M. M. Bianco, 25–52. Palermo: Flaccovio.

Rau, P. 1967. *Paratragodia: Untersuchung einer komischen Form des Aristophanes*. Munich: Beck.

Ribbeck, O. ed. [R.³] 1897. *Scaenicae Romanorum poesis fragmenta*. Vol. 1, *Tragicorum Romanorum fragmenta, tertiis curis*. Leipzig: Teubner.

——, ed. [R.³] 1898. *Scaenicae Romanorum poesis fragmenta*. Vol. 2, *Comicorum Romanorum praeter Plautum et Syri quae feruntur sententias fragmenta, tertiis curis*. Leipzig: Teubner.

Rychlewska, L., ed. [Ry.] 1971. *Turpilii comici fragmenta*. Leipzig: Teubner.

Schierl, P. 2006. [S.] *Die Tragödien des Pacuvius: Ein Kommentar zu den Fragmenten mit Einleitung, Text und Übersetzung*. Berlin and New York: de Gruyter.

Schmidt, E. A. 2003. "Die Tragikomödie *Amphitruo* des Plautus als Komödie und Tragödie." *MH* 60: 80–104.

Sedgwick, W. B. 1927. "Parody in Plautus." *CQ* 21: 88–89.

Segal, E. 1975. "Perché Amphitruo." *Dioniso* 46: 247–267. Repr. as "Why Plautus Chose Amphitruo" in *Roman Laughter: The Comedy of Plautus* by E. Segal, 2nd ed., 171–191. New York and Oxford: Oxford University Press, 1987.

——. 1987. "Is the *Captivi* Plautine?" In E. Segal, *Roman Laughter: The Comedy of Plautus*, 191–214. 2nd ed. New York and Oxford: Oxford University Press. Also in *Studi di filologia classica in onore di Giusto Monaco*. Vol. 2, 553–568. Palermo: Università di Palermo, 1991.

Seidensticker, B. 1982. *Palintonos Harmonia: Studien zu komischen Elementen in der griechischen Tragödie*. Göttingen: Vandenhoeck & Ruprecht.

Sharrock, A. 2009. *Reading Roman Comedy: Poetics and Playfulness in Plautus and Terence*. Cambridge, UK: Cambridge University Press.

Shaw Hardy, C. 2005. "The Parasite's Daughter: Metatheatrical Costuming in Plautus' *Persa*." *CW* 99: 25–233.

Sheets, G. A. 1983. "Plautus and Early Roman Tragedy." *ICS* 8: 195–209.

Skutsch, O., ed. [Sk.] 1985. *The Annals of Q. Ennius*. Oxford: Clarendon Press.

Slater, N. W. 1990. "*Amphitruo, Bacchae*, and Metatheatre," *Lexis* 5–6: 101–125. Repr. in *Plautus in Performance: The Theatre of the Mind*, by N. W. Slater, 181–202. 2nd ed. Amsterdam: Harwood Academic, 2000.

——. 1992. "Plautine Negotiations: The *Poenulus* Prologue Unpacked." *YClS* 29: 131–146. Repr. in *Plautus in Performance: The Theatre of the Mind*, by N. W. Slater, 149–162. 2nd ed. Amsterdam: Harwood Academic, 2000.

Stärk, E. 1982. "Die Geschichte des Amphitryonstoffes vor Plautus." *RhM* 125: 275–303.

Stewart, Z. 1958. "The *Amphitruo* of Plautus and Euripides' *Bacchae*." *TAPA* 89: 348–373.

Swoboda, M. 1972. "Elementy satyryczne i parodystyczne w komediach Plauta" = "De argumentis satiricis et parodiam redolentibus apud Plautum obviis" (summary in Latin). *Eos* 60: 51–69.

Thierfelder, A. 1939. "Plautus und römische Tragödie." *Hermes* 74: 155–166.

Vahlen, I., ed. [V.²] 1903. *Ennianae poesis reliquiae*. 2nd ed. Leipzig: Teubner (= 3rd ed. Leipzig 1928, Amsterdam: Hakkert, 1963, 1967).

Warmington, E. H., ed. [W.] 1935. *Remains of Old Latin*. Vol. 1, *Ennius and Caecilius*. Cambridge, MA: Harvard University Press (rev. and repr. 1967; several repr.).

——, ed. [W.] 1936. *Remains of Old Latin*. Vol. 2, *Livius Andronicus, Naevius, Pacuvius and Accius*. Cambridge, MA: Harvard University Press (repr. 1957, with minor bibliographical additions; several repr.).

——, ed. [W.] 1938. *Remains of Old Latin*. Vol. 3, *Lucilius, The Twelve Tables*. Cambridge, MA: Harvard University Press (rev. and repr. 1979).

Zwierlein, O. 1992. *Zur Kritik und Exegese des Plautus*. Vol. 4, *Bacchides*. Stuttgart: Steiner.

III

Roman Comedy and Society

CHAPTER 30

ROMAN COMEDY AND THE SOCIAL SCENE

ERICH GRUEN

ROMAN comedy emerged and flourished in a time of extraordinary change in the history of the Roman republic. The republic fought its most terrifying fight in the war with Hannibal and was nearly brought to its knees, but survived to become the most powerful nation in the west. That pivotal contest brought in its wake an explosion of expansionism that took Rome across the eastern Mediterranean, embroiled the state with Hellenistic kings and Greek poleis, and made it a conspicuous, if not dominant, presence in the world of Hellas. The extant plays of Plautus and Terence span that remarkable era from the pivotal Punic War to the point when Polybius announced that Rome had brought the entire *oecumene* under its sway. Roman coffers swelled, and war captives, whether through direct import or the trade market, entered Italy as slaves, bringing profound change to the economy of the land and a new shape to society as they entered citizen ranks through manumission. Roman leaders took full advantage of the glories and the wealth that such expansion accorded them, but also competed fiercely for the political and social gains that multiplied in value and intensified rivalries. The stakes were high and the contentions more contentious.

How far did Roman comedy engage with the turbulent contemporary scene? An old and contested problem, in the end perhaps not altogether soluble. The playwrights eschewed express comments and avoided direct reference to any contemporaries. The genre had its own character and rationale, modeled explicitly and unashamedly on Greek comedies, with plots set in Hellas and characters nearly all Greek, not a Roman among them. Further, the genre had a host of conventions and stereotypes duly followed for the edification of audiences who could readily anticipate them. Social and political commentary was not an expected part of the bargain.

That fact has hardly discouraged modern scholars from discerning a host of disguised topical references and ingenious parallels to contemporary Roman events, circumstances, and individuals. Certainly there is *Plautinisches in Plautus*. Allusions to law, institutions, and practices distinctively Roman, quite foreign to anything Hellenic, can be found in the plays. That has long since been acknowledged and stands uncontested (Leo 1912; Perna 1955; Fraenkel 1960; Gaiser 1972). It is something else altogether, however, to scour the scripts in order to detect direct connection with individuals or with current events, to propose dates for the plays or political affiliations for the playwrights. That particular parlor game has largely (and happily) been abandoned (Harvey 1981: 480–489; Harvey 1986: 297–304; Gruen 1990: 124–157; Leigh 2004: 20–23).

It does not follow that comic drama exists in a cocoon, divorced from the realities of late-third- and early- to mid-second-century Rome, trapped in a self-enclosed genre that abides strictly by its own rules and appeals to an audience interested only in escapism or a condescending contempt for Greeks. The plays may not be reflections of reality, but they do present the playwrights' reflections on reality. And that is no small part of their significance. A brief essay cannot pretend to demonstrate this with thoroughness or depth. A selective treatment of certain themes and issues will have to suffice. But they can illustrate the engagement of the dramatists with contemporary discourse on Roman values, attitudes, and demeanor that lend important dimensions to the plays and may have raised the consciousness of their audiences.

In the heyday of Plautine productions, Roman armies not only emerged victorious from the fearsome contest with Hannibal but defeated the two most powerful and formidable Hellenistic monarchies, Macedon under Philip V and Syria under Antiochus III ("the Great"). Fighting in Italy and abroad for three pivotal decades from Hannibal's crossing of the Alps to the Peace of Apamea in 188 meant nearly continuous contests, martial heroes, an influx of material and psychological rewards, and a heightened sense of both individual accomplishment and collective superiority. It is tempting to see the nearly ubiquitous *miles gloriosus* in Plautus's plays as index to the puffery of Roman officers intoxicated with achievement abroad and throwing their weight around at home (Hanson 1965: 51–67). But matters are not so simple. The stock character was stock already in Greek New Comedy, readily adaptable by Plautus but not necessarily an allusion to the Roman military. The figure generally corresponds to a mercenary captain, common in the fluid world of Hellenic warfare but rare in Rome's military service. This, of course, does not rule out indirect swipes at boastful Roman leaders (while retaining "deniability" through conventional Greek characters). But Plautus may have been more subtle. The comedies call attention to wider matters, not restricted to jabs at wacky warriors.

A striking statement issues from the mouth of the central character in Plautus's *Persa*. Toxilus is no military man; he is in fact a slave, though not the standard *servus callidus*, a complex and in some ways even appealing character. He manipulates the entire plot in his own interests, not those of his master, who is absent throughout the play. Having successfully orchestrated his scheme, routing and humiliating the thwarted pimp Dordalus, Toxilus pauses to revel in his victory. Not for the first time in Plautine drama, the successful slave borrows the terminology of triumphant generals. But here he goes beyond the standard chest-thumping. Toxilus maintains not only that enemies have been conquered and citizens saved, but calm has descended, peace been guaranteed, war extinguished, the task well accomplished, the army and garrisons kept intact.

He thanks Jupiter and all the other gods for their aid in exacting vengeance upon the enemy, and promises now to share the loot with participants and to take his own share (Plaut. *Persa* 753–757; cf. Fraenkel 1960: 226–232 and McCarthy 2000: 153). This, of course, delivers a parodic version of a Roman general's triumphant return, thanksgiving to the gods, and generosity with plundered goods (cf. Plaut. *Bacchides* 1067–1071; see Fraenkel 1960: 228–230; note also similar jabs in Plaut. *Asinaria* 269, 278–279; *Epidicus* 208–218). But the words suggest something more. Toxilus appears to declare the termination of war and the arrival of a secure peace. If this echoes contemporary sentiments, it may represent the pride in imperial success and a celebration of Roman dominance in the Mediterranean. Polybius has Scipio Africanus issue such a boast in 187, praising Romans as masters of Asia, Africa, and Spain. The defeat of Philip and Antiochus, according to Polybius, had given them rule and dominion over all the world (Polyb. 21.4.4–5, 23.14.10; cf. 3.3.5, 21.16.8, 21.4.4–5; 21.23.4, 24.11.3). One need not conclude that the *Persa* was composed in the wake of one or the other of those contests or that the passage made direct reference to individual commanders in the eastern wars. Polybius's own comments, in fact, were retrospective judgments and can be used only with caution in assessing the outlook of Plautus's contemporaries. Nevertheless, the string of successful victories that humbled the great powers of west and east can only have engendered élan and self-assurance among leaders and populace alike. The idea that the *oecumene* had been tamed by Roman arms and that peace (or pacification) was now guaranteed by the nation's power would hardly be surprising in those heady times. Toxilus's assertion, therefore, may well capture that sense of national accomplishment pervading the atmosphere of early-second-century Rome.

What was Plautus's purpose here? Surely not to parade the state's imperial achievement. The parodic character of such a speech in the mouth of a slave, albeit a skillful and capable one, who had just outwitted an incompetent pimp, can hardly be plainer. Nor, on the other hand, should one imagine some Plautine form of antiwar advocacy. A more nuanced message lurks in these lines. The playwright evidently holds up to scrutiny an overblown and premature sense of international authority or Mediterranean security engendered by temporary military success (cf. also *Truculentus* 73–75).

The theme of moral decline plays a notable part in the comedies. It is, of course, a hackneyed theme in ancient literature. Perhaps it came more intensely to the fore when Roman expansionism brought exorbitant wealth to public coffers and the fruits of conquest lined the pockets of officers and enlisted men alike. Exhilaration and overconfidence may have given stimulus to lavish living, a shattering of traditional restraints, a disturbing generational gap that divided earlier frugality from contemporary excess, and a severe compromise of the *mos maiorum*. So at least the strictures of moralists like Cato the Elder would suggest. The motif appears with some frequency in the dramas of Plautus. To what end? Does the playwright embrace the stance of those who lament the erosion of ancient values and assault the moral laxity of the younger generation? Does he here take sides in contemporary debate?

Once more the search for a Plautine moral, social, or political position misses the mark. Nor will it do to finesse the issue by considering it a mere reproduction of

Menandrian New Comedy. Plautus plays with the platitudes. He moves easily between a Greek setting and Roman practice, dropping broad hints to his audience that the differences only highlight the pervasiveness of the cliché.

When the veteran slave Lydus, tutor to his master's son in the *Bacchides*, bewails the decline in morals between the generations, the Greek context is unmistakable. Lydus reminds his elderly master that he had undergone serious training in his youth, the demanding discipline of the gymnasium and the stern lessons of the gymnasium director. He makes a pointed contrast between the rigorous exercises of the playing fields for the earlier generation and the luxuriant lolling with ladies for the present one. Students paid attention to their teachers in the old days, learned their lesson or got thrashed for it; at present, the brats hold the whip hand over their tutors, and fathers egg them on because they consider it a sign of lively spirit (Plaut. *Bacchides* 419–448). The *senex* Philoxenus can only sigh in resignation: customs are different nowadays (Plaut. *Bacchides* 436). Explicit reference to the gymnasium, to activities like wrestling, boxing, throwing the spear and the discus, leave no doubt that Plautus underscores the Hellenic character of the scene.

By contrast, a dialogue in the *Trinummus* between the *senex* Charmides and the slave Stasimus on the same subject makes clear allusion to a Roman context. Stasimus pronounces on the days when old customs and old frugality were held in higher esteem than the wicked habits of the present. Charmides (listening, but speaking to himself) reacts with glee at the slave's upholding of ancient virtues in the manner of his ancestors. Stasimus then waxes eloquent on the degradation of current morals that sanction corruption and ignore laws. Present practices subject the law to custom even more than parents are subject to children (Plaut. *Trinummus* 1028–1048). That cynical comment links the passage to that noted above in the *Bacchides*. The Roman echoes, however, predominate in this case. Both characters refer again and again to *mos* or *mos maiorum* with such repetition that it cannot be accident (fourteen times in the space of eighteen lines: Plaut. *Trinummus* 1028–1045). But with a sardonic twist: current *mos* has subjected even *leges* to its control, a reversal of the proper order of society (Plaut. *Trinummus* 1037, 1043; cf. 28–38, 284–300).

It may be no accident that Plautus plies this platitude in two separate contexts, the one palpably Greek, the other Roman. In each instance, a lowly slave mouths the clichés, the first instructing his master, the other delighting him. Once again, it would be simplistic to interpret this as Plautus taking sides in contemporary arguments about moral decline. The playwright draws attention instead to the tiresome hypocrisy inherent in moralistic pronouncements that forever contrast the older and younger generations, the good old days of the past with the dissoluteness of the present. By having closely comparable moralisms uttered by characters in altogether distinct societies, Plautus underscores the banality of such discourse that crosses cultural divides and renders it ridiculous.

Religion constitutes an area of considerable interest, a central ingredient in Roman society, inseparable from a range of political, social, and cultural activities and alluded to with notable frequency in the comedies. The subject plainly intrigued Plautus (Duckworth 1952: 295–300; Hanson 1959: 48–60). His own stance, however, is tantalizingly elusive. The combination of reverence and irreverence in the plays could leave audiences guessing. And Plautus probably preferred it that way.

Ostensible mockery of the gods or of those who believe in them occurs repeatedly, in a variety of ways and a variety of contexts (Tolliver 1952: 49–57; Hanson 1959: 82–101; Segal 1968: 29–31). A number of examples can serve as illustration. Agorastocles, the *adulescens* in *Poenulus*, his ends achieved, boasts that Jupiter does his bidding and holds him in awe (Plaut.*Poenulus* 1190–1192). He proceeds subsequently to praise his girlfriend by affirming that were he Jupiter he would take her as his wife and boot Juno out of the house (Plaut. *Poenulus* 1219–1220). The cook in *Pseudolus* maintains that his seasonings are so marvelous that their odors waft to heaven and Jupiter would not dine without them; if he fails to cook, the god goes hungry (Plaut. *Pseudolus* 840–846). Sosia the slave in *Amphitruo*, impatient while waiting for daybreak, rails at the sun for his delay, probably sleeping off a drunken binge (Plaut. *Amphitruo* 281–282). In the *Casina,* a dialogue between the *senex* and his slave has the old man express his trust and hope in the gods, only to have the *servus* undercut him by asserting that all mortals rely on the gods but are regularly deceived by them (Plaut. *Casina* 346–349). A comic exchange between a pimp and a fisherman in *Rudens* involves the swearing of a solemn oath to Venus to pay a promised price. Having sworn, the pimp offers an aside: my tongue may swear, but my mind decides (Plaut. *Rudens* 1355). And the pimp later underscores his cynicism by announcing his willingness to swear readily and at any time, for swearing serves only to preserve property, not to lose it (Plaut. *Rudens* 1373–1374). His counterpart, the irrepressible Ballio in *Pseudolus*, parades a parallel impiety. He flaunts his dedication to profit by declaring that, even if he were in the midst of performing sacrifice to Jupiter himself, he would drop the very entrails at the altar if a chance of material gain presented itself: you can't resist that form of piety (Plaut. *Pseudolus* 265–268).

Calling on the gods for assistance is a common feature in the plays. But the practice can be taken to excess and subjected to mockery. So, for example, Chrysalus, the slave in *Bacchides,* in seeking authorization for a statement about his master's whereabouts, summons the support of Jupiter, Juno, Ceres, Minerva, and a dozen more deities and divine personifications by name, and then adds "all the gods" (Plaut. *Bacchides* 992–997). Toxilus, in the *Persae*, having proclaimed the success of his scheme as if it were a glorious military triumph and the arrival of peace to the world, gives thanks to Jupiter and all the gods who dwell in heaven for granting him vengeance upon his enemy, the pimp (Plaut. *Persa* 752–756). In the *Captivi*, the parasite parodically likens himself to Jupiter and adds identification also with a roster of abstract divinities, Salus, Fortuna, Lux, Laetitia, and Gaudium, thus to expand his claims on dinner (Plaut. *Captivi* 863–865). The *senex* Charmides in *Trinummus* heaps praise upon Neptune for bringing him back home safely after a dangerous sea voyage. Fair enough. But a strong irony clings to the passage. Charmides feels the need to repair Neptune's general reputation by denying a host of charges commonly brought against the god: his savagery, harshness, avariciousness, cruelty, madness, filthiness, infidelity, and a variety of other defects. The fact that Neptune's badly bruised image needed defense at such length leaves a more vivid impression than the strained efforts to exculpate him (Plaut. *Trinummus* 820–831; cf. *Rudens* 485–486).

Tongue-in cheek jabs appear in diverse forms and places. The *adulescens* of the *Bacchides* twits his tutor by rattling off a series of variants on the concept of Venus and love, claiming them all as divinities, and when rebuked by the tutor rebukes him in turn for ignorance of the expanded pantheon (Plaut. *Bacchides* 114–124). In the *Trinummus*, the *sycophanta* spins a fancy yarn about visiting Jupiter, who, according to other gods, happened to be away visiting his villa, where he went to fetch food for his slaves (Plaut. *Trinummus* 943–944). The love-struck and hungry *adulescens* in the *Rudens* seeks his girl at the temple of Venus and is told that he should go to Ceres, who can supply food, not to Venus, who has responsibility only for love (Plaut. *Rudens* 144–146). The conventional attributes of the gods come in for as much fun as their character.

The dramatist can also take a swipe at Greek (Roman) mythology—or at least those who embrace its fancies. So Mercury himself, in the prologue to the *Amphitruo*, with reference to his father Jupiter's latest sexual conquest, observes to the audience: "I think you already know how my father is, how freewheeling he is in many matters of this kind, and what a lover he is once he is turned on" (Plaut. *Amphitruo* 104–106). This light-hearted reference to divine amours delivered to a knowing audience has the delicious character of a mythological figure poking fun sympathetically at mythology—or, more probably, at those who swallow its sillier side. Similarly, the pimp in *Rudens* makes reference in passing to the marital tension between Vulcan and Venus, for reasons that no one in the audience needed to be reminded of (Plaut. *Rudens* 761).

What is to be made of all this? Plautus certainly conducts no campaign to discredit the gods. Mockery and playfulness abound, but the characters who scorn divinity are hardly admirable or meritorious. The pimps in *Rudens* and *Pseudolus* declare the worthlessness of oaths and sacrifices, preferring profit to piety. A slave in *Casina* declares that men are deceived by gods, and another in *Amphitruo* scolds the sun. A cook claims that Jupiter would not dine without the sweet aromas that he sends to heaven. And a parasite professes identity not only with Jupiter with an entire array of divine abstractions. Plautus further aims his barbs at those who believe naively in fanciful myths about Jupiter's philandering, Vulcan's jealousies, or Neptune's savagery rather than at the objects of their beliefs. The spectators might be prompted to rethink their persuasions and practices, but the gods emerge unscathed.

Reverence for divinity, by contrast, is not so funny. Its relatively rare appearance in the comedies is scarcely surprising. But it does appear, and when it does it needs to be taken seriously. The prologue to the *Rudens* is spoken by a divine figure, the celestial constellation Arcturus. The star begins with a solemn statement, an ascription of omniscience to the supreme deity. He attributes to Jupiter knowledge of the good and the wicked, a knowledge impervious to falsehood and perjury, resistant to supplication, gifts, or offerings by the guilty. Prayers of the pious will be heard; those who do evil are ignored. Arcturus then issues an invocation to piety and fidelity, urging his listeners to maintain that course from which they will find joy (Plaut. *Rudens* 13–30). That profound pronouncement does not stand alone. Tyndarus, the once prosperous free man, now a captive and slave, in the *Captivi* consoles Hegio, whose own son had suffered the same fate. Tyndarus echoes the convictions of Arcturus and offers a profound assurance: there is a god who hears and sees what we do, who rewards the meritorious and punishes the undeserving (Plaut. *Captivi* 313–315). There is no mockery in any of this. Plautus's own sentiments may well receive expression here. Most of the action of the *Rudens* takes place at the shrine of Venus, an altogether benign and magnanimous divinity in the play who, through her priestess, protects the shipwrecked girls and effects the happy outcome. Her praises are sung on several occasions and genuinely (Plaut. *Rudens* 261–262, 305, 349–350, 694–696). Authentic devotion to divinity gains strong reinforcement from the *Poenulus*. Its central figure, the admirable Carthaginian Hanno, repeatedly exhibits his homage to the divine. He offers a sublime paean to Jupiter, whom he describes as cherishing and nourishing humankind, one through whom we live and draw vital breath, on whom depend the hopes and lives of all persons (Plaut. *Poenulus* 1186–1187). Once reunited with his daughters, Hanno lifts a prayer of thanksgiving to the gods, who have earned eternal gratitude by bringing the family back together, a sign of their gracious favor and a recognition of the piety that had been paid them (Plaut. *Poenulus* 1253–1255). And near the end of the play, he reiterates his gratitude, this time to all gods and goddesses for according him such happiness and joy (Plaut. *Poenulus* 1274–1276). These were heartfelt invocations by a commendable character, no comic caricature.

The comedies thus supply a mixture of reverence and irreverence, in uneven quantities and differing weights. Can they be reconciled? Should they be reconciled? The playwright was not interested in doing so. They may, in some fashion, bear upon diverse attitudes in Roman society, where religion was a primary element in civic and cultural life and drew a range of reactions. More importantly, they reflect the mentality of a shrewd observer who discerned (and probably shared) authentic piety but also witnessed hypocrisy, manipulation, and simplistic credulity that lent itself readily to comic parody.

Plautus's reflections on religious matters, however, penetrate still further. This is no mere contrast or balance between reverence and irreverence, to be settled either by statistics or by relative magnitude. The playwright offers some key passages that suggest a deeper probe.

A character in *Miles Gloriosus* ruminates on the relation of divine purpose to humankind. He expresses regret that the gods fixed matters so that all lead lives according to a single standard. It would be preferable if they operated more like a fair market assessor who sets prices in terms of the value of the merchandise, higher for the meritorious and lower for the deficient. Similarly, the gods ought to extend the lives of admirable men and diminish those of scoundrels who should be cut off early. If such had been the divine scheme, the world would have seen far fewer evildoers and their opportunity for villainy would be reduced, whereas good men would enjoy a cheaper cost of living (Plaut. *Miles* 725–735). The *senex*, an object of admiration for the speaker, then responds with a mild rebuke: anyone who indicts the wisdom of the gods or criticizes them is foolish and ignorant (Plaut. *Miles* 736–737). The matter is then dropped. We need not speculate on where Plautus stands on this. He has, in any case, had a character raise the issue of the gods' impartiality. They are, on this reckoning, too impartial. Instead of rewarding virtue and discouraging vice, they prefer an evenhandedness that the speaker regrets, only to be chastised by his interlocutor for folly in censuring divine counsels. The speaker himself hardly exhibits profundity. His criterion for the benefit of virtue amounts to little more than material gain. And the question remains unresolved. But the dramatist has put in the minds of his audience the problem of divine justice— and its limitations.

Two intriguing passages spoken by two different characters in the *Rudens* provoke parallel thought along these lines. Near the beginning of the play, one of the two ship-wrecked girls, having been washed ashore after much buffeting and misfortune, in despair and with little hope for the future, issues a remarkable indictment of the gods for her undeserved sufferings. Is it divine will, she laments, that I be cast, frightened and helpless, upon forbidding shores? Should I think that I was born for this wretched fate? Is this the reward for my preeminent piety? I could understand it if I had been dis-respectful to a parent or to the gods. But, since I have taken care to avoid such impiety, o gods, you treat me shabbily, unjustly, and impudently. If this is how you honor the innocent, what signal does it give to the guilty? If I knew that I or my parents had com-mitted iniquities against you, I would have fewer grounds for self-pity. But it is the guilt of others, not my own, that has been inflicted upon me (Plaut. *Rudens* 188–198). This is a harsh and unequivocal verdict on the justice of the gods, their apparent indifference to good and evil, and their imperviousness to acts of piety or impiety. The girl, of course, eventually enjoys a happy ending. But her impassioned declaration once more puts the spotlight upon the troublesome issue of the gods' often inscrutable behavior—which remains unsettling to mortals.

Toward the end of the play, a much more positive statement issues from the mouth of the *senex* Daemones, who has just been happily reunited with his long-lost daughter. Its import, however, actually reinforces rather than contravenes the sentiments of the ship-wrecked girl. Daemones heaps praise upon the immortal gods for the unexpected good fortune that allowed him to find his daughter once again. But his emphasis rests heavily and precisely upon the unexpectedness. Is it not the case, he asks, that if the gods wish to bring benefit to a man, this desired end comes in some fashion to the pious? I never expected or believed that it would happen.Nevertheless, I unexpectedly discovered my daughter (Plaut. *Rudens* 1191–1196). The upshot of this seems to be that divine justice descends in unpredictable fashion. The pious may be favored, but only if the gods will it so. Daemones can rejoice in his good fortune and express gratitude for it. Acts of piety may help. But one cannot bank on them. If things work out well, that is a nice surprise, rather than a quid pro quo for devotion.

In short, Plautus's repeated references to religion carry a complex and thoughtful message. He shows respect for the reverent and makes sport of the irreverent. But the former do not always comprehend the ways of the divine, and the latter are belittled to expose the broader misconceptions in Roman society. Plautus delivers a nuanced assessment that distinguishes credence from credulity, contrasts a superficial and a per-ceptive grasp of divinity, and reaffirms the value of veneration even while mocking its misuse. In a social setting where religion plays so central a part, these intuitions carry significant meaning.

Plautus lived through an era of the highest importance for Roman history and Roman identity: the Second Punic War, the titanic struggle for survival with the Carthaginians and their fiercely formidable leader Hannibal. It could hardly fail to have left a powerful impression. Nothing in the comedies makes explicit reference to that momentous contest—not surprisingly, as the nature of the genre would nearly foreclose that possibility. But one noteworthy play does open a revealing window on contemporary Roman attitudes toward Carthage in the immediate aftermath of the bitter and bloody conflict.

The *Poenulus* ("The Little Carthaginian") presents Hanno as the principal figure around whom the entire drama revolves. That itself is cause for astonishment. The play hit the stage only a decade or so after the end of the war. Bitterness and hostility toward the enemy ought to have been at a high level of intensity at that time. To be sure, here, as elsewhere, a Hellenic comedy served as model for the Plautine play. But Plautus chose to put a Carthaginian character on the stage at this time, a time when the war carried recent and powerful resonance, hardly an accident. How does one interpret this?

The comedy does contain a number of snide remarks about Hanno's exotic clothing, his unintelligible language, his dissembling, and a variety of alien peculiarities (Plaut. *Poenulus* 111–113, 975–981, 990–1034, 1298–1318). Ostensibly this points to stereotypes of the Punic trickster and unwelcome outsider, and caters to the biases of a Roman audience still scarred by the wounds of the Hannibalic conflict (cf. Leigh 2004: 28–56). But an important point needs to be noted. The persons who cast nasty aspersions upon Hanno are the more despicable characters in the play: the scheming slave and the swaggering soldier. If Plautus alludes to contemporary slurs against Carthaginians, he seems to subvert rather than to endorse them. Hanno, in fact, defies the caricatures. Plautus presents him as a man of erudition, understanding, and forgiveness, whose determined search for his kidnapped daughters ultimately brings success, a thwarting of the wicked, and a happy ending. Not only does Hanno challenge the Punic stereotype, he challenges the comic stereotype: a worthy and respected figure, not the standard comic *senex*.

Plautus subtly undermines the "otherness" of Hanno. He associates the Carthaginian four times with *pietas*, that quintessentially Roman quality (Plaut. *Poenulus* 1137, 1190, 1255, 1277). Moreover, he has Hanno refer to an equally quintessential Roman virtue, that of *fides* (Plaut.*Poenulus* 967). By having a Carthaginian exemplify Roman values, Plautus sends a striking message. His audience will certainly have noticed that. The playwright plainly plays with inversion here, a standard feature of Roman comedy. He may have upset the expectations of the prejudiced. But he must have anticipated a broadly sympathetic audience for such thrusts. Hanno, in the end, is a complex and paradoxical character, with a range of qualities moving from the questionable to the estimable. But the fact that Plautus could toy whimsically with such a figure, parodying purported Punic practices while puncturing Roman prejudices, within just a decade of the Hannibalic war, constitutes the most significant and meaningful feature of the *Poenulus*. The dramatist has his eye fixed on the contemporary scene here. And he discloses an intriguing mixture of Roman feelings in the wake of the fearsome conflict. Hostile stereotypes circulated, but sufficient sentiment existed to back a play that presented a largely sympathetic portrait of a Carthaginian. The Roman populace could keep its ferocity toward the Punic enemy on the battlefield separate from its estimate of the character of the nation. *Poenulus* offers powerful testimony to that important attribute of the Roman mentality.

Plautus was alive to current issues, controversies, and developments, even when he did not make any direct reference to them. They might come disguised in Hellenic garb, but that facade was conventional, not designed to deceive. A swift sketch of a few pertinent matters can illustrate the point.

Increasing number of victories on the battlefield sparked more intensive competition among conquering generals to claim showy triumphs at home. And their efforts in turn provoked reaction among rival political and military leaders to challenge those claims through principled or questionable means. Debates over what constituted legitimate requests for triumphs grew more heated. Criteria shifted and fluctuated. Did subordinate officers merit them? What numbers of killed or captured would qualify? What was needed to obtain a triumph rather than an *ovatio*? Was it necessary to lead back the army largely intact? Charges flew back and forth about false claims or exaggerated stories, provoking sharp exchanges in the senate or even trials in public. Major figures like Cato the Elder weighed in on the debates. Cato published a blistering speech entitled *De Falsis Pugnis*, and attacked generals who sought triumphs even when they had not taken territory by force. The battles made a major splash on the public scene (see, e.g., Cato, *ORF*, fr. 58,148; Gellius, 10.3.17; cf. Fontaine 2010: 125–126; in general, Gruen 1990: 129–133; Pittenger 2008: 33–53, 84–103, and *passim*). In conjunction with them came controversies over who should control the spoils of war. As cash and booty accumulated from foreign wars, exhibited in lavish triumphs, distribution of the loot became a divisive issue. The line between a general's prerogative to dispose of spoils and the public claim on these treasures was fuzzy and disputed, and the disputes became more vehement as the amounts increased, prompting challenges in the senate and charges in the courts, including the celebrated (and inconclusive) trials of the Scipios. It is no coincidence that Cato delivered speeches entitled *De Pecunia Regis Antiochi* and *De Praeda Militibus Dividenda* (for details, see Gruen 1990: 133–137).

Plautus refrains from reference to individual episodes. But some indirect intimations are unmistakable. The *servus* Chrysalis in the *Bacchides* conducts a mock *ovatio* to proclaim victory for his deception, picturing himself weighed down with booty, boasting that he captured a city by guile while bringing his army home intact, disdaining a triumph on the grounds that they are all too common, and offering to entertain his troops with food and drink all the same (Plaut. *Bacchides* 1068–1075). One could hardly miss the allusions here to contemporary wrangles over triumphs and booty. Nor would Plautus's audience regard as purely innocent Amphitryon's remark about his soldiers acquiring booty, land, and glory, Toxilus's blatant characterization of his deception as military victory with spoils to be distributed to his followers in lavish fashion, and Pseudolus's boast that his successful scheme meant booty for himself and his partisans (Plaut. *Amphitruo* 193; *Persa* 757–758; *Pseudolus* 588). Further, references to false testimony and overzealous informers would readily bring to mind the increasing recourse to the courts in challenges to returning commanders and their excessive claims (Plaut. *Persa* 62–73; *Curculio* 470; *Menaechmi* 838–839). Plautus did not need to be explicit. The plays mocked ambition, lampooned overblown scenarios, deflated braggart conquerors, and likened the acquisition of plunder to the duplicitous guile of slaves.

One other matter merits note. A plethora of laws surfaced in this period, particularly to curb usury and exploitation of lending practices, and to check excessive display of luxury, the sumptuary legislation (Livy, 34.1.3, 34.1.8, 34.7.2–5, 35.41.9–10). The multiplication of measures, of course, did not assure their enforcement. And comedy proved to be a convenient means to mock the ineffectiveness of legislators. Plautus on several occasions calls attention to laws that were ignored, unenforced, or violated with impunity. He belittles both father and son in the *Asinaria* for squandering their labors in senate and legislative activity to no good purpose: the activity debilitates those who engage in it, and the legislation appeals to the debauched (Plaut. *Asinaria* 599–602, 871–875). A character in the *Poenulus* makes reference to laws passed repeatedly by the people against the same offense, one that is committed again in the play. The statutes obviously lacked force (Plaut. *Poenulus* 725). The pimp Labrax in the *Rudens* expresses himself as altogether unrestrained by laws (Plaut. *Rudens* 724–725). Curculio blasts bankers for breaking every law passed to hold them in check: they can always find a loophole (Plaut. *Curculio* 509–511). Plautus places the most extensive tirade in the mouth of the slave Stasimus in the *Trinummus* who laments that contemporaries run roughshod over *leges* that are without force, subservient to *mores mali* (Plaut. *Trinummus* 1028–1044). The issue is reduced to farce when an *adulescens* in the *Mercator* proposes a measure to prohibit all men over sixty from using the services of courtesans (Plaut. *Mercator* 1015–1024)! An equally unenforceable bill to curtail informing is suggested by the parasite Saturio in the *Persa*. He advances the proposition that a successful informer should yield up half his earnings to the public treasury and that any defendant should be permitted to sue his accuser for the same sum sought from himself (Plaut. *Persa* 62–76). The playwright appears to be parodying legislation on the books that could command no obedience. The plague of moneylenders also offered fodder for comedy. Curculio's broadside against the whole tribe of *faeneratores* associates pimps with bankers as objects of revilement: the first tear men apart with baneful solicitation and debauchery, the second with exorbitant interest rates. Bankers are even worse, for they unscrupulously violate a host of laws, and they can count on lack of enforcement and escape clauses (Plaut. *Curculio* 506–511; cf. *Casina* 25–28; *Pseudolus* 296–300; *Mostellaria* 532–538; *Aulularia* 527–531; *Epidicus* 53–54, 114–115). These caustic comments are not simply copied from Greek New Comedy. The tight credit and straitened economic circumstances that prevailed in the aftermath of the Hannibalic war, as well as the frustration engendered by inept and fruitless legislation, lent some immediacy to Plautus's parodies.

The comic dramatist avoided targeting individuals or specific events. His topicality operated on a broader plane. The plays caricatured practices, attitudes, and temperaments that would have resonance with his audience and provide insight into the disposition of his contemporaries.

The comedies of Terence, by contrast, offer little that counts as comment on the current scene. As has long been recognized by scholars, his plays hew more closely to their originals, keep attention focused on the Hellenic setting, and have far greater concern with domestic interplay than with social commentary. But they may not be altogether devoid of the latter.

Terence's play, *Hecyra* ("The Mother-in-Law"), merits mention in this regard. The plot is complicated and engaging. It employs ostensibly stock characters and stock situations, misapprehensions and misunderstandings. But the familiar features are overshadowed or subverted in ingenious ways that lend real suspense to the course of events, the shifts are unexpected, the outcome not forecast, and the revelations only partial (Konstan 1983: 130–141; Goldberg 1986: 150–169; Sharrock 2009: 233–249). The characters do not fit the usual molds. The audience as well as the individuals are kept in the dark for much of the drama, as the dramatist plays with expectations and increases the intrigue. Most important, key figures shatter the stereotypes. The mother-in-law, though subjected to standard abuse, reacts with dignity and stature, the most admirable person in the play. And the courtesan breaks even the "prostitute with heart of gold" stereotype, rising above it as a woman of integrity and discernment.

The women are decidedly more admirable than the men in this play. Each of the fathers is a blustering angry *senex* who repeatedly misconceives the situation. The *adulescens*, in addition to reaching hasty and incorrect conclusions, is an unrepentant rapist. And the *servus*, far from being *callidus*, is largely ineffective and clueless. The mother-in-law, mother, courtesan, and daughter/wife (even though she never appears on stage) earn our sympathy.

A subtle undertone exists here regarding male authority and the ascendancy of the paterfamilias. Of course, it is comic convention to make sport of fumbling fathers and foolish youths and to invert social hierarchies for whimsical purposes. But the *Hecyra* does not engage in Plautine topsy-turvy, nor does it render its characters ridiculous in farcical fashion. Honest mistakes and foolish decisions drive the story. But Terence does call attention to, and indeed calls into question, societal circumstances that made all this possible (Slater 1987–1988: 249–260; Barsby 2001: 140–142). The young man Pamphilus, long the lover of the courtesan Bacchis, found himself pushed into an unwanted marriage by his father Laches. Pamphilus's reluctant concession to filial piety caused him immediate misgivings. He went through with the wedding but did not consummate the marriage, ignoring the feelings of his new bride. The paterfamilias prevailed, leaving no one satisfied (Ter. *Hecyra* 114–137; cf. 686–688). Philumena, the bride, it appears, lacked all recourse except to carry out the expected part of the modest, submissive wife, nobly bearing in silence the injuries and insults inflicted by her husband (Ter. *Hecyra* 164–166). Similar injustices were suffered by Sostrata, mother of Pamphilus, lacerated by Laches as a typically spiteful mother-in-law who hates her daughter-in-law and has thus caused friction between the spouses. Her response, like that of Philumena, is demure and amicable, protesting her innocence but unwilling to quarrel with her husband (Ter. *Hecyra* 198–242; cf. 513–515). A comparable clash occurs in the household of the bride's father and mother. The *pater* Phidippus reminds his daughter Philumena that it is his right to compel her to obey his commands, but he elects not to exercise it (Ter. *Hecyra* 243–245). Phidippus does, however, rail at his wife Myrrina with a similar insistence on his patriarchal authority—although Terence gives it a twist by having him concede that his insistence will be ignored. Myrrina, hamstrung by a secret that she cannot disclose (that Philumena is pregnant with a child that she thought could not be that of her husband), prefers, like Sostrata, amiability to hostility (Ter. *Hecyra* 522–565; cf. 631–633). Pamphilus, the *adulescens*, having yielded to paternal power, is pressed also by filial duty to his mother, thereby preventing reconciliation with his wife (Ter. *Hecyra* 293–305, 470–481). The conflicting pressures increase tensions in a situation where ignorance and misunderstandings prevail. The resolution (at least for some, but not all) comes when the *meretrix* Bacchis clears up the misapprehension of the two fathers that she is still having relations with Pamphilus and generously agrees to make the case to the two mothers in order to remove suspicion from the *adulescens* (Ter. *Hecyra* 743–797). That act of generosity brings about the denouement of the drama, once it is discovered that the baby is actually Pamphilus's own—even though as consequence of a rape (Ter. *Hecyra* 816–840)!

Terence's point is not that the female characters are commendable and the men's actions are dubious or despicable. There was enough self-deception and jumping to conclusions to go around for all parties concerned. A broader issue manifests itself. The exercise of paternal authority in a patriarchal society can have unanticipated and unintended consequences, disruptive to family and social relations. Terence's sensitivities were attuned to such matters. Of course, Hellas had no immunity to these problems, and we cannot tell how far the dramatist drew plot and characters from his model. But the centrality of the paterfamilias on the Roman political and social scene was something to which the playwright could hardly have been impervious. The *Hecyra* puts a bright and striking light on that institution. The quiet comic genius of Terence, in short, might also prompt his audience to look again at their own circumstances and surroundings. Roman drama did not constitute a hermetically sealed compartment. It conducted its own special interplay with Roman society.

FURTHER READING

The general study of Duckworth (1952), a sound and judicious survey, is the ideal starting point for this subject. Fraenkel's classic work in the revised Italian edition (1960, now translated into English as Fraenkel 2007), remains fundamental and unsurpassed in teasing out the Roman features in Plautine comedy that departed from Hellenic models. Gaiser (1972) carried the subject further and found comparable features in Terence. Segal's important book (1968), while somewhat one-sided in interpreting Plautus's comedy as inversion of Roman values, remains required reading. The perceptive essays of Konstan (1983) treating six plays of Plautus and two of Terence bring numerous sensitive insights to bear. Goldberg's book (1986) holds its place as the best treatment in English on the whole range of issues associated with Terence's plays. The chapter in Gruen (1990) on Plautus sketches links between the comedies and contemporary historical developments. Leigh (2004) treats that topic with reference to three of Plautus's plays and one of Terence's with some stimulating but occasionally overconjectural suggestions.

BIBLIOGRAPHY

Barsby, J. 2001. *Terence: Phormio, The Mother-in-Law, The Brothers.* Cambridge, MA: Harvard University Press.

Duckworth, G. E. 1952. *The Nature of Roman Comedy: A Study in Popular Entertainment.* Princeton: Princeton University Press.

Fontaine, M. 2010. *Funny Words in Plautine Comedy.* Oxford and New York: Oxford University Press.

Fraenkel, E. 1960. *Elementi Plautini in Plauto.* Translated by F. Munari. Florence: La Nuova Italia. = Fraenkel, E. 2007. *Plautine Elements in Plautus.* Translated by T. Drevikovsky and F. Muecke. Oxford: Oxford University Press. Originally published as *Plautinisches im Plautus* (Berlin, 1922).

Gaiser, K. 1972. "Zur Eigenart der römischen Komödie: Plautus und Terenz gegenüber ihren grechischen Vorbildern." *ANRW* I.2: 1027–1113.

Goldberg, S. M. 1986. *Understanding Terence.* Princeton: Princeton University Press.

Gruen, E. S. 1990. *Studies in Greek Culture and Roman Policy.* Leiden: E. J. Brill.

Hanson, J. A. 1959. "Plautus as a Source Book for Roman Religion." *TAPA* 90: 48–101.

——. 1965. "The Glorious Military." In *Roman Drama*, edited by T. A. Dorey and D. R. Dudley, 51–85. New York: Basic Books.

Harvey, P. B. 1981. "Historical Allusions in Plautus and the Date of the Amphitryo." *Athenaeum* 50: 480–489.

——. 1986. "Historical Topicality in Plautus." *CW* 79: 297–304.

Konstan, D. 1983. *Roman Comedy.* Ithaca, NY: Cornell University Press.

Leigh, M. 2004. *Comedy and the Rise of Rome.* Oxford: Oxford University Press.

Leo, F. 1912. *Plautinische Forschungen: Zur Kritik und Geschichte der Komödie.* 2nd ed. Berlin: Weidmann.

McCarthy, K. 2000. *Slaves, Masters, and the Art of Authority in Plautine Comedy.* Princeton: Princeton University Press.

Perna, R. 1955. *L'originalità di Plauto.* Bari: Leonardo da Vinci.

Pittenger, M. R. P. 2008. *Contested Triumphs: Politics, Pageantry, and Performance in Livy's Republican Rome.* Berkeley: University of California Press.

Segal, E. 1968. *Roman Laughter: The Comedy of Plautus.* Cambridge, MA: Harvard University Press.

Sharrock. A. 2009. *Reading Roman Comedy: Poetics and Playfulness in Plautus and Terence.* Cambridge, UK: Cambridge University Press.

Slater, N. W. 1987–1988. "The Fictions of Patriarchy in Terence's *Hecyra*." *CW* 81: 249–260.

Tolliver, H. M. 1952. "Plautus and the State Gods of Rome." *CJ* 48: 49–57.

CHAPTER 31

··

LAW AND ROMAN COMEDY

··

JAN FELIX GAERTNER

1. INTRODUCTION

THE relation between law and literature has played an important role in the study of Roman comedy at least since the late nineteenth century, when legal historians began to exploit the remains of Roman comedy as sources for the reconstruction of Attic and Roman law and scholars interested in classical literature tried to explain the legal scenarios of the plays or used our knowledge of Attic and Roman law as an analytical tool to determine the relation between Greek and Roman comedy. Over the last thirty years, new avenues of research have been opened up by debates in other disciplines. Literary theorists, sociologists, and philosophers have emphasized that literature does not simply mirror law and legal practice, but is influenced by legal norms (e.g., rules regarding intellectual property) and in turn also influences the public perception of law and legality. Furthermore, international commerce and the development of supranational institutions have led to numerous studies on the problems of legal translation, which offer a new methodology for analyzing how Roman poets adapted the legal scenarios of their Greek originals. The present chapter must be selective. It begins with a brief sketch of the research of earlier scholars and an outline of the problems posed by the analysis of the Roman *comoediae palliatae*. This is followed by three sections which describe how Plautus, Terence, and some of the fragmentary comic poets employ legal content and legal language in their plays.

2. THE *COMOEDIAE PALLIATAE* BETWEEN ATTIC AND ROMAN LAW

All the transmitted comedies of Plautus and Terence and most of the plays of which we still possess fragments are so-called *comoediae palliatae* which are situated in Greek-speaking cities of the Hellenistic world. In addition, testimonies in ancient grammarians, production notices (*didascaliae*), and the plays themselves indicate that all six comedies of Terence and Plautus's *Asinaria, Casina, Mercator, Miles, Mostellaria, Poenulus, Rudens, Stichus, Trinummus*, and *Vidularia* are adaptations of Greek plays of Attic comedy. This raises the question whether the remaining eleven Plautine plays, too, are based on Greek originals and how closely the Roman playwrights followed their Greek models. Since it is unlikely that an Athenian poet should have written a play that conforms to Roman law or that a Roman playwright should have been so familiar with Attic law that he could compose a comedy that accurately depicted the legal situation in Athens, the analysis of legal scenarios could shed some light on these questions. However, our knowledge of Attic law is incomplete, and there are few reliable sources on the law and legal practice in Rome around 200 BCE. Some of the first studies on the topic of law and Roman comedy simply postulated that the plays represented Roman (e.g., Bekker 1892, Pernard 1900) or Attic law (e.g., Green 1929); they did not take into account that the Roman poets may have altered their Greek models or could have considered it dramatically effective to confront their audience with a scenic reality that did not conform to their expectations. An important step forward was taken by Otto Fredershausen, who differentiated (Fredershausen 1906: 15–19, Fredershausen 1912: 200) between (a) elements that were incompatible with our knowledge of contemporary or later Roman law and hence probably came from the Greek originals; (b) elements that were incompatible with our sources on Attic law and so must have been altered or added by the Roman dramatists; and (c) elements which were equally consistent with Greek and Roman law and whose origin could not be determined (see also Dareste 1892, Girard 1893, Pringsheim 1950: 419–429). Fredershausen's work was continued by Paoli (1962, 1976), Witt (1971a, 1971b) and Scafuro (1993, 1997, 2003–2004), who expanded Fredershausen's methodology and used dramatic conventions of Greek New Comedy as further criteria for determining the provenience of plot elements (cf. Scafuro 1997: 424–427). The research of these scholars shows that the Roman *comoediae palliatae* are a hybrid mix of Greek and Roman elements and that the key elements of the plots presuppose Attic law. This fact, which can be substantiated by many further observations (cf. Gaertner 2011: Vol. 2, *passim*), strongly speaks against recent attempts (e.g., Lefèvre et al. 1991) to show that some of Plautus's plays may not have been based on Greek originals. At the same time, however, it should also make us wonder how and why the Roman poets constructed such a hybrid scenic reality that is neither entirely Greek nor Roman. In the following sections, I shall first give an outline of Plautus's use of legal contents and legal language and later contrast this with the approach of other Roman playwrights.

3. PLAUTUS

A. The Adaptation of Legal Scenarios from Attic Comedy

To understand Plautus's use of legal scenarios and language, we must first turn to his choice of Greek models. If we compare the twenty-one transmitted comedies with the remains of Menander's oeuvre and the six surviving plays of Terence, we see that Plautus avoids Greek scenarios that involve institutions that are completely alien to Roman law, such as the epiclerate. Instead, he prefers scenarios that present Attic law but can be associated with current debates and problems in Rome. A good example of this is the criticism of opulent dowries in the *Aulularia* (especially 475–495), which is influenced by Greek political philosophy (cf. Aristot. *Pol.* 1266a39–b6, Plat. *Leg.* 742c, 774c), but of course also touches a nerve of the Roman audience (cf. Cato *orat.* fr. 158, p. 60 Malcovati[4]). More important, however, is Plautus's fondness for turbulent plots in which the protagonists achieve their goals by means of legal loopholes and traps: the characters use false identities to obtain money or goods (e.g., *Asinaria* 407–503, *Curculio* 406–461, *Pseudolus* 594–666, 956–1016), feign the purchase of a house (*Mostellaria* 615–654), sell a freeborn girl as a slave (*Persa* 492–710), or frame their enemies by constructing charges of adultery (*Miles Gloriosus* 1394–1437), illegal enslavement (*Persa* 738–752), or theft (*Poenulus* 761–816). This stands in stark contrast to the practice of Menander and Terence, in whose plays law tends to function as an obstacle: legal regulations stand in the way of the young couple's marriage (e.g., *Kitharistes* 83–91), and lawsuits (e.g., *Sikyonioi* 272, *Samia* 717–718) or claims of a third party (e.g., *Aspis* 180–189, *Sikyonioi* 133–140) often threaten the happy ending.

Plautus's Technique of Adaptation

In adapting plays for the Roman stage, Plautus was prepared to confront his audience with a scenic reality that was in several ways unlike its everyday life:

1. The legal capacity of Plautine sons is incompatible with Roman *patria potestas*: without the permission or collaboration of their *pater*, Roman sons could not squander the family fortune (*Mercator* 40–60, *Trinummus* 106–139), manumit slave-girls (*Epidicus* 236–305), leave their home and emigrate (*Mercator* 644–660), or choose their own way of life (*Cistellaria* 312, 314, 319, 481–482, 485, 497–498).

2. Various economic activities of the slaves reflect the legal and social reality at Athens; e.g., in *Persa*, Toxilus manages the household and affairs of his master, who is on a business trip (*Persa* 29–31, *passim*); as far as we know, Roman slaves did not have such far-reaching responsibilities.

3. The transactions by proxy are incompatible with the Roman concept of indirect representation: at *Curculio* 616, 618–619, the soldier argues that the girl is his property because she was bought with his money. This reflects the Greek law of sale, according to which "the provenance of the money used for the payment of the price is decisive for the acquisition" (Pringsheim 1950: 205). Hence, someone could obtain property even if not personally present at the sale. Roman law, on the contrary, only allowed for indirect representation by which the proxy enters a legal relation with the other side and later has to account for his action to the person he represented (cf. Kaser 1971: 264–265). One may compare *Epidicus*, where the Theban banker is the legal owner of the girl until the young man returns the loan (cf. *Epidicus* 607–609, 648).

4. Some details concerning dowry and marriage conform only with Attic law; thus, e.g., the criticism of the law of divorce at *Mercator* 817–829 has close parallels in Greek literature and refers to Attic law (Leo 1912: 118–119, Enk 1932: Vol. 2, 163–164). Likewise, it was Greek, not Roman, practice to provide a dowry for someone else's daughter (*Trinummus* 157–159, 734–743, cf. Erdmann 1934: 308).

Despite this apparent fidelity to the Greek originals, there are many passages where Plautus changes or suppresses legal content. These alterations do not follow a strict pattern. Nevertheless, one can discern three tendencies or factors that prompted the Latin poet to depart from his models.

1. *The distance between the Roman audience and the legal scenarios on the stage*: In order to bring the action closer to the spectators and render it more meaningful to them, Plautus occasionally romanizes the linguistic surface. For example, he styles old men as *senatores* or speaks of *patroni*, *clientes*, or *liberti*, although none of these categories has an exact equivalent in Attic law or features in the remains of Greek New Comedy. A similar effect is created in *Poenulus* 504–816, where Plautus turns the witnesses of the Greek original, who may have been represented as Athenian sycophants, into Roman *advocati* and thus transforms the whole episode into a satire of Roman legal practice (cf. Lofberg 1920: 62–63, Lowe 1990).

2. *Comic potential*: In *Epidicus*, the intrigue becomes much funnier because the two old men who will be fooled by the clever slave are introduced as two experienced lawyers and members of the Senate (188, 292, 359, 522–525). In *Asinaria*, Plautus exploits the terminology of the Roman patronage system to increase the comic effect of a role reversal between a young master and his slaves (621, 649–653, 689–690; cf. also *Captivi* 444, *Casina* 734–740, *Mercator* 996, *Mostellaria* 244, 406–408, *Rudens* 1265–1266).

3. *A different sense of justice in Rome*: In view of the differing notions of incest and its horrors, Plautus may have suppressed the half-sister marriage at the end of *Epidicus* (634–654, cf. Dziatzko 1900; *contra* Keyes 1940). Likewise, the different perception of *suppositio* ('fraudulent introduction of a child into a family'), which was a capital crime in Rome (cf. Kleinfeller 1931: 952), may account for some drastic cuts in *Truculentus*. Moreover, Plautus tends to stiffen the punishment of the antagonists. In *Poenulus,* the pimp is threatened not only with insolvency (as is likely to have happened in the Greek original) but with the Roman penalty of debt bondage (cf. *Poenulus* 185–186, [1341]), and in *Pseudolus* Plautus has altered the plot so that the pimp loses both the girl and her cash value (cf. Lefèvre 1977: 443–444). Unlike the poets of his Greek originals, Plautus seems to have felt that dubious characters such as pimps did not deserve a moderate punishment. Plautus also inserts numerous references to crucifixion, which was the typical punishment of slaves in Rome. In some instances, he may merely replace other forms of capital punishment; in others, he may stiffen the penalty.

Far more frequent than these cuts and changes are passages where Plautus expands the legal scenario and inserts elements referring to Roman law. Again, there is no overarching principle, but a variety of motives and factors:

1. *Plautus occasionally adds elements of Roman law in order to make his plays appear more familiar and meaningful to his Roman audience.* A good illustration of this phenomenon is *Poenulus* 832–833, where Plautus romanizes the description of the pimp's household by inserting Roman legal categories (*equitem, peditem, libertinum*) and punishments (debt bondage).
2. *References to Roman law may also clarify the parameters of the action.* In *Persa,* the pretty slave girl is once manumitted informally (according to Attic law) and once in front of the Roman *praetor* (437–448, 474–475, 483–491). The references to Roman procedure signal to the audience that, once the pimp finds out that he has been deceived, he cannot simply drag his former slave home and pretend that she had never been freed.
3. *Ethical evaluation of the action is frequent.* The best example of this phenomenon is the fantasy law at the end of *Mercator* (1017–1024), which limits the sexual activity of old men and serves as a moral to the entire play. Since the passage is tinged with Roman legal language and is far more relevant to a state which is primarily run by the older generation (cf. 985–986) and in which fathers control the sexual life of their sons (cf. 1021), it suits Rome far better than Athens and is likely to be an invention of Plautus.
4. *The legal elements added by Plautus sometimes structure the plot and mark a closure.* At the end of *Asinaria* (937) and *Bacchides* (1205), comparisons between Roman debt bondage and sexual relations underscore the complete defeat and submission of the father(s) and thus signal the end of the action. Similarly, the mock-pompous legal language of the fantasy laws at the end of *Casina*

(1001–1003) and *Mercator* (1017–1024, see above) functions like a fermata and brings the plays to a halt.

5. *Plautus exploits Roman law to render the plot more lively.* In *Amphitruo*, he inserts Alcumena's wish for a divorce to heighten the tension of the intramarital dispute.[1] In *Asinaria* (131–133) and *Truculentus* (759–763), Plautus makes the disappointed lovers threaten to report their beloved or her mother to the Roman police (*tres viri*). More complex is Plautus's adaptation of the summons in *Persa* (738–752). Apart from replacing the Greek procedure of *apagoge* by the formulae of the corresponding Roman procedure of *in ius vocatio* (cf. Witt 1971a: 233–234), Plautus also adds a reference to the *antestatio* (calling of witnesses), which was a necessary part of the Roman summons but had no equivalent in Attic law. Eventually, however, the *antestatio* is not carried out, because the plaintiff claims that the defendant has no right to be treated according to the law and drags him off to court by force. Thus Plautus deliberately creates and later flouts the expectation that the scene will follow Roman law, and thereby produces a highly turbulent scene (cf. Scafuro 1997: 419–423). The same technique also underlies Plautus's adaptation of the summons in *Curculio* 620–628.

6. Finally, and most importantly, Plautine expansions serve to increase the comic effect. Plautus often inserts Roman institutions and terminology to create legal absurdities. At *Pseudolus* 117–118, a slave promises by means of a *sponsio* to fulfill his master's wishes, although such *sponsiones* could only be given by Roman citizens (cf. Kaser 1971: 169 n. 25), and at *Pseudolus* 1322 the old master absurdly begs his clever slave not to insist on the payment of the wagered amount. Just as entertaining is the parody of a Roman edict on spectacles at the beginning of *Poenulus* (16–45; cf. *CIL* 6.32332). Furthermore, Roman law and legal language are exploited for various puns: e.g., Plautus plays with the double-meaning of *intestabilis* ("disqualified from calling witnesses"/"without testicles," cf. *Curculio* 30–31, *Miles Gloriosus* 1416–1417, 1420–1421, 1426) or the metaphorical use of *vendere* ("to fool someone," cf. *Bacchides* 976–977). Another source of entertainment is riddle-jokes based on Roman law such as the Roman punishment of patricides (*Epidicus* 349–351), the typically Roman institution of *auctio* (*Poenulus* 410–413), or the castration of adulterers caught in the act, which was permitted by Roman but probably not by Attic law (*Poenulus* 862–863). Particularly common is the comic "juridicization" (Zagagi 1980: 106–131) of nonlegal topics: a rendezvous with the beloved is presented as a meeting with one's opponent for a trial (*Curculio* 3–6, 162–164), the relations between a prostitute and her customers are compared to the Roman tax farming system (*Truculentus* 141–151, 214), a thrashing is described as a bequest or an attempt to

---

[1] The fact that Athenian women needed the assistance of a male relative or friend to file a divorce (Erdmann 1934: 391–397, Gatti 1957: 62–63), while Roman women did not (cf. Kaser 1971: 82 n. 11, 326–327), is a strong argument in favour of a Plautine addition.

obtain property by usucaption (*Asinaria* 306, *Amphitruo* 375), and a successful trickster styles himself as a Roman general handing over the booty to the *quaestor* (*Bacchides* 1075).

All the preceding examples of Plautine expansions concern only the dramatic effect of motifs or scenes but do not affect the general structure of the plot. There are, however, a few exceptions to this rule. In *Trinummus* (223–275a), Plautus has the young Lysiteles weigh the advantages of love and virtue in a sort of court hearing; the monologue does not fit the structure of the play and is likely to have been inserted by the Roman playwright (cf. Leo 1913: 117, Fraenkel 1922: 56, 140). In *Poenulus*, the slave Milphio concocts a second intrigue against the pimp Lycus, which is based on Greek law but incompatible with the legal parameters of the play; probably Plautus has contaminated his original with motifs from another play (possibly Menander's *Sikyonioi*, cf. Gratwick 1971: 30–31, Gratwick 1982: 99–100). A third exception can be found in *Bacchides*. There, the main intrigue concerning the contract between the prostitute and the soldier comes from the Menandrian model, but Plautus has added a second trick which has a much feebler legal substance and merely serves to supply Pistoclerus and Mnesilochus with some cash for a jolly time with Bacchis and her sister (cf. Fraenkel 1912: 100–102, Fraenkel 1922: 61 n. 1).

If we connect the various observations to create a coherent picture, we see that Plautus sticks to the scenarios of his Greek originals but is not interested in presenting his audience with a coherent and realistic image of the legal practice in Athens or other Hellenistic poleis. Instead, he inserts Roman institutions and legal language and thereby brings the action closer to the *Lebenswelt* of his audience and occasionally plays with its expectations. The result is a heterogeneous scenic reality that Gratwick (1993: 15) aptly termed "Plautopolis."

B. Plautus as a "Legal Translator"

The creation of "Plautopolis" has a lot to do with the linguistic surface of the plays and the use of Roman legal terminology. These issues had already been touched on by Mommsen (1887: Vol. 2, 500 n. 2, *al.*) and Fredershausen (1906: 17–18, *passim*), but the first scholar to approach them in a more systematic fashion was Witt (1971a, 1971b), who, in his analysis of the Plautine summons to court, drew from modern studies on legal translation. There are basically four ways of translating legal texts: one may (1) employ (or, in our case, transliterate) the legal terminology of the source language; (2) use loanwords that are uncommon in the target language, but convey a sufficiently clear idea of the content of the source text; (3) paraphrase the content of the source by means of general, nontechnical expressions; or (4) use the legal terminology and formulae of the target language. Two further options available to Plautus but not the modern legal translator are (5) the suppression of legal content and (6) the juridification of general, untechnical vocabulary found in the Greek originals. Plautus rarely employs the first two of these six translation methods: we find few transliterated terms, such as *arrabo* ("earnest money," *Mostellaria* 645, 918, 1013, *al.*), *syngraphus* ("passport": *Captivi* 450, 506; "written contract": *Asinaria* 238, 746, 802), and *dica* ("legal action," *Aulularia* 760, *Poenulus* 800); likewise, there are few loan translations, such as *legirupa* (*Pseudolus* 364, 975, *Rudens* 652) for παρανομῶν / παράνομος, *sector zonarius* (*Trinummus* 862) for βαλλαντιοτόμος, *perfossor parietum* (*Pseudolus* 979–980) for τοιχωρύχος, *dimidium* (*Persa* 69) for τὸ ἥμισυ ("half" / "reward paid to a denouncer"), and *iusta facere* (*Cistellaria* 176) for τὰ νόμιμα ποιεῖν (e.g., Menander, *Heros* 34). Equally infrequent are circumlocutions for Greek terms such as *magister curiae* (*Aulularia* 107, ~ δήμαρχος), *moribus praefectus mulierum* (*Aulularia* 504, ~ γυναικονόμος), or *gymnasi praefectus* (*Bacchides* 425, ~ γυμνασίαρχος).

More often, Plautus employs general, nontechnical expressions such as *allegare* (used at *Epidicus* 427 for a proxy relation), *facinus* (used at *Aulularia* 733 for a rape), and *argentum* (used at *Pseudolus* 1183 and 1091 both of the full price and of the difference between the full price and the earnest money). The most characteristic translation method, however, is the use of Roman legal terminology to represent Greek legal practice. Witt has argued persuasively that Plautus applies the formulae of the Roman *in ius vocatio* when representing Greek *apagogai* for *andrapodismos* ("illegal enslavement") in *Persa* and *Curculio* (cf. Menander *Sikyonioi* 272); this is all the more striking because the *vindicatio in libertatem*, not the *in ius vocatio*, would have been the normal procedure, and there may not have been a specific legal category "illegal enslavement" at Rome in Plautus's day.[2] In a similar fashion, Plautus uses the Roman term *tres viri* when adapting an imaginary law against Athenian sycophants (*Persa* 72, cf. Leo 1912: 124–125), and when dealing with contracts he employs the Roman terminology of *sponsio* and *fide promissio* and pays close attention to the fact that the former procedure was only available to citizens, whereas the latter was also open to foreigners (Kaser 1971: 168–171); notably, the phrase *fide promitto* occurs only once in Plautus at *Men.* 894, where it is put into the mouth of a doctor, thus reflecting the fact that in Plautus's day medical personnel in Rome consisted mostly of foreigners.

Slightly more complex is Plautus's depiction of marriage. The key element of Greek marriage was *engyesis*, a contract between the *kyrios* ("person in charge") of the woman and her future husband to create a marriage. Although many of the details concerning *engyesis* are unclear, it is certain that it was an essential element of many types of marriages and thus should not be identified with a mere promise of a future marriage (cf. Harrison 1968–1971: Vol. 1, 8–9). In Rome, there was no exact equivalent; instead, Romans only differentiated between the formal promise of a future marriage (*sponsio*) and the marriage itself. Despite the differences, Plautus regularly puts the terminology of the *sponsio* in place of the *engyesis*: cf. *Trinummus* 1157–1158: *sponden ergo tuam gnatam uxorem mihi? - spondeo, et mille auri Philippum dotis* ("So, do you promise to

---

[2] Cf. Witt 1971a: 233–234, 236 n. 51. Scafuro (1997: 406–409) suggests that the Roman legislation on *plagium* could go back to Plautus's lifetime, but most historians of Roman law date it to the first century BCE.

give me your daughter as wife?" "I promise that and also a thousand gold Philippi/ as a dowry") and Menander *Dyskolos* 842–844: ἀλλ' ἐγγυῶ παίδων ἐπ' ἀρότῳ γνησίων / τὴν θυγατέρ' ἤδη, μειράκιον, σοί, προῖκά τε / δίδωμ' ἐπ' αὐτῇ τρία τάλαντ' ("But to you, young man, I now give my daughter for the procreation of legitimate children, and in addition I also give you three talents as a dowry").

While serving the same function, the different translation methods have different advantages and drawbacks. Foreign terminology, loan translations, and circumlocutions offer a high degree of precision, but are less familiar to the recipients. Hence, they are less suitable for a comedy which should be immediately comprehensible.[3] Moreover, circumlocutions have the disadvantage of being bulky. Both considerations suggest why Plautus generally avoids these translation methods and prefers general, nontechnical expressions or Roman legal terminology. A disadvantage of the latter two methods is that they do not indicate the foreign character of the legal content but invite the recipients to approach the text with preconceptions that are shaped by the target culture. This quickly leads to misunderstandings, because there are no true equivalents between different legal systems and their terminologies. Even the English "marriage," the French "marriage," and the Italian "matrimonio," which all refer to a formal relationship, imply different requirements, rights, obligations, and procedures. Because of this, modern studies on legal translation generally discourage their readers from the use of technical terms of the target language and advise them to use annotations and explanations. The latter advice is of course not particularly appealing to a poet whose primary objective is to entertain and not to instruct.

Plautus does not seem to have been bothered by minor inaccuracies and may have even consciously exploited the confusion caused by the use of Roman terminology. While discussing Plautine additions to *Persa* 738–752 (*p. 620*), we saw that the poet combines Roman terminology with Attic legal procedure in order to transform the correct procedure of his Greek original into a turbulent scene of illegal coercion. Something similar occurs in *Persa* 470–682. There, the slave Toxilus and his friend Sagaristio, who pretends to be a Persian salesman, want to sell a girl to a pimp, and they stress that neither the traveling salesman nor Toxilus nor his master will offer warranty if the slave should be vindicated as a free girl. To express this, Plautus employs the Roman legal term *mancipium* (525): *mancipio neque promittet neque quisquam dabit* ("No one will promise or give her to you for lawful ownership [sc. as acquired by the procedure of *mancipatio*]"). His usage is patently incorrect, for *mancipium* refers to the handing over of the goods from one legitimate owner to the next. It implies that the vendor will guarantee that the goods are free from defects or claims of a third party, but it cannot denote the concept of warranty, let alone refer to guarantees offered by persons other than the vendor. The Attic original probably referred to a πρατὴρ καὶ βεβαιωτής "(additional)

---

[3] A good illustration is Plautus's translation of ἥμισυ ("half" / "reward paid to a denouncer") with *dimidium* ("half," *Persa* 69), which is likely to have been misunderstood by his audience and has been misinterpreted by many modern readers.

vendor and guarantor," cf. Partsch 1910: 606–610). Knowing that the *mancipatio* (i.e., the act of laying hold on a thing in front of witnesses) had a similar effect as the Attic βεβαίωσις, Plautus simply extended the range of meaning of *mancipium*. For the Roman spectators, who have witnessed the preparations for the sale and know that it is a scam, the misapplication of the Roman terminology may have sounded suspicious and could have made the fooled pimp appear even more gullible and laughable, thus increasing the comic effect of the scene. In addition, the mix of Greek law and (misapplied) Roman legal terminology also conveys the impression of a scenic reality that is neither Roman nor Greek. Thus, Plautus's choice of translation method also plays a crucial role in his construction of the scenic reality of "Plautopolis."

The last point can be further corroborated if we take a closer look at the distribution of Greek or Greek-sounding expressions on the one hand and Roman terminology on the other. Shipp (1955: 139–141) and Andreau (1968: 469–477) have shown that *trapezita / tarpezita* only occurs in passages that concern key elements of the plot and go back to Plautus's Greek originals, whereas the Latin equivalent *argentarius* is used when Plautus expands his models (*Casina* 25 may be an exception: cf. Skutsch 1900: 278–280). In view of Plautus's creative refashioning of the Greek originals, the use of *trapezita / tarpezita* is unlikely to result from slavish imitation. Rather, Plautus uses the Greek terms to remind his audience of the Greek setting of the play. In the same fashion, he may also employ other Greek and Roman terms as markers of "Greekness" and "Romanness." This raises a question concerning the types of subject matter Plautus wants to present as typically Greek and Roman. Looking at the linguistic evidence, it is quite striking that the Greek words and Greek-sounding loan translations comprise several expressions for crimes (cf. *p. 622*), while the Roman terminology primarily points to the administration of justice (e.g., *tres viri*, *aediles*, *praetor*) and legal procedures (e.g., *in ius vocare*, *antestatio*). Thus, linguistically, in the heterogeneous scenic reality of "Plautopolis," disorder and crime are sometimes marked as Greek, whereas the establishment of order regularly appears as something Roman. Although the number of attestations does not allow for a statistical evaluation, the phenomenon may nevertheless be significant, for it closely corresponds to the Romans' self-perception as a well-organised commonwealth and their prejudices against chaotic and unreliable *Graeculi*. One may compare *Stichus* 670 and *Casina* 68–74, where the shocking image of slaves partying on stage is explicitly marked as a Greek custom (cf. also the derogatory reference to *Graeca fides* at *Asinaria* 199).

C. Law, Legal Language, and Plautine Humor

In the extant remains of Menander, law functions as a source of humor mostly through the mechanisms which Bergson (1995: 71–78) termed "inversion" and "interference." A good illustration of the former is the plot of *Aspis*, in which the legal strategy of the old Smicrines is turned against him by the clever slave Davus; the latter technique plays a prominent role in the fourth act of *Samia*, where different interpretations of the same conversation overlap and create a comic interference. These strategies can also be found in the comedies of Plautus. In *Persa* and *Pseudolus,* the spectators can laugh over a funny inversion because the pimp, the shady businessman par excellence, becomes the victim of fraudulent schemes. A good illustration of comic interference is the conversation between Euclio and Lyconides (*Aulularia* 731–776): the former has just found out that his treasure has been stolen, while the latter wants to make amends for the rape of Euclio's daughter. Since both are using fairly vague terms, the comic ambiguity lasts for some time before they realize they are speaking of completely different things.

As we have seen above (*p. 620*), Plautus tends to increase the comic effect of his plays by inserting references or allusions to Roman law. Particularly characteristic of his dramatic technique are riddles, legal absurdities, the juridicization of nonlegal contents, and the caricature of legal experts. The prominent role of the latter in Plautine comedy contrasts sharply with the remains of Attic New Comedy and partly reflects two important differences between the two legal systems: in Athens, law was not interpreted and applied by specialists only (cf. Pringsheim 1950: 1–5, Wolff 1957: 63) and did not involve a technical language that was distinct from general usage (cf. Willi 2002: 72–79); in Rome, on the contrary, the interpretation of laws was traditionally put into the hands of experts, and there was a more developed legal language that differed from general usage with regard to vocabulary, syntax, and morphology (cf. Leo 1913: 22–23, Wieacker 1988: 318–340, 519–551). These phenomena were the necessary preconditions for the comical misapplication of legal language and the invention of the ridiculous *advocatus* that we find in Plautine comedy.

D. Plautine Law and the Roman Audience

After analyzing Plautus's handling of law and legal language, we can finally consider how his plays influence the Roman audience's perception of law and justice. Although Greek New Comedy often problematizes the relation of law and ethics or draws attention to deficiencies of the Athenian legal system (cf. Menander's *Aspis* or *Samia* 134–143), such reflections do not play a prominent role in the extant plays of Plautus. The main reason for this is Plautus's extensive use of legal humor and his misrepresentation of Greek law, which obfuscate the philosophical dimension of the scenarios. In *Captivi*, for example, an attentive reader can still discern that the role reversal of master and servant and the eventual recognition of Tyndarus as Hegio's son were originally intended to make us think about the justification of different legal statuses (Kraus 1984: 324). This idea, however, is almost completely lost in the Roman adaptation because of the various legal and nonlegal jokes which Plautus has added to the play. Something similar happens in *Mercator.* There, the Roman playwright expands the scene in which father and son pretend to act as proxies and bid for the same slave girl. By inserting legal absurdities and increasing the comic effect, Plautus directs our attention away from the ethical and legal questions concerning the relation of father and son. Plautus indulges far too much in comic effect and topsy-turvydom to be a serious mediator of Greek legal thought.

As far as Roman law is concerned, it is remarkable that the magistrates who are responsible for the administration of civil order and justice (*tres viri, aediles, praetor*) are presented as efficient and reliable (e.g., *Stichus* 352–353, *Rudens* 372–373), whereas the Roman senators (cf. *p. 618 above*), the *advocati* and *patroni* (e.g., *Casina* 563–573, *Menaechmi* 571–595, *Poenulus* 504–816), and the "civil service machinery" (cf. *Persa* 143, *decuriae apparitorum*) are often characterized as ill-informed, incompetent, negligent, or lazy. Thus, the plays on the one hand function as a kind of safety valve to relieve some of the tensions in Roman society, but on the other hand emphasize the reliability of the Roman institutions and thereby underpin the legal system. A similar affirmative effect is also created by Plautus's stiffening of poetic justice (cf. *p. 619*), which leaves little room for mercy or "do-goodery" (χρηστότης, cf. Menander K-A fr. 771), but propagates the view that misconduct must and will be punished.

Criticism of Roman law is extremely rare. Plautus adapts the attacks on bribery and perjury (*Rudens* 22–25) or the dowry system (*Aulularia* 475–495), which he found in his Greek models and which may have also appealed to Roman spectators. In *Miles Gloriosus* (211–212), he reminds his audience of the incarcerated poet Naevius, but he does so in a joking manner and neither supports nor attacks his colleague. More serious criticism can be found in *Pseudolus* (303–304) and *Rudens* (1381–1382), where Plautus highlights the negative side effects of the *Lex Laetoria*, which may have been intended to protect young citizens from fraudulent transactions but in practice curbed their economic and legal capacities (cf. Mommsen 1899: 181–182 n. 6, Kaser 1971: 276, Paoli 1976: 68, 151). Moreover, in *Curculio* (506–511) Plautus makes the parasite criticize Roman legislation on usury as ineffective and call for more severe measures.

4. Terence

The legal scenarios and use of legal language in the comedies of the younger Roman playwright Terence generally appear more homogeneous (Schwind 1901: 24–25, 83–84) and have less dramatic effect than those of Plautine comedy. This partly results from the fact that Terence mostly adapted comedies in which legal loopholes or traps do not play a prominent role; the only exceptions are the plot of *Phormio* and the trick developed at *Heauton Timorumenos* 600–613, 790–804. As in Plautus, the plots presuppose Attic law and in many ways conflict with Roman concepts. In particular, Terence's fathers lack the Roman *patria potestas*, and this becomes most obvious when slaves are torn between their loyalties to father and son (*Andria* 210–211, *Phormio* 74–76), when a son almost goes abroad against his father's will (*Heauton Timorumenos* 115–117, 524–529, *Phormio* 548–551; cf. Zagagi 1988), or when fathers have no other means to discipline their sons than to disinherit them (*Andria* 889–892; cf. Harrison 1968–1971: Vol. 1, 75 on ἀποκήρυξις). Moreover, unlike Plautus (cf. *p. 617 above*), Terence does not hesitate to confront his audience with the Attic institution of the epiclerate (*Phormio* 125–134, 407–410, *Adelphoe* 650–652).

Like Plautus, Terence occasionally inserts typically Roman institutions and concepts, such as the relation between former masters and their *liberti* (*Andria* 35–39, *Eunuchus* 608), the terminology of patronage (*Eunuchus* 885–888, 1039–1040, *Adelphoe* 455–458), Roman *advocati* (*Phormio* 441–464; cf. *Eunuchus* 335–344, 764), or litigation and grain usury on the Forum (*Andria* 745–746). However, he does so more rarely and in a fashion that does not disrupt the course of the action. At *Phormio* 331–336, for example, Terence deftly fuses the figure of the voracious parasite with the concept of Roman debt bondage.[4]

In addition, Terence tends to avoid characteristic features of Plautus's legal dramaturgy such as the juridicization of nonlegal contents (but cf. *Heauton Timorumenos* 516, *Phormio* 72–73) or the insertion of legal absurdities (cf. *Andria* 370, *Heauton Timorumenos* 350–357, *Phormio* 217–218 and contrast *pp. 620–621 above*). Whereas Plautus almost makes his plays explode with such inventions and thus obscures the ethical issues contained in them, Terence tries to construct a consistent whole and preserves the ethical focus. Occasionally, he even increases the ethical focus by suppressing legal contents: at *Heauton Timorumenos* 61–64, he departs from his Menandrian model and does not mention that Menedemus's land is not mortgaged (contrast Menander K-A fr. 77.6).

One factor that greatly contributes to the homogeneous appearance and ethical focus of Terence's plays is his handling of legal language. Unlike Plautus, he carefully avoids using Roman terminology for Greek legal content and prefers Greek terminology. For example, Terence's *Phormio* features several attestations (127, 329, 439, 668) of the Greek loanword *dica* ("written charges," "statement of claim"), which occurs only twice in the much larger oeuvre of Plautus (*Aulularia* 760, *Poenulus* 800). Furthermore, Terence often employs general expressions which imply no particular legal system or procedure: instead of equating Greek marriage agreements and *engyesis* with the form and terminology of the Roman *sponsio* (cf. *pp. 622–623*), he often employs the phrases *uxorem dare* (e.g., *Andria* 99–102), *committere* (e.g., *Andria* 241), or *ducere* (e.g., *Andria* 254–255; cf. also the informal marriage negotiations at *Heauton Timorumenos* 935–948). Occasionally Terence employs *(de)spondere* in the general sense of "promise" when referring to the fact that someone has agreed to give his daughter to someone else or will do so in the future (e.g., *Andria* 102, 980); however, he never uses *(de)spondere* as part of a formal marriage agreement or an *engyesis* that is made on stage. The cancellation of the marriage agreement, too, tends to be expressed in nonlegal language (but cf. *repudium renuntiare* "declare the repudiation of one's bride or wife" at *Phormio* 677).

The same preference for nontechnical language can also be observed in Terence's depiction of sale and property. Unlike Plautus, Terence employs *mancipium* only twice in the sense of "piece of property" (*Eunuchus* 274, 364), but never employs *mancipio dare* (Plautus *Curculio* 494, *al.*), *mancipio accipere* (*Curculio* 495, *al.*), or any other

---

[4] An exception is the inconsistency between the relation of patronage mentioned at *Eunuchus* 1039–1040 and the end of *Eunuchus*, where the soldier and the patron's son agree to "share" the services of the prostitute.

reference to the Roman *mancipatio* (cf. *pp. 623–624*); instead, he simply uses *emere* (e.g., *Adelphoe* 191) and *vendere* (e.g., *Eunuchus* 134). Likewise, Terence avoids the terminology of the Roman summons to court: whereas Plautus sometimes takes up the wording of the *Twelve Tables* (cf. *Lex XII Tab.* 1.1: *si in ius vocat...*) and uses *in ius vocare* (*Curculio* 683, *Persa* 745 al.), Terence only employs *in ius ducere* (*Eunuchus* 768), *in ius ambulare* (*Phormio* 936), and *in ius ire* (*Phormio* 981), which sound less legalistic and do not point specifically to Roman law. Moreover, Terence usually does not classify crimes according to legal categories: he refers to "rape" as *facinus* (e.g., *Eunuchus* 644), *scelus* (e.g., *Eunuchus* 645), *vitium* (e.g., *Eunuchus* 722; cf. also *vitiare* at *Eunuchus* 654), *flagitium* (e.g., *Eunuchus* 1013), or *indigne factam iniuriam* (*Hecyra* 401), but never employs the terms *stuprum* or *adulterium*, which we find in Plautus (e.g., *Amphitruo* 883, *Miles Gloriosus* 90) and Caecilius (cf. *p. 629 below*). Finally, Terence also inserts explanations to make the Greek legal scenario comprehensible to his audience; in *Phormio* he gives some orientation on the Attic epiclerate, which is clearly aimed at a Roman rather than Athenian audience (*Phormio* 125–134, 407–410, 412).[5]

Since Terence makes fewer Romanizing additions or changes and avoids Roman terminology, his plays remain closer to their Greek originals, but are also more remote from the *Lebenswelt* of Terence's Roman audience. Apart from the satirical representation of *advocati* at *Phormio* 441–464, there is little comment on Roman law. If Terence's plays had any effect on the Roman perception of law and justice, it is by castigating loose morals (e.g., *Phormio* 55–56) or propagating images of remorse (e.g., *Adelphoe* 681–683) and forgiveness (e.g., *Heauton Timorumenos* 1045–1055, *Adelphoe* 51–58). Unlike Plautus (cf. *p. 619 above*), Terence does not seem to stiffen the punishment suffered by the antagonists. Hence Neumann's claim (1958: 182) that Plautus and Terence do not differ in the application of poetic justice is inaccurate.

5. The Fragments of *Comoediae Palliatae*, *Comoediae Togatae*, and Literary Farces

Our knowledge of the other poets of Roman comedy is far more sketchy. The surviving fragments suggest that the lost *palliatae* written by Naevius, Caecilius, and others, as well as the "plays in Roman dress" (*fabulae togatae*) composed by Titinius, Atta, and Afranius, and finally, the literary farces of Pomponius and Novius, all shared many legal themes and motifs with the extant comedies of Plautus and Terence and

---

[5] Interestingly, *Adelphoe*, which was staged one year later, does not offer an explanation but assumes that the audience is familiar with the epiclerate: cf. *Adelphoe* 650–652.

focused primarily on the relation between husbands and wives or fathers and sons. Most of the fragments of the *fabulae palliatae* do not allow for a reliable reconstruction of the plays, let alone an analysis of how the poets adapted Greek law and legal terminology. Exceptional are the passages of Caecilius's *Plocium* (*com.* 142–157, 158–162) that Aulus Gellius (2.23) compares to the corresponding lines of the Menandrian original (K-A fr. 296–297). In both comic texts, an old man laments that his rich wife has forced him to expel a young slave-girl. Whereas, however, the Greek original describes the wife as an ἐπίκληρος, the Roman poet avoids this Greek legal term and speaks more vaguely of a rich old woman. The rather free adaptation and disinterest in the details of Greek law seem fairly Plautine, and generally both Naevius and Caecilius bear a closer resemblance to Plautus than to Terence in that they employ similar calques (e.g., Naev. *com.* 17: *nocturnos ... praemiatores* "night-time reward collectors") and absurd legal metaphors (e.g., Caecil. *com.* 70: *mihi sex menses satis sunt vitae, septimum Orco spondeo* "six months of life are enough for me, the seventh I promise to the god of the underworld"), classify misdeeds according to Roman legal categories (e.g., Caecil. *com.* 166: *stupri*; but contrast 254–255: *nomen virginis /... deintegravit* "he destroyed the good reputation of a virgin"), are fond of plots involving tricks and loopholes (e.g., Caecil. *inc. fab.* fr. xxxvii: fraudulent plot to gain a *dos*), and freely insert references to Roman institutions into their Greek scenarios (e.g., Naev. *com.* 107: *dictator*).

Quite different must have been the effect of the *fabulae togatae*, which were not adaptations of Greek plays but independent compositions with a Roman setting. In accordance with Roman law, slaves played a much more subservient and less prominent role in the *fabulae togatae* (cf. Donat. Ter. *Eun.* 57). Likewise, the greater degree of legal capacity of women and the rise of Roman jurisprudence are reflected by the appearance of a *iurisperita* ("female legal expert") at Titin. *com.* 62–64; also, at Titin. *com.* 15–16, a wife complains about her husband squandering the *dos*, and at 91–92, someone investigates the husband's (?) sexual relations with female slaves. Moreover, the Roman *aediles* may have been a central topic of Atta's *Aedilicia*. Guardì's view (1984: 17, 103–105) that Titinius's *Barbatus* and Afranius's *Vopiscus* respond to the abrogation of the *lex Oppia* and to Caecilius Metellus's attempts to regulate the demographic development of Rome could be correct, but it has no firm basis in the transmitted texts. References to Greek law and institutions seem to have been completely absent from the *fabulae togatae*. Since law and its exegesis were a strictly male domain in Rome, the title of Titinius's *Iurisperita* can be taken as evidence that Plautus's fondness for legal absurdities must have lived on in some of the *fabulae togatae*.

Other typical features of Plautus's legal humor may recur in the literary farces of the late second and first centuries BCE. Thus in Pomponius's *Pictores*, the verse *ipsus cum uno servo senex intestato proficiscitur* ("Without witnesses and accompanied by just one slave the old man sets out"; *com.* 113) may have been linked with a typically Plautine pun on *testis* (cf. *p. 620 above*). Moreover, isolated references to Greek institutions suggest that literary farces may have occasionally mixed Greek and Roman elements to create a hybrid scenic reality that was similar to that of Plautine comedy: one of

Pomponius's plays was called *Synephebi,* and also the title *praefectus morum* (Pompon. *com.* 145–147) may remind one of Plautus's reference to a *moribus praefectum mulierum* (~ γυναικονόμος) at *Aulularia* 504.

The social and political impact of the fragmentary authors is difficult to determine. Naevius's criticism of the Metelli and his incarceration (cf. Gell. 3.3.15) suggest that his plays may also have commented freely on issues of legislation and jurisdiction and that later poets may have deliberately avoided political statements because they were afraid of prosecution (cf. Leo 1913: 143). However, neither of these hypotheses can be verified, and some remarks about the Roman election system in literary farces suggest that comic poets would still raise political and legal issues (cf., e.g., Pompon. *com.* 105–106, Nov. *com.* 75–76).

6. CONCLUSION

As we have seen, law and legal language serve a variety of functions in Roman comedy. Despite this diversity, two general conclusions can be drawn. First, the extant comedies of Plautus and Terence, but also some of the literary farces, combine elements of Greek and Roman law and constitute a problematic source for the reconstruction of Attic or Roman law. Secondly, the use of law and legal language in Roman comedy is not simply an adaptation of similar phenomena in Greek New Comedy. The Roman poets, especially the authors of *comoediae palliatae,* adopted and adapted the dramatic structures of their Greek predecessors and with these also some of the dramatic functions of law in Greek New Comedy; at the same time, however, they realized that the professionalization and greater exclusiveness of law and legal practice in Rome and the existence of a linguistically marked terminology and fixed formulae also offered new opportunities for legal humor. As a result, entertaining word plays and the absurd juridicization of nonlegal contents play a far more prominent role, and there is a new comic figure: the bumptious but incompetent jurist. These innovations have had a strong influence not just on later Roman literature, but also on medieval and modern drama.

FURTHER READING

The literature on law and Roman comedy is vast. The most important studies are mentioned in section 2; in addition, cf. also Schwind 1901, Radin 1910, Neumann 1958, Kupiszewski 1960, Zagagi 1980: 106–131, Rosenmeyer 1995, Karakasis 2003, and Pieczonka 2008. For the sociological and literary-theoretical dimension of the topic, see especially Derrida 1992, Luhmann 1981, Bourdieu 1986, and Habermas 1992. Useful discussions of the problems of legal translation can be found, e.g., in Weisflog 1996 and de Groot and Schulze 1999.

BIBLIOGRAPHY

Andreau, J. 1968. "Banque grecque et banque romaine dans le théâtre de Plaute et Térence." *Mélanges d'Archéologie et d'Histoire* 80: 461–526.

Bekker, E. I. 1892. "Die römischen Komiker als Rechtszeugen." *Zeitschrift der Savigny-Stiftung für Rechtsgeschichte. Romanistische Abteilung* 26: 53–118.

Bergson, H. 1995. *Le rire: Essai sur la signification du comique*. 8th ed. Paris: Presses universitaires de France. First pub. 1899.

Bourdieu, P. 1986. "La force du droit: Éléments pour une sociologie du champ juridique." *Actes de la recherche en sciences sociales* 64: 3–19.

Costa, E. 1890. *Il diritto privato Romano nelle comedie di Plauto*. Torino: Fratelli Bocca.

Dareste, R. 1892. Review of *Il diritto privato Romano nelle comedie di Plauto,* by E. Costa. *Journal des Savants* 1892: 145–154.

de Groot, G.-R., and R. Schulze, eds. 1999. *Recht und Übersetzen*. Baden-Baden: Nomos.

Derrida, J. 1992. "Before the Law." In *Jacques Derrida: Acts of Literature*, edited by D. Attridge, 181–220. New York: Routledge.

Dziatzko, K. 1900. "Der Inhalt des Georgos von Menander (Schluss)." *RhM* 55: 104–111.

Enk, P. J. 1932. *Plauti Mercator: Cum prolegomenis, notis criticis, commentario exegetico*. 2 vols. Leiden: A. W. Sijthoff.

Erdmann, W. 1934. *Die Ehe im alten Griechenland*. Munich: C.H. Beck.

Fraenkel, E. 1912. *De media et nova comoedia quaestiones selectae*. Göttingen: Dieterich.

———. 1922. *Plautinisches im Plautus*. Berlin: Weidmann.

Fredershausen, O. 1906. *De iure Plautino et Terentiano*. Göttingen: Goldschmidt & Hubert.

———. 1912. "Weitere Studien über das Recht bei Plautus und Terenz." *Hermes* 47: 199–249.

Gaertner, J. F. 2011. "Das antike Recht und die griechisch-römische Neue Komödie: Untersuchungen zu Plautus und seinen griechischen Vorbildern." 2 vols. Habilitationsschrift, Leipzig University.

Gatti, C. 1957. "Alcuni aspetti della posizione giuridica della donna ateniese nel V e IV secolo a.C." *Acme* 10: 57–65.

Girard, P. F. 1893. "Droit romain." *Nouvelle revue historique de droit français et étranger* 17: 789–797.

Gratwick, A. S. 1971. "Hanno's Punic Speech in the *Poenulus* of Plautus." *Hermes* 99: 25–45.

———. 1982. "Drama." In *Cambridge History of Classical Literature*. Vol. 2, *Latin Literature*, edited by W. V. Clausen and E. J. Kenney, 77–137. Cambridge, UK, and New York: Cambridge University Press.

———. 1993. *Plautus: Menaechmi*. Cambridge, UK: Cambridge University Press.

Green, W. M. 1929. "Greek and Roman Law in the *Trinummus* of Plautus." *CPh* 24: 183–192.

Guardì, T. 1984. *Fabula togata: I frammenti*. Milan: Jaca Book.

Habermas, J. 1992. *Faktizität und Geltung: Beiträge zur Diskurstheorie des Rechts und des demokratischen Rechtsstaats*. Frankfurt: Suhrkamp.

Harrison, A. R. W. 1968–1971. *The Law of Athens*. 2 vols. Oxford: Clarendon Press.

Karakasis, E. 2003. "Legal Language in Plautus with Special Reference to *Trinummus*." *Mnemosyne* 56: 194–209.

Kaser, M. 1971. *Das römische Privatrecht. Das altrömische, das vorklassische und klassische Recht*. 2nd ed. Munich: Beck.

Keyes, C. W. 1940. "Half-Sister Marriage in New Comedy and the *Epidicus*." *TAPA* 71: 217–229.

Kleinfeller, G. 1931. "Suppositio partus." In *Paulys Real-Encyclopädie der classischen Altertumswissenschaft*, IV A, Vol. 1, edited by A. Pauly, G. Wissowa, and K. Ziegler, col. 952.

Kraus, W. 1984. "Die Captivi im neuen Lichte Menanders." In *Aus Allem Eines: Studien zur Antiken Geistesgeschichte*, by W. Kraus, 317–26. Heidelberg: L. Stiehm. First pub. 1977.

Kupiszewski, H. 1960. "Das Verlöbnis im altrömischen Recht." *Zeitschrift der Savigny-Stiftung für Rechtsgeschichte. Romanistische Abteilung* 77: 125–159.

Lefèvre, E. 1977. "Plautus-Studien I: Der doppelte Geldkreislauf im *Pseudolus*." *Hermes* 105: 441–454.

——, E. Stärk, and G. Vogt-Spira. 1991. *Plautus barbarus: Sechs Kapitel zur Originalität des Plautus*. Tübingen: Narr.

Leo, F. 1912. *Plautinische Forschungen: Zur Kritik und Geschichte der Komödie*. 2nd ed. Berlin: Weidmann.

——. 1913. *Geschichte der römischen Literatur*. Berlin: Weidmann.

Lofberg, J. O. 1920. "The Sycophant-Parasite." *CPh* 15: 61–72.

Lowe, J. C. B. 1990. "Plautus' Choruses." *RhM* 133: 274–297.

Luhmann, N. 1981. "Kommunikation über Recht in Interaktionssystemen." In *Ausdifferenzierung des Rechts: Beiträge zur Rechtssoziologie und Rechtstheorie*, by N. Luhmann, 53–72. Frankfurt: Suhrkamp.

Mommsen, T. 1887. *Römisches Staatsrecht*. 3 vols. Leipzig: S. Hirzel.

——. 1899. *Römisches Strafrecht*. Leipzig: Duncker & Humblot.

Neumann, M. 1958. *Die poetische Gerechtigkeit in der Neuen Komödie: Untersuchungen zur Technik des antiken Lustspiels*. Speyer: Pilger-Druckerei.

Paoli, U. E. 1962. *Comici latini e diritto attico*. Milano: A. Giuffrè.

——. 1976. *Altri studi di diritto greco e romano*. Milano: La Goliardica.

Partsch, J. 1910. "Römisches und Griechisches Recht in Plautus' *Persa*." *Hermes* 45: 595–614.

Pernard, L. 1900. *Le droit romain et le droit grec dans le théâtre de Plaute et de Térence*. Lyon: A. Rey.

Pieczonka, J. 2008. "Jurilinguistic Research on the Comedies of Plautus." In *Laetae segetes iterum*, edited by I. Radová, 254–263. Brno: Masarykova univerzita.

Pringsheim, F. 1950. *The Greek Law of Sale*. Weimar: H. Böhlaus Nachfolger.

Radin, M. 1910. "Greek Law in Roman Comedy." *CPh* 5: 365–367.

Rosenmeyer, P. A. 1995. "Enacting the Law: Plautus' Use of the Divorce Formula on Stage." *Phoenix* 49: 201–217.

Scafuro, A. C. 1993. "Staging Entrapment: On the Boundaries of the Law in Plautus' *Persa*." In *Intertextualität in der griechisch-römischen Komödie*, edited by N. W. Slater and B. Zimmermann, 55–77. Stuttgart: M & P.

——. 1997. *The Forensic Stage: Settling Disputes in Graeco-Roman New Comedy*. Cambridge, UK: Cambridge University Press.

——. 2003–2004. "The Rigmarole of the Parasite's Contract for a Prostitute in *Asinaria*: Legal Documents in Plautus and his Predecessors." *Leeds International Classical Studies* 3: 1–21.

Schwind, A. 1901. *Über das Recht bei Terenz*. Würzburg: Scheiner.

Shipp, G. P. 1955. "Plautine Terms for Greek and Roman Things." *Glotta* 34: 139–151.

Skutsch, F. 1900. "Ein Prolog des Diphilos und eine Komödie des Plautus." *RhM* 55: 272–285.

Weisflog, W. E. 1996. *Rechtsvergleichung und juristische Übersetzung: Eine interdisziplinäre Studie*. Zürich: Schulthess Polygraphischer Verlag.

Wieacker, F. 1988. *Römische Rechtsgeschichte: Quellenkunde, Rechtsbildung, Jurisprudenz und Rechtsliteratur. Erster Abschnitt, Einleitung, Quellenkunde, Frühzeit und Republik*. Munich: C. H. Beck.

Willi, A. 2002. *The Languages of Aristophanes: Aspects of Linguistic Variation in Classical Attic Greek.* Oxford: Oxford University Press.

Witt, P. 1971a. "Die Übersetzung von Rechtsbegriffen, dargestellt am Beispiel der *in ius vocatio* bei Plautus und Terenz." *Studia et Documenta Historiae et Iuris* 37: 217–260.

——. 1971b. "In ius vocare bei Plautus und Terenz: Zur Interpretation römischen Rechts in klassischen Übersetzungen." PhD diss., University of Freiburg.

Wolff, H. J. 1957. "Die Grundlagen des griechischen Vertragsrechts." *Zeitschrift der Savigny-Stiftung für Rechtsgeschichte. Romanistische Abteilung* 74: 26–72.

Zagagi, N. 1980. *Tradition and Originality in Plautus: Studies of the Amatory Motifs in Plautine Comedy.* Göttingen: Vandenhoeck & Ruprecht.

——. 1988. "Exilium Amoris in New Comedy." *Hermes* 116: 193–209.

CHAPTER 32

....

RELIGION IN
ROMAN COMEDY

....

BORIS DUNSCH

THE LUDIC CONTEXT OF ROMAN COMEDY
....

ALTHOUGH students of ancient drama regularly assume as a matter of course that performances of Greek tragedy and comedy were closely related to religion and ritual, scholars acknowledge a similar relation for Roman drama far less often. Yet since no play in Rome could be produced outside the context of a *ludus*, a festival or "games" (Versnel 1998: 101f.), the dramatic impact of Roman comedy unfolded in a decidedly ludic context. To form an adequate idea of Roman comedy, therefore, it is imperative to see how close the link between religion and Roman theater actually was (cf. Edwards 1993: 107–109; Dupont 2010: 451; see also Gruen in this volume).

The main occasions for festival performances (*ludi scaenici*) were the *ludi Romani* in September (in honor of Jupiter; probably held beginning as early as 509 BCE, with scenic performances perhaps since 364), *plebeii* in November (also in honor of Jupiter; probably from 220; in 200 performance of Plautus's *Stichus*), *Ceriales* in April (in honor of Ceres, Liber, and Libera; attested for 202/201, but probably introduced around 220), *Apollinares* in July (in honor of Apollo; from 212), *Megalenses* in April (in honor of the Magna Mater/Cybele; established in 204, including scenic performances since 194, made annual in 191, the year when Plautus's *Pseudolus* was performed; 166 performance of Terence's *Andria*, 165 aborted performance of *Hecyra*, 163 *Heauton Timorumenos*, 161 *Eunuchus*), and *Florales* in late April (in honor of Flora; introduced in 238). From 173 BCE, the year when the *ludi Florales* were made annual, Rome boasted six public *ludi* each year, thus offering many opportunities for regular dramatic performances (cf. Bernstein 1998 and Bernstein 2007; Dunsch 2009: 25f.; Manuwald 2011: 41–49).[1]

---

[1] Although Plautus's plays are often described metaphorically as "Saturnalian" (see Fontaine on Plautus in this volume), they have nothing to do with the festival of the *Saturnalia* itself (Jocelyn 2001: 263), which did not feature scenic performances.

One could argue that the performance of a play had little to do with the festival as such and nothing at all with its eponymous deities. The tacit assumption underlying this view is that a meaningful distinction can be made between performing a play in honor of a deity and performing it for purely "worldly" ends—for "entertainment." Yet it is unhelpful to project this conceptual divide back upon the ancient world. Establishing a dichotomy between "the sacred" and "the profane" with regard to drama only became possible in later antiquity, after the Christian condemnation of theatrical performances as an immoral pagan institution (cf. Edwards 1993: 108). The ludic character does not attach itself to the plays from the outside, so to speak, but the plays themselves help to constitute it. It is wrong to argue that they alone constitute it, but it would be similarly wrong to say that they are completely detachable from their ludic context. Rather, one could regard "Roman worship—the repetition of carefully defined exemplary gestures and verbal formulae" as "a repertoire of proto-theatrical acts" (Beacham 1995: 2f.).

The close proximity of the performance sites to the temples of the respective deities is another indication of the close relation between theater and cult. It has been shown that the space in front of the temple of the Great Mother was used for performances during the *Megalenses* (Goldberg 1998); for the *ludi Florales,* the area *ante ipsum delubrum* could have had a comparable function (Hanson 1959: 16). A similar assumption can be made for the *ludi Apollinares* (Hanson 1959: 18–24). The religious character of the games becomes obvious also in the practice of *instauratio,* the restarting of a play in cases when it had been interrupted somehow or when even the smallest omission or disturbance had occurred during its performance. In such a case a play, like any ritual, had to be reperformed from scratch (Bernstein 1998: 85). For example, the *ludi Romani* were repeated seven times in 205 BCE, possibly due to the popularity of Plautus's *Miles Gloriosus:* "It cannot be a coincidence that during Plautus' lifetime the *ludi Romani* were repeated more often than at any time before or after" (Graf 2007: 57).

The life of an ancient Roman was saturated with religious festivals in a way hardly comprehensible to us. The number of days dedicated to *ludi* amounted to more than forty by the end of the republic—more than there had ever been in Athens—and toward the middle of the fourth century CE comprised as many as 101 (Blume 1991: 116 n. 39). And to the official, calendrically fixed and state-sanctioned public holidays (*ludi publici*) one must add the private festivals (such as *ludi funebres, triumphales,* and *votivi,* or funereal, triumphal, and votive games): though hard to pin down in numbers, they were certainly not insignificant (Bernstein 1998: 84–116). Terence's *Adelphoe* and *Hecyra,* for instance, were staged at the *ludi funebres* for Aemilius Paullus (160 BCE).

PREVIOUS RESEARCH

Over and above the ludic character of the performances, it has been noted that "[n]o other Latin author, with the possible exception of St. Augustine" can match Plautus for the sheer number of references to religion. More importantly, "this material is almost entirely non-analytic, even accidental in quality, in contrast to the more organized but artificial reasoning of Cicero and Varro or the poetic remolding of Vergil and Ovid" (Hanson 1959a: 50f.). Thus, for example, the first instances of the words *religio* and *religiosus* in Latin literature can be traced to Plautus (*Asinaria* 782; *Curculio* 350; *Mercator* 881) and Terence (*Andria* 730, 941; *Heauton Timorumenos* 650; cf. Bergmann 1998: 13–32), as can the first statements about the gods. An almost postmodernist definition of divinity appears in Plautus (*Asinaria* 712f., see Feeney 1998: 89, and cf. *Captivi* 860–865 and *Pseudolus* 326–328); reflections on the gods' existence are found in Terence (*Eunuchus* 583–591, 1025–1027; *Heauton Timorumenos* 1035–1037), and thoughts on mankind pleasing the gods through moral behavior in Plautus (*Captivi* 313–315).

Despite this wealth of material, the role of religion in comedy was dealt with in relatively few scholarly studies in the twentieth century. These were mainly concerned with specific questions, such as the relation between Greek and Roman mythology, mythological travesty, the terminology of religious specialists, and the parody of sacred acts. There have also been attempts to investigate the cultic realities and the historical background of references to religious practices. Possible allusions to the cult of Dionysus and traces of the "Bacchanalian Affair" (186 BCE) in Plautus have attracted particular interest. Attention was unevenly divided among the plays, and syntheses were hardly attempted (cf. Dunsch 2009: 18–25). Similarly, relatively few and brief references to comedy can be found in studies on Roman religion (cf., e.g., Beard, North, and Price 1998; notable exceptions are Feeney 1998, Liebeschuetz 1979, and Rüpke 2012). Studies on prayers and hymns in literature deal in some depth with Roman comedy (cf. Kleinknecht 1937: 157–178; Swoboda/ Danielewicz 1981; Guittard 1992; Hickson 1993; La Bua 1999: 105–110; Chapot and Laurot 2001: 240–248).

The idea that Roman comedy is of little value as a source is ultimately founded, it would seem, on the basically correct assumption that these texts are the result of the cultural encounter between Greece and Rome and thus find their place between the poles of Greek (literary) and Roman (unscripted and improvised) drama (for the implications of this, see, e.g., Vogt-Spira 2001), and that they therefore occupy a kind of no man's land and do not correlate in any meaningful way with the daily life of either culture. A more optimistic appraisal of what we can learn about Roman religion from Roman comedy is required. One advantage of envisioning a potentially nonanalytical portrayal that does reflect everyday life is that it brings into focus matters that often remain unappreciated, such as notions or actions familiar to an ancient audience.

Previous studies have paid attention primarily to the surface of the text, e.g., by looking into the frequency of gods being named and of oaths addressed to them or the formation of routine formulae of thanksgiving or cursing. By contrast, little attention has been paid to the physical dimension of what is actually going on while a religious ritual is performed onstage, and even less to the question whether there may have been certain formal conditions for sacred acts on the Roman stage and how Plautus and other playwrights might have reacted to these.[2] The latter question is particularly pertinent when one considers that the formal aspects of rituals were always of great importance to the Romans (cf. Rüpke 2012: 62–81). In similar fashion, older scholarship did not devote detailed discussion to mythological detail, ritual acts, references to "Oriental" deities, auspices, omens, sacrifice, and so on, as research tended to draw a clear distinction between "the verbalization of religious concepts" and "religious acts" (cf. Hanson 1959a: 53 n. 12; 97). Yet, this distinction is not convincing for the world of pre-Christian antiquity. On the contrary, religious concepts in the ancient world are constitutively reflected in religious acts; they find their expression in religious practices, and are modified by them. Conversely, religious acts may at the same time come under the influence of language and concepts written for the stage (Slater 2011: 298).

Ritual in Drama, Drama in Ritual: The Performative Turn

The considerations above make it clear that there are links between religion, ritual, and drama. This idea is not new. Its main outlines were developed in the wake of the performative turn in the cultural sciences, which constituted a move away from the explanatory metaphor of "culture as text" that had dominated research into the 1980s by its claim that culture as a whole, as well as individual cultural phenomena, can be regarded as the structured correlation of individual elements to which specific meanings can be attributed. In performance theory, it depends chiefly on context and intended function whether one labels a certain performance a "ritual" or a "drama," on the questions of who carries it out, where it takes place, and under what circumstances. If the aim of the performance is to effect transformations, then the performance is a ritual. If the aim is entertainment, then it is theatrical drama, although perhaps no performance is ever purely ritual or exclusively entertainment (Schechner 1990: 68f.). In principle, all drama can also (and is often expected to) effect transformations, and every ritual can be effective in entertaining. Both forms of performance are concerned with "other worlds" (Diller 1998). Thus, the boundary between staged and nonstaged ritual, so to speak, between "ritual in drama" and "drama in ritual," is fluid. The external framework, the stage and the theatrical context as a whole, shows the informed viewer that the dramatic action is not meant to be taken seriously—in contrast to a sacred act, which, if carried out correctly, would actually be valid (for more on theatrical framing, see Dunsch on prologues in this volume and Carlson 2004: 35f.). However, the moment a participant

---

[2] Cf., e.g., *Amphitruo* 1093f.: *Invocat deos immortales, ut sibi auxilium ferant, / manibus puris, capite operto.* ("She invokes the immortal gods to bring her help, / with clean hands, with her head duly covered.") The focus put on interruptions that could invalidate a sacred act, in this case a prayer, is also interesting: *Cistellaria* 512–520.

breaches the rules of the drama, the dramatic process is over, the world of the stage becomes the real world, and the merely "staged ritual" becomes a "ritual on stage," thus potentially effective and no longer therefore simply part of the theatrical action.[3] This is illustrated by the fact that, for example, Christian sacred acts, like baptism, that were commonly portrayed on stage in late antiquity for the purpose of ridiculing Christian beliefs had the potential of turning from mere parts of the theatrical action into real and binding sacraments (cf. Binder 1998: 118f.). By corollary, if a sacred act is portrayed on stage, then an actor in the context of a *ludus scaenicus* (thus within the execution of a ritual realized as a result of the *ludi*) finds himself standing on a stage on which he plays a character who carries out a sacred act in a ritual context. In a way, this is a mise en scène of a ritual within a ritual—almost performance squared.

This remarkable circumstance makes it astonishing that virtually no studies have examined the mise en scène of sacred acts, parodic or nonparodic, on the Roman stage. As noted, the most comprehensive study of religion in Plautus to date (Hanson 1959a) still subscribed to a text-oriented approach. Nevertheless, the religious practices to which the texts attest are potentially still within the reach of our comprehension. To achieve a better understanding of the complex rituals that lie behind the texts, we should subject them as far as possible to a cautious hermeneutical reading that puts them in their proper sociocultural and performative contexts. This interpretation will then, in turn, have to be calibrated against the cognitive and emotional dimensions of these rituals. The following pages will present possible methods of contextualization as a necessary prerequisite for understanding religious references in Roman comedy, drawing on examples from Plautus's *Mercator*. Although the play is not primarily concerned with religious questions, it does contain many passages that explicitly or implicitly deal with "the religious," and rituals are used to accentuate decisive turning points in the dramatic action. In other plays, religious motifs and themes are perhaps more prominent, e.g., in *Amphitruo* or *Rudens*. No play, however, is entirely devoid of them. On the whole, fewer and more isolated references to religion and ritual are found in Terence (an overview is now provided by Gellar-Goad 2013). Apart from standard invocations of the gods, there is little to be gleaned from the fragments of other *palliata* playwrights, even less from *togata* and *Atellana* (López 2000).

RELIGION IN ROMAN COMEDY: A SYSTEM OF CATEGORIES

In the following remarks, I suggest a system of classification consisting of seven categories (examples for six of them are found in *Mercator*). These categories are not mutually

---

[3] The ontologically precarious status of a theatrical performance, which Plautus on one occasion calls "making lies probable" (*Pseudolus* 401–404), is referred to in amazingly similar terms in modern drama theory: Pavis 1988: 55 states that in the theater fiction assumes its form by using real things, namely the stage and the actors, so that it becomes impossible to attribute the elements of the performance directly and exclusively to one domain (reality) or the other (fiction).

exclusive, since elements are often found in clusters matching two or more of these categories. They are as follows (the successive numbering does not imply gradations of quantity or quality):

I: statements about the gods and their actions; statements about their characteristics and behavior, often containing descriptive detail (e.g., *Mercator* 3–8, 37f., 225–228, 285, 319–321, 625–628, 844, 854–856, 908);

II: references to individual mythological figures or groups of figures, often in hyperbolic comparisons with mortals (e.g., 469f., 488f., 689–691, 956);

III: communications with the gods, such as prayers, oaths, or the enactment of sacred actions on stage (e.g., 675–680, 789–791, 830–835);

IV: brief invocations, pleas, and curses (e.g., *hercle*, *edepol*, including slightly longer ones like *o Apollo, quantus es!*); communications with the gods less complex than those in category III (e.g., 709f., 762, 842f., 850, 864f., 865, 966f.);

V: personifications or identifications, including momentary deities prevalent in the comic merging of human and divine spheres (867–871); these overlap not infrequently with category II;

VI: individual pieces of information, isolated references to cultic rules or ritual systems; often used by the playwright to add "local color" (e.g., 66–68, 274, 606, 879–881).

VII (not found in *Mercator*, but in several other plays): appearance of gods on stage, who visibly participate in the action or reveal and comment on future occurrences in the play (e.g., *passim* in *Amphitruo*; frequently as prologue-speakers: Mercury in *Amphitruo*; the Lar familiaris in *Aulularia*; Auxilium in *Cistellaria*; Arcturus in *Rudens*; see also my chapter on prologues in this volume).

This system contains categories devoted to discourse *about* the gods (I, II, V, VI), discourse and interaction *with* the gods (II, IV), and discourse or action *by* the gods (VII). An underlying structural principle is the relative proximity to, or distance from, the gods. If one extended this approach with a view to theatrical semiotics, then the gestures associated with the religious (postures and actions), props, and other (real or imagined) ritual objects (an altar, a cultic knife, etc.) should also be considered.

Admittedly, questions concerning the cultural relationship between Greece and Rome and the relationship between deities and the action on stage, and between the world of the stage and the real world (in other words, on the *Sitz im Leben* of the religious language and actions enacted on stage), are problematic in all categories; so too are questions about potential influence of parodic exaggeration on that which is portrayed. I now turn, therefore, to explain the categories in greater detail.

CATEGORY I

An exemplary instance appears at the beginning of *Mercator*. The young lover Charinus, who—unusually for a *palliata*—simultaneously acts as the narrator of the prologue (see my chapter on prologues in this volume), addresses himself directly *ad spectatores* (*Mercator* 3–8):

> *non ego item facio ut alios in comoediis*
> *<vi> vidi Amoris facere, qui aut Nocti aut Die*
> *aut Soli aut Lunae miserias narrant suas:*
> *quos pol ego credo humanas querimonias*
> *non tanti facere, quid velint quid non velint;*
> *vobis narrabo potius meas nunc miserias.*

> *I* don't just do what I've seen others in comedies
> do under Cupid's spell, who tell either Night or Day
> or Sun or Moon their miseries.
> These, I think, by Pollux, don't care *that* much [*gesturing with his hand*]
> about the complaints of mortals—what they want, what they don't.
> Rather, I'll now tell my miseries to *you*.

Reference is made here to a common dramatic convention, the *amekhania* monologue of the typical ill-starred lover, and the widespread comic practice of lovers addressing monologues to deities or natural phenomena (Holzberg 1974: 34). This convention is linked to theological speculations about the scope of the influence the gods exert on human life: they are not interested in the wishes or affairs of men. They perceive these, but stand above them. A *captatio benevolentiae* is attached, too, which the audience will undoubtedly appreciate: they are more worthy than the gods to hear what the narrator has to say.

This passage is also a fine illustration of the fact that individual categories are rarely found on their own; thus, besides category I, category IV is represented by a short exclamation (6: *pol*), as is category VI (3: if the conjecture <*vi*> is correct, then Cupid is presented as a deity wielding a considerable power over our state of mind). The popular topos of "the power of love" recurs later, where one might hesitate whether it should be included in category I or VI (854–856). Statements such as these should nonetheless ultimately be assigned to category I, since in such cases divine power is not simply stated, but explained in descriptive detail.

CATEGORY II

Statements in category I such as those just mentioned should be distinguished from verses such as these (469f.):

> *Pentheum diripuisse aiunt Bacchas: nugas maximas*
> *fuisse credo, praeut quo pacto ego divorsus distrahor.*

> They say that the Bacchae tore Pentheus to pieces: I believe that was the greatest trifle, compared with the way in which I'm torn apart.

The young lover Charinus compares himself to a mythological figure: Pentheus, King of Thebes, who was gruesomely dismembered by the Bacchants for scorning Dionysus. The comparison is hyperbolic: the suffering experienced by the unhappy lover, who is "torn apart" by his passions, is (tendentiously) far greater than anything suffered even by Pentheus, whose very name evokes notions of archetypal suffering. Such exaggerations should not routinely be invoked as evidence for a declining "belief" in the gods. Rather, they are intentionally comic attempts to exploit the mythological inventory known to the audience (cf. Fraenkel 2007: 45–71). To savor such comparisons, some knowledge of mythology and religion is required; otherwise, the remark is pointless.

A comparison voiced by the elderly nurse Syra is similar. Having just returned to town, her mistress, Dorippa, will in a few moments catch sight of an alleged love-rival in her own home, whom Syra has already seen (689–691):

> SY. *ei hac mecum, ut videas semul*
> *tuam Alcumenam paelicem, Iuno mea. –*
> DO. *ecastor vero istuc eo quantum potest.*

> Sy. Come this way with me, so that you too may see
> the rival—your Alcmene, my Juno.
> Do. By Castor, I shall indeed come inside as fast as I can.

Only a spectator at least generally familiar with Jupiter's family relations will catch the allusion to the famous love triangle hinted at here. Thus, while category II texts do not contain explicit statements about the gods, they nonetheless do enable a modern reader to make inferences about the quantity and quality of knowledge about gods and mythological figures that a Roman audience would commonly be expected to have had.

Category III

Examples in category III arouse unusual interest because of their pragmatic complexity and semantic density. This is particularly true for prayers, which closely resemble theatrical play-acting, insofar as they are also performances that "involve actors and an audience" (Hickson Hahn 2007: 237). Witness Dorippa's homecoming prayer, initially spoken while accompanied by Syra (675–680):

> DO. *aliquid cedo*
> *qui hanc vicini nostri aram <ad>augeam, <Syra>.*
> *da sane hanc virgam lauri. abi tu intro. SY. eo. –*
> DO. *Apollo, quaeso te ut des pacem propitius,*
> *salutem et sanitatem nostrae familiae,*
> *meoque ut parcas gnato pace propitius.*

> Do. Give me something
> with which I can decorate this altar of our neighbor's, Syra.
> Yes, give me this laurel branch. You go inside. Sy. Of course.
> Do. Apollo, I ask you to graciously grant us peace,
> health, and well-being for our family,
> and may you graciously spare my son with your peace.[4]

An important general question that arises when such texts are looked at from the perspective of performance criticism is: to whom are such prayers addressed? They are not spoken *ad spectatores*, but they are not spoken to other characters on stage, either, nor to the speaker him- or herself. Instead, they are addressed to entities whose presence can only be as certain to the person speaking as it is to the audience, unless the address is to an onstage statue or other representation of the gods. Research has thus struggled slightly with how best to categorize invocations to the gods in Menander and Terence (Blundell 1980: 73; Denzler 1968: 155f.), though in this case we can be more specific, since Apollo's altar likely forms part of the stage scenery.[5]

Many other questions of staging remain unanswered. For instance, where does the laurel branch come from? Is it real, and if so, has Syra been holding it in her hand? Or does she produce it from her luggage on Dorippa's request? The expression *hanc virgam lauri* (677) suggests that Syra is already holding it, but what happens when Dorippa takes it in her hand? Should it be laid on the altar and burned?

Furthermore, is Dorippa's prayer to Apollo a parody of a prayer or is it, as it were, a "real" prayer, nonetheless brought onto the Roman (or originally, Greek) stage? Since the context does not suggest parodic intent (cf. Averna 2009: 32), it seems to be the prayer offered by a wife returning home to the tutelary deity of the house entrance. It thus characterizes Dorippa as devout and concerned with the well-being of her family,

---

[4] In liturgical phrases like *pacem peto* (particularly, as here, in conjunction with religiously charged words like *propitius*), *pax* means primarily "grace, divine favor." (Despite its frequent occurrence in Plautus, it is never used in this sense in Terence, where it always refers to relationships between human beings.) Yet Dorippa's words could equally mark another of the many wartime allusions found in *Mercator*, notable among them *Mercator* 829 (a pun on *viduae* "without husband"/"widow" and *vidui* "without wife"/"widower"), on which see now Dunsch 2014. It is therefore tempting to suggest that the play was first performed during the Second Punic War—years that took a heavy toll on the Roman population—and, further, at the *ludi Apollinares* in particular. The latter would help explain Apollo's great prominence in *Mercator* as well as why in particular Syra hands Dorippa a laurel branch—the main prop in this passage: such branches were burnt on an altar in sacrifices to Apollo, and in 207 BCE a supplicatory procession was organized in Rome for the first time, a procession at which all suppliants wore laurel branches (Schuhmann 1975: 180).

[5] A stage altar was a regular feature of Greek and Roman theater, even if its exact position onstage remains unclear (cf. Duckworth 1952: 83f.; Marshall 2006 : 38–40; Manuwald 2012: 72). In theatrical performance, the altar was usually represented by a pillar (Barsby 1991: 112 on *Bacchides* 172). It was not, however, invariably associated with Apollo. It is associated with other deities (*Curculio* 71f.; *Miles Gloriosus* 411f.; *Truculentus* 476) or is used anonymously (Menander, *Perikeiromene* 999; Terence, *Andria* 72f.), and among other purposes it occasionally served as the sanctuary of a fugitive (Menander K-A fr. 893; Plautus, *Mostellaria* 1094, *Rudens* 688).

particularly her son. All this suggests that Dorippa's is the prayer of a reverent and pious Roman wife (or indeed, a Greek one: cf. Lefèvre 1995: 46f.).

More can be said regarding the tone of Dorippa's prayer by comparing another from the *Synephebes* of Caecilius, which is quoted by Cicero (*De nat. deor.* 1.13f.)—the heart-felt groan of a frustrated young man. Unlike Dorippa's, context easily identifies this prayer as an exaggerated parody:

> *Itaque mihi libet exclamare ut in Synephebis:*
> *"pro deum, popularium omnium, <omnium> adulescentium*
> *clamo, postulo, obsecro, oro, ploro, atque inploro fidem,"*
> *non levissuma de re, ut queritur ille in civitate fieri facinora capitalia:*
> *"ab amico amante argentum accipere meretrix non vult,"*
> *sed ut adsint, cognoscant, animadvertant, quid de religione, pietate, sanctitate,*
> *caerimoniis, fide, iure iurando, quid de templis, delubris, sacrificiisque sollemnibus,*
> *quid de ipsis auspiciis, quibus nos praesumus, existimandum sit, haec enim omnia*
> *ad hanc de dis immortalibus quaestionem referenda sunt. Profecto eos ipsos, qui*
> *se aliquid certi habere arbitrantur, addubitare coget doctissimorum hominum de*
> *maxuma re tanta dissensio.*

> Therefore, I would like to exclaim, as in *Synephebes*:
> "The protection of the gods, of all citizens, of all young men,
> I call on, demand, beseech, beg, cry out, and implore,"
> and not because of some trifle, like a man who complains of the occurrence of capital crimes in society:
> "The courtesan does not want to take money from her friend, her lover,"
> but so that they attend, become acquainted with, and assess what opinions should be held about religion, piety, worship, rites, faith, oaths, about temples, shrines, and solemn sacrifices, about the very auspices over which I myself preside; for all of these matters must be considered in our investigation into the nature of the gods. Surely such wide diversity of opinion among men of the greatest learning on a matter of the highest moment must affect even those who think that they possess certain knowledge with a feeling of doubt.

Here Cicero (who, it seems, knew the *Synephebes* at first hand) states that the man who laments so heart-wrenchingly to the gods (and a few other addressees) does this because of a mere trifle. The context evidently makes the difference: while Dorippa does not pray because of a mere trifle, the unknown youth in *Synephebes* certainly does. One should therefore assume that a Roman comedian is writing with a parodic intent only in cases where boundless exaggerations cluster—not in the case of such consciously crafted private prayers as Dorippa's.[6]

Let us therefore assume that Dorippa's prayer to Apollo is not parodic, but "real," albeit portrayed on stage. How does Plautus deal with a character carrying out an act

---

[6] A similar distinction can be drawn between prayers and parodies of prayer in Aristophanes (Horn 1970: 60).

of prayer that is, so to speak, effective "in reality"—a sacred act within the framework of a play, the dramatic action identified above as "ritual within a ritual"? The answer is simple and yet surprising: Dorippa's request is fulfilled in the course of the play. Recall that Dorippa prays for the well-being of her family and the whole household, but in particular her son. In fact, a courtesan (*meretrix*) is discovered in her home, and her husband Lysimachus must eventually eat humble pie—the family home, the *oikos*, which was in danger of becoming dysfunctional, regains its functionality. So Dorippa's wish has, in a way, been granted—but by Apollo?[7] Was it really believed that Dorippa's prayer during the performance of the play had been carried out "in reality" and with religiously binding force?

In reply to these questions, one conspicuous fact seems significant: Plautus has Dorippa's prayer interrupted. It ends abruptly, as soon as Syra rushes back on stage, wailing and disrupting the *preces* with her noise—about which her mistress has already complained twice, thus distinctly interrupting the ritually required *silentium* (in principle also required in Greek ritual, cf. Montiglio 2000: 9–17). What is more, it may be that even Syra's very presence compromises the execution of the ritual. This would certainly explain why Syra is permitted to pass Dorippa the laurel branch but not to join in laying it on the altar (she is sent inside the house instead). It is true that dramaturgy necessitates Syra's withdrawal (it enables the *hetaira*, Pasicompsa, to be discovered in Dorippa's house), but such technical reasons alone are not decisive: after all, Plautus could have removed the scene entirely. Perhaps Plautus thought it pointless to complete a nonparodic passage—or rather, the speech act codified by precisely such a passage—onstage and according to rite.

This hypothesis is supported by the fact that a similar interruption of a sacred act recurs in *Mercator*, when Lysimachus tries to swear an oath to his wife Dorippa that he had no business with the courtesan. Lysimachus himself interrupts the speech act of this *iusiurandum*, after both his wife and her maid have left the stage (789–794):

> LY. *nescis negoti quid sit, uxor, obsecro.*
> *conceptis verbis iam iusiurandum dabo*
> *me numquam quicquam cum illa—iamne abiit Syra?*
> *perii hercle. ecce autem haec abiit. vae misero mihi!*
> *at te, vicine, di deaeque perduint,*
> *cum tua amica cumque amationibus.*

> Ly. You do not know the situation, my wife, I beg.
> I'll now take an oath in solemn words
> that I never had anything to do with her—has Syra gone already?
> By Hercules, I'm doomed! See, even my wife has gone. O, wretched me!
> But you, neighbor, may all the gods and goddesses ruin you,
> with your mistress and your affairs together!

---

[7] The notion that the prayers of the pious rather than those of the impious are answered can incidentally be found in a number of passages in Plautus (cf., e.g., *Rudens* 26f., 1193f.; *Poenulus* 869, 1137, 1190, 1252ff., 1277).

There are many instances of oath-taking in Plautine comedy (e.g., *Asinaria* 23; *Bacchides* 771; *Casina* 670; *Cistellaria* 512ff.: an accumulation of gods of oath, equally *Bacchides* 892ff.; *Rudens* 1332ff.); the mentions of *concepta verba*, oath formulae, which are not uncommon, form a specific group mostly found in contexts that thematize perjury (*concepta verba*: *Asinaria* 562, *Bacchides* 1028, *Cistellaria* 98, *Mercator* 790, *Pseudolus* 353, 1057, 1077 [*concepisti verba*], *Truculentus* 767; implicitly with wordplay [*consutis dolis*]: *Pseudolus* 540). A failed oath is portrayed in detail at *Cistellaria* 492–527 (particularly 512–527). Interestingly, sacred acts, at least in Plautus, are generally presented under the conditions of their failure, with their incompletion and lack of end constituting an aspect of this failure.[8]

What then is the reason for the interruption of the prayer in *Mercator*? It must be noted that Lysimachus would perjure himself if he completed the oath, and in particular with *concepta verba*. The consideration of who actually swears the oath—or conducts the speech act—is interesting here: is it the actor standing on stage or the character played by him? From a modern point of view, one might reflexively argue that it is the character on stage who takes the oath, and not the actor himself (cf. Elam 1980, 169f.). Yet the very fact that "Lysimachus" interrupts his oath before he perjures himself on stage creates doubt whether this modern distinction was made in Plautus's Rome.[9]

The last examples for category III texts are a slightly different case. In utter desperation, Charinus resolves to leave his father's house and try his luck as a mercenary. Upon his departure—entering the stage (as emerges in a later passage) in his full travel gear—he prays for the well-being of his parents, whom he now wants to leave behind (830–841):

> CH. *Limen superum inferumque, salve, simul autem vale:*
> *hunc hodie postremum extollo mea domo patria pedem.*
> *usus, fructus, victus, cultus iam mihi harunc aedium*
> *interemptust, interfectust, alienatust. occidi.*
> *Di Penates meum parentum, familiai Lar Pater,*
> *vobis mando, meum parentum rem bene ut tutemini.*
> *ego mihi alios Deos Penatis persequar, alium Larem,*
> *aliam urbem, aliam civitatem: ab Atticis abhorreo;*
> *nam ubi mores deteriores increbrescunt in dies,*
> *ubique amici qui infideles sint nequeas pernoscere*
> *ubique id eripiatur animo tuo quod placeat maxume,*
> *ibi quidem si regnum detur, non cupitast civitas.*

> Ch. Lintel high and threshold low, greetings, and likewise goodbye:
> Today for the last time I lift this foot from my paternal home.
> The use and fruition, sustenance and nurture of this abode

---

[8] Moore (2004): 66 remarks on Alcesimarchus' prayer in *Cistellaria* that while Plautus does use the traditional Roman language of prayer as a source of parodic exaggeration, he is equally "not critical of that language" but "rather of someone who tries without success to recreate the language of prayer."

[9] It is interesting to compare cases such as *Bacchides* 892f., where a long litany of gods commences with Jupiter, Juno, Ceres, and Minerva—precisely in a way that does not have the Capitoline triad come in immediate succession, but "defuses" them by the interruption of naming Ceres (cf. Moore 2004, 54 n. 3).

> are cut off from me, dead to me, estranged from me! I am done!
> Divine Penates of my parents, Father Lar of this abode,
> I charge you to protect my parents' fortunes well.
> I will seek for myself other divine Penates, another Lar,
> another city, another country: I abhor Athens!
> For where customs decay more day by day,
> and where one cannot distinguish friend from foe,
> and where that which is your heart's greatest delight is snatched away from you,
> there I desire no citizenship, even if I should be king there.

Appropriately in the circumstances, the utterance is tragic: a snippet of paratragedy in the comic context, a technique with which Plautus was well acquainted (see Manuwald in this volume). In content and form, the monologue is structured in three sections: strophe, antistrophe, and epode (830–833, 834–837, 838–841). Deities are invoked at the start of the strophe and antistrophe respectively—lintel and threshold (830), *Penates* and *Lar* (834). In the epode, Charinus states his reasons for leaving. The body of the text is carefully weighted, structured, and cautiously phrased.[10]

Why does Plautus not have Charinus interrupt his monologue—and thereby the act of prayer onstage? Lysimachus stops short in the middle of his oath when he realizes that he is now alone onstage, and Dorippa is interrupted by external circumstances (Syra's disruption). But Charinus seemingly recites his carefully structured farewell prayer through to the end. Is it therefore possible that this prayer was regarded as being carried out just as genuinely as one which would, for example, be carried out in public and in earnest?

Charinus's request, forcibly expressed at the end of his prayer, that the *Lar* and the *Penates* should protect the fortune and possessions of his parents, is one-sided: he does not pray for his parents' well-being but for the preservation of their purse, which would fit with the description of things seemingly of most importance to him in his parental home: *usus, fructus, victus, cultus* (832). It is at least to this extent that one might suspect this prayer is parody, namely as part of the characterization of the young lover as irresponsible, irrational, and egocentric. Yet as with Dorippa's prayer, it is striking that Charinus's prayer is also eventually fulfilled: the parental fortune is protected by his father, who must renounce his affair with the courtesan Pasicompsa before it has even begun (that is, before he has had the opportunity to spend even more money on her: cf. 966, 989).

---

[10] A two-line fragment of Novius's *Maccus exul*, an Atellan farce, contains a strikingly similar greeting to lintel and threshold (fr. 49 R.³): "Lintel high, on which, wretched me, I often bashed my head, and threshold low, where I broke all my toes" (*Limen superum, quod mihi misero saepe confregit caput, / inferum autem, digitos omnis ubi ego diffregi meos*). Yet comparison shows that Novius's text is far less serious in tone than Charinus's monologue: the inappropriate combination of an address to the threshold of the house—which, taken on its own, is not peculiar, particularly in a Roman context—with Maccus's evidently disagreeable experiences on his way abroad decisively reveals this prayer as parody.

One might therefore even say that the prayers in *Mercator* function as a vehicle of poetic justice, or rather that the favorable outcome of the onstage action is already anticipated in the request—if the request is uttered by the right person (a respectable Roman matron; a young man truly in love). As with the prayers to Pan in Menander's *Dyskolos*, one can regard these rituals (or rather, the execution of these rituals) within the ritual (that is, the play itself) as a kind of catalyst for stage action, without necessitating any physical intervention of the deities themselves onstage.

CATEGORY IV

In contrast to category III, category IV contains only short cases of communications with the gods, usually unproblematic in their interpretation, not greatly elaborated, and which tend to be isolated instances. For example (762f.):

> CO. *mihi quidem hercle.* LY. *ita me amabit Iuppiter,*
> *uxor, ut ego illud numquam dixi.* DO. *etiam negas?*

> Co. Yes, to me personally, by Hercules! Ly. For the love of Jove,
> my dear wife, I've never said anything of the kind. Do. Denying it, now?

The cook employs the expletive *hercle* to substantiate his statement; Lysimachus uses the more elaborate *ita me amabit Iuppiter*, in order to surpass the cook and his claim ("Of course I know this man; he wants to have a party here with his lady friend!") with the longer form of substantiation, not only qualitatively (moving up from Hercules, born a demigod, to Jupiter, the father of gods and men, particularly of Hercules) but also quantitatively (four words instead of one). Taken in isolation, the value of such short exchanges as evidence for Roman religion is rather small. Viewed collectively, however, such texts can help us gain important insights, particularly with the help of statistical investigations and the methods of sociolinguistics and gender studies (see Stockert 2004 on the gender-specific use of *hercle* and other expletives).

Short expressions can nonetheless be integrated into the action with great virtuosity, for instance by having several of them follow one after another for comic effect, as here (966–967):

> LY. *di me servant!* EV. *tibi amicam esse nullam nuntio.*
> DE. *di te perdant! quid negotist nam, quaeso, istuc?* EV. *eloquar.*

> Ly. The gods are saving me! Eu. To you I announce that you have no mistress.
> De. May the gods ruin you! Do tell, what do you mean by that? Eu. I'll tell you.

As Eutychus announces a message that is good for one *senex* but bad for the other, Lysimachus and Demipho—the two *senes*—say exactly what they think of it. They do so with contrary intentions (joy and praise on the one hand, reproof and bad temper on the other), but with exclamations constructed in parallel (in meter and by assonance), with the gods' actions as their aim (the first a statement, the second a curse).

CATEGORY V

Roman comedy is rich in personifications and identifications of gods with men. A great deal of material that may prove fruitful for statistical investigation falls into this category. The occasional facetious naming of momentary deities, such as *Suavisaviatio*, "Sweetkiss" (*Bacchides* 116, 120), also belongs to this group. One example from *Mercator* demonstrates how abstract nouns, which are not documented as deities worshiped with genuine cults in Plautus's time, appear in long enumerations, which, though funny enough in themselves, become even funnier through the sheer accumulation of the names of these "gods" (866–871):

> *EV. ilico*
> *sta, Charine. CH. qui me revocat? EV. Spes, Salus, Victoria.*
> *CH. quid me voltis? EV. ire tecum. CH. alium comitem quaerite,*
> *non amittunt hi me comites qui tenent. EV. qui sunt ei?*
> *CH. Cura, Miseria, Aegritudo, Lacrumae, Lamentatio.*
> *EV. repudia istos comites atque hoc respice et revortere.*

> Eu. Stop where you are,
> Charinus! Ch. Who calls me back? Eu. Hope, Health, Victory.
> Ch. What do you want of me? Eu. To go with you. Ch. Seek another companion,
> these companions in whose grip I am, will not let me go. Eu. Who are they?
> Ch. Worry, Misery, Sorrow, Tears, and Lamentation.
> Eu. Renounce such vile companions, look back here, and return.

The second list of "gods" (*Cura, Miseria, Aegritudo, Lacrumae, Lamentatio*) is structurally reminiscent of catalogues of deities not uncommon in ancient literature (particularly epic poetry), as in for instance the second line of the famous catalogue of the Olympians in Ennius's *Annals* (fr. 240 Sk.):

> *Iuno, Vesta, Minerva, Ceres, Diana, Venus, Mars,*
> *Mercurius, Iovis, Neptunus, Vulcanus, Apollo.*

CATEGORY VI

When contextualized systematically and situated in their historical environment, religious details that seem uninformative in isolation can occasionally reveal much to us.

One of the first mentions of the word *religio* in Roman literature, for instance, appears in connection with sea travel (878–881):

> (EV.) recipe te ad terram, Charine, huc. nonne ex advorso vides,
> nubis atra imberque <ut> instat? aspice ad sinisteram,
> caelum ut est splendore plenum atque ut dei is<tuc vorti iubent>?
> CH. religionem illic <mi> obiecit: recipiam me illuc. EV. sapis.

> Eu. Come back to land, Charinus, here. Do you not see behind,
> how a black cloud and rain threatens? Look to the left,
> do you not see how the sky is aglow and how the gods bid you turn your course?
> Ch. He has filled me with *religio* there. I'll return that way! Eu. Very wise.

The scene in which these words are spoken is performed neither on a ship nor at the harbor, but rather in front of Charinus's parental home on a street in "Athens," where Eutychus wants to prevent his friend Charinus from turning his back on his home and becoming a mercenary abroad. To achieve this, it is important for Eutychus firstly to incite Charinus to turn around altogether, which he manages to do by indicating the weather conditions, urging that he should return "to land" (that is, to his parents' house). Charinus then paraphrases this indication with the term *religio*, "awe." It is precisely such passages from category VI that require extensive contextualization in order to be fully understood.

Category VII

Although one could argue that Apollo is indirectly present in *Mercator* because the altar consecrated to him appears onstage (and thus, not unlike Pan in Menander's *Dyskolos*), the play does not contain any true examples of this category. Yet the gods do appear repeatedly in Plautus's other plays, either as divine prologists (see my chapter on prologues in this volume) or in the form of actors onstage throughout the play (such as Jupiter and Mercury in *Amphitruo*); nothing similar is found in Terence.

Conclusion

This chapter has sought to demonstrate how the study of Roman comedy can be made productive for the study of Roman religion. It remains to be said that Plautus's treatment of religious themes and of the gods themselves is largely unified and classifiable rather than coincidental and disorganized. Future research should especially take note that, expressly or by implication, Plautus often thematizes the formal conditions for the successful completion of ritual acts and, conversely, that he often interrupts these acts or otherwise leaves them incomplete. Further research may also shed light on what relation, if any, exists between divine justice and poetic justice in Roman comedy and whether this relation leads to a particular behavior onstage being remunerated or cultivated while another is penalized or hampered. Such a study would enable us to investigate the gods' influence on the action more closely, and in particular their possible function as a controlling authority imagined as standing, as it were, beyond the drama, "to favour the good and to punish the wicked" (Liebeschuetz 1979: 44). To be more precise, the gods are not so much part of a philosophically saturated unfolding of a certain worldview that is constantly redefined by the comic playwright, but rather "actors" themselves, forming part of the hydraulics of the dramaturgical and theatrical background.

The occasions on which comedies were performed, the *ludi*, possessed a religious and equally a political character (see Gruen in this volume). In the very period when the cultural relations between Greece and Rome were put on a new basis, *ludi* came to be of great importance to the Romans, providing them with strategies of tuning in to and aligning themselves religiously and culturally with the Greeks (cf. Bernstein 1998: 353; Gruen 1990: 157). Beyond this, however, references to religion and cult in comedy naturally underlie actualities specific to the literary genre. Thus, in the case of sacred acts (and primarily in prayers) onstage, we can see in Dorippa's prayer to Apollo that religious speech acts are more than just ornamental decoration, and that Plautus employs references to religion within the framework of the whole drama, not only to characterize the people involved in them but at times even to foreshadow the eventual resolution of plot lines.

BIBLIOGRAPHY

Averna, D. 2009. "La suasoria nelle preghiere agli dei: Percorso diacronico dalla commedia alla tragedia." *Rhetorica* 27: 19–46.

Barsby, J., ed. 1991. *Plautus: Bacchides*. 3rd corr. impr. Warminster: Aris & Phillips.

Beacham, R. C. 1995. *The Roman Theater and its Audience*. London: Routledge.

Beard, M., North, J. and Price, S. 1998. *Religions of Rome*. 2 vols. Cambridge, UK: Cambridge University Press.

Bergmann, A. 1998. *Die 'Grundbedeutung' des lateinischen Wortes Religion*. Marburg: Diagonal-Verlag.

Bernstein, F. 1998. *Ludi publici: Untersuchungen zur Entstehung und Entwicklung der öffentlichen Spiele im republikanischen Rom*. Stuttgart: Franz Steiner Verlag.

——. 2007. "Complex Rituals: Games and Processions in Republican Rome." In *A Companion to Roman Religion*, edited by J. Rüpke, 222–234. Malden, MA: Blackwell.

Binder, G. 1998. "Pompa diaboli—Das Heidenspektakel und die Christenmoral." In *Das antike Theater: Aspekte seiner Geschichte, Rezeption und Aktualität*, edited by G. Binder and B. Effe, 115–147. Trier: Wissenschaftlicher Verlag Trier.

Blume, H.-D. 1991. *Einführung in das antike Theaterwesen*. 3rd ed. Darmstadt: Wissenschaftliche Buchgesellschaft.

Blundell, J. 1980. *Menander and the Monologue*. Göttingen: Vandenhoeck & Ruprecht.

Carlson, M. *Performance: A Critical Introduction*. 2nd ed. New York and London: Routledge.

Chapot, F. and Laurot, B. 2001. *Corpus de prières grecques et romains*. Turnhout: Brepols.

Denzler, B. 1968. *Der Monolog bei Terenz*. Zürich: P.G. Keller.

Diller, H.-J. 1998. "Religion, Theater, and the "Other World." In *Theater and Religion*, edited by G. Ahrends and H.-J. Günter/Diller, 25–38. Tübingen: Gunter Narr Verlag.

Duckworth, G. E. 1952. *The Nature of Roman Comedy: A Study in Popular Entertainment*. Princeton: Princeton University Press.

Dunsch, B. 2009. "Religion in der römischen Komödie: Einige programmatische Überlegungen." In *Römische Religion im historischen Wandel: Diskursentwicklung von Plautus bis Ovid*, edited by A. Bendlin and J. Rüpke, 17–56. Stuttgart: Franz Steiner Verlag.

——. 2014. "*Lege dura vivont mulieres*. Syra's Complaint about the Sexual Double Standard (Plautus *Merc.* 817-29)." In *Ancient Comedy and Reception. Essays in Honor of Jeffrey Henderson*, edited by S. D. Olson. Berlin and Boston: de Gruyter.

Dupont, F. 2010. "Theater." In *The Oxford Handbook of Roman Studies*, edited by A. Barchiesi and W. Scheidel, 450–463. Oxford: Oxford University Press.

Edwards, C. 1993. *The Politics of Immorality in Ancient Rome*. Cambridge, UK: Cambridge University Press.

Feeney, D. 1998. *Literature and Religion at Rome: Cultures, Contexts, and Beliefs*. Cambridge, UK: Cambridge University Press.

Fraenkel, E. 2007. *Plautine Elements in Plautus*. Translated by T. Drevikovsky and F. Muecke. Oxford: Oxford University Press (Italian ed. *Elementi Plautini in Plauto*, Florence, 1960; German ed. *Plautinisches im Plautus*, Berlin, 1922).

Gellar-Goad, T.H.M. 2013. "Religious Ritual and Family Dynamics in Terence." In: *A Companion to Terence*, edited by A. Augoustakis and A. Traill, 156-174. Malden, MA and Oxford: Wiley-Blackwell.

Goldberg, S. M. 1998. "Plautus on the Palatine." *Journal of Roman Studies* 88: 1–20.

Graf, F. 2007. "Religion and Drama." In *The Cambridge Companion to Greek and Roman Theater*, edited by M. McDonald and J. Walton, 55–71. Cambridge, UK: Cambridge University Press.

Gruen, E. S. 1990. *Studies in Greek Culture and Roman Policy*. Leiden: Brill.

Guittard, C. 1992. "Formes et fonctions de la prière dans les comédies de Plaute et de Térence." In *Actes du XXIVe Congrès International de l'Association des professeurs de langues anciennes de l'enseignement supérieur*, 75–99. Tours: Université François Rabelais.

Hanson, J. A. 1959. *Roman Theater-Temples*. Princeton: Princeton University Press.

——. 1959a. "Plautus as a Source-Book for Roman Religion." *Transactions and Proceedings of the American Philological Association* 90: 48–101.

Hickson, F. V. 1993. *Roman Prayer Language: Livy and the Aeneid of Vergil*. Stuttgart: Teubner.

Hickson Hahn, F. 2007. "Performing the Sacred: Prayers and Hymns." In *A Companion to Roman Religion*, edited by J. Rüpke, 235–248. Malden, MA: Blackwell

Holzberg, N. 1974. *Menander: Untersuchungen zur dramatischen Technik*. Nürnberg: Hans Carl.

Horn, W. 1970. *Gebet und Gebetsparodie in den Komödien des Aristophanes*. Nürnberg: Hans Carl.

Jocelyn, H. D. 2001. "Gods, Cult and Cultic Language in Plautus' *Epidicus*." In *Studien zu Plautus' Epidicus*, edited by U. Auhagen, 261–296. Tübingen: Gunter Narr Verlag.

Kleinknecht, H. 1937. *Die Gebetsparodie in der Antike*. Stuttgart: W. Kohlhammer. Repr. 1967.

La Bua, G. 1999. *L'inno nella letteratura poetica latina*. San Severo: Gerni Editori.

Lefèvre, E. 1995. *Plautus und Philemon*. Tübingen: Gunter Narr Verlag.

Liebeschuetz, J. H. W. G. 1979. *Continuity and Change in Roman Religion*. Oxford: Clarendon Press.

López, A. 2000. "Los dioses en los subgéneros cómicos del teatro romano." In *Estudios sobre comedia romana*, edited by A. López and A. Pociña, 89-95. Frankfurt: Peter Lang.

Manuwald, G. 2011. *Roman Republican Theater*. Cambridge, UK: Cambridge University Press.

Marshall, C.W. 2006. *The Stagecraft and Performance of Roman Comedy*. Cambridge, UK: Cambridge University Press.

Montiglio, S. 2000. *Silence in the Land of Logos*. Princeton: Princeton University Press.

Moore, T.J. 2004. "Meter and Meaning in *Cistellaria* I 1." In: Studien zu Plautus' *Cistellaria*, edited by R. Hartkamp and F. Hurka, 319–333. Tübingen: Gunter Narr Verlag.

Muth, R. 1998. *Einführung in die griechische und römische Religion*. 2nd ed. Darmstadt: Wissenschaftliche Buchgesellschaft.

Pavis, P. 1988. *Semiotik der Theaterrezeption*. Tübingen: Gunter Narr Verlag.

Rüpke, J. 2012. *Religion in Republican Rome: Rationalization and Ritual Change*. Philadelphia: University of Pennsylvania Press.

Schechner, R. 1990. *Theater-Anthropologie: Spiel und Ritual im Kulturvergleich*. Reinbek bei Hamburg: Rowohlt.

Schuhmann, E. 1975. "Die Stellung der Frau in den Komödien des Plautus." PhD diss., Karl-Marx-Universität Leipzig.

Slater, N. W. 2011. "Plautus the Theologian." In *Sacred Words: Orality, Literacy and Religion*, edited by A. P. M. H. Lardinois, et al., 297–310. Leiden and Boston: Brill.

Stockert, W. 2004. "Schwören auch Frauen bei Herkules? Bemerkungen zu *Cist.* 52 und anderen Plautus-Stellen." In *Studien zu Plautus' Cistellaria*, edited by R. Hartkamp and F. Hurka, 363–369. Tübingen: Gunter Narr Verlag.

Swoboda, M., and J. Danielewicz. 1981. *Modlitwa i hymn w poezji rzymskiej*. Poznań: Uniwersytet im. Adama Mickiewicza.

Versnel, H. S. 1998. "Komödie, Utopie und verkehrte Welt." In *Das antike Theater: Aspekte seiner Geschichte, Rezeption und Aktualität*, edited by G. Binder and B. Effe, 93–114. Trier: Wissenschaftlicher Verlag Trier.

Vogt-Spira, G. 2001. "Traditions of Theatrical Improvisation in Plautus: Some Considerations." In *Oxford Readings in Menander, Plautus, and Terence*, edited by E. Segal, 95–106. Oxford: Oxford University Press.

PART THREE

··

TRANSMISSION AND
ANCIENT RECEPTION

··

CHAPTER 33

THE TRANSMISSION OF ARISTOPHANES[*]

NIGEL WILSON

THOUGH there are many studies of the textual transmission of Greek authors, Aristophanes must be said to have received less attention than he deserves. There is no overall survey of the manuscript tradition along the lines of those dedicated to the three tragedians by Alexander Turyn, and despite the advances in our knowledge made in recent decades, more work is needed before a full account can be attempted. However, much important information is supplied by recent editions of several plays which give fairly detailed reports about the papyri and medieval manuscripts available for the play in question; a gap that remains to be filled is the evaluation of some of the more recent manuscripts of the *Plutus*. In addition, there is a good and accessible recent survey of the history of Aristophanic textual scholarship in Nan Dunbar's edition of the *Birds*.[1] The purpose of the account that follows here is to offer a sketch from the vantage point of an editor who can claim to be better acquainted than his predecessors with problems of textual transmission, Greek paleography, and Byzantine studies. The absence of a reference work for Greek texts corresponding to *Texts and Transmission: A Survey of the Latin Classics*, edited by L. D. Reynolds (Oxford: Clarendon Press, 1983), is to be regretted; my remarks are designed to be similar to an entry in such a volume.

The history of a text begins with the author's autograph or master copy. Such copies do not survive for the text of any ancient author of note. In a few cases, inferences can be made about the character of such copies. The incoherent state of certain passages in the text of two comedies, *Clouds* and *Frogs*, forces us to the conclusion that after the first performance the author decided to modify the text, perhaps with a view to a second performance, which is attested for the *Frogs* by the remark of the Peripatetic scholar

---

[*] This chapter originally appeared as the introduction to Wilson (2009: 1–14). Minor changes of format have been introduced.

[1] Dunbar (1995).

Dicaearchus quoted at the end of one of the Arguments. Alternatively, the author may have wished to allow a revised version to circulate through the book trade, which developed gradually in the second half of the fifth century BCE and may have been quite vigorous by the time of the poet's death.

Though I have used the term "book trade," it should probably be assumed that initially access to the master copy was obtained only by direct contact with the author or his family. There is no sign at this date of authors offering their works to booksellers, who would also have fulfilled the role of publishers. When Aristophanes died, it would appear that the text of at least the two plays just mentioned had not been fully revised. He is not the only author to have left some of his work unfinished. When investigating the text of Aelian's *Varia Historia,* I came to a similar conclusion.[2] The same explanation will account for some other alleged instances of second or revised editions.[3]

It has been claimed that there is other evidence of disorder in the texts that Aristophanes kept as master copies. The suggestion has been made that in the *Wasps* two sections of text, 290–316 and 266–89, need to change places; also—and less plausibly—1265–1291 and 1450–1473; similarly, that in the *Lysistrata* 1273–1294 and 1295–1321 should be read in reverse order. The errors allegedly occurred because the passages in question were written out on separate sheets for the benefit of the actors, and these sheets were subsequently put together in the wrong order. In other words, either the faulty order was transferred into a copy made on a papyrus roll, perhaps by or for the author, or the author was content to have a bundle of sheets rather than a roll as his master copy, and the sheets were not numbered. The latter hypothesis seems very implausible, but the former cannot be entirely ruled out.[4] In recent commentaries on the plays, the problem is usually discussed not so much in terms of the history of ancient books as the coherence of the context. It is difficult to come to a definite conclusion, and the editor should probably err on the safe side by accepting the transmitted text. Yet it is interesting to note that one modern commentator of generally conservative tendency admitted that the first transposition proposed in the *Wasps* is quite possibly right.[5] An uncertain light is thrown on the question by the recent publication of a papyrus (P.Oxy. 4546, i BCE/i CE) containing Euripides, *Alcestis* 344–382, but with omissions: the scribe wrote only the lines spoken by Admetus. Was this an actor's copy?

There is not much that can usefully be said about the circulation of texts of the plays between the early fourth century BCE and the end of antiquity. But one unexpected testimony to knowledge of our author is provided by an inscription from Rhodes. On the base of a cylindrical column are inscribed ll. 454–458 of the *Frogs,* with the author's

---

[2] See my Loeb edition (Wilson 1997), 18.

[3] For discussion of Isocrates and some other fourth-century authors who appear to have revised their texts, see Pinto (2003: 153–160).

[4] A recent discussion can be found in the latest version of C. F. Russo's monograph *Aristophanes: An Author for the Stage* (Russo 1994), 243–245, 263. These cases were raised in Srebrny (1959–1960: 43–45) and Srebrny (1961).

[5] D. M. MacDowell in his edition (MacDowell 1971), 169.

name given above. The inscription would appear to be from a dedication by one or more members of a guild of initiates. Their text avoids two errors that occur in most of the medieval witnesses, one a minor detail involving a connecting particle, the other a substitution of ἱλαρόν for ἱερόν, a mistake induced by recollection of a well-known phrase in a Christian hymn.[6] But epigraphic evidence for literary texts is extremely rare.[7]

The papyri have not brought a generous harvest of fragments from plays that failed to survive until the Middle Ages, and their contribution to the extant plays is also relatively modest.[8] In this latter respect, they are on a par with the Sophoclean papyri. They reveal few serious textual divergences, with the possible exception of P. Colon. 14 of *Lysistrata* dating from the fourth century CE, which in ll. 182–199 has a lacuna and some lines in the wrong order. This fact has been taken to suggest that a second authorial version of the scene existed or that an actor or producer wished to abbreviate the scene. But the arguments against these possibilities are strong.[9] We are probably safe in assuming that the text of the comedies was stable and that Alexandrian editors played their part by making their library's exemplar available for transcription, as is supposed to have been the case with Homer. The number of published papyri continues to increase. It is noticeable that many are from late antiquity. This may reflect the influence of the Atticist movement with its interest in many aspects of Athenian life in the fifth and fourth centuries BCE, for which Aristophanes was an excellent source. It is possible that as a result Aristophanes began to occupy a larger place in the school curriculum, so as to rival Menander. Some of the quotations which constitute a part of the secondary tradition are a result of the Atticist movement. Educators of late antiquity, unlike many of their modern counterparts, did not expound their principles, and so we have to guess as best we can to what extent and when the syllabus of the schools was modified.

Although statistics derived mainly from papyrological evidence can never be entirely satisfactory, because of the unpredictability of future publications and because almost all the evidence comes from Egypt, where the reading habits of the public were not necessarily identical in all respects with those typical of other regions, it is still worth quoting figures from a recent survey. Among the extant books written in the period from the fourth to the seventh century CE there are thirty-six containing Aristophanes and thirty-four of Menander. For the sixth and seventh centuries, the figures are respectively three and four, probably too low to be reliable, and one of the four in any case results from a significant redating. But the general picture is clear.[10]

Aristophanes's place in the curriculum was apparently not affected during the so-called Dark Age. Menander, though a few of his plays seem to have been still available in Byzantium at the end of the sixth century and perhaps figured in the curriculum,

---

[6] See G. Pugliese Carratelli (1940), with plate.
[7] Some examples are given in Reynolds and Wilson (1991: 199–202, 287).
[8] See Austin (1973:, 7–32); Gelzer (1970, cols. 1552–1554); Mertens (1996); Gonis (1999).
[9] See J. Henderson in his edition (Henderson 1987), 91–92.
[10] Crisci (2003: 90–93, 113 n. 107, 115 n. 113). The relative popularity of the two poets as attested by the papyri has also been studied by A. Blanchard (Blanchard 1997).

can no longer be traced at the end of the eighth century, when the first signs of a cultural revival began to appear. The most notable product of that revival, the patriarch Photius (ca. 810–93), displays in his correspondence a knowledge of *Plutus* and *Frogs*, and he would not have made the allusions if he had not hoped that his addressees would follow them. From that time onward, it is clear that educated Byzantines had read some Aristophanes at school. Since the Byzantines had no theater, their reading of ancient drama can only have given them a limited appreciation of the texts, and quite possibly these were regarded as little more than a quarry for telling examples of rhetorical devices or vocabulary suitable for use in their own archaizing literary compositions. Notwithstanding this unpromising cultural background, there are a number of medieval copies of the plays. About thirty-five are datable before ca. 1400. If one adds those transcribed between that date and ca. 1600, the total rises to about 170. Of these, the vast majority contain at most three plays, *Clouds*, *Frogs*, and *Plutus*, often referred to as the triad, and some have only one or two, reflecting the reduction of the curriculum.[11]

Very few classical authors are transmitted in more than a handful of manuscripts that date from the middle Byzantine period, which began with the revival just mentioned and continued until the capture and destruction of the capital by the Crusaders in 1204. Aristophanes is no exception to this rule. The witnesses that belong to this period can be counted on the fingers of one hand. Pride of place goes to MS Ravenna, Biblioteca Classense 429 (R), from the second half of the tenth century, which alone (apart from a Renaissance apograph now in Munich) contains all eleven plays. Though it is rather carelessly written, many of its errors are trivial and it often preserves the true reading or something close to it, so that the quality of its text overall entitles it to be considered the best manuscript. It was first used systematically by Invernizi at the end of the eighteenth century.[12] Consultation of the facsimile[13] has enabled me to correct reports of its readings in a few passages. For practical purposes the *Suda* lexicon, compiled at much the same time as the Ravenna manuscript was written, is to be regarded as its incomplete twin. The extremely numerous quotations from the plays and accompanying scholia exhibit an almost identical text.

Not much later is a tiny fragment of the *Birds*, a single leaf surviving in Florence (MS Laurentianus 60. 9). But the only other substantial witness from this period, i.e., one that contains more than the three plays normally read in the schools, is in Venice: MS Marcianus gr. 474 (V) contains seven plays and on paleographical grounds is to be dated to the second half of the eleventh century rather than to the twelfth.[14] Though I am inclined on balance to rate V as slightly inferior to R overall, it should be recognized that

---

[11] They were listed by J. W. White (White 1906); his sigla are generally accepted. Six others that remained unknown to him are listed by K. J. Dover in his edition of the *Clouds* (Dover 1968: c n. 2). See also Gelzer (1970: cols. 1560–1563) and Eberline (1980).

[12] His edition appeared at Leipzig between 1794 and 1834.

[13] Edited by J. van Leeuwen (van Leeuwen 1904).

[14] This was the view expressed by T. W. Allen in his preface to the facsimile (Allen 1902) and confirmed in my discussion in Wilson (1977), 237.

its merits are considerable, and for instance in many passages of the *Wasps* it alone offers the correct readings.

A witness of uncertain date which probably belongs to the twelfth century is now in Madrid, Biblioteca Nacional de España MS 4683 (formerly N 53) (Md1). It contains the triad and *Knights* 1–306, but parts of it, including the fragment of the *Knights*, are leaves restored by its fifteenth-century owner Constantine Lascaris and another unknown hand; the original scribe is responsible for *Plutus* 1–528, *Clouds*, and *Frogs* 1–959. A later date was proposed by W. J. W. Koster on the ground that certain of its readings look like emendations of a kind to be expected from scholars of the Palaeologan period (1261–1453).[15] He was followed by Sir Kenneth Dover in his edition of the *Clouds*. The key point is that at l. 728, Md1 is one of several witnesses that make the metrically necessary change of ἐξευρετέος for ἐξευρητέος and all the others are of the later date.[16] Could the reading be attributed to a fortunate slip or to superior metrical knowledge displayed by a twelfth-century scholar such as John Tzetzes or his brother Isaac? Although these men did not greatly distinguish themselves as metricians, one or other of these two explanations may have to be accepted in the light of the paleographical evidence.[17]

Another important manuscript is in Milan, Biblioteca Ambrosiana MS C 222 inf. (K). It is now in very poor condition, so that collation from microfilm is barely possible. An up-to-date description has been published by C. M. Mazzucchi, who concludes that it is to be dated between 1180 and 1186.[18] His paleographical analysis, supported by close study of some informative marginalia, results in a substantially earlier dating than was accepted in the past; in my opinion it is correct, and this manuscript therefore becomes one of the very few that predate the disaster of 1204. Some of its readings in *Plutus* were reported by Holzinger in his commentary; I examined it in situ in October 2003 in order to be able to give a fuller report of its variants in that play, but even so I do not feel absolutely confident that I have extracted every detail that might be useful. For its readings in the other plays of the triad, I have accepted the reports in Dover's editions.

As is well known, the return of the Byzantine government to its former capital in 1261 was followed by a notable artistic and cultural revival, especially in the years ca. 1280–ca. 1350. One of the early signs of this is the corpus of classical poetry collected in what is now the Florentine MS Laurentianus 32. 16, produced under the auspices of the monk Maximus Planudes ca. 1280. Manuscripts of classical authors written between that date and ca. 1350 survive in relatively large numbers—no doubt this is due in part to the shorter time that they have been exposed to the hazards of war and natural

---

[15] Koster (1956).

[16] See his edition (Dover 1968: ciii, cxx).

[17] In his edition of *Frogs* (Dover 1993: 79), Dover contented himself with the remark that the dating is controversial and referred to earlier discussion. The later date has also been proposed by Holwerda (1977: vii-viii, xxxi-xxxii), but his attempt to find analogous scripts in MSS of ca. 1320–1345 did not convince me.

[18] Mazzucchi 77 (2003), with two plates, and Mazzucchi (2004).

disaster—and the activities of several scholars can be traced in varying degrees of detail. For Aristophanes, the main figures are Thomas Magister and Demetrius Triclinius.

Thomas's contribution is very difficult to assess, as no autograph copy has yet been identified. He may have confined himself to the triad. For the *Plutus,* there is no modern study of the transmission which might throw light on his contribution. In his edition of *Frogs,* Dover refers to Thomas Magister as the author of some scholia identified as his by Triclinius.[19] But Thomas is not described as having prepared a recension of the text. In Eberline's monograph on the MSS of the play, a number of Thoman manuscripts are identified (they are Cr O3 P25 V2 and Ln3 L2 Vv18).[20] It is noted that there are "gaps and inconsistencies" in this group, and Eberline remains uncertain whether Thomas edited the text.[21] If he did, "it is certain that many of the readings cited above for Th(omas) are not his own conjectures." This conclusion explains why Dover did not attempt to cite Thoman readings in this play. In his edition of *Clouds,* he uses the siglum *f* to refer to one or more Thoman MSS and mentions some good readings that first occur in them, while admitting that the class is difficult to define.[22] They are found at 87 πίθωμαι in Vv2, 654 ἔτ' in Ct1 P25 V2 Vv2(pc) and 1046 δειλόν in Ct1 O3 P20 P25 V2. Thomas is also cited at 647, 711–715, 733, 811, and 886. Whether we accept any of these readings or not, are we entitled to speak of a Thoman recension? Though he wrote a fresh version of the short life of the poet and hypotheses to the triad plays, it does not follow that he did more. Given the uncertainties about Thomas's work, I have found it difficult to be consistent in reporting. In some places, where I know of only one MS carrying an allegedly Thoman reading I record the fact in the form, e.g., Vv2 (Thomas Magister); where the attestation is apparently wider, the sigla of the MSS are omitted.[23]

Triclinius is more easily dealt with. His definitive recension of eight plays is represented by Oxford, Bodleian Library, Holkham gr. 88 (L) (almost complete, lacking only the end of *Peace*), its damaged twin, MS Vaticanus gr. 1294 (the three plays of the normal school curriculum of that date, followed by *Knights* 1–270) and MS Vaticanus gr. 2181.[24] His earlier edition, of the triad only, is in Paris, Bibliothèque nationale de France, MS suppl. grec 463; the text, which is not in his hand, is said to be Thoman in

[19] Dover (1993: 81).

[20] Eberline (1980: 78).

[21] Eberline (1980: 86).

[22] Dover (1968: cxvii–cxix).

[23] In his essay "Explorations in the History of the Text of Aristophanes" in Vol. 2 of his collected papers (Dover 1988: 223–265), Dover does not deal with Thomas. The Cremona MS has been studied by D. Harlfinger and M. Chantry in their contributions to the proceedings of the 1998 Cremona congress on Greek palaeography (Harlfinger 1998; Chantry 1998).. It turns out to be earlier than previously supposed (a watermark hints at a date as early as ca. 1320–1325); but there is no evidence that it is an autograph, and other Thoman MSS may conceivably be equally early. The forthcoming dissertation on Thomas by Dr. Niels Gaul [now published in revised form as Gaul 2011] will help to place him clearly in context.

[24] Sicherl (1997: 125 n. 63) argues that this MS is a copy of the Holkham MS. For the latter, see my paper "The Triclinian Edition of Aristophanes" (Wilson 1962).

character. Triclinius attributes some of the scholia to Thomas, which is another matter.[25] Triclinius's understanding of some basic principles of meter enabled him to make a more significant contribution to the textual criticism of the plays than any other scholar in the Middle Ages or Renaissance. We do not know how many copies he was able to use as the basis for his text, but from his work on *Birds* we can make some inferences. At l. 809, it would seem that he depended on a manuscript like Laurentianus 31. 15 (Γ), which omits the word χρή, because he there remedied the lacuna of one syllable in a totally inappropriate way, which he would have avoided had he been able to use any better source. It also appears that towards the end of the play he was using a witness akin to MS Vaticanus Urbinas gr. 141 (U), because he shares readings with it at ll. 1437, 1514, 1666, and 1712. At ll. 1543, 1548, 1566, 1575, 1624, 1670, 1693, and 1736, he has a reading shared with both U and Γ, and at 1579 his correction presumably derives from a faulty reading found in those two codices.

Approximately contemporary with Triclinius are a small number of other manuscripts that contain at least one play from outside the triad and are of some importance to editors. They are Θ (Laurentianus, Conventi Soppressi 140, triad and *Knights*), U (Urbinas gr. 141, triad and *Birds*), M (Ambrosianus L 39 sup., triad and *Knights*), E (Modena, Estensis 127 = α. U. 5. 10, triad, *Knights*, *Birds*, and *Acharnians*), Γ (Laurentianus 31. 15 + Leiden, Vossianus gr. F 52, *Knights*, *Birds*, *Acharnians*, *Ecclesiazusae*, *Lysistrata*, and *Peace*), and A (Paris, grec 2712, triad, *Knights*, *Birds*, *Acharnians*, and *Ecclesiazusae* 1–444). The sum total of what these manuscripts contribute to the text is modest; to put it another way, if they had not come down to us the task of the editor would not have been significantly more difficult. Other manuscripts of this date or a little later occasionally need to be cited, usually for no more than an isolated reading; an exception is MS Perugia, Biblioteca Augusta, H 56, a fifteenth-century copy of the *Ecclesiazusae*; there are also manuscripts of modest value containing scholia only (Bodleian Library, Barocci 38, *Lysistrata* and Naples, Biblioteca Nazionale II. D. 49, a copy of Γ which supplies some lacunae in that manuscript).[26]

Triclinius does not appear to have had any worthy successor among later Byzantine teachers, and in general it is not common to find much of value in manuscripts copied after ca. 1350. But it is worth saying that there is some hope of further research that would enable us to give a fuller picture of the handling of the text in the Palaeologan period, which might overturn this negative judgment. Progress will depend on detailed

---

[25] A detailed study of this MS is provided by Koster (1957); his assertions about the extent of Triclinius's part in the production of the MS cannot be accepted in full.

[26] I mention in passing a recent article by A. Bravo García (Bravo García 1998) which deals with MSS of Aristophanes in the libraries of Madrid. It does not appear to have findings of note for the textual critic, but refers to the work of I. Pérez Martín (Pérez Martín 1996: 99–113); she discusses excerpts in Escorial MS X.I. 13 (355) which amount to some 17% of *Plutus*, 13% of *Clouds*, 10% of *Frogs*, and 9% of *Knights*. These turn out not to offer anything of importance, in striking contrast to similar excerpts from Sophocles in the same MS. A leaf from A (Paris, grec 2712) which was extant in the eighteenth century and then disappeared has now been recovered by Förstel and Rashed (2003).

study of all the surviving fourteenth-century manuscripts, so as to obtain an assessment of their variant readings. Extra precision may be achieved in two ways: many of these manuscripts are written on Western paper, in which the watermarks often permit a fairly accurate dating, and it may also be possible to identify the hands of some of the scribes.

The next important phase in the transmission of texts begins early in the fifteenth century, when refugees from the declining empire brought their books and their notions of education with them to Italy. Though some parts of the text are far from easy for students, the plays were recommended by at least one of the most eminent humanists of the day. Aldus Manutius's preface to the editio princeps of 1498 reports that Theodore Gaza (1400–ca. 1476), when asked his advice about the best authors to read, replied "Just Aristophanes, because he is very acute, fluent, learned and pure Attic." But at this stage in the history of Greek scholarship, no more than a tiny handful of readers or copyists, whether refugees or their Italian pupils, were expert enough in the niceties of the classical language to be able to make a contribution to the criticism of what was by now a rather corrupt text. It is not wholly surprising that Aristophanes tends not to be mentioned in educational treatises by humanists, who give few specific recommendations about Greek authors to be read.[27] Manuel Chrysoloras might have been expected to introduce Aristophanes to his Florentine audience in the years 1397–1400. The youthful Guarino, while studying with him and his nephew in Constantinople, had acquired a copy of some comedies (MS Vaticanus Palatinus gr. 116) and equipped it with Latin glosses. But there seems to be no proof that the master on arrival in Italy included this standard text in the range of authors to be studied.[28]

Early traces of an interest in the *Plutus* can be found. It served as part of the inspiration for a work entitled *Fabula Penia* by Rinuccio di Castiglione, composed in Crete in 1415–1416. Acceptance of the comedies as essential reading came slowly. In Vittorino da Feltre's celebrated school at Mantua, which flourished in the second quarter of the century, it is reported that the master omitted or toned down passages that seemed to him obscene or otherwise objectionable.[29] In the meantime, an attempt had been made, perhaps ca. 1439, to translate *Plutus* into Latin: Leonardo Bruni, perhaps following up an initial effort by Giovanni Tortelli, produced a version of ll. 1–239. It is worth noting that here again a reference to sexual practices in ll. 153 ff. is suppressed. A later version of the play has been credited to the Paduan scholar Pietro da Montagnana (d. 1478); it is in MS Marcianus lat. XIV. 10 (4659), fos. 41–65ᵛ. Elsewhere, one can see the study of the plays being undertaken at a far from exalted level, which I suspect may have been typical, in a MS now in Vienna (phil. gr. 204). This is a copy of *Plutus* and *Clouds* commissioned from a Greek scribe in 1458 by Alexander of Otranto, later a professor of theology and vicar-general of the Dominicans in his province. Having obtained his copy, Alexander

---

[27] See, e.g., the useful collection edited by Kallendorf (2002).
[28] This is the negative inference I draw from the fact that there is no other mention of our author in the up-to-date surveys provided by Maisano and Rollo (2002); see p. 136.
[29] Platina as cited by Garin (1958: 680).

entered in the margins a Latin version and notes on *Plutus* and ll. 1–205 of *Clouds*. But it is clear that though he may have consulted other copies while making his version, he did not have the ambition to undertake scholarly work on the text, and there is only one passage where he shows awareness of a textual variant. His Latin is literal and not at all elegant, but no doubt he was less concerned with elegance than with the practical requirements of the schoolroom.[30] The use of *Plutus* as a university text is attested by some short extracts in MS Laurentianus 66. 31,[31] the contents of which seem to represent the program of instruction given by Andronicus Callistus during an academic year at Florence.

There are three exceptions to this general picture of gloom. One is Marcus Musurus, who produced the editio princeps for Aldus Manutius. It will be seen from my apparatus criticus that he tidied up details, not, however, achieving nearly as much as he did later in his career when editing some other authors.[32] His edition included nine plays; *Lysistrata* and *Women at the Thesmophoria* had to wait until 1515, when they were issued in Florence by the Juntine Press. The second bright light is found in MS Paris, grec 2715 (B), traditionally regarded as mysterious because it contains a number of good readings of unexplained origin. The situation can now be clarified. Not long ago, when examining some photostat prints taken from it I realized that, despite the misleading effect created by a substantial enlargement, the hand must be that of the prolific copyist Andronicus Callistus, and this identification was confirmed by the new standard reference book on Greek scribes.[33] It was already known that this scribe was capable of making useful suggestions for the improvement of texts, and it is therefore no surprise that he should have been able to do the same for Aristophanes.[34] Nor is it necessary to toy any longer with the hypothesis that B represents, albeit very imperfectly, the result of work undertaken by Triclinius after his completion of the recension that we see in L.

The third figure of some note in this period is an Istrian humanist called Andreas Divus. He was born in Capodistria (now Koper), but it is not clear whether he was Italian or Slovenian, and his vernacular name has never been discovered. His Latin version of the comedies was issued in Venice in 1538 and reprinted in Basle in 1542; from time to time it is clear that he has successfully emended the Greek. The version was perhaps made from Zanetti's 1538 text, if the reading at *Lysistrata* 600 is any guide; there Divus has *opportunum est*, corresponding to Zanetti's proposal. But as the translation appeared in the same year as the edition, one may prefer to suppose that there was collaboration.[35]

Other early printed editions of the Greek text issued during the sixteenth century exhibit occasional improvements. It should be noted that few contain all eleven plays;

---

[30] See Chirico (1991), esp. p. 36.
[31] Information kindly provided by Professor G. N. Knauer.
[32] For an account of his career see Wilson (1992: 148–155). The materials used by him for the edition have been identified by Sicherl (1997: 114–154 with pl. iv).
[33] Gamillscheg and Harlfinger (1989: 34).
[34] On the quality of some of his other proposals, see my remarks (Wilson 1992: 117, 182 n. 13).
[35] The interest of Divus's version was noted by Colin Austin (Austin 1987: 69).

the majority offer only one, doubtless chosen as a set text for school or university use. One such edition, which contains the triad only, is a bibliographical rarity, details of which deserve to be clarified; see my note on *Plutus* 216. It is also interesting to note that the edition of the *Plutus* by the French scholar Girardus, issued in Paris in 1549, arranges the material in an intelligent way: a short passage of the Greek text, anything from four to twenty-two lines, is followed first by a Latin version in ordinary type, then by notes, where the Latin is in italics and a smaller typeface. It may be that this arrangement was a didactic innovation.

The progress of textual scholarship since the Renaissance is adequately known in its general outlines. Interesting additions to our knowledge are made from time to time when the work of previously obscure or anonymous scholars comes to light. A case in point is the discovery that Biset, Daubuz, and an anonymous French scholar made useful suggestions which anticipate proposals by Bentley and others.[36] One result of my experience in editing Sophocles is the conviction that there is potential for further discoveries if it is possible to compile a repertory of conjectures. Many of those published in the nineteenth century appeared in pamphlets that are exceedingly difficult to consult, and it can even happen that contributions to well-known periodicals are lost sight of.

BIBLIOGRAPHY

Allen, T. W. 1902. Ἀριστοφάνους Κωμωιδίαι.*Facsimile of the Codex Venetus Marcianus 474.* London and Boston: Printed for the Archaeological Institute of America and the Society for the Promotion of Hellenic Studies.

Austin, C. 1973. *Comicorum graecorum fragmenta in papyris reperta.* Berlin and New York: de Gruyter.

———. 1987. "Textual Problems in Ar. *Thesm.*" *Dodone* 16: 61–92.

Austin, C. and S. D. Olson. 2004. *Aristophanes: Thesmophoriazusae.* Oxford: Oxford University Press.

Blanchard, A. 1997. "Destins de Ménandre." *Ktema* 22: 213–225.

Bravo García, A. 1998. "El Aristófanes de las bibliotecas de la Comunidad de Madrid: una ojeada a los fondos de El Escorial." In *La comedia griega y su influencia en la literatura española*, edited by J. A. López Férez, 369–386. Madrid: Ediciones Clásicas.

Chantry, M. 2000. "Le manuscrit Cremonensis 171." In *I manoscritti greci tra riflessione e dibattito*, edited by G. Prato, 665–667. Florence: Gonnelli.

Chirico, M. 1991. *Aristofane in Terra d'Otranto.* Naples: Università degli studi di Napoli Federico II.

Crisci, E. 2003. "Papiro e pergamena nella produzione libraria in Oriente fra IV e VIII secolo d.C.: Materiali e riflessioni," *Segno e testo* 1: 79–127.

Dover, K. J. 1968. *Aristophanes: Clouds.* Oxford: Clarendon Press.

---

[36] For a convenient conspectus, see Austin and Olson's edition of *Women at the Thesmophoria* (Austin and Olson 2004), pp. xcix–civ. Korais's notes in the plays have been published from MSS in the library at Chios by N. Kalospyros (Kalospyros 2001).

——. 1993. *Aristophanes: Frogs*. Oxford: Clarendon Press.

——. 1988. "Explorations in the History of the Text of Aristophanes." In The Greeks and their Legacy: Collected Papers, volume 2: Prose Literature, History, Society, Transmission, Influence, 223–265. Oxford: Basil Blackwell.

Dunbar, N. 1995. *Aristophanes: Birds*. Oxford: Clarendon Press.

Eberline, C. 1980. Studies in the Manuscript Tradition of the Ranae of Aristophanes. Meisenheim am Glan: Hain.

Förstel, C. and M. Rashed, 2003. "Ein neues Aristophanes-Fragment (Ekkl. 283-444) aus Paris." *Museum Helveticum* 60: 146–151.

Gamillscheg, E. and D. Harlfinger. 1989. *Repertorium der griechischen Kopisten 800–1600*, Vol. 2. Vienna: Verlag der Österreichischen Akademie der Wissenschaften.

Garin, E. 1958. *Il pensiero pedagogico dell'Umanesimo*. Florence: Giuntine.

Gaul, N. 2011. *Thomas Magistros und die spätbyzantische Sophistik: Studien zum Humanismus urbaner Eliten der frühen Palaiologenzeit*. Wiesbaden: Harrassowitz.

Gelzer, T. 1970. "Aristophanes 12." In *Paulys Real-Encyclopädie der classischen Altertumswissenschaft*, edited by A. Pauly, G. Wissowa, W. Kroll, K. Ziegler, and H. Gärtner, Supplement-Band XII: *Abdigildus bis Thukydides*, cols. 1392–1569. Stuttgart: J. B. Metzler.

Gonis, N., ed. 1999. "4508-4521." *The Oxyrhynchus Papyri LXVI* (London: Egypt Exploration Fund).

Harlfinger, D. 2000. "Codices Cremonenses Graeci: eine kurze Neusichtung anlässlich des V Colloquio internazionale di paleografia greca." In *I manoscritti greci tra riflessione e dibattito*, edited by G. Prato, 763–769. Florence: Gonnelli.

Henderson, J. 1987. *Aristophanes: Lysistrata*. Oxford: Clarendon Press.

Holwerda, D. 1977. *Scholia vetera in Nubes*. Groningen: Bouma's Boekhuis.

Invernizi, P. 1794-1834. *Aristophanis Comoediae auctoritate libri praeclarissimi saeculi decimi emendatae a Philippo Invernizio*. Leipzig: Weidmann.

Kallendorf, C. W. 2002. *Humanist Educational Treatises*. Cambridge, MA: Harvard University Press.

Kalospyros, N. 2001. Ὁι κριτικές επιστάσεις του Αδαμαντίου Κοραή στον Αριστοφάνη και στα αρχαία αριστοφανικά σχόλια (Τα χειρόγραφα Χίου αριθ. 404 και 490)'. In *Πρακτικά ΙΑ΄ Διεθνούς Συνεδρίου Κλασσικών Σπουδών Fédération Internationale des Associations d' Études Classiques (F.I.E.C.) Καβάλα 24-30 Αυγούστου 1999*, vol. 1, *Εις μνήμην Νικολάου Α. Λιβαδάρα*: 444–467. Athens: Α. Ν. Κυριαζόπουλος.

Koster, W. 1956. "De codice Aristophaneo Matritensi 4683." *Mnemosyne* 9: 225–231.

——. 1957. *Autour d'un manuscrit d'Aristophane écrit par Démétrius Triclinius: Études paléographiques et critiques sur les éditions d'Aristophane de l'époque byzantine tardive*. Groningen: J. B. Wolters.

MacDowell, D. M. 1971. *Aristophanes: Wasps*. Oxford: Clarendon Press.

Maisano, R. and A. Rollo, eds. 2002. *Manuele Crisolora e il ritorno del greco in Occidente*. Naples: C.I.S.C.S.F.

Mazzucchi, C. 2003. "Ambrosianus C 222 inf. (Graecus 886): il codice e il suo autore." *Aevum* 77: 263–275.

——. 2004. "Ambrosianus C 222 inf. (Graecus 886) : il codice e il suo autore. 2: L'autore." *Aevum* 78: 411–440.

Mertens, P. 1996. "Les papyrus d'Aristophane. Actualisation des données bibliologiques et bibliographiques." In Ὁδοὶ διζήσιος: Le vie della ricerca: studi in onore di Francesco Adorno, edited by M. Serena Funghi, 335–343. Florence: L. S. Olschki.

Pérez Martín, I. 1996. *El patriarca Gregorio de Chipre (ca. 1240–1290) y la transmisión de los textos clásicos en Bizancio.* Madrid: Consejo Superior de Investigaciones Científicas.

Pinto, P. M. 2003. *Per la storia del testo di Isocrate: La testimonianza d'autore.* Bari: Dedalo.

Pugliese Carratelli, G. 1940. "Versi di un coro delle Rane in un epigrafe rodia." *Dioniso* 8: 119–123.

Reynolds, L. D. and N. G. Wilson, 1991. *Scribes and Scholars.* Oxford: Clarendon Press. 3rd ed.

Russo, C. F. 1994. *Aristophanes: An Author for the Stage.* London: Routledge.

Sicherl, M. 1997. Griechische Erstausgaben des Aldus Manutius: Druckvorlagen, Stellenwert, kultureller Hintergrund. Paderborn: Schöningh.

Srebrny, S. 1959–1960. "Aristophanea." *Eos* 50: 43–51.

Srebrny, S. 1961. "Der Schluss der Lysistrate." *Eos* 51: 39–43.

van Leeuwen, J. 1905. *Aristophanis Comoediae undecim cum scholiis: Codex Ravennas 137, 4, A: Phototypice editus.* Leiden: A. W. Sijthoff.

White, J. W. 1906. "The Manuscripts of Aristophanes." *Classical Philology* 1: 1–20, 255–278.

Wilson. N. G. 1962. "The Triclinian Edition of Aristophanes," *Classical Quarterly* n.s. 12: 32–47.

——. 1977. "Scholarly hands to the middle Byzantine period." In *La Paléographie grecque et byzantine,* 221–239. Paris: Éditions du Centre national de la recherche scientifique.

——. 1992. *From Byzantium to Italy: Greek Studies in the Italian Renaissance.* London: Duckworth

——. 1997. *Aelian: Historical Miscellany.* Cambridge, MA, and London: Harvard University Press.

——. 2009. *Aristophanea: Studies in the Text of Aristophanes.* Oxford: Oxford University Press.

CHAPTER 34

....

LATER GREEK COMEDY IN
LATER ANTIQUITY

....

HEINZ-GÜNTHER NESSELRATH

1. PRELIMINARY REMARKS

THE fate of an ancient author is determined by the transmission of his texts, and this can take a number of forms.

a. If the author is lucky, at least a part of his work will make it into the manuscript tradition and thus endure (though never without some deterioration) until our times.
b. If the author is popular in the times subsequent to his life, at least a part of his work will be widely read and quoted, and it will leave substantial traces in the papyrus record, which gives it a good chance to be rediscovered in modern times (at least in more or less extensive scraps).
c. If an author's work is interesting to subsequent times for aspects of its content or its language, it will be excerpted and find its way into scholarly literature, anthologies (of various orientations), and lexica.

All three cases can be found in connection with ancient Greek comedy (though case "a." only in connection with Aristophanes). It is, in any case, the interest of later ancient times that has determined what we still know about this genre; especially in the case of Middle Comedy, the peculiar interests of some of its "transmissors" determine its perception up to the present day.

2. The Great Unknown? Athenian Middle Comedy in Hellenistic and Later Antique Times

Middle Comedy is conventionally dated between the times of Aristophanes (whose last fully extant play dates from 388 BCE) and those of Menander (for whom the first stage production is attested for 321 BCE).[1] It is the least well-attested phase in the development of Greek comedy, and some scholars have even doubted its very existence. As not a single complete play has survived from this period, we have only a heap of often very disheveled fragments to tell us something about Middle Comedy's later fortunes. Nevertheless, even these fragments can help us to make out at least something about the specific ways Middle Comic poets still appealed to some later readers, long after they had vanished from the stage.

For a long time, there was an extended debate about whether the label "Middle Comedy" was already coined in Hellenistic times (i.e., in the third or second century BCE) or was actually only invented in the second century CE (for a history of this debate see Nesselrath 1990: 3–27). At first sight, one might feel inclined to the latter position, as securely dated texts explicitly speaking of Middle Comedy or of poets belonging to it cannot be found before 100 CE. There are, however, also texts about Middle Comedy whose origins clearly go back to Hellenistic times although they themselves were written only much later; this is surely the case with the so-called *Prolegomena de Comoedia* No. 3 (according to the numbering in Koster 1975), which exhibit so much well-founded knowledge about the three periods of Attic Comedy and their poets that scholarship of high Hellenistic times must be the ultimate source for these judicious remarks (see Nesselrath 1990: 45–51). Another such gem of Hellenistic scholarship seems to be preserved in *Schol. Ar. Plut.* 515, where we find the interesting remark "this verse [i.e., *Plut.* 515] smells of the Middle Comedy" (see Nesselrath 1990: 57 and 241–242).

The earliest securely datable and explicit attestation of Middle Comedy is found in the paroemiographer Zenobius, who collected his material in Hadrianic times (117–138): he characterizes the playwright Eubulus as "the poet of Middle Comedy" (Zenob. Ath. 1.42 = Eubulus K-A fr. 134: Εὐβούλῳ τῷ τῆς μέσης κωμῳδίας ποιητῇ). A few decades later, Apuleius calls the poet Philemon *mediae comoediae scriptor* (*Florid.* 16 p. 24,7 Helm), and about the same time the Emperor Marcus Aurelius (121–180) in his *Meditations* (170–180) mentions both Middle and New Comedy within a short survey of Greek dramatic genres and their usefulness for real life (11.6.2: μετὰ δὲ τὴν τραγῳδίαν ἡ ἀρχαία κωμῳδία παρήχθη, παιδαγωγικὴν παρρησίαν παρέχουσα… μετὰ ταῦτα τίς ἡ μέση κωμῳδία καὶ λοιπὸν ἡ νέα πρὸς τί ποτε παρείληπται,… ἀλλὰ ἡ ὅλη ἐπιβολὴ τῆς τοιαύτης ποιήσεως καὶ δραματουργίας πρὸς τίνα ποτὲ σκοπὸν ἀπέβλεψεν;). Marcus

---

[1] In Nesselrath 1990: 331–340, I have argued for a somewhat modified chronology of Middle Comedy.

Aurelius's son Commodus (161–192) appointed the sophist and grammarian Julius Polydeuces / Pollux professor of rhetoric at Athens, and Pollux wrote the still extant *Onomasticon*,[2] a kind of lexicon of Attic synonyms in ten books, in which he quite often quotes from comic poets (especially in book 10). In seven passages of his work (1.232, 233, 2.197, 7.17, 69, 71, 162), he speaks of μέσοι κωμικοί and μέση κωμῳδία as a kind of genre; thus either Pollux himself or at least the sources he drew on still seem to have had a fairly distinct notion of such a genre and its existence. Probably a few years after Pollux, an author set to work who is by far our most important source of information regarding Middle Comedy: the famous (some people might say infamous) deipnological poly-math Athenaeus of Naucratis, who toward the end of the second century CE avidly col-lected everything he could find on eating, drinking, and all kinds of items somehow related to these activities and put it all together in his fifteen books of *Deipnosophistai*.

In Athenaeus, the label "Middle Comedy" appears seven times, too. In one of these passages (8.336d), one of his speakers boasts that he has read—and excerpted!—more than eight hundred plays "of the so-called Middle Comedy"; in another (11.482c), Athenaeus cites a treatise "On the poets satirized in Middle Comedy" (Περὶ τῶν ἐν τῇ μέσῃ κωμῳδίᾳ κωμῳδουμένων ποιητῶν) by Antiochus of Alexandria, very probably a Hellenistic author (see Nesselrath 1990: 59 and 75–77); in the five remaining passages, lesser-known comic poets are provided with a frame of reference by being called "poet of Middle Comedy" (7.293a: Σωτάδης…ὁ τῆς μέσης κωμῳδίας; 329d: Μνησίμαχος…· ποιητὴς δ᾽ ἐστὶν καὶ οὗτος τῆς μέσης κωμῳδίας; 9.387a: Μνησίμαχος…εἷς δὲ καὶ οὗτός ἐστιν <τῶν> τῆς μέσης κωμῳδίας ποιητῶν; 10.422f: Ἐπικράτης…μέσης δ᾽ ἐστὶ κωμῳδίας ποιητής; 13.387d: Νικόστρατος…ὁ τῆς μέσης κωμῳδίας ποιητής). To see, however, the real importance of Athenaeus for the preservation of (at least some aspects of) Middle Comedy, we must go beyond these few passages and look at the impressive numbers of Middle Comic fragments that Athenaeus's pages are teeming with.

Probably the most prolific poet of Middle Comedy was Antiphanes, whose stage career seems to have lasted from the 380s until the last decades of the fourth century BCE (for these dates, see Nesselrath 1990: 193–194). Of his astonishingly high output of several hundred plays (for the various numbers transmitted see Nesselrath 1996: 781), 327 fragments have been preserved (ten doubtful ones included). More than half of these (184 or 185)[3] are found in Athenaeus, and no other source even comes close to this: Johannes Stobaeus, the author of a massive late antique anthology containing

---

[2] It is often thought that this work has come down to us only in epitomized form, but the evidence for this is rather slight; see Nesselrath 1990: 101–102 n. 93.

[3] This is a major difference compared with the source-distribution for Old Comic poets: of, e.g., Cratinus's 514 fragments, about two-thirds are found in lexicographical works of later antique and Byzantine times (for more exact numbers, see Nesselrath 2010: 424–425), while these account for only seventy-three items in Antiphanes's case (Nesselrath 2010: 431). Athenaeus, on the other hand, provides "only" sixty-one Cratinus fragments (Nesselrath 2010: 427). With Eupolis, we get a similar picture: more than half of his 494 fragments are found in texts belonging to the lexicographical tradition, while Athenaeus provides just forty-nine (Nesselrath 2010: 430).

innumerable quotations from otherwise lost works of many Greek writers (poets, historians, orators, philosophers and others), preserves fifty-one quotations from Antiphanes, or 15.5% of the total; thirty-five are found in Athenaeus's slightly younger contemporary Pollux. Other authors quote Antiphanes only very rarely (see Nesselrath 2010: 431–432): Plutarch quotes Antiphanes just twice (and one of these quotes is doubtful), and there are only four more quotations in other Greek authors of the imperial age. There is only one Antiphanes quote each in the paroemiographers and in Byzantine authors. The papyrus yield is meager: though eight papyri provide Antiphanean material, only one may have preserved a small part of an actual manuscript of an Antiphanes play (Antiphanes K-A fr. 34; all other papyrus quotations of Antiphanes—K-A fr. 247, 257, 263, 281, 315–317—were once part of gnomologia or florilegia). Thus evidence that Antiphanes—after his time as author for the stage—ever served as a source for reading (like some Old Comic poets and Menander) is next to nil.

Another major poet of Middle Comedy (in fact the one most often explicitly called a writer "of Middle Comedy"; see Nesselrath 1990: 60) is Eubulus, who was active from (probably) the 370s until Demosthenic times (see Nesselrath 1990: 195–196) and wrote more than 100 plays, of which 150 fragments (three doubtful ones included) have been preserved. Of these, Athenaeus provides 100 fragments (two-thirds of the total!) and thus an even bigger part than in the case of Antiphanes, while the lexicographical tradition yields only forty-two (see Nesselrath 2010: 433). The only other imperial Greek author who cites Eubulus more than once is Pollux; he has preserved thirteen Eubulus fragments. Other imperial Greek authors provide only two. Even Stobaeus—and this is quite different from Antiphanes—comes in for only one fragment. No papyrus provides any additional material (for Eubulus's presence in other sources—which can be neglected here—see Nesselrath 2010: 433).

Regarding the third major author of Middle Comedy, Alexis, the source-distribution is similar: again, Athenaeus is by far the most important source for fragments for this very prolific writer, providing 212 (= 62%) of all 342 items; much less are provided by Pollux (twenty-six) and Stobaeus (twenty-seven; for these—and other—numbers, see Arnott 1996b: 34–44 and Nesselrath 2010: 433 n. 42). Alexis, of course, is a sort of special case; since his career probably extended beyond the end of the fourth century, he may at least in part be considered also a New Comic poet (see Nesselrath 1990: 199 and Arnott 1996b: 15–17).

Other authors of Middle Comedy owe their survival even more to Athenaeus's almost insatiable lust for collecting deipnological material: of Amphis's forty-nine fragments, thirty (61.2%) are quoted by Athenaeus (five are found in Pollux, six in Stobaeus); of Anaxandrides's eighty-two, forty-one (50%; five are quoted by Pollux, ten by Stobaeus); of Anaxilas's forty-three, twenty-three (53.4%; we owe seven to Pollux and just one to Stobaeus); of Aristophon's fifteen, nine (60%; one is found in Pollux, three in Stobaeus); of Axionicus's eleven, seven (63.6%; Pollux and Stobaeus provide one each); of Crobylus's eleven, nine (81.8%; exactly the same numbers apply also to Epicrates); of Dionysius's nine, five (55.5%; the other four are provided by Stobaeus); of Epigenes's eight, six (75%); of Eriphus's seven, six (85.7%); of Heniochus's five, four (80%;

the remaining one is found in Stobaeus); of Mnesimachus's eleven, seven (63.6%); of Nicostratus's (a son of Aristophanes) forty, twenty-four (60%; four fragments are found in Stobaeus, none in Pollux); of Ophelio's six, five (83.3%); of Philetaerus's (another son of Aristophanes) twenty, sixteen (80%; Pollux has preserved just one fragment, Stobaeus none); of Sophilus's eleven, ten (90.9%); of Theophilus's twelve, eleven (91.6%; the remaining one is quoted by Pollux); of Timocles's forty-two, twenty-nine (69%). For some Middle Comic poets, Athenaeus is the sole preserver of fragments: this is the case for Antidotus (four fragments; a further, but very dubious one is attested by Pollux), Clearchus (five), Ephippus (twenty-eight), and Xenarchus (fourteen). (Athenaeus is also the only preserver of fragments in the case of some later comic poets: Athenio: one; Damoxenus: three; Epinicus: two; Sopater: twenty-five.)

These numbers illustrate the paramount importance of just one author, Athenaeus, for our knowledge of Middle Comedy. All other sources for comic fragments provide us either with only very meager Middle Comic material or with none at all. Relatively few fragments of these plays made it into the lexicographical tradition, because they did not hold enough interest for people who looked for linguistic models to reconstruct the "authentic" Attic speech of old. Likewise, there are almost no remnants of papyrus manuscripts of those plays (contrary to New Comic plays and especially Menander; see below), because these plays were apparently not deemed interesting enough to be preserved as reading material after their time on the stage had passed. Even their content of noteworthy aphorisms or morally edifying sayings was rather limited, and therefore only rather few Middle Comic fragments made it into Stobaeus's collection of excerpts.

What they did contain, however, was obviously sufficient to whet the all-encompassing gastronomical interests of Athenaeus: ample descriptions of elaborate dinner preparations and subsequent festivities, mouth-watering catalogues of fish and other delicacies, and depictions of the multifarious activities of all sorts of people somehow connected with the dinner table (slaves, cooks, parasites, *hetairai*). It may also be called a lucky coincidence that Athenaeus indulged these interests at a time when the resources to satisfy them were still available (at least in the places where he probably lived and wrote, Alexandria and Rome): the big lexica and glossaries still bulging with full and exhaustive references put together by meticulous Alexandrian scholarship in preceding ages. What Athenaeus could still read in such sources is tellingly illustrated by the fact that he provides us with by far the longest verse quotations not only from Middle Comic poets, but from some of New Comedy as well. Here are some examples: Anaxandrides K-A fr. 42 contains seventy-one anapaestic dimeters; Anaxippus K-A fr. 1, forty-nine iambic trimeters; Athenion K-A fr. 1, forty-six iambic trimeters; Damoxenus K-A fr. 2, sixty-eight iambic trimeters; Diphilus K-A fr. 42, forty-one iambic trimeters; Epicrates K-A fr. 10, thirty-seven anapaestic dimeters; Mnesimachus K-A fr. 4, sixty-five anapaestic dimeters; Sosipater K-A fr. 1, fifty-seven iambic trimeters; Straton K-A fr. 1, forty-seven iambic trimeters (interestingly, a papyrus version of this fragment is more concise, extending over "only" thirty-seven verses). The length of these excerpts is no sure argument that Athenaeus would have made them from the whole text of plays (see

Nesselrath 1990: 67–68 with n. 7). Only comic papyri sometimes contain longer (but usually also more mutilated) comic texts.

It has, of course, to be recognized that for all the richness of his materials, Athenaeus provides us with only a very distorted view of what really happened in Middle Comic plays; by reading him, one might easily get the impression that in these plays all that mattered were busy slaves going to the market to buy items for the next big feast, boastful cooks bragging about their inventiveness in producing elaborate dinners, hungry parasites yearning to be part of the gastronomical action, and *hetairai* providing for other needs after dinner-guests had eaten their fill. This, however, is barely conceivable as the only subject matter of these plays, because then they all would have looked more or less the same, and spectators' patience would (after some initial titillation) quickly have been exhausted. On the other hand, the characters just mentioned (slaves, cooks, parasites, *hetairai*) must certainly have loomed large in these plays—in any case, larger than in plays from other periods—or Athenaeus would very probably have preserved more quotations from, e.g., New Comedy, which, however, is not the case (see below). In an earlier publication (Nesselrath 2010: 434), I have therefore ventured to call Athenaeus the "savior" of Middle Comedy: without his very peculiar (though admittedly one-sided) literary interests, the numerous productions of comic poets between Aristophanes and Menander would be even more of a mystery for us than in many respects they still are.

3. Just Menander and Nothing more? New Comedy after its Heyday in Hellenism

If it were not for Menander, New Comedy might be a heap of uncontextualized fragments, just as Middle Comedy is. In fact, the situation was (almost) like this, until by the later nineteenth century papyrus finds started to bring Menander back, so that now we can once again read one complete play, substantial parts of seven others, and at least single scenes of another ten (for a survey of these plays see Nesselrath 1999: 1216–1217 and Blanchard and Bathrellou in this volume). Apart from this, one other important difference between the fates of Middle and New Comedy in antiquity is the considerable number of New Comic plays (both by Menander and by other authors) that served as models for Roman comedies in Latin between the latter part of the third and the latter part of the second century BCE; from this process of adaptation, twenty-seven plays are still extant (twenty-one by Plautus and six by Terence). Thanks to indications in their prologues, we still know the Greek models for many of them: Plautus adapted his plays *Aulularia*, *Bacchides*, *Cistellaria*, and *Stichus* from Menander (perhaps *Apistos* or *Thesauros*, *Dis Exapaton*, *Synaristosai*, and *Adelphoi I* respectively), *Casina*, *Commorientes*, *Rudens*, and *Vidularia* from Diphilus (*Kleroumenoi*, *Synapothneskontes*, a play of unknown title, and *Schedia*), *Mercator*, *Mostellaria*, and *Trinummus* from

Philemon (*Emporos*, *Phasma*, and *Thesauros* respectively), and *Asinaria* from the otherwise almost unknown Demophilus (*Onagos*); Terence used Menander as a model in *Adelphoe*, *Andria*, *Eunuchus* and *Heauton Timorumenos* (the originals had all the same titles), and the "Menanderizing" poet Apollodorus for *Hecyra* (with the same title for the Greek original) and *Phormio* (*Epidikazomenos*), and he incorporated a scene from Diphilus's *Synapothneskontes* in his *Adelphoe*.

By being thus transported into another linguistic medium, all three major poets of Attic New Comedy were present on the stage of Republican Rome,[4] and as their texts were transmitted across the Middle Ages, they have continued to be present on the stage to the present day. The Greek originals did not fare so well; the following paragraphs will try to trace their fate through later Hellenistic and then Imperial times.

While in their lifetime Philemon and Diphilus had not been less but actually more successful than Menander (see Nesselrath 2011: 119), things changed after their death: just as in Greek tragedy Euripides eclipsed Aeschylus and Sophocles during the subsequent history of theater, so now Menander began to outshine Philemon and Diphilus and finally became more or less the sole representative of New Comedy. This development took some time, and there is not much evidence to show how exactly it came about, but one telling indicator is the already-mentioned phenomenon of Roman adaptation of Greek comedy. As we have seen, Plautus—the preeminent Roman comic poet in the last decades of the third and the first decades of the second century BCE—apparently derived his plays in about equal numbers from all three major New Comic poets (see above). A few decades later, the picture had considerably changed: Plautus's younger rival Caecilius was the first to draw massively on Menander's plays as models, adapting at least eight and possibly thirteen (if not more) of his plays from them, while there is no evidence that he also used Diphilus's or Philemon's comedies. Terence's focusing on Menander and a Menander epigone has already been mentioned, and other contemporary Roman poets (see Nesselrath 2011: 121) looked to Menander as their main inspiration as well. By the middle of the second century BCE, the Roman comic stage had become a very "Menandrian" affair, and Diphilus and Philemon seem already then to have all but vanished as providers of models for Roman comic plays.

Even when New Comic plays were no longer performed on the stage (either in their original language or in Roman adaptations), they apparently continued to be read (unlike their earlier colleagues from Middle Comedy). For the last centuries BCE, this must have been the case not only for Menander but for poets like Philemon and Diphilus as well, as seems to be attested by an interesting passage in the treatise "On Style" by an author called Demetrius, who most probably still belongs to the first century BCE. In this passage (ch. 193 = Menander K-A test. 84), Demetrius compares the so-called "disjointed style" (*lexis dialelymene*) and the "written style" (*lexis graphike*): the first "is also called the actor's style since the asyndeton stimulates dramatic delivery, while

---

[4] In imperial times, comedy gave way to the mime on the stage. Nevertheless, Plautus and Terence remained in the manuscript tradition and so could be read until the end of antiquity and beyond.

the written style is easy to read," and Demetrius then associates the "disjointed style" with Menander, "while Philemon is read" (translations by D. Innes). These remarks might lead us to believe that at least in Demetrius's time (about two hundred years after Philemon's death) Philemon's comedies were considered good reading material. There may be some sort of confirmation for this in the papyrus record: K-A VIII (adespota) presents 156 papyri, most of which are the remains of papyrus manuscripts of comic plays that were once written for a reading public in Hellenistic and Roman Egypt. Probably most of these papyri have to be attributed to Menander (see below), but among them there might also still lurk a number of plays written by his New Comic rivals, and that this is a plausible assumption may be shown by the following considerations (see also Nesselrath 2011: 126–127). Of the 156 papyri just mentioned, thirty[5] are more substantial. Of these, fifteen were written in the third to first centuries BCE, with ten of them belonging to the third century. Of those ten, six have in the past been tentatively attributed to poets other than Menander and two to him (with two undecided); of the remaining five, non-Menandrian authorship has been proposed for three and Menandrian authorship for the other two. Now for the other fifteen papyri, which belong to CE centuries, numbers are perceptibly different: five of them have been claimed for Menander, one (not very convincingly; see Kassel-Austin ad loc.) for Philemon (adesp. 1047f.; actually two short fragments, possibly from different plays), and two or three have had both Menandrian and non-Menandrian ascriptions (with the remaining six more or less undecided). These numbers suggest that the rate of non-Menandrian papyri of New Comedy diminishes the later we get in antiquity.

This impression may be supported by another interesting piece of literary evidence. In the late first or early second century CE, Plutarch wrote a "Comparison between Aristophanes and Menander" (unfortunately, only an epitome of it has been preserved), and the very title of this treatise seems to indicate that already by Plutarch's times, the only comic authors that were still circulated widely enough to warrant such a comparison were Aristophanes and Menander. By the way, Plutarch himself quotes Menander about thirty times, which is double the number of his Aristophanes quotes.

There is, in fact, sufficient further evidence for Menander's slowly but surely increasing preeminence among the poets of New Comedy. Already around 200 BCE, one of the greatest Alexandrian philological scholars, Aristophanes of Byzantium, wrote an important treatise about him and praised his outstanding skill in depicting human life (Menander K-A test. 76 and 83); later Alexandrian scholars wrote commentaries on

---

[5] They are: adesp. 1000 (second cent. BCE), 1001 (second cent. BCE), 1006 (second/third cent. CE), 1007 (first/second cent. CE), 1008 (first or second cent. CE), 1014 (third cent. BCE), 1017 (third cent. BCE), 1018 (first cent. BCE), 1027 (second/first cent. BCE), 1032 (third cent. BCE), 1047f. (second cent. CE), 1063 (first cent. CE), 1064 (third cent. BCE), 1073 (third cent. BCE), 1084 (third / fourth cent. CE), 1089 (third cent. BCE), 1091 (second / third cent. CE), 1092 (third cent. BCE), 1093 (third cent. BCE), 1094 (third cent. BCE), 1096 (fourth cent. CE), 1097 (first cent. CE), 1103 (second cent. CE), 1112 (second cent. CE), 1129 (second cent. CE), 1132 (first cent. CE), 1141 (third cent. CE), 1146 (third / second cent. BCE), 1147 (third cent. BCE), 1152 (second / third cent. CE).

parts or even the whole of his work (Menander K-A test. 77–79). We still have more than seventy representations of the poet in art (busts and reliefs; see Menander K-A test. 25–40), and many paintings and mosaics all over the Roman Empire depicted scenes of his plays (see Nesselrath 1999: 1218). For many Greek and Roman authors of imperial times, he was the very embodiment of comedy,[6] and his plays continued to be read until the end of antiquity, as is abundantly shown by the papyri to which we owe the reemergence of a great part of his work (see above; for further details see Arnott 1979: xxvi–xxix). For some of these reemerged plays, not just one but several witnesses on papyrus (sometimes already parchment) have come to light, documenting an impressive number of reading editions of Menandrian plays between the second and the seventh centuries CE. Here are some examples: *Aspis* is found in two papyrus codices from the third and the fifth centuries (Arnott 1979: 2–3); *Georgos* in three papyrus codices from the first century BCE, the fourth century CE, and the fourth–seventh century CE (Arnott 1979: 98–99); *Dyskolos* in five manuscripts from the third or second century BCE, the second CE, third CE, fourth CE, and sixth–seventh centuries CE (Arnott 1979: 176–177); and *Epitrepontes* in four manuscripts from the second, fourth (two), and fifth centuries CE (Arnott 1979: 380–381); of *Perikeiromene*, we still have remains of six manuscripts from the second, third, and fifth centuries CE (Arnott 1996a: 367–368), and of *Misoumenos* remains of ten from the second through the fifth centuries (Arnott 1996a: 246–249). For the Roman West, we have the remarkable testimony of the fifth-century Gallo-Roman nobleman, poet, politician, and bishop Sidonius Apollinaris, who still read Menander's *Epitrepontes* together with his son in the Greek original (Arnott 1979: xxiii; see also Menander K-A test. 133–134).

Still, for all his success with the reading public until the very end of antiquity, Menander (unlike Aristophanes) did not make it into the medieval manuscript tradition, and the main reason for this is that in the eyes of hard-core Atticists (who came to dominate the discussion about the right standards for "correct" written Greek from the second century CE onwards), Menander's linguistic standards were not "Attic" enough. "By Heracles, I do not see what is the matter with the people who think highly of Menander and prefer him to everything else Greek! And why am I astonished? Because I see that the elite of Greeks is crazy about this comic poet" (Phryn. ecl. 394 = Menander K-A test. 119). This rant by the second-century sophist and grammarian Phrynichus shows how highly esteemed Menander was at that time, but also how resistance was being built up by people who thought this esteem totally misguided—even the more "relaxed" Atticist Pollux did not accept every usage he found in Menander (see 3.29 in his *Onomasticon* = Menander K-A test. 120). Ultimately, this resistance led to Menander's disappearance from the manuscript tradition at some point during the seventh to ninth centuries CE.

---

[6] Ovid: Menander K-A test. 90–92; Manilius: Menander K-A test. 94; Martial: Menander K-A test. 98; Theon: Menander K-A test. 108; Quintilian: Menander. K-A test. 100f.; Dio of Prusa: Menander K-A test. 102; Apuleius: Menander K-A test. 114; Hermogenes: Menander K-A test. 116.

Even without the papyri, however, the fragments of Menander's works preserved in quotations are much more numerous than those of other New Comic poets, namely 894 in K-A VI.2[7] versus only 198 for Philemon and even less, namely 135, for Diphilus (see below). Now the source-distribution of these 894 fragments shows remarkable differences compared to the poets of Middle Comedy discussed above: almost one-third (293) are provided by Stobaeus and 207 (a bit less than a quarter) by the lexicographical tradition, while Athenaeus is responsible for only 58 (6.4%) and Pollux for 40 (4.4 %).

A similar source-distribution can be found in the 198 extant fragments (with four doubtful ones included) of Philemon. According to the *Suda* (= K-A test. 1), Philemon wrote 97 plays, slightly less than Menander, to whom between 105 and 109 are attributed (Menander K-A test. 1, 3, 46, 63). Here, Athenaeus again is a source for only 27 fragments, 14% of the total—more than in Menander's case, but a far cry from his importance for Middle Comic poets. Again Stobaeus has the lion's share with 87 items, 44% of the total. Apparently, both Menander and Philemon were poets with a strong liking for memorable moralizing phrases, and thus could provide much material for Stobaeus's *Eclogae*. In the case of Menander, another result of this is the similarly gnomic *Menandri Monosticha*. Both Menander and Philemon are also much more present in paroemiographical collections than other comic poets (with the remarkable exception of Cratinus, who has twenty entries there; see Nesselrath 2010: 428 n. 22), namely sixteen (Menander) and twelve times (Philemon). On the other hand, Philemon is much less present in the lexicographical tradition (with forty-eight items altogether; see Nesselrath 2010: 436 n. 49) than Menander and other poets considered earlier in this chapter.

The third major New Comic poet, Diphilus—he wrote 100 plays (Diphilus K-A test. 1), roughly the same number as Menander and Philemon—shows a source-distribution for his 135 preserved fragments that comes closer to what we saw in Middle Comedy. Once again Athenaeus has the biggest share of any single quoting author, but with fifty-one fragments (38% of the total) his presence seems not as overwhelming as in the case of many Middle Comic poets. To Stobaeus we owe the preservation of twenty-seven Diphilus fragments, 20% of the total; this is much higher than in the case of most Middle Comic authors (only Antiphanes comes close; see above). The presence of other source categories in Diphilus is comparable to that in Middle Comic authors: the lexicographical tradition comes in for a number similar to those found in the cases of Antiphanes and Eubulus, namely fifty-six items altogether (for a more detailed breakdown, see Nesselrath 2010: 435 n. 47). Pollux provides nine items, Plutarch just one, and other Imperial authors four more, the paroemiographers five, and there is only one certain quote (not from the manuscript of a play) on a papyrus.

---

[7] In the preceding Körte edition there were even more, namely 951, and yet more in Kock's *Comicorum Atticorum Fragmenta*, namely 1,082 (not counting 48 *dubia* and *spuria*). This remarkable "shrinking" in the more recent editions is explained by the fact that with increasing papyrus finds an increasing number of secondary quotations could be integrated into their former contexts within plays.

All in all, these numbers for New Comedy confirm what was said above about the outstanding importance of Athenaeus for Middle Comedy; apparently no other period of Attic Comedy provided so much material of the sort that Athenaeus could draw upon for his gastronomic-symposiastic encyclopedia in dialogue form.

Interestingly, the strong gnomological current detectable in New Comic authors (especially in Menander and Philemon, as attested by Stobaeus) also made possible their use by a group of people whom so far we have not yet considered: Christian authors. As is well known, Christian opinion was very much divided regarding the question whether Christians should make use of pagan literature (and culture in general) or not, and we find the same fundamentally divided attitude also with regard to (pagan) comedy. In Christian circles that were open towards pagan culture, however, several authors were prepared to accept and make use of comic quotations that might lend support to Christian ethical (and also religious, e.g., regarding monotheism) viewpoints.

Already the important Jewish philosopher Philo of Alexandria (20 BCE–50 CE) very occasionally uses comic quotes in his argumentation: in *Quis rer. div. her.* 5, he cites Menander K-A fr. 273.1–2 (without naming the poet), and in *Vit. cont.* 43 he again quotes an unnamed κωμικός (*adesp.* K-A fr. 475). From the second century onwards, we find such quotes also in Christian literature. The apologists Justinus Martyr and Theophilus are the first: in *Apol.* 1.20.5, Justinus quotes Menander (K-A fr. 501) in support of the Jewish/Christian teaching forbidding the veneration of idols made by human hands; Theophilus (*Ad Autol.* 3.7) adduces Philemon (*dub.* K-A fr. 197) to underline the necessity of fearing God in the right way. In the treatise *De monarchia*, which was transmitted under the name of Justinus, Menander is quoted four and Philemon three times.

It is Athenaeus's contemporary Clement of Alexandria (ca. 115–215) who makes very extensive use of quotations from comedy to combat wrong perceptions of God and to inculcate moral and theological teaching. Interestingly, Clement—and contrary to pagan authors (e.g., Plutarch)—shows no explicit preference for Old or for New Comedy (he quotes Aristophanes seven times, Cratinus four, and Philemon and Diphilus five times each), but nevertheless a noticeable liking for Menander (seventeen quotations; for details see Nesselrath 2005: 349–350). It may be more remarkable that he also quotes fourteen other comic poets. In most cases, these quotes will have been taken from already existing collections, though Clement may also still have read whole plays of Menander and perhaps Aristophanes.

Another aspect of Clement's citations is remarkable, too: not all of them are genuine, as some are clearly fakes. Take, e.g., Strom. 5.119.2–120.1 (Menander *spur.* K-A fr. 1001): after citing a passage from the Prophet Isaiah, which stresses that God is not in need of many sacrifices but prefers human beings who live without sin, Clement adds a longish quote (twelve iambic trimeters) from "the comic poet Menander," in which a speaker (addressing a young man called Pamphilus) makes just the same point: "if someone offers a sacrifice, Pamphilus, / a lot of bulls or lambs or, by Zeus, / of other such animals, or products of craftsmanship, / having made golden or purple garments, / or animal statues of ivory or emerald, / and then believes that he can procure God's goodwill (by these things): / that man is mistaken and has a very shallow mind. / For Man needs to be morally just: / he must not rape girls or commit adultery, / or steal and kill for possession. / Do not even desire the eye of a needle, Pamphilus: for God is (always) near and sees you." This piece of pious admonition (with a markedly monotheistic slant) agrees much too well with Isaiah's words to be an authentic piece of a Menandrian comedy. Soon afterwards (Strom. 5.121.1 – Diphilus *spur.* K-A fr. 136), Clement adduces two quotes allegedly taken from the comic poet Diphilus to support the Christian notion of the Last Judgment: "Do you believe, Niceratus, that the dead, / after having had their fill of pleasure in life, / can evade divine power, because they have remained undetected? / There is the Eye of Justice that sees everything! / For we believe that there are two roads in Hades: / one for the just, the other for the wicked." The immediately following quote adds further emphasis: "If the earth covers the two (i.e. the just and the unjust) for all time, / then go and plunder, steal, rape, create havoc! / But don't fool yourself: there is a judgment also in Hades, / which will be held by God, the lord of all, / whose name is terrifying and I would not pronounce it..." Especially in the last lines, the transparently Jewish attitude vis-à-vis the unspeakable name of God is unmistakable.

Who made up these fakes? Clement need not necessarily have been the culprit himself: he could already have found them in the Judeo-Christian tradition. In any case, he apparently felt that such quotes from comedy (whether genuine or fake) might bolster his arguments. Interestingly, the two "Diphilus" passages quoted here are attributed by another source (Ps.-Justin, De monarchia 3) to the poet Philemon: apparently it had to be a New Comic poet with enough reputation to endow such lines (created by a Judeo-Christian forger) with sufficient authority.

Other Christian authors in the third to fifth centuries CE followed Clement in this line of reasoning: Eusebius of Caesarea, Epiphanius of Salamis, Palladius, and Theodoretus (for details, see Nesselrath 2005: 350–351). Usually these later authors took their quotes simply out of Clement's works (both the genuine and the fake ones). Perhaps the most telling evidence for the esteem in which these authors held Greek New Comedy and especially Menander is the following event (related by Sozomenus, *Ecclesiastical History* 5.18.2): when the pagan Emperor Julian forbade Christian teachers to use non-Christian texts for their teaching in 362, Apollinaris of Laodicea undertook the task of creating a Christian "substitute" literature, to which also belonged comedies in the style of Menander.

4. A CONCLUDING COMPARISON: THE PERCEPTION OF LATER GREEK COMEDY IN ROMAN IMPERIAL TIMES AND OURS

Around 200 CE (the age of Athenaeus and Clement of Alexandria), the perception of later Greek comedy was in many respects remarkably similar to ours today (and the reason for this is, of course, that we have to rely heavily on texts of just that age for our knowledge of it). At that time, Middle Comedy already seems to have been available only in excerpts and quotations, and the same seems true for the greatest part of New Comedy as well, with the difference that the excerpts and quotations from New Comedy are not as preponderantly focused on activities and characters revolving around the dinner table (thanks to Athenaeus), but also contain moral observations and aphorisms which appealed to Christian authors open to pagan culture (Clement of Alexandria in particular). The one big difference between that age and ours concerning comedy is the fact that contemporaries of Athenaeus and Clement were still able to read many plays of Menander, which we cannot. It is true that the papyrus finds of the last one and a half centuries have done much to narrow this gap, but it will probably never completely vanish.

BIBLIOGRAPHY

Arnott, W. G. 1979. *Menander.* Vol. 1, *Aspis—Epitrepontes.* Cambridge, MA: Harvard University Press.
——. 1996a. *Menander.* Vol. 2, *Heros—Perinthia.* Cambridge, MA: Harvard University Press.
——.1996b. *Alexis: The Fragments: A Commentary,* Cambridge, UK: Cambridge University Press.
Koster, W. J. W. 1975. *Prolegomena de Comoedia (= Scholia in Aristophanem,* Pars 1, Fasc. 1A), Groningen: Bouma's Boekhuis.
Nesselrath, H.-G. 1990. *Die attische Mittlere Komödie: Ihre Stellung in der antiken Literaturkritik und Literaturgeschichte* (= UaLG 36), Berlin and New York: de Gruyter.
——. 1996. "Antiphanes." In *Der Neue Pauly.* Vol. 1, edited by H. Cancik and H. Schneider, 781–782. Stuttgart and Weimar: J. B. Metzler.
——. 1999. "Menandros [4]." In *Der Neue Pauly.* Vol. 7, edited by H. Cancik and H. Schneider, 1215–1219. Stuttgart and Weimar: J. B. Metzler.
——. 2005. Komödie, in: *Reallexikon für Antike und Christentum.* Vol. 21, edited by T. Klauser et al., 330–354. Stuttgart: Anton Hiersemann,
——. 2010. "Comic Fragments: Transmission and Textual Criticism." In *Brill's Companion to the Study of Greek Comedy,* edited by G. Dobrov, 423–453. Leiden: Brill.
——. 2011. "Menander and His Rivals: New Light from the Comic Adespota?" In *Culture in Pieces: Essays on Ancient Texts in Honour of Peter Parsons,* edited by D. Obbink and R. Rutherford, 119–137. Oxford: Oxford University Press.

CHAPTER 35

THE REBIRTH OF A CODEX: VIRTUAL WORK ON THE AMBROSIAN PALIMPSEST OF PLAUTUS[1]

WALTER STOCKERT

I. THE PALATINE TRADITION

WE do not know how many plays Plautus wrote. An edition of the 130 comedies transmitted under his name was made at the end of the second century BCE (Deufert 2002: 44 ff.). When Varro was drawing up his canon in about 40 BCE, he claimed that of that number, twenty-one plays were, by general agreement, considered genuine (Gellius 3.3.3; Leo 1912: 18 ff.). These twenty-one have come to be known as the *fabulae Varronianae*, and they are the plays that were passed down into late antiquity as the received corpus of Plautus's work. At some point in the fourth century CE, a copy of the twenty-one plays was made in codex form (Questa 1984: 23–129). From that lost codex (which modern scholars have given the name Ω) are descended the two *recensiones* that are at our disposal: the *Ambrosianus* (A) and the antique ancestor of the *recensio Palatina*, called Π, both written in the fifth century. The transcription of the majuscule codex Π into minuscule seems to have taken place during the ninth century in Carolingian France (P, now also lost[2]); besides P, a second manuscript was copied

---

[1] This translation is a corrected and slightly amplified version of Stockert 2008. A number of the photos published there are republished here (autorizzazione veneranda biblioteca Ambrosiana, numero F 008/11); for the remainder, I must refer to that paper. I thank Keith Maclennan for substantial help, especially with the translation, and for the pictures in black and white I am grateful to Giovanni Martellucci of Florence.

[2] According to Questa 1985: 93, P was already copied from a codex in minuscules.

from Π, the so-called *codex Turnebi* (T), which is known only from the notes made by Adrien Turnèbe in his *Adversaria* (Lindsay 1898) and from the collation that Duaren wrote in the margins of his printed Gryphius edition of Plautus (see now Clementi 2009). From the *archetypus* P depend all the "old Palatine manuscripts" of Plautus: the "second half" (twelve comedies)[3] descends directly, while the "first half"[4] (eight comedies) reaches us via a lost intermediate codex (usually, with Lindsay, called P^{BD}). The Middle Ages and the early Renaissance knew only manuscripts with the "eight comedies": there was a *Vossianus Leidensis* of the eleventh century (V), the learned author of the so-called *Gallica recensio* (eleventh century), the ancestor of both the *Londinensis* J (about 1100) and of the late *Parisinus* K (early fifteenth century), as well as the *Ambrosianus* E (about 1200).

The situation changed substantially when, in 1429, the so-called *codex Ursinianus* (D) was found in Cologne (it had been written in a German monastery in the tenth century). This codex attracted the closest interest of the greatest scholars of the time (Poggio, for instance); the vicissitudes of its circulation in these years are documented in detail by Questa (1985: 169 ff.; Tontini 2002: 57ff.). This manuscript consists of the twelve comedies of the "second half" plus four of the "eight comedies." All the manuscripts of the humanists, the highly contaminated *Itala recensio*, for instance, are descended from the *codex Ursinianus* (Cappelletto 1988: 185 ff.; Tontini 1996: 33 ff.).

In the sixteenth century, a manuscript was found that would prove even more important for the constitution of our text. In his editions, Joachim Kammermeister, called Camerarius, made use of a codex that had also been written in the tenth century in a German monastery: this is the so-called *codex vetus* or *codex Camerarii* (B), containing all twenty comedies. As already noted, its "second part" is descended directly from P; the first part was from an intermediate codex (P^{BD}), which was copied from P. Additionally, the rubricator had corrected this manuscript in its prior part with the help of a much better codex, possibly even P (this hand is designated B^3 in modern editions). For the "twelve comedies," Camerarius also had at hand another old manuscript, the so called *Decurtatus* C, a *gemellus* of D.

At this point, discovery of medieval manuscripts ended; up to the discovery of the palimpsest in 1815, the "Palatine group" remained the only basis of all the many printed editions of Plautus (Ritschl 1868: 34–161). After Merula's editio princeps (1472), for instance, Pylades (1506) was of major importance, while the Aldine in this case has less value (1522). Taubmann's and Pareus's competing editions were almost contemporary (early seventeenth century). Gronovius's edition (1664, etc.) became the vulgate until Bothe's first edition (1809–1811) appeared, which was the last to depend exclusively on the *Palatini*.

---

[3] *Bacchides, Menaechmi, Mercator, Miles, Mostellaria, Persa, Poenulus, Pseudolus, Rudens, Stichus, Trinummus,* and *Truculentus.*

[4] *Amphitruo, Asinaria, Aulularia, Captivi, Casina, Cistellaria, Curculio,* and *Epidicus.*

II. The Ambrosian Palimpsest: Earlier Studies

It caused one of the greatest sensations in classical philology in the early nineteenth century when, in a manuscript in the Ambrosian library,[5] the later Cardinal Angelo Mai discovered parts of an ancient fifth-century Plautus codex beneath the *scriptio superior* (Reges, lib. I 13–IV 23; sixth century: Lowe CLA III 345). An assistant of Joh. Bapt. Franca, vice president of the library, had realized even earlier that underneath the badly damaged biblical text were concealed substantial remains of other texts: fragments of Plautus and Seneca's tragedies.

To bring out the suppressed *scriptio inferior*, Mai used a reagent made of gallnuts. It did appalling damage to the parchment, as Ritschl writes (Ritschl 1868: 166 ff., on p. 169): "Mai's reagents have discolored the pages of the *codex* with every shade of yellow, brown, and black. In the *Cistellaria* they are particularly shocking to see. As a result, much of what Mai was able to read is now totally unrecognizable, revealing its former presence only by a barely distinguishable blur." And he added that at his time better results could be achieved by liver of sulphur, "an utterly foul smelling substance." He also added the crucial fact that the biblical text was written exactly above the *scriptura inferior*, which resulted in further destruction by the aggressive reagent. Much more than Ritschl, who worked on the codex for a few months, Wilhelm Studemund so occupied himself with the palimpsest that deciphering the badly damaged manuscript finally became the important scholar's life's work.[6] While some of his contributions had been published earlier, he left us the record of his life's work in his *Apographum*. In the short *praefatio,* we read about the most important discoveries of earlier research; the structure of the medieval codex and the relation of its layers to the *quaterniones* of the ancient codex are documented with extreme precision. O. Seyffert tells us in a footnote (Studemund 1889: xii) that Studemund worked for about twenty-five years on the codex. In his effort to show the degree of certainty of every single letter, he designed a subtle system that enables us to see which parts of a letter are readable and which letters are covered by the *scriptura superior* and therefore completely unreadable; alternatives are given above single letters, and supplements are proposed here and there. At the bottom of a page, we find notes containing other possible readings, and statements about the condition of the page. At the bottom of fol. 235r, for instance, we read, "Pagina interior passim cribri in modum lacera partim non facile, partim difficillime legitur" ("The interior of the page is as full of holes as a sieve; parts can be read with

---

[5] Codex bibliothecae Ambrosianae G 82 sup.; now S. P. 9/13–20; the relevant edition is Studemund 1889.

[6] We know that Studemund stressed his eyes to such a degree in carrying out the work that he finally lost his sight; in his *Apographum* we therefore find the motto: *ni te plus oculis meis amarem.*

difficulty, other parts with the greatest difficulty"). Studemund had had to use chemical substances as well (Giobert's cyanide of potassium, for instance), since there were no other means of making these texts visible, and we can be certain that he applied these substances several times. In very difficult cases, sometimes he offers no reading at all ("nimis incertos ductus describere nolui"), giving later scholars a faint chance of finding out new readings by using better (chemical) substances: "paulo plura fortasse...leget cui novis medicamentis uti licebit" ("It may be that someone who obtains permission to use new chemicals will be able to read a bit more"). As far as we know, nobody else has applied better chemical substances, but today, thanks to modern technical equipment, we have instruments which, despite later, post-Studemundian damage to the codex (nobody knows how many scholars had a look at the part which contains the *Cistellaria*), give us some hope to find out a little more.

As far as I know, after Studemund only Friedrich Schoell, editor of the *Cistellaria* for the major Teubner edition, worked intensively on the pages of the palimpsest that contain the *Cistellaria*. In 1888, he did some work on the manuscript (Schoell 1894: xv), and after the edition of Studemund's *Apographum* he took a second look at the relevant pages, and sometimes he even corrected Studemund's readings. In *Cistellaria* 261, for instance, he seems to read *EXEMERI* correctly. On the other hand, his independence from Studemund does not go as far as one would expect from his words (cf. Leo, 1894: 201f.). As far as we know, with the publication of Schoell's edition, independent research on the Ambrosian palimpsest came to an end. The two most important editors of Plautus, Friedrich Leo and Wallace Martin Lindsay, depend for the palimpsest on the *Apographum* (partly also on Schoell), as does W. Suess in his two important contributions on the *Cistellaria* (Suess 1935 and Suess 1938); but he sometimes gives risky supplements based on just a few uncertain letters. Particularly hazardous, however, is the approach of Gonzales Lodge, who in his *Lexicon Plautinum* sometimes accepts even the absurd conjectures of Schoell.[7]

III. A New Study of the Palimpsest

After this little survey I will now briefly explain the origin of my own work on this manuscript. The particular interest of this project lies in the fact that this was the first application of modern techniques to the Ambrosianus.

Some years ago, the editor of the *editiones Sarsinates*, Cesare Questa, commissioned me to edit the *Cistellaria* (Stockert 2009), a play whose central part is only transmitted by the palimpsest (Stockert 2008: n. 25). The badly damaged manuscript (and its damage is at its worst in the *Cistellaria*) was universally agreed to have been deciphered as far as

[7] I refer to *Cistellaria* 340, where Lodge accepts Schoell's supplement *inicias* without any discussion, and *Cistellaria* 488, where he prints Schoell's rash conjecture *camum* ("necklace," as in Accius, *Trag.* 302).

humanly possible by Studemund in his *Apographum* (Gratwick 2000: 327). But precisely in the case of the *Cistellaria*, where the Ambrosianus is *codex unicus*, we should at least try to find out something new. From several scholars I had also heard that it might be possible to detect the *scriptura inferior* of palimpsest manuscripts by multispectral photography and further elaboration at the computer. Outstanding in this field is the fundamental project "Rinascimento Virtuale," whose members (led by Harlfinger / Hamburg) cooperated in the digital elaboration of Greek palimpsests (see Escobar 2006). So after having been encouraged by many scholars, I decided to present my *Cistellaria* project to the "Forschungsfonds für Wissenschaft, Wien" (FWF). I was delighted when this institution took over the costs for the digital photographs and the computer elaborations, along with additional funds to carry out further work. Meanwhile the Board of the Biblioteca Ambrosiana[8] gave permission under strict conditions for multispectral photographs to be made by Fotoscientifica—Parma. Of the twelve pages of the codex where I saw the possibility of some chance of success, photos were taken in ultraviolet and infrared.[9] The results were sent to me on two DVDs and on marvelous prints: here we can see in juxtaposition a photo of the codex in its present condition, an elaboration of the medieval *scriptura superior*, and also of the *scriptura inferior*, which contains the text of Plautus written in antiquity (see Stockert 2008, plate II). These elaborations are of very different quality. While some pages show results similar to Studemund's *Apographum*, in other parts the readings are only fragmentary in comparison with the *Apographum*. With the help of Cesare Questa, I also found a specialist for palimpsests, the Florentine professor Teresa De Robertis; the codex being in a terrible state, the help of such a specialist was indispensable.

Finally, in Vienna we tried to achieve better results from the digital material. Paul Kammerer, assistant at the Institute of Computer-Aided Automation at the school of Technology, had the idea of simulating the original situation of the codex by laying the recto page over the verso page. Because of the enormous amount of data on the original DVDs, it was expedient to "cut out" the digital material line per line and to overlay recto and verso lines mirror-wise, so that they relate to each other as they do in the actual codex. With the help of the computer program Adobe Photoshop, we were now able to achieve the exact overlay of the two layers as well as the clarification of the pictures, and further refinements. And so we could exclude characters that might possibly belong to the page on the reverse, which must be eliminated in the decipherment if the editor wants to avoid major mistakes. In a laborious effort, all the texts were scrutinized at the School of Technology and in some cases "read" for the first time. In a second step, all the results had to be checked with the specialist at Florence. There, over the course of several weeks, Teresa De Robertis generously gave me a hand with her superior knowledge. The

---

[8] Overall I have to thank Monsignor Cesare Pasini for all his help; and I have also to thank Monsignor Pier Francesco Fumagalli and Don Francesco Braschi for their help and the rights of publication.

[9] The photographs in ultraviolet, however, did not give any results; specialists told me that useful photos are only possible for an ink that contains some ingredients of iron.

result of this common work at the computer (I cannot thank her enough for all her kindness) is the documentation given in the appendix to this chapter.

Essentially, our expectations were confirmed: Studemund's *Apographum* is reliable, and we must follow him in doubtful cases. He had enormous experience in this special field (as I said earlier, he worked on the Ambrosianus for some twenty-five years), and the codex was certainly in a much better condition at that time than today. But the digital photographs sometimes enable us to see material that Studemund did not detect. This project is the first modern effort to make the readings of this badly damaged codex once again visible (in the case of the *Cistellaria,* it looks rather like a carbonized papyrus roll). Complete documentation of the material will therefore be given at the end of this chapter. I need hardly say that errors in detail cannot be excluded.

Before listing the new material I will briefly treat some significant passages.[10] All of these texts belong to the long lacuna in the medieval manuscripts. Firstly I must remind the reader of the content of the *Cistellaria* and put the special passages in their respective context.

In the initial scene of the comedy, which is set in Sicyon, we see a tableau with three women of the demimonde: the young Selenium and her two guests, her friend Gymnasium and Gymnasium's mother, a procuress, who in Plautus remains anonymous. Some time ago, Selenium began a relationship with a rich young man, Alcesimarchus, and their love is mutual. But now his father has ordered him to leave the courtesan and to contract a legitimate marriage. Therefore, Selenium's mother Melaenis has called her back to her house. Selenium now asks Gymnasium to stay for a few days in the house where she lived together with Alcesimarchus, and to inform him delicately when he returns from the countryside. Before her exit, the procuress, like a Prologue, reveals some information: she found Selenium as an exposed baby and passed her over to her friend Melaenis. The real Prologue, the god Auxilium, confirms the suspicion of the audience, who will surely have already been struck by the noble character of the girl: Selenium is of good descent and even daughter of the rich neighbor, Demipho, and—who would think it possible?—of his current wife, whom he long ago raped when drunk. After a first marriage on Lemnos (thanks to the working of Fortune, his daughter from that marriage is now Alcesimarchus's bride), he has married Phanostrata and tasked her slave Lampadio, who had exposed the baby, with finding the woman he saw picking up the child. The central part of the drama that the remains of the palimpsest more or less cover, and which are therefore of most interest for us, consists of two sequences featuring Alcesimarchus on either side of a longer confrontation scene between Gymnasium and the young man's father. Alcesimarchus makes his first entry with a desperate *canticum* (the last scene still available in the Palatine codices), and in a tragicomic scene he afterwards orders his slave to insult him (examples 1 and 2). Then young Gymnasium joins the two and tries to dissuade

---

[10] See Stockert 2008, plates III–VIII, where some of the photographs of these passages are published; in the present chapter, a subset of these are reproduced as figures 1–5 (see below).

Alcesimarchus from his love (examples 3 and 4), but in the end is forced to recognize that the boy is deadly serious about it. She accordingly advises him to beg the girl's mother, Melaenis, for forgiveness. In the next scene, we see Alcesimarchus's father, who wants to free his son from his sweetheart—but instead he finds Gymnasium, who makes a fool of him (examples 6 and 7); at length he falls into the pretty woman's trap, though he ultimately fails in his mission, since she is taken away by her mother, the procuress. In the third sequence, which can also be partly read in the medieval transmission, Alcesimarchus meets Melaenis, who does not give any credit to his oaths (examples 8, 9, and 10). In the final part, which is not relevant here, the search for the lost girl has nearly reached its goal so that Melaenis feels forced to return the girl to her real parents, along with the basket containing the little tokens that show her descent. The young people's marriage is hindered no more.

With the help of this short sketch of the contents of the *Cistellaria*, the reader should now be able to judge the passages where, with the help of the new photographs and the expertise of Teresa De Robertis, new readings have been deciphered.

EXAMPLE 1: V. 249 (F. 235R [P. 297], 18)[11]

Here *laetor*, which was read by Studemund and not questioned by Schoell, has always prompted surprise. According to the traditional reading, after the words of the slave who had been ordered by his master to insult him fiercely *Ob istuc unum verbum dignu's deciens qui furcam feras* (v. 248) "Because of that one word you deserve to carry the fork ten times" (tr. de Melo), Alcesimarchus (with light irony?) reacts with *laetor* "what a joy." But such a response is completely inadequate for his earnest/pathetic persona. Leo and Lindsay register their doubt in the *apparatus criticus*, but could not find a plausible solution. Some years ago Roberta Strati discussed this problem in an article (Strati 1989) and proposed an excellent conjecture: *fateor* "I confess it." As the letters of this verb are quite close to *laetor*, I first supposed this represented a scribal confusion of *laetor* with an original *fateor*, and it was a great surprise when Teresa De Robertis and I saw in the manuscript an F instead of an L, rather easily recognizable by the form of its "head" and by the thickening in the middle of the vertical *hasta* (see figures 35.1a and 35.1b).

Since it is not easy to distinguish T and E in our manuscript and original TE look very much like ET, Studemund's error can be explained. FATEOR, therefore, is now the transmitted reading and it fits the context exactly: with the words "I completely agree," the *adulescens* accedes to this further punishment humorously proposed by his slave.

---

[11] In this chapter correct readings are given in majuscules, all other letters in minuscules; for a survey of all the new readings, see the *Index lectionum* at the end of the chapter.

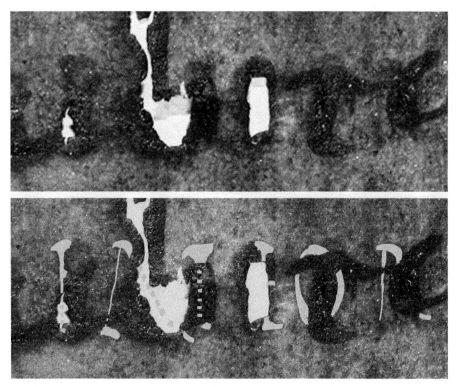

FIGURE 35.1 a) Codex Ambrosianus fol. 235r lin. 18 (detail) b) Codex Ambrosianus fol. 235r lin. 18 (reconstruction: T. De Robertis)

Example 2: v. 260 (f. 235v [p. 298], 11)

This verse belongs to the same scene (the dialogue between young Alcesimarchus and his slave). The context is completely lost because of the holes in the parchment. At the end of the line (we cannot even be certain of the speaker) Studemund read, with some hesitation, *exemii*; and because of the uncertainty of reading and sense, he gave a series of alternative letters. Schoell, on the other hand, read EXEMERI, and in this case seems to be right (see figures 35.2a–c); possibly, we should read EXEMERI<T> rather than his *exemeri<m>*. Before EXEMERI<T> a Q<U>A<M>QU<AM> can be read with some plausibility.

Example 3: v. 272 (f. 238r [p. 299], 6)

Here the first half of the verse is undoubtedly corrupt: after SEMPER appears the sense-less series of letters SITUIUTUX (still recognizable on the photographs), which Schoell

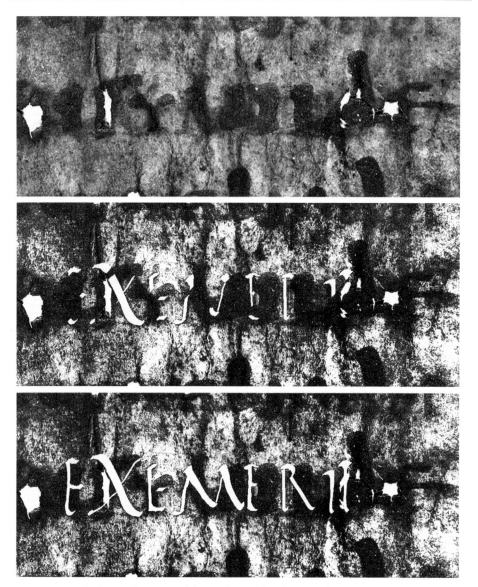

FIGURE 35.2 a) Codex Ambrosianus fol. 235v lin.11 (detail) b) Codex Ambrosianus fol. 235v lin. 11 (deciphering: T. De Robertis) c) Codex Ambrosianus fol. 235v lin. 11 (reconstruction: T. De Robertis)

corrected to *sic ut tu uxor* (the final OR is perhaps still visible). Schoell's correction seems to fit the dialogue between Alcesimarchus and Gymnasium about his two women— Selenium and his fiancée—very well, when Schoell restores the second half with *quibus data a patre est*, but our decipherment of the verse has led to a completely different result. Schoell himself thought he could see an *es* here, which would fit his reconstruction of the verse, but the uncertain letters that can be seen in the infrared photographs do not coincide with this suggestion (see Stockert 2008, plate V): after FEC (possibly FEC<I>), ID seems to follow, as well as a series of letters whose reading is still very uncertain: an EM seems at least possible, and FEC<I> IDEM paleographically conceivable. But these two words would be unusual at the end of a trochaic *septenarius*, even if we have a parallel in *Epidicus* 32 (*fecerunt idem*). And metrically some doubt remains, too, since this kind of synaloephe is very rare at verse end (Questa 2007: 315–316). Additionally, I had no success when I tried to fit these words into the context (in the next line, v. 273, we have a QUIDSIAM<O> of the young hero).

EXAMPLE 4: V. 278 (F. 238R [P. 299], 12)

Here we tried a conjecture that may seem a bit risky, but it is compatible with the paleographical situation. After an easily recognizable MIHINUNQUAMQUISQUAM, a form of *credere* would be welcome, a *credat* for instance, or (with a glance at *Truculentus* 307) a *credit*: "nobody (in this case) should/could give me any credit." The paleographical situation is not unequivocal, but traces of the R and the D seem to be recognizable, possibly even more (see Stockert 2008, plate V). The young *hetaira* Gymnasium seems to have suggested to Alcesimarchus an antidote for his love: if Alcesimarchus shuts himself together with the woman for some days, he would be healed of this love. If she should prove wrong with her prediction, nobody ought to credit her henceforth (*mihi numquam quisquam credit*). The end of the verse, which I think should be read differently from Studemund, remains a riddle (see Stockert 2009).

EXAMPLE 5: V. 323 (F. 241V [P. 310], 2)

Here in the margin, immediately before a shadowy N, we find a little sign that can most easily be interpreted as a *signum personae*, or indication of speaker (see figure 3; on *signa personae* in the Plautine manuscripts, see Wahl 1974). In his *praefatio* (Studemund 1889: xxix), Studemund explains that in the ancient manuscript of Plautus, *signa personae* were written in Greek letters in red color; they were later destroyed when the ancient writing was washed away. The little A that we recognize here, being written with black ink, is certainly not the original (red) symbol, but an addition or a correction in the margin. But we should not conclude from the fact that in the so-called numerical system the speaker of the words (apparently Alcesimarchus's father) could not have the symbol A, which would be given to the first speaker of the drama: in the "nonnumerical system" the first speaker of a scene or series of scenes can also be given this symbol (Wahl 1974: 12ff.). But it could also be the correction of a Greek symbol by Latin letters; Studemund (1889: xxix) identified this procedure at work for *Miles* 790. After the letter A follows something that might be the remains of an L, and is thus possibly a sign for

FIGURE 35.3 Codex Ambrosianus fol. 241v lin.2 (detail)

Alcesimarchi pater in an abbreviated form, the rest of the name being covered by the enormous *e* of the *scriptura superior.*

EXAMPLE 6: V. 340/341 (F. 241V [P. 310], 19 AND F. 242R [P.321], 1)

Schoell and all editors after him connected the reading BONU at the beginning of fol. 242r with a *testimonium* from Nonius (p. 773 Lindsay), where we find the following citation from the *Cistellaria*: *malum aufer; bonum mihi opus est.* The second part of the citation (*bonum mihi opus est*) can easily be added to verse 341, since the rest of the verse has been lost in the tradition. At the other side, *malum aufer*, as far as Teresa De Robertis and I see, does not coincide with the remains of the verse 340 (which concludes the page before). Studemund reads an uncertain CIA here, but autopsy of the *codex* produced an uncertain A, then after one or two letters possibly an I, and after a further lost letter a little S (small letters are typical at the end of a longer line). But one thing seems to be clear: contrary to Schoell's note in the apparatus criticus of his edition, there is no room for *aufer malum* in v. 340. If we want to refer the *testimonium* to our passage, we are forced to insert *aufer malum* after *bonum mi(hi) opust /opus est* and, because of its rhythmical form, at the end of the iambic septenarius. If this were correct, Nonius, contrary to his normal usage, would have transposed the words. Because of the new readings, it has at least become risky to put them in the usual position (in Stockert 2009, I set them under the *Fragmenta incertae sedis*; see also Stockert 2012: 177).

EXAMPLE 7: V. 356 (F. 242R [P. 321], 17)

This case offers a special surprise. After a certain N and about six other letters that are not visible, we find a complete word (the pronoun QUOD), whose letters—except for the first—are certain (see figures 35.4a–b).

These letters, which are written in a very fine script, were not seen by Studemund, though we might also suspect they were lost during the vicissitudes of the publication of the *Apographum*. Unfortunately, the codex is so thoroughly damaged here that despite another series of letters (UMTUOS), a plausible supplement has not been possible.

EXAMPLE 8: V. 468 (F. 247V [P. 312], 3)

Not far from the end of a mostly damaged line, the *Apographum* gives an INS, then after about four letters an S and MUST at the end of the line. After the INS we may have an A, so that a form of the adjective *insanus* can be suspected. INSA<NIS>S<U>MUST would fit the context very well: it could be a (verbal) insult by Melaenis, the foster mother of

FIGURE 35.4 a) Codex Ambrosianus fol. 242r lin. 17 (detail) b) Codex Ambrosianus fol. 242r lin. 17 (reconstruction: T. De Robertis)

the drama's heroine, directed against Alcesimarchus, who in this scene wants to effect the pardon of the old woman and the return of Selenium to their common home. It would also go well with the following words (v. 469), QUE<M> (or possibly *quia*) SINE<O>MMI (*que<m> sine< o>mni*): "A fool is a man, who/whom without any...." But there remains some doubt, since after INSANISSU there seems to be room for a further letter before MUST (see Stockert 2008, plate VII). The adjective *insanus* would fit very well for the young man, who seems to be crazy more than once in this comedy. Memorable in this regard are his scene of "melancholia" in discussion with his slave, his oaths at the end of our scene, and, overall, the suicidal scene (whether feigned or authentic) in a later part of the drama.

Example 9: v. 485 (f. 248r [p. 323], 2)

Alcesimarchus vows, as he has done before (v. 98 f.), that he will marry Selenium, although that is against the law: *Quin equidem illam ducam uxorem*. Since after these words we read a certain DUCASSID (see figures 5a–b), a supplement *detu<r tib>i* seems adequate; Melaenis would then be pointing out to the youngster that he could only marry the girl if she were given to him. Studemund, however, rejected this solution

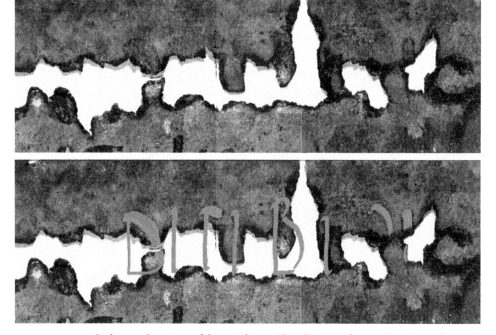

FIGURE 35.5 a) Codex Ambrosianus fol. 248r lin. 2 (detail) b) Codex Ambrosianus fol. 248r lin. 2 (reconstruction: T. De Robertis)

explicitly, so that major doubts arise about it. The paleographical situation is not altogether clear. After the securely read D, an *etu* would go quite well with the obscure letter remains (the final *r* being concealed in the lacuna); at the other side of the *tibi* we would see only the final I, while the letters *tib* could only be inserted in the remaining space with difficulty. Studemund's suggestion SIDITIB<I>DU<INT> (Studemund 1889: 491) seems to be supported by the fact that after DITI (or -TE) and before the lacuna, a B (TIB<I>) seems to be the most reasonable reading, while of the DU<INT> only remains of the first letters would be visible. As Teresa De Robertis has confirmed, Schoell's reading *si dei siuerint* is incompatible with the remains of the letters. Such a reference to the gods, which Studemund's suggestion implies ("if the gods wanted to give her to you"), would fit very well after v. 484 (*deis numquam* [sc. *verba*] *dares*).

EXAMPLE 10: V. 488 (F. 248R [P. 323], 5)

The beginning (SIQUIDEMAMABASPROINDE [or PROINDI]) and the end (ILLIINSTRUI) of the verse can be read with certainty. Melaenis certainly says to Alcesimarchus that it has been his obligation to provide for his sweetheart in a reasonable way; he should not speak of any merit on his side. Studemund, in the damaged part of the verse (after two lost letters) gives just C . MU (*camum* Schoell); instead of the C, we rather read an O, immediately followed by the M (see Stockert 2008, plate VI); afterwards, after the U and a few letters, we thought we could read a T. In this discussion about Alcesimarchus's provisions for Selenium, a text with *uestem* seems reasonable; therefore one might accept a half line ending *proin <fuit> dignom* or *proin<de erat> dignom*. The double hiatus suggests that another word has been lost in the second half; a supplement analogous to 487 (*instruxi illi aurum atque vestem*), for instance *v<es>tem et aurum> illi instrui*, at least seems possible.

These ten examples show both the possibilities and the limits of computerized elaboration of digital infrared photographs in the Ambrosian palimpsest, especially in an extremely damaged passage. These pages are full of lacunae, which are caused partly by the chemical treatment given them by Angelo Mai and others, partly by the extremely aggressive ink of the *scriptura superior*, the biblical text being written exactly above our Plautus. In those passages Studemund's "softer chemicals" might still lead to better results, but because of the terrible condition of the codex, such a treatment is out of the question. On the other hand, there are definitely passages in which the cleansed text of the *scriptura inferior*, our Plautus, was not visible for Studemund, while on the infrared photographs we recognize at least traces of some letters. However, these traces are for the most part in such a deplorable state that we had better refrain from documentation. Sometimes even letters of the reverse side can lead to mistakes. Moreover, considered as a whole, the achievements of the great scholar Studemund have not been diminished by the modern methods applied to this codex for the first time, only modified here and there. He did not have the resources of powerful enlargement, variation of color, brightness and contrast, computer-aided procedures in general, and certainly not digital photography, which allows us to take perfect photographs of the actual state of a manuscript in a careful way. But we would need a scholar of the quality of Wilhelm Studemund to make adequate use of the results of this new autopsy. One thing at least has become clear by our work: anyone preparing an edition of a Plautine comedy should use digital photography at least in those passages where the Ambrosian palimpsest is the *codex unicus*. In the European Union, with its generous institutions, certainly the necessary sponsors can be found who are willing and able to contribute to the recovery of such an important heritage.

APPENDIX

NOVARUM IN CODICE AMBROSIANO LECTIONUM, QUAS ADIUVANTE TERESA DE ROBERTIS DISPEXI, INDEX

Sigla

A	Codex Ambrosianus G 82 super., nunc S. P. 9 / 13-20, saec. V (CLA III 345) secundum Guilelmi Studemund Apographum
Apographum	T. Maccius Plautus, Fabularum reliquiae Ambrosianae, codicis rescripti Ambrosiani apographum, confecit et edidit Guilelmus Studemund, Berolini 1889

In hoc indice his formis ad certitudinem singularum litterarum illustrandam usus sum
B	littera certa
Ḅ	littera minus certa
(b)	littera incerta
(ḅ)	littera incertissima et coniecturae similior
.	spatium unius litterae

f. 235r (p. 297) vv. 233–250

l. 18 (249)   *post 6 litt.* FAṬEOR

f. 235v (p. 298) vv. 251–266

l. 1 (251)	QUIAṆL *[spat. ca. 12 litt.]* (l) . (l) *[spat. ca. 15 litt.]* A … AM
l. 2	(*cauda versus bipartiti, quam scriptura vacuam esse Studemund affirmavit*) Ḷ(e)
l. 3 (252)	QUIḌṬUEṚGO . I
l. 4 (253)	*post ca 8 litt.* ṾE(a) *[spat. fort. 7 litt.]* Ọ(*vel* c) . (.) (ṇ)

l. 5 (254)   *post fort. 26 litt.* D(ạṛ) .. (ụ)SṢI . (.)P(a)(t)ER
l. 6 (255)   (*init.*) UỤ(*vix* o) [*spat. ca. 30 litt.*] S(s . o[*vel* d]). ẸRMIHI
l. 7 (256)   (*init.*) S (.) . A (*vel* ṛ). Ẹ
l. 8 (257)   (*init.*) ṢẠ(ṇụ)Ṣ
l. 11 (260)   (*init.*) QUỊ. DỤ [*ca. 14 litt.*] Q . Ạ . . (.)QU .... ẸXẸMẸRỊ
l. 12 (261)   (ị)NLA *vel* (ẹ)NLẠ
l. 13 (262)   U . LḶ [*spat. ca.10 litt.*] MḶLẠ [*spat. ca. 17 litt.*] ORẸS (*vel* oṛẹịṣ) *litteris*
              minusculis ascendentibus
l. 16 (265)   (*finis*) SUS . ST

f. 238r (p. 299) vv. 267–285

l. 2 (268)   CẸNSẸ(*vel* i)NTỤẸS ... AR [*spat. ca. 18 litt.*] LỤ(*vix* ạ)
l. 4 (270)   UBIẸA(m [*vel* . a])U .... (o)
l. 5 (271)   Ị(*vel* t)AN(tẹ)
l. 6 (272)   *post 17 litteras* UX(oṛ) [*spat. fort. 13 litt.*] F̣(ẹ[*vel* i]c̣) (.) ỊD(eṃ)
l. 8 (274)   (n[*vel* ṛ]) ... (.) DỤ. (.) Ụ
l. 11 (277)   *post ca. 25 litt.* MỊỤMỌ
l. 12 (278)   *post 19 litt.* (c̣)R(ẹ)D(uịṭ) ... OṢTỊLL (.). D(ẹ)
l. 13 (279)   NONẸS(ẹ) .. (.) Ạ(*vel* ṃ) .... (ẹ)M
l. 14 (280)   *post 34 litt.* ỊN(p). Ọ(b)Ẹ
l. 15 (281)   *post ca. 12 litt.* Ṇ(*vix* ṛ)NẸ

f. 241r (p. 309) vv. 306–321

l. 14 (317)   *post 8 litt.* CORRUMPỊ(ṭ)

f. 241v (p. 310) vv. 322–340

l. 2 (323)   N(ẹ)Q [*spat. fort. 8 litt.*] Ạ [*spat. fere 10 litt.*] RṚ(ẹ)Ọ(*vel* s *vel* c?)
              in mg. sin. A(l), *fortasse personae nota.*
l. 3 (324)   [*spat. fort. 20 litt.*] Q(ụ)AẸRẸ(ṭ)
l. 5 (326)   *post fort. 23 litt.* F̣ESṆ
l. 6 (327)   .... S [*spat. fort. 15 litt.*] S
l. 7 (328)   *post fort. 35 litt.* ṚICLIS
l. 12 (333)   *post fort. 32 litt.* MẸAMQ·
l. 13 (334)   *post fort. 25 litt.* (f)
l. 15 (336)   (ṛ[*vel* a]ị). DS
l. 16 (337)   (ạ)S [*spat. fort. 16 litt.*] (ẹṣ) . Ụ ..... S
l. 17 (338)   Ạ [*spat. fort. 6 litt.]* U(ea)Ḷ
l. 18 (339)   *post fort. 35 litt.* ỊL ... (eṗ)
l. 19 (340)   *post fort. 35 litt.* (ạ . ị). S

f. 242r (p. 321) vv. 341–358

l. 1 (341)   *supra* ḄONU *signum quoddam apparet:* B̃N
l. 4 (344)   NIṢ(i)(.)UṆCT . (pr̲)
l. 7 (347)   *post fort.* 25 *litt.* ΓẸC̣(*vel* o)
l. 9 (349)   *post fort.* 17 *litt.* PỤ(*fort.* i) [*spat. fort.* 14 *litt.*] Ọ
l. 11 (351)   . Ạ. . . . (c)Ạ(*vel* r)
l. 13 (353)   ṆO [*spat. fort.* 7 *litt.*] P̣(*vel* d). (a) . . . . Ṣ(iṭ)
l. 17 (356)   N [*spat.* 6 *litt.*] QUOD [*spat. fort.* 8 *litt.*] (u)MṬU(ọ)
l. 18 (357)   NẸ(t)U . (.) Ṇ(*fort.* r)

f. 242v (p. 322) vv. 359–372

l. 6 (362)   A . U . . . UT (.) Ṃ . . Ị(*vix* t) [*spat. fort.* 13 *litt.*] LUSẸGỌ . (.) (*pro* ḶO *fort.*
              ỊC̣; *spatium parvum pro* uolo, *magnum pro* hic) QUIDUIS
l. 7 (363)   *post fort.* 38 *litt.* Ụ (*fort.* c)

f. 247r (p. 311) vv. 449–465

In hac pagina multo plura legit Studemund quam hodie in imaginibus phototypice depictis etiam suspicari possumus; ubique igitur virum doctissimum sequi necesse est.

f. 247v (p. 312) vv. 466–483

l. 1 (466)   *post fort.* 30 *litt.* CONS(pịc̣ . ṣ)
l. 2 (467)   *ante* Q *signum quoddam:* ˜Q
l. 3 (468)   *post fort.* 11 *litt.* RF̣(u) [*spat. fort.* 14 *litt.*] (ụi)INS(ạ) . . . S . (.) MUST
l. 4 (469)   QUI. (.) SINE . ṂMỊ [*spat. fort.* 18 *litt.*] (ụ)EṬ(u)Ṇ(*vel* r)DIE . . .
l. 13 (477)   *post fort.* 24 *litt.* P̣ (*fort.* r) . Ị (*vel* t) . . ATQ·ILLI . (ẹ)
l. 16 (480)   QUAEDẠ(ṃ)

f. 248r (p. 323) vv. 484–501

l. 2 (485)   *post* 28 *litt.* DUCASSIDITIB<ID>Ụ<INT> (*sic Studemund in Addendis
              Apographi*) *potius quam* DUCASSIDETU<RTIB>I
l. 3 (486)   *post* 23 *litt.* QUAE . Ọ(*vel* c *vel* d)
l. 4 (487)   *post* 21 *litt.* UEṢ. (ẹ) [*spat. fort.* 8 *litt.*] MAGIS(t) . . (rạ *vel* ịụi)
l. 5 (488)   *post* 15 *litt.* P̣ROINDỊ(*vel* ẹ) . . . ỌP̣(*vel* c) (.)Ṃ(*fort* . . r)U . . . Ṭ . . (.)ILLI
l. 7 (490)   ỊṆṢ . . . . Ṭ. . EAM . . C(*vel* s)EP̣(*vel* d)(o) . Ọ(*vel* s *vel* c)TẸNESQUIA(*vel*
              QUA) . . ỊṆḌUṬA . Ụ

l. 8 (491)   *post 17 litt.* QUIDAM…Ç(*vel* o *vel* d)T . Ṭ
l. 13 (496)   *post 21 litt.* SCIAS *potius quam* SCIES
l.18 (500)   *post 24 litt.* ALIQUANDO

f. 248v (p. 324) vv. 502–522

l. 8 (509)   *post 5 litt.* IST . T

FURTHER READING

I first suggest a few titles on modern techniques applied to palimpsests; I then refer to some articles and books that can introduce students to Plautine transmission and editorial technique.

A) ON MODERN TECHNIQUES:

Above all, I recommend two internet websites: www.archimedespalimpsest.org and www.rinascimentovirtuale.eu.

Additionally:

Escobar, A. (2006), *El palimpsesto grecolatino como fenómeno librario y textual* (Zaragoza); Grusková J. (2010), *Untersuchungen zu den griechischen Palimpsesten der österreichischen Nationalbibliothek* (Wien), 17–28.

B) ON MANUSCRIPTS AND EDITIONS OF PLAUTUS:

Lindsay (1900) 1–12 on the medieval *codices* of Plautus; Chelius (1989) on the "minor codices"; Clementi (2009) on the "*codex Turnebi*"; Deufert (2002) on the tradition of the text from Plautus to late antiquity; Gratwick (2000) on a new edition of Plautus; Questa (2001) on the ongoing *Editiones Sarsinates*; Calderan (2004) on the transmission of the *Vidularia* (transmitted only by the palimpsest like the *Cistellaria*).

BIBLIOGRAPHY

Calderan, R. 2004. *Tito Maccio Plauto, Vidularia; Introduzione, testo critico e commento* Rev. ed. Urbino: QuattroVenti.

Cappelletto, R. 1988. *La "lectura Plauti" del Pontano*. Urbino: QuattroVenti.

Chelius, K. H. 1989. *Die Codices minores des Plautus: Forschungen zur Geschichte und Kritik*. Baden Baden: Koerner.

Clementi, G. 2009. *La filologia plautina negli* Adversaria *di Adrien Turnèbe*. Alessandria, Italy: Edizioni dell'Orso.

Deufert, M. 2002. *Textgeschichte und Rezeption der plautinischen Komödien im Altertum: Untersuchungen zur antiken Literatur und Geschichte.* Berlin. New York: de Gruyter.

Gratwick, A. S. 2000. "Brauchen wir einen neuen Plautus?" In *Dramatische Wäldchen: Festschrift für Eckard Lefèvre zum 65. Geburtstag,* edited by E. Stärk and G. Vogt-Spira, 321–344. Hildesheim: Georg Olms.

Leo, F. 1894. "Ueber einige Palimpsestverse der Cistellaria." *Nachrichten der Königl. Gesellschaft der Wissenschaften zu Göttingen: Philologisch-historische Klasse* 1894: 201–207.

——. 1895. *Plauti comoediae.* 2 vols. Berlin: Weidmann.

——. 1912. *Plautinische Forschungen zur Kritik und Geschichte der Komödie.* 2nd ed. Berlin: Weidmann.

Lindsay, W. M. 1898. *The Codex Turnebi of Plautus.* Oxford: Clarendon Press.

——. 1900. *The Captivi of Plautus.* London: Methuen.

——. 1910. *T. Macci Plauti comoediae.* Oxford: Clarendon Press.

Lodge, G. 1924–1933. *Lexicon Plautinum.* 2 vols. Leipzig: Teubner.

Lowe, E. A. 1934–1971. [CLA] *Codices Latini Antiquiores: A Palaeographical Guide to Latin Manuscripts Prior to the Ninth Century.* 11 vols. plus supplements. Oxford: Clarendon Press.

Mai, A. 1815. *M. Acci Plauti fragmenta inedita.* Milan: Regiis Typis.

Pasquali, G. 1971[2]. *Storia della tradizione e critica del testo.* 2nd ed. Florence: Le Monnier.

Questa, C. 1984. *Numeri innumeri.* Rome: Edizioni dell'Ateneo.

——. 1985. *Parerga plautina.* Urbino: QuattroVenti.

——. 2001. "Per un'edizione di Plauto." In *Giornate Filologiche "Francesco della Corte."* Vol. 2, *Atti, 4–6 ottobre 2000,* 63–83. Genoa: D.Ar.Fi.Cl.Et.

——. 2007. *La metrica di Plauto e di Terenzio.* Urbino: QuattroVenti.

Ritschl, F. 1868. *Opuscula philologica.* Vol. 2, *Ad Plautum et grammaticam Latinam spectantia.* Leipzig: Teubner.

Schoell, F. 1894. *T. Macci Plauti comoediae.* Vol. 4, fasc. 5, *Cistellaria.* Leipzig: Teubner.

Stockert, W. 2008. "Die Wiedererweckung eines Codex (Virtuelle Arbeit am Codex Ambrosianus des Plautus)." *Rendiconti della Classe di Scienze morali, storiche e filologiche dell'Accademia dei Lincei* 19: 407–434.

——. 2009. *T. Maccius Plautus: Cistellaria.* Urbino: QuattroVenti.

——. 2012. *T. Maccius Plautus, Cistellaria: Einleitung, Text und Kommentar.* Munich: C. H. Beck.

Studemund, W. 1889. *T. Macci Plauti fabularum reliquiae Ambrosianae: Codicis rescripti Ambrosiani apographum.* Berlin: Weidmann.

Suess, W. 1935. "Zur Cistellaria des Plautus." *RhM* 84: 161–187.

——. 1938. "Nochmals zur Cistellaria des Plautus." *RhM* 87: 97–141.

Tontini, A. 1996. "Il codice Escorialense T. II. 8: Un Plauto del Panormita e di altri?" In *Studi Latini in ricordo di Rita Cappelletto,* edited by C. Questa and R. Raffaelli, 33–62. Urbino: QuattroVenti.

——. 2002. "La tradizione manoscritta umanistica di Plauto: Novità e problemi." In *Due seminari plautini: La tradizione del testo, i modelli,* edited by C. Questa and R. Raffaelli, 57–88. Urbino: QuattroVenti.

Wahl, K-U. 1974, *Sprecherbezeichnungen mit griechischen Buchstaben in den Handschriften des Plautus und Terenz.* Tübingen: Narr.

CHAPTER 36

THE TRANSMISSION OF TERENCE

BENJAMIN VICTOR

OVERVIEW OF THE TRADITION; DIRECT ANCIENT WITNESSES

By the time of Varro and Cicero, Terence's comedies could be enjoyed through books, and books would thenceforth be the principal medium of their enjoyment. The conventions of presentation in these copies—their indications of speakers, headings of scenes, and so forth—must have followed much the same evolution as in those of Plautus, described in chapter 40 of this volume. In some respects, though, the two stories do not run parallel. Plainly, Terence's text entered the literary tradition in a more orderly state, for doublets and interpolations are far fewer in it. Nor did it present the problems of authenticity that attached to Plautus, occupying Varro and others.

Modern scholarship for some time assumed that a learned edition—specifically by Valerius Probus, a scholar of the late first century CE—underlay the extant tradition. This idea, put about by Jachmann 1924: 75–76, was not well grounded. To be sure, extant scholia ascribe diorthotic comments on Terence to Probus, and there are sources attributing to him diorthotic methods of Alexandrian inspiration (most explicitly, *Grammatici Latini* VII.534.5, 534.19, 536.23). That given, it may be imagined that in saying things like *distinxit Probus (ad An. 720)* and *Probus annotauit (ad Ph. 49)* Donatus was speaking of an edition of Terence by Probus accompanied, in Alexandrian style, by a volume of adversaria. However, absolute proof is lacking that the Probian edition strictly so called (as opposed to the volume of notes) in fact existed. And if it did, its influence is likely to have been small. The textual criticism of Virgil ascribed to Probus, for which evidence is fuller, had only a limited impact on the Virgil text in circulation, and such impact as it had would seem to have come about largely through the intermediary of

Servius (Zetzel 1981: 53–54). In the end, there is no reason to think the Terence text that reached late antiquity to have been significantly marked by conscious and systematic editing.[1]

Between the second century CE and the fourth, the school curriculum of the western empire came to be dominated by a canon of four writers: Cicero, Sallust, Virgil, and Terence. Terence's place in this company, which might well surprise, was owed to a confluence of factors: as the nearest thing in Latin to Menander, he was guaranteed prestige at the outset (see further chapter 27 of this volume); his popularity among archaizers of the second century carried over into later times; his language, nearer the classical norm than that of other *comici*, suited him better to the schoolroom; and his rhetorical approach to writing endeared him to a system that made synonyms of "educated man" and "polished speaker." As a result, copies of Terence were to be found wherever children were taught to read and write Latin. This made him prime matter for the grammarians, who repertoried his deviations from the linguistic standard, and also cited as example much in him that was perfectly normal. A thick deposit of scholia was laid down: beside two ancient commentaries that survive, six others, whole or partial, are known of.

Terence's ubiquity in the fourth to the sixth centuries caused several copies of the period to survive to the present day, albeit for the most part in fragments. These direct ancient witnesses to the text are:

A   Vatican City, BAV Vat. lat. 3226. Ca. 500. Known commonly as the "codex Bembinus" after the humanist Pietro Bembo, who owned and publicized it in the early sixteenth century. Lacks *Andria* 1–786, *Adelphoe* 915–end, *Hecyra* 1–57; some of the remainder is fragmentary.

Π[a]   Wien, Papyrussammlung der ÖNB L 103 = *CLA* X.1537. Fragments of *Andria* III.2–III.4.

Π[b]   P. Oxy. 2401 = *CLA* Suppl. 1717. Substantial fragments from the latter half of *Andria*.

Sa   Sankt Gallen, Stiftsbibl. 912 = *CLA* VII.974. Eleven lines of *Heauton Timorumenos*.

A is by far the most remarkable of them, not only for the extent of its text but also for the quality of its readings. The scribe was of the ideal sort: conscientious, steady of hand, and without interest in what he wrote. And his model had escaped, for some reason, much trivialization then current: A's text is visibly purer than those underlying the medieval tradition (on which see below) and those used by most grammarians of late antiquity.

---

[1] On Probus, see further note 9. In saying that the ancient text was not visibly marked by editing, we must except certain features not belonging to the text proper, namely the indications of speakers and the scene headings, plainly the work of scholarly thought, and the *didascaliae*. In late antiquity, one does encounter, notably in the black-ink corrections to manuscript A, interpolation thorough enough to suggest a systematic endeavor. On Calliopius and his (possible) recension, see below under "Relations among Δ, Γ and A."

A perhaps makes its most distinctive contribution in the didascalic notices, which it preserves in a redaction unique to it, sometimes (among other things) naming the festivals and magistrates differently than do other sources. It carries a few corrections by the scribe in his own brown ink, a few in brown ink by another writer, and a great many in black ink, mostly cursive. The black-ink corrections, though antique, are of shockingly low worth, being drawn from a highly interpolated source or sources. These are the corrections reported in the Oxford apparatus as "Iov." for *Ioviales*, a name signed to some of them.

Now the Carolingians saw reflections of the intensive late-antique study of Terence, particularly in the numerous quotations of his work by grammarians. They accordingly made a point of reading Terence themselves, and of teaching him to children alongside a small number of other poetic texts. Medieval manuscripts are therefore very abundant, running to well over seven hundred. We shall best find order among them by distinguishing three points of origin for medieval tradition:

- Γ, the ancient ancestor to be assumed for an (initially) tight group of manuscripts ("γ"), first seen between the Rhine and Seine in the earlier ninth century;
- Δ, the ancient ancestor to be assumed for a looser but no less real family of medieval manuscripts ("δ") with a broad geographical distribution;
- the vulgate, a hybrid and slightly interpolated form of the text, created (to some extent consciously) in the first half of the ninth century.

The γ Family of Medieval Manuscripts

Γ, the ancient manuscript that gave rise to this class, was extensively illustrated: each scene was preceded by a painting of masked actors making stereotyped gestures; there was also before each play a display of masks in an architectural structure (*aedicula*), and an impressive frontispiece at the beginning of the volume. The date when the illustrations were first conceived may, of course, long precede that of Γ's execution; both have been much discussed (Jones and Morey 1931, text vol. 200–212; Dodwell 2000: 1–21; Wright 2006: 209–211), as has their relation to stage practice (see especially Jachmann 1924: 10–44; Dodwell 2000, 22–33, noting however the criticisms of Wright 2002). Γ presented the plays in the order *Andria-Eunuchus-Heauton Timorumenos-Adelphoe-Hecyra-Phormio*. It lost two leaves before the propagation of its descendants began, for the oldest and purest of them leave a long lacuna in *Andria*, at the end of act IV and beginning of act V, at the same time omitting front matter to *Eunuchus*. The γ class has generally been studied on the basis of the following:

C   Vatican City, BAV Vat. lat. 3868. Early or middle ninth century. Origin disputed. A carefully calligraphed, deluxe copy, reproducing the paintings of the original.

Y   Paris, BnF lat. 7900. Mid-ninth century, probably Corbie. Includes clumsy pen reproductions of some illustrations.

P   Paris, BnF lat. 7899. Late ninth century, Rheims. The full cycle of illustrations is reproduced in pen and wash.

O   Oxford, Bodleian Libr. Auct. F.II.13. Twelfth century, St. Albans provenance and probably origin. The full cycle of illustrations is reproduced, quite skillfully, in pen and wash.

F   Milan, Bibl. Ambrosiana H 75 inf. Tenth century, Rheims. The full cycle of illustrations is reproduced in pen and wash. Now incomplete, lacking *Andria*, the beginning of *Eunuchus* and the end of *Phormio*.

λ   Lyon, Bibl. Municipale 788. Early to middle ninth century, northern France. Seven leaves containing lines 522–904 of *Heauton Timorumenos*. Unillustrated.

The last detailed work on the γ class, with regard to the text, is Grant 1986: 136–159. Grant concluded that Γ generated the principal hyparchetypes of the γ class during antiquity itself. These ancient books would then have all surfaced in Carolingian times between the Rhine and the Seine, giving rise there respectively to F, CYλ, and PO. Such a scenario is to be rejected, for it looks nothing like the history of texts as otherwise known. It was already an uncommon event for any ancient copy of a pagan classic to survive into the ninth century; in France and Germany it was a very rare one. The chances that three nearly identical such books should all be discovered in one and the same transalpine region, or all arrive there from elsewhere, must approach those of winning a lottery. Surely it was Γ itself that emerged from obscurity in the Carolingian Renaissance, and then that the copies at the base of the γ class were executed.[2]

The γ manuscripts have also been studied by art historians, most recent among them David Wright (Wright 2006). Wright believed (without attempting detailed proof) that C, Y, P, and F were all produced directly from Γ. This idea, too, should be rejected, for two reasons. First, colometric errors (of which more will be said shortly) show that P belongs to a textual subgroup within the γ class in large parts, if not all, of the corpus (Victor and Quesnel 1999); so, for that matter, does F in places. Second, C and Y show unmistakeable signs of copying from antecedents in minuscule script, an impossibility if their scribes worked directly from an ancient exemplar:

An. 699 credat *ex* tredat C
An. 744 It seems that the scribe of C began to write *abut* for *abiit*, then corrected himself. A classic confusion of minims.
An. 854 The majority of manuscripts have *ex me audias*. C before correction wrote *ex mem diccs*. Its model therefore used an *a* resembling two *c*'s.
Haut. 746 harunc] harunt C
Hec. 200 ullam] ullum C[1]

---

[2] The date when Γ was discovered would be known more precisely if it were certain that fifteen lines of *Heautontimorumenos*, copied before 828 into Paris, BnF lat. 2109 (on this manuscript of Eugippius, prepared for Lotharius of Saint-Amand, see Villa 1984: 3, 393) were taken from it. As luck would have it, the γ class as a whole makes no error in the passage in question; hence no affiliation is possible.

Hec. 377 percitus *ex* peccitus C

Hec. 561 aderam] amderam C[1] The scribe of C must have seen a stray mark over the
a, which he took for an abbreviation stroke; in all likelihood, then, his model
used abbreviation strokes.

Hec. 852 feceris] fereris C

An. 388 tu] ut Y

An. 669 defetigatus *ex* defecigatus Y

An. 689 atque] acqui Y

An. 869 miseret] miserer Y

An. 917 huic credundum] huicreddndum Y Was the model in one of those
minuscules with an *en* ligature?

Eun. 308 pollicitum] pollicitam Y

Eun. 702 abierunt] abierant Y

Hec. Per. 11, *Hec.* 445, 523, 541, 560: in all these places Y writes *mrthina* or *myrthina*
for *Myrrhina*

Hec. 298 abstrahat *ex* xbstrahat Y, *ut videtur*

Hec. 803 es tu] ettu *vel fort.* ectu Y. The scribe has misread a common minuscule
ligature.

If the illustrations in C and Y were really copied directly from those of Γ, then textual
errors such as those above could only be explained on the supposition that text and pictures followed different paths. That would be uneconomical, to say the least. Very well
then, what really happened?

Study should begin with the relative positions in the stemma of manuscripts C, Y, and
P, which (among extensive witnesses) are plainly the closest to Γ and the sincerest. The
following are to be observed at the outset.

- The pattern of error excludes that any of the three was copied from any other.
- C and Y share numerous errors against truth in P (Grant 1986: 141). These errors
  often create *voces nihili* (examples: *Haut.* 952 *dericulo*; *Haut.* 967 *sempeperit*). Their
  presence in C and Y cannot therefore be due to horizontal processes.
- Cases of CP or YP agreement in error are much rarer, and the error in question
  is never of such a mechanical sort or results in such nonsense. Examples: *An.* 349
  paues Y, *caue* CP[1]; *Hec.* 357 *cotidiana* C[1], *cotidianan* YPC[2] (with most mss.); *Hec.*
  406 *es* Y, *est* CP

All, then, points toward the following stemma shown in fig. 36.1. From Ψ likewise
derives the fragment λ. There is some reason to place it closer to Y than to C (Grant
1986: 144–145). An intermediate node or nodes must be supposed between Γ and
P to account for certain phenomena, among them the twin status of P and O (see
below).

Was Ψ really a manuscript, or could it just be an illusion created by successive layers
of correction to Γ? This is a question always to be asked in stemmatic research. If the
intermediary underlying P was copied from Γ after correction, but C and Y before, then
C and Y would share errors against P, giving the impression of a hyparchetype where in

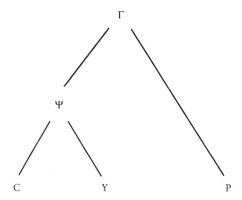

FIGURE 36.1 Stemma of the principal γ manuscripts

fact there was none. But the errors common to C and Y include some hard to explain by such a process:

An. 495–496   edixin tibi?
              interminatus sum ne faceres? num ueritu's? quid re tulit?

                    quid re tulit? P, codd. cett. praeter CY: quid rem tulit? CY

Ad. 412–413 DE Syre, praeceptorum plenust istorum ille SY phy!
                    domi habuit unde disceret.

                    phy P, codd. cett. praeter CY: hy CY

Ad. 432 num quid uis? P, codd. cett. praeter CY: nunc quid uis? CY

Ad. 974–975   et quidem tuo nepoti huius filio
                    hodie prima mammam dedit haec

                    hodie P, codd. cett. praeter CY: hoc die CY

Since P shares with C and Y the long lacuna of *Andria*, its tradition lacked access to sources outside Γ; if, then, correction to Γ were responsible for the divergences between CY and P seen above, this correction would have been entirely conjectural. Such conjectures, however, would require as motive a finer attention to details of usage than the Carolingian world knew. Ψ is therefore to be accepted as a hyparchetype in the full and literal sense.

There is a glitch. Among the errors unique to C are many that betray a model in a majuscule script, more specifically in rustic capital. I give examples, to which numerous others could be added:

    An. 501 renuntiatum] denuntiatum *C*
    An. 780 Atticam] attigam *C*
    An. 949 mutat] mutae *C¹*
    Eun. 585 gremium] cremium *C*
    Haut. 1062 adunco] adungo *C*

Ph. 120 indotatam] inpotatam *C*
Ph. 444 re dicat] redigat *C*
Ph. 783 orationem] grationem *C*
Ph. 882 rape] pape *C*
Hec. 218 ero fama] pro fama *C*
Hec. 429 hunc] nunc *C¹*
Hec. 667 difficultas] difficuitas *C¹*

It has been claimed Y also shows error unique to it and due to misreading of capitals. The following are the best examples adduced:

Eun. 215 poteris] poteres *Y*
Eun. 220 ut] ui *Y*
Eun. 715 me] mi *Y*
Eun. 716 oiei] oli *Y*
Ad. 564 uirum] uerum *Y*

It would be unwise to attribute weight to these last data. Confusions of *i* and *e* can have a phonetic base (Salmon 1944–53, 1: L–LI). The error at *Eun.* 716 may have been due to a tall *i* in a minuscule model, that at *Eun.* 220 to a minuscule *t* crowded against the next word in a *scriptura continua*. Other errors cited by Grant 1986: 143 are not worth consideration.

Of scenarios that can be imagined, the following involves the least implausibility: Ψ was written in minuscule, in the late eighth or early ninth century, with many errors due to misreading of Γ's capitals; shortly after Ψ's execution, C (or an intermediary underlying C) was copied from it; thereafter Ψ underwent a light correction, eliminating most careless misreadings of the model; only then would Y or (more probably) the intermediary underlying Yλ have been produced.

The status of O was for a long time in doubt. Both the illustrations and text of O are very close to those of P—surprisingly so, given O's late date. Was O simply a copy of P? Art historians thought so, and the evidence of illustrations is indeed suggestive (Wright 2006: 197). Recent investigation, however, has adduced evidence that O is not derived from P, namely that it does not reproduce P's scholia and that it conserves errors of word-division not found in P but occurring in other early γ manuscripts (Muir and Turner 2011, Introduction 5.3). This last point is very telling. P and O should henceforth be considered older and younger sibling, not parent and child.

Confusion sets in once additional manuscripts are brought into the picture. Investigators have felt obliged, notably, to make room somewhere for F. This manuscript has long been cited by editors; this fact, and its illustrations of high quality, have caused it to be assumed an important textual witness to Γ. Yet though F's text has everywhere a strong γ character (so much is undeniable), it cannot be fixed to any one point in the γ stemma, sometimes sharing characteristic readings of C,[3] sometimes of Y,[4] sometimes

---

[3] E.g., *Hec.* 236 ais] agis *CF¹*
[4] E.g., *Hec.* 630 reuereatur *ApCP*: reueatur *D*: uereatur *YF*.

of P,[5] sometimes of a δ source.[6] On occasion, it has truth where not only γ, but also δ so far as it is known, present error.[7] Above all, its text is heavily infiltrated by readings of the new vulgate, on which see below.

A tool is at hand to clarify F's situation somewhat. Since comic versification was not understood in the Middle Ages, errors in the colometry, or division of verses, could not be rectified. Rather they remained and were compounded, leaving a record of the text's history in its purely vertical aspect—that is to say, a record of direct ancestry only, excluding influences of collation and correction. This evidence is available only sporadically (since scribes only sporadically commit this sort of error) and then not for all manuscripts (since some are written as prose). But all such evidence as we have confirms F's status as a γ manuscript. The colometry also shows F to change positions in the stemma, sometimes belonging with PO to a subgroup of γ, sometimes deriving from a high point in the γ stemma, possibly descending straight from Γ and sharing no hyparchetype with others (Victor and Quesnel 1999, especially 159, on *Adelphoe* 172–434, and 161–165, on *Hecyra* and *Phormio*).

Because the vulgate adopted γ features of presentation and a text with more γ than δ elements, no clear distinction is possible between the vulgate and the less pure members of γ. But whatever one chooses to call them, a good many later manuscripts with γ credentials (tenth- and eleventh-century) are known. The following have appeared in apparatus critici during modern times:

B   Vatican City, BAV, Arch. S. Pietro H 19. Cluny, eleventh century. An apograph of C.

E   Florence, Bibl. Riccardiana 528. Germany, tenth century.

e   Escorial, Bibl. del Monastero S III 23. Catalonia, tenth/eleventh century. Has a text very close to F's.

ε   Einsiedeln, Stiftsbibl. 362-I + Sankt Gallen, Stiftsbibl. 1394-VIIIa. Trier (?), tenth century.

η   Einsiedeln, Stiftsbibl. 362-II + Sankt Gallen, Stiftsbibl. 1394-VIIIb. Einsiedeln (?), tenth century.

v   Valenciennes, Bibl. Municipale 448. St-Amand, tenth/eleventh century. Used by editors since Lindsay and Kauer. In *Hecyra* and *Phormio* this manuscript is an apograph of F.

A number of later manuscripts continue the γ cycle of illustrations, treating it however more freely than do CYPOF; descriptions and photographic reproductions will be found in Jones and Morey 1931.

---

[5] E.g., *Eun.* 879 magis nunc] nunc magis *PF*; *Hec.* 603 non] nam P[1]*F*.

[6] E.g., *Eun.* 825 certe] certo *Dp*[1]*F* (the OCT apparatus is inaccurate); *Hec.* 294 duxi] dixi *p*[1]*F*; *Hec.* 480 a me est *ACYP*: est a me *DpF*.

[7] E.g., *Hec.* 65 quemque *AF*: quemquem *cett.*

The δ Family of Medieval Manuscripts

The δ family of medieval manuscripts is defined by features both of text and of presentation (among other things, the plays come in the order *Andria-Adelphoe-Eunuchus-Phormio-Heauton Timorumenos-Hecyra*). Δ, the late-antique codex that was its fountainhead, would seem to have followed a pattern common for ancient manuscripts that survived the Dark Ages, being kept in Italy and first beginning to generate copies there, at some time in the eighth or very early ninth century. One of these copies was a source for an Italian glossary (=Goetz, *Glossaria latina* V.529–539), for the Terence glosses there conserve in places the order of plays characteristic of δ. Another copy moved north of the Alps, where its influence can be seen in the vulgate version of the Terence text (attested by the middle of the ninth century; see below). The most important representatives of δ were, however, executed somewhat later:

D   Florence, Bibl. Medicea-Laurenziana 38.24. Ca. 900. Origin near Lake Constance; St-Gall provenance. The best δ manuscript.
p   Paris, BnF lat. 10304. Beauvais provenance and origin, tenth (?) century.

Several other manuscripts, though in some cases giving the plays in the γ order, nevertheless are affiliated with δ through one or more parts of the corpus:[8]

G   Vatican City, BAV Vat. lat. 1640.
L   Leipzig, Universitätsbibl. Rep. I 37.
    Florence, Bibl. Medicea-Laurenziana 38.27.
    Florence, Bibl. Riccardiana 531.
    Leiden, University Libr. Voss lat. Q 38.
    Paris, BnF lat. 7900A.
    Paris, BnF lat. 9345.
    Vienna, ÖNB lat. 85.

All these bear the impress of the vulgate. Though some have had a place in critical apparatuses (G, L), their value to the editor is slight.

No meaningful internal stemma of the δ group as a whole can be drawn. Stemmata based on colometry are feasible in parts of the text, though they can never include p, written throughout as prose, and only seldom D, written mostly as prose. Such colometric stemmata as are possible will be unreliable for the relations among manuscripts in regard to their text (as opposed to their division of verses), owing to constant contamination, particularly from the vulgate.

---

[8] Leiden, University Libr. BPL 109 could be mentioned in this group, since its colometry is in places that of δ; its text, however, cannot be called anything but vulgate. On it see below, under "Formation and spread of the medieval vulgate."

FORMATION AND SPREAD OF THE MEDIEVAL VULGATE

The medieval vulgate has by now been mentioned several times. It corresponds roughly to the "mixed" class of Webb 1911. Vulgate sources present the plays in the γ order and indicate changes of speaker by abbreviations like those of the γ class. They lack the long lacuna in *Andria*. They also show the phrase *Calliopius recensui* ("Revised by me, Calliopius") at the end of each play. The majority of vulgate manuscripts, including the earliest ones, are unillustrated. As for their text, it is hybrid with a predominance of γ readings, and slightly banalized by comparison to that of good γ and δ manuscripts; however, there is much textual variation among them, so that I doubt if a "vulgate text" could be rigorously defined. The vulgate features become standard throughout Europe by the middle of the tenth century.

It might be thought that the vulgate came about through a slow process of haphazard encounter among manuscripts, were there not signs that much of the development occurred at the same time and early on. The first witnesses to it are: the correcting hands in manuscripts Y and (especially) C, the latter contemporary to the scribe; the *Commentum Brunsianum* to Terence, a work of the early to middle ninth century; the quotations from Terence found in writings of Sedulius Scotus about 850; and the manuscript Leiden, University Libr. BPL 109, the oldest copy of Terence whose first hand writes the vulgate (the date of this manuscript, open to dispute, may be as early as the mid-ninth century; it will have been executed in central France).

The vulgate in its main lines would therefore seem to have been created by a Carolingian editor. It is probably this man, then, who placed the phrase *Calliopius recensui* at the ends of plays, where it would remain standard right through the Middle Ages. The words are commonly assumed to be a subscription, inherited from antiquity, but the circumstances of their occurrence tell against it. Calliopius was indeed a person of late-antique date and was named in Γ, in the final explicit after *Phormio (feliciter Calliopio bono scholastico)*, copied by the first hands of C, Y, and P, likewise in a line of the title page (*feliciter Calliopio*), copied by the first hands of C and P (the beginning of Y is lost). *Calliopius recensui*, however, was copied with the text in P alone (among the best γ manuscripts), and there not after every play; it would be written into C and Y only after their execution. The Leiden manuscript, University Libr. BPL 109, is the first to carry it after all plays by the first hand. No mention whatever of Calliopius is likely to have figured in Δ, since none appears in the first hand of its best representative, D (none appears either in the ancient manuscript A, though that need guarantee nothing, since the beginning and end of A's text are not conserved). In writing *Calliopius recensui*, the anonymous Carolingian editor would seem to have been interpreting the mentions of Calliopius at the very beginning and end of his γ source, reasoning that Calliopius must be named there because he had edited the text.

OTHER SOURCES OF THE MEDIEVAL TRADITION; THE *ALTER EXITUS ANDRIAE*

We have seen that two ancient copies of Terence (Γ and Δ) provided, either in pure or in hybrid and doctored form, the base for the medieval tradition. Now, did the Carolingians ever transcribe other ancient codices of Terence? They did so at least once, and one or more of this book's descendants had a limited but palpable influence, leaving among its marks a spurious scene of ancient date (the *alter exitus Andriae*), the rare *Vita Ambrosiana* (Vita #206 in Munk Olsen 1982–, also known as the "Vita II," edited in Deufert 2003) and certain isolated readings. The principal vectors of the *alter exitus* and *Vita Ambrosiana* have been described and their history traced (Reeve 1983: 418–419; Villa 1984: 99–136 *et passim*; Deufert 2003; Victor 2007: 7–10). These texts appear both to have spent the Dark Ages in one and the same manuscript of Terence, itself housed in an Italian library, and first been transcribed in Italy. Copies of Terence carrying them, more than one in number, were then taken into Germany in the late tenth century, along with a great many other Italian books. Manuscripts in contact with this tradition repay collation. A case in point is Erlangen, Universitätsbibl. 391 (s. XI), likelier than not produced at Bamberg (it carries an early ex libris of the Michelsberg), where resided important carriers of the *alter exitus* (Reeve 1983: 418–419; Victor 2007: 8–10). Though presenting for the most part a typical vulgate text of the eleventh century, it also contains rare readings of ancient origin. It is the only direct source not to interpolate *iam* at *Eunuchus* 422; it also reads with an ancient source (manuscript A) against the whole or very nearly the whole medieval tradition at *Eun.* 153 (*tibi* om.); *Eun.* 510 (*se*); *Eun.* 545 (*adeo*); *Eun.* 803 (*ego tibi caput hodie*); *Eun.* 569 (*fuerat frater*); *Eun.* 929 (*et sine dispendio*); and *Eun.* 952 (*esse* non habet). Likewise, its correcting hand shares unique readings with A at *Eun.* 558 (*aut* non habet) and 1063 (*scis*). No such manuscript has yet been used by editors for the text itself of Terence (as opposed to the *alter exitus* and *Vita Ambrosiana*).

Relatively late Italian Terences (twelfth century and on), even when not equipped with the *alter exitus* and *Vita Ambrosiana*, often show occasional good readings unknown in the earlier medieval sources (Ceccarelli 1992, Victor 2007). They also tend to have the *periocha* to *Eunuchus*, absent from all the most important medieval manuscripts. This raises the possibility that yet another ancient book leaked material into the Italian tradition. Like manuscripts in contact with the *alter exitus* tradition, the Italian Terences of the high and later Middle Ages have not received adequate attention from editors.

RELATIONS AMONG Δ, Γ AND A

Relations are customarily supposed between Γ and Δ so as to assign them a common source "Σ", sometimes called the "Calliopian recension" in the belief that the Calliopius named in medieval manuscripts had edited its text; Σ is then imagined to share an ancestor ("Φ") with A (Jachmann 1924: 72–90; Grant 1986: 1–17, 160–176). Editors or readers will reject readings limited to one or other of Γ and Δ in proportion to their confidence in this scheme; the more they doubt it, on the other hand, the more eclectic must be their method. I have warned elsewhere that the common errors adduced for Σ and Φ do not in fact support their existence: these errors are either trivializations, which tend to migrate horizontally through collation of copies, or else mechanical errors which can be made independently, hence of no use for stemmatics (Victor 1996). Now, even if resemblances between Δ and Γ are due to genetic relation, no one called Calliopius was responsible. We have seen that proper evidence for Calliopius's connection to a manuscript is limited to γ. Moreover, this evidence leaves it uncertain that the connection had anything editorial about it. The mentions of Calliopius that must be ancient, on the title page and in the explicit following *Phormio* in the best γ manuscripts, read only *feliciter Calliopio* ("with best wishes to Calliopius") and *feliciter Calliopio bono scholastico* ("with best wishes to Calliopius the good schoolmaster/the good scholar"), respectively. It is the words *Calliopius recensui* that make of him the corrector, but we have seen that these words are nowhere original to C or to Y and that they are unlikely to be older than the ninth century.

THE INDIRECT TRADITION: DONATUS AND OTHER SOURCES

Some six dozen lines of Terence are cited by Cicero and Varro. These earliest quotations show one wide divergence from the direct tradition: at *Adelphoe* 117, where the manuscripts give

> Obsonat, potat, olet ungenta de meo;
> amat

> He banquets, he carouses, he smells of perfume—at my expense. He has love-affairs.

Varro *DLL* VII.84 reads *scortatur, potat*... "He has flings with tarts, he carouses..." It would be tempting to see in *scortatur* an acting variant suppressed by the manuscript tradition, or in *obsonat* a bowdlerizing intervention by a reader/editor, were not Varro's practice in quoting literary texts well documented. He is guilty elsewhere of sloppy citation from memory (Deufert 2002: 139–143) and will be here, too.

The Latin of Terence was of relatively minor interest to Verrius Flaccus, the Augustan lexicographer who served as source to Pompeius Festus in the late second century; hence the remains of the latter are not the important testimony that they are for a number of other archaic writers. Our extensive indirect sources are of more advanced date, from the fourth century to the early sixth for the most part. The major grammarians of late antiquity, as well as the scholiasts of Virgil, Horace, and Statius, cite Terence abundantly. Some of these late-antique writers worked carelessly from memory, Priscian being especially disappointing in that regard. With one exception, they also bear witness to a text of Terence little different, and no better on the whole, than that of good extant manuscripts. The exception is Aelius Donatus, whose floruit of CE 353 is somewhat deceptive. His *Commentum Terenti* being largely a secondhand product, much of its content will date to the time of intense scholiastic activity in the late second and early third century CE, some to even remoter periods. It would be surprising if the contribution of Probus, a Flavian figure, were limited to those places that name him directly.[9] And a few notes appear to go all the way back to the republic.[10] Parts of the commentary are thus based ultimately on copies of Terence older by centuries than any of the direct witnesses or the great bulk of the indirect. It often preserves just the strikingly attractive readings we should expect of such a source: we have Donatus to thank for *quoi mi expurgandus* at *Andria* 167, where all manuscripts read *qui mihi exorandus*: likewise for the remarkable archaism *sum*, meaning *eum*, at *Phormio* 1028, for *fortasse* governing an infinitive at *Hecyra* 313, and for much more besides.

The *Commentum Terenti* has a complicated history. After its compilation by Donatus about the middle of the fourth century CE, it was often excerpted and paraphrased. Abridgement during this phase clouded much that had once been clear. At some time later, two sets of extensive excerpts/paraphrases were recombined to make a single commentary again. It is likely that many shorter scholia, alien to Donatus's fourth-century work, also found their way into the new composite before or during recombination. The lemmata need be no earlier than the recombination, and in any case they were especially vulnerable afterward to contamination from manuscripts of Terence; hence the tendency of variants among Donatus manuscripts in the lemmata to reflect disagreements within the direct tradition of the playwright. The quotes embedded in the commentary itself are affected, to a lesser degree, by this same influence of Terence manuscripts. And I have not yet mentioned simple miscopying, of which the commentary received more than the usual dose. Two passages will illustrate the problems.

Andria 69–70, in the consensus of the older manuscripts:

interea mulier quaedam abhinc triennium
ex Andro commigrauit huic uiciniae.

In the meantime, three years ago, a certain woman moved to this neighborhood from Andros.

---

[9] It is disputed whether observations on Terence and Virgil ascribed to Probus are really due to him and, if so, by what paths they reached commentators of the fourth and fifth centuries: Aistermann 1909, 28–30 may be taken to represent the standard view, Jocelyn 1984-5 a skeptical extreme.

[10] The scholia on *Ph*. 182, 190, and 233 name the late-republican polymath Nigidius Figulus as their source (=Nigidius frags. 35–37 Funaioli). Ritschl 1845: 363–364 has been followed in denying that Nigidius wrote a Terence commentary. But Ritschl appealed to no more than a similarity of interest between the Nigidian scholia in Donatus and Nigidius's grammatical work, the *Commentaria*. Donatus on *Ph*. 233 (*hic Nigidius annotauit*) univocally implies a commentary, at least partial, on Terence.

A, Y, p, and F are not available. A correcting hand of C transmits the variant *huc* for *huic* in line 70. *Viciniam* for *uiciniae* is legible in the first hand of C; it was subsequently altered to *uiciniae*; the original reading of P cannot be made out (in it the final *e* is written over an erasure). Other manuscripts read *huic uiciniae*, as do Nonius p. 802 Lindsay and Priscian *GLK* III.187.

> *Phormio* 367–368, as given by A:
>
> (PHORMIO) at quem uirum! quem ego uiderim in uita optumum.
> GETA uideas te atque illum ut narras. PHORMIO i in malam crucem!
>
> (PHORMIO) And what a man he was! About the best I've ever seen.
> GETA May you live to find yourself as you describe him. PHORMIO Go be hanged!

The δ group read *in hinc in malam crucem*, the γ group and medieval vulgate *abi hinc in malam crucem*. Here now are the scholia as transmitted:

> *Ad An.* 70 HVIC VICINIAE uiciniae A·PEΛKON est ut huic locorum.
> VICINIAE *TCV*: NVPERNAE *A* | uiciniae *TCV*: uicinae *A* | A·PEΛKON est *A*: n·a·p·e·a·c·o·n·e *TC: om. V*

> *Ibid.* HVIC VICINIAE legitur et 'uiciniam'.
> uiciniam *A, V ante corr.*: uicinia *TC, V post corr.*

> *Ad Ph.* 368 IN MALAM CRVCEM aduerbialiter, ut 'huic uiciniae'.

In the first scholion to *Andria* 70, it is clear that we must correct to παρέλκον *est*. The scholiast, then, understood *uiciniae* to be appended pleonastically. Since *huic locorum* is not Latin, the parallel he cited will have been *huc locorum*. He therefore read *huc uiciniae* at *Andria* 70. The scholion to *Phormio* 368 only makes sense if its author had before him an unusual adverbial use of a noun. He must then have read *in'* (i.e., *isne*) *malam crucem?* at *Phormio* 368. Now, the parallel he cites should contain a similar adverbial noun. This scholiast therefore knew *Andria* 70 in the form *huc uiciniam*. Thus the commentary of Donatus transmits valuable evidence for an otherwise unknown but likely right variant at *Phormio* 368, and for two weakly attested variants, again likely right, at *Andria* 70. But one of these variants—*in' malam crucem?*—is no longer easily recognized: presumably the scholion was fuller and clearer in its fourth-century form. Another—*huc*—is nowhere written as such in manuscripts of Donatus. The third—*uiciniam*—has been replaced by a commoner one in much of the Donatus tradition. Such contamination of the indirect tradition by the direct has even affected the citation of *Andria* in a scholion to *Phormio*, where it might have been thought safe from interference. It will have been noticed as well that the authors of the two scholia on *Andria* 70 used different texts of Terence; such contradictions are common. And it is altogether typical that the lemmata do not match the text commented. All that to say: the *Commentum Terenti* is not like most ancient works. The reconstruction of its anterior states is no side issue, but a necessary step in its intelligent use. The apparatus, too, must be read at least as carefully as what is printed above it, and it is advisable to supplement the standard edition, Wessner 1902–1908, with new evidence collected in Zwierlein 1970.

Many of the scholia are explicitly concerned with diorthosis. These often present competing textual possibilities and their justifications, sometimes expressing a preference for one of them. In such cases, the voice of the summarizer/arbiter may be assumed to be that of Donatus himself. Though the Romans never articulated more than the crudest notions of method in matters of textual criticism, a good many tendencies can nonetheless be discerned in their practice. For one thing, they did not share with us the scruple reserving conjecture for a late stage of the critical process, after all variants transmitted have been weighed and rejected. Variant and conjecture might therefore be considered on something closer to an equal footing, so that the distinction between them held less importance. Terminology was accordingly imprecise. So *emendare* may designate correction by comparison of exemplars or by the critic's wits alone. *Legere* is vaguer still: *X legit Y* may be said if the scholiast X expressed a preference for the variant Y, if he conjectured Y, or if he simply commented the expression Y, whether or not he considered or even knew other possibilities. Under these conditions, it is very hard to estimate the proportion of conjecture in the distinctive readings of Latin scholiasts. James Zetzel has found reason to think it significant (1973, 1974, 1981) and deserves a more sympathetic hearing than he has been given (for the reaction at its most elaborate, see Timpanaro 1986). As regards Terence specifically, Donatus *ad An.* 592 and *ad Hec.* 58 implies that some had proposed conjectures to bring Terence closer to his Greek models (Zetzel 1981: 152); likewise, *ad Ph.* 249 records a conjecture to regularize grammar (*usque*: see just below), as do *ad An.* 55 (*quae*) and *ad An.* 653 (*altercatus es*): Zetzel 1981: 153, 163–164, 166. Now, again limiting discussion to the commentary of Donatus on Terence (the ancient commentaries on Virgil are more problematic), nothing suggests that it drew on critics who had conjectured in an archaizing or otherwise denormalizing direction. Those Donatian scholia recording archaisms and other linguistic anomalies, which are in any case the most valuable, may accordingly be followed with fair confidence.

Alongside the conjectural tendency, there is also among scholiasts a highly conservative one. It predominates in those of the third and later centuries, and Donatus stands squarely within the trend. The scholiastic tradition of this period was concerned to defend its authors, presenting them as artistically successful in nearly all respects. With this tendency came another—that of defending their received text. Terminology encouraged such a development and to a degree evolved in consequence of it: many scholiastic terms covered a great deal of ground and, when they brought with them an excuse, excused much. So the phrase *figura per modos* described, and by implication justified, any anomaly in the use of moods, *figura per genera* in the concord of genders, and so on.

The concept of *ethos*, or character type (the most overworked tool in Donatus's kit), proved useful in defending the transmitted text. *Phormio* 248–250 with Donatus's comments:

> Meditata mihi sunt omnia mea incommoda erus si redierit:
> molendum esse in pistrino, uapulandum, habendae compedes,
> opus ruri faciundum.

I've thought of all the trouble I'll have if master comes back: there will be grinding to do at the mill, there will be beating, shackles to be worn, labor to do on the farm.

HABENDAE COMPEDES uitiosam locutionem seruili personae dedit Terentius; nam integrum esset, si diceret 'habendas compedes'. unde quidam non 'esse' sed 'usque' legunt.

SHACKLES TO BE WORN (*HABENDAE COMPEDES*) Terence gave a faulty expression to a servile character. It would be correct if he said *habendas compedes*. That is why some read not *esse* but *usque*.

Thus Donatus notes that a conjectural emendation (*molendum usque* for *molendum esse*) has been proposed to remedy the change of construction. He in no way endorses the emendation, and one has the impression that he thinks it the inferior choice. That is not remarkable in itself; any modern philologist would prefer the traditional reading as well. What startles is rather the reasoning: *molendum esse... habendae compedes* is fine, it is implied, because spoken by a slave, of whom rough grammar may be expected. The same note demonstrates that conjecture in the scholiastic tradition could have an effect on the text circulating among the public: *usque* would find its way into manuscripts of Terence, some of which have *molendum mihi esse usque* and the like. However, the other readings that Donatus indicates to have been conjectural do not appear in extant manuscripts.

Living in a world without punctuation and where voice and gesture had much importance, the scholiasts were also sensitive to the possibilities of redividing sentences, reinflecting them, or working the face and hands so as to make them interrogative, ironical, and so on. These, too, tend to be privileged first resorts, invoked to excess. Thus for the difficult and perhaps corrupt *scio quid conere* at *Andria* 703, irony is one of the explanations recorded by Donatus. Similarly *lectulos in sole* at *Adelphoe* 585 is taken—with much liberty—to mean "dining couches for outdoor use," and excused on grounds that the speaker is improvising frantically, as the actor's face and gestures, we are told, would make clear. Assigning a special sense to some one word was another way to rescue a text otherwise intolerable, as at *Hecyra* 307–308, saved by understanding *faciunt* to mean *ostendunt*.[11] We should not accept such explanations with unqualified gratitude but evaluate them as if proposed by a scholar of our own time, asking what parallels there are and, if none, whether the circumstances justify rewriting the dictionary. Rewriting the dictionary, after all, may well be what the scholiast was up to.

FURTHER READING

Villa 1984 is a rich collection of observations, by an outstanding medievalist, on manuscripts of Terence from the Carolingian Renaissance to the time of Petrarch, with a particular concentration on reception and annotation. This work also contains, on pages 295–454, a thorough

[11] For a discussion of the last two passages (*Ad.* 585 and *Hec.* 307–308), with a repertory of conjectures and a suggestion of my own, see Victor 2010: 48–49, 54.

census of manuscripts. Another census, with more detailed descriptions of the manuscripts and a repertory of paratexts (though not covering the later Middle Ages), will be found in Munk Olsen 1982–, Vol. 2: 583–653. Jones and Morey 1931 can also be valuable as a repository of data, though few of its conclusions are to be accepted. Among more recent investigations centered about the text itself, those of largest scope are Grant 1986, Ceccarelli 1992, and my own articles Victor 1996, Victor and Quesnel 1999, and Victor 2007. On the art-historical side, note Dodwell 2000 and Wright 2006. Jakobi 1996 provides an introduction to Donatus; pages 19–46 treat the diorthotic scholia, as does Zetzel 1981: 148–167.

BIBLIOGRAPHY

Aistermann, J. 1909. "De M. Valerii Probi Berytii vita et scriptis." PhD diss., University of Bonn.

Ceccarelli, L. 1992. *Primi sondaggi sulla tradizione manoscritta di Terenzio*. Rome: Bagatto.

Deufert, M. 2002. *Textgeschichte und Rezeption der plautinischen Komödien im Altertum*. Berlin: De Gruyter.

——. 2003. *Eine verkannte Terenzbiographie der Spätantike: Untersuchungen zur Vita Ambrosiana*. Göttingen: Vandenhoeck & Ruprecht.

Dodwell, C. R. 2000. *Anglo-Saxon Gestures and the Roman Stage*. Cambridge, UK: Cambridge University Press.

Grant, J. 1986. *Studies in the Textual Tradition of Terence*. Toronto: University of Toronto Press.

Jachmann, G. 1924. *Geschichte des Terenztextes im Altertum*. Basel: Reinhardt.

Jakobi, R. 1996. *Die Kunst der Exegese im Terenzkommentar des Donat*. Berlin: De Gruyter.

Jocelyn, H. D. 1984–1985. "The Annotations of M. Valerius Probus." *Classical Quarterly* 34: 464–472; *ibid.* 35: 149–161, 466–474.

Jones, L. W., and Morey, C. R. 1931. *The Miniatures of the Manuscripts of Terence Prior to the Thirteenth Century*. Princeton: Princeton University Press.

Muir, B., and A. Turner. 2011. *A Facsimile Edition of Terence's Comedies. Oxford, Bodleian Library MS Auct. F.2.13*. CD ROM. Oxford: Bodleian Library.

Munk Olsen, B. 1982–. *L'étude des auteurs classiques latins aux XIe et XIIe siècles*. Paris: Éditions du Centre National de la Recherche Scientifique.

Prete, S. 1970. *Il codice di Terenzio Vaticano latino 3226*. Vatican City: Biblioteca Apostolica Vaticana.

Reeve, M. R. 1983. "Terence." In *Texts and Transmission: A Survey of the Latin Classics*, edited by L. D. Reynolds, 412–420. Oxford: Clarendon Press.

Ritschl, F. 1845. "De veteribus Plauti interpretibus." In *Parerga zu Plautus und Terenz*, by F. Ritschl, 357–387. Leipzig: Weidmann.

Salmon, P. 1944–1953. *Le lectionnaire de Luxeuil*. Rome: Abbazia San Girolamo.

Timpanaro, S. 1986. *Per la storia della filologia virgiliana antica*. Rome: Salerno.

Victor, B. 1996. "A Problem of Method in the History of Texts and Its Implications for the Manuscript Tradition of Terence." *Revue d'Histoire des Textes* 26: 269–287.

——. 2007. "New Manuscript Sources of the Terence-Text." In *Terentius Poeta*, edited by P. Kruschwitz, W.W. Ehlers, and F. Felgentreu, 1–14. Munich: C. H. Beck.

——. 2010. "Terence's Greek: Observations on Certain Cruxes in His Comedies." *Bulletin of the Institute of Classical Studies* 53: 45–54.

Victor, B., and B. Quesnel. 1999. "The Colometric Evidence for the History of the Terence-Text in the Early Middle Ages." *Revue d'Histoire des Textes* 29: 141–168.

Villa, C. 1984. *La "lectura Terentii."* Vol. 1, *Da Ildemaro a Francesco Petrarca.* Padua: Antenore.

Webb, R. H. 1911. "An Attempt to Restore the γ Archetype of Terence Manuscripts." *Harvard Studies in Classical Philology* 22: 55–110.

Wessner, P., ed. 1902–1908. *Aeli Donati Commentum Terenti.* Leipzig: Teubner.

Wright, D. 2002. Review of *Anglo-Saxon Gestures and the Roman Stage*, by C. R. Dodwell. *The Classical Bulletin* 78: 230–234.

——. 2006. *The Lost Late Antique Illustrated Terence.* Vatican City: Biblioteca Apostolica Vaticana.

Zetzel, J. E. G. 1973. "*Emendavi ad Tironem*: Some Notes on Scholarship in the Second Century A.D." *Harvard Studies in Classical Philology* 77: 225–243.

——. 1974. "Andria 403 (II. 3. 29)." *Hermes* 102: 372–376.

——. 1981. *Latin Textual Criticism in Antiquity.* New York: Arno Press.

Zwierlein, O. 1970. *Der Terenzkommentar des Donat im Codex Chigianus H VII 240.* Berlin: de Gruyter.

CHAPTER 37

GRAPHIC COMEDY: MENANDRIAN MOSAICS AND TERENTIAN MINIATURES

SEBASTIANA NERVEGNA

In the Byzantine period, Menander's comedies dropped out of the school curriculum and were no longer copied. Until the nineteenth century, Menander was known only through the maxims attributed to him ("Menander's Maxims"), through excerpts cited by ancient authors, and through Roman adaptations of his comedies. Luckily, to make up for this huge loss we now have a host of papyri preserving portions of Menander's plays and a wealth of artifacts illustrating scenes from them. Considering only those that can be more or less securely assigned to a specific comedy, we have about ninety Menandrian papyri. This high number accords well with the claims made by authors such as Quintilian (*Inst.* 10.1.69–71) and Dio Chrysostom (*Or.* 18.6–7): Menander's plays were in wide circulation, both in and out of schools.

Something new can also be learned from the rich visual record. We have over 3,500 artifacts reproducing scenes, characters, or masks from New Comedy. They come in all kinds of artistic media, from small terracotta figurines to large mosaics, and were produced in every corner of the Roman Empire, with dates ranging from the late fourth century BCE well into the sixth century CE. To judge from the extant inscribed scenes, the iconographic tradition of New Comedy invariably coincides with Menander's comedy, and this rich pictorial record complements the wide popularity of illustrations of Menander himself in ancient art. With over seventy portraits derived from the same early-Hellenistic archetype statue that stood in Athens' Theater of Dionysus, and with many other independent portraits, Menander is the single Greek author most commonly represented in the plastic arts in antiquity.[1]

---

[1] Fittschen 1991 (reconstruction of Menander's early statue and collection of related portraits); Bassett 2008 (tradition and innovations in Menander's portraits). See also Richter 1965: 229–234; Richter 1984: 159–164.

Ancient viewers everywhere thus saw Menander and his dramas in their daily surroundings. The iconographic tradition of Menander's comedy was longstanding, persistent, and trendsetting. When ancient artists (and ancient viewers) envisioned later comedy, they did so within the iconographic conventions of New Comedy. This is true whether they were illustrating brand new comedy, comedy in general, or Roman adaptations of Greek plays.

MENANDER'S COMEDIES AND THEIR ICONOGRAPHIC TRADITION

Illustrations self-identified by "inscription"—that is, by labels within a composition identifying the scene depicted—are but the tip of the iceberg. We have a total of twenty-two New Comedy scenes, all from the imperial period and the Greek East. Priority of mention goes to our richest and best-preserved assemblage of artifacts relating to drama, the House of Menander in Mytilene. Variously dated to the late third or, more likely, to the later fourth century CE, seven mosaics depicting Menandrian comedies (*Plokion, Samia, Synaristosai, Epitrepontes, Theophoroumene, Encheiridion,* and *Messenia*) decorated the dining room of this house, and four more were set in the portico (depicting *Kybernetai, Leukadia, Misoumenos,* and *Phasma*). Illustrations also belong to the decorative program of private houses elsewhere. A house in Zeugma (in Syria) is named after a mosaic of *Synaristosai* found in it (first half of the third century CE). A mosaic reproducing *Plokion* comes from the House of Dionysus and Ariadne in Chania (on Crete), where it was set with an unlabeled mosaic, now fragmentary, that may reproduce *Sikyonioi* (possibly fourth century CE). The reception room of a terrace house in Ephesus was graced with several dramatic illustrations, including two paintings titled *Sikyonioi* and *Perikeiromene* (late second century or early third century CE). Our latest inscribed scene may be a fourth- or fifth-century CE mosaic from the ancient Roman colony of Ulpia Oescus (in Bulgaria), where a building yet to be identified displayed a large mosaic labeled "Menander's *Achaioi*." Very little is known about two recent findings. Four mosaics (*Synaristosai, Theophoroumene, Perikeiromene,* and *Philadelphoi*) have been uncovered in Daphne (a wealthy suburb of Antioch), and two more (*Theophoroumene* and *Sikyonios*) at Kastelli Kissamos (on Crete).[2] By stark

---

[2] For important discussions of the inscribed illustrations of Menander's plays, all accompanied by generally good photographs, see Charitonides, Kahil, and Ginouvès 1970 (Mytilene mosaics); Abadie-Reynal, Darmon, and Manière-Lévêque 2003 (Zeugma *Synaristosai*); Markoulaki 1990 (Chania mosaics); Strocka 1977 (Ephesus wall paintings); and Ivanov 1954 (*Achaioi* mosaic). The preliminary publication of four new Daphne mosaics by Çelik (2009) is now superseded by Gutzwiller and Çelik 2012, which includes extensive discussion and color plates. The *Sikyonios* mosaic from Kastelli Kissamos, which is to be published with its companion piece by Stavroula Markoulaki, provides yet further evidence that this comedy circulated as both *Sikyonios* and *Sikyonioi*.

contrast, with only two scenes identified by inscriptions, the iconographic tradition of Greek tragedy is no match for that of Menander's comedy.[3]

Labeled illustrations are important for several reasons. They help us trace the popularity of individual plays in the visual record, they furnish clues to their archetypes, and they shed light on the processes that kept this iconographic tradition alive. For example, artists began labeling the comedies they depicted only in the imperial period, in the late second or early third century CE, whereas earlier artifacts are unlabeled (early viewers apparently had no need for identification tags). By comparing these early scenes with the inscribed ones, many anonymous scenes can now be identified as illustrations of specific comedies. A prominent example of this procedure are the two mosaics executed by Dioscurides of Samos around the late second century BCE to grace the so-called Villa of Cicero in Pompeii: comparison with the Mytilene mosaics has conclusively shown that they depict Menander's *Synaristosai* (figure 37.1) and *Theophoroumene* (figure 37.2). Likewise, the comic scene reproduced on a set of molds (of disputed purpose) in Ostia of the third century CE is strikingly similar to the Mytilene *Misoumenos*. And both a Pompeian painting now in Bonn and a fragmentary mosaic from Avenches of ca. 200–250 CE resemble the Mytilene mosaic of *Samia*.[4] Similarly, several terracotta statuettes can be identified by their resemblance to labeled scenes. Examples could be multiplied (see *MNC³* 1.85–98).

This is not to say that we are dealing in every case with images faithfully copied across media and time. Exact replicas are in fact relatively rare among our comic scenes. The surviving *Synaristosai* mosaics, for example, do not all reproduce precisely the same illustration. Dioscurides's mosaic, which is the earliest and finest example, depicts three women seated around a table; the young woman in the middle is speaking (note her speaking gesture), flanked on the left by a second young woman and on the right by an old woman holding a drinking cup in her right hand and a servant beside her. The same basic composition—two young women and an old one seated around a table—recurs in the Mytilene mosaic, but here the old woman, though still holding her cup with a servant nearby, is now on the left and sitting in a high-backed chair. The single attendant in the Pompeii and Mytilene mosaics becomes two attendants in Zeugma and three in Daphne. In Zeugma, the composition is less compact than on Dioscurides's mosaic and is also set against a backdrop resembling a *scaenae frons*. Interestingly, while this latter element emphasizes that this is a theatrical scene, the characters seem to have lost their masks, as their mouths are not obviously open. Meanwhile the scene opens up even more in Daphne, with the table now moved to the right and the three women seated one next to the

---

[3] The two tragic illustrations are murals in Ephesus of Euripides's *Orestes* and an *Iphigenia*, set alongside illustrations of Menander's comedies. For our mosaic and mural illustrations of tragedy, see Nervegna 2013, ch. 3 with Appendix 3.

[4] Dioscurides's *Synaristosai* and *Theophoroumene*: Naples, Museo Archeologico Nazionale 9987, 9985; *Misoumenos* molds: Ostia, Museum 3532, 3799–3800, 3801–3802 (Charitonides, Kahil and Ginouvès 1970, pls. 5, 2; 6, 2; 26, 3). Avenches, Roman Museum (Lancha 1997: 271–272 with pl. CXVI); Bonn, Akademisches Kunstmuseum E 108 (Csapo 1999: 188, fig. 13).

FIGURE 37.1 *Synaristosai* mosaic signed by Dioscurides. Naples, Museo Archeologico Nazionale 9987. After M. Bieber, *Die Denkmäler zum Theaterwesen im Altertum* (Berlin and Leipzig: Vereinigung wissenschaftlicher Verleger, 1920), pl. 93

other. And the old woman keeps switching sides: she is on the right in Zeugma, but on the left in Daphne.

More conspicuous changes characterize our record of the iconography of *Theophoroumene*, the comedy of Menander's that is most often illustrated. Generally speaking, a fundamental gap divides early depictions from later ones. Dioscurides's mosaic includes two young men, one in the center playing the cymbals and the other beating a *tympanon* on the right, in front of a door. A female *aulos* player is on the left, with her assistant carrying the *aulos*'s case. Though not in every last detail, this image is essentially replicated in a series of various artifacts. These include a fresco from Stabia, a battered mosaic from an area near Vesuvius (both probably executed in the first century CE),[5] and a few terracotta statuettes of the *tympanon* player and cymbal player. Coming from Asia Minor and dated possibly to the second century BCE, these terracottas survive as single items because they were placed individually in tombs. Originally, however, they were intended to be displayed as a set. Because one of the terracotta cymbal players (figure 37.3) has a vent hole on its left

---

[5] Naples, Museo Archeologico Nazionale 9034 (fresco from Stabia); Ufficio Scavi di Pompei 17735 (fragmentary mosaic). For illustrations, see Nervegna 2010, plates 4 and 5.

FIGURE 37.2 *Theophoroumene* mosaic signed by Dioscurides. Naples, Museo Archeologico Nazionale 9985. After M. Bieber, *Die Denkmäler zum Theaterwesen im Altertum* (Berlin and Leipzig: Vereinigung wissenschaftlicher Verleger, 1920), pl. 92.

FIGURE 37.3 Terracotta statuette from Myrina reproducing the cymbal player from *Theophoroumene*. Athens, National Museum 5060. Photo: D-DAI-ATH-NM 194. Courtesy of the Deutsches Archäologisches Institut Athen.

side, it was meant to be seen from the right. This is the same stance and position that the cymbal player has on Dioscurides's mosaic and on related monuments.

Later depictions depart from this largely coherent tradition in a number of details. From left to right, the Mytilene *Theophoroumene* has a male figure inscribed "Lysias," a slave, "Parmenon," and a young man called "Kleinias" with a small figure, a mute, next to him. Unique elements are found on the *Theophoroumene* mosaic from Kastelli Kissamos, such as a fourth actor and a full-sized piper's assistant, now playing a single *aulos*. On the Daphne mosaic, we find a character playing the *tympanon* at the center, one playing the cymbals on the right, a slave on the left, and a small figure playing a pipe—and this is, we learn from the inscription, the third act of the play. Moreover, the two figures playing music on the right are quite remarkable. At first sight they seem female, but rather than reaching to their ankles, as female dresses invariably do, their costumes reach only mid-calf, in the manner of those worn by young men and slaves. Costume is an issue with the Mytilene *Theophoroumene* as well; here Lysias has the name of a free person but is dressed like a slave. Nevertheless, although variously arranged, dressed, and positioned within the scene, the actor-musicians are invariably the core of the tableau.

For all the iconographic and interpretative problems that they raise, surviving artifacts do offer a few important clues about their models. In the past it was supposed that they were enlargements of pictures found in papyrus rolls, but a number of features—the quality of composition, the painterly technique, the precise reproduction of masks and other details—point rather to an archetype from the major arts, most likely paintings. Given the wide diffusion of these images, moreover, the original paintings must have been located in a conspicuous and probably public setting. Furthermore, illustrations of New Comedy proliferated as early as they did widely. Since our earliest surviving artifact is a terracotta statuette from Halae, in Boeotia, dated to before 300 BCE, the iconographic tradition of New Comedy dates back to Menander's lifetime and thus challenges the famous claim that Menander became popular only after his death. Since, too, the original paintings were so close to the first performance of the comedies they illustrated and were on display to viewers who must have seen these plays in the theater, the original paintings must have also provided good evidence for contemporary masks, costumes, gestures, and stage action for later artists and illustrators.[6] As Csapo (forthcoming) notes, these early-Hellenistic paintings and the examples that most faithfully follow them make up our best source for the visual impact of Menander's comedy.

Extant artifacts also shed light on the subject matter of their lost archetypes. Judging from the plays that we have or can reconstruct, artifacts typically depict either the opening scene of a play (as with *Perikeiromene, Synaristosai, Philadelphoi* and

---

[6] Discussion of original paintings: Webster, Green, and Seeberg 1995, esp. 57, 85–86; Green 1994, esp. 112, Csapo 1999: 48, Nervegna 2013. The Boeotian terracotta, now in the Museum of Thebes, is an excerpt of the scene reproduced on several artifacts, with the Naples relief as the best-known example (Naples, Museo Archeologico Nazionale 6687; see also below). See Green 1985 for photographs and discussion.

probably *Leukadia*) or its key scene (*Epitrepontes, Phasma, Theophoroumene, Sikyonios* or *Sikyonioi, Samia* and probably *Encheiridion* and *Misoumenos*). Ancient artists captured moments that had captivated the audience: the angry Demea chasing his mistress Chrysis out of his house in *Samia* and the unique tableau of three women conversing over a meal in *Synaristosai*. Since New Comedy has less music than Old Comedy, the relatively rare musical scenes were particularly impressive. Consider the actor-musicians in *Theophoroumene* or the female piper in the scene reproduced on a first-century CE marble relief and on several other monuments (Naples, Museo Nazionale 6687; see Green 1985 and Csapo 2010: 151–153 with illustrations). In all likelihood, the piper is playing in accompaniment to the song of the drunken young man—whose own unusual antics, incidentally, also made for good theater on the New Comedy stage. In our plays, there are only a couple of tipsy young men who can be compared to him, the singing Callidamates early in Plautus's *Mostellaria* (313–348) and Chremes in the fourth act of Terence's *Eunuchus* (esp. 727–729).

In every case, the scenes that we find in our record are distinctive and easily recognizable. Indeed, some of them are even the title scenes. Rather than illustrating scenes, however, our artifacts illustrate plays, with one play represented by one scene (see Csapo 1999, Nervegna 2010, and Nervegna 2013, ch. 3, where other views are discussed). This observation squares with the hypothesis that the originals on which they are based were conceived of as a set. Similar illustrations, in other words, do not copy different archetypes. The differences that they show can rather be explained by each artist's individual alteration of the model. A corrupt image, the wishes of patrons commissioning the artifact, and constraints imposed by the overall composition within which our scenes came to be set are some of the reasons that help explain such alterations.

It can no longer be doubted that painters and mosaicists relied on copybooks. Their existence and use were already strongly suggested by replicas and extant scenes in which an image is shown in reverse, and they are now confirmed by the identification of two examples on papyrus. Copybooks made artists' work easier and faster, but they also made image transmission subject to simplification and corruption. Dioscurides's *Theophoroumene*, for example, includes a door on the left and shows the shadow that the *tympanon* player casts on the back wall, two details both omitted on other depictions. We can, however, still catch a glimpse of the shadow cast by the *tympanon* player: already misinterpreted on the Stabian fresco, it became a full-fledged altar on the battered mosaic from the Vesuvian area. On the whole, however, while copybook sketches can be blamed for corrupting some details, such as masks and costumes, they can be credited with at least occasionally preserving consistency in the use of color.[7]

Menander's plays continued to be reproduced long after they disappeared from the stage. The illustrations took on a life of their own, independent both of performance

---

[7] Donderer 2008; Csapo 1999 (use of copybooks); Green 2008: 231 (misinterpretation of the shadow). See also Nervegna 2010, which identifies a fragmentary painting from Pompeii (Ufficio Scavi di Pompei 20545; pl. 1) as an altered excerpt of the *Theophoroumene* illustration.

tradition, whether public or private, and of textual transmission. The popularity of scenes such as *Synaristosai* and *Theophoroumene* in the material record can be explained by their subject matter. As these illustrations represent a convivial scene and a scene of entertainment, they made appropriate decorations for the public areas of the houses they graced. Even after the third century CE, when Menander's texts circulated less widely and lost ground to Aristophanes's comedies, homeowners kept commissioning illustrations of them, especially in the Greek East, while making sure to identify them as scenes from Menander's comedies. By then, these images had long become a symbol of Greek culture and learning.

VISUALIZING COMEDY UNDER THE EMPIRE

It is not easy to reconstruct the details of dramatic activities under the empire. Surviving inscriptions record performances of comedy and tragedy at Greek festivals held in both the Greek East and Roman West well into the third century CE. They include two main categories for comic performances: "brand new" (*kaine*) comedy, i.e., original dramas by contemporary authors, and "old" (*palaia*) comedy—that is, our New Comedies, which are specifically recorded until around the mid-second century CE. Although we know very little about new plays—their authors' names survive only sporadically, and their texts have all but disappeared—we still can piece together snippets of information from a range of sources. We can be sure, for instance, that Menander remained the unsurpassed comic model throughout antiquity. Various intellectuals entertained themselves with comedy writing. Active under Trajan or Hadrian, for instance, was one Marcus Pomponius Bassulus, a politician who took care to record on his tombstone that he had both adapted some of Menander's plays and composed original ones so as not to spend his leisurely hours "like a sheep" (*CIL* 9.1164). Apuleius authored a (partial?) Latin adaptation of Menander's *Anechomenos* (*Anth. Lat.* 712 R; see May's chapter in this volume). When in the fourth century CE the Emperor Julian forbade Christian professors to teach classical studies, the grammarian Apollinarius of Laodicea composed his own classics; these included Christian comedies fashioned after Menander (Sozomenon, *Historia Ecclesiastica* 5.18.4).

What happened on public stages is harder to gauge, but the picture is similar. Time and again we hear of plays resembling New Comedies. Manilius, who wrote his *Astronomica* probably in the last years of Augustus's reign, could purportedly foresee a man's inclinations by reading the stars. According to him, those born when the constellation of Cepheus is rising beside Aquarius may display an interest in staging comedies with "ardent young men and maidens abducted and loved, old men tricked, and all-resourceful slaves" (*ardentis iuvenes raptasque in amore puellas / elusosque senes agilisque per omnia servos*). These are, of course, New Comedy plots—a point Manilius makes clear when he names Menander and the reputation he won through this kind of drama (5.470–476). Dreams and their meanings are the subject matter of Artemidorus's

Interpretation of Dreams, a work of the second century CE. If your dreams involve old comedies, Artemidorus warns, expect abuse and problems, but if they deal with "our comedies," a happy ending is ahead, as in the comic plots (1.56). For Artemidorus, there were only two types of comedies: one with personal abuse ("old comedy") and the other with happy marriages ("modern comedy"). According to Cassius Dio, the emperor Caracalla killed his brother Geta, condemned him to *damnatio memoriae*, and sufficiently terrified playwrights that they avoided including any character named Geta in their dramas (78.12.5). Fictitious as it may be, this anecdote suggests that the name Geta, a standard name for New Comedy slaves, was still familiar to comic poets. By contrast, plays in the style of Old Comedy are vanishingly hard to find in either the Hellenistic period or under the empire. With its family-oriented and politics-free plots, its moralizing stance and edifying maxims, New Comedy and New Comedy–style plays were well suited for the citizenry of a monarchical government.

New Comedy also set the leading iconographic model for later comedy, or so at least it can be argued by considering comic illustrations that cannot be traced to specific early-Hellenistic models. The best examples of dramatic illustrations that are independent of iconographic tradition are found in three composite pictures of episodes from a festival of Greek type: a funerary painting from the Tomba dei Ludi in Cyrene (late second century CE), a frieze from Patras in Greece (second or third century CE), and a mosaic from the Villa di Piazza Armerina in Sicily (fourth century CE).[8] Encircling the tomb from left to right, the Cyrene decorations begin and terminate in hunting scenes. In between are gladiatorial combats, chariot racing, athletic events, and musical and dramatic performances. In a very rare example of a dramatic illustration that includes verse—whether it is actually a quotation from the play or not is debated (see Perusino 1993)—a puzzled slave (his left hand is at his chin) figures in the comic scene, where he is addressed by a young man. Above the door to the young man's right a caption reads, "the door has creaked, the father is coming out." More words were originally written next to the young man; although they cannot all be deciphered, they have been plausibly reconstructed as, "I will knock myself." Since door-knocking scenes appear frequently in the Greek and Roman comic tradition, this painting seems to illustrate a common scenario; and yet if the young man here is indeed about to knock on the door of his beloved girl, there may be something special about it. In Greek and Roman New Comedy, young men in love often discuss knocking on their ladylove's door but stop short of doing so. This is the case of both the (to us) anonymous young man in Menander's *Georgos* (17) and Sostratus in *Dis Exapaton* (23–24). In Plautus's *Curculio*, Phaedromus stands before the door of the house where the pimp keeps his beloved girl, but he does not knock: he first pours wine over the door to have the doorkeeper come out, then sings a song to the door bolts (75–95; 147–157). In *Dyskolos*, Sostratus sends Pyrrhia to approach Cnemo,

---

[8] Bacchielli 2002: 295, fig. 14C (painting from Cyrene); Waywell 1979, no. 38 fig. 32; Dunbabin 2006: 198–199 with fig. 5 (frieze from Patras); Carandini, Ricci, and De Vos 1982: 284–291, pl. XLII.87; Duval 1984 and Dunbabin 2006: 205 with fig. 10 (frieze from the Villa di Piazza Armerina).

and then, after Pyrrhia's failure, he tries to enlist the services of his father's slave, Geta. It is only when everything fails that Sostratus himself goes up to Cnemo's door: ready to knock, he is held back by Gorgias's arrival (267–268). For these young lovers, knocking on the door can be considered a test of character. This test is successfully undergone by Aeschinus in Terence's *Adelphoe,* when he has finally decided to take responsibility for his actions (633–634; Cleostratos in the fourth act of Menander's *Aspis* is a different case: Csapo 1986: 199–204; see also Brown 1995). If the scene in Cyrene does represent a specific, brand new comedy, it may in turn suggest that the contemporary play reworked an old motif and provided another example of a mature young man in love. And like Menander's comedies, this play may also have been alluded to by an illustration of its most memorable scene.

Roughly contemporary with this funerary painting is a frieze from Patras, a polychrome mosaic currently preserved in the Archaeological Museum in Patras. The composition is divided into two registers, with the lower section taken up by athletic contests. In the upper level, ranged around a table with prizes are actors and assorted musicians—namely, two different kinds of cithara players, two different kinds of *aulos* players, a chorus, two groups of comic and tragic actors, a trumpeter, and a herald. The comic scene is damaged, but it includes one woman gesturing and two other figures, possibly a youth and an old man or a slave. Identifiable illustrations suggest that these three characters should comprise the entire dramatic cast; as far as we know, only excerpts include fewer figures.

Unlike the frieze from Patras, the entertainers' mosaic in the Villa di Piazza Armerina can be placed in its original display context, a bedroom (room no. 45). In keeping with other mosaics in this part of the villa, the entertainers are depicted as children engaging in various activities. In addition to performing as pipers and cithara players, for instance, they are also portrayed as putting on comedy and tragedy. The dramatic scenes are both damaged (only the bottom part of the tragic one survives) and the actors do not seem to be wearing masks, but their stage costume marks them as performers. The tragic performers have their typical high-soled boots, while the comic ones have their padding and their comic outfit underneath their costumes. Interestingly, the best-preserved comic character from Piazza Armerina seems to mix iconographic conventions. He sports the padding and scarf typical of late comic slaves, the same scarf worn by slaves on the Mytilene mosaics and on Terence miniatures—but he is holding the stick of an old man.

As with the comic scenes from Cyrene and Patras, we do not know if the illustration from the Villa di Piazza Armerina relates to a brand new comedy or if it simply stands for comedy. Given its late date, however, the case for seeing this mosaic as a reflection of contemporary dramatic production is hard to make. In all three compositions, a table with prizes is invariably present and, although the details are hard to make out, crowns and palms seem to be included both in Cyrene and in Patras. In the Villa di Piazza Armerina, the artist represented palm branches and wreaths of roses placed inside two prize crowns. He also set next to them, on either side, one money bag marked by the symbol XIIa, with a superscript bar indicating 12,500 denarii. Conspicuously placed within the frieze, the victory prizes arrest the viewer's attention and clearly signal that the *agon* alluded to is an *agon* of Greek type. Regardless of their official names, *agones* of the Greek type had cash prizes. In the letter that he wrote to regulate festivals, for instance, the emperor Hadrian took care to specify that prize money was to be "put in a bag, sealed, and put beside the crown," and, to prevent the possibility of embezzlement, the successful performer was to accept it in full sight of everyone. These cash prizes are slower to appear in the artistic record, making their way onto coins only in the late second century CE and into private artifacts slightly earlier: in symbolizing victory, crowns were evidently preferable to vulgar bags of money.[9]

The dramatic performances shown in Cyrene, Patras, and Villa Armerina are related to Greek tragedy and Greek comedy. As far as we know, Roman drama was not performed in a competitive framework either during the republic or later on.

ILLUSTRATING TERENCE'S COMEDIES

As with Roman drama in general, the Latin-language plays first staged under the republic did not enjoy an enduring appeal in ancient theaters. Late republican actors did still entertain public audiences with the revived "classics" of early Roman theater—Roscius, for instance, was famous for his role as the pimp Ballio in Plautus's *Pseudolus* (Cic. *Q. Rosc.* 20). And several emperors did sponsor varied and elaborate forms of entertainment, including dramatic performances, but our sources are frustratingly vague and the details of what plays were staged are beyond recovery. The composition of Roman comedy featuring Greek subject matter—the *palliata*—virtually died out already in the late republic. Turpilius, who died in 103 BCE, is the last author included in standard textbooks of Latin literature, and after him writers of *palliatae* are attested but sporadically.

The genre was, however, to retain great popularity in Roman schools, especially in the works of Terence. Prized for their language, they entered the school curriculum and remained favorite texts well beyond the end of antiquity. As Terence's illustrated manuscripts are the only Roman counterpart to our extraordinarily rich visual record for Greek New Comedy and Greek drama in general, they also represent the entirety of the iconographic tradition of Roman comedy.

At some point in late antiquity, Terence's comedies were copied in a manuscript beautifully decorated with miniatures illustrating their scenes. Although this original edition is lost, it can be reconstructed with some accuracy through Carolingian copies and, in particular, through four key editions. The best is a very large and essentially complete book produced in Aachen at the court of Louis the Pious at about 825 and

[9] The newly published letters by Hadrian from Alexandria Troas are conveniently translated by Slater 2008 (§§1.B, 2.E 617–618). On crowns and victory prizes, see Dunbabin's detailed and well-illustrated discussion (Dunbabin 2010).

currently preserved in the Biblioteca Apostolica Vaticana (Vat. Lat. 3868, known as C). This manuscript bears the signature of its scribe, Hrodgarius, while three hands, including that of one Aldericus, who recorded his name early in the book, decorated it with color paintings of generally skilled execution. Two other important exemplars are kept in the Bibliothèque Nationale in Paris. The most famous one, known as P (Lat. 7899), was produced at Reims in the second half of the ninth century and was illustrated by two artists. At times, their ink drawings compare well with those of the Vatican Terence, but their tendency to exaggerate figures' features and their unreliability in iconographic details impair their value for reconstructing their archetype. Similar faults impair the other Paris Terence (Lat. 7900; also known as Y or J), a manuscript of modest quality attributed to Corbie and dated to the middle of the ninth century. Its ink drawings are often crude and careless—two of them, for instance, omit a whole figure—and while the sequence of scenes is easy to follow, gestures and facial and body features can be distorted. Color drawings characterize the fourth key witness, the Ambrosian Terence (Milan, Biblioteca Ambrosiana H 75 inf. [S.P. 4bis]; also known as F) produced in tenth-century Reims. This is a fairly elaborate book, but its illustrations tend to reelaborate and often modernize their archetype rather than copy it.

Important clues to the original edition, its layout and general features, can be gathered not only from these manuscripts but also from comparison with the unillustrated Bembine Terence (Biblioteca Apostolica Vaticana, Vat. Lat. 3226; fourth or fifth century CE), our only Terence manuscript produced in antiquity. The original illustrated edition of Terence, now lost, included 6,074 lines of text and 147 regular illustrations requiring about half a page each, for a total length of some 220 folios. It was meant to be an elegant and sumptuous book, with three display pages for each comedy. Placed right after the title page and set in a frame held by two comic slaves, a portrait of Terence opened the work—presumably, given his short career and premature death, an imaginary portrait. In it, Terence was, interestingly, given the beard typical of classical and early-Hellenistic Greek authors (and of later Hellenizing figures, such as Hadrian). Placed before each comedy were a production notice (*didascalia*) recording the details of the play's first performance and, on the facing page, an aedicula containing the characters' masks, arranged in their order of appearance. Then followed the plot summary (*argumentum*), written in verse and attributed to the second-century CE scholar Sulpicius Apollinaris. Finally came the beginning of the play under the title *prologus*, which featured a miniature illustrating the prologue speaker. The only exception to this pattern is *Andria*. Its production note went unrecorded, leaving a blank page, and the title *prologus* was never added, either.

In the archetype, Terence's text was probably written in rustic capitals and with proper verse division. When copying the lines, the scribe left an appropriate space for the illustrations; later on, after the artist had completed his work, he went back to label the characters. The Bembine Terence has a list of characters at the beginning of each scene, with the characters' names arranged in the order in which they first speak. When the painter created his miniatures, all of which he placed above the first verse of each scene, he tended to follow the same order that we find in the characters lists found in the Bembine

Terence. Although some scholars have sought to link these illustrations to theatrical performances at the time when the original edition was produced, the miniatures are in fact pictorial renderings of these cast lists.[10] They do not follow earlier models but are instead invented according to some basic principles. The artist generally chose to illustrate each scene by its opening action and to add minimal stage property; a door, often decorated with a curtain, is included in several instances. The artist also distinguished characters by costume rather than mask.

For several reasons, characters' masks in the illustrated manuscripts cannot be easily categorized. First, they are not consistently reproduced in later miniatures in the way they first appear in the aedicula introducing the play. Nor are they necessarily consistent with the text. In *Phormio*, for instance, the slave Davus is said to be red-haired, but color illustrations give him brown hair.[11] A large mouth characterizes both old men and slaves, whose masks are often interchangeable. Also interchangeable are the masks worn by young men, female slaves, and women both young and old: all share the same light complexion and small mouth, with hairstyle often their only differentiating feature (women's hair is normally parted). Since each category of characters sports its own specific attire, costumes are more easily classified. A long-sleeved fitted undergarment, a tunic with vertical stripes (*clavi*), and the Greek cloak (*pallium*) comprise the outfit of both old and young men, but young men tend to wear their cloak in a different way. Slaves have only an undergarment and a tunic, with a belt over their padded belly and a scarf over their shoulder or around their neck. Unlike men, women wear a tunic reaching down to their ankles; this hides their slippers (men wear sandals instead). Yet details of costume are not always above confusion. As Wright (2006: 100–101) notes, we may be able to identify at least one instance of misrepresentation in the original edition by comparing the miniatures that show *Adelphoe* 2.1, the scene that Terence famously claims (6–11) to have incorporated "word-for-word" from Diphilus's *Synapothneskontes*. By this point in the play, Aeschinus, who is a young man, has already abducted from the pimp Sannio the music girl loved by his brother Ctesipho. Sannio asks for financial compensation; Aeschinus responds by having his slave Parmeno hit him. The miniature for this scene—including, in what would be the correct order, Parmeno, Sannio, the music girl (a mute character), and Aeschinus right next to her—displays confusion at several levels. The artist's decision to reject the speaking order has resulted in incorrect labeling in C and other manuscripts; moreover, in two of our main editions, C and P (figure 37.4), Aeschinus is given a long tunic—he has, that is, been turned into a woman.

Our illustrated editions of Terence preserve the name of Calliopius in several places. It appears on the title page, in the final colophon, and at the end of each comedy, normally in the formula *Calliopius recensui*. From these notes we conclude the only fact

---

[10] The connection between the original miniatures and theatrical activities has been most recently defended by Dodwell 2000 (esp. ch. 2) and Dutsch 2007; see also the chapter by Demetriou in this volume.

[11] Terence *Phormio* 51 (*rufus*). See Wright (2006: 219), who also discusses other discrepancies between how characters are described in the text and how they are reproduced in the miniatures.

FIGURE 37.4 Terence, *Adelphoe*, act 2, scene 1. P; fol. 100ʳ. After Jones and Morey 1931, Vol. 2, fig. 465.

we can know about Calliopius—that he supervised the quality of the text. The original edition was produced at his scriptorium, probably in Rome and probably around 400 CE, as indicated by features such as the style or shape of figures.[12] This original edition was a wonderfully imaginative work of art and a pioneer of its kind. The artists who copied its illustrations in later editions tended to reproduce their late-antique features, but occasionally created new, original miniatures. The best examples are found in a Terence manuscript (Vat. Lat. 3305; also known as S) probably produced just after 1100 in the Loire valley and only partially illustrated with ten miniatures. The frontispiece of this book is elaborately decorated with a composite picture set within a frame resembling an aedicula (Jones and Morey 1931: 163–174 with fig. 10). On the bottom level, the artist drew two original illustrations containing two characters each (Simo and Davus on the left, Pamphilus and Glycerium on the right). The two drawings are both related to *Andria* but, surprisingly, do not illustrate any specific episode in it. On the top level, the artist created a remarkably imaginative debate scene set before an audience labeled

---

[12] Wright 2006, esp. 209; Dodwell (2000, ch. 1), however, argues that the date of the original should be lowered to the third century mostly because of the hairstyle of Terence's portrait and the use of ground lines in our miniatures. Since ground lines are also found in North African mosaics dated to the second and third centuries CE, Dodwell suggests that the original manuscript was produced in North Africa.

"Romans." On the left sits Terence himself, confronted by two figures on his right: they are his "rivals" (*adversarii*), named "Luscius" and "Livinius." Between them, higher up, sits Calliopius. The artist had read both Terence and works on Terence. He knew of the controversy between Terence and other contemporary poets from Terence's prologues and he was familiar with Luscius Lanuvinus, whose name he must have mistaken, from scholarly tradition. Terence never mentions Luscius, but Donatus took care to record his identity in his commentary on Terence's plays. Finally, the artist was also acquainted with Calliopius. He came across him in the illustrated editions that he saw and followed in some of his miniatures.

With his left hand pointing to Terence and his right to Terence's rivals, Calliopius is here crossing his arms. The prologue speaker of *Andria* also points in both directions; he is, like Calliopius, a medieval figure. They bear comparison with an original miniature from the *Heauton Timorumenos* that reproduces Chremes and Syrus in the Ambrosian Terence (figure 37.5; see also Wright 2006: 200 with fig. 10). The oddity of this illustration stands out sharply. Both characters are speaking in the wrong way—they are gesticulating with their left hands— and, by covering his right arm, Chremes's cloak is also misplaced. Here too the artist has created medieval figures, but even in his misunderstanding he betrays some familiarity with the classical tradition. He has given his characters their standard comic costumes: Chremes has his undergarment, tunic, and cloak, while Syrus sports the scarf typical of late comic slaves.

FIGURE 37.5 Invented miniature for Terence, *Heauton Timorumenos* 593. F. fol. 36ᵛ. After Jones and Morey 1931, Vol. 2, fig. 385.

FURTHER READING

The single most important work on the iconography of New Comedy is Webster, Green, and Seeberg (1996), a two-volume study that combines a thorough collection of our monuments reproducing New Comedy with careful and insightful discussion. The chapter titled "Survey of the Evidence" is particularly valuable. Readers should also consult Green (forthcoming), which updates the collection. Important contributions on the visual record for Greek New Comedy and Greek theater in general are Green (1994), Csapo (1999), Csapo (2010), and Dunbabin (2006). Nervegna (2013) includes a chapter on the iconographic tradition of both Menander and his comedies. Green and Handley (1995) and Moraw and Nölle (2002) provide expert and beautifully illustrated discussion of our visual record for Greek drama in general. The definitive study on the lost original of our illustrated editions of Terence's comedies is Wright (2006), which includes a full description of our key witnesses. Jones and Morey (1931) remains valuable for its illustrations.

BIBLIOGRAPHY

Abadie-Reynal, C., J.-P. Darmon, and A.-M. Manière-Lévêque. 2003. "La maison et la mosaïque des *Synaristôsai* (*Les femmes au déjeuner* de Ménandre)." In *Zeugma: Interim Reports: Rescue Excavations (Packard Humanities Institute), Inscription of Antiochus I, Bronze Statue of Mars, House and Mosaïc of the Synaristôsai, and Recent Work on the Roman Army at Zeugma*, edited by R. Early et al., 79–99. Portsmouth, RI: Journal of Roman Archaeology.

Bacchielli, L. 2002. "La «Tomba dei Ludi a Cirene»: Dai viaggiatori dell'Ottocento alla riscoperta." *Quaderni di Archeologia della Libia* 16: 285–312.

Bassett, S. E. 2008. "The Late Antique Image of Menander." *GRBS* 48: 201–225.

Brown, P. G. McC. 1995. "Aeschinus at the Door: Terence *Adelphoe* 632–43 and the Traditions of Greco-Roman Comedy." In *Papers of the Leeds International Latin Seminar*. Vol. 8, *Roman Comedy, Augustan Poetry, Historiography*, edited by R. Brock and A. J. Woodman, 71–89. Leeds: F. Cairns.

Carandini, A., A. Ricci, and M. De Vos. 1982. *Filosofiana: La Villa di Piazza Armerina: Immagine di un aristocratico romano al tempo di Costantino*. Palermo: S. F. Flaccovio.

Çelik, Ö. 2009. "Yukarı Harbiye mozaik kurtarma kazısı (Perikeiromene, Philadelphoi, Syaristosai, Theophorosmene)." In *17. Müze çalışmaları ve kurtarma kazıları sempozyumu (28 nisan–1 mayıs 2008, Side)*, edited by A. N. Toy and C. Keskin, 41–52. Ankara: T. C. Kültür ve Turizm Bakanlığı.

Charitonides, S., L. Kahil, and R. Ginouvès 1970. *Les mosaïques de la Maison du Ménandre à Mytilène*. Bern: Francke.

Cribiore, R. 2001. *Gymnastics of the Mind: Greek Education in Hellenistic and Roman Egypt*. Princeton: Princeton University Press.

Csapo, E. 1986. "Stock Scenes in Greek Comedy." Ph.D. diss., University of Toronto.

——. 1999. "Performance and Iconographic Tradition in the Illustrations of Menander." *Syllecta Classica* 10: 154–188.

——. 2010. *Actors and Icons of the Ancient Theatre*. Malden, MA: Wiley-Blackwell.

——. Forthcoming. "The Iconography of Comedy." In *The Cambridge Companion to Greek Comedy*, edited by M. Revermann. Cambridge, UK: Cambridge University Press.

Dodwell, C. R. 2000. *Anglo-Saxon Gestures and the Roman Stage*. Cambridge, UK: Cambridge University Press.

Donderer, W. 2008. "Antike Musterbücher und (k)ein Ende: Ein neuer Papyrus und die Aussage der Mosaiken." *Musiva et Sectilia* 2–3 [2005–2006]: 81–113.

Dunbabin, K. M. D. 2006. "A Theatrical Device on the Late Roman Stage: The Relief of Flavius Valerianus." *JRA* 19: 191–212.

———. 2010. "The Prize Table: Crowns, Wreaths and Moneybags in Roman Art." In *L'argent dans les concours du monde grec*, edited by B. Le Guen, 301–345. Saint-Denis: Presses Universitaires de Vincennes.

Dutsch, D. 2007. "Gestures in the Manuscripts of Terence and Late Revivals of Literary Drama." *Gesture* 7: 39–71.

Duval, N. 1984. "Les concours sur les mosaïques de Piazza Armerina: Prix et tirage au sort: L'influence de l'agonistique grecque." In *La villa romana del Casale di Piazza Armerina: Atti della IV Riunione scientifica della Scuola di perfezionamento in archeologia classica dell'Università di Catania (Piazza Armerina, 28 settembre–1 ottobre 1983)*, edited by G. Rizza, 157–169. Catania: Università di Catania, Istituto di archeologia.

Fittschen, K. 1991. "Zur Rekonstruktion griechischer Dichterstatuen. 1.Teil: Die Statue des Menander." *MDAI(A)* 106: 243–279.

Green, J. R. 1985. "Drunk Again: A Study in the Iconography of the Comic Theatre." *AJA* 89: 465–472.

———. 1994. *Theatre in Ancient Greek Society*. London and New York: Routledge.

———. 2008. "Theatre Production: 1996–2006." *Lustrum* 50: 1–390.

———. Forthcoming. "Additions and Alterations to *MNC³*." *BICS*.

Green, J. R., and E. Handley. 1995. *Images of the Greek Theatre*. London: British Museum Press.

Gutzwiller, K., and Ö. Çelik. 2012. "New Menander Mosaics from Antioch." *AJA* 116: 573–623.

Ivanov, T. 1954. *Une mosaïque romaine de Ulpia Oescus*. Sofia: Académie bulgare des Sciences.

Jones, L. W., and C. R. Morey. 1931. *The Miniatures of the Manuscripts of Terence*. Princeton: Princeton University Press.

Lancha, J. 1997. *Mosaïque et culture dans l'Occident romain (Iᵉʳ–IVᵉ s)*. Rome: L'Erma di Bretschneider.

Markoulaki, S. 1990. "Ψηφιδωτά 'Οικίας Διονύσου' στο Μουσείο Χανίων." In *Πεπραγμένα του ΣΤ΄ Διεθνούς Κρητολογικού Συνεδρίου 24–30 Αυγ. 1986*, 449–463. Chania, Greece: Philologikos Syllogos Chanion "O Chrysostomos."

Moraw, S., and E. Nölle, eds. 2002. *Die Geburt des Theaters in der griechischen Antike*. Mainz: Von Zabern.

Nervegna, S. 2010. "Menander's *Theophoroumene* between Greece and Rome." *AJPh* 131: 23–68.

———. 2013. *Menander in Antiquity: The Contexts of Reception*. Cambridge, UK: Cambridge University Press.

Perusino, F. 1993. "Commedia nuova a Cirene." In *Tradizione e innovazione nella cultura greca da Omero all'età ellenistica: Studi in onore di B. Gentili II*, edited by R. Pretagostini, 735–40. Rome: Gruppo Editoriale Internazionale.

Richter, G. M. 1965. *The Portraits of the Greeks*. Vol. 2, *The Fourth and Third Centuries: The Third and Second Centuries*. London: Phaidon Press.

———. 1984. *The Portraits of the Greeks*. Abridged and revised by R. R. R. Smith. Oxford: Phaidon Press.

Slater, W. 2008. "Hadrian's Letters to the Athletes and Dionysiac Artists concerning Arrangements for the 'Circuit' of Games." *JRA* 21: 610–620.

Strocka, V. 1977. *Die Wandmalerei der Hanghäuser in Ephesos*. Vienna: Verlag der Österreichische Akademie der Wissenschaften.

Waywell, S. E. 1979. "Roman Mosaics in Greece." *AJA* 83: 293–321.

Webster, T. B. L, J. R. Green, and A. Seeberg. 1995. *Monuments Illustrating New Comedy*. 3rd ed. London: Institute of Classical Studies.

Wright, D. H. 2006. *The Lost Late Antique Illustrated Terence*. Vatican City: Biblioteca Apostolica Vaticana.

....

CHAPTER 38

GREEK COMEDY, THE NOVEL, AND EPISTOLOGRAPHY

....

REGINA HÖSCHELE

PART I: THE RECEPTION OF COMEDY IN THE NOVEL

....

CHARITON's *Callirhoe* (mid-first cent. CE), the oldest of the five love novels to survive from Greek antiquity,[1] contains a scene of stunning theatricality featuring a rapid-fire exchange between two men who are rivals in love for a woman. Were it not for the fact that their verbal altercation begins with the introductory formulae Χαιρέας μὲν ἔλεγε ("Chaereas said") and Διονύσιος δὲ ("but Dionysius") before switching into virtual *antilabai*, and were it not that it is written in prose instead of iambic trimeters, one might think that the episode came straight out of comedy. To illustrate just how closely it is related to comic stichomythia, let me rearrange the layout of the passage (5.8.5) so that it assumes the aspect of a dramatic text—the change is a very slight one, indeed:

CHAER.	"I am her first husband."
DION.	"I am a more steadfast one."
CHAER.	"Did I divorce my wife?"
DION.	"No, but you buried her."
CHAER.	"Show me the divorce certificate!"
DION.	"You can see her tomb."
CHAER.	"Her father gave her to me in marriage."
DION.	"She gave herself to me."
CHAER.	"You are not worthy of Hermocrates's daughter!"
DION.	"You even less so, having been kept in chains by Mithridates!"

---

[1] Some scholars even view Chariton as the inventor of the genre; cf. most recently Tilg 2010.

CHAER.   "I demand Callirhoe back."
DION.   "I am keeping her."
CHAER.   "You're seizing another man's wife."
DION.   "You killed yours."
CHAER.   "Adulterer!"
DION.   "Murderer!"

This clash between Dionysius and Chaereas follows the latter's miraculous appearance during a trial after he had been declared dead, which the author characterizes as a spectacle worthy of the stage: ποῖος ποιητὴς ἐπὶ σκηνῆς παράδοξον μῦθον οὕτως εἰσήγαγεν οὕτως ἔδοξας ἂν ἐν θεάτρῳ παρεῖναι μυρίων παθῶν πλήρει ("What poet ever put such an astounding story on stage? It was like being in a theater filled with thousands of emotions," 5.8.2). The narrator's question here, with its reference to the theater, serves almost like a cue to readers to think back to analogous situations in earlier drama. Our attention is similarly drawn to the narrative's theatricality when the audience is said to have listened to the quarrel of the two rivals "not without pleasure" (οὐκ ἀηδῶς, 5.8.6), a reaction which underlines the dialogue's closeness to comparable scenes in comedy.

Chariton's theatrical references[2] and his imitation of an antilabic exchange are not coincidental: they point to an affinity between Greek comedy and the amatory novel that extends far beyond the above-quoted passage. Notoriously polyphonic, the novel has absorbed distinctive elements from a great variety of genres (Fusillo 1989: 17–109), but the thematic and structural matrix to which it adheres most closely is taken from New Comedy; in either case, the text's telos is the union of two lovers, who need to overcome a series of obstacles—be it a misunderstanding, the opposition of a parent or physical separation—before living happily ever after. As the novel presents a particularly complex case of *Gattungskreuzung*, comedy is, of course, not the only model operative here, but the confines of the present chapter do not allow me to discuss the textual dynamics resulting from this fusion of multiple genres in greater detail.

Limiting our observations to the relationship of comedy and the novel, then, we may first of all note that they both follow a rather formulaic narrative scheme and feature a number of stock characters. However, stereotypical though the plots may be, a good deal of variation is possible, as individual texts may alter standard motifs and invert generic convention. Even if we know only a tiny fraction of the plays available to Imperial authors, the inspiration they drew from New Comedy is unmistakable (cf. Corbato 1968, Borgogno 1971, Fusillo 1989: 43–55, Paulsen 1992, Crismani 1997, Brethes 2007: 13–63, Smith 2007: 104–110). It is important to recall that Menander was widely read at the time and considered second only to Homer.[3] The two authors were indeed

---

[2] The novel with the greatest number of such dramatic references is Heliodorus's *Aethiopica* (Walden 1894; Paulsen 1992: 21–41).

[3] The two second-century CE herms of Menander and Homer from the so-called Villa of Aelian, each inscribed with three epigrams in honor of the respective poet (IG XIV 1183 and 1188), are a case in point. According to one of the poems, the ranking of Menander after Homer goes back to the Hellenistic grammarian Aristophanes.

frequently paired, in both poetic and rhetorical contexts, as the two main representatives of Greek literature, their works being considered the pinnacle of elevated poetry on the one hand and of the lighthearted tradition on the other (Pini 2006). It should thus not come as a surprise to us that the novelists were intimately familiar with the world of New Comedy and turned to the plays of Menander as a primary model when writing romantic tales of their own.

This influence manifests itself not so much through direct allusions, though these do exist, as through the appropriation of typically comedic elements and the novels' overall "Menandrian spirit." The parallels adduced below are thus not necessarily meant to suggest that a scene or character is based on a specific play, but rather serve to illustrate the genre's general impact. As we shall see, the novelists not only imitated many standard elements of plot such as mix-ups, intrigues, coincidences, or the misconception of status, but their character portrayal is also strongly inspired by that of Menandrian drama.

Since Old Comedy, with its bawdy humor, political satire, and fantastic plots, has little in common with the world of romance and played no significant role in the composition of these amatory tales,[4] my discussion will focus on the novels' engagement with Menander. It should, however, be noted that Aristophanic influence is a great deal more palpable in certain "fringe" novels, i.e., fictional prose texts of the postclassical age that offer novel-like narratives.[5] Among them we find, for instance, Antonius Diogenes's *Wonders Beyond Thule* (probably second cent. CE), which recounts the miraculous travel adventures of a pair of siblings. The text itself has not come down to us, but we do have a summary by the ninth-century patriarch Photius (*Bibliotheke* 109a–112a), according to which its narrator presented himself as a poet of "Old Comedy," though the precise meaning of κωμῳδία παλαιά in this context is disputed (Morgan 2009: 135–136). Lucian's *True Stories*, in turn, a science-fiction-like travelogue from the second cent. CE, marks its debt to Old Comedy by having the narrator sail by Cloudcookooland (*VH* 1.29), whose sight makes him remember "Aristophanes the poet, a wise and truthful man, who was wrongly disbelieved for what he had written" (on this text cf. Möllendorff 2000).

But let us return to the novels proper. Set in a bourgeois world and not in the mythical realm of epic or tragedy, both novel and comedy are concerned with the private lives and sentiments of citizens. Of course, there are also remarkable differences. The novel's narrative form, for one, allows it to move far beyond the spatiotemporal boundaries of drama, its protagonists sent to exotic places and their adventures stretching out over months, if not years. Another important aspect is the active role of the female protagonist, which differs greatly from the silence characterizing comic *parthenoi* (Brethes 2007: 51–53). In comedy, women only appear as agents if they are courtesans, not citizens (think, for instance, of Chrysis in the *Samia* or Habrotonon in the *Epitrepontes*;

---

[4] The passage in Achilles Tatius (8.9.1) where a character is said to "rival with the comedy of Aristophanes" and to speak "in the witty style of comedy" (ἀστείως καὶ κωμῳδικῷ) is exceptional; cf. Brethes 2007: 21–23.

[5] For the term, cf. Holzberg (1996); see also the recent edited volume Grammatiki (2009).

on women in Menander, cf. Traill 2008). By way of contrast, the novelistic heroines do everything to protect their virginity or preserve their chastity, courageously fending for themselves and devising ways to escape their various predicaments (often more success-fully than their male counterparts, whose masculinity is cast into doubt by the females' greater agility and cunning; cf. Egger 1999, Haynes 2003). Theirs is, as Konstan (1994) describes it, a *symmetrical* relationship,[6] which has little to do with the amorous entan-glements that are the stuff of New Comedy, even if both genres in their own way do pro-mote marriage as a civic ideal (Egger 1994; Lape 2004).

With their portrayal of eternal love and unwavering fidelity, the five erotic novels— Chariton's *Callirhoe*, Xenophon of Ephesus's *Ephesiaka* (second cent.), Achilles Tatius's *Leucippe and Clitophon* (second half of the second cent.), Longus's *Daphnis and Chloe* (late second/early third cent.) and Heliodorus' *Aethiopica* (third or fourth cent.)— are commonly characterized as idealistic and distinguished from the comic-realistic novel, which is represented by Petronius's *Satyrica*, Apuleius's *Metamorphoses,* and Ps.-Lucian's epitome of the Greek *Ass*-story.[7] A remarkable analogy between these erotic narratives and comedy is drawn by Macrobius in his commentary on Cicero's *Somnium Scipionis* (1.2.8): "Comedies [*comoediae*], such as Menander and his imita-tors brought to the stage, please the ear, as do narratives [*argumenta*] filled with the fictional calamities of lovers [*fictis casibus amatorum referta*], at which Petronius often tried his hand and with which also Apuleius, to our amazement, played from time to time." The relation of the Latin novels to their Greek counterparts and their own engagement with the comic tradition has been discussed elsewhere and will not be of concern to us here (cf. May 2007 and in this volume; on mimic and other the-atrical elements in Petronius, cf. Panayotakis 1995). What is crucial in our context is Macrobius's perception of a close affinity between comedy and erotic prose fiction; he, in fact, subsumes both under the same category by characterizing them as "a class of stories [*genus fabularum*], which exclusively displays things that delight the audience [*delicias aurium*]".

In addition, it is worthy of note that later readers such as Photius referred to the nov-els, for which the ancients had no standard name, as *dramata* or *dramatika,* the word *drama* being used synonymously with *plasma* to describe stories that, although made up, could in fact have happened (cf. Rohde 1876: 350–352). Even if this label should not be taken to mean that the novel was identified with theatrical drama, it certainly points in the same direction as Macrobius's juxtaposition of comedy and erotic prose fiction: the two genres were obviously thought to belong to the same literary sphere.

It is, of course, not only their common wish to entertain that invites such an asso-ciation. As mentioned above, the novel essentially follows the same pattern as New

---

[6] According to Lalanne 2006, this symmetry represents a pre-adult stage and the novels portray a form of *rite de passage*, by the end of which the male protagonists take on their dominant role; on initiation and its narrative function in the novel, see also Bierl 2007.

[7] For treatments of the genre, cf. Perry 1967, Hägg 1983, Fusillo 1989, Reardon 1991, Holzberg 1995, and Whitmarsh 2011; see also the edited volumes Tatum 1994, Schmeling 1996, and Whitmarsh 2008.

Comedy, in which a series of intrigues and mix-ups typically precedes the happy union of two lovers. In both genres, the force that drives most happenings is Tyche, who, according to the intrinsically Hellenistic concept of fortune, interferes with human intentions and brings about unexpected twists and turns (Vogt-Spira 1992; Fusillo 1989: 43–47; Brethes 2007: 39–45). Functioning, for instance, as the prologue goddess of Menander's *Aspis*, Tyche reveals that Cleostratus, whom everybody believes to be dead, is actually alive (97–148): the body that his slave discovered after a surprise attack by the barbarians belonged to his neighbor, who had accidentally grabbed the other's shield when running out to battle (105–108). It is this initial confusion and subsequent mis-identification that sets the plot of the play in motion.

In the novels, too, Fortune often directs the order of events and is responsible for many of the calamities befalling their protagonists. Let us take *Leucippe and Clitophon* as an example. The hero's father Hippias was making plans to betroth him to his half-sister when, we are told, "Tyche initiated the drama" (ἤρχετο τοῦ δράματος ἡ Τύχη, 1.3.3)— the debt to comedy could hardly be signaled in stronger terms! Since his city is at war, Hippias's half-brother sends his wife and daughter to stay with the former's family, and Clitophon immediately falls in love with the girl. The two elope—only to end up in a shipwreck and be separated by brigands. After various trials, the lovers are reunited, but not for long, as the girl is once more kidnapped and Clitophon once more witnesses what he believes to be her execution.

Six months later, he discovers that one day, after they had run away, a letter of Leucippe's father arrived proposing an engagement between the two (5.10.3). The lover bitterly bewails Fortune's cruel joke (5.11.1). "What bride is Tyche giving me," he asks, "a bride whose corpse she did not even give me in its entirety?" (5.11.2). We thus learn, halfway through the novel, that "none of these things would have happened if the letter had been delivered faster" (5.10.4): had the mail arrived one day earlier, there would be no adventures to tell. Fortune thus appears virtually in an authorial role, as the existence of the story itself is entirely dependent on an ill-fated coincidence—as Hunter (1994: 1063) put it, "in such a narrative even random 'chance' is planned."

Chariton, in turn, has Aphrodite interfere with the machinations of Tyche so as to put an end to the sufferings of Chaereas and Callirhoe. At the beginning of Book 8, just as the two lovers are to be reunited, we learn that "Tyche was about to accomplish something as grim as it was unexpected […] but this seemed too cruel to Aphrodite" (8.1.2). Read as a metaliterary comment, this passage seems to suggest that the story could go on, the author/Fortune could introduce still more surprising twists, the list of misadventures could basically be expanded ad infinitum, but enough is enough, love must be satisfied and an idealistic novel needs to reach its conclusion (on this passage and the novels' narrative telos, cf. Whitmarsh 2009: 144–146). Significantly, the narrator declares that this final book will be the most pleasant for his readers (τὸ τελευταῖον τοῦτο σύγγραμμα τοῖς ἀναγινώσκουσιν ἥδιστον, 8.1.4) and announces a happy ending strongly reminiscent of comedy: "No more piracy or slavery or trial or battle or suicide or war or captivity in this one, but genuine love and lawful marriage!"

At this point in the narrative Aphrodite has forgiven Chaereas for his "ill-timed jealousy" (ἄκαιρον ζηλοτυπίαν, 8.1.3), which had caused the lovers' separation in the first place. It is worth recalling this initial conflict, since it shows the hero behaving under the influence of anger (ὀργή) in a way akin to that of certain characters in comedy (Borgogno 1971: 258–259). Out of envy, Callirhoe's former suitors make Chaereas believe that she is committing adultery. He tries to catch the supposed perpetrator, but only stumbles upon his unsuspecting wife. In a jealous rage, he kicks her so hard that she faints, is believed dead, and is actually buried (this is the murder Dionysius refers to in the dialogue quoted above). Compare Polemo's behavior in Menander's *Perikeiromene*: when Glycera embraces her brother Moschio, Polemo misconstrues the situation and angrily shaves off her hair. Charisius, in the *Epitrepontes*, similarly directs his fury against his wife, when he learns that she has exposed a baby, which he believes to be by another man, while he himself is the one who had raped Pamphile before their wedding. Like Chaereas, both protagonists quickly come to regret their impulsive reaction. Notably, Menander's first play was entitled *Orge*, and it is a fair guess that it featured Anger personified and dealt with someone seized by this emotion, just as Polemo's behavior is inspired by Agnoia (Misapprehension), who functions as prologue goddess in the *Perikeiromene* (in both genres, the characters' ignorance of things known to the audience tends to produce dramatic irony). The type of the rash young man represented by Chaereas may serve as an example of the various stock figures, for whose depiction the novelists clearly drew inspiration from New Comedy, while Menander himself seems to have been inspired by the *Characters* of Theophrastus.

In his despair over Callirhoe's supposed death, Chaereas tries to take his own life, but is held back by his friend Polycharmus, whose main function over the course of the novel seems to be just that: to stop the hero from killing himself (1.5.2, 1.6.1, 5.10.10, 6.2.8, 6.2.11). This too is a stock motif in comedy, where spurned lovers often indulge in pathetic laments and suicidal fantasies. To name just one example: in the *Misoumenos*, Thrasonides contemplates suicide when faced with the hatred of his beloved, which leads his slave Geta to remove all swords from the house as a precautionary measure. Though a soldier, Thrasonides does not behave like the *miles gloriosus* type so often ridiculed in Plautine comedy (Mastromarco 2009). His noble character traits, in fact, seem to have provided a model for Chariton's Dionysius, the only male rival in the Greek novels to be portrayed in a positive light (Brethes 2007: 32–35) and functioning as an embodiment of Hellenic *paideia* (1.12.6). Where Thrasonides refuses to use force on Crateia, even though she is under his power, Dionysius is outraged at his steward's suggestion that he inflict violence on Callirhoe, whom he has bought as a slave: "Shall I rule as a tyrant over a free body? Shall I, Dionysius, famed for his temperance [σωφροσύνη], violate a woman against her will?" (2.6.3).[8]

Chariton significantly marks the association between the two by inserting into his narrative a line from the opening scene of the *Misoumenos*, which features Thrasonides

---

[8] This speech implicitly contrasts two forms of political rule: democracy (associated with Greece) and tyranny (associated with Persia); cf. Smith 2007: 76–86. On Menander's reinforcement of democratic values, cf. Lape 2004.

pacing to and fro in front of his own house, ἐξὸν καθεύδειν τήν τ᾽ ἐρωμένην ἔχειν ("when I could be asleep and hold my darling in my arms," A9 Sandbach). This same iambic verse is used to underline Dionysius's regret at having brought Callirhoe to Babylon, where he finds himself at risk of losing her to any number of rivals, when "he could be asleep and hold his darling in his arms" (4.7.7; note how the absence of personal pronouns facilitates the transfer of Menander's phrase from a first-person monologue to a third-person account). Of all the novelists, Chariton most frequently intersperses his prose with poetic quotations, taken primarily from Homer (Fusillo 1990; Robiano 2000). This mingling of prose and poetry might seem somewhat inorganic, but the intertextual effects are often subtler than they appear at first sight, as is the case here. By featuring Dionysius in the role of Thrasonides, Chariton, I suggest, not only invites us to draw a parallel between their noble characters, but to perceive a further analogy in their respective situations: just as Crateia mistakenly believes her brother to have been killed by Thrasonides, Callirhoe is wrong to think that Chaereas has perished. Even if the revelation that those presumed dead are alive leads to diametrically opposed results in each case (marriage in one, separation in the other), Chariton's quotation of Menander's line implicitly highlights this structural correspondence and might be read as a foreshadowing of Chaereas's unexpected "comeback."

Scheintod ("apparent death") in fact is a common element in both genres. Apart from Chaereas and Crateia's brother, we might, for instance, think of Cleostratus's alleged death in the *Aspis*, Callirhoe's burial, or the two "executions" of Leucippe mentioned above. Another instance of misapprehension may relate to social status. If the beloved in comedy is a *hetaira*, a legitimate union in wedlock can be facilitated through a lucky coincidence identifying her as the long-lost daughter of a citizen (Traill 2008: 14–78). This recognition, or anagnorisis, is often brought about by birth tokens or *gnorismata* (Hähnle 1929). In the *Perikeiromene*, for instance, it is a box of ornaments that lets Pataecus recognize Glycera as the daughter whom he had exposed, together with her twin brother, after the death of his wife and his sudden loss of fortune.[9] Longus's pastoral novel offers a variation on this motif by culminating in a double anagnorisis, which reveals first Daphnis and then Chloe to be the offspring of rich, city-dwelling parents (each was exposed at birth and found by a farmer, while being suckled by a she-goat/sheep).[10] Daphnis's identification temporarily creates a social difference between him and Chloe that threatens to stand in the way of their marriage—an obstacle well known from comedy. The introduction of a city milieu at the end, moreover, transfers Longus's "rural comedy" into the typical urban setting of New Comedy. While the countryside, which forms the background of Daphnis and Chloe's romance, closely connects the

[9] On Glycera's role between courtesan and wife, cf. Konstan 1987.
[10] On comic and comedic elements in *Daphnis and Chloe*, cf. Heiserman 1977: 130–145, Bretzigheimer 1988, Hunter 1983: 67–70, and Crismani 1997: 87–101.

narrative with the pastoral genre, it also brings to mind Menander's *Dyskolos*, where Pan, a crucial deity in Longus, makes Sostratus fall in love with a peasant girl.

Heliodorus's Charicleia, too, was exposed as a baby together with birth tokens: her mother, the Ethiopian queen Persinna, had been afraid her husband would suspect her of adultery when their child was miraculously born with white skin. The final recognition of Charicleia as the king's daughter, which saves her and Theagenes from being sacrificed to the gods, has a much more "dramatic" flair to it than the conclusion of *Daphnis and Chloe* (Fusillo 1989: 53–55; Bretzigheimer 1999: 72–84). One is, for example, reminded of Euripides's *Ion*, where an anagnorisis prevents mother and son from killing each other. The *Aethiopica* does have a happy ending, and its finale is marked as comedy-like not least by the phrase ὥσπερ λαμπάδιον δράματος (10.39.2), which evokes the use of torches in Old and New Comedy endings (Arnott 1965). Altogether, however, the narrative seems to have incorporated more elements from tragedy than comedy (Paulsen 1992; on Heliodorus's use of pseudo-tragedy, cf. Bretzigheimer 1999). But then New Comedy, too, is strongly influenced by the late dramas of Euripides, and Satyrus, in his *Vita* of the poet (P.Oxy. 1176, fr. 39, col. 7.8–22), significantly remarks that Euripides had brought to perfection the typical devices of the νεωτέρα κωμῳδία, including "peripeties, violations of virgins, swappings of children, recognitions through rings or necklaces."

As this close association between tragic and comedic features serves to remind us, we should not try to determine a single generic paradigm for the novel, and the present discussion does not suggest that the various motifs mentioned above reminded the ancient reader exclusively of comedy. The concept of Tyche, for instance, likewise played a crucial role in the dramatic historiography of the Hellenistic age, while historiography as a genre provided another important matrix for the Greek novelists (Morgan 1982; Fusillo 1989: 57–68; Hunter 1994). Recognition, in turn, is an essential motif in Homer's *Odyssey*, the travel narrative par excellence, which functions as a primary model for the novels' tales of adventure and clearly stands behind the narrative structure of Heliodorus's *Aethiopica* (Whitmarsh 1998). It would also be a misconception to think that each author engaged with comedy and the comic in the same way. As Brethes (2007) shows, they all employ different comic devices: where Chariton's novel is full of irony, Xenophon indulges in sensationalism, Heliodorus focuses on textual *enigmata* and surprise effects, while Achilles Tatius, with his special taste for the exaggerated and grotesque, exploits the limited perspective of his first-person narrator for comic purposes.[11] But even if the novelists have brought together and appropriated elements from a great variety of genres in composing their erotic narratives, there can be no doubt that New Comedy is to be regarded as one of their most influential models.

---

[11] Brethes excludes *Daphnis and Chloe* from his analysis, since it transposes the novelistic genre into the realm of pastoral.

PART II: THE RECEPTION OF COMEDY IN EPISTOLARY COLLECTIONS

We have seen how various characters in the novels are based on figures from comedy. Significantly, one of its most amusing stock types, the parasite (Nesselrath 1985: 15–121; Tylawski 2002; Antonsen-Resch 2005), makes his appearance in the fourth book of *Daphnis and Chloe*: Gnathon ("Jaws"), bearing the same name as the parasite in Terence's *Eunuchus*, who is modeled on the titular character of Menander's *Kolax* (*Eunuchus* 30), follows his host Astylus ("City Slicker") to the countryside, where he is seized by desire for Daphnis and tries in vain first to seduce, then rape the boy (4.11–12). While homosexual passion is not featured in New Comedy (Plut. *Quaest. Conv.* 7.11), Gnathon's representation as "nothing more than a jaw [*gnathos*], a belly, and those parts below the belly" (4.11) perfectly emblematizes the voracity of the comic parasite. While Longus uses this stock figure to create an entertaining scene within a much larger narrative, Alciphron, another Second Sophistic author, offers us a whole series of vignettes illustrating the ups and downs of parasitic life in a very different genre, the epistle. Probably sometime between 170 and 220 CE, he composed a collection of some 120 fictive letters in four books.[12] Firmly anchored in the world of Menandrian comedy and written in the classical Attic dialect, his *Letters of Fishermen, Farmers, Parasites, and Courtesans* grant the reader glimpses into the private concerns of people living in and around an imaginary fourth-century Athens. As Rosenmeyer (2001: 257) put it, "[w]hile Menander was praised for showing scenes of 'real life' to his audience, Alciphron creates for his readership a 'reality' based on the literary representations of Menander, so at a second degree of distance."

The letters' perceived artificiality and their persistent appropriation of earlier literature, not least of all comedy, brought the works of Alciphron and other epistolographers, such as Aelian (ca. 175–235), Philostratus (ca. 170–ca. 244/49), and Aristaenetus (ca. 500 CE), into discredit with previous generations of scholars, who repeatedly criticized the texts for their lack of originality and failed to perceive the appeal of the erudite game that their authors are playing. Suffice it to quote the damning statement of Volkmann, who collected Alciphron's borrowings from comedy in his Latin dissertation of 1886, only to conclude (p. 36): *quid multa? satis superque nonne vidimus quo iure contemptim de Alciphrone iudicetur?* ("Why lose many words? Have we not seen enough and more than enough by what right Alciphron is judged with contempt?"). The past few decades, however, have seen a fundamental reappraisal of such texts, and recent contributions

---

[12] We have no firm evidence for dating Alciphron; any attempt to position him chronologically in relation to other authors has to remain speculative (cf. n. 18). The transmission of the letters, too, is a complicated issue, as manuscripts present them in differing order and none contains all of the texts. My discussion follows the arrangement proposed by Schepers in his 1901 edition (*Alciphronis rhetoris epistularum libri IV*, Groningen: Wolters).

draw our attention to Alciphron's sophisticated creation of a thoroughly "lettered" universe and his self-conscious use of the epistolary medium (Anderson 1997; Rosenmeyer 2001: 255–307; Schmitz 2004; König 2007; Hodkinson 2007). Though these treatments have substantially advanced our understanding of Alciphron's oeuvre, a more comprehensive and systematic analysis of the letters' allusiveness against the backdrop of their literary-cultural context is still a desideratum.

While the novelists have, so to speak, mapped the basic scheme of comedy onto extended narratives that move far beyond the spatiotemporal boundaries of drama, Alciphron has created small sketches in the mode of rhetorical *ethopoieai*, which feature comic characters expressing their anxieties and desires. Reardon (1971: 182) aptly characterizes Alciphron's miniature technique as "literary pointillism," comparing the individual letters to dots of color in a painting à la Seurat, which, taken together, constitute a fascinating tableau of Menandrian Athens. Half a millennium after the playwright's time, Alciphron recreates the world of New Comedy[13] by giving voice to fishermen, farmers, parasites, and courtesans not as characters on stage but as letter writers.

Time and again scholars have wondered about the significance of the epistolary medium, whose use often seems rather artificial. Even if it would be wrong to assume that people in the countryside were by definition illiterate, it is indeed hard to imagine the country folk of Books 1 and 2 with pen in hand, unlike the more cultivated city-dwellers of the following two books. Why would, for instance, Glaucippe, a fisherman's daughter, communicate with her mother through letters when they live in the same house (1.11 and 12)? König (2007) connects the general precariousness of epistolary communication—the fact that letters can be delayed, get lost, or remain unanswered—with the frustrated desires of Alciphron's figures, who dream about escaping their personal lot, but never do.

Another important aspect is, I believe, the transition of drama from its original performance context into the medium of the book. We may, after all, assume that Alciphron and his contemporaries mostly encountered comic speeches on the written page—not in the theater, that is, but mediated through the literary tradition. It is tempting to view the letter form as a reflection of precisely this "writtenness." Alciphron's transformation of comic stock figures into letter writers might mirror the genre's passage from stage to page: after having become *written* figures, the characters of comedy can now be seen as *writing* their own speeches.[14] Since letters, moreover, seem to have been a favored comic device, the epistolary activity of Alciphron's characters is at least partly prefigured in the plays themselves. Admittedly, we do not know whether letters were as integral to the

---

[13] While New Comedy once again plays a more important role as model, it should be noted that Alciphron's letters also contain allusions to Aristophanes; cf. Volkmann (1886: 3–22). Aristaenetus likewise engages with Old Comedy, for instance in *Ep.* 2.3, where the orator Strepsiades, who refuses to have sex with his young wife, is modeled on the homonymous character from Aristophanes's *Clouds* (cf. Arnott 1973: 203).

[14] As I have argued in a paper on Aristaenetus (Höschele 2012), the letter may also function as a means to bridge the spatial, temporary and cultural gulf between the author and his literary models.

plots of New Comedy as they are to Plautine drama (Scafuro 2003–2004, Jenkins 2005), but the title "Letter" or "Letters" is attested for several Greek comedies, and it is fair to assume that Alciphron's letter-writing characters also had predecessors on the comic stage.[15]

The incongruity between the writers' social status and their literary skills is a deliberate one; indeed, one may say that the texts flaunt their own artificiality. They do so, for instance, through their ubiquitous use of *redende Namen*, a comedic feature that is taken to extremes by Alciphron (Schmitz 2004: 99–100). One parasite named Gnathon (3.8) may be fine. But what about, say, Cothylobrochthisus ("Cup-Guzzler," 3.5), Psichodialectes ("Crumb-Discusser," 3.9) or Dipsanapausilypus ("Thirst-Assuager", 3.31) and their countless peers with similarly grotesque names? In this fictive universe, name and profession are inextricably linked, and characters, like those in a play, hardly ever escape the role they have been assigned (König 2007: 278). How can the farmer Phyllis ("Leafy") in *Letter* 3.13 be surprised at his son's military ambitions, when he baptized him Thrasonides ("Daredevil"), like the soldier of Menander's *Misoumenos*? Or consider the example of Polybius, who, after losing his fortune, becomes a parasite and is compelled to change his name to Scordosphrantes ("Garlic-Sniffer," 3.25.4)—an anecdote that serves to highlight the name's very artificiality.[16]

An even greater degree of literary self-awareness is to be found in *Letter* 3.29, whose writer, after quoting a line from Theocritus (without indication of his source), "justifies" his erudition by the fact that he is from Athens, "where there is not a single man who hasn't had a taste of these things". As Schmitz (2004: 98) remarks, "the Athens where everybody has part in παιδεία is not any real landscape, it is located in the nostalgic imagination of the πεπαιδευμένοι of the Second Sophistic." Similarly, Claudius Aelianus, or Aelian, who followed in Alciphron's footsteps in composing a collection of twenty *Rustic Letters* (Rosenmeyer 2001: 308–321; Hodkinson 2013), sealed his corpus by implicitly addressing his readers through the mouth of a farmer: "If this letter sent to you sounds too smart to be supplied by the country, don't be surprised: for we are not Libyan or Lydian, but *Athenian* farmers" (20).

Alciphron furthermore marks the closeness of his oeuvre to comedy by envisioning a parasite-turned-actor (3.35): fed up with the insults he commonly experiences at banquets, Philoporus ("Mr. Materialistic") follows the invitation of the comic poet Lexiphanes to join his troupe and take on the role of—slave! A marvelous instance of play-within-the-play: the character acting as parasite in the mini-drama of Alciphron's letter is "degraded" to an even lower status, presumably connected with yet greater insults, in the context of an inlaid comic performance. This epistle, moreover, enters

---

[15] Cf. Athenaeus 124B on a comedy by Euthycles (Ἄσωτοι or Ἐπιστολή), Macho K-A fr. 2 (Ἐπιστολή) and Timocles K-A fr. 9–10 (Ἐπιστολαί). On the epistolary intrigue in Menander's *Dis Exapaton* and Plautus's *Bacchides*, cf. Lefèvre (1978). For the use of letters in Euripidean drama, where this device is especially prominent, cf. Rosenmeyer (2001: 61–97); on letters in ancient drama, see also Monaco (1965).

[16] One may compare the following exchange from Plautus's *Stichus*, which is based on Menander's first *Adelphoi* (239–242): CROC.*Gelasime, salve*. GEL.*Non id est nomen mihi.* / CROC. *Certo mecastor id fuit nomen tibi.* / GEL. *Fuit disertim, verum id usu perdidi: / nunc Miccotrogus nomine e vero vocor.*

into an interesting dialogue with the preceding one (3.34), where Limopyctes ("Famine-Fighter") assumes that he can become a countryman by dressing up "farmer-fashion, sheepskin around the shoulders, mattock in hand, like a real trench digger." His description makes one wonder whether he simply went to a costume shop for the outfit.[17] At any rate, he soon discovers that his new profession, quite contrary to his expectations, does involve hard work, to which he is as unaccustomed as Sostratus in Menander's *Dyskolos* (523–545). In both cases, Alciphron presents us with a parasite trying out another role—one in "real" life, and one in the theater. This juxtaposition, I submit, amusingly invites us to reflect on the relation between reality and fiction in a world where everything is invented.

There can be no doubt that the utterances and experiences of Alciphron's figures are modeled on comedy, whether by way of direct allusion or through the evocation of comedy-like scenarios. In his attempt to demonstrate the dependence of Alciphron and Lucian from a common source,[18] Kock (1888) even went so far as to reconstruct lost comic models by turning the author's prose into iambic trimeters! Take a sentence like οὐ γὰρ βούλομαι χείρων φανῆναι τῶν κυνῶν, αἳ τῶν τρεφόντων προφυλακτοῦσι καὶ κήδονται (3.26.2), twist it a little—and you have: χείρων φανῆναι τῶν κυνῶν οὐ βούλομαι, / αἳ τῶν τρεφόντων παραφυλάττουσιν θύρας (Kock 1888: 38–39). While Kock's procedure as such is rather dubious, it is certainly true that many an unknown text lurks behind the lines of Alciphron and his peers, the loss of which will forever prevent us from a full understanding of their compositional technique.

Kock's transformation of prose into iambic trimeters admittedly bears a certain resemblance to my own adaptation of Chariton's words into comic stichomythia at the beginning of this essay. But whereas my aim was simply to provide a heuristic device that underlines the commonalities between comedy and novel, Kock's procedure is an earnest attempt to reconstruct a lost and completely conjectural model. Questionable though this method may be, we should not exclude that some of the texts *might* derive directly from passages in comedy, as is shown by the following example: already back in 1888, Otto Ribbeck (1888: 11–15) suggested a relation between the Cnemo of Menander's *Dyskolos* and the homonymous character we encounter in a series of letters by Aelian (13–16), which pose as an epistolary exchange between a misanthrope and his neighbor. Just how close a relation it is was revealed decades later through the play's rediscovery on papyrus. In response to a note from Callipides (13), urging him to be friendlier to his fellow men, Aelian's Cnemo admits to hating mankind and declares himself envious of Perseus (14):

μακάριον δὲ ἥγημαι τὸν Περσέα κατὰ δύο τρόπους ἐκεῖνον, ὅτι τε πτηνὸς ἦν καὶ οὐδενὶ συνήντα, ὑπεράνω τε ἦν τοῦ προσαγορεύειν τινὰ καὶ ἀσπάζεσθαι. ζηλῶ δὲ αὐτὸν καὶ τοῦ κτήματος ἐκείνου εὖ μάλα ᾧ τοὺς συναντῶντας ἐποίει λίθους· οὗπερ οὖν εἴ μοί τις εὐμοιρία κατατυχεῖν ἐγένετο, οὐδὲν ἂν ἦν ἀφθονώτερον λιθίνων ἀνδριάντων, καὶ σέ γ' ἂν εἰργασάμην τοῦτο πρῶτον.

---

[17] This observation is owed to Owen Hodkinson's paper "Typecast? Speaking Names in Alciphron," presented at the 2008 meeting of the Classical Association of Canada in Montréal.

[18] Their relative chronology has been the subject of much scholarly debate; for a summary cf. Benner and Fobes (1949: 6–18) and Hunter (1983: 6–15).

I think Perseus—that famous one—was fortunate in two ways: because he had wings and didn't encounter anybody; he was too high up for having to address or greet people. I also envy him right well for that possession with which he turned into stone whoever came his way. So, if by a lucky strike of fortune I were to get hold of this, there would be nothing more plentiful than statues fashioned from stone, and you'd be the very first I'd turn into one.

In a footnote Ribbeck (1888: 13 n. 1) cautiously proposed a link between these lines and the *Dyskolos*, for which the use of the word ἀνδριάς was attested (the fragment in question was 139 Meineke; cf. now *Dyskolos* 159). And his intuition would prove right, for—lo and behold—these are what turned out to be Cnemo's opening words in the newly rediscovered play (vv. 153–159):

> εἶτ' οὐ μακάριος ἦν ὁ Περσεὺς κατὰ δύο
> τρόπους ἐκεῖνος, ὅτι πετηνὸς ἐγένετο
> κοὐδενὶ συνήντα τῶν βαδιζόντων χαμαί,
> εἶθ' ὅτι τοιοῦτο κτῆμ' ἐκέκτηθ' ᾧ λίθους
> ἅπαντας ἐπόει τοὺς ἐνοχλοῦντας; ὅπερ ἐμοὶ
> νυνὶ γένοιτ'· οὐδὲν γὰρ ἀφθονώτερον
> λιθίνων γένοιτ' ἂν ἀνδριάντων πανταχοῦ.

While Menander's Cnemo utters these words to the audience, addressing nobody in particular, Aelian's grouch writes to Callipides, threatening his correspondent with instant petrification. The epistolary situation adds an amusing twist to the misanthropic outburst: first Cnemo claims that he only replies because the medium of the letter permits him to do so without having to lay eyes on Callipides (Rosenmeyer 2001: 316; Hodkinson 2007: 293–295), then he envisions a retaliatory measure that would require a face-to-face encounter—Medusa's head can, after all, hardly be sent by mail. Cnemo's *makarismos* of Perseus, which Aelian reproduces almost verbatim, while adding the direct threat to Callipides, is not the only parallel between the two works (Thyresson 1964); the neighbor's observation in *Ep.* 13 that Cnemo hurls clods of earth and pears at everyone, for instance, recalls the misanthrope's attack of Pyrrhia (*Dyskolos* 103–123; see also 365). In thus replicating scenes of Menander's play, Aelian reimagines the uncommunicative and cantankerous farmer as a letter writer, with the focus of his textual appropriation lying on the portrayal of the misanthrope's character rather than the play's plot.

   While it is fair to say that comedy serves as the primary paradigm (if not the only model) for both Alciphron and Aelian, the collection of Aristaenetus, which contains fifty fictive erotic letters[19] in two books, is less closely linked with comedy, as its letters overall engage with a greater variety of genres (Drago 2007: 36–77). However, he too envisions comedic

---

[19]   Many of the texts are not love letters proper but erotic narratives cast in epistolary form, comparable to Ps.-Aeschines *Letter* 10, which tells of how Cimon tricked a girl into giving him her virginity by posing as the river-god Scamander (Mignogna 1996). Note how Cimon explicitly characterizes his act as something one might find ἐν κωμῳδίαις (10.9).

scenarios, and it is of particular interest in our context that he does so not least in a pair of letters that feature as correspondents none other than Alciphron and Lucian! As Zanetto (1987: 198–199) has observed, *Ep.* 1.5 (Alciphron to Lucian) and 1.22 (Lucian to Alciphron) form a thematic diptych: both tell of a woman who cunningly regains a man's affection with the help of another female. Aristaenetus, I submit, not only pays homage to his literary predecessors by incorporating them into his oeuvre as letter writers, but his insertion of Menandrian echoes in both letters attests to his awareness of how closely Alciphron modeled his own epistles on New Comedy.

In the first of the letters, 1.5, a married woman secretly attends a banquet, where she is almost discovered by her husband. She hurries home and, to divert his suspicions, teams up with a friend, who pretends to have borrowed the woman's robe. Their trick has the desired effect, the furious man lets go of his anger, which had been triggered by seeing his wife's garment at another's house, and asks for her forgiveness. As Arnott (1973: 203–5) has shown, Aristaenetus seems to be drawing here on the vocabulary of Menander's *Samia*: the Greek word used to express the women's deceit (βουκολέω = "bamboozle"), for instance, twice appears in the play (530, 596), where it is employed by Demea and Niceratus in the midst of heated arguments. In addition, the conduct of the jealous husband, who is described as leaping over the threshold (εἰσπεπήδηκεν) and screaming (κεκραγώς), closely resembles the furious behavior of Menander's Niceratus (εἰσπεπήδηκεν, 564; κεκράξεται, 549; κέκραγε, 553; κέκραχθι, 580). Aristaenetus, then, does not reproduce a specific plot, but does highlight the comedy-like atmosphere of his letter by verbally echoing the playwright's depiction of angry old men in his own representation of a raging husband.

Letter 1.22, in turn, may be said to have as its generative nucleus Menander's *Perikeiromene* (Drago 1997). In both texts, the lover, who is portrayed as rash and arrogant, is filled with jealousy toward an imagined rival. But while in Menander it is Polemo's misdirected jealousy which sets off the crisis, Glycera and her slave Doris, whose names are identical to those of Menander's females, deliberately provoke Charisius's jealousy by pretending that she is crazy about Polemo (!) so as to rekindle Charisius's passion for her. As in 1.5, the trick works, the duped lover asks for forgiveness, and the two are happily reconciled. Aristaenetus, I think, draws our attention to this structural reversal in relation to the *Perikeiromene* by his switch of names, turning Polemo from lover into rival, a switch that is moreover paralleled by the letter's reversal of sender and addressee (Lucian to Alciphron) in relation to *Ep.* 1.5.

We have seen how Aristaenetus marks his literary debt to these authors by featuring them as correspondents in his own collection (he does the same with Philostratus at 1.11 and Aelian at 2.1). This procedure is prefigured by Alciphron's invention of an epistolary exchange between Menander and his beloved Glycera, which serves as *sphragis* to his work (Bungarten 1967; Rosenmeyer 2001: 301–306). Book 4, at whose end we find this pair of letters (18 and 19), distinguishes itself from the preceding parts by presenting epistles of historical individuals (fourth-century courtesans, intellectuals, artists and politicians); its texts are also more tightly interwoven, as several revolve around the same issues, offering mini-narratives of sorts (Rosenmeyer 2001: 272–274). In 4.18, Menander writes to Glycera to inform her that Ptolemy has invited him to Egypt; though honored by this proposal, he reassures his beloved that he will never leave her and Athens. In her reply, Glycera shows herself proud of her lover; not doubting his commitment, she wavers between her wish to keep him in Athens and her reluctance to stand in the way of his success.

This Glycera is, of course, not a historical *hetaira* involved with the real Menander (against this view cf. already Körte 1919). No, she is one of his comic characters who, in a witty play reminiscent of Hermesianax (fr. 7), is envisioned as the beloved of her own creator. In fact, she even highlights her status as a literary figure by mentioning a drama about herself (τὸ δρᾶμα ἐν ᾧ με γέγραφας, 4.19.20), which she wants Menander to present to Ptolemy besides his *Thais, Misoumenos, Thrasyleon, Epitrepontes, Rhapizomene,* and *Sikyonios.* Whether this is a reference to the *Perikeiromene*, whose female lead is called Glycera, or to another play, the image of Menander taking his beloved to Egypt in her written manifestation betrays a high degree of self-consciousness and points to the easy mobility of the written word as opposed to that of individuals, mingling once more reality and fiction ("so that the king may see how great his influence is with you—to make you bring your darling in writing [γεγραμμένους . . . τοὺς ἔρωτας] while leaving your real love [τοὺς ἀληθίνους] behind in the city").

While Glycera, a literary figure, is pictured as a quasi-historical character, the playwright Menander is in a way fictionalized, as he is turned into a letter writer within Alciphron's universe, which itself is based on the world of Menandrian comedy: the model author is intriguingly absorbed into the epistolary discourse of the collection. "O Menander, O Life, who of you imitated the other?" Aristophanes of Byzantium famously asked, suggesting a blending of reality and fiction, from which, I submit, Alciphron might have taken his cue for his perpetual play with imitation, invention, and "authenticity." "What indeed is Athens without Menander? What is Menander without Glycera?" wonders the courtesan in her letter (4.19.5). And what, indeed, would Alciphron be without Menander? Like the poet's plays, the epistolographer's oeuvre is unthinkable without its Athenian context, mediated though it is through the genre of New Comedy.[20]

BIBLIOGRAPHY

Anderson, G. 1997. "Alciphron's Miniatures." *ANRW* II 34.3: 2188–2206.
Antonsen-Resch, A. 2005. *Von Gnathon zu Saturio: Die Parasitenfigur und das Verhältnis der römischen Komödie zur griechischen.* Berlin: de Gruyter.
Arnott, W.G. 1965. "Ὥσπερ λαμπάδιον δράματος." *Hermes* 93: 253–255.
———. 1973. "Imitation, Variation, Exploitation: A Study in Aristaenetus." *GRBS* 14: 197–211.
Benner, A.R., and F. H. Fobes. 1949. *The Letters of Alciphron, Aelian and Philostratus.* Cambridge, MA: Heinemann.

[20] I wish to thank Anton Bierl, Peter Bing, Owen Hodkinson, Niklas Holzberg, David Konstan, and Silvia Montiglio for their generous comments on this essay.

Bierl, T. 2007. "Mysterien der Liebe und die Initiation Jugendlicher: Literatur und Religion im griechischen Roman." In *Literatur und Religion 2: Wege zu einer mythisch-rituellen Poetik bei den Griechen*, edited by A. Bierl, R. Lämmle, and K. Wesselmann, 239–334. Berlin: de Gruyter.

Borgogno, A. 1971. "Menandro in Caritone." *RFIC* 99: 257–263.

Brethes, R. 2007. *De l'idéalisme au réalisme: Une étude du comique dans le roman grec.* Salerno: Helios.

Bretzigheimer, G. 1988. "Die Komik in Longos' Hirtenroman *Daphnis und Chloe.*" *Gymnasium* 95: 515–555.

——. 1999. "Brudermord und Kindesmord: Pseudotragik in Heliodors Äthiopika (mit einer Appendix zum Beginn des Romans)." *WS* 112: 59–86.

Bungarten, J. J. 1967. "Menanders und Glykeras Brief bei Alkiphron." PhD diss., University of Bonn.

Corbato, C. 1968. "De Menandro a Caritone: Studi sulla genesi del Romanzo Greco e i sui rapporti con la Commedia Nuova." *Quaderni Triestini sul Teatro Antico* 1: 5–44.

Crismani, D. 1997. *Il teatro nel romanzo ellenistico d'amore e di avventure.* Alessandria, Italy: Edizioni dell'Orso.

Drago, A. T. 1997. "Due esempi di intertestualità in Aristeneto." *Lexis* 15: 173–187.

——. 2007. *Aristeneto: Lettere d'amore.* Lecce: Pensa Multimedia.

Egger, B. 1994. "Women and Marriage in the Greek Novels: The Boundaries of Romance." In *The Search for the Ancient Novel*, edited by J. Tatum, 260–280. Baltimore: Johns Hopkins University Press.

——. 1999. "The Role of Women in the Greek Novel: Woman as Heroine and Reader." In *Oxford Readings in the Greek Novel*, edited by S. Swain, 108–136. Oxford: Oxford University Press.

Fusillo, M. 1989. *Il romanzo greco: Polifonia ed Eros.* Venice: Marsilio.

——. 1990. "Il testo nel testo: La citazione nel romanzo greco." *Materiali e discussioni* 25: 27–48.

Grammatiki, K. ed. 2009. *Fiction on the Fringe: Novelistic Writing in the Post-Classical Age.* Leiden: Brill.

Hägg, T. 1983. *The Novel in Antiquity.* Oxford: B. Blackwell.

Hähnle, A. 1929. "Γνωρίσματα." PhD diss., University of Tübingen.

Haynes, K. 2003. *Fashioning the Feminine in the Greek Novel.* London and New York: Routledge.

Heiserman, A. 1977. *The Novel before the Novel: Essays and Discussions about the Beginnings of Prose Fiction in the West.* Chicago and London: University of Chicago Press.

Hodkinson, O. 2007. "Better than Speech: Some Advantages of the Letter in the Second Sophistic." In *Ancient Letters: Classical and Late Antique Epistolography*, edited by R. Morello and A. D. Morrison, 283–300. Oxford and New York: Oxford University Press.

——. 2013. "Aelian's Rustic Epistles in the context of his corpus: A reassessment of Aelian's literary programme and qualities." In *Lettere, Mimesi, Retorica: Studi sull' epistolografia letteraria greca di età imperiale e tardo antica*, edited by O. Vox, 257–310. Lecce: Pensa Multimedia.

Höschele, R. 2012. "From Hellas with Love: The Aesthetics of Imitation in Aristaenetus' *Letters.*" *TAPA* 142: 157–186.

Holzberg, N. 1995. *The Ancient Novel: An Introduction.* Translated by C. Jackson-Holzberg. London: Routledge.

——. 1996. "The Genre: Novels Proper and the Fringe." In *The Novel in the Ancient World*, edited by G. Schmeling, 11–28. Leiden: Brill.

Hunter, R. 1983. *A Study of* Daphnis and Chloe. Cambridge, UK: Cambridge University Press.

——. 1994. "History and Historicity in the Romance of Chariton." *ANRW* II 34.2: 1055–1086.

Jenkins, T. 2005. "At Play with Writing: Letters and Readers in Plautus." *TAPA* 135: 359–392.

Kock, T. 1888. "Lucian und die Komödie." *RhM* 43: 29–59.

König, J. 2007. "Alciphron's Epistolarity." In *Ancient Letters: Classical and Late Antique Epistolography*, edited by R. Morello and A. D. Morrison, 257–282. Oxford: Oxford University Press.

Körte, A. 1919. "Glykera und Menander." *Hermes* 54: 87–93.

Konstan, D. 1987. "Between Courtesan and Wife: Menander's *Perikeiromene*." *Phoenix* 41: 122–139.

——. 1994. *Sexual Symmetry: Love in the Ancient Novel and Related Genres*. Princeton: Princeton University Press.

Lalanne, S. 2006. *Une éducation grecque: Rites de passage et construction des genres dans le roman grec*. Paris: Ed. la Découverte.

Lape, S. 2004. *Reproducing Athens: Menander's Comedy, Democratic Culture, and the Hellenistic City*. Princeton: Princeton University Press.

Lefèvre, E. 1978. "Plautus-Studien II: Die Briefintrige in Menanders *Dis exapaton* und ihre Verdoppelung in den *Bacchides*." *Hermes* 106: 513–538.

Mastromarco, G. 2009. "La maschera del *miles gloriosus*: Dai Greci a Plauto." In *Lecturae Plautinae Sarsinares XII. Miles gloriosus (Sarsina, 27 settembre 2008)*, edited by R. Raffaelli and A. Tontini, 17–40. Urbino: QuattroVenti.

May, R. 2007. *Apuleius and the Drama: The Ass on Stage*. Oxford: Oxford University Press.

Mignogna, E. 1996. "Cimone e Calliroe: Un 'romanzo' nel romanzo: Intertestualità e valenza strutturale di Ps.-Eschine *Epist.* 10." *Maia* 48: 315–326.

Möllendorff, P. v. 2000. *Auf der Suche nach der verlogenen Wahrheit: Lukians Wahre Geschichten*. Tübingen: Narr.

Monaco, G. 1965. "L'epistola nel teatro antico." *Dioniso* 39: 334–351.

Morgan, J. 1982. "History, Romance, and Realism in the Aithiopika of Heliodoros." *ClAnt* 1: 221–265.

——. 2009. "Readers Writing Readers, and Writers Reading Writers: Reflections of Antonius Diogenes." In *Readers and Writers in the Ancient Novel*, edited by M. Paschalis, S. Panayotakis, and G. Schmeling, 127–141. Groningen: Barkhuis & Groningen University Library.

Nesselrath, H.-G. 1985. *Lukians Parasitendialog: Untersuchungen und Kommentar*. Berlin: De Gruyter.

Panayotakis, C. 1995. *Theatrum Arbitri: Theatrical Elements in the* Satyrica *of Petronius*. Leiden: Brill.

Paulsen, T. 1992. *Inszenierung des Schicksals: Tragödie und Komödie im Roman des Heliodor*. Trier: Wissenschaftlicher Verlag.

Perry, B. E. 1967. *The Ancient Romances: A Literary-Historical Account of Their Origins*. Berkeley: University of California Press.

Pini, L. 2006. "Omero, Menandro e i classici latini negli *Apophoreta* di Marziale: Criteri di selezione e ordinamento." *RFIC* 134: 443–478.

Reardon, B. P. 1971. *Courants Littéraires Grecs des IIe et IIIe siècles après J.-C.* Paris: Les Belles Lettres.

——. 1991. *The Form of Greek Romance*. Princeton: Princeton University Press.

Ribbeck, O. 1888. *Agroikos: Eine ethologische Studie*. Leipzig: Hirzel.

Robiano, P. 2000. "La citation poétique dans le roman érotique grec." *REA* 102: 509–529.

Rohde, E. 1876. *Der griechische Roman und seine Vorläufer*. Leipzig: Breitkopf & Härtel.

Rosenmeyer, P. A. 2001. *Ancient Epistolary Fictions: The Letter in Greek Literature*. Cambridge, UK: Cambridge University Press.

Scafuro, A. 2003–2004. "The Rigmarole of the Parasite's Contract for a Prostitute in *Asinaria*: Legal Documents in Plautus and his Predecessors." *Leeds International Classical Studies* 3.4: 1–21.

Schmeling, G., ed. 1996. *The Novel in the Ancient World*. Leiden: Brill.

Schmitz, T. 2004. "Alciphron's Letters as a Sophistic Text." In *Paideia: The World of the Second Sophistic*, edited by B. Borg, 87–104. Berlin: De Gruyter.

Smith, S. D. 2007. *Greek Identity and the Athenian Past in Chariton: The Romance of Empire*. Groningen: Barkhuis & Groningen University Library.

Tatum, J., ed. 1994. *The Search for the Ancient Novel*. Baltimore: Johns Hopkins University Press.

Thyresson, I. L. 1964. "Quatre lettres de Claude Elien inspirées par le Dyscolos de Ménandre." *Eranos* 62: 7–25.

Tilg, S. 2010. *Chariton of Aphrodisias and the Invention of the Greek Love Novel*. Oxford: Oxford University Press.

Traill, A. 2008. *Women and the Comic Plot in Menander*. Cambridge, UK: Cambridge University Press.

Tylawski, E. I. 2002. *Saturio's Inheritance: The Greek Ancestry of the Roman Comic Parasite*. New York: P. Lang.

Vogt-Spira, G. 1992. *Dramaturgie des Zufalls: Tyche und Handeln in der Komödie Menanders*. Munich: C. H. Beck.

Volkmann, W. 1886. "Studia Alciphronea. Partic. I: De Alciphrone comoediae imitatore." PhD diss., University of Breslau.

Walden, J. W. H. 1894. "Stage-Terms in Heliodorus's *Aethiopica*." *HSPh* 5: 1–43.

Whitmarsh, T. 1998. "The Birth of a Prodigy: Heliodorus and the Genealogy of Hellenism." In *Studies in Heliodorus*, edited by R. Hunter, 93–124. Cambridge, UK: Cambridge Philological Society.

——, ed. 2008. *The Cambridge Companion to the Greek and Roman Novel*. Cambridge, UK: Cambridge University Press .

——. 2009. "Desire and the End of the Greek Novel." In *Plotting with Eros: Essays on the Poetics of Love and the Erotics of Reading*, edited by I. Nilsson, 135–152. Copenhagen: Museum Tusculanum Press.

——. 2011. *Narrative and Identity in the Ancient Greek Novel: Returning Romance*. Cambridge, UK: Cambridge University Press.

Zanetto, G. 1987. "Un epistolografo al lavoro: Le *Lettere* di Aristeneto." *SIFC* 5: 193–211.

CHAPTER 39

ROMAN COMEDY IN THE SECOND SOPHISTIC

REGINE MAY

THE Second Sophistic (ca. 100–230 CE) was a time of renewed interest in the comic genres of Athens and Rome. In the Greek-speaking world, New Comedy begins to be associated with the literary elite. Although evidence for actual performance of comedies, which would imply a wide spread of knowledge of comedy throughout the Second Sophistic, is vague and sparse (Green 1994: 145; May 2006: 16–44), it is nevertheless sufficient to indicate that the plays were studied, recited, and performed. Archaeological evidence ranges from possible entrance tokens (cf. Arnott 1979–2000 ii.51–52) through inscriptions to famous actors and the eminence of their organizations (Jamot 1895, Mette 1977). Above all, the literary symposium, during which excerpts from comedy could be performed, contributed to the popularity of Menander among the elite. Plutarch (*Moralia* 854b) asks why an educated man should go to the theater unless to see Menander, and in *Moralia* 712b he notes that a symposium without wine is more imaginable than one without Menander. Continued performance during the Second Sophistic is also attested by Aelius Aristides, Marcus Aurelius, and Phrynichus, although it is not always clear whether this was in a public or a private, perhaps, symposiastic, context (Friedländer 1919–1921 appendix 14, Jones 1993: 40–41). Sophists like Philostratus are claimed by the Suda to have written plays themselves: in his case, forty-three tragedies, fourteen comedies, and a three-book treatise on tragedy (cf. Philostratus II K-A test.; for comedy in the Greek novel and epistolography, see Höschele in this volume). Menander especially became the comedian of choice for the literary elite, as he provided good examples for *ethopoiia* and the use of the apt word. Lucian (e.g., *How to Tell a Flatterer from a Friend*) and Alciphron use material from Menander in their works, e.g., by using the stock character of the parasite (cf. Nesselrath 1985: 120–121). A similar interest in stock characters can be found in Pollux's *Onomasticon*, dedicated to Commodus. New Comedy begins to be associated with the literary elite of the Second Sophistic, whose interest in the text of Menander was essential to its survival (see Nesselrath in this volume).

This interest in New Comedy in the Greek world finds its parallel in the Latin-speaking world of Rome. In fact, even among the Latin populace Menander himself had never ceased to be read in schools; consummately Latin writers such as Ovid and Manilius (5.471–476) continued to cite Menander rather than Plautus or Terence. Like Menander, Terence was read as a school author throughout antiquity. Even when his popularity among rhetoricians in the first century CE took a dip during the second, he remained a standard school text in studies with the *grammaticus*.

It was, however, Plautus who returned to center stage during the archaizing Second Sophistic. The Latin sophistic movement was characterized by the archaists' predilection for the single word rather than the *sententiae* of Seneca or the period of classical times (Traina 2010: 217), and this predilection triggered and contributed to a renewal of interest in Plautus. This new popularity was due to interest in him first as a text to be studied for its language, for words fit for an archaizing orator to use (Vessey 1994: 1863–1867), and finally as a literary inspiration. This chapter takes a look at Plautus's popularity and reception in this period.

THE REDISCOVERY OF PLAUTUS

Scholars have traditionally attributed the revival of interest in Plautus to Probus. This Flavian grammarian (cf. Suetonius *gramm.* 24) had been credited by Leo 1895 with "rescuing" an all but extinct Plautine text from the provinces. Interest in the *veteres* had indeed disappeared during the Augustan period and the early first century CE, but the supposition that Plautus had to be rescued from extinction is too pessimistic (Deufert 2002: 176–183). Plautus's comedies were still being read in Rome during the early Empire (see Hor. *Ep.* 2.1), although not as widely as Terence's, whose text was edited by Remmius Palaemon at the time of Tiberius and Claudius. The text of Plautus that Probus had access to did not vary greatly from Varro's edition and thus our own texts.

From the late Flavian and Trajanic period on, moreover, interest in rhetoric, and especially in choosing the right words, began to bring the *veteres* back into the mainstream. Examples of this trend include Tacitus's *Dialogus* 23.2–3 and the *Institutio Oratoria* of Quintilian, who, however, does not regard Plautus particularly highly and recommends instead the study of Menander (10.1.69–72; 10.1.99–100; cf. Deufert 2002: 194–195). Quintilian's interest was mainly in *ethopoiia*, a technique he judged Menander to excel in. Quintilian paid relatively little attention to Plautus because his greater obscenity made him less suitable for use as a school author. Studying comic stock characters was part of Roman education, too, even before the archaizing movement (Quint. 10.1.71–72; 11.3.73; 11.3.91; cf. Beacham 1991: 237 n. 28).

Scholars assume that Latin comedies were performed, either complete or as excerpts together with other genres (tragedies, pantomimes etc.), during the rapidly increasing number of days dedicated to scenic entertainments in the Roman empire (Jory 1986: 144, Blänsdorf 1990: 12). The Emperor Hadrian, too, ensured the performance of plays both publicly and privately, to strengthen his credentials in the archaizing taste (*SHA* 16.5– 6; 19.6). His interest in the *veteres* encouraged a widespread renaissance of interest in Plautus during his time. This allowed the archaizing movement to flourish, with its three primary authors Fronto, Gellius, and Apuleius valuing the language of Plautus over that of his contemporaries, although their interest included, but to a lesser extent, some mimographers and tragedians of the early Latin period, too.

Plautus's unusual and experimental language facilitated his increasing popularity during the archaizing movement; he eventually overtook Terence as the author of choice. The works of Terence were largely neglected by the elite authors of the second century CE, although school editions of his comedies continued to flourish in the period. Because of his rich language, it is Plautus who started to become the object of study for grammarians. A renewed interest in Plautus's language and morphology, connected with the interest in Plautus as a source for rhetorical embellishment, created a need for guides for students of rhetoric, as the works by Charisius and Priscian, heavily based on Second Sophistic analyses of Plautine language, testify (cf. Deufert 2002: 208).

The need to offer guides for students of rhetoric reading comedies fueled a revived scholarly interest in comedy in the second century; for example, Gellius's teacher C. Sulpicius Apollinaris wrote *periochae* (metrical plot summaries) for the comedies of Terence and possibly Plautus, and Aemilius Asper produced commentaries on Terence. Terentius Scaurus produced a commentary or at least wrote on *Poenulus* (*NA* 11.15; sceptical: Deufert 2002: 210 with n. 63).

FRONTO, GELLIUS, AND APULEIUS

Evidence suggests that all three frontrunners of the archaizing movement made use of grammarians' excerpts from comedies to locate interesting words, although they most likely also studied (and possibly watched) plays themselves. Many direct quotations in Apuleius, for example, are from the beginning of plays (*Truc.* 1–3 in *Flor.* 18.7; *Mil.* 4 in *Socr.* 145).

Fronto (ca. 90/5–ca. 167 CE) was from 139 to 145 the teacher of Marcus Aurelius, whose preference for philosophy over rhetoric he resented. As a literary conservative, he peppered his rhetoric in his letters with archaizing words, mostly drawn from Plautus, who is the most cited and referenced *poeta vetus* in his work (cf. Marache 1957, May 2006: 30; generally on Fronto and the *veteres* cf. Keulen 2009: 54). Fronto made Marcus Aurelius promise to study more Plautus to improve his diction; cf. Fronto p. 68.10–11 *meque ad istum histrionum poetam totum convertam lecteis prius orationculeis Tullianeis*, "When I have finished reading some of Cicero's little speeches first, I will immerse myself completely into that stage poet of yours" (Fronto is cited according to van den Hout 1988). In Fronto's oeuvre, Plautine imitation is mainly restricted to his private correspondence and is little found in his published speeches (Van den Hout 1999: x; Deufert 2002: 204). He never quotes from or even mentions Terence (p. 133 *Terentius* is a conjecture). His main interest is rhetoric and the choice of the right words, the *insperata atque inopinata verba* ("unexpected and surprising words," Fronto 57.16; cf. Marache 1952: 128–137; Steinmetz 1982: 174). Plautine language is used to polish one's style (cf. p. 227.11–12: *ut te Plauto expolires*) and provides a good model for innovative word formations (p. 160, with Deufert 2002: 200–202).

Fronto also prescribes the correct usage of archaic words, drawn from Plautus and at times explicitly signposted as such; thus, for example, *exradicitus* "completely" is described as *Plautinotatum*, "most Plautine" (p. 153.14), but unmarked examples also exist (see below). Archaism is not a goal in itself but a means to finding the right word, and Fronto's interest in archaizing authors was a further development from the niche interest in the first century CE shown in Tacitus's *Dialogus* (Mayer 2001: 163–164, cf. also Brock 1911: 25–35 and Marache 1952: 15–78). Fronto's contribution was to systematize and spearhead the emerging archaizing movement. He integrated Plautine words and phrases seamlessly into his own style. For example, p. 77.3–4 *M. Lucilius tribunus pl(ebis) hominem liberum, civem Romanum, cum collegae mitti iuberent, adversus eorum sententiam ipsius vi in carcerem compegit* ("M. Lucilius, a tribune of the people, *cast into prison* a Roman citizen, although his colleagues ordered him to be released, and against their decree") uses a Plautine phrase quite naturally (it appears at *Amphitruo* 155 *in carcerem compegerint*, "they cast (me) into prison,") and at *Menaechmi* 942, *Poenulus* 1409, and *Rudens* 715). Plautus provides succinct, archaizing, but elegant vocabulary, while the context of the comic quotation is secondary, and not at all intended to comicize Fronto's own context.

Plays other than the twenty-one now extant were available during the Second Sophistic, and Gellius discussed the genuineness of some of them (*NA* 3.3). Our modern selection may have been created either in the late Hadrianic or early Antonine age, with Deufert 2002: 200–237 arguing for the later date. Calling the twenty-one plays still extant through our manuscript tradition the *fabulae Varronianae* is somewhat misleading (Gratwick 1993: 5–6), as the term should rather be applied to the approximately nineteen additional plays that Varro wanted to include in the list of genuine plays on stylistic grounds, but the term is commonly (and consequently also here) used to identify the extant twenty-one plays.

The Plautine plays Fronto concentrates on are the twenty-one Varronian *fabulae*, possibly because they are assuredly "genuine" and will provide his students with proper archaic words to use. Only two passages in the corpus of his correspondence are possibly from non-Varronian plays, and Fronto is not responsible for either: they are both in Marcus Aurelius's letters to Fronto. One (p. 28.9–13) is a quotation from *Colax* (fr. ii Lindsay, cf. May 2006: 33–34), a non-Varronian play, which Marcus seems to cite from memory, as it is slightly unmetrical. The fragment bears some resemblance to a fragment of Menander's *Kolax* ca. lines 195–199, which also mentions kings and flatterers, although there the sentiment is somewhat different (cf. Arnott 1979–2000 ii.155 and 176–177).

The other (p. 26.6–7) may be an adaptation of a passage in *Mostellaria*. Marcus colorfully describes the love between himself and Fronto as rivaling that of Fronto's wife Cratia for her husband, whose love he facetiously compares to "a storm of love that not only drenched her clothes but flowed into her very marrow" (*amoris imber grandibus guttis non vestem modo permanavit, sed in medullam ultro fluit*)." In *Mostellaria* 138–143, a young man compares love to hail and rain entering his breast and penetrating to his very heart; this suggests that Marcus may be drawing from the play or, if not, perhaps from another play in which similar themes featured (so Van den Hout 1999: 66; May 2006: 33f.). Importantly, even in this personalized passage, the phrase is used decoratively only; the writer does not engage with the content of the play itself. This kind of elegant game with Plautine phrases would have pleased Marcus Aurelius's teacher: Fronto has reduced comedy, especially Plautine comedy, to a teaching tool and a quarry for elegant phrases, disregarding his source's literary merits. Still, Fronto's interest in Plautus contributed immensely to the revived interest in and survival at least of the twenty-one plays during the second century, and made the use of Plautine language not only legitimate but desirable to imitators of the emperor's teacher, after Terence's long hegemony in the field.

Evidently, Marcus Aurelius has indeed read Plautus on his teacher's advice, albeit more reluctantly than Fronto had hoped. Fronto prefers to select his words from the twenty-one plays that were already becoming canonical. Marcus however was less enthusiastic about Plautus, and his inclusion of plays from outside the Varronian canon of twenty-one may be a sign of his reluctance to follow Fronto's lead.

Aulus Gellius (ca. 125–180 CE), Fronto's younger contemporary and student, similarly interested in rare words, appreciates both Greek and Roman comedy. His knowledge of Menander overshadows his knowledge of Aristophanes, who had never been popular with Latin authors, and he cites several Latin *poetae veteres* in his *Noctes Atticae* (Mattiacci 1986; Holford-Strevens 2003: 213–220; Keulen 2009: 6). Like Fronto, Gellius is primarily interested in Plautus as a source for words, and within these parameters Gellius believes him to be the most elegant ancient author available (*NA* 1.7.17; 6.17.4 etc.). In his *Noctes Atticae*, a miscellany of intentionally random information ostensibly based on conversations between Gellius and his friends and teachers, Gellius discusses how to source the correct words and integrate them properly into one's discourse. Unlike Fronto, however, Gellius also discusses the content and literary value of Plautus's comedies with some frequency, though these aspects still seem to be of secondary importance to him. He and his circle particularly admire Plautus for his diction, language, and grammar (he calls Plautus *linguae Latinae decus*, "the ornament of the Latin language," at *NA* 19.8.6), for his life (*NA* 3.3.14), but above all for his learning—he cites Plautus, for example, as evidence for the length of animal gestation (*NA* 3.16). Gellius mainly disregards Terence, whose language he does not find interesting (*NA* 6.14.6; Marache 1952: 231). Gellius admires Varro's scholarship, which influences his own taste; his interest is overwhelmingly in the twenty-one Varronian *fabulae*, although he gives the impression that he has read several plays outside the canon, e.g., the *Boeotia*, *Nervolaria*, and *Fretum* (*NA* 3.3). This claim is sometimes seen as artistic license, for example by

Holford-Strevens 2003: 67, but Gellius strives for realism and credibility throughout the *Noctes Atticae*. Deufert 2002: 214 leaves the question open. Anderson 2004: 116 offers a differentiated analysis of Gellius's claims for authenticity. Even if Gellius had not read these plays, his claim to have done so does not undermine his striving for credibility: these and other plays must have still been available to read, but were clearly not at the forefront of his attention. Other non-Varronian plays are mentioned or cited in the corpus, too: a lawyer quotes *Astraba* in *NA* 11.7, *Trigemini* is quoted in *NA* 6.9, and an unknown play is cited in *NA* 18.12. Jocelyn 1988: 68, who is generally skeptical about the transmission of Plautus, argues that Varro's *De comoediis Plautinis* or grammarians like Verrius Flaccus are Gellius's source here.

Gellius 3.3 is our main source for the fate of Plautus's comedies and the concept of the *fabulae Varronianae* and their authenticity. The latter concept, important to Gellius, was determined by the archaists' ideas of Plautus's *elegantia*. Gellius argues in *NA* 3.3 that the *Boeotia*, *Nervolaria*, and *Fretum*, although not part of the twenty-one comedies, are genuinely Plautine: the authenticity of the *Nervolaria* can be proved by a single verse because of its elegance (*NA* 3.3.6). Pseudo-scholars who use the "wrong" archaic words from Plautine plays that Gellius (and Varro) consider unquestionably inauthentic are, however, derided for their ignorance. Thus Gellius makes an example of the Roman knight who justifies his use of *apluda* ("bran") with the word's occurrence in *Astraba*, a play Gellius regards as non-Plautine (*NA* 11.7). Even though Gellius was willing to consider plays beyond the twenty-one as genuine and therefore deserving of discussion, excerption, and use, a narrowing of the canon of plays at the disposal of rhetoricians is notable. The fact that the vast majority of lexical references and discussions refer to canonical plays is the natural consequence of the archaists' orientation towards Plautus for linguistic embellishment and use in argumentation: Plautine words could enhance their style and thus reputation as knowledgeable rhetoricians, whereas non-genuine or spurious words sourced from non-Plautine plays would fatally undermine a rhetor's elegance and credibility; as the case of the knight in *NA* 11.7 shows, this was an unforgivable error.

Although Gellius, along with the grammarians, is one of our main sources for fragments of non-Varronian plays, his treatment of them is symptomatic of the time's obsession with establishing the pedigree of a genuinely archaic word. Because non-Varronian plays thus carried an intrinsic risk for the rhetor, they began to be neglected by the cautious archaists.

On the other hand, Gellius is also curious and knowledgeable about other playwrights and plays outside the canon, such as Caecilius (ca. 220–160 BCE), whom he rates second only to Plautus. When he compares Caecilius's *Plocium* and Menander's *Plokion*, however (*NA* 2.23), Menander emerges as the more simple and delightful author, whereas the Roman play taken on its own is considered enjoyable enough but suffers by comparison. This comparison reveals much of what Gellius thinks of Roman comedy; although he discusses Caecilius, this playwright's similarity to Plautus allows us to extrapolate Gellius's attitude toward both authors. Gellius criticizes Caecilius for adding farcical elements to Menander's simpler plot and making the characterization less subtle (cf. May 2006: 37): *quae Menander praeclare et apposite et facete scripsit, ea Caecilius, ne qua potuit quidem, conatus est enarrare, sed quasi minime probanda praetermisit et alia nescio qua mimica inculcauit,* "what Menander wrote clearly, aptly, and wittily, Caecilius has not attempted to expound, even where he could have done so; but he has not mentioned it, as if it could be considered as rather bad, and has forced in some other stuff from mime." Before the discovery of the *Dis Exapaton* papyrus, this was our only available direct juxtaposition of a Greek play and its Latin adaptation, and Gellius's judgments on the differences are on the whole borne out by the newly available material. For example, the characters in *Plocium* are more farcical and somewhat vulgar, e.g., Caecilius l. 162 Ribbeck *ut devomas volt quod foris potaveris,* "She wants you to throw up what you had drunk when you were away," finds no equivalent in *Plokion* K-A fr. 297, where the rich wife is merely described as lording it over the whole family. The change in characterization does, however, add comic force. Gellius here does not treat Caecilius's play as an adaptation for a Roman audience but criticizes it for its shortcomings as a translation, which explains his displeasure and negative judgment. Caecilius is probably chosen instead of Plautus to avoid a necessarily unfavorable judgment of Plautus in this comparison of a Greek original and its Roman adaptation.

Gellius's judgment must, however, be qualified. He considered Greek superior to Latin in many ways and believed that a true intellectual must understand and appreciate Greek (Swain 2004); a comparison of a Greek and a Latin comedy could therefore for Gellius only result in evaluating the Greek play as superior. The choice of Caecilius over Plautus in *NA* 2.23 facilitates this without jeopardizing his high esteem for Plautus, but as far as characterization and coherence of plot are concerned, he praises Menander over his Roman imitator. Plautus is thus reduced to a source of words and information that might occasionally be useful. Gellius's limited engagement with Plautus's plays as literary works influenced scholarly approaches to Plautus until relatively recently, inviting as it did the study of Plautus primarily for his archaism and his value for reconstructing lost Greek models over his originality as a playwright in his own right.

The most prolific admirer of Plautus in the second century is Apuleius of Madaurus in Northern Africa (ca. 125–185 CE). He probably knew Gellius and may have shared his teacher in Athens. As a student in Carthage and Rome, and later in Athens, he studied Plautus, who, together with Ennius and Accius, is his favorite archaic author for quotations. The fact that these quotations are not always marked suggests that Apuleius assumes his audience, the learned elite of Northern Africa and Rome, could recognize his quotations specifically as Plautine (Marache 1952: 329).

Apuleius shows a remarkable interest in Plautus not only as a linguist but also as a writer of literature, and his imitation of Plautus ranges from single words to stock characters in speeches (notably the *Apologia*) to adaptations of plotlines in his novel, *Metamorphoses* or *The Golden Ass*. For Apuleius, studying comedy would not only have been part of his education and training (cf. Green 1994: 145; Bonner 1977: 215–216), but as a rhetorician he made use of *ethopoiia* inspired by comedy in the *Apologia*. As the author of a novel, however, he utilized comedy imaginatively as an important literary device.

For example, his twenty-four-line poem *Anechomenos,* "The one who holds himself back," purports to be a translation of an otherwise unknown Menandrian comedy. In it, Apuleius has not translated but adapted and entirely transformed a typically comic statement by a disappointed lover into something entirely different. The first two lines, *Amare liceat, si potiri non licet / Fruantur alii; non moror, non sum invidus* ("May I be allowed to love, if I am not allowed to possess! / Others may enjoy it: I do not hinder them, I am not envious") sound innocuous and echo such lines as *Samia* 349–351, where Demea contemplates forgetting his desire and love for Chrysis, and *Heauton Timorumenos* 322: *vis amare, vis potiri, vis quod des illi effici* ("You want to love her, you want to possess her, you want the means to give her presents"). Yet the sentiment completely changes after this. Lines 4–22 describe in colorful Plautine language and great detail a sexual act between lovers, which the speaker enviously observes while himself being excluded from erotic fulfillment: l. 6f. *Olli purpurea delibantes oscula / clemente morsu rosea labia vellicent,* "Nibbling someone's dark-red kisses / With soft biting let them peck rosy lips." The poem's final line repeats the first, giving a Plautinesque ring composition but creating a self-contained poem. This change of sentiment echoes the observations Gellius made on Caecilius's adaptations of Greek comedy exactly; in both Latin versions the characters seem very much transformed (cf. May 2006: 63–71).

Apuleius is, however, to some extent different from Fronto and Gellius. He is happy to use noncanonical comedies, which perhaps underlie his portrait of the murderous wife in *Met.* 10.23–28 (see below). Moreover, unlike Fronto and Gellius, Apuleius uses comedy argumentatively even in his rhetorical and philosophical works. He mainly ignores Terence, with one interesting exception in *De Deo Socratis,* a Middle Platonist treatise on the nature of Socrates's *daimonion.* In *Soc.* 165, he refers to a Terentian *meretrix* in connection with his explanation of the invisibility and luster of Socrates's *daimonion,* the only mention of Terence's name in the whole of Apuleius (May 2006: 50–53), citing Terence, *Eunuchus* 454: *audire vocem visa sum modo militis* ("Just now I seemed to hear the soldier's voice"). The context is a discussion of Socrates's ability to hear and see his *daimonion,* which is parallel to the situation in the comedy, where Thais comes on stage after first hearing the soldier and consequently can see him.

In the same work, in *Soc.* 145, Apuleius had previously used a paraphrase from Plautus, *Miles Gloriosus* 4 (*prorsus quod Plautinus miles super clipeo suo gloriatur, praestringens oculorum aciem hostibus,* "This is just what Plautus's soldier brags about his shield, it 'dazzles the sharpness of the eyes of the enemy' "). The passage alluded to is *Miles Gloriosus* 1–4:

> *Curate ut splendor meo sit clupeo clarior*
> *quam solis radii esse olim quom sudumst solent,*
> *ut, ubi usus veniat, contra conserta manu*
> *praestringat oculorum aciem in acie hostibus.*

> Make sure that the splendor of my shield is brighter than the rays of the sun in the clear sky, so that, when it needs to be used in the thick of combat, it dazzles my enemies' eyesight in battle with them.

Here it is much clearer than in Apuleius's actual phrase that the shield is indeed bright and shiny, and thus an apt comparison for the *daimones*. The reference to the play is veiled, as *miles... gloriatur* paraphrases the title *Miles Gloriosus*, but easily recognizable. The paraphrase is from the famous first few lines of the play, but the argument is complicated: only the reader's knowledge of the context of the Plautine passage makes it clear that Apuleius's argument is about the *daimonion's* fine luster, which causes its invisibility. The way the quotation is employed actually avoids a direct comparison, but invites the reader to recall the rest of the passage. Although the splendor is the point of comparison, crucially the word itself is not cited in *Soc.* 145, but only alluded to. A quotation from Plautus thus becomes part of a philosophical argument, but more important here is the fact that Apuleius can assume that his readers think associatively, and are knowledgeable and educated enough to add information from the context of the Plautine passage which is actually missing in his direct quotation. For Apuleius, the knowledge of Plautus among the learned elite of his time is so embedded in their mindset that this allusive argument actually works. Plautus has become part of the intellectual discourse of the second century to an extent that perhaps could be matched only by Shakespearean allusions in modern thinking and argumentation, making Plautus—not only his language and grammar but also his comedies as literature—a shortcut for intellectualism, but an intellectualism of a kind to which a relatively large part of the population could aspire. This is in sharp contrast to Fronto's decontextualizing approach of using Plautine phrases for embellishment and as a sophistic marker. Apuleius's method of allusive intertextuality transcends Fronto's mere linguistic approach.

Apuleius goes beyond his fellow archaists in making use of the noncanonical plays of Plautus, and consequently his use of comedy in his rhetorical and philosophical works, but especially the *Apologia* and the *Metamorphoses*, is more multilayered and imaginative.

Apuleius is able to quote from comedies and tragedies no longer available today but known to him from his rhetorical training and from memory. Apuleius's *Apologia sive Pro Se de Magia* (158/9 CE) is his speech in self-defense against accusations of having used magic to make his wife Pudentilla fall in love with him, a dangerous accusation which could result in his execution under the *lex Cornelia de sicariis et veneficis*. In the speech, quotations and allusions become part of the argument. In this only complete Latin defense speech extant from antiquity outside the corpus of Cicero, the accusing parties and their witnesses are laughed out of court with the help of Plautine language and characterization. The judge Apuleius needed to convince was an intellectual himself, C. Claudius Maximus, a teacher of Marcus Aurelius for Stoicism and at home with poetry (Bradley 1997: 216; May 2010), but the ubiquity of comedy, specifically Plautine comedy, indicates a certain awareness of comedy among the rest of the speech's audience as well.

Apuleius the sophist turns against his opponents magnificently and goes on the counterattack against his accusers by associating them with comic stock characters, especially blocking characters who need to be overcome to ensure a satisfying, happy, comic ending, in which the good persons are rewarded and the blocking characters thwarted

(May 2006; Hunink 1998). For example, he associates (*Apol.* 66–101) members of the opposition with the roles of the *leno* (his main opponent Rufinus, the father-in-law of Apuleius's dead stepson Pontianus), the experienced *meretrix* ensnaring the foolish young man (Rufinus's daughter, Pontianus's widow, who goes on to marry Pontianus's younger brother Sicinius Pudens and, according to Apuleius, corrupts him), and the greedy *parasitus* Crassus, the main witness for the prosecution, who is characterized as fat, as good only at smelling out food, and as having wasted all his money (*Apol.* 57.5 *ructus popinam. Patrimonium omne iam abligurrivit, nec quicquam ei de bonis paternis superest.* "He reeks of cheap eateries. He has squandered already his entire inheritance, and nothing at all remains of his father's property."). Both Crassus's characterization in general and the language specifically are taken from Plautine descriptions of parasites, e.g., Ergasilus, *Captivi* 82–87, which describes the fate of parasites who commonly sponge off people (*homines quos ligurriant*). Apuleius's tactics in the *Apologia* pay off—the judge must have been swayed by Apuleius's attempts to associate himself and Pudentilla with a serious and blameless noncomic relationship and his enemies with blocking characters who need to be overcome to achieve a happy ending. Apuleius evidently was acquitted, and although the transmitted *Apologia* is probably embellished and edited rather than a mere transcript of the actual speech (as claimed, e.g., by Winter 1969), given its length and elaboration, its original shape cannot be reconstructed and is of secondary importance for our merely literary approach (cf. Sallmann 1995: 140; Schindel 1996). Along with learned citations from other, mainly archaic, poetry, knowledge of comedy and its typical plot lines and language formed a bonding mechanism between Apuleius on trial and his audience, which included the sophistically educated judge, and was one of his most effective defense mechanisms (cf. May 2010). The language and characterization used are those of Plautus rather than Terence.

Similarly, Apuleius's *Florida*, excerpts of his sophistic speeches, some of which were held in Carthage's theater as popular entertainment for the gathered audience, contained frequent allusions to and quotations from Plautus (e.g., *Flor.* 2, 18 etc., cf. May 2006: 55–58). Plautine comedy must therefore have become not only fashionable for the elite to appreciate again, but also familiar enough for the normal populace of the Roman provinces to follow Apuleius's defense strategy and enjoy his display speeches as entertainment.

Apuleius's most important literary achievement is the *Metamorphoses,* or *The Golden Ass.* It is the one work in which he uses comedy to best effect. This novel charts the progress of the young man Lucius, who sets out on a journey to Thessaly to learn about witchcraft, and is accidentally turned into a donkey by a witch's apprentice. In his asinine form, Lucius travels from owner to owner and experiences contemporary Greek society's underbelly, until at long last he is rescued by the goddess Isis, who transforms him back into his human form. The novel ends with Lucius becoming her devoted initiate.

In the novel, too, Apuleius follows Fronto's lead in adding Plautine words to his language (cf. Pasetti 2007), but even more subtly and manipulatively: e.g., *cordolium* ("heartfelt grief") in *Met.* 9.21, otherwise found only in Plautus *Cistellaria* 65 and *Poenulus* 299, may be primarily decorative, but often enough these comic words carry an additional comicization of the passage, e.g., *mea festivitas* ("my delight") used in the love scene between the novel's hero Lucius and the girl Photis at *Met.* 2.10 recalls Plautine endearments between lovers, cf. *Casina* 135f., *Poenulus* 389 (Callebat 1968: 499), and together with other linguistic markers throws a Plautine light on the love scene between the young man and the (in some ways unsuitable) slave girl. This association at once directs the attentive reader, comparing comedy plots, toward assumptions about the centrality of the love scene to the rest of the novel and its outcome, which Apuleius then intentionally sets out to thwart. The love plot will in fact turn out to be of only secondary interest in the novel, although Lucius has been portrayed as an *adulescens amans* in that scene, and the whole setting of this scene in the novel so far recalls a comic household in which a young man's dalliance with a pretty slave girl who shares many characterizations with a comic *meretrix* might be a comic possibility (cf. May 2006: 156–181).

In addition to a sign of literariness and characterization, the use of comedy becomes a fundamental part of Apuleius's poetics. Much of the comicality of the novel is actually derived from this concept of recognizable Plautine features set up for the reader to discover. Certain audience expectations are created based on the recognizability and often predictability of the features of Plautine comedy, only to be thwarted by a twist in the plot that turns the comic setup into a tragedy. One example of this comic inversion is the drunken old woman who tells the captured girl Charite (and the protagonist Lucius, who has now turned into a donkey and listens in on her story) the famous tale of *Cupid and Psyche*. The old woman is the housekeeper of the robbers who have kidnapped the girl, and Apuleius calls her *Met.* 6.25 *delira et temulenta* ("crazy and drunken"). Drunken old women are stereotypical, as Athenaeus 10.440e argues, who says that women are fond of wine. Especially old ladies in comedy are prone to drinking a lot, e.g., Terence *Andria* 228–230 (the midwife Lesbia), Plautus *Curculio* 77–81 and 96–109 (the door-keeper Leaena even sings a song about wine), *Truculentus* 903–904 (a drunken nurse), *Casina* 638–640 (Pardalisca is fond of her mistress and wine; for more examples, see Oeri 1948). The fact that Apuleius makes the old woman fond of drink, just at a time when she is about to assume, in Charite's mind at least, the role of a nurse about to give her advice, is a generic marker intended to recall comedy (May 2006: 260–262). The reader's assumptions about the close relationship between a comic nurse and her charge are set into place—in *Truculentus* 903–904 the nurse is a drinker, too; Canthara in Terence *Adelphoe* and Staphyla in Plautus *Aulularia* are both confidantes to their charges—only to be thwarted when after Charite's escape the old woman hangs herself. This makes true the threats uttered but never enacted by old women in comedy: In Plautus, *Aulularia* 76–78, Staphyla contemplates killing herself by hanging after having been abused by her employer Euclio, just as Apuleius's old woman had been harangued by her employers in drastically comic language when the readers first encounter her (*Met.* 4.7; cf. Desertine 1898: 107; Deufert 2002: 207; May 2006: 251): "You last corpse from the funeral pyre, first disgrace of life, and the only reject from Orcus (. . .), you who day and night do nothing but eagerly pour undiluted wine into your mad belly" (*Quae diebus ac noctibus nil quicquam rei quam merum saevienti ventri tuo soles aviditer ingurgitare*).

Apart from the put-upon Staphyla, the language also recalls Leaena in *Curculio* 128, another drunken old woman, who is described thus: *hoc vide ut ingurgitat impura in se merum avariter* ("look how that dirty old woman greedily pours undiluted wine into herself"). The old narrator of *Cupid and Psyche* is set up as a comic old woman through this allusion to a comic stock character, and the reader's knowledge of comedy is intended to trigger certain expectations about that character's future behavior, expectations that Apuleius subsequently manipulates and plays with.

For Apuleius's novel, using Plautine clichés is an essential part of his writing technique. The novel is titled *Metamorphoses*, and apart from delineating the progress of the young man Lucius turned into a donkey by magic and his retransformation into a human being with the unexpected help of the goddess Isis, it also depicts metamorphoses of a more metaphorical manner, here the metamorphosis of literary genres. Comedy, especially Plautine comedy, is predictable in its plot lines, which nevertheless allow for significant surprise and variations of stock scenes and plots within comic parameters. For instance, the young *meretrix* in *Mercator* will not be recognized as a marriageable young freeborn girl, whereas the one in *Cistellaria* will. Using comedy allows Apuleius to play with his audience's literary knowledge and expectations. It is telling that Apuleius does not restrict himself to the twenty-one *fabulae* for this kind of intellectual-intertextual game. In *Met.* 10.23–25 he seems to be using either the prologue of a lost comedy by Menander or one of his Latin imitators, or an intelligent reconfiguration of stock characters inspired by them, to set up a plot directly taken, it seems, from comedy: a mother was ordered to kill her girl child at birth by her husband, but has her secretly brought up by the neighbors instead. When she tells her son about his unrecognized sister, he arranges her marriage to his best friend. Similar plot lines are found in, e.g., Menander's *Phasma, Perikeiromene,* and *Epitrepontes* and Terence's *Heauton Timorumenos* (more detailed analysis in May 2006: 275–290), and readers may be forgiven for assuming that based on this outline they are about to read a comedy with a comic happy ending. The use of especially Plautine language throughout the scene enhances this expectation. Unfortunately, the son's jealous wife, who assumes her husband has a relationship with the girl next door, proceeds to kill the girl, her husband, and other members of her family in the most atrocious manner, only to be found out and condemned to the beasts in the amphitheater in Corinth, where she is to encounter the novel's hero Lucius (still in his asinine form), who is to take part in her execution but flees before this can happen. Again, knowledge of comedy offers an essential clue to how the novel is to be read and interpreted, and the novel in itself is an indication of the ubiquity of comic knowledge in the literary circles of the second century. Comedy is an important, perhaps the most important, tool in the Latin sophist's box of literary games and manipulation.

During the archaizing Latin Second Sophistic, the interest in comedy moved from the margins to the center of attention. It was triggered by the archaists' interest specifically in Plautus as a source of unusual words and information, and turned him into one of the most important authors for the Latin sophistic movement. This contributed to Plautus's popularity both as a text to be studied for its language and as a literary inspiration, and returned him to center stage again after a long period of relative neglect.

BIBLIOGRAPHY

Anderson, G. 2004. "Aulus Gellius as a Storyteller." In *The Worlds of Aulus Gellius,* edited by L. Holford-Strevens and A. D. Vardi, 105–117. Oxford: Oxford University Press.

Arnott, W. G., ed., trans. 1979–2000. *Menander.* 3 vols. Cambridge, MA: Harvard University Press.

Barchiesi, A., and W. Scheidel, eds. 2010. *The Oxford Handbook of Roman Studies.* Oxford: Oxford University Press.

Beacham, R. C. 1991. *The Roman Theatre and Its Audience.* London: Routledge.

Betts, J. H., J. T. Hooker, and J. R. Green, eds. 1986. *Studies in Honour of T. B. L. Webster.* Bristol: Bristol Classical Press.

Blänsdorf, J. 1990. "Einführung: Theater und Gesellschaft im Imperium Romanum." In *Theater und Gesellschaft im Imperium Romanum,* edited by J. Blänsdorf, 7–18. Tübingen: Francke.

——, ed. 1990. *Theater und Gesellschaft im Imperium Romanum = Théâtre et societé dans l'empire romain.* Tübingen: Francke.

Bonner, S. F. 1977. *Education in Ancient Rome: From the Elder Cato to the Younger Pliny.* London: Methuen.

Bradley, K. P. 1997. "Law, Magic and Culture in the *Apologia* of Apuleius." *Phoenix* 51: 202–223.

Brock, M. D. 1911. *Studies in Fronto and his Age: With an Appendix on African Latinity Illustrated by Selections from the Correspondence of Fronto.* Cambridge, UK: University Press.

Callebat, L. 1968. *Sermo Cotidianus dans les Métamorphoses d'Apulée.* Caen: Université de Caen.

Desertine, A. H. J. V. M. 1898. "De Apulei studiis Plautinis." PhD diss., Utrecht University.

Deufert, M. 2002. *Textgeschichte und Rezeption der plautinischen Komödien im Altertum.* Berlin: de Gruyter.

Friedländer, L. 1919–1921. *Darstellungen aus der Sittengeschichte Roms in der Zeit von August bis zum Ausgang der Antonine.* Rev. ed. Leipzig: S. Hirzel.

Gratwick, A. S., ed. 1993. *Plautus: Menaechmi.* Cambridge, UK: Cambridge University Press.

Green, J. R. 1994. *Theatre in Ancient Greek Society.* London: Routledge.

Handley, E. W. 1968. *Menander and Plautus: A Study in Comparison.* London: Lewis.

Harrison, S. J. 2000. *Apuleius: A Latin Sophist.* Oxford: Oxford University Press.

Holford-Strevens, L. 2003. *Aulus Gellius: An Antonine Scholar and his Achievement.* Oxford: Oxford University Press.

——, and A. D. Vardi, eds. 2004. *The Worlds of Aulus Gellius.* Oxford: Oxford University Press.

Horsfall, N., ed. 1988. *Vir Bonus Discendi Peritus: Studies in Celebration of Otto Skutsch's Eightieth Birthday.* London: University of London.

Hunink, V. 1998. "Comedy in Apuleius' Apology." *Groningen Colloquia on the Novel* 9: 97–113.

Jamot, P. 1895. "Fouilles de Thespies." *BCH* 19: 321–385.

Jocelyn, H. D. 1988. "Studies in the Indirect Tradition of Plautus' *Pseudolus* III: The 'Archaising Movement,' Republican Comedy and Aulus Gellius' *Noctes Atticae.*" In *Vir Bonus Discendi Peritus: Studies in Celebration of Otto Skutsch's Eightieth Birthday,* edited by N. Horsfall, 57–72. London: University of London.

Jones, C. P. 1993. "Greek Drama in the Roman Empire." In *Theater and Society in the Classical World,* edited by R. Scodel, 39–52. Ann Arbor: University of Michigan Press.

Jory, E. J. 1986. "Continuity and Change in the Roman Theatre." In *Studies in Honour of T. B. L. Webster,* edited by J. H. Betts, J. T. Hooker, and J. R. Green, 143–152. Bristol: Bristol Classical Press.

Keulen, W. H. 2009. *Gellius the Satirist: Roman Cultural Authority in* Attic Nights. Leiden: Brill.

Konstan, D. 1983. *Roman Comedy.* Ithaca: Cornell University Press.

Leo, F. 1912. *Plautinische Forschungen: Zur Kritik und Geschichte der Komödie.* 2nd ed. Berlin: Weidman. (1st ed. 1895.)

Marache, R. 1952. *La critique littéraire de langue latine et le développement du gout archaïsant au IIe siècle de notre ère.* Rennes: Phihon.

———. 1957. *Mots nouveaux et mots archaïques chez Fronton et Aulu-Gelle.* Paris: Presses universitaires de France.

Mattiacci, S. 1986. "Apuleio e i poeti latini arcaici." In *Munus Amicitiae: Scritti in memoria di Alessandro Ronconi.* Vol. 1, 159–200. Florence: F. Le Monnier.

May, R. 2010. "The Function of Verse Quotations in Apuleius' Speeches: Making the Case with Plato." In *Form and Function in Roman Oratory,* edited by D. H. Berry and A. Erskine, 175–192. Cambridge, UK: Cambridge University Press.

———. 2006. *Apuleius and Drama: The Ass on Stage.* Oxford: Oxford University Press.

Mayer, R., ed. 2001. *Tacitus, Dialogus de Oratoribus.* Cambridge, UK: Cambridge University Press.

Mette, H. J. 1977. *Urkunden dramatischer Aufführungen in Griechenland.* Berlin: de Gruyter.

Mölk, U., ed. 1996. *Literatur und Recht: Literarische Rechtsfälle von der Antike bis in die Gegenwart.* Göttingen: Wallstein-Verlag.

Nesselrath, H.-G. 1985. *Lukians Parasitendialog: Untersuchungen und Kommentar.* Berlin: de Gruyter.

Oeri, H. G. 1948. *Der Typ der komischen Alten in der griechischen Komödie: Seine Nachwirkungen und seine Herkunft.* Basel: B. Schwabe.

Pasetti, L. 2007. *Plauto in Apuleio.* Bologna: Pàtron.

Sallmann, Klaus. 1995. "Erzählendes in der *Apologie* des Apuleius, oder Argumentation als Unterhaltung." In *Groningen Colloquia on the Novel.* Vol. 6, edited by H. Hofmann, 137–168. Groningen: Forsten.

Schindel, U. 1996. "Die Verteidigungsrede des Apuleius." In *Literatur und Recht: Literarische Rechtsfälle von der Antike bis in die Gegenwart,* edited by U. Mölk, 13–24. Göttingen: Wallstein-Verl.

Scodel, R., ed. 1993. *Theater and Society in the Classical World.* Ann Arbor: University of Michigan Press.

Steinmetz, P. 1982. *Untersuchungen zur römischen Literatur des zweiten Jahrhunderts nach Christi Geburt.* Wiesbaden: F. Steiner.

Swain, S. 2004. "Bilingualism and Biculturalism in Antonine Rome: Fronto, Gellius and Apuleius." In *The Worlds of Aulus Gellius,* edited by L. Holford-Strevens and A. D. Vardi, 3–40. Oxford: Oxford University Press.

Traina, A. 2010. "Style." In *The Oxford Handbook of Roman Studies,* edited by A. Barchiesi and W. Scheidel, 203–219. Oxford: Oxford University Press.

Van den Hout, M. P. J., ed. 1988. *M. Cornelii Frontonis Epistulae: Schedis tam editis quam ineditis Edmundi Hauleri.* Leipzig: Teubner.

———, ed. 1999. *A Commentary on the Letters of M. Cornelius Fronto.* Leiden: Brill.

Vessey, D. W. T. 1994. "Aulus Gellius and the Cult of the Past." *ANRW* 2.34.2: 1863–1917.

Winter, T. N. 1969. "The Publication of Apuleius' *Apology.*" *TAPhA* 100: 607–612.

··

CHAPTER 40

THE RECEPTION OF PLAUTUS IN ANTIQUITY

··

ROLANDO FERRI

1. PHASE IA: REPERFORMANCE

···

THE earliest, as well as probably the liveliest and most creative, phase of the reception of Plautus in antiquity must have started immediately after the playwright's lifetime, if not even earlier.[1] The first hint of an active reception of Plautus through performance was long recognized (Ritschl 1845: 180–238) in the initial lines of *Casina*, where the prologue speaker addresses the young members of the audience, who never had an opportunity to enjoy this play:

> nos postquam populi rumore intelleximus studiose expetere uos Plautinas fabulas, antiquam eius edimus comoediam, quam uos probastis qui estis in senioribus: nam iuniorum qui sunt, non norunt, scio.

> Since the rumor has reached us that you long to see Plautus's plays, we are putting onstage one of his old comedies: it was well received by you, I mean you older folks—for I know the younger ones among you are not acquainted with it.

Here the words *antiquam eius...comoediam* and *non norunt* suggest that these lines were pronounced long after the play's first production, and that Plautus was no longer directly involved as a producer or actor. Although we are in no position to reconstruct the way in which these repeat performances shaped the reception of Plautus at the level of stage action and setting, or of actors' interpretation (we have basically no clear idea of these features even for Plautus), we know with some certainty that these shows provided occasions for some extensive reworking of the plays. Plautus's scripts had not yet

---

[1] Very important discussion of the problem in Deufert 2002: 29–43, who however champions the mid-second century BCE as the period in which Plautus's plays underwent extensive revision.

attained the status of unmodifiable classics, and it was easy for them to undergo revisions, sometimes simply to fit a director's taste, others to match the size and expertise of the company putting up the play (see below). Indeed, intellectual property was feebly protected in Rome at this time, especially in the case of dramatic scripts: comedies were not published as books but passed on in the form of stage scripts from one stage director to the next. Plautus himself was thought by later critics to have put on stage earlier dramatists' plays after giving them a veneer of his own style (Gellius *N.A.* 3.3.13), and it is likely that he did the same to his own plays when they were reperformed after the premiere.

Unfortunately, only rarely can we isolate the authentic from the "revamped" or reperformed Plautus ("Revival" text was the definition of the great Plautus scholar W. M. Lindsay in Lindsay 1904) and use the latter in a literary-historical perspective. Were it not so, we could add to our history of the Latin theater a substantial new chapter, much more consistent than the entire body of fragments of Roman comedy collected in Ribbeck 1898.[2] What has come down as "Plautus" derives from ancient editions—the earliest presumably from the end of the second century BCE—in which critics collected and, in the course of time, merged, even competing versions of the same scene, or of single lines inside the same scene (Deufert 2002: 54–62). Unfortunately, whatever marks these ancient critics placed in the margins by way of signposting suspected interpolation all but disappeared in transmission.

Sometimes the modernization of language or metrics clearly was the motive for a later adapter's rewriting (the humor of a joke is lost on an audience that has difficulty in understanding the grammar of a phrase),[3] but many short interpolations may just as well be unintentional copying errors, or corrections introduced by later scholars who did not understand early Latin phraseology or meter. It is mostly from some suspected longer sections that we seem to glean interesting clues to the history of Plautus' *Nachleben*.[4]

---

[2] In recent years, the debate about later interpolations came into renewed prominence in a series of books by the German scholar Otto Zwierlein, who devised criteria for distinguishing authentic from spurious and later passages and advanced the thesis that most such interpolations stemmed from the hand of a single writer who was active after Terence and knew the *Togata* (Zwierlein 1991a: 228–235). Even if some of Zwierlein's analysis is very acute, his conclusions have not gained much consensus, both in the matter of detailed analysis, with too much emphasis on repetition and rational organization of thought and plot linearity as authenticity blueprints—always weak assumptions in comedy—as well as his proposal to date the doublets in the post-Terentian period.

[3] The two most typical examples for each category, obsolete language or obsolete metrics, are *Pseudolus* 523–523a, *studeo hercle audire, nam ted ausculto lubens.* / *[agedum nam satis libenter te ausculto loqui]* and *Trinummus* 788–788a, *sed epistulas quando opsignatas adferet* / *[sed opsignatas quando attulerit epistulas].*

[4] The search for interpolated sections was a constant concern of German nineteenth-century scholarship, which deployed great acumen and energy in this area (see for example Langen 1886: 233–387, Thierfelder 1929, and, more recently, Zwierlein 1990, Zwierlein 1991a, Zwierlein 1991b, and Zwierlein 1992). By contrast, the most recent series of editions of single plays of Plautus, the important Urbino-Sarsina series, shows much greater restraint. If we compare the list of suspect passages in Lindsay 1904: 43–45 with the practice of, e.g., Danese 2004, we see that most athetized passages have disappeared from the text.

For example, in his edition of *Poenulus* (Leo 1896: 240) the German scholar Friedrich Leo, athetized 1372–1397. In his view they were written to replace 1315–1354, "by some-one, as it seems, who wanted to increase the role of the *leno*"—a ribald character's role, but one which, to judge from the great actor Quintus Roscius's preference for Ballio part in Cicero's day (*Pro Q. Roscio comoedo* 20), was not unsympathetic to audiences and attracted good performers. Indeed, the entire very long ending of *Poenulus* reveals more than one loose joint between scenes written by different hands, for example when similar punch lines occur in succession or when entrance and contact announcements for the same character are inconsistent (the *leno*, for example, appears to enter the stage three times without ever exiting it, at 1342, 1387, and 1398).

In *Cistellaria* 671–748, the "Casket comedy," the maid Halisca is desperate because she has lost the "casket" containing small toys and other tokens needed to prove the status of the young *meretrix* Selenium. While Halisca frets onstage (singing a lively aria), even asking the audience if they have seen the casket, Lampadio, an old servant, and his mistress Phanostrata appear. Phanostrata has recognized in the casket the tokens of her own long lost daughter, and for this reason the two decide to listen aside. When they finally approach Halisca, the maid speaks so uninhibitedly of what is supposed to be a confidential family matter that she seems to be speaking to herself, or to address the audience once more. Then, at ll. 723–740, Halisca imparts again the same information, this time more reticently, with half-answers: she is looking for "signs" (*uestigium*) of something which "fled" somewhere, and gave the family "affliction"—a stalling tactic that irritates Lampadio. Only after some further comic banter with Lampadio does Halisca come to the point. Here the feeling of having a duplicate scene is impossible to overcome, and Thierfelder 1929: 120 persuasively suggested that the iambic septenarii at 708–718 were a later substitute for Halisca's song at 671–707. The reason for the substitution may have been that Halisca's role was not important enough for the ambitious aria (Goldberg 2004: 390–392), or simply that the actor impersonating this character (even allowing for role doubling, which we think was the rule) lacked the requisite expertise in singing.

2. PHASE IB: THE COMIC TRADITION

Closest in time, if not contemporary, to the elusive reperformances of Plautus comes the activity of the lesser-known authors of *comoedia palliata,* through and beyond Terence, and of the other comic subgenres. The latter are mainly *togata,* set in Rome or its whereabouts, and *Atellana,* distinguished by the use of fixed stock types and possibly by looser language and obscenity. However, study of these fragments in an intertextual, reception-focused perspective is hampered by the limited amount of extant material available for comparison. Fragments of Roman comedy outside Plautus and Terence are numerous but very short, and selected by their transmitting sources for their verbal rarities, which tends to distort our image of this tradition (see de Melo, this volume). Finally, even if a great deal of linguistic parallels between Plautus and the other comic authors is in evidence, *comici minores* were also probably drawing on a common tradition of comic verse writing, with a shared repertoire of near-formulaic verse forms, verbal jokes, and metaphors (Wright 1974). Hence it is never quite clear when we are dealing with a "reception" of Plautus in the strict sense. For example, it is difficult to decide whether the line end at Turpilius (who died in 103 BCE, according to Jerome's *Chronicon*) 101 R.[3] *ut fastidit carnufex,* "look at the rascal, how he scorns us" is influenced by Plautus *Mostellaria* 886 *ut fastidit simia* "look at the ape, how he scorns us." The same may also be true of Afranius (active ca. 150 BCE) 330–331 R.[3] *quis hic est Simia / qui me hodie ludificatus est,* "who is this Simia who's made a laughing stock of me today?" and Plautus *Pseudolus* 1017–1018 *peiorem... nunquam... uidi quam hic est Simia/* "I never saw a worse man than this Simia," though it is tempting to see a close parallel between what must have been a clever slave figure and the impertinent Simia who helps Pseudolus to cheat Ballio with an able disguise plot. Terence too seems to share formulaic expressions with Plautus; Terence, *Phormio* 166: *iam depecisci morte cupio: tu conicito cetera* ("I'm keen to settle for death in return, you can work out the rest") is almost identical to Plautus, *Casina* 93–94: *etiam in crucem / sequi decretumst: dehinc conicito ceterum* ("I'm determined to cling to you even on the scaffold—you can work out the rest from this"). In this case (*hinc*) *conicito cetera* (*-um*) seems a common conversational move in lively dialogue, and also prosodically convenient as a line end in iambic verse.

Even with these cautionary remarks, close linguistic analysis of the fragments suggests that the other comedians were closer to Plautus's verbal exuberance than to Terence's restraint and naturalism (see Karakasis, this volume), though on such tattered evidence the swing of individual variation between these two extremes is bound to be invisible to us.

A close relationship seems to exist between Plautus, *Asinaria* 307–308: *uerbis uelitationem fieri compendi uolo:/quid istuc est negoti?* "let us make an end to all this cut-and-thrust—what's the matter?" and Turpilius 145 R.[3]: *comperce uerbis uelitare: ad rem redi* "stop this guerrilla of words—come to the point," not only because of the metaphorical use of *uelitare,* literally "to attack with the light-armed infantry," but also because the expression is used in both passages to end a comic exchange and move on with the action (*quid istuc... negoti?/ ad rem redi*). Another passage possibly under direct influence from Plautus is Turpilius 132 R.[3]: *inuitauit uini poculis plusculum hic se in prandio* "this guy has indulged himself a little more over lunch with his wine." It seems to draw on Plautus, *Amphitruo* 282–283: *credo edepol equidem dormire Solem, atque adpotum probe: / mira sunt nisi inuitauit sese in cena plusculum* "I really think the sun is asleep, and full of wine to the brim: he really must have indulged himself a bit last night over dinner." The exhilarating scene in *Mostellaria* 157–312, in which the old servant Scapha advises the naive young courtesan Philematium on how to make the best of his young lover's affection, may have had an impact on two later authors. The joke in *Mostellaria* 268: *ut speculum tenuisti, metuo ne oleant argentum manus* "since you held the mirror, I am worried that your hand may smell of silver" is similar to that in Pomponius ("well known" as a poet in 89 BCE, according to Jerome), 6 R.[3] (from *Aleones,* "The gamesters"): *aleo non ludam sane, ne meae male olant manus* "I don't want to play with garlic, because I am worried that my hands may smell badly." (This is presumably said by a rustic who confuses the words *alium* "garlic" and *aleo* "gambler," which may separately suggest Plautine influence[5].) Likewise, Plautus, *Mostellaria* 261: *tum tu igitur cedo purpurissum* "then give me the purple makeup" resembles Afranius 231 R.[3] (from *Omen*, "The sign"): *cedo purpurissum*, "give me the purple makeup."

Ancient critics themselves sometimes provide other comparisons and parallels. To the otherwise almost unknown comedian Aquilius were ascribed nine lines from a play titled *Boeotia* in which a parasite complains against the inventors of sundials, presumably because he has to wait till midday before he can turn up at his patrons' doors. According to Gellius, who transmits the lines (*Noctes Atticae* 3.3.3), the parasite's tirade is stylistically so Plautine that the fragment would provide a very telling example of the reception of Plautus—except that, beginning with Varro *apud* Gellius, many have thought the play was actually by Plautus. (Indeed, the lines are normally ascribed to Plautus in many modern editions (cf. Monda 2004: 61).) Gellius again, in 13.23.11 and 16, quotes in close proximity Plautus, *Truculentus* 515: *Mars peregre adueniens salutat Nerienem uxorem suam* ("The home-coming Mars greets his wife Nerio") and the similar greeting formula in the obscure comic poet Licinius Imbrex, *nolo ego Neaeram te uocent, set Nerienem, /cum quidem Mauorti es in conubium data* ("let your name be not Neaera, but Nerio, since you were given as wife to Mars"). The similarity of situation, a boastful mercenary saluting his mistress with ridiculous pomp, and the recherché mythological imagery, suggests that Imbrex echoed Plautus's passage.

Less can be said at the level of plot structure or invention and characterization. It is extremely difficult to establish whether the rest of the comic tradition was oriented more closely toward Plautus's metatheatrical and verbally exuberance and thematic preference for plot types centered on deception, or toward Terence's greater naturalism in language and predilection for romantic plot types.

Titinius, a younger contemporary of Plautus, represented the (presumably) joking banter of fellow slaves in fr. 131 R: *lassitudo conseruum, reduuiae flagri* (spoken verse, probably iambics), "you sweating ground of fellow slaves, you residue of the whip," which has parallels in the abusive exchange between Libanus and Leonida in Plautus, *Asinaria* 297–298: *gymnasium flagri, salveto. :: quid agis, custos carceris? :: o catenarum colone. :: o uirgarum lascivia*, "hail to you, sporting ground of the whip! :: How are things, guard of the gaol? :: / Hail to you, tenant of the fetters. :: Hail to you, delight of the rod!," and in the greeting that the *leno* Dordalus offers the slave Toxilus in *Persa* 419–420: *scortorum liberator, suduculum flagri, compedium tritor, pistrinorum ciuitas*, "You freer of whores, you wearer-out of whips and fetters, you citizen of the mill" (tr. Bovie).

With a poetic program at the other end of the comic spectrum, Terence certainly knew Plautus's scripts, and probably even studied them in a company's or magistrate's

---

[5] To make the intertextual network even more tight-fitting, the same wordplay, and caricature of substandard rustic pronunciation, has been shown to occur in Plautus, *Mostellaria* 47: *sine me aleato fungi fortunas meas*: cf. Fontaine 2010: 52.

archives (Deufert 2002: 27).[6] In the prologue of *Eunuchus,* Terence admits having gone back to a Plautine script when an antagonist accused him of plagiarism: "He said that there was a play called *The Toady* [*Kolax*] by Naevius and Plautus, an old play, and that the characters of the parasite and the soldier had been lifted from it" (tr. P. Brown).

Plautus's *Colax* has not survived, so the truth of the charge cannot be checked, but critics ancient and modern have often remarked on the presence of "Plautine" features in *Eunuchus,* sometimes seen as a concession to the "unsophisticated" taste (true or supposed) of Roman popular audiences. Influence from Plautus is seen especially in the more conspicuous adoption of expressions of abuse and of inorganic speeches holding up the plot (Karakasis 2005: 121–123), particularly in the scenes in which the soldier and the parasite appear, where even Donatus, Terence's fourth-century commentator, mentions Plautus as a parallel for the characterization of Thraso the soldier (*Comm. in Ter. Eun.* 432—in Donatus's view, both Thraso and Plautus's soldier, Pyrgopolynices, express themselves in incorrect Latin as a mark of their stupidity). One example of a Plautine feature in *Eunuchus* occurs at 256–257: *concurrunt mi obuiam cuppedinarii omnes,/ cetarii, lanii, coqui, fartores, piscatores* "up there rushed, glad to meet me, all the sellers of fancy foods, the tunny-sellers, butchers, cooks, poulterers, and fishmongers" (tr. Brown), where Gnatho, the cunning parasite, is met by a colorful crowd of Roman market traders—his purveyors when he is in luck. This Roman intrusion is uncharacteristic for Terence, who aims at recreating a consistent, self-contained dramatic illusion (all his plays are set in Greece), so in this case he seems to have been inspired by Plautus, where such Roman vignettes are abundant: compare the satire of the traders coming to the house of the rich lady in *Aulularia* 508–513: *stat fullo, phyrgio, aurifex, lanarius;/ cauponiones, patagiarii, indusiarii, flammarii, violarii, carinarii; stant manulearii, stant murobatharii, propolae linteones, calceolarii; sedentarii sutores diabathrarii* "here come the cloth-fuller, the embroiderer, the goldsmith, the wool-weaver, the designers of fringes, makers of underwear, inventors of veils, dyers in purple and saffron, sleeve-stitchers, linen-weavers, perfumiers, shoe-makers and slipper-makers, sandal-fitters, and leather-stainers" (tr. Watling). In fact, the enumeration in Plautus is much longer, with a clear relish for the heaping up of more and more names effectively conjuring up the rich woman's world; Terence shows greater restraint and, typically for his linguistic purism, shuns traders' names of Greek etymology.

Later in the play, an interesting comment on the Plautine character of *Eunuchus* comes from Donatus's commentary.

---

[6] No explicit information about the availability of previous comic writers' scripts is extant prior to the learned activities of second and first century scholars such as Accius, Stilo, and Varro, which in itself shows that Plautus at least was entering a literary canon designed to compete with those of the Greeks. However, the close verbal echoes illustrated here and elsewhere (see Fontaine on Terence in this volume) suggest perusal of scripts, not merely some aural acquaintance with a performance; perhaps more decisively, Terence himself hints at a careful analysis of a number of written dramatic texts in his famous defense against the charge of plagiarism (*furtum*) in *Eunuchus* 19–33.

Don. *Comm. in Ter. Eun.* 694 AGEDVM HOC MIHI haec Plautina sunt, cum in iisdem longa sit disputatio; sed mire a Terentio proferuntur ad eius exemplum et, quod est plus, carent Plautinis nugis.

PAY ATTENTION, THEN—all of this is in the Plautine manner, because there is a long altercation about the same topic. At the same time, Terence ably sets the scene in Plautine manner and, what is more, without any of Plautus's idle jesting.

Donatus's note was probably in origin a comment on the entire scene in which young Phaedria grills the unhappy eunuch Dorus for allegedly raping the girl in his care. Since Phaedria refuses to believe his own brother is the real culprit, Dorus gets some heavy shaking, and Donatus must have felt that the questioning of the eunuch was too long-winded and repetitive and held up the action (*in iisdem...longa disputatio*). At the same time, Terence "adapts his model oddly" (*mire...ad eius exemplum*, which is, incidentally, a unique admission of influence from a Latin comic model in Terence), with no recourse to *nugae*. Donatus does not explain what in his view counts as Plautine *nugae*, but the word conjures up the emphasis on *ioci*, "verbal humor," as the main qualifying feature of Plautus in other critics (e.g., in Gellius, *Noctes Atticae*,3.3.3; Macrob. *Saturn.* 2.1.11). Wessner 1902: 418 suggested that Donatus had in mind Plautus *Menaechmi* 601–662, where Menaechmus tries in vain to pacify his wife for having stolen one of her dresses (a *palla* he has brought to his mistress) in a long-drawn-out series of evasions and denials which at some point the wife qualifies, in five successive lines, with *nugas agis* "all avails nothing." The passage in Donatus is doubly relevant both for the admission of Plautus as a model for Terence and for the hint of the dominant critical idea about Plautus, namely the preponderance of the comic, purely linguistic element over plausibility of action and characterization.

In 160 BCE, one year after staging *Eunuchus*, Terence wrote *Adelphoe*, where study and imitation of Plautus seems quite prominent. Plautus is mentioned in the prologue (22–24), and several echoes are in evidence, especially of *Miles Gloriosus*.

Old Micio in his initial monologue gives voice to his worries because his adopted son has not yet returned from a nocturnal escapade, and he starts to fear that his tolerant approach to education has not been well thought out (34–38): *ego quia non rediit filius quae cogito et / quibus nunc sollicitor rebus! ne aut ille alserit / aut uspiam ceciderit aut praefregerit / aliquid.* "But look what I'm suspecting and worrying about now because my son hasn't returned! I'm afraid he may have caught a chill, or fallen over somewhere, or broken something" (tr. Brown; on Micio's monologue, see Dunsch on prologues, this volume). Micio's lament seems inspired by the long tirade of old Periplecomenus in *Miles Gloriosus*, another satiric passage expatiating on the advantages of remaining a childless bachelor (*Miles Gloriosus* 718–722): *Pol si habuissem, satis cepissem miseriarum e liberis: / continuo excruciarer animi: si ei forte fuisset febris, / censerem emori; cecidis-setve ebrius aut de equo uspiam, / metuerem ne ibi diffregisset crura aut cervices sibi,* "children, if I had any, would have brought me a peck of trouble. I should never have had a moment's peace. If a child were ill, I should have thought he was dying; if my son fell off

his horse, or fell down drunk in the street, I'd be afraid he'd broken his leg or his neck."
(tr. Watling). Although the ethos of the words is different (Terence's father is deeply concerned, Periplecomenus speaks of a danger he has shunned), the borrowing is certain,
especially in the description of the possible mishaps (catching cold, a fall from a horse, a
bone fracture, *cecidisset... uspiam, metuerem ne ibi diffregisset...* and *ne... uspiam ceciderit aut praefregerit aliquid*), and reveals the extent of Terence's study of Plautus. At the
same time, the lack of specific details in Terence shows his greater concern for characterization (Micio speaking of his own son refrains from imagining grisly details), while at
the same time highlighting Plautus's taste for comic schadenfreude.

In *Adelphoe* 785–786, the frightened slave Syrus goes into hiding to escape from
Demea, the strict father who has just caught his own son holding a courtesan in his
brother's house: *nisi, dum haec silescunt turbae, interea in angulum / aliquo abeam atque
edormiscam hoc villi: sic agam* "All I can think of is to go off into a corner somewhere
while this rumpus quietens down and sleep off my little drop of wine: that's what I'll do"
(tr. Brown). The words Syrus pronounces while exiting the stage recall closely a passage
in Plautus, *Miles Gloriosus* 582–583: *nam iam aliquo aufugiam et me occultabo aliquot
dies, / dum haec consilescunt turbae atque irae leniunt*, "I'll do a bunk and lie doggo for a
day or two, until tempers have cooled and all this commotion died down" (tr. Watling).
In Plautus, the speaker is Sceledrus, also a slave, who has been convinced that the woman
he has seen in the arms of another is not Philocomasium, his master's mistress, and now
fears punishment for his rash accusations. The parallel is verbally close, especially *dum
haec (con)silescunt turbae*, although its intertextual relevance has never been explained.
Whereas Sceledrus all but disappears from the rest of *Miles Gloriosus* (evidently because
the actor impersonating him was later engaged in a different role), it is possible that
Terence, by reusing the Plautine exit cue with a more plausible motivation in naturalistic terms (dozing away the wine drunk during the incriminated party), is casting some
retrospective criticism over Plautus's more cavalier treatment of plot consistency and
dramatic unity.[7]

3. PHASE II: LATE REPUBLIC AND EARLY IMPERIAL PERIOD: SWING PHASE

By the end of the second century BCE, Plautus's plays began to be canonized.
Grammatical writers had become interested in his work and had collected the plays in
an edition, circulating in rolls (*uolumina*) that contained one or more plays (Deufert
2002: 44–62). The availability of an extensive Plautine corpus in turn triggered scholarly

---

[7] For an innovative discussion of intertextual phenomena in *comoedia palliata*, notably between
Plautus and Terence, cf. Fontaine 2014.

engagement with text and interpretation as well as critical debate at a literary-historical level. Traces of these early debates are visible in the work of later scholars (Varro, Gellius). Performances, too, certainly continued at least to the age of Cicero or a bit later, but little can be made of them in terms of reception. More generally, theatrical shows became more and more detached from what upper-class intellectuals regarded as "literature," for which crowded theaters were in their view an unsuitable venue.

Lucilius is the earliest author outside the comic tradition to have used this new Plautus in book form as a literary model. Indeed, among the literary genres of the later period it is satire that inherits many of the qualifying features of comedy, such as verbal humor and aggression, caricature, lively dialogue, and the use of colorful language, even mixtures of Latin and Greek. Unfortunately, owing to the fragmentary state of his *Satires*, Lucilius's debt to Plautus is not easy to evaluate. Nevertheless, at least fr. 736 Marx (from a satire recommending venal love) is worth mentioning, because it is an exact quotation of Plautus *Mercator* 396, *lignum caedat pensum faciat aedis uerrat uapulet* (describing the duties of a decent maidservant), "she must know how to cut wood, weave, mop the floor...take a beating."

Among Republican scholars interested in Plautus, M. Terentius Varro stands out. He fostered the critical appreciation of the playwright. He discussed issues of authenticity, exegesis, and literary history, and he recreated some of Plautus's spirit in his *Menippean Satires*.

Varro's *Menippean Satires* are a literary hybrid of prose and verse in various meters, including dramatic. They were probably narratives with much dialogue, perhaps sometimes even fully dialogic, in the manner of Horace's *Sermones*. We do not know if Varro had a marked preference for Plautus over all other comic writers. However, in the *Menippeans*, his debt to Plautus is certainly relevant. Varro quotes Plautus explicitly as a linguistic source, usually for made-up, inventive vocabulary (*ut ait Plautus*, 522 Astbury). In the satire *Agatho*, set at a symposium, a servant is addressed in iambic senarii: *quid tristiorem uideo te esse quam antidhac, / Lampadio? numquid familiaris filius / amat, nec spes est auxili argentaria, / ideoque scapulae metuunt uirgidemiam?* "Why do I see you so much sadder than you were wont to be, Lampadio? Is it that the young gentleman is in love, with no hope of finding help in money, and therefore your shoulders fear a harvest of flogs?" Here, an explicit allusion to Plautus is the final word *uirgidemia*. It is an invented compound from *uirga* "rod" and *(uin)demia* "vintage," a one-off verbal coinage found in Plautus, *Rudens* 636 *tibi ulmeam ni deesse speres virgidemiam* "may you never fail to receive a harvest of elm-tree bruises," where the comic slave's expectation of beatings for misbehavior humorously becomes his staple, something he prays for to live up to his comic role.[8]

---

[8] Another possible allusion to Plautine language is *spes auxili argentaria*, literally "silvery hope of help." The facetious misuse of the adjective also appears in *auxilium argentarium* in *Pseudolus* 105 and *inopia argentaria* in *Pseudolus* 300, both at line end.

Unmistakable adaptations of Plautine language are recognizable also in fr. 133–134 Astbury (from the *Eumenides*), where a spoiled young gentleman, who was probably cured of his bad temper at the end (hence *Eumenides*), shouts at one of his servants, perhaps his teacher, and even administers him a beating in the course of the scene: *quin mihi caperratam tuam frontem, Strobile, omittis?* "why don't you take away that frown of yours, Strobilus?" With *caperrata*, compare Plautus, *Epidicus* 609: *quid illud est quod illi caperrat frons severitudine?* "what is the reason that his brow is wrinkled from severity?" and 133 *apage in dierectum a domo nostra istam insanitatem,* "take this madness away from our house, to hell with you," where the adverbial *in dierectum* occurs only in Plautus, although typically in the form *i* (or *abi*) *dierecte* (e.g., *Mostellaria* 8).

A prose extract from *Menippeans* fr. 385 Astbury ushers us into a different aspect of the reception of Plautus, one in which comparison within the Roman comic tradition is the means of judgment and aesthetic evaluation: 399 Astbury *in quibus partibus, in argumentis Caecilius poscit palmam, in ethesin Terentius, in sermonibus Plautus* "for what regards the elements (of comedy), Caecilius comes first in writing plots, Terence in characters, Plautus in style."[9] The passage suggests that there were discussions about the literary accomplishments of early Roman comic writers, and these discussions centered on the three critical categories of language (choice of words), characterization, and plot structure. The fragment adumbrates a criticism against Plautus in some quarters, and seems to suggest that even Varro's endorsement of Plautus was not unrestricted. These standards of judgment were modeled on Greek New Comedy, and it may be argued that they were inadequate for a proper aesthetic appreciation of Plautus—yet even Varro, to all appearances, did not bring up new criteria to assess Plautus.

At least in terms of language and style, Plautus's prestige was rarely challenged. One generation before Varro, recognition for Plautus's style had been expressed in a famously eloquent dictum by the grammarian Aelius Stilo, according to whom "if the Muses had spoken Latin, they would have spoken the language of Plautus" (*apud* Quintilian, *Institutio oratoria* 10.1.99).

The works of Cicero mark a different stage of the reception of Plautus in the next century and a half. In Cicero, Plautus, with only five quotations, is vastly outnumbered by quotations of Terence (Deufert 2002: 151–158). In addition, four of the quotes are from *Trinummus,* one of the plays more suitable for education. For Cicero, Plautus is a paradigm of good, old-fashioned Latin—one step further from admiration as a creative, influential writer. In *De oratore* 3.45, the leading character of the dialogue, Crassus, describes his mother-in-law's more conservative manner of speaking as something that reminds him of Plautus. In this passage of Cicero, Plautus is synonymous with upper-class as well as highly educated diction (in particular, he is opposing urban to rustic and nonnative linguistic usage)—not the most immediate connection for a modern

---

[9] There is some controversy in the translation of *sermonibus*, which used to be taken to allude to lively dialogue rather than specifically to "style." In fact, this is much too specific: study of ancient critical vocabulary shows that style means primarily lexical choice (Jocelyn 1995: 241).

reader of Plautus, and presumably this has to do with the above-mentioned process of canonization of Plautus's works into literary (book) form. In the passage, Cicero is probably paying lip service to received critical opinion about Plautus's excellence in language. By his time, Plautine comedy was cultural heritage rather than pure entertainment. The compliment is echoed much later by Pliny the Younger, where letters written by a friend's young wife are compared to Plautus or Terence without the meter (cf. Plin. *Epist.* 1.16.6: *legit mihi nuper epistulas; uxoris esse dicebat: Plautum uel Terentium metro solutum legi credidi*).

A more peculiar, though interesting, comment on Plautus is preserved in Cicero *De officiis* 1.29. In it, two sorts of humor are enumerated, "the one, coarse, rude, vicious, indecent; the other, refined, polite, clever, witty," and Plautus is placed on a level with Greek New Comedy and Plato's dialogues as an example of the latter sort (no examples are provided for the former). The Greek examples probably come from a Greek source, with Plautus thrown in to add Roman color. We see in Cicero the two main high points of Plautus for the later tradition, his skill in making *ioci* and the elegance of his vocabulary.

Sometime at the beginning of the Augustan period, a radical break occurs in school practice. Teachers of grammar and rhetoric and schoolmasters begin to use near-contemporary literature in the educational curriculum, ousting the ancients. In fact, use of Plautus as a school author used for practicing correct word-division, punctuation, reading aloud, analysis of grammar and rhetorical figures, and so on, as we know was done for Vergil and Terence, may never have been extensive. However, the new interest in modern writers, such as Vergil, seems to lie behind the harsher evaluation of early drama expressed by critics of the Augustan and early imperial period, for example Quintilian, *Institutio oratoria* 10.1.99: *in comoedia maxime claudicamus* ("in comedy we are very deficient").

The new trend is clearly reflected in Horace's damning judgment of Plautus in the *Epistle to Augustus,* written probably around the year 12 BCE (*Epistulae* 2. 1.170–174):

> adspice, Plautus
> quo pacto partis tutetur amantis ephebi,
> ut patris attenti, lenonis ut insidiosi,
> quantus sit Dossennus edacibus in parasitis,
> quam non adstricto percurrat pulpita socco.

> Look at how badly[10] Plautus handles
> a youthful lover's part, or a tight-fisted father,
> or treacherous pimp, what a Dossennus he makes,
> sly villain, amongst his gluttonous parasites,
> how slipshod he is in sliding about the stage.
> (tr. Kline)

---

[10] I take the phrase *partis tutetur* as ironic, hence the need for "badly" in the translation.

In this passage of Horace, Plautus himself, keen to make easy money (175–176), walks the stage taking up farcical roles (Dossennus was a fixed type in *Atellana,* buffoonish or cartoonish rather than a character proper)—a criticism against Plautus's contamination of new comedy realism with the more surreal tradition of Roman farce, which in Horace's view was a debasement of the Greek tradition. Horace's criticism of Plautus centers mainly on Plautus's failure to maintain the (ultimately social) distinction between the dramatic roles of young lovers, strict fathers, pimps, and servants. In spite of the graphic, highly effective language in which this judgment is couched, Horace's opinion is not original in the context of ancient criticism. Donatus, for example, constantly praises Terence for maintaining distinctions (*seruare*) between *honestiores* and *humiliores,* between *liberale* "what is proper for free individuals" and *seruile.* In Donatus's comment *in Ter. Ad.* 986, the foil against which praise of Terence is outlined is Plautus. According to Donatus, Demea, though forced to accept the failure of his educational plan, maintains his dignity when he lays bare the compromises of his brother's leniency—he is different from the earlier Demea, but not so inconsistent with himself "as the character of Truculentus in Plautus": *bene in postremo dignitas personae huius seruata est, ne perpetuo commutata uideretur, ut Truculenti apud Plautum.* Donatus has in mind the rustic servant in *Truculentus,* who undergoes a complete change of attitude in the play, from uncouth misogynist to victim of the courtesans' charms.

For the early imperial period, the use of Plautus in the schoolroom is suggested (Deufert 2002: 177) by an interesting fragment that refers to Annaeus Cornutus, the teacher of the satirist Persius, who lived in the Neronian period. The passage was transmitted by the grammatical writer Charisius, active in the second half of the fourth century: Charisius, *Ars* 261.17 Barwick: *in mundo pro palam et in expedito ac cito: Plautus in Pseudulo* (500) *"quia sciebam," inquit, "pistrinum in mundo fore" ut Annaeus Cornutus libro tabularum ceratarum patris sui,* "The expression *in mundo* means 'openly' and 'quickly', or 'soon', as Plautus says in *Pseudolus,* (500), 'as I knew punishment in the mill was soon to come to me', as Annaeus Cornutus explains in the *Father's Wax-tablets."* Commentaries, or more probably exegetical writings, did exist in the republican period.[11]

4. PHASE III: SECOND CENTURY CE: REVIVAL

The critical fortunes of Plautus thereafter seem to have been at their lowest until the Antonine period (II century CE), when there was a revival of early Roman literature. In the figure of Apuleius, this so-called archaizing movement coincided with one of

---

[11] In late antiquity, there are traces of school use of Plautus, but such use was probably limited to a few very selective schools, like Donatus's, where Jerome studied. Commentaries on Plautus are mentioned in Jerome, *Apologia, PL* Migne 23.410B. One of these was the work of the otherwise unknown Sisenna (Deufert 2002: 245–256), active in the third century. Interestingly, this work contained many interpretations of metrical and prosodic phenomena, a rarity for this later period.

the most significant phases of the creative reception of Plautus in antiquity (see May in this volume). The archaizing movement in fact developed a trend never absent from Latin, the love for solemn obsolete language, for example in epic poetry and historical writers and in some orators. In this context, Fronto, *Epistulae ad Caes.* 4.3.2, includes Plautus in a catalogue of Roman early writers committed to the "peril of seeking out words with excessive diligence" (*periculum uerba industriosius quaerendi*); he opposed him to Cicero, whom Fronto saw as an author less devoted to such concentration over language. It is almost certainly in this context that a new critical edition of twenty-one plays of Plautus (the so-called Hadrianic edition) was put together, one in which for the first time the plays were divided into separate episodes called "scenes." This selection went back to Varro's own canon of the authentic Plautine plays, and it is responsible for the survival of Plautus into the Middle Ages.

5. PHASE IV: LATE RECEPTION

Second-century authors of the second sophistic, namely Gellius and Fronto, were fundamental in elevating Plautus to the status of a recognized linguistic authority in the works of later lexicographers (especially Nonius Marcellus, ca. 400 CE) and other grammatical writers. So, for example, at the end of the fourth century, Servius's commentary of Vergil largely resorts to Plautus to defend the use of archaic language in Vergil, and even goes so far as to argue, without much regard for genre or register expectations, that Plautus is the source of a passage in the *Aeneid* (Serv. *In Verg. Aen.* 6.62). Close in time to Servius, Macrobius mentions Plautus in his *Saturnalia* as one of the two most eloquent ancient Latin writers, on a par with Cicero (Macr. *Saturnalia* 2.1.10 *duos quos eloquentissimos antiqua aetas tulit, comicum Plautum et oratorem Tullium*).

The school tradition, however, remains firmly dominated by Terence and the particular type of dramatic illusion his works promoted. In the treatise *On Comedy* by the grammarian Evanthius (Cupaiuolo 1992), active in the first half of the fourth century and perhaps author of a commentary on Terence antedating Donatus, Plautus is viewed only against the model of Terentian dramatic qualities: his work suffers from stylistic disunity (presumably a reference to Plautus's paratragic and parodic sections), is replete with obscurities (because of allusions to customs and topic events in need of explanation, for later generations, by the *historici*), and frequently *facit actorem uelut extra comoediam loqui* ("shows actors breaking the dramatic illusion"), which Terence does not allow and which, in Evanthius's view of comedy, is a flaw.

Little pagan or profane literature survives after Apuleius, and therefore the reception of Plautus is harder to follow for the later periods, except in grammatical writers.

Among Christian writers, Jerome is the only one who seems to have had an extensive knowledge of Plautus, commonly attributed to his school years at Donatus's school in Rome. Jerome mentions Plautus several times, for example in his list of translators aiming at correct idiom in translation from a foreign language (in his letter 57, to

Pammachius, also known as *De optimo genere interpretandi*). Jerome uses Plautus as a source of sarcastic allusion, especially in his polemical writings, for example in *Aduersus Iouinianum* 1.1. Here he describes the contortion of Jovinian's argument with the words *has quidem praeter Sibyllam leget nemo*, paraphrasing *Pseudolus* 23–24, *has quidem pol credo nisi Sibylla legerit / interpretari alium posse neminem* ("I don't think anyone but the Sibyl will be able to decipher this letter"). In Minucius's *Octavius,* the expression *homo Plautinae prosapiae* is synonymous with buffoon or charlatan. Decimus Ausonius, a court notable, imitates and adapts Plautus in the *Ludus septem sapientum*, written in 390, in iambic senarii exhibiting a fairly expert understanding of Plautine metrics.

A little-known chapter in the history of Plautus reception in antiquity is the play *Querolus siue Aulularia,* probably written in fifth-century Gaul. It is not known whether the play was intended for reading or for performance. *Querolus* ("The grumpy man") is written in prose imitating the iambic and trochaic rhythms of *palliata.* The play takes its name from the title figure, who is the son of Plautus's miser Euclio in *Aulularia.* When the play begins, Querolus has received news of his father's death while abroad. He is upset, though mainly at the thought that his father has left him penniless. The wheeler-dealer Mandrogerus, presented in the play as a "parasite" though he claims to be an astrologer and a magician, knows that Euclio has left his son a treasure in a pot kept inside the house, and manages to obtain it from Querolus through a stratagem. However, when he finally opens the pot, Mandrogerus finds only a funerary urn in it. In a fit of anger and spite, he throws the urn through a window into Querolus's house. The urn breaks apart and reveals a treasure inside, to the great joy of Querolus, who is thus cured of his bad temper.

Querolus is a middle-class malcontent in search of his way in life. The initial dialogue with *Lar familiaris,* another character taken from Plautus's *Aulularia,* is the occasion of much satire against various contemporary professions, especially lawyers. Plautus's *Aulularia* provides a rough background and the odd turn, especially short answers and greetings, but the main character is very different from the original Euclio, and nothing of the more subversive elements of Plautus has survived. Querolus's slave Pantomalus takes no initiatives, and in fact only appears briefly to fill in details of the psychological profile of the grumpy protagonist. The old *Aulularia* has been turned into a neat morality play, in which a young man of neither shining intellect nor flawless character is helped by a friendly deity to a little fortune which also makes his temper less sour in the end. Curiously, the author's initial declaration to be writing "in Plautus' footsteps" seems to echo the "revival" prologue to *Casina* (see p. 768): *Aululariam hodie sumus acturi, non ueterem at rudem* "we are going to put up today *Aulularia,* not the old but a new one," yet memory of Plautus is watered down by school reminiscences of all the major classics, down to Cicero's *o tempora o mores.*

BIBLIOGRAPHY

Cupaiuolo, G., ed. 1992. *Evanzio: De fabula.* Naples: Loffredo.

Danese, R. M. 2004. *Titus Maccius Plautus: Asinaria.* Urbino: QuattroVenti.

Deufert, M. 2002. *Textgeschichte und Rezeption der plautinischen Komödien im Altertum.* Berlin: de Gruyter.

Fontaine, M. 2010. *Funny Words in Plautine Comedy.* Oxford: Oxford University Press.

——. 2014. "Dynamics of Appropriation in Roman Comedy: Menander's *Kolax* in Three Roman Receptions (Naevius, Plautus, and Terence's *Eunuchus*)." In *Ancient Comedy and Reception. Essays in Honor of Jeffrey Henderson,* edited by S. D. Olson. Berlin and Boston: de Gruyter.

Goldberg, S. 2004. "Plautus and His Alternatives: Textual Doublets in *Cistellaria.*" In *Studien zu Plautus' Cistellaria,* edited by R. Hartkamp and F. Hurka, 385–395. Tübingen: Gunter Narr Verlag.

Jakobi, R. 1996. *Die Kunst der Exegese in Terenzkommentar des Donat.* Berlin and New York: W. de Gruyter.

Jocelyn, H. D. 1988. "Studies in the Indirect Tradition of Plautus' *Pseudolus* III: The 'Archaising Movement,' Republican Comedy and Aulus Gellius' *Noctes Atticae.*" In *Vir bonus discendi peritus: Studies in Celebration of Otto Skutsch's Eightieth Birthday,* edited by N. Horsfall, 57–72. London: Institute of Classical Studies.

——. 1995. "Horace and the Reputation of Plautus in the Late First Century BC." In *Homage to Horace,* edited by S. J. Harrison, 228–247. Oxford: Oxford University Press.

Karakasis, E. 2005. *Terence and the Language of Roman Comedy.* Cambridge, UK: Cambridge University Press.

Langen, P. 1886. *Plautinische Studien,* Berlin: Calvary & Co.

Leo, F., ed. 1896. *Plauti comoediae,* 2 vols. Berlin: Weidmann.

Lindsay, W. M. 1904. *The Ancient Editions of Plautus.* Oxford: Parker.

Monda, S., ed. 2004. *Titus Maccius Plautus: Vidularia et deperditarum fabularum fragmenta.* Urbino: QuattroVenti.

Ribbeck, O., ed. 1898. *Comicorum Romanorum praeter Plautum et Syri quae feruntur sententias fragmenta.* Leipzig: Teubner.

Ritschl, F. 1845. *Parerga zu Plautus und Terenz.* Berlin: Weidmann.

Blänsdorf, J. 2002. "Antike Rezeption." In *Handbuch der lateinischen Literatur der Antike.* Vol. 1, *Die archaische Literatur: Von den Anfängen bis zu Sullas Tod: Die vorliterarische Periode und die Zeit von 240 bis 78 v. Chr.,* edited by W. Suerbaum. Munich: C. H. Beck. 225–227.

Thierfelder, A. 1929. *De rationibus interpolationum Plautinarum.* Leipzig: Teubner.

Wessner. P., ed. 1902. *Aeli Donati quod fertur commentum Terenti.*2 vols. Leipzig: Teubner.

Wright, J. 1974. *Dancing in Chains: The Stylistic Unity of the Comoedia. Palliata.* Rome: American Academy.

Zwierlein, O. 1990. *Zur Kritik und Exegese des Plautus.* Vol. 1, *Poenulus und Curculio.* Stuttgart: Franz Steiner.

——. 1991a. *Zur Kritik und Exegese des Plautus.* Vol. 2, *Miles gloriosus.* Stuttgart: Franz Steiner.

——. 1991b. *Zur Kritik und Exegese des Plautus.* Vol. 3, *Pseudolus.* Stuttgart: Franz Steiner.

——. 1992. *Zur Kritik und Exegese des Plautus.* Vol. 4, *Bacchides.* Stuttgart: Franz Steiner.

....

AELIUS DONATUS AND HIS COMMENTARY ON TERENCE'S COMEDIES

....

CHRYSANTHI DEMETRIOU

LITTLE is known of the life of Aelius Donatus, one of the most famous grammarians of Rome. Although he was probably of African descent (Kaster 1988: 276, based on evidence from Syme 1978), there is no certain evidence that verifies his origin (Holtz 1981: 19–20). We can infer from Jerome's writings that Donatus was his teacher as a schoolboy (*Comm. Eccl.* 1) and that he was active around the middle of the fourth century (Jer. *Chron.* s. a. 354); we can also infer from a treatise by Jerome (*C. Ruf.* 1.16) that both he and his contemporary Rufinus had read Donatus's commentaries as boys. Donatus was the author of two *artes grammaticae*, the *minor* in one book and the *maior* in three. He also composed a variorum commentary on Vergil's works, from which only a few fragments survive; it constituted a valuable source for Servius and Macrobius, and important parts were included in the commentary of Servius Danielis. And he also composed a commentary on Terence's comedies (consult Kaster 1988: 276).

Donatus's commentary on Terence is found in about forty manuscripts of the fifteenth century, and in two manuscripts of the eleventh and thirteenth centuries that preserve only a part of the work; it survives as well in two later editions that are based on manuscripts about which we know little (see Reeve 1983: 153). The commentary treats five of the six comedies of Terence; we possess no scholia on *Heauton Timorumenos*. Not only is the commentary we possess today incomplete, but the state in which it has survived is problematic. As Benjamin Victor explains in this volume, Donatus composed his commentary in the fourth century, drawing from material of earlier sources. At some point, scribes copied the commentary into the margins of manuscripts of Terence, where it was folded in with other scholia. Later, the original commentary was lost, and still later, someone attempted a "reconstruction" of the commentary by copying the scholia found in the margins of the manuscripts that preserved Terence's comedies. We cannot confirm how many sources were used for this composition. The fact that comments on lines

348–440 of *Phormio* survive in the manuscripts in two successive forms makes it likely that the scribe used two sources (Grant 1986: 61; Barsby 2000: 492–493). The exact date of this "reproduction" of Donatus's commentary on Terence is unknown, but the sixth century has been regarded as the terminus post quem (Grant 1986: 60–70).

The long and complex process by which the commentary survived has inevitably influenced the material we now possess. As Benjamin Victor points out, the process is evident in the inconsistencies found between the lemmata and corresponding scholia (e.g., the scholiast to *Phormio* 368 must have read a variant here). In addition, some references appear twice (e.g., a similar remark on Gnatho's speech at *Eunuchus* 232.3 and 233), whereas some comments contain contradictory statements (e.g., the scholia on *Hecyra* 670, discussed in Jakobi 1996: 31, are clearly drawn from two different models, since they discuss two variant readings); certainly not all scholia are of the same quality. The commentator is sometimes imprecise, as on *Eunuchus* 283, when he suggests that Parmeno (and thus the reader) should deliver the line in a lower tone so that "secrets are not revealed" (283.2 *et hoc lentius; nam si aliter pronuntiaueris secreta produntur*), failing to notice that there is no one on stage with the slave. Michael Reeve pointed out that the reconstruction of Donatus's original commentary is an "impossible task," partly because citations that are not included in the surviving version are found in other sources, as in Priscian, and the scholia on the *Bembinus* and *Victorianus* of Terence; these scholia, in turn, may not have been excerpted from the original commentary but from shortened versions (Reeve 1983: 156).

The commentary is preceded by three introductory texts: a *Life of Terence* (the author of the commentary indicates that the first seven paragraphs were copied from Suetonius—*Vita Terenti* 8 *Haec Suetonius Tranquillus*), and two treatises, *De Fabula*, assigned to Evanthius (Ruf. *GL* 6.554), and *Excerpta de Comoedia*, assigned to Donatus. The first treatise outlines the origins of tragedy and comedy and then focuses on the genre of comedy, beginning with its evolution from Old Comedy, which is then contrasted with New Comedy. A discussion of some basic features of comedy follows (chorus and division into five acts, action and stage machinery), with particular reference to Terence's characteristics (often in comparison with Plautus). Subsequently, the genres of Roman comedy are briefly explained (*togata, praetexta, Atellana, Rinthonica, tabernaria, mimus*) and a comparison is made with tragedy. Finally, the treatise discusses the three types of comedy (*motoria, stataria,* and *mixta*) and the division of each play into four parts (prologue, *protasis, epitasis,* and *catastrophe*). The second treatise, *De comoedia*, provides a definition for comedy, discusses its function, and then takes up particular themes: origin of the genre and its name, history and development, types and subdivisions, the use of masks, its four parts (as listed above), the games in which comedies were performed, costumes and stagecraft, and the division between *diverbia* and *cantica*.

After these two treatises, a running commentary on the five comedies appears. A preface to each play comes first, which usually discusses: the name of the play and its Greek original, its plot, the four divisions (as mentioned in the introductory treatises), the type of play (*motoria, stataria,* or *mixta*), the *didascalia*, the roles (and protatic characters), and a brief outline of what happens in each act. The main corpus of the commentary for each comedy is divided into five acts and then into scenes. The first observation on the first verse of each scene often provides a brief summary of that scene, with reference to dramatic technique and the arrangement of plot. Finally, there are scholia on each verse, and these are preceded by a lemma, i.e., the part of the text discussed by the commentator.[1] The scholia on the corpus of verses are varied in content: interpretations and analyses of text, variant readings, and discussions of grammar (including linguistic matters), delivery, stage action, and Terence's use of rhetorical figures.

Overall, despite its problems in transmission, the commentary that survives under the name of Donatus plays a prominent role in the study of Terence. It serves, for example, as one of the most important sources for editors of Terence's text.[2] It has enabled scholars to interpret linguistic and social aspects of Terence's comedies (e.g., Citti 2008) and to illuminate traditional Roman legends and stories (e.g., Williams 1970; Jocelyn 1971). Furthermore, by discussing Terence's relationship to the Greek originals, the commentary often suggests approaches to this thorny issue and has consequently led to fruitful scholarly discussion, including whether the commentator's accounts of Greek sources are accurate (e.g. Barsby 2000: 497–502, Turner 2010). However, a basic problem we face when studying the commentary concerns the identity of the author of the scholia we now possess. The surviving commentary is certainly not Donatus's original work; nevertheless, the person(s) who worked on this compilation aimed at reconstructing the original commentary and in all likelihood tried to preserve its original aims. Accordingly, in this chapter, I use the name Donatus to refer to the author(s) of the corpus of the surviving scholia, the core of which is undoubtedly Donatus's original commentary.

1. Identifying Donatus' Readers: Delivery, Gestures, and Linguistic Characterization

A brief examination of some recurrent topics in the Commentary—namely, vocal delivery, the use of facial expressions and gestures by the comic characters, and linguistic characterization—may aid in identifying its audience and purpose. The commentator often seems to be addressing readers in an instructive way, explaining how a line or specific word should be delivered. For instance, a scholium on *Hecyra* 640 refers to

---

[1]   In this essay, lemmata are omitted. Donatus's text is taken from Wessner 1902–1908; in translating Donatus's passages, I have consulted Bureau et al. (2007–2011).

[2]   Barsby 2000: 494–497 examines some instances in which Donatus's testimony was used by Terence's editors in texts of the *Eunuchus*. Victor 2002, on the other hand, draws attention to the problem of Donatus's reliability, mainly in relation to his translations and interpretations.

Phidippus's delivery: *hoc totum cum indignatione in uxorem pronuntiandum est* (640.3, "all this must be pronounced with indignation against his wife"); another on *Andria* 663 refers to Charinus's delivery: *"Dauus" cum admiratione pronuntiandum* (663.1, " 'Davus' must be pronounced with surprise"), and later in the same play, a scholium again gives instruction for Charinus's delivery, this time when he accuses Davus of scheming: *cum odio hoc pronuntiandum est* (667.3, "this must be delivered with hatred"). Similar scholia appear frequently (e.g., on *Adelphoe* 949.3 and on *Hecyra* 595.1).

Additionally, Donatus often calls for the use of specific facial expressions; e.g., in *Phormio*, as Davus describes the frivolous expenses that his slave-friend Geta will have to pay for, the commentator remarks *hoc uultuose pronuntiandum* (49.1, "this must be delivered with a face full of grimaces"), and in *Andria,* when Davus addresses his young master Pamphilus, explaining how difficult his situation will be if refuses his father's bidding to marry (380–381: *pater est, Pamphile: difficilest*), the commentator offers the same remark: *hoc uultuose pronuntiandum est* (380.3). On other occasions, he suggests the appearance of particular emotions; thus, on Micio's facial expression in *Adelphoe*, we find *haec interrogatio quasi subtristi uultu est proferenda* (596.2, "this question must be uttered with a kind of sad facial expression").[3]

The commentator often calls for the use of gesture in delivery. Most cases are associated with the delivery of demonstrative adverbs and pronouns, as in *Phormio* 145.1 *"sic" dicendum est cum aliquo gestu* (145.1, " 'sic' must be said with some sort of gesture"). On a few occasions, Donatus instructs the speaker to use his fingers or hands, as in the scholia on *Adelphoe*: *Et hoc "tibi" et "tu" pronuntiandum est intento digito et infestis in Micionem oculis* (97.2, "and this 'tibi' and 'tu' must be delivered with an extended finger and hostile eyes towards Micio"; cf. on *Eunuchus* 859.4). In *Adelphoe*, while focusing on a grammatical point, he explains how an imitative hand gesture accompanies delivery: *Et TANTILLVM δεικτικόν est: uidetur enim manu fingere quam paruulum* (563.2, "and 'tantillum' is demonstrative: indeed, it seems that he represents with his hand how small [it was]").

Some calls for gestures suggest a deeper understanding of stage action and characterization. When commenting on Charinus's remark to his slave Byrria in the *Andria* ("If you were in this situation [*hic*], you'd think otherwise!"), Donatus again focuses on a demonstrative pronoun and observes, *"hic" gestu scaenico melius commendatur, nam haec magis spectatoribus quam lectori scripta sunt* (310.1, " 'hic' is better designated by a gesture of the stage, since these are written more for the spectators' benefit than for the reader's"). In *Eunuchus*, regarding Phaedria, who has just conceded to Thais's pleas that he leave town for a couple of days (188, "it's been decided to act just so: Thais must be humored!"), the commentator emphasizes the importance of vocal delivery and gesture for the expression of this lover's sentiments: *cum pronuntiatione et gestu, ut ostendat*

---

[3] On Donatus's references to facial expressions and the use of masks in theater, see section ii of this essay.

quae uis amoris sit, ut Thaidi mos geratur (188.2, "with a verbal delivery and gesture to show what the power of love is so that he humors Thais").

As the previous comment suggests, scholia on the characters' nonverbal behavior elucidate their reactions to dialogue and/or the dramatic situation and are surely consistent with their roles. The commentator's interest in characterization is especially evident in remarks on the linguistic usage of stock characters (more examples in Reich 1933 and Dutsch 2008: 188–194). In the commentary on *Eunuchus*, for example, Donatus discusses the courtesan's language and use of blandishments. At 95.2, he comments on her repeated use of the vocative *mi* (*anime mi, <mi> Phaedria*) as she prepares to petition her young suitor to leave town for two days: *Vide quam familiariter hoc idem repetat blandimentum; uult enim Terentius uelut peculiare uerbum hoc esse Thaidis* ("see how familiarly she repeats this same blandishment; indeed, Terence wants this word to serve as Thais' own idiom"), and cites other examples of the usage. Of particular interest is the term *blandimentum*, usually, but not always, referring to expressions such as *mea, mea tu, amabo*, as well as repetition of the interlocutor's name. Thus (keeping to *Eunuchus*), Donatus comments on Thais's speech when she first espies the slave Parmeno at the opening of III2 and says *ehem Parmeno: bene fecisti*; here he asks: *quid bene fecit Parmeno? an quasi perturbata haec loquitur et iam de nihilo blandiens, utpote meretrix et faceta?* (463.1: "What has Parmeno done well? Or does she say this as being somewhat troubled and now flattering for no reason, inasmuch as she is a savvy courtesan?"). Thais's praise of Parmeno is not explained by the action, and so the commentator suggests that she may be setting the tone for a kindly reception of the slave upon his inopportune intrusion. Elsewhere Donatus acknowledges the distinct nature of a courtesan's speech, reflecting a long tradition of interest; scholarly attention to the subject is prominent today (e.g., Dutsch 2008: 49–66).

Donatus is also interested in the language and sentiments of comic slaves, pointing out what is both appropriate *and* inappropriate for their characterization. Thus in the *Phormio scholia*, he contrasts the language of comic slaves to that of slaves of tragedy: *garrulos seruos et sententiosos amat comoedia, tristes et parce loquentes tragoedia* (41.4, "comedy likes its slaves to be garrulous and pompous moralizers, tragedy likes them to be unhappy and reserved"). At *Eunuchus* 926.1, he finds Parmeno's diction appropriate for gladiators. In some instances, he recognizes "slave style" even when commenting on the language of nonslaves: e.g., when Chaerea approaches Thais in *Eunuchus* and begs her to pardon him, the commentator points out that Chaerea pretends to be her slave and uses the language of a (runaway) slave (853.1 *uerba seruorum*; 855 *uerba fugitiuorum*). Linguistic characterization is firmly connected even with textual criticism, since the commentator sometimes makes his choice of a variant reading on the basis of what is appropriate for the speaking character and his *ethos* (e.g., on *Phormio* 249, he explains that grammatical mistakes are common for slaves—see Victor in this volume). Serious sentiments, on the other hand, are inappropriate for slaves— unless they are meant for comic effect; thus in the scholia on *Phormio*, the commentator explains Geta's remarks this way: *hae graues sententiae ex persona seruorum cum dicuntur, ridiculae sunt et eo consilio interponuntur* (138.1, "these serious maxims, when expressed by a slave character, arouse laughter and are introduced for this purpose"; and cf. Don. *ad Eunuchus* 789.1, where he makes a similar statement about the soldier's speech: *animaduerte, quantam uim habeant ad delectandum in comoediis seuerae sententiae, cum ab ridiculis personis proferuntur* (789.1, "observe what power serious maxims have for entertaining in comedies, when uttered by funny characters"). Similarly, he makes an effort to justify the use of a serious proverbial statement by the freedman Sosia in *Andria* by claiming that this particular *sententia* is well-known: *sententia non incongrua seruo, quia et peruulagata* (61.2, "the saying is not inappropriate for the slave, since it is very common"). So sensitive is Donatus to correct linguistic characterization that not only does he offer special pleading for an inappropriate characterization (as he does with Sosia's sentiment in *Andria*), but he also, on occasion, gently chides the author; thus, regarding Chremes's speech at *Eunuchus* 736, he writes: *hoc videtur sapientius et facetius dici quam ebrio rustico adulescentulo debuisset. hoc vitium tunc fit, cum ingenium suum poetae in personas conferunt* (736.3, "this seems more clever and witty than what should have been said by a drunken young man. This fault is evident in those instances in which poets assign their own braininess to their characters").

Scholia on delivery and linguistic characterization have elicited much modern discussion about Donatus's sources and purposes; this discussion, in turn, is intimately connected with questions about his audience. Jakobi (1996: 10–14), for example, suggested that scholia on characters' delivery, facial expressions, and gestures were most likely products of a literary analysis of the text. And most scholars, for that matter, think that the purpose of Donatus's scholia on acting was related to his profession as a *grammaticus*. Comments on gesture and vocal delivery were a part of the students' practice in *lectio/anagnosis*, "reading," "recitation" (Blundell 1987: 180–181). Likewise, comments on linguistic characterization have been viewed as a grammarian's instruction about different registers of diction (Maltby 2007: 23–24). From a practical perspective, as Benjamin Victor points out in this volume, Donatus's references to nonverbal components would facilitate reading a text that had no punctuation. And on a more general level of praxis, we can turn to Quintilian (*Inst. Or.* 1.11.12–13), who points out that a professional actor (*comoedus*) was employed to teach recitation at schools and that comedy passages are the most suitable for practice in delivery. Terence continued to be among the standard four Latin authors studied in schools after Quintilian's lifetime and was certainly studied in late antiquity (Pugliarello 2009: 606–607). The study of comedy and tragedy in recitation exercises as well as the observation of professional comedians formed a vital part of Roman education; the study of drama is attested even in the fifth century CE (e.g., Augustine, *C.D.* 2.8). Viewed in this light, the purpose of Donatus's teaching is manifest: the *Commentum Terenti* is addressed primarily to his students as a part of their study of Latin literature and language and their practice in rhetoric and public speaking.

Numerous instances in the scholia, however, suggest that Donatus's purpose went beyond the exercises of *anagnosis*. The scholia on nonverbal expressions are not always instructions addressed to a reader with a view to reciting a passage; rather, they often seem to analyze the action and to aim at assisting the reader in understanding and interpreting particular scenes (see also Csapo-Slater 1995: 29). Consider comments on a scene from *Andria* in which the slave Davus directs a scheme to deceive Chremes, giving instructions to the female slave Mysis on how to act in front of the old man. Here Donatus has perceived the need for quick changes in voice modulation on the part of the slave characters, depending on what Chremes is meant to hear. First he refers to Mysis's lower tone when addressing Davus (752.2 *summissa uoce*—"in a low voice"), and then, two verses later, when Davus addresses Mysis, he refers to his "urgent tone" (*hoc pressius dixit*, 754.4); the "lower voice" is required so as not to be overheard by Chremes, but the "urgent tone" is meant to elicit a response from Mysis that *will* be overheard. After a few more lines, Donatus points to another change in delivery style: *hic uersus clare dicitur, sequens, ne senex audiat, presse* (759, "this verse is said aloud, the following in a low voice, so that the old man does not hear"), i.e., Chremes must hear the first verse (759), where Davus orders Mysis to remove the infant from the doorstep, but must *not* overhear the next, when he bids her not to move an inch. The commentator's observations in these instances not only look to a possible recitation but also vividly suggest the way he understood how action onstage was conveyed by the modulation of voice.

Analysis of action and stage movement is also apparent in Donatus's commentary on *Eunuchus*, where he depicts Pythias's approach to Chremes with a gesture: *Et apparet illum manu tactum esse, qui sic irascitur, quia dixit "mi Chremes" quasi: meus indignatus est adulescens* (536.2, "and it's clear that she has touched him with her hand, and that he then becomes irritated, because she said 'my Chremes' as if saying 'my young man is indignant'"); indeed, so indignant is he that he responds with a curse (*malam rem hinc ibi?*); we might infer, with Donatus's assistance here, that Pythias has touched him to prevent him from turning away. Later in the play, when the maids repeatedly fail to recognize the wretched eunuch who has been hauled onstage before their very eyes ("Where is he?" "You ask? Don't you see?" "Me? See? I beg of you, see whom?" 675–676), Phaedria exclaims, *hunc scilicet* ("This man, of course!"). Donatus remarks, with an eye to onstage action, *hoc iam tangens eunuchum dicit Phaedria* (676, "Phaedria says this while touching the eunuch"), presumably thrusting the eunuch before them. And still later in the play, the commentator outlines the overall movement of the soldier: *hic rursus inepti uanitas militis demonstratur ad amicam tamquam ad hostilem exercitum pergentis irritato animo, concito cursu, undanti chlamyde, trepidi et quatientis caput* (771.1, "once again here we are shown the vanity of the stupid soldier, advancing against his mistress as if against a hostile army, full of anger, with headlong speed, cloak rippling, quivering and shaking his head").

While scholia that give instruction for delivery are not always clearly distinguishable from those that offer analyses of action (often the same scholium does both), nevertheless, Donatus's interest in reconstructing the action for readers is evident and should be understood within the larger framework of his interest in the plots of plays and the exegetical character of his work; after all, his commentary belongs to the grammarian's task of the "exegesis of the poets" (*enarratio poetarum*)—combined with the study of grammar (Holtz 1981: 25; Kaster 1988: 18)—and discussion of the nature of the text would be a part of this task (Holtz 1981: 32). In this context, apart from visualizing the action in ways that have been discussed (recall, e.g., his remarks on Davus's instructions to Mysis in the *Andria*, or his interpretations of gesture based on demonstrative pronouns, as in Phaedria's *hunc scilicet* in *Eunuchus*), the commentator often explicitly reminds his readers that what is being discussed is a *dramatic text*. In a scholium from *Andria*, he observes that a saying is condemned at school but used in theater (67 *sed in theatro dicitur, non in schola*). In another scholium from the same play, he explains how Terence presents a courtesan's death: "notice that on every occasion comic deaths are introduced by the playwright in such a way that, although they are mentioned in accord with the requirements of the plot, yet they are not tragic" (105.3 *animaduerte ubique a poeta sic induci comicas mortes, ut cum ad necessitatem argumenti referantur, non sint tamen tragicae*).[4] Such remarks, demonstrating as they do an interest in theatrical genres, share an intellectual context with theories associated with the nature of comedy and theater that are found in the introductory treatises attached to the main corpus of the commentary. Comments on Terence's successful management of the comic plot that are found throughout the commentary (e.g. on *Andria* 228.1–2, 404.1; *Eunuchus* 440.2, *Hecyra* 415.1) also share that context.

What, then, is the purpose of Donatus's scholia on stage action, and why does the commentator offer so many remarks on it as well as on conventions of the comic genre? Comments on linguistic characterization and stage action can certainly be a part of the commentator's exegesis, since the commentator, apart from providing instruction on ideal diction, could also view his task as to offer deeper insights into the plot and characters of each play. Does this mean that the different strands of his exegesis contradict each other in terms of purpose and audience? I would say no. Observations on delivery are successfully blended with the commentator's interpretation of Terence's text. Although Donatus's interest in aspects of performance finds its starting point in delivery exercises, he extended that fundamental interest, incorporating comments on action and characterization, most likely to help more advanced students to interpret Terence's dramaturgy and to visualize the stage action. Donatus's audience, then, will have been heterogeneous to some extent, including both novices and advanced students of rhetoric and dramatic literature.

2. DONATUS'S GESTURES AND GRAPHIC ILLUSTRATIONS

A return to Donatus's remarks on gesture will lead to a comparison with graphic illustrations in the manuscript tradition. More examples are at hand, this time of gestures that are more generally characteristic of a specific behavior and sometimes suggestive

---

[4] The scholium continues: "For it's the death of a prostitute, or an old man, or one wife when someone has two at the same time. And so deaths of this sort are met with moderate sadness or even joy." Donatus here refers to the other two deaths in Terence's comedies (*Hecyra* 171 and *Phormio* 750), which are presented in a similar way.

of different postures for the character's body. In the scholia on *Hecyra*, Donatus depicts the entrance speech of Phidippus (who had been ignorant of his daughter's condition and has now learned she has given birth) in this way: *mirantis est gestus et dictum* (522.2 "his is the gesture and language of a character who is astonished"). In *Andria*, he points to another gesture, that of someone (here, Simo) "in meditation": *si dixisset "hoc cogitabam," sensum tantum cogitationis dicere debuit; sed quia "sic cogitabam" dixit, ipsum gestum cogitantis exponit* (110.1, "if he had said 'I was thinking this' he would have to tell only the sense of his thought; however, since he said 'I was thinking in this way,' he shows the very gesture of thinking"). Later in the same play, Charinus's slave Byrria enters the stage surreptitiously, announcing to the audience that, at his young master's bidding, he is following Pamphilus and keeping an eye on him; he now spots him with Davus and says, *hoc agam* (415). Donatus interprets: *in gestu est, nam est figura corporis obseruantis, quid agatur* (415, "it [the meaning] is in the gesture, for he is a figure of someone observing what happens")—that is to say, Byrria is eavesdropping.

Donatus's interest in the onstage motion and gestures of characters is especially evident in comments on comic slaves; often he attributes a servile habitude to them. For instance, in *Andria* I2, Davus, unaware that his master Simo is nearby, deduces his scheme to trip up Pamphilus, articulates it aloud, and designates it "clever!" (*astute*); the commentator remarks on the last word: *hoc in gestu et uultu seruili et cum agitatione capitis dixit* (183.1, "he said this with the gesture and facial expression of a slave and while shaking his head"). Next, Davus realizes his master is present and suspects that his monologue (not especially kindly toward Simo) has been overheard; Simo calls upon Davus and the latter asks in response, *hem quid est*? (184); the commentator observes:

> (1) *quasi correptio totius corporis* and (4) *more seruili et uernili gestu: sic enim uocati a dominis secum uultuose agunt* (184.1, '[he speaks] as if [Simo's summons had been] a shock to his entire being' and 184.4, '[he speaks] according to the nature of a slave and with fawning gesture: in fact, this is how they behave, with affected and exaggerated expression, when called by their masters').

The commentator uses similar expressions of slaves elsewhere: in *Eunuchus* he says of Parmeno, *similiter et Parmeno secum seruili gestu* (274.5, "in the same way, Parmeno also talks to himself with a gesture appropriate for slaves"); and in *Adelphoe*, he says of Syrus: *hoc gestu seruili et nimis leuiori personae congrue dictum est* (567.2, "this is said with a gesture of a slave and in a very suitable way for an insignificant person"). In these cases, the commentator has a uniform notion of the "habitude" of slaves; he may also be referring to a specific posture. The *gestus servilis* is described by Quintilian as a "contraction of the shoulders" that causes a "shortening of the neck" (11.3.83) and "the chin to be pressed to the chest" (11.3.82). Such a posture is evident in the illustrated representations of slaves in medieval manuscripts of Terence (for instance, Davus in *Andria* II2 and Syrus in *Adelphoe*

FIGURE 41.1 Bodleianus Auct. F. 2. 13 fol. 13v

IV2, in the scene referred to in this paragraph).[5] The illustrated contortion of the slaves' body and Donatus's references to a gesture that distinguishes slaves (since it is related to the "contraction" of a body) seem to reflect the same visual notion.[6] Nonetheless, the question must be raised: can these illustrations be useful for interpreting Donatus's comments?

The group of illustrated manuscripts that preserve Terence's comedies comes from a period between the ninth and the twelfth centuries (see Nervegna, this volume). Nevertheless, they are based on a late antique original; its date has been debated, but it is commonly regarded as belonging to the late fourth or early fifth century CE (e.g., Jones and Morey 1930–1931 II: 19–24; Wright 2006: 209–211).[7] An important question involved in the study of the illustrations concerns their possible dependence on stage practices. Many scholars have argued for their *independence* from

[5] The figures come from the digital edition of Muir—Turner 2010 of the Bodleian illustrated manuscript which is assigned the siglum O (twelfth century). The editors note that although the illustrations are influenced by contemporary architecture and clothing, the figures are faithful to the antique original in regard to the gestures of the characters (p. 15). Since the aim of this chapter is not to focus on the illustrations but rather to look at some examples briefly, the illustrations from O have been used. The figures are similar in other illustrations (see especially P and C, Jones and Morey nos. 56 and 57 for Andria II2, and nos. 514 and 515 for Adelphoe IV2). For the representation of slaves in the illustrated manuscripts, see Dodwell 2000: 29–30 and Dutsch 2007: 62.

[6] Possible correspondences between Donatus's scholia and the illustrations have long been identified (e.g., Leo 1883: 338). See especially Basore 1908: 7–9 and 37–38 on the *gestus servilis* (in Quintilian, the illustrations, and Donatus).

[7] Dodwell (2000: 4–21) assigned their archetype to the third century, but this thesis has been largely rejected (e.g., Wright 2002: 230–231 and Lateiner 2003–2004: 462).

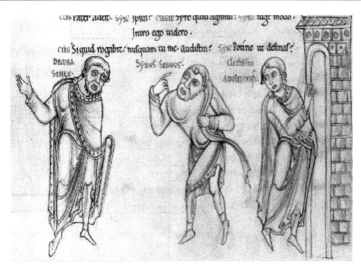

FIGURE 41.2 Bodleianus Auct. F. 2. 13 fol. 111v

Terence's staging and have regarded the illustrations as an "imaginative" product (e.g., Jachmann 1924: 10–44; Jones and Morey 1930–1931: 203–204; Csapo and Slater 1995: 77–78; Wright 2006: 212–214; Nervegna, this volume). Some have suggested that the illustrations were (to a certain extent) influenced by stage practices, but not necessarily in connection with the staging of Terence (e.g., Aldrete 1999: 54–67; Wright 2006: 216, 218); some have gone so far as to argue that they demonstrate knowledge of professional productions of Terence (e.g., Dodwell 2000: 86–100). On the other hand, Dutsch (2007), based on the hypothesis that the illustrations may have been produced for another manuscript and then inserted into the lost archetype (Grant 1986: 39–42), accepts possible connections of the illustrated figures with earlier artifacts, given that the model for the illustrations could have derived from a date earlier than that of the prototype for the Calliopian manuscripts. She further argues that the gestures in the illustrations often present practices condemned by rhetoricians such as Quintilian, and concludes that the illustrations seem to reflect gestures used in stage revivals of classical drama.

How, then, are we to interpret Donatus's correspondences (if that is what they are) with the manuscripts' illustrations? If, for the sake of argument, we accept the possibility that the manuscripts were influenced by theater, can we assume the same for Donatus, i.e., that his observations on specific gestures and postures reflect theatrical and well-known performance practices? And, if that is so, could a reference to a "gesture showing admiration" be recognized and visualized by the readers of the commentary? We might then extend the speculation further: if references to specific gestures reflect real theater practice, then would not the same apply to similar scholia on different aspects of nonverbal communication? In that case, they too would reflect the influence of theater. Against such speculation, however, stands the absence of evidence for the commentator's familiarity with professional theatrical performances of Terence, if any existed at his time.[8] On the other hand, Donatus's remarks could have been influenced by contemporary performances of any kind, including mime (see Jakobi 1996: 171 on parasites' gestures).

A different argument, however, can be made that would remove Donatus as an autoptic source for theatrical visualizations but at the same time insert those visualizations into a theatrical tradition. We do know that Donatus's commentary made use of previous commentaries.[9] We can reasonably infer that their creators were familiar with or interested in stage practices—Terence, after all, is attested to have been popular and staged in late revivals of classical drama (Dutsch 2007: 44). Indeed, in some cases we can demonstrate familiarity: consider, for example, Donatus's reference to an anecdote from Terence's lifetime regarding his reaction to the actor playing the parasite in *Phormio* (315.2), which is probably drawn from the earlier commentary of Aemilius Asper in the second century CE (as is evident from Rufinus *GL* 6.555; Maltby 2007: 22). Moreover, Donatus refers to the use of stage masks in Terence's time (e.g., *Adelphoe* Praef. I.6). Similarly, in the well-known passage from the scholia on *Andria* (716.1), he explicitly contrasts the earlier performances of female roles by masked male actors and the practice of his time, which relied upon the participation of female actors in stage performances. It is not clear whether Donatus here compares earlier with contemporary stagings of Terence (as Kragelund 2012 argues) or whether his remark is influenced by contemporary performance practices, principally mime (Jakobi 1996: 12–13). Nevertheless, while this example does not clearly specify Donatus's theatrical references, it certainly reveals the interest of the preserved scholia in the staging of Terence's comedy. Similarly with the illustrations: although the artist might not have witnessed an actual stage performance himself (see, e.g., Gutzwiller and Çelik 2012: 580–581, on the influence of the Hellenistic "dramatic illustration" tradition), he may well have used reliable sources that reflected stage practices. This, of course, does not mean that the illustrator's or the commentator's work is not "imaginary"—we expect that they both worked in a unique, independent way (see also Gutzwiller and Çelik 2012: 614, on the process of producing visual representations of comedy); yet our interest lies in the nature of possible theatrical influences found in these works. And in cases in which both Donatus and this late antique illustrator seem to "visualize" a similar situation, we might reasonably think that both sources reflect a certain informed knowledge of how Terence would (or should) have been presented on stage, even if neither had ever seen a performance. For instance, it is reasonable to expect a comic slave to bear a "typical," "servile" habitude. But when there is such an emphasis on this in both visual and literary sources

---

[8] Evidence for performances of literary drama in the imperial period is limited. Augustine refers to the staging of tragedies and comedies (*C.D.* 2.8; *Conf.* 3.2), but the precise content of such plays cannot be specified, even if we accept a certain level of continuity of interests through the centuries (Jory 1986: 144; Beacham 1991: 195). Kragelund 2012: 420 thinks that Donatus's references strengthen the possibility that Terence was performed in his time.

[9] Some scholia explicitly refer to earlier scholars (e.g., *Ad.* 323, 875; *Ph.* 49.3, 233.2).

(i.e., in the illustrations and Donatus), we would expect this to be a well-known, traditional stage convention.

To return, then, to the question raised earlier regarding the extent to which the illustrations aid in the study of Donatus, it seems that the relationship throws further light on Donatus's sources and his interest in theater and the comic genre; on the other hand, it does not contradict what was posited earlier in regard to the makeup of the commentator's audience. Advanced students (see section i) would be interested in the reconstruction of stage action and depiction of theater conventions in the scholia; these, after all, offer a guideline for interpreting the physical reactions of characters to dramatic situations.

3. CONCLUSION AND FURTHER CONSIDERATIONS

Donatus's scholia on delivery, linguistic characterization, and performance must be perceived within the framework of the commentary's educational purpose and his own profession. The framework adduced here of Donatus's purpose and profession allows for a broad envisioning of the commentator's (and possibly his students') interests. Scholia that show a deep interest in a character's or performer's nonverbal expression demonstrate that, at least in the instruction of Terence, performance (both as training in oratorical delivery and as imagined delivery onstage) was not neglected. At the same time, the possible parallels and similarities with the illustrations found in the medieval manuscripts of Terence based on a late-antique archetype, although not verifying any certain relationship with the stage, at least demonstrate that both these sources had an interest in—and possibly a high level of knowledge of—the way Terence was supposed to have been staged. In the case of Donatus's commentary (and the treatise "On Comedy"), this interest is expansive and embraces the comic genre, both as a literary and a dramatic genre: readers are again and again reminded that what they are looking at is not a narrative text but a text designed to be presented on stage. Viewed in this larger framework, the scholia on performance, along with observations on comic characters and rules governing the genre, illuminate the commentator's understanding of Terence's comedy as a system based on particular themes and traditional axes that included its staging. Donatus suggests that, in order to read a play or scene properly and to grasp its atmosphere, we should envisage it in the way it would have been performed.

Excursus: Donatus and Eugraphius

We have briefly looked at some basic issues involved in the study of the commentary preserved under the name of Donatus, focusing on the challenging scholia on "performance" and simultaneously exploring the functions and purposes of the commentary. Our examination of Donatus will be enriched if we look at a similar work, the commentary of Eugraphius.[10] Our knowledge about this commentator is even more limited than that about Donatus. We know nothing about his person, but he is generally assumed to have been a grammarian.[11] We know that he used Donatus, and so composed the commentary *after* the mid-fourth century but probably used an early version (Wessner 1907: 225). The scholia in Eugraphius's commentary show dependence on Donatus, but they also show, now and again, signs of individuality: for example, deeper interest in Greek matters (e.g., on *Andria* 473, 621) or longer discussions (see, e.g., Blundell: 1987 on Donatus and Eugraphius on *Eunuchus* 480 and 606).

Eugraphius's commentary is mostly of an exegetical character, elaborating on the comedies and in many instances simply paraphrasing. Its aim is stated in the first lines to *Andria*: *Cum omnes poetae uirtutem oratoriam semper uersibus exsequantur, tum magis duo uiri apud Latinos, Virgilius et Terentius. Ex quibus, ut suspicio nostra est, magis Terentii uirtus ad rationem rhetoricae artis accedit, cuius potentiam per comoedias singulas ut possumus explicabimus* ("While all poets always pursue the oratorical virtue in verses, two men among the Romans, Virgil and Terence, do this to a higher degree. Of these two, as my notion has it, the excellence of Terence more closely approximates the principles of rhetoric, whose force I shall treat analytically in each play, one after another, as well as I can"). Indeed, the main focus is Terence's rhetoric, and the commentator often makes use of terms used in rhetorical textbooks.

Although a certain connection between Donatus's and Eugraphius's commentaries is generally accepted, it is impossible to attempt a direct and thorough comparison because of the textual problems involved. A more limited one, of observations on performance, however, can illustrate similarities and differences of focus, purpose, and method, though a caveat is in order from the start: whereas Donatus' introductory theoretical treatises enlighten certain features of the scholia, such treatises are absent from Eugraphius's corpus. Given these constraints, my aim is to provoke questions rather than to give answers; through a brief study of somewhat parallel passages in Donatus and Eugraphius, I ask, where do Eugraphius' "rhetorical" interests lie? Does Donatus differ from Eugraphius because the former's scholia are more concerned with performance? And if that is the case, do the works have different purposes?

A striking observation can be made at the outset: the kind of explicit references to the importance and use of nonverbal expressions that we find in Donatus are largely absent from Eugraphius. Nevertheless, in the latter's scholia, we do find occasional references to the characters' nonverbal behavior, mainly in regard to voice and face. *Andria* IV 4 provides a good case study; it is an active scene, which, as mentioned earlier, was extensively commented on by Donatus, since the asides (between Davus and

---

[10] The third volume of Wessner (1908) remains the standard edition of Eugraphius.

[11] Kaster (1988: 234 n.1), however, excludes Eugraphius from his detailed prosopography because of the absence of solid evidence in regard to his profession.

Mysis, away from Chremes's hearing) and changing tones of the characters required a significant level of exegesis. We do not find anything in Eugraphius that corresponds to Donatus's comments on delivery in 752.2, 753.2, 754.1, 754.4, and 764. Note, however, that Donatus's comment on line 751 explains why Davus orders Mysis to come to his right: "because Chremes is coming from the left" (751.2 *bene "ad dexteram": sinistra enim uenit Chremes*). Eugraphius comments differently: he recommends that Davus should address Mysis in a calm tone, obviously to prevent Chremes from overhearing him (*leni hoc voce pronuntiandum est*). Line 759 also attracts the attention of both commentators; here Davus asks Mysis to remove the infant from his master's doorstep (whereas earlier, before Chremes's arrival onstage, he had ordered her to set him there); and in the following line, he tells her not to move an inch. The contrasting lines beckon for exegesis. Donatus comments: *hic uersus clare dicitur, sequens, ne senex audiat, presse* (759, "this verse is said aloud, the following in a low voice, so that the old man does not hear"), and Eugraphius, similarly: *imperat, uti ab ianua puer qui est positus auferatur. Verumtamen post summissa voce, ne Chremes audiat, imperat Mysidi, ut loco maneat nec recedat* ("he orders the infant who has been placed before the door to be removed from it; nevertheless, afterwards, in a low tone, so that Chremes does not hear, he orders Mysis not to leave but to stay in place"). Both commentators have perceived the unfolding of the drama and have called for voice modulation; however, given Eugraphius's familiarity with Donatus's scholia, the possibility that Eugraphius has used Donatus here cannot be rejected.

Although Donatus's scholia engage with the style of delivery more consistently, Eugraphius, as we have just seen, is attentive to delivery techniques. If we continue to search Eugraphius's commentaries for such observations, we shall find more scholia, sometimes similar to Donatus's (e.g., cf. Donatus and Eugraphius on *Adelphoe* 425) and sometimes different. As for examples of the latter, we might consider a scholium of Eugraphius that points to an ironic tone of delivery (*ad Hecyra* 233, *hoc per ironiam pronuntiandum*), another to a pause in delivery (*ad Adelphoe* 196, *cum mora igitur pronuntiandum est "leno"*), and a third to an angry, passionate manner (*ad Adelphoe* 569, *hoc iracunde pronuntiandum*). In a scene from *Andria*, Simo makes an indirect reference to Davus as being a "dangerous teacher" for his son (192–193); Davus subsequently pretends that he has not understood the reference (194), and Simo then accuses him openly. On line 192, Eugraphius's α scholium reads: *siquidem senex et uultu et uerbis agebat, ut Dauum deciperet* ("if indeed the old man was performing by both face and speech in order to entrap Davus"). This is a rare instance in Eugraphius of a comment that touches upon the importance of acting style (with reference to the use of face and delivery), and here again we do not find a similar reference in Donatus.

Although striking references to specific gestures are absent (in contrast to Donatus) and references to the importance of delivery for understanding the action of a scene or the utterance of a line are limited, nevertheless, delivery observations are made. The question then arises: what was the purpose of these comments? Are such "performance" scholia by Eugraphius to be perceived as part of his examination of Terence's use of rhetoric? In that case, "rhetoric" must be viewed more broadly as encompassing Eugraphius's analyses of linguistic style *and* delivery techniques for Terence's characters—a study that can be a useful tool for students and readers of the commentary. Eugraphius, then, provides mere glimpses of what is a more established habit in Donatus, whose "rhetorical" discussion more often moves from diction to delivery and shows an interest in the latter that is deeper and more consistent. This particular contrast between the two surviving corpora (and their scopes) suggests the different composition of their audiences. It adds cogency to the hypothesis that Donatus's students were heterogeneous, including students of literature and rhetoric, as well as more advanced students interested in understanding the plays as performances.

When identifying the aims of the ancient scholia by examining their interest in both rhetoric and theater, we should recall the close relationship between the two realms. As mentioned in the introduction to this chapter, comic texts and actors were used in exercises of delivery; furthermore, rhetoricians often likened themselves to actors, while they also took pains to make a clear distinction between their profession and that of the stage actor (e.g., *Rhet. ad Her.* 3.26, *De Orat.* 3.220, *Inst.* 11.3.182)—indeed, the very insistence on the differences between the one profession and the other suggests that the boundaries were opaque. Nevertheless, the connecting point of rhetoric and theater is the element of performance, used to enliven a passage, to make it more persuasive, to punctuate it, so to speak, with pauses, gestures, and modulations of voice both on the stage and before the court. We should thus assume a profound commerce between the two realms that must have also influenced the development of drama by rhetorical perspectives (Enders 1992: 19–128).

Further Reading

An effort to draw a distinction between original scholia and later insertions was made by Karsten 1912–1913; his methods have often and rightly been criticized (e.g., Blundell 1987). A comprehensive study of the commentary was made by Jakobi (1996), who focuses on Donatus's sources and methods in using Terence in his instruction. Blundell (1987), although examining only a part of the *Eunuchus* commentary, offers a good discussion of basic issues concerned with the commentary as a whole; similarly, Barsby (2000) uses his commentary on *Eunuchus* to introduce some of the basic themes of the full commentary. Some scholars have viewed more positively the possibility that the "performance scholia" might have a "stage value"; e.g., Basore 1908 briefly discussed the problem of the origins of the scholia and made a detailed classification of Donatus's references to characters' nonverbal behavior, and a classification was also devised by Madyda 1953. Thomadaki 1989 concludes that the commentary is useful in reconstructing the scenic space of Terence's comedies. A detailed study on Donatus's references to plot composition was produced by Moorhead 1923. Hilger 1970 examined references to comic theory under the spectrum of rhetorical instruction.

An electronic edition of the commentary, with translation and notes, is found on *Hyperdonat* (Bureau et al. 2007–2011).

BIBLIOGRAPHY

Aldrete, G. S. 1999. *Gestures and Acclamations in Ancient Rome*. Baltimore: Johns Hopkins University Press.

Barsby, J. A. 2000. "Donatus on Terence: The *Eunuchus* Commentary." In *Dramatische Wäldchen: Festschrift für Eckard Lefèvre zum 65. Geburtstag*, edited by E. Stärk and G. Vogt-Spira, 491–513. Hildesheim: Olms.

Basore, J. W. 1908. *The Scholia on Hypokrisis in the Commentary of Donatus*. Baltimore: J. H. Furst.

Beacham, R. C. 1991. *The Roman Theatre and its Audience*. London and New York: Routledge.

Blundell, J. 1987. "A Commentary of Donatus, *Eunuchus* 391–453 and 471–614." PhD diss., University of London.

Bureau, B., M. Ingarao, C. Nicolas, and E. Raymond, eds. 2007–2011. *Hyperdonat, une édition électronique des commentaires de Donat aux comédies de Térence*. CEROR, Université Lyon III, ENS de Lyon. Available online at http://hyperdonat.ens-lyon.fr (accessed Aug. 21, 2012).

Citti, F. 2008. "*Legitimos filios faciunt partus et sublatio* (Don. *ad* Ter. *Andr.* 464): Nota lessicale." *Eikasmos* 19: 273–278.

Csapo, E., and W. J. Slater. 1995. *The Context of Ancient Drama*. Ann Arbor: University of Michigan Press.

Dodwell, C. R. 2000. *Anglo-Saxon Gestures and the Roman Stage*. Cambridge, UK: Cambridge University Press.

Dutsch, D. 2007. "Gestures in the Manuscripts of Terence and Late Revivals of Literary Drama." *Gesture* 7.1: 39–71.

——. 2008. *Feminine Discourse in Roman Comedy: On Echoes and Voices*. Oxford: Oxford University Press.

Enders, J. 1992. *Rhetoric and the Origins of Medieval Drama*. Ithaca: Cornell University Press.

Grant, J. N. 1986. *Studies in the Textual Tradition of Terence*. Toronto and London: University of Toronto Press.

Gutzwiller, K., and Ö. Çelik. 2012. "New Menander Mosaics from Antioch." *AJA* 116.4: 573–623.

Hilger, M. J. 1970. "The Rhetoric of Comedy: Comic Theory in the Terentian Commentary of Aelius Donatus." PhD diss., University of Nebraska.

Holtz, L. 1981. *Donat et la tradition de l'enseignement grammatical: Étude sur l'Ars Donati et sa diffusion (IVe–IXe siècle) et édition critique*. Paris: Centre national de la recherche scientifique.

Jachmann, G. 1924. *Die Geschichte des Terenztextes im Altertum*. Basel: F. Reinhardt.

Jakobi, R. 1996. *Die Kunst der Exegese im Terenzkommentar des Donat*. Berlin: de Gruyter.

Jocelyn, H. D. 1971. "Donatus ad Ter. *Ad.* 537." *Mnemosyne* 24: 90–91.

Jones, L. W., and C. R. Morey. 1930–1931. *The Miniatures of the Manuscripts of Terence prior to the Thirteenth Century*. 2 vols. Princeton: Princeton University Press.

Jory, E. J. 1986. "Continuity and Change in the Roman Theatre." In *Studies in Honour of T. B. L. Webster*. Vol. 1, edited by J. H. Betts, J. T. Hooker, and J. R. Green, 145–152. Bristol: Bristol Classical Press.

Karsten, H. T. 1912–1913. *Commenti Donatiani ad Terenti fabulas scholia genuina et spuria probabiliter separare conatus est*. 2 vols. Leiden: Sijthoff.

Kaster, R. A. 1988. *Guardians of Language: The Grammarian and Society in Late Antiquity*. Berkeley: University of California Press.

Kragelund, P. 2012. "Evidence for Performances of Republican Comedy in Fourth-Century Rome." *CQ* 62.1: 415–422.

Lateiner, D. 2003–2004. "Gestures: The Imagined Journey from the Roman Stage to the Anglo-Saxon Manuscript." *IJCT* 10.3–4: 454–464.

Leo, F. 1883. "Die Überlieferungsgeschichte der terenzischen Komödien und der Kommentar des Donatus." *RhM* 38: 317–347.

Madyda, W. 1953. *De Donato histrionum praeceptore.* Wrocław: Zakład im. Ossolińskich.

Maltby, R. 2007. "Donat über die Stegreifelemente in Terenz' *Phormio.*" in *Terentius Poeta,* edited by P. Kruschwitz, W.-W. Ehlers, and F. Felgentreu, 15–28. Munich: C. H. Beck.

Moorhead, P. G. 1923. "The Comments on the Content and Form of the Comic Plot in the *Commentum Terenti* Ascribed to Donatus." PhD diss., University of Chicago.

Muir, B. J., and A. Turner, eds. 2010. *A Facsimile Edition of Terence's Comedies: Oxford Bodleian Library MS Auct. F. 2. 13.* Oxford: Bodleian Library.

Pugliarello, M. 2009. "A lezione dal *grammaticus*: La lettura degli *auctores.*" *Maia* 61.3: 592–610.

Reeve, M. D. 1983. "Aelius Donatus." In *Texts and Transmission: A Survey of the Latin Classics,* edited by L. D. Reynolds, 153–156. Oxford: Clarendon Press.

Reich, V. 1933. "Sprachliche Charakteristik bei Terenz (Studien zum Kommentar des Donat)." *WS* 51: 72–94.

Syme, R. 1978. "'Donatus' and the Like." *Historia* 27: 588–603.

Thomadaki, M. 1989. "La mise en scène du theatre de Terence dans le commentaire de Donat." *Dioniso* 59: 365–372.

Turner, A. 2010. "Unnoticed Latin Hypotheses to Two Plays Mentioned by Terence: The 'Phasma' of Menander and the 'Thesaurus.'" *Hermes* 138.1: 38–47.

Victor, B. 2002. Review of *Terence I: The Woman of Andros; The Self-Tormentor; The Eunuch,* by J. Barsby. *BMCR* 2002.06.08. Available online at http://bmcr.brynmawr.edu/2002/2002-06-08.html (accessed May 6, 2013).

Wessner, P. ed. 1902–1908. *Aeli Donati quod fertur Commentum Terenti.* 3 vols. Leipzig: Teubner.

——. 1907. "Der Terenzkommentar des Eugraphius." *RhM* 62: 203–228, 339–365.

Williams, T. 1970. "The Vestiges of a Roman Nursery Rhyme at Donatus in Ter. *Adel.* 537." *Mnemosyne* 23: 62–67.

Wright, D. H. 2002. Review of *Anglo-Saxon Gestures and the Roman Stage,* by C. R. Dodwell. *CB* 78: 230–234.

——. 2006. *The Lost Late Antique Illustrated Terence.* Vatican: Biblioteca Apostolica Vaticana.

APPENDICES

APPENDIX 1

···

NEW TEXTS: GREEK COMIC PAPYRI 1973–2010[1]

···

EFTYCHIA BATHRELLOU

THIS Appendix aims to present the Greek comic papyri published since 1973—the year of publication of the first comprehensive collection of comic papyri, Colin Austin's *Comicorum Graecorum Fragmenta in Papyris Reperta* (*CGFP*). It is in two parts. Part I introduces the material and, by means of a few case studies, draws attention to some of the ways the post-1973 papyri have enriched our understanding of ancient comedy. Part II is a table which synoptically presents the post-1973 comic papyri one by one.

PART I

···

1. The Origin of New Comic Texts

Our access today to the texts of ancient Greek comedy is through three main channels. The most substantial and best known of these consists of copies of plays in medieval and early modern manuscripts (tenth–seventeenth centuries CE). Of all Greek comic poets, only Aristophanes, and only eleven plays of his, have survived through such copies. Consequently, these eleven plays of Aristophanes were the only comic texts to appear in the printed editions of the Renaissance and are, with one exception, the only Greek comedies known to us in their entirety.[2]

---

[1] While a few exceptional citations of post-2010 material appear here, the end point of this survey is the year 2010. That year saw the death of Colin Austin, whose work was pivotal for the study of comic papyri; the Appendix is dedicated to his memory. For its completion, I am much indebted to the corrections and insightful suggestions of Peter Brown and Peter Parsons. I also thank Tania Demetriou, Timothy Duff, and Kyriaki Konstantinidou for their comments and help. Any remaining mistakes and other shortcomings are, of course, my own responsibility.

[2] On the manuscripts of Aristophanes, see the summary presentation of Sommerstein 2010: 412–420; also Wilson 2007: 5–13. The exception is Menander's *Dyskolos*.

The second channel consists of quotations from comedy in ancient and medieval authors and, accordingly, is often called "the indirect tradition." Despite its indirect and fragmentary character, this channel is actually quite rich, in that it offers thousands of passages, from one word to almost seventy lines long, from a great number of plays by many different comic poets.[3]

Unlike the first two channels, which to a lesser or greater extent have been available at least since the Renaissance, the third channel involves material discovered only in the last 150 or so years. It includes copies of plays, or of excerpts from plays, mainly on papyrus, but also on parchment and other materials, like pottery shards (ostraca), which were, in their majority, found in Egypt and which date from roughly the third century BCE to the early seventh century CE. Information and bibliography on these documents can most conveniently be found in the online database Mertens-Pack[3] (henceforth MP[3]) and the Leuven Database of Ancient Books (henceforth LDAB).[4]

Due to their antiquity and the conditions of their discovery, these documents, often summarily referred to as "papyri," are more often than not in extremely fragmentary form, sometimes consisting of only a few letters each and often barely legible. Only once in the last 150 years has a papyrus yielded an entire play—the *Dyskolos* of Menander.[5] Nevertheless, the papyri are often our main access to the texts of plays previously thought lost, and they preserve thousands of comic lines, most of which are otherwise unattested.

The papyri, then, are an invaluable source of new comic texts—a source which, moreover, is still growing. Not only do more papyri continue to be discovered, but also so many have already been discovered that they are only gradually being read, identified, and published. This third channel, then, has the potential, far more than the other two, to continuously increase and enrich our understanding of comedy.

2. The Significance of Papyri

Many of the comic texts preserved on papyri cannot be securely attributed to a specific play or author.[6] Those which have been identified come from a limited range of authors,[7] of whom Aristophanes and Menander are incomparably better represented. In fact, Menander is indisputably the comic poet about whom we have learned the most from these discoveries: it is

---

[3] On the indirect tradition of comedy, see Nesselrath 2010. These quotations, few of which are much longer than ten lines or so, are now most conveniently collected and accurately edited by R. Kassel and C. Austin in the eight volumes of *Poetae Comici Graeci* (1983–2001). For the quotations of Old Comedy, see also Storey 2011.

[4] http://promethee.philo.ulg.ac.be/cedopal/index.htm and http://www.trismegistos.org/ldab. For catalogues available in print, see Mertens 1992 and Mertens 1996; they have, however, been superseded by the online databases.

[5] It is preserved in P. Bodmer 4, the middle part of a papyrus codex of the late third or early fourth century CE, first published in 1959. For bibliography on the Bodmer papyrus, see MP[3] no. 1298.

[6] For a list of tentative attributions of papyri which cannot be securely identified, see *Poetae Comici Graeci*, vol. 8, pp. 519–520.

[7] Anaxandrides, Antiphanes, Apollodorus, Aristophanes, Epicharmus, Eupolis, Cratinus, Menander, Pherecrates, Philemo, Plato, Posidippus, Strato, Strattis, and Timocles. For the following comic poets,

because of the papyri that we today have access to one whole play of his and substantial parts of about twenty more.[8]

The significance of these discoveries for comedy, however, is not limited to the comic texts they carry on their surface, but has another, equally important, side. They are sources of valuable information about the reception of Greek comedy from the Hellenistic through the Roman to the early Byzantine periods. The date of the documents, the archaeological context in which they were found, the type of material used, the script, the layout, any notes or reading aids that might accompany the text, etc., can often be suggestive about the uses and importance of comedy to individuals and communities for almost a millennium after the first productions of the plays. Even when containing already attested passages, a new papyrus has the potential to throw new light on and increase our understanding of ancient comedy. The following sections aim to highlight this double significance of comic papyri, while focusing on those published after 1973.[9]

3. The post-1973 Papyri of Aristophanes and their Original Readers

Of securely identified authors, only Aristophanes and Menander are represented in the post-1973 material. The Aristophanic papyri in particular have increased substantially since 1973, by nearly thirty items. The post-1973 papyri have confirmed, rather than upset, the trends in chronological distribution of Aristophanic papyri as set by the pre-1973 ones.[10] The earliest known Aristophanic papyri are of the first century BCE, but it is to the second century CE that the earliest known witnesses for most plays are dated.[11] The latest documents come from the sixth century CE.[12] The largest proportion comes from the fifth century CE, thus confirming that century as a period of increased interest in Aristophanes.[13]

the only contribution of the papyri has so far been lists of titles: Ameipsias, Apollonius, Apollophanes, Ararus, Archippus (but see below, Part II, table no. 6), possibly Aristomenes (see K-A test. 6), Autocrates, Dinolochus, Demetrius, and Diocles.

[8] For a summary presentation of the Menandrian discoveries, see Casanova 2004.

[9] In the following sections, references of the type "no. 1" etc. are to the table in Part II.

[10] For an overview, see Cavallo 1986: 113–117 (reprinted in Cavallo 2002: 94–99); Manfredi 2000: 96–98; and, briefly, Sommerstein 2010: 410–412. It should be noted, however, that most comic and, indeed, other literary papyri cannot be dated with absolute precision, but are assigned to a century on paleographic and other grounds. For factors taken into account when dating papyri, see, e.g., GMAW, pp. 18–23. It should also be noted that the chronological distribution of the papyri of any given author must be seen in the light of the general survival rate and chronological distribution of all papyri; see the tables in Habermann 1998, especially table 11.

[11] Earliest known Aristophanic papyri: nos 7, 8, and, of the pre-1973 material, MP^3 142.2, with *Knights* 1057–1076.

[12] The one Aristophanic papyrus for which a seventh-century date has been considered possible, P. Strasbourg inv. 621 (from the pre-1973 material), has been recently dated to the late sixth century by Montana (in CLGP I 1.4, Ar. no. 16, p. 102).

[13] See Cavallo 1986: 114 (reprinted in Cavallo 2002: 95); also Barrenechea 2006: 50, Fournet and Gascou 2008: 1051–1052. The prominence of Aristophanes in the fifth century is all the more remarkable given

The major contribution of the post-1973 material is not so much the discovery of otherwise unattested Aristophanic passages. In fact, most of these papyri, with the exception of nos. 8 and 32, preserve parts of one or other of the eleven plays already known to us through medieval copies. Rather, the importance of this material lies elsewhere. First, it confirms further the impression formed by scholars very early, on the basis of only few papyri,[14] namely that the text of the papyri for the eleven plays does not diverge much from that in the medieval manuscripts. The papyri thus speak for a more or less consolidated tradition of the text of these plays from the second century CE, the date of most of the earliest Aristophanic papyri, to the time of the medieval manuscripts.[15] The same is true for the colometry, that is, the ways lyric verses are organized into metric units: the colometry of the papyri is more or less identical with that transmitted by the medieval manuscripts.[16]

Secondly, the post-1973 material suggests a quite varied set of contexts for the reception of Aristophanes in Egypt in the time of the papyri. For example, the post-1973 Aristophanic papyri include books of varying levels of craftsmanship, which suggests a range of different uses. For example, we find "luxury" books, beautifully made and calligraphically written, intended, presumably, not only to be read but also to please aesthetically and impress (e.g., no. 91). We also find less luxurious but most likely professionally made copies, written by competent, practiced hands, and often revised (e.g. 8, 95, 111),[17] as well as copies which give the impression that they were made by nonprofessionals, perhaps for their own use (e.g., possibly, 99). Or, to use a different criterion, the post-1973 Aristophanic papyri range from books which suggest more or less advanced scholarly activity, such as commentaries on plays (33, 34, 107, 108) or copies of plays with marginal annotations of various degrees (28, 30, 66, 92, 94, 99, 102, 104),[18] to a humble, reused ostracon, with text marred by a series of spelling mistakes which made it unrecognizable to its first editor (7: ?perhaps a personal message, or a school exercise; see Litinas 2002). However, whether as a luxury item, an object of serious study, or a text to be used in education (?104),[19] the Aristophanes

the general decline in the overall number of papyri in that century; for the numbers, see Habermann 1998: 157, which stresses that the decline is sharper among the documentary papyri.

[14] Grenfell 1919: 22; Grenfell knew of twelve papyri.

[15] See Gonis 1999: 120–121, Wilson 2007: 3–4. For divergences from the medieval tradition in the post-1973 papyri, see particularly nos 29, 99, 104, 106.

[16] See Parker 1997: 98–99, Gonis 1999: 121. For the few divergences, see Parker 1997: 99–102, Gonis 1999: 138–139, on our no. 106.

[17] Specifically on no. 111, a papyrus codex containing at least four (most likely more) plays of Aristophanes, dated to the late fifth or early sixth century, see Maehler 1998: 85. It was found, along with other "classics" (Sophocles, Euripides, Isocrates, Apollonius Rhodius, Theocritus), among the papers of a prominent Hermoupolitan, who in 510 CE was also "presbyter of the catholic church" at Hermoupolis: see Maehler 1998: 84.

[18] The marginal annotations on Aristophanic papyri, as well as commentaries on Aristophanic plays found in papyri, are most recently edited and discussed in *CLGP* I 1.4, pp. 3–240. See also Trojahn 2002, Montana 2005, Montana 2006a.

[19] See Gonis 1999: 161. At line 679, the papyrus has ἅπα [, not απα [, as in the editio princeps. The ink, different in colour from that of the text, suggests that accent and breathing have been added by a second hand.

of the papyri remains an author to be *read*; nothing in the post-1973 material suggests performance of any kind.[20]

4. Papyri and Performance

Evidence for performance, although unclear of what type, can better be seen in two other
items, both from Roman Oxyrhynchus: one of the first century CE, with animated dialogue
in iambics with content that suggests New Comedy (no. 15), and one of the third century CE,
with line 796 of Menander's *Perikeiromene* (no. 76). In no. 15, the ordinal number $\bar{\Gamma}$ (*sic*) is written in mid-line, between the end of a word and the beginning of another and at a point where
a change of speaker is possible.[21] Such ordinal numbers, written to designate a new speaker,
occur in other dramatic papyri too and have been interpreted as indicating which actor was to
speak the line and, hence, as suggestive of a text produced not for reading but for performance
by a troupe.[22] In the case of no. 15, $\bar{\Gamma}$ suggests that the speaker would be the third actor, the
so-called *tritagonistes*. But was no. 15 actually used in the theater, or in any other kind of performance involving a troupe of actors,[23] or was it rather a reading copy, but deriving from one
used by a troupe? Although no certainty can be claimed, the fact that $\bar{\Gamma}$ has been copied as part
of the text, in a completely unconspicuous way, with nothing, apart from the horizontal above
it, to distinguish it from the rest, speaks against a copy actually used by performers.[24] The same
can be said of the fact that a correction has been made in such a way that it could in practice
confuse a performer. The correction aims to replace the last word of fragment 1, line 2, νέου
(?new), with λίθον (stone). The correct word has been written above the mistaken one, but not
only has the mistaken word not been deleted but the correct word appears at first sight as part
of the previous line: it has been written immediately after the last word of that line, without any
gap, in letters of similar size to the rest.[25]

  If no. 15 might attest performance indirectly, as deriving from a copy used by a troupe,
no. 76 seems to do so in a more direct way. But what kind of performance? And how much
more directly? No. 76 is a rectangular piece (7.5 cm width × 4 cm height) from a papyrus roll
which was most probably initially used for another text. On what would originally have been
the outer side of the roll, but turned by ninety degrees, an informal third-century hand has

[20] The same is, in fact, true for all Aristophanic papyri. For the possibility of performance of Old
Comedy and, hence, probably, Aristophanes in the period of the papyri, see Jones 1993: 47, on *MAMA* 8,
420 (Aphrodisias, late second century CE).

[21] Fragment 1, l. 4:]γοη$\bar{\gamma}$ματουϲθεουϲ.

[22] Gammacurta 2006: 240–247.

[23] For example, in a symposium: see Jones 1991: 192–193; also Handley 2002: 169–170.

[24] Contrast how the ordinal numbers are marked out by blank spaces in P. Oxy. 3.413→, very probably
a copy used by performers: see Gammacurta 2006, no. 1. I thank Dr. Bruce Barker-Benfield, of the
Bodleian library, for allowing me to examine this papyrus (Bod. Ms. gr. class. b 4 (P)). For a miniature
photograph of part of the → side, see the cover of Gammacurta 2006.

[25] For a photograph, search http://www.papyrology.ox.ac.uk for P. Oxy. 3218.

written, in a decisive, rather rapid manner, three, possibly four, times, one below the other, the same Menandrian iambic trimeter (*Perikeiromene* 796), each time with a different musical setting written above.[26] It seems then that the line, which comes from the recognition scene between Glycera and Pataecus in Menander's *Perikeiromene*, was here set to music in four different ways.

In Menander's time, as indeed generally in the classical period, iambic trimeters of either tragedy or comedy would not have been sung but recited, without music. For the later Hellenistic and Roman periods, however, there is evidence, which includes several papyri, that scenes in iambics from classical tragedy, which would have been spoken, not sung, when they were originally produced, were sometimes set to music.[27] A similar practice for the iambics of comedy had been postulated,[28] and no. 76 seems to be our first piece of direct evidence for it.[29]

However, the fact that none of the other dramatic papyri with musical notation known to us contains comedy, and that no. 76 does not preserve a whole scene but a single line repeated several times, has led some scholars to suggest that the notes in 76 do not actually represent song, but the risings and fallings of the pitch in spoken—i.e., not sung—delivery.[30]

Nevertheless, whether the different musical settings in no. 76 represent different styles of sung or of spoken delivery, it is clear that they suggest performance; or, at the very least, that the possibility of performance was conceivable to the author and user (or users) of this piece. Moreover, the fact that the same line is set to more than one musical setting suggests experimentation—someone trying, or proposing, different ways of delivery (sung or not). Is the author possibly a professional, who on a spare piece of reused papyrus is experimenting with how to sing or speak the line?[31] If so, for what kind of performance is he (or she?) preparing? A public one, at, say, a festival, or one for a more limited audience—for example, a symposium?[32] And, would it be a performance of the whole play, or of, say, only the recognition scene between Glycera and Pataecus, whence *Perikeiromene* 796 comes? Although many questions remain, no. 76 is an illustration of how much light the tiniest piece of papyrus can throw onto the reception of comedy, and at the same time how limited and provisional our understanding can ultimately be. It is also a good reminder of the fact that comedies, as indeed other literary works, can have been used in ways unintended by, or even

---

[26] The significance of one of the note-symbols, found in three of the four different settings, is unknown; see Pöhlmann and West 2001: 154, 185.

[27] See West 1992: 377–378; also Gentili 1979, mainly 26–31.

[28] Gentili 1979: 31; restated, with reference to no. 76, in Gentili 2006: 49, with n. 53.

[29] Huys 1993. Notice that the line, although from a comedy, is versified in the manner of tragedy; see Gomme and Sandbach 1973: 519.

[30] Pöhlmann and West 2001: 185. Their reservations are far from decisive; see the criticism of Pernigotti 2005a: 76.

[31] See also Pernigotti 2005a, n. 38, which advances a very similar interpretation. For other interpretations, see the summary presentation in Nervegna 2007: 39, and, below, Part II, no. 76, under "Use".

[32] The first possibility is advanced by Huys 1993, the second by Perusino 1995; see the criticism of Pernigotti 2005a.

unimaginable to, their author, but no less meaningful to their users or worthy of our attention and interpretation.

5. "New" Menander

Unlike the Aristophanic papyri, most Menandrian papyri offer passages otherwise unattested.[33] Two plays in particular have greatly benefited from the post-1973 papyri: *Misoumenos* (at least six, possibly eight, items) and *Epitrepontes* (ten items). When the pre-1973 material too is taken into account, these two plays appear to have been the most popular Menandrian plays that we know of: parts of *Misoumenos* are preserved in twelve, possibly fourteen,[34] different papyri, and parts of *Epitrepontes* in fifteen.[35]

The most spectacular contribution of the post-1973 papyri to our knowledge of the text of *Misoumenos* (*The Hated Man*) concerns the first scene of the play. In the 1972 edition of Menander by Harry Sandbach for the Oxford Classical Texts (OCT), only the first eighteen lines of the play's first scene were known, but the most recent edition of the play (Arnott 1996), which makes use of the post-1973 papyri, includes no fewer than the first hundred lines. This breathtaking increase is due to the publication of four papyri (nos. 57, 72–74), some of which partly overlap and which compose, in the manner of a jigsaw, the beginning of the play: the desperate invocation to the Night by Thrasonides, the male protagonist, before his house in the middle of a cold wintry night (1–14), and his dialogue with his slave Getas (15–100), which reveals the cause of Thrasonides's desperation: his mistress, with whom he is madly in love, hates him.[36] Tellingly for the fate of some papyri after their modern discovery in the late nineteenth and early twentieth centuries, the two fragments which constitute no. 72, although they were originally adjacent pieces, from the same column, ended up in different collections. The first fragment, containing lines 1–18, remained in Cairo, in the Institut Français de l'Archéologie Orientale (IFAO), and was published in 1970 (and was hence included in Sandbach's 1972 edition mentioned above); the second, containing lines 18–30, ended up in Cologne and was published twenty years later, in 1991.[37]

The papyri of the *Epitrepontes* (*Men at Arbitration*) are a very clear illustration of how the discovery and publication of ancient material can create a constant flow of new texts and how gradually, papyrus by papyrus, publication by publication, they can transform our knowledge of a play's text. Since the 1972 OCT edition, no fewer than ten papyri have contributed towards the reconstruction of at least five scenes of the play.

---

[33] For a play-by-play overview of the papyri published in the 1990s, see Arnott 2004a.

[34] See nos. 13, 42. They are both included in the most recent edition of the play: Arnott 1996.

[35] For the text of the *Epitrepontes*, see the recent editions, Furley 2009 and Ireland 2010; also Bathrellou 2009. Specifically for lines 690–701 and 786–823, see Römer 2012a, Römer 2012b, and Furley 2013.

[36] I follow the line-numbering of Arnott 1996. For a recent discussion of this scene, see Lamagna 2004.

[37] For similar examples, compare nos 1, 36, 99, 111; also 8, 46, 59: fragments from the same collection, but not filed together and hence published separately. For another example of confusion caused by filing, see no. 50.

a. No. 39 most probably comes from the opening scene: Chaerestratus, Onesimus the slave, and Cario the cook make arrangements for the party that is to follow. The papyrus allowed its editor, Eric Handley, to reassess the evidence for this scene and propose a very probable reconstruction of Act I of the play (Handley 2009).

b. No. 71 contributes to the reconstruction of the last scene of Act I.

c. No. 55 has offered the beginning of the arbitration scene, where Smicrines, an old Athenian who is asked by two slaves to act as arbitrator, unwittingly decides the fate of his baby grandson.

d. Nos. 36, 90, and 109 have immensely increased our knowledge of the end of Act III.

e. Nos. 36, 37, and 38, three partly overlapping papyri of the second century CE, have allowed us to gauge the structure and character of the entire first scene of Act IV—Smicrines's effort to persuade his daughter Pamphila to leave her husband. Before their discovery, we knew of only twenty-five lines from this scene, all but two of which came from Smicrines's speech to Pamphila. The three papyri offer substantial parts of the initial dialogue between father and daugher, the end of Smicrines's speech, and a good part of Pamphila's: a total of at least sixty more lines.[38]

Apart from thus increasing our knowledge of *Epitrepontes*, these last three documents are a good illustration of the potential insight papyri can offer to comedy's reception. No. 37 is a probably professionally made manuscript, written on an unused roll, in monumental hand-writing, and found among other literary texts. Is this perhaps a copy made to order for an Oxyrhynchian library? No. 38, again from Oxyrhynchus, was written on the back of an already used roll, in informal handwriting. The space between the lines is remarkably wide, and oblique dashes, usually followed by blank spaces, have been written at clause endings, prob-ably to aid delivery, a layout that suggests performance of some kind.[39] Finally, no. 36 is writ-ten on the back of an already used roll, in a somewhat irregular but not unskilled bookhand with cursive elements.[40] It was found, along with other literary works, among the papers of Socrates, a prominent second-century CE tax collector from Karanis, in Northern Fayum (see van Minnen 1994, esp. 237 ff.). Is this perhaps a copy made in Socrates's house by a member of his family, several of whom, as we know from the papyri found in Socrates's house, were not only literate, but very actively taking part in a writing and reading culture?[41]

[38] For recent analyses of the scene, which, however, do not take into account the fragments published in 2012, see Arnott 2004a, 43–46, and Arnott 2004b: 276–281; Traill 2008: 177–188, 205–223; Bathrellou 2009: 216–233, and Bathrellou 2012: 179–181.

[39] See Turner 1983: 43.

[40] This early-second-century roll consists of several fragments, some of which are now in Michigan, while others are in Cairo. Some of the Cairo fragments were published by Cornelia Römer (Römer 2012a and Römer 2012b). Of the Michigan fragments, only two have been published (Gronewald 1986). The editors of the rest, Ludwig Koenen, the late Traianos Gagos and René Nünlist, made available to some scholars a preliminary edition of some of these other fragments. They have been included in the editions Martina 1997, Furley 2009, and Ireland 2010.

[41] See van Minnen 1994, esp. 248–249. Several blank papyri were found among Socrates's papers as well as three inkwells in two of the house's rooms—discoveries which "well attest the presence of someone actively engaged in the process of producing written texts": van Minnen 1994: 248. See also van Minnen 1998 (for no. 36, see p. 126).

6. Codices and the Popularity of Menander

Another papyrus preserving *Epitrepontes*, no. 35, suggests that Menander's works were among the first pagan works copied into the new book format which gradually replaced the roll, the codex. No. 35 is a papyrus codex from Oxyrhynchus, dated to the second century CE. It is, then, one of the earliest codices and, in fact, the earliest known codex to bear a comic text.[42]

Of the other Menandrian codices in the post-1973 material, two are particularly noteworthy, as they attest the existence of major editions of Menander. No. 97, dated to the fourth century CE,[43] comes from what would have been a very luxurious codex. It consists of two parchment leaves which have been overwritten twice: once in the seventh or eighth century, to bear a work of Nemesius, and a second time in the ninth century, when each leaf was used as a sheet for a composite codex with Syriac texts of an ascetic and hagiographical character.[44] This codex was found in St Catherine's monastery in Sinai and now is in the Vatican library. Under the upper two layers of writing, one of the two leaves preserves 195 lines of the *Dyskolos*; the other leaf preserves 196 lines of an unknown, most likely also Menandrian, play.[45] Because of the difficulties in deciphering text thus doubly overwritten, the edition of no. 97 is still under preparation.[46] However, the minute size of the script, which is a very elegant biblical majuscule, the layout in two columns, and the leaves' overall appearance have led its editor to compare no. 97 with the grand biblical Sinaitic manuscripts of the fourth century CE and to suggest that the codex may have been a full edition of Menander, including all hundred or so plays attributed to him (D'Aiuto 2003). This possibility substantially modifies our understanding of the transmission of Menander, since the possibility of an edition of all his plays had been rejected by earlier scholars even for the third century.[47]

No. 100, dated to the late fourth or early fifth century CE, also comes from a luxurious codex. What has been preserved is the upper right corner of a high-quality parchment leaf, with *Dyskolos* 529–531 and 557–561 written in an elegant biblical majuscule. A gathering number (27) on the upper right corner of the page written first (the recto) makes it probable that this codex contained at least eleven, probably twelve, plays, if its gatherings were quaternia (four sheets = eight leaves = sixteen pages per gathering), or a couple or so less if the gatherings were a mixture of quaternia with smaller gatherings.[48]

---

[42] No. 35 is also important because it is, along with nos. 59 and 116, among the few Menandrian and other New Comedy papyri with comments written in the margins. Most of the marginal annotation in 35 is illegible, but what has been deciphered suggests it might have included delivery directions.

[43] See Orsini 2005: 295.

[44] See van Lantschoot 1965, no. 623, pp. 151–153.

[45] It has tentatively been suggested by Colin Austin that this play might have been Menander's *Titthe*.

[46] By Francesco D'Aiuto and Nigel Wilson.

[47] This point is made by D'Aiuto 2003: 276–277, which cites Cavallo 1986: 118 (reprinted in Cavallo 2002: 99–100).

[48] The gathering number on the leaf with *Dyskolos* 529 ff. is 27, and the front page of that leaf had twenty-eight lines of text. If the gatherings were quaternia, this leaf would have been preceded by roughly $26 \times 16 \times 28 = 11,648$ lines of text. Assuming about 1,000 lines per play, *Dyskolos* would have probably

The post-1973 material also includes Menandrian codices which probably predate only by a few decades the Arabic conquest of Egypt. Nos. 116–118 have been dated to the late sixth or the early seventh century CE.[49] Page numbers at the top of a surviving leaf suggest that no. 116, with Menander's *Aspis*, was a substantial codex, including at least five plays. Whatever the reasons why Menander, unlike Aristophanes, was not copied in the ninth century, to survive in medieval manuscripts,[50] it seems that at least in Egypt, substantial editions of his plays were in circulation at least till the beginning of the seventh century.[51]

7. Unattributed Papyri and New Comedy

About a third of the post-1973 papyri cannot be attributed with certainty to a specific author or play. Few of these are in the style of Old Comedy—notably, nos. 17, 20, 54, and 101. No. 101 in particular, dated to the late fourth or early fifth century CE, is of a relatively late date for an Old Comedy papyrus containing text unattested in the medieval manuscripts. With very few exceptions, the papyri suggest that after 300 CE, "Old Comedy in effect meant Aristophanes, and Aristophanes meant the eleven plays," i.e., those preserved in medieval manuscripts.[52]

New Comedy, however, is incomparably better represented, by about three-quarters of the unattributed comic papyri. Given the vast popularity of Menander in Hellenistic and Roman times and the paucity of papyri that can be securely attributed to other New Comedy authors, many of the unattributed papyri are likely to have been Menandrian. In fact, some have tentatively been included in the latest edition of Menander's works (Arnott 1996 and Arnott 2000a): for example, no. 13, probably from the *Misoumenos*, nos. 12 and 18, probably from the *Leukadia*,[53] or nos. 14 and 81, probably from the *Synaristosai*.

For most unattributed papyri, however, the evidence is even less secure, and we can only guess at their possible authorship and context.[54] This uncertainty makes the interpretation of these papyri extremely challenging and, necessarily, highly provisional. Still, the content of these fragments can enrich our understanding of New Comedy and even throw light upon the social and historical context in which the plays were first produced and would originally have been performed. No. 59, for example, consists of several fragments from a beautifully written and relatively extensively annotated papyrus roll,[55] dated to the late second or early third

---

been the eleventh or twelfth play of the codex. On gathering numbers (or, as they are sometimes called, quire signatures), see Turner 1977: 77–78.

[49] At no. 118, flesh side, l. 2, read ἥκετε — not ηκετε, as the editio princeps. The accent and breathing are in the same ink as the text.

[50] For some thoughts, see Blanchard, this volume.

[51] See further Handley 1990, esp. 146–148.

[52] For the quotation, see Sommerstein 2010: 411.

[53] On these two papyri and *Leukadia*, see further Ferrari 2004: 143–148.

[54] For the value of making hypotheses when confronted with fragmentary texts, see, for example, Handley 1990: 135.

[55] On the paucity of annotated papyri of New Comedy, see above, n. 42. The few known examples are presented in *CLGP* II 4, pp. 121–138. Unlike no. 59, the annotation in most New Comedy papyri consists mainly of glosses.

century CE. The larger fragments preserve about forty-four lines of animated dialogue between two characters (one possibly a slave, the other possibly an Athenian called Aeschro), who challenge one another about their financial dealings.[56] References to the polemarch and to a *prostates* suggest that the scene is set in Athens and that metics are involved in the plot. Money, some possibly as part of an inheritance, is referred to repeatedly and seems to be at the heart of the matter. There are references to secret sales, to sums of money lent out to different borrowers, and to money hoarded in the house. The pervasiveness of the theme suggests, as the editors note, a financial plot, or at least a plot where one of the main threads was financial.[57] Although the fragmentary condition of the material does not allow a more detailed reconstruction, the surviving lines seem to offer a vivid representation of everyday financial dealings involving metics, citizens, and slaves in Athens, which is reminiscent of the world depicted in the Attic orators or in the vignettes in several of Theophrastus's *Characters*. No. 59 then is full of potential both for the New Comedy scholar and the historian.[58]

8. Papyri and Roman Comedy

The Greek papyri preserving New Comedy have given a great impetus to the study of Roman New Comedy. The most important landmark in this respect was the presentation by Eric Handley in 1968 of parts from a late-third-century roll from Oxyrhynchus which preserves a sequence of scenes from the Greek model of Plautus's *Bacchides*: Menander's *Dis Exapaton*. The papyrus was published in full in 1997 (see no. 69). This is the longest available piece from a Greek New Comedy which can be compared to its Latin adaptation. Its great significance lies in the fact that it allowed scholars to explore Plautus's methods of adaptation.[59]

---

[56] See Handley 1975; Austin, Handley, and Parsons 1995; Thür 2001. Full text in *adespota* K-A fr. 1152.

[57] Austin, Handley, and Parsons 1995, 4. See also Handley 1975. They mention, as a possible comparison, the plot suggested by the title and some of the surviving fragments of Menander's *Parakatatheke* (*The Deposit*). One could also compare the plot suggested by the title of Philippides's *Argyriou aphanismos* (*Vanished Money*). The one surviving fragment from this play (K-A fr. 9) is understood by Athenaeus, who quotes it (VI p. 230 A), to be referring to metics. (Whitehead 1977: 40 is, in my opinion, too skeptical.)

[58] Aspects of the potential historical significance of no. 59 are explored in the fascinating study Thür 2001. In line with Thür's interpretation, it can be noted that *triobolon*, at l. 3, might be a reference to the sum that freedmen had to pay in addition to the *metoikion*; see Whitehead 1977: 16–17 and Zelnick-Abramovitz 2005: 308–312. Harpocration (μ 27 Keaney), the main source for this tax, says that Menander referred to it in two of his plays, the *Anatithemene* (probably: *The Girl Who Dedicated Herself to a God*) and the *Didymai* (*Twin Sisters*); see Menander K-A fr. 33. However, Thür's suggestion that the owner of the slave (who, as we saw, is one of the interlocutors in the larger fragments) had a bank because sums of money are presented as hoarded in her house and other sums as having been lent out (see p. 151) is far from certain. The Attic orators provide several examples of Athenians and metics who do not run a bank but have substantial sums of money kept in the house, in addition to sums lent out. See, for example, the cases listed in Millett 1991: 167–168 and Lysias 12.10–11. On hoarding as a pervasive practice in classical Athens, see Millett 1991: 169–171.

[59] The bibliography is vast. To the works cited in Handley 1997: 18, one may add Anderson 1993, esp. ch. 1, Damen 1992 and Damen 1995, and the essays in Raffaelli and Tontini 2001.

No. 43, although much shorter and in an extremely fragmentary condition, might preserve another such piece. It is dated to the late second century CE and consists of five very damaged fragments from a roll. The three larger fragments contain dialogue in iambics. In frs 2–3, which are adjacent and belong to the same column, one speaker (A) seems to reassure his (or her) interlocutor (B) that B too will have a share in something (l. 21),[60] which, it transpires, was given to B's sister (23). This "share" seems to consist of B's ability to go to his sister's house to have dinner (24–25) and to be provided by her with a garment (25–26). B seems to find all this "wicked" (25). References to "daughter" and "son" a few lines below (38) suggest that A might be their father. References are made to "mocking" (36: he or she "will mock") and to somebody being deceived (41); someone is referred to as "sophist" (44, 45). The first editor, Susan Stephens, has pointed out the similarities of this scene to the second scene in Act V of Terence's *Heauton Timorumenos*.[61] There, Chremes justifies to his son Clitipho his decision not to leave him any property but to give it all to his future son-in-law as dowry for his daughter (Clitipho's sister). Stephens observes how Chremes too, like A, mentions food and clothing as what the husband of Clitipho's sister will offer (Ter. *HT* 968). "Sophist," "deceit," and "mocking," although without exact equivalents in the Terentian scene, are not out of place in the context of Terence's play. "Sophist" might be a reference to the Greek equivalent of the slave Syrus, who has tirelessly devised scheme after scheme in the course of the play. "Being deceived" would be appropriate either to Chremes, who has been deceived by Syrus and his son, or to Clitipho, who is being "deceived" out of his inheritance by his father. The concept of "mocking" too is present in Terence; see *HT* 952 and, perhaps, 982.

Might no. 43 then preserve, as Stephens tentatively suggests, the Greek original adapted by Terence for Chremes's punishment of his son in Act V of the *Heauton Timorumenos*?[62] If this is right, then no. 43, most probably from Menander's *Heauton Timoroumenos*, which Terence adapted in his own homonymous play, would be the first papyrus preserving a passage which would allow us to compare Terence's adaptation to its Greek original.[63]

PART II

The table that follows (see p. 818 ff.) includes all papyri identified as preserving Greek comedy, as well as titles of and commentaries (*hypomnemata*) on comedies, published since 1973.[64] It also includes comic papyri which were first published before 1973 but have since then been

[60] I follow the line-numbering of K-A (*adespota* fr. 1129).
[61] Stephens 1982.
[62] Paradoxically, although this scene from Terence's *Heauton Timorumenos* has been the subject of much scholarly debate concerning whether it is an adaptation of a scene in Menander's homonymous play or Terence's own invention, Terentian scholars have completely ignored the papyrus. For the debate, compare, for example, Lefèvre 1994, especially 82–84, and Steidle 1974, especially 272–275; also Lowe 1998. Specifically on Act V, see also Maltby 1984.
[63] For another tentative attribution, much less persuasive in my opinion, see Dedoussi 1980 on *adespota* K-A fr. 1054.
[64] The data are based on the records of MP³, which I last consulted on 31/3/2011. MP³ 1637.3 is more likely to come from a satyr play rather than from a comedy, and is therefore not included here: see

augmented by more fragments (e.g., 40) or reidentified as, for example, comedy (e.g., 7), or as of a specific play (e.g., 14), or as from the same roll as another papyrus (e.g., 8).

The presentation is primarily by date of the papyrus (see first column: the date suggested in the first edition, unless otherwise stated), and only secondarily by author (second column), so that diachronic trends in the reception of comedy as a whole can be observed more easily. Attention is drawn both to the type of comic text the papyri preserve (e.g., second column: sub-genre or, where possible, author; col. 4: content and, where possible, play; col. 11: presence of act-break and/or lyric parts) and to elements potentially illuminating reception (bibliological information: columns 6–8; provenance: col. 9; presence of reading aids and annotation: columns 10 and 12 respectively). Columns 13 and 14 contain, where possible, tentative suggestions about the papyri's original use and their significance for our understanding of comedy. The third, fifth, and last column offer basic (not exhaustive) bibliographical information.

Notes on the Table:

"Date": Chronological indications of the type, for example, 2/3 CE are used for papyri estimated to have been written late in the second or early in the third century CE.

"Author": In the case of papyri that cannot be securely attributed to an author but are in the style of New Comedy and could conceivably have been Menandrian, my classification sometimes differs from that of MP³. In general, I have used a more descriptive system of classification: e.g. "?Menander," "New Comedy (?Menander)", "New Comedy," "Comedy (?New)," in declining degree of certainty.

"MP³ no": In the case of no. 97, not listed in MP³, the item's number in LDAB is given instead.

"Content/play": For identified fragments, I give specific references. For unidentified fragments, I give very brief descriptions and/or key words. Words in quotation marks are translations of words on the papyrus. Tentative attributions are of the editio princeps unless otherwise stated.

"Main publication": To save space, details of the papyrus's main publication (usually its first edition) are given in an abbreviated manner and are normally not included in the Bibliography. For example, in no. 10, "P. Oxy. 49.3433 (Bingen 1982)" means that the papyrus was published with ID P. Oxy. 3433 in 1982, in volume 49 of the Oxyrhynchus papyri series, and that its editor was Jean Bingen. Also to save space, information regarding photographs of papyri has been included only if a papyrus does not belong to a digitized collection available online. For photographs of the Oxyrhynchus papyri, see: http://www.papyrology.ox.ac.uk/POxy. For the papyri at Cologne, see: http://www.uni-koeln.de/phil-fak/ifa/NRWakademie/papyrologie. For those at Heidelberg, see: http://aquila.papy.uni-heidelberg.de/Kat.html. For the papyri in Vienna, see: http://aleph.onb.ac.at/F?func=file&file_name=login&local_base=ONB08.

Krumeich et al. 1999: 635–638; cf. Storey 2011, vol. 3, pp. 421, 423. Neither is MP³ 1320.71, as it is unclear whether it comes from a tragedy or a comedy.

"Form": The abbreviation "pap." without further clarification is used when it is not clear whether the fragment might have come from a roll or from a piece of papyrus. → indicates that the writing is along the fibers; ↓ that it is across.

"Reading aids, etc.": Additions, corrections, signs or notes indicating change of speaker and punctuation, and other signs are noted systematically. So is the presence of accents and breathings. But the use of apostrophes and tremata (that is, diacritics, usually in the form of two dots, placed over a vowel—usually an ι or an υ) is remarked upon only selectively.

"Other publications": "Wilson" refers to the 2007 edition of the eleven plays of Aristophanes by Nigel Wilson for Oxford Classical Texts; "Arnott" to Geoffrey Arnott's Loeb edition of Menander (Vol. 1: 1979, Vol. 2: 1996; Vol. 3: 2000). "Blanchard" to Alain Blanchard's Budé edition of *Sikyonioi* (2009). For "Austin", "Dedoussi," "Furley," "Ireland," "Pöhlmann and West," and "van Rossum-Steenbeek," see Bibliography.

In the other columns, when a reference to a modern author is made by name only (rather than by name and date of publication), then the reference is to the work of this author cited in the fifth and/or the last columns.

With the exception of the fourth column, the source of passages in quotation marks is the first edition, unless otherwise indicated.

The bibliography on each papyrus is not exhaustive.

I have examined photographs of all papyri if publicly available and have inspected in person many of those belonging to the Oxyrhynchus collection. I thank its recent and present curators, Drs. Daniela Colomo, Nikolaos Gonis, and Ben Henry, for their patience and help.

Table app.1 Greek Comic Papyri 1973–2010

No.	Date	Author	MP³ no.	Content/Play	Main Publication	Form	Reused Material
1	3 BCE (mid.)	New Comedy (?Menander)	1645.01	244 ll. Young man in love with girl whose face he has not seen; Ephesus. ?Menander *Ephesios* (Arnott, Laplace 1997) ?*Dis Exapaton* (Nünlist)	P. Köln 5.203 (Maresch 1985) +P. Köln 6.243 (Maresch 1987) +P. Mich. inv. 6950 (Nünlist, *ZPE* 99, 1993, 245-78: edition of all)	roll, from cartonnage→	NO
2	3 BCE	New Comedy	1668	Comic dialogue in iambics. "κόπτω" joke; "tokens." ?Recognition of daughter.	P. Vindob. 29811 (=P. Rain. 3.22: Oellacher 1939=*CGFP* 261). Identification and edition of col. 1: Römer, *ZPE* 167, 2008, 1-2.	roll →	↓: document
3	3 BCE (mid/ 2nd half)	Comedy (?not Old Comedy)	1665.01	12 beginnings of iambics. ?Cook monologue (ed. pr.).	P. Petrie Mus. UC 31915 (Handley, *Studies in honour of T. B. L. Webster* II, 1988, 51-55, with plate 5.1)	pap. sheet, from cart. →	NO
4	3/2 BCE	Menander	1300.2	*Dyskolos* 766-773	P. Oslo 3.168 (Eitrem– Amundsen 1936, p. 259). New ed. and ident.: Lenaerts, *Papyrus littéraires grecs* ("Papyrologica bruxellensia 13," 1977), no. 7, with pl. 1	tiny scrap of pap. →	NO

Bibliological Details	Provenance	Reading Aids etc.	XOPOY or Lyric Parts	Annotations	Use	Special Significance	Other Publications
3 nearly full columns plus more frs. 18-21 ll. per col. "Large, unskilled, uneven hand."	Unknown	Paragraphoi/ double points. ?Sometimes spaces for change of speaker.	**XOPOY:** End of Act I, beginning of Act II. Unique in New Comedy introduction of the chorus by a character with the word χορός.	NO			*ad.* K-A fr. 1147, *Fabula Incerta* 8 Arnott
Column of 26 ll., plus traces from right end of previous column. ?Stichometric in left margin (?400: Römer).	Unknown	Paragr./ blank spaces: for change of speaker.	**XOPOY.** If Δ= stichometric 400: ?end of Act II, beginning of Act III (Römer).	NO (see Römer)	?Professional copy (see stichometric number)		*ad.* K-A fr. 1081 (superseded by Römer)
Large size letters—if roll containing the whole play, of unusually large proportions: ed. pr.	Gurob	NO	NO	NO	?Excerpt (ed. pr.)	?Early attestation of cook speeches as "souvenirs of comedy" (ed. pr.).	*ad.* K-A fr. 1138
	Unknown	NO	NO	NO		Earliest doc. for *Dysk.* Better text than the main source (P. Bodmer 4).	

No.	Date	Author	MP³ no.	Content/Play	Main Publication	Form	Reused Material
5	3/2 BCE	?Menander	1306.2	Dialogue in iambics. ?Menander *Phanion* (φανιον, i.e., probably Φάνιον, at line end: ed. pr.)	P. Carlsberg 50 (previously P. Haun.: Bülow – Jacobsen, *BICS* 24, 1977, 64-66, with pl. 1)	small scrap of pap. →	↓demotic
6	3/2 BCE	Comedy (?written in 390s; not in the style of New Comedy)	1638.21	50 trochaic tetrameters, many in para-dithyrambic language (see Csapo, *ZPE* 100, 1994, 39–44). One of the interlocutors, a cook, is justifying his decision to compose the encomium of a fish. ?Archippus *Fishes*. ?Cratinus the younger *Giants*. ?Alexandrian play. (See ed. pr. 336-337, Csapo, and Storey 2011, vol. 3, p. 411.)	P. Duk. inv. 313 R (b) (Willis, *GRBS* 32, 1991, 331–53, with tables 1-3).	pap. sheet, from cart.→: palimpsest	Cut from a larger sheet (or roll), already used on both sides. →a. Underwriting: doc.=P. Duk. inv. 313 R (a) →b.=no. 6 ↓ Accounts (P. Duk. inv. 313 V)
7	?1 BCE	Aristophanes	148.01	*Clouds* 974-975 (From after the *diairesis* of 974 to the *diairesis* of 975, with many mistakes and a form of ἐπαχθές instead of ἀπηνές at 974.)	O. Bodl. 1.279 (Tait, *Greek ostraca in the Bodleian library* 1930, vol. 1, p. 46, no. 279. Ident. Litinas, *ZPE* 141, 2002, 103–105).	ostracon (palimpsest)	Underwriting: ?Ptolemaic bank receipt

Bibliological Details	Provenance	Reading Aids etc.	XOPOY or Lyric Parts	Annotations	Use	Special Significance	Other Publications
	Unknown	NO	NO	NO			*ad.* K-A fr. 1124
3 full cols. 16/17 lines per col. Scribe: "not a beginner, not yet professional." Copying errors.	Fayum (on Fayum and its papyri, see van Minnen, *JJP* 28, 1998, 99–184)	NO (although a dialogue)	NO	NO	?Copying exercise for apprentice scribe (ed. pr.). ?Copied from an anthology of excerpts.	?Another (compare no. 3) early testament for cook scenes as suitable for excerption.	*ad.* K-A fr. 1146
Each metrical half-line starts at the left edge. The rest: indented.	?Thebes	NO	NO	NO	?Part of a series of ostraca with a school exercise. ?A personal (?erotic) message. (Litinas 2002)	Earliest doc. for *Clouds*.	

No.	Date	Author	MP³ no.	Content/Play	Main Publication	Form	Reused Material
8	1 BCE (end: Ronconi, *HB* no. 69; 1/2 CE: ed. pr. P. Oxy. 212; 1 CE: ed. pr. P. Oxy. 2808)	?Aristophanes	156	?Aristophanes (see l. 35 in Ar. fr. 592 K-A). ?*Clouds i* (Ronconi), ?*Lemnian women* (Ciriello 1989), ?*Thesmo. ii* (ed. pr. of P. Oxy. 212)	P. Oxy. 2.212 (1899)+37.2808 (1971)=*CGFP* 62+233. Identified as of the same hand and roll: Ronconi, *APF* 51, 2005, 197-204, pls xvi-xvii (of P. Oxy. 212, photo of fr. a only)	roll →	NO
9	1 BCE	Comedy	1641.01	30 beginnings of iambics. ?Cook monologue (ed. pr.).	P. Köln 7.284 (Gronewald 1991)	?roll, from cart.→	NO
10	1 BCE/1CE	Menander	1320.2	740 K-T+shreds of 12 more lines: Admonitions of slave to young master.	P. Oxy. 49.3433 (Bingen 1982)	?roll →	NO
11	1 CE (Turner Handley)/1 BCE (Koenen)	?Menander	1297.31	Loutrophoria for nuptial bath. ?*Karchedonios*, ?*Kres*, ?*Phasma* (see in Handley and Hurst 1990, 138-43, 162-66).	P. Oxy. 59.3966 (Handley 1992)	roll→	NO
12	1 CE	Menander	1302.52	?*Leukadia* (ed. pr.). Dialogue: priestess and younger person.	P. Oxy. 60.4024 (Parsons 1994)	?roll↓	→: cursive
13	1 CE	Menander	1304.11	?*Misoumenos* (?'[Cra]teia', ?'Deme[as]', ?'Cle[inias]')	P. Oxy. 60.4025 (Parsons 1994)	?roll→	NO
14	1 CE	?Menander	1308.5	?*Synaristosai* (Webster 1974, 187; Arnott *ZPE* 72, 1988, 23-25: comparing Plaut. *Cist.* 95-103)	P. Baden 6.175 (Gerhard 1938)=P. Heid. inv. G 200b *recto*=*CGFP* 265	pap.→	?NO

Bibliological Details	Provenance	Reading Aids etc.	XOPOY or Lyric Parts	Annotations	Use	Special Significance	Other Publications
Six frs. The two larger ones: each holds upper parts of 2 consecutive columns. 1 col. intact in height: 20 ll. "Upright, regular, well-controlled hand" (*HB*).	Oxyrhynchus	Double points, paragr. High and middle stops. Some accents. Some corrections and additions, probably by different hand.	NO	NO			Ar. K-A fr. 592 + *ad.* K-A fr. 1111
Upper left part of col., with left and upper margins. Towards the end, the writing becomes more cursive (?excerpt: ed. pr.).	Unknown	NO	NO	NO	?Excerpt with cook monologue (compare nos 3, 6).		*ad.* K-A fr. 1140
Upper right part of col., with right and upper margins. At least 30 ll./col.	Oxyrhynchus	NO. Two additions, by first hand.	NO	NO	Unclear whether part of a play or excerpt.		Men. K-A fr. 602
Parts of 16 lines from bottom part of column, with lower margin. Same hand as "Hand 1" of P. Oxy. 2654, with M's *Karchedonios.*	Oxyrhynchus	NO	XOPOY, and, probably, 1 line in lyric metre written in reverse indentation.	NO		?Song (l. 12). ?2 days of dramatic action (Brown, in Handley and Hurst 1990, 162).	Perusino and Giacomoni 1999, *Fab. Inc.* 9 Arnott, *Karch.* 70-84 Austin
10 lines of iambics, with upper margin. See also under no. 18.	Oxyrhynchus	Paragraphoi, double points. Some additions, corrections.	NO	NO		?Beginning of *Leukadia.*	*Leukadia* 1-10 Arnott, Austin
Scrap with parts of 7 lines.	Oxyrhynchus	NO	NO	NO			*Misoum.* fr. 3 Arnott
Parts of 12 last lines of col., with lower margin.	Unknown	Possibly space (?and double point) for change of speaker.	NO	NO			*ad.* K-A fr. 1074, Arnott *Synar.* pp. 332-333

No.	Date	Author	MP³ no.	Content/Play	Main Publication	Form	Reused Material
15	1 CE	New Comedy	1671.4	Animated dialogue in iambics. "Moschio."	P. Oxy. 45.3218 (Stephens 1977)	roll→	↓: ?novel: MP³ 2641.1
16	1 CE	?New Comedy	1627.1	Expository speech: "twin daughters," "nurse," "countryside." ?Prologue of New Comedy. ?Calligeneia's prologue in Aristophanes' *Thesmo. ii* (ed. pr.).	P. Oxy. 50.3540 (Handley 1983)	roll→	NO
17	1 CE (first half)	Comedy (?Old)	1637.31	?Character speaking to another character, in either iambic trimeters or trochaic tetrameters. ?'Archias'. ?Old Comedy (see ed. pr. and Storey 2011, vol. 3, p. 417).	P. Köln 8.330 (Gronewald 1997)	roll→	NO
18	1 CE (ed. pr.), or 2 CE (Cavallo in MP³)	?Menander	1308.6	?*Leukadia* (ed. pr.; Mette, *Lustrum* 25, 1983, 29; Arnott), ?*Synaristosai* (Gaiser, *ZPE* 39, 1980, 99–111).	P. Oxy. inv. 50 4B 30 H (5)a, fr. 1 (Handley in *BICS* 26, 1979, 84–87). No photo available.	roll↓	→: doc. (upside down in relation to ↓)

Bibliological Details	Provenance	Reading Aids etc.	ΧΟΡΟΥ or Lyric Parts	Annotations	Use	Special Significance	Other Publications
Parts of 13 lines, from upper right corner of col., with upper margin. Well-made papyrus. Informal, uneven round hand, with cursive elements.	Oxyrhynchus	Double point. Ordinal number Γ in text: ?for *tritagonistes*. Corrections, one by a second hand, which added the correct form but did not delete the error.	NO	NO	?Copy ultimately deriving from copy used by a theater troupe.	?Attesting performance.	*ad.* K-A fr. 1125
Right part of full column (36 lines), with upper, lower and right margins.	Oxyrhynchus	1 grave	NO	NO			*ad.* K-A fr. 1132
Ends of 12 bottom lines of col., with right and lower margin. Unskilled, uneven hand.	Unknown	NO	NO	NO			*ad.* K-A fr. 1148
1 of several unpublished fragments, in a 'small, round and fluent' hand. ?Same roll as no. 12 (ed. pr. of no. 12, p. 42: but different hand, different orientation of writing at the back).	Oxyrhynchus	Double point.	?	?			*ad.* K-A fr. 1127, Arnott *Leuk.* pp. 234-237

No.	Date	Author	MP³ no.	Content/Play	Main Publication	Form	Reused Material
19	1 or early 2 CE	?Menander	1650.02	Animated dialogue between Smicrines and an interlocutor. "daughter"	P. Oxy. 59.3969 (Handley 1992)	roll→	NO
20	1/2 CE	Old Comedy (?Eupolis)	1638.11	Dialogue in iambics. "Cleonymus," "Demaratus." ?Eupolis *Prospaltioi* (ed. pr., tentatively; see also Storey 2000, 166-71).	P. Oxy. 62.4301 (Austin–Parsons 1995)	roll→	NO
21	1/2 CE	?Menander	1297.51	?End of monologue, followed by entry of "Phania" and "Parmeno." Ph. is reassured by P. that some people he cares about (?his family) are alive and well. "Ship to Crete," "betrayal." *?Kitharistes* (ed. pr.)	P. Oxy. 68.4642 (Nünlist 2003)	roll→	NO
22	1/2 CE	?Menander	1302.51	?Menander *Hymnis* (ed. pr.: *nota pers.* starting with **Y**). Dialogue: ?Hymnis, Parmeno, ?young master.	P. Oxy. 68.4643 (Austin–Parsons 2003)	roll→	NO
23	1/2 CE	?Menander	1308.4	*?Sikyonioi.* "Malthake," "grievious absence from home."	P. Oxy. inv. 33 4B 83E (8-11) (Handley in *BICS* 31, 1984, 25–31 with pl. 1)	roll→	NO

Bibliological Details	Provenance	Reading Aids etc.	XOPOY or Lyric Parts	Annotations	Use	Special Significance	Other Publications
4 frs. Larger: parts of 12 lines from end of col. with lower margin.	Oxyrhynchus	Change of speaker: double points with space.	NO	NO			*ad.* K-A fr. 1142
2 frs, 1 with left margin, in Roman uncial. "Elegant, decorated hand": ?same as PSI 1213 (=Eupolis, *Prospaltioi* fr. 260 K-A)	Oxyrhynchus	Paragr. (?by second hand)	NO	NO			*ad.* K-A fr. 1151
Parts from 16 first lines of col., with upper and some left margin. Minimal traces from previous column (ed. pr.).	Oxyrhynchus	Change of speaker: paragr. and blank spaces (no double points). Later additions (?by same hand): some *notae personarum.* Acute.	NO	NO		?New fragment from *Kitharistes*.	*Kith.* 102-117 Austin
Parts of 23 first lines of column, with upper margin. "Round, calligraphic" hand.	Oxyrhynchus	Double points, copied with the text (i.e. not inserted later). Interlinear *notae pers.,* one with ∫ sign, by second hand.	?XOPOY (see ed. pr. p. 34)	NO			Men. *Hymnis* K-A fr. 361a (in K-A vol. 1, p. 395)
29 line-ends with right margin.	Oxyrhynchus	Double points in mid-line, copied with the text.	NO	NO			*Sik.* fr. 3 Arnott, fr. 12 Blanchard

No.	Date	Author	MP³ no.	Content/Play	Main Publication	Form	Reused Material
24	1/2 CE	?Menander	1320.7	?Monologue. "Chrysis," "pulling of hair." ?*Samia* (ed. pr.)	P. Berol. 8450 (Luppe–Müller, *APF* 29, 1983, pp. 5–7 with plate 1).	roll→	NO
25	1/2 CE	?Menander	1324.23	Probably end of play with invocation to "goddess" (?Nike).	P. Oxy. 66.4522 (Handley 1999)	roll→	NO
26	1/2 CE	New Comedy	1667.25	Dialogue in iambics.	P. Oxy. 68.4645 (Handley 2003)	roll→	NO
27	1 or 2 CE	?Comedy ?Satyr play	1650.03	"Piraeus," "Attica," "sailing," "small ship," "Poseidon"	P. Oxy. 68.4644 (Austin and Parsons 2003)	roll →	NO
28	2 CE	Aristophanes	137.01	*Ach.* 55–60, 165–80, 234–40, 278–83, 291, 308, 316–35, 345–47, 380–85, 417–19, 506–09, 539–42, 655–58, 695–704, 822–25 and 8 frs unplaced (frs. 16–23)	P. Oxy. 66.4510 (Gonis 1999). For fr. 6, see also Savignago 2008, 15.	roll→	? ↓: Ink traces on some frs.
29	2 CE	Aristophanes	140.02	*Birds* 1661–1676	P. Oxy. 66.4516 (Gonis 1999: a preliminary edition was available to Dunbar 1995)	roll→	NO

Bibliological Details	Provenance	Reading Aids etc.	XOPOY or Lyric Parts	Annotations	Use	Special Significance	Other Publications
Parts of 21 lines from top of column, in "beautiful large script," with upper margin.	Fayum	Apostrophes and high stops (?for punctuation), added later.	NO	NO			*ad.* K-A fr. 1131, *Samia* fr. 2 Dedoussi
22 ends of lines, with upper and very deep lower margin (?end of play with rest of col. left blank).	Oxyrhynchus	Double point and space for change of speaker.	NO	NO			Men. K-A fr. *910
Ends and beginnings of 2 consecutive columns, written in a fluent cursive.	Oxyrhynchus	Double points and high stops: written with the text. 1 paragraphos, of unclear import: see ed. pr. p. 42.	NO	NO	?Copy made for one's own use (ed. pr.).		
Parts of 8 lines from end of column, with lower margin.	Oxyrhynchus	Space with double point (?and spaces alone) for change of speaker.	NO	NO			
23 frs. Lyric parts are written in various forms of indentation.	Oxyrhynchus	Frequent diacritical marks, probably by first scribe: paragr. (to separate dialogue from lyric), double points, *nota pers.* (?"chorus": fr. 9).	YES (lyric parts). Colometry similar to the medieval: see Perusino 2007, Savignago 2008.	In cursive: only traces are visible. See *CLGP* I 1.4, Ar. no. 2.		Earliest doc. of *Ach.* In some "suspect readings…", it confirms the antiquity of the transmitted text."	P73 Wilson
"Handsome" roll. Lower and right margin survive.	Oxyrhynchus	1 middle point, written with the text (for ?punctuation, or ?word- division).	NO	NO			Oldest of *Birds*. "Important testimony to the constitution of the text": unique variants; confirms some emendations; confirms that Estensis gr. 127 provides at least some access to ancient readings.	P69 Wilson

No.	Date	Author	MP³ no.	Content/Play	Main Publication	Form	Reused Material
30	2 CE (?mid)	Aristophanes	152.12	*Wealth* 687–705, 726–31, 957–70	P. Oxy. 4521 (Gonis 1999)	roll→	NO
31	2 CE	Aristophanes	154.001	*Thesm.* 1043–51 and 1202–10	P. Oxy. 73.4935 (Benaissa 2009)	roll→	NO
32	2 CE (late: ed. pr.; late 1 CE: N. Lewis)	Aristophanes	155.2	*Poiesis* (ll. 4–5=fr. 451 Kock) ?From first scene (Lloyd-Jones, *ZPE* 42, 1981, 23-25)	P. Turner 4 (=P. Yale 1625: Stephens, in *Papyri Greek and Egyptian… In honour of E. G. Turner* 1981, with plate iii)	roll→	↓: accounts.
33	2 CE (2nd half)	Aristophanes (*hypomnema*)	154.02	Commentary on *Wasps* 36–41	P. Oxy. 66.4509 (Gonis 1999)	roll→	↓: cursive on frs 2-3

Bibliological Details	Provenance	Reading Aids etc.	XOPOY or Lyric Parts	Annotations	Use	Special Significance	Other Publications
3 frs from "elegant roll." See ed. pr. 166–167	Oxyrhynchus	Double points for change of speaker, 1 accent, 1 breathing, 1 high point for punctuation.	NO	Unusually extensive for the date, in "exceptionally formal" handwriting. Glosses, notes on myth, etymology, and identification of speakers/ addressees. Affinities to the medieval scholia. ?Ultimately derived from a *hypomnema* (ed. pr.). See *CLGP* I 1.4, Ar. no. 22.		Earliest of *Wealth*. Earliest extensively annotated pap. of Ar.	P83 Wilson
2 small frs, one with upper margin. Same scribe as P. Oxy. 5084 with Plato's *Crito*.	Oxyrhynchus	Perhaps a high stop (for punctuation).	YES, some lines possibly in reverse indentation. Colometry similar to the medieval one.	NO			
Narrow strip with central part of 18 top lines of a col. with upper margin+a tiny scrap.	Unknown	Some accents, some stops (?for punctuation).	NO	NO			Ar. K-A fr. 466
5 frs, one with lower margin, in semi-cursive ("scholiastic") hand.	Oxyrhynchus	NO		Lemmata set off by blank space. Combines notes which appear separately, in distinct families of mss, in the medieval scholia.		Earliest comm. on a play of Ar. known from the medieval tradition.	*CLGP* I 1.4 Ar. no. 25; Trojahn (2002, 43-44)

No.	Date	Author	MP³ no.	Content/Play	Main Publication	Form	Reused Material
34	2 CE	Aristophanes (title to commentary)	157.11	] ου (=author's name in the genitive) | Ἀ[ριστο]φανείων | ς ὑπ(όμνημα)	P. Oxy. inv. 51B44/G(b) (Caroli, *Titolo iniziale*, 2007, P12, with table xx)	pap.↓	→:blank
35	2 CE	Menander	1301.01	*Epitrepontes* 290-301, 338-345, 376-400, 421-447	P. Oxy. 60.4022 (Parsons 1994)	pap. codex	
36	2 CE (early)	Menander	1301.04	*Epitr.* 676-710, 786-823, 1128-1144, and Furley pp. 77-79	P. Mich. inv. 4733, 4752, 4800, 4801, 4805, 4807. P. Mich. inv. 4733 fr. 1-2: Gronewald, *ZPE* 66, 1986, 1-13, with pl. 1. P. Mich. 4752, frs A, B and C: Römer 2012a. P. Mich. 4805: Römer 2012b. Rest unpublished. Preliminary edition of some of the unpublished fragments, prepared by Koenen and Gagos, in Martina 1997.	roll↓	→: documents partly washed or rubbed off

Bibliological Details	Provenance	Reading Aids etc.	XOPOY or Lyric Parts	Annotations	Use	Special Significance	Other Publications
	Oxyrhynchus				Papyrus tag with title, probably to be glued on roll.	*Hypomnema* on the 6th play (or: ?on 6 plays) of Aristophanes, by ?Aristarchus/ ?Symmachus/ ?Didymus. See ed. pr. and Montana in *CLGP* I 1.4, pp. 6–7, n. 23.	
2 frs, from 2 consecutive leaves. Very little side margin survives. 45–47 lines per page. → page facing ↓page.	Oxyrhynchus	Rough breathing (to distinguish a rarely attested particle). Change of speaker: paragr., blank space/ blank space and punctuation (high oblique dash or stop)/stop without space. Marginal and interlinear *notae pers.* Corrections. ?All by same hand (ed. pr.).	NO	?YES. Perhaps note on delivery to the left of 293–294 (written in cursive: ?different hand). Character assigned by both name and profession: Nünlist, *ZPE* 126, 1999, 75–76.		Earliest codex of Menander. Many variant readings and attributions (?livelier text). ?"Theatrical origins" (Sisti 2000, 634; 2004, 161–62). Unique direct evidence for particle ἦν.	
Many frs., from at least 3 columns. C. 50 lines per col. Irregular but not unskilled bookhand, with cursive elements.	Karanis	Double points and *notae pers.* written with the text when in mid-line.	YES. End of Act III.	NO	Found among the papers of Socrates (probably not in his hand), a 2nd cent. collector of money taxes in Karanis. See van Minnen 1994, 237–246.	Crucial for end of Act III and the Smicrines-Pamphila scene early in Act IV.	

No.	Date	Author	MP³ no.	Content/Play	Main Publication	Form	Reused Material
37	2 CE	Menander	1301.1	*Epitr.* 788-811, 812-835	P. Oxy. 50.3532 (Turner 1983). See now Furley 2009, pp. 86-89, Römer 2012a, Furley 2013.	roll→	NO
38	2 CE	Menander	1301.2	*Epitr.* 790-809	P. Oxy. 50.3533 (Turner 1983). See now Furley 2009, pp. 86-88, Römer 2012a, Furley 2013.	roll↓	→: ?Latin register
39	2 CE (2nd half)	Menander	1302.01	*Epitr.* Act I: Furley pp. 39-41.	P. Oxy. 73.4936 (Handley 2009)	roll↓	→: cursive doc. (2 CE)
40	2 CE	Menander	1305	*Perikeiromene* 162–179+ 182–191	Prk. 162-179 (=*CGFP* 175)+182-191 (Salewski, *ZPE* 129, 2000, 12)	roll	?
41	2 CE	Menander (hypothesis)	1321.21	Hypothesis to *Epitr.*	P. Oxy. 60.4020 (Parsons 1994)	pap.→	↓: Accounts
42	2 CE	Menander (title)	1303.1	Title with ornamentation Μισού[μενος] (or ? Μισογ[ύνης]) | Μενά[νδρου]	P. Oxy. 48.3371 (Turner 1981)	papyrus scrap→	?NO

Bibliological Details	Provenance	Reading Aids etc.	XOPOY or Lyric Parts	Annotations	Use	Special Significance	Other Publications
3 frs, from upper part of 2 consecutive cols. Fr. 3 precedes frs 1-2.	Oxyrhynchus	NO	NO	NO	?From "library" (found together with other literary texts).	End of Smicrines's speech and beginning of Pamphila's in Act IV.	
Central part of upper half of col., with upper margin.	Oxyrhynchus	Elision systematically marked. Oblique dashes in the line plus blank space: ?"reading marks", aiding delivery (ed. pr.; see also Gammacurta 2006, p. 30).	NO	NO	?Copied from an acting edition or selection (ed. pr.).	End of Smicrines's speech in Act IV.	
Ends and beginnings of 2 cols. C. 35 lines per col.	Oxyrhynchus	Paragr., marginal *notae pers.*	NO	NO		New piece from (?) first scene of Act I.	
2 frs, probably from the same column.	Unknown	Only a trema survives.	NO	NO		In 187, the end of the line has been omitted.	
Upper left corner of a ?leaf. Heading: title (?written twice—cf. Austin 2010, 10; Handley 2011, 51) and incipit in large capitals (some letters overwritten). Below, hypothesis in smaller handwriting.	Oxyrhynchus	NO			?Copying exercise (ed. pr.).		Van Rossum-Steenbeek no. 25
	Oxyrhynchus	NO	NO	NO	NO	?End-title	

No.	Date	Author	MP³ no.	Content/Play	Main Publication	Form	Reused Material
43	2 CE (late)	New Comedy (?Menander)	1667.1	?Menander *Heauton Timoroumenos* (ed. pr., comparing fr. 2–3, 22 ff. to Ter. *Heaut.* 964 ff.; see also Luppe, *CR* 34, 1984, 113)	P. Oxy. 49.3431 (Stephens 1982)	roll→	NO
44	2 CE	New Comedy	1297.1	?Daughter reported as crying over dead father. ?Menander *Aspis* (Gaizer, *ZPE* 51, 1983, 37–43).	P. Berol. 21145 (Kannicht in *Festschrift für U. Hausmann* 1982, pp. 374–376, with table 79; see also Ioannidou 1996, no. 47)	roll→	NO (but traces of ink)
45	2 CE (?2nd half)	New Comedy	1667.26	Dialogue. Betrothal formula. ?Dowry of half a talent (?or consisting of both cash and other revenues: see ed. pr. p. 46).	P. Oxy. 68.4646 (Handley 2003)	roll→	↓ and other way up: "literary or subliterary text" (late 3rd)
46	2 CE	New Comedy	1671.1	Dialogue. "All-night festival." ?ephebes, ?rape (Henry).	P. Oxy. 66.4523 (Henry 1999) Fr. 1: P. Oxy. 38.2827 (Weinstein 1971=*CGFP* 283)	roll→	NO
47	2 CE (mid- late)	Comedy (?New)	1687.01	Rapid dialogue in iambics. ?Between 3 slaves. "epiclerus"	P. Oxy 59.3972 (Handley 1992)	roll→	NO

Bibliological Details	Provenance	Reading Aids etc.	XOPOY or Lyric Parts	Annotations	Use	Special Significance	Other Publications
5 frs, 2 tiny, 3 from 2 columns. Fr. 1: beginnings of 20 first lines of col. Frs. 2–3: col. (26 lines) with upper and lower margins.	Oxyrhynchus	Paragr., double points with blank space, high stops added later. Some corrections (same hand). At the foot of frs 2–3, stichometric κοτ (=26), by different hand.	NO	NO	?Professional copy (see stichometric number).	?Greek model for Ter. *Heaut.* 960 ff.	*ad.* K-A fr. 1129
Lower part of col., with lower margin, in irregular semi-cursive script.	Fayum	NO	NO	NO		?Speech within speech.	*ad.* K-A fr. 1128
Frs from 2 cols, at least 24 lines long each, with upper margin, in Roman uncial.	Oxyrhynchus	Paragr. High and middle points (one added afterwards). Rough breathing. Circumflex bridging the two vowels of a diphthong. ?Same hand.	NO	NO	"Professionally made copy of a well-known play."	Example of belated recycling (ed. pr.: almost a century).	
5 frs, one with lower margin, in semi-cursive "scholiastic" hand.	Oxyrhynchus	Double points. A high stop. Accents. A rough breathing. Some corrections.	NO	NO			fr. 1=*ad.* K-A fr. 1116
Beginnings of 14 last lines of col. in Roman uncial. Left and lower margin.	Oxyrhynchus	Paragr., marginal and interlin. *notae pers.* High points (punct.), some accents, a hyphen above 2 letters to assist word articulation (see ed. pr. p. 83, and add *ad.* K-A fr. 1149.13): by second hand.	NO	NO	"Handsome roll," corrected copy.		*ad.* K-A fr. 1145

No.	Date	Author	MP³ no.	Content/Play	Main Publication	Form	Reused Material
48	2 CE (early)	?Comedy	1673.11	Very little survives. Names of 2 fish.	P. Freiburg 46 (Gronewald, *Griechische und demotische Papyri der Universitätsbibliothek Freiburg* 1986, pp. 5–6, table 1)	pap., tiny scrap	?NO
49	2 CE (?middle)	?Comedy	1687.04	Dialogue. σκώμματα. (?Old Comedy: ed. pr., *CLGP* II 4, p. 93, n. 1)	P. Oxy. 64.4410 (Haslam 1997)	roll→	NO
50	2 CE (?middle)	?Comedy	1687.05	?Old Comedy (ed. pr.)	P. Oxy. 64.4411 (Haslam 1997). For some of the frs as from a different roll, with poems of Sappho, see Steinrück 2000, Ucciardello 2001 (=MP³ 1450.01).	roll→	NO
51	2 CE (second half: ed. pr.; 2/3: *CLGP*)	?Comedy (?*hypomnema*)	1637.01	If commentary on a comedy (see, e.g.: ἡ σκηνή, κ]ωμωιδουν[), the play included mythological elements.	PSI inv. 13 *verso* (Pernigotti in *Comunicazioni dell'Istituto Papirologico 'G. Vitelli'* 8, 2009, 5–9, with table I)	roll↓	→: damaged surface—only traces are visible.
52	2 (late)/3 (first half) CE	Aristophanes	152.02	*Wealth* 210–219	Bodl. Libr. inv. MS.Gr.cl.g.44(P) (Luiselli, *APF* 48, 2002, 7–12: photo on p. 9)	roll↓	→: unidentified cursive of 2ⁿᵈ cent. CE

Bibliological Details	Provenance	Reading Aids etc.	XOPOY or Lyric Parts	Annotations	Use	Special Significance	Other Publications
1 small fr. from bottom of column.	Unknown	NO	NO	NO			*ad.* K-A fr. *1136
8 frs, some with margin, in Roman uncial. "Prime product."	Oxyrhynchus	Paragr., double points. Middle stop. A grave. Some corrections.	NO	NO	Luxury roll; "should carry a work of high literature."		
Luxury roll, in Roman uncial. Ed. pr.: 95 frs. 5 of them have proven to be from a different roll. Confusion due to filing: ed. pr. p. 59, Ucciardello 2001, 167.	Oxyrhynchus	Paragr., double points. Some accents and breathings. High and middle point (?for punctuation).	NO	YES. See *CLGP* II 4 no. 10. 1 gloss, 1 longer note (?metaphrase, ?historical).	Luxury roll		
Central part of 27 last lines of column, with lower margin.	Unknown	Double point: ?to distinguish lemmata.	NO	YES		?*Hypomnema* on comedy.	*CLGP* II 4 no. 13
Upper part of col. with upper margin.	Fayum	Some elisions. A stop for punctuation. At 215, ?high stop for change of speaker (ed. pr.: incidental).	NO	NO		Earliest, possibly with MP^3 152.2 (of *Wealth* too, but nothing written can be seen at the front), Aristophanes written on recycled papyrus.	

No.	Date	Author	MP³ no.	Content/Play	Main Publication	Form	Reused Material
53	2/3 CE (early third: Orsini)	Aristophanes	153.1	*Thesm.* 25, 742–66, 941–56	P. Oxy. 56.3839 (Cockle 1989) (Fr. 1 listed as *CGFP* 48)	roll→	↓: Apollonius the Sophist, *Alphabetic lexicon to the* Iliad *and the* Odyssey (2nd half of 3rd)
54	2/3 CE	Old Comedy	1631.11	?Choral song. ?Chorus takes an oath regarding their future attitude towards ?"the man of Acamantis" and "Sosia son of Parmeno." ?Cratinus *Ploutoi* (ed. pr., taking "the man of Acamantis" as a reference to Pericles).	P. Oxy. inv. 101B. 169/F(d) (Handley, *AAntHung* 48, 2008, 49-54, with photos on p. 52).	roll→	?NO
55	2 (late) or 3 CE (Furley: probably 3rd)	Menander	1300.52	*Epitr.* 195-216 Nünlist (see Nünlist 2004 and Ireland)	P. Oxy. 68.4641 (Nünlist 2003)	roll→	NO
56	2/3 CE	Menander	1297.5	*Kitharistes* (includes (?another version of: Pernigotti 2005b) fr. 1 Sandbach)	P. Turner 5 (Handley in *Papyri…edited in honour of E. Turner,* 1981, with pl. 3)	pap. →	NO

Bibliological Details	Provenance	Reading Aids etc.	XOPOY or Lyric Parts	Annotations	Use	Special Significance	Other Publications
3 frs, 1 with col. in full height (25 lines) with upper and lower margin, in biblical majuscule. ?The same scribe as MP³ 142.3 with *Knights* (=*CGFP* 27) from Karanis (Turner, in ed. pr.; Johnson 2004, 27; *contra*: Orsini 2005, 107).	Oxyrhynchus	Change of speaker: paragr. (?and a horizontal stroke below the writing in mid-line: fr. 1), blank spaces. High points for punctuation (?to mark questions).	YES. Lyric parts, written with indentation. Colometry same as the medieval mss.	NO	Good text. ?Luxury edition, by a popular scribe.		P14 Wilson
3 small frs. Larger: Beginnings of 9 bottom lines of col., with left and lower margin. In biblical majuscule.	Oxyrhynchus	?Paragraphos	YES. ?Dactylo-epitrites (ed. pr.).			?Fragment from choral song of Old Comedy.	
21 lines, ?from bottom of col., with lower margin, in biblical majuscule.	Oxyrhynchus	Double points, copied with the text. Single points (?punctuation) added afterwards. Corrections.	NO	NO		Beginning of arbitration scene. Name "Syriscus." ?Speech within speech.	
Fragments of 19 ll., written clearly and well-spaced, but in a "not expertly calligraphic" hand. Poetry written as prose.	Oxyrhynchus	NO lectional signs, but a few corrections/additions in the same hand.	NO	NO	?Excerpt of a dramatic *rhesis* (rather than copy of the whole play) (ed. pr.).	Adds a new line. *Kith.* Offers a different fr. 1 version of ll. 6-10 of fr. 1 Sandbach. Austin (Pernigotti 2005b. Cf. ed. pr.: copying mistake, rather than different tradition.)	Arnott,

No.	Date	Author	MP³ no.	Content/Play	Main Publication	Form	Reused Material
57	2/3 CE	Menander	1303.5	*Misoum.* 29-43 Arnott	P. Oxy. 48.3370 (Turner 1981)	roll↓, upside down in relation to →	→accounts. A strip of pap., with writing, is stuck on the accounts, for support. See Puglia 1997, 52.
58	2/3 CE	Menander	1303.71	Contributes to *Misoum.* 552-559 Arnott	P. Oxy. 64.4408 (Gonis 1997)	roll?→	NO
59	2/3 CE	New Comedy	1297.2	Parts of c. 90 lines. Financial plot involving non-Athenians (probably metics). Reference to slave-torture. ?Menander (Handley)	P. Oxy. 4.678 (Grenfell–Hunt 1904 = *CGFP* 269; ident. Handley *BICS* 24, 1977, 132-134, with photo)+Handley (*Proceedings XIV Intern. Congr. Papyrologists* 1975, 133–148)+P. Oxy. 62.4302 (Austin, Handley, and Parsons 1995) First full edition: *ad.* K-A fr. 1152.	roll→	NO
60	2/3 CE	New Comedy	1658.01	Dialogue. ?A letter reveals the real paternity of a character. (?Menander: ed. pr.)	P. Köln 7.283 (Gronewald 1991)	pap. →	NO

Bibliological Details	Provenance	Reading Aids etc.	XOPOY or Lyric Parts	Annotations	Use	Special Significance	Other Publications
	Oxyrhynchus	*Notae pers.* Middle and high stops (?punctuation).	NO	NO		Contributes, with nos 72-74, to the first scene of *Mis*.	
Nearly full length of lines, with side margins, but in very bad condition.	Oxyrhynchus	Double point (copied with the text). Interl. *notae pers.*, ?by different hand.	NO	NO		Contributes, with MP^3 1303.7, to a dialogic scene in Act III, which is still very unclear. Text seems different in places from that of MP^3 1303.7.	
12 frs, from at least 3 different cols. 22 lines per col. Generous margins. In biblical majuscule.	Oxyrhynchus	Paragr., double points (some with blank space, some squeezed in): perhaps by another hand. Some accents and breathings. Occasional punctuation (high points).	NO	YES, in the margins, in semi-cursive, with abbreviations, by a different hand. Some extensive, interpretative. See *CLGP* II 4 no. 14. For the note next to l. 50 K-A, see K-A—not McNamee (2007, 297).	"A scholar's text of high calligraphic order" (Handley 1975, 133).	Rare example of annotated New Comedy. (For other examples, see *CLGP* II 4 pp. 127-138.) For the potential historical significance of the play: see Thür 2001.	*ad.* K-A fr. 1152
16 line-beginnings of iambics. No margins survive. Semi-cursive script.	Unknown	Paragr.: change of speaker. Mid-points and blank space: ?delivery aids, ?punctuation. One correction.	NO	NO			*ad.* K-A fr. 1139

No.	Date	Author	MP³ no.	Content/Play	Main Publication	Form	Reused Material
61	2/3 CE	New Comedy	1667.23	?Young man in love is advised to give over his father's gold to get the "maiden". (Most likely not Menander's *Dis Exapaton*.)	P. Oxy. 61.4093 (Handley 1995)	roll↓	→: much earlier (of mid-1 CE) document
62	2/3 CE	Comedy (?New)	1667.22	?"Doris"; "night"; "tears"	P. Oxy. 59.3971 (Handley 1992)	roll→	NO
63	2/3 CE	Comedy (?linguistically 4th cent. but pre-Menandrian: ed. pr.)	1687.03	?Monologue in iambics with quoted dialogue (ed. pr.). Luxurious living, parsimony. ?Husband and wife in need of reconciliation.	P. Oxy. 62.4304 (Handley 1995)	roll→	NO
64	2/3 CE	Comedy	1676.1	Iambic tetrameters catalectic, referring to a storm in an allegorical manner. ?New Comedy (Perusino, based on metre and the storm-motif).	P. Mich. inv. 4925 *recto* (Koenen, *BASP* 16, 1979, 114–116; see also Perusino, *ZPE* 51, 1983, 45–49, with table Ib)	roll→	↓: MP³ 2640.3 (4 CE)
65	3 CE	Aristophanes	142.01	*Knights* 736–746	P. Oxy. 66.4511 (Gonis 1999)	pap.→	NO
66	3 CE (early)	Aristophanes	152.01	*Wealth* 1–16	P. Oxy. 66.4519 (Gonis 1999)	roll→	NO

Bibliological Details	Provenance	Reading Aids etc.	XOPOY or Lyric Parts	Annotations	Use	Special Significance	Other Publications
Central parts of 16 bottom lines of col. with lower margin, in "mixed hand."	Oxyrhynchus	Double points with space, copied with the text. Single points (?punctuation) added afterwards. Hyphen above letters (?to assist with word articulation).	XOPOY. Probably not end of Act I.	NO		Rare example of late recycling of roll (see also no. 64).	*ad.* K-A fr. 1149
Middle part of 11 top lines of col. with upper margin.	Oxyrhynchus	Double points copied with the text. Single points (most high) and high short oblique added afterwards (?punctuation).	NO	NO			*ad.* K-A fr. 1144
Right half of first 15 lines of col., with big upper margin. A roll of some "bibliographical pretensions." In formal handwriting.	Oxyrhynchus	Single points, for punctuation.	NO	NO			*ad.* K-A fr. 1154
Fragments of 10 lines, from the right part of a column, with some right margin. In a "semi-cursive bookhand."	Unknown	?NO (perhaps a double point, but the pap. is torn). Median *diairesis* is marked, when first half ended in *sigma*, by prolonging the *sigma*'s upper right edge.	NO	NO			*ad.* K-A fr. 1126
10 line-beginnings, without margins. "Rather informal" severe style script.	Oxyrhynchus	Paragr. Rough breathing and accent on ἔψοντος.	NO	NO			P74 Wilson
Upper left corner of col., with upper and wide left margin.	Oxyrhynchus	Breathings	NO	In upper left margin, in cursive, of obscure import. See *CLGP* I 1.4 Ar. no. 33.		Beginning of play. Line 1: at column's top (no title etc.).	P81 Wilson

No.	Date	Author	MP³ no.	Content/Play	Main Publication	Form	Reused Material
67	3 CE (1st half)	Aristophanes	154.03	*Wasps* 96-116	P. Oxy. 66.4512 (Gonis 1999)	roll→	NO
68	3 CE	Menander	1297.8	*Kolax* fr. 12 Arnott (parts of 6 lines of dialogue between Bias, Strouthias and a third person: slave ?Trachelion-Arnott).	P. Oxy. 50.3534 (Handley 1983)	?roll→	NO
69	3 CE (late)	Menander	1297.91	*Dis exap.* 11-30, 47-63, 89-112 Sandbach+ll. 1-10, 31-46, 64-88, 113	P. Oxy. 64.4407 (Handley 1997). See also Jacques, *REA* 106, 2004, 38-48. First edition of 11-30, 89-112: Handley 1968.	roll↓	→docum. of 241/2 CE.
70	3 CE	Menander	1300.12	*Dysk.* 739-750	P. Oxy. 60.4019 (Parsons 1994)	roll↓	→: cursive
71	3 CE	Menander	1300.51	*Epitr.* 150-164, and fr. 8 Martina (=ll. 180a-180u in Nünlist 2004; pp. 44-45 in Furley; p. 134 in Ireland)	P. Oxy. 60.4021 (Parsons 1994). New edition of fr. 3: Nünlist in *ZPE* 144, 2003	roll↓, upside down in relation to →	→: documents from 3 different pap. sheets.
72	3 CE	Menander	1303.2	*Misoum.* 1-30 Arnott	P.IFAO inv. 89v (=*CGFP* 147; photo: *ZPE* 6, 1970, pl. 1)+P. Köln 7.282 (inv. 96v: Gronewald 1991)	pap.↓	→: documentary register

Bibliological Details	Provenance	Reading Aids etc.	XOPOY or Lyric Parts	Annotations	Use	Special Significance	Other Publications
Upper part of col. with upper margin, in severe style script.	Oxyrhynchus	Blank space (?for punctuation: ed. pr.).	NO	NO			P75 Wilson
	Oxyrhynchus	Double points, copied with the text. Interlinear *notae pers.*	NO	NO			Pernerstorfer 2009, pp. 64–65
3 consecutive cols with upper and lower margin. 51 ll. per col., in professional but not elegant script.	Oxyrhynchus	Breathings, accents. Single point (punctuation). Paragr., double points, *notae pers.* Some corrections. All written in the process of copying (i.e. not added afterwards).	**XOPOY** at top of col. 3 (between Acts II and III). End of col. 2, to the left and right of last line of column/ Act: coronis and stichometric number 364 respectively.	NO	Professional copy (see stichometric number), on reused roll.	"The longest piece of a comedy available for direct comparison with its Latin version" (=Plautus *Bacchides*). First attestation of so long Act II (364 lines).	*Dis exap.* 1–113 Austin
12 line-beginnings from bottom of col., with left and lower margin. In an informal, rapid hand.	Oxyrhynchus	*Notae personarum* in the left margin, by the same hand.	NO	NO		Offers the beginnings of 740–745, confirming earlier supplements, with the possible exception of 740.	
3 frs. Fr. 3: a narrow strip with beginnings of 21 iambics (no margin). Frs. 1–2: parts of the lower 15 lines of col., with left and lower margin. Sloppy script. Very damaged.	Oxyrhynchus	Change of speaker: paragr., blank space, and (once) oblique line taking up space for *c.* 2 letters. Marginal and interlinear *notae pers.* All by the same hand.	NO	NO	"Amateurish copy," on the back of a roll made up from at least 3 different sheets of papyrus.	Confirms Habrotonon as interlocutor of Chaerestratus at end of Act I.	
Middle part of col. with upper margin	Unknown	Some marked elisions. Some corrections, but mistakes remain.	NO	NO	?School exercise (see Cribiore 1996, no. 290).	Contributes to beginning of play.	

No.	Date	Author	MP³ no.	Content/Play	Main Publication	Form	Reused Material
73	3 CE	Menander	1303.3	*Misoum.* 1–18, 33–45, 51–68, 85–100, 241–248 Arnott	P. Oxy. 48.3368 (Turner 1981)	roll↓	→: 3rd c. documentary register
74	3 CE	Menander	1303.4	*Misoum.* 12–54, 78–94 Arnott	P. Oxy. 48.3369 (Turner 1981)	roll→	?NO. Another sheet of papyrus, also →, has been glued at the back, ?for support.
75	3 CE	Menander	1304.01	*Misoum.* 784–821 and fr. 2 Arnott	P. Oxy. 59.3967 (M. Maehler 1992)	roll↓	→: accounts
76	3 CE	Menander	1305.21	*Perikeiromene* 796 (written 3, perhaps 4 times, with different musical notations)	P. Oxy. 53.3705 (Haslam 1986). Identified as *Prk.* 796: Huys, *ZPE* 99, 1993, 30-32.	Pap.→, but at the length of a *kollesis*. So, actually, on the back of a roll (↓), but turned 90°.	Nothing is visible on the other side, but it is a small piece.

Bibliological Details	Provenance	Reading Aids etc.	XOPOY or Lyric Parts	Annotations	Use	Special Significance	Other Publications
Several frs. forming parts of 2 consecutive cols, of 50 ll. each, in a fast, inconsistent hand. Play starts at top of col. Left margin: wider than the intercolumnium.	Oxyrhynchus	Sparing in lectional signs. Change of speaker: paragr., occasional blank spaces and *notae pers.*	NO	NO	?Professional but not very able scribe (careless copying, many mistakes, letters formed in different ways).	Adds substantial parts to the first scene of the play.	
Parts of 2 consecutive cols. No outer margins survive. ?Around 57 lines per col. Not very consistent hand.	Oxyrhynchus	Change of speaker: double points, paragr. Often *notae pers.* Occasionally high stop for punctuation.	NO	NO	?Not top quality copy.	Contributes to first scene of the play. More careful copy, but not without mistakes. Rare example of restoration by gluing another sheet at the back (see Puglia 1997, 32, 51).	
Middle parts of lines. No margin. Very damaged.	Oxyrhynchus	One small dash at high level: ?reading aid.	**XOPOY:** End of Act IV, beginning of Act V.	NO		Contributes to Thrasonides' monologue.	
"Informal" hand with cursive elements.	Oxyrhynchus	?Musical notation (ed. pr., Huys, Bélis 1988, Perusino 1995, 156–157). ?Musical notation used to illustrate different ways of speech intonation (Pöhlmann–West 2001, p. 185).	An iambic from a dialogue, set to music in 4 different ways.		?Copy of "*komodos*" (Huys). ?Copy used by musical teacher, illustrating "wrong" ways to sing the line (Bélis). ?Amateur's copy for performance at symposion (Perusino 1995). ?Not music, but illustrating different intonations (Pöhlmann–West no. 56). ?Individual in a private setting trying different modes of delivery (Pernigotti 2005a, 74–77).		Pöhlmann–West no. 56

No.	Date	Author	MP³ no.	Content/Play	Main Publication	Form	Reused Material
77	3 CE (early)	Menander (title)	1308.7	Ἰσιδώρωι | Μενάνδρου Θαῖδα	P. Turner 6 (Roberts in *Papyri edited for E. Turner* 1981) (no photo)	pap.→	Other side (also →): document
78	3 CE	?Menander (title)	1320.01	ονειρος | ή (*sic*, with rough breathing) | προγαμων	P. Oxy. 60.4026 (Parsons 1994)	roll↓. Upside down in relation to →	→: land register
79	3 CE	?Menander	1320.21	End of play	P. Harris 172 (Bastianini 1985 (=vol. 2), with pl. xvi)	roll→	?NO
80	3 CE	New Comedy (?Menander)	1650.01	"Phania," "Sosia," "Thais." Menander's *?Kitharistes, ?Thais* (ed. pr.)	P. Oxy. 59.3968 (Handley 1992)	roll↓	→: document
81	3 CE	New Comedy (?Menander)	1308.61	?Dialogue between old man (Demea) and slave (Pythias). ?Menander's *Synaristosai* (ed. pr.).	P. Oxy. 62.4305 (Handley 1995)	roll→	NO
82	3 CE	New Comedy (?Menander)	1320.02	End of Act I. Dismissal of interlocutor and announcement of departure to the market. ?Menander *Thais* (K-A: on thin grounds)	P. Oxy. 62.4303 (Brown and Parsons 1995)	roll→	NO
83	3 CE	New Comedy (?Menander)	1324.21	A young man complains to Laches for denying him his daughter. ?Same play as the *Fabula Interta* in the Cairo papyrus (ed. pr.)	P. Oxy. 64.4409 (Handley 1997)	roll→	NO

Bibliological Details	Provenance	Reading Aids etc.	XOPOY or Lyric Parts	Annotations	Use	Special Significance	Other Publications
Strip cut from roll, turned back and 90°. "Large and rounded cursive."	Unknown				Cut piece from used roll, to be used as label or delivery note.	Only direct testimony for *Thais*.	Men. *Thais* K-A test. x
	Oxyrhynchus				?Colophon		*ad.* K-A fr. 13
8 last lines of play in an informal literary hand.	?Oxyrhynchus (see *The Rendel Harris Papyri*, vol. ii 1985, p. vii).	NO	NO			End of a play.	Men. K-A fr. 908
30+20 ends and beginnings of lines from 2 consecutive cols. Upper margin. "Workmanlike hand."	Oxyrhynchus	High points (?punctuation), double points (?change of speaker).	NO	NO			*ad.* K-A fr. 1141, Arnott *Kith.* pp. 146–149
2 frs, from upper part of roll, with upper margin. Bigger: beginnings and endings of first 13+10 ll. of 2 consecutive cols. "Practised" but "not calligraphic" hand.	Oxyrhynchus	Paragr., double points. 1 high point. Traces of 2 marginal *notae pers.*	**XOPOY:** Most probably not end of Act I.	NO			*ad.* K-A fr. 1155, Arnott *Synar.* pp. 338–340
Central parts of 10 first lines of col. in severe style.	Oxyrhynchus	Correction by second hand.	**XOPOY:** End of Act I.			Slight variation from Menandrian formula of closing Act I.	*ad.* K-A fr. 1153
21 lines from bottom of col., with left and lower margin, plus another fr. Lower margin suggests "roll of handsome proportions."	Oxyrhynchus	Paragr., double points. Sparing in reading aids: 1 rough breathing, high points. Correction: ?in the process of copying (i.e. not afterwards).	NO	NO			*Fabula Incerta* 1 Arnott, pp. 466–472

No.	Date	Author	MP³ no.	Content/Play	Main Publication	Form	Reused Material
84	3 CE	New Comedy	1324.22	Dialogue: "daughter," somebody takes an oath.	P. Oxy. 64.4412 (Brown and Parsons 1997)	roll↓ (upside down in relation to →)	→prose =MP³ 2273.01
85	3 CE (early)	New Comedy	1667.2	?A character explains the paternity of a baby. ?Reference to recognition token (?torn garment: see ed. pr., p. 10, on l. 12, rather than K-A). "Moschio"	P. Oxy. 49.3432 (Stephens 1982)	pap.↓	→accounts from 2 joined pieces
86	3 CE (early)	New Comedy	1667.21	First: 2 characters on stage (?one admonishing the other). ?Then: 1 (but see ed. pr. 77). "Micio"	P. Oxy. 59.3970 (Handley 1992)	roll→	NO
87	3 CE	Comedy	1673.1	? "Farcical" dialogue ("if you hit me...")	P. Berol. inv. 17041 (Müller, in *Mitteilungen aus der Ägyptischen Sammlung* vol. 7 (=*Festschr. zum 150jähr. Bestehen d. Berl. Ägypt. Mus.*), 1974, p. 396 (without photo)	roll→	?NO
88	3 CE	Comedy	1687.02	Dialogue. At least one interlocutor is a woman (oath to "the two goddesses"). "Hippostrate"	P. Oxy. 61.4095 (Austin and Parsons 1995)	pap.→	NO
89	3 CE	?Comedy (list of names)	1698.1	5 names, written one next to the other, with the indication "female"/"male" above each, written probably by a different hand.	P. Berol. inv. 18115 (Luppe-Müller, *APF* 29, 1983, 7-8, with photo)	pap.↓	nothing on the →, but small strip

Bibliological Details	Provenance	Reading Aids etc.	XOPOY or Lyric Parts	Annotations	Use	Special Significance	Other Publications
9 frs. The larger: 18 line-ends from foot of col. In severe style.	Oxyrhynchus	NO	NO	NO			Men. K-A fr. *909
Bottom left corner of a piece, with left and lower margins. Iambics written as prose. Coarse papyrus.	Oxyrhynchus	Tremata	NO	NO	?From anthology (see ed. pr. p. 10, on l. 10). ?School exercise (Luppe in *CR* 34, 1984, p. 113).	Example of drama written as prose (compare also no. 56).	*ad.* K-A fr. 1130
Frs. of 23 lines.	Oxyrhynchus	High points (?punctuation), copied or inserted along with the text.	NO	NO			*ad.* K-A fr. 1143
Upper left corner of col.	Hermoupolis	Paragr. Circumflex on an *alpha* followed by *upsilon*.	NO	NO			*ad.* K-A fr. 1123
8 line ends, "in a decent…severe style."	Oxyrhynchus	Double points/ high points: added afterwards.					*ad.* K-A fr. 1150
	Unknown						*ad.* K-A fr. *71

No.	Date	Author	MP³ no.	Content/Play	Main Publication	Form	Reused Material
90	3/4 CE	Menander	1301.02	*Epitr.* 657–67 and fr. 14 Martina. On fr. 14, see Arnott 2000b, 155.	P. Oxy. 60.4023 (Turner and Parsons 1994)	parchm. codex	
91	4 CE	Aristophanes	138.1	*Ach.* 446–455 (→), 474–494 (↓)	P. Mich. inv. 5607a (Renner 1974, no. 7 and *ZPE* 31, 1981, pp. 1–7 with table Ia).	pap. codex	
92	4 CE (end)	Aristophanes	142.1	Scholia on *Knights* 998ff. (flesh)+*Knights* 1040-1058 (hair)	P. Bingen 18. (Manfredi in *Papyri in honorem Johannis Bingen* 2000, no. 18, pl. 10)	parchm. codex	
93	4 CE	Aristophanes	144.1	*Clouds* 1–7	PL III/18 (Pintaudi, *ZPE* 27, 1977, p. 107 with pl. V)	pap.↓	→: blank (but very small piece).

Bibliological Details	Provenance	Reading Aids etc.	XOPOY or Lyric Parts	Annotations	Use	Special Significance	Other Publications
Small very damaged piece from top of leaf. Ed. pr. estimates *c.* 50 lines per page. Top of both sides: ?page numbers. One: ?81. If so, ?*Epitr.* perhaps 4th play in codex.	Oxyrhynchus	Many accents, added by a second hand: ?some misplaced.	NO	NO		Codex with *Epitr.* as (?) 4th play.	
Upper right corner of leaf, from "deluxe" book, with wide margins, in careful, experienced elegant hand. Corrected.	Unknown	Paragr., double points, high points: by original scribe. Second hand/ink: corrections, breathing, some elisions. Third hand: *notae pers.* ?Fourth hand: "chorus"/ "semi-chorus."	Lyric part, separated by paragr., deep indentation and indications "Chorus," "Semi-chorus." Colometry/ attribution to semi-chorus: similar to the medieval one.	NO	"Deluxe" codex	"One of the more polished and ornate examples of…sloping oval with…biblical uncial features."	P59 Wilson
From the front page (flesh), only the right margin survives (with scholia). Text+scholia: same hand, in severe style, quite uneven. Estim.: 1 col. of *c.* 40 ll. per page.	Unknown	Double points. Some accents.	NO	YES, in the margin. Similarities with medieval scholia. See *CLGP* I 1.4 Ar. no. 9	?Text used (?and written: see uneven writing, not in straight lines) by scholar.		P64 Wilson
Small piece. No margin survives. Small, "uniform" writing "with characteristics of biblical majuscule."	Unknown	A trema	NO. L. 1, an *extra metrum* exclamation, *might* have been indented (difficult to judge). Lines 2, 4: not in reverse indentation (*pace* ed. pr.)	NO			

No.	Date	Author	MP³ no.	Content/Play	Main Publication	Form	Reused Material
94	4 CE	Aristophanes	150.01	*Peace* 1195–1211 (→), 1233–1247 (↓)	P. Oxy. 66.4514 (Gonis 1999)	pap. codex	
95	4 CE	Aristophanes	153.01	*Frogs* 592–605 (↓), 630–647 (→)	P. Oxy. 66.4517 (Gonis 1999)	pap. codex	
96	4 CE	Aristophanes	154.01	*Thesm.* 1185–1193, most probably including 1187b as part of the text.	P. Oxy. 56.3840 (Parsons 1989)	pap.→	NO
97	4 CE (late: Orsini; early: Escobar; late 3/early 4: D'Aiuto)	Menander	not in MP³. LDAB: no. 10072	*Dysk.* 305–500 (ff. 212+217) and 196 lines from another comedy (ff. 211+218). "bride," "child," "old woman," rape.	Vat. Sir. 623, ff. 211+218, 212+217. First underwriting: D'Aiuto and Wilson, under preparation. Description with 2 photographs: D'Aiuto 2003, with pl. 13, 14, pp. 266–283. See also: Escobar in *Euphrosyne* 33, 2005, 447–451; Orsini 2005, 294–296.	From a parchm. codex, overwritten twice.	a. no. 97. b. Nemesius *On human nature* (7 or 8 CE). c. ascetic Syriac texts (9 CE)
98	4 CE (Cavallo in MP³). 4 or 5 (ed. pr.).	Aristophanes	140.1	*Ekkl.* 600–614 (↓), 638–654 (→)	P. Mich. inv. 6649 (Renner 1974, no. 8; *ZPE* 31, 1981, pp. 7–12 with pl. Ib and c)	pap. codex	

Bibliological Details	Provenance	Reading Aids etc.	XOPOY or Lyric Parts	Annotations	Use	Special Significance	Other Publications
Right edge of leaf, with side margin. 36 ll. per page, in "plain" hand with an "informal stance."	Oxyrhynchus	Change of sp.: paragr., double points. Some errors in attribution (to those in ed. pr. p. 143, add the double point at the end of 1195). Breathing, accents, low point (punctuation).	NO	YES, in near-cursive script, in the right margin. Mostly glosses. ?From a *hypomnema* (ed. pr.). *CLGP* I 1.4 Ar. no. 20.			P77 Wilson
Lower part of leaf, with lower and side margins. 42 ll. to page. "Practised hand."	Oxyrhynchus	Rich in lectional signs, by same hand: Paragr., double points, *nota pers*. Single points, accents, breathings. Some additions/ corrections.	Lyric parts. Not considerable differences from medieval colometry: ed. pr. 154.	NO (?but possibly "relics" from a gloss in some antecedent: see ed. pr. on 603b)			P79 Wilson
Tiny scrap with line-ends.	Oxyrhynchus	Double-point.	NO	NO		?Suggesting that a scenic direction (1187b) had already intruded into the text.	P68 Wilson
2 leaves. 2 cols per page, 49 ll. per col., in minute, very elegant biblical majuscule. Comparable to the grand biblical 4th-century mss.	?Palestine (D'Aiuto) (found in St Catherine's monastery in Sinai)	?	?YES	?NO	?A full edition of Menander (c. 200 lines per leaf, 5 leaves per play), for a library (D'Aiuto).	"Extraordinary" luxurious major edition from the same environment as the Codex Sinaiticus: attests to the importance of Menander in 4th-century Palestine.	F. D'Aiuto and N. Wilson: under preparation
Lower left corner of leaf, with lower margin. Bottom left: binding hole. Experienced but "utilitarian" hand.	Unknown	Paragr., double points. Single points (punctuation). Accents, breathings. Marked elision and crasis. All same hand.	NO	NO		Only pap. for *Ekkl.* "Rather good text."	P60 Wilson

No.	Date	Author	MP³ no.	Content/Play	Main Publication	Form	Reused Material
99	4/5 CE (second half of 4: *GBEB* no. 10a)	Aristophanes	141	*Knights* 36–47 (↓), 86–95 (→), with scholia	Bodl. Ms. Gr. class. f. 72 (P) (Grenfell and Hunt, in *Mélanges Nicole* 1905, 212–217=*CGFP* 22)+P. Acad. 3/4 (Fournet and Gascou in *CRAIBL* 2008, 1051-1052, 1060-1066: full ed. with photo)	pap. codex	
100	4/5 CE (ed. pr., Orsini). 5/6 (D'Aiuto 2003, 279)	Menander	1300.11	*Dysk.* 529–531, 557-561	P. Oxy. 60.4018 (Parsons 1994)	parch. codex	
101	4/5 CE	Comedy (?Old)	1638.01	10 beginnings of iambics with change of speaker, in elevated style. ?Audience address. "theater" ?Reference to a demagogue. Ed. pr.: from prologue.	P. Columbia inv. 430 (Barrenechea in *ZPE* 158, 2006, 49–54) Photo: http://www.papyri.info/apis/columbia.apis.p1550	pap.→	NO
102	5 CE (Maehler in Athanassiou 1999, p. 126)/3 CE (ed. pr.)	Aristophanes	149.21	*Peace* 474 (↓), 476 (↓), 507–523 (→), with scholia	P. Duk. inv. 643 (Smith in *APF* 42, 1996, 155-160 with pl. 17. New edition of the *recto*: Luppe in *APF* 43, 1997, 7–10.)	pap. codex	

Bibliological Details	Provenance	Reading Aids etc.	XOPOY or Lyric Parts	Annotations	Use	Special Significance	Other Publications
4 frs, from lower part of leaf with lower margin. 46-49 ll. per page. Main text: in a clear but cursive hand. Annot. by same hand.	?Lykopolis ?Hermoupolis Magna: See *CRAIBL* 2008, 1045-1046	Most lectional signs: added later (?by second hand). Breathings, accents, punctuation, double points, quantity marks.	NO	YES, in the margins, some glosses, 1 extensive explanatory, 1 historical. Similarities with the medieval scholia. See *CLGP* I 1.4, Ar. no. 5.	?Private copy (Fournet and Gascou, based on the cursive tendencies of the script) of scholar.	?Did not have l. 96 (present in the Ravennas 429, but deleted by Thiersch).	P2 Wilson (did not know of P. Acad. 3/4)
Top outer corner of leaf. Upper margin of *recto*, to the right: gathering number 27 (by third hand). 28 lines per page, Turner group ix (same as another Menandrian codex: PSI ii 126=see MP³ 1318). Fine quality parchm. In biblical majuscule.	Oxyrhynchus	Rich in lectional signs: accents, breathings, apostrophes: second hand.	NO	NO	?High-quality edition of Menander. If gatherings= quaternia, *Dysk.* would be ?12th play.	?Example of major luxurious and scholarly edition of Menander.	
Small fragment with some left margin. Large, uneven hand, with cursive elements. Lines waver.	Unknown	Paragr. *iota* adscript inserted above the line (same hand).	NO	NO	?Private copy of excerpt (space between lines is more compressed towards the end: ed. pr.)	?Example of excerption from Old Comedy.	
Semi-cursive script.	Unknown	Paragr., double points.	Lyric parts written in indentation. Colometry similar to the medieval.	YES, extensive, with similarities to the medieval scholia. See *CLGP* I 1.4, Ar. no. 18.		If 3rd c. (ed. pr., McNamee 2007, Wilson), an early codex and early example of extensive annotation. But *CLGP* accept Maehler's 5th c. date.	P70 Wilson

No.	Date	Author	MP³ no.	Content/Play	Main Publication	Form	Reused Material
103	5 CE	Aristophanes	149.3	*Peace* 609–619 (↓) and 655–667 (→)	P. Vindob. G 29354. (Carlini, in *SCO* 22, 1973, 37–40, with table ii (*verso* only). See also Carlini in *Athenaeum* 52, 1974, pp. 4-5.	pap. codex	
104	5 CE	Aristophanes	152.11	*Wealth* 635–679 (↓), 698–738 (→)	P. Oxy. 66.4520 (Gonis 1999)	pap. codex	
105	5 CE	Aristophanes	153.02	*Frogs* 1244–1248 (↓), 1277–1281 (→)	P. Oxy. 66.4518 (Gonis 1999)	pap. codex	
106	5 CE	Aristophanes	155.01	*Wasps* 1066–1108	P. Oxy. 66.4513 (Gonis 1999)	parch. codex	
107	5 CE	Aristophanes (*hypomnema*)	146.1	Commentary on *Clouds* ?186-213 (→) and ?170s (↓: Montana, *CLGP* I 1.4, p. 101: almost illegible)	P. Vindob. G 29423 (P. Rain. 3.20: Oellacher 1939). Ident. and new edition: Gronewald, *ZPE* 45, 1982, 61-64, with table I.	pap. codex	

Bibliological Details	Provenance	Reading Aids etc.	XOPOY or Lyric Parts	Annotations	Use	Special Significance	Other Publications
3 frs forming parts from outer bottom right corner of leaf.	Unknown	Paragr., double points.	NO	NO		?663 assigned to Peace (?or paragr. used to signal change of addressee)	P61 Wilson
About 2/3 of the width of a leaf's bottom 35 ll., with lower and one side margin. 58-59 ll. to page. Informal, occasionally cursive writing.	Oxyrhynchus	Abundant reading aid, esp. accents and breathings, by original and another hand. Paragr., double points. One *diple obelismene* (?to mark monologue).	NO	YES. Glosses. See *CLGP* I 1.4 Ar. no. 23	Probably not a scholar's text (uncorrected errors left: ed. pr.) ?"Close affiliation with the school" (ed. pr. 161, *vis-à-vis* abundant accentuation).	?Attesting to a branch of the tradition with 1 line less (omits 648—see ed. pr.).	P82 Wilson
Tiny piece, no margins. c. 33 ll. per page.	Oxyrhynchus	NO	NO	NO			P80 Wilson
8 frs from the same leaf. 31 lines of text per page. No margins survive. "Handsome codex." "Sloping pointed majuscule."	Oxyrhynchus	Some apostrophes only.	YES. Colometry similar to the medieval one. Metrical cola, usually counted as single verses, often appear here split in 2 lines, the second indented. Difference of division between epirrhema and antepirrhema.	NO		7 different readings. Ed. pr.: not different tradition, but idiosyncratic.	P76 Wilson
Narrow vertical strip from upper part of page, with upper margin.	Fayum					Only *hypomn.* of *Clouds.* Some similarities with the medieval scholia.	*CLGP* I 1.4 Ar. no. 15

No.	Date	Author	MP³ no.	Content/Play	Main Publication	Form	Reused Material
108	5 CE	Aristophanes (*hypomnēma*)	149.2	Commentary on *Peace* 106-415 (↓), 457-466 (→)	P. Vindob. inv. G 29780 (=P. Rain. 1.34: Gerstinger 1932)+29833c. Full edition, with photo: Gronewald in *ZPE* 45, 1982, 64-69, table II.	pap. codex	
109	5 CE	Menander	1301.03	*Epitr.* 664-668 (↓) and 690-694 (→) Martina	PL III/310 A (Pintaudi-López García, in *ZPE* 124, 1999, pp. 15-16, with table 1)	pap. codex	
110	5 CE	Comedy	1645.02	End of Act. Extremely little survives.	P. Montserrat 127 (López García in *Misc. Pap. R. Roca-Puig*, 1987, pp. 177-179 with photo)	roll→	?
111	5/6 CE	Aristophanes	139	*Ach.* 593-601, 608-625, 631-641, 646-663, 686-689, 725-728, 747-758, 762-786, 791-803, 807-829, 904-936, 941-976; *Frogs* 234-262, 273-300, 404-410, 607-611, 1458-1460, 1493-1496; *Birds* 819-829, 859-864; *Wealth* 134-138, 140-144, 171-173, 289-293, 311-319, 327-331, 347-355	P. Berol. 13231 (BKT 5.2: Schubart–Wilamowitz 1907=*CGFP* 20)+21201+21202 (Maehler in *APF* 30, 1984, 18-20; see Ioannidou 1996, nos 105, 106, plates 51, 52)+P. Vindob. inv. G. 42250 (=P. Sijp. 1: Harrauer, in *Papyri in memory Sijpesteijn*, 2007, pp. 1-3 with plate 1)	pap. codex	
112	5/6 CE	Aristophanes	140.01	*Birds* 1324-1328 (→), 1357-1361 (↓)	P. Oxy. 66.4515 (Gonis 1999)	pap. codex	
113	5/6 (ed. pr., Porro in *S&C* 9, 1985, p. 173) 2/3 (Cavallo: MP³)	Aristophanes	152.2	*Wealth* 1135-1139	P. Laur. 4.132 III 319 (inv. iii 319: ed. pr. Pintaudi, *ZPE* 27, 1977, 108, plate V)	pap. ↓	→: blank (but small piece).

Bibliological Details	Provenance	Reading Aids etc.	XOPOY or Lyric Parts	Annotations	Use	Special Significance	Other Publications
Two small adjacent frs. ?c. 50 ll. per page	Unknown	*Diple obelismene*				Only *hypomnema* for *Peace*. Similarities, and differences, with the medieval scholia.	*CLGP* I 1.4 Ar. no. 17
	Unknown	?Paragr. and indentation for change of speaker.				Led to the -incorporation of *ad.* K-A fr. 78 (see Nünlist 1999, 54-56).	
Tiny scrap from end of page.	Unknown	Double points. An oblique without space: ?change of speaker.	**XOPOY**	NO			*ad.* K-A fr. 1137
Many fragments from different leaves and gatherings. On the leaf beginning *Ach.* 904 (*recto*): gathering number 9 on the left, leaf number 65 on the right. *c.* 37 lines per page. 3 plays preceding *Ach.* See also under no. 115.	Hermoupolis (on Byzantine Hermoupolis and its papyri, see Maehler 1998)	Double points, paragr. *Notae pers.* Few accents. Some corrections, by different hands.	Includes lyric parts.	NO	?Edition of Aristophanes for library of prominent Christian Hermoupolitan. In the same archive: Sophocles, Euripides, Isocrates, Apoll. Rh., Theocr. See Maehler 1998, 84-85.	Edition of several plays of Aristophanes. Arrangement different from the Ravennas.	P19 Wilson (did not know of P. Sijp. 1)
'Coarse' hand.	Oxyrhynchus	1 acute, by same scribe.	YES. 1325: 1 line, as in modern editions; medieval mss: in 2 lines.	NO		?Different colometry to the medieval. (ed. pr.: probably not)	P78 Wilson
Small piece without margins. Ed. pr. compares with Coptic uncial. Consecutive letters occasionally combined with curve at line level.	Unknown	Trema, apostrophe.	NO	NO			P63 Wilson

No.	Date	Author	MP³ no.	Content/Play	Main Publication	Form	Reused Material
114	6 CE	Aristophanes	137.02	*Ach.* 76-78 ($\downarrow$). Unrecognized ($\rightarrow$)	P. Berol. 21200 (Luppe in *APF* 41, 1995, pp. 40-41; see also Ioannidou 1996, no. 104, plate 50)	pap. codex	
115	6 CE	Aristophanes	149.1	*Peace* 141-152 ($\downarrow$), 175 ($\rightarrow$), 178-187 ($\rightarrow$), 194-200 ($\rightarrow$). Fr. 1 $\downarrow$: unidentified traces. Fr. 3 $\downarrow$: blank (?lines indented deeply: ed. pr. p. 17)	P. Berol. 21223 (Maehler, *APF* 30, 1984, pp. 17–18; see also Ioannidou 1996, no. 127, plate 58)	pap. codex	
116	6 (2nd half)	Menander	1297.01	*Aspis* 170-198 (omits 189 but offers 193a) ($\rightarrow$); 199–231 ($\downarrow$)	P. Oxy. 61.4094 (Handley 1995)	pap. codex	
117	6/7 CE	Menander	1307.11	*Samia* 312-315 (hair), 341–350 (flesh)	P. Bingen 23 (=P. Ant. inv. 4, Gonis, in *Papyri in hon. Bingen* 2000, 125-128, with pl. 12)	parch. codex	
118	6/7 CE	New Comedy (?Menander)	1650	Dialogue: dowry, betrothal of sister, "Gorgias," "Chaer[eas]" (or "Chaer[estratus]"). ?Menander *Georgos* (ed. pr.)	P. Oxy. 73.4937 (Handley 2009)	parch. codex	

Bibliological Details	Provenance	Reading Aids etc.	XOPOY or Lyric Parts	Annotations	Use	Special Significance	Other Publications
Tiny scrap. →: line beginnings	Hermoupolis						P71 Wilson
Three frs. Hand "a little bit different" from MP³ 139 (= no. 111), but same format and layout: ?same codex (thus Maehler in *Gaia* 3, 1998, 85).	Hermoupolis	Paragr., double points, *notae pers.* Tremata in the form of horizontals (see West in *ZPE* 60, 1985, 10, n. 1; also *GMAW* no. 60).		NO		Only direct attestation of exclamation ἰηῦ (West, *ZPE* 60, 1985, 10; *ZPE* 94, 1992, 230)	P67 Wilson
Several frs forming 1 leaf, with upper/lower margins. 29/33 ll. per page. Tall and relatively narrow format. Page numbers at the top: 142, 143.	Oxyrhynchus	Double points, paragr., *notae pers.* Some punctuation. Corrections and accentuation: some copied with the main text, some added later.	NO	?Interlinear glosses: see McNamee 2007, p. 297.	Codex with at least 5 plays (5th=*Aspis*). Not very elegant script, but signs of scholarly activity.	Some variants in comparison to the Bodmer papyrus.	
Small scrap from side edge of text. No margins survive. In Coptic uncial.	Antinoopolis (On Antinoopolis and its papyri, see Del Francia Barocas 1998, esp. 49–55.)	Double points, by original scribe. Circumflex, apostrophe: by another hand.	NO	NO	?Edition of Menander for library. Probably found along with other literary texts. See ed. pr. 126.		
Small piece from edge of leaf, with side margin marked off by vertical rulings. Text written on ruled lines.	Oxyrhynchus	Double points, *nota pers.*: second hand. Rough breathing and acute (?by first hand: not in the ed. pr.)	NO	NO			*Georg.* 168–178 Austin

ABBREVIATIONS

CGFP	Austin, C. *Comicorum Graecorum Fragmenta in Papyris Reperta*. Berlin: de Gruyter. 1973.
CLGP	Bastianini, G. et al. *Commentaria e Lexica Graeca in Papyris Reperta*. Munich: K. G. Saur. 2004–.
GBEB	Cavallo, G., and H. Maehler. *Greek Bookhands of the Early Byzantine Period*. London: University of London, ICS. 1987.
GMAW	Turner, E. G., and P. J. Parsons. *Greek Manuscripts of the Ancient World* (2nd ed., revised and enlarged). London: University of London, ICS. 1987.
HB	Cavallo, G., and H. Maehler. *Hellenistic Bookhands*. Berlin: de Gruyter. 2008.
K-A	Kassel, R., and C. Austin. *Poetae Comici Graeci*. Berlin: de Gruyter. 8 vols.: 1983–2001.
Kock	Kock, T. *Comicorum Atticorum Fragmenta*. Leipzig: Teubner. 3 vols.: 1880–1888.
K-T	Körte, A. *Menandri quae supersunt: II. Reliquiae apud veteres scriptores servatae* (2nd, posthumous, edition, with additions and revisions by A. Thierfelder). Leipzig: Teubner. 1959.
Sandbach	Sandbach, F. H. *Menandri reliquiae selectae* (OCT: 2nd ed. with appendix). Oxford: Clarendon Press. 1990.

BIBLIOGRAPHY

Anderson, W. A. 1993. *Barbarian Play: Plautus' Roman Comedy*. Toronto: University of Toronto Press.

Arnott, W. G. 1996. *Menander*. Vol. 2. Loeb Classical Library 459. Cambridge, MA: Harvard University Press.

——. 2000a. *Menander*. Vol. 3. Loeb Classical Library 460. Cambridge, MA: Harvard University Press.

——. 2000b. "Notes on Some New Papyri of Menander's *Epitrepontes*." In *Dramatische Wäldchen: Festschrift für Eckard Lefèvre zum 65.Geburtstag*, edited by E. Stärk and G. Vogt-Spira, 153–163. Hildesheim: Olms.

——. 2004a. "New Menander from the 1990's." In *Menandro—Cent'anni di papiri: Atti del convegno internazionale di studi, Firenze, 12–13 giugno 2003*, edited by G. Bastianini and A. Casanova, 35–53. Florence: Istituto papirologico G. Vitelli.

——. 2004b. "Menander's *Epitrepontes* in the Light of the New Papyri." In *Law, Rhetoric and Comedy in Classical Athens: Essays in Honour of D. M. MacDowell*, edited by D. L. Cairns and R. A. Knox, 269–292. Swansea: Classical Press of Wales.

Athanassiou, N. 1999. "Marginalia and Commentaries in the Papyri of Euripides, Sophocles and Aristophanes." PhD diss., University College London.

Austin, C. 2010. "Varia Menandrea." *ZPE* 175: 9–14.

——. 2013. *Menander: Eleven Plays*. Cambridge: Proceedings of the Cambridge Philological Society, Suppl. volume 37.

Austin, C., E. W. Handley, and P. Parsons. 1995. No. 4302 [New Comedy]. *The Oxyrhynchus Papyri* 62: 3–8.

Barrenechea, F. 2006. "A Fragment of Old Comedy: P. Columbia inv. 430." *ZPE* 158: 49–54.

Bastianini, G., and A. Casanova, eds. 2004. *Menandro—Cent'anni di papiri: Atti del convegno internazionale di studi, Firenze, 12–13 giugno 2003*. Florence: Istituto papirologico G. Vitelli.

Bathrellou, E. 2009. "Studies in the *Epitrepontes* of Menander." PhD diss., University of Cambridge.

——. 2012. "Menander's *Epitrepontes* and the Festival of the Tauropolia." *ClAnt* 31: 151–192.

Bélis, A. 1988. "Interprétation du Pap.Oxy. 3705." *ZPE* 72: 53–63.

Casanova, A. 2004. "Cent'anni di papiri menandrei." In *Menandro—Cent'anni di papiri: Atti del convegno internazionale di studi, Firenze, 12–13 giugno 2003,* edited by G. Bastianini and A. Casanova, 1–7. Florence: Istituto papirologico G. Vitelli.

Caroli, M. 2007. *Il titolo iniziale nel rotolo librario greco-egizio.* Bari: Levante.

Cavallo, G. 1986. "Conservazione e perdita dei testi greci: Fattori materiali, sociali, culturali." In *Società romana e impero tardoantico, IV: Tradizione dei classici, trasformazioni della cultura,* edited by A. Giardina, 83–172. Rome: Editori Laterza. Reproduced in G. Cavallo, *Dalla parte del libro: Storie di transmissione dei classici* (Urbino: QuattroVenti, 2002), 49–175.

Ciriello, S. 1989. "Aristofane, fr. 592 K.-A.: *Lemnie?*" *Sileno* 16: 83–88.

Cribiore, R. 1996. *Writing, Teachers and Students in Graeco-Roman Egypt.* Atlanta: Scholars Press.

D'Aiuto, F. 2003. "*Graeca* in codici orientali della Biblioteca Vaticana (con i resti di un manoscritto tardoantico delle commedie di Menandro)." In *Tra oriente e occidente: scritture e libri greci fra le regioni orientali di Bisanzio e l'Italia,* edited by L. Perria, 227–296. Rome: Università di Roma "La Sapienza."

Damen, M. L. 1992. "Translating Scenes: Plautus' Adaptation of Menander's *Dis Exapaton.*" *Phoenix* 46: 205–231.

——. 1995. " 'By the gods, boy, . . . Stop bothering me! Can't you tell Menander from Plautus?' or How *Dis Exapaton* Does *Not* Help Us Understand *Bacchides.*" *Antichthon* 29: 15–29.

Dedoussi, Ch. 1980: "An Illustrated Fragment of Menander's Εὐνοῦχος." *BICS* 27: 97–102.

——. 2006. Μενάνδρου Σαμία. Athens: Academy of Athens.

Del Francia Barocas, L., ed. 1998. *Antinoe cent'anni dopo.* Florence: Istituto papirologico G. Vitelli.

Dobrov, G. W., ed. 2010. *Brill's Companion to the Study of Greek Comedy.* Leiden: Brill.

Dunbar, N. 1995. *Aristophanes: Birds.* Oxford: Clarendon Press.

Ferrari, F. 2004. "Papiri e mosaici: Tradizione testuale e iconografia in alcune scene di Menandro." In *Menandro—Cent'anni di papiri: Atti del convegno internazionale di studi, Firenze, 12–13 giugno 2003,* edited by G. Bastianini and A. Casanova, 127–149. Florence: Istituto papirologico G. Vitelli.

Fournet, J.-L., and J. Gascou. 2008. "Un lot d'archives inédit de Lycopolis (Égypte) à l'Académie des Inscriptions et Belles-lettres." *CRAIBL* 2008: 1041–1075.

Furley, W. D. 2009. *Menander:* Epitrepontes. London: Institute of Classical Studies.

——. 2013. "Pamphile Finds Her Voice: On the Newly Published Fragments of Menander's *Epitrepontes.*" *ZPE* 185: 82–90.

Gammacurta, T. 2006. *Papyrologica scaenica: I copioni teatrali della tradizione papiracea.* Alessandria, Italy: Edizioni dell'Orso.

Gentili, B. 1979. *Theatrical Performances in the Ancient World: Hellenistic and Early Roman Theatre.* Amsterdam: Gieben. Originally published in Italian as *Lo spettacolo nel mondo antico: Teatro greco e teatro romano arcaico* (Rome: Laterza, 1977; rev. ed. 2006).

Gomme, A. W., and F. H. Sandbach. 1973. *Menander: A Commentary.* Oxford: Oxford University Press.

Gonis, N. 1999. Nos. 4510–4521 [Aristophanes]. *The Oxyrhynchus Papyri* 66: 118–172.

Grenfell, B. P. 1919. "The Value of Papyri for the Textual Criticism of Extant Greek Authors." *JHS* 39: 16–36.

Gronewald, M. 1986. "Menander *Epitrepontes*—Neue Fragmente aus Akt III und IV." *ZPE* 66: 1–13.

Habermann, W. 1998. "Zur chronologischen Verteilung der papyrologischen Zeugnisse." *ZPE* 122: 144–160.

Handley, E. W. 1968. *Menander and Plautus: A Study in Comparison*. London: University College.

——. 1975. "Some New Fragments of Greek Comedy." In *Proceedings of the XIV International Congress of Papyrologists*, 133 148. London: Egypt Exploration Society.

——. 1990. "The Bodmer Menander and the Comic Fragments." In *Relire Ménandre*, edited by E. Handley and A. Hurst, 123–148. Geneva: Droz.

——. 1997. No. 4407 [Menander, *Dis Exapaton*]. *The Oxyrhynchus Papyri* 64: 14–42.

——. 2002. "Acting, Action and Words in New Comedy." In *Greek and Roman Actors: Aspects of an Ancient Profession*, edited by P. Easterling and E. Hall, 165–188. Cambridge, UK: Cambridge University Press.

——. 2009. No. 4936 [Menander, *Epitrepontes*]. *The Oxyrhynchus Papyri* 73: 25–36.

——. 2011. "The Date of Menander's *Epitrepontes*." *ZPE* 178: 51.

Handley E., and A. Hurst, eds. 1990. *Relire Ménandre*. Geneva: Droz.

Huys, M. 1993. "P.Oxy. LIII 3705: A Line from Menander's *Periceiromene* with Musical Notation." *ZPE* 99: 30–32.

Ioannidou, G. 1996. *Catalogue of Greek and Latin Literary Papyri in Berlin (P. Berol. inv. 21101–21299, 21911)*. Mainz am Rhein: P. von Zabern.

Ireland, S. 2010. *Menander: The Shield and The Arbitration*. Oxford: Oxbow Books.

Johnson, W. A. 2004. *Bookrolls and Scribes in Oxyrhynchus*. Toronto: University of Toronto Press.

Jones, C. P. 1991. "Dinner Theatre." In *Dining in a Classical Context*, edited by W. J. Slater, 185–198. Ann Arbor: University of Michigan Press.

——. 1993. "Greek Drama in the Roman Empire." In *Theatre and Society in the Classical World*, edited by R. Scodel, 39–52. Ann Arbor: University of Michigan Press.

Krumeich, R., N. Pechstein, and B. Seidensticker. 1999. *Das griechische Satyrspiel*. Darmstadt: Wissenschaftliche Buchgesellschaft.

Lamagna, M. 2004. "Note critiche ed esegetiche alle scene iniziali del *Misumenos*." In *Menandro—Cent'anni di papiri: Atti del convegno internazionale di studi, Firenze, 12–13 giugno 2003*, edited by G. Bastianini and A. Casanova, 185–203. Florence: Istituto papirologico G. Vitelli.

Laplace, M. M. J. 1997. "P.Köln V 203." In *Akten des 21. Internationalen Papyrologenkongresses: Berlin, 13.–19. 8. 1995*. Vol. 1, 570–577. Stuttgart: Teubner.

Lefèvre, E. 1994. *Terenz' und Menanders Heautontimorumenos*. Munich: C. H. Beck.

Litinas, N. 2002. "Aristophanes on a Bank Receipt?" *ZPE* 141: 103–105.

Lowe, J. C. B. 1998. "The Intrigue of Terence's *Heauton Timorumenos*." *RhM* 141: 163–171.

Maehler, H. 1998. "Élites urbaines et production littéraire en Égypte romaine et byzantine." *Gaia* 3: 81–95.

Maltby, R. 1983. "The Last Act of Terence's *Heautontimorumenos*." *Papers of the Liverpool Latin Seminar* 4: 27–41.

Manfredi, M. 2000. "Un frammento di Aristofane, *I Cavalieri*, con scolî." In *Papyri in honorem Johannis Bingen octogenarii (P. Bingen)*, edited by H. Melaerts, 95–104. Leuven: Peeters.

Martina, A. 1997. *Menandri* Epitrepontes: *Introduzione, testo critico e traduzione*. Rome: kepos.

McNamee, K. 2007. *Annotations in Greek and Latin Texts from Egypt*. New Haven, CT: American Society of Papyrologists.

Mertens, P. 1992. "Les témoins papyrologiques de Ménandre: Essai de classement rationnel et esquisse d'étude bibliologique." In *Mélanges publiés par les Classiques de Liège à l'occasion du 175ᵉ anniversaire de l'Université*, 331–356. Liège: Serta Leodiensia secunda.

——. 1996. "Les papyrus d'Aristophane: Actualisation des données bibliologiques et bibliographiques." In Ὁδοὶ διζήσιος: *Le vie della ricerca: Studi in onore di Francesco Adorno*, edited by M. S. Funghi, 335–343. Florence: Olschki.

Millett, P. 1991. *Lending and Borrowing in Ancient Athens*. Cambridge, UK: Cambridge University Press.

Montana, F. 2005. "L'esegesi ad Aristofane su papiro." In *Interpretazioni antiche di Aristofane*, edited by F. Montana, 1–53. Sarzana: Agorà.

——. 2006a. "L'anello mancante: L'esegesi ad Aristofane tra l'antichità e bisanzio." In *I classici greci e i loro commentatori: Dai papiri ai marginalia rinascimentali*, edited by G. Avezzù and P. Scattolin, 17–34. Rovereto: Accademia reveretana degli Agiati.

——. 2006b. "Aristophanes." In *Commentaria e lexica graeca in papyris reperta*, edited by G. Bastianini et al. Vol. 1, fasc. 4, 3–12. Munich: K. G. Saur.

Nervegna, S. 2007. "Staging Scenes or Plays? Theatrical Revivals of 'Old' Greek Drama in Antiquity." *ZPE* 162: 14–42.

Nesselrath, H.-G. 2010. "Comic Fragments: Transmission and Textual Criticism." In *Brill's Companion to the Study of Greek Comedy*, edited by G. W. Dobrov, 423–453. Leiden: Brill.

Nünlist, R. 1999. "Ein neu identifiziertes Buchfragment aus Menanders *Epitrepontes*." *ZPE* 128: 54–56.

——. 2004. "The Beginning of *Epitrepontes* Act II." In *Menandro—Cent'anni di papiri: Atti del convegno internazionale di studi, Firenze, 12–13 giugno 2003*, edited by G. Bastianini and A. Casanova, 95–106. Florence: Istituto papirologico G. Vitelli.

Orsini, P. 2005. *Manoscritti in maiuscola biblica: Materiali per un aggiornamento*. Cassino: Edizioni dell'Università degli studi di Cassino.

Parker, L. P. E. 1997. *The Songs of Aristophanes*. Oxford: Clarendon Press.

Pernerstorfer, M. J. 2009. *Menanders Kolax: Ein Beitrag zu Rekonstruktion und Interpretation der Komödie*. Berlin: de Gruyter.

Pernigotti, C. 2005a. "Menandro a simposio? P. Oxy. III 409 + XXXIII 2655 e P. Oxy. LIII 3705 riconsiderati." *ZPE* 154: 69–78.

——. 2005b. "P. Turner 5: Testi e lettori di Menandro." *Eikasmos* 16: 135–144.

Perusino, F. 1995. "Menandro e il simposio: Nota al *POxy* 3705." In *Atti del V seminario internazionale di papirologia, Lecce 27–29 giugno 1994*, 151–157. Galatina: Congedo.

——. 2007. "Colometria dei papiri di Aristofane: Nota al *P. Oxy.* 4510, fr. 6." *QUCC* 85: 125–129.

Perusino, F., and A. Giacomoni. 1999. "Un canto di risveglio nella commedia nuova: Nota al *P.Oxy.* 3966." *Cuadernos de Filología Clásica (Estudios griegos)* 9: 155–162.

Pöhlmann, E., and M. L. West. 2001. *Documents of Ancient Greek Music: The Extant Melodies and Fragments*. Oxford: Clarendon Press.

Puglia, E. 1997. *La cura del libro nel mondo antico: Guasti e restauri del rotolo di papiro*. Naples: Enzo.

Raffaelli, R., and A. Tontini, eds. 2001. *Lecturae plautinae sarsinates IV: Bacchides*. Urbino: QuattroVenti.

Römer, C. 2012a. "New Fragments of Act IV, *Epitrepontes* 786–823 Sandbach (P. Mich. 4752 a, b and c." *ZPE* 182: 112–120.

——. 2012b. "A New Fragment of the End of Act III, *Epitrepontes* 690-701 Sandbach (P. Mich. 4805)." *ZPE* 183: 32–36.

Savignago, L. 2008. "Rilettura di P. Oxy. 4510." In *Didaskaliai II: Nuovi studi sulla tradizione e l'interpretazione del dramma attico*, edited by G. Avezzù, 1–36. Verona: Fiorini.

Sisti, F. 2000. "Osservazioni sui nuovi papiri degli *Epitrepontes* di Menandro." In *Poesia e religione in Grecia: Studi in onore di G. Aurelio Privitera*, edited by M. Cannatà Fera and S. Grandolini, 631–637. Naples: Edizioni scientifiche italiane.

——. 2004. "Varianti equipollenti e varianti di esecuzione nella tradizione papiracea di Menandro." In *Menandro—Cent'anni di papiri: Atti del convegno internazionale di studi, Firenze, 12–13 giugno 2003*, edited by G. Bastianini and A. Casanova, 151–163. Florence: Istituto papirologico G. Vitelli.

Sommerstein, A. H. 2010. "The History of the Text of Aristophanes." In *Brill's Companion to the Study of Greek Comedy*, edited by G. W. Dobrov, 399–422. Leiden: Brill.

Steidle, W. 1974. "Menander bei Terenz." *RhM* 117: 247–276.

Steinrück, M. 2000. "Neues zu Sappho." *ZPE* 13: 10–12.

Stephens, S. A. 1982. No. 3431 [Anon., New Comedy]. *The Oxyrhynchus Papyri* 49: 1–7.

Storey, I. C. 2000. "Some Thoughts on *POxy*. 4301." In *The Rivals of Aristophanes: Studies in Athenian Old Comedy*, edited by G. D. Harvey, and J. Wilkins, 166–171. London: Duckworth and Classical Press of Wales.

——. 2011. *Fragments of Old Comedy*. 3 vols. Cambridge, MA: Harvard University Press.

Thür, G. 2001. "Recht im hellenistischen Athen." In *Symposion 1997: Akten der Gesellschaft für griechische und hellenistische Rechtsgeschichte*, edited by E. Cantarella, and G. Thür, 141–164. Cologne: Böhlau.

Traill, A. 2008. *Women and the Comic Plot in Menander*. Cambridge, UK: Cambridge University Press.

Trojahn, S. 2002. *Die auf Papyri erhaltenen Kommentare zur Alten Komödie: Ein Beitrag zur Geschichte der antiken Philologie*. Munich: K. G. Saur.

Turner, E. G. 1977. *The Typology of the Early Codex*. Philadelphia: University of Pennsylvania Press.

——. 1983. No. 3533 [Menander, *Epitrepontes*]. *The Oxyrhynchus Papyri* 50: 35–48.

Ucciardello, G. 2001. "Sapph. frr. 88 e 159 V. in *POxy*. LXIV 4411." *ZPE* 136: 167–168.

Van Lantschoot, A. 1965. *Inventaire des manuscrits syriaques des fonds Vatican (490-631): Barberini oriental et neofiti*. Vatican: Biblioteca Apostolica Vaticana.

Van Minnen, P. 1994. "House-to-House Enquiries: An Interdisciplinary Approach to Roman Karanis." *ZPE* 100: 227–251.

——. 1998. "Boorish or Bookish?: Literature in Egyptian Villages in the Fayum in the Graeco-Roman Period." *JJP* 28: 99–184.

Van Rossum-Steenbeek, M. 1998. *Greek Readers' Digests?: Studies on a Selection of Subliterary Papyri*. Leiden: Brill.

Webster, T. B. L. 1974. *An Introduction to Menander*. Manchester: Manchester University Press.

West, M. L. 1992. *Ancient Greek Music*. Oxford: Clarendon Press.

Whitehead, D. 1977. *The Ideology of the Athenian Metic*. Cambridge, UK: Cambridge Philological Society.

Wilson, N. G. 2007. *Aristophanea*. Oxford: Oxford University Press.

Zelnick-Abramovitz, R. 2005. *Not Wholly Free: The Concept of Manumission and the Status of Manumitted Slaves in the Ancient Greek World*. Leiden: Brill.

APPENDIX 2

....

POST-MENANDRIAN COMIC POETS: AN OVERVIEW OF THE EVIDENCE AND A CHECKLIST

....

BENJAMIN MILLIS

In the latter part of the twentieth century and the beginning of the twenty-first, work on theatrical antiquities and dramatic production of the Hellenistic and Roman periods proliferated. Scholars are now well informed about artistic representations of theatrical artifacts and dramatic production and about many aspects of acting and actors, professional organizations, and much else, reaching far into the Roman period.[1] In contrast, modern scholarship on Greek comic poets who postdate Menander is virtually nonexistent.[2] The fragments of this material have been gathered in the successive collections of Greek comic fragments, but little attention has been given to them.[3] Relative

---

[1] The following bibliography is highly selective and meant only as a starting point. Artistic representations: the successive editions of *MNC* (Webster 1961; Webster 1969; Webster 1995); Green 1994. Actors: Easterling and Hall 2002; Csapo 2010b (a selection of earlier work, some revised). Fundamental for actors and other performers (except poets) is Stephanis 1988. Professional associations: Le Guen 2001; Aneziri 2003. Dramatic production in the imperial period: Jones 1993; Heldmann 2000. As important as all this work has been in documenting continued dramatic production throughout the Hellenistic and Roman periods, it also shows a notable reticence in suggesting the production of new plays; a notable exception is Jones, who almost alone argues strenuously for the continued production of newly written comedies and tragedies into at least the second century CE.

[2] Statements once routinely made about "Middle Comedy" might with some justice be taken as representative of current views on later comedy: e.g., Rose (1934): 242 "a somewhat dreary period whereof not much is known" (see Lever 1956: 183–184 notes 1–2 for further examples).

[3] One of the very few in-depth studies of a post-Menandrian comic poet is Belardinelli's commentary on Diodorus in Belardinelli et al. 1998. The only substantial treatment for most other post-Menandrian poets (his immediate contemporaries excepted) remains Meineke 1839: 457–487, 492. Brief accounts derived largely from Meineke appear in various handbooks: e.g. Schmid and Stählin (1920–1924): 48–50, 178, 336, 685; Susemihl (1891): 262–269; Bergk (1887): 224–237; Bernhardy (1880): 696–699.

neglect of later periods in favor of the extant authors Aristophanes and Menander would not be surprising; the lack of almost any scholarship on later comedy is. That the work of Aristophanes cannot necessarily be understood as emblematic of fifth-century comedy has long been recognized, and has led to attempts to contextualize his comedies by studying his contemporaries.[4] Oddly, the same has been less true for Menander.[5] Even for the middle of the fourth century, where there are no extant plays, much work has been done, and it is possible to discuss the comedy of the period in general terms.[6]

In contrast, many scholars, including a fair number who work primarily on comedy, remain largely unaware that the evidence for Greek comic poets continues for centuries past the death of Menander. Attention has concentrated on the century and a half preceding Menander's death, i.e., from about the middle of the fifth century until shortly after 300 BCE, despite the fact that original comedies[7] continued to be written and produced until at least the second century CE. This neglect becomes more glaring with the realization that almost exactly half of the ca. 250 comic poets in K-A postdate Menander.

The reasons for this lack of attention are varied and include the following. The paradigm of literary history as a narrative of postclassical decline, and thus decreasing worth, is difficult to escape even for those aware of its pernicious effects. The fragments of earlier comedy often lend themselves to treatment similar to that provided by the best modern commentators on Aristophanes, while the fragments of later comedy are mostly less conducive to the sorts of questions asked by modern scholars of Menander. Scholarship on a subject breeds more scholarship on the same, even while other potentially fertile areas remain neglected. But the most important point is that, for whatever reason, post-Menandrian comedy has been largely ignored.[8] One result is that modern scholars'

---

[4] See, for example, Harvey and Wilkins 2000 for essays on a variety of authors. Commentaries or extended studies on individual poets include several of the contributions in Beladinelli et al. 1998; Storey 2003; Pirrotta 2009; Orth 2009; Bakola 2010. Olson 2007 provides commentaries on selected individual fragments of this and later periods.

[5] An exception was the tendency in the beginning of the nineteenth century and earlier, before the advent of comprehensive collections of comic fragments, to discuss Menander and Philemon together. Webster 1970 devoted a chapter each to Philemon, Diphilus, and Apollodorus Carystius, but more typical is Ireland 2010, which, in a lengthy treatment of "New Comedy" (not Menander), gave no more than a page or two each to these three, compared with fifty pages on Menander. See now, however, Bruzzese 2011 for a study of Philemon; Scafuro, chapter 9, this volume, for the period more generally. Important contemporaries of Menander such as Diphilus and Philippides, both of whom survive in a substantial number of fragments, remain largely neglected. Interestingly, scholarship prior to the rediscovery of Menander showed much more interest in Menander's contemporaries than is typical subsequently; Menander's rediscovery resulted in a focus on that poet to the exclusion of others instead of increased work on the period generally.

[6] For general accounts, see Webster 1970 (outdated and often overspeculative, but with many valuable observations); Nesselrath 1990. For commentaries on individual poets, see Hunter 1983; Arnott 1996; Papachrysostomou 2008. In addition, several of the commentaries on Aristophanes's contemporaries concern poets whose careers extended well into the fourth century.

[7] "Original comedy" is used here as a translation of καινὴ κωμῳδία, a newly written comedy, in contrast to the ancient scholarly term νέα κωμῳδία ("New Comedy"), the comedy of the late fourth and early third centuries. Similarly, a sharp distinction must be maintained between the occasional ancient scholarly use of παλαιὰ κωμῳδία, "Old Comedy" in the modern sense of comedy of the late fifth century, and the contemporary epigraphic use of the same term with the meaning "a revival of a previously performed comedy."

[8] Exceptional only in its explicitness is Dobrov's statement (Dobrov 2010: 20): "the 270s marked the end of the productive era of Greek comedy."

understanding of the genre's trends and development is focused on barely a quarter of a tradition that lasted nearly a millennium.

Leaving aside trends in scholarship, perhaps the greatest reason for the neglect of post-Menandrian (or more precisely, "post-Philemon") comedy is the nature of the evidence. Except sporadically, it does not involve Athenaeus, Stobaeus, the lexicographers, or the other usual sources of book fragments. Moreover, the contribution of papyri is not as great as it might be, because, although some greater or lesser number of papyri might preserve post-Menandrian comedy, it is impossible for us to make confident attributions.[9] Instead, nearly all the certain evidence is from epigraphy, a field with which few scholars of ancient comedy have more than a passing familiarity. What is more, epigraphy offers not new fragments, the primary interest of literary scholars, but only names of poets and, very occasionally, of plays. The difference in the nature of the evidence, however, ought not to obscure its importance; it merely means that the scholarly focus must be different.

Seen through the lens of the extant plays and major fragments, comedy comes into focus in the second half of the fifth century and has an efflorescence of several decades before lapsing into relative obscurity, only to rise again at the end of the fourth century in the seemingly very different work of Menander. In this paradigm, the route from the earlier poets to Menander remains unclear,[10] while the production of poets later than Menander is irrelevant and thus largely ignored. In contrast, the epigraphic evidence offers an unbroken chain of comic production from the early history of the genre in Athens to Menander and beyond. Viewed this way, figures such as Aristophanes and Menander, otherwise known to have been influential or important, may remain leading emblems of their time but are no longer necessarily the defining artists of the genre; in contrast to the literary evidence, which offers an implicit correlation between the extent of survival and importance, the epigraphic evidence presents a randomly selected multitude. Equally important, comic production at the major Athenian festivals, the City Dionysia and the Lenaea, did not limp on in a post-Menandrian decline, but continued unabated for a century and a half;[11] at the same time, festivals elsewhere in the Greek world became important and showcased comedy for nearly five centuries more.[12]

Modern knowledge of ancient Greek comedy is the product of a historical process that privileged the earlier periods. Collection and study of comedy began early in the Hellenistic period; it thus a priori excluded post-Menandrian authors.[13] Subsequent ancient scholarship,

---

[9] For a similar conclusion, see, e.g., Sommerstein 2002: 76, "It is highly probable that we possess papyrus fragments of plays by Diphilus or Philemon, but we cannot identify any"; cf. Nesselrath, chapter 34, this volume. Not mentioned here is by far the greatest source for post-Menandrian comedy, the extant plays of Plautus and Terence together with the fragments of Roman comedy. As for Apollodorus of Carystus, it should be remembered that apart from Terence's *Hecyra* and *Phormio*, Donatus's commentary offers some information and excerpts from this playwright. For this material as essentially Hellenistic Greek comedy written in Latin, see Fontaine 2010, esp. 253–256.

[10] For discussion, see Csapo 2000.

[11] Note, however, that around the middle of the third century BCE the schedule of dramatic production at the two major Athenian festivals changed, and the City Dionysia and Lenaea seem to have gone to a schedule that alternated between comedy and tragedy: each year plays in one genre were performed at one festival and plays in the other genre at the other festival. On this point, see Millis and Olson (2012): 76.

[12] The same point is true for the even more maligned and less studied postclassical tragedy. For the increase in the number of festivals, whether offering dramatic production or not, see Chaniotis 1995.

[13] Modern scholars continue to rely on the periodization of comedy that was developed in antiquity and is exemplified by the anonymous *De comoedia* (III Koster). This tradition defines "New Comedy" as the period of Menander, his contemporaries, and his immediate successors. The marginalization of

being in many ways inherently conservative, accepted the canon that had been developed, and declined to add to it. Even centuries later, in the Roman imperial period, scholars continued to quote earlier comedy while largely ignoring post-Menandrian comedy. As a result, comedy of the third century and later, although theoretically available to the authors who are our major sources for fragments, seldom appears as book fragments. This paucity of fragments leads directly to the appearance that later comedy is insignificant and derivative.

The epigraphic evidence, although not offering new fragments,[14] presents a corrective to this misleading picture. Side by side with reproductions of "old" comedy,[15] i.e., comedy that had been previously produced, original comedies continued to be written and produced. At the same time, venues for the production of comedy, as well as of other drama, proliferated and were now even less restricted to the traditional Athenian festivals than they had been in the fourth century. Indeed, there is reason to believe that the Athenian festivals were not the preserve of the most successful poets, with festivals elsewhere in the Greek world offering a stage to lesser lights. Philemon is exemplary: he produced a play on Delos at the height of a successful career.[16] Comparable are poets such as Ariston, who in the second century produced plays both at the Athenian Lenaea and the Samian Heraea, and Alexander, a member of the Athenian Artists of Dionysus in the late second/early first century, who produced plays at two different festivals in Orchomenus and was honored several times at Delphi.

Most importantly, perhaps, original comedies were produced across the Greek world[17] at a variety of festivals; no longer was Athens, or the two major festivals there, the preeminent venue.[18] Late comedy ought not, therefore, to be read as a uniformly Athenian product written for an Athenian audience but with much of the local flavor suppressed to create international appeal. Instead, comedies were written expressly for competition in central Greece, the islands, Asia Minor, and elsewhere as well as in Athens. Whatever is the case for comedy of the fifth and fourth centuries, in the third century and later, comedy cannot be assumed to have been

Greek comedy from later periods exists in part because later Greek comedy falls outside this scheme and thus remains undefined.

[14] Titles are occasionally recorded, albeit rarely, and suggest a continuity between what scholars label "New Comedy" and the comedy of the post-Menandrian period. Nevertheless, caution is necessary, since trends in titles may well be distinct from trends in plots.

[15] See note 7 above. There is no evidence that the use of παλαιὰ κωμῳδία, the term uniformly used for revivals, refers to what modern scholars understand as "Old Comedy." The earliest attested comic revival at the Dionysia is the Θησαυρός ("Treasure") of Anaxandrides, which was revived in 312/1, although revivals had been produced at that festival since 340/39 (IG II² 2318.317–318 [= 1564–1565 M–O). Nothing certain can be said about the plot of Anaxandrides's play, but the title suggests a plot of the sort associated with New Comedy. All other attested revivals are of works of poets from the mid-fourth century or later, and all plays are either known New Comedy plays or have titles that suggest stereotypical New Comedy plots.

[16] IG XI.2 107.25. This potentially affects how the poets listed with him should be interpreted: since he is a successful poet at the peak of his career, perhaps the more obscure Nicostratus II and Aminias are as well.

[17] And even beyond, if one includes the Roman comedies; see note 9 above. For the spread of comedy outside Athens in the fourth century, see Konstantakos 2011.

[18] In the checklist below, the apparent preeminence of Athens is due to the existence of IG II² 2325 and, to a lesser extent, 2323. If we lacked either of these inscriptions or if a comparable inscription were to be found outside of Attica, the appearance would be strikingly different.

written and produced within the context of an Athenian religious festival.[19] The often-noted generic nature of much of Menander's comedy may be one response to this changing situation. The melding of Athenian comedy and local tradition in Plautus and Terence may be another, perhaps one that was far more widespread than is observable in the fragments of Greek plays. In any event, original Greek comedies continued to be written and produced for a half-millennium after the death of Menander and for centuries after the records for the Athenian City Dionysia and Lenaea cease. A literary history that ignores everything outside the period from the early fifth century to the death of Menander does injustice to the chronological and geographical scope of the genre.

CHECKLIST OF POST-MENANDRIAN COMIC POETS (ARRANGED GEOGRAPHICALLY AND BY FESTIVAL)

Included are all poets whose careers appear, largely or entirely, to postdate ca. 300 BCE. Also included are all those who appear subsequent to Menander in IG II² 2325, i.e., with an initial victory at one of the two major Athenian dramatic festivals subsequent to Menander's first victory at the same festival. The arrangement is alphabetical by location, with the festival specified where known. Locations with multiple dramatic festivals receive multiple headings, e.g., Athens: City Dionysia and Athens: Lenaea. Comic poets attested in a specific location but without a connection to a specific festival are listed under the name of the location alone (e.g., Athens as opposed to Athens: City Dionysia). Poets who cannot be connected with a specific location are listed at the end under "uncertain location." Names of comic poets are given in the Latinized form preferred by K-A and are alphabetized by the form given there: e.g., L. Marius Antiochus is alphabetized as Antiochus, L. Marius. In each entry, the name of the poet is followed by up to three pieces of information in parentheses: (1) date by century, normally as given by K-A; any change to that date is expressly marked (for the sake of convenience, minor disagreement with the dating of K-A is ignored); (2) test. [lit.; ep.] = testimonia (literary and/or epigraphic) not explicitly mentioned subsequently in the entry (test. [ep.] does not include occurrences of the poet solely as a patronymic); (3) frr. = one or more fragments (with or without titles) are known; the instances where only titles are known are marked as tit. [lit; ep.]. A poet attested at multiple festivals but with titles known from only one has the designation tit. [lit.; ep.] only in the entry at the relevant festival. A statement of how the poet is connected with the location together with the reference follows the parenthetic information. Poets known from more than one festival or location are listed under each with cross-references to the others.

Acraiphia: Soteria
Protarchus (I): victorious in the 1st c. BCE: IG VII 2727.28.
Alexandria
Macho (III; test. [lit.]; frr.): produced his comedies not in Athens but in Alexandria: Ath. 14.664a.

---

[19] A point already made (in a somewhat different context) by Green (1994): 68–69 and emphasized by Csapo (2010a): 106.

Athens: City Dionysia

Agathocles (II; tit. [ep.]): 5th in 155/4: IG II^2 2323.242 (= 519 M-O). See also Athens: Lenaea.

Aminias (IV/III; tit. [ep.]): 3rd in 312/1: IG II^2 2323a.46 (= Col. I.12 M-O). See also Athens: Lenaea; Delos: exhibitions.

[Λn?]tigenes (II). See Epigenes.

Apollodorus Carystius (III; test. [lit.]; frr.): victorious two times: IG II^2 2325.73 (= 2325C.82 M-O).

Aristocles (III): 5th in 186/5: *SEG* XXXVIII 162.151 (= IG II^2 2323.277 M-O)

Aristocrates (III/II; tit. [ep.]) 1st in 216/5: IG II^2 2323.102 (= 16 M-O); victorious an unknown number of times: IG II^2 2325.83 (= 2325C.100 M-O).

Biottus (II; tit. [ep.]): 3rd in 168/7: IG II^2 2323.212 (= 417 M-O); 3rd in 155/4: IG II^2 2323.238 (= 515 M-O). See also Athens: Lenaea.

Chaerion (II; tit. [ep.]): 2nd in 155/4: IG II^2 2323.236 (= 513 M-O); possibly victorious an unknown number of times: IG II^2 2325.86 (= 2325C.111 M-O [reading Χα[- - -]]).

Cleo[- - -] (III/II^{20}): 3rd in 201/0: IG II^2 2323.121 (= 145 M-O).

Crito (II; frr.): 2nd in 184/3: IG II^2 2323.151 (= 287 M-O); 2nd in 168/7: IG II^2 2323.210 (= 415 M-O).

Damoxenus (III; test. [lit.]; frr.): victorious one time: IG II^2 2325.75 (= 2325C.84 M-O).

De[- - -]^{21} (II): victorious an unknown number of times: IG II^2 2325.87 (= 2325C.112 M-O).

Epicr[ates] II (II): 5th in 168/7: IG II^2 2323.216 (= 421 M-O).

Epigenes (II^{22}): 6th in 158/7: IG II^2 2323.227 (= 504 M-O).

G[- - -] (III/II^{23}): 5th in 201/0: IG II^2 2323.125 (= 149 M-O).

Iolaus (II): 2nd in 176/5: IG II^2 2323.178 (= 351 M-O).

Laines (II): 1st in 186/5: IG II^2 2323.148 (= 269 M-O); victorious three times: IG II^2 2325.84 (= 2325C.101 M-O).

Lampytus (II): 4th in 168/7: IG II^2 2323.214 (= 419 M-O).

Nicarchus (III/II): victorious one time: IG II^2 2325.81 (= 2325C.98 M-O).

Nicomachus II (III/II): victorious one time: IG II^2 2325.82 (= 2325C.99 M-O).

Nicostratus II (IV/III; tit. [ep.]): 2nd in 312/1: IG II^2 2323a.43 (= 9 M-O); possibly 5th in ca. 302/1: IG II^2 2323a Col. II.13 (= Col. II.16 M-O). See also Athens: Lenaea; Delos: exhibitions.

[Ni]costratus III (III/II): 6th in 186/5: *SEG* XXXVIII 162.153 (= IG II^2 2323.279 M-O). See also Athens: Lenaea.

---

[20] This man is placed in the second century by K-A on the assumption that his one recorded production was ca. 192; the reconstruction of the relevant inscription in M-O moves this date back by a decade into the end of the third century.

[21] Not in K-A, who read Δι[- - -] (= Diomedes test. 5).

[22] K-A follow Ruck in reading [Σω]σιγένης at IG II^2 2323.227; [Eπ]ιγένης is preferable not only epigraphically, but because no comic poet named Sosigenes (or Antigenes, another suggested restoration here) is otherwise attested, whereas an Epigenes is referred to as a poet of "New Comedy" (K-A test. 2). The date assigned to Epigenes by K-A should be adjusted accordingly (from IV to II).

[23] See above on Cleo[- - -].

O[- - -] (II[24]): victorious an unknown number of times: IG II² 2325.87bis (= 2325C.116 M-O [reading Οὐ[- - -]]).

Oly[mp - - -] (III/II[25]): 4th in 201/0: IG II² 2323.123 (= 147 M-O).

Paramonus (II; tit. [ep.]): 3rd in 184/3: IG II² 2323.153 (= 289 M-O); 6th in 170/69: IG II² 2323. 202 (= 407 M-O); 1st (posthumously) in 168/7: IG II² 2323.208 (= 413 M-O).

Philemo (IV/III; test. [lit.; ep.]; frr.): 1st in 328/7: Marm. Par. *FGrHist* 239 B 7; 1st in 307/6: IG II² 3073.5. See also Athens: Lenaea; Delos: exhibitions.

Philemo Iunior (III; test. [lit.]; frr.): victorious six times: IG II² 2325.74 (= 2325C.83 M-O).

Philemo III (II; tit. [ep.]): 6th in 184/3: IG II² 2323.159 (= 295 M-O); victorious an unknown number of times: IG II² 2325.85 (= 2325C.102 M-O).

Philippides (IV/III; test. [lit.; ep.]; frr.): 1st in 312/1: IG II² 2323a.41 (= 7 M-O). See also Athens: Lenaea.

Philocles (II; tit. [ep.]): 1st in 155/4: IG II² 2323.234 (= 511 M-O).

Phoenicides (III; text. [lit.]; frr.): victorious two times: 2325.76 (= 2325C.85 M-O). See also Athens: Lenaea.

Po[- - -] (II[26]): victorious an unknown number of times: IG II² 2325.86bis (= 2325C.115 M-O).

Posidippus (III; test. [lit.; ep.]; frr.): victorious five times:[27] IG II² 2325.71 (= 2325C.80 M-O).

[Posi]dippus II (II): victorious two times: IG II² 2325.79 (= 2325C.95 M-O).

Satyrion (III): victorious one time: IG II² 2325.72 (= 2325C.81 M-O).

Sogenes (II; tit. [ep.]): 5th in 184/3: IG II² 2323.157 (= 193 M-O).

[So?]sigenes (II). See Epigenes.

Strato (IV ex.; test. [lit.]; frr.): possibly 4th in ca. 302/1: IG II² 2323a. Col. II.11 (= Col. II.14 M-O [reading Στ[- - -]]).

Timostratus (II; test. [ep.]; frr.): 6th in 189/8: IG II² 2323.141 (= 262 M-O); 4th in 184/3: IG II² 2323.155 (= 291 M-O); possibly 3rd in 176/5: IG II² 2323.180 (= 353 M-O [reading Τιμο[- - -]; cf. Timotheus II]). See also Athens: Lenaea (under Nicostratus III).

Timotheus II (III/II[28]): 2nd in 201/0: IG II² 2323.119 (= 143 M-O); possibly 3rd in 176/5: IG II² 2323.180 (= 353 M-O [reading Τιμο[- - -]; cf. Timostratus]); possibly victorious one time: 2325.78 (= 2325C.94 [reading [. ....]θεος]).

Timoxenus (II; tit. [ep.]): 4th in 155/4: IG II² 2323.240 (= 517 M-O).

[- - -]nes[29] (III/II; tit. [ep.]): 1st in 198/7: IG II² 2323.131 (= 173 M-O).

[ca. 7]us[30] (II): victorious one time: IG II² 2325.77 (= 2325C.93 M-O).

---

[24] K-A assign this man a date of II/I, but this portion of the Victors Lists does not postdate by much, if at all, the middle of the second century.

[25] See above on Cleo[- - -].

[26] See above on O[- - -].

[27] *Pace* previous editors (followed by K-A), Posidippus was victorious five times, not four; an orignal IIII was erased in order to be replaced by Π. Posidippus was thus still active when this section of the Victors Lists was inscribed, and the list was later corrected to include a subsequent victory.

[28] See above on Cleo[- - -].

[29] The poet himself is not in K-A, but cf. adesp. fr. 2.

[30] Apparently not in K-A.

[4-5]yk[- - -]³¹ (II): victorious an unknown number of times: IG II² 2325.80 (reading [. .. 6...] III) (= 2325C.96 M-O).

Athens: Lenaea

Agathocles (II): victorious one time: IG II² 2325.186 (= 2325E.132 M-O). See also Athens: City Dionysia.

Aminias (IV/III): victorious one time: IG II² 2325.167 (= 2325E.67 M-O). See also Athens: City Dionysia; Delos: exhibitions.

Apollodorus Gelous (IV/III; test. [lit.]; frr.): victorious an unknown number of times: IG II² 2325.162 (= 2325E.62 M-O).

Archid[- - -]³² (III): victorious an unknown number of times: SEG XXVI 207.19 (= 2325E.106 M-O).

Archicles (II): victorious two times: IG II² 2325.187 (= 2325E.133 M-O). Doubtfully restored as 1st at the City Dionysia in 182/1: IG II² 2323.165 (= 301 M-O), whence K-A test. 2.

Ariston (II): victorious three times: IG II² 2325.183 (= 2325E.129 M-O). See also Samos: Heraea.

Aropus (III): victorious two times: SEG XXVI 207.2 (= IG II² 2325E. 87 M-O).

Biottus (II): victorious one time: IG II² 2325.188 (= 2325E.134 M-O). See also Athens: City Dionysia.

Calliades (IV ex.): possibly 5th in 286/5: IG II² 2319.56 (= Col. I.3 M-O); victorious one time: IG II² 2325.166 (= 2325E.66 M-O).

Callimachus (III; test. [lit.]): possibly victorious an unknown number of times: SEG XXVI 207.18 (= IG II² 2325E.105 M-O [reading Καλλ[- - -]]).

Chariclides (III; frr.): possibly victorious one time: SEG XXVI 207.9 (= IG II² 2325E.94 M-O [reading [3–4]κλείδης]).

Dexicrates (III; test. [lit.]; frr.): victorious an unknown number of times: SEG XXVI 207. 23 (= IG II² 2325E.110 M-O).

Diodorus (III; test. [lit.; ep.]; frr.): 2nd and 3rd in 285/4: IG II² 2319.61, 63 (= Col. I.8, 10 M-O); victorious one time: IG II² 2325.170 (= 2325E.97 M-O [reading [. .]όδωρος]).

Dionysius III (II): victorious two times: IG II² 2325.185 (= 2325E.131 M-O).

Diosc[uride]s (III): victorious one time: IG II² 2325.178 (= 2325E.115 M-O).

Diphilus (IV/III; test. [lit.; ep.]; frr.): victorious three times: IG II² 2325.163 (= 2325E.63 M-O).

[Emm]enides (II): victorious one time: IG II² 2325.182 (= 2325E.128 M-O).

Erato[- - -] (III): victorious an unknown number of times: SEG XXVI 207.17 (= IG II² 2325E.104 M-O).

Eteagoras (III): victorious one time: SEG XXVI 207.3 (= IG II² 2325E.88 M-O).

Eubu[lide]s II (III): victorious one time: IG II² 2325.179 (= 2325E.116 M-O).

Eumedes (III): victorious two times: IG II² 2325.171 (= 2325E.98 M-O).

---

³¹ Not in K-A.
³² K-A list the poet as Archi . [- - -], but the *delta* is certain.

Euthycrates (III): victorious two times: *SEG* XXVI 207.1 (= IG II^2 2325E.86 M-O).

Menestheus (III): victorious one time: IG II^2 2325.173 (= 2325E.100 M-O).

[M?]nesi[- - -] (III ex.): victorious three times: IG II^2 2325.181 (= 2325E.18 M-O [reading [.]νησι[.....].]).

Neanthes[33] (III): victorious two times: *SEG* XXVI 207.6 (= IG II^2 2325E.91).

[Ne]leus (III): victorious one time: *SEG* XXVI 207.7 (= IG II^2 2325E.92 [reading [2–3] λεύς).

Nici[as] (III): victorious an unknown number of times: *SEG* XXVI 207.22 (= IG II^2 2325E.109 [reading Νικι[- - -]]).

Nicodemus (II): victorious two times: IG II^2 2325.189 (= 2325E.135).

Nicostratus II (IV/III): victorious an unknown number of times: IG II^2 2325.165 (= 2325E.65 M-O). See also Athens: City Dionysia; Delos: exhibitions.

Nicostratus III (III/II): possibly victorious one or two times: *SEG* XXVI 207.10 (= IG II^2 2325E.95 M-O [reading [3-4 σ]τρατος]). See also Athens: City Dionysia.

Novius (II): victorious three times: IG II^2 2325.184 (= 2325E.130 M-O).

[O?]nesi[- - -]. See **[?M]nesi[- - -]**.

Pandaetes (III): victorious one time: IG II^2 2325.172 (= 2325E.99 M-O).

Philemo (IV/III; test. [lit.; ep.]; frr.): victorious three times: IG II^2 2325.161 (= 2325E.61 M-O). See also Athens: City Dionysia; Delos: exhibitions.

Philippides (IV/III; test. [lit.; ep.]; frr.): victorious two or more times: IG II^2 2325.164 (= 2325E.64 M-O); possibly 5th in 286/5: IG II^2 2319.56 (= Col. I.3 M-O). See also Athens: City Dionysia.

Philiscus II (III): victorious one time: *SEG* XXVI 207.5 (= IG II^2 2325E.90 M-O).

Philom[- - -] (III): victorious an unknown number of times: *SEG* XXVI 207.21 (= IG II^2 2325E.108 M-O).

[Philos]tratus (III). See Nicostratus III.

Phoenicides (III; text. [lit.]; frr.): 4th in 285/4: IG II^2 2319.65 (= Col. I.12 M-O); possibly 5th in 286/5: IG II^2 2319.56 (= Col. I.3 M-O). See also Athens: City Dionysia.

P[o]ly[- - -] (III): victorious an unknown number of times: IG II^2 2325.174 (= 2325E.111 M-O).

Polyclitus (III): victorious one time: *SEG* XXVI 207.4 (= IG II^2 2325E.89 M-O).

Pythod[- - -] (III): victorious an unknown number of times: *SEG* XXVI 207.16 (= IG II^2 2325E.103 M-O).

Simylus (III; frr.): 1st in 285/4: IG II^2 2319.59 (= Col. I.6 M-O).

Soc[- - -] (III): victorious an unknown number of times: *SEG* XXVI 207.20 (= IG II^2 2325E.107 M-O).

Themis[- - -] (III): victorious an unknown number of times: IG II^2 2325.175 (= 2325E.112 M-O).

Theod[- - -] (III): victorious an unknown number of times: IG II^2 2325.177 (= 2325E.114 M-O).

---

[33] K-A, following the original editor, list the poet as [N]eanthes, but the *nu* can be read.

[The]odorus (III): victorious one time: *SEG* XXVI 207.8 (= IG II² 2325E.93 M-O [reading [. .]όδωρος]).

Theodor[us] (III): victorious an unknown number of times: IG II² 2325.180 (= 2325E.117 M-O).

Theo[n] (III): victorious an unknown number of times: IG II² 2325.176 (= 2325E.113 M-O [reading Θεω[- - -]]).

[5–6]ε[s]³⁴ (II): victorious one time: IG II² 2325.169 (= 2325E.96 M-O).

Delos

Nicomachus (III; frr.): honored on Delos in the mid 3rd c. BCE: IG XI.4 638. See also Delos: exhibitions; Samos.

Delos: exhibitions³⁵

Aminias (IV/III): produced an exhibition for Apollo in 280: IG XI.2 107.25. See also Athens: City Dionysia; Athens: Lenaea.

Aristides³⁶ (III): produced an exhibition for Apollo in 236: IG XI.2 120.53.

Chrysippus (III; frr.): produced an exhibition for Apollo in 259: IG XI.2 115.26.

Nicomachus (III; frr.): produced an exhibition for Apollo in 263: IG XI.2 113. See also Delos; Samos.

Nicostratus II (IV/III): produced an exhibition for Apollo in 280: IG XI.2 107. See also Athens: City Dionysia; Athens: Lenaea.

Philemo (III; test [.lit.]; frr.): produced an exhibition for Apollo in 280: IG XI.2 107. 25.³⁷ See also Athens: City Dionysia; Athens: Lenaea.

[- - -]as³⁸ (III): produced an exhibition for Apollo twice in 236: IG XI.2 120.53.

Delphi

Alexander (II/I; frr.): honored in his role as *epimeletes* of the Athenian Artists of Dionysus at Delphi in 106/5: *F.Delphes* III.2 48.3–4; likewise honored in 97/6: *F.Delphes* III.2 49.1; 48; See also Orchomenus: Charitesia; Orchomenus: Homoloia.

Crito II³⁹ (I): member of the Athenian Artists of Dionysus honored in Delphi in 97/6: *F. Delphes* III.2 49.33.

Diomedes (II/I; test. [ep.]): member of the Athenian Artists of Dionysus honored in Delphi in 97/6: *F.Delphes* III.2 49.33. See also Epidaurus; Magnesia on the Maeander: Romaia. Cf. De[- - -] (Athens: City Dionysia).

---

³⁴ Apparently not in K-A.

³⁵ Included under this heading are references to productions in honor of the god but apparently outside the bounds of a specific festival competition even if they may have coincided closely in time with a festival such as the Dionysia; see Sifakis (1967): 24.

³⁶ There is some doubt whether this man should be identified as a comic poet; see Sifakis (1967): 25.

³⁷ K-A assign this testimonium to Philemo Iunior, but the date makes this attribution difficult; see Millis and Olson (2012) on IG II² 2325.74 (= 2325C.83 M-O).

³⁸ If Aristides is correctly identified as a comic poet (see note 36 above), this man is as well; apparently not in K-A.

³⁹ The identification of this man as a comic poet depends entirely on the fact that the name following his is that of the comic poet Diomedes.

Epidaurus

Diomedes (II/I; test. [ep.]): honored by the Epidaurians in the 2nd c.: IG IV².1 626. See also Delphi; Magnesia on the Maeander: Romaia. Cf. De[- - -] (Athens: City Dionysia).

Isthmia: Caesarea

Anubion (IIp): victorious in CE 127: *Hesperia* 39 (1970): 79–83, line 48.

Magnesia on the Maeander: Romaia

Agathenor (I; tit. [ep.]): victorious in the early 1st c. BCE: *I.Magnesia* 88d Col. I.4.

Diomedes (II/I; test. [ep.]): victorious in the second half of the 2nd c. BCE: *I.Magnesia* 88b Col. II.4–5. See also Delphi; Epidaurus. Cf. De[- - -] (Athens: City Dionysia).

Metrodorus (II; tit. [ep.]): victorious in the second half of the 2nd c. BCE: *I.Magnesia* 88a Col. II.4.

Neapolis

Germanicus (Ip; test. [lit.]): victorious posthumously in the 1st c. CE: Suet. *Claud.* 11.2.

Orchomenus: Charitesia

Alexander (II/I; frr.): victorious in the 1st c. BCE: IG VII 3197.32. See also Delphi; Orchomenus: Homoloia.

Orchomenus: Homoloia

Alexander (II/I; frr.): victorious in the 1st c. BCE: IG VII 3197.50. See also Delphi; Orchomenus: Charitesia.

Oropus: Amphiaraia

Ariston II (I; test. [ep.]): victorious in the mid-1st c. BCE: IG VII 416.30 (= *I.Oropos* 523.30).

Ariston III (I): victorious in the mid-1st c. BCE: IG VII 419.32 (= *I.Oropos* 526.32).

Chionnes (I): victorious in the mid-1st c. BCE: IG VII 420.34 (= *I.Oropos* 528.34).

Dieuches (I): victorious in the mid-1st c. BCE: IG VII 417.3 (= *I.Oropos* 525.3).

Ptolemais (Egypt)

Musaeus (III): member of Artists of Dionysus in Ptolemais, 269–246: *OGIS* 51.36 (= *I.Prose* 6.36).

Stratagus (III): member of Artists of Dionysus in Ptolemais, 269–246: *OGIS* 51.35 (= *I.Prose* 6.35).

Samos

Nicomachus (III; frr.): honored on Samos: IG XII.6 122. See also Delos; Delos: exhibitions.

Samos: Heraea

Ariston (II): victorious in the first half of the 2nd c. BCE: IG XII.6 173.10. See also Athens: Lenaea.

Thespiae: Musea

Amphichares, P. Aelius (IIp): victorious in the 2nd c. CE: *BCH* 19 (1895): 343–345 no. 17.26 (also victorious in the same festival as tragic poet [line 22]).

Antiochus, L. Marius (IIp): victorious in ca. CE 160: *SEG* III 334.40 (also victorious at the same festival as tragic actor [line 46]).

Antiphon (IIp; test. [ep.]): victorious in the 2nd c. CE: IG VII 1773.23 (also victorious at the same festival as ποιητὴς προσοδίου[40] [lines 7–8] and as the actor of original comedy [line 24].

[Bo]iscus (I): victorious in the 1st c. BCE: IG VII 1761.8.

Tanagra: Sarapiea

Poses (I; test. [ep.]): victorious in ca. 85 BCE: IG VII 540.14.

Unknown performance location

Antiphanes II (III; test. [lit.]; frr.?[41])

Apollinaris (IVp; test. [lit.])

Athenio (I?; frr.)

Bato (III; test. [lit.]; frr.)

Demetrius II (III; frr.)

Demophilus (III–II?; tit. [lit.])

Epinicus (III/II; test. [lit.]; frr.)

Euangelus (III?; test. [lit.]; frr.)

Euphro (III; test. [lit.]; frr)

Eudoxus (III vel II; test. [lit.]; frr.): doubtfully restored as 1st at the City Dionysia in 182/1: IG II² 2323.165 (= 301 M-O), whence K-A test. 2.

Hegesippus (III; test. [lit.]; frr.)

Hipparchus (III; test. [lit.]; fr.)

Laon (III; frr.)

Lynceus (IV/III; test. [lit.]; frr.)

Mnasicles (II): member of the Artists of Dionysus at Athens: IG II² 1331.

Moschio (III vel II?;[42] frr.)

Nico (IV vel III?; frr.)

Nicolaus (II?; frr.)

Nicolaus Damascenus (I; test. [lit.])

Onesicles (Roman):[43] funerary (?) inscription of the Roman period from Hierapolis in Cilicia: *JHS* 11 (1890): 249 no. 23 (the man was also an epic poet, an iambic poet, and a panegyrist as well as a jurist).

Philonides II (inc.; frr.)

Philostephanus (III–II?; frr.)

Philostratus II (II vel III; test. [lit.])

Sosicrates (III?; frr.)

Sosipater (III; frr.)

Sosippus (IV/III?; frr.)

Stephanus (IV/III; test. [lit.])

---

[40] For the meaning of this term, see Rutherford, *ZPE* 130 (2000): 147–148.

[41] For two possible fragments, see Antiphanes K-A fr. 81 and 185 with K-A ad loc.

[42] K-A date Moschio as "saec. incert." The name is common only from the late fourth century, so the poet is most likely Hellenistic.

[43] K-A's designation of the man's dates as "saec. incert.," while strictly true, is misleading in that the inscription clearly belongs to the Roman period, perhaps to the third century or so.

Theognetus (III; test. [lit.]; tit. [lit.])

Thymoteles (II; test. [ep.]): possibly sent to Delphi as an ambassador from the Athenian Artists of Dionysus: IG II² 1132.45, 71 ≈ *F.Delphes* III(2) 68.31 (both with the restorations of Sifakis [1967] 94).

Timon (III; test. [lit.])

Xeno (III; frr.)

BIBLIOGRAPHY

Aneziri, S. 2003. *Die Vereine der dionysischen Techniten im Kontext der hellenistischen Gesellschaft: Untersuchungen zur Geschichte, Organization und Wirkung der hellenistischen Technitenvereine*. Wiesbaden: F. Steiner.

Arnott, W. G. 1996. *Alexis: The Fragments*. Cambridge, UK: Cambridge University Press.

Bakola, E. 2010. *Cratinus and the Art of Comedy*. Oxford: Oxford University Press.

Belardinelli, A. M., O. Imperio, G. Mastromarco, M. Pellegrino, and P. Totaro. 1998. *Tessere: Frammenti della commedia greca: Studi e commenti*. Bari: Adriatica.

Bergk, T. 1887. *Griechische Literaturgeschichte*. Vol. 4, *Aus dem Nachlass herausgegeben von Rudolf Peppmüller*. Berlin: Weidmann.

Bernhardy, G. 1880. *Grundriss der griechischen Literatur*. 3rd ed. Vol. 2, *Geschichte der griechischen Poesie*. Part 2, *Dramatische Poesie, Alexandriner, Byzantiner, Fabel*. Halle: Anton.

Bruzzese, L. 2011. *Studi su Filemone comico*. Lecce: Pensa Multimedia.

Chaniotis, A. 1995. "Sich selbst feiern? Städtische Feste des Hellenismus in Spannungsfeld von Religion und Politik." In *Stadtbild und Bürgerbild in Hellenismus: Kolloquium, München, 24. bis 26. Juni 1993*, edited by M. Wörrle and P. Zanker, 147–172. Munich: Beck.

Csapo, E. 2000. "From Aristophanes to Menander? Genre Transformation in Greek Comedy." In *Matrices of Genre: Authors, Canons, and Society*, edited by M. Depew and D. Obbink, 115–133. Cambridge, MA: Harvard University Press.

——. 2010a. "The Production and Performance of Comedy in Antiquity." In *Brill's Companion to the Study of Greek Comedy*, edited by G. W. Dobrov, 103–142. Leiden: Brill.

——. 2010b. *Actors and Icons of the Ancient Theater*. Malden, MA: Wiley-Blackwell.

Dobrov, G. W. 2010. "Comedy and Her Critics." In *Brill's Companion to the Study of Greek Comedy*, edited by G. W. Dobrov, 3–33. Leiden: Brill.

Easterling, P. E., and E. Hall, eds. 2002. *Greek and Roman Actors: Aspects of an Ancient Profession*. Cambridge: Cambridge University Press.

Fontaine, M. 2010. *Funny Words in Plautine Comedy*. Oxford: Oxford University Press.

Green, J. R. 1994. *Theatre in Ancient Greek Society*. London: Routledge.

Harvey, D., and J. Wilkins, eds. 2000. *The Rivals of Aristophanes: Studies in Athenian Old Comedy*. London: Duckworth and the Classical Press of Wales.

Heldmann, G. 2000. "Die griechische und lateinische Tragödie und Komödie in der Kaiserzeit." *WJA* 24: 185–205.

Hunter, R. L. 1983. *Eubulus: The Fragments*. Cambridge, UK: Cambridge University Press.

Ireland, S. 2010. "New Comedy." In *Brill's Companion to the Study of Greek Comedy*, edited by G. W. Dobrov, 333–396. Leiden: Brill.

Jones, C. P. 1993. "Greek Drama in the Roman Empire." In *Theater and Society in the Classical World*, edited by R. Scodel, 39–52. Ann Arbor: University of Michigan Press.

Konstantakos, I. M. 2011. "Conditions of Playwriting and the Comic Dramatist's Craft in the Fourth Century." *Logeion* 1: 145–183.

Le Guen, B. 2001. *Les associations des Technites dionysiaques à l'époque hellénistique*. Nancy: Association pour la diffusion de la recherche sur l'antiquité.

Lever, K. 1956. *The Art of Greek Comedy*. London: Methuen.

Meineke, A. 1839. *Fragmenta comicorum graecorum*. Vol. 1, *Historia critica comicorum graecorum*. Berlin: Reimer.

Millis, B. W., and S. D. Olson. 2012. *Inscriptional Records for the Dramatic Festivals in Athens: IG II² 2318–2325 and Related Texts*. Leiden and Boston: Brill.

Nesselrath, H.-G. 1990. *Die attische mittlere Komödie: Ihre Stellung in der antiken Literaturkritik und Literaturgeschichte*. Berlin: de Gruyter.

Olson, S. D. 2007. *Broken Laughter: Select Fragments of Greek Comedy*. Oxford: Oxford University Press.

Orth, C. 2009. *Strattis: Die Fragmente: Ein Kommentar*. Berlin: Verlag Antike.

Papachrysostomou, A. 2008. *Six Comic Poets: A Commentary of Selected Fragments of Middle Comedy*. Tübingen: Narr.

Pirrotta, S. 2009. *Plato comicus: Die fragmentarischen Komödien: Ein Kommentar*. Berlin: Verlag Antike.

Rose, H. J. 1934. *A Handbook of Greek Literature from Homer to the Age of Lucian*. London: Dutton.

Schmid, W., and O. Stählin. 1920–1924. *Geschichte der griechischen Literatur. Zweiter Teil: Die nachklassische Periode der griechischen Literatur*. 6th ed. Munich: C.H. Beck.

Sifakis, G. M. 1967. *Studies in the History of Hellenistic Drama*. London: Athlone.

Sommerstein, A. H. 2002. *Greek Drama and Dramatists*. London: Routledge.

Stephanis, I. E. 1988. Διονυσιακοὶ τεχνῖται: Συμβολὲς στην προσωπογραφία τοῦ θεάτρου καὶ τῆς μουσικῆς τῶν ἀρχαίων Ἑλλήνων, Heraklion, Greece: Panepistemiakes Ekdoseis Kretes.

Storey, I. C. 2003. *Eupolis: Poet of Old Comedy*. Oxford: Oxford University Press.

Susemihl, F. 1891. *Geschichte der griechischen Literatur in der Alexandrinerzeit*. Vol. 1. Leipzig: Teubner.

Webster, T. B. L. 1961. *Monuments Illustrating New Comedy*. London: Institute of Classical Studies.

——. 1969. *Monuments Illustrating New Comedy*. 2nd ed. London: Institute of Classical Studies.

——. 1970. *Studies in Later Greek Comedy*. 2nd ed. Manchester: Manchester University Press.

——. 1995. *Monuments Illustrating New Comedy*. 3rd ed. Revised and enlarged by J. R. Green and A. Seeberg. London: Institute of Classical Studies.

Index

acting troupes 415–18, 467
actors, Greek and Hellenistic 51–2, 65–7
    (illusionism, virtuoso acting), 359–77
    See also Artists of Dionysus
  Roman 420–2
adespota K-A fr. 71 533
adespota K-A fr. 1027 528–9
adespota K-A fr. 1147 526
Aeschylus 127, 194, 266–8, 272
aischron 38
Alcaeus (Comicus) 162, 192, 194, 264
Alciphron 743–9
Alexander the Great 360–2
Alexandrianism 542–5, 553
Alexis 165–7, 176, 185, 187–8, 192–5, 200, 203–
    4, 205, 209–10, 271, 280, 284, 286, 289–90,
    293, 308–11, 313, 670
Ameipsias 186, 191–2, 279
Amphis 174, 184–5, 188, 191–3, 280, 286, 311
Anaxandrides 167, 169, 173, 185, 187, 192–5,
    200, 201, 203, 205, 212, 264. *See also*
    virtuoso speeches
ancient grammarians 450–60, 549, 550,
    700–1, 711, 754–5
Anderson, W.S. 426–7
Anechomenos 760
Antiphanes 164, 168, 175, 185–8, 191, 193–5,
    270–1, 288–9, 308, 310–11, 502–3, 505,
    669–670, 676
Apollodorus of Carystus 205, 207–8, 541. *See*
    also Terence
aprosdoketon 140, 155
Apuleius 755–64
Archedicus 189–90, 203, 301
Aristophanes (Comicus)
  audience address 141, 143, 144, 233–4
  chorus 138–9, 141–5, 147, 148, 150, 152, 154–5
  comic themes 149–56

dramatis personae 145–9
fragmentary plays: *Aeolosicon* 146, 162,
    270, 298; *Babylonians* 302–3;
    Cocalus 162, 194, 271, 298; *Dramas*
    or The Centaur 165
influence on the comic canon 113–15;
    critique of other poets 96, 99, 104, 117
language 64, 135–7; neologisms 149
life 132–3, 194
linguistic characterization 136–7
meters 40, 137–40, 141–3
parabasis and constituent elements
    (*kommation*, *parabasis* proper,
    epirrhematic syzygy [ode, antode,
    epirrhema], *pnigos*, *sphragis*) 141–3, 263
papyri 804–7
poetics 156–7
as school author, 657
structure 51, 141–5, 150–1
surviving plays: *Acharnians* 146, 148–9,
    151–4, 156, 265, 292, 342–3; *Assembly*
    women 151, 186, 286, 292, 299; *Birds* 154–
    5, 163, 261; *Clouds* 113–14, 154–6, 262,
    279, 284, 292, 341, 343–5; *Frogs* 148, 155–7,
    163, 168, 266, 344; *Knights* 96, 116, 146,
    154–5, 305; *Lysistrata* 150; *Peace* 150, 343;
    Wasps 145; *Wealth* 299; *Women at the*
    Thesmophoria 153, 155, 163–4, 265
textual tradition, 655–66
works, 133–4
See also Athenian law, Athenian religion
Aristophanes of Byzantium 542, 549,
    552, 674
Aristophon 188, 288
Aristotle
  Metaphysics, on the word *holos* (1023b12–37)
    503
  Nicomachean Ethics 155, 184, 291–2

Aristotle (*Cont.*)

  Poetics, on the relationships among
    Comedy, Tragedy, and Epic (1448a16–19,
    b35–1149a6, 1449a2–6, a9–14, 1453a35–39)
    34–5; actions follow from character
    (1454a33–b2) 293; comedy distinctive
    (1448a31–38, 1449a32–b27, 1449a32–b27,
    1449b2–8, 1451b12, 1449b5–9) 36–8; on
    prologues (1452b19f.) 503; themes not
    discussed about comedy (1449b21–22,
    1449a37–b6) 36, 72–3

  Politics 184, 286–8, 314

  Rhetoric 291

  on prologues (1414b19–21, 1415a11–19)
    501–2, (1415a7–25) 502

Arnott, G. 4, 5, 6n12, 16, 19

Artists of Dionysus 362–4, 368, 373,
    530, 533

asides 473–4

Atellan farce, 404–7, 424–5, 430–40, 534
  influenced by Rhinthon, 404 (*see also*
    masks)

Athenaeus of Naucratis 34, 166, 259, 279–81,
    283–4, 287–9, 669–72, 676–9

Attic demes 74 and n1, 76 and n2, 80, 81–7. *See
    also* festivals, Greek, Rural Dionysia

Atticization 163, 165–8, 169

audience, Greek
  internal 229, 232, 233
  international, at the Dionysia 53; activity
    of 55; size of 54, 200
  audience address 209 (*see also under*
    Aristophanes)

audience, Roman 410–18
  effect on, of asides 473–44
  internal 468
  participation of 469–70
  perceptions and expectations of 464–6, 473
  reading audience also presumed 544

audience response theory 429

Austin, C. 6n12, 13, 15, 17, 18, 803

Axionicus 271

Bakhtin, M. 283, 429

Baton 188, 283, 285, 289–90

Bierl, A. 46

Blanchard, A. 15

Bowie, A. M. 45

Caecilius of Calacte 522

Caecilius Statius 448–52, 455–7, 540, 541, 546,
    550, 557–9
  in Gellius 758–9

Callias 101, 107, 165

Callimedon 309–10

Callistratus 308, 310

Callopian recension. *See under* Terence

canon, of comic poets 113–14
  of school authors 777–80
  of Roman authors 533, 540
  of Homer and Menander 549

Carthage 609–10

Cato the Elder 428
  as Roman Demosthenes 551

chance. See *Tyche*

Chariton, *Callirhoe* 735–42

Chionides 95

choregos (pl.: choregoi) 70
  appointed by archon, later nominated by
    tribe for City Dionysia 73–5, 300
  appointed by *basileus* for Lenaea 75
  metic choregoi and chorus members at the
    Lenaea 76

choregia ("agonistic liturgy") 70
  beginning of the institution 73
  its end 86–9

choregic monuments (dedications) 79–87

chorus (comic)
  Aristotle's view of 38–9
  characterization of 147–8
  description of 51
  in fourth century 201, 203, 271
  interaction with actors and audience 141–5,
    262–3
  See under Aristophanes, Menander

Christian reception of Greek comedy 677–9

Chrysoloras, Manuel 662

City Dionysia. *See* festivals, Greek, City
    Dionysia

Clement of Alexandria 290, 677–679

Cleon 114, 182–3, 301–3, 305, 308–9

Cleonymus 303, 305

Cleophon 305–6

Comedy, Greek. *See also* names of Greek
    Comic poets under "Comic poets, Greek"
  origins 33–47 *passim*
  treatment by Aristotle (*see* Aristotle)

ancient tripartition of ("Old," "Middle," "New") 181, 207, 298–301

Old Comedy, demagogues in 98–9, 125, 304–6, 310–12; political humor 98–107, 182–3; personal jokes (*to onomasti komoidein*) 96–108, 114, 304 (*see also* humor, personal); mythological burlesque 100–3 (Cratinus), 106 (Hermippus), 109–10 (Pherecrates), 160–77 *passim*; domestic comedy 109–10 (Pherecrates) (*see also* Magnes, Cratinus, Crates, Hermippus, Callias, Teleclides, Pherecrates, Aristophanes)

"Middle Comedy," domestic comedy 190–5; *hetaira* comedy 183–4, 186–8, 190–5; myth comedy and mythological burlesque 193–5; political comedy 182–90, 300, 310; reception of in later antiquity, 667–79

"New Comedy" settings 298; visual record 717–27 (*see also* papyri)

continuity in 181

post-Menandrian 871–5; names of poets 875–83

productions, in Athens 50–6

productions outside Athens 219, 362–5; non-Dionysiac, in eastern Mediterranean 365–70; outside Greece 52, 201, 362–5; in western 372–4 (*see also* festivals, Greek, Rural Dionysia)

See also Greek law, Greek religion, Greek festivals: City Dionysia, Lenaea, Rural Dionysia

Comedy, Roman

acting troupes 415–18, 467

actors 420–2

Artists of Dionysus, relation to 370–3, 530, 533

Atellan farce, relation to, 404–7, 424–40, 534 (*see also* Atellan farce)

audience (*see under* audience, Roman)

canon of 533, 540

exposition 501–13

interpolation (*see* Plautus, interpolation)

intertextuality (*see* intertextuality in Roman comedy)

linguistic characterization in 569–72

literary language of 568–9

piety 605–12

prologues 413–20, 498–513

prologue speakers 413–20, 501–13

production 462–6

production notices (*didascaliae*) 422, 471

visual record 727–31 (*see also* gesture)

See also festivals, Roman; metrics, Roman; reception; Roman law, Roman religion

comic fragments 13, 16, 17–19, 115–29 *passim*, 162

Roman 449–60

See also papyri *and* individual poets

comic language. *See* Aristophanes; Menander; Plautus; Terence; comic patter; linguistic characterization

Comic poets, Greek. *See under* individual names: Alcaeus (Comicus), Alexis, Ameipsias, Amphis, Anaxandrides, Antiphanes, Archedicus, Aristophanes (Comicus), Aristophon, Axionicus, Baton, Callias, Callimedon, Callistratus, Chionides, Cleonymus, Cleophon, Crates, Cratinus, Damoxenus, Dinolochus, Diodorus, Diphilus, Ecphantides, Ephippus, Epicharmus, Eubulus, Eupolis, Hegesippus, Heniochus, Hermippus, Magnes, Menander, Pherecrates, Philemon, Philippides, Philyllius, Phrynichus, Plato Comicus, Posidippus, Strattis, Susarion, Teleclides, Theognetus, Theophilus, Theopompus, Timocles, Xenarchus. *See also* Artists of Dionysus, Rhinthon

Comic poets, Rome. *See under* individual names: Afranius, Caecilius Statius, Ennius, Livius Andronicus, Naevius, Plautus, Terence, Titinius

comic patter 208–14

comic reversal 175–6

commentaries, ancient, on Plautus and Terence 755

comoedia palliata 409–10, 425, 427, 432, 447–9

masks of 433–40

Comparison of Aristophanes and Menander 674

contaminatio 526–9
    criticized by Horace 777–8
    See also Plautus
Cornford, F. M., on the origin of Comedy in
        ritual 45
costume, Greek Comedy 57–9
Crates 107–8, 125, 157, 190–1, 194, 287–8
Cratinus 96–105, 116–18, 120–1, 128, 157, 164,
        182–3, 194
    All-Seers 279
    Dionysalexander, 100–2, 125, 182
    Odysseus and Company, 102–3, 164–5, 299
    source of fragments 669n3
    Wealths 287
    Wine-Flask 104–5, 116, 191, 307–8
cult 341–5

Damoxenus 188, 194, 281
de Robertis, Teresa 684–94 *passim*
Demetrius of Phalerum 184, 188, 189,
        218, 219
Demetrius Poliorcetes 185, 190, 218, 219
Demetrius *On Style* 673–4
Demetrius Triclinius 660–1, 663
democracy, Athenian 300–7
Democritus 282–3
didaskalos 50
didascaliae 422, 471
Dinolochus 264
Diodorus 311
Dionysiac Festivals. *See* festivals, Greek
Diphilus, 184, 191, 194–5, 200, 205, 207, 208,
        210–13 (*Zographos* K-A fr. 42, *Emporos*
        K-A fr. 31 vv.2–11), 310–11, 672–3, 676–8,
        874–5
Divus, Andreas 663
Donatus, Aelius 711–15, 782–97
dramatic illusion 65–7, 104
    nature of, in Plautine comedy 529–34

Ecphantides 97
ekkyklema 55, 222
Ennius 545–9, 588–91 *passim,* 648
Ephippus 170–2, 185, 188, 191, 195
epic 120, 127, 160, 546
Epicharmus 280
Epicrates 188, 191–2, 280

Epicurus 281–3, 285
epistolography 743–9
ethos (character type) 713–14
Euanthius. *See* Evanthius
Eugraphius 794–7
Eubulus 164, 167, 169, 172–3, 175–6,
        184–7, 192–5, 299, 308, 311, 350, 668,
        670, 676
Eupolis 113–21, 128, 186–7, 192, 279
    Demes 118–20
    Dyers 115, 117, 299
    Maricas 113, 125, 183, 305–6, 309
    source of fragments 669n3
Euripides 121–4, 163–4, 194, 264–6, 267–9,
        271–3
"euripidaristophanize" 121, 157
"euripidize" 208, 214
Evanthius 253, 582, 779, 783

fabula Atellana. *See* Atellan farce
fabula palliata 409–10, 425, 427, 432, 447–9
    masks of 433–40
fabula togata 447–9, 459–60
    Terence familiar with 768n2 (*see also*
        Titinius)
Fasti (IG II² 2318) 73
Fescennine verses 404, 405
festivals, Greek
    in Athens 341–5, 875–6
    City ("Great") Dionysia 260–1, 268, 270,
        302–3; beginning in 487/486 BCE 33,
        72, 74–5
    Lenaea 70, 72, 76–77, 98, 260–1, 268
    outside Greece 52, 362–5, 876–7 (e.g.
        Dionysia-Antiocheia, Dionysia-
        Attaleia); non-Dionysiac, in
        eastern Mediterranean 365–70; in
        western 372–4
    Rural Dionysia (celebrated in the demes of
        Attica) 70, 80, 81–4
festivals, Roman 409–14, 634–5
    ludi Megalenses 465, 466 (of 191 BCE)
five-act rule 252–3
Fraenkel, E. 5, 7, 425–7, 433, 456, 519, 527, 529
Fragmentum Grenfellianum 382–3, 490
Fredershausen, O. 616, 620
freedom of speech (*parrhesia*) 302–7

Freiburg School 431–3, 441
Fronto 755–7, 779

Gaza, Theodore 662
Gellius, Aulus 755–60, 771, 775, 779
genre/s 46–47, 121, 258–73 *passim*
gesture, in Roman comedy 784–97
gods, in Old Comedy 345–9
  in New Comedy 349–53
Goldberg, S. 545
Green, J. R. 10–12, 21
Groningen edition 12, 14

Halliwell, S., and aischrology 46
Handley, E. 6n12, 8n15, 12, 14n25, 15, 17 and
  n32, 220, 222, 426, 519, 520n5, 529, 809, 813
hedonism 286–7
Hegesippus 188, 191, 283
Heniochus 185, 191, 195
Henderson, J. 4, 13–14, 19, 20, 21
Hermippus 105–8, 113, 182–3, 194, 305–6, 308
hero, comic 142–5, 145–9
Herodas 379, 381–2, 385–93. *See also* mime
humor, personal 96–108, 114, 115–18, 136, 151
  political, 98, 101–2, 106, 115–21
  verbal 40
Hyperbolus 303–6, 309
hypocrisy 284

iconography 717–28
illustrated manuscripts 701–8, 727–31,
  789–94. *See also* Terence
images. *See* comedy, Greek, New Comedy,
  visual record; comedy, Roman, visual
  record; iconography; illustrated
  manuscripts
impersonation 471–2
improvisation 428–33
infrared photography 684, 688, 693
intertextuality in Greek comedy 115n2, 119,
  121, 272
  in Roman comedy 543–4, 588–9 (*see also*
  paratragedy)
indirect tradition of Terence 710–14 (*see also*
  Menander)
interpolation. *See* Plautus, interpolation
irony 151, 154–5, 714

Kassel, R. 18
Konstan, D. 426

Laberius, Decimus 385–90. *See also* mime
Latin language
  archaizing language 754–9, 778–9 (*see also*
  Second Sophistic)
  early Latin (EL) 563–5
  colloquial spoken Latin 568–9
law, Athenian
  and Aristophanes, legal terminology
  in 322–6; as a source for law
  324–5; effect of Aristophanes' critique
  of the courts on the audience 326–33
  passim; excessive litigiousness 312,
  332–3; parody of law-making
  protocols 328–9; parody of laws ("legal
  intertextuality") 326–8; using laws out of
  context ("transcontextulization")
  329–31
  and Aristophanes' rivals 333–4
  and Menander, private law, family
  relationships, arbitration and the
  law 334–6
law, Roman
  and comedy, earlier scholarship 616–17
  and the fragments of *comoediae palliatae*,
  comoediae togatae, and literary
  farces 628–30
  and Plautus, adapting legal scenarios from
  Attic Comedy 617–21; comic effect
  of legal language in Plautus 624–5;
  methods of translating legal texts 621–4;
  Plautine law and the audience 625–6;
  satire of lawyers in Plautus 780
  sumptuary laws 546, 548n8, 611
  and Terence 626–8
Leigh, M. 427
Lefèvre, E. 431. *See also* Freiburg School
Lenaea. *See* festivals, Greek
Leo, F. 426, 526
letters, fictional. *See* epistolography
lexicography 779–80
linguistic characterization, in Roman
  comedy 569–72. *See also* Aristophanes,
  Menander, Plautus, Terence
linguistic correctness, Latin 772, 779

liturgies, military and festival (= "agonistic liturgy", i.e. *choregia*) 70
Livius Andronicus 544, 548, 580, 534
love plots 160, 173–4
ludi. See festivals, Roman
    ludi scaenici 19

MacDowell, D. M. 332n2, 324–5, 326, 335 and n11, 337
Magnes (comic victor at City Dionysia in 473/2) 73, 96–7, 157
Mai, Cardinal 682, 693
Marshall, C.W. 428, 430–3, 436–8
"marvelous motifs" 169–70
masks
    generally 201 and n4, 206 and n9
    in New Comedy 60–4
    in Old Comedy 58
    in Roman Comedy, 425, 433–41
Manutius, Aldus 662–3
Matius, Cnaeus 386–90. *See also* mime
Mazon, P., theory of the origin of Old Comedy's structure 44–5
McCarthy, K. 427, 429
Menander
    Anechomenos 760; *Aspis* 293; *Dis Exapaton* (as model of Plautus' *Bacchides*) 426–7, 519–26; *Dyskolos* 227–8 (vv.104–15), 228–9 (vv.487–99), 224–5 (play's conclusion), 252–3, 350, 811; *Epitrepontes* 193, 229 and n11, 230, 271–2, 809–11; *Misoumenos* 230, 809; *Perikeiromene* 272; *Samia* 230–1, 272, 290–1; *Sikyonios/oi* 231, 272, 313–14; *Synaristosai* 269
    ancient biography 551–3 (*see also* as character in fictitious letters)
    as character in fictitious letters 205, 748–9
    as preeminent author of New Comedy 674–5
    audience address 232–4
    author of model of Plautus' *Pseudolus* 526–9
    chorus 221–2
    linguistic characterization 225–9, 234
    maxims 717, 725
    meters 202n5, 222, 224–5

monologues 221, 223, 226, 229–31, 232–4
mosaics. *See* visual record
papyri 15, 16, 17, 220–1, 247–51, 804–5, 807–12, 818–62
personal address 226–9
and philosophy 292
politics 189, 301, 312–13
prologues 223–4
reception in ancient novels 736–42; in epistolary collections 743–9; in later antiquity 670, 672–9 (*see also* relationship to Homer *and* visual record)
relationship to Homer 549–53, 736–7; to Terence 241–2, 539–41, 549–51; to tragedy 271–3
"speech within speech" ("quoted speech") 227, 230–1
text of 239–55 *passim*; fragments 242–3; indirect tradition 242–7, 249–50, 254–5; titles 243–7
"three-actor convention" 222–3
visual record 717–27
metatheater, 5, 65, 67, 116, 124, 127, 128, 265, 428–31, 440
metrics, Greek
    music, of a piper 64
    in Aristophanes (*see under* Aristophanes)
    in Menander (see under *Menander*)
metrics, Roman 477–93
    accompanied verses 477–80, 484, 491
    alphabetic notation 483, 484
    cantica, polymetric 487–91
    change of meter 491
    of Early Latin (EL) 565
    iambic senarius 482–4
    laws 478n1, 480–4
    long verses 480, 484–8
    music 477–91, 517–19
    Plautus vs. Terence 491–2
    song (*see* cantica, polymetric *and* music)
    trochaic septenarius 484–7
    unaccompanied verses 477–82
Middle Comedy. *See* comedy, Greek
mime 378–93, 405–6. *See also* Herodas; Laberius, Decimus; Matius, Cnaeus; Syrus, Publilius; Sophron; Vergilius Romanus

mimiamb 379, 381–2, 385–91

monuments of New Comedy. *See* comedy, Greek, New Comedy, visual record

Moore, T. 428, 518

mos maiorum 428, 603–4

Mosaics. *See* comedy, Greek, New Comedy, visual record

MS Ravenna 658

Musurus, Marcus 663

mythological burlesque. *See under* Comedy, Old

Naevius 448, 452–5, 556–7, 531

neologism 135–6, 149, 156–7, 530

New Comedy. *See* comedy, Greek

non-Athenians 184–5

novel, Greek 735–42

Old Comedy. *See* comedy, Greek

P. Freiburg 12 527–9

papyri 664, 670–9 *passim*, 803–16, 818–65. *See also* Menander *and* P. Freiburg 12

parabasis. *See under* Aristophanes

paratragedy 119, 121–4, 194, 264–6, 273
Roman comedy 546, 580–98

parody
in Aristophanes 135, 138, 140, 153–4, 157
of philosophy 279
of prayer 636, 642–6
See also law, Athenian *and* paratragedy

paterfamilias 612–13

Pellio 414–17

performance, of *Eunuchus* vv.46–206 470–3; *Hecyra* vv.623–726 473–4; *Menaechmi* vv.1050–1152 468–70; *Pseudolus* vv.129–229 466–8
discussed by ancient commentators 783, 789, 792–7
performance grammar 260–3
performance studies 6–8

Petrone, G., 429

Pherecrates 108–10, 125, 186, 190–2, 287, 345

Philemon 185–6, 188, 192, 200, 202, 203, 204–5, 207, 208–9 and n11 (*Adelphoi* K-A fr. 3), 211, 214, 280, 290, 309–10, 352, 668, 673–4, 676–8, 874–6

in Roman comedy 530, 551, 673

Philippides 188–90, 203, 205, 219, 283, 301

Philo of Alexandria 677

philosophy 278–93 *passim*

Philyllius 173, 185, 187, 192

Phrynichus 113–14, 191

piety 605–12

Plato Comicus 124–8, 167, 174, 183–4, 186, 191, 194, 305–6, 308–9

Plato Philosophus 184, 188, 259, 268, 279–81, 283, 285–7, 290, 293, 305

"plautinisches" in Plautus 424–8

Plautus
Amphitruo 264, 413, 583–5, 596n1, 605, 606, 610–11, 637n2; vv.282–3 as model for Turpilius 770; *Asinaria* 415, 436, 611; vv.307–8 as model for Turpilius 770; *Aulularia* vv.508–13 772; *Bacchides* 426–7, 519–26, 591, 603–6, 610, 645n9; *Captivi* 438, 585–7, 605–7; *Casina* 417–18, 590, 605, 606; prologue 767–8, 780; *Cistellaria* 269, 527n10, 637n2, 645, 682–97, 769; *Curculio* 416, 419, 434–6, 533, 589, 611; *Epidicus* 414, 435; *Menaechmi* 416, 531, 590; model for Terence 773; vv.1050–1152 468–470; *Mercator* 506–8, 590, 516n1, 611, 638–49; v.396 as model for Lucilius 775; *Miles Gloriosus* 420, 527, 602, 607, 635; vv.1–4 760–1; as model for Terence's *Eunuchus* 773–4; *Mostellaria* 516n1; vv.138–143 adapted by Gellius 757; vv.157–312 as model for Pomponius 770; v.261 as model for Afranius 771; *Persa* 416, 533, 591, 602–5, 611; vv.419–420 as model for Titinius 771; *Poenulus* 413, 526, 588–9, 605–10 *passim*; ancient commentary on 755; interpolations in 769; *Pseudolus* 409, 413–21 *passim*, 436–8, 589, 634, 638n3; vv.23–4 imitated by Jerome 780; vv.129–229 466–8; model of 526–9; *Rudens* 436–7, 516n1, 586–8, 605–8, 611, 638; *Stichus* 412; *Trinummus* 530–2; quoted by Cicero 776; *Truculentus*, quoted by Donatus 778; fragmentary plays 516, 756–60 (*see also* Varronian canon)

Plautus (*Cont.*)
  ancient biography 533–4
  audience (*see* audience, Roman)
  contaminatio 526–9
  Hellenistic paradigm 529–34
  imperialism 603
  interpolation 768
  intertextual allusions 516n1
  language 448–52, 556–62, 645n8
  law 604, 611 (*see also* law, Roman)
  linguistic characterization 556–62
  metrics (*see* metrics, Roman)
  models, possible, *adespota* K-A fr. 1027
    528–9; *adespota* K-A fr. 1147 526;
    Menandrian 241–2, 519–29, 540, 813;
    P. Freiburg 12 527–9; of
    Pseudolus 526–59
  morality 525–6, 603–4, 635–6
  mos maiorum 603–4
  palimpsest 680–98
  "plautinisches" in Plautus 424–8
  politics 413, 427, 453, 601–5, 610–11, 650
  relation to Old Comedy 125–8
  relation to tragedy 124, 413, 415, 580–92,
    646 (*see also* paratragedy)
  religion 412–13, 634–50 (*see also* religion,
    Rome)
  Saturnalian paradigm 412, 428–9, 529–34,
    634n1
  Second sophistic, reception in (*see* Second
    sophistic *and* reception of Plautus)
  "speech within speech" 521
  Textual tradition 418, 526, 680–98, 699
plot construction. *See* Aristophanes;
    Menander; Plautus; Terence
Plutarch, as source of fragments 670, 674,
    676, 677
  *Comparison of Aristophanes and
    Menander* 674
Pollux, *On Masks* 60, 62, 64, 66, 201n4, 435–8
  Onomasticon: 669–71, 675
"popular" theater 424–33, 439, 440
populism 182–3
Posidippus 284–5
prizes
  for tragic actors at the Dionysia and
    Lenaea 52

  for comic actors at the Dionysia and
    Lenaea 52
producers, Roman 414–18
production. *See under* comedy, Greek *and*
    comedy, Roman
prologue. *See under* Menander *and* comedy,
    Roman
Publilius Syrus 385. *See also* mime
Pythagoras 283, 288–9

Querolus 780
Questa, C. 16–17, 434

rationalization 169
reception
  of Caecilius Statius 758–60
  of Diphilus 672–3, 676–8
  of Greek comedy by Christian and Jewish
    authors 677–9
  of Menander, by Apuleius 760; in
    ancient novels 736–42; in epistolary
    collections 743–9; by Ovid and
    Manilius 754 (*see also* Menander, visual
    record)
  of Middle Comedy in antiquity 667–79
  of New Comedy by authors of the
    palliata 672–3 (*see also* Comedy, Roman)
  of Philemon 668, 673–4, 676–8
  of Plautus, in the Second Sophistic 753–
    65; in late antiquity 779–80; in late
    republic 774–8; by other comic
    authors 543–4, 769–74
  of Terence 756–7, 760; by ancient
    scholars 754–5
religion, Greece 340–53 *passim. See also* cult,
    gods, religious attitudes, ritual, sacrifice
religion, Rome 604–9, 634–50
  curse 639, 647
  instauratio 635
  interrupted rituals 635, 637, 644–6
  oath 605–6, 644–6
  performance theory 637–8
  prayer 606, 636–7, 641–50
  religious festivals 634–5 (*see also* festivals,
    Roman)
  speech act 644–5
  staged rituals 637–8

religious attitudes 343–9, 350–1
revivals 200–1, 205, 207 and n10
    of Plautus and Terence, immediate 767–9;
      in 2nd c. AD 778–9
Rhinthon 403–4
ritual 349
role division 468–70
romances, Greek 735–42
Römer, C. 809–10

sacrifice 341–5, 350–1
Saturnalia 530, 634n1. *See also* Plautus,
    Saturnalian paradigm
satyr play 259–61, 268–9
Satyrus 262
Scafuro, A. 336n12, 337, 616, 620
scholia
    Aristophanic 12–14, 658, 660–1 (*see also*
      Groningen edition)
    Latin 699–700, 705, 711–15, 782–97
school syllabus. *See* canon of school authors
Second Sophistic 735–52 *passim*, 753–66, 779
Seeberg, A. 10–11
Segal, E. 427–9, 529
semiotics, theater 639
Slater, N. 427–32
Socrates 279–81, 284, 292. *See also* Plato
    Philosophus
Sommerstein, A. 4, 13–14, 19
Sophron 379n2, 385–6, 393. *See also* mime
"speech within speech." *See under* Plautus,
    Terence, *and* Menander
stage properties 464–5
Stärk, E. 431. *See also* Freiburg School
stock characters 171–2, 386, 753–4, 759, 761,
    764
Strattis 121–4, 192, 194
Studemund, W. 682–94
sublime 118–21
Susarion 95
Süss, W., prototypic figures of comic plots 44
Syrus, Publilius, 385. *See also* mime

Teleclides 106–8, 287, 312
Terence
    Adelphoe 414, 509–12, 542; modeled
      on *Miles Gloriosus* 773–4; *Andria*,

alternate ending 709; *Eunuchus* 411n2,
    413, 414, 542–52 *passim*, 559–62,
    589–90; vv.46–206 470–3; Plautine
    quality of 772–3; *Hecyra* 410, 540–5
    passim, 551, 612–13; vv.623–726: 473–4;
    Phormio 414–16, 540–1, 546–8, 551, 590
Alexandrianism 542–5, 553
ancient biography 549–53, 709
Apollodorus of Carystus, relation to 541
Aristophanes of Byzantium, influence
    of 542, 549, 552
Callopian recension 708–10
commentaries. *See* Donatus; Eugraphius;
    scholia, Latin
Ennius, relation to 545–9
illustrated manuscripts 701–8, 727–31,
    789–94
intertextual allusions 543–4, 589–90
Lex Fannia, allusion to 546, 548n8
language 555–63
law. *See Lex Fannia and* law, Roman
linguistic characterization 569–72
manuscripts 699–715
metrics. *See* metrics, Roman
neotericism 539, 544
politics 413, 612–13
religion 412–13, 636, 638, 642, 649
as Roman Menander 539–41,
    549–51, 814
as school author 539–40, 700, 754, 779
"speech within speech" 472
textual tradition. *See* Terence, manuscripts
See also reception of Terence
theater buildings, Greek 53–6
    Roman 463–4
theater semiotics 639
theater spaces, Roman 418–21
Theocritus 379n2
Theognetus 289
Theophilus 192–3, 309
Theophrastus 155, 292, 313, 351
Theopompus 185–6, 188, 191–2, 280, 308
Thomas Magister 660–1
Timocles 184–5, 187–8, 192–5, 202, 259, 301,
    308, 310
    Dionysiazousai (*Women at the Dionysia*,
      K-A fr. 6) 185, 213–14, 258, 270

Titinius 448, 457–60, 771
tragedy 194, 258–73 *passim*, 297
   Roman 546
   See also festivals; paratragedy; tragicomedy;
      Aeschylus; Euripides
tragicomedy 583–5
Turpilius 558–9, 770
Turpio 414–17, 422
Tyche 293, 350–2

utopia 286–8

Varro, creative imitator of Plautus 775–6
Varronian plays 754–8, 771–2
vase paintings, South Italian and Sicily ("West
   Greek") 56, 162, 169–71, 174–5, 370
   virtuoso speeches 201 (Anaxandrides
      Protesilaus K-A fr. 42), 203

(Mnesimachus *Hippotrophos* K-A
   fr. 4), 211 (Straton *Phoinikides* K-A
   fr. 1), 521
Vogt-Spira, G. 428, 430–2

wealth 182, 185–6
Webster, T.B.L. 7–12, 21, 23
Wiles, D. 428, 434–9
Witt, P. 616, 620, 621–2

Xenarchus 184, 186, 311
Xenocleides (victorious *choregos* at City
   Dionysia in 473/2) 73

Zieliński, T., theory of the origin of
   Old Comedy's structure
      41–3
   folk-tale comedy 44